GunDigest
2020

74th EDITION

Edited by
JERRY LEE

Published by

Gun Digest® Books, an imprint of Caribou Media Group, LLC

Gun Digest Media
5600 W. Grande Market Drive, Suite 100
Appleton, WI 54913
www.gundigest.com

To order books or other products call 920.471.4522
or visit us online at www.gundigeststore.com

ISBN-13: 978-1-946267-82-5

Edited by Jerry Lee, Corey Graff & Chuck Smock
Cover Design by Jordan Matuszak
Interior Design by Dave Hauser, Jeromy Boutwell,
& Jordan Matuszak

Printed in the United States of America

10 9 8 7 6 5 4 3 2 1

John T. Amber LITERARY AWARD

GEORGE LAYMAN

George is shown with an SKS, his favorite rifle for collecting, next to the Remington Rolling Block. This is his most coveted, a lightweight 1989 Navy Arms Chinese Type 56 imported variant known as the "Cowboy's Companion." It has a 16.5-inch barrel and no provision for the cruciform bayonet. Never used by China's military, it was made strictly for the U.S. market. They are no longer easy to locate.
Photo by Dianna Kelly.

I am pleased to announce the recipient of the John T. Amber Award this year is George Layman. Every year the award is presented to an author in recognition of a contribution to the previous edition of *Gun Digest.* George's fine story in the 2019

73rd edition titled "Russia's Mosin-Nagant Model 1944: Last of the Cold War Favorites that Continue to Serve" is based on his very thorough knowledge of Com Bloc rifles and handguns. He has been a frequent contributor to *Gun Digest* in recent years with stories on unusual firearms, such as the Brown-Merrill bolt action, and diverse models ranging from Remington Rolling Blocks to Thompson Submachine Guns and British Bulldog revolvers.

George has been a life-long gun collector, beginning with his first Rolling Block at the age of 12.

He considers Remington Military Rolling Block rifles and the handguns of the American West to be his specialties in the world of firearms.

George has a fascinating background, having served 21 years in the U.S. Army as an intelligence analyst and foreign-language interrogator specializing in oriental languages. He is fluent in Japanese, Korean, Hungarian, Russian, German and Spanish, and is also an expert at reading Chinese. George also has a working fluency in Romanian and Bulgarian. These linguistic skills have been very helpful in his research into the history of military weapons in the various countries.

George has written hundreds of magazine articles and columns in titles such as *Rifle, Man at Arms, Gun Journal, Black Powder Hunting, The Gun Report* and others. He has had 10 books published, the latest being *Communist Bloc Handguns,* Mowbray Publishing in 2018. Having spent most of his Army intelligence career in Asia, he says he was fortunate to have had access to many

The John T. Amber Literary Award is named for the editor of Gun Digest from 1950 to 1979, a period that could be called the heyday of gun and outdoor writing. Amber worked with many of the legends in the business during his almost 30 years with the book, including the great shooting and hunting writer, Townsend Whelen. In 1967, Amber instituted an award to honor each year an outstanding author of Gun Digest, which he named for Whelen. In 1982, three years after Amber's retirement, the award was renamed in his honor.

of these handguns during those years. After his retirement, George worked as a government contractor in the Balkans, where he continued to do research on these firearms at a time when access by others was very limited.

His expertise in firearms has also played a role in taking George's career into the world of television. He has been seen in numerous TV programs including appearing as a guest panelist on the History Channel's *Old West Tech* series and as an actor played four roles on a special called *The Wild West's 10 Most Wanted* on Discovery Channel. He's also had acting roles in three episodes of *Deadwood* on HBO and in a theatrical film, *The Last Shot,* a comedy/crime drama about the FBI and the mob.

Born and raised in Connecticut, today George and his significant other, Dianna, live in Florida. He has become one of our regular contributors and is a fine gentleman to work with. Again, it's a pleasure to honor him with the 38th Annual John T. Amber Award.

— Jerry Lee, Editor

GunDigest
2020

2020 FIREARMS CATALOG

WELCOME

TO YEAR 2020, AND THE 74TH ANNUAL EDITION OF *GUN DIGEST!*

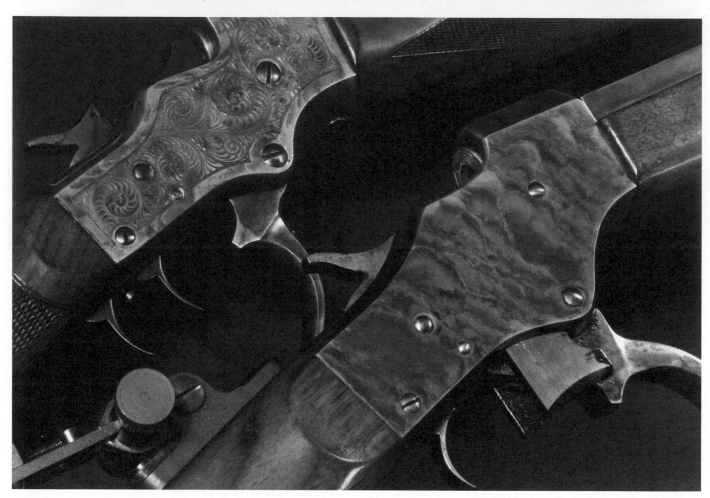

A s we wind down the second decade of the 21st century, our staff is very proud to present the 2020 edition of *Gun Digest*. Not long ago, 2020 sounded like a time that was a long away and suddenly, we are in the future!

Within these pages you will find a mix of stories about virtually every type of firearm. No matter what your interest is in relation to guns — hunting, collecting, personal defense, history, militaria, target shooting, or all the above — there's something here for you. We continue our long tradition of presenting hunting stories about the best guns for the game, historical profiles of great firearms from the past, test reports on some of the year's new models, how-to articles for the do-it-yourself gunsmith, and professional photos showcasing the works of America's best custom gunmakers.

It is still 2019 as this edition goes to press, a year that marks the 70th anniversary of Sturm, Ruger & Co. The anniversary was celebrated with a special edition of the Mark IV, the latest version of the .22 semi-automatic pistol that started it all back in 1949. Ruger today, of course, is recognized as one of the most successful companies in the industry, having sold more than 30 million firearms.

It has been a year of expansion and relocation for several major manufacturers. Weatherby officially opened its new headquarters in Sheridan, Wyoming, in June, after having been located in California since 1945. Needless to say, a gun company is more than welcome in Wyoming, especially in comparison to California. In other moves, Kimber is expanding and reaching into friendly southern territory for its sixth location in Troy, Alabama. The company has locations in New Jersey and headquarters in Yonkers, New York, where it will remain. Another handgun manufacturer and importer, Taurus, has announced plans to move from Miami to Bainbridge, Georgia in 2020. Kahr Arms is planning to leave New York for the more gun-friendly state of Pennsylvania and Stag Arms is looking to relocate from Connecticut to South Carolina.

HIGHLIGHTS OF THIS EDITION

We've collected articles from some of the best writers in the shooting sports for this edition. In the hunting-rifle category, we have three fine stories on the right gun and cartridges for the pursuit of dangerous game. Phil Massaro covers the history and performance of John Rigby's .470 Nitro Express, still getting the job done since 1898. Joe Coogan tells the tale of a wealthy hunter from Beverly Hills who wanted Holland and Holland to build him a .600 Nitro Express. They declined, and then he talked them into a .700, laying out the cash himself for the research and development. And then we have Brad Fitzpatrick making the argument that the .375 H&H is a superb choice for taming big beasts the world over.

Looking back at great guns of the past, Jeff John profiles some of the world's finest single shots, illustrated with his excellent photography. Terry Wieland writes about the history of the Stevens Arms and Tool company and its high-grade *Schutzen* rifles that dominated that shooting sport early in the last century. Have you ever heard of the .35 Smith & Wesson, the revolver and the cartridge? Charlie Petty knows all and shares it in his feature article. I would bet that many readers of *Gun Digest* began their shooting years with an Old Model Ruger Single Six. Rick Hacker admits he didn't own one until he became an old model himself. But he has a great story on the little .22 that was introduced by a very wise Bill Ruger in 1953, when millions of young cowboys like Rick and yours truly were watching all those westerns on TV.

There are more fine stories by writers including Wayne van Zwoll, Jon Sundra, George Layman, John Taffin and others — too many to list here. Also, you'll find in this edition our annual updates of ballistics tables, our huge catalog sections and Web Directory of the industry.

It is with much sadness that I report the passing of Nick Sisley. He died in February 2019 at his home in Pennsylvania after a long bout with cancer. A wonderful man and one of the experts in the field of shotguns, he was one of the good guys. We're publishing his last story submitted to *Gun Digest* just a short time before his passing. It's about his pick of 12 great American shotguns, which is appropriate for his farewell story. Don't miss the tribute by Jon Sundra at the end of Nick's story.

As this edition was about to be shipped to the printer, we learned that S.P. (Steve) Fjestad, publisher and author of the Blue Book of Gun Values, had passed away on July 15, 2019. He had just published the 40th Edition of the gun values book, one of the more than 160 titles Steve had edited or published about firearms and other collectibles since the 1980s. Steve was a very popular and highly respected colleague in the firearms industry and a dear friend of this editor and many contributors to Gun Digest. May he rest in peace.

At his State of the Industry speech at the SHOT Show in February 2019, Steve Sanetti, president of NSSF, the National Shooting Sports Foundation, made some comments we would like to share.

"I would respectfully suggest that the ownership of firearms is a lifestyle choice for many millions of good Americans who hunt, target shoot, enjoy outdoor recreation, and want the means to protect their families. They do not deserve to be made into political enemies or to be marginalized for the choices they have made or the activities they pursue safely, responsibly and legally. They are good people who don't harm anyone and have the same right to the American Dream as everyone else. We ask nothing more than respect for our traditions that may differ from theirs. We ask for that same tolerance and appreciation for the liberty and rights and freedoms our great American way of life and laws have provided, so long as we harm no one. We ask that they acknowledge our experiences with family and friends and neighbors that bring us together, and for an honest appreciation that ours is a nation of diverse interests, activities and lifestyles, which include our own. And that we care about the sanctity of human life as much as they do. And we grieve for the loss of decency and all the anger and hatred that so permeates society today."

— Jerry Lee

ABOUT THE COVER

On the following three pages, you'll find a detailed look at this edition's cover gun: a stunning Boyds At-One Adjustable Thumbhole Gunstock holding a Remington 700 action and barrel from the company's SPS Varmint line. The Boyds At-One Adjustable Gunstock delivers a true custom fit by allowing adjustments for length of pull and comb height with the simple push of a button. The cover rifle is topped with a Crimson Trace CSA-2416 2-Series Sport 4-16x50mm mid-range rifle scope, a first focal-plane scope from a company known for producing quality laser sights and tactical lights. Also pictured is a Champion Vanquish Electronic Hearing Protection muff designed specifically for the shooting sports.

Gun Digest Staff

Jim Schlender — **Group Publisher**
Jerry Lee — **Editor-in-Chief**
Chuck Smock — **Features Editor**

CONTRIBUTING EDITORS

Wayne van Zwoll: Rifles
John Haviland: Shotguns
Robert Sadowski: Handgun/Semi-Auto
Max Prasac: Revolvers & Others
Mike Beliveau: Muzzleloaders

Phil Massaro: Ammunition, Ballistics & Components
Tom Tabor: Optics
Tom Turpin: Custom and Engraved Guns
Jim House: Airguns

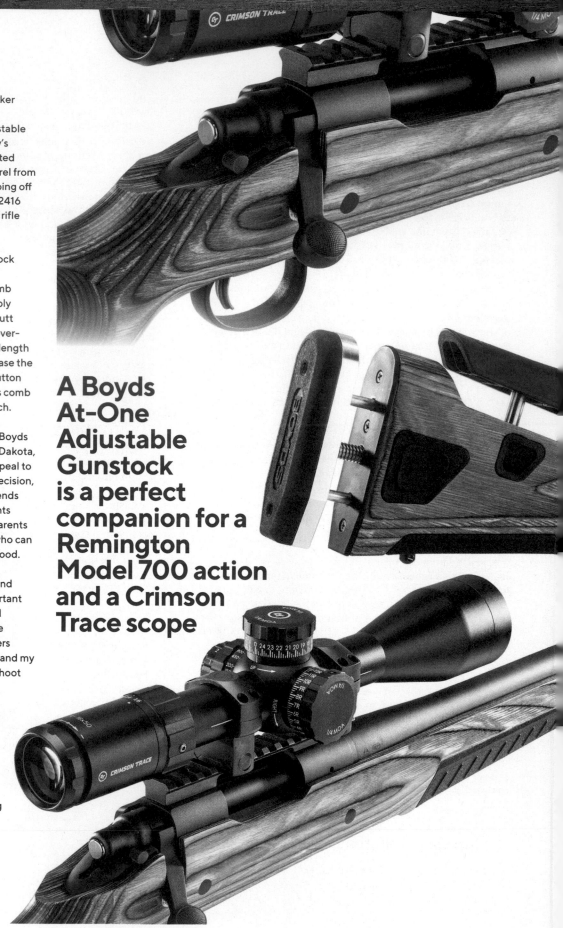

This year's cover gun is a looker and a shooter. The foundation of this amazing rifle is a Boyds At-One Adjustable Thumbhole Gunstock in the company's Pepper laminate color. The stock is fitted with a Remington 700 action and barrel from the company's SPS Varmint line. Topping off the cover rig is a Crimson Trace CSA-2416 2-Series Sport 4-16x50mm midrange rifle scope.

The Boyds At-One Adjustable Gunstock delivers a true custom fit by allowing adjustments for length of pull and comb height with the push of a button. Simply push in the Bring-It button near the butt of the gun, slide the half-inch-thick, over-molded rubber buttpad to the adjust length of pull from 12.5 to 14 inches, and release the button to set the length. A Bring-It button near the top of the cheek piece allows comb height to be raised up to 9/16 of an inch.

Dustin Knutson, general manager for Boyds at its headquarters in Mitchell, South Dakota, said the At-One Adjustable stocks appeal to a wide range of shooters, including precision, long-range shooters, to couples or friends and family members of different heights who want to shoot the same gun, to parents looking to buy a rifle for a youngster who can shoot it as he or she grows into adulthood.

"Precision shooting is really popular, and people are educated about how important it is to have a properly fitted rifle," said Knutson, who has personal experience relating to the second group of shooters mentioned above. "And, I'm 6-foot-6 and my wife is 5-foot-5, and we never could shoot the same rifle. Now we can."

Knutson also said the quick and easy adjustability is convenient for people who want to change shooting positions during the same range session, as well as for transitioning from shooting in warmer weather to winter conditions, when extra clothing layers or heavy jackets could affect length of pull.

A Boyds At-One Adjustable Gunstock is a perfect companion for a Remington Model 700 action and a Crimson Trace scope

All Boyds At-One stocks are constructed of up to 37 individual sheets of top-grade hardwood that are dried to exacting specifications to ensure rigidity and stability, dyed in the desired color, and dried again. The sheets are then laminated together, using a process that involves a special adhesive, heat and extreme pressure, to form a three-foot-long block that will yield two stocks.

After the block is sawed in half, each of the two blanks is CNC-machined to a close approximation of the finished product and then hand-sanded to the final detail. The stocks are also hand-sprayed with chemical-resistant varnish finishes for long-lasting durability in all weather conditions.

The At-One stock includes a Traditional Grip, with a swept-back, pistol-grip design. An optional Target Grip with a thicker, more vertical grip, designed for prone shooting, is sold separately. It also includes a Traditional Forearm, a sleek and slender standard forearm, while a Target Forearm, with a beaver-tail style, fat and flat design, is available as an option. At-One Adjustable Gunstocks are available in an almost infinite number of configurations based on make, model and action of the firearm they are intended for.

Customers can visit the Boyds website (www.boydsgunstocks.com) and use the Build & Price feature to see available options for firearms they might be interested in, as well as all the different color choices. And the Pepper color seen in the cover gun is just one of 11 colors, from mild to wild, available in the Boyds At-One line.

All Boyds At-One Adjustable stocks are built to order, and they won't break the bank. Prices start at $199, compared to other custom stocks on the market that can cost as much as $600 to $800, or more. Average weight is about three pounds.

In all, Boyds offers 19 colors and 19 different stock shapes for more than 255 gun brands and more than 1,200 different models within those brands.

We chose to pair our At-One Adjustable Gunstock with a Remington Model 700 action and barrel, chambered in .308 Win., from the Remington SPS Varmint collection. It has a short action, blind magazine and bull barrel. The SPS Varmint is available in nine calibers, from .204 Ruger up to .308.

Introduced in 1962, the Remington Model 700 has spent nearly 60 years earning its reputation as one of the most solid, dependable and trusted bolt-action rifles ever invented.

The Remington website reports: "(The Model 700) is the number one bolt-action of all time, proudly made in the U.S.A. For over 50 years, more Model 700s have been sold than any other bolt-action rifle before or since. The legendary strength of its three-rings-of-steel receiver paired with a hammer-forged barrel, combine to yield the most popular bolt-action rifle in history."

Long known for producing quality laser sights and tactical lights, Crimson Trace has entered the riflescope arena with an impressive collection of quality sporting and tactical optics. Our cover gun is topped with a Crimson Trace CSA-2416 2-Series Sport scope, a 4-16x50mm first-focal-plane rifle scope built with impressive, multi-coated Japanese ED glass for clarity and true color transmission in all light conditions.

This scope features a custom MR1-MOA advanced reticle that is fully illuminated and offers quick hold-over points for windage and elevation. All Crimson Trace scopes are part of the company's free batteries for life program and are covered under a lifetime protection guaranteed warranty.

The 30mm main tube is constructed of a single piece of anodized aluminum and is nitrogen-purged and O-ring-sealed to make it waterproof and fogproof. Exposed .25 MOA tactical turrets deliver precise adjustments.

Also shown in the cover photo is a Champion Vanquish Electronic Hearing Protection muff. Designed specifically for the shooting sports, each muff is acoustically modeled on gunshot reports to achieve the optimal balance of comfort and noise reduction. They feature Safe Level Sound Compression Technology with a refresh time of less than one millisecond, and two HD speakers with omnidirectional microphones that allow in natural sounds while minimizing wind noise.

America's 12 GREATEST SHOTGUNS

WE ARE SORRY TO REPORT THAT NICK SISLEY PASSED AWAY AT HIS HOME IN PENNSYLVANIA ON FEB. 6, 2019. HE WAS A FREQUENT CONTRIBUTOR TO GUN DIGEST AND WAS WIDELY RECOGNIZED AS ONE OF THE LEADING EXPERTS IN SHOTGUNS AND THE SHOTGUN SPORTS. THIS ARTICLE WAS SUBMITTED JUST DAYS BEFORE NICK'S PASSING AND IS PRESENTED AS A FOND FAREWELL TO ONE OF OUR GREAT OUTDOOR WRITERS.

Outstanding shotguns come from all over the world, but the dozen described here are **America's best** BY NICK SISLEY

ngland's great shotgun makers come from Birmingham and London, the Scots gave us the round-body action, Brescia in Italy is perhaps the king in great shotguns these days, Spain has been in the limelight and for about 15 years, Turkish-made shotguns are being bought here in the U.S. at an astonishing rate. But American-made guns continue to capture the hearts of American shotgunners. If you put three or four hunters together in a room, each of them would probably have a similar but somewhat differing list of favorites. Let's look at one man's take on the great American shotguns.

REMINGTON 870

One shotgun that will probably be on most everyone's list is the Remington Model 870 pump gun. This model saw its first clay target field in 1950. Master Shotgunner Rudy Etchen soon ran a 100-straight in Doubles Trap — perhaps the first ever with a pump.

Sales for Remington's outstanding Model 31 pump gun were sagging after World War II, playing second fiddle at the time to another great American shotgun, Winchester's Model 12. The 870 took those post–World War II days by storm. In only 13 years Remington had sold 2 million 870s. By 1983, three million. By 1996, seven million. By 2009, over 10 million. And the number given today by Remington is 11 million.

"Pull!" The author shooting skeet with a .410-bore Remington 870.

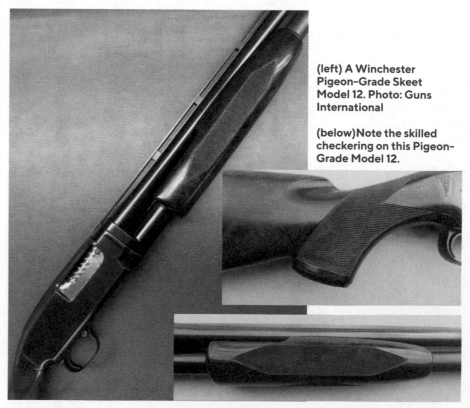

The Remington 870 is the best-selling shotgun of all time. More than 11 million have been sold since its introduction in 1950. Photo: Guns America

A member of my local gun club, John Smith, has killed 62 different bird species with his 12-gauge 870. He's looking to add more. Both his sons shot their first ducks with this same 870. It is a 3-inch version. John had a 2 ¾-inch 870 but bought this one in the late 1970s when the steel shot wind first began blowing.

From the onset, the 870 was reliable, rugged, had a streamlined look — plus was relatively inexpensive. It was made in 12, 16, 20 and 28 gauges and .410 bore, but maybe not all five gauges at the same time. Further, the model had several special "commemorative" runs. Bottom line — it was one smooth-operating pump. Sales numbers don't lie. The 870 is one super-popular American-made shotgun, and they are still being made 70 years later.

WINCHESTER MODEL 12

As popular as the 870 Remington is, on the used market another pump gun, the Winchester Model 12, sells for more dollars. There are far fewer Model 12s than 870s, and it's one heck of a shotgun. The year of introduction was 1912 (some say a year later) and the gun's original name was the Model 1912. It was introduced originally as a 20 gauge. Later, Winchester added 12 and 16 gauges to the line.

> **SKEET SHOOTING CAME ALONG AROUND 1930 AND SOON BECAME A COMPETITION GAME. IN 1934, WINCHESTER CAME OUT WITH THE MODEL 12 IN 28 GAUGE.**

Skeet shooting came along around 1930 and soon became a competition game. In 1934, Winchester came out with the Model 12 in 28 gauge. These days the 28-gauge Model 12 is the most valuable of the four gauges by far. In 1933 the

Model 42 Winchester was introduced, only in .410 — another answer to the hue and cry of skeet shooters. The 42 is a kissin' cousin to the Model 12. Some were produced with 3-inch chambers. Early skeet shooters shot 3-inch .410 shotshells in 28-gauge events (3/4 ounce of shot) and 2 ½-inch .410 (1/2 ounce) in the .410 events. This saved buying a 28-gauge Model 12.

Six 2 3/4-inch shells could be loaded into the 12-gauge Model 12's magazine. Add one in the chamber, and it's no wonder it became so popular with waterfowlers prior to the Migratory Bird Treaty, which limited magazines to two shells. Early 20 gauges wore 2 1/2-inch chambers and early 16s had 2 9/16-inch chambers. The Model 12 Duck Gun had 3-inch chambers.

Model 12s had especially slick actions. I always marveled at the pump gun shooting of two members at my gun club. John Schoen shot 870s, Paul McConville shot the 28-gauge Model 12 at skeet. They would break the first bird. Standing behind either man I never heard the pumping action. That sound was lost in the reverberation of the first shot. Those two pump gunners were that fast. With no pump-action noise, the second bird would break. To me this seemed magical.

(left) A Winchester Pigeon-Grade Skeet Model 12. Photo: Guns International

(below)Note the skilled checkering on this Pigeon-Grade Model 12.

The author getting ready to shoot a 20-gauge Ithaca Model 37.

(below) The Ithaca's most familiar feature is the ejection/loading port at the bottom of the receiver.

ITHACA MODEL 37

The Ithaca Model 37, another pump gun, was one of many designs by John Browning. Remington had bought Browning's patent, or at least the right to make that design. In 1917 Remington made it in 20-gauge only and called it the Model 17 (for the year of its introduction). By 1937, two patents on the Remington Model 17 were expiring. That's when Ithaca jumped on the pump-gun bandwagon. With the Great Depression hanging on, 1937 wasn't ideal timing for Ithaca. But after World War II, 37s started getting out of the gate with gusto. By 1963 the books showed 1 million had been sold. By 2003 the company had produced 2 million.

Ithaca has not been without its financial problems. The company has changed hands many times. The guns are now being produced in Sandusky, Ohio, and high-quality pump guns they are. The originals were typified by rolled-on engraving — a flushing duck/ marsh scene on the receiver's left side, flushing pheasants on the right with a pointing setter in an upland scene. If there are any aspects that typify the Ithaca 37, they would be bottom-ejection, light weight and slickness of the action.

MOSSBERG MODEL 500

The basic Model 500 pump shotgun from Mossberg was introduced in 1960 with a single-action slide bar. When Remington's patent on its dual-action bar expired in 1970, Mossberg incorporated that feature into this shotgun. The 500 and its many iterations have been sold all over the world. Production numbers total over 10 million and counting. Militaries and police departments in 76 countries use or have used the model 500.

From a cost standpoint, the 500 is very inexpensive. Mossberg's Maverick model, made just across the border in Mexico, costs even less. The 500 is easy to clean and

Mossberg celebrated its 10-millionth Model 500 with this very exceptional high-grade gun.

(top) The Model 500 is one of the most popular shotguns in the world.

(above) This young lady is set to flush a bird with her Model 500 at the ready.

intended for use in harsh conditions. These days most models have receivers drilled and tapped for the addition of some type of rear sight or scope. Barrels interchange easily. The receiver is made of aluminum, so 500 pumps are light. Action bars are of steel.

Like the model 500, the beefed-up version — the 835 Ulti-Mag — was the first shotgun designed for the then-new Federal 12-gauge 3½-inch Magnum, both introduced in 1988. The 835 uses overboring to reduce recoil and improve patterns. The 835 has the same internal boring as a 10-gauge shotgun. With its steel receiver, the 835 is heavier than the 500. Both the many 500 and 835 versions are hard-working and can take all the punishment serious shotgunners can dish out.

REMINGTON MODEL 1100

When it comes to American-made semi-auto shotguns, the Remington 1100 is undoubtedly at the head of its class. Introduced in 1963, the 1100 replaced the company's Model 58 — the first ever gas-operated autoloader. The 1100 was an instant success because of its outstanding handling qualities. Further, it was also very reliable — probably the most reliable semi-auto to that time.

> **WHAT CERTAINLY TOOK THE 1100 OVER THE TOP WAS ITS RECOIL-TAMING ASPECT. ... BECAUSE OF THE GAS OPERATION, RECOIL WAS STRETCHED OUT OVER A LONGER PERIOD. THAT PERIOD WAS ONLY MILLI-SECONDS, BUT A HUGE DIFFERENCE RESULTED IN FELT RECOIL.**

What certainly took the 1100 over the top was its recoil-taming aspect. The true recoil with the 1100 is the same as, say, a pump gun or double gun of the same weight and shooting the same shells. But it was "felt" recoil shotgunners were looking for. How did the 1100 reduce felt recoil? Pretty simple. Because of the gas operation, recoil was stretched out over a longer period. That period was only milliseconds, but a huge difference resulted in felt recoil. Today a high percentage of semi-autos, no matter where produced, use this or a similar gas-operated system.

Introduced in 12 gauge, a year later in 1964 a 16 gauge and 20 bore were offered. The 16 was never a big seller — in the 1100 or most any shotgun design, whether pump, semi-auto, side-by-side or over/under. For years, the 20-gauge 1100 was built on the 12/16-gauge frame and was heavier than today's 20. Years after its introduction, the 20-gauge 1100 was built on a smaller and lighter 20-gauge frame. Serious clay target buffs still look for the original, heavier version as most shooters are recoil conscious, pounding thousands of rounds downrange at clay each year.

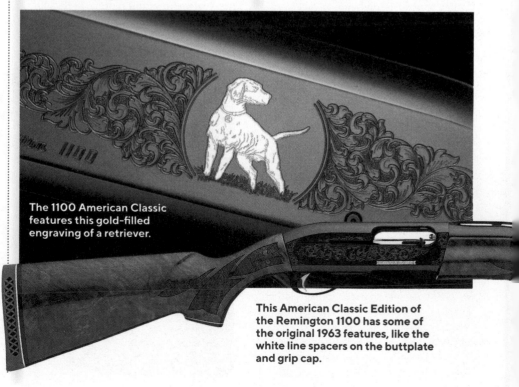

The 1100 American Classic features this gold-filled engraving of a retriever.

This American Classic Edition of the Remington 1100 has some of the original 1963 features, like the white line spacers on the buttplate and grip cap.

A .410 version came on the scene in 1969, and a Matched Pair .410 and 28 in 1970. There have been many, many 1100 models over the years, from 3-inch Magnums to the 11-87 series. It is still being produced today, and it is still sell-

A quartet of Parkers are given a break on a woodcock hunt. Photo: Art Wheaton

(right) Nothing serious. Just a brier scratch — one of the hardships of woodcock hunting. His double is a 28-gauge Parker.

ing, despite inroads from gas-operated models made overseas.

PARKER

No top shotgun discussion could ever take place without serious coverage of America's Golden Boy side-by-side, the Parker. Production started way back in 1867 — the blackpowder era. Eventually these side-by-sides were made in all gauges — and I mean all; 8, 10, 12, 14, 16, 20, 28 and .410. Yes, even 14 gauge.

Wouldn't you love to have one of those in mint condition? Sell it and you could probably buy a new house! Most Parkers, even with Damascus barrels, still bring mighty dollars on the used market.

In 1888 Parker introduced what might have been the first hammerless side-by-side. Parker also made single-barrel trap

guns — not many, so these are much sought after by collectors, and there are thousands of Parker collectors. The smallest gauge Parkers are very much in demand on the used market. Further there are many grades, plus those that were specially made for individual customers.

The basic grade was the Trojan, which lacked engraving and came with extractors. Grades above the Trojan featured increased levels of engraving, quality of wood and ejectors. The pick of the litter, if you could find one in this latter day, would be the A1-Special. Fewer than 80 were made, and if you find one in very good condition or better be prepared to spend six figures.

Before World War II, Remington bought the rights to produce Parker shotguns. But the war soon started, and Remington only made a few. Years later Remington brought the Parker back in a super-high grade that retailed for $50,000. These were made by Tony Galazan's Connecticut Shotgun Manufacturing Company.

A.H. FOX

The entry-level Fox was the Sterlingworth. From there the grades went upward — the AE, BE, CE, DE, etc. Mainly these grades increased in price and value due to more and intricate engraving. Nash Buckingham shot one of the first Fox doubles with 3-inch chambers

John Taylor with his original Super Fox. The mallards were taken in one of Nash Buckingham's favorite duck haunts: Beaver Dam in northwest Mississippi, just south of Memphis, Tennessee.

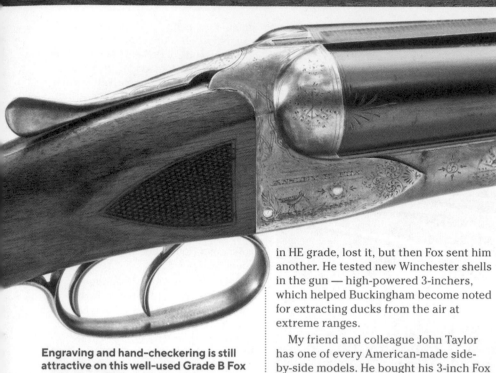

Engraving and hand-checkering is still attractive on this well-used Grade B Fox made circa 1910.

in HE grade, lost it, but then Fox sent him another. He tested new Winchester shells in the gun — high-powered 3-inchers, which helped Buckingham become noted for extracting ducks from the air at extreme ranges.

My friend and colleague John Taylor has one of every American-made side-by-side models. He bought his 3-inch Fox because it still had the tag on it from the gun shop in Memphis where Buckingham worked from time to time. Taylor wondered if Nash had put his hands on that one, perhaps while showing it to a customer. Taylor has both 3 and 2 3/4-inch versions. He shoots this unique duo regularly.

There are plenty of Fox doubles up for grabs on various Internet auction sites. Connecticut Shotgun has its own version of the A.H. Fox. Not inexpensive, these are made exactly like the originals. Three grades are offered by Connecticut Shotgun: CE, XE and DE, the first starting at $19,500. Years back Fox billed its shotgun as "The Finest Gun in the World." Today Connecticut Shotgun hails its A.H. Fox as having "The Finest Craftmanship in the World."

WINCHESTER MODEL 21

At a Remington writer's seminar in Wyoming, one of the side trips during that long weekend was a trip to the Winchester Museum in Cody. There were many great Winchester shotguns on

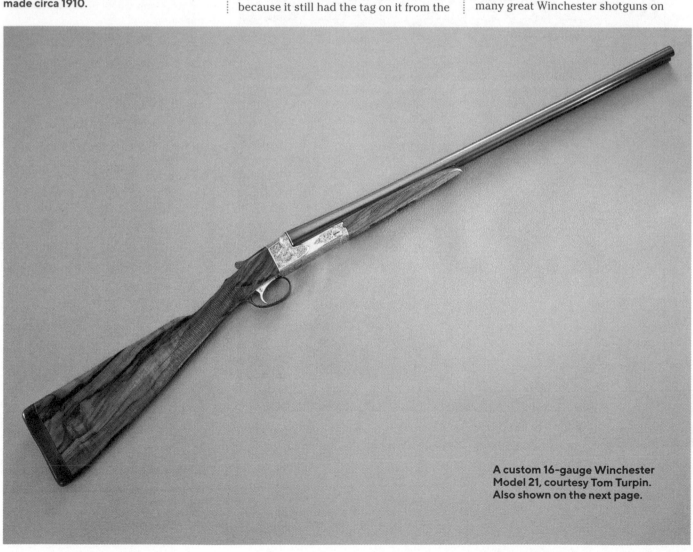

A custom 16-gauge Winchester Model 21, courtesy Tom Turpin. Also shown on the next page.

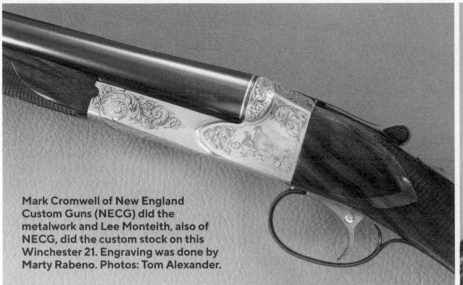

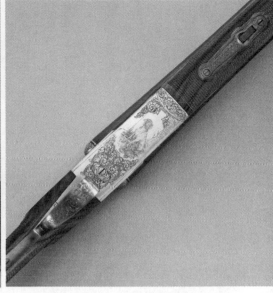

Mark Cromwell of New England Custom Guns (NECG) did the metalwork and Lee Monteith, also of NECG, did the custom stock on this Winchester 21. Engraving was done by Marty Rabeno. Photos: Tom Alexander.

display there, but the one I remember most was a Model 21 side-by-side in .410. It was ornately engraved, wore beautiful wood and was under heavy glass — displayed vertically and turning. It was a shotgun that would never be taken into the brambles.

But lots of Model 21s have seen the brambles and worse. One of my grouse hunting buddies, Leonard Reeves, owned several 21s and he hunted with them all. This double gun was almost handmade — one reason they are so cherished today by collectors.

The receiver is longer than most side-by-sides, so there's a little more engraving room, though few 21s ever saw the engraver's tools. They were made in 12, 16, 20, 28 and .410 — the smaller gauges being the rarest. Manufactured from 1931 to about 1960, even the latter 21s are 60 years old. The Winchester Custom Shop made a few during the '60s, '70s and later. Plus, the 21s are still being produced and sold through Connecticut Shotgun. Prices there start at about $15,000.

L.C. SMITH

Dubbed as the only American-made sidelock side-by-side (until Connecticut Shotgun's A-10 American), this L. C. Smith is often called the "Elsie," mimicking the first two letters in the company name. Lyman Cornelius Smith started the company in about 1880, but by the

The author with a handsome customized L.C. Smith.

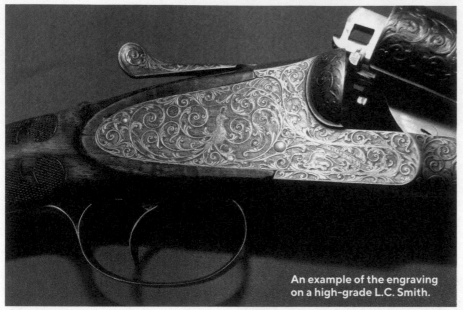

An example of the engraving on a high-grade L.C. Smith.

Financial woes were a part of L.C. Smith from almost the beginning to its end. But if you own an L.C. Smith today, count yourself lucky. You own a significant part of American shotgun history.

The "Elsie" was one of the first American double guns to incorporate ejectors, as opposed to extractors. It did this way back in 1892. Many grades were offered: Field, Ideal, Trap, Olympic, Deluxe, Specialty, Monogram, Premier, Eagle and Crown — not necessarily in escalating order. Regarding the higher grades, those sidelocks offered lots more room for engravers to show their art.

RUGER RED LABEL

Now to move to over/under double guns. Like the Remington Model 17, which was introduced in 20 gauge, Bill Ruger rolled out his Red Label over/un-

time this full sidelock was born he was already out of the gun industry and was making waves with a guy named Corona in the newly invented typewriter business.

The L. C. Smith was finely made — even the internal parts were well-polished. The receiver, fore-end iron and all the metal parts were time-consuming to make. This made the shotgun more expensive than the other side-by-sides of that era, but ardent sportsmen, like grouse and waterfowl hunters, were willing to pay the few extra dollars. Unfortunately, in 1910 not many Americans had the extra dollars to spend.

(above) A grouse is about to flush and this hunter is ready with a 28-gauge Ruger. The author was a big fan of the Red Label and owned models in all three gauges, 12, 20 and 28.

Ruger's Red Label was in production from 1977 to 2011.

der also in 20 gauge, hitting the market in 1977. His idea, as with all the Ruger guns, was to make the Red Label of high quality but at an affordable price. The original price was only $480. While the Red Label was a dandy over/under for the money, even more important was the gun's great looks. The appearance of the receiver and the style of the wood stock and fore-end were, to this writer's eyes, very good.

The first 20-gauge Red Labels wore blued-steel receivers. That material was eventually exchanged for stainless steel.

It also had the second-best safety idea on any double — the switch on the top tang, which you pushed right or left for barrel selection, then forward to fire. (The Remington model 3200 O/U had the best safety: when the selector lever was centered it was on safe; you moved that lever right or left for barrel selection to fire.) The 12-gauge Red Label arrived in 1979. The 28 gauge, built on its own smaller-size receiver, came out in 1994. In my view this was the best hunting Red Label of all and I owned all three gauges. The 28 Red Label was a grouse gun I

carried frequently.

The Red Label could be had with pistol or straight grip. I've seen few of the latter. Prices kept escalating as Ruger found it difficult to produce this high-quality gun at such low prices. By 2000 and a bit beyond, prices at retail were around $2,000 — a big difference compared to the $480 intro. Sales began to slump. In 2013 the "New" Red Label was introduced at $1,399. Despite cost savings by new production processes, Ruger could not make money on the Red Label. Production ended about 18 months later. These great-looking O/Us are readily available on the used market. As a side note, Ruger also made a side-by-side dubbed the Gold Label from 2002 to 2008. Again, production costs were too high, and it was taken out of production with very few made.

KOLAR

While many shotguns can be used in both hunting and various competitions, the Kolar, made in Racine, Wisconsin, is strictly a clay target gun, designed exclusively for trap, skeet, sporting clays, 5-Stand and ZZ birds. When the Kolar was introduced in the 1990s it was

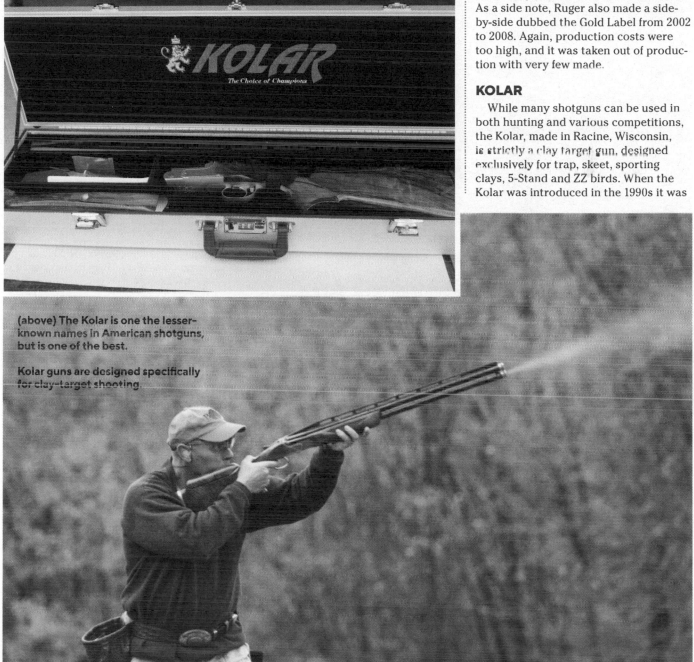

(above) The Kolar is one the lesser-known names in American shotguns, but is one of the best.

Kolar guns are designed specifically for clay-target shooting.

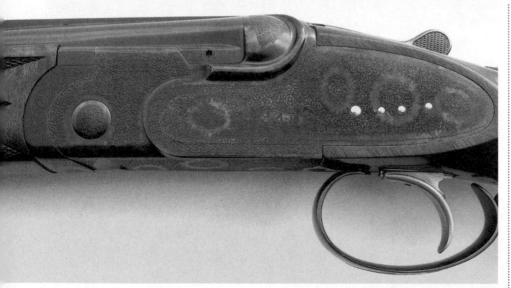

(above) The Inverness is one of the top-of-the-line models from Connecticut Shotgun Manufacturing Co. It's offered only in 20 gauge.

(left) The intricate engraving on the author's A-10 American sidelock.

the thicker receiver concept.

There are no underlocking lugs. Barrels pivot on trunnions. Two round bolts protrude from the receiver face to engage matching milled-out areas adjacent to the top barrel. Dual recoil lugs add to the strength of the lockup system, which is somewhat like the Boss over/under design of yesteryear. Of course, the thicker receiver is a major reason for the Kolar's strength. Everything about the Kolar spells strong. Don Mainland, the gun's original designer says, "I overbuild everything." When it comes to American-made competition shotguns, Kolar has captured the market.

CONNECTICUT SHOTGUN

As Kolar is a relative upstart in America-made shotguns, Connecticut Shotgun Manufacturing Co. in New Britain, Connecticut got its figurative barrel rolling a few years later. Its over/

named the Kolar Competition. These days, with even more specialty built into this over/under, various models are called the Max Sporting, the Max Trap and the Max Skeet.

These serious shotguns are seen increasingly in all three target sports, including receiving numerous laurels in the winner's circle. What makes the Ko-

lar tick? It is one beefy smoothbore with wide receiver walls. Initial criticisms revolved around the added weight because of the thicker receivers. More and more gun designers are coming around to this heavier receiver concept — as such a design puts more weight between the hands, and this helps with gun balance. The relatively new Perazzi Hi Tech uses

under shotgun models didn't arrive until this decade, but now there are three: The Inverness, the A-10 American and now the Revelation. This trio is not only U.S.-made — these O/Us are handmade. There's no assembly line in New Britain.

Where can you buy a handmade shotgun these days? Maybe England but be prepared to mortgage your house and wait two years. Spain would be another consideration for handmade. As in England, Spain's choices are limited to side-by-sides for the most part. Such double guns have merit and a following, but compared to over/under sales they are a very distant second. For most Americans buying double guns it's the over/under hands down.

The Inverness! A round-body O/U, the Inverness name came from Scotland where the round body was born, though in a side-by-side. Lockup is standard for most over/unders built these days. Barrels pivot on trunnions, a bolt moves forward from the bottom of the receiver to engage lugs milled into the base of the monobloc. Dual recoil lugs add to the strength.

The Inverness is a hunting gun, 20-gauge only and weighs a tad over 6 pounds. There are 28- and 30-inch barrels, bone charcoal casehardening of the receiver and other metal parts, nicely engraved, plus other features many buyers want as well as add-on options. The just-announced Revelation model is a dead ringer for the Inverness, mechanically identical, without engraving and other Inverness features at a much-reduced price.

The A-10 American was introduced between the Inverness and the Revelation. Connecticut Shotgun makes other models, like exact duplicates of the Winchester Model 21, the A. H. Fox in several grades and a host of others. I consider the A-10 American to be this company's crowning achievement. It is a full sidelock, handmade, initially offered in 20 gauge, but now available in most other gauges. To me it is spectacular, sporting fine engraving all over the receiver and sidelocks, bone charcoal casehardening, gold-washed internal parts and more. You simply can't buy a handmade gun anywhere for the prices of these three beauties.

Outstanding shotguns are available from many parts of the world, but the 12 described here are all American-made. They are also rugged, dependable and good looking.

★ ★ ★ ★ **A Tribute to Nick Sisley** ★ ★ ★ ★
BY JON R. SUNDRA

HARRIS D. "NICK" SISLEY
1937 - 2019

Nick Sisley and I met quite by chance some 45 years ago in a restaurant in Coudersport, Potter County, Pennsylvania. We were both living in the greater Pittsburgh area at the time and were both fledgling gun writers. We were in the area shooting groundhogs — they were plentiful back then, and we had stopped for lunch in town. I can't recall how we actually contacted each other in that restaurant, but we did. What followed was a lifelong friendship with one of the best human beings I've ever known.

Nick never had a bad thing to say about anybody, ever. And, in turn, I've never heard a bad thing said about Nick. Writing-wise, he was primarily a shotgun guy; he forgot more than I'll ever know about 'em. Whenever I had a question about smoothbores, he had the answer. His knowledge was immense, and his wingshooting experience unmatched. On dove shoots alone Nick made 52 trips to Argentina and Uruguay.

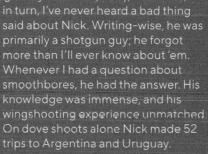

One day in 1987 we were in Sonora, Mexico, on a dove shoot, the guest of the outfitter who also owned a golf course and who put us up in one of the cottages there on the course. To make a long story short, we had several hours to waste before the afternoon shoot, so Nick suggested I try my hand at golf. I had caddied a little when I was a kid, but I never actually played the game. Nick had been playing since high school. One round of golf and I was hooked. 'Til the day he died, I chided him that I'd never forgive him for that.

Several years later Nick had the good sense to give up the game and took up flying. I, however, was not imbued with that same wisdom, and I've been plagued to this day with the golf game — that most frustrating of pursuits.

Last year proved extremely fortuitous for me because I had the opportunity to spend quite a bit of time with Nick. In May, we traveled to Cinque Terre, Florence and Venice together, and in September to Santorini and Athens. The accompanying photos — one taken at an Irish pub in Athens, the other in my kitchen of Nick playing with my Siamese cat, Sidney — may be the last ones taken of him.

Nick died at home peacefully on Feb. 6, 2019, after a long bout with cancer. The industry, and this old gun writer, are vastly diminished by his passing. See ya' soon, old friend.

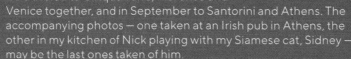

ELEGANCE
of Purpose

Finding original 19th-century actions suitable for remodeling as performed to the Ballard No. 6 (top) in .32-40 is now difficult and expensive, but reproductions of original actions are better. This Steve Earle Wesson No. 1 has a Krieger Barrel in .45-90, and is far stronger than the 19th-century Ballard. The modern steels used in today's actions and barrels are far safer in the long run, and the results just as pleasing to the eye, as is performance on the range.

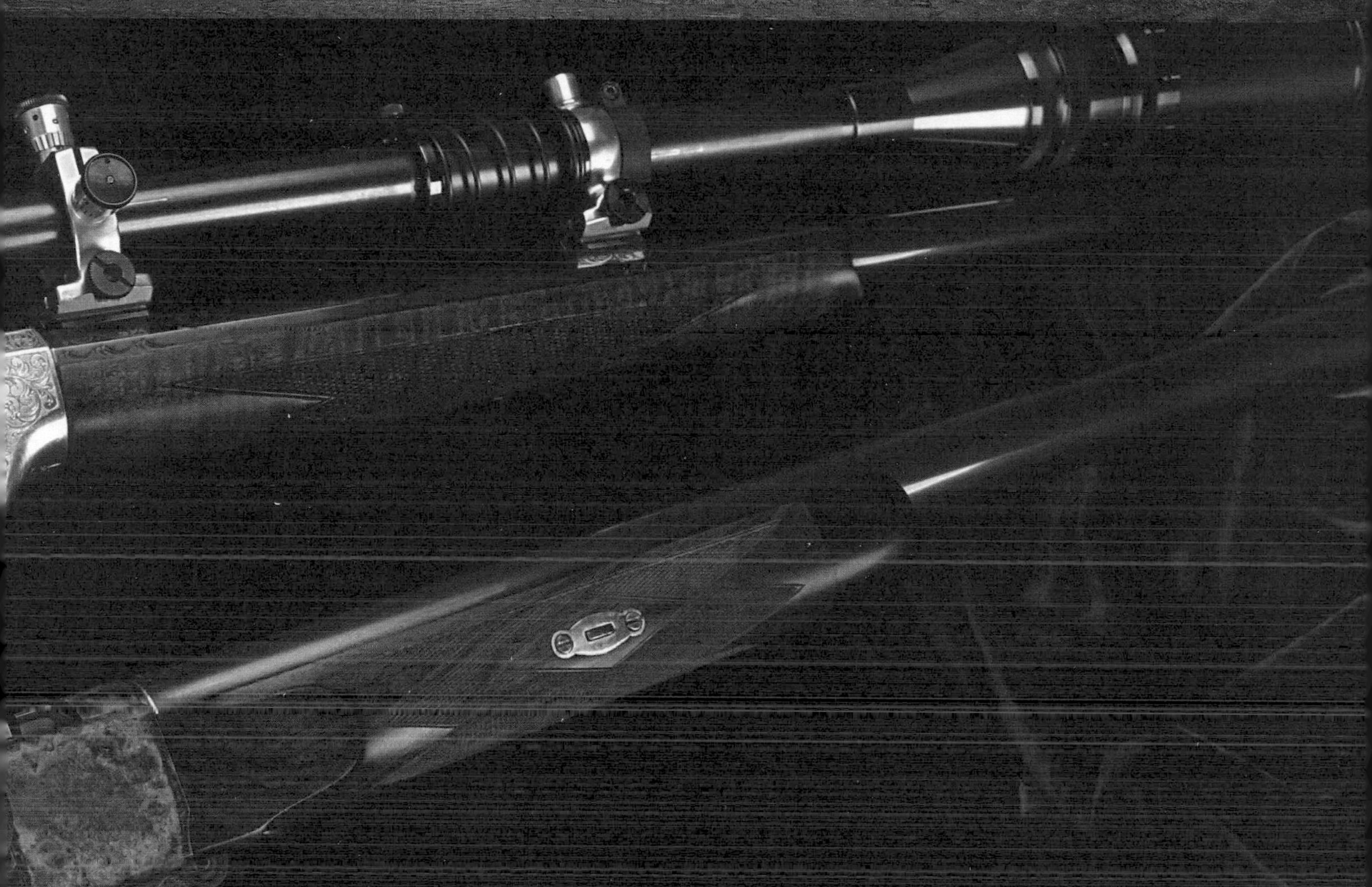

No other arm focuses marksmanship skill better, and with such incomparable beauty, as does a single-shot rifle

BY JEFF JOHN

As long as men appreciate the simplicity of firing one good shot at a time through arms richly embellished with fine engraving, extravagantly figured wood hand-rubbed with oil, endowed by the wild no-two-alike vivid patterns of traditional color case-hardening, subtle, satiny, rust blue and bright, vivid peacock blue, the single-shot rifle will always rise to become the centerpiece of a collection. Afield, the single-shot rifle focuses the hunter's mind on the shot like no other arm while providing contemplative beauty while he awaits his game.

The single-shot rifles under discussion here are the ones that blossomed with the creation of the metallic cartridge after our Civil War, utilizing falling or tilting breechblocks, and featuring two-piece wooden stocks, rather than today's single-shot turn-bolt rifles in solid one-piece synthetic stocks, or a poorly maintained self-loader with a clogged gas system. We'll leave the other rifles for a turn of the page of this Gun Digest, and simply recommend a good scrub behind the ears for the semis that aren't.

LET'S NOT ARGUE ABOUT WHICH SINGLE-SHOT RIFLE MECHANISM IS BETTER THAN ANOTHER. EVERY ONE HAS UNIQUE STRENGTHS AND WEAKNESSES, ALL OF WHICH ADD TO THEIR CONSIDERABLE CHARM (OR PUT A THUMB IN YOUR EYE, DEPENDING ON YOUR POINT OF VIEW).

Let's not argue about which single-shot rifle mechanism is better than another. Every one has unique strengths and weaknesses, all of which add to their considerable charm (or put a thumb in your eye, depending on your point of view). For me, the bug bit when I saw the 1969 Gun Digest cover with an engraved Ruger No. 1 at a friend's house. The fever would take longer to hit — almost 20 years. When it did, I weighed the advantages of the actions by reading James J. Grant's Single Shot Rifles. It's still the best overview of single-shots.

To sum up the whole game simply, accuracy will be found in the barrel, and any single-shot action will deliver the bullets on target if it breaches up good and tight with a well-made barrel and a tight stock. Some are stronger than others, yet all provide vast potential for beauty on top of accuracy within their strength parameters. Better, each one gives us a pleasurable way to slow down life and enjoy a relaxing day at the range. If you gravitate to original 19th century arms, sticking with blackpowder in a suitable caliber will give you an arm capable of taking the world's largest animals, or make targets worthy of framing. If you gravitate to the 20th and 21st centuries preferring smokeless powder firing high-velocity bullets, there are even more choices. Whichever you choose, the single-shot rifle brings about a different way of going about hunting and target shooting.

THE ZEN OF SHOOTING

Younger people are usually annoyed by the slow-paced action firing one shot at a time, finding more entertainment haphazardly rending the earth with bullets. But as people age, they usually find a single shot allows them to better enjoy the Zen of shooting. Placing one shot exactly where you desire, and repeating as soon as you are comfortable doing so is highly relaxing. There is nothing else to concentrate on except sight picture and trigger squeeze. Making the gun safe is as simple as opening the action and withdrawing its single cartridge. There's

The J. M. Marlin Ballard No. 6 Schuetzen action offers a rich canvas for the engraver (Phil Quigley did this one based on an original pattern) and is showcased by silver plating. Silver not only looks good, the engraving takes on depth as it tarnishes, and silver provides lubricity for the action. This one is wonderfully smooth and silent in operation.

If you look carefully in the center of Mike Gouse's engraving on the Wesson No. 1, you will see the author's cat peeking out from the center. He gets into everything, seemingly. Engraving should be fun. Note also the fore-end is fitted off the receiver just the thickness of a dollar bill. Free floating the wood off the face of the receiver helps accuracy, and it doesn't take much.

Steve Earle's Wesson No. 1 has modern improvements such as a radius in the corners for the breechblock to ride in rather than the square corners of originals. This reduces the chances of cracking, operates more smoothly and is one reason why modern-made actions are superior for a custom rifle. Rather have an Alex Henry? Go ahead and make one. Henry sued Wesson and forced him to stop making No. 1 rifles because of their similarities.

The action of Marlin Ballards is a heavy 2 pounds, 10 ounces, moving the center of gravity back, and balance very nicely between the hands, even with heavy barrels. This Ballard Pacific No. 5 has the optional pistol grip and a 32-inch Ron Long barrel in .40-65 Sharps Straight (aka .40-70 SS). The reproduction 6X Malcolm Telescope is by RHO. Currently, only MVA and Hi Lux offer Malcolms. Another key Ballard advantage is a through-bolt for the buttstock. Rifles with two-piece stocks are inherently less accurate than those with one-piece stocks, unless they have a through bolt. Jeff's Ballard suffers from "lever droop," a common malady. It could use a new link, and Distant Thunder BPCR is now making a link set, one of which should do the trick. DT makes a variety of other hard-to-find single-shot rifle parts, too.

Somehow, all of the author's Ballards wound up scoped. The late-model Marlin Firearms Co. 3PG .22 LR (top) has an original Marbles tang sight in addition to the MVA Lyman A5 reproduction. The early J. M. Marlin Ballard No. 6 in .32–40 (bottom) was barreled by Bo Clerke in the beginning of this century, and now sports a 20X Unertl Programmer over a Jim Kelley Vernier tang and Riflesmith windgauge front. The Ballard falling block actions, whether cast or forged, have always been highly regarded for target shooting because they do something quite simple and well: As the breechblock is raised, it tilts and cams the cartridge into the chamber with the same amount of pressure the same way each time. Headspace is consistent, and remains so for a lot of shooting. Few other actions achieve this. Both guns and calibers are very relaxing to shoot, offering superb accuracy and little recoil — a perfect recipe for an enjoyable day.

no brass to pick up, no rounds lurk deep in hidden cavities within the action, and few if any buttons or switches require a push.

The adrenaline rush of fast-paced competition with its heart-racing action is usually won by the young, but in the relaxed atmosphere of the single-shot rifle, many elderly folks can shoot competitively well into their twilight years with younger folks. But whatever your age, a slow day concentrating just on accurate shooting can be as relaxing as it is rewarding, since you re-enforce good trigger and sighting habits.

In the scheme of things, a single-shot rifle is about the same price as any other elite arm carefully crafted, but one that lends itself best to higher embellishment. Once in hand, single-shots are exceptionally easy to feed, even if you favor obscure calibers from bygone eras. Once you have the brass, dies and a mold or two, you'll be shooting for pennies, since you really can have just as much fun shooting 20 rounds carefully placed on the target in the same amount of time 200 rounds once was barely satisfactory.

Which brings us to the fun and frustration of single-shots. I've never been able to afford the ones I want, since I favor ones more or less unique. Cost of such desirable originals is astronomical. An 1874 Sharps remodeled by J. P. Gemmer,

The Marlin Firearms Co. Ballard 3PG Model .22 is very similar to the 3F (Fine Gallery Model) and was likely just a parts cleanup at the very end of Ballard production, since they were never cataloged by Marlin, but only by a distributor. Its key characteristic is a rifle buttplate on a pistol grip stock, instead of the 3F's small Schuetzen plate. This one was stocked with a set from Crossno's Gun Shop. Original Ballard .22s are in .22 Short and Long, by the way, the Ballard being discontinued before the .22 Long Rifle was introduced. This one has a correct length and profile barrel for a 3F/3PG at 26 inches, but in .22 Long Rifle. Longer and heavier than barrels used for sporting versions, balance is about perfect, although the rifle's weight is 9 pounds, 9 ounces scoped.

or the Freund Bros., is the elusive Holy Grail for me, and one I still don't possess. Even original plain 1874 Sharps rifles have been either too well-used or priced far beyond my means (sometimes both). So my Sharps urge was satisfied with the 1878 Borchardt model, and I built a mid-range from a military action somebody else had dismantled, and purchased a nice hunting model for less than a quarter of what a comparable sidehammer Sharps cost.

Hunting rifles were bread-and-butter tools and had to work far from civilization. Remington Rolling Blocks (top) saw much action in the Old West, and was one of the first rifles to see extensive customization for the new jobs at hand. Carlos Gove of Denver was one such gunsmith, and he modified the Remington by adding an underlever, wiping rod and sights. The author and gunsmith John King of Montana built this one in .45-90 Sharps with a Badger Barrel. The Ballard Pacific No. 5 was built for the West and had a wiping rod added in addition to set triggers. This one replicates one that left the factory with a Malcolm telescope. The late Al Perry, who owned the original rifle, graciously sent the author a tracing of the original stock. Single-shot aficionados are a friendly lot. The original rifle was a .45-100, but Jeff acted almost sensibly by having Ron Long chamber the rifle in .40-65 Sharps Straight. One weakness of Ballards is primary extraction is short, which is why most Ballards were chambered for cartridges with plenty of body taper. Thus the long, straight .40 Sharps has to be plucked out, rather than falling out. While the wiping rod was once essential, they tend to walk out under recoil and will disrupt accuracy.

I still don't have an 1874 Sharps, but someday I will. I should just order a Shiloh or C. Sharps in the meantime, but my style and caliber preferences keep changing mid stride. But someday…

Having some basic gun making skills allowed me to build some interesting rifles from parts, since I could let the treasury refill while I was doing something else pertinent to the build. Some projects drag on for years as the better barrel makers and gunsmiths have long lead times. Sometimes all that did was encourage me to greater finery!

Ballard rifles became a favorite, but none of mine are original. They were built from actions, and comprise a hunting, target and gallery model. Desirable originals (there were probably fewer than 37,000 ever made) are beyond my finances. Ones I could afford were in models or calibers of little interest to me.

The days when you could find suitable actions have paused for now. If you think of gun collecting as a living, breathing thing, the interest in single shots was like a deep inhale over the last 35 years that vacuumed up all rifles and actions, but the exhale as generations pass or interests change is causing them to resurface.

For us cranks starting with gun bits, parts are a perennial problem. If you're lucky, you'll have a friend like Tom, who has the uncanny ability to look at a 55-gallon barrel of scrap metal, shout with glee, and plunge his hand deep inside and pluck out the plum (whether it's a Winchester set trigger or a '56 Chevy headlight bezel). It was always fun going to gun shows with him! Otherwise, be careful before buying a "parts gun." The hunt for parts is fun, but are catch as catch can. Patience is required, and the search can't be reliably hired out.

HUNTING OR TARGET?

Why you need a single-shot is always the fun part of the equation, too. I discovered I "needed" hunting and target models. This is a large requirement, since target games are as plentiful as the types of game. I found hunting models in .22 Long Rifle, .40-65 SS, .45-70 and .45-90 Sharps fill the bill. For targets, the .22 LR, .32-40, .45-70 and .45-90 equally satisfy. So I'm covered for whatever Walter Mitty

hat winds up on my head on a given day. Other calibers always beckon, and a .38-55 Stevens 44-1/2 is in the works to fill the gap. For that one, I'll combine target and hunting. For now, anyway.

Most of these calibers are all blackpowder ones, and I stay with black most of the time. Dirty as it is, it is still a hoot to shoot, safer in original actions, and sometimes all you can use. In both Sharps Borchardts, for instance, the firing pin hole is so big, use of modest smokeless powder loads causes the primer to flow back just a little and cause difficulty opening the breechblock. Long articles on bushing the firing pin hole for these '78s have been written over the last 75 years or so, but I'll leave the actions alone and stay with black. In my factory original 1878, the throat is slightly enlarged to boot, and hard bullets over smokeless don't shoot well, on top of the action being hard to open. Soft bullets over blackpowder shoot well. The original's main detraction is the sights are vestigial at best, and I've resisted the temptation to "improve" them, too, since it is increasingly valuable as-is. Rifles in

good-plus original condition aren't cheap enough to monkey with anymore, but are if you build from parts, or choose among the excellent reproductions. Those you can wrench on to your heart's delight.

The Stevens 44-1/2, is one action both strong and versatile, with a small firing pin already. It will be equally pleasant shooting blackpowder or smokeless loads and my build in the works sports a Badger Barrel in .38-55. The caliber will handle either powder with aplomb. My .45-90 was built on a Remington Rolling Block No. 5 model, which was designed for smokeless powder and has a small firing pin. So far, I've only shot blackpowder from it, and it shoots black so well I haven't experimented with smokeless.

THE MILITARY MODELS

Accessible single-shots doubling as "shooting collectibles" are one of the many types made for domestic and foreign militaries. Best are U.S. Springfield Trapdoors, since ammunition components are readily available. Remington Rolling Blocks, once a staple

(above) The Remington/Gove underlever (top) addressed a problem unique to hunters in the Old West who very often reloaded ammunition in the field. Early dies neck sized only, and the shooter's thumb provided little leverage when closing the block to seat the cartridge if it didn't chamber freely. The underlever gave the necessary leverage in and out of the chamber. This was of little concern in military actions (bottom), since factory ammunition was used in the field.

(below) The 30-inch-barreled .45-70 Sharps Borchardt Mid-Range (top) weighs just 10 pounds, which meets the rules set by the NRA in the 1870s. The horn-paneled action has a Riflesmith reproduction Sharps Borchardt Tang base and staff along with a spirit level windgauge front. The Steve Earle Wesson No. 1 with a 34-inch .45-90 Krieger barrel weighs 12 pounds, 1.8 ounces with sights, which include a Jim Kelley Soule-style rear and MVA spirit level windgauge front. It might seem strange to have windage at both front and rear, but it can be necessary at extreme range if windy.

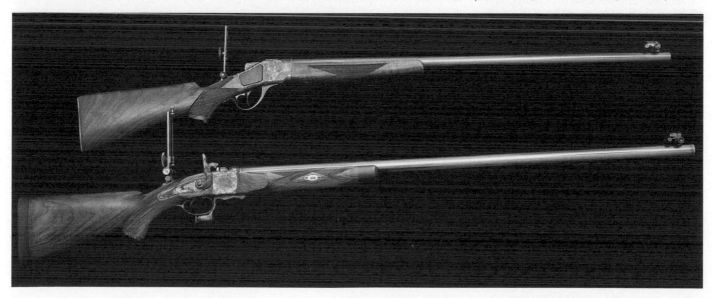

The Sharps Borchardt Mid-Range Target had a removable rear sight base screwed into a milled recess in the receiver. The Borchardt sight is unique in that a center wheel is rotated to adjust for range, using the staff as a ratchet rather than a long screw. Windage is adjusted at the front sight. Target Model 1878s had the receiver further lightened by machining the sides of the receiver and installing panels of lighter material such as wood, or in this case, buffalo horn.

catches to operate. After firing you cock the hammer, flip open the "trapdoor" and the cartridge case comes whizzing out.

Recoil of the U.S. M1881 load, with a 500-grain bullet over 70 grains of blackpowder (and the load the sights are regulated for), can become brutal shooting from the bench due to the design of the buttplate, a hangover from the Civil War. The recoil is perfectly acceptable standing upright. The original 405-grain rifle load is fine, and the carbine load of the 405-grain bullet over 55 grains of powder positively pleasant. Stick with blackpowder and cast bullets, and you'll be able to do some fine shooting.

The Martini-Henry, on the other hand, is one of the world's most boring single shots. This in no way diminishes its historical value! It's just you only pull down the lever, load a cartridge, pull up the lever and shoot, and perhaps fix bayonet. No, the Trapdoor is at the high end of operating fun, the Martini-Henry at the other end, and all the others somewhere in-between. Nevertheless, Martini actions are fast to use, strong and dependable. Facing 4,000 Zulus, the simple manual of arms would quickly become appreciated over the multiple machinations of the Trapdoor or the Snider (a design meant to convert England's P1853 Enfields from muzzleloaders to cartridge). You can add to the fun of the Martini at the range by shouting as loud as you can, "At 100 yards, volley fire PRESENT! … FIRE!" just before shooting. I'm sure no one will mind.

England's American-designed Snider has a much higher fun factor. You cock the hammer, flip over the breech to load, and after firing, cock the hammer, flip over and pull back on the breechblock extracting the cartridge so you can fish out the empty. Many Sniders are found in pretty good shape, and prices are still fairly reasonable.

One thing: While civilian models often have superb triggers, military arms have triggers only a drill sergeant could love. Their heavy pulls usually break crisp and clean, thankfully. Unless it's the .45-70, most military models will be chambered for cartridges now expensive and hard-to-find. But bewildering your friends with expert knowledge of obscure cartridges and other bits of arcana adds to the charm.

THE SINGLE-SHOT LIVES TODAY!

Winchester High and Low Wall reproductions from Browning/Winchester

of many of the world's armies, are relatively inexpensive, too, but are harder to load for. All can be found in various conditions from sublime to ridiculous, and many of the least expensive—Rolling Blocks in relic condition—have seen new life as custom sporters (such as the Gove Underlever pictured nearby).

Many old military single-shots can be found with pristine bores, good wood and are capable of excellent shooting, even if the gun's point-blank zero is apparently better suited for lobbing bullets at the moon than 100-yard groups. There is often no good fix for poor sights without considerable effort. But it doesn't mean you can't have fun shooting it once

you learn where it shoots (and learn to squint a bit to clear up the hazy sight picture, like I do with that old Borchardt sporter).

The U.S. M1884 Trapdoor with its Buffington rear sight is one exception, and it is designed for marksmanship. The point-blank setting is high, but upon raising the staff, the low setting is 200, and a peep is set into the leaf along with an open notch. The peep is just a teensy hole, but the front sight is also very fine, and combined, subtend an 8-inch bull's-eye at 100 yards well, and is capable of delivering fine groups. The Trapdoors have a high fun factor since there are a lot of manipulations and flipping of

(left)Sharps Model 1878 Sporting rifles (top) were often profiled the same as target model actions (below) but without the panels. The top tang of standard Borchardt rifles was machined integrally with the receiver and drilled and tapped for a conventional tang sight. Target models (bottom) had a separate tang as a base installed for the unique Vernier sight. Borchardt actions are uncommonly strong for the 1800s, and many have been turned into high-power varmint or hunting rifles, but require a small firing pin in a bushing to contain the higher pressures. Borchardts use a draw-bolt to attach the stock, giving them the foundation for accuracy. Both these rifles have the standard trigger, always considered another downcheck by custom makers, sin ce it is usually heavy and gritty, although sporting and target models are better than the more common military rifles used for high-power conversions. The rear trigger is an automatic safety pushed "on" as the breechblock is opened.

(below) U.S. military single-shot rifles can provide plenty of shooting fun. They shoot best with soft lead bullets over blackpowder, and later ones like the M1884 .45-70 (top) have sights delivering fine accuracy. Rolling Block military rifles abound in a variety of calibers. This New York Militia Model 1872 in .50-70 (middle) is one of the easier ones to find components for. Yes, the rear sight is backward. A clever gunsmith modified it for target shooting. The Springfields in .50-70 (here, bottom, a Model 1870) are fun to collect since many use Civil War parts, and subtle changes were made as the trapdoor system was perfected. This one has a lockplate dated 1863. Many .50-70 Springfields went buffalo hunting, since they were sold surplus after adoption of the .45-70 in 1873. Slings on the bottom two are from C&D Jarnigan.

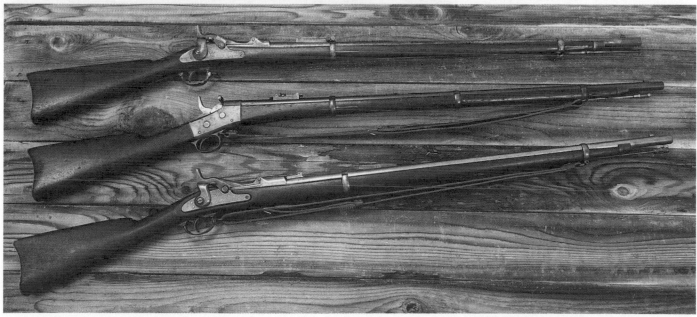

The U.S. Trapdoor's Buffington rear sight allows for very precise shooting with the 500-grain M1881 load and is adjustable for windage and elevation with range markings in 25-yard increments from 200 to 1,400 yards, and 100-yard increments out to 2,000 yards. Folded, most of these rifles shoot high. "R" on the upper right of the staff indicates the sight is for the "rifle" (carbine sights have "C"). Note the staff is on an angle to automatically adjust for the bullet's drift as the range increases.

come in a wide variety of modern smokeless and old-timey calibers, and the menu changes regularly. The modern Browning Arms Co. has kept a single-shot in the line for a long time, and it has always had an excellent reputation for accuracy. Today, under Fabrique Nationale, the Winchester-marked Model 1885 is similar to the one long sold by Browning and still made by Miroku in Japan. They are an excellent first choice in a single shot, featuring modern metallurgy with subtle design tweaks to better adapt them for today's high-performance cartridges, and are ready for optical sights.

Finely crafted Sharps 1874 rifles are available from C. Sharps and Shiloh Sharps in a wide variety of original and modern calibers. Italian reproductions of the 1874 Sharps and Remington Rolling Blocks, Springfield Trapdoors and High Walls from Pedersoli and Uberti are imported through Cimarron and others, but the caliber choice is very limited. C. Sharps also makes High Walls and Remington Hepburns, and the slimmer target model 1877 Sharps are available from both C. Sharps and Shiloh.

Currently, the Ruger No. 1 is only in limited editions each year. Specialty ones are available from distributors like Lipsey's and Talo in exotic calibers like .30-30 or .475 Ruger. The Ruger No. 1 once had a reputation for not always shooting well, but newer ones made in the 21st century shoot very well without any voodoo. I haven't done anything to my No. 1 in .405 Winchester except add a 1-3X Weaver (and shoot a hog). Hornady factory ammo delivers 1-inch 100-yard groups. Expensive new, used No. 1 rifles are reasonable, found in almost any caliber, and lend themselves to customization.

Savage discontinued the very reasonably priced Favorite (again) in .22 LR, .22 WMRF and .17 HMR. If one crops

up used, don't pass it by. The modern ones shoot very well, and are very lightweight. It's the perfect starter single shot for child or adult, and a true delight to carry afield for bunnies or squirrels. A reproduction Marbles Tang Sight is just the ticket to improve the sights, but requires drilling and tapping.

Thompson/Center wrote a whole new chapter on single-shot handgunning with the Contender. Today's T/C G2 Contender and Encore carry that tradition forward into the rifle realm as well, and they come in many useful calibers. They are very reasonably priced, and the interchangeable barrels keep down costs. For the budding experimenter, a barrel in one of J.D. Jones' calibers can't be beat, since you have all the pleasures of exotic reloading on top of shooting satisfyingly

small groups.

"KNOWING YOU HAVE BUT ONE ROUND MEANS NOT TAKING A SHOT WHERE THERE IS UNCERTAINTY. A PRACTICED SHOOTER CAN RELOAD A WINCHESTER 1885 OR RUGER NO. 1 ABOUT AS FAST AS WORKING A BOLT, BUT THAT'S NOT THE POINT. NOW THE GAME INCLUDES THE STALK, AND WORKING IN AS CLOSE AS POSSIBLE TO ENSURE A CLEAN, ONE-SHOT KILL."

For those wanting to reach out and touch animals at a distance, a rifle in a modern smokeless powder cartridge will

(left) This New York Militia Remington Rolling Block had a clever target sight grafted onto its coarse military rear. Turning the rear sight around allowed engraving of finer graduations on the blank underside of the staff. Adding a windgauge to the slider gave the shooter a sight more amenable for "military match" target shooting, the pleasure of which is somewhat dampened by a 6-pound military trigger pull.

(below) Stock Ruger No. 1s, such as the No .405 (top) are excellent introductions to the single-shot rifle and exotic calibers. One might encourage you to take another to the next level, such as the Ruger (bottom) extensively customized by gun maker Roger Renner. Removal of the fore-end's complex hanger system along with the ejector (this rifle extracts only) allows the fore-end to be slenderized significantly, which also pares weight to 6 pounds, 6 ounces. Elimination of the hanger simplified installation of the custom John Taylor Germanic-style octagon barrel in .338 Federal with integral rib (and has led to two-barrel sets). The theme for the engraving on this No. 1 Stalking Rifle is St. Hubertus, the patron saint of hunters.

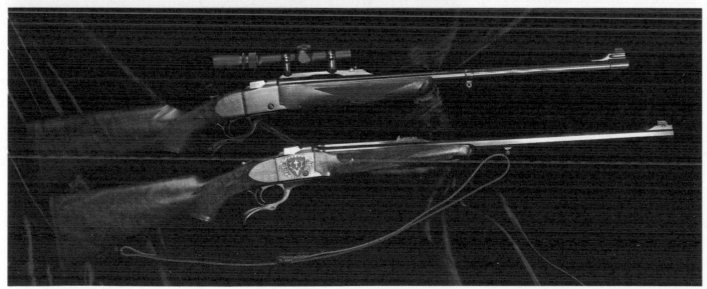

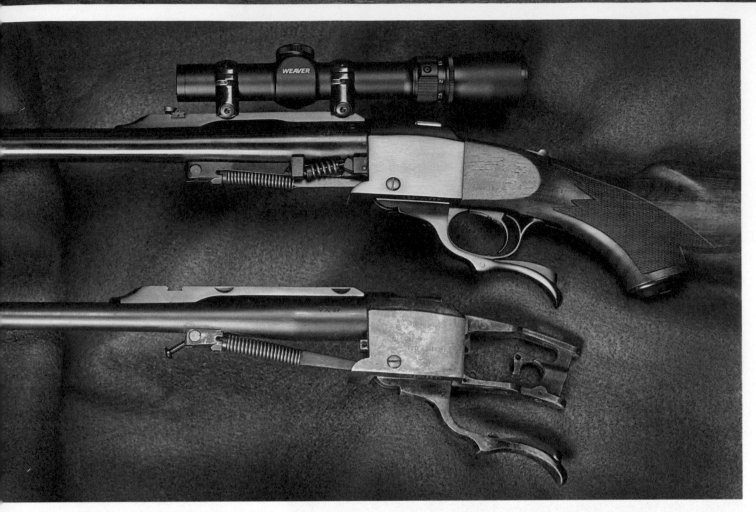

Gun maker Roger Renner gets a slim profile on the Ruger by eliminating the fore–end hanger entirely, and the fore-end now is attached to the barrel and free floated from the receiver. This also eliminates the ejector, and extracts only. Best choices for such a conversion are cartridges with plenty of body taper designed for lever actions and semi-autos, such as the 9x49 (.35 Remington) chosen for this one.

be best, since trajectory is substantially flatter than 19th century cartridges, but I would council thinking over your hunting strategy beforehand. Knowing you have but one round means not taking a shot where there is uncertainty. A practiced shooter can reload a Winchester 1885 or Ruger No. 1 about as fast as working a bolt, but that's not the point. Now the game includes the stalk, and working in as close as possible to ensure a clean, one-shot kill.

If you like the old timers, brass and dies are available for almost every one, sometimes reasonably priced, most often

not, though, since they entail odd bullet sizes and their large, capacious cases aren't made in a volume to keep prices down. Always ask Lee first, since it offers many obscure dies and molds. CH/4D is another great source, and if it doesn't list it, it's really obscure!

Almost any old-time cartridge can be fabricated with a little effort, and sometimes no effort. Custom loaders like Buffalo Arms offer many of these rounds as loaded ammunition, and while the tariff is high, one box might be enough. If it's fun, try handloading to satisfy future itches, and you'll have a start with properly formed brass, since Buffalo Arms often redraws obsolete brass from modern cases. The company has many molds for the old-timey bullets in their correct profiles, and diameters, too.

FINAL NOTES

I purposely didn't want to confuse the issue with pictures of groups, since the best groups only prove the loose nut behind the trigger was tight that day. All the rifles I've built have first-class barrels. The Ballards in .22 and .32 deliver

MOA and 1/2-MOA 100-yard groups, and sometimes better. The big bores, including the Ballard Pacific, Remington/Gove, both Sharps and Wesson deliver five-shot groups of 1-1/2 to 2-1/2 MOA at 100 yards. The Gove is a surprise, since I can shoot those small groups with open barrel sights!

Sighting systems are as varied as the rifles. The best Vernier tang sighting systems have finely tuned movements that would make a watchmaker proud, and will deliver the big, long bullets with consistency from 100 to 1,000 yards and beyond. They can cost as much or more than a good, modern telescopic sight, too. The reproduction scopes have much better optics than originals, and work well as long as you respect the fragility of their external adjustments. These sights are mechanical marvels all, and as fun to collect and study as the arms themselves. Even the simple barrel sight can deliver payloads accurately, and are fast to use and easy to adjust (for cave-men, anyway, since it usually involves a club and a stick of some sort).

I still have plans for an 1874 Sharps, if

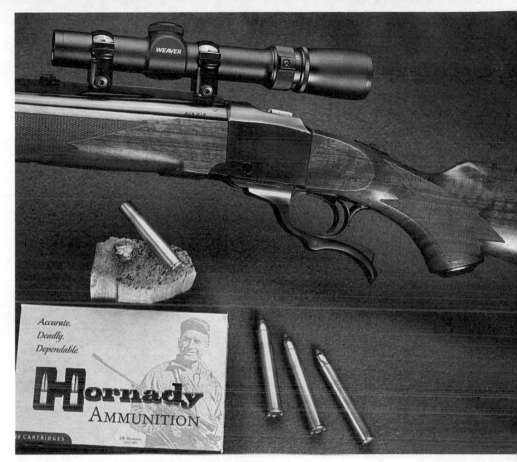

not my preferred Gemmer or Freund. I'll be satisfied with an early one from the late 1860s/early 1870s, a Hartford model with a 30-inch heavy barrel, straight stock with military butt in .50-70 Gov't of the type once made with leftover parts from the Civil War. I'm beginning to have quite a bit of respect for the 50-70's accuracy and abilities within the limits of its modest range, and barrel sights will be just fine. Why I haven't ordered it yet is the .44-77. It was there in the beginning, too, and I bounce between the two cartridges. The .50's edge is I have dies and brass. The .44's edge is I don't have one, and it gives me another caliber to play with. And better ranging. Oops! Better add a tang sight. You see my problem.

After all, both calibers were there at the start of the big buffalo-hunting era and racked up plenty of buffalo. It made me think about how many of today's climate-change acolytes who obsess over cow flatulence should also worship at the statue of Christian Sharps holding his eponymous rifle. Just think how much greenhouse gas the huge buffalo herds generated in the Old West. So much so, I think the motto for the Sharps Rifle should be: "Saving the World From Global Warming Since 1874."

One of the finest single-shots available today is the Ruger No. 1. This one, topped with a 1-3X Weaver, is in .405 Winchester, and has taken one 265-pound boar so far, with one shot of Hornady Factory 300-grain Soft Point (the recovered bullet weighs 207 grains). The single-shot rifle lends itself to limited runs in exotic calibers like the .405.

SOURCES

Brownells
200 South Front St.
Montezuma, IA 50171
(800) 741-0015
www.brownells.com

Buffalo Arms
660 Vermeer Court
Ponderay, ID 83852
(208) 263-6953
www.buffaloarms.com

C&H/4D Dies
711 N. Sandusky St.
Mt. Vernon, OH 43050
(740) 397-7214
www.ch4d.com

Cimarron Arms
P.O. Box 906
Fredericksburg, TX 78624
(830) 997-9090
www.cimarron-firearms.com

Dave Crossno Gun Stocks
23380 N. Anderson Road
Arcadia, OK 73007
(405) 396-8786
www.angelfire.com/ok5/crossnostocks

CPA Corp.
RR 2 Box 1012
Dingmans Ferry, PA 18328
(570) 828-1669
www.singleshotrifles.com

C. Sharps Arms
100 Centennial Drive
Big Timber, MT 59011
(406) 932-4353
www.csharpsarms.com

Distant Thunder BPCR
O'Hare Tool
P.O. Box 138
Niagara, WI 54151
(715) 251-3839
www.distantthunderbpcr.com

Graf & Sons
4050 S. Clark
Mexico, MO 65265
(573) 581-2266
www.grafs.com

C & D Jarnagin
113 North Fillmore St.
Corinth, MS 38834
(662) 287-4977
www.jarnaginco.com

Jeff John
www.jeff-john.com

Leatherwood Hi-Lux, Inc.
3135 Kashiwa St.
Torrance, CA 90505
(888) 445-8912
www.leatherwoodoptics.com

Lee Precision
4275 Highway U
Hartford, WI 53027
(262) 673-3075
www.leeprecision.com

Lyman
475 Smith St.
Middletown, CT 06457
(860) 632-2020
www.lymanproducts.com

Marble Arms
420 Industrial Park
P.O. Box 111
Gladstone, MI 49837
(906) 428-3710
www.marblearms.com

Montana Vintage Arms (MVA)
61 Andrea Drive
Belgrade, MT 59714
(406) 388-4027
www.montanavintagearms.com

RCBS
605 Oro Dam Blvd.
Oroville, CA 95965
(800) 553-5000
www.rcbs.com

Rotometals
865 Estabrook St.
San Leandro, CA 94577
(800) 779-1102
www.rotometals.com

Sturm, Ruger & Co., Inc.
Customer Service Department
411 Sunapee St.
Newport, NH 03773
(336) 949-5200
www.ruger.com

S&S Firearms
74-11 Myrtle Avenue
Glendale, New York 11385
(718) 497-1100
www.ssfirearms.com

Steve Earle Products, Inc.
24 Palmer Road
Plympton, MA 02367
www.steveearleproducts.com

Shiloh Rifle Mfg. Co.
P.O. Box 279
Big Timber, MT 59011
(406) 932-4454
www.shilohrifle.com

Thompson/Center
2100 Roosevelt Ave.
Springfield, MA 01104
(866) 730-1614
www.tcarms.com

Uberti USA
Stoeger Industries
901 8th St.
Pocomoke, MD 21851
(800) 264-4962
www.uberti.com

Winchester Repeating Arms Co.
275 Winchester Ave.
Morgan UT 84050
(801) 876-2711
www.winchesterguns.com

THE RUGER OLD MODEL SINGLE SIX

INSTRUCTIONS and PARTS LIST for RUGER "BEARCAT" REVOLVER

NATIONAL RIFLE ASSOCIATION
1600 RHODE ISLAND AVENUE N.W.
WASHINGTON 6, D.C.

BUSINESS REPLY CARD

Postage Will be Paid by Addressee

No Postage Stamp Necessary if Mailed in the United States

STURM, RUGER & CO., INC.
SOUTHPORT, CONNECTICUT
U.S.A.

OCTOBER 1, 1965

22 LONG RIFLE HIGH VELOCITY
50 CARTRIDGES
50 CARTOUCHES
WINCHESTER
SUPER X

WARNING
Keep out of reach of children. Read all Warnings on package.

AVERTISSEMENT
Gardez hors de la portée des enfants. Lisez tous les avertissements sur l'emballage.

The success of the Ruger Single Six led to the introduction of the smaller-framed Ruger Bearcat in 1958, which, in turn, was inspired by the design of the 19th-century Remington .44 percussion revolvers. The "brass" triggerguard is an anodized aluminum casting. The stag grips were made by Eagle Grips.

A sixgun so good you can't buy just one

BY **RICK HACKER**

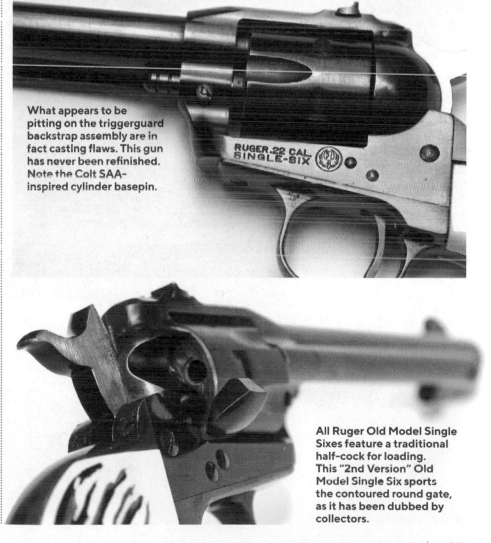

The author's first Ruger Old Model Single Six features aftermarket, but period-correct, plastic "staghorn" grips and retains 98 percent of its original finish, even though it was made in 1959.

Millennials might have the Ruger Precision Rifle, Gen Xers the Ruger 10/22, but as far as I'm concerned, the Ruger that defines the Baby Boomer Generation (of which I happen to be a charter member) is the Ruger Single Six, a scaled-down single-action revolver that straddled both the past and future of American gunmaking technology. Yet ironically, although I have fired a few of them while stalking through the dry washes of the Arizona desert during my youth, I never actually had a Single Six of my own until I finally became what the current news media condescendingly likes to refer to as "an elderly person." But let's start at the beginning.

Inspired by the legendary lines of the Colt Single Action Army (SAA) — an 1873-designed firearm that even Colt considered passé when it announced its discontinuance in 1947 — the Single Six was just 7/8th the size of the heftier Model P. It came riding fast out of the gate, hard on the heels of the success that Sturm, Ruger & Company was enjoying with its first offering, the .22 semi-automatic Mark 1 Standard pistol.

Long a fan of the classic "B" western movies and their tall-in-the-saddle sixgun-totin' heroes, Bill Ruger convinced his partner, Alexander Sturm, they needed to make a scaled-down version of the Peacemaker in the caliber that they knew best — the .22 rimfire.

And, as an antique automobile devotee and collector, Bill Ruger decided to name the new pistol after the classic Packard 1920 Single Six Model 116 Sedan.

Unfortunately, Alex Sturm became suddenly ill and passed away in 1951, leaving Ruger to continue with the development of the Single Six. Even though he was mechanically gifted and entrepreneurial by nature, Ruger ran into technological obstacles that kept the Single Six tethered. For one thing, he did not want to simply make a smaller duplicate of the Colt Peacemaker, even though the gun he eventually fashioned would bear a strong resemblance to it externally. His goal was to make a better gun.

After creating a few prototypes by trying to mill the frames out of a solid block of steel as Colt had done, Ruger soon

What appears to be pitting on the triggerguard backstrap assembly are in fact casting flaws. This gun has never been refinished. Note the Colt SAA-inspired cylinder basepin.

All Ruger Old Model Single Sixes feature a traditional half-cock for loading. This "2nd Version" Old Model Single Six sports the contoured round gate, as it has been dubbed by collectors.

The original Single Six sported a drift-adjustable notched rear sight.

realized that this would make his single action too expensive to manufacture. After much experimentation, he found the solution by using investment castings for the major components, including a chrome-molybdenum steel frame. As a result, Sturm, Ruger & Company pioneered the use of this technology for the firearms industry.

Another weak point of the Single Action Army was the flat springs in use at the time, which would occasionally break, especially on guns that had seen hard use. Ruger solved this dilemma by switching to piano wire and using an unbreakable coil mainspring. This was secured inside a cast Alcoa aluminum one-piece backstrap and triggerguard, which helped keep manufacturing costs down and made assembly quicker. But the traditional SAA-style upswept knurled hammer, angled ejector rod housing, and plow handled grips remained, although the topstrap-groove rear sight of the SAA was changed to a drift-adjustable fixed notch rear sight on the Single Six.

Another design change on the Single Six that deviated from the original Colt's was reconfiguring the SAA's rounded loading gate to a unique flat loading gate with a shallow groove, so that the gate could be flipped open with the thumbnail. This was another cost-savings

device, as a flat loading gate required less metal and machining to make. In later years, these earliest versions would be dubbed by collectors as Flat Gate Rugers, for obvious reasons. They were the progenitors of things to come.

With a 5 1/2-inch barrel and two-piece checkered hard rubber grips inletted with the Ruger "rising Phoenix" (not an eagle, as is now widely miswritten), the Ruger Single Six finally made its appearance in June 1953, right on the eve of The Golden Age of Television Westerns. Less than 100 Single Sixes were produced that first year, but it set the stage (pun intended), and the timing could not have been better, as families throughout America were busily acquiring that latest "must have" appliance for their households: the TV set. Thus, millions of children, having been lured from the B westerns of the cinema, to instead ride the range in the comfort of

The Old Model Super Single Six has an adjustable rear sight, round loading gate and a half-cock for loading.

(below) The author's Super Single Six has an adjustable rear sight and included an extra .22 Magnum cylinder.

The rear sight of the Super Single Six is adjustable for windage and elevation.

A Flat Gate Old Model, showing the thumb indentation on the loading gate for ease of operation.

their own homes, were devotedly tuning in weekly to watch the exploits of the earliest cowboy heroes, which included Hopalong Cassidy, Gene Autry, The Lone Ranger and The Cisco Kid.

Suddenly, every kid — and their brothers, fathers, uncles, and grandfathers — wanted to strap on a sixgun, just like the television gunslingers. Consequently, although conceived as a handy and economical handgun for plinking and small game hunting, the Single Six was soon adopted by devotees of the rapidly growing sport of fast draw.

Due to all of these factors, and aside from buying a used, original Colt Single Action Army (and shelling out

for boxes of its much more expensive ammunition), the only lookalike alternative on the market was the Ruger Single Six, which was chambered for the inexpensive .22 Short, .22 Long, and .22 Long Rifle rimfire cartridges, and was priced at an affordable (even back then) $57.50. It was a hard handgun to resist. There was no other competition — even a few years later, when Great Western introduced a full-sized single action chambered in .22 rimfire. But that rimfire was much too heavy and did not have the distribution network that Ruger had

already amassed, thanks to the success of the company's original Mark 1 semi-automatic pistol.

The Ruger company improved its Single Six in 1955 by adding non-loosening Nylok screws. That same year an aluminum-framed Lightweight Single Six was introduced, featuring a steel-sleeved aluminum cylinder and a 4 5/8-inch barrel; later guns were offered with optional all-steel cylinders. But Ruger's near-monopoly on the .22 single-action market ended in 1957, when Colt — realizing the

The author re-converted his Super Single Six back to its Old Model mechanism. The replaced parts are shown alongside the gun.

Flat Gate Single Sixes are easily identified by their flat loading gates, hence the name.

Frontier Scout was introduced Ruger replaced its flat loading gate with a more traditionally styled rounded version, like Colt's. This change, now known to collectors as "Round Gate" Single Sixes, occurred around serial number 70,000, after approximately 60,000 "Flat Gate" models had been produced. Today, the Flat Gate version has become a Single Six collecting sub-category of its own. However, most of those early guns encountered are usually worn, which attests to their initial popularity.

Also reflecting the popularity of the Single Six when coupled with the equally popular TV westerns, a fast draw-inspired 4 5/8-inch barrel, and a Wyatt Earp-influenced 9 ½-inch barrel version of the steel–framed gun was introduced in 1959. Both are somewhat rare today. A .22 Rimfire Magnum chambering was brought out in 1961, and in 1964 Ruger premiered its Super Single Six, featuring adjustable sights. It also came with an extra cylinder chambered for the .22 Magnum.

It was about this time, having already developed a deep fascination for everything connected with firearms and the Old West, that I began paying closer attention to the Ruger ads. I also had the pleasure of plinking at a few wayward tin cans and unsuspecting jackrabbits with

error of its ways and seeing the success that Ruger was enjoying — brought out its Frontier Scout, a similarly scaled-down .22 version of the Single Action Army. Initially offered with an aluminum alloy die cast "duo-tone finish" frame, and priced at only $49.50, there was no denying that Ruger now had some serious competition. Plus, it was a real Colt, as ads rightfully proclaimed, "… a .22-caliber version of the world-famous

Single Action Army …(with) the same classic lines … fundamentally the same foolproof action, and though lighter … the same superb balance and feel."

Just as telling was the fact that the Frontier Scout sported a "full-formed" loading gate, a not-so-subtle dig at the flat gates of the Single Six and the Lightweight Single Six. It was because of this — no doubt coupled with consumer feedback — that in the same year the

The Ruger Super Single Six is a versatile .22, with an adjustable rear sight, ramp front sight and a .22 Magnum supplementary cylinder.

The author's first two Ruger Single Sixes: A Flat Gate model (top) made in 1955, and a Round Gate version (bottom), produced in 1959. Both fixed-sight guns shoot very close to point of aim. Interestingly, the anodized "bluing" on some of these early guns turned purple over time.

Single Sixes owned by my more fortunate high school buddies. But it would be many decades before I finally acquired my first Single Six, and which, in turn, would ultimately inspire me to acquire a few more.

But the days were numbered for what has now been dubbed the Old Model Single Six. In 1973 Ruger introduced a transfer bar safety system for all of its single actions, the Single Six included. Henceforth, these post–1973 guns would be known as the New Model Single Six, while the pre–'73 guns were now christened as the Old Models. That meant the New Model single actions could be safely carried with all six rounds in the cylinder, unlike the earlier guns that, like the Colts, you would load only five rounds in the cylinder, with the hammer resting over the empty sixth chamber in order to prevent an accidental discharge.

Coupled with this, Ruger offered (and still does) a free service to convert any Old Model Single Six into a New Model by factory-installing the new transfer bar parts and returning both the gun and the Old Model parts back to the owner. However, many collectors today prefer unaltered Old Models, while shooters obviously opt for the New Model (the only version now being produced by the company) due to the convenience of having that extra sixth shot.

Ironically, it was a used round gate Old Model Single Six that I bought from the original owner at a gun show that prompted me to purchase a New Model Ruger Blackhawk in .357 Magnum. After all, one of Ruger's selling points was that once a shooter got used to the Single Six, it was a natural progression to step up to

its big-bore brother. And it worked, for me, at least, although I still have muscle memory problems when loading my New Model Blackhawk, which only requires the loading gate to be flipped open to free the cylinder for chambering a round. The Old Models have a traditional half-cock for loading, and I am constantly finding that I draw the hammer back on my New Model Ruger in a vain search for this non-existing half-cock notch. Of course, I have no such problems with my Old Model sixguns.

I distinctly remember my excitement, having purchased my first Old Model contoured-gate Single Six. Even though I was a bonafide adult, it was almost like the Christmas present I had always wanted as a kid but never got. The first thing I did was leaf through all of my old gun magazines, searching for those

His acquisition of a Ruger Single Six was directly responsible for the author acquiring a Ruger Blackhawk in .357 Magnum, proving Ruger's adage that buying one of its guns will lead to buying another.

familiar full-page Ruger Single Six ads I remembered so well. At last I found one, circa 1958, depicting the "new" round gate version, and listing its price at $63.25 — a slight jump from the original $57.50 price tag. Interestingly, the ad stated, "…Because it is not built to a price, the 'Single-Six' incorporates every useful mechanical refinement, and yet because it is produced in a factory that is famous for efficiency, it is not a costly gun to own. That is why the Single Six is not only the prestige gun, but also the value gun in the revolver field."

To be honest, I don't recall what I paid for my first Single Six. I subsequently learned that my gun was made in 1959, even though it still retained 98 percent of its original finish, which put it in "NRA Excellent" condition. I was glad the origi-

nal owner had taken such good care of it. And even though my Old Model Single Six sported aftermarket period-correct plastic "staghorn" grips, current prices indicate it would fetch around $550 today. By comparison, on January 27, 2019, an 80 percent Old Model Single Six, with factory original two-piece walnut grips and which was also made in 1959, sold for $257 at an online auction by Lock, Stock and Barrel (www.lsbauctions.com). With so many guns produced, condition is everything.

Of course, now that I had what is known as a "2nd Version" Old Model Single Six with the contoured loading gate, I just naturally had to have a Flat Gate. But even considering that approximately 60,000 of them were made between 1953 and 1957, there just

didn't seem to be many around — at least not in any kind of condition that I would consider owning or shooting. I do remember seeing a Flat Gate a few years back at the Las Vegas Antique Arms Show, new in the box, for what seemed to me at the time to be an outrageous price, so I passed on it. Considering that these 100 percent boxed guns now fetch anywhere from $750 to $850, in hindsight I probably should have bought it. But instead, in a somewhat convoluted trade, I finally ended up acquiring a nice, shootable 70 percent Flat Gate Single Six that was made in 1955, the third year of production.

Years later, I obtained a three-screw Super Single Six with a 6 1/2-inch barrel. The previous owner had it factory converted with Ruger's transfer bar system, but the gun still had its original box and extra .22 Magnum cylinder and it came with its original Old Model parts. I immediately took it down to my local gunsmith and had those parts put back into the

(left) Although other .22 rimfire single actions existed, including a full-sized (and much heavier) Great Western, the only real competition to the Single Six was the Colt Single Action Frontier Scout, which came with an "official" Colt screwdriver and a bore brush. Shown here is an early 1958 version, with its two-tone "duotone" aluminum frame. It was a contemporary of the Round Gate Old Model Single Sixes.

(below) This November 1958 Guns Magazine ad from the author's collection touts the internal mechanism of the Single Six, and notes "...it was not built for keeping in a bureau drawer," but should be "carried and used by practical shooters ...."

RUGER
BUILDS THE BEST IN SINGLE ACTIONS

The Patented Ruger Mechanism Cannot Be Copied

"SINGLE-SIX" REVOLVER

There is no single action revolver made, nor has a gun of this kind ever been made, which can compare with the RUGER Single-Six. We mean this on the basis of durability, reliability, accuracy, and accurate fitting of component parts. Materials throughout are the best for the purpose that can be obtained. The finish is neat and uniform, as only the most experienced polishers can make it. The lines of the gun are handsome—its balance superb. Grips, sights, trigger, every detail, in fact, which contributes to real performance has been designed by and for experts.

Although it conforms to tradition in appearance, the Single-Six is no mere reproduction of an older gun, nor is it an antique collectors substitute for the real thing. It was not built for keeping in a bureau drawer. The idea behind the RUGER Single-Six is that it should be carried and used by practical shooters who will fire many thousands of rounds a year and who judge guns by performance and by sensible design.

Write for literature on the entire line of RUGER firearms.

Retail list price **$63.25**

Uses .22 short, long or long rifle ammunition.

All prices subject to change without notice.

manufactured entirely in the United States of America by
STURM, RUGER & COMPANY, INC.
SOUTHPORT, CONNECTICUT.

gun, as I wanted to bring it back to its original condition. Besides, I reasoned, if you can't hit what you're aiming at with five shots, you shouldn't be shooting.

To that point, I have found these Old Model Single Sixes to be surprisingly accurate, even the fixed-sight models, which I find shoot close to point of aim. They're not target guns, by any means, but for close-range tin can popping and small game hunting, these Old Model Single Sixes are quite rewarding. And for me, shooting them produces a heavy dose of nostalgia with every shot.

Although I have yet to acquire the 9 1/2- and 4 5/8-inch Old Model versions, for now I am quite content with the three Single Sixes that I do own. And while the New Model Rugers offer numerous variations and retain their legacy of being great values, packing an Old Model — albeit with "only" five rounds in the cylinder — is like stepping back in time with a gun I coveted as a kid.

THE .470 NITRO EXPRESS

CLASSIC DANGEROUS-GAME MEDICINE

The classic .470 NE makes a perfect choice for any and all dangerous game.

The most popular of the rimmed, double-rifle cartridges has been getting the job done, worldwide, since 1907

BY **PHIL MASSARO**

We had run for more than a half-mile, nearly recklessly, along the elephant paths which were parallel with the shore of the Sengwa River, inattentive to the numerous thorny vines and creepers. We had split up, with our head tracker and the Zimbabwean game ranger being caught on the far side of the dried up pan when we spotted the herd of Cape buffalo, and it was then the mayhem ensued.

It was Day Eight of a seven-day safari in Zimbabwe's Chirisa Safari Area, and Brian van Blerk, my Professional Hunter, refused to give up, in spite of the fact that I was scheduled to leave camp no later than noon. We cut the buffalo's spoor at first light, in the sand of the Sengwa River, and the father-and-son tracking team of Albert and Proud Ndlovu were hot on the trail. Brian and I were following Proud, with Albert examining the spoor on the far side of the pan, when Proud extended his right arm, dropped to one knee and made the hissing sound which stopped us in our tracks. They'd seen us, and thundered off along the river's edge; van Blerk snapped his head back at me, and uttered a single word: "*Run.*"

The author with an Australian water buffalo taken with a Heym .470 in Graham Williams' Arnhemland concession, with 500-grain North Fork Cup Solids

Twice we had pulled up, easing to the edge of the thick vegetation, and seeing the herd still moving, but slower each time. The third time, Proud's sharp eyes found them across the waist-high cover, interspersed with stunted trees, giving us just enough cover to crawl into effective range. Brian van Blerk brought his binocular up, and then pointed, instructing me to shoot the bull he was pointing to. The big Heym rifle came to my shoulder, the bead settled on the bull's shoulder and I broke the trigger of the right barrel. The bull dropped to the shot, and immediately gave its death bellow. BvB then pointed further to the right, and excitedly instructed *"There's his brother, take him too."* The left trigger broke, and the sound of the bullet's impact came back to our ears. A handful of follow-up shots – out in that sand riverbed, at distances greater than I personally care to shoot an iron-sighted rifle – sorted out the second bull, and I had done something I had only ever dreamed of – taken two buffalo with a double rifle.

A DOUBLE OF MY OWN

That rifle – a fine Heym Model 89B – had quickly become a dear friend. Double rifles are – and shall remain to be – an undeniably romantic means of hunting dangerous game; they are chambered for a wide variety of cartridges suitable for the largest game on earth. I had been fortunate enough to have used a couple of the new 89Bs on both African Cape buffalo and Australian water buffalo, both with good success. I enjoyed hunting with the double rifle so much that I decided I needed to purchase one of my

The author's Heym Model 89B .470 NE and a Zimbabwean buffalo.

can be taken with the .375s, I feel the .450-class cartridges handle them better. I knew I wanted at least a 500-grain bullet, so I got to chatting with some of my African PH friends about the differences in performance between the .450, .470 and .500s; most of them indicated that for the PH, the .500 made an excellent choice – as most of their work is at very close quarters – though they all agreed that a 500-grain slug at 2,150 fps made an excellent choice for a client's rifle.

The final decision came at the Heym booth at the Dallas Safari Club convention; my buddy Chris Sells of Heym USA had a good selection of rifles on hand. We spent some time not only measuring my frame for a proper rifle fit, but comparing and contrasting the balance and feel of the Model 89B in various calibers. As you've figured out from the article's title, I settled on a .470 Nitro Express, with 26-inch barrels, and I'm very happy I did.

THE .470 3 1/4-INCH NITRO EXPRESS

John Rigby & Company's 1898 release of the .450 Nitro Express (fueled by smokeless powder) pretty well defined the standard for big-game hunting in both Africa and India. Driving a 480-grain, .458-inch diameter bullet at 2,150 fps, it worked very well, no matter the game. Insurrections in Sudan and India saw the use of the British military .577/450 Martini Henry rifles against His Majesty's own soldiers, so a ban on .450 caliber ammunition went into effect in 1907, in order to deprive the insurgents of ammunition. The British gun makers

own, and I knew I wanted a Heym 89B, but the main question was the cartridge. Heym offers a wide selection, from the .375 H&H Flanged and .450/400 3-inch NE, up to the huge .577 NE. I pondered long and hard, as I enjoyed the lightweight, mild recoil and striking power of the .450/400 – with it I took an excellent buffalo in Mozambique – as well as the horsepower of the .470 NE and .500 NE, which so many Professional Hunters rely upon daily.

The decision would be based on the species I'd be using the rifle for, the feel and balance of the rifle/cartridge combination, and the balance of bullet weight/velocity/recoil. With regard to the first issue, I wanted a cartridge that would handle the full gamut of huntable species, including elephant. Though I know full well even the largest pachyderms

The North Fork Cup Solids make a good choice for the .470 NE for almost all dangerous game.

(left) These .470 cartridges were loaded with 500-grain Peregrine BushMaster soft points.

(below) With a proper handload, the .470 NE can be a very accurate cartridge, as this 100-yard target shows.

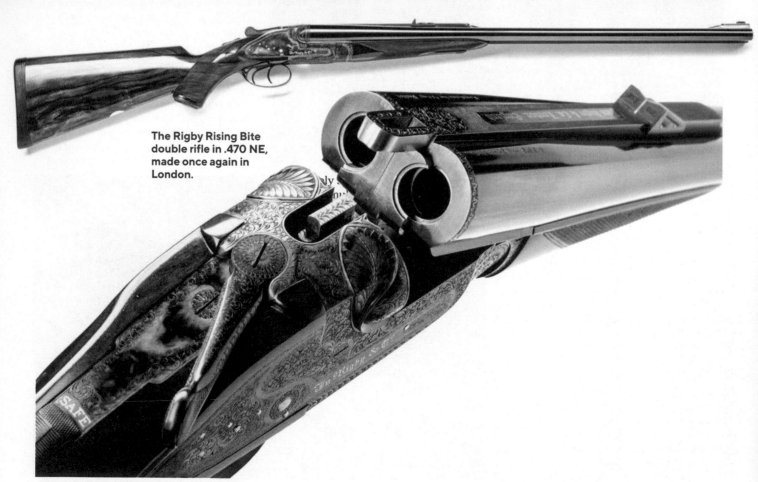

The Rigby Rising Bite double rifle in .470 NE, made once again in London.

Three Peregrine VRG-3 BushMasters recovered from a Zimbabwean Cape buffalo. With weight retention in the high 90-percent range, these are an excellent and accurate choice for the .470.

(below) Norma's African PH line of ammunition uses the Woodleigh Weldcore soft points and Woodleigh FMJ (shown here) to mimic the bullet profile of the older Kynoch ammunition, in order to shoot well in the older double rifles.

But the availability is only one of the reasons the .470 NE is one of the most popular of the double-rifle cartridges; more about that in just a minute. The .470 produces 5,140 ft.-lbs. of energy at the muzzle, perfect for any and all game on earth. With a solid (non-expanding) bullet, it will penetrate even the largest bull elephant's skull from any angle, as well as the entire length of a buffalo. With expanding, soft-point bullets – especially the modern monometals and bonded core designs – it will kill anything shy of elephant. The .470 has been most popular in the double rifles, which are most often equipped with traditional iron sights, making the effective range of the cartridge – for most shooters – about 125 yards. The sedate muzzle velocity equates to a manageable level of recoil, about on par with the .458 Lott, especially when the rifle fits the shooter properly. In theory, the .470 NE is no better, or worse, than any of the cartridges in the .450 to .475 class, as they all generate the same muzzle energy, or so close that an animal won't care.

The .470 Nitro Express is based on the .500 Nitro Express 3 1/4-inch case, necked down to hold the .474-inch-diameter bullets. The Cartridge Overall Length is specified at 3.98 inches, the rim diameter is 0.665 inches, and the slight shoulder — 7 degrees, to be precise — makes for easy feeding in a double rifle, yet gives enough neck ten-

them were the .500/465 NE, the .475 NE, the .475 No. 2, and of course the .470 NE. All will drive a 480- or 500-grain bullet at a muzzle velocity of 2,150 fps (or thereabouts), though the bullet diameter will vary.

> **JOSEPH LANG RELEASED THE .470 NE IN 1907, USING A .474-INCH-DIAMETER BULLET OF 500 GRAINS, AND UNCOMMON FOR THE TIME, MADE THE DESIGN AVAILABLE TO ALL, AND THE FIRST RIGBY DOUBLES CHAMBERED FOR THE .470 WERE PRODUCED IN NOVEMBER OF 1907.**

Joseph Lang released the .470 NE in 1907, using a .474-inch-diameter bullet of 500 grains, and uncommon for the time, made the design available to all, and the first Rigby doubles chambered for the .470 were produced in November of 1907.

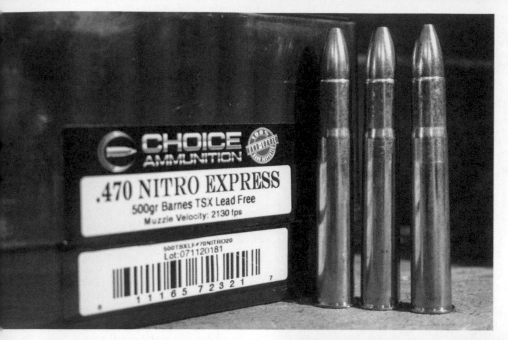

Choice Ammunition makes a great load for .470 shooters, using the .500-grain Barnes TSX all-copper hollowpoint. It shot very well in the author's rifle.

the British ammunition for the double rifles dried up, and quickly. Many of those classic double rifles were taken out of commission, or at the very least shot very seldom, as ammunition was unattainable.

The period from the late 1950s through the late 1980s was certainly the Dark Ages for double rifles, with few produced, but thanks to a few devoted aficionados, the phoenix would rise from the ashes. *Gun Digest* contributor Tom Turpin had a big hand in the resurgence of the double rifle, its ammunition, and the .470 NE. While stationed in Germany in the early 1970s, Mr. Turpin befriended the folks at Heym rifles and over the next decade they decided to make a modern double rifle. To keep a long tale as short as possible, they decided on the .470 (as it was a sensible choice, both ballistically and logistically) for the first cartridge, and relied upon the talents of

sion so as not to need a heavy roll crimp. Pressures are on the lower side — 35,000 psi on average — which is an important consideration in the heat of the tropics.

The sectional density of the .470's 500-grain bullet is 0.316, while the .450 NE's 480-grain bullet has an S.D. of 0.327, so in theory the .450 should penetrate better than the .470; as a result of the numbers game, I've had some colleagues go so far as to insist that the .470 lacks the necessary penetration for a proper elephant stopper. This is a ridiculous theory, as for the last 113 years the .470 NE has been relied upon by both Professional Hunters and safari clients alike, with very, very few unsatisfied customers. Looking at the .475 No. 2 Jeffery, which uses a 480-grain bullet of .483-inch diameter, having an SD value of 0.294, and yet it has a stellar reputation. Yes, sectional density does play a role in penetration, that is irrefutable, but any bullet with an SD value at or approaching 0.300 makes a sound choice for danger-ous game.

MODERN AVAILABILITY

The .470 is the most popular of the lineup of the rimmed double-rifle cartridges, but why? Surely the effects of that ammunition ban — more than a century old — are long passed. Well, you must understand that as popular as the safari industry was in the post-WWII era,

The famous Trophy Bonded Sledgehammer solid – with trademark 'T' on the meplat – is now available from Federal as a component bullet. It worked perfectly as a backup bullet on the author's Zimbabwe safari over a charge of Reloder-15.

Jim Bell and his Brass Extrusion Laboratories Limited (B.E.L.L.) to produce the ammunition. The double rifle, as well as the .470 Nitro Express, was reborn.

It would take a while for the wave to reach shore, but the late 1980s saw a resurgence of safari cartridges and rifles, with Ruger chambering the .416 Rigby in its RSM rifle, Remington releasing the .416 Remington Magnum, and Federal's loading of .470 Nitro Express ammunition. The wave crashed on the shore, and with it brought a renewed interest in rimmed, big-bore cartridges. Undeniably, the .470 NE has the widest selection of factory ammunition of any of the double-rifle cartridges, with factory ammunition available from Federal, Hornady, Norma, Nosler, Swift, Barnes, Doubletap and Choice, as well as a wide selection of component bullets. The Swift A-Frame and Breakaway Solid; Barnes TSX and Banded Solid; Woodleigh Weldcore, FMJ and Hydrostatically Stabilized Solid; Peregrine BushMaster and Solid; Nosler's Solid; NorthFork softs and Cup Point Solids, and Federal's Trophy Bonded Bear Claw and Sledgehammer solid are a sampling of the component bullets available for the .470 NE. I think you see the picture: The cartridge can be customized to include your favorite bullet, whether by shooting factory ammunition or handloading the cartridge.

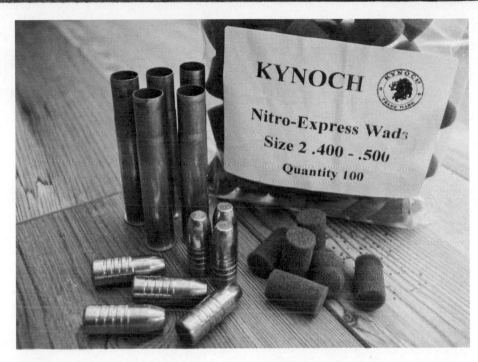

> 66 A DOUBLE RIFLE IS REGULATED FOR A SINGLE BULLET WEIGHT AT A SPECIFIC MUZZLE VELOCITY. ANY VARIATION FROM THAT FORMULA AND YOU'LL SEE THE RESULTS CHANGE ON THE TARGET. 99

While using faster burning powders like Reloder-15, a Kynoch foam wad will keep the low-density powder column in place, resulting in very uniform results.

REGULATION AND MODIFICATION

A double rifle is regulated for a single bullet weight at a specific muzzle velocity. Any variation from that formula and you'll see the results change on the target. The right-left combination of shots might rise, separate, shift to the left or the right, so if purchasing a double rifle — of any caliber — make sure and find out what the regulation ammunition was, in order to either purchase ammo of the same specifications, or handload the ammo to those specs.

My Heym 89B was regulated with Hornady ammunition, using the 500-grain DGX and DGS bullet profile. To illustrate my point, Federal's Trophy Bonded Bear Claw load runs a bit hotter (2,098 fps for the Hornady vs. 2,251 fps for the Federal) than the regulation velocity, and accordingly, the impact moves up and to the left. Accuracy was maintained, but if I wanted to use that load, I'd need a taller front sight, and would have to drift the rear sight a bit. Should you find a rifle which fits you well, yet you wish to use different ammunition than the regulation ammo, you'll have to do some experimentation. I have spent some time at the range with a variety of different ammunition, and have included the data herewith.

The Swift A-Frame – one of the best premium soft points on the market – now has the Swift Break Away solid for backup, for an excellent one-two punch.

.470 NE LOAD DATA HORNADY CASES | FEDERAL GM215M PRIMER | RIFLE: HEYM 89B

Powder	Charge Weight	Bullet	Velocity	Accuracy (right and left barrel at 100 yds)
H4831SC	110.0 grains	500-grain Trophy Bonded SledgeHammer	2,140 fps	1"
H4831SC	109.0 grains	500-grain Swift A-Frame	2,155 fps	1.35"
Reloder-15	87.0 grains*	500-grain Peregrine VRG-3	2,107 fps	1.75"
Reloder-15	88.0 grains*	500-grain Peregrine VRG-3	2,130 fps	1"
Reloder-15	89.0 grains*	500-grain Peregrine VRG-3	2,190 fps	2.5"
Reloder-15	87.0 grains*	500-grain Trophy Bonded SledgeHammer	2,134 fps	2"
Reloder-15	88.0 grains*	500-grain Trophy Bonded SledgeHammer	2,145 fps	1.15"
Hornady	Factory Load	500-grain DGX	2,098 fps	1.75"
Federal Premium	Factory Load	500-grain Trophy Bonded Bear Claw	2,251 fps	1.95"
Choice Ammunition	Factory Load	500-grain Barnes TSX	2,125 fps	1.6"
Norma African PH	Factory Load	500-grain Woodleigh Weldcore	2,160 fps	2"
Norma African PH	Factory Load	500-grain Woodleigh FMJ	2,145 fps	2.5"

* denotes use of a Kynoch No. 2 foam wad

If you've read much of my work, you're aware that I am an avid handloader, and as good as our modern factory ammunition is, I still prefer to handload my own safari ammunition. Handloading for a double rifle requires a different mindset, as you essentially have two barrels welded together, and are imparting forces upon them that single-barreled rifle don't see. The regulation process involves wedging, and then securing the two barrels in place, in order to have them strike the same (or as near as is acceptable) point at a specific distance, usually 75 yards.

In order to achieve the best results when handloading for a double, I advise you use a good chronograph, as it will be the easiest means of finding the accuracy. What you're looking to do is replicate the regulation velocity, as that will — usually — give the best accuracy. I start by observing the accuracy and velocity of the regulation ammunition, and begin trying to replicate the velocity with the handloads.

Now, in the case of my .470, the rifle printed an average of 1 3/4 inches — one shot from each barrel — at 100 yards with the Hornady ammunition, with an average muzzle velocity of 2,098 fps. Keep in mind iron-sighted rifles, combined with a set of eyes in their late 40s, and the rather stout recoil of the .470 at the bench might require several pairs of shots to verify group size, taking an average of both size and location in relationship to the bull.

I grabbed a good set of RCBS dies and headed to the bench. The .470 should be sparked by a large rifle magnum primer, and I like the Federal Gold Medal Match GM215M primer for my loads. Powders for the .470 include H4350, H4831SC, RL15, RL19, RL22, RL25 and Norma 204. Looking at these, you'll see the big case prefers powders on the slower side of things, and those will indeed work well. I had excellent results with 110.0 grains of H4831SC under a 500-grain Trophy Bonded Sledgehammer Solid, printing just about 1-inch apart, at 2,140 fps. I suspect this is Hornady's powder of choice for its factory load.

However, speaking with my friend Chris Sells from Heym USA, he goaded me into trying something new: a lighter charge of Alliant's Reloder-15, compressed with a Kynoch foam wad. Federal's factory load uses Reloder-15, though minus the foam wad. Instead they use a 216 primer — unavailable to the consumer — relying on a hotter spark to consistently ignite the low-density powder charge. I had fantastic results using Reloder-15 and that foam wad, with a number of bullets.

I loaded several pairs of bullets, in one-grain increments from 87.0 to 90.0 grains of RL15. Watching things progress on both the chronograph and the target, I found that 87.0 grains of RL15 matched the Hornady factory velocity almost perfectly, but the 88.0-grain load gave the best accuracy and velocity balance, with the two shots hitting 1-inch above the bullseye at 2,130 fps, with the Peregrine VRG-3 BushMaster soft point and the Federal Trophy Bonded Sledgehammer solid, both of which I took on my safari.

But, the best feature of the Reloder-15 loads was the reduction in felt recoil. You see, the faster powder reduces the felt recoil — in my rifle at least — by about 15 percent, and when it comes to accurately placing a shot on dangerous game, that's an appreciable difference. The Kynoch wad kept things very uniform, giving me velocities that had an extreme spread of 9 fps for the pair. Reloder-15 also worked very well in the Zimbabwean heat, where temperatures approached 114-degrees Fahrenheit in the afternoon.

WHY THE .470 OVER OTHER CARTRIDGES?

According to Sells, the three best-selling cartridges among the Heym double rifles are, in order, the .450/400 3-inch

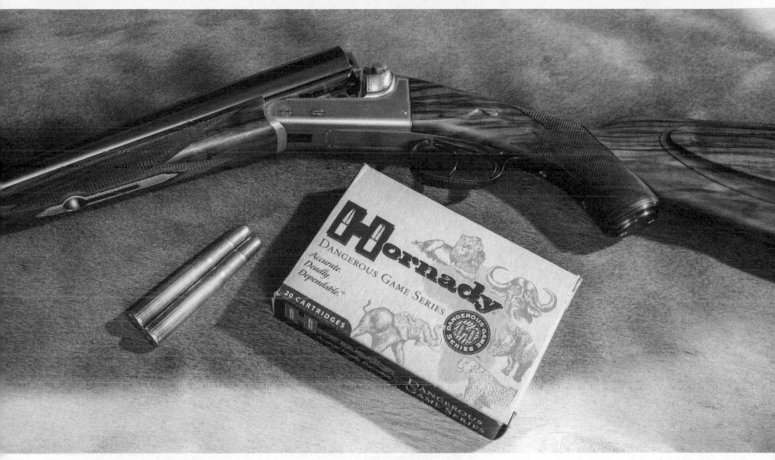

The author's Heym double rifle was regulated with Hornady ammunition, and with the new DGX Bonded bullet, it's even better than before.

NE, the .470 NE and the .500 3-inch NE. John Rigby & Company have brought back the Rising Bite double rifle, with the majority of them being chambered for the .470 NE; both statements are representative of the popularity of the cartridge.

It's true, the .450/400 offers both lighter recoil and a lighter rifle (10 lbs. vs. 11 lbs.), but the 400-grain .411-inch-diameter bullets at 2,050 fps just don't produce the energy figures the .470 does. Is the .450/400's 3,900 ft-lbs. enough for all game? I'd have to say yes, as the cartridge is certainly a near-perfect choice for buffalo, and has taken a good number of elephant, but I also feel the .470 NE is a better choice for elephant. The additional energy and bullet weight come at a price, being a rifle that is a bit heavier — yet still balances nicely — and a recoil level that is still tolerable. The .500 NE remains extremely popular among the Professional Hunters — Brian van Blerk swears by his Heym .500 — yet offers another step up in both rifle weight and recoil.

> ❝ IF I HADN'T BELIEVED ALL THE THEORETICAL VIRTUES OF THE .470 BEFORE I'D EVER HUNTED WITH ONE, TRIPS TO BOTH AUSTRALIA AND AFRICA HAVE SEALED THE DEAL FOR ME. A LARGE-BODIED WATER BUFFALO AND A TRIO OF CAPE BUFFALO WERE SORTED OUT NEATLY, AT DISTANCES FROM 17 TO 87 YARDS. ❞

If I hadn't believed all the theoretical virtues of the .470 before I'd ever hunted with one, trips to both Australia and Africa have sealed the deal for me. A large-bodied water buffalo and a trio of Cape buffalo were sorted out neatly, at distances from 17 to 87 yards. Using North Fork Cup Point solids, Peregrine VRG3 BushMaster soft points and Trophy Bonded Sledgehammer solids, the century-plus old cartridge worked very well with modern bullet designs, and the modern Heym 89B rifle is both strong and balanced.

Many famous hunters, both client and professional, have embraced Joseph Lang's .470, including John "Pondoro" Taylor, Robert Ruark, Harry Selby and Elmer Keith. I could have chosen any cartridge when I ordered my Heym double rifle, but settled on the .470 for a few reasons. One, I like the performance of bullets producing 5,000 ft-lbs. for dangerous game. Two, its level of recoil still allows me to place my shots accurately; personally, I can't report the same for the .500s. Yes, I can shoot them, but not as fast or accurately as the .450 to .470 class, and if I place the first shot accurately there is usually no need for the PH to shoot at all. Three, because it's the most popular of the double-rifle cartridges, a hunter has the greatest chance of finding ammunition in a pinch when traveling abroad.

If you're in the market for a double rifle — and I highly recommend the experience of hunting dangerous game with the classic design — you could do a lot worse than the .470 Nitro Express. It's been getting the job done, worldwide, since 1907, and will continue to do so.

Springfield's new XD(M) 10mm is capable of excellent accuracy and offers plenty of punch. Yet it's manageable for most shooters, especially with lighter 10mm loads.

SPRINGFIELD ARMORY XD[M] 10MM

From hunting to defense, the Springfield XD(M) 10mm has you covered

BY **BRAD FITZPATRICK**

Springfield Armory has joined the ranks of striker-fired pistol manufacturers offering a 10mm Auto. The brand's XD(M) pistols will now be available in two 10mm versions — one with a 4.5-inch barrel, the other with a 5.25 inch barrel. Once exclusive Glock territory (which helped bolster the 10mm's popularity by offering it in its affordable, polymer-framed G20, G29 and G40), the striker-fired 10mm market is opening up. And if ever there was a striker-fired pistol that was well-suited to be chambered in 10mm it's the Springfield XD(M).

RISE OF THE 10MM

Not too long ago while I was visiting my local gun shop, a patron stopped me to tell me that I was mistaken in a recent article. He went on to challenge my assertion that the 10mm Auto caliber was growing in popularity. The 10mm, he told me, had been replaced by the .40 Smith & Wesson and, as a commercial cartridge, it's life would be short. Soon it would largely be forgotten by the firearms world at large.

If he had made those predictions 25 years ago, he might have been right. After the 10mm was dumped by the FBI in favor of the then-new .40 S&W due to fears about excessive recoil, one could reasonably make the argument that the cartridge was on the way out. Then, after the first Bren Ten pistols — the first commercial 10mm — turned out to be a failure due to issues with magazines, you could almost surely have said that the 10mm was teetering on the brink of obscurity.

The 10mm is growing in popularity, and the new Springfield is already a standout in the field. It's accurate, very reliable and offers the durability of a Melonite finish.

(left) The XD(M) comes with a 5.25-inch match-grade barrel. Like the slide, the barrel is treated with Melonite.

(below) The XD(M)'s bladed trigger offers moderate travel, breaks at around 6 pounds and has a short, positive reset. Also shown is the ambidextrous magazine-release button.

> ## "THE .40 SMITH & WESSON, SAID TO BE THE 10MM'S FINAL COFFIN NAIL, HAS WITHERED IN TERMS OF POPULARITY LATELY."

The cartridge, however, was too good to go away. Conventional wisdom in the 1990s told us that the 10mm was never going to amount to much. But shooters and hunters began to catch on to the cartridge's potential and it continued to gain fans. In fact, it's one of the fastest-growing handgun cartridges in terms of ammunition sold and new firearms offered. The .40 Smith & Wesson, said to be the 10mm's final coffin nail, has withered in terms of popularity lately.

RINGFIELD XD(M) 10MM

I'm an unabashed 10mm loyalist, but I'm also a Springfield fan. Springfield's Croatian-made XD pistols are extremely durable and have all the features that I've come to expect in the best polymer striker-fired guns, including a crisp, but safe, trigger, a multitude of passive safeties (including a grip safety), adjustable sights, solid finishes and a carrying case that includes lots of extra equipment you'd have to pay extra for from other manufacturers. Plus, these pistols shoot very well and have proven to be reliable. Springfield's XD line remains quite popular with some of the nation's best competition shooters.

The XD(M) that I tested was the 5.25-inch version, which comes with a square-notch rear sight — screw adjustable for both windage and elevation — and a post front sight with red fiber-optic insert that is dovetailed into the slide. The rear sight's adjustment screws are large enough to be easily altered, and there are indicators on the slide that show direction of travel for up and left adjustments. There are also index lines cut into the slide to help you keep track of left/right adjustments as you fine-tune the pistol to your shooting. Both the front and rear sight are secure and solidly constructed — an important consideration on a cartridge that generates the level of recoil of the 10mm Auto.

XD pistols operate on a locked-breech, tilt-barrel design and the XD(M) 10mm comes with a match-grade barrel with a 1:16 right-hand twist. The model I tested features an open cutout in the top of the slide over the barrel that adds a touch of unique styling and cuts down on weight a

bit. The slide and barrel are both treated with Melonite, a ferritic nitrocarburizing treatment that makes the metal corrosion resistant. The slide itself is made from forged steel and comes with deep, angular slide cuts fore and aft for better control when operating the pistol. At the rear of the gun a small, silver cocking indicator tab extends through the rear of the slide to offer both a visual and tactile indicator of the XD(M)'s condition.

If you have large hands and constantly struggle to find a semi-auto pistol to accommodate your mitts, the XD(M) will suit you perfectly. The large polymer grip is spacious and offers plenty of purchase thanks to texturing — Springfield calls it Mega-Lock — on the front, rear and sides. Length of pull on this 10mm pistol is long enough to make shooters with large hands comfortable, but not so great that the average shooter will strain to reach the trigger. My wife has relatively small hands, but she was able to firmly grip the gun and access the trigger, and we were both equally comfortable firing the XD(M). It's rare that a pistol suits us both, but the Springfield does.

The polymer frame comes with a molded front rail that's large enough to accommodate lights and lasers, and there are molded depressions behind the trigger that provide a comfortable and stable hand position when holding the gun.

Like all XD(M) pistols, the 10mm utilizes double-stack magazines that hold 15 rounds of 10mm Auto ammunition. Springfield provides three magazines with each gun, which is a welcome addition. All-metal construction makes the mags very durable, and the spring weight is stout enough to properly feed cartridges without being so heavy that you'll have to grunt and strain to top it off.

Like many polymer-framed, striker-fired guns, the Springfield XD(M) 10mm's controls are minimalistic. There's a serrated slide stop that's triangular in cross-section, and an ambidextrous magazine release and rotating takedown lever on the left side. The trigger has a moderate amount of travel for a striker gun and the test pistol's trigger broke at 6 pounds as measured with a RCBS gauge. Reset is positive and short, so once you're familiar with the XD(M) you can fire very fast, controlled follow-ups.

Field stripping the handgun for routine maintenance is simple: with the magazine removed and an unloaded chamber, simply pull the slide back until

Springfield calls its wraparound polymer texturing pattern Grip-Lock. It's not too aggressive, but offers a firm grip on the gun. There's ample space on the grip for even the largest hands.

The XD(M)'s rear target sight is fully adjustable. A screw on the top of the sight adjusts elevation, and a screw on the right controls windage.

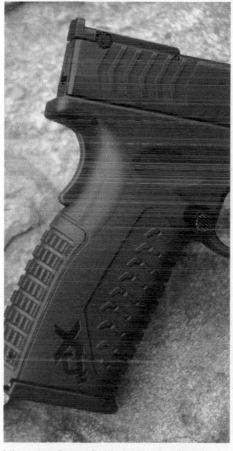

Like other Springfield pistols, the XD(M) features a passive grip safety on the rear of the polymer grip.

The XD(M)'s front sight is dovetailed into the slide and features a fiber-optic insert. The fiber-optic sight works well in low light or when drawing and shooting quickly.

the semicircular cutout on the slide aligns with the rotating takedown lever. The lever is then turned 90 degrees in a clockwise direction (up) and the slide is pushed forward along the rails and removed. The one-piece guide rod, spring, barrel and internal portion of the slide can then be easily accessed for cleaning. Reassembly is a matter of reversing the process, and there's no need to pull the trigger when breaking down the gun for routine maintenance.

The XD(M) 10mm is a large gun, but that's not all bad when firing full-power 10mm loads. Unloaded weight is 32.8 ounces, and overall length is 8.3 inches. Height is 5.75 inches, and the Springfield's grip measures 1.2-inches wide. Big for concealed carry? Yes, this gun wouldn't be my first choice, and it would be quite difficult to hide under light clothing, but I suspect it could be possible since, after all, there are many shooters who carry full-sized 1911s concealed and the Springfield's dimensions aren't that much greater. But this will primarily be an open carry option.

> **MUCH HAS BEEN MADE OF THE 10MM'S RECOIL, AND IF YOU READ ENOUGH ABOUT THE CARTRIDGE, YOU'D ASSUME THAT IT'S NEARLY UNBEARABLE TO TAME THIS BEAST OF A ROUND. NOT SO. THE SPRINGFIELD'S RECOIL IS STIFF, BUT NOT ABUSIVE, AND THE GUN'S WEIGHT, LONG SLIDE AND 5.25-INCH BARREL HELP REDUCE MUZZLE FLIP.**

At the front of the XD(M)'s polymer frame is a large accessory rail for mounting lasers and lights.

The top of the XD(M)'s slide has a cutout above the barrel, which helps keep weight down slightly. Unloaded weight is 32.8 ounces, striking a good balance between portability and recoil management.

The XD(M)'s controls are minimalistic: there's a grip safety, slide stop, takedown lever and magazine-release button. This prevents the pistol from getting hung up when drawn and simplifies operation.

(above) Breaking down the XD(M) is quite simple, and it doesn't require pulling the trigger. With an empty chamber and the magazine removed, simply pull the slide back until the notch aligns with the takedown lever, turn the lever clockwise 90 degrees and remove the slide.

SPECS

Model:	Springfield XD(M) 10mm 5.25 in.
Action:	Striker-fired semi-auto
Caliber:	10mm Auto
Capacity:	15
Barrel:	5.25 in.
Overall Length:	8.3 in.
Weight:	32.8 oz. (empty magazine)
Grips:	Polymer
Finish:	Matte black
Trigger Pull:	6.1 lbs.
Sights:	Adjustable target rear, fiber-optic front
MSRP:	$779
Website:	springfield-armory.com
Phone:	800-680-6866

At the rear of the XD(M)'s slide is a small silver cocking indicator tab. It offers a visual and tactile indication of the condition of the pistol.

AT THE RANGE

Much has been made of the 10mm's recoil, and if you read enough about the cartridge, you'd assume that it's nearly unbearable to tame this beast of a round. Not so. The Springfield's recoil is stiff, but not abusive, and the gun's weight, long slide and 5.25-inch barrel help reduce muzzle flip. With high-power hunting and defense loads — those approaching light .41 Magnum ballistics — the gun is a handful and generates more setback than most novice shooters would care to contend with. But with milder loads in the 1,000 fps range, such as Speer's Gold Dot ammo, the pistol is manageable and can be fired quickly and accurately. And while I couldn't manage the type of splits you would achieve with the same handgun in 9mm, I was able to deliver fast double-taps and three-shot strings in rapid succession and still hit the target.

I'd also venture to say that, despite its prodigious stopping power, the Springfield 10mm (which weighs in the neighborhood of 40 ounces fully loaded) is more pleasant and manageable to shoot than really short-barreled, ultra-light 9mm carry pistols with hot defensive ammunition. Short-barreled carry pistols often produce so much muzzle flip that aimed follow-ups can be tough. The 10mm generates more energy, but its greater size and added weight make it possible to shoot it accurately and quickly with more sedate defensive loads.

When you step up to hotter ammunition — 1,200 feet per second and up — the Springfield becomes more of a handful. Again, not abusive, and more manageable than the short-barreled .44 Magnums that many carry for backup in bear country. Additionally, that added barrel length allows the Springfield to wring more velocity out of those high-power 10mm loads. With such a wide range of 10mm ammo now being offered, you can load the XD(M) as needed — lower-powered loads for competition, practice and defense against two-legged predators and hotter loads for hunting big game or as defense in bear country.

Accuracy from the bench was quite good, the smallest group coming in at 1.4 inches with Hornady's Critical Defense ammunition and average group sizes ranging from 2.05 to 2.63 inches at 25 yards. Bench shooting was aided by a predictable and manageable trigger pull and the Springfield's excellent sights and almost 8-inch sight radius. Recoil was

This 25-yard group measured 1.3 inches with Hornady's 10mm Critical Defense 175-grain load, an ideal choice for personal defense because it produces a great deal of stopping power and manageable recoil.

The XD(M) performed very well with Speer's Gold Dot ammo, averaging 2.11-inch groups from the bench at 25 yards.

more noticeable from the bench but still wasn't painful, and the target rear and fiber-optic front sights were easy to see and align. There weren't any reliability issues to report, the Springfield ran well — feeding, firing, extracting and ejecting every round from five separate manufacturers. That's especially telling since, as previously stated, 10mm Auto ammo ranges widely in terms of velocity and energy. Springfield claims to have fired the gun to 10,000 rounds without failure, stopping every 2,000 rounds to oil the gun and change recoil springs. I've no reason to doubt those claims after what I experienced.

If you're in the market for a backup

pistol in bear country, the Springfield's reliability and accuracy make it a top contender. Many guides in the Great North have traded in their big-bore revolvers in favor of 10mm Auto pistols, and the XD(M) is perfectly suited for the task. It offers a capacity of 15+1 rounds and the bright fiber-optic front sight is ideal for making fast, accurate shots in the most stressful situations. I personally like the grip safety, which acts as one more level of security when carrying a pistol with a round in the chamber (a must in bear country).

The Melonite finish is durable: I've carried the XD(M)'s little brother, The

(above) The 10mm ammo tested included (from left) Hornady 175-grain Critical Duty, Hornady 180-grain Custom, SIG Sauer 180-grain FMJ, SIG Sauer 180-grain V-Crown and Speer 200-grain Gold Dot.

(right) The XD(M) 10mm comes with double-stack magazines that hold 15 rounds of ammunition. Each purchase includes three magazines, adding to the XD(M)'s value.

XD(S), quite frequently for extended periods and the Melonite finish on that gun handles the rigors of daily carry with aplomb, and the polymer frame is capable of taking a serious beating. I also like that the Springfield's controls are easy to operate when wearing gloves, and the large magazine well makes reloads fast and easy. For those who hunt hogs or deer at close range with a 10mm the XD(M) is a valid option.

MSRP on this Springfield is $779, less than you'll pay for most 1911 10mm pistols, and it comes with a hard case with lots of extras, including the trio of magazines and three backstrap inserts that allow you to customize the gun to your hand. As a fan of 10mms in general and Springfield guns in particular, I had high hopes when this gun was announced, and it did not disappoint.

The 10mm is not faltering. As long as there are guns like the Springfield XD(M) chambered for it, I suspect its popularity will continue to grow — and deservedly so.

Table A. Accuracy Test: Springfield XD(M) 10mm

Load	Muzzle Velocity (fps)	Muzzle Energy (ft-lbs)	Average Group (in.)
Hornady Critical Duty 175 gr.	1,142	507	2.05
Hornady Custom 180 gr.	1,238	603	2.63
SIG Sauer FMJ 180 gr.	1,222	597	2.37
SIG Sauer V-Crown 180 gr.	1,239	614	2.15
Speer Gold Dot 200 gr.	1,061	500	2.11

Note: Accuracy results are average of four five-shot groups at 25 yards from a fixed rest. Velocity figures are 10-shot averages recorded on a ProChrono digital chronograph placed 10 feet from the muzzle.

FINLAND'S FINEST

BY **WAYNE VAN ZWOLL**

Her 11th day on the mountain tested her resolve, already worn thin. Public lands give up their elk reluctantly. On traditional ranges like this, Tamar Bartz knew, odds were one in seven she'd kill a bull. Nearing the limit of her allotted time, she climbed early that day, across elk tracks braided deep into the snow, her breath white in the dim promise of dawn. As morning's light sifted through the conifers well above camp, she slowed, looking hard.

There! Tawny forms ghosted behind lodgepoles scant yards away. She shed her pack, dropped to her knees and eased ahead. *Please. Just one brow-tine bull!* A cow caught her movement. The stare-down froze Tamar's fingers to the .270. As the cow turned away, a lighter-hued elk came clear, also quartering off. Branched bone! Eye to the scope, Tamar waited until she saw rib. The bull collapsed to her shot.

Her rifle, a product of Finland, had come to the Rockies by way of the Dakotas and the Namibian desert. "It's like the Sako that took my first kudu," Tamar had enthused when she bought it. I recalled that safari and spotting the bull our last evening afield. Tamar finished with a careful stalk and a perfect shot, one of many she'd make on subsequent trips to Africa. Yes, I agreed, it was time she *owned* a Sako.

By the late 1940s, when reliable, fog-proof scopes appeared, iron-sighted lever rifles were giving way to bolt actions. While most U.S. hunters favored rifles of domestic heritage, enthusiasts dug deeper for imports from Riihimaki, Finland. *Suojeluskuntain yliesikunnan asepaja* had been founded on the first of April 1919. Mercifully — or fearing that name would all but consume the surface of

Sako and Tikka rifles on loan to visiting hunters salvage many safaris. Here: a Sako and a Namibian kudu.

Stoeger brought the first Sako rifles across the Atlantic in 1946. The rifles got fine reviews but sold at a modest pace, given their relatively high price. Also, the short-belted magnums making news in the '40s and '50s bore American names. On the heels of the war, Roy Weatherby developed and ably defined his hot-rod .257, .270, 7mm and .300 Magnums as the future of big game cartridges. Winchester's .458, .338, .264 and .300, and Remington's 7mm arrived between 1956 and 1963. Norma introduced its .308 and .358 Magnums in 1960 and '61 (though costly loaded ammunition came later, and in the U.S. Browning's beautiful High Power was the only rifle of consequence to chamber these two rounds).

Weatherby's cartridges were proprietary in that day, exclusive to Weatherby among commercial gun makers. Sako was quick to sense a tide of demand for Winchester and Remington magnums. It would soon comprise multitudes of hunters, who came to view the 7mm Remington and .300 Winchester almost as their forebears had the .270 and .30-06, especially for elk in the West and tough game abroad.

Sako also offered chamberings destined for less celebrity — like the .264 Winchester Magnum. At its 1959 debut, the .264 was advertised as a brimstone-breathing deer and varmint round that teased 3,700 fps from 100-grain bullets and shot as flat as the curve of the earth. Gun scribes wailed that it ate throats; deer and predator hunters shied from its loud bark and sharp recoil. Tainted by troll-speak, the .264 languished as Remington put final touches on its

(above) This Sako 85 in .416 Remington shows the Finns' attention to line and detail.

(left) A three-lug bolt gives Sako's 85 a short 70-degree lift, and it has smooth, reliable feeding. Controlled? Almost!

> 66 STOEGER BROUGHT THE FIRST SAKO RIFLES ACROSS THE ATLANTIC IN 1946. THE RIFLES GOT FINE REVIEWS BUT SOLD AT A MODEST PACE, GIVEN THEIR RELATIVELY HIGH PRICE. 99

carbine barrels — someone proposed "Sako" as the brand. Delightfully brief, it's pronounced "Socko," not "Sayko."

The company's first rifle of note appeared shortly after the end of World War II. Called the Vixen, it was a lovely arm, elegantly proportioned for its maiden chamberings, the .22 Hornet and .218 Bee. Varmint and full-stocked carbine versions soon followed. The .222, .222 Magnum and .223 joined the Vixen's cartridge roster. In 1957 Sako expanded its rifle offerings with the L-57 Forester, its action sized for the then-new .308 and .243 Winchester. The .22-250 was added in 1965 when Remington gave it a commercial home and factory loads. Sporter, Carbine and Heavy Barrel versions appeared. Then came the long-action L-61 Finnbear, for the .30-06 clan and belted magnums. A limited number of L-61 Carbines were shipped.

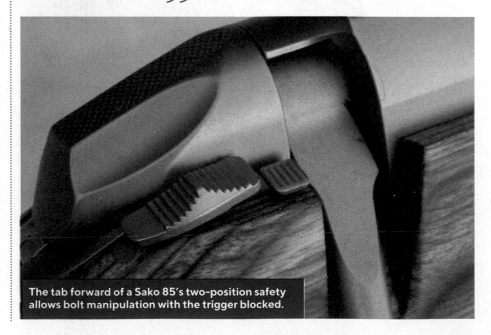

The tab forward of a Sako 85's two-position safety allows bolt manipulation with the trigger blocked.

(left) Sako's 1950s Vixen rifles had actions sized for the .22 Hornet. The later 995 handled the .338 Lapua.

(above) Cartridges as big as the .338 Lapua prove the strength of Sako extractors. Who needs a 98 Mauser's?

(below) Tamar's first kill on safari came by way of a Sako. Many others have followed in Africa and the U.S.

(bottom) Best .375 ever? The author likes Sako's 85 Kodiak. "Nimble, accurate, reliable! Fine sights and trigger!"

7mm Magnum, cleverly marketed with 140- and 175-grain bullets for deer and elk. Oddly enough, these two magnums are nearly identical, neck diameters differing by just .020 inch. In sales, the 7mm buried the .264.

Unfairly maligned or not, Winchester's perky 6.5mm magnum might have showed up too soon. Its fortunes might well have been brighter had it emerged today with other 6.5s, all of which enjoy gushing accolades.

....

Before I began hunting with the .264 Winchester, a Texan named Doug Burris bought a Sako rifle so chambered. On an annual hunt for mule deer in Colorado's San Juan National Forest, he was probing the rim of an oak-brush canyon when he heard a shot. He scrambled to higher ground in time to spot the biggest buck he'd ever seen making for cover 250 yards away. Centering the deer in his 3-9x Leupold, he loosed a handloaded 125-grain Nosler. The animal fell. Its amazing antlers had 18 points and measured 41 inches outside, a real prize. They would fall just shy of Boone and Crockett's minimum score for listing.

In 1972 Burris readied his Sako for a fourth trip to that Colorado plateau. Towing a Jeep behind a Power Wagon, he and three pals drove 22 hours in shifts, then hurried to set up tents on their public land campsite. A gunmetal sky spit drizzle most of opening day but the hunters downed two fine bucks.

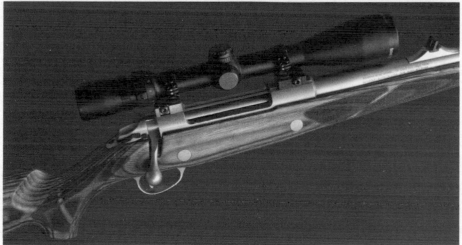

Every Sako 85 must put five shots into 1 MOA. Even big bores deliver groups like this — and better.

(below) This magnificent old eland fell to a Sako. Africa has long been a proving ground for Finland's rifles.

The next morning, under a ceiling that promised more of the same weather, Burris eased along the rim of a familiar canyon. Two distant deer with towering antlers led him through tangles that denied him a better view. When on close approach a doe bounced from cover, he knew any chance for a shot was seconds from gone. He dashed toward an opening and cheeked the Sako as the bucks bounded off. But he gasped as a third animal appeared, even bigger than the others: At 300 yards, Burris' Nosler struck home.

With one shot from his Sako, Burris had killed a new world's record mule deer. The deep-forked antlers were so wide and tall as to diminish at a glance their great mass. Still the top-ranked typical antlers in "the book," they also brought him B&C's coveted Sagamore Hill Award, reserved for trophies and hunts of distinction.

Sako rifles had by then secured for the brand a reputation for fine finish, accuracy and reliability.

The company had improved and grown its bolt-rifle series. In 1961 it announced the front-locking, lever-action Finnwolf, a hammerless rifle with a detachable magazine and a one-piece stock. In .243 and .308, it was succeeded a decade later by the similar Model 73, which lasted into the mid–1970s. By that time Sako had been eight years under new owners with new ideas. Refinements gave way to overhauls. The Model 74 in three action lengths replaced the Vixen, Forester and Finnbear from 1974 until 1978. An "A series" followed: A1, A11 and

A111 rifles with short, medium and long receivers. In the mid–'80s Sako replaced that group with the Hunter, also in three action lengths, and added a left-handed option. A new rimfire, the Model 78, was offered in .22 Hornet and .22 Long Rifle.

Early Sakos wore hand-checkered walnut stocks. Glossy wood finish dates to the late 1950s. I've seen the company's signature fine polish and deep blue on the chrome-moly steel of low-number Vixens. Silky bolt travel and adjustable triggers added to their appeal. Ditto the close, careful mating of walnut to metal. Sako extractors were smaller than the vaunted non-rotating Mauser claw, but so reliable that their type would later serve as replacements for various bolt-face hooks and clips.

In 1993 Sako blessed long-range shooters with the TRG. In sporting and "tactical" form, this rifle was barreled for the .338 Lapua on the Model 42 action and .308 on the more compact Model 22. TRGs would later sire the Model 10. A new Sako sporting rifle arrived in 1997. The Model 75's three locking lugs, a departure from the traditional twin lugs, reduced bolt lift to a low 70 degrees. More controversial was a lock inside the bolt shroud. A twist of the supplied key, separate from the rifle, rendered the action inoperable (or safe, if you prefer euphemisms). Four receiver lengths suited 18 cartridges, from .17 Remington and .22 PPC to 9.3x62 and .340 Weatherby. Like the TRG, the 75 had integral dovetails on top for Sako's finely finished but costly Optilock mounts.

The Model 85 that came along in 2006 was less a new rifle than a $220 upgrade of the Model 75 with a redesigned stock. It had a different magazine catch and a mechanical ejector. A tab in front of the two-detent thumb safety released the bolt for cycling. Triggers adjusted down to 2 ¼ pounds. Hailed as a "controlled-round feed" action, the Model 85s fell short of meeting the standard set by the 98 Mauser. But it was and is a strong, smooth-cycling mechanism you'll try in vain to jam, whether you attempt that with a top-loading magazine or a detachable box. The Model 85 endures as Sako's flagship bolt action, the heart of 11 sporting rifles. Stocks are of carbon fiber on the Model 85 Carbonlight and Carbon Wolf, synthetic on the Finnlight and Finnlight II (with adjustable comb), walnut on the Classic and full-stocked Bavarian, and laminated wood on the Grey Wolf, Varmint, Long Range and Kodiak.

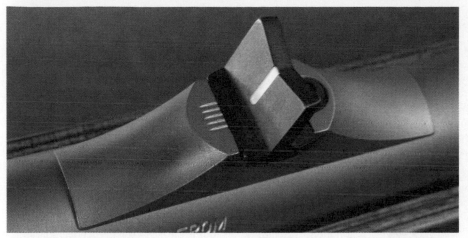

Excellent sights — adjustable
shallow–V rear and concave white bead —
distinguish the Sako Kodiak.

The detachable box mag on the Model
85 Kodiak in .375 H&H must be nudged
up to release the latch, a clever way
to prevent accidental drops without
slowing reloads. Crossbolts reinforce
the Kodiak's gray laminated stock either
end of its four-shot magazine, which
can be topped off through the rifle's
generous port. A superbly engineered
rifle, the Kodiak has a barrel-band sling
swivel, and the best iron sights I've seen
on a big-bore rifle. The wide, shallow
rear V with white centerline is windage-
adjustable and nicely slanted to kill glare.
A fat, white bead under a generous hood
up front is concave so reflection won't
draw your eye off center. Like all other
Sakos, the Kodiak has a hammer-forged
barrel. It has poked sub-minute groups
for me with Federal-loaded 260-grain Ac-
cuBonds. Incidentally, Sako guarantees
that *every* Model 85 shipped has met
an accuracy standard of five shots in a
1-MOA group.

In 2009 Sako unveiled the A-7 bolt
rifle. Two action lengths were paired
with chamberings from .22-250 to .300
Winchester. Weaver-style scope bases
replaced Sako dovetails, a change welcomed by the frugal among us. Discontinued in 2011, the A-7 was resurrected
as the A-7 Roughneck three years later.
It offered hunters a less costly push-feed
rifle in Long Range, Coyote and Big
Game configurations. Alloy-reinforced
synthetic stocks cradled fluted barrels
in a dozen popular chamberings. At the
same time, Sako revisited the Model 78
rimfire and came up with the Finnfire II.
This twin-lug, box-fed rifle in .22 LR and
.17 HMR had a checkered walnut stock, a
single-set trigger adjustable to 2 pounds.
It is no longer listed.

The TRG "tactical" series now includes
22/42 rifles in black or green synthetic
stocks with steep grips, toe hooks and
adjustable combs. They have detachable
box magazines, receiver-length rails. The
M10 is a chassis-style version with fully
adjustable stock, an AR-style fore-end
with rails front-to-back on top and belly.
The newest member of this clan is the
TRG22A1/42A1, essentially the 22/42 with
a stock very much like that on the A10.

> **REMARKABLY SUCCESS-
FUL IN FOREIGN MARKETS,
INCLUDING THE U.S. JUG-
GERNAUT POWERED BY
WINCHESTER, REMINGTON,
RUGER, SAVAGE, WEATH-
ERBY, AND A HOST OF LESSER
GUN-MAKERS COURTING
THE PROLETARIAT, SAKO
HAS FOUND ITS TOUGHEST
COMPETITION ON ITS OWN
FACTORY FLOOR.**

The author cheeks a Sako Grey Wolf 85, his eye centered in the scope by the stock comb.
Note the Sako rings.

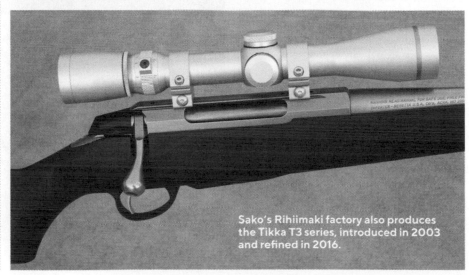

Sako's Riihimäki factory also produces
the Tikka T3 series, introduced in 2003
and refined in 2016.

This 13-year-old huntress borrowed a Sako .270 for her first safari. Three animals fell to three shots.

over/under shotguns. By 1989 Sako-Valmet Oy, Tourula had begun assembling shotguns in Italy, while Tikka's Tikkakoski Works had shifted production to Sako's Riihimaki factory.

In 2003 Tikka announced its T3 bolt rifle. I was blessed with the chance to see early production runs during manufacture. Superb design, high-quality components (including Sako cold hammer-forged barrels) and a retail price of just $549 made it an instant hit in the U.S. and on foreign game fields as well as in Scandinavia. Delightful for its simplicity, the twin-lug bolt comprised four major elements, easily separated by hand. It ran piston-smooth in its race and boasted the 70-degree lift of three-lug Sakos. The trigger adjusted from 2 to 4 pounds with a hex key through the magazine well.

More nimble than Tikka's Whitetail (sold stateside beginning in 1999), the T3 had a stiff receiver courtesy a modest ejection port. Two bolt stops adapted it to short and long cartridges. Top rails accepted 17mm clamp rings, though the rifle was also drilled and tapped for scope mounts. A steel stock insert served as recoil lug, engaging a receiver slot forward of the lightweight detachable polymer magazine. The T3 has chambered cartridges from the .204 Ruger to the .300 Winchester, including Remington's .222, a delightful round that during the 1950s punished foxes, crows and woodchucks when it wasn't winning Benchrest matches.

Tikka refined the T3 action in 2016, adding an "x" to the model designation. The T3x is the T3 intact, with minor improvements. More tapped holes provide additional scope mounting options. A larger port makes single loading easier. Modular moldings at wrist and fore-end of synthetic stocks on Lite and Varmint versions let you modify grip dimensions. A more resilient pad keeps a tighter rein on recoil. Hunter and Forest T3x rifles have checkered walnut stocks with straight and Monte Carlo combs. Three of eight sporters feature stainless steel, including a T3x with laminated wood. The current cartridge roster includes Sweden's own 6.5x55, still a Scandinavian favorite. But the other 14 rounds hail from the U.S. Prices have risen over the last decade and a half, to start at $725 (T3x Lite). Still, the least expensive Sako 85 lists for $1,000 more.

The Tikka line includes two "tactical" rifles. The TAC A1 has a chassis-style stock in both right- and left-handed con-

Remarkably successful in foreign markets, including the U.S. juggernaut powered by Winchester, Remington, Ruger, Savage, Weatherby, and a host of lesser gun-makers courting the proletariat, Sako has found its toughest competition on its own factory floor.

Tikka began manufacturing operations 26 years before Sako, when Finland was a Grand Duchy of Russia. During WWII Tikka turned out submachine guns and sewing machines. Following armistice, it produced Models 55 and 65 hunting rifles and Models 17, then 77 shotguns. In 1983 Tikka collaborated with Sako on the Model 555 bolt rifle. Sako then acquired Tikka — along with Valmet and its six decades of experience building

Lightweight, quiet, almost indestructible, Tikka T3 polymer magazines feed with sunrise certainty.

figurations. New last year was the T1x Multi-Task Rimfire, a 10-shot bolt action with a stiff, short, sight-free barrel and a synthetic stock.

Range trials of several T3 hunting rifles have blessed me with tight groups. A .308 carbine with 19-inch barrel *averaged* .86 with five types of ammo. Rifles in .270 and 7mm Magnum delivered knots almost as snug. Greased-piston bolt travel and triggers that break like glass rods are bonuses. Afield, the fine balance and agile feel of these rifles, and their reliable function, make them standouts.

....

In tall forest on a moose hunt, I turned to the snap of a twig. Then: a hoofbeat! A blur became a bull, galloping across my front, through brush too thick for a shot. By great good luck a slot opened just as he paused on a hill 90 yards off. My T3 already at cheek, I fired offhand, dropping him on the spot. Another time, on a frigid Scandinavian morning, I came suddenly upon a big cow. The T3 that day, a .300 WSM, came instantly on target. Steam erupted from off-side ribs as the moose spun, then collapsed.

Overwhelming favorites of hunters in northern Europe, Sako and Tikka rifles have become hits worldwide. I've found them from Scotland to South Africa, not only in the hands of visiting hunters, but in vehicles of gamekeepers and Professional Hunters, in racks of rifles to loan clients who don't travel with their own, or whose personal rifles develop problems afield — "rifles not so reliable as ours," shrugged one PH, hoisting a Sako that had been beaten about in Land Cruisers, fed a steady diet of sand by clients crawling toward game, sent hundreds of shots without a cleaning, and endured the repeated clasp of sweaty, bloody hands to earn one annual swipe with an oily rag.

Tamar had used one such rifle on her first safari. The evening a big kudu fell to her shot, that .270 got a little more attention than normal. Not that it needed coddling. "I like this rifle," she told me. "Maybe someday I'll own one."

Beretta now handles Sako and Tikka sales stateside: beretta.com.

Finland's rifles are popular abroad. This suppressed Tikka T3 is owned by a Scottish gamekeeper.

A HARD, LOVELY PLACE

Sako, Tikka and the ammunition firm Lapua have given Finland a place in shooting circles, but it's otherwise a little-known country. Swedish missionaries explored this rugged region as early as 1155, establishing Finland as a Swedish protectorate. It remained so until 1809. Surrendered to Russia, it was proclaimed a Grand Duchy by the Czar. In 1919 (Sako's debut year) Finland became an independent republic. Uneasy peace with the USSR ended when the Soviet army invaded in the winter of 1939-40. Hard fighting ensued until 1944. Finns lost land to the Soviets but kept their independence.

Eighty percent of Finland is timbered; 30 percent of its exports are forest products. Woodland and small farms support herds of whitetail deer, descendants of six animals brought from Minnesota in 1934. By 1960 Finns had begun hunting deer. Now they kill 17,500 annually. On a hunt there soon after the T3 appeared, I fired across a small meadow to down a whitetail at 220

yards. That shot drew mixed reactions from my Finnish companions, who thought 150 a long poke.

Finland has only one large native predator: the wolf. Historically considered a threat to children and livestock, it was trapped and shot to extinction by the end of the 19th century.

Hunting in Finland is highly regulated, the game managed by 300 state-sanctioned hunting groups that, at the time of my latest visit, comprised 2,370 clubs and 140,000 members. A Central Association of Hunters administers 15 conservation districts. You needn't be a club member to hunt, but members enjoy access to the best places. Finland's 300,000 moose hunters deliver a healthy boost to the economy, as 84 percent of the 22 million pounds of

game meat sold each year in Finland is moose!

To ensure hunters are capable of safe conduct and clean kills afield, Finland requires each license applicant to pass range tests. Visitors not exempted. All shots offhand.

"Standing, then moving," boomed the truck-shouldered Finn, without a smile. Apprehensively I closed the bolt and hoisted the Tikka. My crosswire bobbed against a black paper moose 80 meters away. Scoring rings were invisible from the line; I knew the "10" was little bigger than my hand.

The buzzer seemed as loud as my shot, too soon on its heels. I ran the bolt, fired again. Too slow! I managed a third just before the moose ducked behind an abutment.

"Now moving."

Palms sweating, I waited. At the buzzer, the moose burst into view and zipped along a rail. On the dewlap! Smoothly now. The bullet sped with a heartbeat to spare. Left to right I swung too fast. That shot would scuttle my chances. After two more runs, the Finn thundered. "You must repeat." That is, if you're a hunter, you must prove you can shoot like one before entering the woods. Eventually, I did.

GEMS FROM THE
STEVENS
LABYRINTH

Looking back at one of the oldest and most famous names in American gun making

BY **TERRY WIELAND**

Stevens has been in business more or less continuously since 1864, interrupted in its civilian production only by two world wars. For most of its 150-plus-years it has produced solid, but low-priced, rifles and shotguns, the vast majority of which were single shots. Stevens never sought to tame the West like Winchester, or attach its name to a great historical event, as with Sharps and the buffalo hunters. Even long-range big-bore target shooting, widely practiced in the late 1800s and dominated by Ballard and Remington, was beyond the ambition of Joshua Stevens.

For 22 years, however, between 1894 and 1916, the J. Stevens Arms & Tool Co. became a name to be reckoned with in the nationally popular sport of *Schützen* (offhand) medium-range target shooting. During that period, Stevens built rifles on its two finest actions, the Model 44, and its successor the 44½, that were the equal of any rifles then being made — even such names as Ballard and Winchester.

And Stevens was a big company. In 1907, it billed itself as the largest manufacturer of sporting arms in the world, and single-handedly put the town of Chicopee Falls, Massachusetts, on the map.

Although Stevens designed and manufactured a wide variety of single-shot actions during its first 50 years, including break actions and solid blocks, the 44 and 44½ were unquestionably its finest, and the best models built on those actions were aimed at the highest levels of American competition shooting. For five years, the most famous barrel maker of the era, Harry M. Pope, was allied with Stevens, lending his expertise to Stevens' production of rifles, barrels, loading tools and the assorted accoutrements vital to a top-flight competitor. The name "Stevens-Pope" lives on to this day as a marque of shooting excellence.

Between 1947 and 1991, rifle collector James J. Grant wrote five volumes on the subject of single-shot rifles, and he was a recognized expert in the field. He stated that, had the Stevens 44½ come on the market a few years earlier, it would have been acknowledged as the finest single-shot action in America — accurate, strong, ergonomic, dependable and beautifully made from the best materials available. It was Stevens' ill luck that the 44½ made its debut just as *Schützen* shooting began its decline. The outbreak of war in Europe in 1914 applied an emphatic end to its production and to Stevens' existence as an independent company. Since 1915, the J. Stevens Arms & Tool Co. has been someone's subsidiary — Westinghouse from 1915 until 1920, and Savage Arms ever since.

No one has ever written a comprehensive, definitive history of Stevens and its products and, frankly, no one in his right mind, knowing even the barest facts about the Stevens company, would attempt it.

First, there are no company records. According to James Grant, around 1920 the U.S. Defense Department began an investigation into war profiteering. Stevens had been a big player in military contracts under the aegis of Westinghouse, but with the war over and contracts canceled, with the big money already made and equipment lying idle, Westinghouse cast Stevens adrift. Just about the same time, the Stevens company records mysteriously went up in flames.

In the absence of such records, an historian's major source of information is company catalogues listing models and variations, with each catalogue, ideally, numbered and dated. While Stevens produced catalogues regularly, there was little logic to them. The company would reuse a catalogue number such as, say, No. 52, reprinting it at a later date, but adding or deleting models as it saw fit. Two catalogues, each numbered "52," might contradict each other, with each claiming to be authoritative and authentic. This did not happen just once or twice; with Stevens, such erratic behavior was habitual.

Then there is the question of models, model numbers and specifications. Such information is the lifeblood of gun collecting, and it was here that Stevens really went off the rails. Frank de Haas, whose *Single Shot Rifles and Actions* (Gun Digest Books, 1969), is one of the standard references, states that Stevens' model numbering system was "completely incomprehensible."

Failing company records and reliable catalogues, the researcher falls back on patent dates and serial numbers stamped on individual rifles. Again, one runs into the Stevens brick wall. De Haas mentioned one instance in which two rifles in his possession were obviously different. Based on the action model, one was later and one earlier, yet the presumably earlier rifle had both a higher serial number and a later patent date stamped on it.

One would think it possible to take a given rifle, study its features and match it up with a catalogue description to at least nail down its model number and possible production date. But no. There were just too many variations and

> **NO ONE HAS EVER WRITTEN A COMPREHENSIVE, DEFINITIVE HISTORY OF STEVENS AND ITS PRODUCTS AND, FRANKLY, NO ONE IN HIS RIGHT MIND, KNOWING EVEN THE BAREST FACTS ABOUT THE STEVENS COMPANY, WOULD ATTEMPT IT.**

....

(opposite) Stevens Ideal No. 47 (top) built on a Model 44½ action, and an Ideal No. 51 on a Model 44 action. The No. 51, probably built around 1902, is a .32–40 and has the original Stevens tang sight. Note that this No. 47, while a 44½ action, has the pin that accommodated the pivoting block in the 44. It was omitted in most 44½ actions but was reinstated later as a base for an optional ejector. The presence or absence of this pin is often used to differentiate between the two actions, so one must be careful.

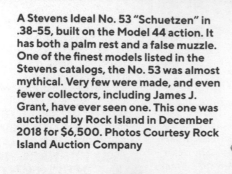

A Stevens Ideal No. 53 "Schuetzen" in .38–55, built on the Model 44 action. It has both a palm rest and a false muzzle. One of the finest models listed in the Stevens catalogs, the No. 53 was almost mythical. Very few were made, and even fewer collectors, including James J. Grant, have ever seen one. This one was auctioned by Rock Island in December 2018 for $6,500. Photos Courtesy Rock Island Auction Company

possible configurations. For example, from catalogue No. 50, dated 1902, referring to its highest-grade target rifle, the No. 54: The purchaser had a choice of 12 cartridges, in four barrel lengths, with seven different sighting systems, a choice of half a dozen buttplates and another half-dozen levers, three different trigger arrangements and two frame sizes. On top of this, custom engraving was available and, if the buyer placed a special order, virtually any of the above, such as barrel length or weight, could be varied.

Since Stevens almost never engraved the actual model name or number on a rifle, physical characteristics are all you have to go on, combined with highly questionable catalogue descriptions.

The foregoing is but a preamble to a mammoth disclaimer. As de Haas pointed out, when it comes to Stevens rifles, the most commonly used words are "generally" and "usually." Two words to be avoided are "never" and "always." As soon as you state an absolute, a rifle is sure to surface and prove you wrong.

Here, however, is the equally mam-

moth irony: Out of this dog's breakfast of inconsistent rifle models and conflicting information, we might be justified in concluding there is no seam of gold amidst the dross. And, we would be wrong. Between 1894 and 1916, the J. Stevens Arms & Tool Co. made some of the finest and most beautiful target rifles ever seen in America, with their accuracy guaranteed by the personal imprimatur of Harry M. Pope himself.

The two actions that made this possible were the Models 44 and 44½. (Because there were rifles with model numbers 44 and 44½, when referring to the actions alone we will use "Model" but identify the rifles by "No.")

Along about 1893 (the date is vague) Stevens introduced a new action that would become the foundation for a line

of top-quality target rifles to compete with the established Maynards, Ballards and the recently introduced Winchester Model 1885. The 44 is sometimes described as a falling-block action, but Frank de Haas calls it a "swinging" block, which is more accurate. The breech-block, manipulated by an underlever, pivots on a pin, rocking back from the barrel. When closed, it's supported by its linkage.

Outwardly, it resembles a cross between the Ballard and the Winchester, and some of its features — notably, the selection of lever designs and even some of the model names — are copied from the Ballard. It's an external-hammer design with a half-cock "safe" position. The 44 made its debut just as the blackpowder era neared its end and was intended for low-pressure blackpowder cartridges such as the .32-40 and .38-55. For these, as well as a plethora of rimfires, from .22 to .32, it was amply strong.

Since about 1885, Stevens had been very active in the field of cartridge

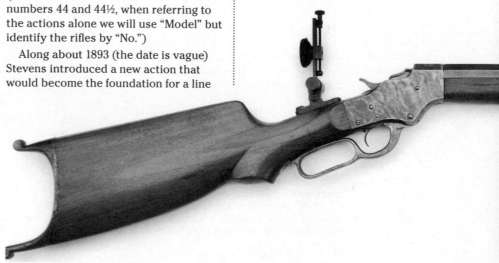

design. Some attribute the .25-20 Single Shot to Stevens, but in fact that was originally a Maynard chambering. The confusion is understandable, given the short-form ".25-20 SS." Later, Stevens itself alluded to the .25-20 SS as being its own development, but since it had bought out the Massachusetts Firearms Co., maker of the Maynard in 1892, perhaps the claim is justified. Either way, the .25-20 SS became popular in the series of rifles named "Ideal," built on the Model 44 action after 1893. Other popular Stevens cartridges included the .25-21 Stevens and the .28-30-120.

The company's great triumph in cartridge design, however, and the one destined to become the all-time most popular and widely distributed cartridge in the world, was the .22 Long Rifle. Stevens originated the design, Union Metallic Cartridge (UMC) made the ammunition, and from its debut in 1888 it scaled one height after another. Thus, having sired the .22 LR and taken over Maynard, in 1893 Stevens was well-positioned to assume a prominent place in the winner's lists at shooting matches across the country.

What it didn't foresee were the dramatic changes to the shooting world soon to be brought about by smoke-less gun powder. Beginning around 1888, smokeless powder proceeded to change everything about rifle shooting: Ballistics, pressures, bullet design and construction, cartridge design and, in-directly, the design of rifles to use them. None of this happened overnight, of course, and serious target shooters did not immediately abandon their beauti-fully made and ultra-accurate single-shot rifles. Quite the contrary: They resisted the change — justifiably, in many ways— so the transition was gradual and gun makers had time to adapt.

In Stevens' case, it realized the Model 44 action was not strong enough to withstand smokeless-powder pressures,

In the Model 44½ action (below) the breechblock protrudes from the action floor when it is open. In the older Model 44, with its rocking block, nothing projects. In the 44, the pin directly beneath the receiver ring is the pivot for the block; although it is unnecessary in the 44½, a pin in a similar position was included on some later actions to provide a base for an optional ejector. For this reason, the lack of a pin definitely denotes the 44½, but the presence of a pin is not an absolute indicator either way.

(above) Rock Island Auction Co. CEO Kevin Hogan, with the "extremely scarce" Stevens No. 53 auctioned by his company in 2018.

This Stevens Ideal No. 47 "Model Range" (sometimes called "Modern Range") in .25-20 Single Shot, is built on a Model 44½ action. It is fitted with Lee Shaver's Soule–style tang sight and globe front sight. James J. Grant considered the Stevens pistol–grip stock to be the most beautiful of any American single–shot rifle. This No. 47 has almost perfect case colors in the distinctive Stevens ripple or "marcel" pattern. The beautiful colors of their casehardened receivers made Stevens rifles very attractive, with or without engraving.

An original Stevens target tang sight. It was a highly regarded sight that incorporated windage adjustments as well as elevation. The J. Stevens Arms & Tool Co. was also a pioneer in the production of rifle scopes and manufactured a line of loading tools and related equipment. Between 1894 and 1916, Stevens was a major player in the world of high-level rifle shooting.

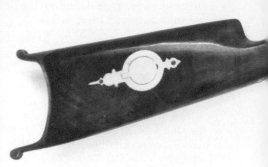

realized that smokeless powder was changing the world and the Model 44 action was not strong enough to adapt. Again, dates are vague, but around 1903 Stevens added a new action to its line: the Model 44½. Whether Pope was involved directly in its design, no one today can say. It would be very strange, however, to bring on board a man of Pope's stature, pay him a king's ransom, lock in his knowledge under contract, and then *not* consult him about such a major development as a new action to transform your line of top-quality target rifles.

Outwardly, the 44½ resembled the 44 in much the same way the Winchester High Wall looks like the Winchester Low Wall. Internally, however, it was quite different. Where the 44 was a rocking block, the 44½ was a true falling block, firmly supported in place by the steel shoulders of the frame, amply strong to accommodate the hottest cartridges of the day and, in fact, the hottest for decades to come.

Beginning with the Sharps in 1848, falling-block actions had been around in many forms for 50 years, but the Stevens 44½ was a falling block with a difference. Most falling blocks require that the cartridge be fully seated as the block slides up behind it. The Stevens block was beveled at the base in such a way that it rocked forward as it closed, seating a cartridge that could be protruding from the chamber by as much as a quarter inch. On opening, it rocked to the rear, pulling the firing pin back from the primer. In an era of soft primers, blackpowder fouling, cartridges of dubious quality, and handloaded bullets seated out to the rifling, these were serious advantages.

The Stevens Ideal rifles had another feature that horrifies modern makers of target rifles, but which worked extremely

which were in the region of 35,000 to 40,000 CUP (Copper Units of Pressure), compared to less than 20,000 CUP for a typical blackpowder cartridge like the .32-40.

However, in the half-dozen years since the introduction of the 44, the Ideal line had established itself on target ranges. Its reputation was good enough that Stevens was able to persuade Harry Melville Pope, barrel maker *extraordinaire*, to merge his business with Stevens,' and come to work for it on a five-year contract at a reputed $5,000 per annum. This was an enormous salary in 1901. Pope

turned over his machinery for making his highly esteemed loading equipment, and taught Stevens employees to make the "Stevens-Pope" line of tools. He also brought his expertise in rifling and fitting barrels and was kept busy imparting these skills to the Stevens craftsmen.

Harry Pope obviously had a high regard for the Stevens 44, else he would not have attached his name to its rifles for any amount of money. (Pope was one of those dedicated men to whom money is unimportant in the greater scheme of things.) However, someone at Stevens, and very likely with Pope's involvement,

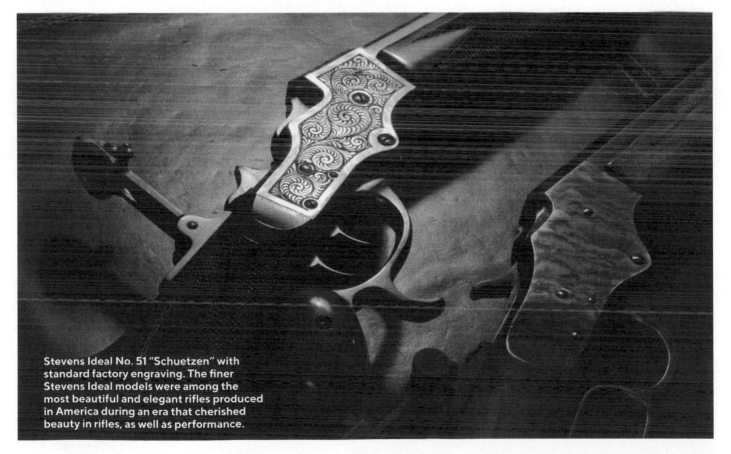

A Stevens rifle built on a Model 44 action, with Stevens scope, in .25–25. It is difficult to determine exactly which model this is, but it's probably a late No. 45 with several special-order items, such as the patchbox and the barrel set up for a scope only and no dovetails for iron sights.

well. (Again, Harry Pope must have approved of it, so who are we to argue?) The barrels were threaded into the action, but not machine-tightened; instead, the barrel was screwed in by hand pressure only. Then, a large set screw in the floor of the action was tightened and its conical tip held the barrel rigidly in place. Although the bore could be cleaned with the barrel on the rifle (unlike many single shots), having a barrel that was easily removed made thorough bore cleaning much easier.

Any other company, having introduced such a radical new action, would come up with an equally new line of distinct models — or at least model designations — to go with it. Not Stevens. Instead, it kept most of the existing model names and numbers, specifications, and optional extras, but henceforth supplied the rifles with the new action

rather than the old. From 1903 onward the high-grade centerfire Stevens target rifles would be built on the 44½ action, with the 44 relegated to low-pressure centerfire and rimfire cartridges like the .22 Long Rifle. It should be noted that the high-end models were numbered, starting at 44 and going up to 56. Some (but not all) also had model names, such as "Schuetzen" (sic) or "Modern Range." Among these was a No. 44 (built originally on the 44 action) and the No. 44½, built on the newer action. To top it all off, they were still called "Ideal." A No. 47, for example, was formally the Stevens Ideal Model 47 "Modern Range." And you could find them with exactly that designation made with either the No. 44 or 44½ action, depending on the year of manufacture — which is impossible to determine exactly from any markings, including the serial number.

We have reproduced schematic diagrams of both the 44 and 44½ actions, drawn by James Triggs and originally published in the 1966 *Gun Digest*. These clearly show the differences, but these differences are not absolute. There were variations to both actions that can be confusing. For example, the usual way to differentiate between them, when viewed from a distance, is the pin (screw) through the upper part of the action, below the receiver ring and forward of the hammer. This is the pivot pin for the 44's breechblock. Since the 44½ breechblock doesn't pivot, it doesn't have a pin in this position.

Or does it? Some later-production 44½ actions have a pin there, used as the base for an ejector, which was not included on all models. Even without an ejector, however, the pin may still be there. How do I know for sure? I know because I have one.

Stevens Ideal No. 51 "Schuetzen" with standard factory engraving. The finer Stevens Ideal models were among the most beautiful and elegant rifles produced in America during an era that cherished beauty in rifles, as well as performance.

Central extractor on a late Model 44 action. This replaced the earlier side extractor and allows us to date this rifle to the late 1890s.

On the 44 the shoulder is slightly lower than on the 44½, just like the Winchester High and Low Walls. But there are differences in appearance among 44s of early and late vintage, as well as between 44s and 44½s. With the action open it's easy to tell because the falling block of the 44½ protrudes from the floor of the action whereas the 44 does not. Still, the only way to be absolutely sure about an action is to have it in your hands.

Although Stevens offered a line of clearly defined models throughout the period in question, like most gun makers of the day it was more than willing to accommodate anything a client wanted. The most common variations, aside from caliber, are barrel length, weight and profile; styles of lever and buttplate; and, of course, engraving. Then as now, there were standard engraving patterns, and there were custom ones to accommodate even the wildest fantasies. One rifle offered for sale at the Rock Island Auction in 2018 had standard scrolling on one side embracing a banner with the name "Lucile," (sic) while on the other side two woodchucks cavorted under a tree. Was "Lucile" a wife, girlfriend, mistress, one of the woodchucks or the rifle itself? Would that I knew.

James J. Grant had almost three-quarters of a century's experience as a connoisseur and enthusiast of Stevens rifles, so what he wrote about them is worth heeding. He said the model number would often be stamped on the face of the action under the fore-end — often, but not always. There were also other marks there that, even with his broad experience, he could not interpret. For example, the letters "O" or "EX." Also under the fore-end, barrels would (or should) be stamped with a number denoting weight and profile, with "1" being the smallest and "5" the heaviest. Well, I have in my possession a No. 51 "Schuetzen" with an extraordinarily heavy barrel — obviously a special order — stamped with a "1" when logic says it should be a "6" or higher. So who knows?

Stevens' grand plan for the transition from the 44 action to the 44½ came to a halt with the outbreak of the Great War.

When it broke out in Europe, the British government cast about desperately, offering contracts to produce everything from rifle barrels to bayonets. Most of Gun Valley's firearms companies snapped at the bait and Stevens was no exception. As an investor-owned company, it was susceptible to fast-cash incentives. In 1915 Westinghouse acquired the J. Stevens Arms & Tool Co. for its gun-making equipment and expertise and began to cash in producing military wares.

Production of civilian rifles ceased by 1916 and the excellent Model 44½ action was never made again. Around 1920, with the war over, contracts canceled, and arms-making facilities standing idle, Westinghouse put Stevens up for sale and it was purchased by Savage Arms. When civilian production resumed, Stevens was relegated to making only low-priced rifles, based solely on the old Model 44 action. Presumably, the production lines for these were still in place, whereas the newer machinery for the 44½ was gone. Whatever the reason, the weaker 44 lived on, through a succession of ever more cheaply made rifles, until the last one left the plant, assembled from parts, around 1947.

....

Although the catalogues do not state it explicitly anywhere that I can find, and James Grant only alludes to it, both the 44 and 44½ actions were made in two (or three) different sizes. In the case of the 44, there was the standard action as well as a larger one used on the higher-grade *Schützen* rifles. Presumably, this same

Stevens put Chicopee Falls, Massachusetts, on the map. The Stevens name on the barrel took various forms over the years. This one dates from about 1900. This barrel is "Nickel Steel," which Stevens began offering as an extra-cost option with the introduction of smokeless powders.

system was applied to the 44½, since Stevens purported to offer in each model the same features as before. The 44½ then added a smaller size, 044½, made especially for the Model 56 or "Ladies" rifle. Nor does Frank de Haas mention this in his chapters on the two actions, wherein he lists their anomalies for gunsmiths and suitability as the basis for custom rifles.

Phil Sharpe, in *The Rifle in America*, states categorically that different action sizes each had an identification number (107, 108, 109, and 110 — he lists only four) but that this system was discontinued in 1896 when management changed. However, also according to Sharpe, there were seven different weights of frames, ranging from 3¼ pounds for the No. 44 to 5¾ pounds for the No. 51, with five in between. This, he says, was "complete with fore-arm." No other writer on the subject confirms this. I suspect he may have been referring to the total weight of an action sans barrel, but with the different buttstock styles, levers and buttplates that were standard for each model.

The heavy Model 44 *Schützen* action also has a lug on the face of the hammer that helps support the breechblock on firing. Again, I know this for certain because I have one.

Aside from Grant, de Haas, and Sharpe, there are books on single shots by Gerald O. Kelver, and the 1987 collaboration by Ned Roberts and Ken Waters. (A bibliography is included at the end.) Anyone wanting to understand Stevens rifles needs them all. Just when you think you have a handle on it, another writer pops up with another bit of heretofore unsuspected information that conflicts with what you think you already know. My suspicion is that each based much of what he wrote about Stevens on specific rifles he had owned or handled, which is the only certain method in the absence of factory records and reliable catalogues.

> **BETWEEN 1900 AND 1920, THE AMERICAN SHOOTING WORLD CHANGED DRAMATICALLY. OFFHAND TARGET SHOOTING WITH SINGLE-SHOT RIFLES LIKE THE BALLARD AND STEVENS FADED, TO BE REPLACED BY MILITARY-STYLE SHOOTING USING BOLT ACTIONS WITH BULL BARRELS, MAINLY SHOOTING FROM PRONE.**

Between 1900 and 1920, the American shooting world changed dramatically. Offhand target shooting with single-shot rifles like the Ballard and Stevens faded, to be replaced by military-style shooting using bolt actions with bull barrels, mainly shooting from prone. Then, in the late 1920s, the creation of the .22 Hornet sparked a rush toward high-velocity varmint rifles and wildcat cartridges. Suddenly, single-shot actions were in demand for building accurate custom varmint rifles, and many a fine old single shot was torn apart and cannibalized for this purpose.

Seeing an opportunity, Stevens chambered its Model 44-actioned No. 417 and 417½ "Walnut Hill" in the .22 Hornet, but it lasted only a couple of years. Stevens quickly learned that the 44 would not take Hornet pressures and the Stevens

Hornet was discontinued. This had an odd connection, however; in the 1930s, my father was a teenager interested in hunting and shooting. Thanks to *Field & Stream*, he developed a yen for a Stevens rifle in .22 Hornet that lasted into the 1960s, and I remember him describing such a rifle with a gleam in his eye.

This experience demonstrated that the 44 action was inadequate for the Hornet, Bee, Zipper Improved or any of that ilk. It developed a reputation for being, to quote one critic, "pitifully weak," but it was hardly that. With its intended cartridges at normal pressures, it stands up well and makes a very fine rifle. You just have to resist trying to turn it into something it's not.

Conversely, the 44½ was not only strong enough to handle the new cartridges, a used one could be had for considerably less money than the glamorous Ballard or Winchester. Fortunately, it seems that during its approximate 12-year life, Stevens made a lot of 44½s.

There are conflicting reports on the quality of steel, or malleable iron, or Norway iron, from which the two actions were made, with some authorities saying one thing and others something quite different. Most agree, however, that the 44½ was made of better steel — drop-forged rather than cast — and was generally better finished than the 44, at least in the lower grades. Stevens' best was always its best, period.

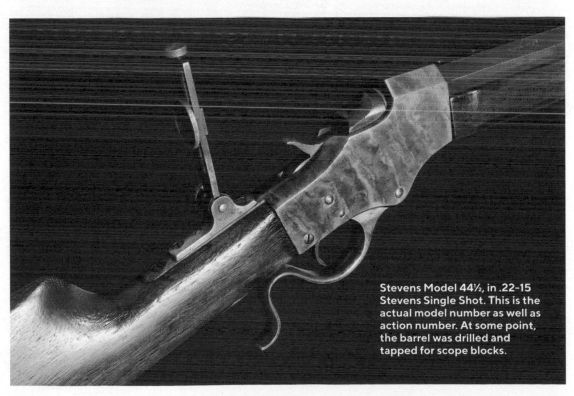

Stevens Model 44½, in .22-15 Stevens Single Shot. This is the actual model number as well as action number. At some point, the barrel was drilled and tapped for scope blocks.

Although he returned to working on his own as soon as his contract expired in 1906, Harry Pope's aura hung on at Stevens (with its contrivance) until war broke out a decade later. The name Pope-Stevens (or Stevens-Pope) is still heard today, in connection with bullet molds, powder measures, powder flasks, lubrication pumps and, of course, a Stevens rifle with a Pope barrel. Harry Pope told James Grant that he personally worked only on rifles up to serial number 1,200, which most take to mean that they were almost all on Model 44 actions.

....

The key Stevens Ideal models were numbered from 44 to 56, built initially on the 44 action and later on the 44½. When this transition began, Stevens dropped some models, amalgamating them with numbers either higher or lower, based on available options. For example, the No. 53 was a full-blown *Schützen* rifle, complete with palm rest. The palm rest was the only feature that differentiated it from the No. 52, so it was made an option on the 52 and the 53 was dropped. So rare was an original 53 that James Grant believed Stevens had never actually made one. Only late in his life did he see a genuine 53. That rifle was auctioned at Rock Island in December 2018, billed as "incredibly scarce…possibly unique…"

The following list is not definitive, but gives an idea of where each model fitted in. It's taken from the 1902 catalogue (#50).

Number 44 was the basic rifle. Many options were offered, but the base price was $10. No. 45 (Ideal Range), at $22, offered many more options, including a wide range of barrel lengths and weights, while the No. 44 was offered in one barrel length only. There was no No. 46 in this catalogue, but it was listed in others. Essentially, it was the No. 45 with a walnut upgrade.

Number 47, the "Model Range" (usually referred to as "Modern Range") was $27 and was the lowest grade to offer the full Stevens panoply of levers, buttplates, calibers, sights and barrels.

Number 49 was the famous "Walnut Hill" ($42). Accuracy was guaranteed: a 10-shot, 4-in. group at 200 yards, in the favorite *Schützen* calibers (.28-30-120, .32-40 and .38-55). This guarantee carried on through the higher grades. Options and variations? Too numerous to list.

With No. 51, the aptly named Ideal "Schuetzen," Stevens was into the realm of serious competition rifles. Its base price was $58, but from there the sky was the limit. No. 52, the "Schuetzen Jr.," was very similar to the 51 except it had a pistol-grip stock and conventional loop lever, rather than the 51's straight stock and lever with wooden panels and finger rest. It was $2 less.

The phantom No. 53 was next, although not listed in this catalogue. The palm rest required a special fore-end with a flat panel to accommodate its base, with checkering around that panel, so it was not merely a matter of screwing a steel base onto the fore-end. (Interestingly, the No. 53 sold at Rock Island does *not* have this panel and differs from the accepted No. 53 specifications in other ways as well. You might say it's a typical Stevens — i.e., an anomaly.)

The "Schuetzen Special," No. 54, was the top of the line at a base of $68. Accuracy was guaranteed at 3½ inches for 10 shots, rather than 4 inches.

After this came the No. 55, called the "Lady Model" in this catalogue, later referred to as the "Ladies Model." It was lighter, with a shorter stock, and was priced at just $25. No mention is made of frame size. In later catalogues, Stevens replaced it with No. 56, a Ladies Model built on the smaller 044½ frame. Naturally, when the 44½ action appeared, model No. 44½ was added to the Ideal line.

From 1894 until 1916, the Stevens 44 and 44½ actions were in a constant process of transition, evolution, expansion and improvement. Although most complaints about the 44½ are minor (or disputed), had the Great War not intervened, it's likely that Stevens would have continued to improve it and iron out any perceived bugs. Had it done so, and had the 44½ still been in production when the great varmint-rifle craze of the 1930s struck, it would have been in a prime position to cash in.

Unlike most single-shot actions, the 44½ was admirably suited for use with a scope, with ample room for loading and unloading. Stevens was a pioneer in the use of scopes for long-range shooting. In 1901, it purchased the Cataract Optical Co. of Buffalo, New York, and produced a line of innovative scopes under the Stevens name. The manager, F.L. Smith, was a highly respected optical engineer, and under his guidance Stevens introduced the focusing reticle (1904) and the first usable variable (1909). The optics division was later sold to Lyman. Similarly, Stevens had its own line of high-quality receiver sights and wind-gauge front sights, employing vernier scales, spirit levels and other features of top-flight competitive rifles.

Like most of its competitors, Stevens had its own unique method of case-hardening its frames, which gave them a distinctive color pattern. James Grant refers to this as "ripple" or "marcel"

Parts List—Stevens 44½
1. Frame
2. Barrel
3. Barrel Screw
4. Rear Sight
5. Front Sight
6. Breechblock Spring
7. Breechblock Spring Plunger
8. Breechblock Spring Screw
9. Breechblock
10. Firing Pin
11. Firing Pin Screw
12. Firing Pin Lever (centerfire only)
13. Firing Pin Lever Pin (centerfire only)
14. Link
15. Breechblock-Link Pin
16. Lever-Link Pin
17. Lever
18. Extractor
19. Lever Bolt
20. Lever Bolt Screw
21. Lever Plunger
22. Lever Plunger Spring
23. Hammer
24. Hammer Fly
25. Hammer Stirrup
26. Hammer Stirrup Pin
27. Hammer Screw
28. Top Stock Screw
29. Bottom Stock Screw
30. Trigger Plate
31. Trigger
32. Trigger Pin
33. Trigger Plate Screw, Long
34. Trigger Plate Screw, Short (2)
35. Trigger Spring

Fore-end, fore-end screw, buttstock, buttplate, and buttplate screws are not shown.

Parts List— Stevens 44
1. Frame
2. Barrel Screw
3. Extractor
4. Hammer
5. Hammer Screw
6. Mainspring
7. Mainspring Screw
8. Trigger Spring
9. Trigger Spring Screw
10. Stock Screw, Upper
11. Stock Screw, Lower
12. Trigger
13. Trigger Screw
14. Breechblock
15. Breechblock Pivot
16. Breechblock Pivot Screw
17. Firing Pin
18. Firing Pin Screw
19. Link
20. Link Pin
21. Lever
22. Lever Pivot
23. Lever Pivot Screw
24. Lever-Link Pin
25. Lever Plunger
26 Lever Plunger Spring

Barrel, front & rear sights, fore-end, fore-end screw, buttstock, buttplate and buttplate screws are not shown.

coloring, and it is quite beautiful and immediately sets any Stevens rifle apart. Lower grades, with no engraving, are still very attractive because of this.

It is possible to roughly date some actions by certain features. For example, around 1898 the side-extractor was replaced by a central extractor, so any rifle with the latter feature is post-1898.

It is only fitting that we give the last word to James J. Grant, who did so much to rekindle interest in America's fine old single-shot rifles. After a lifetime spent collecting, studying, searching for, shoot-

ing, restoring, and converting single-shot rifles, he wrote that "the incomparable Stevens Model 44½ was one of the best falling-block action systems ever to see the light of day."

Col. Townsend Whelen agreed. In the 1953 *Gun Digest*, reflecting on his 60 years' experience with single-shot rifles, he concluded that "A first-rate rifle maker will turn out a larger proportion of gilt-edge shooting rifles when he uses the Stevens 44½ action than with any other."

James Grant especially admired the pistol-grip stock of the Model 47 *et al*,

which he called the most graceful and beautiful of any single shot. He also stated flatly that the Stevens factory barrels, even before Harry Pope, were as accurate as any then made, and he believed the 44½ action to be as strong as any. Overall, he wrote, "The rifles built at Stevens from 1903 until (1916) were the best ever produced by that great company, and among the very finest ever made in America."

These schematic diagrams by James Triggs of the 44 and 44½ actions were originally published in the 1966 *Gun Digest*.

MODEL 44½

MODEL 44

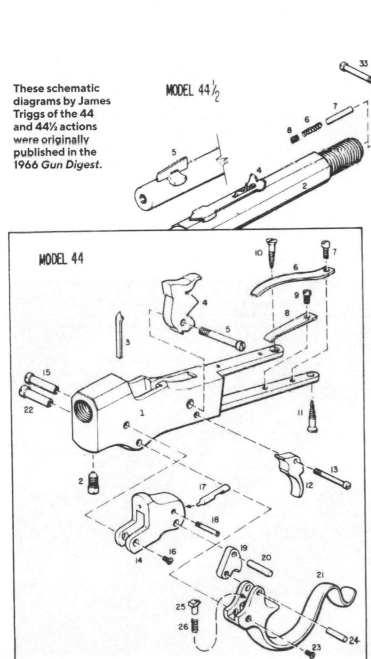

BIBLIOGRAPHY

De Haas, Frank, *Single Shot Rifles and Actions* (1969)

Grant, James J., *Single-Shot Rifles* (1947 and subsequent printings);

Grant, James J., *More Single-Shot Rifles* (1959 and subsequent printings)

Grant, James J., *Boys' Single-Shot Rifles* (1967)

Grant, James J., *Still More Single-Shot Rifles* (1979 and subsequent printings)

Grant, James J., *Single-Shot Rifles Finale* (1992)

Kelver, Gerald O., *Schuetzen Rifles History and Loadings* (1972 and subsequent printings) Kelver, Gerald O., *Reloading Tools, Sights and Telescopes for Single Shot Rifles* (1982 and subsequent printings)

Sharpe, Philip B., *The Rifle in America* (1938 and subsequent editions and printings through 1958)

Waters, Ken, and Roberts, Ned, *The Breech-Loading Single-Shot Rifle* (1987)

CUSTOM 1911s FOR A NEW CENTURY

BY **PATRICK SWEENEY**

As good as the old-time gun-smiths were, if a time machine allowed you to drop today's custom 1911s down on their bench, they would be green with envy. Today, the work on custom guns has reached a new high-water mark in quality. In fact, if you have the chance to look at some of the early work, with few exceptions you risk being disappointed when you closely inspect the details. You'll find unevenly pointed checkering, lines that wander or disappear and other details of craftsmanship that don't measure up to 21st-century standards.

The gunsmiths of earlier eras were diligent, and their products worked well, some fabulously so. But the standards of detail, finish and aesthetics were not as high as they are now, and customers

back then either didn't know, or were unwilling to pay for higher-level details.

Here, we'll look at the top-end custom, bespoke 1911s. The best custom gun-smiths often have clear ideas about what they will and won't do on a gun, but you can discuss it. With some, however, you can have it entirely your way.

Let's say you don't like 20 lpi checker-ing, and 30 is too fine. A full-custom 'smith can do 25 lpi checkering. Or, even something odd, like 27.5 lpi checkering or metric checkering. Of course, the further you wander from the path of the "usual" and the "known," the more you will have to pay for it. If you wish, you can shepherd a gun through several different gunsmiths. It will take a lot of time, but you can get the checkering from one, the sights from another, and the polish, blue and frenched borders

from a third. Not all combinations will be possible. To pick one example, if you ask Les Baer to do some extra work on an Ed Brown 1911, he may or may not do it (and vice versa). And even if he does, he's likely to be a bit grumpy about it.

The full-custom guys may object on aesthetic grounds, but only when you want to make something really heinous. And then, they may leave their name off it if they decide your tastes are simply too outré.

The subject of custom gunsmithing brings with it a few caveats. First, custom gunsmiths are not gun makers. Despite the inability of the various agen-cies involved to figure it out, installing sights, finishing or adding checkering is not "manufacturing." However, it is a gray area and custom gunsmiths work to keep themselves below whatever radar

Dripping with class, the Heirloom Precision look is timeless. Photo: Brady Miller, courtesy Heirloom Precision

The new custom gun is a level of quality so far above previous guns, that the older 'smiths would be green with envy if they knew. Photo courtesy Heirloom Precision and Hernandez Photography

A Delta out of Heirloom, built like a tank, but not as rattly as a tank. Photo courtesy Heirloom Precision and Hernandez Photography

A Dan Wesson 1911, like this suppressor-ready Wraith, comes with a slide-to-frame fit that a pistolsmith of the 1980s would envy.

may be sweeping to look for manufacturers. Basically, if a company can provide you with a finished firearm, and it has its name on it as the maker (Colt, Springfield, etc.), it is a manufacturer. If a gunsmith has you send him a working firearm, or a complete collection of parts, then he's a custom gunsmith and not a maker.

In many cases, top-end custom gunsmiths are one-man shops. If they get swamped with work, they may refuse new work for a while. Time spent on the phone is time not spent on the bench working on guns, so you may find that you can only contact them via email, and even then, you may wait a few days for a reply. As royalty and popes of the

past have discovered, having money and desire is often not enough. In many cases, you must pique the interest of an artist in order to get him or her to accept a commission.

A couple decades ago, before all custom rifle stocks became wispy carbon-fiber creations that weighed mere ounces, there were indestructible, non-magnetic, non-conducting stocks that went through a radical change. The styling became much more refined, traditional, formal and restrained. The white-line spacers and inlays had long disappeared — except for the Weatherby owners — and Monte Carlo stocks were on the wane, but the shape of custom stocks settled down to a mix of European and formal American-style points. If you want to see what the new rifle stock style is like, look at a current Ruger M77 Hawkeye, Mk II Magnum or a Kimber. What you'll see is highly reminiscent of an English African-hunting rifle of three-quarters of a century or more ago. The lines are cleaner, leaner and the details subtler.

The real change was in the

(below) Custom gunsmiths are usually one-man shops. That means that while they are out test firing your new gun, they can't be on the phone talking. And vice-versa.

reject the stock. Diamonds not all pointy? Redo it. Overruns were a near-panic situation and a stock with an uneven finish was a crisis. Of course, prices went up, but you expect to pay for quality.

Within the last couple of decades, the work on custom 1911s has undergone a similar transformation. And, as a bonus, you can get factory-new custom 1911s, as well as "send a gun off to a pistolsmith" custom guns, of the highest quality. In fact, some production guns are the equal in fit to the custom or semi-custom 1911s of the old days. A plain Dan Wesson 1911 will be fitted,

slide to frame, and barrel to the pair, as well as a whole raft of custom guns in the 1990s or later. If you send a Dan Wesson 1911 to a custom gunsmith who works on Dan Wessons, they might not have to do more than a small amount of work to the fit. And that will probably be as much for peace of mind as actual need.

To rehash two previously mentioned examples, consider checkering and slide-to-frame fit. Checkering used to be done by hand with a checkering file. It was a file with a negative impression of the checkering you wanted cut instead of the regular crosscut grooves. If you wanted checkering at 20 lpi, you used a 20 lpi file.

The checkering on a custom gun is often "chased" or touched-up with a hand file and a 10X loupe.

quality of workmanship. One example: back in even earlier days (formally known as "before Reagan") if you had custom checkering cut on your rifle stock, the fact that it was custom was plenty. If the lines were straight, parallel and the diamonds reasonably pointy, well, so much the better. When the quality of custom rifle work suddenly picked up, if the lines weren't straight and parallel, then that was enough to

(top) Once welded, a frame such as this one gets locked into a fixture, and the rails are machined or surface ground to the exact dimensions of the slide rails and slots. This level of work beats the peened-and-lapped approach to fitting hands-down. Photo: Jason Burton

This Best-Grade by Jason Burton was done on a USGI 1943 Colt. While the slide may be too soft for high-volume IPSC competition, it certainly will last 50,000 rounds or more. Photo courtesy Heirloom Precision and Hernandez Photography

A custom 'smith will attend to such details as the slide stop pin. Here, it has been cut flush with the frame, and the frame beveled slightly to allow disassembly.

A full-house gun takes time, planning and patience. A Stan Chen custom is worth every minute of waiting and every penny. Pistol courtesy Stan Chen Custom, photograph courtesy Christopher Marona

You used the file to cut parallel grooves on the frame frontstrap (or mainspring housing) and proceeded until they were evenly cut. Then, you'd go at a right angle and cut the cross grooves. Finally, you'd use a curved, three-sided file to clean things up and make the checkering perfect. Most production guns have a slide-to-frame fit that is OK, or casual. The slide might "float" over the frame rails with a few thousandths of an inch play.

For the modern custom 'smith, the first step in checkering is to see if the frame is dimensionally correct. It may take half a day to measure and compare the parts in order to determine if the frame is within spec (measuring the rails, the top deck, mag well, recoil spring cover, etc.) to proceed. If it isn't in spec, there isn't any point in continuing. If found wanting, the 'smith will send it back with instructions to send another that measures up. Once inspected and declared acceptable, the frame is locked in a fixture, and the frontstrap is ground or milled so the front face is cylindrical and parallel to the mag-well axis. (It may have been buffed to "clean up" a mar or machine tool mark, or it may just be

No blingy touches, no comps, no fads of the moment from Stan Chen. Just a purely perfect 1911, built to last a lifetime.

Note the detail that goes into the rails. They've been relieved where they don't need to do anything and have been precisely fitted where they have to work. Pistol courtesy Stan Chen Custom, photograph courtesy Christopher Marona

A Chen gun, in all its glory: fitted case, nameplate, numbered magazines and a spare extractor, as well as tools. You either leave this to someone in your will, or donate it to a museum once you're done shooting with it. Pistol courtesy Stan Chen Custom, photograph courtesy Christopher Marona

uneven.) Once it's dead-cylindrical, the same fixture is used to machine the basic lines. Then, the gunsmith will go over the lines with the same three-sided finishing file as before, but this time while wearing a magnifying visor or loupe. He'll inspect and even up any and all points and lines while watching through a 10x viewer.

Or, if the gunsmith does a specialty nonslip treatment, like Ned Christensen's Conamyds or Frag, or Chuck Rogers' Golfballs, after the ground-radius surface gets machined, it is closely inspected before it leaves the fixture just in case something needs to be attended to.

Next, the frame- and slide-rail dimensions will be fully mapped. Instead of simply measuring the frame-rail height and the slide-rail slot gap like in the old days, and then peening the former down to close the gap on the latter, the modern gunsmith goes about it as a rebuild. Once he's plotted the pistol's dimensions against the master drawing, he sends the frame off to his welder with detailed instructions. Using a surface grinder or milling machine the frame rails are welded and recut, so they are a perfect fit. The newest step is a laser welder. This adds steel to the rails in a controlled manner without injecting excess heat into the frame. Less heat means less chance of warpage.

Now, all this is dependent on the base gun and on the brand. You could have a wildly out-of-spec Colt and a perfect-fit Norinco and have a dilemma on your hands. Some gunsmiths will take on the Colt, even with the dimensions off,

An Heirloom Precision 1911 with a Swenson-like squared triggerguard and a Bruce Nelson Summer Special holster. Add a tactical folder and a suitable writing instrument, and you have a gentleman's daily carry ensemble. Photo: Brady Miller, courtesy Heirloom Precision

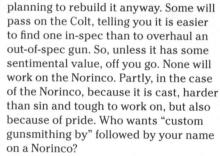

❝ ON TOP, A DETAIL OF THE TOP FLAT SERRATIONS THAT MIGHT PASS UNNOTICED AT THE FIRST VIEWING IS HIS INTERRUPTED LINE PATTERNS IN THE SERRATIONS.❞

The slide top lines end in an arrowhead, and the front sight has a gold line inlaid in it. All executed perfectly. Photo: Brady Miller, courtesy Heirloom Precision

planning to rebuild it anyway. Some will pass on the Colt, telling you it is easier to find one in-spec than to overhaul an out-of-spec gun. So, unless it has some sentimental value, off you go. None will work on the Norinco. Partly, in the case of the Norinco, because it is cast, harder than sin and tough to work on, but also because of pride. Who wants "custom gunsmithing by" followed by your name on a Norinco?

Now, in this book, because it is an illustrated edition, I would love to show you the fixtures, the drawings and the work in process. And so would the prospective competitors to those 'smiths, who would then not have to go to all the work of developing the stuff themselves, refining and fine-tuning their first efforts. To make a fixture that holds a frame, allows the frontstrap to be ground or machined, and allows for adjustments in the settings takes savvy, skill and hard work. You don't just give that kind of stuff away. So instead we look at the results. And if you really want to get a grasp of the difference between what the guy who thinks he knows guns looks for, and what the top hands look

A 9mm Commander out of Heirloom, with perfect 30 lpi checkering and serrations on the underside of the slide stop. Photo courtesy Heirloom Precision and Hernandez Photography

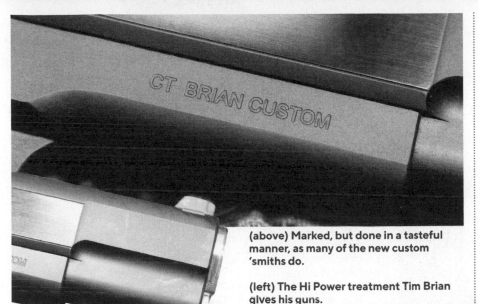

(above) Marked, but done in a tasteful manner, as many of the new custom 'smiths do.

(left) The Hi Power treatment Tim Brian gives his guns.

lines all must be parallel. The checkering on the frontstrap is checked for its "fit" to the frame corner and the grips. If it goes under the grips, it must be a perfect line-to-line fit. If it stops short, it must be an even line on the corner of the frame and evenly spaced from the grips. Again, it needs to be parallel and perfect. Do those details matter in function? No, but if you're going to be among the best, you tend to every detail, no matter how small.

Oh, and one of the details that is tended to is base-gun selection. The

The slide serrations, showing the "arrow to the muzzle" treatment.

for, here's an example: You'll have your local gun club 1911 expert handle a pistol, and he'll of course check the fit of the barrel to the slide and frame — the common "thumb push" check — and a slide-wriggling check.

The top hands will do that (they can't help it, it is part of their genetic code), but then they will look for the slide markings. Is the slide polished, and if so, are the markings crisp? Some of the top hands won't work on a gun if the markings have already been "pulled" or they

find it's thin in spots from prior buffing. Are the slide and frame dehorned? If so, is the edge of the dehorning even along its length? Uneven dehorning is a sign of sloppy work.

And here's an instance where the masters step out from the wannabes: they check the lines of the grips along the frame at the mainspring housing. The grip, frame and mainspring housing

Every surface, every detail, of this Tim Bryan mainspring housing has been planned and attended to.

top gunsmiths, the "name" guys, will insist on a Colt or a Springfield Armory, or they may be willing to accommodate themselves to a Caspian slide and frame if it hasn't already been worked on. They won't work on much else, although some, in a moment of weakness, might take on a project that "looks interesting." They aren't going to salvage someone else's work, they won't work on lesser-name guns, and they most definitely are not going to adjust their schedule for you.

In addition to timing, people often question what a custom gun is, exactly,

(above) The author's Titanium Commander built by Ned Christansen. This is a 10-shot, 30-yard Ransom Rest group. Be envious.

(right) Ned Christiansen's Conamyds grip treatment. This takes a special tool, planning, skill and patience.

and how much does it cost. Custom is as custom does. If you have a gunsmith install a set of adjustable sights and put some checkering on the frontstrap, that's a custom gun. If he was at least competent, and everything on it is straight and level, you have no need to be hesitant about showing off your custom gun. I think I'd have to draw the line at something so simple as slapping a pair of new grips on your 1911. That just doesn't rise to the level of customization even if they are Esmerelda or VZ grips.

A Tim Brian custom, with the slide-edge bevel lighted to show it off.

And he can shoot. Here Christiansen is wringing out a custom comp–carry gun chambered in .357 SIG on long-range targets. It doesn't drop much at 300 meters.

The author with his Ned Christiansen 9mm. He's two hits short of a passing score, shooting a rifle qualification course.

What can it cost? When you think of custom work, get your mind into the pattern of "$100 increments." Checkering? That'll be at least a couple of hundred — add another hundred if you want a non-standard spacing. Installing sights? Another hundred or two. Frenched borders? There's another Franklin or two added to the invoice.

Replacement parts add up, as does basic mechanical work such as fitting slides and frames and installing barrels. The result can be easily over $1,000 for

a light custom job, and the limit is met only after all the details have been attended to, which happens at about the $4,000 to $5,000 figure. Of course, for that you have an object of art, a thing of beauty, and a subject of some envy and/or appreciation. Of course, having done that, you can then completely blow the doors off the down payment for a house by handing the almost-finished pistol over to an engraver. It doesn't take much to add to our previous maximum again, in getting the perfect finish all "scratched up."

Oh, and forward-cocking serrations? That is like arguing religion. Some like them, some love them, some hate them, and some don't care and don't want to get sucked into yet an-

other debate over them. But for heaven's sake, if you do have to have them, at least be sure they match the rear serrations in pitch, angle, shape and depth. Nothing looks cheesier than vertical fronts and angled rears.

Now that all that's out of the way, here's a brief look at some of today's top names in the custom 1911 business.

STAN CHEN

Stan Chen is one of the guys who came to gunsmithing to work on art and make a living. Like many of the new breed of top custom 'smiths, he only does full-house customs. That is, you don't send a gun to Chen asking for a mag funnel and sights. If you are on the list, when you make it to the top, Chen builds you a full-house custom 1911, all the bells and whistles, and your input (like so many custom gunsmiths) is limited to the details like the kind of slide-top matting pattern you'd like, and whether you want it blued, stainless or hard-chrome.

Besides the now-standard exquisite workmanship found among the top 'smiths, Stan Chen is known for a few touches that you won't find elsewhere. One is his frontstrap and mainspring housing treatment. He cuts a diagonal

Bill Laughridge's "pocket" .45. He took a regular 1911, and turned it into a "hammerless" model compact 1911. And you can't see the silver solder seam, even blowing the photo up to 100%.

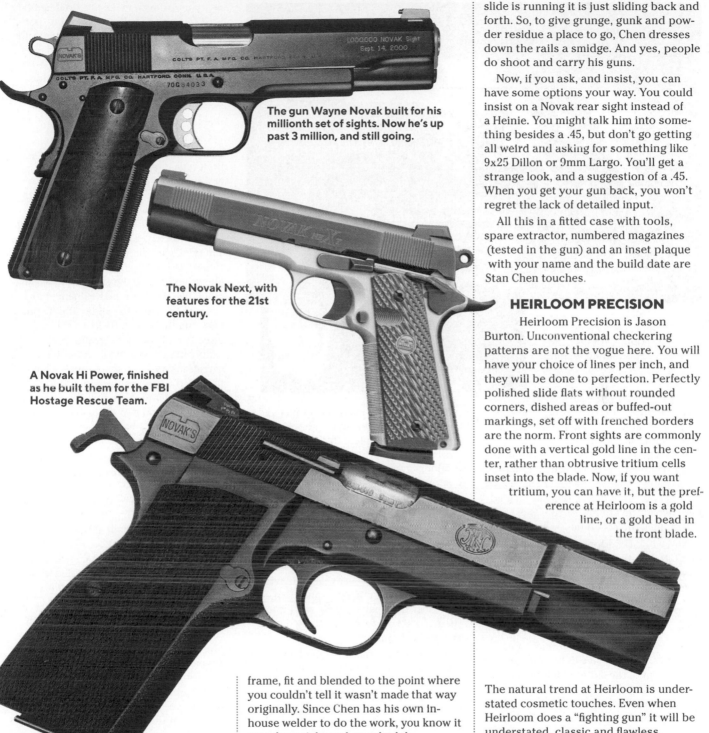

The gun Wayne Novak built for his millionth set of sights. Now he's up past 3 million, and still going.

The Novak Next, with features for the 21st century.

A Novak Hi Power, finished as he built them for the FBI Hostage Rescue Team.

slide is running it is just sliding back and forth. So, to give grunge, gunk and powder residue a place to go, Chen dresses down the rails a smidge. And yes, people do shoot and carry his guns.

Now, if you ask, and insist, you can have some options your way. You could insist on a Novak rear sight instead of a Heinie. You might talk him into something besides a .45, but don't go getting all weird and asking for something like 9x25 Dillon or 9mm Largo. You'll get a strange look, and a suggestion of a .45. When you get your gun back, you won't regret the lack of detailed input.

All this in a fitted case with tools, spare extractor, numbered magazines (tested in the gun) and an inset plaque with your name and the build date are Stan Chen touches.

HEIRLOOM PRECISION

Heirloom Precision is Jason Burton. Unconventional checkering patterns are not the vogue here. You will have your choice of lines per inch, and they will be done to perfection. Perfectly polished slide flats without rounded corners, dished areas or buffed-out markings, set off with frenched borders are the norm. Front sights are commonly done with a vertical gold line in the center, rather than obtrusive tritium cells inset into the blade. Now, if you want tritium, you can have it, but the preference at Heirloom is a gold line, or a gold bead in the front blade.

skip-line checkering pattern that at first seems quite coarse compared to 20 or 30 lpi checkering. Called "Progressive Traction," it provides a non-slip grip that works wonderfully. The mainspring housing pattern goes onto the frame, and it is perfectly symmetric at all edges. He also has his own mag well funnel, a low-profile addition that is welded onto the

frame, fit and blended to the point where you couldn't tell it wasn't made that way originally. Since Chen has his own in-house welder to do the work, you know it gets done right and on schedule.

He does slide-top flattening and matting in various patterns that simply pop your eyes out. Cosmetic details like fluted barrel and chamber, a dead-perfect fit of slide to frame, and a surface finish that is flawless are standard on a Stan Chen 1911. The rails have been relieved in the center, and bear on the slide just on the front and rear loading portions. Those are the areas at work when the gun locks up, and the rest of the time when the

The natural trend at Heirloom is under-stated cosmetic touches. Even when Heirloom does a "fighting gun" it will be understated, classic and flawless.

Grips will be highly figured, checkered or smooth for most guns, or aggressively textured for a fighting gun, but in all instances fitted to perfection. A Burton-built 1911 is an heirloom you will be proud to pass down to succeeding generations. And it will, of course, perform flawlessly. There wouldn't be any other point to it, would there?

Now, Jason Burton is not only a full-house gun guy, he can overhaul or

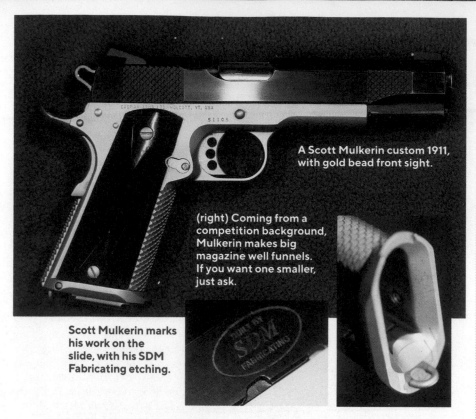

A Scott Mulkerin custom 1911, with gold bead front sight.

(right) Coming from a competition background, Mulkerin makes big magazine well funnels. If you want one smaller, just ask.

Scott Mulkerin marks his work on the slide, with his SDM Fabricating etching.

upgrade other firearms. You can send him a gun built by a name gunsmith or maker and ask him to change something, and he'll be happy to do it. Just be aware, as with so many custom gunsmiths, that he is doing things in the order they came in, and small one-detail jobs are tackled in between the full-house guns. So, the schedule is the schedule.

And while Heirloom prefers to work on Colt, it can and will build on a good base gun, such as a Springfield, Wilson Combat, Caspian or Les Baer.

CT BRIAN

The best way to describe a CT (Tim) Brian 1911 is "radical traditional." He does a very aggressive dehorning to the bottom of the slide, which results in an almost beveled edge. That and the frenched borders set off a flat, square, perfectly buffed slide flat, with scalloped edges to the cocking serrations.

On top, a detail of the top flat serrations that might pass unnoticed at the first viewing is his interrupted line patterns in the serrations. The resulting pattern forms three arrows pointing toward the muzzle to help direct your eye to the front sight.

A beveled barrel bushing, with a concentric-crowned barrel, allows all the accuracy of which the tube and ammo are capable. A huge but not

competition-sized magazine funnel and a flat mainspring housing with wide side-grooves complete this 1911. The matter of mainspring housing patterns is a long-standing discussion between customers and gunsmiths. In the old days, we'd simply cut cross-grooves with a checkering file, using the existing checkering on the mainspring housing and leave the outermost grooves double-wide pyramids. Now, custom gunsmiths often make their own mainspring housings from scratch — easy enough, with CNC machining stations — and then cut the checkering pattern they want into them. So, if you want something out of the ordinary, just ask.

The grips are smooth and highly figured with an inset CTB medallion. CT Brian does only full-house custom guns. However, within the full-house build you do have options. Don't like the Hi Power flats? Brian can be talked out of them. Want straight lines, without inset arrows? Again, Brian can be talked out of them. But it seems kind of pointless to go to a guy who does perfect polishing, matte work, borders and grips and not have him do those things.

NED CHRISTIANSEN

Ned Christiansen is not one to stick to a single pattern. While he is known for his "Conamyds" checkering pattern, he will undertake a task in a wide variety

of styles, or even make one up if need be. Conamyds are like checkering, but he developed a special tool, fixture and process to machine cones instead of pyramids. The cones, left flat-topped (else they'd be far too sharp) provide a distinctive nonslip pattern. Nothing looks like Conamyds, and no one else does them.

Christiansen built a special gun for me, a 9mm Titanium Commander. Built on a Caspian Commander slide and titanium race-ready receiver, he went to town. On it, he put some of his hallmark touches. He designed a new and improved grip safety, one that even those whose hands don't like the grip safety can get along with. He put his "Shield-Driver" sight on it. That design allows you to use the edge of something stout, like a holster, tactical shield or doorway, to work the slide. And he put his Conamyds on it. Because the slide already had cocking serrations, he simply milled a flat on it and put lateral serrations as a non-glare touch. Finally, he added a low-profile lanyard loop that is recessed into the mainspring housing. I've had several people gush over the pistol, and some have not even noticed the lanyard loop.

But Christiansen likes to stretch the boundaries. For one example, he finished a real 1911 as a custom gun. The pistol originally left Colt in 1924. It arrived in 2009 with a finish mostly gone and some minor pitting. He made it real, not retro. He tightened it up, put on hi-viz sights that would not have been considered outrageous in 1924, a low-profile lanyard loop and polished it to the standard of 1924. It was perfect.

At the other extreme, he built a 9mm comp gun, a proof-of-concept project. The comp is the most effective he could devise. The tang was sculpted so that you could place your hand higher than on any other tang. To accommodate the tang, he redesigned the thumb safety, so it pivots at the front end instead of the rear. The result is a 9mm 1911 that cycles like lightning and has so little felt recoil it is like shooting a super-loud .22LR. And as the pièce de résistance, he milled the top of the slide to accept an Optima 2000 red-dot sight. No iron sights at all.

And finally, he is the only one I've ever seen who could take a LAR Grizzly in .45 Win. Mag. and make it look good. Even made it look like a normal 1911, if you didn't have it in your hands to check the actual size.

Rich Dettlehauser makes his squared triggerguards with a much sharper corner to them than previous-era 'smiths had made.

CYLINDER & SLIDE

Bill Laughridge is Cylinder & Slide, and he's been in business for a long time. I first met him at the 1984 Second Chance shoot, where he had his traveling trailer of gunsmithing goodness. Laughridge was relatively new at the time, having opened C&S in 1978. He has all the tools and parts needed in the trailer to do the handwork of gunsmithing. No lathe or mill; that's just too much weight to haul. But he can do all the rest.

He does 1911 work, Browning Hi Power work and is one of the few guys left who still does Colt "V" spring revolver work. (That's the Official Police, Python and Detective Special guns.) Laughridge teaches a 1911 armorers' course that is to die for. You arrive at his class with a box o' parts, and you leave the class with a gun you built.

Located in Fremont, Nebraska, Cylinder & Slide offers upgrade parts, hammers and sears, which often find their way into the custom builds of other gunsmiths. After all, if you can get a perfect trigger pull by dropping in a C&S hammer and sear set, why not? Laughridge does more than just 1911s; he

works on a whole raft of guns, but he has made a national name for himself doing 1911 work.

At the 2007 SHOT show, Laughridge stunned us all with his bravura gunsmithing when he took a base gun — Caspian slide and frame — and turned it into a 1908 pocket model in .45 ACP. Not a 1908 interim test gun, but basically a scaled-up 1908 .380 Auto, it was chambered in .45 ACP. The idea was to make something new and different. In order to make a hammer-enclosing slide, he had to fit and silver-solder a cap on the end of it. Unless Laughridge told you, you would not see the joint — that's how precise it was. Well, things got out of hand, and he had people actually chasing him, checkbook in hand, to make one for them. Despite quoting a staggering sum, he had buyers for identical guns.

So, if a custom 1911 or BHP isn't enough for you, you can have Bill Laughridge make a 1908 pocket model in .45. Me, I think I'd hold out for a 1905 Government-sized model. And, if a "pocket" .45 ACP is a bit much for you, find a clean M1903 in .32 or 1908 in .380, and he can turn it into a pocket 1911 clone, with magazine release in the right

spot, low-profile sights and a thumb safety you can actually work.

A clever fellow, and yes, he's had the handlebar mustache for as long as anyone remembers.

WAYNE NOVAK

Wayne Novak is perhaps most known for his sights. While working with Smith & Wesson to improve hi-cap 9mms, he came up with a sight design that worked so well he patented it. This was back in the days of S&W's "gun of the month" expansion, and a common feature was the Novak sight. Actually, there were two sights and three patents. The one I liked, which did not catch on, is a bit larger and works even better as an impact device.

Novak is also known for his work on the Browning Hi Power. He built me an FN MkIII in 9mm, the model with the cast frame. My instructions from the editor I was working for was to "shoot it until you break it, and then write about it." Well, I had to write about it before I broke it, 23,000 rounds later.

A regular in IPSC from the early days, Novak shot at Nationals and World Shoots. However, when the IPSC world shifted to hi-cap Supers and guns with

Custom guns shoot. The features are nice, but what a custom gun does for you (this is a Nighthawk) is deliver accuracy, reliability, durability and ergonomics, as well as looks.

red-dot sights, he stayed with the single stack, which is what he does a lot of. Novak also does some work on other guns: SIG, S&W, STI, but he prefers to work on single-stack 1911s.

Along the way to making 2 million sights, Novak has also worked on a couple of details that have been head-scratchers for a century now. One is the grip safety, which many shooters have a real problem with. The Novak answer is to replace the grip's safety and mainspring housing with a single, non-moving unit — a solid backstrap, but a removable one. With the grip safety removed, you don't have to worry about a sloppy, weak or hurried grip keeping you from using your 1911. Of course, it does the same for anyone who picks it up, too.

He also addressed a problem that some people have had with the 1911, that you can't work the action with the safety on. You must first check to see if it is loaded, or load and unload it, with the safety off. Having grown up with and used the 1911 as-is for more than 40 years now, I don't break out in a sweat every time I flip the safety off. But some who have grown up using pistols since the peanut farmer left the oval office are just a bit leery of the old way.

Novak modifies the safety — and the slide where the safety rides — so you can work the slide with the safety on. You can't take the slide off the gun with the safety off, but you can unload it before you disassemble it. I wonder sometimes if that alone might have been enough to keep the 1911A1 in government service back in the 1980s.

Probably not, but it would have permitted the 1911 to be considered by police agencies that might not have otherwise given the pistol a second look. Now, everything is not all sweetness and light. To get something, you must give up something. In this case, what you give up is the locked slide. A non-locking safety and a tight holster means your pistol can be pushed slightly out of battery when you holster. Of course, only those of us who worry about minor things worry about the slide failing to re-seat into battery when you draw. In all, it seems like a useful trade-off to me, especially if it allows you to carry a 1911 at an agency or department that might otherwise bar its use.

Novak also does the full range of custom work on single stacks, as long as you aren't looking for something with a compensator. He does sights, trigger work, accuracy jobs and more, generally as a package arrangement.

Oh, and since he was in on the ground floor of the design of the FBI pistol, you can have an exact copy of it as your base gun. After all, the FBI used one of his guns as a model to draw up the specs, and Novak has one of the rare FBI-prefix guns on hand, should he ever need to check a detail.

Scott Mulkerin/SDM Fabricating

I've known Scott Mulkerin for some 20 years now, as he was a heavy hitter at the Second Chance bowling-pin matches. Mulkerin does classic à la carte gunsmithing. That is, you can go down the list of goodies and compose what you want and leave off what you don't. And for that, I have to tip my hat to him. I did

much the same thing when I was getting started as a gunsmith (that was pretty much what we all did back then) and I can tell you it is a pain in the neck for a gunsmith to do it that way. One must carefully calculate the individual labor time and materials for each task and then correctly price it on the worksheet, else you'll find you are doing work that you don't earn a living on.

Mulkerin also offers his own 1911 sights, both a low-profile tactical target rear, and gold-bead front blades. Now, a gold bead front sight is a combination of the fiber optic and the all-steel. It offers a high-vis dot, but one of much greater durability than fiber optic. If you are going to have him install sights, I would suggest that you make every effort to send in your 1911 zeroed. That is, shoot it, and make sure the sights are dead-on because a gold-dot front sight can't be filed or machined to adjust point of impact. It is what it is, and if you don't make sure your 1911 is "on" before you send it to Mulkerin, he can't be sure the gold bead front will be "on" when it goes back to you. This holds for all other gunsmiths, too.

Scott Mulkerin also makes some essential tools. One is his firing pin retaining plate remover. A tight plate means a securely fitted extractor that won't "clock" or rotate slightly. The problem with a tight plate is that it is hard to remove to clean the firing pin tunnel. The SDM tool solves that problem. Another tool is his spring tester. With it, you can measure the spring tension or "life" left in your springs. People who do a lot of shooting find that regular spring replacement makes a difference in reliable function and ensures a long service life. With it, you can measure both the resting and fully compressed force of your springs. Where I find it particularly useful is with the Browning Hi Power. You'll have to make some extra parts to fit the Hi Power springs into the scale, but once you do, you'll be stylin.' You see, the Hi Power, more so than the 1911, needs a really up-to-spec spring to ensure a long life. And the spring really takes a hammering.

I once had a chance to measure a pair of Browning "T" series Hi Powers, guns that were used in daily carry. A standard recoil spring is 17.5 pounds, and I generally run mine with 18.5-pound springs in them. These two T Brownings had springs that measured 9 and 11 pounds. Ouch.

So, you can have everything from a light custom gun, à la carte or package,

up to a competition-ready 1911. Mulkerin also does Smith & Wesson revolver work, for carry or competition.

RICH DETTLEHAUSER

Rich Dettlehauser runs Canyon Creek, a shop that works on 1911s and a couple of other very interesting pistols. Dettlehauser is a USPSA Grand Master, and that is something uncommon in shooting and gunsmithing circles. Yes, many gunsmiths can shoot quite well indeed, and some top shooters can be good at working on guns. But to combine the two is rare. In the 1911 arena, he mostly does competition and combat-ready single stacks, with some hi-caps suitable for Limited thrown in.

He does checkering, serrations, non-slip scales and slide and frame sculpting, with an eye toward pushing the boundaries. One detail he is particularly fond and proud of is the squared triggerguard. However, Dettlehauser squares the guard to a sharper degree and appearance than the old-style Swenson look.

He has also perfected a look I experimented with when I was working on custom 1911s: the low-profile mag well. In most instances the mag well as it is fabricated is as wide as or wider than the grips. As a result, you end up with a frame that has a ring of steel at the bottom instead of ending in the wooden grips. Dettlehauser sculpts the mag-well funnel so its sides are thinner than that of the grips, and then relieves the grip to ride over the mag-well sides. The result is a frame and grips that look proportional and correct.

As a Grand Master, he knows what details matter, and you can count on them being tended to. The frontstrap is lifted and the grip safety has a tight, no-bind grip and clears the trigger early enough so that a somewhat sloppy grip won't preclude a shot. And of course these 1911s are utterly reliable and accurate. You don't make it to Grand Master status running unreliable or inaccurate guns, and having made it, you don't do that to your customers.

The other guns Rich Dettlehauser works on are the EAA and its clones, and the Springfield XD and XDm. The EAA, basically a CZ 75, still has a following. Much more so overseas, but the grip shape is very nice, and the feel of the grip is enough to lure Limited and some Production shooters away from the 1911 hi-caps and Glocks. The Springfield XD is chosen by some Limited shooters (in .40) and the XDm is poised to be the new big kid on the block in Production. (Due to a puzzling rules interpretation, the XD and XDm are precluded from international Production, so if you plan on going to a World Shoot, you'll have to pick something else to take.)

Dettlehauser can tune an old or new CZ/EAA, and he can make your XDm a real Production-winning machine. You could have half of your USPSA/IPSC competition battery built by him, and on Springfields at that: he could build a single stack on a Springfield Armory 1911A1, A Limited/Limited 10 gun on a Springfield hi-cap, and your production gun could be an XDm. If you found an old Springfield P9, you could even have him build it as an Open gun in 9X21. The only thing left out would be Revolver, and that might be asking too much, because Springfield doesn't make revolvers.

WILSON COMBAT

Bill Wilson transformed the 1911 parts aftermarket. Then, he super-charged the "custom gun at a reasonable price and not two presidential elections from now" market. He spends his time on his ranch in Texas shooting pigs, testing loads, developing new products and enjoying life as a successful businessman. He also likes to invent new pistols.

What he did with the X9 is instructive. As I've mentioned before, the STI frame was developed when we were all in thrall to the .45 as the be-all and end-all, but we wanted capacity. So, the magazine tube is big enough to hold .45s, a lot of them.

In the 21st century, while a lot of shooters still want a 1911, many want a 9mm, which lead to the surge in single-stack 9mm 1911s, both for competition and daily carry. Wilson searched for the best high-capacity 9mm magazine that could not hold .40 or .45 cartridges, and once he found the best, he rebuilt the 1911 around

it. That magazine was a Walther PPQ M2, which he modified to work with his pistol (and the OEM magazine supplier, Mec-Gar, can also provide). In fact, he assembled a 1911 pistol around it, but it was a 1911 pistol with all the lessons learned from decades of building the original.

The X9 EDC is a compact 9mm pistol meant for daily carry, with plenty of capacity and all the Wilson Combat skill and knowledge built in. If you want a 1911, but you want 9mm and lots of capacity, well, here is just the pistol for you.

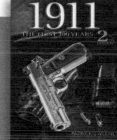

Compact, lots of 9mm ammo on board, a 1911 (at least, 1911 DNA) from Wilson Combat. Rejoice, the 21st century is turning out just fine.

The Search for the PERFECT CARTRIDGE

The author's quest has spanned four decades, but might not be fully realized BY JON R. SUNDRA

I s there such a thing as the perfect cartridge? Of course not, but I've had a lot of fun over a lifetime looking for it, and learned a lot in the process. In many ways though, there actually is such a thing as the perfect cartridge, but it exists only in a moment in time, and it's different for each of us.

The first thing we have to ask is: perfect for what? So that we don't bite off more than we can chew here, let's confine our discussion to hunting applications, because competitive shooting in any of its many forms is a different can of worms entirely.

So, we're considering hunting cartridges, but hunting what? Exactly. Hunting what, as well as where and when, for those are equally important factors. Well, if you'll indulge my starting from the very beginning, it was English sparrows in the exotic environs of urban Cleveland in the late 1940s, and the perfect weapon for me at the time was a Red Ryder BB gun and its .177 cal. spherical projectile. I swear, the iconic 1983 movie *A Christmas Story* is so frighteningly identical to my childhood that little Ralphie Parker and the avarice with which he lusted for a Red Ryder BB gun could have been me. It was the same time, 1949, the same place, Cleveland, and like Ralphie, I was 9 years old and I wanted a BB gun more than life itself.

Anyway, like most of you reading this, my first real gun was a .22, and it was on my 12th birthday, I think, my dad, who was a Cleveland cop, presented me with a little Winchester single-shot bolt action rifle. It was almost a token gesture, howe ver, because living on Cleveland's east side I didn't have any place to shoot a .22. It was only on rare occasions that my dad, or my best friend's dad, would drive us into the country where we could shoot at chipmunks, barn rats, blackbirds, whatever. Sometimes we'd luck out and get a shot at what for us was big game, groundhogs.

Shown here is the chronological progression through the author's search for the perfect cartridge at various stages in his life (l. to r.): .22 LR, .22 WMR, .256 Win. Magnum, .22–250, 6mm Rem., 7mm Rem. Magnum, 7mm JRS and 7mm WSM. At far right is the .375 JRS.

At the time when the author was deciding on which of the two 6mms he'd go with, there were only two, the .243 and .244 Rem. (two center cartridges). Since then the .243 WSSM at left, and the .240 Weatherby have come on the scene. As hunting rounds, the 6mms have lost much of their luster.

It wasn't until I was 17 and had a car that I could actually indulge my developing passion for guns and hunting, albeit still at the squirrel and woodchuck level. Centerfire rifles were not allowed for deer hunting in Ohio even back then, and being an aspiring rifle weenie I had no interest in entering the world of "big-game hunting" with a 12-gauge shotgun and "pumpkin balls."

By the time I entered college at the age of 21, I had graduated first to a Marlin bolt action in .22 Magnum (WMR), followed by a Marlin Model 62 Levermatic chambered in a silly little cartridge known as the .256 Win. Magnum, a misnomer if ever there was one. It was derived by necking down the .357 Magnum pistol round to .25 caliber, but it was my first centerfire rifle and with it I became a handloader. Given the modest cost of the rifle and the varmints-only kind of hunting I was doing at the time, that little .256 was more than enough for skulking around the relatively small farms of northern Ohio where a 150-yard shot on a 'chuck was considered long range.

It didn't take long for me to realize that my .256 was woefully inadequate for the much larger farms and more open country of central Ohio, where I was attending Ohio State. I made the acquaintance of a fellow student whose family lived on a large farm there and who also happened to be an avid 'chuck hunter. He had a Winchester Model 70 in .220 Swift and hunting with him gave me a decided inferiority complex. He was popping groundhogs at distances I wouldn't even try with my mighty .256.

The solution was obvious: I just had to have a .22-250! By then I had become a walking encyclopedia on rifle cartridges and external ballistics. And now that I was a handloader, I could also evaluate a cartridge from that perspective. To my mind the Swift case was old fash-

(above) The author has had what he describes as brief dalliances with the .284 Win., 7.21 Lazzeroni Tomahawk and the 7mm Dakota.

(below) The 7mm is the most populated of calibers (l. to r.): 7mm-08, 7x57, .284 Win., .280 Rem., .280 Ackley Improved, 7mm Rem. Mag, 7mm Rem. SAUM, 7mm WSM, 7mm Weatherby, 7mm Dakota, 7mm STW, .28 Nosler, 7mm Rem Ultra Mag. and 7.21 Lazzeroni Firebird.

The stages in the making of the 7mm JRS (l. to r.): .280 Rem. case; the .30 caliber expander button used to neck up the .280 to .30 cal.; partial necking back down to .284 in a 7 JRS die, but only to where the bulge on the neck provides proper headspace; loaded round ready for fire forming; the finished JRS case.

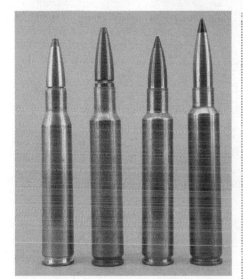

The author's journey to his wildcat started with the .280 Rem., at left, then to the .280 RCBS, .280 Ackley Improved and finally to his 7mm JRS, his "perfect cartridge" for a decade.

ioned; it was semi-rimmed, had a long body with too much taper from head to shoulder, and a shallow shoulder angle. The .22-250 on the other hand, was rimless (better feeding), had a shorter body with less taper and a sharper shoulder for more positive headspacing. I knew I'd be giving up about 100 fps to my friend's Swift, but with velocities approaching 4,000 fps with either cartridge, I figured that was pretty much meaningless. I

went with what I considered to be a better-designed cartridge. Besides, the consensus at the time was that the .22-250 was more tractable from a handloading standpoint.

If there was a fly in the ointment it was the .22-250 was still a wildcat in 1962, so my only option was a custom rifle. The solution was a Remington Model 722 chambered in .257 Roberts that I found

in a pawn shop in Columbus. I sent the barreled action off to Flaig's in Millvale, Pennsylvania, and had it re-barreled to what for me was the perfect cartridge for the hunting I was doing at the time.

That lasted until 1966 when, after graduating the year before, I moved to Pennsylvania. For me it was like the Promised Land because you could hunt deer there with a centerfire rifle. Hell, they even had a black-bear season. What I needed now was a "dual-purpose" rifle. The idea of having one rifle perfectly suited for both varmints and deer was very popular concept back then and by far the one cartridge most synonymous with that way of thinking was the .243 Win. Having been introduced in 1955, the .243 was still a relatively young cartridge, but it was already firmly entrenched as the dual-purpose round, even though there had been another 6mm introduced that same year. I'm referring, of course, to the .244 Remington. While Winchester touted its .24 as varmint/deer cartridge for which it offered factory loads of 80 and 100 grains dictating a 1-10-inch twist rate, Remington saw its .244 as a long-range varmint cartridge and went with 70 and 90 grain bullets and a 1-12-inch twist rate. The gun writers of the day were quick to point out that the slower twist would not reliably stabilize 100-grain spitzer bullets, so handloading wasn't a solution. Perception was a 100-grain bullet was deadly on deer, but a 90-grain bullet was not.

At left the .375 H&H case; the 8mm Rem. Mag., expanded button to neck up the 8 Mag to .375 and the .375 JRS at right.

(above) Many a groundhog fell to the author's stint with the 6mm Remington.

(right) When game no larger than deer and black bear were realistic, the 6mm Rem. proved to be a great choice.

Even though Remington changed the twist rate to 1-10 inches in 1958, the damage had been done. In another attempt to save the round, in 1963 Remington reintroduced the .244 as the 6mm Remington. It was identical and interchangeable with the .244, but it was now being offered in a 100-grain factory load, and the sexy new Remington 700 rifle that was introduced the year before had a 1-9-inch twist.

At that time, I was not yet experienced enough as a handloader to consider a wildcat cartridge, so I had to choose which of the two factory rounds would be the perfect one for me. Despite the .243's dominance in the marketplace, for me it was no contest; I went with the 6mm Rem. The ballistic charts then had the 6mm Rem. 100-grain load at 3,190 fps, while the .243's was listed at 3,070. Even before the name and performance changes of '63, I thought the .244 to be the better cartridge. For one thing, the .244 case held about 7 percent more powder than the .243. To a handloader, that's a lot. Also, the case (which was essentially a necked down .257 Roberts, which in turn was a necked down 7mm Mauser), had a sharper shoulder and a longer neck, which meant that if I used a standard-length instead of a short action

for my build, I'd be able to seat even 100-grain bullets no deeper than the neck/shoulder juncture thereby taking full advantage of the larger case.

As would become my standard MO, I sent an action, a commercial Santa Barbara Mauser, off to have it barreled to the new 6mm Rem., with its chamber throated to a shallow-seated 100-grain Sierra bullet. Ultimately, that rifle, along with a Ruger No.1B also in 6mm Rem., accounted for several hundred woodchucks, a mule deer, two pronghorns and three black bears before I retired them.

> **❝ ALL WHILE THIS DALLIANCE WITH THE 6MM WAS GOING ON, MY REAL AND TRUE LOVE WAS THE SEXY NEW 7MM REM. MAGNUM. ❞**

All while this dalliance with the 6mm was going on, my real and true love was the sexy new 7mm Rem. Magnum. Even before it was introduced in 1962, I had already made up my mind that when I started real big-game hunting — the kind that required something more than a 6mm Rem. — it would be with a 7mm of some sort, not a .30 like everyone else. It was the iconoclast in me that made

me choose the .22-250 over the Swift; the 6mm Rem. over the .243, and now the 7 Mag over the .300 Win. And forget the .30-06; I never even considered it. Too many guys had a .30-06, and too many gun writers fawned over it. And it was the same with the .270; I never considered it, either, thanks primarily to its flacking by Jack O'Connor.

Prior to the birth of the 7 Mag., metric cartridges were not all that poplar here. The best known .28 was the 7mm Mauser (7x57). Remington's 280, which was introduced in 1958, wasn't setting the world on fire, but I considered it to be a better, more versatile cartridge than the .270, and up to that time my perfect cartridge, even though I didn't own a rifle so chambered. Then came the Big Seven and everything changed. In 1963 the major source of external ballistics were the charts of Remington and Winchester, and both were published on opposing pages in what had become my bible, the Gun Digest. Winchester had its .300 magnum, 180-grain load at 3,070 fps, delivering 2,380 ft-lbs of energy at 300 yards, with a midrange trajectory of 5.3 inches. Remington's 150-grain, 7 Mag. loading, however, exited at 3,260 fps, delivering 2,410 ft-lbs of energy at 300 yards, over an MRT of 4.7 inches. Not only did it shoot flatter and hit harder at 300 yards than the .300 Win., it did it with about 20 percent less recoil. How, I asked myself, could any rational human being go with the .300 over the 7mm?

So, for about a 10-year period from 1966 to 1976 the 7mm Rem. Magnum was to me the perfect cartridge for any critter, anywhere, other than dangerous ones. I honestly can't remember how many 7 mags I've owned, but four I do recall were a Ruger No.1B, a Carl Gustaf, a Howa and one built on a Sako action. All saw action in either Africa, South America, Canada, Europe, Alaska or the American West.

In the autumn of '76 I was preparing

THE SEARCH FOR THE PERFECT CARTRIDGE

The 7mm WSM becomes almost a different cartridge when it's chambered in a rifle that will allow seating bullets out to where they don't infringe on usable powder space. Rounds at left are loaded to factory overall length.

One was a Model 70 Safari Grade out of Winchester's Custom Shop, which for a couple years chambered for it. A-Square loaded ammo for it using cases wearing the ".375 JRS" headstamp. The other three guns consisted of a Ruger No.1-B, a Brno magnum Mauser and a Sako, all custom jobs. I used the No. 1 to take my first elephant and Cape buffalo; the Brno for Asiatic buffalo in Australia and an elephant hunt in Malawi, and the Sako for other Cape buffalo and assorted African plains game. I still own two of them.

By 1978 I had become disenchanted with the belted magnum case. As much as I liked 7-Mag performance, I didn't like the belt; from the handloading standpoint it was purely vestigial. On two back-to-back safaris that year to South and South West Africa (now Namibia), I took a stock Ruger 77 in .280 Rem. and killed everything just as dead, but I was used to the slightly flatter trajectory of the 7 Mag. and wanted a beltless case to provide it. In those days, if you wanted a bigger but readily available case than the basic '06, it was pretty much the belted H&H, which I of course didn't want. And so I came down with another case of feline fever. I decided the .280 RCBS was the answer, which was simply an improved .280 Rem. That meant cases could be formed by simply firing factory .280 Rem. rounds in an RCBS chamber. By reducing the body taper and going to a 30-degree shoulder, case capacity was increased by a scant 3 percent. It

for my first African safari, and on my list was Cape buffalo. Obviously, I had to settle on a big bore of some kind. I liked the .375 as a caliber, but I didn't like the H&H's sloping body and shoulder. I decided to go with the .375 Mashburn, a wildcat based on the .375 H&H case, but "improved," in that it had a minimum body taper, a sharper shoulder and a shorter neck, all of which resulted in a case having about 8 percent more powder capacity than the H&H hull. All I'd have to do to get brass was to fire form .375 H&H factory loads in the Mashburn chamber. But just as I was about to go ahead with the project, the Remington Writers' Seminar (by then I was a writer), came up, and there we were shown the brand new 8mm Rem. Magnum. Low and behold, it was essentially the Mashburn case; all I had to do was neck it up to .375. Thus was born the .375 JRS. It bested the H&H by about 125 fps and some 400 ft-lbs of energy. Ultimately, I ended up with four guns so chambered.

The Montana 1999 and Winchester Model 70 short actions are long enough to allow seating bullets in any of the WSM family of cartridges out where they belong.

This Zambian lion fell to two shots from a .284 Win., and a 7x57. A totally unplanned incident.

160-grain bullets could be seated to where they didn't infringe on usable powder space, which is about 10 percent more than that of the .280. My original rifle was built on a Remington 700 action, followed by one built on a Sako action, and a third on a Winchester Model 70. With all three of those rifles I was able to get 3,150 fps with a 150-grain bullet in a 24-inch barrel; that's 7 Mag performance. I used those rifles to take more game in more places than with all other cartridges combined. Well, almost anyway. I still own all three.

Though the 7 JRS was for me the perfect cartridge for about a decade, my affair wasn't totally monogamous because during that time I had a brief dalliance with the .284 Win.; I thought it had the coolest case ever, but its rebated rim caused a jam at an inopportune time on a lion hunt in Zambia, and that cooled my enthusiasm.

took only a few weeks at the handloading bench and shooting range for me to realize the increase in velocity was too slight to justify the cartridge.

> 66 I CONSIDERED THE .280 ACKLEY IMPROVED, BUT I DIDN'T LIKE ITS 40-DEGREE SHOULDER — TOO STEEP IN MY OPINION, AND TOO TOUGH ON BRASS. I CONSIDERED THE 35-DEGREE SHOULDER OF THE THEN-NEW .284 WINCHESTER TO BE IDEAL. 99

I considered the .280 Ackley Improved, but I didn't like its 40-degree shoulder — too steep in my opinion, and too tough on brass. I considered the 35-degree shoulder of the then-new .284 Winchester to be ideal. Also, the .345-inch neck on the Ackley was unnecessarily long for a .284 bullet; a neck length of one caliber, i.e., .284, is considered sufficient for reliable bullet tension. So, I designed my own 7mm, and doing so could not have been easier. All I did was take the specs of the .280 Rem. case and reduced the neck length to .300 of an inch, specified a 35-degree shoulder and a .015 of an inch body taper from head to shoulder. Those specs alone were enough for Clymer to make the chambering reamers and Hornady the dies. The 7mm JRS is not just an "improved" case because brass can't be derived by fire forming a .280 Rem. in a JRS chamber; to do so would be dangerous because my

The WSM family from left: .270, 7mm, .300 and .325. Note how the body of the 7mm is longer than the other three.

cartridge pushes the shoulder more than .140 of an inch forward. The .280 cases must first be necked up to .308, then necked down in the JRS die, but only to where the bulge on the neck acts as the datum line for headspacing. Once that's done, the case can be loaded and safely fire formed in the JRS chamber. For a while a company named Buzztail Brass offered 7mm JRS unprimed brass.

My specs for the 7mm JRS dictated a magnum-length action so 140- to

By the early '90s the industry began to realize the belted H&H case had run its course. Enter the proprietary 7mm Dakota and 7.21 Lazzeroni Firebird (full magnum length), and 7.21 Tomahawk (short magnum), all three of which were beltless cartridges based on the .404 Jeffery. Here was a case that was of larger

The author made one safari to Tanzania using a Ruger No.1 chambered in Lazzeroni's 7.21 Tomahawk.

diameter than the H&H and thus held more powder than comparable-length cartridges.

For the next few years I had a Ruger No.1B in 7mm Rem. rechambered to the Dakota round, then had that same rifle re-barreled to the 7.21 Tomahawk. I don't think I hunted at all with it when it was chambered in the Dakota round, but as a Lazzeroni I hunted Alaska and Africa with it. I liked both, but neither was exactly what I thought would the perfect cartridge to see me to the end of my hunting days.

It took several years for the biggies to acknowledge finally what we rifle weenies already knew: Belted cases were passé. Fatter, beltless cases were the future and Winchester was the first to test the water in 2001 with the introduction of the .300 Winchester Short Magnum (WSM). Actually, we gun writers got to see and shoot the new round in late 2000. I thought it might just be what I was looking for: The perfect case, but

necked down to 7mm. I absconded with about three boxes of empty brass and immediately sent three each to Clymer and Hornady to cut a reamer and dies.

Just about the time Browning and Winchester rifles and ammo were first reaching dealers' shelves, I was in Africa with my wildcat 7mm WSM. I, of course, was sure Winchester would do the same thing the following year, and it did, as well as bringing out a .270 version. Interestingly enough, my friend and colleague Bryce Towsley discovered, if determined enough, one could chamber a 7mm WSM cartridge in a .270 WSM rifle. After all, there's only a .007 of an inch difference in bullet diameter. And since Winchester had to assume there was going to be at least one knuckle-dragging doofus out

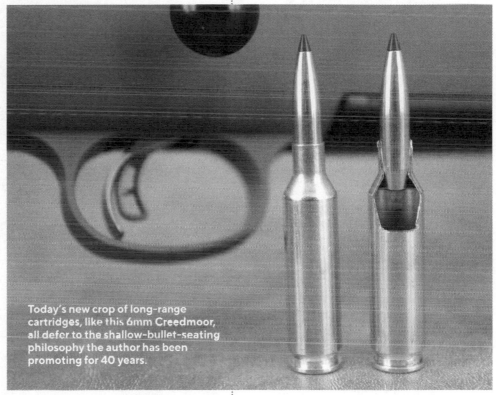

Today's new crop of long-range cartridges, like this 6mm Creedmoor, all defer to the shallow-bullet-seating philosophy the author has been promoting for 40 years.

there who was going to do just that, it recalled what few guns had left the factory and changed the specs, lengthening the body of the 7mm version by .055 of an inch and thereby increasing its volume about 5 percent over its siblings).

The idea behind the WSM concept, of course, was to provide magnum performance in a short-action rifle; therefore, the overall cartridge length of factory ammunition is 2.8 inches, which is the magazine length of most short-actions rifles. However, I knew the magazine length of the Winchester Model 70 and

Montana Rifle Company's short actions to be 3.125 inches. This allows me to continue the philosophy I've always championed: always use an action that will allow for the seating of bullets to where they don't infringe on usable powder space, and have the chamber throated accordingly. That is precisely the thinking behind the 6 and 6.5 Creedmoor twins, the .224 Valkyrie, the 6.5 and .300 PRC, and the best benchrest cartridges. When the base of a bullet is seated well below the shoulder, let alone the neck, it can more easily yaw within the chamber on ignition. That is the major reason why the aforementioned cartridges are noticeably more accurate.

So far, I've built three 7 WSMs; one on the Model-70 action, one on a Montana and one on a standard-length Ruger. With a 150-grain bullet I get 3,225 fps out of a 24-inch barrel with all three of them. That stacks up pretty well against the fire-breathing 7 Ultra Mag and 7mm Nosler, which require gobs more powder to get an additional 100 to 125 fps. I love efficient cartridges and to me the 7mm WSM setup as I've described is about as perfect a rifle/cartridge combination as I can envision. For me. And being in the twilight of my hunting career I don't think I'll look any further, though necking down the .30 Ruger to 7mm does look intriguing!

RETRO BLACK RIFLES

Looking back on a forward-thinking black rifle with a new-production retro AR

BY **ROBERT SADOWSKI**

Jungle warfare helped shape the design of the black rifle. It was also the first time the rifle saw combat. Photo: DoD

An AR-10 rifle that was the precursor to the black rifle produced by the Dutch company of Artillerie-Inrichtengen. Photo: Rock Island Auction Company

By the time the Vietnam War was under way, the main-issue rifle was an M16. Photo: DoD

There was a time when the black rifle, what we've come to refer to as the AR-15 today, might not ever have happened. In fact, in the beginning there were several times when Armalite went back to the drawing board, so to speak. Other U.S. government projects like SALVO and AGILE greatly impacted the development of the so-called black rifle. Truth be told, the AR wasn't even black in the beginning. When the barrels of early prototypes exploded during Army tests, you would think that would have halted any further development. It didn't, it just made Armalite think smarter.

When a new caliber was adopted by the U.S. government, a complete redo of the rifle morphed into a new variant. Then there was trouble brewing in a southeast Asian country no one ever heard of called Vietnam. These events collided in the late 1950s and early 1960s to spawn the "black rifle" moniker — the nickname given to the AR-15 (Armalite's name), the Model 601 (Colt's nomenclature) and the M16 (the U.S. military designation). You see, the story of the black rifle is not cut and dry, but filled will glorious moments of success, the agony of defeat and ultimate perseverance. Perhaps the pivotal moment took place on a warm summer day in 1960 when two watermelons spectacularly demonstrated the effectiveness of the black rifle and the 5.56mm NATO cartridge to a brash Air Force general. But we're getting

Troy meticulously re-creates the XM177 Commando model in the XM177E2. The original XM177 was specifically built for the covert combat needs of MACV-SOG in Vietnam.

The standard-issue M16 was found to be too long in thick jungle combat, so the more compact XM177 version was designed. Photo: DoD

ahead of the story. Let's back up to 1956 and Hollywood, California. That's where and when the black rifle's story starts.

In the mid–1950s, Armalite Corporation was a small machine shop in Hollywood, California, that was immersed in creating cutting-edge weapon designs. Its business model was to design a weapon and then license the design to a manufacturer, and its claim to fame was the AR-5 and AR-7 survival rifles designed for the Air Force. Armalite's ideas needed funding, so it became

a subdivision of Fairchild Engine and Airplane Corporation. It hired Eugene Stoner as chief design engineer. Yes, *the* Eugene Stoner. Under Stoner's direction, Robert Fremont and L. James Sullivan developed and engineered new small arms designs.

In fall 1956, Armalite developed an ultra-modern combat rifle. The prototype was designated the AR-10 and it was unlike any rifle — non-reciprocating charging handle, hinged upper and lower, modular components, select-fire, gas-operated direct impingement system, lightweight aluminum receiver, synthetic stock, aluminum/steel barrel to name just a few unique design characteristics — and it was chambered in 7.62mm. The Armalite promo film shows a soldier emerging from the ocean firing an AR-10 in full-auto as he walks up onto the beach. Think I'm kidding? Google "Armalite promo video" and if you are of a certain age the sound and quality of this video will remind you of movie reels you were forced to watch in high school: except this one will have you glued to the edge of your seat and will give you an idea of what Armalite was up to when communication technology consisted of a rotary dial telephone.

Armalite hurriedly submitted four sample rifles into the U.S. Army's tests for a replacement of the M1 Garand. The

Originally the M16 was not issued with a cleaning kit. That changed when jamming issues caused American soldiers to die in combat. Photo: DoD

competition was Springfield Armory, which submitted the T44E4, and Fabrique Nationale, which entered the FAL. During torture testing, the AR-10's barrel burst and so, one would think, the U.S. government's confidence in Armalite. The AR-10 could have gone down as a footnote in military arms history. The Springfield Armory T44, a more conventional design — basically an M1 Garand with a removable magazine — got the nod from the military and, in 1957, the Army designated it the M14.

Far from licking its wounds, Armalite licensed the AR-10 to Artillerie Inrichtingen in Holland to manufacture the rifles to fulfill contracts with Cuba, Nicaragua, Portugal, Sudan, Guatemala, Italy and Burma. But the real money would be made with a U.S. military contract, not some banana republic or small country that might pony up cash for a paltry 1,000 rifles.

❝ WHILE THE ARMY OPTED FOR THE M14, IT ALSO FUNDED THE SALVO RESEARCH PROJECT IN WHICH HIGH-VELOCITY .22-CALIBER WEAPONS WERE FOUND TO HAVE THE SAME LETHAL POWER AS .30-CALIBER WEAPONS, BUT WITHOUT THE RECOIL OR LACK OF CONTROL IN FULL-AUTO FIRE.❞

These rifles appear to be M16A1s, in use toward the end of the Vietnam War. Note the triangular handguard. Photo: DoD

An example of the XM16E1. Note the tear-drop button, forward-assist button and the three-prong flash hider. Photo: DoD

While the Army opted for the M14, it also funded the SALVO research project in which high-velocity .22-caliber weapons were found to have the same lethal power as .30-caliber weapons, but without the recoil or lack of control in full-auto fire. Plus, a soldier could carry more .22-caliber cartridges than .30-caliber ones — more firepower per soldier.

Armalite shifted gears and developed the AR-15, borrowing many features from the AR-10. The AR-15 was space-age and high-tech compared to other military rifles at the time. Ten AR-15 rifles were tested at Fort Benning, Aberdeen Proving Ground and in the Arctic in 1958. Testing discovered the design needed modifications, but the final reports stated the AR-15 was a viable replacement for the .30-caliber M14. Armalite didn't pop the champagne cork just yet. There were backdoor deals going on and production of the M14 rifle continued. Armalite was hemorrhaging money so Fairchild sold the manufacturing and marketing rights to Colt's Patent Firearms and Manufacturing Corporation in Hartford, Connecticut. Colt

then began the hard sell of the AR-15 to the U.S. military. It wasn't a question of if the AR-15 was going to be adopted by the military but when.

In 1960 in Hagerstown, Maryland, a Colt salesperson demonstrated the AR-15 to General Curtis LeMay, Air Force Chief of Staff. This is where the watermelons come in. LeMay was convinced of the

killing power of the AR-15 and requested an order for 80,000 AR-15 rifles for the Air Force. The military was loathed to have two different caliber rifles in service and President John F. Kennedy nixed LeMay's request. LeMay would not take no for an answer. And then there was this troubling thing in southeast Asia. Before the 1960s, Vietnam was virtually unknown to most Americans. That would soon change.

The goal of Project AGILE was to deter the communist presence in South Vietnam. AGILE was launched in 1961, and a handful of prototype AR-15s designated by Colt as the Model 601 were sent to South Vietnam for testing and evaluation. Design tweaks were made, and the Colt Model 602 — also known as the XM16 — succeeded the 601. These early rifles had a buttstock, pistol grip and handguard with a green finish. They were still not yet black. The test rifles were well received by users. The next year, an additional 1,000 were sent to South Vietnam for use by Special Operations forces and advisors. In combat the rifles proved to be effective, and the power of the 5.56mm cartridge made devastating kills on enemy combatants.

The year 1963 cemented the black rifle's fate. While the military was still stuck on the conventionally designed M14, the reports from AGILE recom-

An Army Specialist fires an M16A2 rifle from the kneeling position during the weapons qualification in 2016. Note the round handguard and birdcage muzzle device. Photo: DoD

Marines take the last objective during a simulated raid as part of urban training. These are M16A4 variants. Photo: DoD

mended adoption of the AR-15 platform and the military ordered rifles. This is when the black rifle got a black eye.

In 1965, the XM16E1 was issued to troops without cleaning supplies or instructions. Two versions of the rifle were made: the M16 without a forward assist for the Air Force and the XM16E1 with a forward assist for the other branches of the military. The Army ordered 85,000 XM16E1 rifles and the Air Force 19,000 M16s. These rifles were the first true black rifles, as they featured black furniture. The XM16E1 sported a fixed buttstock, triangular handguard and a three-prong "duck-bill" flash suppressor on a 20-inch barrel. Standard issue was a 20-round magazine.

In 1964, the .223 Remington/5.56x45mm cartridge was officially adopted by the U.S. Army for use in the AR-15 platform. What caused the black eye and congressional investigations concerned gun powder. There were insufficient quantities of 5.56mm ammo on hand so the military changed the type of gun powder in the ammunition to speed up delivery. The nitrocellulose-based powder the rifle

An American advisor in Vietnam armed with a Colt Model 601. Photo: DoD

was designed to use was replaced with a nitrocellulose and nitroglycerin-based powder that left a residue in the rifle's mechanism.

The AR-15's gas impingement system was designed as self-cleaning, requiring minimal maintenance. Originally the M16

was not issued with a cleaning kit, but that soon changed as U.S. soldiers began to experience stoppages in combat with cartridge cases lodged in the chamber. U.S. casualties were discovered, literally with soldiers killed over rifles disassembled while trying to fix jams. Congress soon intervened as evidence of jamming rifles mounted and an investigation was launched. It was found that the main issue for the failure-to-extract stoppages was the gun powder in the ammunition.

By 1967 the problems with the XM16E1 were addressed and the rifle was standardized as the M16A1 with a chrome-lined chamber, the recoil buffer was modified for the ammo, the "duck-bill" flash suppressor was replaced by the A1 "bird-cage" flash suppressor. The three-prong muzzle device would catch on vegetation and gear. The three-position safety selector on M16A1 is marked "safe," "semi-automatic" and "fully automatic." The firing modes on the A2 are marked "safe," "semi-automatic" and "burst." A cleaning kit was supplied to troops, too. Will Elsner's comic manual, *The M16A1 Rifle: Operation and Preventive Maintenance*, was passed out among G.I.s. With the design changes and maintenance, the reliability of the black rifle increased, and so too did our troops' confidence with the rifle.

> ❝ **A SHORT-BARRELED VARIANT, THE XM177 COMMANDO, WAS ALSO DISTRIBUTED DURING THE VIETNAM WAR. THIS RIFLE WITH A 10-INCH BARREL WAS MORE COMPACT AND MANEUVERABLE IN THICK JUNGLE COVER.** ❞

A short-barreled variant, the XM177

U.S. government photo of the Armalite AR-15 rifle as built by Colt. Note the original waffle magazine. Photo: Springfield Armory Museum

U.S. Army troops on patrol in Iraq circa 2006 with M16A4 carbines. Photo: DoD

Commando, was also distributed during the Vietnam War. This rifle with a 10-inch barrel was more compact and maneuverable in thick jungle cover. The XM177 used a distinct-looking muzzle device to reduce flash and moderate sound. The carbine had a CAR adjustable buttstock, which was the precursor to the M2-style buttstock. The handguard was round. By the mid–1980s, the Marines requested extensive design changes and adopted the M16A2. Some of the requested changes were a thicker barrel with new twist-rate, new sights, different flash suppressor, brass deflector and three-round burst among others. The M16A3 is a full-auto version for use by SEAL forces.

The fourth generation M16 is the M16A4, which has a removable carry handle so optics can be mounted. It features quad rails to mount vertical grips, tactical lights and laser pointers. The M16A4 is what most U.S. troops now use and is the most modern variant.

The most current compact version is the M4 carbine with a 14.5-inch barrel that makes the weapon more easily maneuverable in vehicles and in urban combat situations such as in buildings. With the shortened barrel there are reports

of less-than-stellar terminal ballistics. Remember, the platform was designed around a 20-inch barrel.

While black rifle scholars know there were other, numerous AR models as the design was constantly tweaked, there are also black-rifle enthusiasts who covet original models and hoard original parts kits like gold. There are reproduction retro AR-15 rifles available from Brownells and Troy Industries and I have had some quality trigger time with these rifles. Brownells offers reproductions of the AR-10, AR-15, Model 601, XM16E1 and M16A1. All these rifles are true to the original models down to the fine details. They are a viable option to owning an original. Troy Industries reproduces the XM177 model and calls it the XM177E2 Commemorative. Stag Arms and Rock River Arms make versions of the M16A2.

While the black rifle has been in use with the U.S. military for over 56 years, there is still much life left in this iconic, groundbreaking rifle design. The story of the black rifle doesn't end here.

BIBLIOGRAPHY

Evans, Joseph Putnam, *The Armalite AR-10: World's Finest Battle Rifle*, Collector Grade Publications, 2016

Stevens, R. Blake and Ezell, Edward C., *The Black Rifle*, Collector Grade Publications, 1992, 2015

Bartocci, Christopher R., *The Black Rifle II*, Collector Grade Publications, 2004

Sadowski, Robert A., *The M16A1 Rifle: Operation and Preventive Maintenance Department of the Army,* 1969, Skyhorse Publishing,

21st CENTURY BLACKPOWDER HANDGUNS

The Ruger Old Army is a new/old cap-and-ball revolver BY DICK WILLIAMS

In 1972, almost 100 years after the introduction of the Colt Single Action Army, Ruger's Old Army hit the streets of America. Interestingly, the Colt had become the unofficial poster child for cartridge-loaded handguns over the years, while Ruger's Old Army was a cap-and-ball revolver that was virtually indestructible and could perform as well as most modern revolvers, both in terms of accuracy and power delivered.

According to Harry Sefried in the book *Ruger & His Guns*, Bill Ruger was "interested in antique blackpowder guns ... and had several percussion revolvers in his collection." When Mr. Ruger decided to make a thoroughly modern blackpowder pistol, he did not need a bunch of consultants to tell him the idea was good or bad. By 1972, his Super Blackhawk 44 Magnum (at that time the world's strongest revolver) had been in production for more than a decade, so he had a great deal of tooling and components on hand that could be used in the new/old cap-and-ball revolver. In fact, the Old Army looks very much like the Super Blackhawk except for the loading lever assembly that replaces the ejector rod on the Super and the nipples in the rear face of the cylinder. And like the company's modern single-action revolvers, many of the parts on the Old Army were investment cast at the New Hampshire facility. The end result was a blued, single-action revolver with a 7.5-inch

Shooting blackpowder guns requires lots of gear because you are the ammunition factory assembling your own rounds of ammo in the gun.

The heart of a blackpowder handgun is the loading lever assembly that pushes round balls or bullets into the cylinder from the front end, a slow process.

barrel that weighed just under 3 pounds, had adjustable sights and could be dry-fired without damaging the nipples. I'm a bit s keptical of marketing claims, but I'll go along with the paragraph in the Ruger book introducing the Old Army. "The finest percussion revolver ever made … (integrating) modern mechanical features with the beautiful lines of the classic cap-and-ball models … one of the most accurate cap-and-ball revolvers available in America today." Still true almost 50 years later!

So we have a gun designed in the 19th century, using propellant technology going back well before the introduction of cartridge revolvers, being built in a state-of-the-art, 20th-century production facility. But what makes the weapon system suitable for the 21st century? As stated, Ruger implemented many upgrades in design, metallurgy and manufacturing for the gun. Prior to entering production, destructive tests were conducted at the factory using incredible amounts of Bullseye powder, and the Old Army survived. (Don't try that at home.) The handgun has modern adjustable sights that allow you to "dial it in" for whatever load you select. There is a .005-inch clearance between the hammer face and the nipple when the hammer is down that ensures the nipple is not damaged by either accidental or deliberate dry firing, a great concept for any

gun that might be utilized in a survival situation. There is a safety recess (or notch) between each chamber similar to the 1858 Remington revolver where the hammer nose can rest, allowing the gun to be carried safely with all six chambers charged and capped. A spring-powered, cupstyle loading latch solidly engages the barrel catch preventing the loading lever assembly coming loose from recoil. Unbreakable coil springs, stainless steel nipples and a large lateral retaining pin that secures or releases the cylinder pin

with a half turn complete the upgrades. Adding frosting to the cake, Ruger began manufacturing stainless steel Old Army versions in 1976.

Interior ballistic improvements have been realized by using some blackpowder substitutes like Pyrodex and 777. Both have a higher energy content than old-style, conventional blackpowder, but have less stringent shipping and storage requirements. They are also more tolerant of delays in getting your gun cleaned

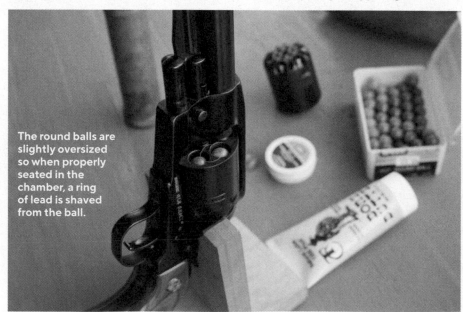

The round balls are slightly oversized so when properly seated in the chamber, a ring of lead is shaved from the ball.

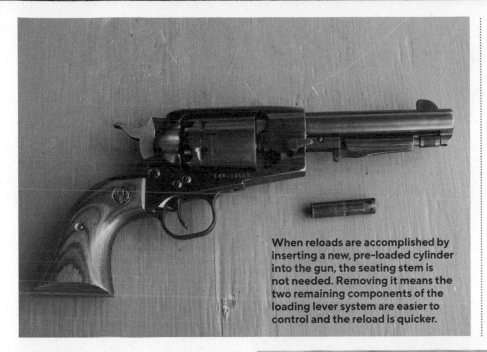

When reloads are accomplished by inserting a new, pre-loaded cylinder into the gun, the seating stem is not needed. Removing it means the two remaining components of the loading lever system are easier to control and the reload is quicker.

If I have a loading stand that holds the Old Army in a vertical position, I prefer to charge all chambers with powder and wad before ramming in the first ball. If I'm reloading in the field without a stand, I load powder and ball one chamber at a time and apply grease after all six are charged. When all chambers are charged, re-latch the front end of the loading lever to the bottom of the barrel. At this point, it's a good idea to run a wire pick through the nipple hole into the powder until it touches the back of the round ball. This will expose more propellant to the percussion cap's flame resulting in more consistent ignition. Point the muzzle downward and you're ready to seat a percussion cap (#11 caps worked well) firmly on each nipple. For me, this is the most difficult step; it's a mismatch of fat fingers trying to manipulate tiny caps. There are "capping tools" available on the market that work

after a shooting session as they seem to be less corrosive, or at least slower to begin the corrosion process. Pyrodex was the first of the two substitute powders commercially available, and I used it initially for hunting small game and javelina in the 1980s. Later, when going after wild boar, I switched to 777 and started using bullets as opposed to round balls. Which leads us to the rather involved loading procedures necessary for blackpowder revolvers.

The first step is to make sure the holes in the nipples are clear. If you oiled or lubricated the gun before storage, which is mandatory, run a pipe cleaner through each nipple to ensure the passage is open. It's also recommended that you fire a percussion cap on each nipple to burn off any remaining lubricant. After the gun is fully loaded, if the flame from the percussion cap doesn't reach the powder, the powder won't ignite and you'll have a misfire. With the hammer at half cock and the muzzle elevated, pour a measured amount of powder into the chamber from the front of the cylinder. Then place a round ball on the mouth of the chamber, and with the ball directly under the seating stem, press the ball firmly into the chamber. Repeat on the other five chambers, after which cover each ball with grease to avoid multiple chambers being ignited by the first round fired. An option here is to place a wad over each powder charge before seating the ball. This also prevents multiple ignition and makes for a much cleaner loading process.

Few things make the author feel as clumsy as trying to place percussion caps on the nipple of a blackpowder handgun. A simple capping tool is a big help.

After powder and ball have been loaded in all chambers, inserting a pin through each nipple and pushing it forward until it contacts the round ball helps ensure quick and thorough ignition of the powder.

Yoke wad, the pistol generated 645 fps and was fairly consistent, but underpowered for my purposes. Using 30 grains of Pyrodex gave 860 fps with a max velocity spread of 55 fps. Jumping to 40 grains of Pyrodex, velocity was 1080 fps with 40 fps variation. The Ruger produced 25 yard, five-shot groups of 2 to 2.5 inches. This was the load with which I took an Arizona javelina.

> **ROUND BALLS ARE MUCH EASIER TO LOAD IN THE RUGER THAN PROPERLY SHAPED BULLETS AS THERE IS NO ORIENTATION REQUIRED WHEN SEATING THE BALL IN THE CYLINDER CHAMBER.**

with varying degrees of success, at least at getting the cap initially seated on the nipple. When caps are on all the nipples, I strongly recommend ensuring all caps are firmly seated, perhaps using a small diameter wood dowel or the eraser on the end of a pencil. Lower the hammer nose until it's resting in one of the notches between cylinders. You're ready to rock.

When you're measuring your powder charge, remember we're dealing with volume measurements, not weights. With the substitute blackpowders I use (Pyrodex and 777), weights run about 75 to 80 percent of volume measurements. My standard load of 40 grains (by volume) of Pyrodex or 777 weighs 30 to 32 grains. To start, you'll need an adjustable powder measure so you can try different loads to determine which work best. Once you've found one or more loads that work, consider buying a batch of brass tubes and trimming them so that each holds exactly the charge you want. Going afield, screw the appropriate spout into your powder flask grab a small tin of CCI percussion caps, a few swaged round balls from either Speer or Hornady, some 44/45 caliber wads (or Bore Butter) and hit the trail.

Recommended round ball size for the Ruger is .457, but I've tried .454 with no noticeable change in performance. A small amount of lead is shaved off either size ball as it is rammed into the cylinder chamber. I didn't spend much time testing lighter loads in the Old Army; the gun is built on a magnum frame and I was going hunting. With 25 grains of Pyrodex and the 148 grain lead ball on top of an Ox-

Firmly (but carefully) seating each cap fully on the nipple improves reliability in igniting the powder with only one strike of the hammer.

The large safety notch between nipples provides the hammer a resting place so the gun can be carried safely with all six chambers charged.

Round balls are much easier to load in the Ruger than properly shaped bullets as there is no orientation required when seating the ball in the cylinder chamber. Not so with real bullets. The bullet must be positioned so the bullet base is centered over the chamber and the nose is engulfed by the cup shape of the rammer. What drove me to "real bullets" was the prospect of hunting wild boars where I wanted heavier weight projectiles with a better ballistic coefficient. Lee makes a 220-grain-bullet mold (it discontinued the same 200-grain hollow-point version of this mold) that is excellent for a blackpowder revolver. A friend of mine cast some of pure lead and lubed them with Alox. It required very little experimentation to home in on 40 grains of 777 covered by the Alox-coated bullet. Five shots produced just under 1,200 fps with no over-powder wad, no added grease and no multiple ignitions due to flashover. In a subsequent hunt using the Ruger Old Army, three pigs were taken with this exact load, and two of them required only one shot each.

Blackpowder purists tend to turn up their noses at the use of "substitute" propellants; if it ain't the real thing, you ain't shooting blackpowder! A hunting partner in Texas hunts with numerous types of muzzleloading firearms and has taken deer with a newer, fixed-sighted Ruger Old Army using round balls over "real" black powder, and there was no doubt about the outcome. But he lives in Texas where he hunts and is much more conscientious than I about cleaning guns thoroughly. I have a long drive home after the hunt and am grateful for the grace period offered by the substitute powders.

Up to now, I've written only about hunting uses of the Ruger Old Army because that was my primary interest when I first acquired Ruger's blackpowder magnum handgun in the 1980s. However, as we rolled into the new millennium there has been a marked shift of interest in the firearm world from recreation/hunting use to self-defense and "tactical" applications. So, what makes a handgun that was manufactured in the 20th century, that is based upon a 19th-century design, viable in the 21st century when we have myriad high-capacity, rapid-firing rifles, shotguns and handguns available?

Two words: Stopping Power. For almost 150 years the description of a fight-stopping handgun always contained the phrase ".45 caliber." Yes, ammo

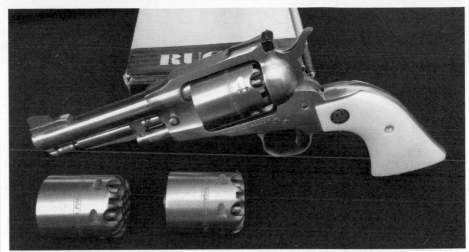

Carrying an extra pair of pre-loaded cylinders that have been fitted to your revolver dramatically speeds up a reload. In a life-threatening situation, it provides an additional 12 powerful rounds in just a few seconds.

This durable leather system from Simply Rugged protects both handgun and extra cylinders, while the holes in the bottom of the cylinder pouches facilitate quick removal for a reload.

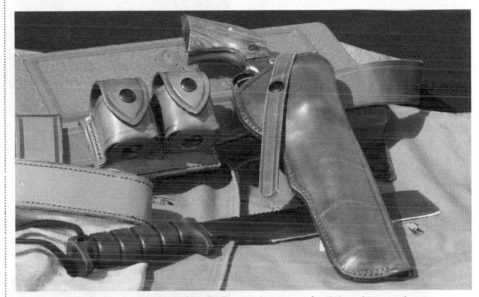

There's no big visual difference between the .480-inch round ball (left) and the .457 round ball (right,) but you do pick up an additional 20 grains of bullet weight in the upgrade. Downside is that your cylinder now holds five shots instead of six.

Acknowledging the slow reloading process for a cap-and-ball revolver, there is a "secret solution" that will allow you

Gary Reeder converted this Ruger Old Army from a six-shot .45 caliber to a five-shot .475 caliber. He'll also build you a .50 caliber, but you'll need to furnish the basic gun.

manufacturers have devoted large amounts of time and money improving the terminal ballistic performance of smaller handgun calibers. The results have been outstanding; bullets with diameters ranging from .22 inches up to .40 inches are expanding more consistently in a soft target. To sum it up, they are all trying to become .45-caliber projectiles after entering the target. The Ruger Old Army delivers a projectile that arrives on target with a diameter of .45 inches. Whatever else transpires, it will not shrink regardless of whether it's a round ball or bullet shape.

The main issue with self-defense using a cap-and-ball revolver is the incredibly slow reloading time. Point taken, but keep in mind that a number of people use/carry smaller caliber guns with a five-round capacity and no reloads. I'm not advocating this, just noting that the Old Army delivers considerably more stopping power and carries six shots rather than five. It's also important to consider possible scenarios and your primary objective. As a civilian, your purpose is not to subdue legions of enemy combatants, but rather to survive a hostile encounter. There isn't room in this article to cover the subject of tactics and mindset. Instead, I recommend anyone looking at the use of firearms for self-defense attend a reputable training class or classes such as taught at Gunsite Academy. While Gunsite doesn't recommend blackpowder revolvers for self-defense, the Academy doctrine and mindset apply to whatever weapon you have in hand when trouble finds you.

Reeder's .475 was equipped with an express rear sight and red-dot front. Slightly quicker to see and faster to acquire than the conventional pistol sight originally on the Ruger.

The fancier .475–caliber Reeder got a new measure and some larger capacity tubes befitting its bigger caliber. Combining a charge from both the 30 grain and 21 grain tubes for a total of 51 grains produced promising results.

The author's old powder measure and premeasured tubes are looking a bit gnarly from ventures afield. For the most part, it's the 40-grain tube that permanently rides atop the measure for the original three-cylinder, .45 caliber Ruger.

to reload your Old Army in a reasonable amount of time, perhaps as quickly as a single-action revolver using cartridge ammo. First, have a couple extra cylinders fitted to your Old Army. Once you've emptied the first cylinder, place the hammer at half cock, rotate the cylinder retention pin 90 degrees, slide the loading lever assembly out of the cylinder, remove the empty cylinder and replace it with a fully loaded spare. It sounds more complicated than it is, but it does require a certain amount of dexterity, and it's definitely a skill you need to develop/practice before you find yourself facing a deadly threat. The first time I tried the cylinder swap it required around 16 seconds and included some fumbling with the three loading assembly parts. A couple more efforts to eliminate the fumbling brought the time down to about

nine seconds. Since you won't be loading any individual cylinders during the fight, you can save some time and simplify things by removing the ramming/seating rod from the loading assembly leaving only two pieces to handle. Remember where you put the seating rod; it's essential when you're finally ready to reload all the individual cylinders.

With Ruger out of production on the Old Army, it's not likely you'll find any extra cylinders in a conventional shopping endeavor. The answer is to send your Old Army revolver to Gary Reeder at Reeder's Custom Guns in Flagstaff, Arizona. He builds Ruger cylinders and will fit one or more to your gun. Should you desire, he will also modify your Old Army to a larger caliber and fit it with one or more custom five-shot cylinders. You can choose between two super

calibers: .475 or .51. Commercial swaged lead balls and other blackpowder accessories are available for both calibers, and the weight of the larger diameter round balls goes up dramatically.

But when all the arguments are in and the discussion ends, it's difficult to make a case for use of blackpowder, cap-and-ball firearms for self-defense given all the more efficient choices available in the 21st century. Due to the special blackpowder hunting seasons offered in many states, and the extra challenges in harvesting animals with traditional weapons, there are other, "non-tactical" reasons to stick with the more historical handguns. Re-enactment groups, like cowboy-action shooters, use blackpowder both in cartridge guns and "front-end" loaders, and while some of them might actually keep an "old hog leg" handy for home defense, for most folks the guns are all about fun.

Author's note: Although my first "big-bore" handgun was an 1858 Remington blackpowder replica, I've focused on the Ruger Old Army since it is the BP handgun with which I'm most familiar. And as noted, I like the idea of it being a "magnum" handgun, a modernized design and, on my personal gun, having adjustable sights. But nothing says you can't use a replica of an original 19th-century revolver. They dispatched a lot of folks in their day. And as the boogey man explained to me years ago, when things go bump in the night, any firearm at hand is much better than reaching for a broom stick or a ping pong paddle. Stay safe.

This wooden stand facilitates loading cylinders while in the gun, but a trip afield should include a small "possibles" bag with a few extra rounds.

CUSTOM AND ENGRAVED GUNS

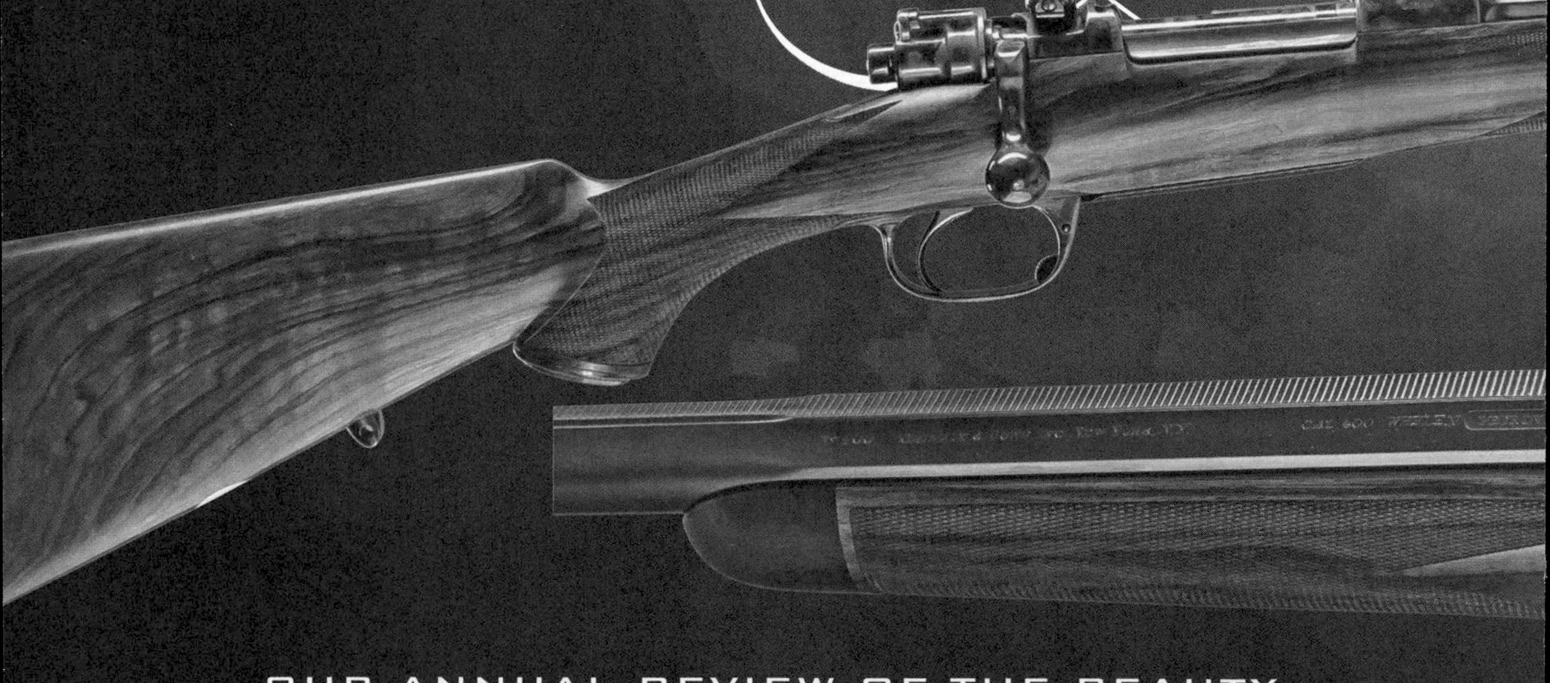

OUR ANNUAL REVIEW OF THE BEAUTY
AND ARTISTRY IN THE WORLD OF
THE CUSTOM GUN

Lee Helgeland

This magnificent rifle is the work of Montana rifle maker Lee Helgeland. He began the project with a large ring/small thread commercial Oberndorf Mauser rifle, which had been engraved. The action was in-the-white and had never been barreled. Helgeland believes it is from the Hoffman shop and the engraving appears to be by Kornbrath. It must have come by way of England as it is stamped "Not English Made," done to comply with export regulations.

Lee fitted a Canjar trigger to the action and installed a Lyman 35 receiver sight. The German-made barrel is 23 1/4 inches long, octagon to round, with a beautiful tapered full-length rib. The barrel had a bad bore, so Lee shipped it to Jim Dubell and had it rebored for the .400 Whelen cartridge.

Lee stocked the rifle in a magnificent stick of California English walnut, checkered it 26 lpi in a point pattern and leather covered the recoil pad. He installed a Dressel English-style grip cap and a gold oval for a monogram. The job was completed with bluing by Michael Baiar and Doug Turnbull did the color case work.

Photos by Creative Photography

C.J. Cai

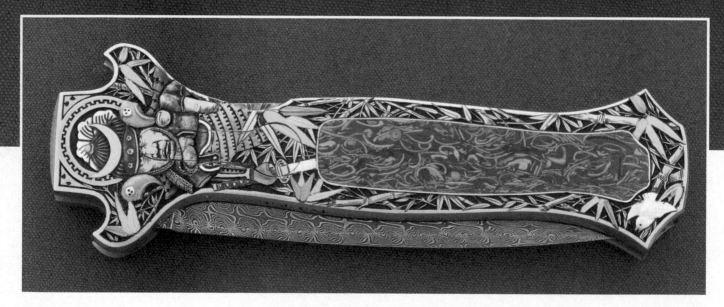

Although the word "knife" does not appear in the Gun Digest title, knives are so closely related to guns that I'd venture a guess that just about every gun owner is also a knife owner. A custom knife is also often on the receiving end of the engravers tools and artistry. That is the case here with this Joe Kious crafted knife and the engraving artistry of C.J. Cai. This example won the Firearms Engravers Guild of America (FEGA) Best Engraved Knife Award at the 2019 FEGA Exhibition in Las Vegas. Photos by Sam Welch

Mike Dubber

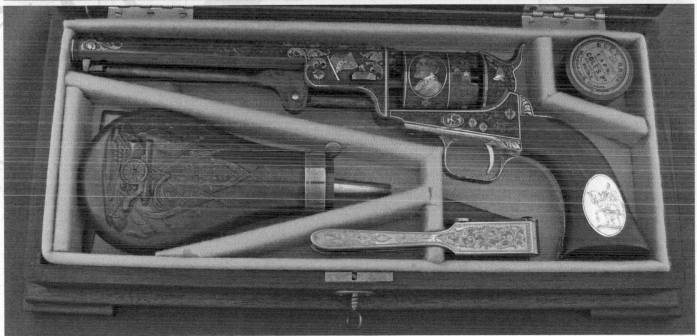

Mike is a recognized master engraver by both the Firearms Engravers Guild of America and Colt Manufacturing Co. Shown here is an example of his superb work. This cased Colt 51 Navy Robert E. Lee Commemorative was engraved and gold inlaid by Dubber and was judged as a runner-up in the FEGA Engravers Choice award at its exhibition in Las Vegas. Photos by Sam Welch

D'Arcy Echols

The action used in crafting the rifle pictured above is, for now at least, if not forever, unique. About 10 years ago, Peter Pi, the long-time owner of CorBon ammunition (it has recently been sold to new owners) approached gun maker D'Arcy Echols to design and arrange to manufacture a new action. He designed an action that basically combined the best features of the Mauser 98 and Winchester Model 70. When satisfied with the design, he went to Central Valley Machine owner Ben Wursten, and chief programmer James Cook, and arranged for the manufacture of five actions.

Two actions were destroyed in the development and testing process, one was sent to HP White Labs where it was rendered unusable due to the high-pressure testing, and Peter Pi donated one action to Safari Club International (SCI) in 2012, where it was placed up for auction as a fundraiser. Sufficient parts to assemble and finish a fifth action are retained at Central Valley Machine. For whatever reason, Mr. Pi did not pursue the project after the five actions.

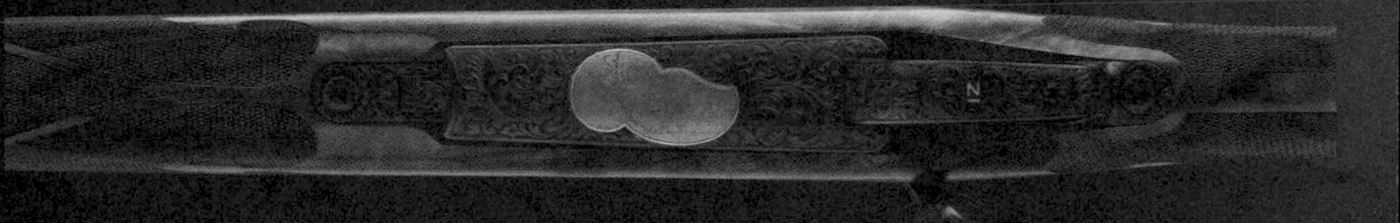

The gentleman who bought the action from the SCI auction did nothing with it for a considerable time and decided to sell it. A client of Echols bought the action and asked D'Arcy to make a rifle out of it. The .375 H&H-chambered rifle shown here is the result. It is the epitome of a classic rifle and most likely, there will never be another just like it. Photos by Kevin Dilley

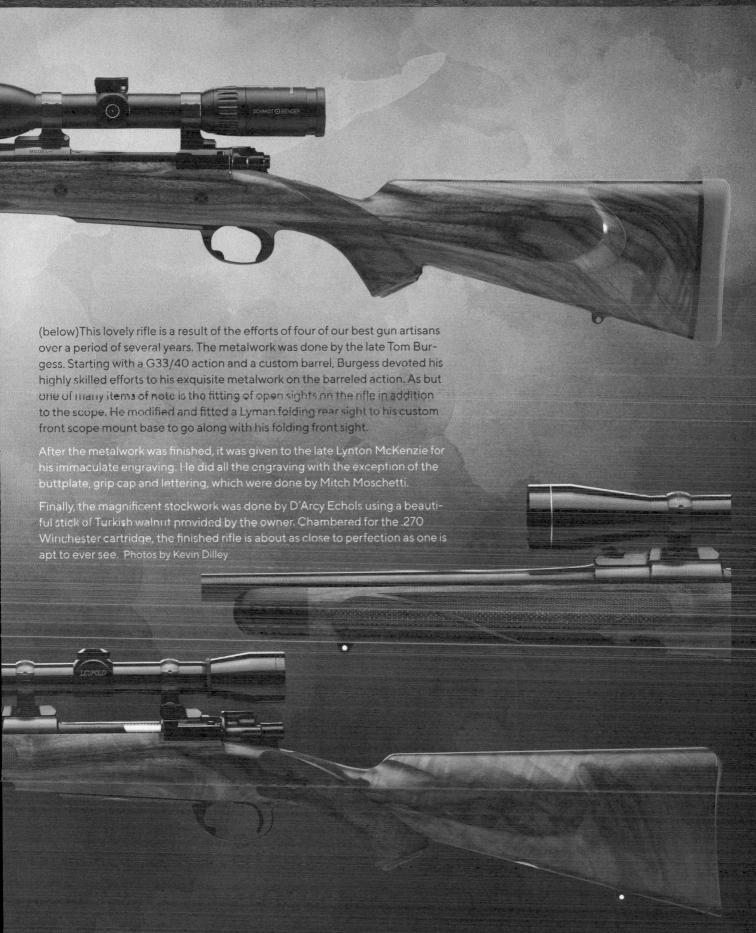

(below) This lovely rifle is a result of the efforts of four of our best gun artisans over a period of several years. The metalwork was done by the late Tom Burgess. Starting with a G33/40 action and a custom barrel, Burgess devoted his highly skilled efforts to his exquisite metalwork on the barreled action. As but one of many items of note is the fitting of open sights on the rifle in addition to the scope. He modified and fitted a Lyman folding rear sight to his custom front scope mount base to go along with his folding front sight.

After the metalwork was finished, it was given to the late Lynton McKenzie for his immaculate engraving. He did all the engraving with the exception of the buttplate, grip cap and lettering, which were done by Mitch Moschetti.

Finally, the magnificent stockwork was done by D'Arcy Echols using a beautiful stick of Turkish walnut provided by the owner. Chambered for the .270 Winchester cartridge, the finished rifle is about as close to perfection as one is apt to ever see. Photos by Kevin Dilley

Lee Griffiths / Steve Heilmann

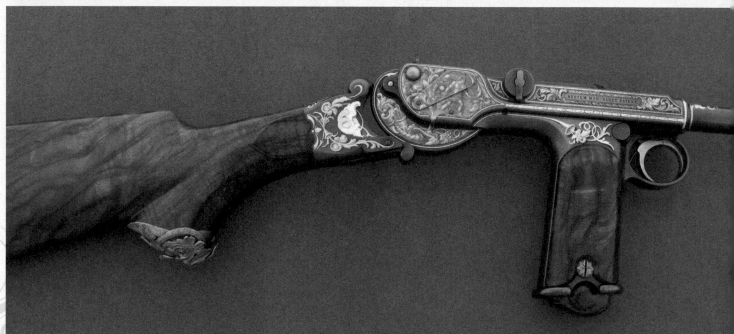

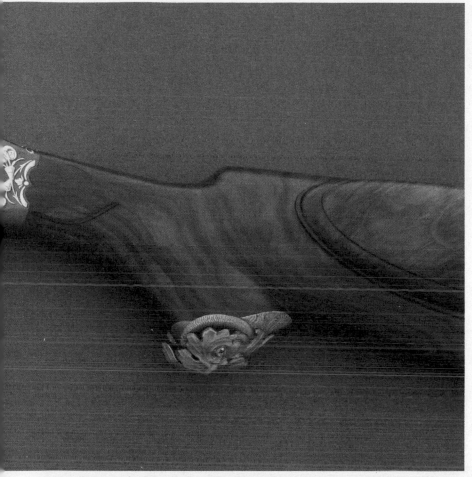

This superb Borchardt is a result of the collaborative efforts of gun maker Steve Heilmann and master engraver Lee Griffiths. It is a safe bet that it is a unique, one-of-a-kind Borchardt. The project began with a nice original specimen, but with no buttstock or attaching iron. Heilmann designed and fabricated the necessary attaching iron as well as wavy grip cap, carbine style buttplate and rising and rotating sling swivel stud. He crafted the buttstock, magazine cap and grips from what he told me was one of the most incredible pieces of California English walnut he had ever worked with. He said it was such a stunning piece of wood that no decision had yet been made whether to carve, checker, or leave the wood as is.

Both Lee and Steve worked on polishing the metal to a flawless finish. Lee then fully engraved the pistol. This project won three major awards at the annual FEGA annual exhibition, including Best Engraved Handgun award, Artistic Uniqueness award, and the FEGA equivalent of the Oscar, the Engravers Choice award. Engraved photos by Sam Welch. Non-engraved photos by Steve Heilmann

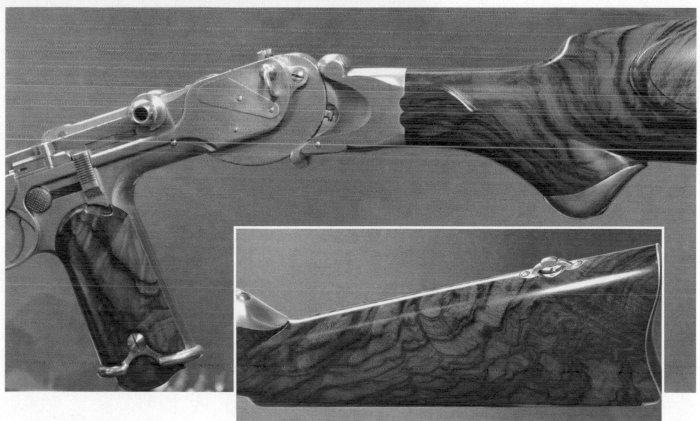

Steve Heilmann

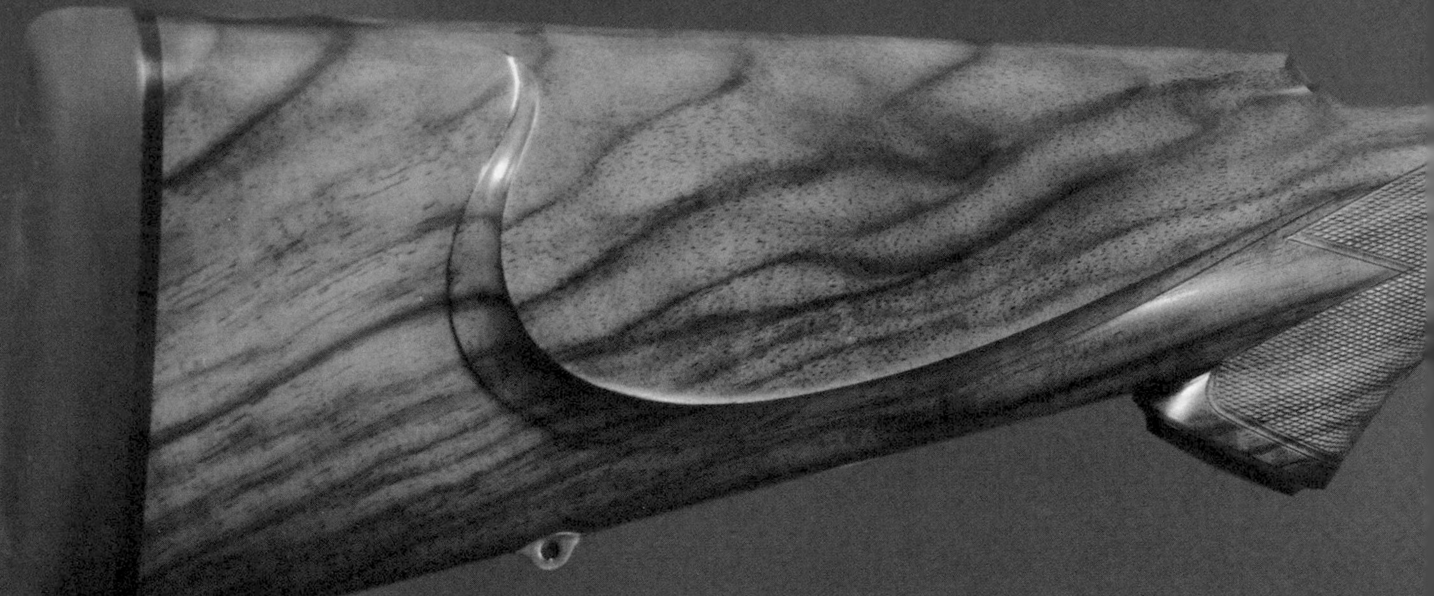

Steve Heilmann built his southpaw client this superb .338 Win Mag rifle on a Granite Mountain Arms (GMA) take on the G33/40 Mauser action. GMA makes the action in both left- and right-hand versions. Steve machined the action square bridges to accept his Heilmann magnum scope rings, re-contoured and checkered the factory GMA bolt handle, refined all the factory metal, and finished up by stoning and polishing all the metal surfaces. He then fitted and chambered a custom-contoured Bartlein barrel. Pete Mazur then did the outstanding fine rust blue job, completing the metal-work.

Steve stocked the rifle in a super-nice stick of California English walnut with nearly perfect layout. He applied a hand-rubbed oil finish and checkered the stock 26 lpi. Photos by Steve Heilmann

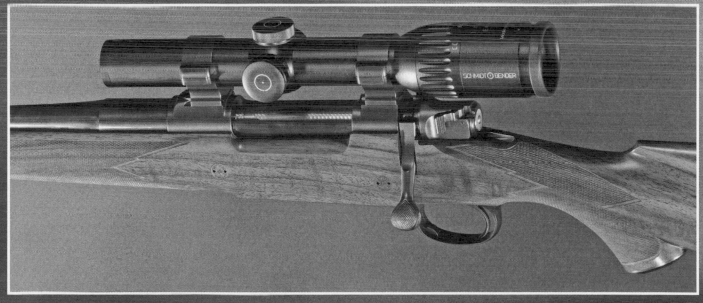

Gordon Alcorn

Gordon Alcorn did the exquisite engraving on the steel Lone Wolf slide, fitted to the Glock handgun shown here. His work on this piece was sufficiently out-standing to be awarded the FEGA award as the Best Engraved Modern Firearm at the FEGA exhibition in Las Vegas. Photos by Sam Welch

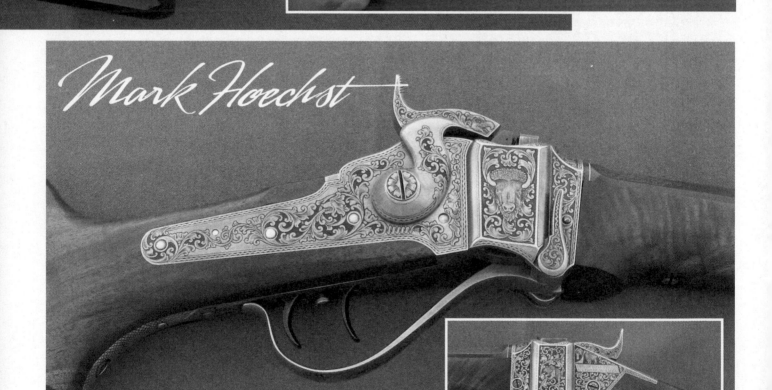

Mark Hoechst

Engraver Mark Hoechst received the FEGA Award for the Best Engraved Single-Shot Rifle at the exhibition in Las Vegas. Mark started with a factory Shiloh Sharps and embellished it nicely with his excellent engraving. Photos by Sam Welch

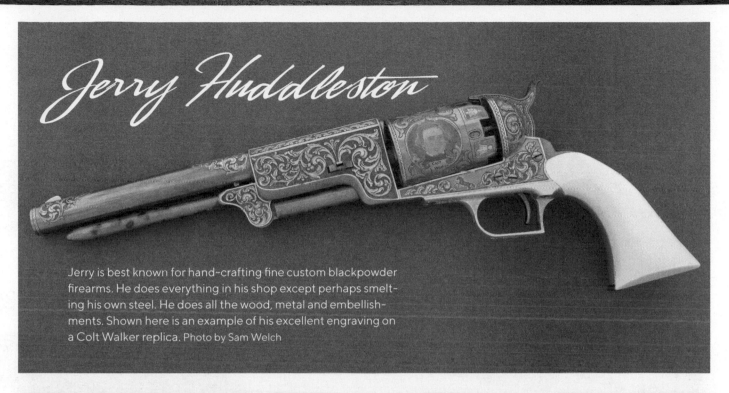

Jerry Huddleston

Jerry is best known for hand-crafting fine custom blackpowder firearms. He does everything in his shop except perhaps smelting his own steel. He does all the wood, metal and embellishments. Shown here is an example of his excellent engraving on a Colt Walker replica. Photo by Sam Welch

Marty Rabeno

Although I'm sure Marty can engrave in many different styles, he seems to have specialized in engravings that would have been right at home in the Old West of the mid-1800s. The only difference is that Marty's work is vastly superior to any work done during that period that I've ever seen. Whether his apparent specialization is on purpose, or, his period work is so outstanding he attracts clients enough to take up most of his time doing period-style work, I can't say. I suspect the answer is somewhere in the middle.

This wonderfully done Winchester Model 73 won the FEGA Best Engraved Rifle Award at the FEGA Exhibition and was a runner-up in the Engravers Choice Award. Photos by Sam Welch

A tale of THREE TRENCH GUNS

A riot gun takes to the battlefields

BY **RICK HACKER**
PHOTOS BY AUTHOR, EXCEPT WHERE NOTED

Before the M16 and the AK-47, in fact even before the M1 Garand, there was a wartime shoulder weapon used by American troops that was so devastating, so deadly and so feared by the enemy that during World War I Germany tried unsuccessfully to get it banned from the battlefields. And yet, in its peacetime guise, it was one of the most popular sporting arms in the country.

The gun I'm referring to is the Winchester Model 1897 – its name shortened to Model 97 in later years – a five-shot, pump-action shotgun that was made from 1897 until 1957, a 60-year lifespan in which 1,024,700 guns were produced. Although the Model 97 was made in many different grades, and came with

a standard barrel length of 30 inches, to me, one of the most fascinating and desirable variations is the Model 97 Trench Gun, a no-holds-barred, take-no-prisoners weapon that earned its stars, bars and stripes through two World Wars, the Korean Conflict and even up through Vietnam. It also fought for law and order on the home front.

That's quite a service record for a shotgun that was conceived by John Moses Browning more than 120 years ago. And while we often look at these venerable weapons and lament, "If only those guns could talk," I found three different versions of the Model 97 Trench Gun that each have a story to tell.

But the individual tales of these three veterans – and the saga of the Model 97 Trench Gun in general – actually begins

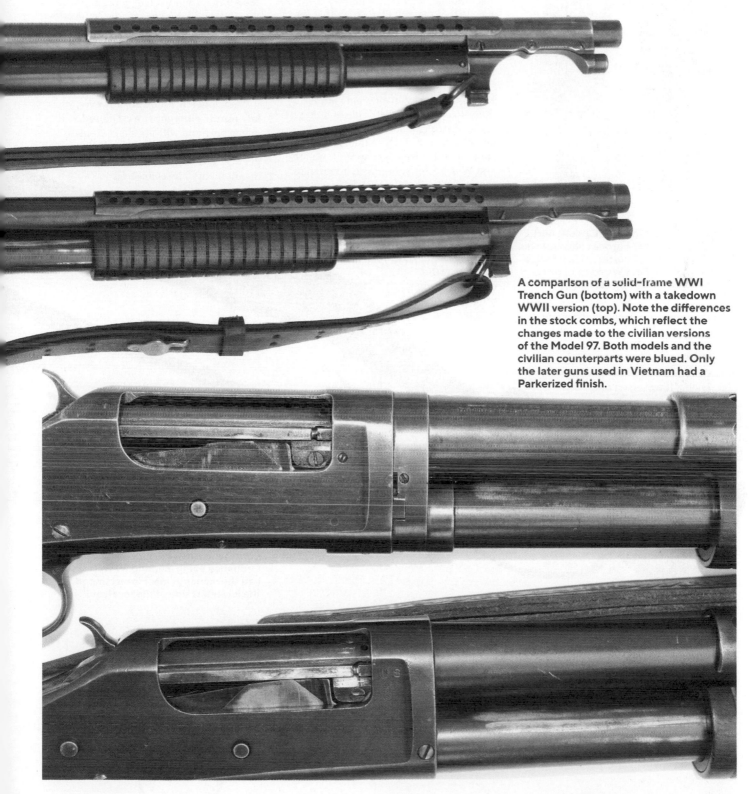

A comparison of a solid-frame WWI Trench Gun (bottom) with a takedown WWII version (top). Note the differences in the stock combs, which reflect the changes made to the civilian versions of the Model 97. Both models and the civilian counterparts were blued. Only the later guns used in Vietnam had a Parkerized finish.

A World War I doughboy stands at port arms with his M1917 bayonet affixed to his M97 Trench Gun. (Courtesy U.S. Infantry Weapons of the First World War; Bruce N. Canfield, Mowbray Publications)

with the Model 1893, which Browning and his brother had designed right on the eve of the smokeless-powder revolution. That was unfortunate, for the '93 was a shotgun made for blackpowder shot shells. It was even offered with Damascus barrels as an option. Consequently,

with its top-ejecting, thin-walled receiver and a penchant for its action to become sluggish midst all that internal black-powder fouling, the Model 93 did not fare very well with hunters, who put far more faith in the side-by-side shotguns of the day. As a result, only 34,176 Model 93s were produced from 1893 until its discontinuance in 1897. The '93's history was further marred by the fact that Winchester offered to buy them back from dealers or swap them outright for their newer and vastly improved Model 1897.

By contrast, the dramatically strengthened and mechanically improved Model 97 was the right gun emerging at the right time. Thick-walled, side-ejecting, made of stronger steel with a fluid steel barrel and, in fact, more than muscular enough for smokeless powder, it was the first Winchester shotgun chambered for the new 2 3/4-inch smokeless ammunition. Consequently, it found a ready audience with sportsmen who now wanted a hard-hitting, smokeless-powder repeater.

By the same token, law enforcement personnel began evaluating the crime-stopping potential of this new pump-action

shotgun. As a result, in 1898 – just one year after its introduction – a 20-inch barreled, cylinder-choked Riot Gun version of the Model 97 was introduced. It is interesting to note a 20-inch barrel riot gun was also offered during the Model 1893's brief existence, but most of these were destroyed by the factory during the 1893-97 shotgun-exchange program, as the '93 was basically considered unsafe to shoot with smokeless powder. Very few factory originals have survived, and, of course, if encountered today, should be used only with low-pressure, blackpowder loads.

The Model 97 Riot Gun, however, was an entirely different story. Offered in 12 gauge only and with its short 20-inch, cylinder-choked barrel, it was quick to get into action and its lack of a detent meant it could be slam-fired just as fast as the shooter could

(above) This WWI Trench Gun was issued to Major E.H. Johnson of Headquarters Company, Medical Corps, 92nd Division of the American Expeditionary Forces. Dr. Johnson subsequently took it home with him to Peabody, Kansas, where it remained in the family until recently.

(below) Most WWI Trench Guns were hand-stamped "U.S." on the upper right-hand side of the receivers plus the Ordnance bomb marking. WWII versions had the markings machine-stamped on the lower left side of the receiver.

work the trombone action. Moreover, its exposed hammer made the Model 97 Riot Gun easy to cock in times of stress. Small wonder it soon became a favorite of law-enforcement agencies such as the Texas Rangers, the Los Angeles Police Department, the Union Pacific Railroad Police and various express companies, to name just a few of the authenticated guns I have examined over the years, although not all of these were so-marked. And as a natural progression, reflecting a change that covered the entire Model 97 line, in October 1898 – at the same time the Riot Gun was

introduced – a take-down version was brought out. Thus, there were now two variations of the Riot Gun – solid frame and takedown.

Law-enforcement agencies aside, the Riot Gun's potential as a battlefield weapon wasn't lost on the U.S. government, which procured a few of them in 1898 for use during the Philippine Insurrection, as our troops were having a hard time putting down the drug-crazed Moro tribesmen. The .38 caliber, double-action Colt New Model Army and Navy revolvers in use at the time were ineffective against the adrenalin-powered Moros, so in addition to re-enlisting the old Colt .45 Single Action Army to help do the job, the 12-gauge Winchester Riot Gun was called into military action for the first time.

The M1917 bayonet, which was made by both Winchester and Remington during WWI, was standard issue for the M1897 Trench Gun.

They proved their close-range effectiveness so well that, a few years later, they were issued to some of the mounted troops riding with Brigadier General John J. "Black Jack" Pershing's Punitive Expedition into Mexico, as they pursued Pancho Villa after his raid on the citizens and soldiers of Columbus, New Mexico. Once again, the Riot Guns were not only deadly at close range, but were psychologically intimidating – even when

shots weren't fired – just by their mere presence. However, all this was only leading up to an even greater chapter in the history of the Winchester 97.

With the advent of World War I – or, more specifically, with Congress finally declaring war against Germany on April 6, 1917 after having unarmed American civilian ships sunk by the Kaiser's navy, coupled with uncovering a secret plot for

The Winchester 1897 had a rugged action, able to handle smokeless ammunition.

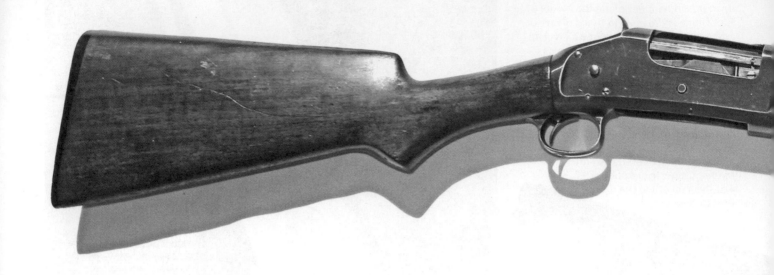

Germany to use Mexico's army to take back Arizona, New Mexico and Texas – we entered the fray. Put in charge of what became known as the American Expeditionary Forces (A.E.F.), now-Major General "Black Jack" Pershing insisted on being in control of the weapons our doughboys were fighting with. Inasmuch as "The War To End All Wars" involved extremely close-range fighting in the trenches of No Man's Land, Pershing, no doubt recalling the success his soldiers had achieved with their Model 97 Riot Guns in Mexico, ordered approximately 200 of the solid frame versions for his troops. It should be noted that none were military marked.

However, it soon became apparent the civilian version of the Riot Gun was not suited for the intense combat situation unfolding in the war. For one thing, during rapid firing, the barrels became too hot to hold. For another, there was no provision for either sling swivels or – when ammo ran out or there was no time to reload – the attachment of a bayonet, which was considered paramount to a soldier's last-ditch defense. Thus, a new batch of modified-for-war, solid frame Riot Guns was requisitioned from Winchester. This resulted in each gun being outfitted with a perforated steel heat shield that featured six rows of holes and covered most of the upper barrel. In addition, a separately secured bayonet lug and sling swivel attachment was mounted on the barrel's muzzle end to accommodate the standard military-issue M-1917 bayonet; a rear sling swivel was screwed into the buttstock, near the heel, as these guns were issued with M-1907 leather slings. The only drawback to this arrangement was that the M-1917 bayonet, with its 16-1/2 inch blade, proved to be unwieldy in the close confines of trench warfare. It also threw off the balance of the short barreled shotgun. As a result, many of these bayonet attachments were discarded in battle.

Nonetheless, this militarized version of the Model 97 Riot Gun received its own designation of "U.S. Model of 1917 Trench Shotgun," or as it was more commonly called – the Trench Gun – as it was literally in the trenches, fighting for freedom. But many of our doughboys also called it the Trench Sweeper, for obvious reasons. With five rounds in the tubular magazine and one in the chamber, each of the military-issued shotshells packed a devastating load of .33 caliber-sized 00 buckshot, which spread a pattern that measured 9 feet horizontally and 3 feet vertically, according to an article in the May 11, 1918 issue of Scientific American Magazine. No wonder Germany tried to get the M97 Trench Gun outlawed, declaring it "inhumane." Their pleas were rebuked by our government, of course, and the Trench Gun continued its march to help eventually win the war, even being employed by skilled wingshooters in our ranks to blast incoming German hand grenades out of the air before they hit the ground.

> **HOWEVER, ONE TRENCH GUN THAT DID MAKE IT TO THE FRONT LINES, SERIAL NUMBER E669695, WAS MANUFACTURED IN 1918 AND WAS SUBSEQUENTLY ISSUED TO A MEDICAL OFFICER. IT IS OUR FIRST TRENCH GUN WITH A TALE TO TELL.**

Interestingly, all of these WWI Trench Guns were solid frame, rust-blued and had no buttstock cartouches. In fact, many WWI Trench Guns encountered today do not bear any military markings at all, although those that were issued were usually hand-stamped with a "U.S." and an ordinance bomb on the upper right-hand side of the receiver. But noted wartime author and authority Bruce Canfield offers a theory that because the Trench Gun came so late to the party, many of them were unissued and hence, remained in storage, unstamped. However, one Trench Gun that did make it to the front lines, serial number E669695, was manufactured in 1918 and was subsequently issued to a medical officer. It is our first Trench Gun with a tale to tell.

It begins shortly after Congress declared war against Germany on April 6, 1917. On August 20, 1917, a Dr. E.H. Johnson from the small town of Peabody, Kansas, along with a number of other patriotic men from the area, enlisted in the Army, most likely at the local recruiting office that had opened there on May

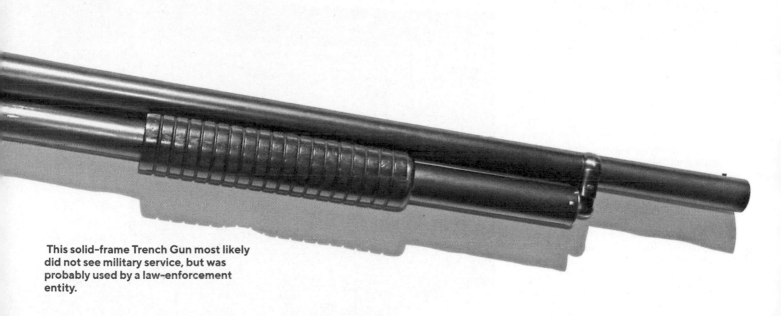

This solid-frame Trench Gun most likely did not see military service, but was probably used by a law-enforcement entity.

31, 1917. Eventually, these new recruits were mustered in as part of Company M of the 3rd Kansas Infantry and were among the first American troops to arrive in France.

Being a medical professional, Dr. Johnson was promoted to the rank of major and eventually was transferred to Headquarters Company, Medical Corps, 92nd Division of the A.E.F. As an aside, he was the first army tuberculosis specialist to be sent overseas. At some point Dr. Johnson was issued a Government 1911, along with this Model 97, which bears the proper hand stamping for a WWI government-issued Trench Gun. Thus, it seems Dr. Johnson was fairly well-armed for any close-in skirmishes he might encounter.

Upon being discharged from the Army on May 23, 1919 at Camp Funston, Kan-

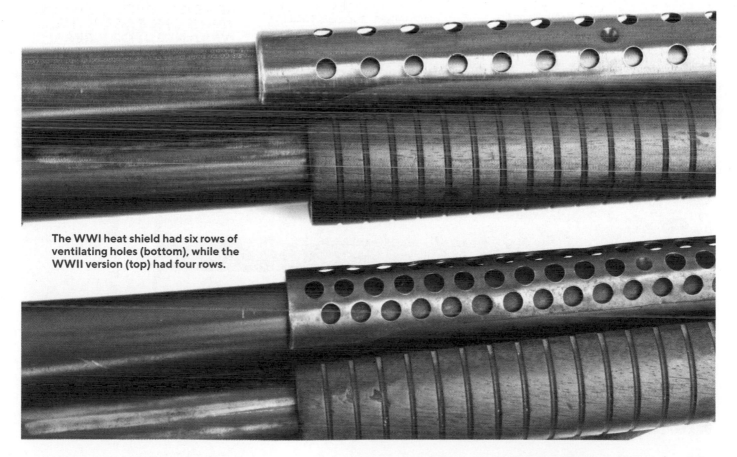

The WWI heat shield had six rows of ventilating holes (bottom), while the WWII version (top) had four rows.

sas, Dr. Johnson returned to Peabody, taking his Model 97 Trench Gun with him. It remained in his possession until 1951, when he sold it to the son of a friend who had served with him in WWI. It is interesting to note this son had just returned from fighting in the Korean War. So, in a way, it was symbolic of one old soldier passing a cherished wartime gun on to a younger veteran. The son, in turn, ended up proudly displaying that Trench Gun in the den of his home. He later sold it to his son-in-law, who, in turn, sold it to the Korean War vet's son, who recalled many years later that, "I was the last one to shoot it around 1971, when my dad and I went dove hunting" (an interesting juxtaposition of the WWI years when those Trench Guns were used to blast incoming enemy grenades out of the air). In 2015, that son eventually sold the gun to a private collector, who researched its history and shared it with me. Thus, this unaltered, completely original Model 97 Trench Gun's story can finally be told.

It is estimated there were somewhere between 19,000 and 25,000 Trench Guns made by Winchester during WWI, and although many were lost due to attrition, as previously noted, an unknown number were unissued and remained in storage. And as shocking as it might seem to collectors of militaria today, after the Armistice many of those surplus Trench Guns were sold on the civilian market for as little as $4.50 each. Consequently, more than a few dealers and other individuals removed the heat shield and bayonet lug attachments and then swapped out the 20-inch, cylinder-choked barrels for longer, more tightly choked tubes. These reconditioned M97s were then resold as sporting arms. This

WWII Trench Guns had their inspector's initials and Ordnance stamps on the left side of the buttstock. The G.H.D. stamp was for Colonel Guy H. Drewry.

is another reason so few authentic WWI Trench Guns have survived, although many of the unissued surplus Trench Guns were subsequently purchased by various police departments and for prison-guard use during the 1920s and '30s. (I emphasize the word "authentic" because due to their rising collector value, many Model 97s have since been converted to Trench Gun configuration – whether or not they were actually Trench Guns in the first place. So buyer beware.)

❝ IN 1941, WHEN THE UNITED STATES ENTERED WORLD WAR II, ONCE AGAIN THERE WAS A NEED FOR FIREARMS THAT FAR EXCEEDED THE EXISTING SUPPLY, AND THOSE FEW M97 TRENCH GUNS THAT REMAINED IN STORAGE WERE FINALLY CALLED INTO ACTION.❞

The same stampings used on the slide of the civilian version of the Winchester 1897 also appear on the Model 97 Trench Gun.

In 1941, when the United States entered World War II, once again there was a need for firearms that far exceeded the existing supply, and those few M97 Trench Guns that remained in storage were finally called into action. In addition, Winchester was again pressed into service to supply the latest iteration of its Trench Gun, but this time the War Department ordered the blued, take-down version of the M97. In addition, the heat shield configuration was changed from the six rows of ventilating holes of the WWI guns to a line of four rows of ventilating holes on the WWII versions. Plus, the stocks of the WWII Trench Guns reflected the lower-comb profile of the current Model 97s in the line, and the left side of the buttstocks were stamped with inspector's cartouches of either WB (Colonel Waldemar Broberg) or GHD (Colonel Guy H. Drewry). In addition, the arsenal markings were now machine-stamped on the left side of the receiver and a small "flaming bomb" was stamped on top of the barrel, near the receiver.

Initially, according to Bruce Canfield in his excellent book *U.S. Infantry Weapons of World War I* (Andrew Mowbray Publishers; www.gunandswordcollector.com), 1,494 of these Model 97 Trench Guns were ordered by the Ordinance Department in 1941. However, as the war escalated, this number was quickly ramped up, with the biggest proponents for the M97 being the U.S. Army and the Marine Corps, which used them extensively in the Pacific Theater. This brings

us to the second of our Trench Gun tales.

This battle-worn Trench Gun, serial number E954635, was made in 1943. It exhibits all the correct markings for a post-May 1942 Trench Gun, including the GHD inspector's stamping of Drewry, who was the chief inspector for Smith & Wesson, Colt, Winchester and Underwood from 1930 through 1946, and who succeeded Broberg as government inspector. But what is especially intriguing are another set of initials that appear on this shotgun – RJM – that had been professionally stamped on both the right and left sides of the buttstock.

Through research with the family, I learned that these stand for Robert J. MacGregor, a U.S. Marine and machine gunner who carried this shotgun throughout the Pacific Theater. After the war, he brought this shotgun back to the states and carried it during his career with the Los Angeles Police Department. (Evidently, and as evidenced by Dr. Johnson's WWI Trench Gun, these "bring backs" were a lot easier to accomplish back then than they are now.) At some point he had his initials stamped on the buttstock, no doubt to ascertain that it was his property, and not the department's. He also outfitted this Trench Gun with a civilian-style sling sometime prior to 1960.

Another intriguing mark on the buttstock is a rather noticeable chunk of wood taken out of the toe of the stock. Was this the result of a well-executed butt stroke during the war? Unfortunately, we may never know, for the tale of this Trench Gun has abruptly ended. But at least a portion of its story can now be told.

That brings us to our final tale, of a Trench Gun with serial number E687071, which puts it right in the same third-and-final batch of WWI Trench Guns as the gun owned by Dr. Johnson. And thanks to firearms records specialist Jessica Bennett of the Buffalo Bill Center of the West in Cody, Wyoming (centerofthewest.org), we know this particular gun's serial number was applied on May 15, 1918 – just over one year after the U.S. entered WWI and only five months before the war ended, on Nov. 11, 1918. However, that fact that this gun has no military markings probably means it was never issued, and was one of those Trench Guns that was put into government storage. The fact that it remained unmarked also most likely means it was

The bayonet lug was a separate piece affixed to the muzzle end of the 1897 Trench Gun.

later sold sometime before WWII, when it otherwise would have been badly needed. Thus, given the fact that it still retains its heat shield and bayonet lug, it was probably purchased for guard duty or by a messenger company. And judging by the 75 percent wear on the metal and wood, it obviously was carried and used, and is consistent with those Trench Guns that saw service in law enforcement. But, sadly, that is all this particular Trench Gun can tell us, other than it was an "attic find" that recently came out of Oregon, and ended up in the collection of a very discriminating firearms enthusiast. And so ends our tale of three Trench Guns, each of them intriguing in its own way.

SMITH & WESSON'S
FIRST AUTOMATIC PIS

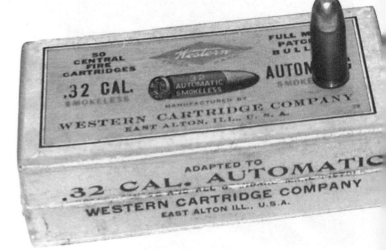

In 1909, Joe Wesson met Charles Clement of Liege, Belgium. Clement had designed a small autoloading pistol chambered for the .25 ACP that had several design elements Smith & Wesson found interesting. S&W purchased the design and patent rights in 1910. One was the location of the bore below the recoil spring channel. Later discussions claimed that this design resulted in more reliable function by reducing the distance the cartridge had to travel to get to the chamber and the lower axis of the bore reduced felt recoil. Thus began S&W's slow and tortuous trip down the semi-auto pistol road. By far the most authoritative information is found in S&W's historian Roy Jinks' book *History of Smith & Wesson*.

The original plan was to make a .32 ACP, but, from a historical perspective, most firearms manufacturers want their name on cartridges, so S&W and Remington developed the .35 S&W Automatic cartridge. It used a .312-inch-diameter bullet, the same as the .32 ACP, and a rimless case only slightly larger in diameter. Jinks reports the factory was concerned about bore life with the jacketed bullets used in pistol cartridges, so the company insisted on a bullet design with a jacketed nose and lead base. While that reasoning is surely flawed in terms of today's knowledge, it wasn't entirely illogical considering Smith & Wesson had only dealt with lead bullets in 1912.

Joe Wesson undertook a revamp of the Clement design beginning with a recoil spring disconnector. The lightweight

On the left, the .32 model that succeeded the .35 on the right.

TOL

The unfortunate .35 S&W

BY **CHARLES E. PETTY**

slide required a very heavy recoil spring that some found impossible to operate. The disconnector was a pushbutton that captured the recoil spring and, when engaged, allowed the slide to move freely. Then came two safeties. The first was analogous to today's grip safety but operated by the shooter's middle finger on the front of the grip frame. The other was a small wheel on the backstrap. There was an arrow on the frame pointing up to the letter "S."

Smith & Wesson chose Remington-UMC to develop the original ammo following its requirement for a two-part bullet. On some of that early ammo you might see a dimple in the nose just above the case mouth. Apparently, this is a form of staking to prevent separation of the two parts. Later ammo from Peters shows similar marks.

Remington ammo of the time bore the legend: "These cartridges have metal point bullets. The lead only coming in contact with the rifling. Specially adapted for the .35 Smith & Wesson automatic." On the other hand, W.H.B. Smith in his *Book of Pistols and Revolvers* writes, "In actual practice the theory does not work very well."

Even though Winchester, Peters and Rem-UMC loaded it, the .35 S&W cartridge was not exactly popular. Ammo production stopped in 1940 even though Smith & Wesson had discontinued the pistol in 1921. The most charitable description of the round is a "barely disguised" .32 ACP. I can find no reference to tell us exactly where ".35" came from.

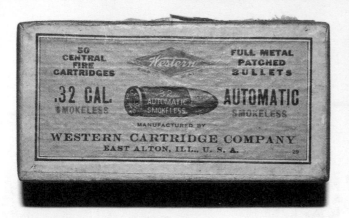

Packaging of ammo for Smith & Wesson's first auto pistols.

> ❝ THE FIRST PISTOLS WERE COMPLETED MAY 3, 1913, AND WERE AVAILABLE IN BLUE OR NICKEL FINISH WITH A RETAIL PRICE OF $16.50. SMITH & WESSON JUSTIFIED THE PRICE, WHICH WAS SOMEWHAT HIGHER THAN THE COMPETITION, BY STATING THAT IT WAS MORE COMPLICATED TO MACHINE. ❞

The first pistols were completed May 3, 1913, and were available in blue or nickel finish with a retail price of $16.50. Smith & Wesson justified the price, which was somewhat higher than the competition, by stating that it was more complicated to machine. Instead of a slide, it has a smaller part called the breechblock, which would have been more intricate to make. At that time, the retail price of the Savage was around $15.

It took a while for Smith & Wesson

to realize the odd cartridge might have done more harm than good. So, in 1921 an order came down to rework the .35 for the standard .32 ACP cartridge. Manufacture of the .35 ended July 5, 1922, with a total production of 8,350 guns.

When I first began research for this story, I was concerned about throwing rocks at Smith & Wesson, but as I read on, it was clear rocks had already been launched. Perhaps the most telling is in Mike Bussard's *Ammo Encyclopedia*: "The .35 S&W Auto remains an example of the danger of allowing a corporate ego to dictate marketing decisions."

The reworked pistol, now a .32 ACP, eliminated some of the complexities that plagued the .35. Most important was to incorporate the breechblock into a conventional slide, which made loading and unloading easier. The recoil spring disconnector was still there, although the slide was much easier to move. The safety on the front of the grip frame of the .35 was eliminated, which made the

grip more comfortable and attractive.

When the .32 was offered to the public in February 1924, there was still one round left in the "foot-shooting" gun. The retail price was set at $33.50. The explanation that it was more difficult to manufacture fell on deaf ears. At that time, both Colt and Savage offered .32 pistols at something nearly half the S&W's price. The consumer today accepts that Ferraris cost more than Fords, but Smith & Wesson did not claim or even hint that it was superior in any way to the competition.

Now, I have long been a fan and collector of Smith & Wessons and when I learned a local shop had one of the .32s, I beat a path to the door. The owner is a longtime friend and while the price tag did not bring on sticker shock, it wasn't cheap. I simply *had* to have it. Before the day was done, the .32 went home with me. The next day I sent a letter off to Roy Jinks. While I had known the .32s were rare I didn't know *how rare* until the reply came.

Roy wrote: "Smith & Wesson's .32 automatic was a well-designed, sleek-looking autoloading pocket pistol. However, its retail price of approximately $11.00 over its competitors, combined with economic factors created by the depression, caused extremely slow sales and seriously damaged the popularity of their .32 automatic." The factory discon-

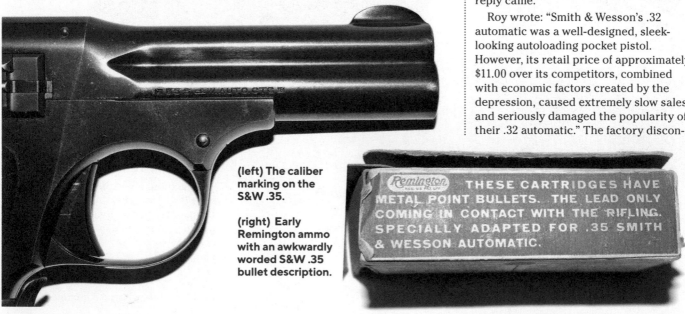

(left) The caliber marking on the S&W .35.

(right) Early Remington ammo with an awkwardly worded S&W .35 bullet description.

tinued production of this model in 1937 after manufacturing 960 units of which 957 were sold."

They could hardly have chosen a worse time to introduce the model. In addition to the cost, economic conditions in the country were faltering, perhaps in anticipation of the Great Depression, which was soon to come. Speaking with the wonderful clarity of hindsight, Smith & Wesson management could or should have anticipated some of the issues their decisions produced. Seen from another angle though, the event created three rarities for collectors.

A muzzle view with a .35 on left and .32 with new slide on the right.

Over the years, I had seen .35s at many gun shows but never wanted one until got the .32. I found several at online auctions and bid on one that looked nice and got it. When the gun came the only mark on it was a scratch caused by inept operation of a screwdriver on the screw at the rear of the barrel assembly.

If I had ever seen a round of .35 ammo I didn't know it. Once more, the Internet produced results and I now have four rounds, for which I paid dearly. Others have written that one can fire .32 ACP ammo in the .35. That might be true, but I haven't tried it.

> ## 66 BY TODAY'S STANDARDS, A PRODUCTION OF 8,350 GUNS MIGHT NOT BE CALLED "RARE," BUT IT SURELY IS A SMALL NUMBER. THE .32S AT 957 ARE ULTRA-RARE AND .35 S&W AMMO MIGHT AS WELL BE MADE OF 'UNOBTANIUM.' 99

By today's standards, a production of 8,350 guns might not be called "rare," but it surely is a small number. The .32s at 957 are ultra-rare and .35 S&W ammo might as well be made of "unobtanium."

I've wrote about "corporate ego" and

another way to express this might be "know your customers." Smith & Wesson's history provides a great example from the 1990s when the political climate was strongly anti-gun. S&W president Ed Schultz, fearing legislation from the Clinton Administration, entered into an agreement designed to appease the political opposition and stave off legislation harmful to the company. The immediate result was a customer campaign under the banner, "S&W Must Die."

I had gotten to know Schultz pretty well and visited the factory regularly. He spoke candidly with me and was taken

Early .35 S&W ammo from Remington, Peters and Winchester.

aback by the outcry and expressed amazement at the reaction. I told him it was absolutely predictable, knowing the company's customer base. Ruger made the same mistake and got a similar response.

The fallout was swift and serious. The British owners, Thompkins PLC, had a fire sale and the company was purchased by a group headed by VP Robert L. Scott. Eventually the furor calmed down and today Smith & Wesson has a strong position in both commercial and law-enforcement markets.

The *Ammo Encyclopedia* from Blue Book Publications has ballistic data and case measurements for both cartridges. For those of us who would like to find a round of .35 S&W ammo, the best clue is the rimless case. One critic mused, "This was the only thing they got right."

Another very important reference is W.H.B. Smith's *Book of Pistols and Revolvers*. First published in 1946, it has beenwfrequently revised. Mine is the Seventh Edition from 1968. There are lengthy chapters on both the .32 and .35 that cover both operation and assembly/disassembly that are too lengthy to repeat here. While it is technically out of print, I found used copies for as little as $5 from online sources.

The author would like to offer special thanks to Roy Jinks, retired Smith & Wesson historian and longtime friend. His little book is a priceless resource

This left side view of .35 S&W pistol shows the odd little wheel safety on the backstrap.

MARKET HUNTING
PUNT GUNS

If it sounds like a dangerous proposition—firing an oversized shotgun from a fragile craft in frigid conditions at night—it was.

BY **JOE ARTERBURN**

P unt guns were oversized black-powder shotguns used by market hunters in the late 1800s and early 1900s. They were capable of downing scores of ducks with a single shot. However, to impugn them is to misunderstand the purpose, economic demands of the time and the world in which market hunters lived.

These were specialty guns, relatively rare, singular and deadly effective in purpose in the hands of skilled hunters plying their trade in a time of flocks of ducks so thick they darkened the sky.

A 1914 listing of "owners of big guns in the vicinity of Susquehanna Flats, Maryland," listed 16 owners, three of them with two big guns each, for a total of 19 guns.

A description of the guns stated, "These guns are all about the same weight—100 to 125 pounds; length, 12 feet; diameter of bore from 1½ to 2 ins [inches]."

These guns of awesome dimensions are often associated with Chesapeake Bay and the Atlantic seaboard, where many were employed in feeding the seemingly insatiable demand for wildfowl in the finest restaurants in the East.

The listing of big-gun owners is published in one of two definitive works on marketing hunting. [[The Outlaw Gunner]] by Harry M. Walsh (1971; Tidewater Publishers) focuses on the Chesapeake Bay area, home of the market-hunting heyday. The second book, [[Texas Market Hunting: Stories of Waterfowl, Game Laws and Outlaws]] by R.K. Sawyer (2013; Texas A&M University Press), covers the rise and fall of market hunting along the Texas coast.

(above) An up-close view of a typical flintlock punt gun. Early flintlock punt guns were usually converted to fire percussion caps as firearms improved. (Photo: Lori Burskey Bouchelle, Upper Bay Museum)

You can see just how huge these punt guns were and how much support they required to do their duck market-hunting job. Pulling the trigger set off a charge that could be heard far and wide, and the boat would be forced backward 40 feet or more. (Photo: Lori Burskey Bouchelle, Upper Bay Museum)

Although punt guns were more common with hunters on the Atlantic seaboard, some Texas market hunters, quick to pick up on successful tactics of the Chesapeake Bay watermen (shooting from sink boxes was another), manhandled cumbersome punt guns. As Sawyer states, the punt gun "was the most infamous, considered 'the deadliest weapon known to waterfowl bagging.'"

Walsh said that even in the heyday, around the turn of the century, there were probably fewer than 100 guns in operation around Chesapeake Bay— more than on the list because, undoubtedly, many went unreported.

MARKET-HUNTING HEYDAY

The culinary demand, along with the market hunting trade, picked up after the Civil War, thanks to post-war advances in technology—particularly advancements in rail and water transportation.

Market hunting developed, or at least was perfected, around Chesapeake Bay, located relatively close to large population centers to which rail and water routes provided ready transportation. As rails connected other parts of the country, such as the Texas coast, the market-hunting trade sprang up. Hunters filled thousands of barrels with ducks bound by train for northern cities (and, with the advent of refrigeration aboard

steamships, Europe).

To be sure, when pump and semi-automatic shotguns (many side-by-sides served as well) came onto the scene, market hunters were quick to set aside their muzzleloading fowling pieces: Rapid-firing and rapid-reloading firearms that could be held to the shoulder had obvious advantages over punt guns.

PUNT BOATS

Many punt boats were brought to the United States from England, where market hunters employed them with similar results, according to Jack Manning, curator of the Upper Bay Museum in North East, Maryland.

The name comes from the type of boat, a sneak skiff called a "punt" in England. It was a shallow-draft, flat-bottom craft designed particularly for getting the big gun in position to kill as many ducks as possible with one shot, he explained.

In his book, Walsh describes these boats. They were usually custom made by the watermen who understood the requirements.

Punts were generally one-man boats (although some two-man boats were used) from 16 to 18 feet long and with a 3½- to 4-foot beam, with boards running the length of the boat to reduce friction. Both bow and stern were sharp, Walsh said, to prevent gurgling in dead water as the hunters silently paddled toward a raft of sleeping or feeding ducks.

If it sounds like a dangerous proposition—firing an oversized shotgun from a fragile craft in frigid conditions at night—it was. "Here, one thin plank and 6 inches of freeboard were all that separated the hunter from eternity," Walsh wrote.

THE BIG GUN

Everything about punt guns is oversized—the barrel, the hammer, the trigger and the stock. Stocks, Manning said, "were pretty crude, because they were just a tool," not fine hunting pieces. Many were homemade, but some, such as the one in the Upper Bay Museum, show touches of gunsmith craftsmanship, such as a tapered, 1½-inch barrel and a "pretty well-made stock, with a dip in it; made almost like a real gunstock."

Manning pointed out that they were nicer than many of the crudely fashioned ones. And, he added, stocks often had a drilled hole through which the hunter could run a rope tied to a cork so if a

game warden showed up, he threw the gun overboard—because, if he wasn't caught with the gun, he wasn't charged. The hunter would come back later to look for the floating cork and pull up the gun.

One gunner went a step further to foil game wardens wise to this practice, Manning said. He tied on a heavy block of salt, which kept the cork submerged until the salt melted away. This allowed the cork to bob to the surface a couple

days later, when the hunter would row out and retrieve his gun.

Market hunting was legal—a respected profession of watermen who made their living on the bay, fishing and crabbing in season. These men would hunt during the waterfowling months; and many of them guided sport hunters by day and market hunt at night. Night hunting, however, was illegal. And because punt gunning required carefully approaching a large raft of ducks, it was most effec-

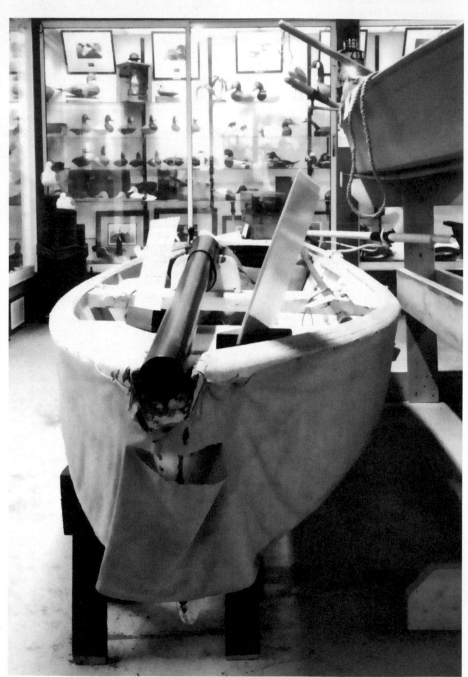

This front view of a punt boat shows a huge punt gun's barrel resting in chocks on the bow. Burlap bags filled with sea grass were positioned to absorb recoil and (hopefully) not take the stern out of the boat. (Photo: Upper Bay Museum)

Robin Hoods of the Water

Market gunners sometimes acquired a Robin Hood status, delivering ducks to needy families, as well as local markets.

In Texas Market Hunting, Sawyer reports that "Leonard Moss Fisher, the 'first flying sheriff of Texas,' fed the town (of Seadrift) from a punting rig during the Depression."

Although laws came into being that prohibited big guns, set limits and forbade the sale of wildfowl, outlaw gunners continued to operate surreptitiously, early game wardens being few and far between.

Jack Manning said when punt gunner Ralph Murphy's big gun boomed at night, residents across Chesapeake Bay knew where to walk the shores the following morning to pick up ducks carried away by the tide before Murphy could gather them.

"They'd say they got all the ducks they needed," Manning said.

tive just at last light, when the gunner would silently slip into range.

"The best time to get on them was just before a storm, because they feed really heavy and don't hear you sneaking up—because they make so much noise when they're feeding," Manning said (not that he knows from first-hand experience, although he did make a non-firing punt gun from patterns of the gun used by a local gunner).

Aiming was accomplished by shifting body weight to lower or raise the muzzle, which protruded over the bow. There was no need to finely sight the gun; just point it in the direction of the thickest part of the flock. There were tricks to get into range for what was mostly likely one shot a night.

Once rowed or push-poled to the vicinity of the resting flock, the hunter lay atop the big gun and, using short hand paddles, worked his way toward the flock, often guided by the sound of thousands of feeding and murmuring ducks. Some hunters used kerosene lamps in a reflective box on the bow, which produced a "duck-in-the-headlights" effect. White was the most effective camouflage, blending better in faded light on the water than a dark silhouette, which would stand out.

The gun muzzle protruded a few inches past the bow, the barrel resting in chocks on the bow and about mid-barrel. Burlap bags filled with sea grass were positioned to absorb recoil and "hopefully not take the stern out of the boat," Manning said. Kickerboards provided reinforcement to "keep the gun from going out through the side of the boat," he explained.

When in position, the gunner would slap the side of the boat, causing ducks to raise their heads and some to take wing. Pulling the trigger set off a charge that could be heard across the bay, and the boat would be forced backward 40 feet or more.

Manning cited an example of a punt gunner who once slid his skiff across ice, pulling it forward with ice hooks, toward an opening packed with ducks. Upon firing, the recoil of the big gun spun the boat three or four revolutions. The shot killed 80 ducks.

THE LOAD

There are accounts of punt gunners loading their guns with as much as a pound of powder and 2 pounds of shot, but Manning believes this, like many stories of past gunning exploits (such as hundreds of ducks being killed with one shot, when 40 to 60 were more likely), is an exaggeration.

"A pound of powder is way more than what you'd put in one of those guns," Manning pointed out. More likely, the load was a pound of shot propelled by a like volume of black powder. So, whatever the volume of a pound of shot—usually No. 4s—was the volume of powder; so maybe one-third of a can of powder. As big as they were, the guns could take only so much pressure, he explained.

Over the powder, the gunner rammed wadding to compact the powder and build pressure as the powder ignited. Oakum—teased-apart rope fibers—were used, Manning said. (He also heard of cork balls wrapped with oakum being rammed down on the powder charge.) Then came the shot, over which was placed a cardboard disk cut to fit tightly and hold the shot in place. Early flintlock punt guns were usually converted to fire percussion caps as firearms improved. Some didn't bother with a trigger and hammer mechanism; they were fired by striking the cap with a common hammer, Manning said.

Ducks were bringing $2 to $3 per pair—except for the highly prized canvasbacks, which would bring $8 to $9 dollars a pair. That was good money for a waterman trying to keep his family fed. (In fact, during the Depression, "The people who made money around here were the market gunners and moonshiners," Manning said.)

THE END OF MARKET HUNTING

The passage of the Migratory Bird Treaty Act of 1918 effectively put an end to market hunting. It was followed by additional conservation legislation well into the 1930s.

Bear in mind, however, that market hunters weren't the only hunters racking up large daily kills. Sport hunters were also shooting hundreds of ducks a day, many of which undoubtedly were bound for restaurants. The combination of sinkboxes and easily reloaded cartridge shotguns—both pumps, such as Winchester's Model 1897, and semi-autos, such as John Browning's Remington Model 11s—were taking an enormous toll in the hands of market gunners and sport hunters alike.

Manning said sportsmen in New York and other Eastern states first sounded the alarm of declining duck populations, and states began clamping down with limits outlawing the sale of wildfowl and other regulations, but enforcement was sparse.

However, restrictions on bore size meant the end of punt guns, many of which were confiscated and destroyed (the result was that surviving punt guns became highly sought-after collectables). Sawyer's book admirably details the fight for game laws in Texas and the push for federal legislation.

And it would take federal legislation, in the form of the MBTA, to put real teeth and resources behind the new laws. "Practically," Sawyer summarizes, "the most essential part of the MBTA was allocation of federal funds for enforcement."

Market gunners were forced into an outlaw existence that lasted for years—well through the Great Depression—but the death knell of market hunters and punt guns had sounded.

We haven't even talked about other market-gunner tools, such as swivel guns, multi-barreled battery guns and pipe guns made of ½-inch-thick boiler pipe ... but that's another story.

THE VERSATILE

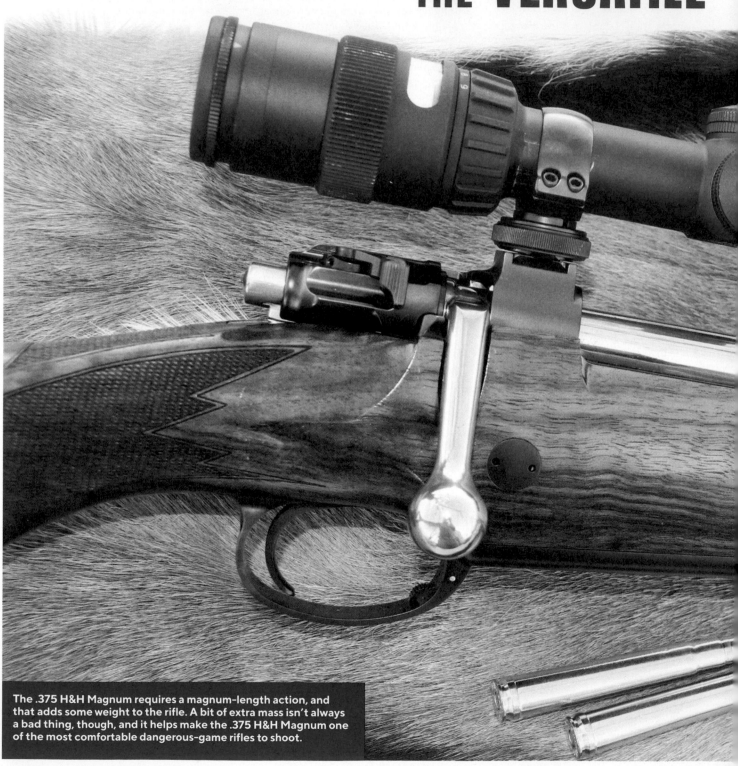

The .375 H&H Magnum requires a magnum-length action, and that adds some weight to the rifle. A bit of extra mass isn't always a bad thing, though, and it helps make the .375 H&H Magnum one of the most comfortable dangerous-game rifles to shoot.

.375 H&H MAGNUM

Now more than a century old, the .375 H&H Mag is still a favorite cartridge of big-game hunters the world over

BY **BRAD FITZPATRICK**

For the better part of an hour, my Professional Hunter Julian Moller and I had been wading through the sawgrass swamps of Mozambique's Coutada 11, guided by a circling flock of white cattle egrets. Visibility in the swamp was minimal, 40 yards or less, and the birds were our only point of reference regarding the location of the herd of Cape buffalo we were

following. Soon we drew close enough to the buffalo that we could hear them sloshing through the black water, and occasionally we would hear one of them bawl or bellow, but they still remained out of sight. Finally, I caught sight of a dark backline through the sawgrass, and then a ragged ear. And then, in a gap left by a hippo path, I saw the first shining black curve of a horn.

(above) The .375 H&H Magnum was one of the first cartridges to wear a belt. It's been chambered in single-shots and double rifles, but this is primarily a bolt-action cartridge.

(below) Four versatile .375 H&H loads (from left): Hornady 250-grain Superformance GMX, Nosler 260-grain Partition, Federal 300-grain Swift A-Frame, Norma 350-grain African PH Woodleigh Weldcore. The two loads on the left shoot flat and hit hard, making them ideal for elk, moose and African plains game. The 300- and 350-grain loads are suitable for the largest game, such as brown bear and Cape buffalo.

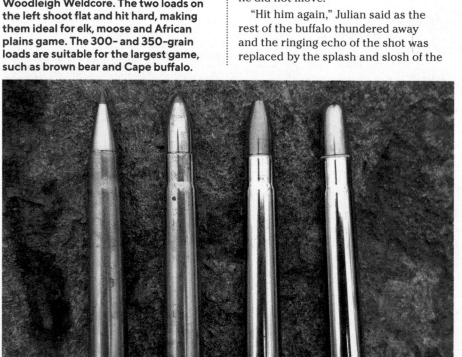

At such a time no gun feels like too much gun, but I was thankful to have a Winchester .375 H&H Magnum beside me. Hunting in the swamp meant shot opportunities would be fast and few, and I needed to know the rifle I was firing would place the bullet exactly where I wanted. There likely wouldn't be time for a follow-up shot, so it was critical the first bullet landed in the right spot and performed well.

After another hour of jockeying around the herd, Julian, the trackers and I slipped into the rear flank of the ranks of buffalo and located an old, wide bull. The buffalo was 40 yards ahead, but I was more than a little distracted by a buffalo cow who was feeding in our direction and was half that distance away.

"Behind the shoulder," Julian said and lifted his .470 double to back my shot. "He's angling away."

66 THE RIFLE CRACKED, AND I HEARD THE SOLID *THWACK* OF THE 350-GRAIN WOODLEIGH WELDCORE BULLET STRIKE. THE BULL SHRUGGED, BUT HE DID NOT MOVE. 99

The rifle cracked, and I heard the solid *thwack* of the 350-grain Weldcore bullet strike. The bull shrugged, but he did not move.

"Hit him again," Julian said as the rest of the buffalo thundered away and the ringing echo of the shot was replaced by the splash and slosh of the

From left: .30-06 Springfield, .375 Ruger, .375 H&H Magnum. The .375 Ruger fits in a shorter action and bests the H&H in ballistics, but the .375 H&H Magnum remains more popular and ammunition is more widely available.

retreating herd. I put a second shot in the bull, which had moved a few yards, and although he was beginning to topple Julian ordered me to work the bolt and fire once more. The bull went down.

It was a hunt dreams are made of, and the .375 H&H Magnum was perfectly suited for my adventure in the swamps of Mozambique's Zambezi Delta. In fact, the .375 H&H Magnum has been synonymous with far-flung lands and wild adventures since its inception in 1912, when it was known as the .375 Belted Rimless Nitro-Express. The cartridge was a favorite of many of the great African hunters including John "Pondoro" Taylor, Harry Manners and Wally Johnson. Manners, who earned a living shooting elephants for ivory in the early and mid-20th century, trusted nothing but the .375 H&H Magnum and owned four off-the-shelf Winchester Model 70s chambered for the cartridge during his career. Despite more than 100 years of cartridge development since the .375 H&H Magnum first came to pass, it still remains a favorite of African PHs, including Julian (whose .375 I used to shoot my buffalo) and several others with whom I've spoken.

But the .375 H&H Magnum isn't just an African gun. It's popular among Western big-game hunters for elk, and it's earned a loyal following in the Great North. The

legendary writer Jack O'Connor carried a .375 H&H in India while hunting tigers. Indeed, the .375 H&H Magnum has proved itself in every corner of the world among some of the most hard-to-please critics, hunters who rely on their rifles to protect them from dangerous game. But what makes the .375 H&H Magnum so great?

DYNAMIC DESIGN

The .375 H&H Magnum was of the first belted magnum cartridges and was originally designed for use with Cordite powder. Long of body and with minimal shoulder taper, the .375 H&H Mag case was perfectly suited for those older powders, but that gently sloping case design had another advantage that made the H&H a favorite of dangerous game hunters: It fed smoothly and reliably. Compared to more modern, sharp-shouldered case designs, the old .375 slides smoothly from the magazine to the chamber. As you might expect, this means there are very few misfeeds, which automatically earns any dangerous-game cartridge a gold star. The .375 H&H does require a magnum-length action, but a little extra rifle weight isn't always a bad thing when firing dangerous-game loads.

With 300-grain loads at a muzzle velocity more than 2,500 fps, the .375 H&H Magnum generates around 4,300

ft-lbs of energy, plenty of punch for even the largest game at moderate ranges. In addition, 300-grain, .375-caliber bullets have a sectional density of .305, which means the H&H Mag penetrates better than other magnum hunting cartridges. Modest velocities keep muzzle blast relatively light and recoil quite manageable, especially considering this cartridge was used extensively as an elephant-hunting round. A 9-pound, .375 H&H Magnum rifle generates between 40 and 50 ft-lbs of recoil, which is substantially less than the larger .416s and .458s, which range from 60 to 100 ft-lbs, depending upon gun weight and load. Most experienced shooters in good physical condition can easily handle the setback of the .375.

The H&H's modest velocities also mean you don't have to be as careful with bullet selection on non-dangerous game. I've hunted zebra, kudu and hartebeest in Africa with a .375 H&H Magnum and found that most cup-and-core soft-point bullets will expand reliably without the risk of bullet blowup. The H&H is also, at least by big-bore standards, a flat-shooting round. A 300-grain bullet at 2,530 fps sighted in 3-inches high at 100 yards will be dead-on at 200 yards and will drop about a foot at 300 yards. If you opt for a lighter bullet at a higher velocity you can improve upon those numbers. Hornady's 250-grain GMX Superformance .375 H&H Magnum load, for

This beautiful .375 H&H Magnum from Montana Rifle Company comes with the company's Model 1999 controlled-feed action and a walnut stock with ebony fore-end. It's a reasonably priced, and stunning, dangerous-game rifle.

(below) Who says the H&H is just a dangerous-game cartridge? The author took this large hog in California with a Weatherby Vanguard in .375 H&H Magnum and the cartridge worked perfectly.

Weatherby's Mark V Dangerous Game Rifle in .375 H&H Magnum looks good, but it's also very accurate for a big bore. With its excellent laminated stock there's no risk of stock warpage or cracking, either.

example, has a muzzle velocity of 2,890 fps and, when sighted in at 200 yards, drops just 7.4 inches at 300 yards. That's a trajectory that mimics a .30-06 while carrying about twice the energy.

In recent years the .375 H&H Magnum's position atop the heavy-medium calibers has been challenged by another, newer cartridge, the .375 Ruger. Unlike the .375 H&H Magnum, the .375 Ruger lacks a belt and, perhaps most importantly, it fits into a standard (.30-06-length) action while the .375 H&H Magnum does not. Ballistics are similar and both cartridges perform, essentially, the same role, though the Ruger does shoot flatter. But the .375 H&H Magnum has that smooth-feeding case and there are lots of rifles chambered for it. Additionally, the .375 H&H Magnum's long history and continued popularity mean that, even in the most remote corners of the globe, there's a good chance you'll be able to find a box of H&H Magnum ammo should the need arise.

BULLS AND BEARS

Even if your hunts never take you outside the United States, the .375 H&H Magnum will serve you well as a big-game cartridge. Many elk hunters swear by the cartridge, saying the .375 combines a flat enough trajectory for cross-canyon shooting, yet delivers bone-crushing impact even at extended distances. I used a Weatherby Vanguard in .375 H&H for a California hog hunt and

66 EVEN IF YOUR HUNTS NEVER TAKE YOU OUTSIDE THE UNITED STATES, THE .375 H&H MAGNUM WILL SERVE YOU WELL AS A BIG-GAME CARTRIDGE. MANY ELK HUNTERS SWEAR BY THE CARTRIDGE, SAYING THE .375 COMBINES A FLAT ENOUGH TRAJECTORY FOR CROSS-CANYON SHOOTING, YET DELIVERS BONE-CRUSHING IMPACT EVEN AT EXTENDED DISTANCES. 99

took a mature boar at 160 yards. The 300-grain bullet struck on the point of the shoulder and the pig dropped where it stood. The .375's modest velocities translate to quick kills with minimal risk of bullet blowup, so it's possible your .375 H&H Magnum, when shooting proper bullets, will actually damage less meat than lighter, faster bullets.

The .375 H&H Magnum is, of course, most suited for our largest and toughest northern game. The H&H Magnum is an ideal moose cartridge, especially when you're hunting in bear country and you need a rifle that can double as a charge

The author with a community buffalo harvested in the swamps of Mozambique. The .375 H&H Magnum is ideal for large, heavy, dangerous game like this. Also pictured is PH Julian Moller

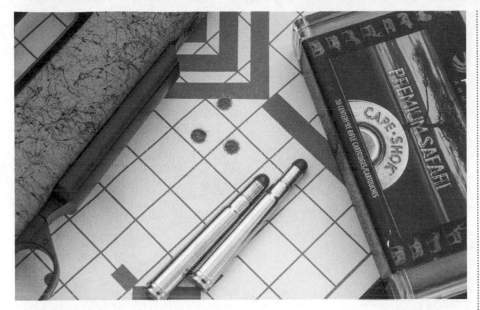

If you think big bores don't shoot well, think again. This Weatherby Mark V DGR in .375 H&H Magnum regularly prints 1-inch groups at 100 yards with both Woodleigh Hydro Solids (shown here) and Woodleigh Weldcore softs.

stopper. And, the .375 H&H Magnum is a natural choice for anyone who is planning on hunting big bears. It even has a place as a black-bear round. You don't need .375 punch on *Ursus americanus*, but the .375 H&H makes a larger hole than smaller-caliber guns and that translates to a better blood trail and a shorter follow-up. Place a well-constructed .375 H&H magnum bullet in a black bear's boiler room and you'll have no tracking job at all.

RIFLES AND LOADS

The .375 H&H Magnum is traditionally chambered in bolt guns. It's sometimes seen in double rifles, but cartridges with larger rims are more commonly used in side-by sides, and the cartridge was originally designed with turnbolt rifles in mind. However, there are a number of really good .375 bolt guns available today. The Winchester Model 70 helped cement the .375 H&H's reputation and you can still purchase a new controlled-round-feed Model 70 Safari Express for about $1,500. Winchester also offers the Model 70 Alaskan in .375 H&H Magnum, and Browning offers two different X-Bolt rifles, with iron sights, chambered for the round. Weatherby offers the newly updated Mark V in .375 H&H Magnum, and the company also offers several accurate Vanguard models in .375 with prices starting at less than $1,000. CZ's superb 550, based on the old BRNO 602

that was extremely popular with African hunters, is an affordable .375 option that's ultra-reliable and surprisingly affordable. Kimber offers both the walnut-stocked Caprivi and stainless/synthetic Talkeetna rifles in .375, and Montana Rifle Company chambers both the American Vantage and Extreme Vantage rifles for this round.

If you aren't limited by budgetary constraints, there are also some truly outstanding top-end .375s available today from some of the most respected gun makers in the world. Rigby is once again offering bolt guns for sale, and Mauser sells its exquisite M98 Magnum, both of which are drool-worthy guns that cost five figures, yet are built to the highest standards and are truly works of art in blued steel and walnut. You can also have a custom .375 H&H built by companies such as Hill Country Rifles and Rifles, Inc., both of which produce very accurate and refined guns.

Over the years, ammo manufacturers have offered .375 loads with bullet weights ranging from 235 to 350 grains. Most common are the 300-grain loads, and there are a number of great options including Swift's A-Frame load, Nosler's Partition, Hornady's DGX Bonded, Federal's Trophy Bonded Bear Claw. Norma offers a 350-grain Woodleigh Weldcore load in its African PH line, and that's the load I used to take my buffalo. If you're looking for lighter, flatter-shooting loads, Hornady's Superformance GMX and Outfitter loads come with 250-grain GMX bullets, and Nosler offers ammo with its Partition and Accubond bullets in 260 grains for the .375.

TAMING THE BEAST

The .375 H&H Magnum is a superb choice for hunting big game, yet it remains affordable and manageable to shoot. Having a .375 H&H makes sense if you already own a medium-caliber hunting rifle, such as a .30-06, .270, or 7mm Remington Magnum, since the .375's power curve complements these lighter guns well. But even if you never reach Africa or the Great North and you simply take your .375 to the range from time to time, this is still a cartridge that you can enjoy shooting. For more than a century it's been a favorite of big-game hunters the world over, and it doesn't seem the .375's glory will be fading any time soon.

The Mauser M98 in .375 H&H Magnum comes with a CRF Mauser 98 action, grade 5 wood, a drop magazine that holds five rounds and, perhaps, the best iron sights of any big bore. Though this rifle isn't cheap, it's beautiful, accurate and extremely reliable.

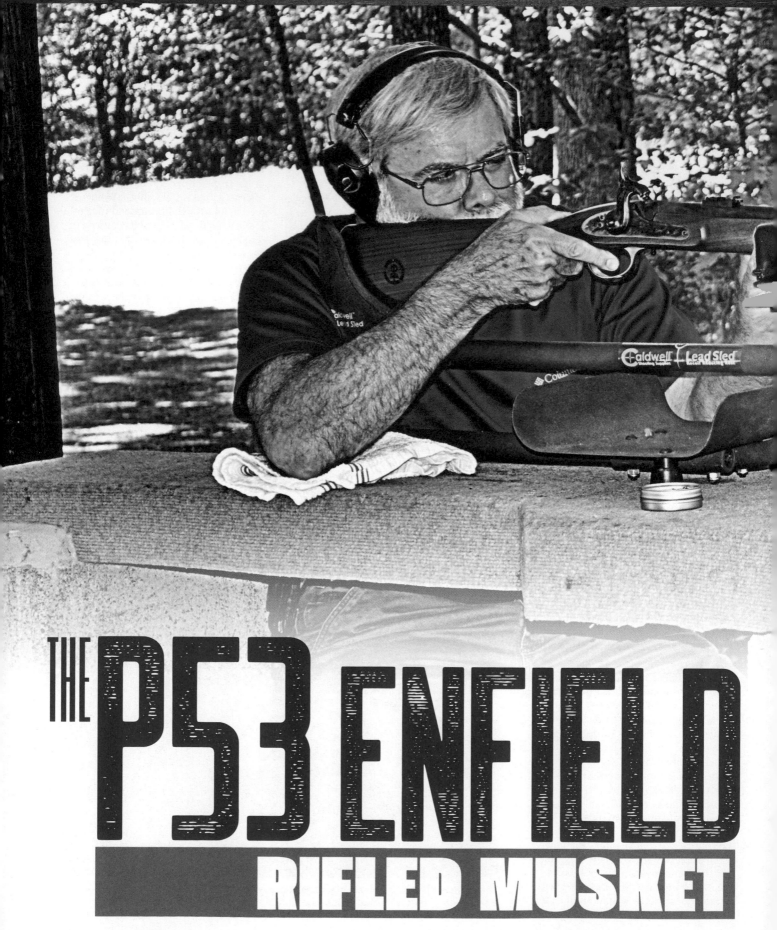

THE P53 ENFIELD
RIFLED MUSKET

The P53 Rifled Musket was developed in the 1850s at the Royal Small Arms Factory (RSAF) in the London Borough of Enfield. (Courtesy James D. Julia Inc., a division of Morphy Auctions)

Some say it was the military muzzleloader perfected

BY **PAUL SCARLATA**

Cpl. Horry Colleton sat his horse as still as he could, and did not let any of the emotions raging inside him show on his face. He calmly waited his turn to dismount and add his Enfield musketoon and two Colt Navy revolvers to the growing pile of weapons in front of the platoon of Yankee soldiers. While it galled him that this was the end result of four years of whipping these Bluebellies, he felt no disgrace because the 6th Virginia Cavalry had shown these Yanks what real cavalrymen were like.

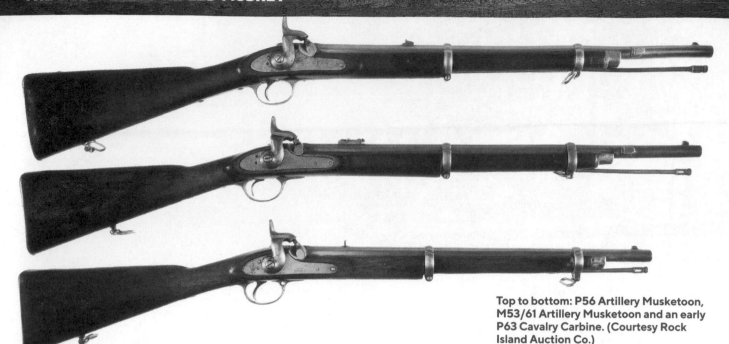

Top to bottom: P56 Artillery Musketoon, M53/61 Artillery Musketoon and an early P63 Cavalry Carbine. (Courtesy Rock Island Auction Co.)

Trooper for trooper, they'd never been outfought. It was only the North's unlimited number of men and supplies that had finally forced Gen. Robert E. Lee to ask for terms. He guessed they should consider themselves lucky in that they were going to be allowed to at least keep their horses. Colleton almost laughed out loud when he saw the scowling Union captain grudgingly return Lt. Drayton's revolver. It had belonged to the lieutenant's older brother, who had been killed outside Petersburg the past winter, and it meant a lot to the 18-year-old officer. As they formed columns one last time and rode off, Colleton thought to himself, "One thing's for sure. They know they've been in a fight!"

> **❝THE AMERICAN CIVIL WAR IS GENERALLY ACKNOWLEDGED AS THE FIRST "MODERN WAR." WHILE AT THE START OF HOSTILITIES, MOST MILITARY COMMANDERS, BOTH NORTH AND SOUTH, STILL ADHERED TO WHAT WERE BASICALLY 18TH-CENTURY TACTICS, NEW WEAPONS QUICKLY CHANGED THE FACE OF WARFARE.❞**

The American Civil War is generally acknowledged as the first "modern war."

While at the start of hostilities, most military commanders, both North and South, still adhered to what were basically 18th-century tactics, new weapons quickly changed the face of warfare. As far as the average infantryman was concerned, the most revolutionary of these arms was the rifled musket.

While the rifled musket aped the appearance of its smooth-bore predecessors, the rifled barrel provided far superior accuracy. No longer did the foot slogger carry a weapon that could not be counted upon to hit a man-sized target past 50 yards; the new rifled muskets were

Shown in 19th-century Afghanistan, Afridi warriors armed with a mixture of Jezails and, what appear to be, P58 Short Muskets.

accurate out to 300 yards and beyond.

Up until this time, the rifle had been the weapon of small units of specialists who used its long-range accuracy to harass artillery crews, pick off the enemy officers, and act as skirmishers and scouts. But while the rifled musket gave the average solider previously unheard range and accuracy, it still retained the old smooth bore weapon's greatest attribute; it could be reloaded rapidly. This was because the rifled musket fired a new projectile, commonly known as the Minie ball after the French officer Capt. Claude Minié, who invented it.

The so-called Minie ball was a cylindro-conoidal lead projectile that had a hollow base fitted with a metal plug. It was undersized to the bore's diameter, so it could be loaded down the rifle barrel easily, but the force of the exploding gunpowder would drive the plug into the bullet's hollow base causing it to expand and engage the rifling. So while the new rifled musket could be loaded as fast as the old smooth bore, it had three or four times the effective range of its predecessor.

In addition, percussion-cap ignition made the weapon even faster to reload and more reliable, especially in windy or wet weather. While breech-loading, metallic-cartridge and repeating long arms were to make their appearance during the Civil War, the muzzleloading rifled musket was to remain the basic weapon of the vast majority of infantrymen, and the weapon that inflicted the horrendous casualties suffered by both sides.

At the outbreak of the war, the standard arms of the U.S. Army were the Model 1855 and 1858 Rifled Muskets, but the rapid expansion of the Army quickly outstripped the ability of Springfield Arsenal to supply sufficient arms. Southern forces captured the other national arsenal at Harper's Ferry and moved its equipment to Virginia Manufactory of Arms in Richmond, where it was used to produce weapons for Confederate forces.

While some of the newly raised Confederate units had Model 1855 rifles, most were equipped with a miscellany of older models, including smoothbore and even some flintlock muskets. Shortly after the war began, the Union adopted the Model 1861 Rifled Musket, which was produced at Springfield Arsenal and also by a number of commercial subcontractors.

Union and Confederate agents were dispatched to Europe to procure arms

The makings of ammo for the Dixie replica P53 Enfield field-tested by the author. The target was shot at 75 yards from a rest, plenty accurate for close-range battle.

where they desperately bought up just about anything that would produce clouds of white smoke while launching projectiles in the enemy's direction. The shoulder weapon that was to become the second most widely used by the North and the most popular with Southern troopers was soon on its way from Europe in the holds of numerous ships and blockade runners.

The .577-caliber Enfield Pattern 53 Rifled Musket (P53) was developed at Royal Small Arms Factory at Enfield (RSAF) in the early 1850s by William Pritchett to replace the .75-caliber Pattern 1842 smoothbore Musket and the .702-caliber Pattern 1851 Rifled Musket. The rifle's cartridges contained 70 grains of blackpowder and a 530-grain modified Minie ball, known as the Pritchett or Burton-Minié bullet, which was driven to about 850 to 900 fps.

The original Pritchett-designed projectile was modified by Col. Edward M. Boxer of the Royal Artillery, who reduced the diameter of the projectile

Comparing a P53 Enfield (top) to a U.S. Model 1861 (bottom) rifled musket. (Courtesy Garry James, photography by Jill Marlow)

to 0.55 of an inch after troops found the original 0.568-inch projectile difficult to load. He changed the projectile's mixed beeswax/tallow lubrication to pure beeswax for the same reason, and added a clay plug to the base to facilitate expansion. The original Pritchett design, which did away with the metal cup in the base of the projectile and relied upon the explosion of the powder charge to expand the skirt of the bullet, was found to cause excessive fouling as its slow expansion allowed unburnt powder to escape around the bullet.

The resulting weapon is considered by many to be the finest example of the rifled-musket genre and, while in British service only a little more than 13 years, it was to become one of the most influential muzzleloading military rifles ever developed. The P53 first saw service in the Crimean War (1853 to 1856), the Great Indian Mutiny (1857) and the New Zealand Land Wars (1845 to 1872). It was also used by the Spanish and Portuguese armies, in addition to being sold to several Latin American, African and Asian nations.

The P53 was first issued to Sepoys (native soldiers) in India in 1856. When Hindu soldiers discovered the cartridges lubricant included beef tallow, which was offensive and forbidden to them, they refused to use them. Rumors also spread that the waterproofing included lard, which was forbidden to Muslim troops.

While the British instituted production of ungreased cartridges to placate the Sepoys, it proved too late. This incident was one of the many causes of the Great Indian Mutiny of 1857.

There were five basic models: the Three Band Pattern 53 musket, with a 39-inch barrel; the Two Band Pattern 58 short musket, with a 33-inch barrel; the Pattern 53 and Pattern 53/61 Artillery Musketoon, both with 24-inch barrels; and the Pattern 56 Cavalry Carbine, with a 21-inch barrel. Late production cavalry carbines were stocked almost to the muzzle and had a swivel retained ramrod.

The various P53 and P58 muskets used a socket-style bayonet with a 21.75-inch triangular blade. The P53/61 Musketoon were also issued with the Pattern 56 saber-style bayonet with a fearsome 23.5-inch curved blade.

The Enfield became the most common, and popular, rifle carried by Southern troops. No less an authority than "Marse Robert" (Gen. Robert E. Lee) is quoted as saying a Confederate soldier could consider himself properly equipped if he had "...an Enfield rifle, 60 cartridges and a bayonet."

In the Union Army, the P53/58 was second only to the Springfield Model 1861 rifled musket in total numbers issued. To meet this demand, besides Enfield arsenal, they were produced under contract by a half dozen British gun makers and by firms in Belgium, Spain and the United States.

The Enfield's cartridge was a paper tube into which a lubricated 530-grain, .577 caliber Minie ball was inserted with the nose of the projectile facing into the tube. A second paper tube containing a charge of approximately 70 grains of black powder was placed inside the first and above the bullet, and the ends twisted and sealed.

To load the Enfield, the soldier first placed the hammer at half cock, then removed a cartridge from his pouch and tore off the twisted end with his teeth (which is why one physical requirement for enlistment was that the recruit have "several" opposing teeth on his upper and lower jaws) and poured the powder charge down the barrel. Then the Minie ball, still encased in the cartridge paper was placed in the muzzle and rammed down with the ram rod, the paper serving as a wad to keep the undersized Minie ball in place. The shooter placed a percussion cap on the rifle's nipple, pulled the hammer back to full cock, aimed the rifle and pulled the trigger. The fearsome wounds inflicted by the soft lead Minie ball accounted for the high number of amputations performed on wounded soldiers during the war.

The Enfield's .577-caliber bore size allowed the use of standard U.S. issue .58-caliber Minie balls (and vice versa), simplifying supply for the Union, and allowing Southern troops to utilize

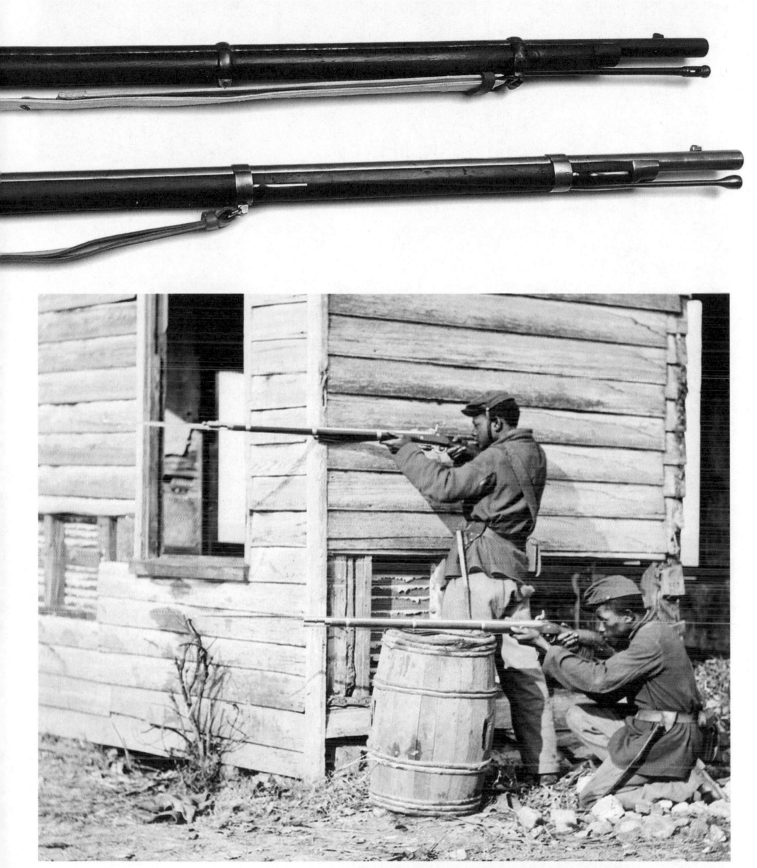

In this 1865 photo, two members of the 10th USCI (U.S. Colored Infantry) fire on Confederates with P53 Enfield rifled muskets.

Well-experienced with blackpowder guns, the author's shooting buddy Butch Simpson was happy to lend a hand with the shooting tests.

captured ammunition. The Pattern 53/61 Musketoon (P53/61) was a favorite weapon of the Southern cavalrymen as it gave them a light, handy weapon with range and accuracy similar to the standard rifle. In an infantry-type engagement, they were at little, or no, disadvantage to opposing troops, while, if fighting on foot against Union cavalry, which at the beginning of the war were armed only with saber and revolver, they had a distinct advantage in range and firepower.

The P53/61 became the preferred shoulder weapon of the fast-moving, hard-fighting Confederate cavalry and partisan units led by such famous officers as Gen. Nathan Bedford Forrest, Gen. J.E.B. Stuart, and Col. John Singleton Mosby. An Oct. 7, 1862 requisition written by Stuart reads in part: "Application from General Stuart,

commanding cavalry, to exchange rifles, for the Enfield carbines (artillery) in the hands of our infantry."[1]

These units often fought as mounted infantry and the P53/61 provided them with long-range accuracy similar to the infantry's rifle muskets and superior to that of Union cavalry. It wasn't until Union Cavalry troopers began receiving large numbers of breech-loading and repeating carbines that they were able to best the Southern horsemen.

Blockade runners continued to bring Enfields into Southern ports until January 1865 and they remained Johnny Reb's primary weapon until the end of the war. They were also the second mostly widely used rifled musket in the Yankee arsenal and were the rifles issued to the first official African-American unit of the Union army, the 54th Mas-

sachusetts.[2]

> **AFTER THE CIVIL WAR, U.S. INFANTRY GARRISONING WESTERN FORTS CONTINUED TO BE ISSUED RIFLED MUSKETS, INCLUDING THE P53, UNTIL THEY WERE REARMED WITH METALLIC CARTRIDGE TRAPDOOR SPRINGFIELD RIFLES IN THE LATE 1860s.**

After the Civil War, U.S. infantry garrisoning Western forts continued to be issued rifled muskets, including the P53, until they were rearmed with metallic cartridge Trapdoor Springfield rifles in the late 1860s.

The P53 continued to see service

---

[1] www.civilwartalk.com/threads/p-1853-artillery-carbine.127205/
[2] Reportedly the U.S. purchased over 500,000 shoulder arms from England while the Confederacy obtained between 300,000-400,000. The majority were P53 rifle muskets with lesser numbers of musketoons and carbines.

around the world during and after our fraternal bloodletting, including the Boshin War (Japan, 1868-1869), War of the Triple Alliance (South America, 1864-1870), the Fenian raids (U.S./Canada, 1866-1871), Red River Rebellion (Canada, 1869), the Second Schleswig War (Denmark 1864) and the War of the Pacific (South America, 1879-1883).

Preparing to do a test fire, I placed a call to Dixie Gun Works. Dixie imports a series of reproduction weapons of the 18th and 19th century that are produced in Italy by Pedersoli to specifications as close to the originals as is possible. Although with modern materials and production methods, they are structurally superior to the originals. Dixie kindly shipped me one of its Enfield Pattern 53/61 Musketoons and a supply of .58 caliber Minie balls. Hodgdon Powder Company chipped in with a quantity of Triple Se7en blackpowder substitute propellant, while CCI sent along a supply of Four Wing Musket percussion caps.

Being I've had little experience with blackpowder weapons and found all these materials and preparations just a bit overwhelming, I called my good friend Butch Simpson. Butch, a "charcoal burner" of long standing, agreed, with only a faint air of condensation to come to my assistance.

My wife (and photographer) Becky and I met Butch at our gun club on a humid May morning. While seeing all the paraphernalia that was required proved a bit daunting, a quick tutorial from Butch on the intricacies of muzzleloading firearms caused my doubts to disappear. Walking down the range I placed a target on the 50-yard backstop and a pair at 75 yards. In order to reduce the negative effects of recoil, I decided to fire the musketoon from a Caldwell Lead Sled.

We loaded the musketoon with 50 grains of Triple Se7en and rammed a lubricated Minie ball down on top of it. Placing a percussion cap on the nipple, I took a six o'clock hold on the 50-yard target and carefully pulled the trigger. This produced a loud boom; the musketoon pushed back against my shoulder and I was wreathed in clouds of white smoke. Peering through the spotting scope, Butch told me I was shooting about a foot high and he suggested we increase the powder charge to 60 grains. The next shot impacted dead center in the bullseye.

I then switched to the 75-yard targets and fired five rounds at each. We were pleased to see they all impacted in the center of the targets producing groups in the 6-inch range, which Butch assured me was more than acceptable accuracy from such a weapon. Then,

A New Zealand militiaman with a P53 Enfield rifled musket. (Courtesy Peter Maxwell)

SPECIFICATIONS

P53 Enfield Rifled Musket

Caliber	.577
Overall length	55 in.
Barrel length	39 in.
Weight (unloaded)	9 lbs.
Magazine	single shot
Sights front:	inverted V blade
rear:	V notch adj. by tangent from 100 to 900 yards
Stock	walnut
Bayonet	socket style with 21.75 in. triangular blade

P58 Enfield Rifled Short Musket

Caliber	.577
Overall length	49 in.
Barrel length	33 in.
Weight (unloaded)	8.5 lbs.
Magazine	single shot
Sights front:	inverted V blade
rear:	V notch adj. by tangent from 100 to 900 yards
Stock	walnut
Bayonet	saber bayonet with 23.5 in. blade

P53/61 Enfield Musketoon

Caliber	.577
Overall length	40.25 in.
Barrel length	24 in.
Weight (unloaded)	7.5 lbs.
Magazine	single shot
Sights front:	inverted V blade
rear:	V notch adj. by tangent from 100 to 600 yards
Stock	walnut
Bayonet	saber bayonet with 23.5 in. blade

P63 Enfield Cavalry Carbine

Caliber	.577
Overall length	37 in.
Barrel length	21 in.
Weight (unloaded)	6.7 lbs.
Magazine	single shot
Sights front:	inverted V blade
rear:	V notch set for 100 yards, fold up leafs for 200 & 300 yards
Stock	walnut
Bayonet	none

Butch instructed me to fire five rounds offhand at the 75-yard target. While the Enfield's tiny sights were a bit of trial for my 60-something-year-old eyes, when the smoke cleared, I was pleased to see five shots in four holes. While I enjoyed shooting the musketoon, after arriving home the onerous task of cleaning it reminded me why I had avoided test-firing blackpowder firearms for two decades!

The Enfield P53 series of weapons served with distinction around the world for more than two decades and is considered by many the nadir of development of the rifled

POINTER

The Phenoma autoloader was right at home in the pheasant fields, and had plenty of reach to bring down eager birds that launched early.

THE POINTER PHENOMA CAN SHOOT!

A Turkish-made autoloader powders some clays BY COREY GRAFF

We marched like ants into the green jungle that marked the beginning of the wooded sporting clays course. Mosquitoes the size of small hummingbirds plowed bloody beaks into exposed skin. "Pull!" The autoloader cycled once, then twice, as the sporting clays machine launched bright clay into the wild blue yonder. Orange discs sailed off into the far brush like frisbees. What a glide ratio! As far as missing goes, it was spectacular. We were shooting the Blue Course, which is supposed to be like the bunny slope. Regardless, things did get better as I warmed up and got a feel for the shotgun —

a 12-gauge autoloader from Pointer called the Phenoma, made by Armsan of Turkey and imported by Legacy Sports International. When it was all said and done, the Phenoma would bring down clays and birds like nothing I'd ever shot.

The Pointer Phenoma is not unlike other gas-operated semi-automatic shotguns. When you yank the trigger, a shell pukes its load and a bunch of gas down the tube, some of which is detoured into two gas ports situated midway down the barrel. That gaseous excrement bores down through the gas cylinder and shoves the gas piston — jacking the spring-loaded action arm and bolt rearward, ejecting the shell. The spring that rides the magazine tube returns the bolt to battery, but not before it plucks another shell and drives it home.

It's a typical gas system. But two things made eyebrows shoot skyward: First, reliability was perfect, no hiccups or jams, and that was right from the box with no cleaning. It ran as smooth as any well-broken-in shotgun ever ran. And second: cleaning was a breeze. Most of the time when I crack an autoloader open for cleaning I find it's dirtier than an anti-gun politician, but the Phenoma ran clean as a whistle.

The Phenoma is available in 12- and 20-gauge configurations and is chambered to handle the big 3-inch shells if you must take a turkey's head clean off (see sidebar) or need to down some high-flying mallards. Barrels are chrome-moly lined and proofed for steel shot and come in lengths that span the gamut from 22 to 28 inches. The youth 20-gauge model carries either a 22- or 28-inch barrel. In addition to a hard case, there is a nifty little choke kit included with F* (full), IM** (improved modified), M*** (modified), IC**** (improved cylinder)

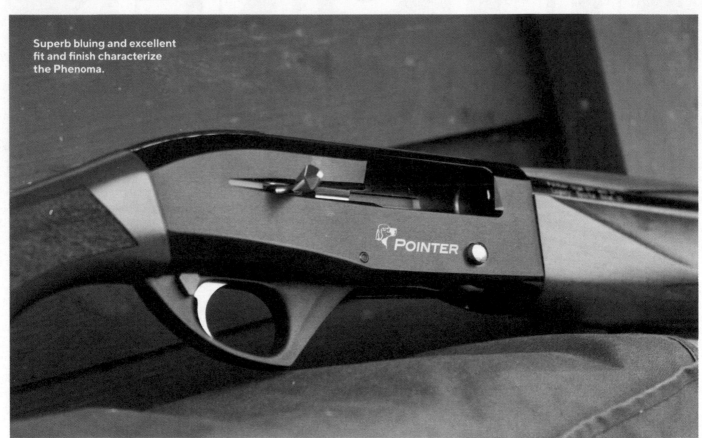

Superb bluing and excellent fit and finish characterize the Phenoma.

The Phenoma is available in a variety of styles, including laminate and camo stocks.

and SKEET***** (skeet!). For the record, the choke I began missing with was the modified one, which proved a little tight for my skill level and the short ranges involved (which could explain the misses, or maybe it was just simple incompetence). A shim kit is also included with the shotgun, but the 14-inch length of pull was perfect for me, so I didn't monkey with it.

One note about shotshell specs: Pointer recommends 2 3/4-inch 1 oz. and 3-inch 1 7/8 oz. shells and includes two gas pistons. The stainless steel piston

that comes installed on the gun is for 1 to 1 1/2 oz. loads, while the red-colored one marked "HEAVY DUTY" is for 1 1/2 oz. loads and heavier. One ingenious thing Pointer has done is to place the extra gas piston inside the forearm. It sits snugly just under the magazine cap, so it's always there if you need it. The Phenoma's payload is 5+1 standard 2 3/4-inch shells or 4+1 of the big 3-inchers. The camo versions of the Phenoma are chambered for 3.5-inch shells, for those who just have to do things the hard way. There is a 24-inch slug barrel available,

with an attached cantilever-style Weaver rail for attachment of optics. The rifled 12-gauge slugger has a 1:33-inch twist, but one was not included with the test gun. There is also a 3/8-inch dovetail machined into the top of the receiver, so adding optics is easy if that's your cup of tea.

The Phenoma has a magazine cut-off system. Clearly a nod to the Phenoma's general use design as a waterfowl and field gun, the cut-off switch is located on the lower-left side of the receiver. Activating it keeps the shells in the magazine

The author tested the blued walnut model, and found the quality of manufacture to be very high.

A look at the Phenoma's magazine tube after a full day of shooting. Autoloading shotguns don't typically run this clean.

Disassembly and cleaning of the Pointer Phenoma was straight forward. The shotgun never failed to feed or run, even after a full day of busting clays.

the Phenoma. Aesthetically speaking, it sports Italian-looking lines, without the Italian price tag. It carries a swept-back triggerguard, an angled walnut forearm that transitions from a deep belly to a sleek, narrow section that wraps about the hexagonal-machined magazine cap, an art deco-looking barrel rib and a buttstock with a cut-chiseled appearance that looks to have been inspired by some futuristic German concept car you might see zipping around on the Autobahn.

The Phenoma is a looker for sure — and that bluing! Receiver, magazine cap and barrel reveal a blued finish that is truly heads and shoulders above so many shotguns in this price range. It's a superb finish that carries into the receiver's inside surfaces — making cleaning the action's interior when the bolt and trigger groups are removed a sweet dream. I also suspect that the smooth finish on the interior grooves of the receiver contribute to the shotgun's silky cycling, noticeable each time you send a load down range. The Phenoma is also available in laminated, straight black and green synthetic, and camo finishes including Realtree Max-5, Bottomland and Obsession.

On the right side of the barrel just in front of the receiver is engraved, "Pointer 12ga 2 3/4 and 3" Legacy Sports Reno NV." Opposite that (inspiring) inscription is, "Made in Turkey by Armsan." On the right side of receiver is the Pointer brand name and logo — yep, you guessed it, a pointer dog's head — etched in white. It's simple, but looks clean. The brand "Pointer" is also engraved into the buttstock just behind the grip.

Functionally, the bolt release button didn't require big Russian farmer hands to operate (which I appreciated) and the bolt handle and bolt were smooth, slamming home with authority when a shell was dropped into the action and the bolt release depressed. The only issue I encountered was, frankly, on me. If I failed to push shells far enough to catch the shell stop while loading the bottom tube mag, they'd slip back under the elevator. This never caused any jams, though, as I always noticed it and cleared before shooting.

WHAT'S NOT TO LIKE?

I didn't throw any parties about the Phenoma's plastic triggerguard, which seems out of place given the quality of the finish and bluing on the rest of the gun. In addition, I found the manual safety, which is also a plastic part, to

tube from cycling into the action after the shot. With such a contraption you can keep your standard payload at bay while you slip a special application shell into play quickly if the need arises. Say, for example, a heavy load to sort things out with a cranky, incoming goose, while you're out on a morning duck mission. The feature is a neat one that hearkens back to the good ol' days of waterfowling when cut-offs were more commonly found on shotguns. It's a swell detail and added value for the shotgunner.

> **ONE THING ABOUT WHICH THERE CAN BE NO QUESTION IS THE EXCELLENT FIT AND FINISH OF THE PHENOMA. AESTHETICALLY SPEAKING, IT SPORTS ITALIAN-LOOKING LINES, WITHOUT THE ITALIAN PRICE TAG.**

FIT AND FINISH

One thing about which there can be no question is the excellent fit and finish of

> **YOU REALLY HAVE EARNED YOUR CURMUDGEON CARD WHEN YOU START BELLY ACHING ABOUT FIBER-OPTIC SIGHTS ON FIREARMS. MAYBE IT'S JUST ME, BUT I LIKE A GOLD OR WHITE BEAD MADE OF STEEL AND SCREWED INTO PLACE.**

be quite stiff. I get that it should require intentional manipulation; it just seemed "sticky" at the firing line. Whether that was due to binding of plastic on plastic, or its large, triangle-shaped design, I can't say.

You really have earned your curmudgeon card when you start belly aching about fiber-optic sights on firearms. Maybe it's just me, but I like a gold or white bead made of steel and screwed into place. However, if you have vision issues, you'll appreciate this feature. I must admit that the little bugger really pops out there, illuminating like a Christmas tree light against all different types of sky — from whitish-gray overcast to bluebird days. Then again, with an MSRP

SPECS	
Model	Pointer Phenoma
Gauge:	12 ga., 3 in.
Barrel:	28 in.
Length of Pull:	14 in.
Length:	48.5 in.
Weight:	7.2 lbs.
Color:	Walnut/Blued
MSRP:	$751

www.legacysports.com

The author's only gripes about the Phenoma were a sticky safety switch, plastic triggerguard and fiber-optic front sight. With a street price of around $500, these nit-picks were easily overlooked.

Kent Elite Target Shotshells

Tested in the Pointer Phenoma autoloader, Kent's Elite Target 12-gauge load of 1 oz. of #7.5 shot at 1,200 fps inspired confidence on the sporting clays range.

For sporting clays, the shotshells tested in the Phenoma were Kent Cartridge's new Elite Target loads. Available in 12 and 20 gauge, from 7/8 oz. to 1 1/8 oz. — the purple-hull shotshells (20 gauges are yellow) are packed with a custom-blended powder that promotes consistency, according to Kent. The 12-gauge loads — #7.5 shot, 1 oz. load at 1,200 fps — ran with perfect consistency through the Phenoma and gobbled up clays like a champ.

The competition-quality shells use Kent's proprietary Diamond Shot technology coupled with a shot polishing process that improves pellet formation for reliable patterns and superior target-breaking performance on trap, skeet and sporting clay ranges. The shells also feature 10mm nickel-plated heads. Learn more at kentgamebore.com.

Reliability was rock-solid, and the author shot the Phenoma better than any other shotgun ever tested. He found it to be light-recoiling and pointed as a natural extension of his hand-eye coordination.

of $751, and a street price around $500, these nit-picks seem kind of petty.

ARMSAN HISTORY

Manufacturer Armsan, proper name *Armsan Silah Sanayi ve Ticaret AS*, is situated in Istanbul. The concern focuses on shotguns, exporting models to over 40 countries on six continents. And these are no off-name oddities, either, with well-known American firms like Tristar (Viper G2), Mossberg (International SA-20) and Weatherby (SA-08 and PA-459 tactical, among other models) entrusting Armsan to manufacture autoloader lines in various gauges and styles.

Armsan was established in 2006 and today cranks out upward of 5,000 scatterguns monthly from its 22,000-plus-sq.-ft. facility. More than 150 craftsmen make metal chips and assemble parts at the plant, churning shotguns that have gained almost a cult following wherever they are owned, but especially in Europe, and the American South. And it's no wonder, for they are well-built shotguns at incredible price points.

IN THE FIELD

The Phenoma is sized like a cannon. Redefining what it means to be a slow

learner, it's taken me nearly 30 years to figure out why old timers prefer small, lightweight grouse guns. While the 12-gauge Phenoma can certainly be pressed into service for grouse and woodcock shooting, it might not be the best tool for those jobs. It is, after all, a full-size autoloader. I learned this lesson on a Central Wisconsin grouse hunt, lugging it around for several hours brush-busting like a deranged sasquatch. Just as I was beginning to tear my shirt off and mumble incoherently somewhere in the middle of a massive dead sea, things came to life as I spotted movement and thought for a second the Phenoma would soon thunder. Alas, it was not to be, for it was only two ladies riding through on horses.

It didn't help matters that our geriatric K9, George — a 13-year-old yellow lab who isn't happy unless he's giving puppy hugs or unleashing thermonuclear farts — was at home snoring in his cozy couch. The point is, if grouse hunting is your thing, get the 20-gauge Phenoma. The 20 is stocked in black synthetic, weighs just 6.6 pounds, and tapes at 42.5 inches, while the big 12 weighs in at 7.2 and measures 48.5 inches. I'm sure the full-size Phenoma is the business in the

duck blind when you need to put the horsepower to an incoming flock of greenheads, which perhaps explains the shotgun's popularity in the South.

However, the Phenoma is perfectly at home in the pheasant fields. We proved that when *Gun Digest* publisher Jim Schlender unleashed his heat-seeking gun dog, Birdie, on some farmland pheasant. Shooting Winchester Rooster XR #6s and Federal Hi-Bird #5s, we unleashed a volley of anti-aircraft fire on the cackling characters and filled the game pot — almost as if we knew what we were doing. However, the last rooster got away scot-free after the shotgun's sticky safety required a transition to thumb power to disengage; with that nanosecond delay, the big rooster reached cruising altitude and sailed off into a far-away field.

WARMING UP THE CLAY BUSTER

Back on the sporting clays course, I'd installed the improved cylinder choke and had a little breeze to keep the squadrons of biting bugs grounded. With a vest full of Kent's new Elite Target shotshells, the clays didn't make it very far before the diamond-coated swarm of shot connected. I was shooting well. The Phenoma was on fire as clays turned to dust. It was the supremely gratifying hit-what-you're-looking-at game. A game that a good shotgun makes possible.

After shooting my personal best, it was impossible not to be left impressed with Legacy's Pointer Phenoma. For almost half the cost of comparable American-made brands — and quality on par with or even better than many of the most popular models — the Phenoma autoloader is a sleeper to put on your shotgun bucket list.

Phenoma Field Test:
South Dakota Turkey

BY JIM SCHLENDER

There's nothing traditional about South Dakota turkey hunting. At least not to a Wisconsin guy like me. I learned that last April on a hunt near White River in south-central South Dakota when Keith Randall of Prairie Knight Guide Service introduced me to the art of "fanning" a gobbler. Fanning means you locate the birds, try to sneak within 150 yards or so, and then tease them with a turkey fan mounted to a plastic decoy.

Catch a tom who's ready to fight and he'll come running to take on the intruder. Shots are typically close, and by that I mean 30 yards would be a long shot. Pulling the trigger on a turkey at 10 yards or less is not uncommon for fanning practitioners.

Since I was breaking with tradition by letting Randall talk me into trying this new hunting method, I also changed up my shotgun and shotshell choices. I decided to try out a Pointer Phenoma shotgun outfitted in

> **THE PHENOMA'S NICE BALANCE AND QUICK-HANDLING QUALITIES FAVORED BY WINGSHOOTERS ARE WHAT MAKE IT IDEAL FOR QUICK-DRAW TURKEY HUNTING.**

Realtree Max-5 camo for our prairie stalk. The trim autoloader is relatively light for a gas gun at slightly over 7 pounds, a contrast to the heavier "super magnum" class of turkey guns I've frequently used.

The Phenoma's nice balance and quick-handling qualities favored by wingshooters are what make it ideal for quick-draw turkey hunting. When a tom comes charging in, but slams to a stop as he realizes he's eyeball-to-eyeball with some bad guys, his next move is to run. Which direction? You never know, but you have just a few short moments to pop up from the prone position, get a bead and touch off a shot at a quickly departing bird.

I paired the Phenoma with Hornady's 3-inch turkey loads in No. 6 shot. I purposely went with the factory-modified choke because our whole plan revolved around getting up close and personal with an angry bird — no need for a choke and shell combo lethal to half a football field. After a couple of shots at paper to verify the gun's point of aim, I knew I was good out to 35 yards or so with my setup.

Schlender found the Phenoma's light weight to be the ticket while trying a new fast-shooting turkey hunting method known as "fanning." He took this Merriam's gobbler on the swing.

After glassing a pair of toms strutting for a hen, Randall and I sneaked through a river bottom, popped up onto the bank, belly-crawled nearly 200 yards to get within comfortable range, and tried to melt into the short, dead grass. When the toms spotted Randall's decoy "strutting," they stared for a couple minutes and then came on a dead run.

When the lead bird got to within 15 yards, he knew something was wrong and let up on the gas. Just as he turned to break to the right, I rolled to my side, rose to a knee and took aim. I painted a stripe through the tom's fat red head just as he kicked it back into gear. The shot was not unlike swinging on an early-season teal, and the result was a very dead Merriam's gobbler.

Whether there's such a thing as a do-it-all turkey and wingshooting gun is open for debate, but for South Dakota hunting, the Phenoma is a remarkably ideal choice.

The Pointer Phenoma in Realtree Max-5 camo digested Hornady Heavy Magnum #6 Turkey and proved its versatility on the South Dakota prairie.

A combination of a full-size grip and short slide make for an easy handling combat pistol.

GLOCK PERFECTION — FINALLY

The Generation 5 M45 9mm

BY **ROBERT K. CAMPBELL**

G lock's footprint on the world market is huge and the company differs greatly from most firearms manufactures. Diversity is not Glock's key selling ingredient. There are no Glock rifles or carbines. Very few gun companies manufacture only handguns or only rifles, and none of these specialty makers are the size of Glock.

Glocks aren't collectible; emotional attachment and a sense of history are not the strong points of the Glock. All Glocks share the same manual of arms, the same sight set and the same trigger action. Almost all are black. It was a big deal when one was offered in Coyote Brown.

There are different frame sizes and calibers. Glocks are available in .380 ACP, 9mm Luger, .357 SIG, .40 S &W, 10mm, .45 GAP and .45 ACP. The 9mm is by far the most popular caliber. Glock has made gradual improvements in various generations. Glock doesn't introduce a small variation on a model to loud fanfare and advertising. A change is bound to be substantial. When Glock introduces an improved model, it gets our attention.

Glock's generations have been an incremental improvement. The first generation introduced the basic Glock and the Glock 17 9mm. Major changes came later. These included the addition of a light rail for

A new magazine well and a magazine tapered at the top make for rapid reloading in the Generation 5.

Note several differences between the Generation 5 Glock 45 9mm, left, and the Glock 17 Generation 4, right. The support pin in the frame and finger grooves are deleted in the Generation 5 pistols.

mounting combat lights, changes in the grip texture, and adding finger grooves to the frontstrap. An important practical improvement was a change in how the front sight attaches. Early front sights were easily ripped away.

66 THE GENERATION 5 IS BIG NEWS. WHILE EARLIER IMPROVEMENTS WERE INCREMENTAL, THE GENERATION 5 GUNS HAVE MORE SWEEPING IMPROVEMENTS. 99

The Generation 5 is big news. While earlier improvements were incremental, the Generation 5 guns have more sweeping improvements. It is truly a redesign rather than a simple upgrade. While a recent military competition resulted in the adoption of a handgun from another manufacturer (SIG's P230) for the U.S. Army, the Glock 19X was the other finalist. It is now a codified Generation 5 gun.

Glock fared better in competition for the FBI's new service pistol. The 17M and 19M as accepted by the FBI are the primogenitors of the Generation 5 pistol.

Glock had design goals that must be met with these handguns. The Generation 5 pistol reflects a great deal of research and development.

Even when a certain handgun is at the top of the list there is still a bidding process so the Glock must be affordable. At present the Glock is the baseline service pistol in my opinion. Other handguns should be measured against the Glock. If you pay less you should consider what you are getting at a cut-rate price, and if you pay more there should be advantages gained by the extra cash expended.

When developing the Generation 5 pistol, the primary goal was for the new handguns to retain their notable reliability. Accuracy could be improved if reliability was not affected. There was some concern with a better trigger action. Interchangeability of parts with previous handguns was not a great concern as Glock was gearing up for a big change. Glock tells me there are 20 changes in manufacture. Some changes are easily discernable, others are not.

A big change in the Generation 5 guns

is the 19X. This pistol features a short slide and full-size grip. The Glock 19X is manufactured in Coyote Brown. The model has been popular in a limited sense and generated much interest from law-enforcement and institutional users. But they did not wish to issue brown guns, they wanted a black gun. That gun is the Glock 45. It features the 4.02-inch barrel and short slide of the Glock 19, but the full-size grip of the Glock 17, increasing magazine capacity by two rounds to 17 cartridges.

The Glock 19X is supplied with a single 17-round magazine and two magazines with an extended-magazine base pad, increasing the capacity to 19 rounds. The Glock 45 is supplied with three 17-round magazines. The Glock 45 is the main focus of this report, however, most of the material covered relates to all the Generation 5 Glock pistols. There are similarities to the Generation 4 guns. Four interchangeable backstraps are included with the Glock 45. There is also a Rough Texture Finish that offers excellent abrasion and adhesion. The surface is more like tiny squares than diamonds and offers a great gripping surface. Glock

has eliminated the finger grooves found on previous handguns. Some liked them, but it seems most did not. All of us can live without the Glock finger grooves.

Some of the mechanical improvements have been seen before in special versions of the Glock. The new style magazine release is reversible. The slide lock is now ambidextrous. The controls are slightly larger. A left-handed shooter will be able to use the magazine release by hitting it with the forefinger, but the ambidextrous slide lock is an improvement for southpaws.

The Generation 5 M45 is advertised as being available with standard Glock white outline sights, AmeriGlo self-luminous iron sights or Glock night sights. Every Glock 45 I have encountered so far has had the AmeriGlo sights. They are arguably the best option for all-around personal-defense and duty use. These sights feature three green dots that offer an excellent aiming point in dim light. The front post also features an orange ring surrounding the front dot. This ring consists of fluorescent material. This makes for a bright aiming point in all lighting conditions. The front sight is fairly wide at .14 inch, offering a good combat sight picture. I found these sights offer greater precision than previous Glock sights. I have never liked the standard plastic Glock sight, even after Glock modified the front sight so that it was no longer easily pulled off. The plastic sights are more than adequate for fast shooting to perhaps 15 yards. I demand more accuracy. The AmeriGlo sights provide.

The author found the G5 9mm quite controllable in off-hand fire.

The slide has been given a share of attention. It is tapered slightly more at the front, which allows easier re-holstering. The Glock 45 also has forward cocking serrations which the 19X and other Glock Generation 5 pistols do not. This sets the Glock 45 apart as a tactical service-grade pistol. These forward cocking serrations do not affect holster fit. The Glock Generation 5 fits holsters intended for the Generation 4 pistols without any problem. The beveled front of the slide is an advantage with all holster types.

The differences between the Glock Generation 4 and Generation 5 warrant close attention before you order your Glock. If you own a perfectly suitable, long-serving Generation 4 pistol you might not be so quick to trade it. On the other hand, if you are looking to purchase a new Glock pistol on its own

merits then it should be the Generation 5.

One example of the changes is a deletion rather than an addition. A second pin in the frame was added to the Glock some time ago. This was intended to brace the frame from the sharp recoil of the .40 Smith & Wesson cartridge. Since there will be no Generation 5 .40 pistol, at least any time soon, this pin is deleted. Glock will keep the Generation 4 going in order to provide .357 SIG-, .40-, 10mm- and .45-caliber handguns to those who desire these pieces. That is a big market, but the 9mm market is bigger. The Generation 5 is all 9mm for the foreseeable future. I have seen both .40 and .45 Glock pistols with broken locking blocks, so these things happen. I have never seen a broken 9mm. I prefer a larger caliber for personal use, but then it isn't usually a Glock, but a 1911. However, the Glock is good to have and I have no misgivings trusting my life to the hardy and reliable Glock pistol.

> **"FOR THOSE WHO CANNOT PRACTICE OFTEN, THE 9MM IS A REASONABLE ALTERNATIVE…. IT WILL TAKE A LOT OF TIME, EFFORT AND EXPENSE TO BE APPRECIABLY BETTER-ARMED THAN WITH THE GLOCK 9MM COMBINATION."**

For those who cannot practice often, the 9mm is a reasonable alternative. Combine the most efficient 9mm loadings with marksmanship and you have one of the finest personal-defense systems in the world. It will take a lot of time, effort and expense to be appreciably better-armed than with the Glock 9mm combination.

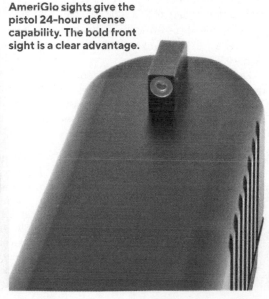

AmeriGlo sights give the pistol 24-hour defense capability. The bold front sight is a clear advantage.

The Generation 5 features a new spring on the takedown lever, although I am unaware of any previous problems with the takedown spring. A hidden change is found in the drop safety, or firing-pin safety. The safety is now oblong instead of round. The result is a stronger contact with the striker. The striker and the striker hole in the slide are modified. The new design is less likely to trap powder and brass particles in the striker channel.

There is little interchangeability of parts other than magazines in the new pistols. The Generation 5 improved parts are unlikely to need replacement, the same as earlier pistols. They are even less likely to give trouble than any earlier Glock and perhaps any other handgun in the world in my opinion. The Generation 5 pistol will not accept aftermarket triggers for earlier generation Glock handguns. God help those who fit aftermarket triggers to personal-defense handguns! I don't see the need to elaborate that point among intelligent readers. There has already been a lawsuit setting precedent for this. Reliability and liability demand the pistol remain as issued if used for

This Werkz inside-the-waistband holster works well for the author.

(above) The new Marksman barrel offers excellent accuracy with its polygonal-type rifling.

(below) Spring-within-a-spring technology aids in function and recoil control.

personal-defense.

Glock has also added an internal magazine well. While the tapered high capacity magazine and original magazine well offered fast reloads, the new design is even faster.

Glock has changed the slide coating from its famous Tenifer to a new type of diamond coating, NDLC. There have been no issues with Tenifer and the new coating looks fine and seems rugged. Glock also introduced a new Marksman barrel. Glocks have always been accurate enough for service use, but left something to be desired among more demanding shooters. Some years ago, I fitted a Bar-Sto barrel to a Glock 22 .40 and also added Novak sights. I changed the Glock 22 from a 25-yard gun to a 50-yard gun.

The Marksman barrel is fitted more tightly than Glocks of the recent past. The less slop in fitting, the less eccentric wear and the greater accuracy. The new rifling is a type of polygonal rifling. The trigger action is different in a good way. While the trigger on my personal Glock

45 breaks at 5.6 pounds — .1 pound over standard — it is lighter than the majority of Glocks I have tested during the past few years, which seem to average 6.0 pounds. The action feels tighter rather than being lighter. The trigger feels better and a smooth trigger is often better than a light trigger.

In order to properly evaluate the pistol, a lot of shooting is needed. This firing cannot be undisciplined, but should involve well-defined goals. The question "Where do I start?" is always easy for a handloader. I began with a good supply of handloads using "range brass," (which, by that, I mean not carefully sorted brass), a good supply of Hornady 115-grain HAP bullets and enough Titegroup in each cartridge case for 1,050 fps. I loaded 500 rounds on the Lyman press to begin. My goal was to see if the long frame and short slide had a clear advantage over either the Glock 19 or the Glock 17. I drew the pistol from a Werkz inside-the-waistband holster. I appreciate the quality and design of this holster and it is my go-to holster when I deploy the Glock 45 9mm.

Frankly, after this test I will be using the Glock 45 often. I have often stated that 500 draws is a realistic minimum for practice with a gun-and-holster combination before you carry it for personal defense. So this was a break-in period for both shooter and holster. I drew the Glock 45 9mm from beneath a covering garment and engaged man-sized targets at 7, 10 and 15 yards. The longer grip allowed a rapid presentation compared to a Glock 19, while the shorter slide allowed the pistol to clear the holster more quickly than a Glock 17.

The combination really works well for

most shooters. Shoot the elbow to the rear, bring the hand up from under the handgun and scoop the pistol from the holster and then meet the support hand in the middle of the body and push it toward the target. This is a fast combination. I fired a combination of single shots for accuracy, double taps, triple taps, hammers and precise fire at 15 yards. Press the trigger, allow the trigger to reset during recoil and then press again as you control the piece and keep your sight picture and you will get a hit. I can discern no practical difference between the Glock 45 9mm and a Generation 4 Glock 17 9mm on hand. The sights and trigger action are an advantage over the Glock 17 with its Glock night sights, I am certain.

Moving to personal-defense loads, the selection of acceptable loads narrows. I have often said when a big-bore cartridge fails it is most often due to inadequate penetration caused by an ill-conceived defense load. When a small bore performs beyond expectation it is due to good penetration. I fired a magazine each of a good quality personal defense loads including the Black Hills Ammunition 115-grain TAC +P, the Hornady American Gunner 124-grain

XTP +P, Speer 124-grain Gold Dot and the Winchester 124-grain PDX +P. Function was good and reliability a constant. There was more push with the +P loads, but the 9mm remained a controllable and accurate handgun to use in fast, reactive fire. I also fired a good quantity of the Federal 147-grain HST to confirm reliability with heavy bullet loads. All went as expected without any type of malfunction.

Probably the least important part of the test program was firing for accuracy from a solid bench-rest firing position. But I did so to satisfy my own curiosity concerning the accuracy potential of the Gen 5 handguns. I fired several five-shot groups with the average of 2.5 inches at 25 yards and a couple of excellent groups slightly smaller. The quality defense loads traded for top honors.

The Glock Generation 5 in general and the Glock 45 in particular are excellent all-around, personal-defense and service handguns. They share the advantages of previous Glock handguns while improving already good performance. The Glock has several advantages that have been proved in service and institutional testing. The first is reliability. The pistol is reliable among all else. The National

Institute of Justice defines reliability as a propensity to fire with each press of the trigger. The Glock is among the most reliable handguns in the world by any standard.

The Glock is a low maintenance firearm. It must be cleaned and lubricated, but it will survive with less care than most handguns. The Glock demands oil only in specific areas including the frame rails and locking block. Glock advises that the trigger bar that makes contact with the connector should be lubricated near the contact point. The barrel should also be lubricated around the barrel hood. Too much oil applied where it will not burn off results in oil pooling in an area. This creates a sludge of unburned powder and cartridge case and jacket debris. It should go without saying that the firing pin channel should never be lubricated. If these instructions are followed, the Glock is an amazingly reliable machine.

The Glock fits most hands better than the majority of high-capacity handguns. Polymer allows a more compact handle even with a double-column magazine. The action of the Glock is relatively compact and this allows for a low bore axis. This simply means the slide rides low over the hand. A double-action, first-shot trigger mechanism means more complication and more space in the frame as required with the SIG P226 and Beretta 92. When the slide is racked, the striker is partially cocked, or prepped as Glock calls it. When the trigger is pressed the striker is moved to the rear against spring pressure until it trips the spring and the striker is released, rushing forward to fire the pistol. The slide moves backward in recoil and resets the trigger action.

Other advantages of the Glock include an easy field strip. The action itself is simple enough and easily maintained. The Glock might accept after-market triggers and there is a large market for aftermarket sights and barrels. With the new Marksman barrel and high-visibility night sights there is less need to modify the Glock. Competition is one thing, but other than adding a good set of sights, the Glock should not be modified if the pistol is intended for personal-defense.

The Generation 5 pistols are the best Glocks ever produced and the Glock 45 9mm is arguably the best Glock service pistol.

Glock pistols strip down easily for cleaning and maintenance.

OLD

The rebuilt Sporting Carbine. It put meat in the freezer.

New Life for an MARLIN

Restoring an American classic

BY **WALT HAMPTON**

The evolution of firearms figures prominently in American history. Any serious student of the gun can generally recite our progression from muzzleloader to what today passes for the "modern" rifle, and the inventions and improvements that have occurred along the way. One style of rifle stands out as uniquely American, even though its roots, of course, came from across the sea, and that is the lever-action repeating rifle. If you are considering starting a collection of American hunting firearms, the lever gun must occupy a place of prominence in that collection.

When I was growing up, generally speaking, a deer hunter was either a "Winchester Man" or a "Marlin Man." Of course, many other makers' guns were recognized and used by deer hunters, but these two companies, in particular, made the most popular

The Marlin 1893 was produced in both rifle and carbine variations. This .30–30 rifle is still taking game for the author.

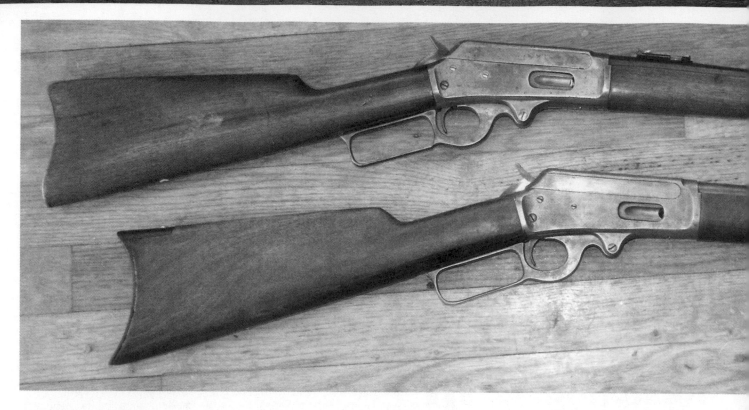

rifles. I was a Marlin Man. On my first deer hunt I carried my great-uncle's Marlin 1893 carbine, chambered for that wonder round, the .30-30, and that day in 1963 is forever imprinted on my mind. The weather was bitterly cold, the only deer we saw was one that had fallen to another hunter (shot with a Winchester 94, by the way), and I got to shoot half a box of cartridges at targets at various ranges. I can vividly remember the thrill of every recoil and muzzle blast and swore an oath that someday, such a wonderful rifle would be my very own.

After some negotiations a few years ago, I became the owner of a Marlin 1893 rifle (with octagon barrel, in .30-30, all original), and two 1893 Marlin carbines, one the standard carbine with the full magazine (also chambered in .30-30) and the remnants of a Sporting Carbine in .32 Winchester Special. The standard carbine and the rifle are substantially complete and original, albeit somewhat scuffed up, and I have left them in their original form, aside from a good cleaning. The Sporting Carbine, however, was a train wreck. The stock was kindling, the metal was solid, but neglected and the magazine tube, nose cap and buttplate were missing; but the bore, by good fortune, had been protected by a packing of heavy gun grease. There were other

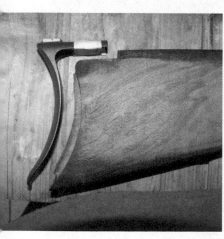

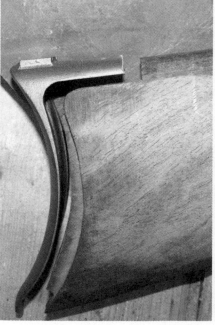

Fabricating a curved steel buttplate for the Sporting Carbine. A rough-cast plate is cut and ground to fit, then drilled and countersunk for screws.

The Sporting Carbine (bottom) has been assembled for function testing, before final finishing of wood and metal. The standard carbine (above) stays just as it is.

parts missing or needing to be replaced, but, I reasoned, because of the excellent bore this rifle should get another chance.

In the early part of the 20th century, the Marlin Company was having problems, and under new management it was scrambling to fill a catalog with workable models. At this time, it was not uncommon to find in stores Marlins that could not be found in the company catalog, and many variations appeared. Adding to this confusion is the fact that Marlin factory records are woefully incomplete, and you have a fertile field for misrepresentation of what exactly is a factory Marlin rifle of this period, and what is not.

> **THE 1893 MODEL WAS THE FIRST MARLIN RIFLE DESIGNED FOR THE NEW, STATE-OF-THE-ART, SMOKE-LESS CARTRIDGES, EVEN THOUGH SOME 1893S WERE MADE FOR BLACKPOWDER-USE ONLY AND MARKED AS SUCH ON THE BARRELS; BUT THE SMOKELESS GUNS MAR-KETED AFTER 1904 WERE MARKED "SPECIAL SMOKE-LESS STEEL" ON THE LEFT SIDE OF THE BARREL.**

The 1893 Model was the first Marlin rifle designed for the new, state-of-the-art, smokeless cartridges, even though some 1893s were made for blackpowder-use only and marked as such on the barrels; but the smokeless guns marketed after 1904 were marked "Special Smokeless Steel" on the left side of the barrel. As with most American gun manufacturers of the period, Marlin offered a wide array of options and custom features that could be ordered directly from the factory. Depending on whose numbers you accept, there were approximately 900,000 Model 1893 and Model 93 rifles and carbines manufactured between 1893 and 1935, when production ended.

In general terms, the 1893 is considered the rifle and the 93 Carbine and 93 Sporting Carbine are the short-barrel guns. The Sporting Carbine had a 1/2 or 2/3 magazine and round barrel chambered in either .30-30 Winchester or .32 Winchester Special (the only factory carbine records I could verify) and might be found in .32-40, .25-36 and .38-55, all three of which were also available in the rifle models. I have seen variations with both the standard "carbine" steel butt-plate and a curved steel buttplate that resembled those found on the rifle model. I have never seen a take-down carbine (there are many examples of take-down rifles), but that does not mean they do not exist; as reported previously, if you got in touch with Marlin in the early days and made an order, with money in hand, I am certain the company would make for you what you wanted. In those days, most American gun makers would work to order on just about any of their models.

There is no doubt that upon its introduction, the .30-30 Winchester round became the standard by which all future smokeless cartridges would be judged. Even today, shooters who have never even held a .30-30 round in hand can relate to its ballistic performance in relation to most "modern" chamberings. In those days of around the turn of the century and the first three decades of the century, the gun and ammo manufacturers (and many, many wildcatters) were in a frenzy to adapt, modify and better the Winchester factory round, including Winchester itself; the .32 Special was one of those attempts and when it was introduced it was an original smokeless-powder design. Pushing a 170-grain, .321-inch-diameter, flat-point bullet in the 2,300-fps neighborhood, it was, on paper at least, slightly more powerful than the .30-30 with its 170-grain .308 slug. You must understand, Winchester was designing the cartridges for the rifle, a short, handy carbine for use in close cover for deer-sized game. Both the .30-30 and the .32 Special were, of course, eventually used on every game animal in North America and under the restrictions of close-range shooting (less than 150 yards), with good shot placement, both would get the job done.

Over the years, the .32 Special has been unfairly maligned as an inaccurate round; actually, there is no such thing. In a good barrel with the proper bullet fit, the Special will do exactly what it was designed to do, deliver groups less than 3 inches at 100 yards from a fast-handling, open-sighted, lightweight rifle. We forget today, in the era of tiny sub-MOA shooting at extreme long range with heavy-barreled, scoped target guns, that even the venerable Holland and Holland firm only guarantees its rifles to shoot less than 3 inches at the 100-yard stripe. The Marlin carbine and the .32 Special (or the .30-30, for that matter) was a match made in heaven for the close-cover deer hunter.

WORKING THE GUN

First, I stripped the rifle to its bare components, even removing the barrel and chasing the threads and cleaning up the receiver/barrel contact shoulder. Amazingly, upon reassembly, the barrel when tightened up still fit with the front

The fore-end is roughed out, bored for the tube, and the tube is fit using the Dremel and hand tools.

Making a new magazine tube for the carbine involved not only coming up with the tube, spring, follower and tube cap, but also the attachment for it (the hanger) to the barrel. For this I consulted old schematics and other drawings of the Sporting Carbine, along with various photos from old catalogs. This project was not so much a restoration as it was a rebuilding. I was not trying to duplicate an original factory gun; I was trying to get "into the ballpark" with a facsimile that would serve as a usable close-range hunting rifle. I found a suitable replacement tube, cut it to length, modified a late-model factory spring and follower and hand-made the tube plug, along with the hanger and associated screws and pins. The existing dovetail under the barrel gave me my fore-end length and I decided to use a barrel band instead of the nose cap usually found on Sporting Carbines. Original fore-end nose caps for the Sporting Carbine are as scarce as common sense in Congress, and if they

sight square to the top of the receiver. I cleaned and examined each part. I did have to replace the spring ejector in the inside of the receiver, using one I hand-made from soft steel and hardened.

The bore of the rifle appeared to be pristine; the rifling was crisp and there was no pitting or erosion, a real surprise considering the rest of the gun. I have many times found this in used guns; a great many have been carried and neglected more than shot and I learned long ago the outward appearance can fool you. For most American guns there are available at least drawings of the parts so a good machinist can usually make what you need, but if the barrel is shot out, a new tube might be the only thing that will work. I have seen, on many occasions, even pitted and damaged barrels can be saved by a good cleaning and a bit of careful work. My Fox Sterlingworth shotguns are good examples of this, and after a bit of tender loving care they are now cherished hunting guns. Don't give up on a good gun!

The top of the receiver had, sometime it its long life, been drilled for a scope mount of the old saddle type. The holes had been filled with cut-off screws and I gave them some attention with a small flat file and some sandpaper, making sure they fit the holes tightly and were not interfering with the internal works of the action. This was a common practice when the first scopes became popular

The fore-end hanger and magazine plug were made by hand to fit the existing dovetail under the barrel and the length of the tube.

and in itself is the killer when it comes to collector value. This is why I acquired the rifle at such a bargain and knowing that I would have to come up with other parts, it didn't bother me in the least.

> **❝ I WAS NOT TRYING TO DUPLICATE AN ORIGINAL FACTORY GUN; I WAS TRYING TO GET 'INTO THE BALLPARK' WITH A FACSIMILE THAT WOULD SERVE AS A USABLE CLOSE-RANGE HUNTING RIFLE. ❞**

can be found are ridiculously expensive, so I went with the sane alternative. It worked.

Restocking a Marlin lever gun is not difficult. Since this was to be a rifle for hard use, I dug around in the woodpile and came up with a very dark, very dense piece of Claro walnut that seemed

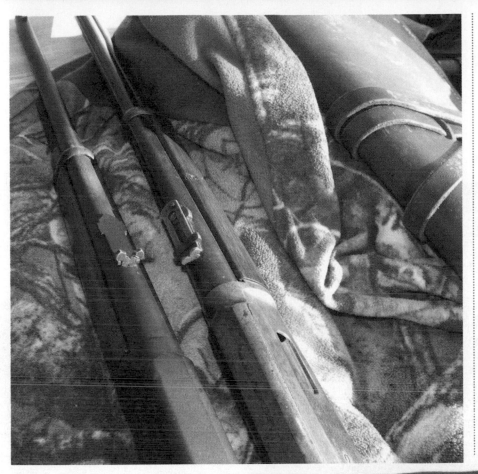

This kind of work takes time. I would file and sand a bit, try the fit, and repeat, until we had things slipping together without any slack or play. In a lever-action rifle, nothing is more disappointing than a fore-end that slips when the action is worked, for invariably the fore-end hand pushes away from the receiver when the lever is actuated. If the fore-end slips forward then all sorts of bad things can happen; the magazine tube can come out of the receiver, the follower and spring can be lost, and a bad day is had all around. This situation is also conducive to the utterance of invectives not suitable for genteel company. Get the fore-end right and tight, and save the aggravation and cussing.

With the action stripped, I started my work on the buttstock by tracing the upper tang on the wood and fit it and the receiver face to the wood. I used my usual cheap red lipstick for inletting marker and carefully scraped away the high spots. When the wood and action metal were together, I fit the lower tang by the same method and on the drill press located the proper angle and position for the tang screw. Go slow here, don't get in a hurry; the screw should not bind in the wood and only fit properly

(above) The rear sights on Marlin carbines were a variety of styles. The author's standard carbine has the ladder style (right), and the Sporting Carbine has the folding leaf buckhorn style.

(right) Both the standard and sporting carbine usually are found in either .30–30 or .32 Winchester Special, although other calibers were available. The .30–30 cartridges on the right with cast bullets are about 175 grains, driven to about 1,000 fps.

in line with what I wanted to accomplish. After the blanks were roughed out, I set about fitting the barrel and magazine tube to the fore-end. This involved some beavering with the Dremel and a hand drill, and reaming with a dowel wrapped with sandpaper, to get the fit close yet leave enough room so there would be no binding between the metal and wood. I cut the barrel channel for full contact with the barrel and, at the receiver end, I sought a tight fit between the face of the receiver and the rear of the fore-end itself.

when the action is fully fit to the stock.

I had on hand some of the rough-cast, unfinished crescent-type buttplates and decided to modify one to fit the carbine. I had to shorten it somewhat, and grind away the sprue, then measure, drill and countersink the holes for the screws. As I have mentioned in previous articles, fitting a curved steel buttplate can be very tedious and changing one aspect of the installation (the angle of the curve in relation to the comb, for instance) can have profound impacts on the shape and length of the butt itself. Plan this part of the work thoroughly before you start your cutting; you will be glad you did. I did have to grind slightly the toe of the buttplate to shorten it and heat it for a gentle bend, to protect the toe of the wood. These operations are not difficult but once again, you must measure, and plan ahead before you start grinding away. Take your time.

I finished the metal with a bead-blasting and baked matte finish using Gun-Coat from Brownell's, a fine company and a great product. No, this finish is not the eye-dazzling color case-hardening or rust bluing, but it is practical and durable, what we want for a close-cover, brier-patch, rain and snow hunting rifle. The wood was sanded, filled, and finished with polyurethane. I like it.

The rebuilt Sporting Carbine and the standard carbine, ready for hard use. Don't give up on a gun because it has some wear; with a little loving care, you might find a new favorite rifle.

If you will be diligent in your search, and visit the gun shows and the used gun stores, you can find 1893 and 93 Marlins on the shelves. Some of these are diamonds in the rough; take the time to give these guns a good look and you might come up with your new favorite shooting iron. Saving a good gun is certainly worth the effort.

In 30 years of gun writing, the author has very seldom put a photo of himself in an article. This morning with the standard 1983 carbine deserved to be an exception. He had been trying to get this piebald doe out of the herd for four years, and finally had to sneak through the impossible cutover to root her out. The carbine was the perfect gun for the close-cover jump shot that put her in the freezer.

If you don't know what this is, and what it signifies, you don't know Marlin.

THE RETURN OF THE
45
LUGER

The .45-cal. Luger from The Luger Man, aka Eugene Golubstov, is a fast-cycling semi-auto in a big-bore cartridge, the .45 ACP. Photo: Eugene Golubstov

The concept of a .45 ACP Luger goes back more than 100 years, and it's an idea that is too good to die   BY **JIM DICKSON**

In 1907, the U.S. Army tested new automatics and revolvers in the first of a series of tests that led to the adoption of the M1911. From the start, the Army's review board favored the Colt and Savage designs but wanted more development work on them. As an interim measure it recommended the .45 Colt New Service revolver, which was adopted as the M1909 for immediate issue against the Moros in the Philippines.

The rim size of the .45 Colt cartridge was increased from .500 to .530 inch to ensure positive extraction with the New Service's star ejector, although it meant that you could only load every other chamber in the Colt Single Actions that were still in service. Later,

Golubstov firing the M1907 Luger. The blurred copper-colored bullet caught streaking through the smoke.

the rim size on all commercial .45 Colt ammo was standardized at .512 inch, the largest size that could be used in the Colt SAA, for better functioning in the new swing-out cylinder guns with their different extractor system.

The German Luger was doing well in these tests, but after the backlash over adopting the foreign-designed Krag rifle, Ordnance was in no mood to look at foreign designs again. This was evident when it permitted the Savage to have a new mainspring installed in the middle of its tests but refused to permit a new hammer spring in the Bergman pistol when it needed one before starting its evaluation, simply refusing to test it

on that count. Army Ordnance recommended against a service test of the Luger because the final seating of the cartridge was not by direct inline spring action and due to its ammo sensitivity.

There was another more urgent reason not to permit a service test, at least if you wanted to prevent a foreign gun from being adopted. The Luger was the fastest and easiest pistol to hit with, and in the 1900 test trials of the earlier .30-caliber Luger many of the troops had fallen in love with it. The only factor mitigating against it was the puny .30 Luger cartridge, which no one thought was big enough. In those days, you not only had to drop crazed Moros on jihad,

you also needed to stop a cavalry horse with one shot. That takes a .45. The new Luger was a .45. Army Ordnance didn't want to deal with troops preferring the German gun.

A look at these tests is interesting. The tested Colt was the M1905, which was hardly recognizable in its perfected M1911 form four years later. In the endurance test the Luger had eight jams in 506 rounds, all of which were easily cleared by simply striking the toggle. The M1905 Colt was a far cry from the later M1911 and had 24 jams in 500 rounds. The Savage was permitted to have a new mainspring after round 151. As previously mentioned, the foreign Bergman was summarily dismissed from the competition when it needed a new hammer spring before tests began — Ordnance favoritism at its finest. The Savage had 18 misfires, eight failures to eject and six jams in 500 rounds. Jams in the Colt or Savage could not be cleared by a simple slap on the toggle but took more time and effort to clear.

The sand box test began with the barrels tightly corked and the magazine empty. A blast of fine sand in a specially prepared box was administered for one minute. The excess sand was removed by blowing, jarring and wiping the piece with the bare hand only. The magazine was then loaded and fired. The Luger had two jams. The Colt had none. The Savage was recorded as firing three rounds. What happened to the other four? Obviously, there was an untold problem.

The dust box test was the same as the sand box test except that fine dust

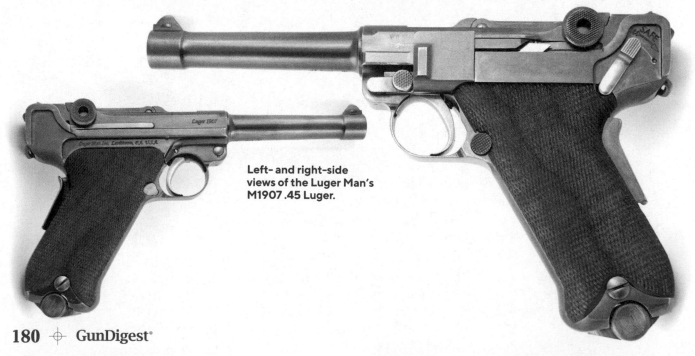

Left- and right-side views of the Luger Man's M1907 .45 Luger.

was used. The Luger had four jams that were easily cleared by striking the toggle. At the inventor's request, another magazine was fired and this time there was only one jam as the Luger's mechanism operating was throwing the dust out of the gun. The Colt had no jams. The Savage had three misfires and one jam.

Significantly, there was no mud test. Such a test would have consisted of dropping the gun into soft, thick, sticky mud, the kind that sticks in clods, not the wet slippery type that can serve as a lubricant. This is the mud that gets in guns when you hit the dirt and artillery is throwing earth everywhere, and the very stuff that stopped the Smith & Wesson Triple Lock revolvers in WWI British service. The Luger is well sealed and throws the dirt off as it operates. If the barrel is plugged it will be bulged on firing, but it will still function. Bulged barrels prevent the slide from coming back, hopelessly jamming the gun. In

> **WITH THE DECK STACKED AGAINST HIM AND NO TROOP TRIALS PERMITTED, GEORG LUGER LEFT THE ARMY TRIALS TO CONCENTRATE ON GETTING THE LUGER ADOPTED AS GERMANY'S OFFICIAL PISTOL THE NEXT YEAR WHEN IT BECAME THE FAMED P08 9MM LUGER. THERE WAS NO POINT CONTINUING IN THE U.S. ARMY TRIALS AS ORDNANCE HAD MADE IT PERFECTLY CLEAR THAT IT WAS NOT GOING TO CONSIDER ANY WEAPONS EXCEPT THE COLT OR SAVAGE PISTOLS.**

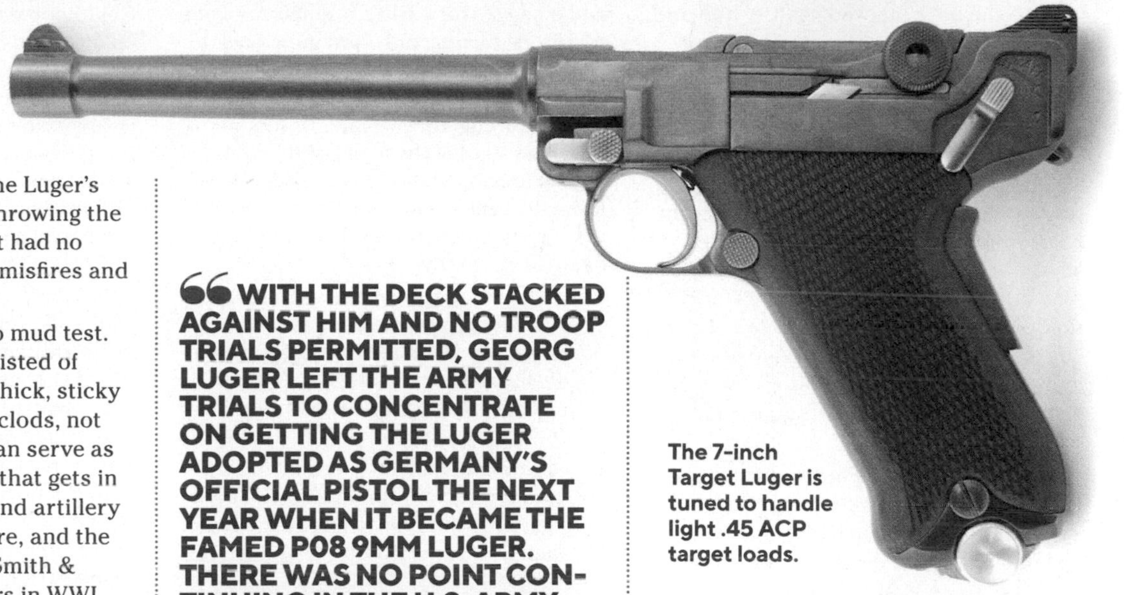

The 7-inch Target Luger is tuned to handle light .45 ACP target loads.

Left-side view of the Baby Luger, an excellent little pistol for concealed carry.

guns with cocked, exposed hammers like the Colt and Savage, mud prevents the hammer fall from firing the cartridge and allows more mud to get inside. When you're in a gunfight, your single-action automatic is kept cocked. Had there been a mud test, it's likely that the Luger would have won and the others failed — unless they were permitted to remove the excess mud before attempting to fire.

The rust test consisted of plugging the bore and soaking the gun in a saturated solution of Salammoniac for five minutes and then hanging it up indoors to rust for 22 hours. The Luger had to be manually cocked and the toggle closed by hand to fire. After applying oil without any rust removal, the gun worked properly. No tools were used to make it work.

That is not to say that it was not the winner of the rust test, as a wooden rod was used on the Colt to manipulate the mainspring and release the slide catch. Also, the slide was worked rapidly back and forth and the hammer snapped several times before starting the test. The Savage had its parts operated by striking on a bench and manipulated by hand before firing. The magazine spring was forced back and forth by a metal rod repeatedly to get it working before firing. (Looks like cheating to me.) If the Luger had also been loosened up it would have functioned without problems as well.

With the deck stacked against him and no troop trials permitted, Georg Luger left the Army trials to concentrate on getting the Luger adopted as Germany's official pistol the next year when it became the famed P08 9mm Luger. There was no point continuing in the U.S. Army trials as Ordnance had made it perfectly clear that it was not going to consider any weapons except the Colt or Savage pistols. It was a great loss to the world that Georg Luger did not offer the .45 Luger commercially. The Luger went on to become the most popular and widely distributed pistol of the first half of the 20th century.

Regrettably, Savage never offered the 1911 version of the .45 to the public, but a scaled-down version in .32 and .380 became one of the most popular pocket pistols of the era, and even saw considerable military use in foreign service.

The Bergman, which Army Ordnance so high-handedly dismissed from the tests, proved a successful design. It was adopted by Denmark in 1910 in 9mm Bayard Long, commonly called the 9mm Bergman Bayard because of its association with the Bergman M1910 pistol. It also saw extensive military and police use in Spain and Greece. Variations were also made in both Germany and Belgium.

THE .45 LUGER BORN AGAIN

The M1907 .45 Luger was just too good of a gun to be lost in the pages of history. Eugene Golubtsov was determined to produce it again. Born in Siberia, Golubtsov immigrated to the U.S. where he pursued his love of handguns. He be-

came one of the world's premier firearms restorers, turning old worn guns back to like-new condition for collectors. Back in 1907, Army Ordnance had blueprints of the M1907 Luger drawn and Golubtsov obtained a set of these drawings from a man who had used them to make copies for collectors. It took him six months to get the gun made from these drawings to function perfectly.

The first magazine made from the original blueprints had rounds stick in the magazine. After reworking the stamping dies, a redesigned magazine would feed all seven cartridges with a light spring when the action was hand-cycled.

Test firing revealed that the gun would not feed the second round with the light springs. After studying the way the bullet interacted with the frame and the barrel,

Golubtsov noted that the Luger had two feed ramps, one on the frame to get the cartridge out of the magazine and the second to feed the round into the barrel. He experimented with different feed ramp designs, welding and reshaping the feed ramp on the frame three times. He ultimately cut, reshaped, and changed the barrel feed ramp five times, destroying two barrels in the process.

Golubtsov purchased a slow-motion camera to see what was actually happening during the feeding cycle and saw that the next round was not being lifted from the magazine before the toggle closed. The magazine spring was then changed three times with each spring stronger than the one before until it would deliver the rounds in position before the toggle could close. The next problem was the recoil spring. The original one was too light and Golubtsov experimented with five different wire sizes before settling on a spring that was strong enough to stop the toggle assembly before it was all the way to the rear. This allowed tuning the gun's action for heavy barrels and light target loads for competition.

Three different toggle designs were tested, each changing the timing of the slide and toggle to the position of the feed ramp during the feeding cycle. During the final stages of research and development, Golubtsov found that Georg Luger had similar problems in the beginning and had experimented with toggle designs and springs as well as grip angles to make his guns function correctly.

The .45 Luger has a different

Comparison of the M1907 and Baby Luger. A chip off the old block.

Eugene Golubstov, a master gun maker and his masterpiece, the M1907 .45 ACP Luger pistol.

case with the Luger. The slow-motion camera reveals that the toggle action cycles so fast that as the last round leaves the bore all 8 ejected cases are still in the air. You can pull the trigger as fast as Ed Mc-Givern and never have to wait on the Luger to load the next round.

The toggle action has a mechanical advantage over conventional heavy slide guns. The size and weight of the moving parts are smaller and lighter, and move faster — plus, the Luger upper assembly only moves ¼ inch. Then the small, light toggle takes over ejecting the cartridge and feeding the next one. It is so fast that even in slow-motion pictures at 2,000 frames per second, the toggle is blurred because it is moving so fast.

Follow-up shots are easier with the Luger because there is less weight moving around and felt recoil is much less.

The classic nose dive of a heavy slide is altogether absent. It is so easy to master the Luger that a new shooter can consistently give good results after only one lesson. This is one of the Luger's strongest points. The gun shoots right where you point it, consistently and accurately.

Golubtsov's first prototype has had over 10,000 rounds fired through it. After the first 1,000 rounds, an overly hardened extractor and ejector broke and were replaced with ones that were properly heat treated. There have been no failures since then and the accuracy has not dropped off, nor has there been any barrel wear that could be measured. He brought three of his Lugers to my farm for me to test — the prototype M1907 Luger, a 7-inch barrel target version and a .45-caliber Baby Luger. All three guns were identical in fit and finish to original DWM commercial Lugers. The deep rust blue of the classic commercial Luger was there in all its splendor.

Rust bluing is done by brushing acid on the metal and letting it rust for one hour, then boiling it in water for half an hour until the rust turns to a black oxide. Any loose rust is then removed by a fine wire brush and the process repeated 8 to 10 times until the desired color is achieved. Since it takes about two hours for each layer it ends up taking 20 hours to blue a gun, but it produces an extremely durable and rust-resistant

A 1900 U.S. Army test trials fixed-sight M1896 Mauser Broomhandle pistol restored by Eugene Golubstov.

grip angle than other Lugers to properly feed the .45 Auto cartridge. Blueprints made by the U.S. Army were from the first prototypes, which were made before the design of the new .45 auto cartridge was standardized. The changes being made in the cartridge at that time and the poor quality of the ammunition provided for the M1907 tests led Luger to demand that his own ammo be used so he would have consistent ammunition performance. The Army found fault with that even though it was perfectly reasonable under the circumstances. Golubtsov had to continue the development process to redesign the gun for today's .45 ACP cartridge.

The best speed shooters, such as the late Ed McGivern, always complained that the semi-auto pistols could not be fired as fast as revolvers because the cycling time was so slow. That is not the

A Webley Green .455 revolver that had heat and water damage from a fire, now fully restored, including heat-treating.

finish. It is so tough that it takes a lot of work with a wire wheel to remove it.

Golubtsov warns people that many modern oils like WD-40 will physically attack rust and because of that feature will degrade a rust blue finish over time. He recommends the original German Ballistol oil, which is the gun oil always used on Lugers in Germany. Ballistol was developed in 1904 for the German army, which wanted one oil for all the soldier's equipment — metal, leather and wood. It does that perfectly. Ballistol forms an emulsion in water and even with 5 percent Ballistol and 95 percent water the water will evaporate leaving the Ballistol behind with no rusting. It prevents rust when moisture condenses on a cold gun brought into a warm house. One part Ballistol to 3 parts water was used as a bore cleaner and 10 percent Ballistol to 90 percent water was used in the German Maxim machine gun water jackets. In the Arctic cold of the WWII Russian front, 3

parts Ballistol to 7 parts kerosene kept the German weapons functioning. You can get Ballistol in the U.S. from Ballistol USA, P.O. Box 900, Kittyhawk, N.C. 27949.

Shooting these three beauties was a joy. We got a 1-inch group at 50 yards with the M1907 prototype Luger. This is the gun that already had 10,000 rounds through it. It certainly doesn't lose accuracy through use. The guns snuggled into your hand like they were a part of you and pointed exactly where you were looking. There was no noticeable recoil, just fun guns to shoot.

The Baby Luger was a .45 ACP version of the original cut-down 9mm Luger that was Georg Luger's personal carry gun. Years ago, I got to handle the original when it belonged to Ralph Shattuck. The Baby Luger has a half-inch shorter frame than the standard M1907, which reduces the magazine capacity to six rounds plus one in the chamber. It sports a 3.2-inch barrel. The gun still fills the hand nicely and the barrel is about the minimum length that you can have without sacrificing ease of hitting. Being more compact, it is a bit easier to conceal, and concealed carry is the Baby Luger's reason for being, both then and now. I found it just as easy to hit with as the full-size .45-caliber Luger.

The 7-inch barrel target model is what you want for match shooting as the Luger is an incredibly accurate design. Golubtsov fits the target gun parts more

closely together than the M1907 and the Baby Luger, which have wider tolerances for reliability in hard service in adverse conditions.

The one drawback to the Luger has always been the small .30 Luger and 9mm Luger cartridges for which it was chambered. While I know of one bear attack stopped and one caribou killed with a 9mm Luger, it is not my idea of a big bore. Making the Luger in .45 caliber changes all that. When Betty and I had Alaskan trappers' licenses and lived in a log cabin deep in the Alaskan interior, we used WWII G.I.-issue M1911A1 .45 automatics with G.I. surplus hardball ammo for everything with perfect satisfaction. Ranges were very short in the thick bush of the Alaskan interior and we had no need for anything longer-ranged than a pistol.

> **THE .45 ACP AND ITS REVOLVER COUNTERPART, THE .45 COLT, ARE TRUE ALL-PURPOSE CARTRIDGES. DESIGNED TO STOP A CHARGING CAVALRY HORSE WITH ONE SHOT, THEY NOT ONLY DO THAT JOB PERFECTLY, THEY WORK EQUALLY WELL ON CHARGING HUMAN FANATICS.**

The .45 ACP and its revolver counterpart, the .45 Colt, are true all-purpose cartridges. Designed to stop a charging cavalry horse with one shot, they not only do that job perfectly, they work equally well on charging human fanatics. They will kill anything in North America so long as you don't use expanding bullets. You need the penetration on the

(below) **This original Naval Luger was so badly pitted it required welding to restore it properly.**

rounds of eight different types of ammo are run through each gun to ensure perfect functioning and reliability. These guns are meant to be carried and used where the Luger's unexcelled speed and ease of hitting can save the customer's life. When the chips are down and it's you or them, having a gun that can give you an edge in speed and accuracy can be the difference between life and death. The handbuilt Luger's price suddenly seems very reasonable.

CONTACT:
Eugene Golubstov
Luger Man, Inc.
1408 Elkins Avenue
Levittown, PA 19057
304-584-3763
Eugene@lugerman.com
lugerman.com

big stuff, you already have a big enough hole. Yet they don't ruin the meat on small game shot for the camp cook pot.

Some people prefer the .44 Magnum cartridge, but the .44 is really not a true .44 caliber as its bullet diameter is only .429, whereas the .45 has a bullet diameter of .451, so you have a significantly larger hole.

Another factor is that pistol cartridges that break the sound barrier at 1,100 fps have a significantly higher noise level that can quickly cause hearing loss when fired without hearing protection. Back when the .32-20 first came out, it was a hot load totally unlike today's puny Cowboy Action loads. There was an old saying that every .32-20 revolver had been dropped the first time it was shot by a new owner as he grabbed his ears in pain. There was a lot of truth in that. This is also the reason that both the Kimball .30 carbine automatic pistol and the Ruger .30 carbine single action were not successful. I have a good friend who quit shooting his .44 Magnum because of the noise level, not the recoil. The big magnums are larger and heavier than the .45s, which makes them less easy to pack. That's why you rarely see them carried as everyday concealed firearms. Personally, I will stick with the .45s. If I need more power, I will pick up a long gun.

Golubtsov makes the .45-caliber Lugers entirely in-house, but as he has a small shop instead of a big factory like Colt or Smith & Wesson, his prices reflect the fact that these are handmade guns turned out by a master craftsman. These new Lugers start out on two CNC milling centers. It takes one or two days to handfit and tune each gun. Then 150

Carrying is where the M1907 Luger's grip safety comes in handy. John Browning always thought a grip safety was all the safety an automatic needed, even though he was required to put a manual safety on all his guns. The Singapore Police issued .380 Colt M1908 automatics with the manual safety locked permanently in the off position by a screw; they relied solely on the grip safety. While the M1907 has a manual safety, you don't have to use it and that means one less thing to do in a gunfight. Golubtsov also makes custom holsters of any style so you can carry your .45 Luger.

I can confidently say that anyone who buys one of these big-bore Lugers is going to learn to love it the more he or she shoots it. These handmade guns are well worth the money. The M1907 costs $6,975 in carbon steel and $7,775 in stainless steel. The Baby Luger runs $8,275, while the 7-inch target model is $7,775. There is also a 16-inch barrel .45 Luger carbine available for $12,975. It's worth remembering that a Luger carbine was Kaiser Wilhelm's favorite hunting rifle.

There is another strong point to the Luger that offsets its price greatly over time: It doesn't wear out like the current crop of automatics. Since WWII,

many prominent new automatic pistols have had a design life of 5,000 to 10,000 rounds. I find this completely unacceptable. The toggle-action Luger, like the Maxim machine gun that inspired it, just goes on and on without fail. Many of the original Swiss Lugers are still in service firing on the range and they have shown no signs of wearing out after well over 100 years. I like that. When you buy a Luger, you are buying a gun to keep and use forever just like best-quality Scottish and British double guns.

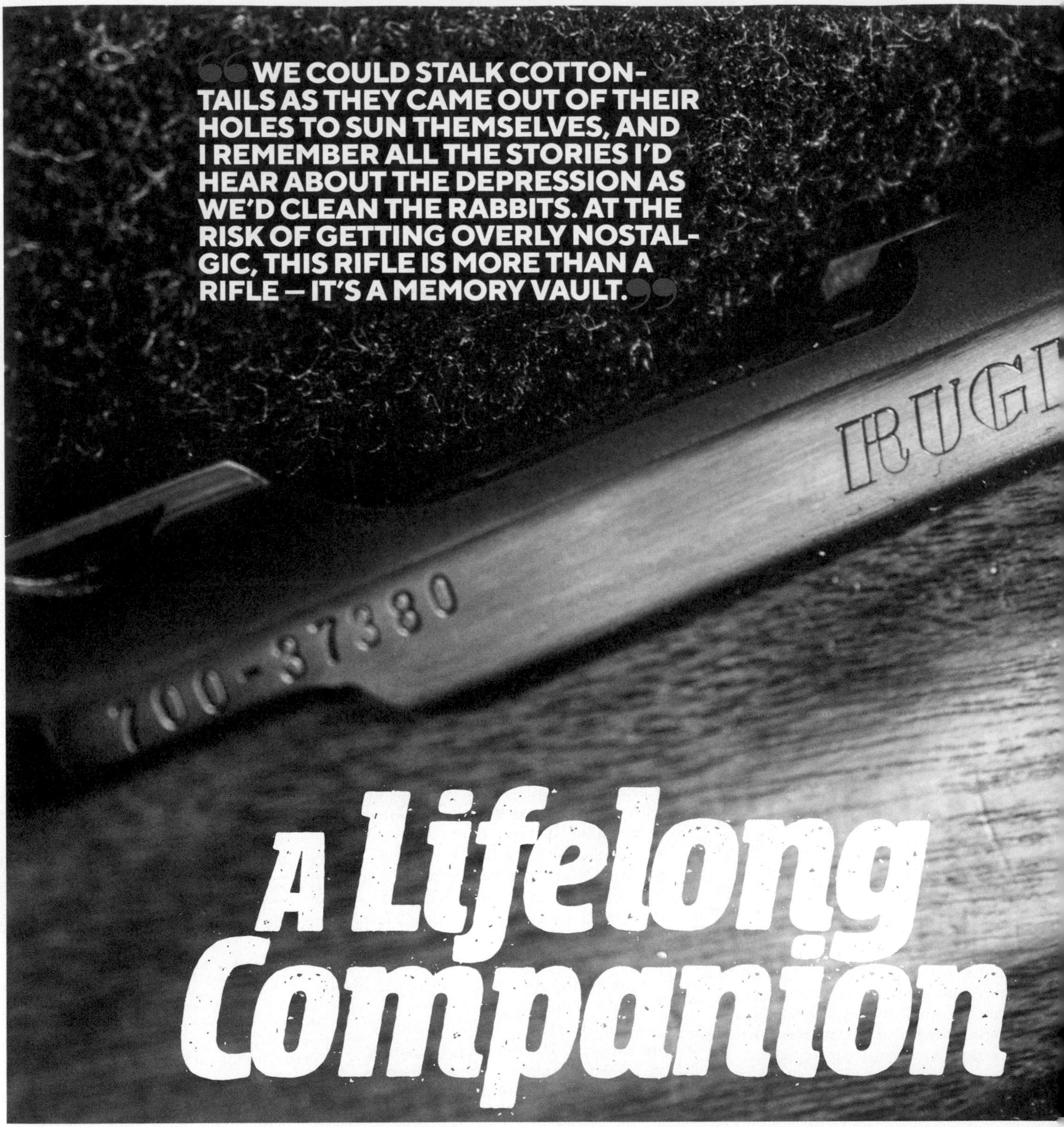

"WE COULD STALK COTTON-TAILS AS THEY CAME OUT OF THEIR HOLES TO SUN THEMSELVES, AND I REMEMBER ALL THE STORIES I'D HEAR ABOUT THE DEPRESSION AS WE'D CLEAN THE RABBITS. AT THE RISK OF GETTING OVERLY NOSTAL-GIC, THIS RIFLE IS MORE THAN A RIFLE — IT'S A MEMORY VAULT."

A Lifelong Companion

Ruger's 77/22 offers big game styling in a rimfire configuration.

BY **PHIL MASSARO**

The Ruger 77/22 is a well-designed bolt action rimfire rifle,

I t was Christmas Day 1985, and I remember vividly as my dad, Ol' Grumpy Pants, produced a long, narrow box, hastily — perhaps clumsily — wrapped. At 14 years of age, as if life wasn't mildly awkward to begin with, I was learning to hunt with him, and each trip to the woods was a new challenge, replete with a healthy dose of nerves because I certainly didn't want to fail in front of my father. In that era, a hunter had to be 16 years old to hunt big game, and until that Christmas Day I hunted with my Fox double barrel .410 ... but all that was about to change.

The Ruger 77/22 features a two-piece bolt with locking lugs at the rear of the first piece.

Inside that amalgam of tape and paper was my first rifle: a Ruger Model 77/22 bolt-action .22 Long Rifle. To me, it was — and still is — a very serious piece of gear. As Dad told me, "It's built just like a big-game rifle, but scaled down. Safety is in the same place, sights are just like the bigger Ruger rifles, and we can easily scope it." Having a rimfire rifle built in the manner of a deer rifle, or even one suitable for dangerous game, would prove very important to me later in life.

Now, I feel that every hunter, old or young, should own at least one good .22 Long Rifle — it's one of the handiest cartridges ever developed, and that rifle has been the only .22 I've owned, because it serves every purpose I've ever asked it to. That rifle has taught me an awful lot

about shooting mechanics, about the way a barrel can behave with various types of ammunition, about trigger control, and about so much more. While there are many different makes and models available — including Ruger's fantastic 10/22, which Grumpy Pants loves — the 77/22 represents everything I want in a rimfire rifle: accuracy, reliability and consistency.

FINDING A FRIEND

My own rifle is in a blued steel/walnut stock configuration, and like the Ruger Model 77, features the integral scope mounts that connect directly to the receiver; 1-inch rings are provided with the rifle. It uses a 10-shot rotary magazine — interchangeable with the 10/22 yet of slightly different dimension in order to mount flush to the stock — that has proved to be very durable over the past 3 decades.

A steel receiver is mated to a 20-inch barrel, complemented by an adjustable, folding rear sight and a barrel band front sight topped with a fine brass bead. Its walnut stock — checkered at the forend and pistol grip — has a plastic grip cap and buttplate in addition to steel sling swivels. A three-position wing safety, identical to the Ruger 77 centerfires, is located at the rear right side of the receiver. A two-piece bolt with spring loaded ears — for proper loading and extraction — runs smoothly at a 90-degree bolt throw. There are two locking lugs just behind the joint in the bolt.

Its trigger, while non-adjustable, is smooth — there's a small amount of creep, but it breaks crisp enough to print accurately. Again, this little rifle has all the attributes of a big game rifle, and for years it mated with my Ruger 77 in .308 Winchester for an effective one-two punch.

I've taken this rifle on enough memorable hunts that it means as much to me as my .404 Jeffery: It has taken coyote, fox, rabbits, squirrels and many more small game species. But, unlike big game, where the conformation of horns or antler comes flooding back to mind, it was the company on those hunts that come back to my mind when I pick the rifle up. Dad would take me in the back woods behind the house we lived in, and

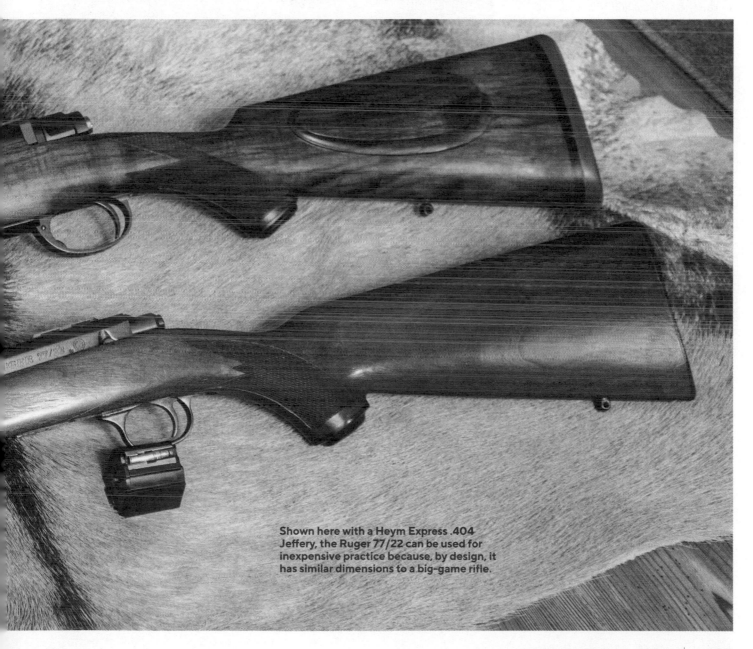

Shown here with a Heym Express .404 Jeffery, the Ruger 77/22 can be used for inexpensive practice because, by design, it has similar dimensions to a big-game rifle.

it was there that I learned how to snipe squirrels in the autumn. Dad insisted on head shots only, so I would practice my marksmanship at our backyard range. Ammunition was cheap then, even for a boy of 14 who only worked weekends. I learned how to properly adjust iron sights with this rifle, as well as sit down with my father to evaluate different brands and types of ammunition to see which performed best in this rifle.

As I got older and was able to join my relatives and friends on deer hunts, the little .22 saw less action, but I always made it a point to join my dad or maternal grandfather for squirrel and rabbit hunts. Those cold, sunny winter days were great fun: We could stalk cottontails as they came out of their holes to sun themselves, and I remember all the stories I'd hear about the Depression as we'd clean the rabbits. At the risk of getting overly nostalgic, this rifle is more than a rifle — it's a memory vault.

As time passed, the rifle became a companion in the truck. Dad's barn suffered the effects of the Great Red Squirrel invasion of 2010: holes were bore into doors and walls, soffits were chewed,

Chambered for the versatile .22 Long Rifle, the 77/22 can fulfill a variety of loads.

property destroyed, war declared. Those reds were reinforced by a battalion of chipmunks — invariably drawn in by the allure of chicken feed — so I called upon the 77/22 to repel boarders. It took nearly a box of Remington Thunderbolts before the enemy was eradicated, but I sure had fun with my rifle. It obtained its fair share of dings and scratches along the way, but was there when opportunity knocked.

The 77/22 uses a 10-shot rotary magazine very similar to the 10/22. Mags from a 77/22 and 10/22 can be interchanged, though they have slightly similar lower dimensions.

I had mounted a Leupold Vari-X 3 6.5-20x40mm AO riflescope for an article I was writing to evaluate accuracy of some Match ammunition, when one snowy afternoon at the office I heard Grumpy Pants holler, "coyote!" Dad and I are business partners, you see, and our land surveying office occupies the basement of his house, in a very rural location, replete with a 100-yard range just out the back door, and behind that is the woods.

The barrel band front sight of the 77/22 is complemented with a fine brass bead.

Ol' G.P. has both homing pigeons and chickens, and they are a constant magnet for predators, so when they're in season, there's a bounty on their heads. Time being of the essence, all I could get my hands on was the 77/22. I saw the coyote as it became aware of what I was up to and was desperately trying to make a hasty exit. I shouldered the rifle.

"Too far," announced G.P., but I pretended not to hear him. I broke the trigger once I had the holdover I wanted, and to even my surprise, the coyote hunched up hard and fell 15 yards later. The shot had been at a measured 158 yards, and while there may have been more than just a little luck involved, the 100-yard targets with that big scope onboard showed me just how accurate a good .22 can be at those distances.

THE GATEWAY CARTRIDGE

As Africa and I entered a committed relationship, the true big-bore rifles became some of my favorites. Shooting them at the range in preparation for a safari can become a challenging proposition, especially when at the bench doing load development. I'm not particularly recoil sensitive, but 30 rounds of .404 Jeffery, .416 Remington or .470 Nitro Express per session can take its toll on any shooter. Oddly enough, I make sure the little 77/22 comes along on each of the big bore sessions. In between groups of the big stuff, I take the time to keep my form proper by shooting a five-shot group with the .22LR; it has been a great help in avoiding the development of a flinch — primarily during bench work.

Additionally, when I'm working with the big iron-sighted guns such as my Heym 89B .470 double, shooting the 77/22 without a scope is an inexpensive and highly efficient means of training for an iron-sighted hunt. Sadly, the art of shooting an iron-sighted rifle is a fading discipline; while I'm a huge proponent of modern high-quality scopes, I do enjoy the close proximity of hunting with a well-stocked iron-sighted rifle. Using my 77/22 at 50 yards on small targets helps me train to stay focused and maintain the proper visual form, without spending $5-$10 per squeeze of the trigger. When it comes time to practice with the big-bore double or bolt gun, the prior work with the 77/22 makes the real deal much more effective.

I've also used a Bushnell Rimfire scope, with an elevation turret marked for the trajectory of a common .22 LR cartridge, as a training tool for shooters who were unaccustomed to dialing for elevation adjustments. I liked the concept from the minute I saw it; I set up a miniature backyard range from 25 to 150 yards with a number of hanging steel targets, and I set the rifle to zero at 25. I would then work with the shooter to identify the target and call the distance for them, have them dial for elevation adjustments and make the shot. It made a world of difference when they headed to the 1,000-yard range, and the exercise cost us very little money.

HERE TO STAY

The Ruger 77/22 has been available in a blued steel/walnut configuration (like my old friend), a stainless-steel/polymer stock configuration, and with a laminate stock, so there's plenty to choose from.

Additionally, it has been chambered in .22 WRM and .17 HMR for those who want a different rimfire experience.

Ruger has, over the years, temporarily discontinued certain models or chamberings, and the 77/22 is currently discontinued, with only the .22 Hornet chambering being available. While this is certainly not good news, I can say that a quick internet search on the common gun auction sites yielded a large number of 77/22 rifles for sale, in all three configurations, so those who would like add one to their collection will certainly have an opportunity to purchase one.

I will be the first to admit that the Ruger 10/22 platform is more popular than is the bolt-action version. However, owning a rifle with so many similar features of a common big game rifle — which you can practice with for pennies on a dollar and which will give a lifetime of hunting service — is definitely a good idea.

Everyone has a rifle that occupies a special place, especially those rifles of our youth. These are the guns that helped us cut our teeth and set us on a path that would — to one degree or another — change our lives. While I've been blessed enough to have spent time with a wide diversity of different rifles, from inexpensive to "she's-going-to-kill-me-for-buying-this," I reach for that little rimfire quite often, and I look forward to another 30 years of our relationship.

ZASTAVA'S M57 QUADRANGLE

Among the few copies of the Russian Tokarev semi-automatic pistol still in sporadic production is the Serbian-made M 57, which spawned two modified versions and two additional calibers

BY **GEORGE LAYMAN**

In spring 1972, *Gun Digest* editor John T. Amber was preparing an article that was to include Yugoslavian-made Zastava sporting rifles and shotguns. In a letter dated May 16, 1972, addressed to Zastava's chief export officer Cabric Miladin, Amber requested black-and-white glossies for use in the upcoming 27th Edition of *Gun Digest*. He also wished to know which autoloading pistols made by Zastava were not importable to the United States in accordance with the Gun Control Act of 1968.

This author never learned the outcome of the inquiry, having only been able to view a copy of the request by Amber for such information. However, I am certain the return letter must have stated that, at the time, none were on the eligibility list.

It wasn't until the end of the Cold War, circa 1991, that any of the Zastava-manufactured pistols made a showing in the U.S. firearms market.

When Yugoslavia's leader Marshal Josip Broz Tito broke off relations with Moscow in 1948, it signaled to Stalin that a united Yugoslavia wished to manage a self-styled communist state on its own terms. One such example of Tito's nationalism may clearly have been seen once Yugoslavia applied for the rights to produce a licensed copy of the Russian Tokarev pistol in mid–1956. Having attained warmer diplomatic relations with the Soviet Union under Premier Nikita Khrushchev, the state arms factory engineers of *Zavodi Crvena Zastava* (Factory Red Star) upon receiving the green flag, were likely making prepara-

The cover of the 1972 Crvena Zastava catalog received by Gun Digest editor John Amber in March of that year. The cover is adorned with an engraved M 70 pistol. From center-left clockwise: The 9mm M 88, 7.62x25mm M 57 (which started the cycle), 9mm M 70A, and at bottom the 62mm (.32 ACP) M 70 pistol.

In the same catalog the Pistols Mod 60 are shown in both 7.62 and 9mm calibers.

Your Ref.: Exp. SAN/MM
Your letter dated: March 13, 1972

May 16, 1972

Zavodi Crvena Zastava
Mr. Cabric Miladin, Ecc.
Chief of the Export Office
29, Novembra St., No. 12
11001 BEOGRAD, Yugoslavia

Dear Mr. Miladin:

Thank you for your March 13 letter and the several brochures.

We will indeed need good glossy black and white photographs if we are to picture Zastava firearms in our upcoming 27th edition. May I suggest that you send me two or three each of such photographs relating to your shotguns, rifles and pistols.

As for your autoloading pistols, please let me know whether any one of the models cannot be imported into the U.S. because of our 1968 Gun Control Act? In other words, if one or another of these Zastava pistols cannot be brought into the U.S., please let me know so that I may write about them accordingly.

Cordially,

John T. Amber
Editor

John Amber's letter to Zastava's export chief Cabric Miladin requesting photographs for use in the upcoming 1973 edition of the Gun Digest.

tions to modify a portion of the Russian-supplied tooling that would improve upon the existing design of the already 27-year-old Russian TT 33 Tokarev.

The result was a noticeably different variation of the Tokarev, which was adopted in 1957 and subsequently coined the Model of 1957, or simply the "*Pistolj M 57.*" Fielded and adopted in August of that year, the 7.62x25mm caliber M 57 may likely be considered in a class of its own as opposed to the standard Tokarev and other licensed copies because of

seven additional differences both physically and mechanically. The most obvious cosmetic deviations are the longer 15mm extended pistol grip, angled striations at the rear of the slide and a windage-adjustable front sight that sits in a dovetailed cut. Internally, the firing pin housing, unlike the exposed cross-pin retainer used on the standard Russian Tokarev and its clones, encompasses an enclosed, four-piece affair that is retained by a U-shaped retainer at the rear of the firing pin channel on the slide. In basic principle, it is like the Colt Model 1911. In addition, the M 57 used a longer recoil spring guide, which is exposed when the slide is locked to the rear.

Perhaps its most notable addition that differs from the original Russian model is the nine-shot magazine, hence the elongated grip. The eight-shot magazine of the standard Russian variant and the nine-round M 57 mag do not interchange. With a round in the chamber, it all adds up to a 10-shot semi-automatic pistol. The Yugoslavian M 57 is the only non-Russian quasi-Tokarev clone that is not stamped with plain digits for year of manufacture. In lieu of this, the serial number along with a letter prefix or a suffix (the latter used only on the second two years of production), allows one to be able to approximate the year of manufacture. An example of this is

shown below. Keep in mind that beginning in 1959, the letter/year prefix has an overlap with each succeeding year.

1957 – No letter prefix on first-year production guns
1958 – A
1959 – A & B (A and B years were used as a suffix following the serial number)
1960 – B&C
1961 – C&D
1962 – D& E
1963 – E & F
1964 – F&G
1965 – G& H
The I through P prefix continue to 1974

Actual full-scale military production slowed to a trickle in 1974 at the P prefix, thus pistols for the army were produced on an "as required" basis for the next 13 years, right through to the end of production in 1992. In late 1962, serial numbers on the M 57 beginning with the E prefix from 1962 to 1963 have a break that resumes the serial number sequence at 10,000. This convoluted anomaly cannot be explained. According to Zastava's Old Foundry Museum curator, Marija Susic, Zastava production records of the M 57 prior to 30 years ago are completely unavailable.

The above partial listing is shown for basic reference, however current factory sources do list 1992 as the final year of manufacture for the Serbian military. Numbers observed thus far end at slightly over the quarter of a million range, however it is believed the actual number exceeds this. It is interesting to note that up to this time, I have yet to observe any pistols with a Q (1975) through Z (1992) prefix.

Military-issue M 57 pistols were stamped on the upper slide with a highly detailed crest commemorating the November 1943 counsel at Jacje, which proclaimed the socialist republic of Yugoslavia. There are two types, however, with either a five- or six-flame torch. The five-flame torch representing Yugoslavia's five ethnic groups was stamped on pistols made from 1957 to 1963–64, when it was then changed to a six-flame torch representing the country's six republics.

When examined closely, there may be two or more stylized details and differences of the latter crest on certain pistols. I was told by Zastava factory historians that some of the original dies of the six-flame torch crest had cracked on one or more occasions and had to be re-cut and engraved, and there were several

Left- and right-side views of the originally configured Zastava M 57 or TETEJAC, adopted by Tito's Yugoslavian military in 1957. Extensively modified from the original Russian TT33, the M 57 is a Tokarev in a class of its own. Hence it went on to spawn three modifications both in size, caliber and design. The three cartridges of the M 57 and its redesigned offspring: from left, the original 7.62x25mm Tokarev; 9mm Luger, which was used in both the M70A and M88; and the 7.65mm (.32ACP), chambered in the smallest of the group, the M 70.

sub-factories within the Zastava arms plant building the M 57. This explains the differences in serial number font styles on pistols produced up to 1974. In addition, the hard rubber grips with a star on pre–1963 pistols have the letters FNRJ, which indicate Federal National Republic of Jugoslavia. After that year, grips were marked SFRJ for Socialist Federal Republic Jugoslavia, when the government changed its national designation.

The M 57 is, and was, affectionately known throughout the Balkans as the "TETEJAC" (pronounced Tay tay yahk), abbreviated as "the tough TulskiyeTokarev." The state-owned Zastava factory is privatized up to a point as it is still funded largely by the Serbian government and produced most regional military arms both in communist times and the present. Manufacture of the M 57 for the commercial market is believed to have begun in 1960 — a marketing feat other communist bloc countries did not undertake. Though it is unknown for certain, M 57 pistols produced for the commercial/civilian market were once thought to have an indigenous serial number range also indicated with the "C" prefix. In-depth research reveals there is only one set of continuous running numbers for both military and civilian variations since production began.

Regarding the military versions, some pistols from 1957 to 1964 have a part number marking on the right frame, slide, trigger and inner hammer assembly flat. Since there were four different plants within the Zastava complex that were building the M 57, it is believed that some of these facilities marked major components with a series of digits — 2-00.01 etc. — a stylized marking that was a blueprint or witness mark indicating a part number. In addition, an inspector mark of BK in a box, which is a Cyrillic "VK," will be found stamped on many early M 57 pistols. This stands for "Vojna Kontrollya," which translates to "military control," and indicates the pistol was inspected by a military ordnance inspector.

Regressing to those pistols intended for the commercial trade, it is very odd that a 1972 catalog received by John Amber lists the civilian 7.62x25mm M 57 as the Pistol Model 60, a term not used in present factory literature. As we shall later see, early production commercial pistols in 9mm Luger were also coined the M 60; however, exactly when this term was dropped in the communist era by Zavodi Crvena Zastava Arms is

not known. Since the "C" prefix was also used on the 1960–61 serial-numbered military M 57 production, the sole method to distinguish the two is the supposed absence of the national crest on the commercial models, a fact yet to be written in stone.

> **TO IDENTIFY A TRUE COMMERCIAL VERSION, LOOK FOR THE OVAL TRADE-MARK, THE "ZASTAVA STAG HORN" CARTOUCHE SIDED WITH A "B1B" MARKING LOCATED TO THE LOWER-RIGHT OVER THE CHAMBER — A MARK NOT PRESENT ON MILITARY VARIATIONS.**

It is quite ironic that several civilian and commercial variants have been discovered stamped with the Yugoslavian communist crest. I own such an example with a post-1964-type six-torch crest and the civilian "C" prefix, and a low five-digit serial number of 25,600. During the military production years, those with the letter "C" serial prefix would have been made at the time of the five-flame torch, thus such a marking is indeed peculiar on a supposed commercial variation having a 1960–61-era serial number. To identify a true commercial version, look for the oval trademark, the "Zastava Stag Horn" cartouche sided with a "B1B" marking located to the lower-right over the chamber — a mark not present on military variations.

The military surplus versions of the M 57 began being imported to our shores in the mid–2000s, advertised as the M 57A. The "A" suffix indicates they had been modified for the U.S. surplus market by the addition of a trigger-block thumb safety located at the rear-left frame. This was demanded by law for any and all pistols of Tokarev design slated for import into the United States. It is odd that the current Zastava Arms catalog does indeed list the legal U.S. import versions as the M 57A. The slide markings however display merely M 57 minus the "A" on all observed thus far. About 10 years following adoption of the M 57 by Yugoslavia, a half-size modified "clone of a clone" was soon to follow.

THE M 70 PISTOL

In 1967, Zastava engineers took the basic M 57 design and introduced something never manufactured by a licensee of the Russian TT 33, a scaled-down, mini Tokarev. An engraved example was

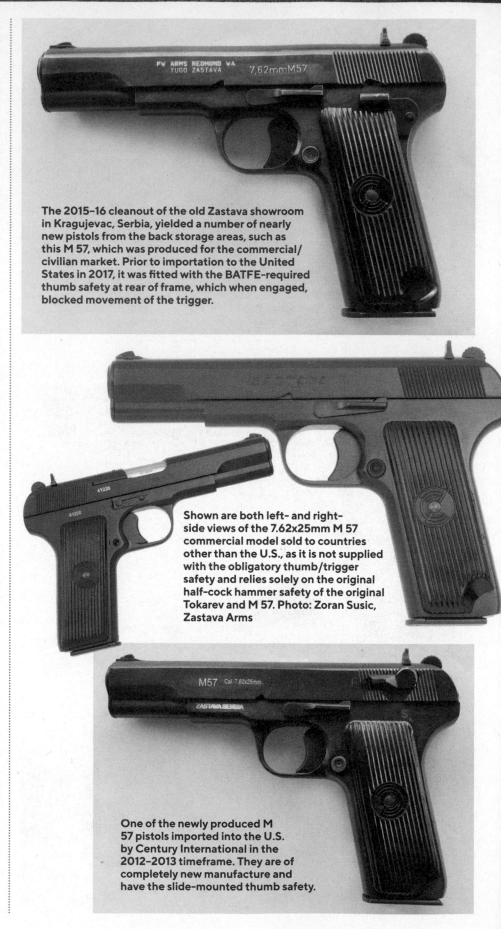

The 2015–16 cleanout of the old Zastava showroom in Kragujevac, Serbia, yielded a number of nearly new pistols from the back storage areas, such as this M 57, which was produced for the commercial/civilian market. Prior to importation to the United States in 2017, it was fitted with the BATFE-required thumb safety at rear of frame, which when engaged, blocked movement of the trigger.

Shown are both left- and right-side views of the 7.62x25mm M 57 commercial model sold to countries other than the U.S., as it is not supplied with the obligatory thumb/trigger safety and relies solely on the original half-cock hammer safety of the original Tokarev and M 57. Photo: Zoran Susic, Zastava Arms

One of the newly produced M 57 pistols imported into the U.S. by Century International in the 2012–2013 timeframe. They are of completely new manufacture and have the slide-mounted thumb safety.

The new production Model 70A in 9mm Parabellum from the 2010s, with slide-mounted safety has an "A" suffix, a necessity as, without it, it would spawn confusion in regard to the more diminutive 7.65mm M 70. Photo: Milos Popovic, Zastava Arms

Among the surprises in Zastava's disposal of inventory from the old showroom was this chromium-plated M 57 that carries a "C" prefix and a six-digit serial number. Its estimated year of production is in the 1965 to 1966 time frame. Still in the original box, it remains in near excellent condition. Slightly more than two dozen identical pistols were reportedly found and imported by PW Arms of Redmond, Washington. Photo: Jude Steele Collection

Though not part of the old showroom inventory disposal, this Exclusive version of the M 88 is part of the current Zastava line. The breathtaking workmanship and finely sculpted and carved walnut grips, together with highly embellished engraving with numerous gold inlays and flower patterns in the European style show just how far Zastava will go to fulfill a customer's wishes. Photo: Zastava Arms

illustrated on the cover of the catalog received by John T. Amber in 1972. In Russia and Eastern European countries, the Zastava M 70 is occasionally referred to as the Zastava M 67/70 simply because it was first introduced in 1967, incorporating the identical M 57 short-recoil system internals. However, by 1970 modifications were soon forthcoming, thus it was redesigned to become the *Pistolj M 70*. Chambered for the 7.65mm Browning, or .32 ACP, it was a major deviation from the larger M 57, aside from being scaled down in size and dispensing with the slide-latch retainer on the right frame. Aside from a period during the Balkan wars of the 1990s when the Zastava factory was once bombed by NATO, production has continued steadily since its introduction.

Details on the background of the Zastava M 70 are elusive at best, but its primary objective was to provide military officers — and perhaps civilian communist *apparatchiks* — with a compact, and handy semi-automatic sidearm. As noted, it originally incorporated a short-recoil locked Tokarev-style system when first manufactured in 1967, but due to the low energy of the .32 ACP cartridge, it was an unnecessary feature. Thus, the M 70 modified to a blowback action was not only simpler, but production-wise was far more cost-effective.

Its greatest enigma is that the 1972 Zavodi Crvena Zastava catalog and other factory literature has it listed as also available in 9mm Kretek or .380 ACP. Upon querying several European collectors who knew of none in circulation, and myself having never observed a single example in .380 ACP, we shall forego any further comment on that version as nothing seems available to discuss on its behalf.

When the great post–Cold War surplus import boom began in the early 1990s the M 70, like its full-size relative the M 57, began arriving on our shores some eight to nine years after the "party" was over, not to mention the end of the decade-plus period of the Yugoslav wars. Unlike many other surplus Com Bloc pistols, the M 70 was at first imported in limited numbers, with quantities suddenly showing up once again mid–2017. Unlike other former communist pistols of Tokarev design, the M 70 doesn't require the addition of an aftermarket safety to enter the U.S. as it was originally equipped with a rotating trigger-block safety. It appears that PW Arms of Redmond, Washington may originally

have been the sole importer of the M 70 in the 2000s, however the most recent arrivals in 2017, surprisingly, were all of a sudden brought into the United States by R Guns of Carpentersville, Illinois, which is believed to be leftover 1970's and '80's stock following Zastava's cleanout of unsold military surplus inventory that began in 2015.

These views of the 7.65mm M 70 semi-automatic pistol show how the M 57 influenced its design. Earlier versions produced in 1967 used the short-recoil system, however three years later it was changed to a blowback. Serial-number prefixes begin on the M 70 with "A" in 1970. This example with an "I" prefix indicates manufacture in 1979. With the action open, the barrel remains stationary. Note the absence of the slide–latch retainer on the right frame, as disassembly of the M 70 begins at the muzzle, similar to that of a Model 1911. Marked with the old communist Crvena Zastava markings on the slide, it is one of the earliest that came out of the old Zastava showroom sometime around 2009, and was imported by PW Arms in limited numbers. This pistol is among three that were imported in the original box with its instruction booklet written, of course, in Serbian. An imported M 70 complete with box is a rare find indeed. The pistol is from the Jude Steele Collection.

Today, current production of the M 70 for sale to the European and Canadian markets has the left slide marked "Zastava Arms, Kragujevac, Serbia." Original communist-era variants, such as those first imported by PW Arms and the second wave from R Guns in 2017, are marked Crvena Zastava (Red Star) on the left-slide flat.

Known users of the M 70 during the Balkan Wars were the former Serbian President Slobodan Milosevic, who was charged with war crimes after the conflict, and Zeljko "Arkan" Raznatovic, leader of a Serbian paramilitary group known as the Tigers. In the old Soviet Union and several Eastern European countries during the Cold War, the M 70 was unofficially coined the "Yovanovitch," which is actually a rare Serbian pistol made in the early 1930s. What the connection is to the M 70 is unknown.

Affectionately nicknamed in Serbia as the "*Pcelica*" (little bee), the Zastava 7.65mm M 70 pistol's official designation should not be confused with the next offshoot of the original M 57 design.

THE M70 A

A true enigma of the Zastava M 57 quadrangle is the 9mm Luger-chambered M 70A. Aside from slide markings, and of course the chambering, it is a dead ringer for the M 57, and not surprisingly the renamed M 70A, originally catalogued the *Pistolj Mod 60* (as listed in John Amber's catalog) received an instant welcome about 2009–2010 when the first are believed to have arrived in the United States. It wasn't until almost 15 years after the Cold War that the M 70A was available in the United States, but for years earlier sold well in Europe and elsewhere.

American Arms imported an unknown quantity of the 9mm Luger M70A pistols sometime in the 2004–06 period, but details on it are sketchy at best. Most importantly, it once more deserves to be mentioned that from the earlier 1960s through the '80s Zastava catalogs continued to list both the civilian version of the 7.62x25 and 9mm variation as the Model 60. It's important to note that though both calibers of the M 60 were catalogued with identical nomenclature, only the 9mm version had its slide stamped as such. The 7.62mm versions were still being marked M 57 on the left slide flat. This enigma defies explanation.

According to Vinicje Ivanovics, a former Zastava employee, the M 60 began production for the commercial Eastern European market in late 1960 in both calibers, and by 1965 limited sales of those chambered in 9mm to countries in Western Europe soon commenced. I was very fortunate to have learned this directly from Mr. Ivanovics as, again, there are no remaining factory records regarding the M 57 and its clones prior to 1988. In any case, this updated full-size 9mm copy of the M 57 has been carried by various U.S. distributors, but appears to have sold out by mid–2018. Many American shooters prefer it due to its easy-to-obtain 9mm caliber, a gun shop staple.

There is a point here that should be addressed concerning its correct nomenclature. The current online Zastava Arms catalog lists it as the Model 70A for the non-U.S. market, but catalogs it as the M 70AA for those destined for export to the United States. Pistols sold outside

European American Armory (EAA) imported the first examples of newly manufactured M 88A pistols in 2008–09 and aside from the omission of the communist-era Zavodi Crvena Zastava markings on the left slide, were supplied with black polymer grips that ergonomically molded to the hands much firmer than the plain wooden grips of the original version. When the EAA supply had been exhausted, Century International imported another batch in the 2012–2013 period, which are still plentiful from some arms distributors. Photo: Zastava Arms

(above and left) The 9mm Zastava M 88 was intended to permanently replace the older 7.62 M 57 pistol in 1989, but would be replaced within two years by the more modern, double-action, high-capacity CZ 99. The M 88 was a single-action semi-auto pistol with a magazine capacity of eight rounds, a design that was practically obsolete. A scaled-down copy of the M 57, its compact size is highly concealable, and it's mechanically identical to the basic Tokarev design. Shown is a left-side view of the author's EAA-imported M 88A which, for reasons unknown, arrived in the U.S. with the original birch or walnut grips and the ZCZ medallion on the base of the left grip. Shown also is a right-side view of a captured M 88 confiscated from one of the Serbian militia groups and is tagged as being slated for destruction by the UN. Photo: Department of Defense/U.S. Army Public Affairs Office

the USA don't require the additional safety equipment. As confusing as this terminology is, the term "Model 70 AA" is never physically seen marked on the pistol, nor mentioned by American distributors, wholesalers or dealers in U.S. catalog descriptions. The Zastava-made pistols with the added BATF required safety are marked solely "M70A" on the left slide, and again, none are imported or marked with the M 70 double-A logo. It is evident Zastava is aware of this, and lists the correct nomenclature in its factory literature, whereas American importers do not. They are sold on the U.S. market as simply the Model 70 A, period!

Zastava also introduced a completely new post–Cold War commercial version of the M 57A in 7.62x25mm along with the 9mm M 70A commencing importation to the United States about the same time. They were apparently manufactured in batches, solely intended for import to this country. Their major, upgraded internal difference is that the once-mandatory frame-mounted trigger safety of the older surplus M 57 has been modified for both pistols with a far more "un-Tokarev-like" slide-mounted, thumb-operated, firing pin block/trigger-block safety machined into the left-rear finger groove of the slide striation. When the latch is pushed downward, the reverse square U-shaped rear retainer traverses 45 degrees forward, acts as a trigger stop and prevents hammer-to-firing pin contact. Incidentally the circular grip logo on the new production pistols have the original Zastava trademark of ZCZ, in lieu of the older communist star of the republic and lettered abbreviation. The new pistols in both calibers are said to have been produced to the estimated tune of about 8,000. Both had been steady sellers since their introduction; however, it is unknown if and when another manufacturing run of both pistols will take place.

THE M 88A

By the late 1980s, a soon-to-disintegrate Socialist Federal Republic of Jugoslavia was searching for a replacement of the 30-plus-year-old Tokarev M 57. In 1987, the Ministry of Defense decided on a newly designed pistol that, ironically, was a scaled-down copy of the Tokarev but in 9mm Parabellum caliber. Upon acceptance, it was christened the *Pistolj M 88*. It was of course built toward the end of communist times by the Zavodi Crvena Zastava factory. The first time

I had ever examined a genuine Crvena Zastava M 88 was in Bosnia in 2000 while on temporary duty working for a U.S. Government contractor.

I observed many of these pistols, most having been tagged by UN forces and piled up awaiting destruction as many were turned in from the recently defunct Kosovo Liberation Army, and other hostile factions when the majority of the Balkan Wars were grinding to a halt. Apparently a popular pistol with police and paramilitary forces during the height of the 1990's conflicts, the eight-shot M 88 pistol is a neat little compact example of a small-framed Tokarev with a few cosmetic modifications. Its adoption took place not long before the breakup of the Yugoslav republics. Overall, the handy, very concealable M 88, unlike the much smaller, M 57-inspired .32-caliber blowback M 70, retains the short-recoil action Tokarev internals and is about the size of one of the Spanish-made small-frame, semi-automatic pistols from Star.

The M 88 didn't enjoy a long service life and was replaced about 1991 by the higher-capacity, double-action Zastava CZ 99. At the present time, the M 88 is still used for training purposes in the Serbian army and remains in use with some modern-day Balkan police forces. It is also used as a second line military pistol in both Slovenia, Macedonia, and other countries in the region, including Moldavia and Hungary. Limited numbers of the first U.S. import versions of the M 88 were introduced to American shooters about 2004–2005 and were primarily brought in by SARCO Distributors, which at the time was located in Stirling, New Jersey. These were the genuine, original production pistols with the left slide marked *Zavodi Crvena Zastava* (Factory Red Star) and were equipped with the original-type stained wooden grips and ZCZ medallion. Some early import pistols slipped into the U.S. and were not equipped with the required left slide-mounted thumb-operated safety, which blocks both trigger and hammer contact with firing pin.

The next showing of the M 88 was around 2009 when European American Armory (EAA) in Rockledge, Florida brought newly manufactured Zastava M 88A models into the U.S. for about three years until inventories had depleted. In regard to the original Zastava-made M 88 Serbian military and police versions, the primary differences between them and the later imported M 88A, (the A in this case indicating a U.S. export version with

the slide safety) were new, previously unseen, ergonomic-styled black polymer grip models. In an odd twist, in 2009 I purchased one of the earliest of the EAA M 88A imported pistols and quite mysteriously it came supplied with the older wood grips of the 1980s-production M 88, complete with the Zastava medallion. Having yet to observe another EAA imported example with this anomaly, it may be among a very small number that arrived as such.

The next shipments of the M 88A to arrive were those manufactured in 2012–13 and were imported by Century International. The M 88/88A is perhaps one of the most underrated 9mm Parabellum pistols, with some complaining of trigger pull, and others who felt it was nothing more than just a low-cost 9mm mini Tokarev with little new to offer. Inventories of these from Southern Ohio Gun Distributors were depleted as of mid–2018. Prices for the new production M 88A were in the low $200 range and it was a high-quality pistol that was very economical and quite sturdy.

In a sudden twist of fortune, early 2018 also saw a limited lot of genuine Yugoslavian/ Serbian-surplus Zastava M 88 pistols imported into the United States. As of this writing they are still available from Classic Arms and are equipped with both wooden and polymer grips, to include the obligatory import slide safety. The ammunition that I regularly use for my own M 88A pistols is the 115-grain round-nosed Czech-made Sellier & Bellot, and Russian steel-cased Tulammo, both of which provide satisfactory performance.

> **THE ALL-STEEL ZASTAVA ARMS M 88A CERTAINLY DEMONSTRATES HOW FAR THE FIRM HAS TAKEN AN OLDER-DESIGNED SEMI-AUTOMATIC AND TRANSFORMED IT INTO A SUPERBLY COMPACT PISTOL, AND ANOTHER VARIANT AT THAT IN 9MM PARABELLUM.**

Noteworthy is the M 88A disassembles for cleaning identically to the full-size M 57 in typical Tokarev fashion. I have found this very slender and comfortable pistol to be a superb concealed-carry handgun, and again, coupled with a very attractive price tag and high-quality blue finish, can honestly say I consider it the hands-down favorite among my 9mm Parabellum collection of semi-automatic

Shown with the Vojvodina Territorial Defense patch, both the 9mm M 88 (top) and the original 7.62x25 M 57 were significant participants in the decade-plus Balkan conflicts from the war in Kosovo to the Croatian civil war. Along with the much smaller 7.65mm M 70, all are still in use in some capacity in all six of the former Yugoslavian republics when this article was written.

pistols. Though practically the entire import inventory may soon be expended, they are regularly available on several auction websites. The all-steel Zastava Arms M 88A certainly demonstrates how far the firm has taken an older-designed semi-automatic and transformed it into a superbly compact pistol, and another variant at that in 9mm Parabellum.

ZASTAVA LUXURY AND EXCLUSIVE PISTOLS

Listed in the current Zastava catalog are variations of Zastava's M 57 quadrangle of pistols in what have been coined as "Lux" or "Exc" versions. The acronyms simply indicate Luxury or Exclusive. Interestingly, once again, unlike any other former communist country

that manufactured the Tokarev pistol, Yugoslavia was the sole nation that for decades offered them commercially either plain, or with highly embellished special-order finishes. Zastava is now located in an independent Serbia. The early Zastava factory literature received by John Amber in 1972 listed these options for either the 7.62x25mm or 9mm in its M 57 and M 70 pistols.

The Lux-grade variations indicate pistols that, to this day, may be ordered with chromium-plated finish, with a choice of custom or walnut grips. The "Exc" grade is available with "... pistols richly engraved by hand with blued or chromium finish with a choice of fine checkered or inlaid walnut grips ..." The 1972 catalog illustrates an engraved M 70 on the cover, displaying on page 8 both an engraved M 70 and "Mod 60" with blue finishes, the latter supplied with. "... handmade walnut sheaths (sic) of the best quality ..."

It was only in the last two years that I had the opportunity to observe three of the Exc copies being offered for sale in the United States, and purchased a Lux-grade M 57 that was chromium plated.

I spoke with Milos Popovic of Zastava in early summer 2017, and as earlier mentioned, was told that after Zastava Arms had in the recent past cleaned out its old showroom had uncovered some 300 pistols of both M 57 and M 70 type that remained unsold since the 1960s to early 1970s. That in addition to surplus components that were assembled into complete pistols and imported.

Needing to make room for new products, it appears that Zastava's export division sold much of the new, used and even shopworn salesman's samples to importers PW Arms of Redmond, Washington and R Guns of Carpentersville, Illinois, which purchased much of the inventory including both civilian surplus and unsold military stock. It wasn't until late 2017 that it began to be cleared for import to the United States. The big surprises were the appearance of perhaps a few dozen or more of both Lux- and Exc-grade M 57 pistols to include a few hundred plain-blue versions of both M 57 and M 70 pistols as well. The limited number of hand-engraved variants all appeared to be one of a kind, with at least two-dozen plus of the chromium-plated

(left and bottom)The ancestor of the Zastava Quadrangle, the M 57 in its original 7.62 Tokarev chambering remains the kingpin of its offspring and is still a handful of power that provides accuracy up to 60 yards. Used with original Czech, Bulgarian and Polish Cold War military surplus ammunition, it produces an impressive muzzle flash that turns heads at most pistol ranges. Using both commercial Sellier & Bellot and 1951 vintage Cold War Bulgarian ammunition, there was a marked difference in accuracy. In a combined shoot with a single silhouette target, the older Bulgarian fodder spread out in a buckshot pattern. The 8, 9 and 10 rings are the results of new S&B ammunition. At 12 yards the latter had practically cut the red out of the picture. Shawn Kelly Photos

Lux versions imported. All the engraved or plain chromium-finished pistols show slight storage wear such as light crazing or rust flaking from years of temperature change, and lack of lubrication or storage maintenance. But for the most part, all appeared in superb condition.

A large quantity of the plain blue M 57 pistols was sold with the "C" or civilian/commercial prefix before the serial numbers, with some oddly having the crest of the republic stamped on the slide. It is believed that many of the stored leftover, military-marked showroom pistols may have been intended for a Yugoslavian government sale that never came to fruition. In any case, they are some of the finest-condition M 57 pistols offered on the U.S. surplus market and most had quickly sold out from distributors by late winter 2017. Many however are still available on an individual basis from online auction sites.

For shooters, collectors, or those with a general interest in Com Bloc pistols, there is no doubt that Zastava Arms has proven to be a most innovative manufacturer. It has created an additional three separate pistols and two different calibers out of the basic, redesigned M 57 variant of the Russian Tokarev TT 33, transforming them into new configurations of the original Tokarev. Remarkably, these are true modifications of models that were already modified, and were kept in the traditional design of the basic concept of Fedor Tokarev's offspring dating back to the early 1930s. All of this speaks volumes about why the Zastava quadrangle has come to be — and endures today among shooters and gun collectors.

THE .700 HOLLAND & HOLLAND NITRO EXPRESS

How one hunter's dream rifle became a reality

BY **JOE COOGAN**

If you ever hunt in Africa, boys, keep a big gun next to you, for it will prevent your friends from remarking, "How natural he looks!"

— John T. Hoover
Outdoor Life
July 1924

Beverly Hills businessman William Feldstein wanted another rifle. He didn't need one, for he already had an eye-popping collection of best-quality double rifles. But of the many rifles he owned, all had been made at earlier times and for other people. So when he approached Holland & Holland in London, check in hand, to order a .600 Nitro Express, the famed gun maker answered Feldstein's request with an unequivocal no.

Not taking "no" for an answer, Feldstein responded with, "Well, if you won't build me a .600, how about a .700?" They thought the silly Yank had lost his mind, wanting to order a Hollands' rifle in a nonexistent caliber. A mirthful outburst erupted from the showroom floor at Feldstein's audacity.

Feldstein's fascination with guns began early. As a youngster he discovered the writings of the early African explorers. Men like Sir Samuel Baker, William Cornwallis Harris and of course Henry Stanley and David Livingston fueled his interest in Africa, and ultimately in big-bore rifles. Reading of their exploits sparked a desire in Feldstein to follow in their footsteps through darkest Africa. He dreamed of one day going there to face the same odds with the same rifles they had carried, and upon which their lives had depended.

When Holland & Holland completed the .700 NE Royal de Luxe, the 18-pound, side-lock-actioned rifle sports 26-inch barrels, the finest deluxe-grade walnut wood and exquisitely ornate engraving masterfully executed by the renowned Brown brothers of Swindon, England.

Finally realizing his lifelong dream, Feldstein journeyed to East Africa with his family on a couple of photo safaris in the early 1970s. These introductory adventures merely stoked the fire of his desire to see more of Africa and to get to know the Dark Continent more intimately. He knew this would mean leaving "the beaten path" for wilder parts of Africa where having a gun in hand was not only recommended, but essential.

Feldstein's first hunting safari happened in 1975 with famed elephant hunter Wally Johnson. It took place in Botswana's Okavango Delta, and for the purposes of that safari Feldstein carried a couple of Winchester magazine rifles — the largest caliber being a .375 Holland & Holland (H&H) Magnum. He hunted buffalo and elephant for the first time and when that safari finished, Feldstein knew he would return to Africa with guns again.

His next safari, also in Botswana, was with Brian Marsh, and for that hunt Feldstein carried a double-barreled, blackpowder 8-bore rifle weighing 17 pounds, and firing conical lead bullets. His aim, as far as practically possible, was to seek similar adventures to those experienced by the Victorian hunter/explorers. On that memorable hunt, he bagged two buffalo bulls with his Charles Osborne 8-bore double — one with an offhand shot. Later, during another safari, he shot two elephants, one with the same 8-bore and one with a 4-bore by Daniel Fraser.

Feldstein began to seek out ever-more

Beverly Hills businessman William Feldstein, featured here in an R.M. McPhale oil painting, was fascinated with guns and hunting from an early age. He began hunting Africa during the mid-1970s, which led to his interest in collecting fine-quality double rifles. In 1985, he initiated the research and development of the .700 NE for the London gun company, Holland & Holland.

Feldstein collected Africana over the years, eventually amassing nearly 400 works of the early explorers. This notable collection of fine books covered a period of African exploration that spanned from the 1800s all the way through to the 1950s. His primary interest lay with the Victorian era of African exploration and he was particularly drawn to the big-bore, blackpowder cartridge rifles used by the men of that period.

Comparing the .700 H&H (left) to these other cartridges: From left: .600 NE, .500 NE, .458 Lott, .416 Rigby, .404 Jeffery and the .30-06 Springfield.

remote and primitive areas of Africa, in which, to "bloody" his rifles, settling on Ethiopia as the ultimate area with the best chances of producing a 100-pound tusker (an elephant old enough and big enough to carry tusks weighing 100 pounds or more, each side). He did four

foot safaris with PH Nassos Russos, solely for big tuskers, emulating the early ivory hunters, mostly using .577 and .600 NEs. Feldstein collected several tuskers, including one that met the 100-pound goal he'd set for himself. Although the tusk weights registered at 100 and 104

lbs., more than sufficient to secure a place in the record books, Feldstein was uninterested in the acclaim coming from the inclusion of his name on a list of records; he hunted purely for the challenge, and his love of Africa — and big-bore rifles.

Holland & Holland completed the first .700 H&H rifle in 1989, establishing it as the most powerful sporting firearm in the world. For the recoil to be manageable, the exquisitely engraved rifle weighs around 18 pounds. As this was being written, the 18th rifle was in production at Holland & Holland's London factory.

> **"MOST MEN WHO PURCHASE ENGLISH BEST DOUBLE RIFLES DO NOT HUNT WITH THEM BECAUSE OF THEIR VALUE. I BELIEVE TO THE CONTRARY. THEY ARE STILL A KILLING WEAPON. MEN HAVE DEVOTED 1,400 TO 1,500 HOURS OF THEIR TIME...IS IT NOT OUR RE-SPONSIBILITY AS A TRIBUTE TO THEIR ARTISTRY TO TAKE THE RIFLES INTO THE FIELD AND USE THEM FOR WHAT THEY WERE BUILT FOR?"**
> — WILLIAM FELDSTEIN

By 1985, with the experience of several safaris in different parts of Africa, Feldstein had developed an affinity for British big-bore Nitro-Express doubles, and had begun collecting them in earnest. His philosophy about the artistry and function of fine double rifles was best summed up in a letter he wrote to Walter Eder, a German friend with whom he'd shared several safaris; "Most men who purchase English best double rifles do not hunt with them because of their value. I believe to the contrary. They are still a killing weapon. Men have devoted 1,400 to 1,500 hours of their time...is it not our responsibility as a tribute to their artistry to take the rifles into the field and use them for what they were built for?"

Feldstein's rifle collection increased to an impressive number by any standard, including 15 blackpowder doubles in 12-, 10-, 8- and 4-bore, and 55 British Nitro Express (NE) doubles, six of them .600s, seven .577s, eight .500s, several .450s as well as many medium-bore and small-bore rifles. He also bought up more than 10,000 Nitro-Express cartridges and used most of the rifles he owned on safari.

Up to 1985, Feldstein's collection consisted of rifles all made "back in the day." That year, he decided he wanted a bespoke British ultra-large bore Nitro-Express double, tailor-made to his personal specifications. He decided on a .600 NE, and he wanted it made by Holland & Holland in Royal grade. So he went to Holland & Holland's prestigious shop in London to place his order and be

A disassembled .700 H&H is displayed in its three main components; the barrels, fore-end and side-lock action and buttstock next to a boxed set of three .700 H&H NE cartridges. Feldstein's initial order of 5,000 rounds of the behemoth cartridge was criticized by denigrators of the .700 project, but the entire lot sold within 18 months — mostly to cartridge collectors for $100 apiece.

measured for his first new double.

David Winks, the showroom manager at the time, explained to Feldstein that they could not entertain his request, as their directors had earlier made the decision to build H&H's very last .600 NE, and having built it in 1975, had announced and certified the rifle as such, which much enhanced its collector's value, and they felt they could not go back on their word to its owner. They had also made the decision to build their last .577 NE. Feldstein then had a meeting with the entire board of directors. They took exception to his suggestion that they were wrong in their decision to make the last .600 and .577, and refused to budge on this.

Feldstein accepted the board's decision, but he was still determined in his pursuit of an ultra-large-bore Holland. So, with his customary nonchalance he suggested, "OK, then build me a .700 NE." When the laughter and mirth abated, the board calmly explained the many reasons why they would be hesitant to even consider his .700 order request.

At the time, the safari market was scaling down because of political problems in several newly independent Africa countries, as well as the effects of increasingly negative attitudes toward trophy hunting taking place worldwide. Consequently, companies such as Kynoch had ceased making center-fire rifle ammunition for doubles and the gun companies creating them were trimming back as well.

Hollands eventually agreed to hear Feldstein's proposal, but they were extremely wary undertaking a scheme they considered to be somewhat impulsive and stipulated conditions which would have proved daunting to a man of lesser means and determination. The design and development of the cartridge, and its provision in sufficient numbers to permit regulation of the barrels, was to be Feldstein's responsibility. Furthermore, the prototype barrels would have to be made at his expense.

H&H could hardly be blamed for being cautious about taking on a double-rifle project involving a completely original, ultra-large-bore cartridge. The .700 would not be based on any known cartridge case, and with no precedent for pressures and recoil energy, they could not be sure it was even feasible. Holland's reply to Feldstein came down to, "Design the cartridge, give us the specs and we'll talk again."

To begin the cartridge research, Feldstein elicited Jim Bell's services.

In 1986, Bell, then president of Brass Extrusion Laboratories Ltd. (B.E.L.L.), and Feldstein drew up plans for an original cartridge design, meaning it was not based on altering the caliber or the configuration of an already existing cartridge. Although Feldstein was a fan of the .600 NE, he realized the blunt shape of the 900-grain bullet was not as effective a penetrator as the more streamline shape of the .577 bullet. So, he decided the .700's bullet should be shaped like the .577.

The .700's case is based on an upscale version of the .600 NE case, but at the same time it's a totally new case of larger diameter. It's also longer by a full half-inch than the .600 case. At the end of their research, Feldstein and Bell had designed a cartridge using a 3 1/2-inch case that accommodates a 1,000-grain, .700-caliber bullet. The loaded case and bullet measure a little more than 4 inches in total length.

> **"ON PAPER, THE BALLISTICS SHOWED THE .700-CALIBER BULLET WOULD LEAVE THE MUZZLE AT 2,000 FPS AND GENERATE MORE THAN 9,000 FT-LBS OF ENERGY. THERE WAS NO DOUBT IT WOULD QUALIFY AS THE MOST POWERFUL SPORTING CARTRIDGE IN THE WORLD."**

On paper, the ballistics showed the .700-caliber bullet would leave the muzzle at 2,000 fps and generate more than 9,000 ft-lbs of energy. There was no doubt it would qualify as the most powerful sporting cartridge in the world.

Two critical questions still needed to be answered before the project could continue. First, could a conventional rifle, weighing what an average man could handle, withstand the tremendous recoil of such a cartridge? And second, would the recoil be within acceptable limits of what an average man could absorb without injury? Even though individuals have a greatly varying amount of tolerance to recoil, a new and powerful .700 cartridge had to remain manageable for the majority of big-game hunters who might fire it.

There are two aspects of recoil to consider: the total recoil energy, which could be described as the overall force, and the "felt" recoil velocity. Shooters will notice the difference in recoil when firing magnum loads in standard field-grade guns. Not only does the overall recoil energy increase, but there is also a noticeably harsher "kick" to the shoulder.

When the muzzle velocity of a bullet of a proposed cartridge has been calculated, it can then be used in an equation to calculate the recoil the cartridge will produce when fired in rifles of different weights. For comparison's sake, consider a .30-06 with a 180-grain load produces nearly 20 ft-lbs of recoil. The .375 H&H generates twice the recoil of the .30-06, and the .460 Weatherby, billed then as the world's most powerful sporting rifle until the advent of the .700 H&H, kicks with 80 ft-lbs of recoil — twice as much as the .375 H&H.

Bell calculated the .700 H&H rifle would have to weigh 17 to 18 pounds, but to be certain he'd have to lathe-turn brass cases, have bullets made, and have a test barrel weighing between 75 and 100 pounds made by a specialist engineering company which would also make a standing breech of some kind. Another company would have to be engaged to make the rifling tools and cut the rifling. The preliminary cost was around $20,000. Feldstein thanked them, picked up the blue-prints and flew back to London to present the plan to the H&H directors.

"They remained stone-faced," Feldstein recalled. They stated the project would have to "pass muster" with

Feldstein hunted elephants in Ethiopia on a number of safaris with PH Nassos Russos. He took his largest tusker in 1988, and met his "tusker" goal of 100 and 104 pounds per tusk. Feldstein collected this elephant with his .600 NE double rifle made by McNaughton.

HOLLAND & HOLLAND

Established 1835

HOLLAND & HOLLAND LTD. 31 & 33 BRUTON STREET, LONDON W1X 8JS
TEL: 071-499 4411. TELEX: 269021 GUNNER G. FAX: 071-499 4544

January 1991

The Royal de Luxe 700-Bore Double Rifle

SPECIFICATION

SERIAL NO: Series 35000

CALIBRE: .700 H&H Nitro Express

BARRELS: 26-inch high grade chrome molybdenum steel chopper lump forgings with sling loop

SIGHTS: Standard foresight with folding moon sight protector on spearpoint block. Standard wide-V rearsight with one folding leaf

ACTION: Forged steel construction with reinforced bar and long top strap; two triggers with hinged front trigger; top lever opening; detachable locks; automatic safety; concealed third grip

STOCK: Finest de luxe grade walnut to client's measurements, with cheek piece, leather recoil pad, pistol hand with cap box, sling loop

FORE-END: Standard English fore-end

ENGRAVING: Royal de luxe scroll engraving (the lettering and numbers in gold if colour-hardened finish)

WEIGHT: Approximately 18 lbs

CASE: Best quality oak and leather case with tools and accessories

AMMUNITION: 100 rounds .700 H&H NE (3 1/2") loaded with 1000 gr Woodleigh bullet

PRICE: £56,500 for full payment in 1991 – inclusive of case and ammunition but exclusive of VAT payable if UK resident

DELIVERY: Approximately three years from confirmation of order

These are the specifications of the .700 H&H double rifle presented on Holland & Holland's official stationary. Since 1991, the original price of the rifle has risen from around $100,000 to around $400,000.

their factory manager, who spoke to Feldstein in a "pontifical manner" that was highly demeaning, frequently referring to "you Americans," even though 50 percent of H&H's annual production went to Americans, and Feldstein knew this. The manager apparently didn't like Americans in general and Feldstein in particular, and wanted the project scrapped. For the next year, the factory manager made Feldstein jump through many hoops. But eventually, when the board stepped in and informed the manager that Mr. Feldstein was willing to place an order for four double rifles with all the bells and whistles, the factory manager backed off.

A number of questions still had to be answered before the project could advance from the drawing board into the Holland & Holland workshops. What levels of pressure and force would the rifle have to withstand? What rate of twist was required for the rifling to stabilize such a bullet? And what degree of barrel convergence was needed to ensure tight grouping?

Furthermore, H&H was not willing to involve itself in the production of the cartridges. For that, Feldstein contacted Australian Geoff McDonald, owner of Woodleigh Gunsmithing (Pvt) Ltd., and put in an initial order of 5,000 bullets: 3,000 solids and 2,000 soft-nose. The solid bullets were made from cupro-nickel over a lead core, and the soft-nose bullets were a soft-lead nose leading into a cupro-nickel cup. B.E.L.L., at the same time, began extruding 5,000 cases for the bullets.

THE PMC/ELDORADO CARTRIDGE

The company undertook the loading of the cartridge — using 160 grains of Du Pont IMR 4064 powder and priming the huge case with Federal's 215 Magnum Primer. Although H&H deemed Feldstein crazy for producing 5,000 .700 NE cartridges, he viewed the cartridge like a proud father, claiming, "It's the most impressive and beautiful cartridge in the world."

Critics of the project felt that producing 5,000 cartridges was extremely excessive and wanted to know what possible need there was for that many cartridges of such a specialized and expensive caliber. Little did they know that besides the potential owners of the .700 H&H, cartridge collectors would snap up the cartridges. Interestingly, within 18 months the entire 5,000 were sold — mostly to collectors for $100 apiece.

By January 1990, a beautifully engraved, double sidelock Holland & Holland Royal de Luxe prototype was completed. Range tests verified what the designers had calculated in the way of recoil: "about on par with a 10-pound, .500 Jeffery Rimless bolt-action with the character of a faster recoiling 8-bore."

The field test for the new .700 H&H was a safari to the game fields of Ethiopia for 21 days to hunt elephant. Feldstein, accompanied by Nassos Russos, collected an elephant on the third day while hunting the Garafurda area. Both cartridge and rifle performed as expected, and Feldstein commented "the fantasy and dream have become a reality."

The official presentation of the .700 began in earnest with it appearing at gun shows and exhibitions all over Europe and the United States. During this time, the rifle had more than 300 rounds fired through it. Holland & Holland soon had orders for several more .700s of the same pattern. At present, Hollands have sold 17 .700 double rifles with number 18 in current production.

Looking back, the original price was quite a deal at $115,000, whereas today you can expect a price of $400,000 for a bare-bones rifle and upward depending on your order requirements. Feldstein's German friend Walter Eder, one of Europe's premier industrialists and international sportsman, ordered and bought three upon initial offering and production.

In June 1992, Feldstein and Eder hunted together in Zimbabwe, with Eder using the .700 prototype and Feldstein choosing a Greener .600 NE. They collected two elephants, one with each rifle. At the end of the hunt, they summed up their feelings about the .700 H&H as an elephant gun. It is heavy, and carrying it for long distances or over a period

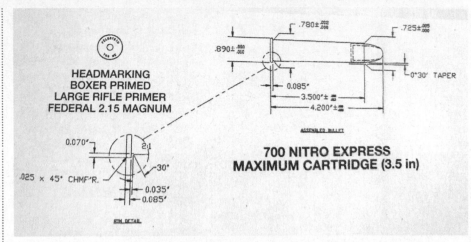

HEADMARKING
BOXER PRIMED
LARGE RIFLE PRIMER
FEDERAL 2.15 MAGNUM

**700 NITRO EXPRESS
MAXIMUM CARTRIDGE (3.5 in)**

Prior to the development of the .700 H&H double rifle, it was first necessary to design the cartridge it would shoot. This is the final blueprint for the 1,000-grain, .700-caliber bullet housed in a 3 1/2-inch case. The .700 NE bullet leaves the muzzle at 2,000 feet per second and generates more than 9,000 ft-lbs of energy.

of time could be problematical, but the weight is absolutely necessary for the rifle to be fired comfortably. Both felt the recoil is not at all unpleasant if the gun is fired like a shotgun and the aim is not held too long. It would be their choice of rifle if transported back in time to the days of professional ivory hunting in Africa.

In this day and age, how often does one get to immortalize oneself and make history by developing something completely original — and at the same time change the punch line of a joke forever? You've heard the one about the old-time elephant hunter, who, when asked why he used a .600 Nitro to hunt elephants, replied, "Because they don't make a .700!" Well, that answer has not applied now for nearly 30 years, due purely to the efforts of Bill Feldstein.

Because his admiration and high regard for guns began early, Feldstein understands the importance of bullet placement. He keeps the .700 in check with the observation that no matter how big the rifle, bullet placement is still crucial — a vital spot must be hit for any rifle to be effective. As large as the .700 bullet is, if it misses an elephant's brain, it might not necessarily knock it down. Feldstein firmly believes the final test for any rifle is when your life is on the line. And if a wounded elephant had to be followed into thick bush, Feldstein would do so confidently, armed with the .700 H&H double rifle.

.700 H&H NITRO EXPRESS

ULTRA-VELOCITY
SOFT POINT

The author's Mark V in .257
Weatherby Magnum. A Leupold
3-9 X 40mm scope in Buehler
rings complements this rifle.

The WEATHERBY Story

How one man changed the rifle industry

BY **STAN TRZONIEC**

If ever there was a man who had a huge influence on both sportsmen and the firearms industry, it had to be Roy Weatherby. For the hunter out there, the chance to own a real Weatherby rifle with all the trimmings, and have a gun that would shoot harder and faster than most of the competition was worth the extra money. For the industry, Roy's idea of how a gun should look with fancy checkering, high gloss finish and a cartridge to match any hunting trip is still envied today by his peers.

Weatherby got the idea for his rifle after wounding a deer on a hunting trip. Thinking it would be much better to have a cartridge that would deliver the goods at a higher, more potent velocity, an idea started to whirl around in his head. Working on the concept of hydrostatic shock, he surmised the animal would die quicker, in a more humane way.

Roy's theory on high velocity and how it relates to hunting occurred around 1945. It was then he wrote a letter to the editor in *Sports Afield* dealing with higher velocities in hunting cartridges. Surprised at the replies from hunters wanting higher velocity cartridges and rifles chambered for them, Roy actually had to hire a secretary to help answer all the replies. At this time in his life, Weatherby was a sales representative with the Auto Club. With new rifles not available because of the war effort, he decided to throw his career to the wind and go with his dream of developing high-velocity rifles and cartridges.

This was nothing new for Roy. As a child growing up in Kansas, he learned to depend upon himself to help the family. They lived off the land with Roy helping with trapping, and other chores around the farm to help raise money. He and his family moved several times, eventually settling down in Florida. Later he would marry, move back to Kansas, go to work for the Auto Club, and finally move to southern California.

In August 1945, Roy was ready to take the plunge. He resigned from the Auto Club and, working out of his garage, began building rifles. With a drill press, small lathe and a bluing tank, he was in business. A friend of his, George Fuller, who had made chambering reamers for Roy, set up loading dies and fire-formed cases for each caliber. One of his first was the .270 Weatherby, followed by the .220 Rocket, a cartridge I had a Ruger Target rifle rechambered for with great results.

Roy opened a sporting goods store, sold guns, ammunition and accessories and of course, his custom-made rifles. Before the notion of ever having a proprietary rifle of his own, he built and rechambered rifles from Mauser, Springfield and Enfield and maybe a Winchester Model 54 or Model 70 that might have been in his shop due to a trade-in or purchase. When it came to his cartridges, they were all based on the .300 Holland & Holland case fire-formed in customer rifles. By calling his .270 Weatherby the .270 PMVF (Powell-Miller-Venturi-Freebore), he started to be recognized as an up-and-comer in the field of sporting arms and ammunition.

While his rifle production was more of a routine operation in his small shop, ammunition was starting to be a problem. He asked Speer to assist in making cases but later turned to Norma in Sweden for final production. With the task of making ammunition off his shoulders, Roy could now turn to his lifelong dream of a true Weatherby rifle chambered for his own ammunition. His requirements were straightforward — he wanted a very strong action with a modern and flowing design, all to be incorporated into a newly designed rifle that would be built around it.

Sounding simple enough, the die was cast. Now came the design and, with it, manufacturing problems for dedicated suppliers who would handle the chore. While Roy didn't have an action of his own, he turned to the likes of Husqvarna, Birmingham Small Arms in England,

As the Mark Vs evolved, the checkering pattern went from the original skip-line to a fine-line pattern complete with a flair toward the rear of the rifle.

The bolt throw on the Mark V is only 54 degrees, which favors a lower-mounted scope and the ability to work the action quicker for follow-up shots.

Sako in Finland and Schultz & Larson in Denmark for help. He planned to have his rifle built in the U.S.A., but because of high wages in California required for skilled craftsmen to make the stock, checker and finish it, along with the action, he began to think about having it all done in Europe.

Within a short period of time around 1954, it was apparent nothing could be firmed up with any of these European arms makers. BSA wanted more money to build and import it into the United States, but declined, as it was unable to build a rifle with nine locking lugs. Later, after another short trip and meeting with the people at Schultz & Larson, Roy did not like the potbellied design of their proposed stock. Additionally,

they too wanted more money to build a new magazine to stagger the rounds of his new .378 case. Sako was another problem with middle men involved in the sales and imports through Firearms International and at the end, Husqvarna declined to give Weatherby prices as its production schedule was all taken up for 1955. As a last shot, he contacted Heym, which said it could build the rifles for Roy, but insisted he pay for all the tooling.

With all this going on and years dribbling away, Roy grew discouraged by all the time and money wasted away on trips to Europe, bad prototypes and companies not willing to take his design to the next level. The future outcome was laid out for him and now it was up to Roy

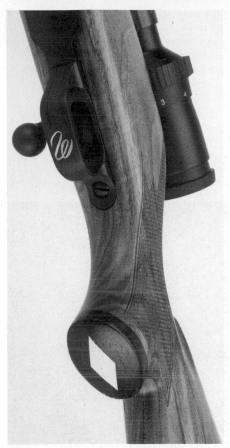

(above) Typical of any Mark V, it's the little extras that make the difference. Here we see the famous diamond inlay on the pistol-grip cap, the flying "W" on the trigger guard and impeccable inletting.

(below) Over the years, the Weatherby line has grown to include not only the famous Mark V (above) but also the popular Vanguard line for budget-minded hunters.

Weatherby to get his own design out in the open and available to the masses. Knowing that hand-loaders were overloading their guns to get better performance, Weatherby looked at the Mauser action, but found it lacking in design features limiting pressure readings to around 70,000 cup (copper units of pressure). His specifications showed he wanted an action to withstand at least 200,000 cup for the safety of handloaders, have a countersunk bolt face, three venting holes on the bolt and most important (and later a trademark of the rifle) was the inclusion of nine lugs on the bolt in three rows similar to an artillery breechblock.

Furthermore, the design incorporated an interrupted screw design the same diameter bolt body from one end to the other without the nine locking lugs adding to the overall diameter with a side benefit of having only a 54-degree bolt lift. With the bolt the same diameter as the inner race of the receiver, there would be no lateral movement inside and between the bolt and the receiver, making this one of the smoothest actions around. Additionally, in a measure for extra safety, the bolt would have an enclosed head to prevent the case head from rupturing due to an overloaded round. Still in the guise of safety, the bolt would have holes drilled around the periphery of the bolt body to allow gases to escape in concert with a shrouded bolt sleeve that would prevent dangerous gases from penetrating the interior of the bolt body and back to the shooter's face.

Roy Weatherby promoted his rifles with full-page ads in virtually all the outdoor magazines. This one is from the late 1950s.

In another round of disappointments, he showed the action to such notables as the H.P White Ballistics Lab, General Hatcher and Colonel Harrison of the NRA for opinions. While all agreed this was "the" action, in the end by way of Walter Howe, then editor of the *American Rifleman* magazine, recommended he take his blueprints to the Mathewson Tool Company in New Haven, Connecticut. The management was happy to see him and work on the project, but as in the past, weeks turned into months and in the end, nothing was accomplished.

❝ AFTER ALL THE TRIALS, MEETINGS AND CHANGES IN THE DESIGN, ROY (WEATHERBY) HAD A RIFLE AROUND 1957, BUT ADDITIONAL CHANGES REQUIRED THE ATTENTION OF A PROFESSIONAL ENGINEER NAMED FRED JENNIE WITH THE BASIC RIFLE GOING THROUGH FOUR MORE MODIFICATIONS. WITH THE FIFTH VERSION OF THE RIFLE BEGINNING THE STANDARD FOR WEATHERBY IN THE FUTURE, THE NAME MARK V (FOR THE FIFTH) IS STILL ASSOCIATED WITH THIS RIFLE TODAY. ❞

For those with deep pockets, the Weatherby Custom Shop has plenty to offer. Shown here is an example of some floral and detail work on the floorplate.

fluting, as this would come later. Another company would finish the parts, still another would do the minor parts to include the trigger sear, thumb safety and the magazine floorplate with everything being delivered to Weatherby's establishment, where final polishing and finishing would take place.

At this time, both the stocks and barrels were being made at Weatherby's plant in South Gate, California. While everything was seemingly going smoothly, the investment-casting process, due to

the porosity of the metal, did not adapt to the high-gloss bluing Weatherby wanted on his rifles. With a rejection rate of more than 50 percent, Roy again was forced to look elsewhere for a dependable vendor capable of delivering quality work.

In the same year, Weatherby traveled again to Europe to make contact with J.P. Sauer & Sohn. Both parties were enthusiastic about the possibilities of working together and the deal was signed with Sauer contracting to do the complete

After all the trials, meetings and changes in the design, Roy had a rifle around 1957, but additional changes required the attention of a professional engineer named Fred Jennie with the basic rifle going through four more modifications. With the fifth version of the rifle beginning the standard for Weatherby in the future, the name Mark V (for the fifth) is still associated with this rifle today.

With the rifle in hand and tossing some of the prior disappointments aside, Weatherby started to put his dream together. He put out bids in 1957 and settled on the Precision Foundry in Leandro, California. Roy, his team and Precision Foundry decided all the major parts, like the bolt, be investment-cast. At this time, the bolt body did not have

When Roy Weatherby was working to get this Mark V established, he also designed and built the VarmintMaster, a smaller, well-proportioned rifle for the .22 calibers. This is from the author's collection and has the original Premier scope as mounted at the factory.

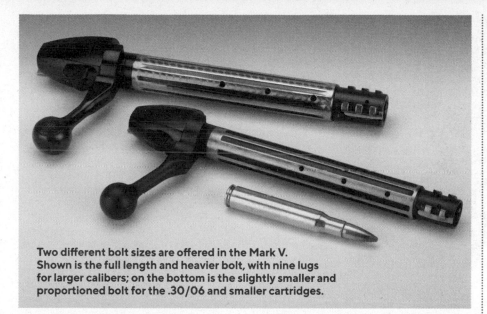

Two different bolt sizes are offered in the Mark V. Shown is the full length and heavier bolt, with nine lugs for larger calibers; on the bottom is the slightly smaller and proportioned bolt for the .30/06 and smaller cartridges.

rifle in 1958. Fred Jennie was sent on ahead to help with the manufacturing process, which it was then decided both the bolt and receiver would be made from forgings, not investment-casts. Barrels would be hammer-forged by Sauer, which then made Weatherby the first company in the United States to offer this unique feature on rifles.

It was at this time Weatherby embarked on the program of stating the Mark V would be the "World's Strongest Bolt Action" with a testing program to substantiate the claim with copper units of pressure amounting up to 200,000. According the history of the company, Roy and his team ran many tests to include a vast overloading of the .300 Weatherby Magnum. Starting out with a typical 180-grain bullet, the case was loaded with 82 grains of Du Pont 4350 powder. This was computed to be in the range of 65,000 cup with no pressure signs. Further testing was done with loads increasing by two grains up to 90 grains, which led to some difficulty in opening the bolt with no expansion of the belt on the case.

Not happy with that, the testing went into some extremes to prove Roy's claim by actually lodging a bullet in the barrel, followed by the firing of the complete cartridge behind it with 75 grains of the same 4350 powder. With the exception of the primer being pierced, both bullets managed to exit the barrel, and with further testing with various bullets and powder charges, in the end, Roy Weatherby did indeed have the world's strongest bolt-action rifle.

When it comes to the bolt itself, Fred Jennie seems to have designed this part of the gun for longevity. Looking back over the years, for the most part the Weatherby action has remained the same. There have been some modifications with the onset of new and high-tech machinery over what they started with Sauer, but overall the action remains the same in appearance and design. While there have always been questions on the nine-lug design (six on lesser calibers) and if they all mated within the receiver walls and took the back pressure the same, the thinking is that if it works after six decades of shooter acceptance, no changes are expected for the future.

Holding the bolt shows this is a heavy piece of forged machinery. The bolt has flutes not only to add to the smoothness of the action by keeping debris out of contact between bolt and receiver as is the friction of the bolt's operation, simply because the body of the bolt does not touch the follower within the magazine. The shorter bolt throw mentioned before allows the shooter not only to mount a scope lower to the receiver, but follow-up shots can be delivered quicker and with less effort.

The bolt face is counter-bored, there is a spring-loaded ejector within the bolt face and a cocking indicator shows when the gun is ready to fire. The safety has not changed with its rocking motion to set the gun to safe or to fire. The bolt handle sits within a machined groove in the receiver and current literature shows the barrels on the Mark V are hand-lapped for accuracy. Except for some of the African-type, heavy-caliber guns with sights, for the most part all models come with a clean barrel with receivers drilled and tapped for scope mounts. Barrel lengths are usually within the 24- to 26-inch range in various contours but the custom shop can tailor just about any rifle to your exact requirements or specifications including various finishes, flutes, muzzle brakes with carbon steel or stainless steel as options. Additionally, all new Weatherby rifles have a guarantee to the shooter to deliver minute-of-angle accuracy with

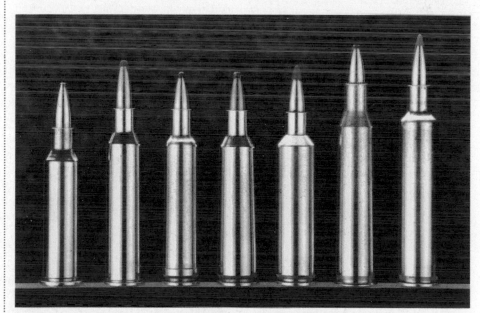

To show how the .224 Weatherby Magnum fits into the scheme of past and present-day varmint cartridges, we see from the left: .219 Wasp, .225 Winchester, .224 Weatherby Mag., .22-250 Remington, .22-250 Rem. Ackley Improved, .220 Swift and the .220 Weatherby Rocket.

With his .224 Weatherby, the author likes to hone the rifle for the best in accuracy. With IMR 4895 powder and Hornady 55-grain bullets, groups were within five-eighths of an inch consistently.

Weatherby factory or premium commercial ammunition.

A new type of trigger is available and can be added to your list of continuing modifications to this famous rifle. Now called the LXX Tigger, it not only has a wider presence on the trigger face but also can be adjusted down to 2.5 pounds for precise shooting.

And, what would a new addition be without the flying W? Yes, it's there right on the face of the trigger. To complete some additional details, there is an Oberndorf-type floorplate latch on the magazine to prevent accidental openings and literally more than a dozen stock options to pick from in the Mark V series of hunting arms.

Before we go any further into the current line of rifles, we should move back a bit to the very late '50s when Roy started to work on a smaller design of the Mark V action complete with a six-locking-lug bolt — which today is available only in calibers up to the .30-06 Springfield. Although it took an additional three years to bring this gun to production, the VarmintMaster was a work of art for the dedicated small-game hunter.

Checking through my records, I purchased my Weatherby VarmintMaster on January 2, 1981. It came equipped at the factory with Weatherby's Premier 3-9X scope, and I just could not wait until the warmer weather came for some range testing with a wide variety of handloads. Throughout the summer and in-between rock-chucking, I finished up in August of

the same year with just over two dozen handloads, some of which grouped under a minute of angle at 100 yards and are still with me today.

In between that time, I was looking for some history on the gun for an article I was writing on chuck hunting almost 40 years ago, so I turned to the source — Roy Weatherby himself. I had met him earlier at the SHOT Show, and as always he was very congenial, talked at length about his products and eager to share information. Although he did not have a proper action and gun to with it at the time, he actually developed the .224 in the late '40's while working on his line of high-velocity proprietary cartridges.

He had to be careful with his money as in those days, tooling for even a small action to hold the .224 could run up into six figures easily. Finally, when the .224 Weatherby was introduced in 1962 as the only belted varmint cartridge in existence, the .225 Winchester came out later, still slightly overshadowed by the .22/250 that was commercialized by Remington Arms. Still, Weatherby does seem to have a cult following, and those in tune with rakish stocks, fancy wood and high polished actions, took the smaller VarmintMaster to their hearts and it made a good run until it was

discontinued in 1994.

With my favorite Hornady 55-grain spire-pointed bullet over 32.0 grains of IMR-4895, velocity is around 3,512 fps. With this load, I can shoot three-shot, half-inch groups all day. Since the tooling was lost in moves some years back, the last time I spoke to Roy's son, Ed Weatherby, the company had no plans to bring back the .224 Weatherby Magnum into the fold. I still have that gun today.

For the what-it's-worth department, you can still buy factory ammunition for the .224 Weatherby but at $75 for 20 rounds, I'd rather buy the brass for $43 per 20 count and handload. Now all you need is a VarmintMaster rifle. Sorry, I am not selling mine.

Back to the Mark V. I can remember a short time back when all the effort at Weatherby seemed to go into the Vanguard. The price point was right, so were the guns. Today however, it's a different tune. Looking at the present lineup, I can count 18 different variations (the Vanguard line boasts one more, 19) of the Mark V in everything from synthetic to wood stocks to various coating and calibers to suit all. Synthetic stocks dominate the line with 13 available in the line, followed by five in traditional higher-grade wood.

> **66 FOR THOSE WHO LIKE THE MORE TRADITIONAL WOOD-STOCKED RIFLES (THIS AUTHOR INCLUDED), THE FLAGSHIP OF THE LINE IS STILL THE MARK V DELUXE. 99**

The .257 Weatherby is the author's favorite for plains game, such as antelope or mule deer.

For those who like the more traditional wood-stocked rifles (this author included), the flagship of the line is still the Mark V Deluxe. With an "AA" fancy grade Claro walnut complete with a Weatherby induced Monte Carlo stock, cut checkering, exotic fore-end tips and spacers, this gun has been in the line the longest and follows the dream Roy had years past. A famous rifle along with a well-designed stock that was made in Germany, then Japan and now the United States, will take the crush out of the most demanding calibers in the field chambered in 11 Weatherby proprietary cartridges from the .240 to the bone-crushing .460 Weatherby Magnum. For those more conservative hunters, the Mark V is also chambered for the .270 Winchester and the .30-06 Springfield.

Prices for the Deluxe now start at $2,700. For the record, my Mark V in 7mm WM that I paid for by working a second job in a lumberyard in 1973, cost me $450 — because I ordered it with a customized action ($35), a rear extension of the checkering pattern ($15), my initials on the floorplate ($25) and a Canjar single set trigger ($20).

Following suit, the Mark V has the Lazermark, Sporter and the Safari complete with a French walnut stock and fleur

The author's .224 Weatherby VarmintMaster ended things for this big rock chuck on a balmy summer day in upper New York State.

de-lis checkering, the latter with a hefty price tag of $6,900. With more and more women getting into the shooting sports, Ed Weatherby introduced the Camilla rifle (named after his mother) especially designed by and for the smaller frames of female shooters with a shorter, slimmer fore-end and other ergonomics that make shooting a rifle more enjoyable for our female partners in the field.

From here the Mark V line is full of various synthetic stocks with colors, textures and design features to suit all. There is the typical black synthetic, a new Kryptek camo, flat dark earth with tones in both light and dark patterns. When it comes to the actions, you have a choice in stainless or carbon steel and some with Cerakote protection. Barrels can be smooth, fluted and come with a muzzle brake if the caliber and your request warrants it. With the addition of the Custom Shop, the list is practically endless allowing you to upgrade a stock, fine-tune a trigger, customize a bolt or floorplate or add a different barrel contour or length. Engraving is available and they are happy to quote you on anything you have in mind. Looking back at some of the older catalogs, Roy himself started this tradition and it continues on today. A nice touch for any rifle.

For hunting in the field, the Weatherby line of belted cartridges from one company certainly has no competition. In the beginning, Roy made the .220 Rocket, which was an improvement on the .220 Swift. Never a big-seller, though I found a gunsmith who would rework one of my rifles for this cartridge complete with the famous Weatherby profile and still enjoy it in the field. As mentioned, the .224 WM has always been a favorite of mine for hunting woodchucks and other small game. From here, you can branch out into the .240 WM that is an excellent medium-game caliber with double-duty as a varmint rig with lighter bullets. Over the years, my preference for plains game has always been the .257 WM. I have several guns chambered for this cartridge and working up handloads leaves nothing to be desired for antelope or mule deer.

The 6.5-300 WM is now the speed demon when it comes this diameter bullet and with velocities moving out to 3,550 fps, it is fast becoming the favorite for long-range shooting. The .270 WM is popular as it exceeds the more traditional .270 Winchester for those who like the versatility of this cartridge, as are some of the Weatherby rifles being

Roy Weatherby, the man who changed the way many hunters looked at rifles and cartridges.

chambered for the .30-06 Springfield. Moving up, the 7mm WM is now skirting the best in a big-game cartridge, the .300 WM is by far the most preferred in the Weatherby lineup and with factory ammunition available in bullet weights from 150 to 200 grains, there is something from this company for all big-game hunters in the field.

Now getting into the harder hitting cartridges, we see the .30-378. While originally developed for the Army in 1959, this cartridge set world records for accuracy and is now another candidate for long-range hunting. Introduced in 1962, the .340 WM falls right between the .300 and .378 Weatherby magnums when it comes to big-game rifles with the latter .378 a perfect match for African game. Finishing up the list, your choices also include the .338-378, .375, .416 and the ultra-powerful .460 Weatherby magnum, and with a cost of more than $10 a round, you had better be good at handloading! With all these choices, if Weatherby has been remiss in filling some of the gaps, you can bet any omission will come later.

With the history, rifles and products growing every year since 1945, the torch was passed to Ed Weatherby and now to his son, Adam. Roy passed away in 1988, but if he were alive now I'm sure he would be very proud of how his company grew from nothing to a prominent place in the firearms field.

The Mark V legend keeps going.

RUGER'S PRECISION MAGNUM RIFLE

The Ruger Precision .338 Lapua Magnum has broken the mold in the bang for your buck concept BY L.P. BREZNY

I first took consignment possession of a heavy .338 Lapua long-range rifle about five years ago during the writing of my second edition *Gun Digest Book of Long Range Shooting.* At that time these rifles required selling the house to own one, and for the most part the military generated shooters were the only shooters seeing a whole lot of service out of these super rifles.

When doing some commercial hunting in Australia and working on my book, I was hooked up with some Australian army dedicated snipers out in the Afghanistan mountains via a real time SAT phone. Some local friends down under and fellow long-range shooters had made contact with these professional warriors, and as a result of that experience I was further educated to the fact that the .338 Lapua was not only their primary go-to weapon, but their knowledge of the gun platform and package was nothing less than indispensable to this shooter and writer. Over time, I was to correspond with these long-range experts as they educated me to the point of building up my own approach to ultra-long range shooting.

Now some four rifles later, and thinking that this whole deal could not get any better, the folks at Ruger have rolled out their idea of a very complete ultra-long range rifle as applied to the Model 18080, Precision .338 Lapua Magnum. It is a well-known fact that the Ruger Precision line has been around for several years, but until now the chambered offerings in the rifle have been directed toward 6.5 mm through .30 caliber game and target offerings. While expansion was a sure thing based on how well the Precision series has been doing for Ruger, when the real hammer hit the nail I was not at all ready for the whole experience. With a very fast call to Ruger I was pleasantly surprised that a test rifle was at my door in under a week's time. It was now "game on" in terms of the big league cartridge, and moving it into my main stream of current test rifles was nothing less than a total pleasure.

NOMENCLATURE

The Ruger Precision in a different rifle from other models, less the .300 Win Mag that uses the same chassis frame. This rifle make use of a completely traditional chassis stock system, and drives recoil straight back at the shooter versus any twisting motion found at times on other rifle-bedding and stock-mounting systems. With an empty magazine weight of 17 pounds, this rifle has a very even balance between the foot pounds of recoil generated by the Lapua round, and the felt pounds of recoil coming back to the shooter's shoulder. In fact, I shoot the Ruger .338 Lapua with one hand and arm, and then rest the left arm over the scope sight much of the time. The recoil as a direct-line system is very manageable, and be advised that I am almost 78

(above) Birchwood Casey "blue Man" long range targets installed in a junk Ford.

(right) The Ruger receiver is over built to take on the stresses of the massive .338 Lapua. Large bolt and easy to use controls.

(below) A variety of loads were shot including every factory offering the author could get his hands on. All current production loads and hand loads returned great results in the new Ruger Precision.

years old. If I can take the .338 Lapua's punch, anyone can as applied to this well-balanced heavy long-range rifle.

Because the barrel is totally free floated along the full length hand guard, there is no contact with any area of the stock save for the receiver itself that is also a one piece section of the breech system. Nothing to cause pressure against, or get out of alignment causing flyers, or in some cases flat out poor overall accuracy.

The cold hammer-forged moly steel barrel is not only accurate based on its R-5 (Russian) rifling system, but also

features of the Ruger Precision .338 Lapua. it becomes obvious that it retains systems and function of some military variants costing upward of $24,000 in boxed sniper kit form. A point in fact is that the Remington Model 2010 .300 Win Mag by example that I was issued for test at a time when only a handful were in existence anyplace on the planet is very close to this rifle's basic design. Being that this new Ruger rifle is also chambered in .300 Win Mag, the new U.S. Army standard regarding sniper weapons, try rolling that around in your brain when you're thinking about buying a new, or even first time purchased

Ruger's in house designed butt stock that can adjust to fit anyone.

In photo at left, A/T steel targets were place at random ranges to simulate real world shooting conditions. This target was addressed at 1,200 yards and as close as 500 yards during a complete series of varied range applications.

heavy hitting long range rifle. Now, at price of $2,000 and change MSRP, you would almost think the Ruger has to be a junk rifle? However not so to be sure. Using any measure you like, the Ruger Precision .338 Lapua is nothing less than a complete well-priced class act.

The barrel on the Ruger Lapua is not standard as found on other models of smaller calibers. This barrel is .875 at the muzzle, making it a true super big bore heavyweight. Tack on the muzzle break that is also massive, but still easily removed, and you have a formidable piece of ultra accurate long range artillery at hand. At a 26-inch length, and the 5R rifling spinning the bullet down range this gun is deadly to 1,500 yards and more, as you will soon see here in print.

In terms of the rifle's action design, the system is field dirt simple with a straight bolt install that can be removed in sec-

(right) Winter day with warm and very much welcomed sun, on one mile range with the new Ruger Precision.

retains a quick detach system in the event a barrel change is necessary, or desired. This barrel is threaded against a barrel nut followed up with the hand guard bushing assembly. This makes for a solid weld to the receiver, but at the same time can be easily removed for inspection or replacement. If you're thinking about the word "military" here you are not alone. As I cross over

Test shooting during the second series in winter conditions.

onds by swinging the butt stock (hinged) away from the receiver, which allows straight away access to the breech and subsequent bolt removal. Cleaning the bore with this access system is straight forward and simple. As I have tested no less than nine different rifles of a similar design, I have found this rifle to be among the easiest to work with in terms of the above indicated maintenance procedures.

This bolt system makes use of a rotating lug with a button extractor. To my way of thinking, this is about the only possible weakness regarding the whole system. I like a Mauser long extractor as is found on Ruger M-77s, even in the heavy target .300 Win Mag model Hawkeye. During the course of reviewing the .338 Lapua in several different rifles, I have come across case web failures that required some stressful application in terms of opening the bolt and extracting the spent brass case. As to the button style extractor holding up well? So far so good, as the rifle has digested 60 rounds of handloaded fodder and 11 boxes of factory manufactured ammunition.

Because the upper, as referenced by Ruger as a section of the receiver is made from a solid block of 4140 chromemoly to minimize possible distortion. The receiver is built unlike a weapon that fits the pattern of a Russian tank it would seem.

The controls on this rifle are AR like.

That is to say, the pistol grip receiver is set up exactly like the AR lower, which includes the ambidextrous safety latch placed where the M-16/M-4 positions theirs. Again, in terms of basic design, there's the very real hint of a military rifle here. With the bolt handle large and well extended away from the receiver, this is a cold weather heavy glove, or mitten shooting system. When shooting cold weather testing for function and ac-

curacy I found these controls easy to use in temperatures as low as -4F with winds and blowing snow a common element to a day on the range in South Dakota.

The five-round magazine on this rifle mirrors the British AI box drop-magazine system very closely. The rifle comes with two magazines, and I found change out function to be good. In most cases I shot the rifle as a single-round weapon, and the push feed action was a nice feature when dealing with single-shot loading on the target range. Utilizing the large extended magazine release was again a welcome addition to this rifle during those very cold and nasty days when running the rifle through rough weather field testing and wearing heavy gloves.

Trigger control on this rifle was excellent by way of the new Ruger Marksman fully adjustable trigger system. This trigger is much like that used on Savage rifles (Accu-trigger) but again if I had set up the rifle it would have made use of the very nice target grade trigger found on the Ruger Hawkeye as applied to the M-77 receiver. When tested by way of my Timney trigger gauge the measured weight straight out of the factory was just under three pounds, and very crisp in terms of let off. At that point I found no need to adjust the trigger any further as with the rifle weight and stock adjustment features, I was in full control

"The Lake." Note the junk cars at the far right side along the water's edge. This is a long-range shooters dream. Bullet splash and correction are fast and effective.

regarding accuracy.

In the area of stock features, this rifle is offered with the unique and a one of a kind system designed and branded by Ruger. The fully adjustable butt stock with that swing-out feature for travel or cleaning is one thing, but the fully adjustable comb and length of pull make this rifle a perfect fit for anyone who shoots. Now add the full-length free-floating fore-end with Magpul M-Lok hard points, the full length AR-style tube, and that tops off the makings for a very well-rounded long-range rifle.

In the sighting department Ruger again was thinking hard during the design period regarding this rifle, because atop the receiver is mounted a full 30 M.O.A Picatinny rail. That means regardless of the optics selected, the down-range application of this rifle now has a major jump on rifles with standard mounting rails when it comes to that final element of effective range. What that means in terms of effective yards is that when equipped with the proper glass — and this rifle was indeed set up with that in mind — the rifles Picatinny rail will add about 300 to 400 additional yards to the effective bullet impact net before a .338 Lapua bullet at 300 grains goes trans sonic (out of gas.) I should add that all this depends on weather conditions, altitude, and load velocity to name a couple of variables.

OPTICS SELECTED

If you're wondering why I have given the subject of optics a sub heading here it is because of the importance regarding the glass selection made in terms of gaining accurate shooting results down range. Select the wrong scope for the job and your shooting as blind as a bat with a rifle that has been designed to shoot 1000 yards to one full mile.

During the first two months of testing the new Ruger Precision .338 Lapua, I had relied on a scope built by Burris as an XTR H-33-15x50. The scope was designed as a long-range optic that made use of m.o.a. turret adjustments for elevation, and also hash marks as applied to the reticle sub-tensions. With a solid 30mm main tube and generous elevation graduations by count due to an extra large adjustment ring, the scope had served me well without question when shooting out to a bit over 1000 yards on barricade targets as in junked

(left) Down range winter conditions on the author's 600-yard course of fire.

(below) Shooting on Blue Man target at 1,200 yards. Note group cluster in white paint on center mass. Five of six rounds found its target. Black Hills Ammunition 285-grain Hornady ELD-M.

motor vehicle targets. Now however, the gunning conditions had changed and range was advancing well out to 1,400 yards or more. Enter the MRAD military system as applied to a second scope built by Tract optics. The scope was a TORIC UHD 4-20x50, and the heavy mil spec steel tube 30mm main frame held the basic pedigree of the famed Leupold M-4 sniper scope.

MRAD systems make use of mils versus m.o.a graduations for elevation and windage. This system is not one inch at 100 yards per full click as used in an m.o.a system, but 3.6 inches of elevation to the same range. Do the math here and you will see MRADS are developed for the next zip code requirements in long-range shooting. Tack on the 30mm Picatinny scope rail and you have one heck of a big league ultra long-range setup in hand. Rough calculations indicate that the scope and paired rifle cartridge is effective to 2,000 yards with ease, and in higher elevations even further. The bottom line is that you will run out of bullet velocity long before you run out of elevation graduations down range.

GOING HOT

The fun part of this review: When taking on the new Ruger Precision .338 Lapua Magnum, the study has two distinct parts. The first part took place during the fall of the year out here in the Black Hills of South Dakota, and the second part was much later when the weather had closed in. Temperatures had fallen below zero on some days, and snow drifts blocked some of my favorite passes and two track trails regarding long-range shooting points.

With the warm weather, I headed directly for my one-mile range setup that included two valleys, a stream bed right in the middle of the half mile point, and a lake at the far eastern end of the property. I had almost everything I needed to study bullets in flight or test a brand new rifle, and after a day's shooting I would often share my results with a couple of real time snipers back in the sand box via e-mail. I was shooting paper and steel, but these Aussie mates were shooting warm targets that shot back. Regardless of the target report, the primary problem always came down to one subject, and that was wind conditions down range. You can "dope" out your shots (data on previous engagement) with perfection, but if anything is going to throw a wrench into the mix it is variable direction and velocity winds. In

Many thanks to the industry for supplying their load offerings in the 338 Lapua Magnum. There were no dogs on the ammo bench regarding group testing or long range applications. The new Ruger liked all of them.

Afghanistan, as well as South Dakota, the wind is always blowing, and to be sure it is not your friend at all.

The Ruger Precision 338 can't do much about the wind, but because loaded it comes in just under 20 pounds, on a bench or bi-pod rest you can study blades of grass at the target, or cat tails half a mile across a valley floor for levels of wind-generated movement. Also, the rifle will not pitch around in gusting wind conditions, and this also gives the shooter a bit of an edge when trying to hit a target a half mile to a mile away. In general, the Ruger Precision rifle handles like a big shoulder-fired .50 caliber BMG. I have several of them and know the feel of the ultra big rifles. When on target they just don't move at all.

On the first day in the field, a fast dead on zero was established at 100 yards, followed by some damage inflicted on medium-range prairie dog lodges that required leveling along with the owners of those abodes. Shooting some general purpose Federal American Eagle 250-grain bullets the event was effortless with shots taken to 400 and 500 yards in most cases.

Out well beyond the dog town was a good size stock tank of water that measured about 500 yards long by 300 yards wide. Along the base of the far side were a series of old junk cars being used as rip-rap filler to hold in the soft gumbo-like clay bank against erosion. The sight was a rifleman's dream come true. Generally, I like to work with gunning scenarios versus static targets on paper or steel.

While these are useful and required much of the time, the junk cars could be set up with Birchwood Casey "Blue Man" targets, being human torsos at full size so as to emulate bad guys on a road that have been taken on by long-range snipers, or police road block situations.

After setting targets down range on an old Ford four-door, I returned to the top of the ridge and set up the Ruger Precision, then loaded the big rifle with one of my favorite handloads that made use of the new Hornady ELD 285-grain bullet, an RL 22 at an 84.6 grains charge of powder, and some Norma once fired brass. Ranging my target I pulled up 811 yards on my Nikon ranging binos, then turned my elevation turret on the Burris glass 19.5 m.o.a clicks according to my pre-established Hornady computer dope on the morning I went into the field.

With the rifle settled into my shoulder and a solid sight picture of a Blue Man in the back seat of the Ford, I pulled for a full value left to right wind just off the edge of the target's shoulder, then touched off my first round. At the shot the rifle just rolled lightly as the target went into a slight blur, then cleared again as I watched the bullet impact 2.3 seconds later. My bullet had hit low on the edge of the back door frame, but if it had been a real shot on a warm target the individual would have taken a hit. After the rusty dust cloud settled around the old car, and the rocks on the back stop along the lake's muddy bank settled down, I pulled for a shot though the passenger side front seat window. Watching

the wave direction on the lake, once again I pulled my windage exactly the same as the first shot, and with another gentle roll of the rifle round two went through the window, hit the dash board panel, then blew off the driver side mirror outside the vehicle. Shooting 800 yards was without question absolutely no effort for this ultra long range gunning tool.

Over the next several weeks I randomly shot across the hills using portable A/T steel targets, Birchwood Casey reactive steel targets, and paper "Blue Men," as well as life size FBI training targets. However, when changing out the optics to the new TRACT TPRIC 4-20X50 MRAD system, phase two of the two part testing went into effect. Now I had MRAD glass on my rifle which enabled me to click major range changes in just a few turns of the elevation turret, and also make use of another well built super optical tool for long range sighting.

The first task assigned to the Ruger with its freshly mounted new glass was to run a series of accuracy tests in terms of group shooting. Due to the cost of .338 Lapua ammunition even when handloaded, my testing was reduced to three-round groups at 100 yards. This would indicate a reasonable level of effectiveness in terms of different bullet weights and brand regarding the rifle's pin point accuracy, as is shown in the Table A.

With tack-driving accuracy testing accomplished it was time to turn to some additional down range work pushing the Ruger Precision to longer limits. Back up in the junk car park and lake, with an additional 400 yards applied to what had already been accomplished with the rifle, I locked onto some strategically place A/T steel targets with a measured range of 1200 yards. With a 10.5 MIL increase off the top turret, the cross hairs settled onto the oversized torso target, and round one consisting of the very new Black Hills 285grain ELD-M load went down range. A few seconds later the big bullet crashed into the hardened steel at 1570 f.p.s. It is not often that I make first-round hits, and rely on bullet splash most of the time for a sight correction. However, with a massive warm front hitting the Black Hills the air was at 68 F, and the wind stood at a totally flat zero velocity. On the first week of January, and dressed in a T shirt, I was sending big bullets into the next zip code from one of the best off-the-shelf long-range rifles I have ever shouldered, bar none.

Next I ran a sweep of three-round strings at 1,200 yards on the four vehicles with a mix of the following: Norma 250-grain Sierra MK's, Federal Premium 250-grain Sierras, Barnes 300-Grain Precision Match OTM-BT's, Black Hills 250-grain Accubond, 300-grain Sierra MK, 285-grain ELD-M in three different loads, and as a final offering the Hornady factory 285-grain ELD Match bullets. The Ruger Precision made accurate direct bullet contact with each and every one of the target vehicles. If the shooting setup had been the real thing as in a military convoy, the line of vehicles would have turned into some additional junk parts. How was I sure I was hitting my targets at that range? Believe me when I say the sound of a .338 Lapua bullet blasting through a large steel mass at a supersonic velocity in dead air leaves no doubt as to what that round is doing down range.

During a selected blue man target run of my self-designed bad guy in the back seat scenario, I zeroed in on that target, and with Black Hills 285-grain Hornady ELD-M's, succeeded in sending five bullets into Mr. bad guy's center mass. The current ammo production for this big rifle is solid as you can see by the number of commercial entries that were taken down range regarding this review, but word has it that other new outfits in the industry are also looking at jumping into the business of selling this caliber of super long-range fodder to interested big bore shooters.

After running out this rifle for over a month's time, and at times several days a week on steel and paper targets I can say for a fact that the Ruger Precision .338 Lapua Magnum is just about the best bang for the hard-earned buck you're ever going to find in a super ultra long-range high-performance rifle.

SPECS

Stock:	Folding, Adjustable Length of Pull and Comb Height
Finish:	Type III Black Hard-Coat Anodized
Barrel Length:	26"
Barrel:	Cold Hammer-Forged, 5R Rifling
Thread Pattern:	5/8"-24
Twist:	1:9" RH
Grooves:	5
Weight:	15.2 lb.
Capacity:	5
Height:	7.50"
Overall Length:	49"–52.50"
Length of Pull:	12.70" – 16.20"
Folded Length:	40.35"
Width:	3.50"
Sugg. Retail:	$2099.00

Table A. Ruger Precision .338 Lupa
100 yards: 3-shot groups. 50 yards: Scope zero group

RL 22, 285 grain Hornady ELD. One hole.	0.419
* Handload RL 22, - 84.6 gr, 285 grain Hornady ELD MATCH	1.028"
Handload RL 25 – 87.8 gr, 285 grain Hornady ELD MATCH	0.919"
Hand load H4831– 87.9 gr, 250 grain Sierra MK	0.810"
* Barnes Precision Match 300 gr OTM BT	1.011"
Federal Premium 250 gr Sierra MK HPBT	1.140"
*Federal American Eagle 250 gr SP BT	1.449
Norma 250 gr Sierra MK HPBT	0.911"
*Hornady 285gr ELD Match	0.983"
Black Hills Ammunition 250 gr AccuBond	1.136
Black Hills Ammunition 300 gr Sierra MK	0.813
Back Hills Ammunition 285 gr 285 gr ELD Match	0.755

* These .338 Lapua loads have made hits on targets at 1,760 yards (one mile).
Wind velocity zero. Temp 68 F– 71 F (Three day shoot). Elevation 3,000 ft. above sea level.
Rest: bench sand bags.

A combination that looks like it came out of the 1870s is actually a replica 1873 Winchester and an antiqued 3rd Generation Colt Single Action, both chambered in .44-40.

SIXGUNS AND LEVERGUNS

Celebrating the 150-year old concept of two guns and one cartridge

BY **JOHN TAFFIN**

It still makes quite a bit of sense and gives a lot of shooting pleasure, to have a sixgun and a levergun both chambered for the same cartridge. This first became possible in 1869 when Smith & Wesson introduced their Model #3 American chambered in not only .44 S&W American, a centerfire cartridge, but also in .44 Rimfire, which was also available in the Model 1860 and Model 1866 Winchesters. We can look back and surmise it was quite handy for someone during the frontier era to have a rifle and a pistol both using the same ammunition. How prevalent was this and especially as more and more sixguns and leverguns arrived that would use the same ammunition, which at the time consisted of .44-40, .38-40, and .32-20?

Sam P. Ridings rode the Chisholm Trail as a young man in the 1880s. He is quoted as saying: "The preferred weapons of cowboys was the 7-1/2" .45 Colt and an 1873 Winchester .44WCF." So at least according to Sam, most cowboys did not opt for the same ammunition in their rifle and pistol. Also in the 1880s Theodore Roosevelt in the Dakotas carried a 7 1/2" Colt Frontier Six Shooter chambered in .44 WCF (.44-40); however he did not choose an 1873 Winchester chambered in the same cartridge. He chose an 1876 Winchester .45-75 as he was a hunter and wanted the best possible hunting rifle.

As Winchesters progressed so did his choice. He went with the 1886 Winchester and then the 1894 Winchester especially in .30-30, which he considered excellent for antelope with its flat-shooting load compared to the black powder loads he was used to. And, of course he especially preferred his Big Medicine Model 1895 chambered in .405 Winchester.

When it comes to the unreal situations we see in western movies, we find both preferences for the .45 Colt Single Action matched up with a .44-40 Winchester, as well as many combination .44-40 sixguns and leverguns. However, we cannot count on western movies to provide us with the real picture. We probably will never know just how popular the idea of having a pistol and rifle both shooting the same ammunition really was. There

Levergun in the hand, sixgun on the hip.

is no doubt that Winchesters Model 1873 and Model 1892 chambered in any of the three Winchester Centerfire cartridges are two of the handiest levergun/cartridge combinations ever offered. The question remains if we were living in that era would we go with a Colt Single Action .45 or would we match our Colt with the Winchester?

Looking at old pictures of two groups who depended upon sixguns and leverguns, namely the Texas Rangers and Arizona Rangers, we see a lot of men who wanted the best possible sixgun and levergun without being concerned if they were both chambered for the same cartridge. The sixgun of choice for many of these Rangers was the Colt Single Action Army .45 while their rifle was either a .30-30 Model 94 or a .30-40 Model 95. After World War I, at least some Texas Rangers began switching from the .45 Single Action to the .45 Government Model semiauto while still opting for a rifle which gave them a lot more possibilities than a Model 1892 Winchester chambered in .44-40, for instance. Some Texas Rangers also opted for double-action sixguns from Smith & Wesson beginning with the .44 Special in the Triple-Lock and Model

1926 and then gravitating to the .357 Magnum. Their rifles of choice remained those chambered for real rifle cartridges as opposed to sixgun cartridges. I know of at least one Texas sheriff who carried a .45 Colt Commander backed up by a .45-70 lever action rifle in the trunk of his car. If he ever had to stop a car this levergun would do the job.

The modern era of sixguns and leverguns chambered in the same cartridge began in the early 1950s. The .357 Magnum had arrived in 1935 and it took a while, however shooters soon discovered how handy it would be to have a levergun chambered in .357 Magnum. Today, if I could have only one centerfire rifle it would be a .357 Magnum, as they are so handy, accurate and easy shooting, and will do almost anything I require of a rifle these days. Over the past half century or so we have had great choices in .357 Magnum leverguns, however this was not true in the 1950s. One gunsmith, Ward Koozer of Arizona, had a brisk business converting Winchester .32-20 Model 1892s to .357 Magnum.

As a teenager my interest was sparked with an early article in GUNS magazine in the 1950s by Kent Bellah. This

article was entitled: "The Two-Gun Man Comes Back." The title alone confirms Bellah's appreciation of a rifle and pistol chambered in the same cartridge and his article paired up the 3-1/2" Smith & Wesson .357 Magnum, a particular favorite of Bellah's, with a Koozer custom .357 Magnum Model 1892. Shortly thereafter, the .44 Magnum arrived and we soon had .44-40 Winchester Model 1892s chambered to .44 Magnum to match up with the new Smith & Wesson and Ruger .44 Magnum sixguns. This gave a powerful sixgun/levergun combination, however the .44-40 itself chambered in the Winchester Model 1892 was and is a pretty powerful performer.

The second boost to having sixguns and leverguns chambered in the same cartridge came with the arrival of Cowboy Action Shooting. With two sixguns and a levergun required for most stages, and since power is not part of the game, it made perfect sense to have all chambered in the same cartridge. Originally there were no Winchesters, be they 1860, 1866, 1873, or 1892 chambered in .45 Colt. Now suddenly we not only had all of these but also the 1894 Winchester shooting the .45 Colt. This matched up perfectly not only with a Colt Single Action .45 which had been around since 1873, but also with Ruger Blackhawks,

Ruger Vaqueros, Ruger New Vaqueros, USFA SAs, and a whole lineup of Uberti replicas coming via Cimarron Firearms.

Why were there no original Winchesters chambered in .45 Colt especially since Colt saw the advantage in chambering their Single Action in .44-40? Two reasons come to mind immediately. The .44-40 is basically a .45 Colt-size cartridge necked down to .44 which gives

it a taper making it much easier and smoother to make the transition from the action into the barrel; the .45 Colt is a straight cartridge and does not feed nearly as smoothly. At the other end of the cycle, ejection of unfired cartridges, the .45 Colt of that era did not have much of a rim for the extractor to grab hold of and reloaders often experienced the rim pulling off, or the shell holder pulling

John's grandkids are well equipped with Marlin .22 leverguns.

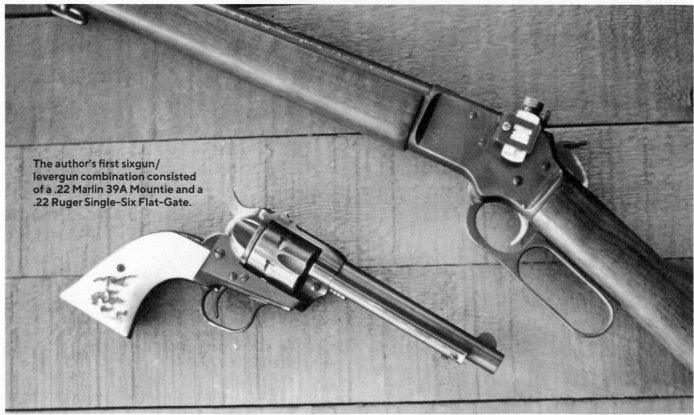

The author's first sixgun/ levergun combination consisted of a .22 Marlin 39A Mountie and a .22 Ruger Single-Six Flat-Gate.

off the rim of .45 Colt cases which were available right up into the 1950s. Today's .45 Colt brass has much stronger rims and a deeper recess all the way around the case above the rim giving something substantial for both the extractor and the shell holder to grab onto.

Whether combination guns were highly popular are not so much so in the frontier era, they certainly are today and are especially handy for relatively close range hunting of deer and deer sized critters, black bear, and especially feral pigs. With this type of hunting we can come up with sixguns and leverguns chambered in such cartridges as .44 Magnum, .45 Colt, and .454 Casull, and if we are extremely lucky we can find a sixgun/lever gun combination chambered in .480 Ruger. Other big bore hunting sixgun/levergun combinations available today for those who wander the fields and forests after game are the .475 and .500 Linebaugh. I am somewhat surprised no one has offered a lever action rifle chambered in any of the SuperMag cartridges, .357, .375, .414, and .445 Maximums.

Other combinations are now found, or can be found in the use gun market, in .22 LR, .22 Magnum, .32 Magnum, .327 Federal, .32-20, .38 Special, .357 Magnum, .41 Magnum, and if one is not tied to a levergun there is the .30 M1 Carbine and if we want to really reach out with a semi-automatic combination of pistol and carbine, we can choose the .45 ACP and the 9 mm. And let us not forget the .44 Magnum chambered in the semi-automatic Ruger carbine, and Ruger has also offered both .357 Magnum and .44 Magnum chambered

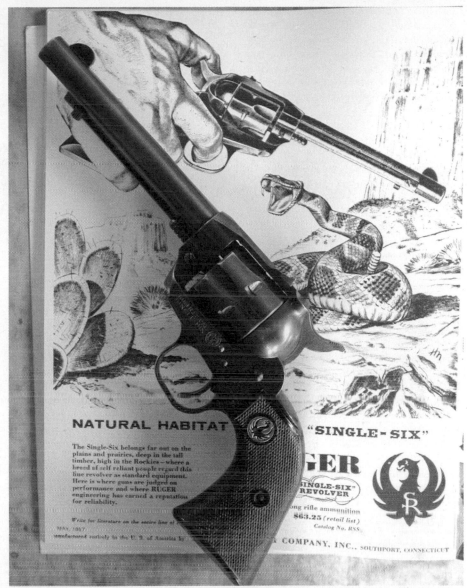

(above) This early magazine ad for the Ruger .22 Single-Six caught the imagination of many a teenager.

Today's Ruger Single-Nine in .22 Magnum (left) makes a good mate with several .22 Magnum leverguns. The Long Rifle model (right) can now be had as a Single-Ten.

bolt guns. There is virtually no end of .22 combinations possible as .22s are offered in abundance in all rifle types, lever, bolt, pump, and semi-auto. Our only boundary is our imagination, however for now we will concentrate on the original sixgun/levergun combo, with the sixgun being a single action.

Before we look at combinations which are available there are some cautions which will help keep us out of trouble and/or going down a dead end: 1) Care must be taken in choosing a sixgun/levergun combination when it comes to loads. The rule of thumb is standard loads only for the Colt Single Action Army and Winchester 1873 replicas; save the heavier loads for Ruger Blackhawks and Winchester 1892 originals or replicas. 2) Sixguns are very forgiving when it comes to bullets chosen and overall length of cartridges; lever guns not so much. It is much easier to find a good load for a levergun and then try it in the sixgun rather than the other way around. 3) When shooting .22 sixguns I use both lead and copper plated bulleted loads, however leading problems can be avoided in the levergun if only copper plated bullets are used. 4) With the centerfires, if cast bullets are used at the very least they should be relatively hard. This only works up to a certain point and then gas-checks are necessary not only to prevent leading but also to help provide accuracy. Plain bases work well with lighter loads, however can be a problem as we increase muzzle

Gary Reeder's contribution to a .32 Magnum sixgun/levergun pairing is this trio of custom .32 Magnum Rugers.

velocity; only experience will tell what works and what doesn't. 5) When starting to reload cartridges for leverguns make several dummies to check ease of feeding and chambering. If the cartridge is too long it may jam the action and in an 1860/1866/1873 pattern levergun a cartridge which is too long will not feed from the magazine tube on to the lifter and if it's too short it will allow the next cartridge to feed through just enough to jam up everything up. 6) For many years Marlins had Micro-Groove barrels which I have found for the most part only work well with jacketed bullets and gas checked bullets driven at certain speeds. Their current Ballard Rifling helps prevent this problem. 7) Bullet diameter can be a problem. Over the years I have found .44-40 sixguns with chamber

throats running from .426" to .434"and .45 Colts have been just as bad from .449" to .457". Trying to pair up a "loose" sixgun with a "tight" levergun can definitely be an exercise in futility. Sixguns produced in the past few decades have been held to much tighter tolerances.

.22 RIMFIRE: My personal shooting life, and by personal I mean owning my own firearm, started the way everyone's should, with a quality .22 rifle. The year was 1956 and I had just graduated from high school. Going to work the first thing I bought was a Marlin 39A Mountie. I doubt if any other firearm through my many years of shooting as ever exceeded the pleasure that first levergun gave me. I spent too much time cleaning it, I've learned better now, however the smell of Hoppe's #9 was intoxicating. Shortly after the Marlin my second firearm was purchased, this time a real sixgun, a Ruger .22 Single-Six which is now known to collectors as a Flat Gate. Now I really had all the bases covered. We worked a half a day on Saturday and then my friends and I would head to the pizza place on the way out of town and spend the afternoon shooting our .22s.

I didn't realize it at the time, but I had begun with just about the best sixgun/levergun combination a kid could have. The Marlin .22 was great for hunting squirrels, rabbits, and varmints while the Ruger .22 Single-Six made a great every-day packin' pistol and both were as good as it could possibly get for the grand old shooting sport of plinking. In those days,

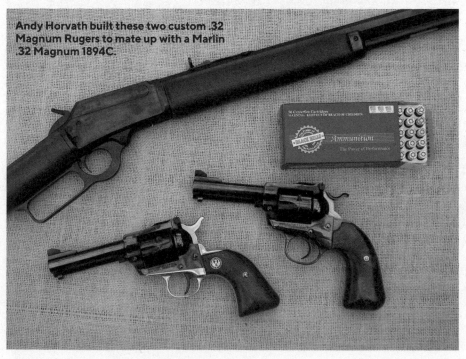

Andy Horvath built these two custom .32 Magnum Rugers to mate up with a Marlin .32 Magnum 1894C.

I was making 90 cents an hour, which meant I had to work one hour to buy two boxes of .22s. The Ruger sold for $63.25 and I believe the Marlin was a few dollars more. Both guns were as sound an investment as I've ever made and both are still in service. I was well on my way to becoming a lifetime shooter.

Today Ruger remains the number one producer of .22 single action sixguns. Great Western produced replicas of the Colt Single Action in Los Angeles for less than 10 years and some of those were .22s. At one time Colt had a .22 Single Action and replicas are available on the Colt pattern today as well as being offered by a couple other manufacturers; however Ruger is still the top choice. Early on Ruger made two important changes to their Single-Six line, namely offering a .22 Magnum auxiliary cylinder with every one they sold and then with the Super Single-Six added adjustable sights. What more could anyone want?

Over the years, other quality .22 leverguns have been offered and can still be found on the used gun market. These include the Browning and the Winchester 9422 which is available in two models, .22 Long Rifle and .22 Rimfire Magnum. Today Henry Repeating Arms offers their lever action .22 in both models also. These little .22s are about as slick handling as a .22 rifle can be.

Arguably the best sixgun/levergun combination for John's use is the Marlin 1894C and the Ruger Old Model Blackhawk, both chambered in .357 Magnum.

.32 W.C.F. (.32-20): This was the first small game and varmint chambering offered by Winchester. It was first chambered in the Model 1873 and then in the Model 1892. Marlin also offered their 1894C in .32-20. Whether one goes with the older 1892 or the newer Marlin, especially when the latter is fitted with a full-length magazine tube, one has an exceptionally easy shooting and accurate levergun. Replicas from both Uberti/ Cimarron and Miroku/Winchester are found rarely and are of the highest quality. For years my most used load for the .32-20 in either a large-frame sixgun or levergun has been the Lyman 120 grain gas checked cast bullet #311316 loaded over 10.0 grains of #2400. For the sixgun half of the combination Colt began chambering their Single Action Army in .32 W.C.F. in the 1880s and also produced some 3rd Generation .32-20s in the past decade and I managed to

This pair of .327 Magnums consist of a Ruger Single-Seven and a custom chambered Marlin.

come up with one with a 5-1/2" barrel that is a well built, finely timed and easy shooting sixgun. Cimarron Firearms offers an excellent Uberti Single Action replica in all three of the traditional barrel lengths, 4-3/4", 5-1/2", and 7-1/2". Ruger also offered the Blackhawk New Model with two cylinders in .32-20 and .32 Magnum. The ultimate single action .32-20 is the Freedom Arms Model 97 which is approximately the same size as a Colt Single Action and it is possible to have one of these Freedom Arms sixguns with three cylinders, .32 Magnum, .327 Federal, and .32-20.

.38 W.C.F. (.38-40): After putting my .22 sixgun/levergun combination together I began looking for something larger, a centerfire sixgun. I found a 1st Generation .38 W.C.F. with a 4-3/4" barrel. It had normal bluing wear one would expect from a sixgun made in 1900 and also a little smoothing off of the checkered rubber grips. It was absolutely beautiful! I was still making 90 cents an hour and this Colt cost me $90. This became one-half of my second sixgun/levergun combination as I found an original Marlin 1894 from the same era chambered in .38-40; Marlin would not write "Winchester" on their barrels. I was not smart enough to hold on to either one of these .38-40s; that's what comes from being a dumb teenager.

Colt has made a few 3rd Generation .38-40s as did USFA in their relatively brief time of existence. Ruger also offered the Blackhawk .38-40 with an auxiliary cylinder chambered in 10mm, and I do believe also chambered the Vaquero for .38-40. I have found the Uberti/Cimarron .38-40 replica Single Actions to be excellent shooters and I also had a Herters .401 PowerMag converted to .38-40 by re-chambering an extra .401 cylinder. The .38-40, 10 mm, .40 S&W, and the .401 PowerMag all use the same diameter bullet.

I let my original .38-40 Marlin get away, but it has been replaced by a Winchester Model 1892 from the same time period. Replica leverguns have been offered on the Model 1873 pattern and even Miroku/Winchester has produced a few Model 1892 leverguns chambered in .38-40. This rifle seems to be an exception when it comes to shooting plain-based bullets. The Lyman #401043 over 10.0 grains of Unique clocks out at 1,500 fps and groups 3 shots in 3/4" at 50 yards. This was my early powerful loading for the Colt Single Action Army, however I now

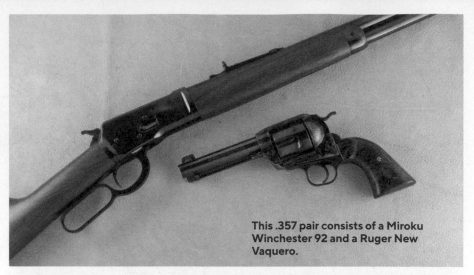

This .357 pair consists of a Miroku Winchester 92 and a Ruger New Vaquero.

Only one of these is what it seems. The bottom sixgun is an 1880s Colt Frontier Six Shooter while the others are a 3rd Generation Colt Single Action and a replica 1860 Henry. All are chambered in .44-40.

A very potent sixgun/levergun combination for hunting deer, black bear, and feral pigs is made up of a Winchester Model 94 and a Ruger Super Blackhawk both chambered in .44 Magnum.

USFA .45 Colt Single Actions go well with a replica .45 Model 1873.

mostly reserve it for Ruger Blackhawks. The .38-40 is not quite as powerful as the .44-40 however it is flatter shooting. How good was/is the .38-40? When the .40 S&W arrived back in the 1980s it was a ballistic dead ringer for the .38-40 of the 1880s.

44 W.C.F (.44-40): This was a very popular cartridge not only in the Colt Single Action Army, where it was second only to the .45 Colt in production numbers, but also in both the Winchester 1873 and 1892. In the latter Winchester it reaches its true potential which is not all that far removed from the .44 Magnum. Colt did not catalog the .44-40 in the 2nd Generation except for the 7-1/2" nickel-plated Frontier Six Shooter which was one half of the Peacemaker Centennial set the other being a blued/case hardened .45 Colt with the same barrel length. However, during the 3rd Generation run which goes back to the 1970s, the .44-40 has been produced in all traditional barrel lengths as well as nickel and blue/case hardened versions, and the New Frontier has also been chambered in .44-40. There was also a Sheriff's Model with two cylinders in .44 Special and .44-40. Ruger chambered the Vaquero for the .44-40 and USFA also offered this chambering in their Single Action. I know I'm being redundant when I say Uberti/Cimarron also offers excellent replicas chambered in .44-40.

Leverguns are relatively easy to

find chambered in .44 W.C.F./.44-40. These include the original Model 1873 and Model 1892 Winchesters, and at the risk of once again being redundant, both of these have been offered by Uberti and are as good, or better than the originals. Uberti also produces both the Model 1860 Henry and 1866 Winchester in .44-40. Henry Repeating Arms has a deluxe, virtually exact replica of the original 1860 Henry chambered in .44-40 rather than .44 Rimfire, and Taurus/Rossi also produces the Model 1892 in .44-40.

For a time in the 1930s the .44-40 Winchester 1892 was made in South America under a contract from Winchester. These guns were known as El Tigres. They came with 22" barrels, a military style ladder sight, and sold for $39.95 in the early 1950s. One found today in excellent condition will cost about 20 times that amount. Mine outshoots my original 1892 Winchester. One of the best .44-40 leverguns offered in recent times has been the Marlin 1894 with an octagon barrel. These are easily fitted with a tang sight making for what may be the best shooting .44 W.C.F. levergun ever. These originally came with 24" octagon barrels, however after measuring I found I could have the barrel cut to 19-1/2" and still have a 10-round capacity magazine tube. That may have been a mistake as it improved the handling quality so much Diamond Dot confiscated it for her own.

The .44-40 in my Marlin 1894 also seems to be an exception to the rule of plain-base bullets shooting well. With the same powder charge as I use for the .38-40, 10.0 grains of Unique under the Lyman #42798, the Marlin clocks out at 1,420 fps and groups its three shots into 1-1/8". This was also my early powerful loading for the .44-40 in the Colt Single Action, as older Lyman manuals list 10.7 grains of Unique as maximum for a sixgun. However, in recent manuals this has been dropped back to 9.0 grains of Unique so I mostly reserve this load for heavier frame sixguns such as the Ruger Blackhawk and the Texas Longhorn Arms West Texas Flat-Top Target. The latter sixgun has been very successful as

a hunting revolver with the 10.0 grains of Unique load.

.45 COLT: The .45 Colt has been chambered in a long list of sixguns for more than 140 years. Colt still offers, at least officially in their catalog, both the Single Action Army and the New Frontier while Ruger has both the Blackhawk and Bisley Model on the Super Blackhawk sized frame, as well as the New Model Flat-Top on the original sized frame from 1955. The Ruger Vaquero was built on large Super Blackhawk frame while the New Vaquero uses the smaller frame; this gives us two basic levels of sixguns when it comes to strength and the rule of thumb is to use standard loads in Colts, New Vaqueros and New Model Flat-Top Rugers and save the heavy loads for the original Vaquero, Blackhawk and Bisley Model.

In addition to these currently produced .45 Colt sixguns, several have been produced in the past and are now only available on the use gun market. These include the Texas Longhorn Arms Improved Number Five, the USFA Single Actions, and the STI Texican. Replicas continue to be offered in Colt Single Action, Remington 1875 and 1890, and Smith & Wesson Schofield versions. All of these replicas are for standard loads only.

More than a century after the .45 Colt arrived in 1873 chambered in the Colt Single Action, we have the use of modern brass and the influence of the Cowboy Action Shooting and the leverguns that never were, are. In the early days of CAS and probably most of the 20th century years the most popular chambering for competition was .45 Colt. This has mostly changed today as serious competitors whose main goal is speed have gone to smaller calibers, however before it happened the influence worked its magic as American gun makers Marlin and Winchester came up with leverguns chambered in .45 Colt as did those who produce replicas of the Winchester 1860, 1866, 1873, and 1892.

The replicas of original Winchesters, the 1860 Henry, the 1866 Yellow Boy, and the 1873 Winchester when chambered in .45 Colt are for standard loads only. The first two were originally brass framed and the 1873 was first iron, then steel. These three "Winchesters" have what is known as a toggle action which means they are not tremendously strong. When John Browning designed the Model 1892 he basically miniaturized his previous

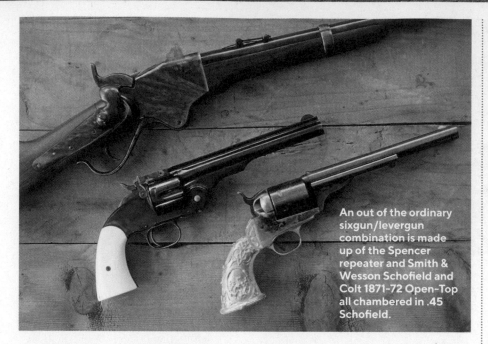

An out of the ordinary sixgun/levergun combination is made up of the Spencer repeater and Smith & Wesson Schofield and Colt 1871-72 Open-Top all chambered in .45 Schofield.

Model 1886 using the twin locking bolts at the back of the frame. Browning's design increased the strength of the Winchester leverguns tremendously.

For a Heavy Duty hunting handgun such as the Ruger Blackhawk or Bisley Model chambered in .45 Colt I normally use 300-grain bullets at 1,200 fps so the long gun I need to side these loads is a Winchester or replica Model 1894 or Model 1892 or a Marlin Model 1894. These leverguns easily handle my heavy duty hunting loads.

The Winchester 1894 is basically a long action designed originally to handle the .38-55, .30-30, and .25-35. When chambered in the .45 Colt round there can be problems with feeding such a short cartridge through such a long action. Personally, I have never had a problem but perhaps I work the lever differently than others do. We have many relatively long 300-grain bullets for the .45 Colt and these are no problem for the Winchester 1894, however overall cartridge length can be a problem in the 1892 replica in .45 Colt or the Marlin 1894. The bullet one plans to use can be the deciding factor in which levergun to choose. With any of these stronger leverguns the .45 Colt is certainly adequate for deer, black bear, and feral pigs at any reasonable distance. In actuality, for close-up hunting — especially for the latter — a .45 Colt in a lever action rifle can be one of the best choices possible. One of my most used loads for these applications is the NEI #310.451, a 300-grain Keith-style bullet, loaded over 22.0 grains of Winchester 296. This load

clocks out at just under 1,500 fps from a Winchester Model 1894 and 1,175 fps from a 4-5/8" Ruger Blackhawk. Although it is a plain-based bullet it provides adequate accuracy for the task at hand from the Winchester Model 1894.

The .45 Colt Marlin Trapper with its 16-1/2" barrel gives identical results with both cast and jacketed bullets and with both heavy and standard weight bullets. Versatility such as this is rare to say the least. Using Lyman's Keith designed 260-grain hard cast #454424 bullet over 9.3 grains of Universal gives a most pleasant shooting 1,130 fps load that stays right at one-inch for three shots at 50 yards. I prefer heavyweight bullets for hunting with the .45 Colt and have had excellent results with both Hornady's 300 grain XTP over 21.7 grains of WW296 and RCBS's hard cast #45-300 SWC-GC over 21.2 grains of H110. Both loads are in the 1,375 to 1,400 fps velocity range and will both shoot right at one inch for three shots at 50 yards.

.32 H&R MAGNUM: When the .32 Magnum first arrived I did not take it seriously. My friend Joe Penner changed this as he acquired one of the first 9-1/2" Ruger Single-Sixes available. We loaded up some JHPs and searched for suitable targets. I found some out of date cans of split pea soup and since I don't like the stuff anyhow, I figured it would be great for experimenting. Putting a jacketed hollowpoint through the first can set at 25 yards changed my mind about the little Mighty Mouse Magnum. The can of split

pea split all right and we had green soup all over us and also on my red Bronco. This cartridge was no toy!

The first factory loads from Federal were very mild as the .32 Magnum arrived in Harrington & Richardson revolvers and that is why it is known officially as the .32 H&R Magnum. The old H&Rs were not what you would call especially strong, however handloads for use in the Ruger Single-Six could be loaded much hotter.

My stable of Ruger .32s does not include a single factory version, but rather customized sixguns by both Andy Horvath and Gary Reeder. Andy is well-known for his L'il Guns and it gives me great pleasure to know I introduced him to sixgunners more than 30 years ago. The first L'il Gun Andy did for me was a 4" round-butted .44 Special followed by a trio of .22s and then the .32 Magnums. Starting with a standard Single-Six and a Bisley Model, he cut the barrels to just under 4" along with the ejector housing and ejector rod, totally tuned the actions, round-butted the grip frames, and finished both in a high bright blue. They make excellent single-action versions of the classic Kit Gun, and fit easily into a backpack or carry nicely in a holster. I mostly use these with the Sierra 90 JHC, Hornady 100 JHP, or Speer 100 JHP over 8.5 grains of #2400 for an accurate shooting 1,060 fps. Even with a short barrel these loads will group right at 1-1/4" for five shots at 20 yards.

Gary Reeder started out with a pair of 6-1/2" Ruger Bisley Model .32 Magnums, one with adjustable sights and the other with fixed sights. Both were fitted with 7-1/2" custom barrels and a special post front sight made for the fixed sighted version resulting in two of the best shooting .32 Magnums one is likely to find. He didn't stop there but then turned to a 4-5/8" Single-Six .32 Magnum. This one has been fitted with a 9-1/2" custom barrel, as found on some of the earlier .32 Single-Sixes, along with a brass grip frame. All three have been highly polished and blued as only Gary Reeder can do it making any one of them an excellent part of a .32 Magnum sixgun/levergun combination that will do yeoman service in plinking or hunting varmints or small game.

It is not been easy to find .32 Magnum leverguns. Marlin offered a 20" octagon barreled version for a short time, however this was dropped even before Remington acquired Marlin. I use the same loads in the Marlin .32 Magnum as I

do in my .32 Magnum Rugers. In the longer barreled Marlin my above-mentioned loads for the .32 Magnum clock out at about 1,600 fps making for a deadly varmint load.

.327 FEDERAL MAGNUM:

The .327 Federal Magnum was introduced in the pocket-sized Ruger SP101 and promoted as a self-defense combination. It may well be a good choice for this application, however it is much more. It didn't take long for reloaders and experimenters to look to custom gunmakers to come up with a longer barreled sixgun designed for field use and varmint hunting. Custom sixgunsmiths such as Alan Harton and Hamilton Bowen began doing conversions on Ruger single actions and Smith & Wesson double actions which opened up a whole new window for the .327 Magnum.

We now have what is about as close as possible to get to a perfect Ruger .327 Magnum and it is the Single-Seven, a stainless steel, seven-shot .327 Magnum. It is offered in the three standard barrel lengths of 4-5/8", 5-1/2", and my favorite choice for this type of sixgun, 7-1/2". With a small-bore cartridge like this I wanted the longest barrel for maximum velocity as well as maximum sight radius. Sights consist of an adjustable Ruger rear sight matched up with a ramp front sight both of which are black as they should be even on stainless steel sixguns. I have not been disappointed as this gun shoots exceptionally well with not just the .327 Magnum but also three other cartridges which are applicable for use in the factory cylinder, namely .32 S&W, .32 S&W Long, and .32 Magnum. With the ability to accept four different .32 cartridges, the Single-Seven is exceptionally versatile.

In handloading for the .327 Magnum I have found Hornady's 85 XTP over 11.0 grains of #2400 is right at 1,400 fps with an amazing 1/2" group. Other noticeable handloads all grouping in one-inch are Hornady's 85 XTP over 12.5 grains of H110 and 1,525 fps; Sierra 90 JHC,11.0 grains of #2400, 1,400 fps, and Speer's 100 JHP over 5.0 grains of Universal at just over 1,225 fps.

Coming up with a .327 Magnum levergun required drastic measures as Marlin did not take the next natural step in chambering their 1894C in .327 but instead went backwards and dropped the .32 Magnum. Something had to be done about this so I talked with my gunsmith Tom at Buckhorn as to whether he thought the Marlin .32 Magnum could be rechambered to the longer .327 Magnum. The problem would not be the re-chambering but actually getting the longer cartridge to feed. Tom thought it could be done and asked me to let him study upon it a mite as I turned over my second .32 Magnum Marlin to him. It did not take him long to come up with a positive response saying he thought it could be. It was.

The .327 Federal Magnum feeds easily through the .32 Magnum Marlin action with the only hitch being extraction is sometimes not always positive. With the .327 Federal Magnum in the Marlin 1894 I can increase the muzzle velocity of the 85-grain jacketed hollowpoint loads by 400 fps over the same bullet in the .32 Magnum. Using the same 10.0 grains of #2400 of my .32-20 loads with the Speer 100 and 115 Gold Dot Hollow Points gives me muzzle velocities over 1,600 fps with the .327 Magnum in the Marlin while 12.5 grains of H110 ups the muzzle velocities to well over 1,700 fps and 11.5 grains of AA9 increases this to over 1,800 fps. For cast bullet loads I use two gas-checked designs both weighing just under 120 grains. These are the RCBS #32-115 FNGC and the old standby Lyman #311316GC. With 12.5 grains of H110 these two bullets clock out at 1,800 fps and group in 7/8" and 5/8" respectively for four shots at 45 yards.

It may now be easier to find a .327 Magnum levergun as Henry Repeating Arms has announced the chambering of their Big Boy in the caliber.

.38 SPECIAL:

Sixgun/levergun combinations in .38 Special? Colt chambered the .38 Special in their 1st Generation run, however these are very rare collector's items today. Colt also made both Single Action and New Frontier 2nd Generation .38 Specials, however these are also very rare. Great Western produced their Single Action in .38 Special in their relatively short run of manufacturing of less than 10 years.

Today my .38 Special Single Action of choice is a 5-1/2" USFA. This is also a relatively rare sixgun and came to me in quite an unusual way. It came into the office of the now long gone SHOOT! Magazine in payment for advertising. No one there had any use for a .38 Special Single Action. I guess I read too much Keith as a budding sixgunner as this heavy-framed .38 Special immediately appealed to me as a single-action version of the .38/44 Heavy Duty. In addition to being in a rare chambering it is also beautifully finished as were most of the now gone USFA sixguns. It is such an excellent shooting and eye-catching single-action sixgun I felt it was worth being stocked with something special which turned out to be flame-grained walnut stocks by the Master Gripmaker himself, Roy Fishpaw. You can bet this combination is one of my prized possessions.

When it comes to leverguns .38 Special versions are rare but not impossible to find. Marlin offered their Cowboy Comp 1894 chambered in .38 Special for a short time and the Uberti 1866 Winchester

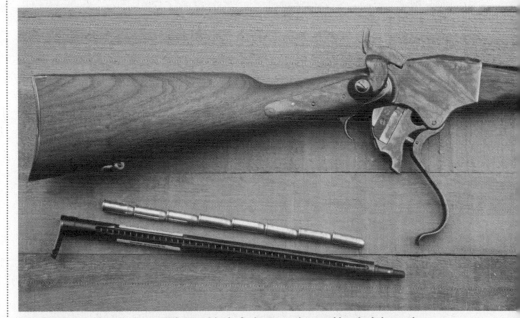

The Spencer repeater was a different kind of a lever action and loaded through a magazine tube in the butt; this replica is chambered in .45 Schofield.

replica has also been available in .38 Special. With a 24" octagon barrel the Uberti version was exceptionally heavy. I had mine cut back to minimum length which makes it much easier to handle. Is such a combination in .38 Special of any practical use? I'd say so as it is a very pleasant plinking combination, works well for varmints and small game, and with proper loads can serve for self-defense.

> ❝ THERE'S SOMETHING ALMOST SUPERNATURAL OR SPIRITUAL ABOUT THE .44 SPECIAL. THOSE WHO UNDERSTAND THIS NEED NO EXPLANATION; THOSE WHO DO NOT PROBABLY WOULD NOT ACCEPT OR UNDERSTAND ANY EXPLANATION. ❞

44 SPECIAL: Over its more than 100-year history the .44 Special has been chambered in some of the finest revolvers ever produced. From Smith & Wesson we had the Triple-Lock, the Model 1926, the 1950 Target, and in more recent times, the Model 24 and Model 624. Colt's contribution has been threefold, the New Service, the Single Action Army, and the New Frontier. For a short period of time Great Western offered their Frontier Model in the .44 Special, as did Texas Longhorn Arms in the West Texas Flat-Top Target and the South Texas Army. Ruger had planned to offer the .44 Special in their original .357 Magnum Blackhawk platform that arrived in 1955. However, the .44 Magnum arrived at the end of 1955 so Ruger jumped directly to the magnum with a slightly larger frame and cylinder than the .357 Blackhawk.

Since Ruger never did chamber for the .44 Special until very recently, several of us writers beginning with Skeeter Skelton in the 1970s and 1980s have diligently searched for Flat-Top and Three-Screw Blackhawks to convert to .44 Special, as these Colt Single Action-sized sixguns convert into an easy packin' and easy shootin' .44 Special. Before the arrival of the 2nd Generation .44 Special Single Action Army in 1957, many shooters converted both the SAA and the Bisley Model to the .44 Special.

The first question someone is going to ask is "Why bother? After all we already had the .44 Magnum." No doubt the .44 Magnum is more powerful, however sixguns made for this excellent Magnum are normally at least 1/2 pound heavier than a comparable sixgun chambered in The Special. Also, most .44 Magnum shooters, if they are honest, will admit their most used .44 Magnum loads are really in the .44 Special class.

The ultimate .44 Special Single Action is the Freedom Arms Model 97 which is only slightly smaller than a Colt Single Action Army. This is a five-shooter which means it is stronger than a six-shot Colt Single Action. The .44 Special is not only easy to load for there is much information available for this great cartridge dating all the way back to the 1920s and Elmer Keith. There's also something almost supernatural or spiritual about the .44 Special. Those who understand this, need no explanation; those who do not probably would not accept or understand any explanation. I was excited to receive my first .44 Special, a 6-1/2" 1950 Target nearly 60 years ago from my teenage bride on the occasion of our first Christmas together. Since then dozens upon dozens of .44 Specials have come my way and that high-level of excitement has never really waned.

The Model 1892 Winchester seems a natural vehicle for the .44 Special, however none have ever been offered that I know of. A few decades back one was announced and I placed my order, however it never materialized. More than 30 years ago gunsmith Andy Horvath sent me his personal custom .44 Special Model 1892. He had picked up a .44-40 Model 1892 as a parts gun and it was so nice he set the barrel back and rechambered it to .44 Special making for a very handy little carbine. Thanks to Cimarron the 1866 Yellow Boy/Winchester has been made available in .44 Special. The .44 Special has been heavy loaded by many experimenters, myself included, over the past 80 years. These loads are not for the 1866 Winchester; standard pressure loads only need apply.

Cimarron's .44 Special 1866 Carbine has a beautiful brass receiver, curved brass butt plate, and a 19" round barrel. Sights consist of a front blade which is part of the barrel band while the rear sight is a standard notch with an added flip-up blade that allows the use of two more settings for long-range shooting. With the regular sight in use this .44

The original cartridges that made for many sixgun/levergun combinations are the .44-40. .38-40, and .32-20.

Small bore cartridges for sixguns and leverguns include .22 Rimfire, .22 Rimfire Magnum, .32 Magnum, and .327 Magnum.

Any of these cartridges will work well for a sixgun/levergun pairing: .38 Special, .44 Special, .357 Magnum, .41 Magnum, .44 Magnum and .45 Colt.

Carbine is pretty much on the money.

The .44 Special can be used successfully in most leverguns chambered in .44 Magnum on the Winchester Model 92 or Marlin Model 1894 pattern. However, they must be loaded to the same recommended overall length of the .44 Magnum cartridge to work in the Model 1873 chambered in .44 Magnum.

> **TODAY, IF I COULD HAVE ONLY ONE CENTERFIRE RIFLE IT WOULD BE A .357 MAGNUM, AS THEY ARE SO HANDY, ACCURATE AND EASY SHOOTING, AND WILL DO ALMOST ANYTHING I REQUIRE OF A RIFLE THESE DAYS.**

.357 MAGNUM: If I could have only one centerfire rifle it would be chambered in .357 Magnum and it would be the Marlin 1894C. This little carbine can do just about anything I want a rifle to do at this time in my life; actually it has that distinction for at least 98 percent of my rifle needs since Marlin introduced it more than 40 years ago. With the Lyman #358156 Ray Thompson-designed gas-checked bullet over 14.0 grains of #2400, muzzle velocity is just under 1,800 fps and goes up to 1,875 fps with one more grain of powder while shooting exceptionally accurately. The same two loads in a 4-5/8" Ruger Blackhawk clock out at 1,300 fps and 1,425 fps respectively. Without fear of anyone arguing the point, I will say this is about as superb a sixgun/levergun combination as one could come up with.

When it comes to .357 Magnum single-action sixguns, we still have the Ruger Blackhawk New Model, which is too big and heavy for my taste, however it has been sided by the 50th Anniversary Model, which is built on the original size frame from 1955 and also is Flat-Topped. Ruger has also offered the 7-1/2" Bisley Model and although it is the same size as the New Model Blackhawk, I do not have the same feelings towards it as far as weight and bulk go. It simply balances differently with the

Bisley grip frame. Colt has produced the .357 Magnum in both the Single Action and New Frontier versions in both the 2nd and 3rd Generation runs. A 7-1/2" New Frontier is a special favorite and just recently I came up with a 2nd Generation Single Action Army .357 Magnum which was not even come close to shooting to the sights. I turned it over to my gunsmith at Buckhorn Gun and had him fit it with a S&W adjustable rear sight and a 5-1/2" New Frontier barrel. To say I like this little sixgun would be a major understatement. It now shoots to point of aim and handles the way a sixgun should.

Beginning in the mid-1950s Great Western offered their Single Action Frontier chambered in .357 Atomic. This cartridge is nothing more than a standard .357 Magnum cartridge with a heavier dose of powder. Over the years I have come up with a pair of .357 Atomics, one is a 5-1/2" while the other wears a 7-1/2" barrel. These are excellent sixguns and were picked up long before the Great Western became so well known to collectors so the price was exceptionally low on both. The ultimate .357 Magnum sixgun is the Freedom Arms Model 97 which is available in both fixed and adjustable sighted versions. Standard barrel lengths are 4-1/4", 5-1/2" and 7-1/2".

In addition to the Marlin 1894C, Winchester has chambered both the Model 1894 and 1892 in .357 Magnum with the latter being made by Miroku in Japan and these are exceptionally well-made, finished and fitted .357 Magnum carbines.

Browning also offered their version of the Model 92 back in the 1980s while Rossi continues to offer their Model 92 in both stainless steel and blued versions. And for those who like a little more weight to reduce recoil, Henry Repeating Arms chambers their brass-frame Big Boy in .357 Magnum. Finally, Uberti now offers the Model 1873 chambered in .357 Magnum.

.41 MAGNUM: Finding a lever action rifle chambered in .41 Magnum borders on the impossible. I recently stumbled over one on the used gun rack and picked it up expecting it to be a .44 Magnum. I discovered on the second look it was actually a Marlin 1894 chambered in .41 Magnum. I wasted no time in purchasing it. However, I am just now beginning to work with it. Ruger has offered both the Old Model and New Model Blackhawks in .41 Magnum, and Freedom Arms also offers the Model 97 as a five-shot .41 Magnum. I have had both a Bisley Model Ruger and an Old Model Ruger Blackhawk cut back to 5-1/2"and they are ready to start working with the Marlin as a sixgun/levergun combination.

.44 MAGNUM: As mentioned earlier custom gunsmiths in the 1950s first began converting Winchester Model 92s to .357 Magnum and then when the .44 Magnum arrived many 44-40 Winchester Model 1892s became .44 Magnums. Ten

This .32-20 combination, a Winchester Model 92 and a Colt Single Action dates back more than 100 years; they still perform exceptionally well.

years later the factory produced .44 Magnum leverguns began to appear. I've been a fan of Marlin leverguns for six decades; ever since I bought a pair of Marlin shooters, original Model 1894s chambered in .38-40 and .25-20. In the foolish time of life known as teenager I let both guns slip through my hands. I would love to have them back now! In the 1960s, Marlin's 336, a long time deer hunter's favorite offered in .30-30 and .35 Remington, was brought forth as the sixgunner's companion in .44 Magnum. I purchased the first one to hit town and it has now served me well for over 50 years. With its 20" barrel, full magazine tube, and straight gripped stock it is the near perfect woods carbine. It was sent off to gunsmith Keith DeHart to make it

even more perfect by having the barrel cut to 18-1/2" and the overly abundant forearm and butt stock, both made of too much quality walnut, were slimmed down. The result is an even easier and faster handling big bore carbine; matched up with my ever present Bear Buster Ruger 4-5/8" .44 Flat-Top it made the perfect sixgun/levergun combination for deep woods hunting. Over the past 50 years a lot of .44 long guns have come, and some have gone, however this Marlin 336 remains a favorite. Micro Groove Marlin rifle barrels are not supposed to shoot cast bullets very well; this one does just fine. The secret is choosing the right cast bullets with gas checked versions giving the best results. The Lyman #431244GC over 20.0 grains of. #2400

clocks out at 1,625 fps and groups three shots in one inch at 50 yards. I would not ask much more than this from a close range deer/black bear rifle.

In 1969, the Marlin 1894 was resurrected and offered in .44 Magnum. This action, being shorter, is better suited to sixgun cartridges than the .30-30-length 336 action. Marlin also made a special run of Trapper-style 1894S carbines in .44 Magnum with a 16-1/2" barrel, full magazine tube that holds seven or eight rounds depending upon the overall length of the cartridge, a recoil pad on its straight gripped stock, checkering on forearm and buttstock , and excellent sights.

Winchester has also offered a Trapper version of the .44 Magnum Model 1894 with a 16-1/2" barrel, full magazine tube, and has been very popular as a woods gun that packs easily and also goes well with pick-up trucks and jeeps. The short barrels and compact size makes it imminently more practical than a long barreled bolt action especially for the 4x4 riding farmer and rancher. Not only is the Winchester 94AE 16-1/2" Trapper extremely convenient it is also quite accurate making it an excellent close range hunting levergun.

Ruger has been offering .44 Magnum sixguns since 1956 beginning with the Flat-Top Old Model Blackhawk, then the Super Blackhawk, which was then followed by the New Model Super Blackhawk and the Bisley Model. The above-mentioned load of the Lyman #431244GC bullet over 20.0 grains of #2400 clocks out of a 5-1/2" Bisley Model at just over 1,225 fps, making it exceptionally well-qualified to be part of the sixgun/levergun combination with the Marlin 1894.

Texas Longhorn Arms offered both their Improved Number Five and West Texas Flat-Top Target in .44 Magnum and although they can be found they are very pricey. The ultimate, that word keeps coming up when talking about Freedom Arms, .44 Magnum is the Model 83. In stainless steel with adjustable sights and a 4-3/4" barrel it also makes an excellent combination sixgun.

Recently Cimarron has offered a ready-made sixgun/levergun combination from Uberti consisting of the 8-inch Bad Boy Single Action with adjustable sights matched up with the 1873 Winchester replica. Several changes have been made to the Model 1873 to handle the .44 Magnum successfully. However, this is definitely a levergun for standard .44 Magnum loads only.

The only successful levergun offered thus far in .454 Casull is the Rossi Model 92. It mates up with this Freedom Arms 4-3/4" .454 Model 83 which is made it exceptionally versatile by having three auxiliary cylinder chambered in .45 Colt, .45 Winchester Magnum, and .45 ACP. Extra interchangeable front sight blades aid in precise sighting for each cartridge.

.454 CASULL: Once the Super Black-hawk arrived Dick Casull and his partner Gene Fullmer offered five-shot conversions chambered for their .454 Magnum. For several years Casull had been working with his cartridge using five-shot cylinders in Colt Single Actions and then building his own custom sixgun. Now all this time with all the experimenting with all the custom guns the brass was nothing more than .45 Colt, standard .45 Colt brass. However, if the .454 Magnum was to have a future it would have to be offered in a factory built sixgun and also with the availability of loaded ammunition. Since 1983, the .454 Casull five-shot revolver has been manufactured by Freedom Arms. Originally Freedom Arms also offered bullets, brass, and loaded ammunition, however this is no longer true and several manufacturers now offer components as well as loaded ammunition. The .454 is a straight-walled cartridge case which is 1/10 of an inch longer than standard .45 Colt brass. Original brass used large rifle primers, however this was soon changed to small rifle primers to give more brass in the head of the case. For my use in loading for the .454 I prefer to use Starline brass and Remington #7-1/2 small rifle primers.

Once again we must use the word "ultimate" as the Freedom Arms Model 83 is the ultimate .454 sixgun and offered in barrel lengths of 4-3/4", 6", 7-1/2" and 10". I've tried about every load level there is in the .454 Casull using both Freedom Arms factory brass and Starline brass.

(above and right) Either one of these 1st Generation .38–40 Colt Single Actions mate up well with either of these .38–40 leverguns — an Uberti Model 1873 or a Miroku Model 1892.

SSK's 340-grain truncated cone cast bullet can be driven over 1,800 fps in a 10" Model 83, however I prefer to stay down around 1,200 to 1,500 fps for shooter comfort. Dick Casull not only developed the cartridge and designed the Model 83 Freedom Arms five-shot revolver to contain it, he also designed an excellent bullet mold for Lyman which is #454629GC. This is a 300-grain, flat-nosed gas-check bullet which can also be driven to a full 1,800 fps with excellent accuracy and also used in the .45 Colt at around 1,200 fps again with excellent accuracy. Ruger has just recently issued five-shot .454 Bisley Models in stainless steel giving sixgun/levergun shooters a second choice as far as a single action .454 is concerned. It handles the 1,200 to 1,500 fps loads with ease.

Several gunsmiths have tried to convert Marlin and Winchester .45 Colt leverguns to .454 Casull. It works up to a point and then the action starts to stretch. In the 1980s Freedom Arms acquired two Winchester 1894AE leverguns with .45 Colt barrels but unchambered. These were converted at the Freedom Arms factory by chambering them to .454. Same song, second verse. The actions were not strong enough and

started to stretch. The Rossi Model 92 in .45 Colt is an exceptionally strong levergun. In fact, it is strong enough it was chambered in .454 Casull. (This does not mean the .45 Colt version can be used with exceptionally heavy loads.) To come up with the .454 Rossi it was necessary to make some changes including some strengthening. In both the 1894 Marlin and Winchester conversions, it did not take much shooting of full house .454 loads for the action to start stretching. The Rossi, built on the Model 92 action seems to be able to handle the .454. On the back end, the shooter is not in such good shape as the .454 in the relatively lightweight Model 92 exhibits extreme recoil.

This gives some idea of the possibilities in coming up with a sixgun/levergun combination for use today. For most of us the .22 combinations serve well, especially if we have kids and grandkids to teach how to shoot. From there we can go with any combination that will suit our needs. The choices are almost endless as is the pleasure derived.

A PUMP FOR A KID

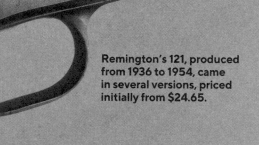

Remington's 121, produced
from 1936 to 1954, came
in several versions, priced
initially from $24.65.

As farms blossomed from homesteads, a borrowed .22 stole my heart

BY **WAYNE VAN ZWOLL**

My parents weren't gun people, so I begged the rifle from a farmer. "I'll buy cartridges and clean the barrel!" He tossed me a box of .22 Shorts, said the tube was full. I skipped down the lane clutching his lovely Remington 121. It wore a Weaver J4 scope a foot long and the diameter of a Magic Marker. On a split rail sniping rats at barn's hem, and under October beeches awaiting squirrels at dawn, I caressed that rifle as a peasant lad might a princess. Our parting left me without a .22. Ensuing decades brought others, but none with the solid feel of that 121, nor its slim, wasp-waist profile, nor the smooth, blink-quick snap of its fore-end.

I longed for a 121 of my own.

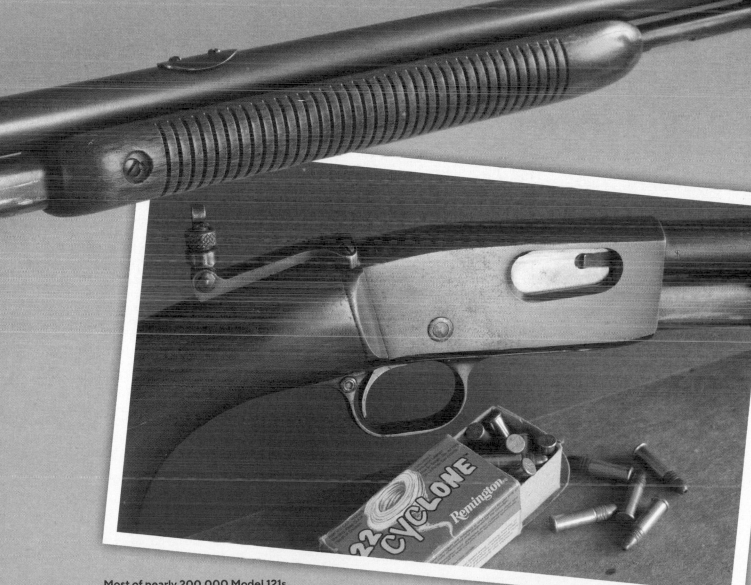

Most of nearly 200,000 Model 121s were bored for .22 Short, Long and Long Rifle cartridges. A few came in .22 Winchester Rimfire (WRF).

My search turned up precious few of these rifles, though the model enjoyed a 15-year production run. Remington's prolific designer Crawford C. Loomis, with George H. Garrison, had re-assessed, then revamped the Model 12 slide-action .22, a John D. Pederson design trotted out in 1909. The 121, dubbed the "Fieldmaster" at its 1936 debut, had a larger, pistol-grip stock, a checkered steel buttplate with lateral grooves and a beefier recoil shoulder on the breech-block. Magazine capacity jumped to 14 .22 Long Rifle cartridges, or 16 Longs or 20 Shorts. The 24-inch barrel (heavier and 2 inches longer than the Model 12's) had open sights borrowed from the Loomis-designed Model 34 bolt-action rifle announced in 1932.

Besides the 121A Standard Grade, which listed initially at $24.65, the Fieldmaster was offered in D (Peerless) and E (Expert) Grades at $78.55 and $122.40. The top-end F (Premier) rifle sold for $152.75.

Less common are 121s barreled for the .22 Remington Special, in Standard, DS, ES and FS grades. This cartridge, by the way, is dimensionally identical to the .22 Winchester Rimfire, or WRF, fashioned for the Model 1890 Winchester slide-action rifle. Both used 45-grain solid bullets — though Remington loaded a round-nose, Winchester a flat-nose — at about 1,450 fps. You could also buy 40-grain hollowpoint ammo. The WRF and Remington Special used flatbase, inside-lubricated bullets, so cases are larger in diameter than those of the .22 Short, Long and Long Rifle with their heel-fitted, outside-lubricated bullets. As .960-inch WRF/Remington Special brass is shorter than that of the 1.052-inch .22 Winchester Magnum Rimfire (also with full-diameter bullet shanks), WMR chambers accept this pair of now-obsolete cartridges.

During the late 1930s and early '40s, miniature clay target games, one dubbed Mo-Skeet-O, became popular. In 1939 Remington announced the Model 121SB Smooth Bore for .22 LR shot cartridges. It retailed for $26.65. At the same time, the company began producing the Routledge-Bored 121A, with a special-order 23 1/2-inch barrel counterbored its forward half to about .40. Patented in 1940 by Fred Routledge of Monroe, Michigan, it was touted to control patterns of .22 shot so 85 percent of the 120-odd #12 pellets struck inside a 6-inch circle at 33 feet. These 121s were not cataloged, just 2,653 were manufactured. Remington also marketed a 25-inch-barreled 121 Skeetrap Rifle with a similar Loewi bore. Its barrels, I'm told, may bear a Mo-Skeet-O inscription.

While the Model 121 survived early post-war changes in rifle manufacture, its days were clearly numbered. Remington dropped the Standard Model in January 1951, and discontinued D, E and F grades in December 1954. At the end of its production run, 199,891 units of this endearing slide-action .22 had shipped. It would be supplanted in 1955 by the Model 572 Fieldmaster, whose receiver profile was shared by Remington's Models 870 shotgun (1950) and 760 centerfire rifle (1960).

***

The 121 had been out of production nearly a decade when, at age 13 and clutching my borrowed rifle, I first slipped around A.I. Root's barn to post myself on weathered rails facing that sad structure. A manure pack four feet thick splayed the splintered walls at their rotting base and forced sheep to climb to enter. Sixteen steps from my perch,

Like many early .22 slide actions, the 121 — including rare smoothbore versions — was a takedown.

surer shot, and less apt to cripple if the bullet didn't hit spot on. The thump of a fox squirrel hitting the forest floor was no less thrilling than, decades later, the tumble of a thundering Cape buffalo.

Slide-operated rimfires, commonly called trombone actions early on, and later widely known as pumps, pre-date the 20th century. Winchester's Model 1890 rifle arrived that year. This exposed-hammer, tube-fed .22 with 24-inch octagon barrel was designed by John Moses Browning as a replacement for the outdated 1873 Winchester lever action — which, despite its great success in .44-40, had sold poorly in .22 rimfire. First offered in .22 Short, Long and WRF (individually), the 1890 was engineered for Long Rifle ammo in 1919. The .22 Short version dominated shooting galleries at county fairs. I used an 1890 in my first efforts to erase a playing-card's diamond with three shots. Alas, diamonds have four points, one of which could always be resurrected by the booth hawker's thumb behind my cloverleaf hole! The Model 1890 would become Winchester's most popular .22 repeater ever. By the time the last of its parts became rifles on the eve of the Second World War, 849,000 had shipped.

Acceding to demand for a more modestly priced slide-action rimfire, Winchester came up with the Model 1906, announcing it in January 1907. It had the 1890's action but a round 20-inch barrel and a composition shotgun-style buttplate. A straight-grip walnut stock

(above) The 121's Fieldmaster name was inherited by Remington's Model 572 pump. A 572 now costs $723!

(left) Early rimfire pumps in .22 Short proved hugely popular in galleries. Hunters then also used Shorts.

I awaited dawn and the first hollow cries of distant crows. As sun fired the horizon, leaves would rustle aloft; a nut would drop. My neck would soon tire of craning to find a squirrel in the colored canopy. When at last I did, I'd as often target the forward ribs as the head. A

rat traffic flickered through holes in the pack, between the straining boards. There I directed my 29-grain solids, each shot an exercise in control as my pulse chattered against my chest and the fuzzy crosswire in that J4 bounced to the beat. A rat that took a bullet at the base of its skull kicked convulsively even as another of the little beasts emerged to gobble the spurting blood. That rodent died too. A double! Breathless, I missed the next shot.

The 121 was also at home while afield. Sneaking through frosted woods in dawn's half-light, I'd search out a dry place under a beech where, shivering,

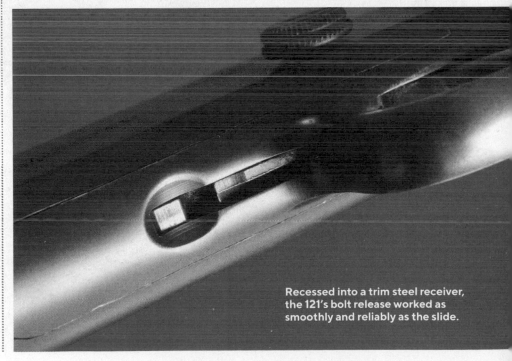

Recessed into a trim steel receiver, the 121's bolt release worked as smoothly and reliably as the slide.

and round, grooved slide handle were common to both models. Early 1906 rifles were listed in .22 Short only, but a year into production they fed Short, Long and Long Rifle rounds interchangeably, an improvement shared by other rimfire pump mechanisms before and after the Great War.

In 1932 Winchester revamped the Models 1890 and 1906. A round 23-inch barrel, shotgun butt and increased magazine capacity defined the new Model 62. It gobbled mixed stacks of .22 Shorts,

Longs and Long Rifles. Three fore-end shapes were used on the Model 62 and, from 1940, the 62-A. Discontinued in 1958, it had a production run of 409,475.

The year the Model 62 appeared, Winchester announced a hammerless counterpart, the Model 61. It came with octagonal barrels in Short only, Long Rifle only and WRF only. Surely more popular was the version with a round 24-inch barrel that fed Short, Long and Long Rifle loads interchangeably. A 61 smoothbore fired .22 LR Shot loads. The

.22 WMR was added to the chambering roster shortly after its 1959 debut. A lovely rifle now pricey on the collectors' market, Winchester's 61 dropped from its catalog in 1963, after 342,000 had shipped.

Savage first entered the slide-action arena with its Model 1903 Hammerless Repeater, fed not by a tube but a detachable box. This takedown rifle had a 24-inch octagon barrel. Initially priced at around $14, it could be had with a rubber shotgun-style butt in an "English"

version for a dollar more. A gallery rifle with "automatic shot counter" in front of the slide handle saw service at the St. Louis World's Fair, where it registered 42,310 rounds. Responding to requests for this specialized .22, Savage sent it to retail outlets in 1907. Price: $25. Four high-grade Model 1903s were listed, the engraved Expert with figured walnut retailing for $40. The 1903 was later joined by the Model 1909 with a 20-inch round barrel but no significant functional change. Both were off the market by 1922.

(above) Bonus! The 121 the author bought wore a proper receiver sight. Standard models came with open sights.

(left) The author found this Remington 121 at a gun show many decades after borrowing one to shoot barn rats.

Savage's tube-fed Model 14 slide-action .22, also hammerless, held 15 Long Rifle cartridges, 17 Longs or 20 Shorts. It had a more substantial pistol-grip stock than the 1903 and 1909, plus mechanical improvements. It was replaced a decade later by the Model 25, with a tang-top cocking indicator, a long-grooved fore-end. A heavy, knurled takedown screw secured its 24-inch octagon barrel. The 25 had a four-year run before it was replaced by the Model 29, with checkered pistol grip and slide handle, a rubber, not a steel buttplate. Savage eliminated the cocking indicator and, eventually, the checkering. Later versions were drilled and tapped for Savage's No. 30 aperture sight, standard equipment on the 29S. The Model 29 left the Savage line in 1967.

Noble Manufacturing, a Massachusetts company in business from 1953 to 1971, offered a slide-action .22 unique for a buttstock that extended forward to house the hammerless mechanism. Fore-end and magazine tube were of conventional appearance.

***

Today the trombone-action .22 is all but a thing of the past. Remington catalogs the 572 Deluxe Fieldmaster, hailing it as "the most popular pump-action .22

The 121's tube accepted 14 .22 LR cartridges, or 16 L, 20 S — more than that of the earlier Model 12.

rimfire made in America today." Unless I'm mistaken, it's now the only U.S.-made .22 pump! It retails for $723.

But my quest wasn't for a new rifle. As I sifted .22s at gun shows, I found a surprising cornucopia of Winchester 1890s and 61s — all at several times the latest list prices, despite honest wear. A few Savage 29s showed up, some Remington Model 12s. The 121 was conspicuously absent. Not so Remington rifles owing their genesis to its designer, Crawford Loomis. Significant among them was the bolt-action Model 37 Rangemaster Target Rifle. A.L. Lowe and Kenneth Lowe helped bring it to prototype stage in 1932. The Depression throttled further development, but this .22 showed up in the hands of a few Camp Perry marksmen in 1937. Production began in earnest the next year. The 12-pound Model 37 featured a heavy 28-inch barrel and match-style stock with front rail. A five-shot box magazine machined from steel, or an equally costly single loading block, fed a dual-extractor bolt. The trigger was adjustable. Remington's micrometer rear sight complemented a Redfield globe front with inserts. At $69.95, the Model 37 was a bargain; but just 1,788

sold before an improved version arrived in January 1940. The new stock had a higher, thicker comb for scope shooting, and a longer fore-end. Several versions appeared, catalog suffixes indicating sight options (e.g. 37AV for rifles with

Wittek Vaver rear sights). After a run of 2,032 improved rifles, WWII interrupted production. The company shipped a total of 12,198 Model 37s before the rifle fell out of the catalog in 1954. The 40x rimfire would replace it two years later.

Crawford C. Loomis, who designed the 121, also fashioned Remington's Model 37 target rifle. The author shot these 50-yard and 50-meter targets, and won a state championship, with a 37. Only 12,000 were built.

I bought an unaltered 37. My friend and fellow competitor Vic Fogle installed a McMillan barrel. That rifle would keep my prone scores near the top of the board and garner two state championships.

Meanwhile I accumulated a handful of sporting .22s, but still none to match the Remington pump growing bigger than life in memory. Then, on a crowded table at a gun show, I spied a slide action with haunting lines. Clawing my way across the aisle, I asked to shoulder it. The action was tight. The slide ran clickety-smooth. A rear aperture sight sat snug on factory-tapped holes. The rifle's original elegance had lost nothing to traces of blue wear on edges, a small wood scar and scraped stock varnish here and there. The seller could have asked more, and I'd have paid it.

These days it's fashionable to check, then report on how well a rifle shoots — to fire groups from a bench until conditions, fate and mathematical probability nudged by repetition give up a one-hole knot. I've yet to put my 121 through such trials, and probably won't. A slide-action rifle properly belongs to a simpler time, when penniless urchins hurried .22 Shorts into magazines, then, over iron sights or through milky, nickel-diameter glass, fought pounding pulse as they crushed the trigger. The value of such rifles is in their ability to flip rats under sagging barns, pull squirrels or crows from high branches and tumble cottontails sprinting through fresh snow. The torn centers of soup cans confirmed zeros; walnuts on fence-posts sifted champion shooters from weekend also-rans.

Surely, the finest .22 sporting rifles date to the first half of the 20th century. While Remington's 121 is only one of several, it was the rimfire that first ushered me afield. Its lethal snap, echoing off barn boards and through beech groves, taught me about killing. Decades later, the thrill and regret of taking a life in fair chase outlasts each faint curl of smoke. Shucking empties from that pump, I shed a little of my innocence. But never did any shot diminish the thrill of the next!

I'm as eager to cheek a Remington 121 now as when begging one from a Michigan farmer half a century ago. In fact, I may pick mine from the rack now, and do just that!

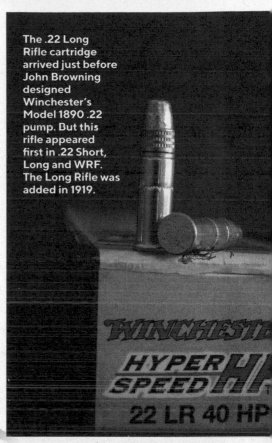

The .22 Long Rifle cartridge arrived just before John Browning designed Winchester's Model 1890 .22 pump. But this rifle appeared first in .22 Short, Long and WRF. The Long Rifle was added in 1919.

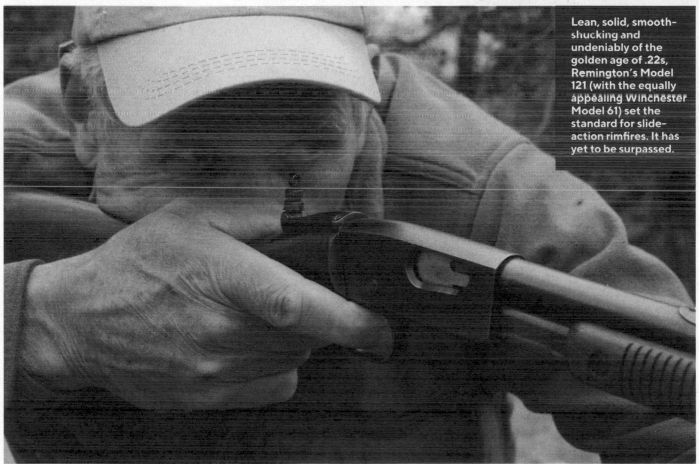

Lean, solid, smooth-shucking and undeniably of the golden age of .22s, Remington's Model 121 (with the equally appealing Winchester Model 61) set the standard for slide-action rimfires. It has yet to be surpassed.

The P6, like all modern SIG pistols, does not use a barrel bushing. In that respect it's like the Browning Hi Power.

THE SIG P6

Remembering a West German icon of the Cold War BY ROBERT SADOWSKI

I did not expect to be drawn into a cult. But that's what happened. In 2000, Germany's police departments were dumping their P6 pistols on the surplus market. There were loads of surplus SIG SAUER P6 pistols suddenly available. Back then, a double-stack 9mm pistol was on everyone's bucket list.

Why would you want a 9mm that held only 8+1 rounds when 15+1 and 17+1 capacity pistols were available? Think girth. I have average-size hands and some double-stack 9mm pistols can be a chore to grasp comfortably. I've always preferred thin-gripped pistols for two reasons: I can grip the pistol better and I usually can shoot them better. When I saw a 9mm SIG SAUER P6 for about $350 I was interested. When I picked it up out of its bright blue plastic box and held it, I immediately knew the gun was going home with me.

The SIG P6 is a compact 9mm handgun that handles like a full-size pistol. The author carried it concealed until, due to fear of having to replace expensive parts, it was "retired" in favor of more modern choices.

The grip was comfortable and easy to control. The P6 was compact yet felt like a full-size pistol. But then there was the trigger, a long stroke that tested finger muscles. It was not as heavy as the trigger pull of a surplus Polish P-64, but in the same neighborhood. I told myself springs were made to be replaced and left with the P6 under my arm. I would soon find out the P6 was an efficient single-stack nine, and little did I know I had just joined the tribe called SIG. I would soon learn why these fantastic pistols garner such a cult-like following. I had become a SIG initiate.

The history of the P6 is like many firearms built for the military or law enforcement: There is a need to sharply cut the production cost of the weapon, yet ensure it is reliable, safe, accurate and easy to operate. In the mid–1970s during the height of the Cold War, when Germany was divided into East and West Germany, the West German police force decided to replace its aging handguns and created a set of specifications for a new pistol. The German police were carrying a Walther PP chambered in .32 ACP. That pistol had been introduced in 1929. It was a good pistol, but was dated and chambered an anemic cartridge. The German police wanted a similar-sized pistol, only chambered in 9mm.

All the big players — Walther, SIG SAUER and Heckler & Koch — ramped up to develop a new pistol that would meet the spec. Back then, steel stamping was a manufacturing method that greatly reduced material and labor cost. Walther offered up the P5, which was basically an updated World War II-era P38. Heckler & Koch overthought the German police

Marking on the right side of the slide indicates this is an authentic German police–issue SIG. "P6" indicates the model, "NW" for Nordrhein-Westfalen state police, and "9/80" means the pistol was proofed in September 1980.

(above) Front grip-strap serrations provide a good hold on the P6. These features, coupled with its 9mm chambering, make it a very controllable handgun, and quite accurate.

specifications and created the P7. This was a compact 9mm with a squeeze cocker, and gas-delayed blowback locking action. The P7 would also become revered among semi-automatic pistol aficionados, but it turned out to be too expensive to build and the German police passed. SIG presented the P225, which was a slimmed down version of its P220. The P225 used all the features of the P220 but in a more compact size. (The P225 is 6.9 inches long and has a 3.6-inch barrel while the P220 sports a 4.4-inch barrel.) At its widest point, the

P225 measures 1.3 inches while the grip is 1.2 inches thick. Unloaded it weighs 30.5 ounces.

The P220 was unique as it used a modified Browning link system, which has since been copied by numerous pistol manufacturers. The SIG system locks the barrel and slide together using an enlarged breech section on the inlet of the barrel lug. Upon firing, the barrel and slide move rearward together, then the barrel tilts as the slide continues rearward to eject the empty case and scrapes a fresh round from the magazine, loading it into the chamber. The P220 also uses a double-action/single-action (DA/SA) trigger system, where the first shot is fired double action and all subsequent shots are fired single action. What SIG added to the P220 was a decocking lever that allowed the right-handed user to decock the hammer and place the pistol in double-action mode.

The P225 had all these features but the

(above) The SIG P6 field-strips quickly and easily. This also endeared it to the German police agencies that used it.

(left) P6 disassembly breaks down into a few components, easy to clean and maintain.

real innovation was the way the pistol was manufactured. The slide was made of stamped steel and welded together with a steel breechblock pined into the slide. It was inexpensive to produce and that ultimately was one of the reasons the German police purchased it.

Safety features on the P225 included an automatic firing pin block that is deactivated when the trigger is pressed fully rearward. It also incorporated a drop safety. The SIG P225 was safe, accurate, reliable, inexpensive and chambered in 9mm. The German government approved pistols for sale to police and designated the models with a "P" for police (Polizei) and, after the P225 was configured to West German standards, it was called the P6.

So what are the differences between the P225 and P6? The P6 has a heavier 24-pound DA trigger pull. That was the trigger pull I first experienced with the P6. A long, heavy trigger pull was considered an added safety feature. It takes real effort to pull it. The P6 mainspring weight was increased to 24 pounds from the 18-pound mainspring in the P225. Perhaps the most noticeable difference is

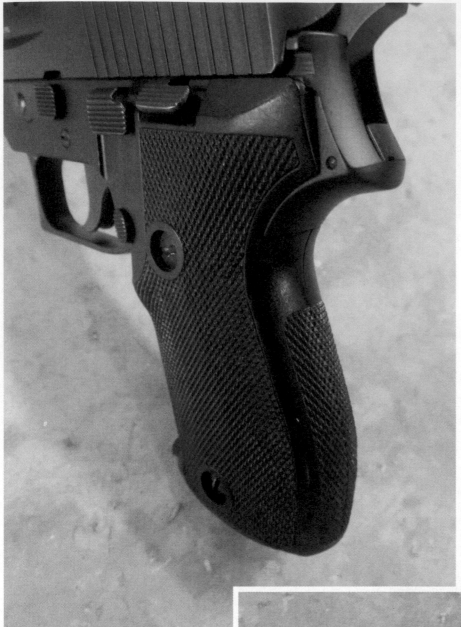

the odd-looking spur hammer, specification for which came directly from the German pistol standard. The notch was intentionally designed to bend or snap off due to an accidental drop. It serves as a visual indicator of a dropped gun incident.

Another difference with the P6 was the barrel feed ramp. The shape of the P6's ramp differed slightly from the P226. The P6 was designed to use FMJ ammunition — the standard ammo of the time. You might find your P6 doesn't tolerate modern JHP ammunition.

Lastly the markings on the P6 differ from the P225. The P6 is void of the SIG P225 rollmarks and has "P6" stamped on the right side of the slide just forward of the ejection port. West German agency markings can also be found on the right side of the slide and are typically two to three uppercase letters. Mine reads "NW" for Nordrhein-Westfalen state police. Toward the muzzle is the date code production in the form of month and year. Mine reads "9/80" which indicates a pistol proofed in September 1980. The side and barrel also share the same last three digits of the serial number, which tells me my P6 has all matching serial numbers.

When I first handled the P6 I experienced its superbly designed grip. It's thin, yet has some palm swell, which was an improvement over the plain-checkered plastic grip. It's compact and points well, and tears down like most SIG DA/SA pistols, which means disassembly for cleaning is fast, simple and intuitive. It is an older pistol so you won't find a

(above) The grip panels come together to form the rear grip strap. This saves weight and uses less metal in the manufacturing process. Being less expensive to manufacture made it appealing to German police agencies of the time.

(right) The P6's sights are large and modern, giving you a good sight picture. This feature was ahead of its time.

Accuracy was good with the P6. Even with JHP ammo it chewed through everything without any mishaps.

captured recoil spring like you will on a modern model. The sights are modern, meaning they are large and allow you to easily acquire the target. As I wrote earlier, the trigger was the feature that dated the P6. Trigger reach was excessive and took too much effort to fire in DA. In SA, pull was about half the weight of the DA pull.

My P6 shows no preference for bullet type and in fact chews through JHPs as easily as it does FMJs. After I purchased the P6 I carried the pistol concealed for a while and retired it only because I was afraid a part would break, and I wouldn't be able to find a replacement, or the parts would cost as much as a new polymer-frame pistol. I've had various SIG handguns pass through my hands and the P6 is the one I've kept.

I tend to speak with reverence about the P6 as do others. It's compact and yet performs like a full-size pistol. As us proud members of the SIG cult know all too well, there are many reasons why the P225 was reintroduced!

(below left) The P6 uses an automatic firing-pin safety.

(below right) The spur hammer on the P6 was specified by the German police. It was used to determine if a pistol had been accidentally dropped.

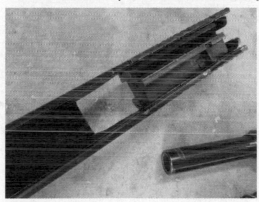

SPECS

Model:	SIG SAUER P6 (P225)
Caliber:	9x19mm Parabellum
Action:	Semi-Automatic, short recoil-operated, locked breech
Trigger:	Single-action/ double-action
Barrel Length:	3.9 in.
Overall Length:	7.1 in.
Weight:	30.4 oz. (unloaded)
Grip:	Checkered polymer
Sights:	Fixed, notch rear/ blade front
Finish:	Blued
Capacity:	8+1, single-stack magazine

Table A. Performace: SIG SAUER P6

9mm Load (grs.)	Velocity (fps)	Energy (ft-lbs)	Best Accuracy (in.)	Avg. Accuracy (in.)
Aguila 124 FMJ	1,007	279	1.67	2.1
Federal American Eagle 115 FMJ	1,155	341	2.0	2.5
Hornady American Gunner 115 XTP	1,070	292	2.7	2.9

Bullet weight measured in grains, velocity in fps and average accuracy in inches for best five-shot groups at 25 yards.

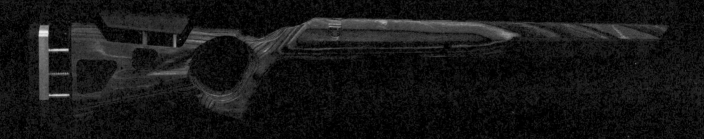

The diminutive Mossberg Shockwave .410 is no slouch for home defense. It packs a wallop and its low recoil makes it easily controllable.

MOSSBERG 590 SHOCKWAVE .410

A Blunt Blaster in .410 is No Pipsqueak

BY **AL DOYLE**

It has to be a Class 3 weapon. That was my first impression upon laying eyes on the Mossberg 590 Shockwave. After all, it is a pump shotgun with a 14-inch barrel and a "raptor" pistol grip (think modified bird's-head design). Surely it would have to be on the ATF's list of National Firearms Act (NFA) weapons, which require a $200 tax stamp and exhaustive background check.

Of course, my assumption was wrong. A March 2, 2017, letter from the Bureau of Alcohol, Tobacco, Firearms and Explosives (ATF) classifies the Shockwave as a "fire-arm" under the Gun Control Act of 1968. At the street level, that means the Shockwave is in the same category as handguns under federal law. That might not be so in certain anti-Second Amendment states and localities, but this compact piece can easily be purchased over the counter at most places in America.

Produced in 12 and 20 gauge and .410 bore, I tested the .410 Shockwave for practical reasons. As a 61-year old, I'm no spring chicken and it doesn't take a crystal ball to see that less recoil could be helpful — even necessary — as the

aging process continues. I also wanted to determine if the .410 version would be up to the task of home defense, as the Shockwave was clearly designed for this crucial purpose. Known for its lack of recoil, the .410 is sometimes scorned as a pee wee by those who swear by the 12 gauge. Only a moron would question the deadliness of the 12, but its recoil and muzzle blast can be too much for many older folks to handle.

It's hard to precisely describe what goes into the "cool" factor, but the Shockwave scores high in that department. It screams

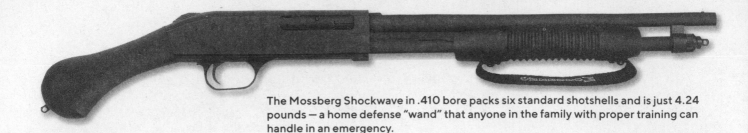

The Mossberg Shockwave in .410 bore packs six standard shotshells and is just 4.24 pounds — a home defense "wand" that anyone in the family with proper training can handle in an emergency.

"Handle me!" and that experience is positive. At 4.24 pounds (the 12- and 20-gauge Shockwaves are heavier), the .410 feels like a deadly wand. A sturdy nylon strap is attached to the "corn cob" fore-end, which makes hanging onto the gun easier. That really isn't an issue with the .410, but it could be useful for the larger Shockwaves. Of course, the real purpose of the nylon strap is for safety — to ensure you keep your hand behind the muzzle.

But how do you hold and shoot such an unusual weapon? The Shockwave's design makes it a natural for hip shooting, but that's a technique with which most gun owners have little or no experience. My limited practice with this technique went no further than gaining a measure of accuracy with .22 pistols, so I was eager to see what would happen with the Mossberg.

It took just a few rounds for the action to become pleasingly smooth, but its light weight caused me to tilt the barrel higher than needed. Shots at 7 to 12 yards — longer than typical home-defense scenarios — went above the target.

More practice and a lower point of aim solved the problem.

Holding the Shockwave like a long gun and looking down the barrel to the brass bead is a familiar practice for anyone with shotgunning experience, but it also requires mental adjustments. Since there is no stock you can forget about getting a good cheek weld. Holding it at eye level with your arms extended is the preferred method.

The .410 proved to be accurate after a brief trigger time. A variety of 3-inch loads of #5 and #6 shot (11/16-ounce payload) displayed even, wide dispersal on small silhouette targets. Winchester 3-inch Xpert steel shot weighs in at a mere 3/8 ounce, and it provided similar accuracy as the heavier loads. I would have preferred something tighter than the standard cylinder bore, but the setup is more than adequate for a short-range shotgun.

The Shockwave fired slugs and 000 buckshot accurately and with ease. Nonexistent recoil and the handiness of the design led to much rapid-fire shooting by me and the other gray-haired testers. It's not a normal range practice for me, but fast firing almost seems natural with this .410.

As one 70-year old described his experience, "This is nice. No recoil, it's smooth

The author tested 000 buck from the .410 Shockwave, and it was no "pee wee." Shot grouped as expected, even when fired from the hip.

and fun to shoot."

According to Linda Powell of Mossberg, "Many people are surprised that it is legal and don't understand why it isn't classified as a short-barreled shotgun," she said. "The Shockwave far exceeded our expectations. We had to revise our forecasted production schedule more than once to accommodate the numbers of orders after the extremely successful launch."

YouTube and gun-related websites are full of videos and reviews of the Shockwave. Its eye-catching looks mean this Mossberg is sure to turn up in numerous places — from low-budget independent films to traditional Hollywood movies. The .410 version will require more initial practice time than a traditional scattergun, but the extra effort will be an enjoyable and almost recoil-free experience. The MSRP of $455 won't break the bank.

The Shockwave pounded .410 slugs into targets accurately and quickly — low recoil gave the author the confidence to unleash volleys of rapid-fire groups from normal self-defense ranges.

SPECIFICATIONS

MODEL: Mossberg Shockwave .410
GAUGE: .410 Bore
CAPACITY: 6
CHAMBER: 3 in.
BARREL LENGTH: 14.375 in.
SIGHT: Bead
CHOKE: Cylinder-bore
BARREL FINISH: Matte blued
STOCK: Raptor Grip/Corn cob fore-end w/strap
WEIGHT: 4.24 lbs.
LENGTH: 26.37 in.
mossberg.com

With the Kimber .22 Conversion Kit installed, this Kimber Stainless II has become a rimfire target pistol.

PROJECT KIMBER RIMFIRE TARGET .22

Taming a 1911 .45 Auto with the Kimber Rimfire Target Conversion Kit

BY JIM HOUSE

When I was a youngster growing up during World War II, the ".45 Automatic" was as easily recognizable to me as was the single-action ".45 Peacemaker" that I saw in so many Western movies. Both handguns were legendary hallmarks of their types, and they continue to be so today. Loosely described as a "model 1911," the single-action, single-stack autoloader in .45 Auto (aka the .45 ACP) is now available in a bewildering array of versions from a very large number of manufacturers other than Colt. Versions from the most basic models to the highly customized and ornate are available.

Long ago, it was realized that the 1911 pistol and .45 Auto cartridge were effective in combat, but such a pistol in a rimfire chambering would be more comfortable to shoot. Many years ago, Colt offered such a pistol, known as the Ace. Later designs have resulted in .22 conversion kits that replace the slide and barrel of a .45 so that the same frame can be used for either caliber. Such kits

The business end of a 1911 autoloader looks quite different when the pistol is configured to shoot .22 LR.

SPECIFICATIONS

MODEL: Kimber .22 Conversion Kit
CALIBER: .22 LR
SLIDE: Aluminum alloy
FINISH: Black or silver
BARREL LENGTH: 5 in. (full size); 4 in. (compact)
BARREL MATERIAL: Stainless steel, match grade
SIGHTS: Adjustable (full size), fixed (compact)
WEIGHT: 13.2 oz.
MSRP: $339
kimberamerica.com

When converted to a .22, this Kimber Custom II performed extremely well.

Attaching the conversion unit involves removing the slide and replacing it with the kit.

are now available from Kimber, Marvel Precision, Ciener and Tactical Solutions. Several manufacturers offer .22/.45 conversion kits in multiple versions. The Ciener kits offer a choice of units with fixed or adjustable sights, whereas those from Tactical Solutions include models that feature different accessory rails, threaded muzzles, etc. Kimber produces a conversion kit with a slide/barrel in black and silver colors.

My handgun collection includes five Kimber 1911s, three of which are .45 Auto models. It was only a matter of time until I would find it almost necessary to convert one of them to a rimfire, and the Kimber Rimfire Target Conversion Kit was the logical choice.

When I first opened the box, I was impressed with the fit and finish of the unit. My plan was to mount the kit on a black Kimber Custom II, so I ordered the black version and chose the one with a 5-inch barrel and target sights. However, the kit has spent a lot of time on a Kimber Stainless II model giving an attractive two-tone look, the same as that of my Kimber Pro Carry II.

Getting the Conversion Kit in place proved to be utterly simple. First, the slide is removed in the conventional manner for a 1911. The kit has the slide and barrel held together so it was a quick job to slide the unit into place and replace the takedown pin. That's it. Kimber says that the unit can be placed in less than one minute and that is not an exaggeration. My Kimber Custom II weighs 38 ounces in the .45 Auto configuration, but the Conversion Kit utilizes an aluminum slide and weighs only 13.2 ounces, so in

The .22 Conversion Kit works well on the full-size Kimber Stainless II (right), but it is shown here installed on the more compact Kimber Pro Carry II (left).

Although magazines that hold .45 Auto cartridges are made of steel, those for use in the Kimber Conversion Kit are made of a rigid polymer.

.22 LR the weight is only 31.9 ounces. Installing the conversion slide on a Kimber .45 Auto basically gives you a Kimber Rimfire Target model. The Kimber unit is available in a 4-inch barrel version with fixed sights, and the 5-inch model with adjustable sights. Both versions have an MSRP of $339.

Although the kit results in moderate weight when mated with the frame of a full-size 1911, when placed into the aluminum-alloy frame of a Commander-size Kimber Pro Carry II, the result is a .22 weighing only 24.7 ounces. Such a combination is a light rimfire pistol that retains all of the functions of a .45 Auto. (Note: the kit will not work on 9mm pistols.) Accuracy is not diminished because the barrel and target sights are not altered.

There are many interesting features of the conversion unit. First, the slide houses a stainless steel barrel and a full-length guide rod. The recoil spring is much less stiff than those used in centerfire pistols, so pulling the slide to the rear requires less force. The barrel does not need to be locked to the slide to shoot .22 LR ammunition, so the kit operates on a simple blowback principle. The kit comes with one 10-round magazine that is made of a rigid polymeric material. Due to mag design, the slide is not held open after the last shot. The tension on the magazine spring is light, so it's easy to load 10 rounds of .22 LR.

As is the case with producers of other conversion kits, Kimber recommends the use of high-velocity .22 ammunition to move the slide smartly and cock the hammer. Even though the slide is made of alu-

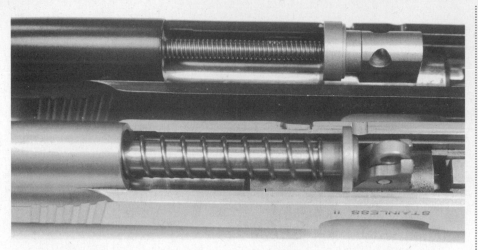

The .22 LR produces very little recoil so the recoil spring in the Conversion Kit (top) is much less robust than the one found in a .45 Auto (bottom).

Feeding of high-velocity .22 LR cartridges was flawless with most types of ammunition.

The fully adjustable rear sight on the .22 Conversion Kit shows clearly how to adjust.

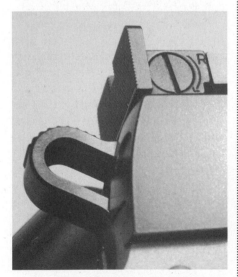

On many autoloaders, the rear sight can be adjusted for windage by moving it laterally by applying pressure, but the Conversion Kit sight can be adjusted by simply turning a screw.

minum and therefore much lighter than the steel one in a .45 Auto, the extra push of a high-velocity .22 LR provides reliable cycling of the action. In that regard, I can say that feeding of several types of high-velocity .22 LR ammo was flawless. Only one type of bulk, value-priced ammunition resulted in any malfunctions.

Accuracy of a handgun can be assessed adequately only with the aid of a machine rest. By any other means, it is the eyes, grip and coordination of the shooter that are being evaluated. Therefore, I am satisfied when a pistol shoots as well as I do and does so with complete reliability. On any of the 1911-type frames, accuracy of the Conversion Kit was more than satisfactory. It outshot me, producing 1.5 to 2-inch groups at 25 yards. I like to carry a .22 when roaming the woods and fields in search of varmints and a converted 1911 is hard to beat.

The Kimber .22 Conversion Kit is a high-quality, durable unit that is easy to install without tools. It provides a low-noise, low-recoil and less intimidating way to gain confidence with the world's most famous pistol.

Converted to a .22, this Kimber Stainless II 1911 is an excellent choice for hunting small varmints with a handgun.

YOUTH SHOTGUN REVIEW:
CZ 720 G2
REDUCED LENGTH

Youth and female shooters found the CZ Model 720 Reduced Length 20-gauge autoloader easy to shoot, getting those critical first hits on clays.

A Handy Little 20-Gauge Autoloader Wins Over First-Time Shooters

BY **COREY GRAFF**

What shotgunner can forget his or her first time touching off a round from a big, bad 12 gauge? For some new shooters, the experience isn't too unpleasant (much like eating a frozen dinner: it's edible, but you do it only when you must) while others seem to suffer deep emotional scars from the surprising snap to the shoulder. The way they tell it, it's as if they've been punched by Evander Holyfield himself. Thankfully, some companies offer reduced-length shotguns in light-recoiling 20 gauge to make that first shotgunning experience go more smoothly. One such shotgun is the 720 G2 Reduced Length youth model from CZ-USA.

The foundation to successful shotgun-

The Model 720 youth model sports a two-tone finish with a polished section of the receiver that transitions to a matte black aluminum alloy. The semi-auto shotgun holds 4+1 shells when the waterfowl plug is removed.

SPECIFICATIONS

MODEL: CZ 720 G2 Reduced Length
GAUGE: 20
BARREL: 24 in.
MAGAZINE CAPACITY: 4+1
MAX SHELL LENGTH: 3 in.
CHOKES: Includes 5 (F, IM, M, IC, C)
STOCK: Turkish Walnut
LENGTH OF PULL: 13 in.
BARREL FINISH: Matte Black Chrome
RIB: 8mm Flat Vent
OVERALL LENGTH: 43.5 in
WEIGHT: 6.3 lbs.
COMB: 1.4375 in.
HEEL: 2.25 in.
SAFETY: Crossbolt Behind Trigger
MSRP: $499.00 USD
cz-usa.com

ning starts with stock fit, and the Model 720 Reduced Length comes in a comfortable 13-inch length of pull. Its 24-inch barrel is long enough for new shooters to point effectively to get those first critical hits on clay to keep up their interest, yet not so long as to be unwieldy. That barrel sports a black hard chrome exterior finish that shrugged off scruff marks from shooting. The 720 comes with five choke tubes (F, IM, M, IC, C). At just a whisker over 43 inches and an honest 6 pounds in weight, this special Model 720 is ideally designed for youth and female shooters. Its trigger trips at about 9 pounds. The shotgun has a 4+1 capacity when the included waterfowl plug is removed.

We tested the 720 Reduced Length this summer with help from my wife Michelle, and daughter Aria, both of whom shot it well. However, because I'd neglected to clean the shotgun from the box, we initially had about a 30 percent jam rate on its first outing. After cleaning the shotgun — it was apparently gummed up with storage grease and cardboard dust — it ran like a Toyota (no issues). Shooting Kent's Elite Target 20-gauge shells (7/8 oz. at 1,200 fps), the little autoloader ran perfectly.

Everyone who tested the shotgun agreed that it was a nice-looking firearm, with a two-tone finish between a polished section of the receiver that transitions to a matte black aluminum alloy portion. The Turkish walnut wood was nice, albeit basic, as has been my experience with previous CZ shotguns.

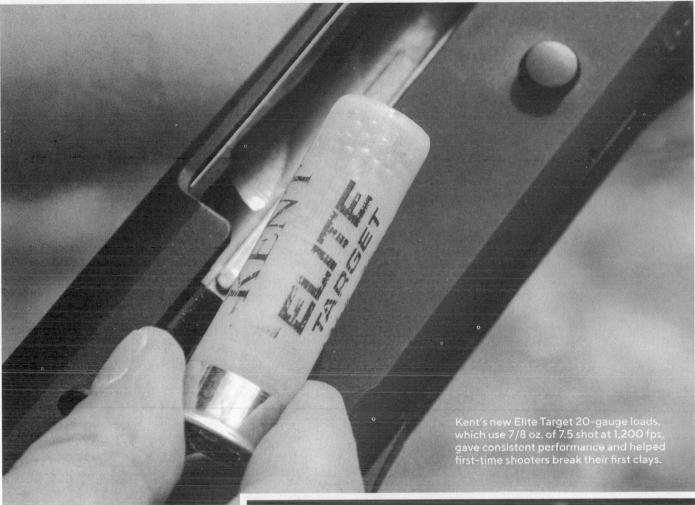

Kent's new Elite Target 20-gauge loads, which use 7/8 oz. of 7.5 shot at 1,200 fps, gave consistent performance and helped first-time shooters break their first clays.

But not all is ferries and pixie dust in Wonderland. Both Michelle and Aria lacked the hand strength to push the bolt release button and had to set the shotgun on the sporting clays stand and leverage downward with all their body weight to release it. Testers also found the cross-bolt safety difficult to push. CZ would do well to lighten up both to improve ease of use for beginners. In the meantime, a trip to a gunsmith would be money well spent and would make a good shotgun great.

Clean up duty with the Model 720 went better than expected. I found it simple to disassemble; there was no guessing which way the gas piston or action arm components needed to be aligned. It was as a no-brainer, fit together intuitively.

The gals found the classic-style stock to be of marginal fit; females tend to have outward curved shoulder pockets and longer necks, and the 720's straight stock

After cleaning, reliability was 100 percent with the CZ Model 720 youth. Just be sure to clean the shotgun as new from the box, as storage grease and oil tend to collect cardboard dust, which can gum up the works on your first outing.

made it somewhat awkward for our new shooters to acquire a natural cheek weld. I'm convinced that, had there been some adjustability in the buttstock angle and cheek weld height, they would have broken more clays and had even more fun.

But fun they did have. First-time shooters won't soon forget their first shotgunning experience — and that's not because it involved a scary whack to the shoulder. With a street price around $350, CZ has delivered a memorable first shotgunning experience at a price point everyone can afford to share.

The CZ Model 720 is covered in a tough, hard-chrome black exterior finish that will give years of service in the game fields as new shooters dish out the abuse.

The CZ 720 Reduced Length 20-gauge shotgun has a 4+1 capacity when the included waterfowl plug is removed. Beginners had no trouble stuffing shells into the magazine loading port.

The BRN-10A feels familiar in hand and, with nearly 9 pounds of rifle, generates mild recoil.

RETRO AR-10: BROWNELLS MODEL BRN-10A

A Vintage Battle Rifle Reproduction Delivers the Goods

BY **ROBERT SADOWSKI**

In the mid–1950s the idea of a combat rifle built of polymer and aircraft-grade aluminum was a completely alien concept to the established military forces of the world. Can't be done, many said. Dumb idea. Today it is common, even normal. But in 1956 Armalite was ahead of the curve and produced a rifle like no other using high-tech materials such as forged aluminum and molded polymer. Modern material meant this new combat rifle weighed a pound less than any other combat rifle at the time. Armalite called it the AR-10. It was truly a modern marvel among the combat rifles of that era and the progenitor of all modern sporting rifles that followed.

The AR-10 was cutting edge, but fewer than 10,000 were produced. Originals are not easy to find. Luckily, Brownells is now producing the BRN-10A, a faithful reproduction of the iconic AR-10.

Brownell's retro AR-10 Model BRN-10A is a faithful reproduction of the 1950s-era gun with some useful upgrades that make it a sweet shooter.

An original AR-10. Brownells tried to replicate the look and function in the BRN-10A. Photo courtesy Rock Island Auction Company

There were several modifications Armalite made to the AR-10 design as it sold it to various military forces around the globe. From my research, Brownells patterned the BRN-10A after the AR-10 sold to Cuba. That rifle was notable for its full-length handguard and its lack of a bayonet lug. Subsequent rifles, such as those sold to Guatemala, Sudan, Portugal and a few more nations, had minor design tweaks that were requested by the military forces purchasing the rifles.

The BRN-10A uses the same direct impingement (DI), rotating bolt mechanism for which the AR-10 and the later AR-15 are known. In DI, gas is siphoned from the barrel when a shot is fired. The gas travels down a gas tube where it pushes back on the bolt carrier group (BCG) to cycle the action. On the upside, this system makes the rifle lighter and more compact. Since the BCG is lighter than one with, say, a piston mechanism, there are fewer parts and less mass moving during cycling so there is less perceived recoil for a follow-up shot. The downside of direct impingement is that the BCG heats up and fouls faster due to gun powder and gas being blown into the mechanism via the gas tube.

The BRN-10A uses a unique trigger-style non-reciprocating charging handle underneath the carry handle. It's retained by an internal detent system that takes some effort to operate. But being

SPECIFICATIONS

MODEL: BRN-10A
CALIBER: .308 Winchester
ACTION: Semi-automatic, direct impingement, rotating bolt
TRIGGER: Single-stage
BARREL LENGTH: 20 in., fluted, 1:10 twist
OVERALL LENGTH: 40.75 in.
WEIGHT: 8.5 lbs. (unloaded)
GRIP: Checkered polymer
STOCK: Fixed polymer
HANDGUARD: Fluted polymer
SIGHTS: Fixed front blade, adjustable rear peep
FINISH: Blued
CAPACITY: 20+1 magazine
brownells.com

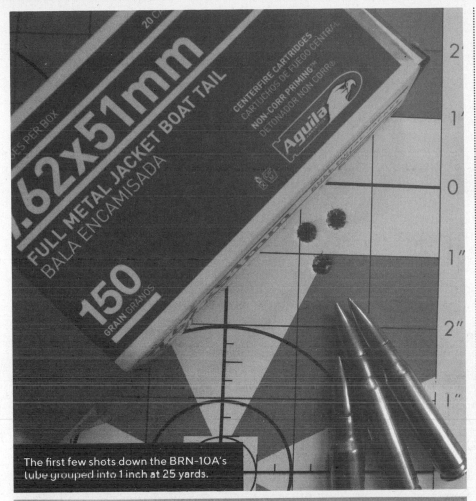

The first few shots down the BRN-10A's tube grouped into 1 inch at 25 yards.

Eugene Stoner holds an AR-10 in this still shot from a promo film circa 1956.

Brownells plans to offer new waffle-pattern magazines to give the BRN-10A an even more retro look.

a new rifle, I'm sure that will break in with use. The upper receiver is also void of a shell deflector and forward assist just like the real deal.

With any reproduction there are differences between it and the original. Brownells has the luxury of 20/20 hindsight and made sure to beef up parts that weren't up to snuff in the original design. The Brownells rifle is a mixture of both old and new, making it a shooter, not a safe queen. One of the modifications was to use a bolt carrier and trigger group based on the DPMS/SR25 pattern. This was to improve the reliability and durability of the rifle and ensured parts would be readily available — a smart move. Another good idea was to modify the BRN-10A to be compatible with modern DPMS/SR25-

TABLE A. PERFORMANCE: BROWNELLS BRN-10A

Load	Velocity (fps)	Energy (ft-lbs)	Best Accuracy (in.)	Average Accuracy (in.)
Aguila 150-gr. FMJ	2,715	2,456	2.0	2.6
Black Hills 168-gr. BTHP	2,554	2,434	2.9	3.1
Sellier & Bellot 150-gr. SP	2,736	2,494	2.1	2.2

A heavy-contoured barrel with fluting is found underneath the two-piece handguard.

pattern magazines, which are easily obtained and inexpensive compared to original AR-10 mags. Plus, this allows you to use any modern AR-style .308 mags you have on hand (except for Magpul PMAGs). The rifle is shipped with one 20-round magazine. Original magazines had a unique waffle pattern, and I've been told Brownells plans to offer waffle-style magazines later. The waffle mags will make the BRN-10A look like the 1956-era rifles.

Other original features on the BRN-10A include a heavy profile, fluted barrel with a three-prong flash hider. The 20-inch barrel has a twist rate of 1:10. Faxon manufactures the barrels for Brownells. The sights are true to the original design. The front post is machined and non-adjustable. The rear sight is adjustable for windage and elevation. Also like original AR-10s are the controls. The magazine release, safety selector and bolt release all mimic orig-

The muzzle device is a three-prong Dutch-style flash hider.

Brown furniture mimics the Armalite AR-10's original fiberglass look. Note the handguard is two pieces and is held in place with a slip ring.

The trigger-style charging handle is located under the carry handle and is non-reciprocating.

The rear peep sight makes for fast target acquisition and is adjustable for both windage and elevation.

inal AR-10s. Following the style of the original is the lower's magazine well. It is squared off giving it a blocky look, and it's flared to more easily insert a magazine.

Brown-colored retro furniture copycats the original fiberglass handguard. Another nice improvement made by Brownells was to use a slip ring to hold the two-piece handguard in place. Original AR-10s required the front sight to be removed to remove the one-piece handguard. The handguard also has the vent holes and fluting like the Cuban version of the AR-10. The buttstock is close to original, but the pistol grip is not. Original pistol grips flared at the butt and were smooth with texture on the backstrap. The buttstock also has sling swivels — another modern improvement. With an unloaded weight of 8.5 pounds, the BRN-10A has some heft, which reduced felt recoil.

I had on hand both FMJ and soft-point ammo: Aguila 7.62x51mm with a 150-grain FMJ, Black Hills .308 Winchester with a 168-grain BTHP and Sellier & Bellot .308 Winchester with a 150-grain soft point. I started out at 25 yards just to see where the BRN-10A was printing. The first three-shot group out of the rifle was shot with Aguila

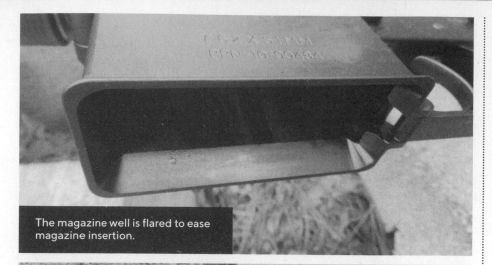

The magazine well is flared to ease magazine insertion.

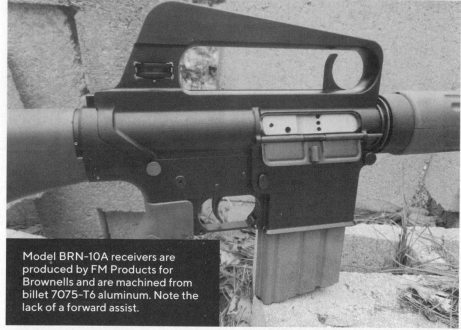

Model BRN-10A receivers are produced by FM Products for Brownells and are machined from billet 7075–T6 aluminum. Note the lack of a forward assist.

Cocking the rifle requires a new procedure and a strong finger to initially rack the bolt carrier group.

FMJs and it measured about 1 inch. Once I had my dope, I moved the target to 100 yards and used my range bag as a rest and an old gym sock filled with sand under the toe of the butt. Moving to 100 yards, I anticipated groups to open up and they did, but the BRN-10A performed well with open sights. The rifle liked 150-grain bullets.

Three-shot groups averaged 2.5 to 3 inches — very acceptable groups with open sights. Recoil was mild thanks to the weight of the rifle and its direct impingement system. Follow-up shots were fast on target. The charging handle is the only issue I had with the rifle. Operating it requires a different procedure. I had to use my strong hand to manipulate the charging handle instead of my support hand. In use, the charging handle should become much easier to manipulate. The trigger pull weight was between 4 and 5 pounds.

Kudos to Brownells for creating the BRN-10A. It's difficult to replicate a rifle like the AR-10 since it went through so many design changes. I like the look and feel, but the real test is putting lead downrange and this rifle performed. Though the rifle is dated compared to modern ARs, the rebirth of the AR-10 into the BRN-10A is more than nostalgia. It is a shooter.

The safety selector looks period-correct and will be familiar to those trained on an AR-15.

The Barrett M107A1 semi-auto .50-caliber sniper rifle modified for use with a suppressor — known as the Quick Deploy Large Caliber Suppressor (QDL). It slashes noise level by 23dB.

A QUIETER .50 CALIBER

The Barrett M107A1 and QDL Suppressor Offer the Most Power for the Least Recoil and Noise

BY **JIM DICKSON**

For those who want a big-bore, high-powered, long-range rifle with lots of firepower, the Barrett .50 caliber has long been the ultimate. The 180dB noise from this beast has put many off, but Barrett offers a silencer — known as the Quick Deploy Large Cali-ber Suppressor (QDL) — that reduces the noise by 23dB (to 157dB), the same as a .45 ACP 1911. You'll still need your hearing protection when you drop the hammer on these massive cartridges, but now the suppressor — coupled with that long overall length — seems quieter to the shooter than firing a .45 automatic.

The M82A1 modified for use with a suppressor is the M107A1. The Barrett is a recoil-operated rifle, so you never have to worry about a gas system clogging up with fouling and jamming. It's a big gun that weighs 28.55 pounds with an overall length of 56.8 inches — that's 4 feet, 9 inches — certainly no pocket

Firing the Barrett without the suppressor. The dust kicked up gives some idea of the muzzle blast.

QUICK DEPLOY LARGE CALIBER SUPPRESSOR (QDL)

The Barrett M82A1 modified for use with a suppressor is the M107A1 and uses the Quick Deploy Large Caliber Suppressor (QDL). Since the suppressor creates a gas back pressure that interferes with the mechanical cycle of the gun, the following changes were made to the suppressor-equipped M107A1:

- The muzzle brake was altered to allow the suppressor to be mounted.
- Due to increased back pressure, the recoil springs were doubled in strength.
- The receiver was changed from steel to a one-piece aluminum extrusion, cutting 4.7 pounds from the standard M82A1.
- The bolt carrier and its subassembly were changed.
- The bolt latch was removed as it was not working fast enough with the suppressor — timing is now set by a bolt extender mounted on the accelerator.
- Due to the increased back pressure, there was more fouling and carbon buildup including hard carbon fouling, so the finish was changed from Parkerizing to NP3 nickel phosphate coating and to Nitride on the bolt carrier. These surfaces are easier to clean than Parkerized surfaces and have improved lubricity.
- The bolt and barrel are a mated set as they are produced. The bolt shape was changed to allow faster operation and reduce weight.
- A polymer cheek piece was added on the top of the buttstock for shooter comfort in extreme heat and cold. This was a huge improvement over the M82A1.
- Polymer handgrips were used on the lower receiver instead of steel.
- Both the trigger components and the transfer bar are NP3 coated.
- The buffer and the buffer spring were redesigned. The buffer now has a sleeve to prevent the bolt from going too far back.
- The magazines were redesigned with a new follower to accommodate the faster cyclic rate with the suppressor.
- Witness holes were added to the back of the magazine to allow instant check of available ammo left in the magazine.
- The bipod is now largely titanium with a polymer foot.
- The impact bumper over the barrel was increased in size, which absorbs some of the recoil.

pistol. The barrel is 29 inches long (a 20-inch variant is available) with a 1:15-inch rate of twist. It sends a 660-grain bullet at 2,750 fps for a maximum range of 8,046 meters. That's about 5 miles. It fires semi-auto from a 10-round magazine. There is a manual thumb-lever safety and the adjustable rear sight adjusts from 100 to 1,500 meters. Disassembly and reassembly is fast and easy.

MSRP is a whopping $15,000 but you get what you pay for.

Telescopic sights are a given on a long-range weapon like this and scopes by Leupold, Nightforce and Vortex have been

A sniper team cocking the M107 .50-caliber Barrett rifle. Despite a nearly 70-pound recoil spring, the enormous .50 is quite easy to cock.

A closeup of the massive QDL suppressor of the M107A1 Barrett .50-caliber rifle. This king of the cans weighs 4.8 pounds and is 14.84 inches long, 2.5 inches in diameter.

successfully used on this rifle. A laser rangefinder is a very useful accessory and highly recommended at these ranges.

The big gun is surprisingly pleasant to shoot. It kicks less than a bolt-action .30-06 with suppressor. Note that suppressors are the world's most efficient muzzle brakes. Gas is forced forward against the suppressor's baffles and drags the gun forward. You feel a very long shove more than a kick as the recoil-operated mechanism spreads out the recoil force throughout the cycling of the action. With a 70-pound recoil spring you would expect this gun to be hard to cock, but I wish the German G3 rifle cocked this easy. Trigger pull is a crisp 8 pounds.

The M107A1 I tested shot 2 MOA. It is a mistake to think that a 2-inch group will expand in an even cone over longer distances. Sometimes it will, or once the bullet stabilizes it can quit drifting off course — accuracy may improve at greater distances. Combine this with the .50-caliber BMG's superior wind-bucking abilities and you can see why this gun has been such a success as an extreme long-range (ELR) sniper rifle.

Even though the Barrett .50 was intended to take out vehicles at ranges to 2,000 yards and farther, it has proven to be a very effective anti-personnel sniper rifle with confirmed kills out to 1,800 meters. There is one unconfirmed kill at 2,200 meters with the earlier M82A1 version. Its effectiveness on vehicles was demonstrated best by Sergeant Kenneth Terry of 3rd Battalion, 1st Marines in the Gulf War when he destroyed an Iraqi BMP-armored personnel carrier at 1,100 meters with two armor-piercing incendiary (API) rounds, causing two other BMPs with it to surrender.

The M107A1 offers the most power for the least recoil and noise of any big bore out there. It is a fun gun to shoot and that is all the justification one needs for a gun. I did not want to quit firing this cannon. As a gun writer I get to shoot a lot of different rifles, but few are as much fun as this one or as pleasant to shoot. Unfortunately, the saying "All good things must come to an end," applies to ammo. When the ammo runs out, buying more is not like run-

IT'S TIME TO DEREGULATE SUPPRESSORS

The Barrett M107A1 is a prime example of the need for silencers — and how effective a suppressor can be — to protect hearing. On the other hand, it completely blows away the myth of suppressors making a gun noiseless. Despite this, efforts continue to regulate suppressors. In the gun-owner camp, many are afraid to own a National Firearms Act (NFA) weapon. Currently, suppressor ownership requires what many consider onerous red tape and invasion of privacy by the ATF. Of course, the anti-gun crowd is in favor of anything that hurts gun owners and they fight tooth and nail against repealing the laws against suppressors.

As of press time of this edition, the Hearing Protection Act of 2019 was reintroduced in congress, which would deregulate suppressors on the federal level. The bill, introduced by Rep. Jeff Duncan of South Carolina, is supported by groups such as The American Suppressor Association and Gun Owners of America (GOA).

ning down to the local sporting goods store and grabbing a box of .30-06 stuff. It often must be ordered and can run around $5 per round.

The Barrett M107A1 is a premier long-range weapon encouraging you to learn the science of long-range shooting. Barrett has its own training programs for people interested in learning this skill. There is an immense satisfaction and feeling of accomplishment at hitting the target at extreme ranges with such a powerful cartridge. The suppressed Barrett M107A1 would be a lot of fun taking out wild hogs ravaging a bean field. You have plenty of power and long-range capability for this work and the semi-auto action is advantageous if you're planning on getting more than one hog.

The Smith & Wesson Model 15 was one of the most popular sidearms for law enforcement a few decades ago.

THE SMITH & WESSON MODEL 15
COMBAT MASTERPIECE

A Revolver Approaching Perfection

BY JIM HOUSE

As a youth, I spent a lot of time looking at gun literature, and during my teenage years an older brother would always buy the latest *Gun Digest* annual book. During those years, I formed opinions about what I liked, what looked good and what others said about firearms. Although I admired single-action revolvers (who doesn't), it was the extensive line of Smith & Wesson revolvers that attracted me. Some had long barrels whereas others were the usual snubnose models with 2-inch barrels. Neither of those extremes attracted me, but what did was the Smith & Wesson Model 15, also known as the Combat Masterpiece. That sleek revolver with a 4-inch tapered barrel and target sights seemed to me to be perfectly proportioned.

The S&W M15 was introduced in 1959 to serve as a high-quality carry gun for law enforcement. It traces its lineage back to the Model 10, which was introduced in 1902 and chambered for the .38 S&W Special, a cartridge that was devel-

Prior to 1977, Smith & Wesson revolvers utilized a pin to lock the barrel, preventing it from rotating with repeated firing.

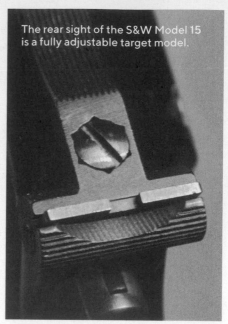

The rear sight of the S&W Model 15 is a fully adjustable target model.

The front sight consists of a square-topped post on a ramp.

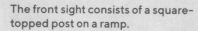

Adding Uncle Mike Boot Grips is the only change made to the author's Model 15.

oped to provide a more effective handgun than those chambered for the earlier .38 Colt, which had been ineffective in several military campaigns. There have been endless debates regarding the effectiveness of the .38 Special as a defense load so I will not add fuel to that fire. I will merely say that given the enormous strides in developing effective handgun ammunition, effectiveness is not as much of an issue today as it was in bygone days when about the only load available was a 158-grain round-nosed lead bullet shot at 850 fps. Today's jacketed lightweight hollowpoint bullets have greatly enhanced the performance of the .38 Special.

Almost 50 years ago, I joined a Sheriff's Reserve Unit and needed a handgun that was capable of firing .38 Special ammunition. Some recruits bought the Model 19 Combat Magnum, but with its heavy barrel, oversized grip, and shrouded ejector rod that model never had the same eye appeal as did the

Model 15. My choice was clear: I bought my Model 15 at a special price of $87. It was not my first centerfire handgun, but it quickly became my favorite. The serial number indicates that it was produced in 1970 and at that time the barrels were pinned into position in the frame. That practice was discontinued by S&W in 1977. Built on the midsize K-frame, the Model 15 is large and heavy enough to be durable, but not so much so that it is burdensome.

For a revolver in .38 Special, a 4-inch barrel is just about right. I have a S&W Model 14 K-38 Masterpiece with a 6-inch barrel and with a considerable number of ammunition loads, the velocity difference between the Model 14 and the Model 15 is normally only about 25 to 35 fps. Both models have cylinder-to-barrel gaps that are similar. With a scope mounted, the Model 14 will shoot very small groups at 50 yards, so it

Ammunition loaded with bullets from 95 to 158 grains assures the versatility and effectiveness of the .38 Special.

This photo shows the dramatic expansion of the 110-grain Winchester Silvertip when fired into water.

The Hornady Critical Defense load provides outstanding terminal performance as shown by this bullet.

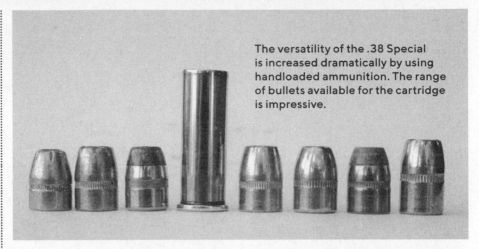

The versatility of the .38 Special is increased dramatically by using handloaded ammunition. The range of bullets available for the cartridge is impressive.

would have an edge in that configuration for hunting, but the Model 15 is much more portable. As a result, it has accompanied me on many outings in many places.

Back in the early 1970s, during one exploratory hike in an area that had both wooded and open areas, it became apparent from the holes dug along banks and near stumps that some critters were lurking nigh. Suddenly, from one of the holes about 35 yards away, appeared an outsized specimen. Slowly I drew the Model 15 from its S&W high-ride holster and took careful aim. At my shot, the animal slid back down into the hole, but I knew that I was successful. I had bagged the largest groundhog that I had ever taken. That day the S&W with a factory 158-grain load won the moment and I became a handgun hunter. Since that day the Model 15 has been used on varmints more than any other handgun I own. It is an excellent tool for those walks while being on the lookout for varmints of opportunity.

This .38-caliber Speer Gold Dot bullet shows clearly why it is considered a premier defense projectile.

My Model 15 has remained stock except for changing grips. In place of the factory wood panels, the discontinued Uncle Mike Boot Grip resides. These panels are made of a checkered rubber-like material that not only provides a comfortable, secure grip but also takes up part of the space behind the triggerguard.

Trigger action on my Model 15 is superb. When firing in single-action mode, let off occurs with no prior travel at a pull weight of 3.5 pounds. In double-action firing, trigger pull requires 9.5 pounds and is very smooth throughout. The Model 15 is provided with a square-topped ramp front sight that is serrated on the rear face. The rear sight is fully adjustable and has a square notch in the blade that mates perfectly with the front sight. The sights are free of gimmicks and, except for those found on

some specialized target revolvers, are as good as any and better than most on any handgun. I do not own a machine rest, but even shooting with the hands propped on a rest, groups at 25 yards measuring 1.5 to 2 inches are routine.

In my knife collection, I have a model that was described in the accompanying literature as "pleasing to the hand and eye." When it comes to the Smith & Wesson Model 15, that description is apt, but I also add, "pleasing in performance." If I had to start dispensing of my handguns, I believe my Model 15 would be the last to go. With it I can accomplish most of the tasks for which a handgun is suitable. Quite frankly, given my experience with the Model 15, I have never been disappointed with my decision half a century ago.

It is readily apparent from this five-shot group fired at 25 yards that the S&W Model 15 lacks nothing in accuracy.

Colt's Finest – THE PYTHON

Why the Colt Python is Still the Cadillac of .357 Magnums

BY ROBERT K. CAMPBELL

The Python is arguably among *the* finest, if not the finest production revolver ever manufactured. It offers both class and style in a beautiful package.

Sometimes things have to get a little age on them before they are fully appreciated. This is the case with both the author and the Colt Python. The Python and I are children of the 1950s, although I don't remember a lot about that decade. I grew up with the trappings of the time, including the '57 Chevy and firearms that had been commonly used since the Depression.

In those days, few shooters used both automatics and revolvers. It was one or the other. The tide was yet to turn, and we were a nation of revolver men. In 1935

There is a certain family resemblance between the Colt Python (top) and the Three Fifty Seven Magnum (below).

the introduction of the .357 Magnum cartridge basically eliminated the need for the .38 Super Automatic. The FBI and its savvy law officers had a high-penetration belt gun and it was a first-class revolver. Prior to World War II there was a great deal of development in custom revolvers. Short, fast actions with better accuracy were custom built and so were heavy barrels and barrel ribs. Improved adjustable sights were developed. After the war, with civilian production gearing up again, these improvements were codified into modern revolvers.

Colt introduced a revolver in 1953 simply called the "357 Magnum," or often in print, "Three Fifty Seven Magnum." It was a deluxe version of the Trooper, which was introduced the same year. Both evolved from Colt's .41-frame Official Police and were excellent heavy-duty Magnum revolvers.

The mid '50s were heady times for handgunners. The .357 Magnum was a popular service cartridge, just 20 years old, and the .38 Special was the most popular target cartridge. Smith & Wesson introduced the Combat Magnum in

1954, a .357 Mag. on a .38 Special frame. Then in 1956 Colt brought back the Single Action Army and Smith & Wesson introduced the .44 Magnum. Meanwhile, Colt improved the Officer's Model Match, a target-grade Official Police revolver — the result was the Python. The new Colt Python revolver scarcely resembled the original, save for the .41

frame. Colt lengthened the cylinder, and strengthened it and the frame to handle the .357 Magnum cartridge. This included a thicker topstrap and a heavier crane. The recoil plate was eliminated and instead the firing pin hole was drilled into the frame. (The Python design is robust but the floating firing pin will not withstand a steady regimen of

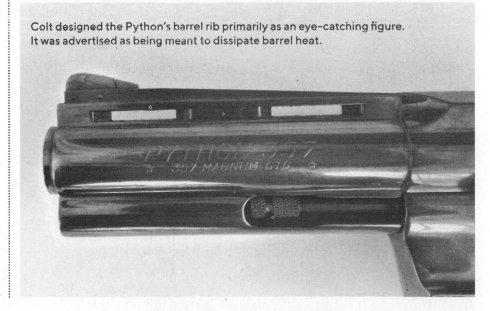

Colt designed the Python's barrel rib primarily as an eye-catching figure. It was advertised as being meant to dissipate barrel heat.

This nickel–finished model proved a tackdriver with Winchester .38 Special ammunition. Note trigger shoe and Rogers grips.

dry fire. If you must dry fire the Python or similar Colt revolver, use snap caps.)

The single most prominent feature of the Python is the bull barrel. This is one of the reasons for its great accuracy. The barrel features a fully shrouded ejector rod. The rib is a flamboyant addition that sets the piece apart as a premium revolver. The rib was advertised as dissipating heat, yet in more than 40 years of revolver shooting and competition I have yet to witness heat mirage from any revolver. But the Python's rib is eye-catching and that was the intent.

Two of the author's most-prized firearms, the Python and Colt 1911 Series 70.

The 1/8-inch front ramp sight is ideal for most uses and the fully adjustable rear makes zeroing the revolver easy. Grips are well designed and have excellent checkering. Early models featured grips with a thicker top that sometimes impeded the ejection of spent cases. I have not experienced this problem, but the stocks may interfere with some speedloaders. The newer cut offers better utility and seems to complement the Colt's flowing lines.

The most common Python barrel length is 4 inches. I like this length, as it doesn't push up on your belt while you're driving a car, and I can discern no accuracy deficit when using this barrel length. The 2.5-inch barrel is rare, a 3 inch very rare, the 6 inch common, and there was an 8-inch hunter version produced. I have never seen a 5-inch barrel Python but I've heard that a few were made, and were available on special order to law enforcement in the early 1980s.

The nickel-finished stainless steel Python was always a strong seller. My 1977 version is blued steel, although "blue" doesn't really describe the beautiful Colt Royal Blue finish. My first experience with the Python involved a trade in which I swapped a Krag Jorgensen rifle. I asked myself: why would anyone trade such a beautiful gun for my old Army rifle? At the time Krags were bringing about $800 in pristine condition and Pythons a little less. It was a trade I don't regret.

I carried the Python on duty as a young officer for several months. My first revolver qualification was shot with it. At the time, after firing the Smith & Wesson for so many years as a young shooter, I did not fully appreciate the hand-honed Python action. And it is truly a hand-fitted, hand-polished action. The action on the Three Fifty Seven was smoother than any modern revolver, but the Python was even slicker. The Lyman electronic trigger-pull gauge shows the Python's single-action trigger breaks at a crisp 4 pounds. The revolver weighs 2.9 pounds overall.

The Python eventually became too expensive to manufacture at an affordable price. Small shops such as Les Baer Custom turn out quality 1911 handguns

that aren't inexpensive but are worth the tariff. Folks seem unwilling to pay for a similar effort when put into a revolver. It seems that a modest number of custom shop Pythons didn't sell that well and Colt could not afford to keep the product line going. Today's price for collector-grade Pythons is stout: An excellent-condition sample is fetching $2,000 to $3,000, about the same as a nice Les Baer or Wilson Combat 1911. Rare Pythons and unfired examples in the original box cost twice that of the shooter-grade ones. There are rough, hard-use and even abused Pythons that folks are asking ridiculous prices for.

What do you get for the price? A Python is one of the few hand-fit revolvers ever made. The care in manufacture and design adds up to a beautiful handgun and the single most accurate revolver I have ever fired. A good, tight Ruger GP100 comes close, but only in benchrest fire. Firing offhand, the smooth double-action Python allows a trained shooter to make hits quickly and smoothly.

The Python action must be understood. If you have heard of an old timer placing a dime on the barrel rib and dry firing the gun without disturbing the dime, it is true. I have seen it and done it myself. The long rolling action is capable of such handling. But you must pull the trigger through and then allow the action to reset. If you do not allow a full reset as the trigger returns and attempt to press it to the rear too soon, you might tie the gun up or break the hand. The Colt rewards a trained shooter. (Remember my previous comment: If you dry fire a Python, use snap caps.)

How accurate is the Python? I've fired excellent groups on a good day and have never been displeased with a Colt Python's performance. Among the single most accurate loads I have shot is the Black Hills Ammunition .38 Special 148-grain wadcutter. This classic target load breaks 750 fps. I've shot a five-shot group at 25 yards that fell into less than an inch when firing off the bench with the aid of a Bullshooter's pistol rest. The Black Hills 158-grain Cowboy Load is good for less than 2 inches. Either would make an excellent small-game load.

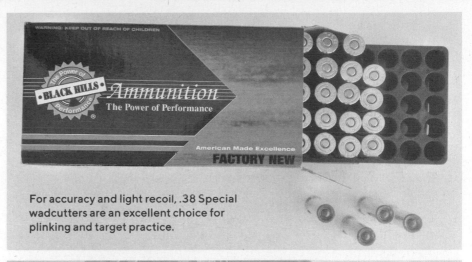
For accuracy and light recoil, .38 Special wadcutters are an excellent choice for plinking and target practice.

A full-power 125-grain JHP is a singularly effective defense load.

The original-style grip panel, left, isn't as friendly to speedloaders.

Offhand fire is rewarding to those who practice it. The double-action trigger pull on the Python is excellent. Superb accuracy and fast shooting are the benefits of this feature.

control the muzzle and bring the front sight back on target for a hit.

I've also engaged in long-range shooting with the Python with excellent results. I've used a 173-grain hardcast SWC from Matt's Bullets loaded in .38 Special cases. At 1,000 fps these bullets are brilliantly accurate well past 100 yards. Theoretically the Python should be good for 4-inch groups at 100 yards, but visual acuity and hand tremors can interfere with this plan. Just the same, I'm able to hold on the neck of a silhouette target and fire a double-action group that destroys the X ring at 100 yards.

Most of my shooting is with .38 Special loads, but among the most useful all-around Magnum loads is one composed of Titegroup Powder and the Hornady 125-grain XTP. Rather than breaking 1,400 fps, this number is loaded to 1,270 fps, plenty fast for most uses. The powder burn is clean and the load is good for a 15/16-inch group at 25 yards. This is what the Python is all about for me: enjoying good ammunition and testing it in an accurate revolver. The Python is certainly up to digesting full-power Magnum loads, though. For personal defense, the Black Hills 125-grain JHP is deployed. This load will break 1,420 fps in my 4-inch Python. Accuracy is excellent. In the .41-frame Python recoil isn't a problem. Take aim, fire, allow the trigger to reset as the barrel rises,

Suffice it to report, the Python is more than suited for use as a go-any-where, do-anything revolver. If you're an accomplished shooter, the type who can coax good accuracy from a Colt Gold Cup National Match 1911 or a SIG P210 9mm, then you will appreciate the Colt Python. There are still some to be found with light bluing wear that make excellent shooters. Remember, the quality remains long after the price is forgotten.

HOLSTERS FOR THE PYTHON

This D.M. Bullard pancake-style holster is ideal for concealed carry.

The Python weighs about 40 ounces in the 4-inch version, so you need a superior load-bearing holster. Even when hiking and hunting I wear the piece covered. DM Bullard offers a first-class pancake-style holster that hugs the body and offers good concealment. This makes packing the Python a joy compared to cheap fabric scabbards. I added basket weave finish to my order and ended up with an exceptional holster. When a holster is dedicated for field use, I like a crossdraw model. The draw is good with practice and the handgun can be drawn quickly while seated or driving.

Galco's cartridge pouch holds six cartridges arranged in twos for quick reloading.

The Galco Phoenix is an interesting design with many good features. These include a sewn-in sight track, reinforced thumb break and retention screw. Some like an easy draw, others like a hard yank to draw. The retention screw allows setting the presentation for what is desired. I added a Galco cartridge pouch. This pouch carries six cartridges in banks of two. For personal defense, the Galco O speedloader pouch is also a good choice.

The author shooting his Ruger .44 Magnum Flattop. It's proven to be an accurate, handy woods gun. It was even carried for specific lawman duties while he was sheriff — namely going on horseback to chase down ruffians who tried to escape into West Texas brush country.

RUGER FLATTOP .44 MAGNUM

A Skeeter–Style Packin' Gun Serves the Sheriff Well

BY **JIM WILSON**

Two of the great gun writers of the past, Elmer Keith and Charles A. "Skeeter" Skelton, are responsible for this big-bore revolver addiction of mine. They were both great advocates of the .44 Magnum cartridge. Since I devoured just about everything these two gentlemen ever wrote, I quickly decided I had to have one.

My first experiences with the cartridge involved the big N-frame Smith & Wesson revolver designated as the Model 29. While it was a wonderfully made and superbly accurate double-action revolver, it just didn't fit my hand. I tried big stocks, little stocks and stocks with a grip adapter, and I just couldn't find anything that would keep the big sixgun from pounding the daylights out of my meat hooks. To be clear, I consider that a personal problem and not a mark against one of the greatest handguns that Smith & Wesson ever built.

Then, back in the early 1970s, I came across one of Ruger's origi-

Ruger Flattop .44 in original Roy Baker Pancake holster. It rides high and carries the Ruger snugly.

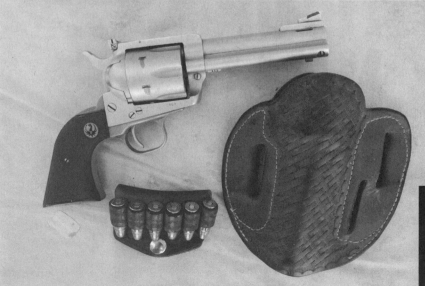

With its 4 5/8-inch barrel, the author's custom Ruger .44 Flattop has served as a genuine packin' piece inspired by gun writers such as Elmer Keith and Skeeter Skelton. With six rounds of heavy hardcast .44 Magnum loads, it is a formidable sidearm.

nal .44 Magnum Blackhawks at a Dallas gun show. Skeeter had used one that sported the rare 7 1/2-inch barrel. The gun that I found had the 6 1/2-inch barrel and was used, but not abused. I figured that it would make a great project gun for some custom work that I had in mind.

There are many stories about how Bill Ruger came to find out about the Smith & Wesson .44 Magnum project. Whatever the true story might be, Ruger quickly jumped on the bandwagon. He took his popular .357 Blackhawk and beefed it up so that it would handle the extra pressures of the new .44 cartridge. The .44 Magnum Blackhawk was introduced in 1956 and was manufactured until 1962. Today, we refer to it as the .44 Flattop because its topstrap was flat, lacking the sight protecting additions that are found on later Blackhawks.

I quickly found I could shoot full-house .44 Magnum ammunition in this single action without it beating my hands to smithereens and causing me to flinch. The curved grip frame fit me very well and caused the gun to roll in recoil, minimizing the felt recoil. It also became quickly apparent that, if I tucked my little finger under the bottom of the grip, I could get off some pretty quick repeat shots.

As a working peace officer, I relied upon my Colt .45 auto to protect my hide. What I wanted in the Ruger .44 was a gun that I could carry when I was out working cattle from horseback, wandering in the woods or while I was rifle hunting. I recalled that Elmer Keith liked the 4-inch Smith & Wesson revolvers because they were out of his way while he went about his ranching and guiding chores. It appeared to me that cutting the Ruger's barrel flush with the end of the ejector rod to 4 5/8 inches would give me the handy yet powerful handgun that I was looking for.

Back in those days, one of the top gunsmiths in the Dallas/Fort Worth area was a fellow by the name of Lou Williamson. He was known for doing excellent work on just about any kind of firearm and was

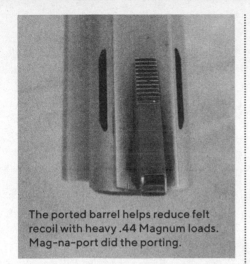

The ported barrel helps reduce felt recoil with heavy .44 Magnum loads. Mag-na-port did the porting.

interested in taking on my packing gun project. Williamson began by tuning the action and giving the gun the light trigger squeeze that I requested. Good sights and an improved trigger go a long way toward making a handgun easy to hit with. And the Ruger already had a very nice micro-adjustable sight on the rear.

The next step was to cut the barrel to 4 5/8 inches. Williamson did just that and also cut the barrel with a recessed crown to protect it from damage. After replacing the front sight, the barrel was shipped off to Mag-na-port. While the porting was not necessary for shooting standard-velocity magnum ammunition, it was a distinct aid in managing the recoil of hotter handloads and heavy bullet loads.

The final step, once the .44 Ruger was reassembled, was to send it to Armoloy for the firm's durable coating. Armoloy was one of the very first electroless chrome-finishing processes. It was originally designed for coating ball bearings to make

them function more smoothly and last longer. One indication of Armoloy's durability is the fact that my old Flattop doesn't have a scratch on it after nearly 50 years of heavy use. It has never needed a tune-up.

In keeping with my idea of the .44 Ruger being a packing gun, I wanted a holster that would carry it high on my hip and out of the way. The Roy Baker pancake holster fit that bill to a "T." It rides high on the hip and snugs the gun into the body like no other holster I have ever found. Simply Rugged Holsters makes a close copy of that original pancake rig to this day, although my Roy Baker is still in good shape and still in service.

Keith and Skelton also influenced the ammunition that I most commonly use in my Ruger. Skelton's load consisted of a .44 Special case, a 250-grain Keith hardcast bullet and a load of Unique powder that would generate 900 to 1,000 fps. Naturally, Keith's load used the same bullet, a .44 Magnum case, and a substantial load of 2400 powder, which probably pushed the bullet out at around 1,350 fps. Both loads were surprisingly accurate.

While I have shot a fair amount of factory JHP ammunition through the gun, my preference still goes for those cast-bullet loads. Being a little lazy in my old age, however, today that ammunition usually comes from Garrett Cartridges or Buffalo Bore Ammunition. Both companies make heavier .44 loads in the 300-grain range and up that are suitable for shooting just about anything on four legs. That's the ammunition that I have chosen when my travels have taken me to big bear country, although I have yet to meet a grizzly

that I was mad enough at — or was upset enough with me — to shoot.

One of the reasons that this .44 Ruger Flattop is such a favorite is that we have shared many very enjoyable adventures. I've taken whitetails, javelina and feral hogs with it as well as several Rio Grande turkeys. One of the nice things about cast-bullet loads is that they don't tear up turkeys, leaving lots of good meat to go into the frying pan. Most of my game shots have been made while I was just bumming around out-of-doors and, of course, if the game was in season at the time.

For a time, I was the elected sheriff of a Texas county down near the Rio Grande. As I mentioned earlier, I generally wore a .45 Colt automatic while doing my sheriff chores. But the problem with our county was that Interstate 10 ran right through the middle of it. Consequently, we would often get after yahoos who were wanted from all over the country. These guys would first try to outrun us in their vehicles, then, failing that, they would dump the vehicle and hit the brush. West Texas brush is very unforgiving and this was rarely a good idea.

In those cases, I often had to go on horseback to find the wandering felons. Now, I just never did like to have an auto pistol while on horseback. If you must shoot from the saddle, Old Dobbin is likely to get gymnastic on you. In which case, while the pistol is drawn and trying to keep yourself and the saddle connected, that auto is liable to go off after you fire your intended shots — mainly when you don't really want it to. My solution was simple. The Ruger .44 Flattop and a cartridge belt were standard equipment carried in the trunk of my county car. I don't care what happens, after you shoot a single action, it is not going to go off again unless you cock the hammer again. It was a handy solution and that big .429 bore seemed to have a soothing effect on most miscreants.

Living with a gun for almost 50 years creates a bond. And that has certainly been the case with my Ruger .44. It's an accurate, powerful and durable sidekick that I have come to rely on. Today, I am blessed to have several very nice guns, many of them custom jobs, but I simply can't imagine keeping house without my Ruger .44 Magnum Flattop revolver.

For comparison: An original, unaltered Ruger Flattop .44 (top) with the author's custom gun (bottom).

NEW RIFLES

Bergara's new Ridgeback and Highlander rifles, on Premier actions, join the B-14-series HMR (here).

More ARs, yes, but more than ARs. Better bolt-actions. A rebirth of levers. And .22s.

BY **WAYNE VAN ZWOLL**

You don't need another rifle? Neither do I. Gun makers get it. You won't see many rifles fashioned to fill an honest-to-gosh *need*. Even "entry level" arms have unnecessary features, and fire more potent, more costly cartridges than called for.

Alberta trapper Bella Twin carried what you might call a basic rifle. One day, deep in the bush, she saw a grizzly

Clean machining to tight tolerances, plus fetching profiles and accurate barrels distinguish Bergara rifles.

then decided to fire as the bear passed, mere feet away. The .22 rimfire bullet from her single-shot Cooey Ace 1 dropped the beast. Many decades later, that grizzly still ranks 28th in Boone and Crockett's all-time records.

The Cooey Ace 1 is long dead. Inexpensive .22s endure, though not built to brook the hardships of Bella Twin's wilderness. Among centerfires, only "dangerous game" rifles wear iron sights. The wants if not the needs of hunters have changed. They want to kill game at longer range. They want sub-minute accuracy. Concurrently, they lust for lighter rifles and more massive scopes.

Target shooters chasing one-hole precision now have the necessary barrels and ammo. The long-range shooting trend has driven rifle design, as well as development of optics with Blue-Tooth wizardry to bring hits at four-figure distances. Such products have found the hunting field. New, short-torso cartridges with long, rocket-shaped bullets are selling to the walls.

But there's plenty on tap for traditionalists, from legendary arms-makers, but also from new firms building rifles with classic mechanisms and profiles. Cartridges once

thought moribund have reappeared, some friskier than ever. And custom-shop rifles wear elegant new iron sights.

Don't *need* another rifle? The industry is playing to your *wants*.

Ashbury Precision Ordinance

The new Saber M700 Tactical Rifle in 6.5 Creedmoor and .308 joins Ashbury's Saber Sport Utility line, built on selected Remington 700 barreled actions. Saber MRCS-AR MOD-1 modular chassis and Rifle Basix triggers distinguish these entries, which offer other modern features and a list of options. Prices start at $2,750. *ashburyprecisionordnance.com*.

Barrett

Fieldcraft rifles from Barrett are commercial versions of the semi-custom rifles designed and built by Melvin Forbes of New Ultra Light Arms. At 5 to 5 3/4 pounds, the Fieldcraft series pares weight to a minimum while maintaining fine balance and the clean, traditional lines of the Forbes stable. With MSRP starting around $1,800, Fieldcraft rifles appear in 10 chamberings, .243 to .30-06, including 6.5x55 and 6mm Creedmoor. Yes, Barrett still makes big .50s. *barrett.net*.

Bergara

New Ridgeback and Highlander Rifles feature Bergara's Cerakoted stainless Premier action with Palma mid-weight and fluted standard-profile stainless barrels, respectively. The cone-shaped "floating" bolt head on these rifles (and on four others in the Premier series) assures smooth feeding and superior lug contact. Bayonet-style bolt design permits tool-free assembly/disassembly. A sliding-plate extractor, non-rotating gas shield (bolt shroud) complement a TriggerTech trigger. Bergara's honed, button-rifled, stress-relieved barrels are true to .0002 inch; the company guarantees sub-minute groups. Four Premier models are available in 6mm Creedmoor. Prices for this series: $1,715 to $2,190. You can order custom rifles with the Premier action.

Bergara's more affordable B-14 family (starting at $825) comprises six models, the popular HMR, or Hunting & Match rifle now available with left-hand action. The Timber and Woodsman feature walnut stocks. All wear Bergara barrels, which, like receivers, are of chrome-moly steel. My 7-pound Woodsman in .270 and an HMR in 6.5 Creedmoor function smoothly and deliver the 1-MOA accuracy Bergara touts for this series. In a cosmetic departure from some "precision" rifles, the HMR's black-flecked, copper-hued prone stock doesn't handle like a piece of 4x6 lumber. Its grip is steep, for sure hold offhand and prone. The adjustable comb puts your eye dead-center behind any scope. Spacers give you just the right length of pull. A toe hook helps you tug the butt into your shoulder from the bench. The stock's alloy internal "mini-chassis" adds rigidity from comb nose to mid-point in the foreend. Synthetic-stocked Ridge and Hunter models are all-weather versions of the Woodsman. The BMP (Bergara Match Precision) rifle suits shooters who prefer an AR-style grip and magazine, a chassis with skeletal look and feel. Bergara offers both the HMR and BMP stocks as accessories. Ditto an AICS magazine. The current catalog also lists a "tactical" bolt knob for B-14s, and an ST1 muzzle brake for threaded Bergara barrels.

Incidentally, the name Bergara is that of the Spanish town where in 1999 a factory was producing rifle barrels for BPI

Outdoors, which had recently bought Connecticut Valley Arms. BPI's CEO Dudley McGarity soon grew that operation to furnish barrels for CVA and other gun makers. Bergara bolt-action rifles followed, most with actions on Remington 700 footprints. Premier- and B-14-based series have sold very well, outpacing the competition. Clean, no-nonsense profiles, fine triggers, and accurate barrels get the credit, insists McGarity, who says new models and chamberings will keep coming! *bergarausa.com.*

Blaser

Introduced in 2008, the Blaser R8 has a radial-head bolt with an expanding collet that locks into the barrel. The straight-pull bolt telescopes, so the receiver is short. A flick of your hand cycles the action. The R8's tang-mounted thumb-piece is a cocking switch, not a safety. Uncocked, the rifle is safe with the chamber loaded. Plasma nitriding on hammer-forged barrels ensures scope base dimples hold Blaser's QD mounts securely and return an optic "on-zero" after you remove it. This claim proved out when I tested it at 600 yards. A feather-light, aramid-reinforced magazine resides in a trigger group that's easily detached, easily locked in place. Load it in the rifle or in your hand. The R8 comes in several versions, the GRS in .338 Lapua with a beautiful prone stock. The R8 Silence in .308 is delightful to fire, courtesy its slim, short suppressor. The Success Ruthenium has a special hard coating on bolt, trigger and bolt knob. A new thumbhole-stocked Success Individual boasts figured walnut with leather at grip and comb. The Carbon Success has leather too, on a carbon-fiber stock with clear finish. The Long Range Professional Success comes in 6.5x47, 6.5/284, .300 Norma as well as .338 Lapua. Prefer European walnut? You can visit Blaser and select your blank from stacks of stunners. All R8s I've fired routinely drilled sub-minute groups. Butter-smooth, sunrise-reliable actions brook 120,000 psi of pressure.

Last year Blaser began offering its own top-quality riflescopes, produced in Wetzlar by German Sports Optics. I've visited the firm. Korsten Kortemeier, also CEO of Minox, shares the title of Managing Director at GSO with Hans Bender, retired from the helm of Schmidt & Bender. He

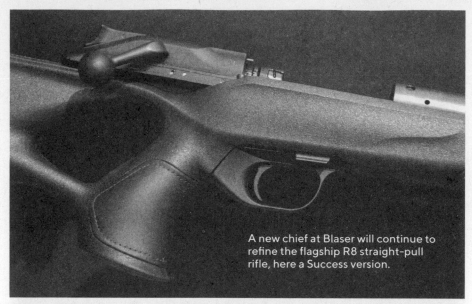

A new chief at Blaser will continue to refine the flagship R8 straight-pull rifle, here a Success version.

With a cocking switch instead of a safety, Blaser's brilliant, quick-cycling R8 is safe to carry loaded.

explained that both companies have benefited from local changes in the optics industry. "Much of Zeiss's operation has gone to Oberkochen headquarters, leaving us a stellar pool of optical designers and engineers. We source our materials from the best suppliers; but what matters most in optics is the lens polishing and fitting, and the quality control." Variation in lens curvatures in the three Blaser-branded Infinity riflescopes are held to .0001 mm. That's finer than mechanical devices can measure, so lasers and reflected light take their place. Tooling and processes at GSO also serve the semiconductor industry, where tolerances run 4,000 times finer than the diameter of a human hair! "Scopes worthy of Blaser's R8 rifle, eh?" smiled my host.

While the R8 is barreled to cartridges as big as the .500 Jeffery, I used a .308 Silence to try out a 1-7x28 Infinity scope at a local range. Four of five 168-grain match bullets chewed a .4 inch-knot at 100 meters. While dogged by that four-in, one-out habit, I was blessed by otherwise fine groups. An R8 in 6.5x47 with a 2.8-20x50 Infinity put a quartet of 123-grain Lapua Scenars inside 1.2 inches at 300 meters!

As I write this, the L&O Group that owns Sauer and Mauser as well as Blaser brands is shuffling administration at its Isny, Germany, campus. No doubt Blaser will have more to report later in 2019. *blaser-usa.com.*

Browning

There's a new BAR this year: the MK 3

DBM with a shim-adjustable, oil-finished walnut stock and an 18-inch fluted barrel, matte-blued. The alloy receiver wears a Picatinny rail, for quick, easy scope mounting. In .308 only, this autoloader lists for $1,530. In bolt rifles, Browning's X-Bolt flagship series now includes the Max Long Range Hunter with adjustable comb and length spacers. The threaded, fluted, heavy 26-inch barrel is bored for nine cartridges, 6mm Creedmoor to .300 UltraMag — including the .26 and .28 Nosler. Prices start at $1,270. Another 2019 entry, the X-Bolt Tungsten, boasts a stainless barrel and receiver, a carbon-fiber stock. Fluted, threaded barrels, 22 to 26 inches, are chambered for a suite of popular hunting rounds. MSRP: from $2,070. These X-Bolts join a growing family, as do the Pro and Pro Long Range. Their "burnt bronze" Cerakoting on stainless barrels and actions also appears on the Hell's Canyon Speed Long Range McMillan, with McMillan Game Scout stock. The Eclipse Hunter, Varmint and Target rifles ($1,200 to $1,400) come with brake-equipped muzzles, laminated thumbhole stocks and stainless barrels on blued receivers. Fluted bolts, rotary magazines and four-screw "X" scope mounting come with all X-Bolt actions. Chamberings include the new 6mm Creedmoor, paired with fast 1-in-7-1/2 rifling to stabilize long bullets. Rimfire enthusiasts will check out the new Buck Mark Target carbine with gray laminate stocks, a heavy fluted barrel. This 10-shot autoloader includes a rail and costs $740. The resurrected T-Bolt now comes in a Laminated Target/Varmint Stainless version. It lists for $940 in .22 LR, $980 in .22 WMR and .17 HMR. The Buck Mark and T-Bolt both weigh 5 1/2-pounds. *browning.com.*

Bushmaster

A quartet of new firearms have appeared under the Bushmaster shingle this year. Carbines in .450 Bushmaster wear 16- and 18 1/2-inch barrels; a 6.8 SPC II features a 16-inch. There's also an ACR pistol in 5.56 NATO. Prices: $2,249 for the carbines, $2,149 for the pistol. *bushmaster.com.*

Christensen Arms

The idea of replacing a traditional rifle barrel with a thin steel tube inside a light-weight carbon fiber shell came to Roland Christensen more than 20 years ago. An accomplished engineer, he proved the concept by making the first carbon-wrapped barrel. In rigidity, strength and accuracy, it matched heavier solid steel barrels. Christensen Arms now builds AR-style and bolt-action rifles with carbon fiber barrels and titanium muzzle brakes. In ARs, the company offers the CA-15 in .204 Ruger, .223 Wylde and .300 Blackout, direct impingement gas mechanisms serving billet-machined receivers. The larger CA-10 DMR comes in 6.5 Creedmoor, .243, .260, 7mm-08, .308. Bolt-action receivers include magnum versions long enough to swallow the .375 H&H and kin. Their pillar-bedded, prone-style stocks with comb and length adjustments make for accurate, comfortable long-range shooting. Even with stiff 27-inch barrels, magnum rifles from the Christensen shop scale less than 7 1/2 pounds. *christensenarms.com.*

CVA

Last fall, in a plum thicket on the steep breaks of Idaho's Salmon River, I sneaked within 20 steps of a black bear and slipped a PowerBelt bullet through its ribs. My black-powder rifle, a CVA fueled by Hodgdon StarFire pellets, had the feel of a centerfire, and save for the loading procedure, performed like one. It had, easily, 150-yard reach. Later a pal using a prototype CVA shot a pronghorn at over 300 steps. That rifle showed up at SHOT, 2019 as the Paramount, a bolt-action 45-caliber muzzleloader designed for powder charges of 150 grains-equivalent, and up. The free-floated Bergara barrel is of 416 stainless steel, rifled for a new PowerBelt ELR bullet with a long, conical, poly-tipped nose. Developed for scope use, the Paramount comes without sights. It does include a compact, folding field rod and a one-piece range rod. The synthetic stock has an adjustable comb; shims change length of pull.

Until now, CVA produced only muzzle-loading rifles. For 2019 it rolls out the Cascade, an entry-level bolt-action centerfire in 6.5 Creedmoor, 7mm-08 and .308. The bolt has a short 70-degree lift; the 22-inch 4140 barrel has a threaded muzzle. Stocked in gray synthetic material with a SoftTouch finish, the new Cascade will list for less than $500. *cva.com.*

CZ

Not long ago the 557 nudged aside the 550 as CZ's flagship bolt rifle. An obvious difference: the 557's bolt-face extractor, in lieu of the 550's non-rotating Mauser claw. The short-action 557 in .308 has a detachable box magazine; the long-action model wears a floorplate. Per the 550, all 557 receivers are machined to accept CZ rings. Now there's a 557 American, synthetic stock or walnut, with 24-inch barrel. Choose from seven popular chamberings, .243 to .30-06, at $871. I like the 557's stock, and the accuracy I've seen from new 557 rifles. The 550 action remains in Safari Magnum and Safari Classics rifles.

In rimfire news, the new 457 is set to replace the 455, which introduced interchangeable barrels to upstage the 452. The 457 receiver is shorter but retains switch-barrel capability. The two-piece

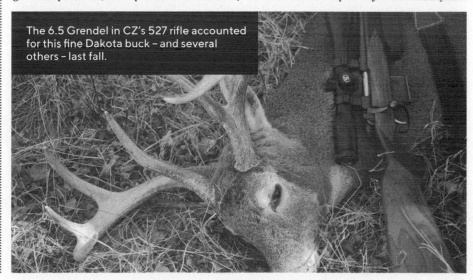

The 6.5 Grendel in CZ's 527 rifle accounted for this fine Dakota buck – and several others – last fall.

bottom metal is fresh. The trigger adjusts for weight, take-up and over-travel. In .22 LR, .22 WMR and .17 HMR, the 457 is priced from $365 (for the Scout model, proportioned for young shooters). The Varmint Pro ($434) wears a synthetic stock, the American ($476) a walnut stock. Training and Lux versions ($449 and $499) feature iron sights and European-style walnut. For small-bore enthusiasts who crave more zip, CZ offers the petite 527 centerfire in .17 and .22 Hornet, .204, .222, and .223, plus 6.5 Grendel and 7.62x39. The rifles, all with adjustable single-set triggers, handle nimbly. Prices: $665 to $787. *cz-usa.com.*

CVA

An ambidextrous thumbhole stock and a 28-inch barrel with CVA's Quick Release Breech Plug might not grab you by the lapels. But if all new Optima V2 LRs shoot like the rifle I used last year, every blackpowder enthusiast should be on the wait list for one. Before hunting black bears with that rifle, I took a few minutes to check its zero and accuracy. Pacing 50 yards, I tacked a paper target to a plywood slab, sandbagged the rifle, settled the crosswire of the 3-9x Konus scope and pressed the trigger. A hole appeared 1 1/2 inches to 11 o'clock. Good. Sliding another PowerBelt bullet into the bore atop three more 35-grain Hodgdon Fire Star pellets, I capped the hinged-breech CVA with another 209 primer, shut it, thumbed the hammer and fired again. The paper looked the same. I loaded and fired again. No change! Optimism has its limits. Walking up, I saw no other mark on plywood or paper. But close examination showed all three bullets had indeed followed one track. Backing off and firing again at a different mark, I got one more hole 1 1/2 inches to 11 o'clock. Those bullets were stacking nose-on-tail at 50 yards — as good as you'll get from centerfire match rifles. Thank that Bergara barrel. Later that day, I killed a bear with this inexpensive 7 1/2-pound CVA. *cva.com.*

Cooper

This small shop in Montana's Bitterroot valley is often overlooked in rifle round-ups. It deserves better. My Cooper rifles, rimfire and centerfire, are remarkably accurate. They also have the conservative lines and attractive walnut that appeal to me. Changes in company ownership have prompted changes in the rifle line, though the bolt actions engineered by Dan Cooper are essentially the same. Stainless and chrome-moly steel are available in a variety of finishes. Repeating rifles have three-round, straight-stack detachable boxes. Cooper has a 5 3/4-pound lightweight in its synthetic-stocked Backcountry. The beefier Excalibur also features a Kevlar-reinforced handle. The Phoenix is a "varmint" rifle with stainless Wilson barrel. Western Classic, Custom Classic, Montana Varminter and Varmint Extreme rifles wear walnut, of which Cooper has a plentiful supply. There's a synthetic-stocked, single-shot Benchrest rifle, even bolt-action muzzleloaders in synthetic and walnut. Prices depend on model and options. Cooper also builds Special Order rifles, rimfire and centerfire. *cooperfirearms.com.*

DPMS

Sparing no refinement to make its new 6.5 Creedmoor Hunter field-worthy, DPMS

Dan Cooper developed the Model 52, still a champ in the Cooper line. This .270 prints .7-inch groups.

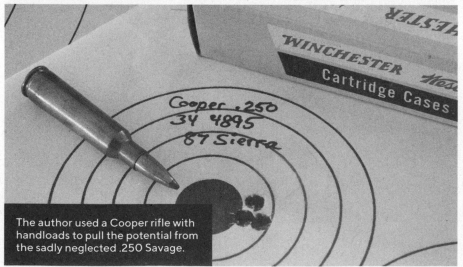

The author used a Cooper rifle with handloads to pull the potential from the sadly neglected .250 Savage.

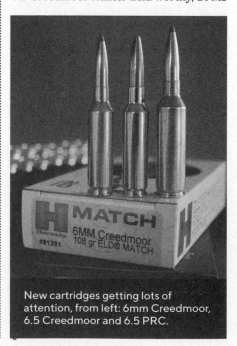

New cartridges getting lots of attention, from left: 6mm Creedmoor, 6.5 Creedmoor and 6.5 PRC.

Dakota's 76 in fine French functions no better than the less costly synthetic-stocked round-action 97.

fitted a 20-inch threaded barrel with 1-in-8 twist, added a floating carbon-fiber handguard and then installed a two-stage match trigger. The rifle, which retails for $1,599, features a Hogue over-molded grip, a Magpul stock, and Teflon-coated metal. The Hunter joins two other new, similar 6.5 Creedmoors, one finished in Kuiu Verdi camo, the other in TrueTimber Strata. Both list for $1,249. In its 5.56 AR line, DPMS has an LCAR with 16-inch, 1-in-8 barrel, a six-position stock and M4 Glacier Guard handguard. Price: $749. dpmsinc.com.

Dakota

The good news: There's no real news. Dakota rifles strike me as the most elegant, most perfectly engineered sporters from a U.S. factory. They're costly — and in truth semi-custom, as shop supervisor Ward Dobler offers many options, accommodates special orders. The Dakota 76 Don Allen wrought from refinements to the early Winchester Model 70 action now comprises several versions, including the take-down 76 Traveler. Now 20 years in production, the affordable round-action Dakota 97 (four variations) still features the non-rotating Mauser extractor for controlled-round feed. Single-shot buffs can order a Dakota Model 10 dropping-block rifle, or a "baby Sharps" built to 80-percent scale on the famous 1874 Sharps design. Remington's acquisition of Dakota and Nesika prompted changes in the Sturgis, South Dakota, shop, which now produces Custom Shop Remington and Marlin rifles too. The talented staff at Dakota have a

full plate. But so far, there's not a hint of slippage in Dakota quality. The company continues to turn out achingly beautiful rifles. They hunt too. A Dakota 97 Outfitter nailed a mountain goat for me in tough country and weather. My Model 10, a .280, must get afield soon. Rifles pretty enough to be rack queens shouldn't be imprisoned. dakotaarms.com.

E.R. Shaw

Operated by the same family for more than 50 years, barrel-maker E.R. Shaw has supplied top-quality replacement and OEM barrels industry-wide. It has also provided thousands of barrels for custom rifles and offered its own. Now known as Shaw, the company lists two bolt-action rifles in dozens of popular chamberings, .17 to .45 caliber. The Mark 7 incorporates a Savage 110 receiver; the Mark 10 is built on a mechanism designed and manufactured on Shaw patents and to Shaw specifications. Barrel configuration, including spiral flutes, is up to the customer, who can design his (her) rifle online. Walnut and laminated stocks wear standard furniture, but options abound. A new chassis stock is in the works. "We've reduced rifle delivery time from eight months to 10 weeks," Bud Shaw told me. "Now, with an additional factory, we're on track for even faster service." All three Pittsburg plants, he said, are equipped with modern CNC machines that can bring barrels from blank to finished product. The firm manufactures other accessories too, such as its

own muzzle brake. Shaw's aim: high quality at affordable prices. shawbarrels.com.

Franchi

Its first bolt-action rifle, the Momentum, appeared at Germany's IWA trade show; but Franchi announced it at SHOT as the Horizon. Minor cosmetic differences aside, both feature a push-feed action with three-lug bolt and internal, three-shot magazine with hinged floorplate. The straight-comb stock has thick recoil pad, textured grip surfaces and a palm-friendly bolt knob. At 6 1/2 pounds in .30-06, this rifle is agile and well balanced. It's available in .308 too. Oopsie: integral sling swivel tabs don't allow swivels to move under sling pressure. At $609, the Momentum costs a bit more than entry-level sporters stateside. But its European competition (Tikka, Mauser) will surely take note. franchiusa.com.

Gunwerks

Capitalizing on — and fueling — the trend in long range shooting, this Wyoming-based company is introducing rifle stocks to complement its GLR and GRB bolt actions. The LR1000 stock introduced in 2006 was refined in 2013. The new Clymr and Magnus Gen II designs have further refinements. Both are developed and produced in-house of carbon fiber (or, by customer order, fiberglass). Both feature a flush-mount bipod rail and flush-cup QD sling mounts. Both incorporate an alloy bedding block and spacers for length adjustment. The Magnus also has a fully adjustable butt assembly. The featherweight Clymr scales just 2.1 pounds, half a pound less than the Magnus, with its longer grip face and fore-end. Gunwerks offers long-range shooters a heavier (4.2-pound), fully adjustable stock for long-range shooters firing magnum loads from long barrels. It's new too. All three complement Gunwerks actions. Based on the Remington 700 receiver, the GLR improves it with a claw-type extractor, dual ejectors and a coned bolt-face. The one-piece bolt has twin cocking cams. The recoil lug is integral with the receiver. Trimming costs in its GLR, Gunwerks used the same 416R stainless steel as the GLR and kept close tolerances, but nixed bolt flutes, dual ejectors, bolt shroud sculpting. The recoil lug is separate, as on the 700. Actions feature detachable-box

The author likes the clean lines and fine balance of H-S Precision rifles, manufactured in South Dakota.

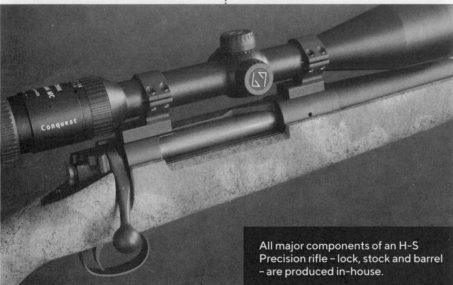

All major components of an H-S Precision rifle – lock, stock and barrel – are produced in-house.

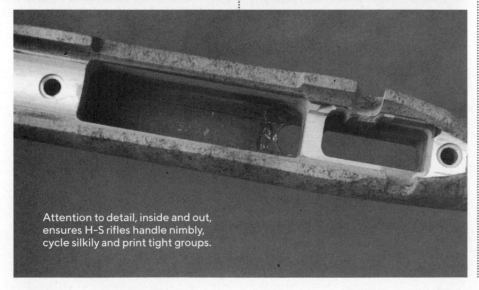

Attention to detail, inside and out, ensures H-S rifles handle nimbly, cycle silkily and print tight groups.

magazines or traditional floorplates. Barrels are cut-rifled with quick-twist rifling to stabilize the long bullets most effective at distance. Pick from stainless and carbon-wrapped barrels in a suite of contours, with threaded muzzles and Gunwerks' own caps and brakes. *gunwerks.com*.

H-S Precision

This Rapid City, South Dakota, firm lists nine bolt-action hunting rifles, include three take-downs. Chamberings: .204 Ruger to .458 Lott. Five "tactical" rifles (one take-down), plus a single-shot Benchrest model and a Varmint bolt-action pistol complete the line. H-S produces all major components, lock, stock and barrel, on site! CNC machining holds gnat's-lash tolerances on the stainless twin-lug actions; triggers adjust to a drag-free 2 1/2 pounds; hand-laid carbon-fiber stocks boast alloy bedding blocks; 416R stainless barrels are cut-rifled. H-S even makes its own detachable box magazines. Given a plethora of options, H-S rifles qualify as semi-custom, and are priced accordingly. *hsprecision.com*.

Henry Repeating Arms

Borrowing the name of the talented young engineer whose work for Oliver Winchester produced the Henry rifle of Civil War fame, today's Henry is a New Jersey-based firm building lever rifles vaguely reminiscent of their 19th-century forebear. At around $470 and $570 in .22 LR and .22 WMR, the Frontier rimfire comes with threaded barrels for an additional $30. Big Boy centerfires for handgun rounds start at $850. Henry fashioned a bigger frame to produce a .45-70. Mine cycles smoothly and prints small groups. The box-fed Long Ranger has more in common with Browning's BLR than with traditional lever rifles. The rack-and-pinion bolt has a six-lug rotating head that bottles pressures from frisky modern cartridges: .223, .243 and .308. That trio appears in a hinged-breech, single-shot Henry announced in 2018 at $427. The company routinely offers cosmetic upgrades and commemorative versions. *henryrifles.com*.

Howa

Legacy Sports International has added to its line of Howa rifles with the Oryx, a

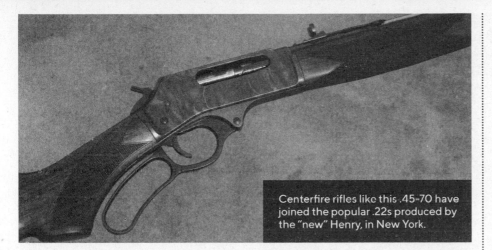

Centerfire rifles like this .45-70 have joined the popular .22s produced by the "new" Henry, in New York.

chassis-stocked short-action in 6mm and 6.5 Creedmoor, and .308. There's a "mini" version in .223, 6.5 Grendel, 7.62x39 and .300 Blackout, and a long-action Oryx barreled to .300 Winchester. Prices start at $1,059. Also new for 2019: a Mini EXCL Lite Chassis rifle, .223 to .300 Blk. At just $699, it's one of the most affordable rifles of its type. Howa lists APC and American Flag Chassis rifles ($999 and $1,499) in a suite of short-action chamberings, and the Bravo ($1,279) a 10-pound rifle in Creedmoor and .308 offerings. Its stock combines features of chassis and traditional "varmint-style" designs. This year Howa introduces "Full Dip Packages" in those chamberings. Favlos and Kratos by name, they wear different camo patterns that cover barrel and receiver. A Nikko Sterling 4-16x44 scope is included with each.

All Howa rifles feature a push-feed action with a twin-lug bolt, two-stage trigger, three-position safety. The cylindrical receiver is very stout. Detachable box magazines have replaced the fixed internal boxes of earlier Howas. I'm not enamored of the protruding latch; it's easy to trip accidentally. Howas are stocked with walnut and laminates, also synthetics mostly from Hogue. Now you can get a rifle equipped with an H-S Precision stock. Choose from 10 chamberings, .223 to .300 Winchester. Through Brownells, Howa is also selling barreled actions with 24- and heavy 26-inch barrels. They come with the subminute accuracy guarantee and a lifetime warranty that applies to all Howa rifles bought stateside. Lithgow Arms has added a Bell & Carlson-stocked Long Range rifle to the Legacy lineup. In 6.5 Creedmoor and .308, the LA105 "Woomera" (Aboriginal for "spear thrower") sports a heavy, threaded 26-inch barrel. Its Pic rail has 20 minutes of gain. Priced at $2,199, the LA105 com-

plements two Lithgow bolt-action rimfires with polymer and laminated stocks (a tad steep at $1,199 and $1,499). *legacysports.com.*

Ithaca

A venerated manufacturer of trap guns and field-worthy doubles, this smoothbore company hit a home run with the Model 37 pump. Its latest offering, though, is a precision rifle, the receiver machined from a billet of 4340 with an EDM-cut race. The bolt, of 4140 chrome-moly, slides like a piston. Three action lengths gobble cartridges as big as the .338 Lapua. The chassis stock is adjustable for length and comb height. Options abound. Ithaca also lists sporting rifles on this action. *ithacagun.com.*

Jarrett

He's still at it, and his "beanfield rifles" are better than ever! Decades after southern farmer and able Benchrest competitor Kenny Jarrett established a shop to produce super accurate long-range hunting rifles (well ahead of the current trend), he's hand-lapping barrels for his own EDM-cut Tri-Lock action. His new single-shot Long Ranger rifle features that mechanism with a Jewell trigger and 27-inch barrel in .300 Jarrett. Its 1-in-9 twist stabilizes long 190- and 220-grain match bullets. Precision? Jarrett demands 4-inch knots at 800 yards. Few shooters consistently hold that tight, even from a bench. *jarrettrifles.com.*

Hill Country Rifles

Among semi-custom shops, this Texas enterprise stands out for the fit and finish of its rifles, and their fine accuracy (half-minute guarantee). The actions are CNC-machined. One-piece fluted bolts with M-16-style extractors are paired with match-quality triggers to ensure you get the potential from barrels by the best: Bartlein, Benchmark, Hart, Krieger, Lilja, Schneider. Pillar-bedded and carefully glassed into McMillan stocks, the rifles come in a wide variety of metal and stock finishes and configurations. Choose Field Stalker, Long Range Hunter, Sheep Rifle, Dangerous Game Synthetic, Genesis Rifle (with walnut stock) or .338 Lapua Hunter (distinctive for its detachable box). There are also three "long-range tactical" models. Hill Coun-

Marketed by Legacy Sports International, Howa rifles are sturdy, well-finished, accurate and affordable.

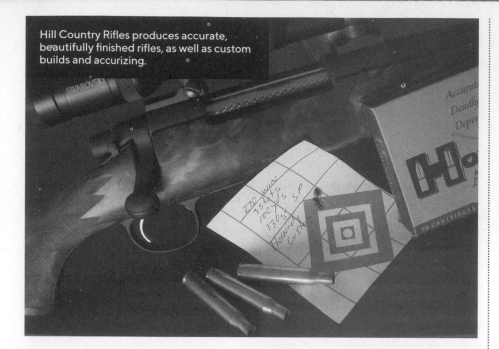

Hill Country Rifles produces accurate, beautifully finished rifles, as well as custom builds and accurizing.

try offers rebuilding and accurizing services as well. *hillcountryrifles.com*.

Kimber

Introduced 20 years ago at this writing, the Kimber 84M short-action bolt rifle has sired a clan of rifles that include 84L (long) and 8400 (magnum) actions. Chamberings range from .204 Ruger to .375 H&H. The actions are delightfully trim, perfectly suited for super-lightweight sporters: the Montana, Adirondack and Mountain Ascent.

Like its svelte 84–series hunting rifles, Kimber's .308 LPT "tactical" rifle produced snug groups for the author.

Kimber's 84M has sired longer actions, more chamberings and new versions. Here: a Custom Select.

Like the heavier Open Country rifles, they have synthetic stocks. Kimber Classic Select and Super America sporters wear walnut, as does the Caprivi. In stainless/synthetic form, the Caprivi becomes the Talkeetna. Both are offered only in .375. Varmint and Pro Varmint 84Ms come stocked in walnut and laminates, respectively. There are three Tactical rifles, on adjustable chassis.

Kimber's most recent new offering, the Hunter, is its first with a detachable box. While it has the mechanism of the 84M, with 8-40 scope mount screws and adjustable trigger, the Hunter costs less. The stock, pillar-bedded to the satin-finished stainless steel action, is of molded polymer. Introduced in .243, .257 Roberts, 6.5 Creedmoor, 7mm-08 and .308, the 6 1/2-pound Hunter soon arrived in long-action form for the .270, .280 Improved and .30-06. *kimberamerica.com*.

Marlin

With 22 lever-action centerfires in the 2019 Marlin catalog, choosing one comes down to details. Newest are the New Model 444 with 2/3 magazine (four shots) and 22-inch barrel. The return of the .444 Marlin to the 336/1895 series will cheer many deer hunters. That straight-walled case will qualify as legal where "shotgun only" seasons have been amended to permit short-range rifle and handgun rounds. The 265-grain bullets succeeding the original 240-grain flat-points are much more effective. Stocked in walnut and scaling a well-balanced 7 pounds, the 444 lists for $769. Short-action Model 1894s have been joined by eight-shot carbines with 16 1/2-inch barrels, stainless (.357/.38) and blued (.44) receivers and laminated stocks. XS Ghost Ring sights include a top rail. There's also a stainless rendition with stainless barrel and black-painted hardwood stock, suppressor-ready and without the rail, in .357/.38 Special. They're priced a few bucks either side of $1,150. The 1894C ($788) and 1894CB ($1,092 with octagon barrel and Marble sights) are straight-grip carbines. Ditto the resurrected Model 336 TDL Texan, with "B Grade" walnut for $999. It comes in .30-30 only. So does a new maple-stocked version of the 336, at $949. The Model 1895 Trapper in .45-70 with 16 1/2-inch barrel has a black-painted

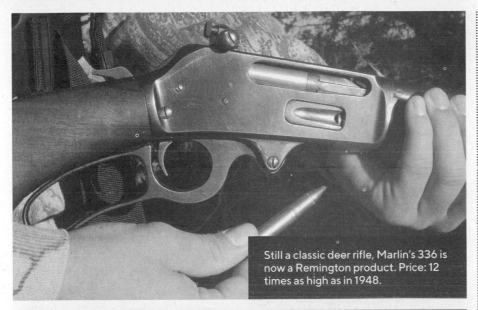

Still a classic deer rifle, Marlin's 336 is now a Remington product. Price: 12 times as high as in 1948.

Marlin's Custom Shop produces fine rifles at Dakota's digs. Here: a CS 1894 with Skinner sights.

The ageless, endearing Marlin 39 rimfire is planned as a Custom Shop rifle. It will, alas, be costly.

hardwood stock and excellent Skinner sights. It retails for $1,146. In my view, Marlins produced by Remington haven't yet matched those from the old North Haven plant in workmanship, but they're getting better. Comb flutes might nudge a kind word from doubters. Marlin Custom rifles, built in Dakota's Sturgis, South Dakota, shop exhibit fine craftsmanship. Actions run silkily. Fit and finish bring a sparkle to my eye. But they're costly. Ditto the CS Model 39, at this writing still a new project on the Sturgis floor. *marlinfirearms.com.*

Mauser

With Blaser and Sauer, Mauser production happens at Isny, Germany. All three brands are owned by the L&O Group, which has recently shuffled the management team and has removed the "M" from the designation of its latest rifle. Named for its model year, like Mauser's M12, the M18 is now simply the Mauser 18. Designed to compete with upscale entry-level rifles in the U.S., it has a synthetic stock and a Spartan appearance, but the action is smooth, with useful features: adjustable trigger, three-detent safety, recessed, three-lug bolt head chiseled from a full-diameter body. The five-shot detachable box feeds 22- and 24-inch barrels. Charitably, Mauser configured the receiver for Remington 700 scope bases. Under a Blaser-branded scope, I used a Mauser 18 to drill 3/4-minute groups with factory loads. Listing for about $650, this new rifle has been well received. The upscale, walnut-stocked M12 endures, as does the 1898 Mauser that earned the German genius worldwide fame. Even Rigby's lovely Highland Stalker begins life at Isny, as a '98 action. In 2015 Mauser re-introduced Magnum and Custom rifles, their actions machined from steel billets. The double-square-bridge Magnum is pillar bedded, with dual recoil lugs and a deep magazine. A height-adjustable, banded front sight pairs with an express sight on an island. The handsome walnut wears point-pattern checkering, a black fore-end tip and steel grip cap. Custom rifles are similar, in chamberings from .22-250 to 9.3x64. Over the last six decades, various Mauser actions have come and gone. Surviving late-model Mausers include the 03, introduced in 2003 as a take-down, switch-barrel rifle

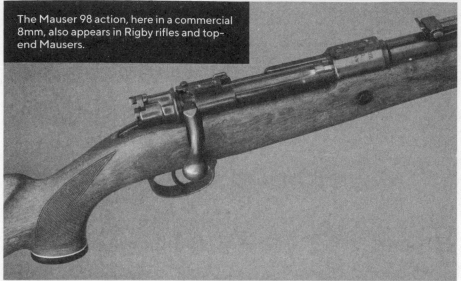

The Mauser 98 action, here in a commercial 8mm, also appears in Rigby rifles and top-end Mausers.

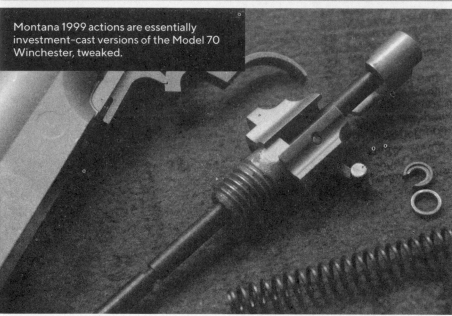

Montana 1999 actions are essentially investment-cast versions of the Model 70 Winchester, tweaked.

in 22 chamberings. Its six-lug bolt has interchangeable heads. *mauser.com.*

Montana Rifle Company

New management at the Kalispell factory has brought new Montana rifles to market, though the foundation for all is still the Winchester M70-style actions Brian Sipe built with investment-cast receivers and the hand-lapped, button-rifled barrels he made for them. The MRC Model 1999 boasts a Mauser non-rotating extractor, a three-position safety and a trigger fashioned after the pre-64 M70s – in my view the best trigger ever on a hunting rifle. Prices start at $1,549 and, with one exception, stop just shy of $3,000. American Standard and Legends rifles have tra-

ditional magazines and walnut stocks. The Xtreme Ascent, X3 and Elite rifles, new for 2019, have floorplates too, but are of stainless steel and wear synthetic stocks. Ditto the "long-range" Xtreme Tactical Hunter and Colorado Buck models. The African is in walnut, with iron sights. The Xtreme Ranch rifle is stainless, with a detachable box. My Montana .375 is The Alaskan, lightweight and nimble, my go-to heavy-game rifle. For elk, my Montana in .280 has excelled. Myriad chamberings run from .243 to .338 Lapua, .460 Weatherby, .505 Gibbs. *montanarifleco.com.*

Mossberg

The trim MVP Light Chassis rifle in .223, 6.5 Creedmoor and .308 joined the MVP Precision last year. MVP Scout, Patrol and Predator rifles have more traditional stocks but accept the same detachable AR magazines. The MVP LR features a heavier prone-style stock with an adjustable comb. The hunter-inspired Patriot line has grown too, with new cosmetics for the Youth Model (spacers adjust stock length) and threaded barrels in the standard version. The .450 Bushmaster chambering has been added to standard and Predator rifles, the latter now available with stocks in Flat Dark Earth and True Timber Strata camo finishes. The Revere is a well-executed deluxe Patriot, with its skip-checkered European walnut stock and rosewood caps. Long action or short, with chrome-moly or stainless steel, synthetic, laminated or walnut stock, the Patriot offers great value. Its LBA trigger adjusts down to two pounds. Chamberings: .22-250 to .375 Ruger. My .375 Patriot handles nimbly, cycles smoothly and reliably, and shoots accurately. It costs less than any other rifle I'd use for dangerous-game. Mossberg still makes its 464 lever-actions in .30-30 and .22 LR. There's a new, appealing synthetic stock on bolt-action 802 and 817 rimfires. *mossberg.com.*

Mossberg's Patriot in its various forms is reliable, smooth-cycling, well-stocked and modestly priced.

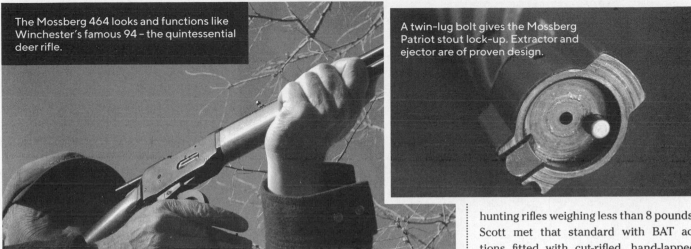

The Mossberg 464 looks and functions like Winchester's famous 94 – the quintessential deer rifle.

A twin-lug bolt gives the Mossberg Patriot stout lock-up. Extractor and ejector are of proven design.

Nosler

The rifle shop at Nosler's Bend, Oregon, digs is growing. The Model 48 series has a new entry in the Mountain Carbon rifle. Scaling 6 pounds with its threaded 24-inch carbon fiber-wrapped barrel, the MC is nonetheless bored for Nosler's potent big game cartridges (.26, .28, .30 and .33), as well as other popular rounds. This rifle complements the Long Range Carbon with 26-inch CF barrel and beefier fore-stock. The Long Range has that Tactical Hunter Carbon/Aramid Fiber "Tactical Hunter" stock, but a stainless steel barrel. The Liberty boasts a slimmer synthetic stock; in 14 chamberings from .22 Nosler to .33 Nosler (including 6mm and 6.5 Creedmoor), it's a popular 48. The Heritage is the Liberty in walnut. All renditions of the Nosler 48 rifle employ a pillar-bedded, push-feed bolt action with a two-position thumb safety, a recessed bolt face with Sako-style extractor and plunger ejector flanked by twin locking lugs lapped for uniform contact. The flat-bottomed receiver (with integral recoil lug) accepts Remington 700 scope bases. The adjustable trigger comes with a 3- to 4-pound pull. Nosler's Custom Shop offers a host of options, which you can specify online. New for 2019 is the Model 48 Independence, a single-shot pistol with 48 action and 15-inch stainless barrel. Stocked in machined aluminum, it's configured for scope use and chambered for half a dozen flat-shooting rounds, .22 Nosler to .308. *nosler.com*.

Proof Research

The triumvirate of Jense Precision, Lone Wolf Rifle Stocks and Advanced Barrel Systems, now Proof Research, builds super-accurate rifles with ABS carbon fiber-wrapped barrels "six times stiffer and 10 times stronger than steel." Its Advanced Composites Division, in Dayton, Ohio, contributes composites developed with defense and aerospace industries. Lawrence Barrels adds conventional stainless barrels to Proof options. Complete rifles from the 27,000-square-foot shop in northern Montana include ARs and bolt-actions whose receivers are wire EDM-cut and hardened before machining to hold tolerances. For long-range shooters, Proof offers an integral Pic rail with 20 minutes of gain. Bolts of 4340 chrome-moly with M16-type extractors accept interchangeable knobs. To ensure they overlook nothing, Proof engineers are blessed with a million-frame-per-second ballistic camera. My first three bullets from a .308 Terminus bolt rifle cut one hole. A custom-built Proof in 6mm Creedmoor delivered a .2-inch five-shot group. Little wonder the company has a half-minute guarantee. *proofresearch.com*.

Quarter Minute Magnums

Moving from Pennsylvania to Idaho to indulge a passion for big-game hunting, Scott and Vickie Harrold brought accuracy standards from the land of Benchrest matches and distant woodchucks. Their goal: half-inch groups at 200 yards, in hunting rifles weighing less than 8 pounds. Scott met that standard with BAT actions fitted with cut-rifled, hand-lapped #5 Krieger barrels, tight-chambered with rifling just steep enough to stabilize long bullets. But he's built super-accurate rifles on Remington 700 actions, with barrels that accommodate factory ammo. He likes McMillan HTG stocks. Customers have many options, including rails, triggers and brakes. To ensure concentricity, he buys BAT brakes undersize, then bores them .020 over groove diameter. For dime-size knots at 200, details matter. *quarterminute-magnums.com*.

Remington

Various renditions of its Model 700 re-

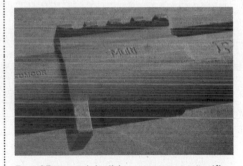

Proof Research builds super-accurate rifles on actions that boast integral recoil lugs and Pic rails.

Beautifully finished, Proof carbon-fiber barrels are lightweight, but stiff. Expect one-hole groups.

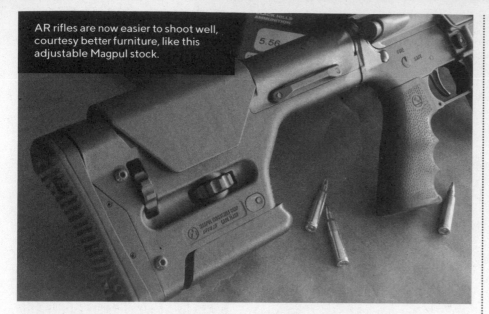

AR rifles are now easier to shoot well, courtesy better furniture, like this adjustable Magpul stock.

main Remington's bread-and-butter centerfires. This year's M700 CDL SF Limited Edition rifle is a .25-06 with 24-inch stainless fluted barrel and walnut stock. It lists for $1,226. Also in stainless: a new Model Seven HS with H-S Precision stock, a 20-inch barrel in .243, 6.5 Creedmoor, 7mm-08 or .308. It's priced at $1,149. The more affordable M783 includes four new versions. The Varmint, with heavy 26-inch barrel and laminated, beavertail stock boasts an oversize bolt knob, a Picatinny rail. In .223, .22-250, .243, 6.5 Creedmoor and .308, it retails for $625. The 783 HBT, or Heavy Barrel Threaded, is a bargain-

priced option, at $459. For the same money you can also get a 783 in .450 Bushmaster, a straight-walled round getting new life for deer hunting in areas previously under "shotgun-only" restriction. This rifle has an 18-inch barrel, an OD green synthetic stock. Finally, there's a bargain-priced 6.5 Creedmoor, a 783 with 22-inch barrel. Remington still catalogs the 7600 pump rifle in .270, .308 and .30-06, and its rimfire counterpart, the 572 Fieldmaster. Autoloaders based on the old 740 pattern are gone, but .22 enthusiasts can still buy a 552 Speedmaster, and the newer 597. Remington and its sister companies are

You can now get Remington's Model Seven with an H–S Precision stock. But it's not cheap: $1,149.

Many rifles share the Remington 700's footprint, with economical tube receiver and washer recoil lug.

still controlled by Cerberus Capital Management. *remington.com*.

Rigby

Short years ago, Marc Newton came on as managing director to revive Britain's oldest gun maker. Newton lost no time getting support in this venture from Isny, Germany, where the L&O Group's Mauser factory produces the famous 98 Magnum action. A century ago in a strange alliance between British and German companies, these actions served as the foundation for Rigby's exquisite magazine rifles. Quickly re-established, that union begat the new Rigby Big Game rifle, finished to prewar standards of quality in London by gun crafters with decades of experience. Dangerous-game rifles in .375, .416 and .450 were followed in 2017 by a slim, lightweight rifle chambered for the .275 Rigby (7mm Mauser) and kin. Called the Highland Stalker, it closely resembles the lithe rifle given celebrated tiger hunter Jim Corbett in 1907, for killing a man-eating cat with his Rigby. Available in chamberings to 9.3x62 and beautifully stocked in Turkish walnut, the Highland Stalker is a lively rifle but steadies quickly on target. It features excellent iron sights, a scope-friendly safety and an adjustable trigger.

Rigby has also revived the "rising bite" double rifle, which first appeared in 1879, 104 years after the first John Rigby opened a Dublin gun shop. His son William joined him to build rifles, shotguns and dueling pistols. Generations of Rigbys kept the business alive. In 1865 the enterprise moved to London as John Rigby & Co., 72 James Street, to sell "breech- and muzzle-loading guns, revolvers and ammunition." In 1887, a third-generation John Rigby worked on Britain's .303 SMLE rifle. Then, with the gunpowder firm of Curtis & Harvey, he developed the .450 NE 3 1/4", a double-rifle cartridge that after its 1898 debut would become a template for loads used in the heyday of African safaris. *johnrigbyandco.com*.

Ruger

While the rush to ARs may have slowed, demand for these autoloading rifles remains strong. It's bolstered by new chamberings like the .300 Blackout, and .450 Bushmaster. Ruger already offers the

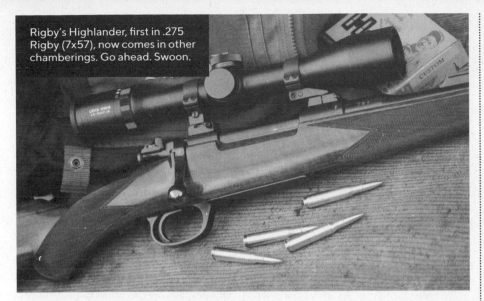

Rigby's Highlander, first in .275 Rigby (7x57), now comes in other chamberings. Go ahead. Swoon.

Ruger's popular RPR now comes in two magnum chamberings: .300 Winchester and .338 Lapua.

.300 Blk in its popular Mini 14 rifles. This year the .450 Bushmaster joins the AR-556 series (with two new variations in 5.56 NATO). The .450 has a Magpul stock and grip, and Magpul M-Lok accessory slots at 3, 6 and 9 o'clock up front on the alloy handguard. The action features a 9310 shot-peened bolt with tapered lugs machined from very stout alloy to support the Bushmaster's large case head. Ruger's Elite two-stage trigger is set at 4.5 pounds pull. A strong spring and lightweight hammer minimize lock time and ensure ignition. The cold-hammer-forged, 18 1/2-inch barrel has 5-R rifling (1 in 16 twist), a black nitride finish. The AR 556 MPR in .450 lists for $1,099. The Bushmaster also appears this year in Ruger's Scout Rifle with black synthetic stock (it's currently the only Scout chambering in walnut). This box-fed bolt action with mid-barrel rail and iron sights at bridge and muzzle seems perfectly balanced. It's one of few rifles that comes naturally to hand and points itself. The 16 1/4-inch barrel has a removable brake. $1,199.

The RPR (Ruger Precision Rifle) comes in two magnum chamberings: .300 Winchester and .338 Lapua. This cleverly designed bolt rifle in .308 and 6.5 Creedmoor, then 6mm Creedmoor, has earned plaudits for its long-range performance. AR-style butt-stock, grip and handguard, and a detachable box magazine, appeal to many shooters who entered competitive shooting in post-Garand years. The RPR would benefit from a single-loading block, for timed events nixing magazine feed. Otherwise, I've found the rifle darned near perfect for pocking plates at distance. The magnum version extends effective reach. At 15 1/4 pounds, it's nearly half again as heavy as the standard RPR — and at $2,099, it costs $500 more. But many riflemen will find it irresistible. As they will the new Hawkeye Long-Range Target in 6mm and 6.5 Creedmoor and .300 Winchester. This 11-pound rifle has a two-stage target trigger, a 20-minute rail, a Hybrid Brake on a 26-inch barrel, and a synthetic prone-style stock with adjustable comb. Price: $1,279.

After a flurry of new Ruger American bolt rifles, that series takes a rest in 2019 — albeit the thick-barreled, threaded Predator has additional sub-models in .243, 7mm-08 and .308, all at $569. American Rimfire rifles with wood, laminated and synthetic stocks are unchanged, from $359. The 77/17 series has added the .17 WSM chambering in blued/walnut ($999) and stainless/green laminate ($1,099). *ruger.com*.

Sig Sauer

New for 2019, the optics-ready SIGM400 Tread is a standout value in AR-type rifles. It has a 16-inch stainless barrel with a mid-length gas system, 15-inch, lightweight,

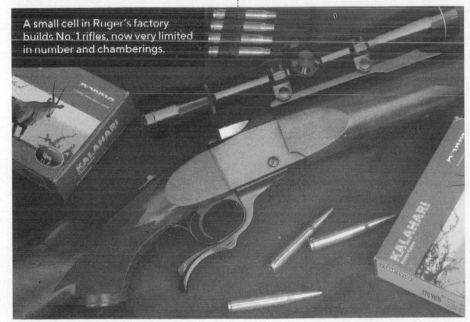

A small cell in Ruger's factory builds No. 1 rifles, now very limited in number and chamberings.

floating M-Lok handguard and Magpul six-position stock. Price: $951. Tread accessories include a vertical grip kit and SIG's Romeo5 red-dot sight, a fine complement to this and other SIG 5.56 NATO rifles. The firm is also introducing the SIGM400 SDI V-TAC, Vanish and SDI Competition, the latter with 16-inch fluted, stainless barrel, .223 Wylde chamber, mid-length direct-impingement gas system, flared magazine well, ambidextrous controls and adjustable stock. There's a new SIG MPX as well, a "sub-gun" in 9mm with 16-inch barrel and five-position telescoping stock – and a SIG716 G2 AR in 6.5 Creedmoor, with 18-inch barrel and Magpul PRS Gen3 stock. Many SIG rifles come with the company's three-chamber compensator. *sigsauer.com.*

Sako

Suojeluskuntain yliesikunnan asepaja was established April 1, 1919. Its founders decided "Sako" was easier to pronounce (it's "Socko," by the way, not "Sayko"). The firm's first rifle of note, the lovely Vixen, appeared shortly after the close of WW II in .22 Hornet and .218 Bee. In 1957 Sako trotted out the L-57 Forester for the then-new .308 and .243. Three years later the L-61 Finnbear arrived, its action long enough for the .375 H&H. The Sako Finnwolf followed, a hammerless, front-locking lever-action with detachable magazine and one-piece stock. New owners pushed Sako to redesign its bolt rifles. The Model 74 in three action lengths replaced the Vixen, Forester and Finnbear. Then came the "A series:" A1, A11 and A111 — short, medium and long receivers. In the mid-

A synthetic stock makes the upscale Sauer 404 just the ticket for Scotland's wet-weather hunting.

1980s Sako replaced that group with the Hunter, the Model 78 .22 rimfire was shipping by then (also in .22 Hornet). The Model 75 arrived in 1997, its three locking lugs reducing bolt lift to 70 degrees. The twist of a key in the bolt shroud rendered the rifle inoperable (or safe, if you prefer the euphemism). Four receivers accepted cartridges from .17 Remington to .340 Weatherby. The Model 85 announced in 2006 was less a new rifle than a $220 upgrade of the 75, with a redesigned stock and magazine latch. It has a mechanical ejector, a tab in front of the sliding two-detent safety to release the bolt for unloading. Triggers adjust to 2 1/4 pounds. The detachable box on my favorite model, the Kodiak in .375 H&H, must be nudged up to release the latch, a clever way to prevent accidental drops without slowing reloads. The 85 is a strong, smooth action. Choose a top-loading three-shot magazine or a de-

tachable box. Stocks are of carbon fiber on the 85 Carbonlight Stainless and Carbon Wolf, fiberglass on the Finnlight II, polymer on the Finnlight, laminated wood on the Black Wolf, Grey Wolf, Kodiak, Varmint and Long Range, walnut on the Classic and Bavarian. Hammer-forged barrels deliver on Sako's MOA accuracy guarantee. Sako TRG 22 (6.5 Creedmoor, .260 and .308) and TRG 42 (.300 Winchester, .338 Lapua) are chassis-stocked "sniper-style" rifles. *beretta.com.*

Sauer

Established in 1751, this German firm now makes firearms for the L&O Group that also owns Mauser and Blaser brands. Many of its current bolt rifles have the looks American shooters have come to consider, well, American. The Model 101 in various forms (like the "Forest" in my rack) has been joined by an expanding line of Model 100 bolt rifles priced from $899 for the CeraTech, in 14 chamberings, .222 to 9.3x62. Its black synthetic stock is sleek and straight, with textured grip panels. The three-lug bolt with 60-degree lift complements a three-position safety, a trigger adjustable down to 2 1/4 pounds. A detachable box holds five rounds in a staggered stack. Long-range shooters will warm to the Fieldshoot and Pantera, stocked for prone shooting and the first rifles commercially bored for Hornady's hot new 6.5 PRC round. Groups I've fired with these Sauers, and the upscale 404, easily kept bullets inside the 1-MOA span Sauer guarantees. *sauer.de.*

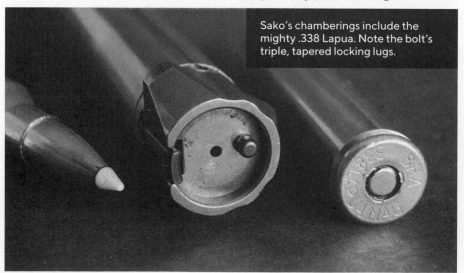

Sako's chamberings include the mighty .338 Lapua. Note the bolt's triple, tapered locking lugs.

Savage

The 110-series bolt rifle, now six decades as Savage's flagship centerfire, is again the 110. Gone (mostly) are the two- and three-digit numbers that served as code for action length, steel type and other details. The 110 no longer sells for $110, but is still built with value in mind. The bolt-face extractor and plunger ejector, and a barrel nut for headspacing, control costs. Synthetic stocks have since replaced now-more-expensive walnut. The tang safety was less a nod to economy than a pitch to southpaws. It now has three positions. In 2003, Savage's jar-proof AccuTrigger sparked an industry-wide search for safe triggers with crisp, lightweight pulls. The projection-free but adjustable AccuStock, whose prototype I used on an elk hunt three years ago, is now a staple of the 110 line. It's a champ. Latest rifle to feature it is the High Country, in 11 short- and long-action chamberings and True Timber Strata Camo. It lists for $1,129. Other rifles on the 110 roster: Hunter, Storm, Lightweight Storm, Brush Hunter, Predator, Varmint, Long-Range Hunter and LRH 338 Lapua, Bear Hunter, Scout, Tactical, Tactical Desert, Engage Hunter, Hog Hunter and Wolverine. Prices: from $599. There are four new 110 Apex rifles: Hunter XP and Hunter XP Muddy Girl, Storm XP and Predator XP, $699 to $749. The walnut-stocked 11/111 Lady Hunter and Lightweight Hunter remain in the line, at $909 and $1,009.

Savage's 220 series of slug-shooting, bolt-action shotguns has a new entry: the smoothbore 220 and 212 Turkey with AccuFit (AccuStock) camo stock. It costs $695 in 20 gauge, $779 in 12. Varmint-series rifles – Models 12 and 25 – remain unchanged for 2019, as do six target rifles on that action. Ditto 10/110 Long Range and chassis-style Stealth rifles. Four Trophy Series package (scoped) rifles continue to offer ready-for-hunting value in 17 chamberings (left-hand versions, too) from $639. Six new Axis rifles bring offerings in that stable to 10. Priced from $325, they include camo and package versions. The new MSR 10 Precision in 6mm and 6.5 Creedmoor and .308 ($2,499), and MSR 15 Long Range .224 Valkyrie ($1,735) are clearly designed for long-range shooting. New Rascal Target, Target XP and FV-SR rimfires bless young shooters with precision-rifle features. Just 3 1/2 to 6 pounds in weight, they're priced from $219 to $405. You'll find dozens of other rimfires in Savage's catalog, from bolt-action Mark II, 93 and B rifles to the autoloading A and 64 series. *savagearms.com*.

Smith & Wesson

Known for handguns, S&W has stormed the AR market with its M&P 15 rifles. A dozen versions in 5.56 NATO/.223, feature Magpul sights, magazines and handguards, and six-position stocks. Two new rifles, in black and camo finish, fire the .300 Blackout. Four M&P 10s are bored to 7.62 NATO/.308. Six M&P 15-22 Sport rifles offer centerfire feel to .22 rimfire shooters. S&W owns Thompson/Center, whose Compass and Venture bolt rifles have replaced the walnut-stocked Icon. The three-lug Ventures I've shot have proved very accurate. This model comes in 11 popular chamberings, .204 Ruger to .300 Winchester. S&W's Performance Center catalogs a new, upscale LRR (Long Range Rifle), also listed by T/C. In .243, 6.5 Creedmoor and .308, it features a chassis-style stock, Magpul M-Lok accessory cuts and a 20-minute Picatinny rail. The Performance Center produces AR rifles in 5.56/.223 and 6.5 Creedmoor, also upscale versions of the T/CR22 autoloading .22. *smith-wesson.com*.

Springfield

Until the Saint, just two years old at this writing, Springfield Armory's rifles were all based on the M1A, civilian version of the M14 service rifle. Springfield still makes a lot of M1As, in 37 versions, from the $1,687 Standard Issue to the $2,143 CQB SOCOM 16 and $2,485 National Match to the Super Match series, $3,018 to $3,785. Chambering is .308, of course, but the 6.5 Creedmoor has been added to some series. Rifles feature chrome moly and stainless steel, walnut and synthetic stocks. The Saint, an AR-15, courts a bigger market. For 2019, new Saint versions outnumber originals, which start at $943. The top-tier Edge lists for $1,559. All are chambered to the 5.56 NATO, save the new Victor Pistol, with a 9-inch barrel in .300 Blk. The Saint features high-quality components, like Magpul magazines and M-Lok floating handguards. Springfield now catalogs 15 Saints, 5 1/2 to 7 1/4 pounds. *springfield-armory.com*.

Steyr

Sadly, the svelte Mannlicher-Schoenauer is a thing of the past. But the firm that produced it, now simply Steyr, continues to offer accurate, high-quality rifles. In a manufacturing coup, Steyr has produced its new Monobloc, a rifle with barrel and action cold-hammer-forged from a single block of steel. There's no way to understand such a feat by handling the rifle or chatting up Steyr representatives. I've tried. But the result is nimble and, logically, accurate. The stock on this box-fed centerfire, in .308 and .30-06, has leather

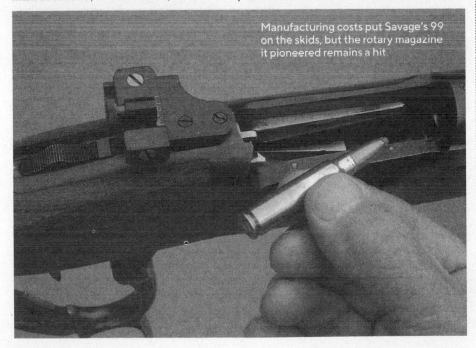

Manufacturing costs put Savage's 99 on the skids, but the rotary magazine it pioneered remains a hit.

Fed by a detachable box, T/C's Venture cycles smoothly and reliably. It's not designed for top-loading.

Arguably the most accurate production-line rimfires, many Volquartsen rifles wear colorful stocks.

inlays. Yes, the technology hikes the price: $5,250. Less costly is Steyr's Pro THB with Manners stock (6.5 Creedmoor and .308) and the SSG 04 (.243 to .300 Winchester). The SSG 08, in a chassis-style stock, also comes in .338 Lapua. Perhaps most appealing in Steyr's stable is the Zephyr II rimfire, in .22 LR, .17 HMR, .22 WMR. At just under 6 pounds with a 20-inch barrel, this rifle brings back the walnut and handling qualities of the original Zephyr (1955 to 1971). The Zephyr II lists for $995. *steyrarms.com*.

Tikka

A manufacturer with a broad product base, Tikka predates its sister Finnish brand, Sako, by 26 years. After WW II the two firms collaborated on a bolt-action hunting rifle. Sako later acquired Tikka and shotgun-maker, Valmet. By 1989 production at Tikkakoski Works had moved to Sako's Riihimaki factory. Tikka's Whitetail rifle sold stateside during the 1990s. A new sporter, the T3 appeared in 2003. Its twin-lug bolt stripped cartridges from a single-stack polymer box. A two-detent safety locked bolt and trigger, adjustable from 2 to 4 pounds. The rifle earned my favor in range trials, and successful hunts for moose and deer. It shares many features with the costlier Sako 75, including Sako barrels. Bolt stops suit the T3 action to various cartridge lengths. A steel bar in the stock serves as recoil lug, mating with a slot in the receiver. The recent, updated T3X boasts a modular synthetic stock whose interchangeable slabs let you customize the grip. A bigger port permits easier single loading. Additional mount holes suit Picatinny rails. Tikka has 12 configurations of the T3X, with walnut, laminated and polymer stocks, .204 Ruger to .300 Winchester. They include stainless and left-hand models, a chassis-based Tac A1. The 10-shot T1X in .22 LR and .17 HMR looks and handles much like a T3X. By the way, Finland's 300 state-sanctioned hunting associations boast 140,000 members, accounting for about half the nation's moose hunters. More than 80 percent of the 22 million pounds of venison sold in Finland comes from moose. *beretta.com*.

Volquartsen

The slick-cycling, super-accurate rimfires from this family-owned business owe much to expert CNC and wire-EDM machining. Now in its 44th year, Volquartsen makes the only self-loaders I know for the frisky .17 WSM rimfire. The tungsten alloy bolt runs in a stainless, rail-equipped receiver. A rotary eight-shot magazine feeds a thick 20-inch stainless barrel. In its Fusion rifle, Volquartsen lets you switch barrels from .22 LR to .22 WMR to .17 HMR without tools. A counter-weighted bolt keeps a leash on the WMR and HMR, and flicks empties reliably. Triggers break like icicles at about two pounds. Volquartsen's colorful laminated stocks are both elegant and futuristic, all sleek and beautifully finished. They're lively in hand and help you wring the one-hole potential of these fine rimfires. Evolution gas-driven centerfires in .204 and .223 feature a nitrided bolt, a stainless receiver. *volquartsen.com*.

Weatherby

Soon to complete its move from California to Wyoming, Weatherby hasn't let the transition hold up development of new rifles. Its Subalpine Mark V, in Optifade camo, weighs as little as 5 3/4 pounds. Its steel wears flat dark earth Cerakoting. Chamberings run from 6.5 Creedmoor to .300 Weatherby. The new First Lite is similar, with different camo. At $2,600, it costs $100 less. The lightweight Camilla, named for Roy Weatherby's wife and proportioned for women, got a field test in Namibia in the hands of six "Safari Sisters." It has a Vanguard action and comes in five chamberings: .240 Wby., 6.5 Creedmoor, .270, .308 and .30-06. Now there's a Camilla Ultra Light with a Mark V action. The stock is pretty much a copy of the original; ditto the cartridge list. At $2,300 it's a jump above the Vanguard's $849 tag. New at $849: a Vanguard Badlands in Approach camo — six chamberings, 6.5 Creedmoor to 6.5-300 Weatherby. The 6.5 mojo is also available in the lightweight Mark V Altitude, introduced last year with carbon-fiber stock in 10 chamberings, 6.5 Creedmoor to .300 Weatherby. Six- and nine-lug rifles ($3,000 and $3,200) carry the company's MOA guarantee. In hot .25s you can't beat the .257 Weatherby. Now there's a Mark V with a barrel accurate enough to

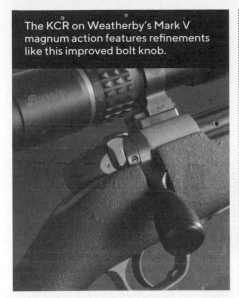

The KCR on Weatherby's Mark V magnum action features refinements like this improved bolt knob.

Well-engineered, Winchester's box-fed XPR draws customers as the Model 70 gets more expensive.

tap its long reach. The KCR (Krieger Custom Rifle) boasts John Krieger's cut-rifled barrel, with an oversize bolt knob, black and Flat Dark Earth Cerakoting. Its carbon-fiber stock has a bedding rail. At $3,600, the KCR also comes in 6.5-300, .300 and .30-378 Weatherby. *weatherby.com.*

Wilson Combat

An ace pistol shot and gifted machinist, Bill Wilson — and now his son Ryan and a talented crew — is renowned for building exquisite 1911 handguns and AR-style rifles. I've hunted with his AR-10 (in .308 and .338 Federal), and AR-15 (seven chamberings, .204 Ruger to .458 SOCOM). The metal-work, fit and finish distinguish these direct-impingement rifles at a glance. Machined from 7075 billets, upper and lower are ripple-free, with crisp edges, flawless detailing. Flash hiders are pinned and welded. NP3 finish on action surfaces sheds debris; the lubricity is so high

Ryan Wilson fires a Wilson Combat carbine, available in many configurations and chamberings.

there's no need for grit-grabbing lube. Five factory loads from Wilson's 9 1/2-pound Super Sniper in .308 drilled groups averaging .85-inch. For long .22 bullets, I'm sweet on the lighter AR-15 SS with a Wylde .223/5.56 chamber, 1-in-8 twist. It costs less than the $3,095 Wilson gets for the AR-10. At this writing, I'm awaiting a Wilson Combat AR in 6mm Creedmoor. Might as well go first class. *wilsoncombat.com.*

Winchester

The XPR bolt-action series, at a lower price point than the flagship M70, gets two new entries this year. The Hunter Strata and Hunter Highlander differ in camo finish on their polymer stocks, but profiles and components are the same. So are prices ($600) and 13 chamberings, .243 to .338 Magnum, including Winchester's new .350 Legend, added as well to other XPRs. Like its brethren, the Strata and Highlander feature a button-rifled, chrome-moly barrel secured by a nut that ensures precise headspacing. The full-diameter bolt recessed behind three lugs runs in a receiver machined from bar stock. Both are of chrome-moly steel, the bolt body nickel Teflon-coated for smooth travel and easy 60-degree lift. Cartridges push-feed from a single stack in a detachable polymer box. A lug-mounted extractor and plunger ejector toss empties. The port is big enough for that occasional top feed. A two-position thumb safety locks the bolt; a tab lets you cycle it safely. The M.O.A. trigger (now also on 70s) adjusts for weight and over-travel. On my XPR in .325 WSM, perceived movement is minimal, consis-

tent and smooth. At 3 pounds, the pull is exceptionally crisp and consistent. Scope-mount holes in the receiver accept stout 8-40 screws, to anchor heavy scopes. The recoil lug is a steel bar that engages a receiver slot. The stock's "Inflex Technology" buttpad has internal ribs that direct the comb away from your face. Fore-end cross-members minimize flex. Textured panels on grip surfaces fore and aft keep cold wet hands from slipping. XPR rifles start at $550.

The Model 70 line, priced from $1,010, is largely unchanged for 2019, though the 6.5 Creedmoor has been added to most cartridge lists. The lever-action series produced by Miroku in Japan now includes the 1866, 1873, 1886, 1892, 1894 and 1895 Winchesters, and the Model 71. The Model 1885 single-shot is a member of this clan too. Production is limited; availability changes, year to year. Just announced: the 1886 Short Rifle in .45-90 and 1892 Short Rifle in .44-40. There's also a new configuration of the '92: A Large Loop Carbine in .357 and .44 Magnum, .44-40 and .45 Colt. (Prices, in order: $1,340, $1,070 and $1,260.) To celebrate its 125th anniversary, Winchester is also offering engraved 94s in .30-30. The High Grade costs $2,400, the Custom $3,450. In rimfire rifles, Winchester has a new $250 Wildcat autoloader, poly-stocked, with receiver rail and simple aperture sight. It uses a 10-shot rotary magazine to feed its 18-inch button-rifled barrel. A rear access port permits bore-cleaning from the breech. *winchesterguns.com.*

NEW SEMI-AUTO PISTOLS

BY ROBERT SADOWSKI

It could be said the trend in the latest semi-auto pistols is a single-stack magazine configuration. Glock, Springfield Armory, Kimber, Ruger, SIG and Mossberg — yes, Mossberg — have all introduced single-stack 9mm pistols designed for conceal carry. Offering economical and affordable pistols is also a trend. Stoeger, another name long associated with shotguns, has introduced a striker-fire 9mm handgun well suited for defense. On the other end of the magazine spectrum is Kel-Tec's quad-stack rimfire pistol. There are also plenty of AR15-platform pistols from SIG, CMMG, Springfield Armory and Wilson Combat. Let's take a look at new semi-auto pistols.

Beretta

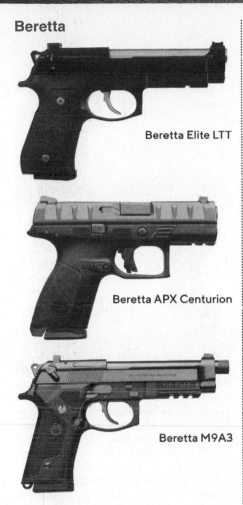

Beretta Elite LTT

Beretta APX Centurion

Beretta M9A3

The striker-fire APX series now includes Compact (MSRP: $575) and Centurion (MSRP: $575) variants. The Compact features a 13+1 capacity in 9mm or 10+1 in .40 S&W with a flush fit magazine. The Centurion is a midsize duty or concealed-carry size pistol that features a 15+1 round capacity in 9mm or 13+1 in .40 S&W with flush fit magazines. Both pistols have a 3.7 inch barrel. The M9A3 (MSRP: $1,099) is now available in a black finish. When Ernest Langdon collaborates with Beretta, the result is some slick, performance paced pistols. The rotating barrel system Storm Px4 Carry (MSRP: $695 to $1,055 depending on options) features a full-size frame and slide with a longer sight plane plus increased capacity along with two 17-round magazines and one extended 20-round magazine. My personal favorite is the Elite LTT (MSRP: $1,100) which is tricked out with a Vertec/M9A3 Slide with front-cocking serrations, dovetail fiber-optic front sight with a square-notch rear sight, stainless 4.7-inch barrel, solid steel guide rod and a beveled rear slide. The frame is built on a M9A1

frame with checkering on frontstrap and backstrap, a beveled magazine well, and radiused trigger guard the ultra-thin G10 grips, oversized magazine release button, a D Model Hammer Spring and skeletonized lightweight hammer. *beretta.com*

Browning

Browning Buck Mark Medallion Rosewood

The newest addition to the Buck Mark line is the Buck Mark Medallion Rosewood (MSRP: $509), which features a blacked stainless steel slab-side 5.5-inch barrel with a fiber-optic front sight. The grip makes this Buck Mark stand out; laminated rosewood with checkering and scroll engraving as well as a gold inlaid Buck Mark logo. *browning.com*

CMMG

CMMG Banshee 100

CMMG has released of a new line of AR pistols chambered in the hot FN 5.7x28mm caliber. The Banshee 100 Series pistol (MSRP: $1,249.95) features an 8-inch barrel, ProMag 20-round magazine, and CMMG RML7 M-Lok handguard. The Banshee 200 Series pistol (MSRP: $1,449.95) is similar to the 100 series pistol, but comes equipped with a Magpul MOE pistol grip and CMMG Ripbrace arm brace. The tricked out Banshee is the 300 Series pistol (MSRP: $1,599.95) with 5-inch barrel, Magpul MOE pistol grip, CMMG Ripbrace arm brace, ambidextrous controls and more. *cmmg.inc.com*

CZ-USA

The new U.S.-made P-10 striker-fire pistols include three models. These pistols feature a modular backstrap, swappable magazine release and crisp trigger. The first is the P-10 F (MSRP: $524), which is a full-size pistol with a 19+1

CZ-USA Bren 2Ms

round capacity and 4.5-inch barrel. The second model is P-10 C (MSRP: $499), a compact pistol with a 15+1 round capacity and 4.02-inch barrel. The third is the P-10 S (MSRP: $577), a subcompact with a 12+1 round capacity and 3.5-inch barrel. All three also come in an optics-ready configuration that allows mounting of a red-dot reflex sight. Also available are suppressor-ready variants in the full- and compact-size models. The next generation of the Bren pistol, the Bren 2 Ms (MSRP: $1,799.00), features multiple barrel lengths, from 8 to 14 inches, and two calibers, 7.62x39mm and 5.56x45mm NATO. The Bren 2 is a completely new design with a lightweight aluminum receiver and a lower made from carbon-fiber-reinforced polymer. *cz-usa.com*

Dan Wesson

Short for Tactical Commander Pistol, the TCP (MSRP: $1,725), is Dan Wesson's latest commander-size 1911 that combines a match-grade bull barrel and railed alloy frame. The TCP is designed for concealed carry and performance, with angled slide cuts and a taper-profiled grip that is slim at the top and flares out at the bottom for ease of use for shooters with small hands. Available in .45 ACP. *danwessonfirearms.com*

FN

FN 509 Midsize

New to the FN 509 series of 9mm striker-fire pistols is the FN 509 Midsize (MSRP: $649), designed as a conceal-carry option with a 4-inch barrel and 15+1 capacity. Also new is the FN 509 Tactical (MSRP: $1,049) with a 4.5-inch

treaded barrel and 17+1 or 24+1 capacity. Both are available in a matte black finish and modular grip inserts. *fnamerica.com*

GLOCK

Glock 43X

Two new additions to the Slimline series are the 43X (MSRP: $479.99) and the 48 (MSRP: $479.99). Similar to the 43, both the 43X and 48 are a single stack 9mm with a 10+1 capacity. They feature a 1-inch longer grip for comfortable balance. Available in a two-tone finish with a silver slide and matte black frame. While the 43x and 48 share the same size frame, they have different slide and barrel lengths. The barrel length for the G43X is 3.4 inches, the 48 is 4.1 inches. Three sight configurations are offered: standard, GLOCK Night Sights, and Ameriglo BOLD. *us.glock.com*

Kimber

The EVO SP (Striker Pistol) series is totally new for Kimber. These are sub-compact 9mm striker-fire pistols built with a metal frame. Yes, you read that right. While other manufacturers produce polymer-frame pistols Kimber goes against the grain with the EVO SP pistols. Designed for concealed carry, the EVO pistols feature a grip system that eliminates screws on the grip surface, a magazine release that can be configured for right- or left-handed shooters, a striker indicator that allows both visual and tactical confirmation, and ledged night sights for single-hand manipulations. The EVO SP TLE (MSRP: $925) features G10 grip panels and a backstrap with an aggressive slant-checkering. The EVO Two-Tone (MSRP: $856) has a matte silver frame and matte black slide. The EVO CDP (MSRP: $949) also features a two-tone finish and checkered G10 grips. The EVO Custom Shop model (MSRP: $1,047) features a contoured slide with Stiplex-inspired slide serrations. Kim-

Kimber EVO SP TLE

Kimber EVO Custom Shop

ber's new 1911 platform models include the Rapide (MSRP: $1,490) with unique stepped cocking serrations, slide lightening cuts for faster lock time, and TiN coated barrels for extreme durability. It's available in 10mm and .45 ACP. The KHX Custom/RL (MSRP: $1,946) has a milled slide to install an optic, a Picatinny accessory rail and Stiplex-style front grip strap stippling for extra grip. *kimberamerica.com*

Kel-Tec

Kel-Tec CP33

Ever hear of a quad-stack magazine? The new CP33 (MSRP: $475) holds a total of 33 rounds of .22 Long Rifle ammo in a quad-stack magazine. This rimfire features a 5.5-inch barrel, is optics-ready and is suppressor-ready. *keltecweapons.com*

Les Baer

The Baer 1911 Gunsite pistol (MSRP: $2,255) is a no-nonsense, custom pistol designed and built with common sense for serious shooter, just like Col. Jeff

Baer Kenai Special

Baer Premier II Heavyweight

Cooper, the founder of Gunsite Academy, would have wanted. The serial number has a GAI prefix (Gunsite Academy, Inc.) and features include the distinctive Gunsite Raven logo engraved on the slide and on the special grips, combat style sights, national match barrel with stainless steel bushing, and a blued finish. The new Kenai Special 1911 (MSRP: $3,630) is a tribute to both power and beauty Alaska. It's based on the Premier II pistol, but includes several upgrades, including 10mm chambering and a hard chrome finish. Each Kenai Special is numbered, beginning with 001, and the numbers will be individually etched on the top of the slide and each slide will also be engraved with a special bear paw logo with the "KENAI SPECIAL" model name. Want performance and reliability? The new Premier II Heavyweight (MSRP: $2,890) includes all the proven features of the popular Premier II series plus it's built on Les Baer's exclusive monolith heavyweight frame, which adds 2.8 ounces of weight, to help reduce muzzle rise and felt recoil, while providing superb balance. It comes with a 3-inch accuracy guarantee at 50 yards. *lesbaer.com*

Magnum Research

The big-bore semi-auto Desert Eagle Mark XIX Pistol (MSRP: $2,278) is now chambered in .429 DE, a caliber based off the .50 AE cartridge case. The .429 DE case is necked down to accept a .44-caliber, 240-grain bullet, with a muzzle velocity of 1,600 fps. That's a lot hotter than your granddaddy's .44

Magnum Research Desert Eagle

Magnum. This model features stainless steel finish with Picatinny bottom rail, Weaver-style top rail, a built-in muzzle brake and black finish controls. Magnum Research recently announced that all Desert Eagle pistols are now being produced in the United States. Besides offering the basic black finish 6-inch pistol, Magnum Research has developed a lineup of Desert Eagle models in a number of distinctive finishes. It currently offers: classic, brushed chrome, Cerakote colors and patterns, "Tiger Stripe" pattern in a Gold titanium nitride-coated finish or black, and case-colored pistols. An all stainless steel Desert Eagle Pistol recently has been added, as well as a 50-ounce, 5-inch-barreled version called the L5. *magnumresearch.com*

Mossberg

Mossberg MC1sc

To celebrate the company's 100th Anniversary, Mossberg released the MC1sc, a 9mm concealed-carry subcompact handgun. The MC1sc weighs a mere 19 ounces with empty magazine, has a 3.4-inch barrel, and a flush 6-round and 7-round extended magazines. Available in five variants: standard (MSRP: $425), cross-bolt safety version (MSRP: $425), TRUGLO Tritium Pro Night Sights (MSRP: $526), Viridian E-Series Red Laser (MSRP: $514), and a Centennial Limited Edition (MSRP: $686) with a production run limited to 1,000 commemorative models. *mossberg.com*

Nighthawk Custom

The Firehawk (MSRP: $4,199) is not your typical 1911. It uses a recoil-taming, single-port compensator and a bull barrel with a full-length guide rod to add weight to the front of the pistol to

Nighthawk Firehawk

reduce muzzle rise. A matte stainless or black nitride finish and is available in 9mm or .45 ACP. A new option on Nighthawk pistol is ISO, or Interchangeable Optic System, (MSRP: $350), which allows users to mount a variety of reflex optics on their 1911. *nighthawkcustom*

Remington

Remington RM380 Micro Executive

Big Green has expanded its RM380 line with the RM380 Micro Executive (MSRP: $405), which features a stainless steel frame and comely Macassar laminate grips. The RM380 Light Blue (MSRP: $415) features a Tiffany-blue Cerakote frame and matte stainless slide. *remington.com*

Ruger

The affordable Security-9 (MSRP: $399) is now available from the factory with a Hogue Beavertail HandALL grip

Ruger LCP II

Ruger Security-9

Ruger Mark IV 22LR

sleeve with Cobblestone texturing, finger grooves and palm swells. The LCP II series now has a model (MSRP: $399) with an extended magazine that seamlessly flows in the grip for a 7+1 round capacity. The Mark IV 22/45 series has three new variants. All feature a receiver made of aerospace-grade aluminum that is ventilated, making the pistol extremely light. All feature adjustable rear sights and a threaded barrel. Model 43921 (MSRP: $599) features a light blue finish and wood laminate target grips. Model 43926 features a gold-and-black, two-tone finish with checkered 1911-style grips. Model 43927 (MSRP: $599) features a matte black finish. *ruger.com*

SIG SAUER

The Legion Series expands with three new pistols: a P229 Legion SAO model (MSRP: $1,200), P238 (MSRP: $850), and P938 (MSRP: $904). All feature the Legion Gray finish, flat trigger, G10 grips and night sights. The P229 is a single-action model equipped with a master-shop flat trigger. The P320 striker-fire series now has a Compact Lima model (MSRP: $750) with an integrated Lima320 red or green laser sight. The P320 M17 MS (MSRP: $768) is similar to what the U.S. Army purchased and is now available to civilians. Like the Government model, this one also has a manual thumb safety. There is also the P320 M17 (MSRP: $768) without a manual safety. I've had the pleasure of running a P320 X-Series and these are reliable handguns. The P320 XCompact

SIG SAUER Legion

SIG SAUER P320 M17

SIG SAUER MPX Copperhead

SIG SAUER P320 Compact Lima

(MSRP: $804) uses a compact grip module, night sights, a slide cut for optics, and a 3.4-inch barrel. The P320 XFull (MSRP: $850) is the opposite end of the spectrum with a long 4.7-inch barrel and full-size grip module. The P320 X-Five Coyote and X-Carry Coyote now come in a Coyote Tan finish.

The P365 line also has two new additions. The Nitron Mirco-Compact (MSRP: $599) features a Nitron stainless steel slide, night sights and 10-round, flush-fit magazine and 11-round extended magazine. There is also a P365 Manual Safety model (MSRP: $599) with an ambidextrous manual thumb safety. SIG's 1911, P238, and P938 lines now have a Spartan II model. The 1911 Spartan II (MSRP: $1,118) is a full-size pistol, with fixed combat sights, chambered in .45 ACP, with an ambidextrous thumb safety. The P938 Spartan II (MSRP: $700) and P238 Spartan II

(MSRP: $630) feature custom Spartan grips. All three Spartan II pistols feature a distressed coyote-tan finish on the slide and frame. MOLON LABE is also engraved on the slide. The newest addition to the SIG SAUER MPX series is the ultra-compact MPX Copperhead (MSRP: $1,835). The Copperhead is built on the MPX platform, but is a radically reduced length, width and size. It features a monolithic upper receiver, with an integrated stock knuckle lower, a 3.5-inch barrel with integrated muzzle brake, and comes equipped with the new SIG SAUER Pivoting Contour Brace (PCB). *sigsauer.com*

Smith and Wesson

Smith & Wesson M&P380 Shield EZ

Smith & Wesson Ported M&P Shield M2.0

The Performance Center is now producing Ported M&P Shield M2.0 pistols in 9mm, .40 S&W and .45 ACP variants. These new pistols feature a ported barrel and slide for reduced muzzle flip, enhanced trigger for a crisp, light trigger pull, and HI-VIZ Fiber Optic Sights (MSRP: $539) or Tritium Night Sights (MSRP: $623). The M&P380 Shield EZ pistol (MSRP: $579) is now available with a Crimson Trace Green Laserguard laser sight with Instinctive Activation installed at the factory. *smith-wesson.com*

Springfield Armory

The 911 is a subcompact 9mm pistol that both shoots and feels like a full-size firearm. This new series of pistols is set up with controls similar to a 1911.

Springfield Armory XD(M) OSP

They come with 6+1 round flush and 7+1 round extended magazines. The 911 Nitride (MSRP: $659) has a matte black finish and green G10 grips. The 911 Stainless (MSRP: $659) has a stainless slide and matte black frame. The 911 Nitride with Hogue Grips (MSRP: $639) has a matte black finish and Hogue rubber wrap-around grips. The 911 Stainless with Laser Grip (MSRP: $849) has a stainless slide and matte black frame and Viridian green grip laser. The 911 Nitride with Laser Grips (MSRP: $849) has a matte black finish and Viridian green grip laser. The 911 Alpha series is similar to the 911 .380 series, and is chambered in .380 ACP, but in a more economical package. They come with a 6+1 round flush-fit magazine. They are slightly smaller than their 911 9mm cousins and come in two models. The Alpha Nitride (MSRP: $429) features a matte black finish and checkered polymer grips. The Alpha Stainless (MSRP: $429) features a matte black frame and stainless slide and checkered polymer grips. The 911 .380 series also has new finishes (MSRP: $729) available: desert FDE, desert FDE/black, platinum/graphite, titanium, titanium/nitride and tactical vintage blue/stainless.

Two new 10mm offering include the RO Elite (MSRP: $1,145) which uses SA's RO Elite series steel frame and fully supported match-grade barrel. Also in 10mm is the XD(M) 4.5-inch (MSRP: $652) and 5.25-inch (MSRP: $779). These two XD(M) take the series to a whole oth-

Springfield Armory 911 .380 Series

Springfield Armory
911 9mm Series

er level of power. Also new to the XD(M) series are XD(M) OSP with threaded barrel (MSRP: $710) and the XD(M) OSP with threaded barrel and Vortex Venom optic (MSRP: $958). These are chambered in 9mm, have a 19+1 round capacity, tall sights, and a 5.3-inch threaded barrel or 4.5-inch non-threaded barrel. The model with the Vortex optic red-dot comes factory installed. The SAINT Edge pistol (MSRP: $1,559) combines premium features, including Maxim Defense CQB, adjustable four-position brace, M-LOK handguard, Bravo Company Mod 3 pistol grip, folding BUIS, match trigger and more. The SAINT Victor Pistol (MSRP: $1,015) is engineered for performance in a potent, compact package in either 5.56mm or 300 BLK calibers. These ultralight pistols feature an interrupted rail to accommodate modern shooting styles, like shooting with a thumb-over grip. They also feature a rugged SB Tactical SBX-K forearm brace, Bravo Company MOD 3 pistol grip, M-LOK handguard, and an SA Forward Blast Diverter at the muzzle. The XD 3 Sub-Compact from SA's Defender Series is designed to bring the most features in a concealed-carry pistol at reasonable price. This is a subcompact 9mm pistol with a 3-inch barrel and 13+1 round capacity.

The SAINT AR-15 pistol (MSRP: $1,059) is now available in a variety of Cerakote finishes including OD green/desert FDE, desert FDE and tactical gray. The hammer-fired XD-E pistol (MSRP: $542) is now available with longer 3.8- and 4.5-inch barrels. The 1911 EMP 4-inch Conceal Carry Contour in 9mm (MSRP: $1,220) is now available in a variety of Cerakote finishes including OD green, desert FDE and tactical gray. New finishes are available on the XD-S MOS2.2 3.3-inch single-stack 9mm pistols (MSRP: $589), including desert FDE, desert FDE/black and tactical gray/black. SA's Custom Shop is now offering the Professional 1911-A1, 9mm (MSRP: $3,363) fully tricked out with fitted frame and slide, match barrel, tuned trigger and more. There is also the Pro-

fessional 1911-A1, 9mm (MSRP: $3,465) with all the features of the other Professional, plus a receiver with a built-in accessory rail. *springfield-armory.com*

Steyr

The A2 MF (MSRP: $675) features a redesigned frame with interchangeable grip panels and backstraps that provide maximum grip, texture and ergonomics. The MF stands for Modular Frame and this new modular grip ensures a proper fit for any hand size. Also new is the flared mag well to reduce reloading time. This new 9mm keeps with the tradition of the A1 series with the high grip-angle, low-bore axis and proprietary trapezoid sights. *steyr-arms.com*

Stoeger

Stoeger STR-9

The affordable STR-9 pistol (MSRP: $349) uses striker-fired mechanism and is chambered in 9mm with a 15+1 capacity. The grip angle is engineered for comfortable grip and a low-bore axis for reduced muzzle flip. *stoegerindustries.com*

Taurus

The TX22 (MSRP: $349) is a full-size semi-auto pistol chambered in .22 Long Rifle. It features a precision-designed Taurus Pittman Trigger System (PTS), which offers a crisp break and short reset, and a built-in safety. The polymer frame has an ergonomic design and is equipped with adjustable rear sights. *taurususa.com*

Walther

The Q5 Match Steel Frame Competition pistol (MSRP: $1499) is Walther's first stall frame pistol introduction in decades. This is a match-ready pistol in 9mm with fiber optic front sight and adjustable rear. It also uses the PPQ Quick Defense trigger system and sport a radically fluted slide for reduced felt recoil. The Q5 Match Steel Frame Pro

Walther Q5 Match

model (MSRP: $1,650) is similar except is equipped with a mag well for faster reloads. *waltherarms.com*

Wilson Combat

Wilson Combat Protector

Wilson Combat
Vertec/Centurion Tactical

WC has taken Beretta's Model 92 Vertec and created the 92G Vertec/Centurion Tactical (MSRP: $1,495). It features a M9A1/Vertec Frame with 92A1 round trigger guard, improved checkering, shortened 92G Vertec slide, steel G model de-cocking levers and other premium components WC is known for like a slide to frame fit as tight as practical within production gun limits to ensure accuracy. The pistol is available in 9mm with a magazine capacity of either 17 or 20 rounds. The Protector Series pistol (MSRP: $1,999.95) uses an AR15 mil-spec upper and lower with an 11.3-inch, match-grade barrel. It uses a mid-length gas system for enhanced reliability. Available in 300 BLK or 300 HAM'R. *wilson-combat.com*

NEW REVOLVERS & OTHERS

BY MAX PRASAC

I was perusing a well-known shooting and hunting website the other day when I came across a thread entitled: Why a Revolver? The premise of the originator of the thread was why, in the modern plastic/ semi-auto/high-capacity world we live in today, would someone deliberately choose a revolver? The discussion went on for days and spanned a number of pages. What was most remarkable was a majority of the responses were pro-revolver and while many of the thoughts expressed were similar in nature, there were some rather unique reasons for revolvers cited. I, being of a rather singular focus, naturally declared that revolvers

are still the best platforms for hunting handguns (over semi-autos) as they can handle much more powerful chamberings. The usual naysayers reared their ill-informed heads, but there's no accounting for bad taste or ignorance!

However, the thread got me thinking. It's not that I haven't embraced autoloaders, I admit a bit of a weakness for 1911s, and I don't dislike semi-autos, I just prefer revolvers — "prefer" perhaps doesn't convey enough emotion.

So, why do I like revolvers so much? I compiled a list.

- First and foremost is reliability. The simplicity of the design is its greatest asset. It's much harder to stop a revolver from going bang than an autoloader. If you want unmatchable reliable ignition, look no further than a revolver. Yes, capacity is limited, but maybe that encourages the shooter to aim more carefully over the "spray-and-pray" crowd. My answer to high-capacity is marksmanship. Let that sink in.

- Aesthetics. There is nothing you can do to some of these plastic bottom-feeders to make them look good. Revolvers, on the other hand... OK, so I'm a little bit biased, but be it stainless steel, or a deep blue, or even color case hardening, you just can't beat 'em. Some revolver designs are timeless and will look good no matter what century we are living in. Smith & Wesson's Model 29/629 is the perfect example of just such a revolver. The same cannot be said for the various "Tupperware" pistols.

- Variety. Variety is the spice of life. Revolvers come in all shapes and sizes, from mini revolvers to double-action-only snubbies, to big, powerful single actions, to reproduction black-powder revolvers of the 19th century, to modern polymer framed revolvers. There is virtually something for everyone, thank you very much.

- Wide range of available cham-

berings. Way more options as far as calibers are concerned in the realm of the revolver, from .17 HMR all the way to the big-daddy .500 Smith & Wesson Magnum. There are also a variety of rifle cartridges available from Magnum Research in their stretch-frame revolver including the .30-30 and .45-70 Government. No shortage of offerings for virtually every need.

- Confuses millennials. Huh? A common quip by young shooters on the range: "Is that an antique?" Yes, a very capable antique.

- Hunting. My personal sub-category puts revolvers in the top position for handgun hunting over auto-loaders. I won't even go into mentioning the superiority of single-shot "specialty pistols" over bottom-feeders, delivering rifle-like performance in a smaller package. There is simply no comparison.

They're seemingly outdated, singularly simplistic, boringly reliable, and they just won't go away. So, with no further delays, I give you the new offerings.

American Derringer

American Derringer was founded in 1980 by Robert Saunders. When Robert passed, his wife Elizabeth took the helm and to this day stays true to Robert's vision of crafting fine handmade derringers. Available in a variety of calibers (from .22 LR to .45 Colt/.410), American Derringer offers a full line of single- and double-action derringers.

American Derringer has a new single-action derringer for 2019, chambered in the popular .327 Federal. Constructed entirely of 17-4PH stainless steel, the overall length of this derringer is 4.82-inches, making concealment a snap. The barrel length is 3 inches and the weight comes in at a paltry 14 ounces. These are limited-quantity, handmade, high-quality firearms that are not mass produced. *www.amderringer.com.*

Charter Arms

Founded in 1964, Charter Arms is headed by the third generation of Ecker family members, staying true to the spirt of this truly all-American firearms company. Known for producing double action revolvers for more than half a century in the heart of New England's "Gun Valley," Charter Arms entered the

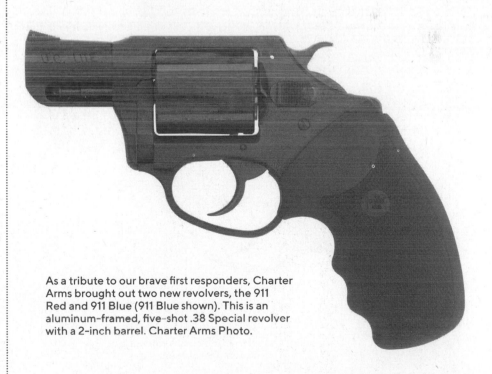

As a tribute to our brave first responders, Charter Arms brought out two new revolvers, the 911 Red and 911 Blue (911 Blue shown). This is an aluminum-framed, five-shot .38 Special revolver with a 2-inch barrel. Charter Arms Photo.

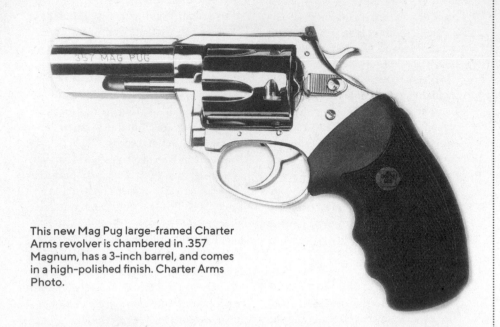

This new Mag Pug large-framed Charter Arms revolver is chambered in .357 Magnum, has a 3-inch barrel, and comes in a high-polished finish. Charter Arms Photo.

gun-building fray with the Undercover, a five-shot .38 Special that weighed in at only 16 ounces.

Every year, we look forward to new models being added to its already impressive lineup of double-action revolvers. Charter Arms revolvers feature one-piece frames (stronger than screw-on side-plate designs), a safe and completely blocked hammer system, and three-place cylinder lock-up. To many, it matters that Charter Arms revolvers are 100-percent American made.

Six new models have joined the line-up starting with two new First Responder series revolvers, the "911 Red" and "911 Blue." The revolvers are finished in black with a red stripe and a blue stripe, respectively. Part of the Undercover Lite series of revolvers, these two are built on the large aluminum frame, are chambered in .38 Special and feature a five-shot capacity. The sights are fixed and the barrel is 2 inches in length. This is a nicely executed tribute to our brave first responders.

A new Mag Pug large-framed revolver graces the Charter Arms lineup this year. This .357 Magnum five-shot features a 3-inch barrel, and an adjustable rear sight. Unlike its Mag Pug stable mates, this new long-barreled model come with an attractive high-polish finish.

Three new revolvers adorn the Pitbull series lineup. The "Tiger IIII" in .45 ACP is a five-shot revolver with fixed sights and a 2.2-inch barrel. This is built on Charter Arms' XL frame and comes with a black finish with green tiger stripes. The other two Pitbull newcomers are built on the large frame in stainless steel. One is a six-shot chambered in .380 and features fixed sights and a 2.2-inch barrel. The other new Pitbull is chambered in .40 S&W in a five-shot configuration with adjustable sights and a 4.2-inch barrel.

Another great reason to buy a Charter Arms revolver is the absolute affordability of the products. You don't need to break the bank to get into a quality revolver. *www.charterarms.com.*

Cimarron

Cimarron imports its revolver line from both Uberti and Pietta and offers a complete line of replica Single Action Army revolvers, black-powder percussion models, open-top and conversion revolvers as well as shotguns — an impressive lineup that offers something for every shooting enthusiast. I receive frequent e-mail updates from Cimarron and I can report, for certain, they are not standing still.

New this year is the 1862 Pocket Navy Conversion revolver. Just looking at it, you would never know it is chambered in the popular (and affordable) .380 ACP. This authentically reproduced, period-correct revolver has been brought to you with the utmost attention to detail and craftsmanship, however with a modern twist. The five-shot revolver is attractively finished in a rich blue with a color case hardened frame, a brass trigger guard and backstrap, and finished off with a beautiful, one-piece varnished walnut grip. The 1862 Pocket Navy Conversion comes with a 6-inch barrel. *www.cimarron-firearms.com.*

The "Tiger IIII" in .45 ACP is a five-shot revolver with fixed sights and a 2.2-inch barrel. This is built on Charter Arms' XL frame and comes with a black finish with green tiger stripes.

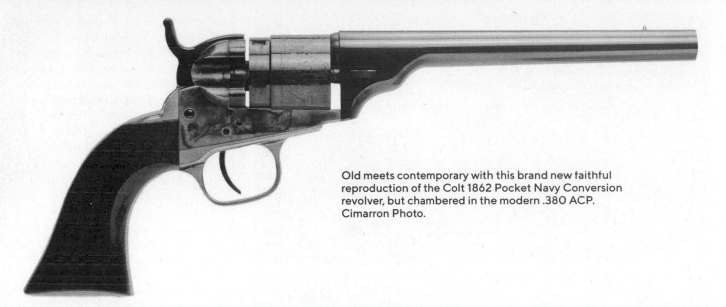

Old meets contemporary with this brand new faithful reproduction of the Colt 1862 Pocket Navy Conversion revolver, but chambered in the modern .380 ACP. Cimarron Photo.

Colt

The company that really started it all still produces a version of the famous Single Action Army (SAA), to which virtually all modern single-action revolvers share DNA with Colt's classic yet timeless design. One of the most iconic pieces of Americana, the Colt Single Action Army is probably the most recognizable gun in American film history and thankfully is still being produced by Colt.

The Single Action Army is available today in only two calibers, .357 Magnum and .45 Colt. There is some discussion of adding more calibers in the future, but for now this is it. The adjustable-sight version, the New Frontier, has been dropped from the lineup for

the time being. The reduction in Single Action Army models is an effort from Colt to get caught up on production, as producing fewer models will enable them to increase the production of the ones they are building. This will enable them to (it is hoped) produce more of these iconic revolvers in a wider variety of configurations in the future.

The big news this year is the all-new King Cobra. Since re-entering the double-action revolver market in 2017 with a .38 Special Cobra model, Colt now has given us the King Cobra in the potent .357 Magnum. The King Cobra features a heavy-duty frame made from American stainless steel. The six-round capacity differentiates the new Colt from

most other small-framed revolvers. The attractive 3-inch barrel has a full lug, a replaceable front sight and a "Linear Leaf" spring trigger (LL2) like the rest of the Cobra line of revolvers from Colt. Rounding out the package is a brushed stainless steel finish and Hogue Over-molded grips. As soon as the Cobra was released, customers began calling for a .357 Magnum version of the new revolver. Colt clearly listens. *www.colt.com*.

Freedom Arms

Freedom Arms has the distinction of making some of the finest single-action revolvers in the industry. Period. These revolvers are the Rolls Royce of the single-action revolver world, and though a traditionally styled single-action revolver, the FA 83 is all modern on the inside and produced of 17-4PH stainless steel, in a five-shot configuration. Freedom Arms prides itself on hand-assembling each and every unit to tight and exacting tolerances. This is a true "custom built" production revolver.

Freedom also produces fine break-open, single-shot pistols designated the Model 2008 (as it was introduced in that year). Available in a variety of calibers, and three different barrel lengths — 10, 15 and 16 inches — the Model 2008 defines practical. All barrels are interchangeable, making caliber switches simple and they feature the excellent grip frame borrowed directly from the FA Model 83, a grip that lends itself

Colt's all-new King Cobra has entered the market, packing .357 Magnum power with six-shot capacity. Colt Photo.

The all-new, first-ever production revolver in the legendary .500 Linebaugh chambering, shown here with Magnum Research's outstanding "Bisley" grip frame.

Big news from Magnum Research is the new Custom BFR Website where you can spec-out your one-off, custom-built revolver from Magnum Research's Precision Center. Some new options are a black nitride finish and full octagon barrels. Magnum Research Photo.

well to heavy recoil. Non-catalog barrel lengths are also available for a fee.

Demand and refinement are so high in Freedom, Wyoming, that Freedom Arms currently isn't releasing anything new on the revolver or single-shot front. Management has made the decision to stay with the status quo of offerings in order to get caught up on production. We eagerly await any and all things new coming out of Freedom, Wyoming.

In summary, these revolvers and pistols have no equals with regard to fit and finish. In all, Freedom Arms produces true modern-day classics. *www. freedomarms.com.*

Iver Johnson Arms

Though the Iver Johnson name has been around since the late 1800s, the brand underwent a complete reinvention in 2003. The new company has not retained any records related to Iver Johnson products produced prior to 2003. The company essentially started with a clean slate and imports a series of 1911-type pistols, several shotgun models and a newly minted four-barrel derringer. This pocket-sized "pepperbox" derringer, chambered in .22 LR, is constructed entirely of steel. It will be available with three different optional grips: Oak Dymondwood, Black Dymondwood and Rosewood Dymondwood grips. *www.iverjohnsonarms.com.*

Magnum Research

Born in 1999, Magnum Research entered the revolver-building business with the introduction of the BFR — the "Biggest Finest Revolver" — chambered in the old warhorse .45-70 Government. The company has since redesigned its revolvers and today produces both long- and short-frame revolvers in a range of calibers to suit just about every shooter's needs. In this author's humble opinion, there is no wider assortment of hunting calibers offered under one roof than that of Magnum Research. There is literally something for everyone and virtually every game animal imaginable.

A subsidiary of Kahr Arms, Magnum Research of Minneapolis, Minnesota, offers a whole line of long-frame and

short-frame stainless steel single-action revolvers in both standard caliber/configurations and a plethora of custom Precision Center offerings.

Last year we reported the first-ever offering in a commercial revolver of the .500 Linebaugh chambering. For the uninitiated, this cartridge started life as a cut-down .348 Winchester case (to 1.40 inches), necked up to .510 bullet diameter. As a big-game cartridge, this one is near the top of the food chain when loaded accordingly. Recoil is expectedly stout with most factory Buffalo Bore loads, but the Bisley grip frame does an outstanding job of taming the large recoil impulse. Why are we reporting about it again? Well, these revolvers are no longer in the planning/development stages and are now actually available and a number are already in customers' hands.

Also, two new six-shot revolvers are being added to the Magnum Research lineup. We announced last year the development of the six-shot, short-framed .44 Magnum, and now they are actually being produced. The other six-shot will be a .357 Magnum to be made available later in the year.

The biggest news out of Magnum Research is the Custom BFR Website (*www.custombfrrevolver.com*). This is where the consumer can build his or her very own custom configured BFR revolver from a host of options from standard catalog calibers as well as a number of Precision-Center only calibers, to barrel length, to barrel type (round or octagon), to fluted or unfluted cylinders to a number of cool finishes like color case hardening and the new black nitride finish. Many more options exist so we recommend you go to the Custom BFR website and look for yourself. I am sure you will be able to find something there that will appeal to you.

These are big, no-compromise, well-built revolvers that offer unparalleled accuracy and strength at a reasonable price point. *www.magnumresearch.com*.

Nighthawk Custom/Korth-Waffen

Nighthawk Custom was established in 2004 by four talented individuals who all shared a true passion for the ubiquitous

The attractive new "True Black Widow" .22 Magnum mini revolver from North American Arms. North American Arms Photo.

1911.The company has grown over the years to become a premier custom 1911 manufacturer/builder, offering more than 40 unique versions of the classic pistol. Nighthawk also offers a line of tactical shotguns based on the Remington 870. However, in the context of this chapter, Nighthawk offers a line of revolvers as well. The legendary German firearms manufacturer, Korth-Waffen, has partnered with Nighthawk Custom to produce a line of high-performance revolvers, the latest being the "Ranger."

The Ranger is a six-shot .357 Magnum double-action revolver with a fully tunable action featuring a trigger-wheel system (alternate wheels are included) that can turn the slick double-action pull into a two-stage, double-action by simply changing the wheels. The single-action pull can also be easily adjusted by turning the screw just rear of the trigger, and as if that isn't enough built-in adjustment, the mainspring can also be manually adjusted by the user.

However, there is even more adjustment built into the package as the cylinder can be swapped with no drama to a 9mm or .38 Special by simply pressing a detent, freeing the cylinder. Pure tenability. The Ranger has a 4-inch barrel with Picatinny rails both top and bottom. The sights are fully adjustable for windage and elevation, and the package is finished with a beautiful set of Turkish walnut grips. With an MSRP of $4,799, the Ranger isn't cheap, but what you get is a

fine machine with many custom touches the end-user can easily tune to perfection. *www.nighthawkcustom.com*.

North American Arms

North American Arms produces small, well-crafted, stainless steel, single-action miniature revolvers available in three rimfire calibers: .22 Short, .22 LR, and .22 Magnum.

New on the mini-revolver front is the "True Black Widow," evolved from the popular .22 Magnum frame series of NAA revolvers. The True Black Widow is equipped with a heavy, vented 2-inch barrel, a bull cylinder, oversized black rubber grips and comes with Marble Arms rear sights adjustable for elevation, or fixed sights. This gun is a special edition of the Black Widow that is finished in a black matte PVD (Physical Vapor Deposition) coating that is not only attractive, but durable and corrosion resistant. The grips are finished with a red hourglass medallion. *www.northamericanarms.com*.

Smith & Wesson

Smith & Wesson has the distinction of building some of the finest double-action revolvers in the world.

New are a number of pocket revolvers with a focus on defensive use. First up is the Model 642CT (Crimson Trace). This J-frame features an alloy frame with a stainless steel 1.88-inch barrel and cylinder. The five-shot revolver is chambered in .38 Special (+P capable) and is

This new .357 Magnum LCRX features a stainless steel frame, a 3-inch barrel and a five-shot cylinder. Ruger Photo.

double-action only (with a snag-free enclosed hammer), comes with a fixed rear sight and is rounded out with robin's egg blue Crimson Trace Lasergrips.

The M&P Bodyguard 38-1 is also new to the lineup and features a gray polymer grip, new updated styling and an integrated Crimson Trace red laser. The newest M&P Bodyguard also comes equipped with a serrated ambidextrous cylinder release, making loading and unloading easy for right- and left-handed shooters.

The newest revolver to come out of Smith & Wesson Performance Center is the Model 442 J-frame "Action Package." This attractive five-shot, .38 Special +P revolver has a stainless steel cylinder with a glass-bead finish and high-polished flutes making for a nice contrast.

The chrome plated trigger has a bright, polished finish and rounded edges. Rounding it out are Crimson Trace LG 105 laser grips. *www.smith-wesson.com.*

Sturm, Ruger & Company

First up is the all new steel LCRX. The monolithic frame is made from 400 series stainless steel, in a matte black finish. The 3-inch barrel is fitted with a replaceable, pinned-ramp front sight, while the rear sight is fully adjustable. Chambered in .357 Magnum, the stainless steel cylinder holds five rounds and is extensively fluted to cut weight. This model is equipped with an external hammer enabling single-action shooting. A comfortable Hogue Tamer grip rounds out the package, and this LCRX weighs in at 21.3 ounces.

There's a new SP101 that Ruger has rolled out, chambered in .357 Magnum in blued steel. Sturm, Ruger & Company is clearly listening to its public. Featuring a 2.25-inch barrel, a fixed rear sight and a black ramp front sight, like its stainless counterpart, this SP101 has a five-shot capacity. The cushioned rubber grips offer some comfort when touching off this little powerhouse.

Ruger offers some real gems as Distributor Exclusives. Two new Redhawks are available from Davidsons (www.davidsonsinc.com) and they are the 4.2-inch and 2.75-inch-barreled .41 Magnums. Like all Redhawks now, these feature a cold hammer-forged sleeve and shroud barrel. The 2.75-inch Redhawk is equipped with attractive hardwood grips while the longer-barreled version gets Hogue Monogrips. Yes, the Redhawk is a lot of gun for such a seemingly diminutive cartridge, but this will enable even the neophyte to handle the recoil a .41 Magnum can generate. Both stainless steel models, both are equipped with adjustable rear sights and a ramp front sight.

Not much new on the Ruger single-action front save for one Distributor Exclusive offered by Lipsey's (www.lipseys.com), a .327 Federal Magnum New Model Single-Seven in a satin-blue finish. An adjustable rear sight adorns this revolver as well as a 4.62-inch barrel, and an unfluted seven-shot cylinder. Attractive black Micarta grips with the Ruger logo round out the 34-ounce package. *www.ruger.com.*

Taurus

Taurus offers a wide range of revolvers for personal defense, recreational shooting and hunting. There is something in their catalog for any handgun endeavor you choose.

Taurus' 856 revolver line has been expanded with the addition of the new Ultra-Lite Model in four new anodized coatings. This six-shot .38 Special + P double-action revolver features an aluminum frame, and matte black carbon steel or matte stainless steel cylinder. The 2-inch barrel is either matte carbon steel or matte stainless steel, with a serrated ramp front sight and a fixed rear

Ruger expanded its SP101 line with this blued-steel .357 Magnum model. The five-shot revolver sports a 2.25-inch barrel. Ruger Photo.

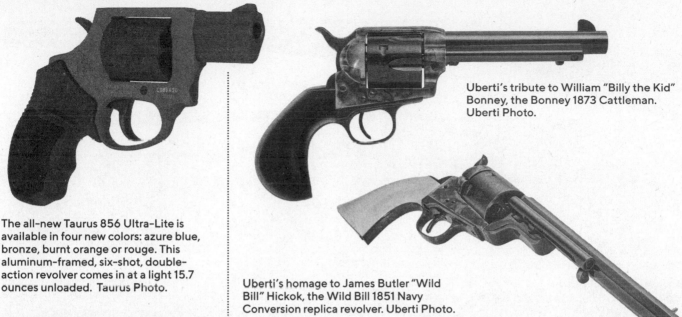

Uberti's tribute to William "Billy the Kid" Bonney, the Bonney 1873 Cattleman. Uberti Photo.

Uberti's homage to James Butler "Wild Bill" Hickok, the Wild Bill 1851 Navy Conversion replica revolver. Uberti Photo.

The all-new Taurus 856 Ultra-Lite is available in four new colors: azure blue, bronze, burnt orange or rouge. This aluminum-framed, six-shot, double-action revolver comes in at a light 15.7 ounces unloaded. Taurus Photo.

sight. Your new Ultra-Lite 856 can be had in azure blue, bronze, burnt orange or rouge finish, and tips the scales at a lean 15.7 ounces empty. *www.taurususa.com.*

Traditions
Performance Firearms

Known for muzzleloader rifles and historic replica muzzleloading pistols, Traditions Performance Firearms also offers a line of imported Single Action Army replicas in two series: the Frontier and, for the more cost-conscious, the Rawhide series. Unlike the original Single Action Army, both lines feature a transfer-bar safety system enabling safe loaded carry in the field with six

rounds. Traditions also sells a full line of black-powder revolvers that are fully functioning, dedicated replicas.

Traditions Performance Firearms has added the Rawhide Rancher series to its line of single-actions. There are three configurations in .22 LR available in this 1873-type model with a 4.75-inch barrel, matte black finish with fixed sights. This easy-to-shoot, six-shot revolver offers inexpensive fun at the range, and comes equipped with a re-bounding hammer safety.

Available with a black checkered PVC grip or a walnut wood grip. Another option comes with a .22 LR cylinder as well as a .22 Magnum cylinder. This new series is perfect for the beginning shooter or the experienced shooter who simply wants a quality revolver that is fun to shoot. *www.traditions-firearms.com.*

Uberti

Uberti, a subsidiary of Benelli, offers a whole line of reproduction Colt 1873 Single Action Army and other western reproduction revolvers, made of modern materials. These fine reproductions are economical, pleasing to look at and of high quality.

There are two new versions of the

limited-edition Outlaws and Lawmen Series of revolvers with the Bonney and Wild Bill models. These two new offerings pay homage to two of the most famous gunfighters of America's Old West: William "Billy the Kid" Bonney and James Butler "Wild Bill" Hickok, with the Bonney 1873 Cattleman, and the Wild Bill 1851 Navy Conversion replica revolvers, respectively.

The Bonney 1873 Cattleman is chambered in the appropriate .45 Colt, and features a color case frame, and a 5 1/2-inch, blued-steel barrel. This new six-shot revolver has an overall length of 11 inches and weighs in at 2.3 pounds. Simulated bison-horn, bird's-head grips round out the Bonney 1873 Cattleman.

The Wild Bill 1851 Navy Conversion revolver is chambered in the much more practical and convenient, and available, .38 Special as opposed to the original muzzleloader configuration of Wild Bill's revolvers. Featuring a color case frame, blued-steel barrel at 7 1/2-inches in length and an engraved, six-shot cylinder, it weighs in at 2.7 pounds with a 13-inch overall length. The Wild Bill 1851 Navy Conversion is equipped with an attractive simulated ivory grip.

The legends of Billy the Kid and Wild Bill Hickok live on thanks to Uberti. *www.uberti.com.*

A member of the new Rawhide Rancher series of revolvers from Traditions with a matte black finish and black checkered PVC grips, chambered in .22 LR. Traditions Photo.

NEW SHOTGUNS

BY **JOHN HAVILAND**

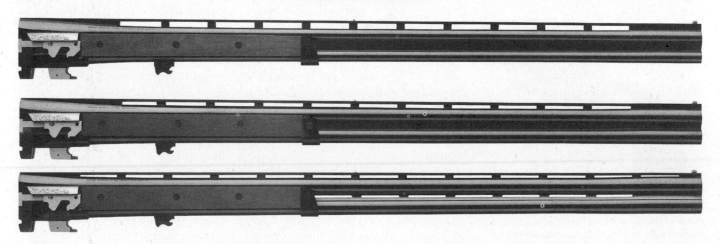

Browning's Citori 525 Field is available in 16 gauge as a Limited Production model.

This year's lineup of new shotguns includes handy short shotguns to utility shotguns to expensive and engraved shotguns with a variety of shotguns tailored to fit young shooters on the range and in the field. Those first shotguns for beginning shooters are good to see as they will be the foundation for a long sporting life. And who would have ever thought the .410-bore would be considered a legitimate turkey hunting gun?

Benelli

Two models have been added to the 828U, Benelli's first over/under. Camouflage and Cerakote have been applied to turkey and waterfowl guns and a featherweight was created by combining two autoloading shotguns.

The 828U Sport is designed for sporting-clay shooters. The Sport weighs a feather over 8 pounds with its steel receiver and 30-inch barrels. The Sport's grip angle and comb height work in union with its wide carbon-fiber rib. The trigger is adjustable for reach. The Progressive Balancing system includes weights to balance the gun. A set of shims positions stock drop and cast. In addition, the Sport comes with a trigger tool, choke wrench and cylinder, improved cylinder, modified, improved modified and full extended, color-coded choke tubes.

The 828U Performance Shop Upland 12 gauge is made for grouse hikes, with an aluminum receiver and 24-inch barrels for a gun weight of 6.9 pounds. Length of pull (LOP) is 14 1/4 inches. Rob Roberts Triple Threat five choke-tube set provides appropriate shot patterns. The removable trigger group makes for easy cleaning. AA-grade walnut stock and fore-end match the anodized bronze/matte blue receiver and carbon-fiber stepped rib. The Upland comes with a case, choke case, choke wrench and trigger removal tool.

Camouflage and Cerakote are the theme of two M2 20-gauge autoloaders for Benelli. The Performance Shop M2 Waterfowl and Turkey shotguns have a lengthened forcing cone, enlarged bolt handle and bolt release lever easy to operate with gloved-hands. ComforTech buttstocks take the edge off recoil and AirTouch checkering on the grip and fore-end provide a sure grip. The Water-

Benelli 828U Performance Shop Upland 12-ga.

Benelli 828U Sport

Benelli M2 20-Ga Performance Shop Waterfowl

Benelli M2 Performance Shop Turkey 20-ga.

Benelli Montefeltro Silver Featherweight 20-ga.

Benelli SBE 3 Performance Shop Waterfowl

fowl weighs an ounce less than 6 pounds, Optifade Marsh camo covers the stock and fore-end and Cerakote Midnight Bronze protects the receiver and barrel. A Rob Roberts Triple Threat Choke System and C, IC, M, IM, F Benelli Crio choke tubes go with the 28-inch barrel. Drop and cast shims make a custom fit. The M2 Turkey weighs 5.7 pounds with a 24-inch barrel that is ported to reduce muzzle rise. A Burris Fast Fire II sight is mounted on the gun. Mossy Oak Bottomlands Camo hides the stock and fore-end and Cerakote Midnight Bronze protects metal. A Rob Roberts extended XFT choke tube and C, IC, M, IM, F Benelli choke tubes along with drop and cast shims complete the gun.

The Montefeltro Silver Featherweight is a combination of the Standard Ultralight and Montefeltro Silver autoloading shotguns. The 12 gauge wears a 26-inch barrel and weighs 6 pounds, 3 ounces, and the 20 weighs 5.3 pounds with its 24-inch barrel. That light weight results

from a shortened fore-end and magazine and carbon-fiber rib. The guns' nickel-plated aluminum receivers are scroll-engraved with gold embellishments that complement a satin-finished walnut stock and fore-end. The shotguns come with C, IC, M, IM and F extended choke tubes, choke wrench and a shim kit to adjust drop and cast.

Benelli's Performance Shop has upgraded the basic Super Black Eagle 3 to the Waterfowl and Turkey. The Waterfowl's barrel and receiver are protected with Cerakote Midnight Bronze and stock and fore-end hidden in Optifade Marsh camo. The Waterfowl's 28-inch barrel comes with three Rob Roberts Custom Triple Threat choke tubes and five Benelli choke tubes. Extra light pipes are available for the front sight, and a 40-position shim kit allows set of cast and drop. The Turkey features a vertical grip and stock and fore-end covered in Mossy Oak Bottomlands camo. The Turkey's 24-inch

barrel comes with a Rob Roberts XFT choke tube and five Benelli choke tubes.

Browning

Browning is always about style with high-grade target and hunting shotguns and also lightweight guns for hunters hiking that additional mile. Six new versions of the Citori include a limited run of the 525 Field 16 gauge.

Browning's High Grade Program continues with the Citori 725 High Grade Side Plate Four Gauge Combo. The receiver's side plates are silver-nitrate finished and extensively engraved with gold bird and dog accents. The receiver is the foundation for interchangeable 12-, 20-, 28-gauge and .410-bore 30- or 32-inch barrel sets. The grade VI/VIII black walnut fore-end and stock are oil-finished and checkered 20 lines per inch. Invector-Plus Flush Choke tubes included in IC, M and F.

The Citori 725 Feather Superlight weighs 6.125 pounds in 12 gauge and 5.4 pounds in 20 gauge. Those light weights can be credited to an aluminum alloy receiver, strengthened with a steel breach face and hinge pin, checkered straight grip black walnut stock and slim fore-end with a Schnabel tip. Barrels are 26 inches with 2 3/4-inch chambers, because no one should shoot magnum shells in such light guns. A large Inflex recoil pad softens recoil and Invector-DS Flush IC, M and F choke tubes are included.

The Citori CX is designed for all clay-target games, yet is plenty light enough for an all-day hike in the field. The 12-gauge CX has 32-inch barrels with high post ventilated top and side ribs and Vector Pro lengthened forcing cones and F, M and IC Invector-Plus choke tubes. The Triple Trigger System provides three different trigger shoe profiles for a perfect finger-on-trigger position. A 60/40 pattern point of impact (POI) makes it suitable for targets and game.

The Citori Adjustable Comb CX wears a Grade II American walnut stock with adjustable comb and Inflex recoil pad. The Citori CXS Micro 12 or 20 gauge have 24- or 26-inch barrels and 13-inch LOP. The longer barrel 12 gauge weighs 7.5 pounds and the 20 gauge 6.6 pounds, POI is flat with F, M and IC Invector-Plus

Browning BT-99 High Grade with Adjustable Butt and Comb

Browning Citori 725 Superlight Feather

Browning Citori CX with Adjustable Comb

Browning Citori CXS Micro

Browning Citori Feather Lightning

Browning Citori Gran Lightning

Midas choke tubes.

Browning is back with three models of the 12-gauge Citori Lightning. The Citori White Lightning's steel receiver is coated with a nitride finish and features intricate engraving offset with polished blued barrels and an oil-finished walnut stock and fore-end. Barrels are 26 or 28 inches with extended black band Invector-Plus F, M and IC choke tubes. The Citori Gran Lightning is highlighted with a satin-finished walnut stock and fore-end, high-polished blued barrel and high relief engraved receiver. The ribbed barrel has an ivory front and mid-bead and Midas Invector-Plus extended black band choke tubes. The Citori Feather Lightning weighs 7 pounds with 26-inch barrels.

Demand for 16-gauge guns builds enough every few years that it's worth chambering a gun to fill the want. Browning has done that with its Citori 525 Field 16 Gauge that weighs 6.7 pounds with 26-inch barrels. The Field features an oil-fin-ished and checkered Grade II/III walnut stock and Schnabel fore-end offset with a silver nitrate finished receiver. Invector Flush chokes tubes include IC, M and F.

The BT-99 Max High Grade trap gun adapts for a perfect fit with a high-post rib with adjustable POI from 50/50 to 100/0 for its HiViz Pro Comp fiber-optic front sight with mid-bead, Graco comb, LOP GraCoil angle/location butt pad plate with a Pachmayr Decelerator XLT recoil pad. Three Midas Grade choke tubes are included.

CZ USA

CZ has reintroduced its side-by-side Bobwhite as the Bobwhite G2. The G2's receiver is machined from a block of steel and is slimmer than the original. Coil springs add longevity and reliability to the gun. Its 28-inch barrels are threaded for C, IC, M, IM and F choke tubes. The Bobwhite is built on gauge-specific frames in 12, 20 and 28 gauge. The 12 gauge weighs 7.3 pounds, while

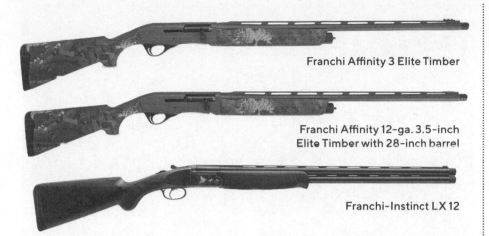

Franchi Affinity 3 Elite Timber

Franchi Affinity 12-ga. 3.5-inch Elite Timber with 28-inch barrel

Franchi-Instinct LX 12

the 28 weighs 5.5 pounds.

The 1012 autoloader uses an inertia operating system and with a retail price of $659, is a direct attempt to undercut similar Benelli shotguns that cost at least twice as much. The basic 1012 wears a Turkish walnut stock and fore-end and 28-inch barrel threaded to accept supplied C, IC, IM and F chokes tubes. Receiver finishes include black chrome, bronze and gray. A synthetic-stocked gun wears a matte black metal finish or full camo.

The All-American Single Trap has a 30-, 32- or 34-inch barrel with a lengthened forcing cone and gas ports at the muzzle. The fore-end and stock are select walnut and comb height adjusts up to 1 3/4 inches.

Franchi

Franchi adds style to one of its over/unders and Cerakote and camo to an autoloader.

Franchi's O/U Instinct LX 12 or 20 gauge combines Italian craftsmanship and American styling. The steel, case-color hardened receiver is engraved with hunting scenes of inlayed gold birds. Checkered AA-grade satin walnut Prince of Wales stock complements a Schnabel-style fore-end. Gloss-blued, 28-inch barrels accept IC, M and F choke tubes, and on top is a red fiber-optic front sight. A safety-mounted selector switch allows choosing barrel firing order. The 12 gauge weighs 7 pounds and the 20 gauge is 6.6 pounds

Affinity Elite autoloading 12- and 20-gauge shotguns withstand tough hunting conditions with a Cerakote Burnt Bronze on the metal and Optifade Marsh camo on the stock and fore-end. The 12 gauge with 28-inch barrel is available with a 3- or 3 1/2-inch chamber. The 20 gauge has a 26-inch barrel with a 3-inch chamber. Extended choke tubes include Close, Mid and Long-Range. Rounding out the features are sling studs, oversized loading port, ambidextrous safety, a ventilated rib, shim kit to set stock drop and cast and receiver drilled and tapped for a mount to install optics.

Mossberg

When Mossberg introduced its 590 Shockwave hand shotgun in 2018, I understood its concept for self-defense and for critters long of teeth that go bump in the night. Recently, I discovered a Shockwave also provides a whole other level of plinking fun. Stuff its magazine full of light-recoiling, 1 ounce of No. 8 shot, 12-gauge shells and ventilating a can or bouncing around a rubber ball is way fun.

Building on that fun, Mossberg has three new models of its 12-gauge 590 Shockwave that include the Nightstick, Shock 'N' Saw and the SPX. All Shockwaves are built with a 14-inch, cylinder-bore barrel above a magazine that holds six rounds and bird's-head shaped grip. The Nightstick is equipped with a hardwood grip and corncob fore-end. It's offered in 12 or 20 gauge, plus .410 bore. (See the Testfire report on the .410 model in that section of this edition. — Editor)

The Shock 'N' Saw's name comes from its chainsaw handle attached to its aluminum M-LOK fore-end. The SPX features a breacher muzzle, heatshield around the barrel and an aluminum side saddle that holds seven shells. A rail on the top of the receiver accepts sights and lights and anything else you can think of to clamp on the gun.

On the long shotgun side, Mossberg has several new models of 500 hunting pumps. The Field/Deer 12 or 20 gauge comes with a fully rifled barrel and smooth-bore barrel with Accu-Set choke tubes. The Retrograde has a walnut stock, ventilated recoil pad and corncob fore-end. The 500 version wears an 18 1/2-inch, cylinder-

The Mossberg Shockwave Nightstick is equipped with a hardwood grip and corncob fore-end.

A fore-end strap on the Mossberg Shockwave helps control recoil when shooting 12-gauge shells in the 5.25-pound gun.

bore barrel and blued-finish. The 590AI model's 20-inch barrel is covered with a heat shield and has a ghost ring rear sight. The Turkey is chambered in .410 and its 26-inch barrel has a fixed full choke. Its synthetic stock and fore-end are covered with Mossy Oak Bottomland camo. The gun weighs 6.5 pounds.

Remington

The V3 autoloader Pro series head-lines Remington shotguns with new camo patterns, and the mainstay 870 pump has a folding stock.

The V3 Field Sport Pro series 12-gauge guns are designed for a specific use and feature a large charging handle, bolt-release button and safety. The V3 Turkey Pro wears a 22-inch barrel with an extended, ported TruGlo Headbanger choke tube. The Turkey is dressed end to end in Realtree Timber camo. LOP is a short 13 inches. Sights are a TruGlo red-dot. The Waterfowl Pro's receiver and barrel are protected with Burnt Bronze color Cerakote and the stock and fore-end are covered with Realtree Max 5 or Mossy Oak Shadow Grass Blades camo. Extended choke tubes include IM, M and F. The V3 Compact weighs a feather under 7 pounds with its 22-inch light-contour barrel. LOP is 13-inches and it can be increased in quarter-inch increments up to an inch with a set of shims.

The V3 Tac-13 is short on both ends, with a 13-inch barrel and Shockwave Raptor grip. A strap on the fore-end helps control recoil. The barrel is cylinder bored and five 2 3/4-inch shells fit in

The Stevens 555 Enhanced over/under, made in Turkey, is now chambered in 16 gauge.

the magazine.

The pump 870 Express Tactical Side Folder 12 or 20 gauge provide a compact carry with the stock folded alongside the right side of the receiver. The extended stock gives the proper cheek weld and comb height for a precise aim shooting slugs. Three different thickness inserts, made of Supercell material, adjust comb height. A Supercell recoil pad soaks up recoil from the 8-pound pump, and a shim kit adjusts LOP. The stock has a Tapco AK-pattern SAW grip. The fore-end has stops at the front and rear that keep the hand in place during recoil. A strap on the fore-end further controls the gun. The 18 1/2-inch barrel has a bead front sight and threaded to

accept a supplied cylinder choke.

Savage

Savage is heavy into utility single-shot and bolt-action turkey shotguns and also a bargain-priced over/under chambered in 16 gauge.

Whoever thought the .410 shotshell would be a serious turkey killer? But hunters have proved the little .410 is deadly on toms out to at least 40 yards shooting Federal's Heavyweight 3-inch, .410 shells loaded with 13/16 ounce of Tungsten Super Shot 9s. Prompted by that success, Stevens has introduced the 301 Turkey break-action, single-shot hammer gun in .410. The 301's extra-full choke is expressly designed to shoot TSS shot. The 301's 26-inch barrel wears a rail for mounted optics. The gun has a camo synthetic stock and weighs only 5 pounds

The Model 212 (12-gauge) and 220 (20-gauge) bolt-action turkey shotguns are based on the Model 110 rifle action. Their receivers are locked in an AccuStock internal aluminum frame and the 22-inch barrels are free-floated. An extra-full turkey choke tube is standard. The AccuFit system includes spacers to adjust LOP and comb height. The one-piece synthetic stock is covered with Mossy Oak Obsession camo.

The Stevens 555 Enhanced over-under, made in Turkey, is now chambered

Remington V3 Field Sport Compact

Remington V3 Field Sport Turkey Pro

Remington V3 Waterfowl Pro Realtree Max5

in 16 gauge. I shot the 555 16 and liked it. Recoil from target loads was mild, even though the gun weighs about 6 pounds and wears a plastic buttplate. A few shots were required to determine pattern impact, which was quite high above aim. Floating targets above the rib powdered the clays. Bores of the 28-inch barrels are chrome-lined and include five choke tubes. The tang-mounted safety doubles as a barrel selector, and case extraction is manual.

Stoeger

The newest M3000 and M3020 autoloaders retain their reliability and durability with a new look featuring a satin-finished walnut buttstock and fore-end paired with a Cerakote Burnt Bronze receiver and barrel. The Inertia Drive action M3000 12 gauge has a 28-inch barrel with a 3-inch chamber and a ventilated, stepped rib and red-bar front sight. The receiver is ready for a Weaver-style rail to mount optics. IC, M, EF choke tubes and a shim kit for adjusting drop and cast are included. The M3020 20 gauge handles 3-inch magnums. It weighs 5.7-pounds and comes with the same barrel style and accessories as the M3000.

Winchester

Winchester has added three models to its SX4 autoloaders and two youth models of SXP pumps.

The SX4 Compact and Waterfowl Hunter Compact are now chambered in 20 gauge; barrel lengths are 24, 26 or 28 inches. Guns weigh 6.25 pounds with the shortest barrel. Length of pull is 13 inches and a Pachmayr Decelerator recoil pad helps prevent flinching. A large safety button, bolt handle and bolt-release tab make it easy for small hands to operate the guns. A TruGlo fiber optic front sight reminds shooters to keep their head down on the comb. IC, M and F Invector-Plus choke tubes are standard. The compact wears a matte black finish on its metal and composite stock and fore-end, while the Waterfowl is covered with Mossy Oak Shadow Grass Blades camo.

The 12-gauge SX4 Upland Field's matte, nickel-finished aluminum receiver complements its satin-finished walnut

Winchester SX4 Compact

Winchester SX4 Upland Field

Winchester SX4 Waterfowl Hunter Compact

Winchester SXP Trap Compact

Winchester SXP Youth

stock. LOP spacers are included and F, M, IC Invector-Plus choke tubes for the 26- or 28-inch barrels.

The SXP Youth Field is chambered in 12 and 20 gauge, and has a 12-inch LOP. Barrel lengths include 20, 22 or 24 inches and an additional 18-inch in 20 gauge. LOP spacers are included as are IC, M and F Invector-Plus choke tubes. An Inflex recoil pad caps the hardwood stock.

The 12-gauge SXP Trap Compact has a choice of a 28- or 30-inch barrel. A Compact weighs 6.25 pounds with the shorter barrel. A 5/16-inch wide rib has a bead in the middle and a TruGlo fiber-optic front sight. M, IM and F extended choke tubes are standard. The stock has a high-profile comb, and checkering on the fore-end provides a sure grip.

This Winchester SX4 Waterfowl Hunter Compact 20 gauge is shooting its way through clay targets.

Bushnell's new TRS-26 is one of the newest additions to the company's AR Optics series sights.

NEW OPTICS

BY **TOM TABOR**

No matter what shooting or outdoor activities you enjoy, optics likely play a significant role. Those products might include a scope or red-dot, reflex-style sight for your rifle, or even in some cases for your handgun or crossbow. Also included in that broad array of products might be binoculars, spotting scopes, rangefinders and various other devices that have the ability to better your chances of success and make your outing just a little better and more enjoyable.

In recent years, all of these products have steadily evolved, advanced and in many cases become more reasonably priced. I personally get a great deal of enjoyment seeing the many innovative breakthroughs that occur each year in this exciting field and thoroughly enjoy covering them in this column. But because of the sheer number and broad array of these products it is an impossible task to cover them all. I can only hope that I have been successful in my endeavor to provide a thorough sampling of these really exciting products.

Bushnell

Bushnell, under Vista Outdoor umbrella, is in the process of greatly expanding its line of optic products. Those products cover a broad array of applications and product lines. Targeting the growing interest in ARs, the company's AR Optic Series has significantly been expanded with riflescopes dedicated to specific calibers, such as the .22 LR, .223/5.56, .308 Win, .300 BLK and even the red-hot 6.5 Creedmoor and the .224 Valkyrie. Each of these scopes comes equipped with a throw-down power-change lever which is adjustable to two different heights. They have fully coated lenses to deliver crisp images no matter what light conditions you are facing. Their Custom BDC reticles, which are purpose-built for each model, allow precise elevation holds based on the caliber. Other features are model-specific, including two options with illuminated reticles and four that boast robust 30mm main tubes. In all, the AR Optics line includes 11 models in configurations from 1-4x24mm through 4.5-18x40 with

Bushnell's new First Strike 2.0 sight offers longer battery life and has a 4 MOA red dot.

The Bushnell Forge Model 4.5-27x50 is a great choice for long-range shooting.

eight different optimized reticle choices.

Also, under Bushnell's AR Optic line are a couple of new red-dot sights. The new TRS-26 model delivers longer battery life, a brighter, crisper dot and push-button operations, all of which have been packed into a very compact design. It features a 3 MOA dot and comes with a 26mm main-tube body. The new First Strike 2.0 also offers longer battery life, but has a 4 MOA red dot and a small reflex-style ruggedized housing. For ease of battery changing, the First Strike 2.0 was designed with a side-battery component and tool-less access. Both the First Strike 2.0 and the TRS-26 offer adjustable brightness settings and are waterproof, fog-proof and shock-proof. The First Strike 2.0 carries a MSRP of $277.45, and the TRS-26 is $194.95.

Bushnell has three new premium high-performance hunting-optic lines: Prime, Nitro and Forge. All of these products were engineered in the U.S., and built with premium components. These three new product lines include a diverse selection of riflescopes, binoculars and

The author found the images through new Bushnell Forge 10x42 binoculars to be crystal clear.

spotting scopes covering more than 100 products, all of which include EXO Barrier external lens coatings. This coating molecularly bonds the lens and fills the microscopic pores in the glass making it one of the best lens-coating technologies. *www.bushnell.com*

FLIR

FLIR engineered and built its new Breach PTQ136 multifunctional, thermal-imaging monocular with the rigors that law-enforcement personnel seek. The Breach PTQ136 is fully capable of displaying the heat signature of people and animals even in total darkness. Featuring the new FLIR Boson core within a compact design, it offers a high degree of tactical awareness when it is needed the most. Using its mini-rail feature, it can be easily mounted to a helmet in a variety of different mounting positions, or its rail can be utilized for mounting additional equipment. Measuring 5.5 x 2.7 x 1.9 inches and weighing only 7.4 ounces allows the Breach to be easily concealed in a pocket for hand use. It has been equipped with onboard recording and seven palettes for fast detection of the targeted images under day or night conditions. The advanced image processing of the internal FLIR Boson thermal core and a bright, high-definition display creates good image clarity, better detec-

FLIR's new Breach PTQ136 is a multi-functional thermal-imaging monocular designed to handle the rigors law-enforcement personnel experience.

tion and classification abilities. Power is provided by a single CR 123A 3V battery with a life expectancy of up to 90-minutes at 68 degrees Fahrenheit. MSRP: $2,495. *www.flir.com*

German Precision Optics

German Precision Optics (GPO) USA recently introduced its new line of premium riflescopes, all of which are German designed and engineered and built on a 30mm, machined-aluminum main tube. The two new offerings within the Passion 4x line come with higher magnification and larger low-light objective lenses. These are available in either 6-24x50 or 3-12x56. The Passion 3-12x56 can be purchased with or without the GPO proprietary iControl illumination on the G4 reticle. The G4i fiber-optic illumination technology system automatically powers down the illumination when the electronic module has been stationary and inactive for more than three hours and alerts the user when

only 15 percent battery life remains. The Passion line of riflescopes optimizes light transmission though the use of double HD glass and the proprietary GPOBright lens-coating technology. Because these scopes are second-focal-plane designs, the reticles will remain the same size throughout all magnification settings. They are waterproof, dust-proof and nitrogen-filled. MSPRs: $685 to $1,140. *http://gp-optics.com*

Hawke

Over the last few decades, Hawke Optics has become a large player within the optics-producing community. The company's growing line of riflescopes, binoculars, spotting scopes and other optical products frequently are priced lower than much of the competition. Hawke's new Endurance ED Compact Spotting Scope is a perfect example of one of those products that encompasses many of the characteristics and traits that other spotting scopes do, but is often more moderately priced. The reduced size of this spotting scope makes it easier to pack while hunting or exploring the backcountry. It features twist-up eyepieces and is available in either an angled or straight design. Each Endurance Spotting Scope is nitrogen purged and is waterproof and fogproof. The compact 12-36x ED scopes have BAK-4 porro prisms for good color transfer and a high degree of contrast. Dielectric coating in the prism and lenses increase light reflectivity and helps increase the sharpness of the images. They come with a close-focusing potential of only 8.2 feet and a 90 to 174 feet

Hawke's new Endurance ED Compact Spotting Scope is available in an angled eyepiece design.

Hawke's Endurance ED Compact Spotting Scope also is available with a straight eyepiece.

Hawke's new first-focal-plane (FFP) scopes are available in several different magnifications including this Frontier FFP 3-15x50.

field of view at 1,000 yards. In order to combat eye strain, extra-low dispersion (ED) glass is used throughout. Each scope comes with a stay-on soft scope cover and flip-up lens covers. They are dig-scope compatible allowing them to be used in conjunction with your camera equipment. MSRP: straight or angled, $329.99.

Hawke's new first-focal-plane (FFP) scopes are dedicated to long-range accuracy and are available in several different models. The FFP design provides constant Mil/MOA values throughout the entire power range of the scope, providing a higher degree of shooter flexibility for different shooting scenarios. Two new models have been added to the company's flagship Frontier line: the Frontier FFP 5-25x56 MIL EXT and the Frontier FFP 3-15x50 MIL EXT. Both models have 21-layer fully multi-coated 5x ratio optics for enhanced clarity with a side-focus, infinite-range parallax adjustment. Both scopes are built on a 30mm mono main tubes, have glass-etched reticles and red illumination with six levels of brightness. Also

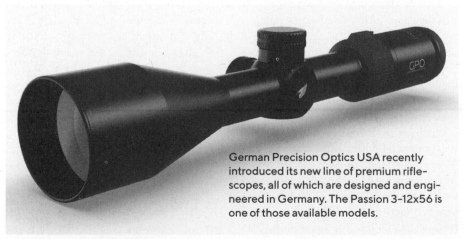

German Precision Optics USA recently introduced its new line of premium riflescopes, all of which are designed and engineered in Germany. The Passion 3-12x56 is one of those available models.

Hawke's new Sidewinder FFP 4-16x50 MIL is equipped with the new FFP MIL glass-etched reticle and has red and green illumination.

For the shooter looking for a bit more magnification, Hawke's new Sidewinder FFP 6-24x56 MIL might be the answer.

new are the Sidewinder FFP 6-24x56 MIL and the Sidewinder FFP 4-16x50 MIL, which are equipped with the new FFP MIL glass-etched reticle with red/green illumination and come with a side parallax adjustment. The glass is 18-layer, fully multi-coated.

Hawke also added a couple new Frontier ED X Binoculars which are available in 8x42 or 10x42 configurations. These come equipped with Hawk's 1.5-turn focus knob with a 6.6 foot close-focus potential. The 8x42 model provides a 426-foot field of view at 1,000 yards and the 10x42s has a field of view of 336 feet at that same distance. For premium optical clarity, these binos are equipped with ED glass and dielectric coatings to provide increased reflectivity of the light, and are covered by lifetime warrantees. MSRPs: 8x42, $389; 10x42, and $399.00. *www.hawkeoptics.com*

Hi-Lux

As part of Hi-Lux's 50th anniversary celebration, the company is offering a new edition Automatic Ranging Trajectory (ART) riflescope, the Hi-Lux ART M1000-PRO. The ART technology is unique in its design. Raising and lowering the rear of the scope, much as you would adjust open or iron sights, allows the shooter to get the first rounds on target up to 1,000 yards without complex distance estimations. The Hi-Lux ART is a 2-10x scope, featuring the HR1 illuminated MOA reticle, available with either red or green illumination. The lower three brightness settings are compatible for use with night vision

optics. Each hash mark on the vertical and horizontal scale represents a 1 MOA sub tension and the longer 2 MOA tick is marked in multiples of 5 MOA. The ART M1000-PRO is built on a 30mm main tube and possesses a total adjustment range of 90 MOA for both windage and elevation in 1/4 MOA increments.

Hi-Lux's MTD30 Red Dot Scope was designed for the turkey hunter and comes in a parallax-free, electronic-reflex design with zero magnification (1x). The built-in sensor automatically adjusts the brightness to ensure the 4 MOA red-dot remains clear and visible in your sight picture without any starbursts. In addition, it comes with an anti-reflective flash-kill device that shields the objective lens from the direct sunlight. This also helps eliminate the possibility of the turkey being tipped off and alarmed by seeing a lens flare. The MTD30 comes with its own solid Picatinny mount, machined right into its housing for quick and easy mounting to any Weaver-style one-piece base or Picatinny rail. *www.hi-luxoptics.com*

Konus

Konus is offering three new riflescopes: the BX, BXE and the BXE-30. The BX model is a 3-9x40mm model with a 1-inch main tube. This scope is available as a stand-alone product or as part of Ruger's gun/scope packages. The BXE also features a 3-9x40mm design with a 1-inch main tube, but it comes equipped with an unbreakable laser engraved reticle. At the top of the line, the BXE-30 boasts a strong, beefy 30mm main tube in a 3-9x42 configuration. This model has an increased MOA adjustment range, a larger 42mm lens and like the BXE it has an unbreakable laser engraved reticle. All three of these scopes have fully multi-coated lenses, fast-focus eye knobs, solid, one-piece tubes, zero-stop adjustments and wide field of view. As with all Konus riflescopes, these scopes are waterproof, fog-proof and shock-proof and are accompanied by the company's very popular lifetime-replacement warranty. *www.konuspro.com*

Leica

Leica's new Noctivid Green Edition

binoculars were designed to set a new standard in wildlife observation and to celebrate that, their armor casings have been colored olive green to blend in with nature. The Noctivid Green binos are compact in design and available in either 8x42 or 10x42. The use of Schott HTTM (high transmission) glass allows better transmission of natural colors. Leica now applies premium lens coatings by way of new high-temperature plasma processes, which help guarantee a balanced light transmission across the entire wave-length. The Noctivid Green's compact dimensions coupled with their balanced weight make one-handed use easier, and the non-slip rubber armoring gives them a comfortable, safe and secure grip. MSRPs: 8x42, $2,749; 10x42, $2,849.

Leica's RangeMaster CRF 2400-R is the company's newest and most advanced handheld rangefinder, with capability of ranging targets up to an astonishing 2,400 yards. This adds an additional 800 yards over the capability of Leica's previous models. The ability of ranging at greater distances is partially made possible by the RangeMaster CRF 2400-R's 7x magnification and its wide field of view. Another remarkable feature is its extremely fast scan mode, which takes measurements every half-second to provide results in decimals of 0.1 yards at distances up to 200 yards. The RangeMaster CRF 2400-R is also capable of providing equivalent horizontal range for distances up to 1,200 yards. A weight only 6.5 ounces and its compact size make carrying this rangefinder in your pocket easy. MSRP: $499.00. *www.us.leica-camera.com/Sport-Optics/Leica-Hunting*

Leupold & Stevens

Leupold has upgraded its award-winning line of thermal imagers with the introduction of the new LTO-Tracker HD and LTO-Quest HD. These units have been designed to be compact and light enough to take on even the most remote backcountry hunting trips. These imagers can be used to show hunters the heat signature of game, and to locate and track blood trails, day or night. The second generation LTO-Tracker HD has

the capability of detecting heat out to 750 yards and temperatures from -40 degrees to 572 degrees F. Its new 390x390 pixel, full-circle display offers improved resolution over the previous model.

The LTO-Quest HD is an all inclusive piece of gear, not only being able to detect heat signatures, but also comes with a built-in camera and a dual-mode 300 lumen flashlight. The LTO-Quest HD uses an advanced thermal sensor to extend its detection range out to 750 yards, provides storage space for up to 3,000 images and is capable of four hours of continuous use. Its 320x240 pixel display is made of durable Gorilla Glass.

Leupold's new SX-5 Santiam HD 55x80mm spotting scope promises premium edge-to-edge clarity and unmatched sharpness and definition. It comes with fully multicoated lenses to eliminate color aberration and distortion throughout the entirety of the magnification range and its rugged, lightweight armor helps protect it against damage in the field. The DiamondCoat 2 and Guard-Ion lens coatings assist in shedding water from the lens surfaces and make them more scratch-resistant. Its porro-prism construction, ultra-fine center focus wheel, adjustable eyecup and indexed rotational tripod ring are just some of the features hunters, shooters and others frequently prefer in their spotting scopes. For versatility and personal preference, the SX-5

Santiam HD 55x80mm is available with either a straight or angled eyepiece and incorporates Leupold's Twilight Max HD light management system. This is the same award-winning system found on the VX-5HD and VX-6HD riflescopes, permitting users to stretch out their viewing time during the dawn and dusk hours. *www.leupold.com*

Meopta

Meopta's new TGA 75 Collapsible Spotting Scope was specifically engineered with the needs of hunters in mind. Its classic draw-tube design allows the length to be shorted from 14.8 inches (when fully extended) to 9.8 inches for ease of packing and carrying. It features a 75mm objective lens and fully multi-coated, premium-grade optics. The TGA 75 is fully rubber-armored and comes in a light-weight aluminum body. There are three interchangeable eyepieces available, which are sold separately: 30x WA-R (wide angle ranging), 30x WA (wide angle) and 20-60x zoom. MSRP: TGA 75 body, $899.95; eyepieces, $399.95 each.

Meopta's newest high-performance 30mm MeoStar R2 riflescope, the 2.5-15x56 RD, features a 6x variable magnification range, a wide field of view and combines the company's most advanced lens coatings with Schott glass. It is available in four illuminated reticle choices: 4C-RD, 4K-RD, BDC 2 and BDC

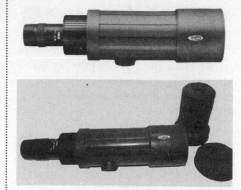

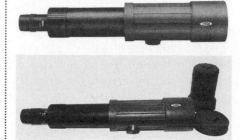

When Meopta's new TGA 75 Collapsible Spotting Scope is collapsed it measures a mere 9.8 inches, making it convenient for packing and carrying in the field.

When the Meopta TGA 75 Collapsible Spotting Scope is fully extended, its length is expanded from 9.8 inches to 14.8 inches.

Meopta's new 30mm MeoStar R2 2.5-15x56 RD riflescope is available in four illuminated reticle choices.

3. Like the other MeoStar R2 scopes, the 2.5-15x56 RD is set to be parallax free at 100-yards and features Meopta's Meo-Drop hydrophobic lens coating which repels rain, snow, skin oils and dirt. MSRP: $1,599.95. *www.meoptausa.com*

Nightforce

Nightforce takes pride in the fact that it is dedicated to listening to shooters and customers and takes action to address their needs. An example of that dedication can be seen in the SHV 3-10x42 riflescope with an illuminated MOAR or Forceplex reticle. Hunters spoke out and now user-adjustable illumination control replaces the paral-

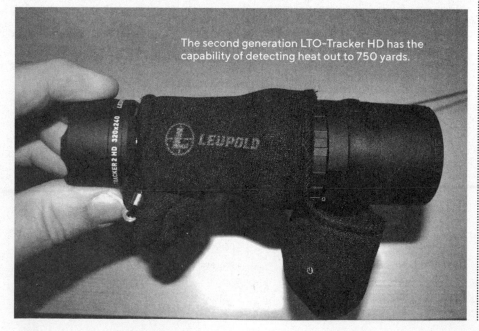

The second generation LTO-Tracker HD has the capability of detecting heat out to 750 yards.

lax adjustment on the 3-10, allowing the reticle brightness to be adjusted manually to fit the needs of the shooter.

Nightforce Optics also recently introduced a new mid-powered riflescope, the ATACR 4-16x50 F1. The 50mm objective lens of this scope, coupled with the company's patented ZeroStop design, is intended to provide better operation under low-light conditions and enhanced viewing for long-range shooting. Other features include: Extra-low Dispersion (ED) glass, optimized intelligent reticles, such as the MOAR and Mil-C, and an integrated Power Throw Lever to make magnification changes quick and easy. It also includes a full 100 minutes, or 30 mils, of elevation adjustment. The built-in digital illumination provides both red and green color options and each scope comes with a set of custom Tenebraex flip-up lens covers. MSRPs: SHV 3-10x42, $985.00; ATACR 4-16x50 F1, $2,500. *www.nightforceoptics.com*

Nikon

Nikon's new Monarch HG 30mm series binoculars follow in the footsteps of Nikon's award-winning 42mm siblings to provide nearly identical performance, but in a smaller size and nearly 8-ounces reduction in weight. The optical system of these Monarch HG 30mm binos has been engineered around its ED (Extra-low Dispersion) glass and its high-quality multilayer coatings, which are applied to all of its lenses and prisms. Nikon's Field Flattener Lens System works in conjunction with the Monarch HG 30mm's wide field of view to provide sharp and clear views.

Nikon also announced a new red-dot sight, the P-Tactical SuperDot Red Dot Sight. This sight includes fully multicoated lenses and Nikon's proprietary Trucolor coating, which was designed to eliminate the bluish tint commonly associated with red-dot sights. The P-Tactical SuperDot comes with a 2 MOA dot that is adjustable to 10 brightness settings, the first two of which are compatible for night-vision viewing. Windage and elevation adjustments are in 1 MOA increments and are adjustable using the integral tool on the top of each cap. The internal adjustment range for both elevation and windage is 100 MOA. This is a compact and light-weight sight measuring only 2.8 x 1.7 x 1.7 inches and weighing a

mere 4.2 ounces. MSRP: $199.95.

Nikon also announced the launch of its black.nikonsportoptics.com website, an all new interactive micro-site developed for its flagship Black precision long-range optics line. *www.NikonSportOptics.com*

Primary Arms

Primary Arms is based in Houston, Texas, but all of the company's riflescopes are fully designed and manufactured in Japan. The Platinum Series scopes are constructed with high-strength aluminum alloy and engineered to be capable of contending with heavy recoil and standing up to abusive handling. Recently the company announced its Platinum 1-8x24mm First Focal Plane (FFP) Scope is now available with three new reticle choices: the ACSS Raptor M2 reticle, which updates and replaces the original ACSS reticle for 5.56 NATO; .308 Winchester, 5.45x39; and 6.5 Grendel chambered rifles. And ACSS Griffin MIL and ACSS Griffin MOA are able to maximize precision and speed with any caliber.

Due to the FFP design of the Platinum series scopes, when set on 1x magnification the appearance through the lens is like a red dot or small ring. This feature encourages a high degree of target acquisition speed and a clear field of view. When turned up to 8x, the reticle grows to display a chevron aiming point, automatic ranging out to 600 yards and includes moving target leads. The ACSS Raptor M2 features bullet-drop compensation and windage hold points at 5 and 10 mph out to 800 yards. ACSS Griffin MIL features a dot grid with 15 MIL vertical and 6 MIL horizontal holdover points, while the ACSS Griffin MOA features a dot

grid with 50 MOA vertical and 20 MOA horizontal holdovers. The Primary Arms Platinum 1-8x24 FFP currently comes with an anodized matte black finish and a lifetime warranty. MSRP: $1,299.99.

Primary Arms' new 3-18x50 FFP scope comes with locking, resettable turrets, a replaceable power ring fin and a choice of the patented ACSS HUD DMR .308 or HUD DMR 5.56 reticles. The unique turret locking system allows the shooter to push the windage and elevation knobs toward the scope tube to lock them. To release the lock, the shooter pulls the knobs away from the scope tube to make crisp, repeatable 0.1 MIL adjustments. The parallax adjustment and the red-reticle illumination can be controlled from the same knob location on the left side. The 3-18x50 FFP comes in a matte black anodized finish, a 30mm main-tube and has a lifetime warranty. MSRP of $499. *www.primaryarms.com*

Pulsar

Four models of the Accolade Thermal Binocular series are now available

Pulsar has four new Trail LRF thermal scope models to select from that are compatible with WiFi remote view via the Stream Vision app. Target distance on the unit's screen is visible up to 1,100 yards. They also feature built-in video recording with sound, eight-hour rechargeable battery and picture-in-picture digital zoom.

Sightmark's new Citadel line of riflescopes currently consists of three variable magnification models: 1-6x24 CR1, 3-18x50 LR2 and 5-30x56 LR2.

Steiner's new M7Xi 4-28x56 riflescope was designed to be capable of handling abusive and unpredictable combat and competition scenarios, yet is reduced in size.

The Steiner P4Xi riflescope was designed as a compact, tactical optic well-suited for patrol rifles and AR platforms.

The Steiner BluHorizons 8x22 binoculars with Autobright weigh only 8.8 ounces and fold up small enough to fit inside the pocket of your shirt.

The slightly larger Steiner BluHorizons 10x26 binoculars also have the Autobright feature and are only slightly larger with a weight of 10.6 ounces.

from Pulsar. Those include models specifically designed and dedicated to hunting, law enforcement and personal use. These feature a dual-eyepiece configuration, which provides comfort and reduced eye fatigue, particularly during long observation sessions. Each unit comes with its own battery pack, charging kit, USB cable, hand-strap, lens cleaning cloth and carrying case.

Pulsar is also offering four new Trail LRF thermal models: XQ38 LRF (PL76516), XQ50 LRF (PL76517), XP38 LRF (PL76518) and XP50 LRF (PL76519). These models offer a high degree of accuracy and include the same useful features the Trail family does. These units are compatible with WiFi, remote view via the Stream Vision app, and target-distance on the unit's screen is visible up to 1,100 yards. They also feature built-in video recording with sound, eight-hour rechargeable battery and picture-in-picture digital zoom. MSRPs: $4,729.99 to $6.599.99. *www.pulsarnv.com*

Sightmark

Sightmark's new Citadel line of riflescopes is an affordable option for the cost-conscious shooter. This line of scopes is comprised of three variable magnification models: 1-6x24 CR1, 3-18x50 LR2 and 5-30x56 LR2. These

Meopta's new 30mm MeoStar R2 2.5-15x56 RD riflescope is available in four illuminated reticle choices.

latter two models are first-focal-plane systems, which come with illuminated LR2 mil-dash reticles to provide precise holdovers at any magnification setting. MSRPs: $359.99 to $515.99.

For crossbow hunters, Sightmark's updated Core SX 1.5-5x32 scope is a rugged, yet lightweight choice, housed in an aluminum body. This scope was designed and tuned for crossbow speeds of 260 to 450 fps and comes with accurate arrow (bolt) drop compensation built-in. Its construction is waterproof, dust-proof, shock-proof and fog-proof. The etched glass reticle is red and green illuminated with variable brightness settings. MSRP: $149.97.

Sightmark's new Core Shot A-Spec Reflex sight is intended to bridge the gap between the more common full-sized and mini red-dot sights used for AR pistols and SBRs. Two models are available: FMS and LQD. FMS features two separate mounts, AR riser mount and a low-profile mount, while the LQD features a quick-detach mounting system. These sights are crafted from dependable and lightweight aircraft-grade aluminum and are shock-proof and water-resistant. Other features include lens coating to discourage and prevent scratches, a wide view lens for quick target acquisition, slotted windage and elevation adjustments, digital switch controls, and eight reticle brightness settings with night vision compatibility. MSRPs: FMS, $155.99; LQD, $179.99. *www.sightmark.com.*

Steiner

Military operations demand the most durable and reliable gear possible. Based on the success of the Steiner M5Xi line of optics used by the elite task forces around the globe, Steiner has added the new M7Xi 4-28x56 riflescope to its M-Series, which

Steiner's Predator AF 8x30 binoculars are compact in their design and come with the unique CAT (Color Adjusted Transmission) lens-coating technology.

The author tested a Steiner Predator AF 8x30 binocular and found the CAT lens coating technology to be quite beneficial, particularly when color contrast is minimal.

The compact size of both the Steiner Predator AF 8x30 and the BluHorizons 10x26 binoculars make them well-suited for field use.

offers enhanced zoom and field-of-view capabilities at mid to long range. This scope is designed to handle abusive and unpredictable combat and competition scenarios, yet is reduced in size. The M7xi coyote brown version is available with the TReMor3 and the new MSR2 reticles, while the black version offers an additional G2B Mil Dot reticle. MSRPs: $3,559.99 to $4,399.99.

Steiner's new P4Xi riflescope was designed to be a compact tactical optic that would be well-suited for rifles used on patrol and AR platforms. It features a proven and versatile 4x zoom with a true 1x viewing potential. The Steiner P3TR illuminated reticle is quick pointing and its high-contrast optic design delivers good results under poor light conditions. The illumination intensity is adjustable in 11 settings. MSRP: $699.99.

Light conditions can vary dramatically from early dawn to high noon to dusk, which poses viewing challenges for all optic products. Steiner has addressed those issues with a newly designed binocular called the BluHorizons with Autobright. This is the very first sunlight-adaptive binocular for all light conditions. The sunlight-adaptable lens technology of these binoculars automatically adjusts the brightness through the lenses to permit the best viewing potential. Whether the sun is shining brightly and located directly overhead, or bouncing off the surface of a body of water or snow covered ground, the BluHorizons lens are engineered to gather just the right amount of light and reduce the glare to produce the optimum viewing possibility. Two models are currently available - the 8.8-ounce 8x22 and the slightly larger 10.6-ounce 10x26. MSRPs: 8x22, $219.99; 10x26.

Also new are the Steiner Predator AF binoculars, which come in either a 19-ounce 8x30 or a 30.3-ounce 10x42. Each unit includes a comfortable neck strap, neoprene outdoor carrying case and the Steiner Heritage Warranty, which is good for the life of the binoculars. These binos feature the unique CAT (Color Adjusted Transmission) lens coating technology, which provides a higher degree of contrast when viewing game. When peering through the lens, the images take on a slight pink or red tinge, but

that affect allows game animals to stand-out better. Unlike many other binoculars, the Predator AF have dual-diopter adjustment rings, allowing precise focus for each eye, and advanced porro prims provide clear in-focus viewing. The AF in the name stands for automatic focus, which allows clear images from about 30 yards out to infinity without any adjustment. MSRPs: 8x30, $344.99; 10x42, $459.99. *www.steiner-optics.com*

Swarovski

Swarovski Optik North America has announced the dS which represents a completely new generation of riflescope. This product is intended to highlight the optical features of a conventional riflescope and combine the technology of digital targeting. The new dS shows not only the correct aiming point, but also the key ballistic data without any distraction and in real time. With a simple press of a button, the dS measures the exact distance to the target, having factored in the magnification setting, air pressure, temperature and angle and takes in the personal ballistic data for the firearm/ammunition being shot. The scope does require networking with a smart phone. *www.swarovskioptik.com*

Zeiss

Zeiss' new Conquest V4 riflescopes are based on a 4x zoom ratio and are built on 30mm main tubes. The second focal-plane scopes are available in four magnification models: 1-4x24, 3-12x56, 4-16x44 and 6-24x50. Each scope delivers 90 percent light transmission and offers .25 MOA click values. The 1-4x24 model is available with either capped or external elevation turrets, while the 3-12x56 comes standard with only capped turrets. The remaining models (4-16x44 & 6-24x50) have external elevation turrets. All of the external elevation turrets include the Zeiss' Ballistic Stop feature to ensure an absolute and positive return to zero under all conditions. Illuminated reticles are standard for the 1-4x24 and optional on the other models. MSRPs: Starting at $799. *www.zeiss.com/us/sports-optics*

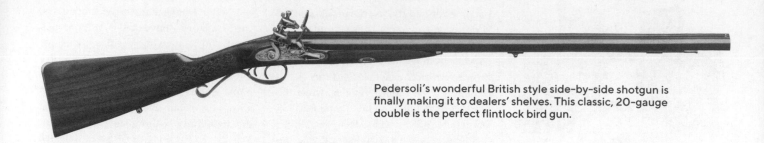

Pedersoli's wonderful British style side-by-side shotgun is finally making it to dealers' shelves. This classic, 20-gauge double is the perfect flintlock bird gun.

NEW MUZZLELOADERS

BY **MIKE BELIVEAU**

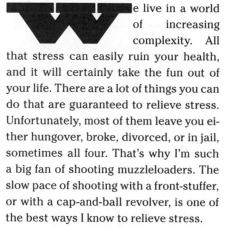

We live in a world of increasing complexity. All that stress can easily ruin your health, and it will certainly take the fun out of your life. There are a lot of things you can do that are guaranteed to relieve stress. Unfortunately, most of them leave you either hungover, broke, divorced, or in jail, sometimes all four. That's why I'm such a big fan of shooting muzzleloaders. The slow pace of shooting with a front-stuffer, or with a cap-and-ball revolver, is one of the best ways I know to relieve stress.

I got my first muzzleloader as a Christmas gift in 1972. It was a brass-framed replica of a Colt model 1851 Navy revolver. Like most rural boys of my generation, I had already been hunting with modern rifles and shotguns for five or six years, but that Navy revolver was my first handgun. Shooting black powder is slow, smoky, smelly and dirty, and it is thoroughly addictive. From the first shot, I was hooked.

It has been nearly 50 years since I took my first shot with black powder. Back in 1972, in-line rifles were barely even a concept, and now they dominate the muzzleloading hunting scene. To the uninitiated, in-line rifles, with their polymer stocks and scoped sights, seem like the antithesis of traditional muzzleloaders. Some people think of them as being no different than modern single-shot rifles. But nothing could be further from the truth.

At their core, in-line rifles, like Thompson Center's popular Omega line, are 100-percent muzzleloaders. Hunters still have to load them from the muzzle, using a ramrod to seat a bullet on a measured powder charge. Even if I was armed with a Trapdoor Springfield, one of the slowest-loading single-shot rifles ever made, I could still easily get off 25 shots while a hunter is reloading an in-line muzzleloader. When you hunt with an in-line, just as when you hunt with a traditional Hawken rifle, you typically get only one bite at the apple. Either that first shot takes down your game, or you might go home empty handed.

The real impact of in-lines has been to make muzzleloading more accessible to modern hunters, and that has led to an explosion of specialty muzzleloader hunting seasons. In 1972, only a handful of states even had hunting seasons specifically dedicated to muzzleloaders. Today, every state has at least one deer season reserved for muzzleloaders, and many states have several seasons dedicated to front-stuffing firearms. In any number of states, dedicated hunters can load up their freezers with venison from three or four deer by hunting throughout archery, muzzleloader and firearms seasons. And a lot of those deer are collected with in-line muzzleloaders.

I think of in-lines as the gateway drug of muzzleloading. While there are some shooters who will harvest a deer with an in-line each year, and never give it a second thought, there are others who will picture themselves standing in the footsteps of Daniel Boone and Kit Carson. Those people will soon be looking for a traditional muzzleloader to add to the gun cabinet.

In-line muzzleloaders using 209 shotgun primers like this Thompson Center Omega, have greatly expanded the popularity of muzzleloader hunting. Every state in the country now offers at least one special hunting season for muzzleloaders.

Despite the tremendous popularity of in-lines, the market for traditional, sidelock muzzleloaders is booming. Pedersoli, the Italian firm that is the largest manufacturer of traditional muzzleloaders, reports strong sales, as does Traditions Firearms, which imports traditional muzzleloaders from Spanish manufacturers.

At the 2018 SHOT Show, Pedersoli unveiled its new side-by-side flintlock shotgun, but, as so often happens, actual models weren't expected until 2019. This is a beautiful shotgun that harkens back to the work of London gunsmith Joseph Manton, who developed the quintessential British sporting gun at the close of the 18th century.

The new Pedersoli flintlock features side-by-side, 27.5-inch, chrome-lined, 20-gauge barrels that are choked improved cylinder on the right-hand barrel and modified on the left tube. The stocks are straight-grained, European walnut. The fore stock is the typical British, splinter style, so if the birds are rising thickly, and your shooting is hot and heavy, you'll feel the heat of the barrels, which can build up quickly with black-powder shooting. The straight-gripped butt stock has a classic English profile that is enhanced by a steel, scroll-shaped trigger guard and basket-weave checkering on the wrist of the stock.

For bird hunters who appreciate flintlocks, this classically British-styled, 20-gauge double will be irresistible. In fact, I fully expect to be carrying one next fall when Mary Pat and I hit the fields with our bird dogs Axel and Cody.

For hunters who are looking for a more basic field shotgun, Pedersoli's Scout 12-gauge might be just what the doctor ordered. This is a single-barrel, cylinder-bore gun and is available in either flintlock or percussion-lock ignition. The walnut half-stock is equipped with a flat rubber recoil pad. The 30-inch, octagon to round 12-gauge barrel,

gives you a handy, hard-hitting shotgun that will serve for both upland game and waterfowl.

The guns you'll see carried at rendezvous and muzzleloading target matches have changed quite a bit since 1972. When I started competing in muzzleloader matches, it seemed like almost every other rifle on the firing line was either a

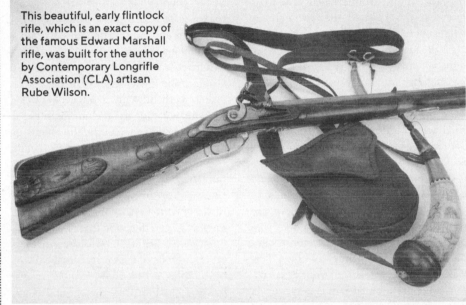

This beautiful, early flintlock rifle, which is an exact copy of the famous Edward Marshall rifle, was built for the author by Contemporary Longrifle Association (CLA) artisan Rube Wilson.

Thompson Center Hawken, or one of the Spanish- or Italian-produced replicas. In those days, everyone imagined themselves as Robert Redford, playing Jeremiah Johnson.

The emphasis today is on more historically accurate reproductions. These days you will still find a healthy interest in the Rocky Mountain fur-trapper era, especially in the western half of the country. Hawken rifle replicas remain popular there. Lyman's Great Plains rifle, a half-stock Hawken copy, has been popular for decades. The Great Plains Rifle is arguably the best value in traditional, sidelock muzzleloaders. Without a doubt, the finest factory built plains

Lyman's Great Plains Rifle is an affordable, historically correct replica of a Hawken Rifle. It is arguably the best value in traditional muzzleloaders.

Pedersoli's Missouri River Hawken Rifle is a traditionally styled plains rifle with fastpitch rifling to stabilize modern conical bullets or sabots.

rifle is Pedersoli's Missouri River Hawken Rifle and Rocky Mountain Hawken Rifle. These rifles are available stocked in either walnut or maple, and are chambered in .45, .50 and .54 calibers. Both models look exactly the same, but the Missouri River model is rifled with a fast pitch to stabilize modern conical bullets and sabots, while the Rocky Mountain model features slow pitched rifling for patched round-ball shooting.

East of the Mississippi, you'll see more interest in the frontiersmen and long-hunters who roamed the 18th-century wilderness. Custom-built, historically correct longrifles are incredibly common at eastern rendezvous and shooting matches. At the events I attend each year, I see very few factory-built rifles being shot. Eighteenth century military re-enactors are most often armed from Pedersoli's extensive catalog of military flintlock muskets, but civilian living historians and target shooters are mostly equipped with custom-built longrifles.

As a consequence of this, there are probably more top-end flintlock rifle builders operating today than there were during the entire century of the 1700s. If you're in the market for your first custom-built flintlock rifle, the first step is to find a builder who can take raw wood and steel, and turn it into the rifle of your dreams. As I mentioned, there are a lot of professional longrifle builders out there, but they don't take out billboards, so finding them can be a challenge.

The best place to start is with the Contemporary Longrifle Association, or CLA. The CLA is an association of contemporary muzzleloading artisans, and enthusiasts. Members include most of the best custom muzzleloading gun builders in the country, as well as artisans who make custom accouterments, like powder horns and hunting pouches. Its ranks also include famous artists of the American frontier like David Wright and Robert Griffing, and lowly writers like me.

Joining the CLA gives you access to its website, www.longrifle.com, which has a searchable database of the thousands of artisans who are CLA members. That's the place to look for your custom-rifle builder. Your CLA membership also entitles you to free access to the annual CLA show in Lexington, Kentucky. The only way I can describe that show is that it is like the SHOT Show for muzzleloaders. Hundreds of custom gun makers will have tables at that show. You can examine and compare their work, and place the order for your dream gun.

Admittedly, a custom-built rifle, made by a top builder is a pricy proposition. That's why so many muzzleloader shooters turn to do-it-yourself kits, which give builders a leg up because the most labor-intensive work is already done. On a typical kit the stock will be shaped close to its final dimensions. The distinctive profile of the school of rifle builders you selected will be clear to see. The barrel channel will be inletted into the stock, and the ramrod channel will be drilled. In many cases, the lock will be at least partially inletted into the stock. All that will save you up to 100 hours of difficult work on the kit.

There are quite a few kit manufacturers. The best selection is available online from Track of The Wolf, which is generally just known as "Track," for short. Track is sort of the Midway USA of muzzleloading. They sell a wide selection of everything you need to shoot black-powder arms. Track offers more than 30 period-correct flintlock and percussion lock-gun kits. A few years ago, I built a Bucks County style flintlock rifle using one of their kits, and I was very happy with the quality. For those who worry that they aren't handy enough with tools to tackle a kit, Track also stocks a good selection of completed rifles, built by professionals.

The best value in kits comes from a relative new comer to the game. Jim Kibler is a custom-longrifle builder, and he is one of the best in the country. But he recognized the cost of a custom longrifle was out of reach for a lot of shooters, and that the high-quality kits on the market took a lot of skill to complete, enough to scare away many shooters. So, Jim developed a different kind of kit. Like most kit makers, he uses top-quality components, such as Rice barrels and Jim Chambers flintlocks. But, instead of roughing out his stocks on a pantograph-duplicating machine, he uses CNC technology which is unmatched for precision. As a result, Jim's kits go together with almost no hand-fitting. Metal parts fit exactly into their mortices in the stock. The really hard work is done, allowing the builder to concentrate on the more enjoyable tasks of embellishing and finishing the wood and metal.

At most muzzleloader shooting matches today, custom longrifles are the most common weapons on the firing line.

The author is on the firing line at the Fort Roberdeau Rifle Frolic, shooting his custom Lancaster County rifle built by CLA artisan Shawn Webster.

Kibler's first kit was a slender, graceful, iron-mounted Southern Mountain Rifle, which was modeled after the work of Joseph Whitson, a rifle maker from western North Carolina. The kit features a 46-inch-long Rice A-weight swamped barrel available in .32, .36, .40 and .45 caliber. This kit makes a beautiful squirrel rifle, or a light deer rifle.

Jim Kibler's newest kit is called the Colonial Rifle Kit. This kit is made with the same CNC technology as the Southern Mountain Rifle kit, but it is modeled on the earlier guns, made from the 1760s to 1770s. The brass-mounted rifle features a 2-inch wide buttplate and a sliding wood patchbox. It is available in .50 and .54 caliber, with a Rice 43.25-inch, custom-profiled swamped barrel. You can order a kit with either square-bottomed or round-bottomed rifling, and there is also a smooth bore, .54-caliber option.

Tennessee Valley Muzzleloading occupies a unique niche between the high-end custom builders and the mass-produced, factory-built rifles. Matt Avance and his crew in Natchez, Mississippi, turn out what I call semi-custom rifles. TVM offers eight styles of rifles and 'fowlers that cover the time frame from the early 18th century through the Rocky Mountain fur-trade era. TVM's rifles are custom-built to your order, for your length of pull, and with any extras you order, but, through the judicious use of power equipment, TVM is able to produce a basic, histori-

The annual Contemporary Longrifle Association Show each August in Lexington, Kentucky, is the place to find a custom gun maker to build your dream rifle.

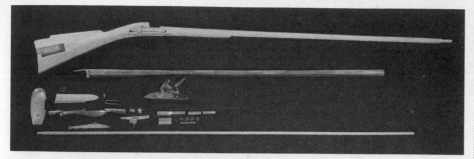

Jim Kibler is using CNC technology to make period-correct longrifle kits that virtually anyone can assemble, regardless of their skill level with tools.

Tennessee Valley Muzzleloading's in-the-white kits make rifle building easy. All the work is done for you except finishing the wood and metal.

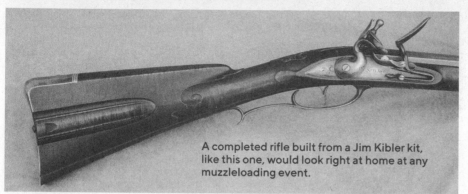

A completed rifle built from a Jim Kibler kit, like this one, would look right at home at any muzzleloading event.

cally correct rifle to your specifications for just a little more than the cost of an Italian mass-produced rifle. Or, you can save even more money if you order your rifle "in the white." Those rifles are fully assembled and functional, but the final wood and metal finishing is left for you to do. Even someone with 10 thumbs can finish an in-the-white kit. It is a great option if you want a great rifle at an affordable price.

Military re-enactors demand complete authenticity in their kit, and that includes their firearms. This is an area where factory-produced weapons prevail, and the top source is the Italian firm of Davide Pedersoli, which makes muskets that cover the entire time frame from the beginning of the 18th century through the Civil War.

A couple years ago, Pedersoli announced it would be producing a replica of the 1854 Lorenz Rifle, and they are starting to appear on the scene. The original Lorenz rifles were developed by Austrian lieutenant Joseph Lorenz. This was the third most-used rifle during the American Civil War. The Union purchased 226,924 Lorenz rifles, and the Confederacy bought as many as 100,000. Most muskets used during the Civil War were .58 caliber, but the Lorenz was .54 caliber, and the Pedersoli reproduction is chambered in the original caliber. With its slow 1:78-inch rifling pitch, the Lorenz should be very accurate shooting patched round balls. The Lorenz is approved by the North/South Skirmish Association, and it has been eagerly awaited by Civil War target-shooting re-enactors.

Pedersoli's Whitworth rifle is another rifle of great interest to Civil War re-enactors. It was developed in 1854 by Sir Joseph Whitworth, a prominent British engineer. Whitworth's great innovation was polygonal rifling in the bore. This proved to be exceptionally accurate. The Whitworth was the rifle of choice for Confederate snipers. The Pedersoli Whitworth has a .451-inch polygonal bore, and it matches the accuracy of the originals.

Blackpowder Revolvers

The cap-and-ball revolver scene has changed quite a bit since 1972, when I shot my first brass-framed, Colt Navy replica. First of all, Armi San Paolo, that gun's manufacturer, has long been out of business. In fact, most of the manufac-

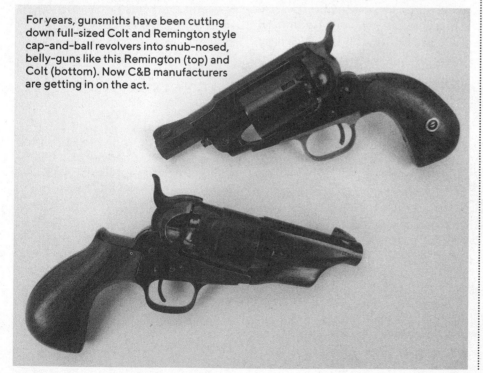

For years, gunsmiths have been cutting down full-sized Colt and Remington style cap-and-ball revolvers into snub-nosed, belly-guns like this Remington (top) and Colt (bottom). Now C&B manufacturers are getting in on the act.

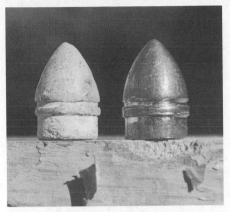

Eras Gone Bullet Molds base their designs for period-correct conical bullets on actual bullets recovered from Civil War battlefields, like this Johnson & Dow .44-caliber conical for Colt and Remington revolvers.

Eras Gone molds are custom made by Lee Precision to Eras Gone's exacting standards.

Pedersoli's 1854 Lorenz Rifle re-creates the third most-used weapon during the American Civil War.

Pedersoli's re-creation of the Whitworth rifle makes the preferred weapon of Confederate snipers available to Civil War re-enactors.

One of the trends in cap-and-ball revolvers has been shrinking barrel lengths. Pietta has taken the standard 7 1/2- and 8-inch barrels on several of its .36- and .44-caliber revolvers and reduced them to 5 1/2 inches, dubbing these more manageable guns, "Sheriff's Models."

turers of the 1970s and 1980s have faded from the scene. Today, two manufacturers of cap-and-ball revolvers remain on the scene, Uberti and Pietta. The good news is that the quality of today's cap-and-ball revolvers is much better than it was in the '70s.

One of the trends in cap-and-ball revolvers is shorter barrel lengths. Back in the 1980s, I started shortening the barrels of cap-and-ball revolvers. At first, I'd shorten the 8-inch-long barrels of Colt 1860 Army revolvers and Remington New Model Army replicas to 5 1/2 inches. When I started cowboy-action shooting in the 1990s, I found these short-barreled guns to be handy for competition shooting. And, since great minds think alike, a lot of other people were doing the same thing. Eventually, cap-and-ball gun manufacturers got on board and Pietta started offering what it calls Sheriff's Models, which are full-sized Army and Navy re-

volvers with 5 1/2-inch barrels.

I also used to radically re-make full-sized, Colt and Remington .44-caliber revolvers into concealable, snubnose revolvers with bird's-head grips. It took a while, but Pietta has begun producing snubnose models of the 1860 Colt Army revolvers. Maybe they'll do the same thing with a Remington someday.

Another change in the cap-and-ball revolver market is the development of better conical bullets. In 1972, round balls were the only game in town, but recently there have been some interesting developments. Eras Gone Bullet Molds designed a line of bullet molds to produce accurate reproductions of the conical bullets used during the Civil War. Mark Hubbs, the owner of Eras Gone, is a professional archeologist. He used bullets recovered from Civil War battlefields to model his Eras Gone mold designs. Currently, Eras Gone offers six authentic molds in calibers ranging from .31 to .50. I use Eras Gone's Johnston & Dow Civil War Era .44 Caliber Bullet to make authentic combustible cartridges that I shoot in my Uberti 1860 Army revolver.

Eras Gone produces a full range of Civil War conical bullets from the tiny .31 caliber, up to the Massive .50 caliber slug for a Smith Carbine.

NEW AMMUNITION, BALLISTICS AND COMPONENTS

BY **PHIL MASSARO**

Winchester 350 Legend is a straight-walled cartridge designed for deer hunting.

The new crop of ammunition-related products gives us all a lot to be happy about. From Winchester's and Hornady's new cartridges to Sierra's loaded ammunition, there are plenty of new products to try at both the reloading bench as well as at the shooting range. Let's take a look at what's new.

Winchester 350 Legend

The 2019 SHOT Show saw the release of the latest cartridge from Winchester, the 350 Legend. The new cartridge uses a .223 case head, and straight walls, making it a perfectly viable choice for those states that require the use of a straight-walled

rifle cartridge for deer hunting. The bullet diameter is listed as .357, and the rimless design will require the cartridge to headspace off the case mouth. Winchester is offering five different loads for the new cartridge: a 150-grain Deer Season XP at 2,350 fps, a 180-grain Power-Point at 2,100 fps, a 160-grain Power Max Bonded at 2,225 fps, a very affordable 145-grain FMJ in the USA ammo line at 2,350 fps and a Super Suppressed 265-grain load at 1,060 fps. At the range, the Deer Season XP load and the USA Full Metal Jacket loads printed such a close point of impact at 100 yards that a shooter could easily use the much more affordable FMJ ammunition for offseason practice as well as

plinking, and switch to the Deer Season XP for hunting. In Winchester's comparison to the veteran .30-30 Winchester, the 350 Legend shows to have an energy advantage of 120 ft.-lbs., yet less recoil than the old deer classic. The new .350 Legend certainly has the potential to catch on in those areas where the shots are close, and a lightweight bolt-action rifle, or AR-platform gun chambered to this cartridge would certainly make sense. I'm sure the 180-grain Power Point would make good hog medicine, and that 265-grain subsonic load would be a ton of fun; couple those with the Deer Season XP load and you have a versatile cartridge that is just plain fun to shoot. *winchester.com*

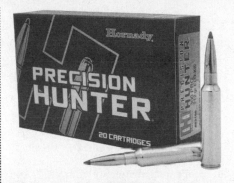

Federal Fusion Component Bullet

More than a decade ago, Federal Premium released what was to become one of the best deer bullets on the market: the Fusion. Accurate, affordable and more than effective, the Fusion employs a rather unique construction method, in which a pressure-formed lead core has a copper jacket molecularly fused to it, and then the overall shape is formed. The ogive is skived, to initiate expansion — which is consistent, and usually at least twice caliber — and the construction method results in high weight retention, even on close shots from fast cartridges. Though the tip is ever so slightly flattened, the boat-tail design will offer attractive trajectories at sane hunting ranges. And, while the Fusion ammunition was, and still is, well-made and accurate stuff, not all rifles like the same powder charge and set of harmonics produced by a single load. Federal has listened to the masses, and has appeased the reloaders by offering the Fusion bullet in component form for 2019; finally we can tailor the load to make the rifle happy, and employ the Fusion projectiles in the less-common cartridges for which Federal didn't provide factory ammunition. The Fusion is available in five very common and highly useable calibers: 6.5mm (140 grains), .277 (130 and 150 grains), 7mm (140, 160 and 175 grains), .308 (150 and 180 grains) and .338 (200 and 225 grains). The 6.5mm, .277 and 7mm bullets are available in 100-count boxes, while the .308 and .388 come in 50-count boxes. *federalpremium.com*

Hornady .300 PRC

The second cartridge to bear the Precision Rifle Competition name, Hornady's .300 PRC gives the long-range shooter plenty to be happy about. Based on the .375 Ruger case — a rimless design with the same case head diameter as the famous .375 H&H Magnum, but without the belt — the .300 PRC was engineered from the start with the idea of handling Hornady's long, high Ballistic Coefficient bullets. The case measures 2.580 inches, and the overall length will range between 3.575 and 3.700 inches, leaving plenty of room outside the case for the longest projectiles. The cartridge features a 30-degree shoulder for headspacing, as well as giving improved chamber alignment, which will result in better concentricity, and will ultimately translate into an improvement in accuracy. Hornady has two loads on the market for the .300 PRC: a 225-grain ELD Match (with a G1 B.C. of .777 and a G7 of .391) load at a muzzle velocity of 2,810 fps and a 212-grain ELD X (with a G1 B.C. of .673 and G7 B.C. of .336) hunting load at a muzzle velocity of 2,860 fps; this pair will handle both long-range target shooting and hunting duties for nearly all game, save the true heavyweights. Both of these bullets are long — too long in fact to be properly seated in the classic .300 Winchester Magnum case — and the .300 PRC will probably be housed in a magnum-length receiver. The case is big enough to have a respectable capacity, yet short enough to allow the long projectiles (which pose an issue in many of the previous .300 Magnum designs) to be properly seated. The Department of Defense has ordered a number of rifles chambered for the new cartridge, which should give an indication of the accuracy and long-range potential of the new .300 PRC cartridge. *hornady.com*

Browning TSS Tungsten Turkey

Tungsten Super Shot (TSS) has proved to be a game-changer in the shotgun world, especially for taking big gobblers. Tungsten's higher density allows for smaller shot size to penetrate as well as a larger size of lead shot, so the pellet count will be higher and patterns will be denser, and that will result in more reliable performance. Browning now loads the TSS in its shotshell line, in 12 gauge (3.5-inch and 3-inch), 20 gauge (3-inch) and 410 bore, using No. 7 shot, No. 9 shot and a blend of 7s and 9s. browningammo.com

Sierra GameChanger Ammunition

Long famous for producing some of the most accurate component bullets on the market, the Sierra name is synonymous with precision shooting. In addition to the benchmark MatchKing bullets, the GameKing, Pro Hunter and the new GameChanger bullets have been serving hunters for decades. Other ammunition companies have offered cartridges loaded with Sierra bullets, but they have been mainly a component part. New for 2019, Sierra has proudly announced its GameChanger loaded ammunition, topped with the polymer tipped boat-tail GameChanger bullet, essentially a Tipped GameKing. The brass casings have the Sierra headstamp, and I'm happy to report that the ammunition carries on the tradition of fantastic accuracy Sierra has so deservedly earned. I've had the opportunity to shoot the 6.5 Creedmoor ammunition, and it has proved to be very accurate out to 900 yards. The new GameChanger ammunition is available in .243 Winchester with a 90-grain GameChanger, 6mm Creedmoor with a 100-grain GameChanger, 6.5mm Creedmoor with a 130-grain GameChanger, .270 Winchester with a 140-grain GameChanger and .308 Winchester with a 165-grain GameChanger. *sierrabullets.com*

Federal Edge TLR Component Bullets

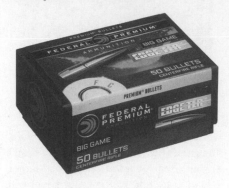

Last year saw Federal release its Edge TLR ammunition, designed to be an excellent choice for hunting at all ranges. Designing a bullet that will deliver consistent expansion at a wide variety of impact velocities, as well as retain energy and velocity, and provide the accuracy that long range shooters want is no easy task. Nonetheless, Federal has checked all those boxes, and for 2019 offers the Edge TLR as a component bullet. I've used the factory-loaded ammunition on a couple of axis deer and small feral hogs, and can attest to its accuracy and terminal qualities; I'm even more excited to test the component bullet this year on safari in Namibia with a .300 H&H handload using the 200-grain, .308-diameter bullet. Using the blue polymer Slipstream tip to both initiate expansion as well as maintain the bullet's Ballistic Coefficient, the Edge TLR has a smaller lead core, which is chemically bonded to the copper jacket and shank, to guarantee deep penetration. As a component, the Edge TLR is available in .277, 136 grains, .284 (7mm) 155 grains, .308, 175 and 200 grains. *federalpremium.com*

Hornady LEVERevolution .348 Winchester Ammunition

In the midst of the Great Depression, Winchester released two of its finest: the Model 70, which we're all familiar with, and the lever-action counterpart, the Model 71. Chambered for the new .348 Winchester cartridge, the Model 71 was designed to replace both the Model 1886 and Model 1895, and the .33 Winchester and .405 Winchester cartridges they were chambered for. The .348 Winchester ammunition used three bullets

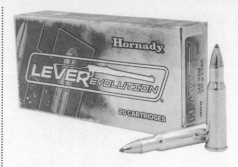

of nominal diameter, weighing 150, 200 and 250 grains. The 250-grain load was fully capable of taking any and all North American game, including the brown bear and bison. Marketed as "the world's newest universal big game rifle," the Model 71 developed, and still has, a devout following, in addition to being highly collectable. The rifle was discontinued in 1958 (having been replaced by Model 88 and the .358 Winchester cartridge), with the exception of a brief run by Browning in 1987, and recent limited reissues by Cimarron and Winchester. Reliable supplies of ammunition have been a problem since the 1960s, when Winchester dropped the 250-grain load, but for 2019 the .348 Winchester gets a facelift. Hornady has added the classic cartridge to the LEVERevolution line, using the 200-grain FTX bullet. With its proprietary Flex-Tip meplat, the FTX bullet is perfectly safe to use in the tubular magazine of the Model 71 (and so many other lever guns) yet offers the downrange benefit of a spitzer bullet, expanding the range of the lever gun cartridges significantly, when compared to the flat-nose and round-nose bullets that are usually employed. Leaving the muzzle at 2,560 fps, the 200-grain Hornady load produces nearly 3,000 ft.-lbs. of energy at the muzzle, and when zeroed at 200 yards, drops 11 inches at 300 yards. Hornady has given the perfect excuse to take that classic Model 71 out to the deer woods this fall. *hornady.com*

Winchester Xpert Snow Goose Shotshells

Snow geese are becoming increasingly popular as a game bird, and Winchester has developed a shotshell load just for them. New for 2019, the Snow Goose shotshells use the Xpert Steel Shot and the Diamond Cut Wad from the Winchester Blind Side shells to create an optimized

shotshell. With a high velocity — 1,425 fps for the 3-inch, 12 gauge (1 1/4 ounce) and 1,550 fps for the 3 ½-inch, 12 gauge (1 3/8 ounce) — and a gray tube and black wad for good concealment, the Winchester Xpert Snow Goose is sure to become a favorite. *winchester.com*

Norma MHP Handgun Ammunition

Norma Precision — long famous for its excellent rifle ammunition — has introduced a line of handgun ammo for 2019. Introduced at the SHOT Show in Las Vegas, the MHP, or Monolithic Hollow Point, is a very forgiving bullet, meaning it will operate and expand reliably across a wide spectrum of barrel lengths and impact velocities. Norma offers the MHP in 9mm Luger, using a 108-grain bullet at a muzzle velocity of 1,312 fps, and that bullet is designed to expand into four sharp petals upon impact. The very design of the MHP gives a quick expansion upon impact, yet the bullet will hold together. Norma has indicated that geometry of the MHP bullet has given reliable feeding in every pistol and carbine it tested. *norma-usa.com*

Remington Premier Scirocco Bonded Ammunition

Among my favorite bullets is the Swift Scirocco. They are wonderfully accurate, they possess a high B.C. value, and their terminal ballistics are excellent. With a polymer tip — used both to initiate expansion, as well as to keep the meplat consistent — secant ogive and a boat tail, the Scirocco will retain a healthy amount of both its initial velocity and energy downrange. The thick, tapering copper jacket is chemically bonded to the lead core, so bullet breakup is absolutely no concern. The Scirocco hits where you aim it, and kills what it hits. I've handloaded the bullet for more than 15 years, without a single issue or lost game animal. Remington saw the wisdom of this bullet as well, and offered it in its Pre-

mier ammunition line, but discontinued it, much to the dismay of many shooters who loved the performance, especially in the Remington Ultra Magnum series of cartridges. Well, Big Green has embraced the Scirocco again, as Remington has announced the reintroduction of the Premier Scirocco Bonded ammunition line. Those hunters who shoot 7mm and .300 Remington Ultra Magnum will finally have the source of ammunition they've missed so much, but there are enough classic cartridges on this list the Scirocco can be enjoyed by the majority of big-game hunters. Available in 20-count boxes, in the following cartridges/bullet weights: .243 Win., 90 grains; .270 Winchester, 130 grains; 7mm Remington Magnum and 7mm RUM, 150-grains; .308 Winchester, 165 grains; .30-'06 Springfield, 150 and 180 grains; .300 RUM, 150 and 180 grains; .300 WSM and .300 Winchester Magnum, 180 grains. *remington.com*

Hornady Outfitter Ammunition

Monometal projectiles are absolutely here to stay, and in some states are required by law. Hornady's GMX (Gilding Metal eXpanding) is among the best monometals on the market, and while Hornady has included them in their loaded ammunition lines before, the Outfitter series is designed around and uses the GMX exclusively. Known for its deep penetration, good expansion and high weight retention, the GMX is a sound choice for the big-game hunter. Hornady's Outfitter line features nickel-plated cases — perfect for sweaty hands or wet environments — and sealed primers and case mouths, to keep things dry as a bone, and perfectly clean to ensure smooth feeding. Lead-free (copper alloy) bullets will be longer than their lead core counterparts of the same weight, so in order to maximize case capacity, Hornady has chosen bullet weights on the lighter side of the spectrum. However, the lighter weight doesn't mean lesser perfor-

mance; due to the structural integrity of a monometal copper bullet, the lighter varieties will often give the performance of the heavier cup-and-core bullets. Hornady's Outfitter line is available in .243 Winchester, 80-grain GMX; 6.5 Creedmoor, 120-grain GMX; .270 Winchester and .270 WSM, 130-grain GMX; 7mm Remington Magnum and 7mm WSM, 150-grain GMX; .308 Winchester, 165-grain GMX; .30-'06 Springfield, .300 WSM and .300 Winchester Magnum, 180-grain GMX; and .375 Ruger and .375 H&H Magnum; 250-grain GMX. *hornady.com*

CCI VNT Rimfire Ammo

Last year saw the release of CCI's .17 HMR load with the Speer VNT bullet; its polymer tip helps to retain velocity at farther ranges, and the thin, frangible jacket gives near-explosive terminal performance on game. For 2019, CCI has expanded the line with two new offerings: the .17 Mach 2 and the .22 WMR. The .17 Mach 2 probably doesn't have the biggest following of the rimfire cartridges, but if you've ever spent a bit of time with one, you quickly realize you might have made a new friend. As for the .22 WMR, I don't think there are many shooters who would deny loving the .22 Mag; it is a flat-shooting, hard-hitting cartridge, which can easily flatten a woodchuck or end a coyote's hunting career. CCI's rimfire ammunition has an impeccable reputation; the priming is utterly reliable — there is nothing more aggravating than the sharp "click" of a misfire once the trigger breaks — and I've relied on this diverse line of ammunition for decades. For the varmint hunter who does most of his or her work within 100 paces, using either one of these rimfire cartridges makes all sorts of sense; they are easy on the ears, as well as on the wallet, yet extremely effective

within that range. The .17 Mach 2 ammo uses a 17-grain VNT bullet at 2,010 fps, and the .22 WMR ammo uses a 30-grain VNT at 2,200 fps; both cartridges come in 50-count boxes. *cci-ammunition.com*

Roberson Cartridge Company

Handloaders are always looking for a reliable source of cartridge cases for those obscure or obsolete cartridges, or for the production of properly headstamped wildcat cartridges. I've met the good folks from Roberson Cartridge Company in Amarillo, Texas, and I'm glad I have. Roberson uses a CNC lathe to cut each individual case, maintaining a unique molecular structure, and avoiding the complications associated with drawn brass cases. Jeff Roberson, president of the company, explained to me his desire to be able to provide his customers with the best product available, and fill those voids in the market, like obscure brass cases for vintage firearms. "We take pride in helping to revive those old firearms; we can make virtually anything with our technique, and it's great to see the .33 Winchesters and other rarities back in business," Roberson said. I've used Roberson cases in .318 Westley Richards and the .17-223 wildcat, with excellent results. I feel their mission statement says it best: "Our mission is to manufacture vintage, obsolete, hard to find, and wildcat calibers for customers across the globe from private use to military applications. With the predominance of Bench Rest and F-Class shooting and the emergence of new shooting sports, like ELR, our new RCC Bench Rest Grade cartridges will help you achieve unprecedented brass performance. We manufacture all our cartridges to SAAMI, CIP or tolerances provided to us. By developing a proprietary process, RCC has the ability to manufacture any caliber in the world, existent or not, on our CNC lathes and mills. We have our brass manufactured

to our exact specifications. Its hammer forged to a high tensile strength and its malleability gives it the flexibility for a longer life span. It is then cold cut to specification and shipped to our customers." If you have a firearm that uses an obsolete cartridge, or you want to see that wildcat you've been dreaming of come to fruition, reach out to Roberson. *rccbrass.com*

Norma BondStrike Ammunition

For 2019, Norma introduces its BondStrike line of ammunition, the third in the Strike series. Norma's TipStrike bullet is a polymer tip cup-and-core flat base design, the EcoStrike is a polymer tip boat tail, of monometal construction, and now the BondStrike is Norma's bonded core bullet. Using a blue polymer tip (to differentiate from the orange TipStrike and green EcoStrike) and a boat-tail configuration, the BondStrike gives the shooter a fantastic all-around ammunition choice, for game of all shapes and sizes. When a bullet's lead core is chemically bonded to the copper jacket, expansion is slowed to allow for deep penetration. Core/jacket separation is nearly eliminated, irrespective of impact velocity. Closer shots — where impact velocities are high — won't destroy the BondStrike's conformation, yet distant shots, where the impact velocities are low, will see the polymer tip act as a wedge, still giving reliable expansion, and a quick, humane kill. Using Norma's excellent brass cases, and state-of-the-art production techniques — I have been to their facility in Amotfors, Sweden, and confess to being highly impressed — the BondStrike ammunition has shown to be accurate, consistent, and reliable. Available initially in .30 caliber in .308 Winchester, .30-'06 Springfield, .300 Winchester Short Magnum, .300 Winchester Magnum and .300 Remington Ultra Magnum, all with the 180-grain BondStrike bullet. *norma-usa.com*

Federal's Shorty Shotshells

New for 2019 is the aptly named Federal "Shorty Shotshell," perfect for a good number of applications, including good, plain fun. At 1 3/4 inches long, the Shorty is available in 12 gauge, in No. 8 bird shot, No. 4 Buck (15-pellet count) and even a rifled slug, in 10-count packs. I see the Shorty Shotshells as an excellent means of teaching a young shooter — or even an adult shooter new to the sport — how to handle a full-sized shotgun, be it a pump, double or autoloader. The No. 8 shot load — with 15/16 ounce of shot — will allow shooters to practice their swings with much less recoil than even light trap loads produce. Using the No. 4 Buck load, a shooter who chooses to use a shotgun as a defensive weapon, the same type of practice or training can be had with the Shorty Shotshells, with a significant reduction in recoil. Though the muzzle velocity is still listed at 1,200 fps, the reduction from 27 pellets to 15 pellets will equate to a significant reduction in recoil. Furthermore, for those who are concerned about over-penetration when using a defensive weapon in the home, the reduced load of Shorty Shotshell makes a comforting choice, as the lighter payload can be used when desired, yet the same firearm can still handle the full house loads of a 12 gauge. The No. 4 Buck load will also make a great choice for coyotes and foxes. The Shorty rifled slug is an excellent means of preparing for the big-game season, without pounding your shoulder, as well as being a sensible choice for young deer hunters, as the 1-ounce slug, even at the reduced velocity, will still kill deer-sized game. *federalpremium.com*

Federal Premium Ammo Loaded with Barnes TSX bullets

Neither of these companies needs any sort of an introduction; Federal Premium has long been an industry standard in the precision ammunition field,

and Barnes was a pioneer in all-copper, monometal-bullet technology. Federal — though it has a lineup of excellent proprietary bullets — has never shied away from embracing the best projectiles available, dating back to the 1980s when they began loading Sierra MatchKing and GameKing bullets. The Barnes TSX is an update of Randy Brooks' original Barnes X design (which gave me absolute fits as a handloader) that offers excellent accuracy, nearly full weight retention and wonderful terminal ballistics. While the original Barnes design had a smooth shank (which led to a large amount of copper fouling in the rifle's bore) the TSX has three or four grooves in the shank — depending on caliber and length — to reduce fouling and improve accuracy. In my experiences, that minor facelift made all the difference in the world in the Barnes TSX; it went from goat to hero. When Federal loads the Barnes TSX, you have a recipe for success, and for 2019, the pair are back together. Federal offers the Barnes TSX in the following calibers and configurations: .223 Rem., 55 grain; .243 Win., 85 grain; .25-06 Rem., 115 grain; 6.5 Creedmoor, 130 grain; .270 Win, 130 grain; .270 WSM, 130 grain; 7mm-08, Rem. 140 grain; 7mm Rem. Mag., 160 grain; .308 Win., 150 grain; .308 Win., 165 grain; .30-30 Win., 150 grain; .30-'06 Sprg., 180 grain; .30-'06 Sprg., 165 grain; .300 WSM, 180 grain; .300 WSM, 165 grain; .300 Win. Mag., 180 grain; and .300 Win Mag. 165 grain. *federalpremium.com*

Hornady Frontier .300 Blackout Ammunition

The Frontier line of ammunition revives an old Hornady brand, now representing the collaboration between Hornady and Lake City. Affordable, accurate and reliable, the Frontier ammunition

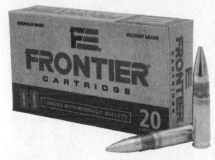

I have tested — in .223 Remington and 5.56mm NATO — has been wonderfully accurate, and represents a great value to the shooter. For 2019, Hornady has expanded the line to include the .300 Blackout cartridge, loaded with a 125-grain Hornady FMJ bullet. Leaving a 16-inch test barrel at 2,175 fps, the Frontier .300 Blackout ammunition is an excellent means of practicing with your rifle, plinking with your rifle and even hunting predators and varmints. *hornady.com*

Speer Impact Component Bullets

Speer announced a new component bullet for 2019: the Impact. Using the same Slipstream polymer tip that the Federal Edge TLR does over a hollow core, the Speer Impact uses boat-tail design and a molecularly fused jacket to give not only a high B.C. value, but the terminal ballistics any hunter will appreciate. The Impact represents a bullet that will not only handle the shots at traditional hunting distances, but those longer shots as well; the Impact is designed to expand at very low velocities. Speer has priced the Impact to be very attractive to the reloader on a budget. Available in 6.5 mm, 140 grains, and .308-inch diameter at 172 and 190 grains. *speer-ammo.com*

Winchester Deer Season Shotgun Slugs

Winchester's Deer Season line of rifle ammunition proved to be a huge hit among deer hunters, and this year Winchester has extended the line to include slugs for those who make their venison with a smoothbore shotgun. Available in

12 gauge, with a 1 1/8-ounce rifled slug, Winchester's unique design includes the Integrated Rear Stabilized Wad, which travels to the target with the slug, separating upon impact. The combination results in greatly improved accuracy, as well as retained velocity to maximize energy downrange. With a muzzle velocity of 1,600 fps, Winchester's Deer Season slugs generate an appreciable amount of energy — more than 3,000 ft.-lbs. — and will most definitely ruin a big buck's day. If you use a smoothbore shotgun for your deer hunting, give the Winchester Deer Season slug an audition; the field reports all indicate it makes the most of the traditional shotgun barrel. *winchester.com*

Aguila 5mm Remington Rimfire Magnum Ammunition

The rarest of the rimfire cartridges — Remington's 5mm Rimfire Magnum — gets a new lease on life with the 2019 release of Aguila's limited run of ammunition. Using a 30-grain jacketed and semi-jacketed hollow point bullets at 2,300 fps, the Aguila ammunition will surely fly off the shelves, to be treasured by those shooters who still enjoy the Model 591 and 592 rifles. No, you can't buy a new rifle chambered for the 5mm Magnum, but thankfully Aguila has provided a means to feed rifles that remain in service. *aguilaammo.com*

Federal Hydra-Shok Component Bullets

Federal is really concentrating on the component-bullet selection for 2019, and for those of us who reload that's a wonderful thing. For 2019, those who reload their pistol ammunition can now get the famous Hydra-Shok bullet in component form. Since 1989, shooters have relied upon the deep penetration and wicked expansion of the Hydra-Shok design as

a self-defense tool, and it has gone on to become one of the standards of the industry. As a component bullet, Federal has made the Hydra-Shok available in the following configurations: .355, 124 and 147 grains; .357, 129 and 158 grains; .400, 165 and 180 grains; and .451, 185 and 230 grains. *federalpremium.com*

Lyman Brass Smith 500 Metal Reloading Scale

Lyman offers a balance-beam reloading scale for 2019, in its Brass Smith line of reloading gear. Using an aluminum body, precision ground knife edges and magnetic damping, the Brass Smith 500 allows a reloader to accurately measure components weighing up to 505 grains. Its high-contrast markings are labeled on both sides of the beam, and the pan has tabs for both right- and left-hand users. *lymanproducts.com*

Redding PR-50 Competition Powder Measure

The Redding name is associated with precision, and that is applicable to the new PR-50 Competition Powder Measure. Any powder measure that works by volume instead of weight will operate most accurately in the middle third of its capacity, and the central target weight for the PR-50 is 50 grains, making this measure perfect for cartridges like the .22-250 Rem., 6mm and 6.5 Creedmoor, .308 Winchester and .30-'06 Springfield. The overall range of the PR-50 is 35 to 70 grains of powder, making it ideal for most mid-capacity cartridges. *redding-reloading.com*

Federal .450 Bushmaster Ammunition

The .450 Bushmaster is gaining quite the following of late, with many states in the Midwest allowing straight-walled rifle cartridges to be used for deer hunting. For 2019, Federal offers three loads for the .450 Bushmaster: the 300-grain Non-Typical soft point, the 300-grain Power-Shok soft point and the 300-grain Fusion bonded-core bullet, all at an advertized muzzle velocity of 1,900 fps. All three bullets will reliably take deer and similar sized animals, giving both good penetration and good expansion. *federalpremium.com*

The Benjamin MAG-Fire loads automatically as the rifle is cocked.

NEW AIRGUNS

BY **JIM HOUSE**

Airguns have been used for centuries, but like many other implements, they have changed enormously in recent years. In the gentler, quieter time of the early 1900s, the most common arms that launched projectiles by compressed air were the BB guns that were charged with a single cocking stroke. Then came the multi-pump models from Benjamin and Crosman, and Daisy produced the Model 880 in 1972. Sheridan entered that market with a .20 caliber multi-pump in 1947. Then came rifles and pistols that fired pellets by means of compressed CO2. Things more or less stayed that way, at least in terms of popularity, for years.

The classic airgun designs are still popular, but the situation has changed enormously in recent years, and there seem to be two general directions in the airgun field. The first is toward models that replicate actual firearms, especially handguns. Operating by means of small cylinders of highly compressed CO2, these models incorporate such a cylinder and some sort of magazine to hold several pellets and make the overall configuration resemble almost any type of pistol. Traditional airguns that are charged by several strokes with an attached handle (multi-pump) are still available and popular. Airguns that are cocked with one stroke of the barrel which functions as the compressing lever abound (break action or break barrel), and they are capable of propelling pellets at 1,000 fps or more depending on caliber and pellet weight.

The second trend is toward larger and more powerful rifles that utilize pellets of .25 to .50 caliber. The quest for more power, more speed and greater range has resulted in a very wide range of airguns that make use of a relatively large reservoir that holds enough air to fire several shots. Known as pre-charged pneumatic (PCP) models, they feature a reservoir that can contain enough air to give a pressure of perhaps 2,000 to 3,000 psi, and that quantity of propellant gas is sufficient to launch

Benjamin Fortitude is a capable PCP rifle that is a good choice for shooting pests.

"pellets" of .25, .30, .35, .45, or even .50 caliber. Such rifles are widely advertised as appropriate tools for hunting even species as large as deer and hogs.

No longer are airguns considered as eliminators for only small pests, but the downside is that some serious pumping, a scuba tank, or a special compressor is needed. The already wide range of airgun models is expanding rapidly with new models from an increasing number of manufacturers and distributors. However, with increased capability comes increased control. Already in some jurisdictions, airguns, especially the more powerful models, come under the same regulations for purchase and use as do firearms. We might not like to think about such things, but these are facts of life in the shooting sports.

Velocity Outdoor

As has happened in other areas of the shooting sports, several brands are consolidated under one umbrella label. This has happened with the long-standing Benjamin, Crosman and Remington airguns that are now part of the Velocity Outdoor group. Of these, the Benjamin and Crosman products have been popular for generations, but airguns bearing the trademarks of firearm companies have also become popular in recent years. Those carrying the Remington label were formerly marketed by Crosman Corporation, so they are now found in the Velocity Outdoor fold. New and exciting are the trio of break action rifles from Benjamin known as the MAG-Fire, Mission, Nomad and Ultra. These rifles feature a rotary 10-round magazine that automatically indexes to the next round as the rifle is cocked. Instead of having to insert a sin-

gle pellet into the barrel when the rifle is cocked, the slow step in loading, a pellet is brought in line with the breech as the rifle is cocked.

Break-action rifles rarely meet the advertised upper limit of velocity except with perhaps the lightest possible alloy pellets. For the .22 caliber rifles, the advertised velocity is 1,100 fps, whereas that of the .177 caliber versions is 1,400 fps. Regardless, these are potent break-action rifles that feature Crosman's Nitro Piston power source rather than a steel spring, and are provided with rails for mounting scopes. None of the three rifles has open sights, but all include rails and a 4X32 CenterPoint scope. The MAG-Fire features a polymer stock that incorporates a vertical pistol grip whereas that of the Nomad is wood and is of a thumbhole design. The Ultra has a polymer stock of more conventional design that has an ambidextrous

cheek piece. All of the MAG-Fire rifles incorporate Crosman's SBD sound suppression system. With the nitrogen-gas propulsion system, rapid reloading capability and sound suppression, the Mission, Nomad, and Ultra are well-suited for serious work on pests and small game.

One of the characteristics of PCP rifles is that as shots are fired, the air pressure in the reservoir decreases leading to a decrease in velocity after a few shots. One of the exciting new rifles from Velocity Outdoor is the Benjamin Marauder Regulated. Standard Marauder rifles are advertised to produce velocities up to 900 fps, 1,000 fps, and 1,100 fps in .25, .22, and .177 calibers, respectively. The Marauder Regulated, one version of which is available with a Lothar Walther barrel, is available in .22 and .177 calibers, but the velocities are specified as 850 and 1,000 fps for the .22 and .177 caliber models. The Regulat-

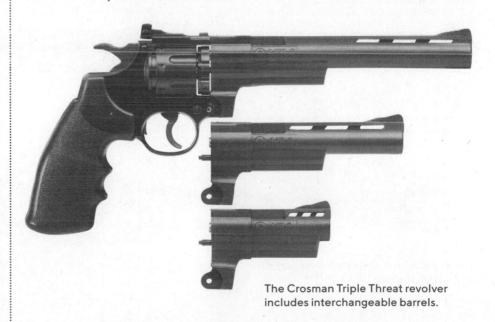

The Crosman Triple Threat revolver includes interchangeable barrels.

Intended for competitive shooting, the Daisy 599 comes with all of the bells and whistles.

ed rifle retains the rotating magazine that has characterized the Marauder for years, but it also has an internal regulator that maintains pressure in such a way that up to 80 to 100 shots can be fired with uniform velocity.

The Marauder Regulated features a hardwood stock with a polymer comb the height of which can be adjusted. Other Marauder rifles are available with either the same stock or one made entirely of a composite material. This is an important consideration because none of the Marauder rifles include open sights and the proper height of the comb depends on the type of scope and mount to be used.

Another new Benjamin product is known as the Fortitude. This rifle includes most of the attributes of the Marauder, but features a valve that can be regulated to control the amount of air released on firing. In that way, the power level can be controlled and on the lower power setting, up to 200 shots can be fired before the reservoir must be refilled. On a medium setting (normal for the model) up to 80 to 90 shots can be fired and on the highest setting up to 60 shots can be fired. This flexibility allows the shooter to choose the power appropriate to the use of the airgun. The Fortitude has a shrouded barrel, but it does not come with the SBD suppressor system.

For many years, Benjamin multi-pump rifles have been offered in .22 and .177 as the models 392 and 397, respectively. These models are now produced with a stock made of a composite material. This configuration certainly gives these classic models a different look.

Although many of the CO2 pistols are of the "me too" variety, a new model from Crosman offers something different. The Triple Threat is a revolver that can be fired in either single or double action mode using either BB or pellet ammunition. A unique feature of the Triple Threat is that it comes with three interchangeable barrels in 3-, 6-, and 8-inch lengths. Ten pellets are held in a pellet magazine but only six BBs can be loaded in the BB magazine. *velocity-outdoor.com*

Gamo USA–Daisy

The reputations of Daisy Outdoor Products and Gamo USA have been highly regarded for many years. Now, under the combined Gamo USA–Daisy label, the entire spectrum of airgun products is spanned. This is especially true when

With a design that imitates the Ruger 10/22 rimfire, the Umarex pellet-firing version is an excellent choice for plinking.

Gamo's Recon G2 is a scaled down version of the Swarm repeater.

one considers that Daisy is also the purveyor of airguns carrying the Winchester brand, which includes break-action models as well as PCP rifles in large calibers. From the legendary Daisy Red Ryder to large bore PCP models, there is something for everyone.

One of the exciting new products from Daisy is not a model designed for hunting, but a rather low-power model for precision shooting. Known as the Daisy 599 Competition, this is a PCP rifle that launches .177 caliber pellets at a velocity of 520 fps. Although the ballistic performance of the rifle is hardly impressive, the accuracy potential is. The 599 features a hardwood stock that can be used by shooters from either side of the stock. Several features found in competition rifles are found on the Daisy 599, including a trigger that can be adjusted to a pull weight as low as 1.5

pounds. Also, the stock is almost infinitely adjustable with a butt that can be moved forward and backward as well as vertically. The comb is a movable section that can be positioned at an appropriate height. Opening the action to insert a pellet is accomplished by pulling back the bolt which has a "T" handle at the rear of the action. Sights on the 599 consist of an aperture rear sight that is fully adjustable and fitted with a rubber eye cup to exclude extraneous light. The front sight is a globe-type that can accept a range of inserts. A scope can be mounted easily owing to the grooved receiver. To top it all off, the appearance and handling qualities of the rifle are enhanced by virtue of the one-piece stock with attractive checkering. This interesting rifle weighs 7.1 pounds and has the MSRP of $595.

The big news from Gamo USA came

last year with announcement of the Swarm Magnum repeating break-action rifle. With an eye to increasing options for youthful shooters, Gamo has introduced the Recon G2 Whisper youth model. This rifle is a break-action model utilizing a gas piston power plant. Sights are adjustable and the stock is made of a composite material and is ambidextrous. The Recon G2 weighs only 4.4 pounds and has a velocity of up to 750 fps so it is suitable for the intended audience. *gamousa.com*

Hatsan

Ever a leader in PCP rifles, Hatsan has new models in .177, .22, and .25 caliber that utilize a large air reservoir. The result is that in .177 caliber the NovaStar and NovaStar QE can fire more than 300 shots, with the first 110 shots at essentially full power from a filled tank. Even the .25 cali-

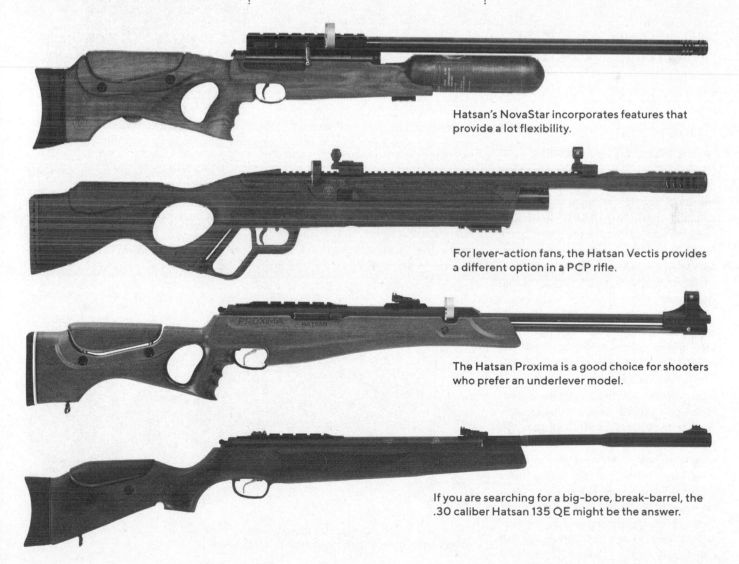

Hatsan's NovaStar incorporates features that provide a lot flexibility.

For lever-action fans, the Hatsan Vectis provides a different option in a PCP rifle.

The Hatsan Proxima is a good choice for shooters who prefer an underlever model.

If you are searching for a big-bore, break-barrel, the .30 caliber Hatsan 135 QE might be the answer.

Owners of a Glock 17 who want to fire BBs should consider the CO2 version from Umarex.

ber version can fire up to 280 shots or 90 full-power shots. The NovaStar rifles have Turkish ambidextrous walnut stocks of the thumbhole design that incorporate adjustable combs. Starting with a filled tank, one of these rifles would be a good choice for a full day of pest popping, which is also facilitated by rotary magazines that hold 14, 12, or 10 pellets in .177, .22 or .25 caliber, respectively.

For those who prefer a more tactical appearance, Hatsan has the Vectis, which also utilizes a rotary magazine, but the action is cycled by means of a lever. The Vectis has a composite stock that features a raised comb and thumbhole design. Because of a smaller reservoir being used, the Vectis delivers fewer shots than the NovaStar models. Perhaps even more of a tactical look is provided by the Flash, which is a bolt action rifle that features a thumbhole polymer stock (either black or wood grain finish) with a cutout section behind the thumbhole. Fanciers of bullpup designs may also choose the Hatsan FlashPup. Performance characteris-

tics of the Flash versions are the same as for the Vectis.

New ground is also broken with the Hatsan Proxima, which is an underlever model that is available in .177, .22, and .25 calibers. It features the rotary magazines used in the PCP models and pellet capacities are identical. The stock is made of

wood, is of a thumbhole design, and provides for adjustments of comb height and length of pull.

Although the muzzle velocity is listed as only 550 fps, the Hatsan Carnivore 135 is an interesting single-shot, break-action airgun in .30 caliber. It has adjustable open sights and a nicely shaped wood

These cast projectiles are .50 caliber bullets that weigh 336 grains, and they are intended for use on large game.

stock. The Carnivore is essentially an upscale version of the Mod 130 QE that comes in .177, .22, .25, and .30 calibers and features a polymer stock. I would be quite happy with the Carnivore 135 as a walk-about pest rifle. *hatsanusa.com*

Umarex

Long known for marketing an incredible array of air and CO2 pistols that mimic actual firearms, Umarex is introducing a rifle that is a replica of the Ruger 10/22, which is probably the most recognizable rimfire of today. The rifle is powered by two 12-gram CO2 cylinders and fires .177 caliber pellets. In reservoirs that hold pellets, the actual magazine itself is a thin cylinder that is essentially a dial with holes. However, in the Umarex version of the 10/22, that cylinder is held in the same location just in front of the trigger guard as is the magazine in a Ruger 10/22. Gas cylinders are placed in the rifle by moving the butt plate and using an Allen wrench to pierce the cylinders. Sights on the Umarex 10/22 are like those on the Ruger firearm, and a barrel band encircles the fore-end of the composite stock and the barrel. For those seeking a pellet-firing rifle that resembles a firearm, the Umarex 10/22 is about as real as it gets.

The Umarex Hammer .50 caliber PCP is billed as the world's most powerful airgun. With an operating maximum pressure of 4,500 psi, measuring almost 44 inches in length and weighing 8.5 pounds without sights or ammunition, there is no question that it is a behemoth airgun. A built-in regulator allows a consistent pressure of 3,000 psi for the first three shots, and velocity produced depends on projectile weight (which can vary from 180 to 550 grains). Muzzle energies are reported to be up to 700 ft-lbs. The Hammer is actually a two-shot rifle because it makes use of a chamber such that only operating the bolt is required for a second shot. Each shot dumps a lot of air and only the first three shots are full power, with the fourth somewhat lower.

For those who fancy having fun with CO2 pistols, Umarex introduces two models that imitate two of the most popular centerfire pistols, the Glock 17 and 19. The Glock 17 version features a blowback action and a magazine that holds 18 BBs.

The replica of the Glock 19 holds 16 BBs, but lacks the blowback feature. With the enormous popularity of the Glock centerfire pistols, the replicas should prove to be quite popular. *umarexusa.com*

Considerations

With large bulbous air reservoirs, stocks having parts that are adjustable, suppressors of large diameter, and other appendages, some airguns are hardly classic looking sporting arms. However, a lack of esthetic appeal in some airguns is likely worth ignoring in deference to their outstanding performance. It should also be kept in mind that an airgun that shoots a 150-grain projectile at perhaps 800 fps just about duplicates the ballistic performance of only a standard load in a .38 Special handgun, so it is no knock-'em dead powerhouse. Some PCP rifles can launch a .45 caliber projectile at approximately 900 fps, which corresponds to approximately muzzle energies of 175 to 200 ft lbs. Such rifles can produce ballistic performance similar to that of a .45 Auto handgun. They are very powerful for an airgun, but there is no way that an airgun that operates at a pressure of 3,000 psi can duplicate the performance of a firearm that operates at 10 times that pressure. When such airguns are used on large game, it should be done carefully and with discretion.

The owner of a .300 Weatherby Magnum should expect to pay more for ammunition than would the owner of a .30-30 Winchester. Specialty items cost more and that is the case with ammunition for large-bore airguns. The air used to power such a rifle might be free, but the ammunition certainly is not. A very cursory check showed some .35-caliber projectiles sell for $17.99 per 100, whereas other specialty types have prices as high as $25.99 for 25. I also found that, in general, .45-caliber projectiles cost around $30 per 50 for several types. In some cases, the pellets might cost more than loaded ammunition for centerfire rifles. The cost of shooting a large-caliber airgun is considerable, and for a big-bore airgun that has uses similar to a firearm, the cost of shooting is comparable to shooting a rifle. As the big-bore airguns have become more common, the variety of ammunition has increased in measure so the shooter has several choices of projectile types in virtually all calibers.

It is an exciting time for airgunners. The equipment available is unprecedented in terms of options and performance. Regardless of whether you prefer a multi-pump, break action or PCP, there are models available that are sure to please.

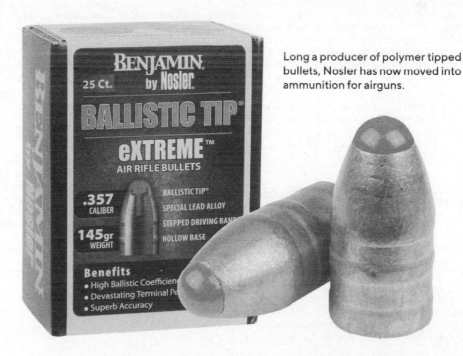

Long a producer of polymer tipped bullets, Nosler has now moved into ammunition for airguns.

ALEXANDER ARMS AR SERIES

Calibers: .17 HMR, 5.56 NATO, 6.5 Grendel, .300 AAC, .338 Lapua Mag., .50 Beowulf. This manufacturer produces a wide range of AR-15 type rifles and carbines. **Barrels:** 16, 18, 20 or 24 in. Models are available for consumer, law enforcement and military markets. Depending on the specific model, features include forged flattop receiver with Picatinny rail, button-rifled stainless steel barrels, composite free-floating handguard, A2 flash hider, M4 collapsible stock, gas piston operating system.

Price: .17 HMR From..**$1,097.00**
Price: 5.56 NATO From...**$1,155.00**
Price: 6.5 Grendel From...**$1,425.00**
Price: .300 AAC From...**$1,275.00**
Price: .50 Beowulf From...**$1,425.00**

ALEXANDER ARMS ULFBERHT

Caliber: .338 Lapua Mag. Custom-designed adjustable gas-piston operating system. **Barrel:** 27.5-in. chrome moly with three-prong flash hider. **Stock:** Magpul PRS. **Length:** 41.25 in. (folded), 50 in. (extended stock). **Weight:** 19.8 lbs.

Price: From...**$6,090.00**

ARMALITE M-15 LIGHT TACTICAL CARBINE

Calibers: .223 Rem., 6.8 SPC, 7.62x39mm. **Capacity:** 30-round magazine. **Barrel:** 16 in. heavy chrome lined; 1:7 in. twist, flash suppressor. (10.3 and 11.5 in. available. NFA regulations apply) **Weight:** 6 lbs. **Length:** 36 in. overall. **Stock:** Green or black composition. **Sights:** Standard A2. **Features:** Forged flattop receiver with Picatinny rail, 10-in. aluminum KeyMod handguard, anodize aluminum supper/lower receiver, flip-up sights. Introduced in 2016.

Price: ....**$999.00-$2,099.00**

ARMALITE AR-10 3-GUN COMPETITION RIFLE

Calibers: 7.62x1mm/.308 Win. **Capacity:** 25-round magazine. **Barrel:** 18-in. stainless steel. **Weight:** 8.9 lbs. **Features:** MBA-1 buttstock with adjustable comb and length of pull, 15-in. free-floating 3-Gun handguard, Raptor charging handle, Timney trigger, ambidextrous safety.

Price: **$2,199.00**

ARMALITE EAGLE-15 VERSATILE SPORTING RIFLE (VSR)

Caliber: .223 Rem/5.56x45 NATO (.223 Wylde chamber). **Capacity:** 30-shot Magpul PMAG. **Barrel:** 16-in. chrome moly with flash suppressor. **Stock:** 6-position collapsible with free-float rail system, rubberized grip. **Weight:** 6.6 lbs. **Features:** Carbine length gas system, 15-in. handguard with Key Mod attachments, forged lower and flat-top upper, Picatinny rail.

Price: **$800.00**

ARSENAL, INC. SLR-107F

Caliber: 7.62x39mm. **Barrel:** 16.25 in. **Weight:** 7.3 lbs. **Stock:** Left-side folding polymer stock. **Sights:** Adjustable rear. **Features:** Stamped receiver, 24mm flash hider, bayonet lug, accessory lug, stainless steel heat shield, two-stage trigger. Introduced 2008. Made in USA by Arsenal, Inc.

Price: SLR-107FR, includes scope rail **$1,099.00**

ARSENAL, INC. SLR-107CR

Caliber: 7.62x39mm. **Barrel:** 16.25 in. **Weight:** 6.9 lbs. **Stock:** Left-side folding polymer stock. **Sights:** Adjustable rear. **Features:** Stamped receiver, front sight block/gas block combination, 500-meter rear sight, cleaning rod, stainless steel heat shield, scope rail, and removable muzzle attachment.

Introduced 2007. Made in USA by Arsenal, Inc.
Price: SLR-107CR...**$1,119.00**

ARSENAL, INC. SLR-106CR

Caliber: 5.56 NATO. **Barrel:** 16.25 in. Steyr chrome-lined barrel, 1:7 twist rate. **Weight:** 6.9 lbs. **Stock:** Black polymer folding stock with cutout for scope rail. Stainless steel heat shield handguard. **Sights:** 500-meter rear sight and rear sight block calibrated for 5.56 NATO. Warsaw Pact scope rail. **Features:** Uses Arsenal, Bulgaria, Mil-Spec receiver, two-stage trigger, hammer and disconnector. Polymer magazines in 5- and 10-round capacity in black and green, with Arsenal logo. Others are 30-round black waffles, 20- and 30-round versions in clear/smoke waffle, featuring the "10" in a double-circle logo of Arsenal, Bulgaria. Ships with 5-round magazine, sling, cleaning kit in a tube, 16 in. cleaning rod, oil bottle. Introduced 2007. Made in USA by Arsenal, Inc.

Price: SLR-106CR...**$1,200.00**

AUTO-ORDNANCE 1927A-1 THOMPSON

Caliber: .45 ACP. **Barrel:** 16.5 in. **Weight:** 13 lbs. **Length:** About 41 in. overall (Deluxe). **Stock:** Walnut stock and vertical fore-end. **Sights:** Blade front, open rear adjustable for windage. **Features:** Recreation of Thompson Model 1927. Semi-auto only. Deluxe model has finned barrel, adjustable rear sight and compensator; Standard model has plain barrel and military sight. Available with 100-round drum or 30-round stick magazine. Made in USA by Auto-Ordnance Corp., a division of Kahr Arms.

Price: Deluxe w/stick magazine......................................**$1,551.00**
Price: Deluxe w/drum magazine.....................................**$2,583.00**
Price: Lightweight model w/stick mag **$1,403.00**

AUTO-ORDNANCE 1927 A-1 COMMANDO

Similar to the 1927 A-1 except has Parkerized finish, black-finish wood butt, pistol grip, horizontal fore-end. Comes with black nylon sling. Introduced 1998. Made in USA by Auto-Ordnance Corp., a division of Kahr Arms.

Price: T1-C...**$1,479.00**

AUTO ORDNANCE M1 CARBINE

Caliber: .30 Carbine (15-shot magazine). **Barrel:** 18 in. **Weight:** 5.4 to 5.8 lbs. **Length:** 36.5 in. **Stock:** Wood or polymer. **Sights:** Blade front, flip-style rear. **Features:** A faithful recreation of the military carbine.

Price: **$1,036.00**
Price: Folding stock...**$1,137.00**

BARRETT MODEL 82A-1 SEMI-AUTOMATIC

Calibers: .416 Barret, 50 BMG. **Capacity:** 10-shot detachable box magazine. **Barrel:** 29 in. **Weight:** 28.5 lbs. **Length:** 57 in. overall. **Stock:** Composition with energy-absorbing recoil pad. **Sights:** Scope optional. **Features:** Semiautomatic, recoil operated with recoiling barrel. Three-lug locking bolt; muzzle brake. Adjustable bipod. Introduced 1985. Made in USA by Barrett Firearms.

Price: From...**$9,119.00**

Prices given are believed to be accurate at time of publication however, many factors affect retail pricing so exact pricing is not possible.

BARRETT M107A1

Caliber: 50 BMG. **Capacity:** 10-round detachable magazine. **Barrels:** 20 or 29 in. **Sights:** 27-in. optics rail with flip-up iron sights. **Weight:** 30.9 lbs. **Finish:** Flat Dark Earth. **Features:** Four-port cylindrical muzzle brake. Quick-detachable Barrett QDL Suppressor. Adjustable bipod and monopod.
Price: $12,281.00

BARRETT MODEL REC7 GEN II

Calibers: 5.56 (.223), 6.8 Rem. SPC. **Capacity:** 30-round magazine. **Barrel:** 16 in. **Sights:** ARMS rear, folding front. **Weight:** 28.7 lbs. **Features:** AR-style configuration with standard 17-4 stainless piston system, two-position forward venting gas plug, chrome-lined gas block, A2 flash hider, 6-position MOE stock.
Price: $2,759.00

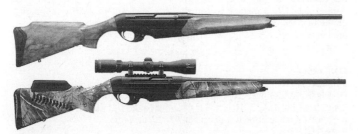

BENELLI R1

Calibers: .30-06 (4+1), .300 Win Mag (3+1), .338 Win Mag (3+1). **Weight:** 7.1 lbs. **Length:** 43.75 in. to 45.75 in. **Stock:** Select satin walnut or synthetic. **Sights:** None. **Features:** Auto-regulating gas-operated system, three-lug rotary bolt, interchangeable barrels, optional recoil pads. Introduced 2003. Imported from Italy by Benelli USA.
Price: $1,019.00

BERETTA ARX 100

Caliber: 5.56 NATO. **Capacity:** 30-round. Accepts AR magazines. **Barrel:** 16 in. with flash suppressor and quick changeability. **Features:** Ambidextrous controls, Picatinny quad rail system.
Price: $1,950.00

BERETTA CX4 STORM CARBINE Calibers: 9mm, 40 S&W, .45 ACP. **Barrel:** 16.6 in. **Stock:** Black synthetic with thumbhole. **Sights:** Ghost ring. **Features:** Blowback single action, ambidextrous controls, Picatinny quad rail system. Reintroduced in 2017.
Price: $700.00

BROWNING BAR SAFARI AND SAFARI W/BOSS SEMI-AUTO

Calibers: Safari: .25-06 Rem., .270 Win., 7mm Rem. Mag., .30-06, .308 Win., .300 Win. Mag., .338 Win. Mag. Safari w/BOSS: .270 Win., 7mm Rem. Mag., .30-06 Spfl., .300 Win. Mag., .338 Win. Mag. **Barrels:** 22–24 in. round tapered. **Weights:** 7.4–8.2 lbs. **Lengths:** 43–45 in. overall. **Stock:** French walnut pistol grip stock and fore-end, hand checkered. **Sights:** No sights. **Features:** Has new bolt release lever; removable trigger assembly with larger trigger guard; redesigned gas and buffer systems. Detachable 4-round box magazine. Scroll-engraved receiver is tapped for scope mounting. BOSS barrel vibration modulator and muzzle brake system available. Mark II Safari introduced 1993. Made in Belgium.

Price: BAR MK II Safari, From $1,230.00
Price: BAR Safari w/BOSS, From $1,400.00

BROWNING BAR MK III SERIES

Calibers: .243 Win., 7mm-08, .270 Win., .270 WSM, 7mm Rem., .308 Win, .30-06, .300 Win. Mag., .300 WSM. **Capacities:** Detachable 4 or 5-shot magazine. **Barrel:** 22, 23 or 24 in.es. **Stock:** Grade II checkered walnut, shim adjustable. Camo stock with composite gripping surfaces available. Stalker model has composite stock. **Weight:** 7.5 lbs. **Features:** Satin nickel alloy with high relief engraving, stylized fore-end.
Price: $1,240.00
Price: Camo $1,380.00
Price: Stalker $1,270.00

BROWNING BAR MK 3 DBM

Caliber: .308 Win. **Capacity:** 10-round detachable magazine. **Barrel:** 18 in. **Stock:** Black composite. Other features similar to standard BAR MK III.
Price: $1,530.00

BUSHMASTER ACR

Calibers: 5.56mm, .300 Blackout, 7.62mm NATO, .450 Bushmaster, .50 BM. **Capacity:** 30-round polymer magazine. **Barrels:** Available with 10.5 in., 14.5 in., 16.5 in. and 18 in. barrels. **Weights:** 14.5 in. bbl. 7 lbs. **Lengths:** 14.5 in. bbl. with stock folded: 25.75 in. with stock deployed (mid) 32.625 in., 10.5 in. bbl. with stock folded: 21.312 in., with stock deployed (mid): 27.875 in., with stock deployed and extended: 31.75 in., Folding Stock Length of Pull — 3 in. **Stock:** Fixed high-impact composite A-frame stock with rubber butt pad and sling mounts. **Features:** Cold hammer-forged barrels with Melonite coating for extreme long life. A2 birdcage-type hider to control muzzle flash and adjustable, two-position, gas piston-driven system for firing suppressed or unsuppressed, supported by hardened internal bearing rails. The Adaptive Combat Rifle (ACR) features a tool-less, quick-change barrel system available in 10.5 in., 14.5 in. and 16.5 in. and in multiple calibers. Free-floating MIl-STD 1913 monolithic top rail for optic mounting. Fully ambidextrous controls including magazine release, bolt catch and release, fire selector and nonreciprocating charging handle. High-impact composite handguard with heat shield; accepts rail inserts. High-impact composite lower receiver with textured magazine well and modular grip storage. Fire Control: Semi and full auto two-stage standard AR capable of accepting drop-in upgrade. Magazine: Optimized for MagPul PMAG Accepts standard NATO/M-16 magazines.
Price: Basic Folder Configuration $2,149.00
Price: ACR Enhanced $2,249.00

BUSHMASTER HEAVY-BARRELED CARBINE

Caliber: 5.56/.223. **Barrel:** 16 in. **Weights:** 6.93–7.28 lbs. **Length:** 32.5 in. overall. **Features:** AR-style carbine with chrome-lined heavy profile vanadium steel barrel, fixed or removable carry handle, six-position telestock.
Price: $895.00
Price: A3 with removable handle $1,420.00

BUSHMASTER 450 RIFLE AND CARBINE

Caliber: .450 Bushmaster. **Capacity:** 5-round magazine. **Barrels:** 20 in. (rifle), 16 in. (carbine). **Weights:** 8.3 lbs. (rifle), 8.1 lbs. (carbine). **Length:** 39.5 in. overall (rifle), 35.25 in. overall (carbine). **Features:** AR-style with chrome-lined chrome-moly barrel, synthetic stock, Izzy muzzle brake.
Price: Carbine $1,285.00
Price: Rifle..$1,300.00

BUSHMASTER TARGET

Caliber: 5.56/.223. **Capacity:** 30-round magazine. **Barrels:** 20 or 24 in. heavy or standard. **Weights:** 8.43–9.29 lbs. **Lengths:** 39.5or 43.5 **Features:** Semiauto AR-style with chrome-lined or stainless steel 1:9 in. twist barrel, fixed or removable carry handle, manganese phosphate finish.
Price: ....$969.00–$1,000.00

Prices given are believed to be accurate at time of publication however, many factors affect retail pricing so exact prices are not possible.

74TH EDITION, 2020 ✛ **353**

BUSHMASTER M4A3 TYPE CARBINE
Caliber: 5.56/.223. **Capacity:** 30-round magazine. **Barrel:** 16 in. **Weights:** 6.22–6.7 lbs. **Lengths:** 31–32.5 in. overall. **Features:** AR-style carbine with chrome-moly vanadium steel barrel, Izzy-type flash hider, six-position telestock, various sight options, standard or multi-rail handguard, fixed or removable carry handle.
Price: $1,100.00

BUSHMASTER QUICK RESPONSE CARBINE
Caliber: 5.56/223. **Capacity:** 10-round magazine. **Barrel:** 16 in. chrome moly superlight contour with Melonite finish. **Features:** Mini red-dot detachable sight, 6-position collapsible stock, A2-type flash hider. Introduced in 2016.
Price: $769.00

CENTURY INTERNATIONAL AES-10 HI-CAP
Caliber: 7.62x39mm. **Capacity:** 30-shot magazine. **Barrel:** 23.2 in. **Weight:** NA. **Length:** 41.5 in. overall. **Stock:** Wood grip, fore-end. **Sights:** Fixed notch rear, windage-adjustable post front. **Features:** RPK-style, accepts standard double-stack AK-type mags. Side-mounted scope mount, integral carry handle, bipod. Imported by Century Arms Int'l.
Price: AES-10, From $450.00

CENTURY INTERNATIONAL GP WASR-10 HI-CAP
Caliber: 7.62x39mm. **Capacity:** 30-round magazine. **Barrel:** 16.25 in. 1:10 right-hand twist. **Weight:** 7.2 lbs. **Length:** 34.25 in. overall. **Stock:** Wood laminate or composite, grip, fore-end. **Sights:** Fixed notch rear, windage-adjustable post front. **Features:** Two 30-rd. detachable box magazines, cleaning kit, bayonet. Version of AKM rifle; U.S. parts added for BATFE compliance. Threaded muzzle, folding stock, bayonet lug, compensator, Dragunov stock available. Made in Romania by Cugir Arsenal. Imported by Century Arms Int'l.
Price: GP WASR-10, From $670.00

CENTURY INTERNATIONAL M70AB2 SPORTER
Caliber: 7.62x39mm. **Capacity:** 30-shot magazine. **Barrel:** 16.25 in. **Weight:** 7.5 lbs. **Length:** 34.25 in. overall. **Stocks:** Metal grip, wood fore-end. **Sights:** Fixed notch rear, windage-adjustable post front. **Features:** Two 30-rd. double-stack magazine, cleaning kit, compensator, bayonet lug and bayonet. Paratrooper-style Kalashnikov with under-folding stock. Imported by Century Arms Int'l.
Price: M70AB2, From..$480.00

CMMG MK SERIES
Calibers: 5.56 NATO, .308 Win., 7.62x39, .300 BLK. This company manufactures a wide range of AR and AK style rifles and carbines. Many AR/AK options offered. Listed are several variations of CMMG's many models. Made in the USA.

Price: MK4 LEM .223..$995.00
Price: MK3 .308 ....$1,595.00
Price: MK47 AKS8 7.62x39 (shown) $1,650.00
Price: MK4 RCE .300 BLK $1,500.00

CMMG MKW ANVIL
Caliber: .458 SOCOM. **Barrel:** 16.1 in. CMMG SV Muzzle Brake. **Weight:** 7.5 lbs. **Stock:** M4 with A2 pistol grip, 6 position mil-spec receiver extension. Introduced in 2017.
Price: From $1,850.00

CMMG Mk4 DTR2
Caliber: .224 Valkyrie. **Capacity:** 10-round magazine (6.8 magazine). **Barrel:** 24 in. threaded. CMMG SV Muzzle Brake. **Weight:** 9.2 lbs. **Stock:** Magpul PRS with MOE Pistol grip4 with A2 pistol grip. **Features:** Model is engineered to deliver on this new cartridge's promise of long-range accuracy and high-energy performance.
Price: From $1,699.95

COLT LE6920 M4 CARBINE
Caliber: 5.56 NATO. **Barrel:** 16.1-in. chrome lined. **Sights:** Adjustable. Based on military M4. **Features:** Magpul MOE handguard, carbine stock, pistol grip, vertical grip. Direct gas/locking bolt operating system.
Price: From..$849.00–$1,099.00

COLT LE6940
Caliber: 5.56 NATO. Similar to LE1920 with Magpul MBUS backup sight, folding front, four accessory rails. One-piece monolithic upper receiver has continuous Mil-Spec rail from rear of upper to the front sight. Direct gas (LE6940) or articulating link piston (LE6940P) system.
Price: LE6940 ....$1,399.00

COLT L36960-CCU
Caliber: 5.56 NATO. **Capacity:** 30-round magazine. **Barrel:** 16-in. **Stock:** Magpul MOE SL with pistol grip. **Weight:** 6.7 lbs. **Features:** Combat Unit Carbine with 30-shot magazine. Aluminum receiver with black finish, mid-length gas system, optics ready.
Price: $1,299.00

COLT EXPANSE M4
Caliber: 5.56 NATO. **Capacity:** 30 rounds. **Barrel:** 16.1 in. **Sights:** Adjustable front post. Comes optics ready. **Weight:** 6.4 lbs. Flattop Picatinny rail. **Stock:** Adjustable M4 with A2-style grip. Economy priced AR. Introduced in 2016.
Price: $799.00

DANIEL DEFENSE AR SERIES
Caliber: 5.56 NATO/.223. **Capacity:** 20-round Magpul PMAG magazine. **Barrels:** 16 or 18 in.es. Flash suppressor. **Weight:** 7.4 lbs. **Lengths:** 34.75–37.85 in. overall. **Stock:** Glass-filled polymer with Soft Touch overmolding. Pistol grip. **Sights:** None. **Features:** Lower receiver is Mil-Spec with enhanced and flared magazine well, QD swivel attachment point. Upper receiver has M4 feed ramps. Lower and upper CNC machined of 7075-T6 aluminum, hard coat anodized. Shown is MK12, one of many AR variants offered by Daniel Defense. Made in the USA
Price: From..$1,599.00
Price: DD5VI 7.62/.308......................................$3,044.00
Price: DDM4V7 ....$1,729.00
Price: DDM4ISR .300 Blackout $3,135.00
Price: DDM4V11 ....$1,729.00-$1,999.00
Price: DDM4V9 ....$1,826.00-$1,999.00
Price: MK12 ....$2,162.00
Price: Ambush Camo......................................$1,946.00

DPMS VARMINT SERIES
Calibers: .204 Ruger, .223. **Barrels:** 16 in., 20 in. or 24 in. bull or fluted profile. **Weights:** 7.75–11.75 lbs. **Lengths:** 34.5–42.25 in. overall. **Stock:** Black Zytel composite. **Sights:** None. **Features:** Flattop receiver with Picatinny top rail; hardcoat anodized receiver; aluminum free-float tube handguard; many options. From DPMS Panther Arms.
Price: .... $939.00–$1,229.00

DPMS PRAIRIE PANTHER
Calibers: 5.56 NATO or 6.8 SPC. **Barrels:** 20-in. 416 stainless fluted heavy 1:8 in. barrel. **Features:** Phosphate steel bolt; free-floated carbon fiber handguard; flattop upper with Picatinny rail; aluminum lower; two 30-round magazines; skeletonized Zytel stock; Choice of matte black or one of several camo finishes.
Price: .... $1,269.00–$1,289.00

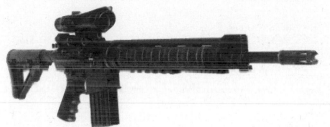

DPMS MK12
Caliber: .308 Win./7.62 NATO. **Barrel:** 18 in. **Weight:** 8.5 lbs. **Sights:** Midwest Industry flip-up. **Features:** 4-rail free floating handguard, flash hider, extruded 7029 T6 A3 Flattop receiver.
Price: $1,759.00

DPMS 3G2
Calibers: .223/5.56, 6.5 Creedmoor. **Barrel:** 16 in. **Weight:** 7.1 lbs. **Stock:** Magpul STR with Hogue rubber pistol grip. **Sights:** Magpul Gen 2 BUS. **Features:** Miculek Compensator, two-stage fire control. M111 Modular handguard allows placement of sights on top rail or 45-degree angle.
Price: From .... $1,129.00–$1,239.00

DPMS LITE HUNTER
Calibers: .243, .260 Rem., 6.5 Creedmoor, .308, .338 Federal. **Barrel:** 20 in. stainless. **Weight:** 8 pounds. **Stock:** Standard A2. **Features:** Two-stage match trigger. Hogue pistol grip. Optics ready top rail.
Price: $1,599.00

DPMS .300 AAC BLACKOUT
Caliber: .300 AAC Blackout. **Barrel:** 16-in. heavy 4150 chrome-lined. **Weight:** 7 pounds. **Stock:** Adjustable 6-position.
Price: $1,199.00

DPMS ORACLE
Calibers: .223/5.56 or .308/7.62. **Barrel:** 16 in. **Weights:** 6.2 (.223), 8.3 (308). Standard AR-15 fire control with A3 flattop receiver. **Finish:** Matte black or A-TACS camo.
Price: .223 ATACS $739, $849
Price: .308 ATACS $1,099, $1,189

DPMS GII SERIES
Caliber: .308 Win./7.62 NATO. **Barrels:** 16, 18 in. **Weight:** From 7.25 lbs. **Features:** promoted as the lightest .308 AR available. Features include new extractor and ejector systems, and improved steel feed ramp. New bolt geometry provides better lock-up and strength. Offered in several configurations.
Price: AP4 (shown) $1,499.00
Price: Recon $1,759.00
Price: SASS $2,379.00
Price: Hunter $1,699.00
Price: Bull $1,759.00
Price: MOE $1,599.00

DSA SA58 STANDARD
Caliber: .308 Win. **Barrel:** 21 in. bipod cut w/threaded flash hider. **Weight:** 8.75 lbs. **Length:** 43 in. **Stock:** Synthetic, X-Series or optional folding para stock. **Sights:** Elevation-adjustable post front, windage-adjustable rear peep. **Features:** Fully adjustable short gas system, high-grade steel or 416 stainless upper receiver. Many variants available. Made in USA by DSA, Inc.
Price: From $1,700.00

DSA SA58 CARBINE
Caliber: .308 Win. **Barrel:** 16.25 in. bipod cut w/threaded flash hider. **Features:** Carbine variation of FAL-style rifle. Other features identical to SA58 Standard model. Made in USA by DSA, Inc.
Price: $1,700.00

DSA SA58 TACTICAL CARBINE
Caliber: .308 Win. **Barrel:** 16.25 in. fluted with A2 flash hider. **Weight:** 8.25 lbs. **Length:** 36.5 in. **Stock:** Synthetic, X-Series or optional folding para stock. **Sights:** Elevation-adjustable post front, windage-adjustable match rear peep. **Features:** Shortened fully adjustable short gas system, high-grade steel or 416 stainless upper receiver. Made in USA by DSA, Inc.
Price: $1,975.00

DSA SA58 MEDIUM CONTOUR
Caliber: .308 Win. **Barrel:** 21 in. w/threaded flash hider. **Weight:** 9.75 lbs. **Length:** 43 in. **Stock:** Synthetic military grade. **Sights:** Elevation-adjustable post front, windage-adjustable match rear peep. **Features:** Gas-operated semiauto with fully adjustable gas system, high-grade steel receiver. Made in USA by DSA, Inc.
Price: $1,700.00

DSA ZM4 AR SERIES
Caliber: .223/5.56 NATO. **Weight:** 9 pounds. **Features:** Standard Flattop rifle features include 20-in., chrome moly heavy barrel with A2 flash hider. Mil-Spec forged lower receiver, forged flattop or A2 upper. Fixed A2 stock. Carbine variations are also available with 16-in. barrels and many options. WarZ series has premium match barrel, 5.56 match chamber developed by Marine Corps, and upgraded fire control group.
Price: Standard Flat-Top $820.00
Price: MRC Multi-Role Carbine....................................$1,275.00
Price: Mid Length Carbine $834.00
Price: Flat-Top with rail $850.00
Price: WarZ Series ....$865.00-$1,150.00

EXCEL ARMS X-SERIES
Caliber: .22 LR, 5.7x28mm (10 or 25-round); .30 Carbine (10 or 20-round magazine). 9mm (10 or 17 rounds). **Barrel:** 18 in. **Weight:** 6.25 lbs. **Length:** 34 to 38 in. **Features:** Available with or without adjustable iron sights. Blow-back action (5.57x28) or delayed blow-back (.30 Carbine).
Price: .22 LR $504.00
Price: 5.7x28 or 9mm.....................$795.00–$916.00

FN15 SERIES
Caliber: 5.56x45. **Capacity:** 20 or 30 rounds. **Barrels:** 16 in., 18 in., 20 in. **Features:** AR-style rifle/carbine series with most standard features and options.
Price: Tactical II (also in .300 BLK) $1,599.00
Price: Standard rifle $1,149.00
Price: Sporting $1,749.00
Price: DMR II $1,999.00
Price: Carbine $1,149.00
Price: Competition..$2,240.00
Price: Military Collector $1,749.00

FN 15 TACTICAL CARBINE FDA P-LOK
Caliber: 5.56x45mm. **Capacity:** 30-shot PMAG. **Barrel:** 16-in. free-floating and chrome-lined with FN 3-prong flash hider. **Stock:** B5 Systems buttstock and grip. **Weight:** 7.2 lbs. **Finish:** Flat Dark Earth. **Features:** P-LOK handguard, M-LOK accessory mounting system, hard anodized aluminum

flat-top receiver with Picatinny rail, forward assist.
Price: $1,499.00

FNH FNAR COMPETITION
Caliber: .308 Win. **Capacity:** 10-shot magazine. **Barrel:** 20 in. fluted. **Weight:** 8.9 lbs. **Length:** 41.25 in. overall. **Sights:** None furnished. Optical rail atop receiver, three accessory rails on fore-end. **Stock:** Adjustable for comb height, length of pull, cast-on and cast-off. Blue/gray laminate. Based on BAR design.
Price: $1,767.00

FNH SCAR 16S Caliber: 5.56mm/.223. **Capacities:** 10 or 30 rounds. **Barrel:** 16.25 in. **Weight:** 7.25 lbs. **Lengths:** 27.5–37.5 in. (extended stock). **Stock:** Telescoping, side-folding polymer. Adjustable cheekpiece, A2 style pistol grip. **Sights:** Adjustable folding front and rear. **Features:** Hard anodized aluminum receiver with four accessory rails. Ambidextrous safety and mag release. Charging handle can be mounted on right or left side. Semi-auto version of newest service rifle of U.S. Special Forces.
Price: $3,299.00

FNH SCAR 17S Caliber: 7.62x51 NATO/.308. **Capacities:** 10 or 30 rounds. **Barrel:** 16.25 in. **Weight:** 8 lbs. **Lengths:** 28.5–38.5 in. (extended stock). **Features:** Other features the same as SCAR 16S.
Price: $3,499.00

FNH SCAR 20S
Caliber: 7.62x51mm. **Capacities:** 10. **Barrel:** 20 in. **Weight:** 11.2 lbs. **Lengths:** 40.6-42.5 in. (extended stock). **Stock:** Precision adjustable for LOP, adjustable cheek piece, Hogue rubber pistol grip with finger grooves. Features: Hard anodized aluminum receiver with four accessory rails, two-stage match trigger, Semi-auto version of newest service rifle of U.S. Special Forces.
Price: $4,499.00

FRANKLIN ARMORY 3 GR-L Caliber: 5.56mm/.223. **Capacities:** 10 or 30 rounds. **Barrel:** 18 in. fluted with threaded muzzle crown. **Weight:** 7.25 lbs. **Stock:** Magpul PRS. Adjustable comb and length of pull. **Features:** Hard anodized Desert Smoke upper receiver with full-length Picatinny rail. One of many AR type rifles and carbines offered by this manufacturer. Made in the USA.
Price: $2,310.00

HECKLER & KOCH MODEL MR556A1

Caliber: .223 Remington/5.56 NATO. **Capacity:** 10+1. **Barrel:** 16.5 in. **Weight:** 8.9 lbs. **Lengths:** 33.9–37.68 in. **Stock:** Black synthetic adjustable. **Features:** Uses the gas piston system found on the HK 416 and G26, which does not introduce propellant gases and carbon fouling into the rifle's interior.

Price: $3,399.00

HECKLER & KOCH MODEL MR762A1

Caliber: Similar to Model MR556A1 except chambered for 7.62x51mm/.308 Win. cartridge. **Weight:** 10 lbs. w/empty magazine. **Lengths:** 36–39.5 in. **Features:** Variety of optional sights are available. Stock has five adjustable positions.

Price: $3,999.00

HECKLER & KOCH MODEL USC

Caliber: .45 ACP. **Capacity:** 10-round magazine. **Barrel:** 16 in. **Weight:** 6.13 lbs. **Length:** 35.4 in. **Features:** Polymer construction, adjustable rear sight, ambidextrous safety/selector, optional Picatinny rail. Civilian version of HK UMP submachine gun.

Price: $1,499.00

HI-POINT CARBINE SERIES

Calibers: .380 ACP, 9mm Para. .40 S&W, 10mm, (10-round magazine); .45 ACP (9-round). **Barrels:** 16.5 in. (17.5 in. for .40 S&W and .45). **Weight:** 4.5–7 lbs. **Length:** 31.5 in. overall. **Stock:** Black polymer, camouflage. **Sights:** Protected post front, aperture rear. Integral scope mount. **Features:** Grip-mounted magazine release. Black or chrome finish. Sling swivels. Available with laser or red-dot sights, RGB 4X scope, forward grip. Introduced 1996. Made in USA by MKS Supply, Inc.

Price: .380 ACP, From $315.00
Price: 9mm (995TS), From $315.00
Price: .40 S&W (4095TS), From $325.00
Price: .45 ACP (4595TS), From $349.00
Price: 10mm (1095TS), From $389.00

INLAND M1 1945 CARBINE

Caliber: .30 Carbine. **Capacity:** 15 rounds. **Barrel:** 18 in. **Weight:** 5 lbs. 3 oz. **Features:** A faithful reproduction of the last model that Inland manufactured in 1945, featuring a type 3 bayonet lug/barrel band, adjustable rear sight, push button safety, and walnut stock. Scout Model has 16.5-in. barrel, flash hider, synthetic stock with accessory rail. Made in the USA.

Price: $1,299.00
Price: Scout Model $1,449.00

JP ENTERPRISES LRP-07

Calibers: .308 Win., .260 Rem., 6.5 Creedmoor, .338 Federal. **Barrels:** 16–22 in., polished stainless with compensator. **Buttstock:** A2, ACE ARFX, Tactical Tactical Intent Carbine, Magpul MOE. **Grip:** Hogue Pistol Grip. **Features:** Machined upper and lower receivers with left-side charging system. MKIII Hand Guard. Adjustable gas system.

Price: From $3,299.00

JP ENTERPRISES JP-15

Calibers: .223, .204 Ruger, 6.5 Grendel, .300 Blackout, .22 LR. **Barrels:** 18 or 24-in. **Buttstock:** Synthetic modified thumbhole or laminate thumbhole. **Grip:** Hogue Pistol grip. Basic AR-type general-purpose rifle with numerous options.

Price: From $1,999.00

KALASHNIKOV USA

Caliber: 7.62x39mm. **Capacity:** 30-round magazine. AK-47 series made in the USA in several variants and styles. **Barrel:** 16.25 in. **Weight:** 7.52 lbs.

Price: KR-9 Side-folding stock $1,249.00
Price: US132S Synthetic stock $799.00
Price: US132W Wood carbine $836.00

KEL-TEC RFB

Caliber: 7.62 NATO/.308. 20-round FAL-type magazine. **Barrel:** 18 in. with threaded muzzle, A2-style flash hider. **Weight:** 8 lbs. **Features:** A bullpup short-stroke gas piston operated carbine with ambidextrous controls, reversible operating handle, Mil-Spec Picatinny rail.

Price: $1,927.00

KEL-TEC SU-16 SERIES

Caliber: 5.56 NATO/.223. **Capacity:** 10-round magazine. **Barrels:** 16 or 18.5 in. **Weights:** 4.5–5 lbs. **Features:** Offering in several rifle and carbine variations.

Price: From .... $682.00–$900.00

LARUE TACTICAL OBR

Calibers: 5.56 NATO/.223, 7.62 NATO/.308 Win., .260 Rem. **Barrels:** 16.1 in., 18 in. or 20 in. **Weights:** 7.5–9.25 lbs. **Features:** Manufacturer of several models of AR-style rifles and carbines. Optimized Battle Rifle (OBR) series is made in both NATO calibers. Many AR-type options available. Made in the USA.

Price: OBR 5.56 .... $2,245.00
Price: OBR 7.62, .260 .... $3,370.00

LEWIS MACHINE & TOOL (LMT)

Calibers: 5.56 NATO/.223, 7.62 NATO/.308 Win. **Barrels:** 16.1 in., 18 in. or 20 in. **Weights:** 7.5–9.25 lbs. **Features:** Manufacturer of a wide range of AR-style carbines with many options. SOPMOD stock, gas piston operating system, monolithic rail platform, tactical sights. Sharpshooter Weapons System includes Harris Bipod and case, eight 20-shot magazines, FDE finish. Made in the USA by Lewis Machine & Tool.

Price: Standard 16 .... $1,649.00
Price: Comp 16, flattop receiver $1,685.00
Price: CQB Series from $2,399.00
Price: Sharpshooter Weapons System $6,499.00
Price: Valkyrie $2,299.00
Price: 6.5 Long Range $2,999.00

Prices given are believed to be accurate at time of publication however, many factors affect retail pricing so exact prices are not possible.

74TH EDITION, 2020 ✛ **357**

LWRC INTERNATIONAL M6 SERIES

Calibers: 5.56 NATO, .224 Valkyrie, .6.5 Creedmoor, 6.8 SPC, 7.62x51mm, .300 BLK. **Capacity:** 30-shot magazine. Features: This company makes a complete line of AR-15 type rifles operated by a short-stroke, gas piston system. A wide variety of stock, sight and finishes are available. Colors include black, Flat Dark Earth, Olive Drab Green, Patriot Brown.

Price: M6-SPR (Special Purpose Rifle) $2,479.00
Price: REPR (Shown).. $5,139.00
Price: SIX8 A5 6.8 SPC.............................. $2,600.00–$2,750.00
Price: IC-DI 224 Valkyrie $1,995.00

MOSSBERG MMR SERIES

Caliber: 5.56 NATO. **Capacity:** 10 or 30 rounds. GIO system. **Barrel:** 16 or 18 in. with A2-style muzzle brake. **Features:** Picatinny rail, black synthetic stock, free-floating stainless barrel. Offered in several variants. Pro and Optics Ready have JM Pro match trigger. Optics Ready has 6-position stock with FLEX pad, Magpul MOE grip and trigger guard. Introduced in 2016.

Price: MMR Carbine... $938.00
Price: MMR Tactical Optics Ready................................ $1,253.00
Price: MMR Pro... $1,393.00

ROCK RIVER ARMS LAR SERIES

Calibers: 204 Ruger, .223/5.56, .243 Win., 6.5 Creedmoor, .300 AAC Blackout, 7.62x39mm, .308/7.62, 6.8 SPC, .450 Bushmaster, .458 SOCOM, 9mm and .40 S&W. **Features:** These AR-15 type rifles and carbines are available with a very wide range of options. Virtually any AR configuration is offered including tactical, hunting and competition models. Some models are available in left-hand versions.

Price: .... $760.00–$2,200.00

RUGER AR-556

Caliber: 5.56 NATO, .350 Legend, .450 Bushmaster. **Capacity:** 30-round magazine (5.56), 5 rounds (.350 and .450). **Features:** Basic AR M4-style Modern Sporting Rifle with direct impingement operation, forged aluminum upper and lower receivers, and cold hammer-forged chrome-moly steel barrel with M4 feed ramp cuts. Other features include Ruger Rapid Deploy folding rear sight, milled F-height gas block with post front sight, telescoping 6-position stock and one 30-round Magpul magazine. Introduced in 2015. MPR (Multi Purpose Rifle) model has 18-in. barrel with muzzle brake, flat-top upper, 15-in. free-floating handguard with Magpul M-LOK accessory slots, Magpul MOE SL collapsible buttstock and MOE grip.

Price: $799.00
Price: MPR (5.56) $899.00
Price: MPR (.350 Legend, .450 Bushmaster) $1,099.00

RUGER PC CARBINE

Caliber: 9mm, .40 S&W. **Capacity:** 17 rounds (9mm), 15 (.40). Interchangeable magazine wells for Ruger and Glock magazines. **Barrel:** 16.12-in. threaded and fluted. **Stock:** Glass-filled nylon synthetic. **Sights:** Adjustable ghost-ring rear, protected-blade front. **Weight:** 6.8 lbs. **Features:** Reversible magazine release and charging handle. Dead-blow action reduces felt recoil. Receiver has integrated Picatinny rail. Available with aluminum free-floating handguard.

Price: $649.00
Price: With handguard... $729.00

RUGER MINI-14 RANCH RIFLE

Calibers: .223 Rem., .300 Blackout (Tactical Rifle). **Capacity:** 5-shot or 20-shot detachable box magazine. **Barrel:** 18.5 in. Rifling twist 1:9 in. **Weights:** 6.75–7 lbs. **Length:** 37.25 in. overall. **Stocks:** American hardwood, steel reinforced, or synthetic. **Sights:** Protected blade front, fully adjustable Ghost Ring rear. **Features:** Fixed piston gas-operated, positive primary extraction. New buffer system, redesigned ejector system. Ruger S100RM scope rings included on Ranch Rifle. Heavier barrels added in 2008, 20-round magazine added in 2009.

Price: Mini-14/5, Ranch Rifle, blued, wood stock $999.00
Price: K-Mini-14/5, Ranch Rifle, stainless, scope rings $1,069.00
Price: Mini-14 Tactical Rifle: Similar to Mini-14 but with 16.12 in. barrel with flash hider, black synthetic stock, adjustable sights $1,019.00

RUGER MINI THIRTY

Caliber: Similar to the Mini-14 rifle except modified to chamber the 7.62x39 Russian service round. **Weight:** 6.75 lbs. **Barrel:** Has 6-groove barrel with 1:10 in. twist. **Features:** Ruger Integral Scope Mount bases and protected blade front, fully adjustable Ghost Ring rear. Detachable 5-shot staggered box magazine. 20-round magazines available. Stainless or matte black alloy w/synthetic stock. Introduced 1987.

Price: Matte black finish $1,069.00
Price: Stainless $1,089.00
Price: Stainless w/20-round mag $1,139.00

SAVAGE MSR 15/MSR 10

Calibers: AR-style series chambered in 5.56 NATO (Patrol and Recon), 6.5 Creedmoor or .308 Win. (MSR 10 Hunter and Long Range). **Barrels:** 16.1 in. (Patrol and Recon), 16 or 18 in. (Hunter), 20 or 22 in. (Long Range). Wylde

chamber on Patrol and Recon models. Hunter and Long Range models have muzzle brake.

Price: Patrol **$869.00**
Price: Recon (shown) **$994.00**
Price: MSR 10 Long Range **$2,284.00**
Price: MSR 10 Hunter...................................... **$1,481.00**

SIG-SAUER MCX VIRTUS PATROL

Calibers: 5.56 NATO, 7.62x39mm or .300 Blackout. **Features:** AR-style rifle. Modular system allows switching between calibers with conversion kit. Features include a 16 in. barrel, aluminum KeyMod handguards, ambi controls and charging handle, choice of side-folding or telescoping stock, auto-regulating gas system to all transition between subsonic and supersonic loads.
Price: **$2,233.00**

SIG 516 PATROL

Caliber: 5.56 NATO. **Features:** AR-style rifle with included 30-round magazine, 16-in. chrome-lined barrel with muzzle brake; free-floating, aluminum quad Picatinny rail, Magpul MOE adjustable stock, black anodized or Flat Dark Earth finish, various configurations available.
Price: From.. **$1,888.00**

SIG-SAUER SIG716 TACTICAL PATROL

Caliber: 7.62 NATO/.308 Win., 6.5 Creedmoor. **Features:** AR-10 type rifle. Gas-piston operation with 3-round-position (4-position optional) gas valve; 16-, 18- or 20-in. chrome-lined barrel with threaded muzzle and nitride finish; free-floating aluminum quad rail fore-end with four M1913 Picatinny rails; telescoping buttstock; lower receiver is machined from a 7075-T6 Aircraft grade aluminum forging; upper receiver, machined from 7075-T6 aircraft grade aluminum with integral M1913 Picatinny rail. DMR has free-floating barrel, two-stage match-grade trigger, short-stroke pushrod operating system.
Price: **$2,385.00**
Price: Designated Marksman (DMR) **$3,108.00**

SIG-SAUER M400

Caliber: 5.56 NATO. AR-style rifle with Direct Impingement system, 20-in. chrome-lined barrel with muzzle brake; free-floating M-LOK handguard with lightening cuts, 3-chamber compensator, Magpul SLK 6-position adjustable stock, various configurations available.
Price: **$900.00**

SIG-SAUER MPX PCC

Caliber: 9mm. 30-round capacity. **Barrel:** 16 in. **Features:** M-LOK handguard, 5-position folding telescoping stock. **Weight:** 6.6 lbs. Sights: none.
Price: From **$2,016.00**

SMITH & WESSON M&P15

Caliber: 5.56mm NATO/.223. **Capacity:** 30-shot steel magazine. **Barrel:** 16 in., 1:9 in. twist. **Weight:** 6.74 lbs., w/o magazine. **Lengths:** 32–35 in. overall. **Stock:** Black synthetic. **Sights:** Adjustable post front sight, adjustable dual aperture rear sight. **Features:** 6-position telescopic stock, thermo-set M4 handguard. 14.75 in. sight radius. 7-lbs. (approx.) trigger pull. 7075 T6 aluminum upper, 4140 steel barrel. Chromed barrel bore, gas key, bolt carrier. Hard-coat black-anodized receiver and barrel finish. OR (Optics Ready) model has no sights. TS model has Magpul stock and folding sights. Made in USA by Smith & Wesson.
Price: Sport Model................................. **$739.00**
Price: OR Model................................... **$1,069.00**

Price: TS model **$1,569.00**

SMITH & WESSON M&P15-300

Calibers: .300 Whisper/.300 AAC Blackout. **Features:** Other specifications the same of 5.56 models.
Price: **$1,119.00**

SMITH & WESSON MODEL M&P15 VTAC II

Caliber: .223 Remington/5.56 NATO. **Capacity:** 30-round magazine. **Barrel:** 16 in. **Weight:** 6.5 lbs. **Length:** 35 in. extended, 32 in. collapsed, overall. **Features:** Six-position stock. Surefire flash-hider and G2 light with VTAC light mount; VTAC/JP handguard; Geissele Super-V trigger; three adjustable Picatinny rails; VTAC padded two-point adjustable sling.
Price: **$1,949.00**

SMITH & WESSON M&P15PC CAMO

Caliber: 223 Rem/5.56 NATO, A2 configuration. **Capacity:** 10-round magazine. **Barrel:** 20 in. stainless with 1:8 in. twist. **Weight:** 8.2 lbs. **Length:** 38.5 in. overall. **Features:** AR-style, no sights but integral front and rear optics rails. Two-stage trigger, aluminum lower. Finished in Realtree Advantage Max-1 camo.
Price: **$1,589.00**

SMITH & WESSON M&P10

Caliber: .308 Win., 6.5 Creedmoor. **Capacity:** 10 rounds. **Barrel:** 18-20 in. **Weight:** 7.7 pounds. **Features:** Magpul MOE stock with MOE Plus grip, 15-in. free-float Troy M-LOK handguard, black hard anodized finish. Camo finish hunting model available w/5-round magazine.
Price: .308.. **$1,619.00**
Price: 6.5 Creedmoor.................................... **$2,035.00**

SPRINGFIELD ARMORY M1A

Caliber: 7.62mm NATO (.308). **Capacities:** 5- or 10-shot box magazine. **Barrel:** 25.062 in. with flash suppressor, 22 in. without suppressor. **Weight:** 9.75 lbs. **Length:** 44.25 in. overall. **Stock:** American walnut with walnut-colored heat-resistant fiberglass handguard. Matching walnut handguard available. Also available with fiberglass stock. **Sights:** Military, square blade front, full click-adjustable aperture rear. **Features:** Commercial equivalent of the U.S. M-14 service rifle with no provision for automatic firing. From Springfield Armory.
Price: SOCOM 16............................... **$1,987.00**
Price: Scout Squad, From **$1,850.00**
Price: Standard M1A, From **$1,685.00**
Price: Loaded Standard, From **$1,847.00**
Price: National Match, From **$2,434.00**
Price: Super Match (heavy premium barrel) about **$2,965.00**
Price: Tactical, From .... **$3,619.00–$4,046.00**

SPRINGFIELD ARMORY SAINT

Caliber: 5.56 NATO. **Capacity:** 30-round magazine. **Barrel:** 16 in., 1:8 twist. **Weight:** 6 lbs., 11 oz. **Sights:** AR2-style fixed post front, flip-up aperture rear. **Features:** Mid-length gas system, BCM 6-position stock, Mod 3 grip PMT KeyMod handguard 7075 T6 aluminum receivers. Springfield Armory's first entry into AR category. Introduced 2016.
Price: **$899.00**

Prices given are believed to be accurate at time of publication however, many factors affect retail pricing so exact prices are not possible.

74TH EDITION, 2020 ✦ **359**

STAG ARMS AR-STYLE SERIES
Calibers: 5.56 NATO/.223, 6.8 SPC. **Capacities:** 20- or 30-shot magazine. **Features:** This manufacturer offers more than 25 AR-style rifles or carbines with many optional features including barrel length and configurations, stocks, sights, rail systems and both direct impingement and gas piston operating systems. Left-hand models are available on some products. Listed is a sampling of Stag Arms models.
Price: Model 15 Tactical $969.99
Price: Model 15L Tactical $1,019.99
Price: Model 15 Bones $539.99
Price: Model 15 SBR $999.99
Price: Model 15L ORC $619.99
Price: Model 15 L LEO $1,114.99
Price: Model 15 M4 .... $649.99

STONER SR-15 MOD2 LPR
Caliber: .223. **Capacity:** 30-round magazine. **Barrel:** 18 in., free-floated inside M-LOK URSx handguard. **Weight:** 7.6 lbs. **Length:** 38 in. overall. **Stock:** Mag-Pul MOE. **Sights:** Post front, fully adjustable rear (300-meter sight). **Features:** URX-4 upper receiver; two-stage trigger, 30-round magazine. Black finish. Made in USA by Knight's Mfg.
Price: $2,700.00

STONER SR-25 ACC E2
Caliber: 7.62 NATO. **Capacities:** 10- or 20-shot steel magazine. **Barrel:** 16 in. with flash hider. **Weight:** 8.5 lbs. **Features:** Shortened, non-slip handguard; drop-in two-stage match trigger, removable carrying handle, ambidextrous controls, matte black finish. Made in USA by Knight's Mfg. Co.
Price: $4,900.00

WILSON COMBAT TACTICAL
Caliber: .204 Ruger, 5.56mm NATO, .223 Wylde, .22 Nosler, .260 Rem., 6.8 SPC, .300 Blackout, .300 Ham'r, 7.62x40mm WT, .338 Federal, .358 Win. **Capacity:** Accepts all M-16/AR-15 Style Magazines, includes one 20-round magazine. **Barrel:** 16.25 in., 1:9 in. twist, match-grade fluted. **Weight:** 6.9 lbs. **Length:** 36.25 in. overall. **Stock:** Fixed or collapsible. **Features:** Free-float ventilated aluminum quad-rail handguard, Mil-Spec Parkerized barrel and steel components, anodized receiver, precision CNC-machined upper and lower receivers, 7075 T6 aluminum forgings. Single-stage JP Trigger/Hammer Group, Wilson Combat Tactical muzzle brake, nylon tactical rifle case. Made in USA by Wilson Combat.
Price: Protector, Ranger $2,000.00
Price: Recon Tactical from $2,225.00
Price: Hunter from $2,365.00
Price: Ultimate, Ultralight Hunter $3,210.00
Price: Super Sniper $3,020.00
Price: Urban Sniper $2,200.00
Price: Ultralight Ranger $2,750.00

BIG HORN ARMORY MODEL 89 RIFLE AND CARBINE
Caliber: .500 S&W Mag. **Capacities:** 5- or 7-round magazine. **Features:** Lever-action rifle or carbine chambered for .500 S&W Magnum. 22- or 18-in. barrel; walnut or maple stocks with pistol grip; aperture rear and blade front sights; recoil pad; sling swivels; enlarged lever loop; magazine capacity 5 (rifle) or 7 (carbine) rounds.
Price: $2,424.00

BIG HORN ARMORY MODEL 89B RIFLE AND CARBINE
Caliber: .475 Linebaugh. **Capacities:** 7-round magazine. **Barrel:** 16, 18 or 22-in. barrel. **Stock:** walnut or laminate buttstock and fore-end with pistol grip. **Sights:** Aperture rear and blade front. Features: Color case hardened finish.
Price: $3,699.00

BIG HORN ARMORY MODEL 90 SERIES
Calibers: .460 S&W, .454 Casull. Features similar to Model 89. Several wood and finish upgrades available.
Price: .460 S&W $2,849.00
Price: .454 Casull, .45 Colt $3,049.00
Price: .500 Linebaugh $3,699.00

BROWNING BLR
Features: Lever action with rotating bolt head, multiple-lug breech bolt with recessed bolt face, side ejection. Rack-and-pinion lever. Flush-mounted detachable magazines, with 4+1 capacity for magnum cartridges, 5+1 for standard rounds. **Barrel:** Button-rifled chrome-moly steel with crowned muzzle. **Stock:** Buttstocks and fore-ends are American walnut with grip and forend checkering. Recoil pad installed. **Trigger:** Wide-groove design, trigger travels with lever. Half-cock hammer safety; fold-down hammer. **Sights:** Gold bead on ramp front; low-profile square-notch adjustable rear. **Features:** Blued barrel and receiver, high-gloss wood finish. Receivers are drilled and tapped for scope mounts, swivel studs included. Action lock provided. Introduced 1996. Imported from Japan by Browning.

BROWNING BLR LIGHTWEIGHT W/PISTOL GRIP, SHORT AND LONG ACTION; LIGHTWEIGHT '81, SHORT AND LONG ACTION
Calibers: Short Action, 20 in. Barrel: .22-250 Rem., .243 Win., 7mm-08 Rem., .308 Win., .358, .450 Marlin. **Calibers: Short Action, 22 in. Barrel:** .270 WSM, 7mm WSM, .300 WSM, .325 WSM. **Calibers: Long Action 22 in. Barrel:** .270 Win., .30-06. **Calibers: Long Action 24 in. Barrel:** 7mm Rem Mag., .300 Win. Mag. **Weights:** 6.5–7.75 lbs. **Lengths:** 40–45 in. overall. **Stock:** New checkered pistol grip and Schnabel forearm. Lightweight '81 differs from Pistol Grip models with a Western-style straight grip stock and banded forearm. Lightweight w/Pistol Grip Short Action and Long Action introduced 2005. Model '81 Lightning Long Action introduced 1996.
Price: Lightweight w/Pistol Grip Short Action, From.....................$1,040.00
Price: Lightweight w/Pistol Grip Long Action $1,100.00
Price: Lightweight '81 Short Action $990.00
Price: Lightweight '81 Long Action $1,040.00
Price: Lightweight '81 Takedown Short Action, From $1,040.00
Price: Lightweight '81 Takedown Long Action, From $1,120.00
Price: Lightweight stainless $1,120.00
Price: Stainless Takedown $1,260.00

CHIAPPA MODEL 1892 RIFLE
Calibers: .38 Special/357 Magnum, .38-40, .44-40, .44 Mag., .45 Colt. **Barrels:** 16 in. (Trapper), 20 in. round and 24 in. octagonal (Takedown). **Weight:** 7.7 lbs. **Stock:** Walnut. **Sights:** Blade front, buckhorn. Trapper model has interchangeable front sight blades. **Features:** Finishes are blue/case colored. Magazine capacity is 12 rounds with 24 in. bbl.; 10 rounds with 20 in. barrel; 9 rounds in 16 in. barrel. Mare's Leg models have 4-shot magazine, 9- or 12-in. barrel.
Price: From $1,329.00
Price: Takedown..$1,435.00
Price: Trapper $1,329.00
Price: Mare's Leg, from...$1,288.00

CHIAPPA MODEL 1886
Caliber: .45-70. **Barrels:** 16, 18.5, 22, 26 in. Replica of famous Winchester model offered in several variants.

Price: Rifle..$1,709.00
Price: Carbine $1,629.00
Price: Kodiak $1,909.00

CIMARRON 1860 HENRY CIVIL WAR MODEL
Calibers: .44 WCF, .45 LC. **Capacity:** 12-round magazine. **Barrel:** 24 in. (rifle). **Weight:** 9.5 lbs. **Length:** 43 in. overall (rifle). **Stock:** European walnut. **Sights:** Bead front, open adjustable rear. **Features:** Brass receiver and buttplate. Uses original Henry loading system. Copy of the original rifle. Charcoal blued finish optional. Introduced 1991. Imported by Cimarron F.A. Co.
Price: From..$1,495.00

CIMARRON 1866 WINCHESTER REPLICAS
Calibers: .38 Special, .357 Magnum, .45 LC, .32 WCF, .38 WCF, .44 WCF. **Barrels:** 24 in. (rifle), 20 in. (short rifle), 19 in. (carbine), 16 in. (trapper). **Weight:** 9 lbs. **Length:** 43 in. overall (rifle). **Stock:** European walnut. **Sights:** Bead front, open adjustable rear. **Features:** Solid brass receiver, buttplate, fore-end cap. Octagonal barrel. Copy of the original Winchester '66 rifle. Introduced 1991. Imported by Cimarron F.A. Co.
Price: 1866 Sporting Rifle, 24 in. barrel, From $1,255.00
Price: 1866 Short Rifle, 20 in. barrel, From $1,255.00
Price: 1866 Carbine, 19 in. barrel, From $1,331.00
Price: 1866 Trapper, 16 in. barrel, From $1,235.00

CIMARRON 1873 SHORT RIFLE
Calibers: .357 Magnum, .38 Special, .32 WCF, .38 WCF, .44 Special, .44 WCF, .45 Colt. **Barrel:** 20 in. tapered octagon. **Weight:** 7.5 lbs. **Length:** 39 in. overall. **Stock:** Walnut. **Sights:** Bead front, adjustable semi-buckhorn rear. **Features:** Has half "button" magazine. Original-type markings, including caliber, on barrel and elevator and "Kings" patent. Trapper Carbine (.357 Mag., .44 WCF, .45 Colt). From Cimarron F.A. Co.
Price: $1,299.00
Price: Trapper Carbine 16-in. bbl. $1,352.00

CIMARRON 1873 DELUXE SPORTING
Similar to the 1873 Short Rifle except has 24-in. barrel with half-magazine.
Price: $1,485.00

CIMARRON 1873 LONG RANGE SPORTING
Calibers: .44 WCF, .45 Colt. **Barrel:** 30 in., octagonal. **Weight:** 8.5 lbs. **Length:** 48 in. overall. **Stock:** Walnut. **Sights:** Blade front, semi-buckhorn ramp rear. Tang sight optional. **Features:** Color casehardened frame; choice of modern blued-black or charcoal blued for other parts. Barrel marked "Kings Improvement." From Cimarron F.A. Co.
Price: $1,385.00

EMF 1866 YELLOWBOY LEVER ACTIONS
Calibers: .38 Special, .44-40, .45 LC. **Barrels:** 19 in. (carbine), 24 in. (rifle). **Weight:** 9 lbs. **Length:** 43 in. overall (rifle). **Stock:** European walnut. **Sights:** Bead front, open adjustable rear. **Features:** Solid brass frame, blued barrel, lever, hammer, buttplate. Imported from Italy by EMF.
Price: Rifle..$1,175.00

EMF MODEL 1873 LEVER-ACTION
Calibers: .32/20, .357 Magnum, .38/40, .44-40, .45 Colt. **Barrels:** 18 in., 20 in., 24 in., 30 in. **Weight:** 8 lbs. **Length:** 43.25 in. overall. **Stock:** European walnut. **Sights:** Bead front, rear adjustable for windage and elevation. **Features:** Color casehardened frame (blued on carbine). Imported by EMF.
Price: $1,250.00

HENRY ORIGINAL RIFLE

Caliber: .44-40, .45 Colt. **Capacity:** 13-round magazine. **Barrel:** 24 in. **Weight:** 9 lbs. **Stock:** Straight-grip fancy American walnut with hardened brass buttplate. **Sights:** Folding ladder rear with blade front. **Finish:** Hardened brass receiver with blued steel barrel. **Features:** Virtually identical to the original 1860 version except for the caliber. Each serial number has prefix " BTH" in honor of Benjamin Tyler Henry, the inventor of the lever-action repeating rifle that went on to become the most legendary firearm in American history. Introduced in 2014 by Henry Repeating Arms. Made in the USA.
Price: $2,415.00
Price: Deluxe Engraved Edition $3,670.00
Price: Silver Deluxe Engraved Edition $3,817.00

HENRY .45-70

Caliber: .45-70. **Capacity:** 4-round magazine. **Barrel:** 18.5 in. **Weight:** 7 lbs. **Stock:** Pistol grip walnut. **Sights:** XS Ghost Rings with blade front.
Price: $850.00

HENRY HENRY SIDE GATE LEVER ACTION

Caliber: .30-30, .35 Rem., .38-55. **Capacity:** 5-round magazine. **Barrel:** 20 in. **Weight:** 7 lbs. **Stock:** Pistol grip walnut. **Sights:** Semi-buckhorn rear, ivory bead front. Removable tube magazine plus side loading gate.
Price: $1,045.00

HENRY BIG BOY LEVER-ACTION CARBINE

Calibers: .327 Fed. Magnum, .357 Magnum/.38 Special, .41 Magnum, .44 Magnum/.44 Special, .45 Colt. **Capacity:** 10-shot tubular magazine. **Barrel:** 20 in. octagonal, 1:38 in. right-hand twist. **Weight:** 8.68 lbs. **Length:** 38.5 in. overall. **Stock:** Straight-grip American walnut, brass buttplate. **Sights:** Marbles fully adjustable semi-buckhorn rear, brass bead front. **Features:** Brasslite receiver not tapped for scope mount. Available in several Deluxe, engraved and other special editions. All Weather has round barrel, hardwood stock, chrome satin finish. Made in USA by Henry Repeating Arms.
Price: $945.00
Price: All Weather $1,050.00
Price: Engraved Special Editions from $1,470.00

HENRY .30/30 LEVER-ACTION CARBINE

Same as the Big Boy except has straight grip American walnut, .30-30 only, 6-shot. Receivers are drilled and tapped for scope mount. Made in USA by Henry Repeating Arms.
Price: H009 Blued receiver, round barrel $893.00
Price: H009B Brass receiver, octagonal barrel $998.00

HENRY LONG RANGER

Calibers: .223 Rem., .243 Win., 6.5 Creedmoor, 308 Win. **Capacities:** 5 (.223), 4 (.243, .308). **Barrel:** 20 in. **Stock:** Straight grip, checkered walnut with buttpad, oil finish, swivel studs. **Features:** Geared action, side ejection, chromed steel bolt with 6 lugs, flush fit detachable magazine.
Price: $1,066.00
Price: Deluxe Engraved model $1,850.00

MARLIN MODEL 336C LEVER-ACTION CARBINE

Calibers: .30-30 or .35 Rem. **Capacity:** 6-shot tubular magazine. **Barrel:** 20 in. Micro-Groove. **Weight:** 7 lbs. **Length:** 38.5 in. overall. **Stock:** Checkered American black walnut, capped pistol grip. Mar-Shield finish; rubber buttpad; swivel studs. **Sights:** Ramp front with wide-scan hood, semi-buckhorn folding rear adjustable for windage and elevation. **Features:** Hammer-block safety. Receiver tapped for scope mount, offset hammer spur; top of receiver sandblasted to prevent glare. Includes safety lock. The latest variation of Marlin's classic lever gun that originated in 1937.
Price: $635.00
Price: Curly Maple stock $899.00

MARLIN MODEL 336SS LEVER-ACTION CARBINE

Caliber: .30-30 only. **Capacity:** 6-shot. **Features:** Same as the 336C except receiver, barrel and other major parts are machined from stainless steel. receiver tapped for scope. Includes safety lock.
Price: $779.00

MARLIN MODEL 336W LEVER-ACTION

Similar to the Model 336C except has walnut-finished, cut-checkered Maine birch stock; blued steel barrel band has integral sling swivel; no front sight hood; comes with padded nylon sling; hard rubber buttplate. Introduced 1998. Includes safety lock. Made in USA by Marlin.
Price: $548.00

MARLIN 336BL

Caliber: .30-30. **Capacity:** 6-shot full-length tubular magazine. **Barrel:** 18-in. blued with Micro-Groove rifling (12 grooves). **Features:** Lever-action rifle. Finger lever; side ejection; blued steel receiver; hammer block safety; brown laminated hardwood pistol-grip stock with fluted comb; cut checkering; deluxe recoil pad; blued swivel studs.
Price: $667.00

MARLIN MODEL 336XLR

Caliber: .30-30. **Features:** Similar to Model 336C except has a 24-in. stainless barrel with Ballard-type cut rifling, stainless steel receiver and other parts, laminated hardwood stock with pistol grip, nickel-plated swivel studs. Chambered for .30-30 Win. with Hornady spire-pointed Flex-Tip cartridges. Includes safety lock. Introduced 2006.
Price: Model 336XLR $969.00

MARLIN MODEL 1894C

Caliber: .44 Special/.44 Magnum, 10-round tubular magazine. **Barrel:** 20 in. Ballard-type rifling. **Weight:** 6 lbs. **Length:** 37.5 in. overall. **Stock:** Checkered American black walnut, straight grip and fore-end. Mar-Shield finish. Rubber rifle buttpad; swivel studs. **Sights:** Wide-Scan hooded ramp front, semi-buckhorn folding rear adjustable for windage and elevation. **Features:** Hammer-block safety. Receiver tapped for scope mount, offset hammer spur, solid top receiver sandblasted to prevent glare. Includes safety lock.
Price: $789.00

MARLIN MODEL 1894 COWBOY

Calibers: .357 Magnum, .44 Magnum, .45 Colt. **Capacity:** 10-round magazine. **Barrel:** 20 in. tapered octagon, deep cut rifling. **Weight:** 7.5 lbs. **Length:** 41.5 in. overall. **Stock:** Straight grip American black walnut, hard rubber buttplate, Mar-Shield finish. **Sights:** Marble carbine front, adjustable Marble semi-buckhorn rear. **Features:** Squared finger lever; straight grip stock; blued steel fore-end tip. Designed for Cowboy Shooting events. Introduced 1996. Includes safety lock. Made in USA by Marlin.
Price: $1,093.00

MARLIN 1894 DELUXE

Caliber: .44 Magnum/.44 Special. **Capacity:** 10-shot tubular magazine. **Features:** Squared finger lever; side ejection; richly polished deep blued metal surfaces; solid top receiver; hammer block safety; #1 grade fancy American black walnut straight-grip stock and fore-end; cut checkering; rubber rifle buttpad; Mar-Shield finish; blued steel fore-end cap: swivel studs; deep-cut Ballard-type rifling (6 grooves).
Price: $950.00

MARLIN 1894 SBL
Caliber: .44 Magnum. **Capacity:** 6-round tubular magazine. **Features:** 16.5-in. barrel, laminated stock, stainless finish, large lever, accessory rail, XS Ghost Ring sights.
Price: $1,146.00

MARLIN MODEL 1895 LEVER-ACTION
Caliber: .45-70 Govt. **Capacity:** 4-shot tubular magazine. **Barrel:** 22 in. round. **Weight:** 7.5 lbs. **Length:** 40.5 in. overall. **Stock:** Checkered American black walnut, full pistol grip. Mar-Shield finish; rubber buttpad; quick detachable swivel studs. **Sights:** Bead front with Wide-Scan hood, semi-buckhorn folding rear adjustable for windage and elevation. **Features:** Hammer-block safety. Solid receiver tapped for scope mounts or receiver sights; offset hammer spur. Includes safety lock.
Price: $745.00

MARLIN MODEL 1895G GUIDE GUN LEVER-ACTION
Similar to Model 1895 with deep-cut Ballard-type rifling; straight-grip walnut stock. Overall length is 37 in., weighs 7 lbs. Introduced 1998. Includes safety lock. Made in USA by Marlin.
Price: $750.00

MARLIN MODEL 1895 TRAPPER
Similar to Model 1895 with deep-cut Ballard-type rifling, threaded muzzle, pistol-grip black synthetic stock with large-loop lever, matte black finish. **Barrel:** 16.5 in. **Overall length:** 35 in. **Weight:** 7 lbs. **Sights:** Skinner peep, blade front..
Price: $1,123.00

MARLIN MODEL 1895 DARK SERIES
Similar to Model 1895 with deep cut Ballard-type rifling; pistol-grip synthetic stock with large-loop lever, matte stainless finish, full length magazine. **Barrel:** 16.25 in. **Overall length:** 34.5 in. **Weight:** 7.65 lbs. **Sights:** XS lever rail with ghost-ring receiver sight.
Price: $949.00

MARLIN MODEL 1895GS GUIDE GUN
Caliber: .45-70 Govt. **Capacity:** 4 rounds. **Features:** Similar to Model 1895G except receiver, barrel and most metal parts are machined from stainless steel. Chambered for .45-70 Govt., 4-shot, 18.5 in. barrel. Overall length is 37 in., weighs 7 lbs. Introduced 2001. Includes safety lock. Made in USA by Marlin.
Price: $896.00

MARLIN MODEL 1895 SBLR
Caliber: .45-70 Govt. **Features:** Similar to Model 1895GS Guide Gun but with stainless steel barrel (18.5 in.), receiver, large loop lever and magazine tube. Black/gray laminated buttstock and fore-end, XS ghost ring rear sight, hooded ramp front sight, receiver/barrel-mounted top rail for mounting accessory optics. Chambered in .45-70 Government. Overall length is 42.5 in., weighs 7.5 lbs.
Price: $1,232.00

MARLIN MODEL 1895 COWBOY LEVER-ACTION
Similar to Model 1895 except has 26-in. tapered octagon barrel with Ballard-type rifling, Marble carbine front sight and Marble adjustable semi-buckhorn rear sight. Receiver tapped for scope or receiver sight. Overall length is 44.5 in., weighs about 8 lbs. Introduced 2001. Includes safety lock. Made in USA by Marlin.
Price: $899.00

MARLIN 1895GBL
Caliber: .45-70 Govt. **Features:** Lever-action rifle with 6-shot, full-length tubular magazine; 18.5-in. barrel with deep-cut Ballard-type rifling (6 grooves); big-loop finger lever; side ejection; solid-top receiver; deeply blued metal surfaces; hammer block safety; pistol-grip two-tone brown laminate stock with cut checkering; ventilated recoil pad; Mar-Shield finish; swivel studs.
Price: $786.00

MOSSBERG 464 LEVER ACTION
Caliber: .30-30 Win. **Capacity:** 6-round tubular magazine. **Barrel:** 20 in. round. **Weight:** 6.7 lbs. **Length:** 38.5 in. overall. **Stock:** Hardwood with straight or pistol grip, quick detachable swivel studs. **Sights:** Folding rear sight, adjustable for windage and elevation. **Features:** Blued receiver and barrel, receiver drilled and tapped, two-position top-tang safety. Available with straight grip or semi-pistol grip. Introduced 2008. From O.F. Mossberg & Sons, Inc.
Price: $574.00
Price: SPX Model w/tactical stock and features $574.00

NAVY ARMS 1873 RIFLE
Calibers: .357 Magnum, .45 Colt. **Capacity:** 12-round magazine. **Barrels:** 20 in., 24.25 in., full octagonal. **Stock:** Deluxe checkered American walnut. **Sights:** Gold bead front, semi-buckhorn rear. **Features:** Turnbull color case-hardened frame, rest blued. Full-octagon barrel. Available exclusively from Navy Arms. Made by Winchester.
Price: $2,500.00

NAVY ARMS 1892 SHORT RIFLE
Calibers: .45 Colt, .44 Magnum. **Capacity:** 10-round magazine. **Barrel:** 20 in. full octagon. **Stock:** Checkered Grade 1 American walnut. **Sights:** Marble's Semi-Buckhorn rear and gold bead front. **Finish:** Color casehardened.
Price: $2,300.00

NAVY ARMS LIGHTNING RIFLE
Calibers: .45 Colt, .357 Magnum. Replica of the Colt Lightning slide-action rifle of the late 19th and early 20th centuries. **Barrel:** Octagon 20 or 24 in. **Stock:** Checkered Grade 1 American walnut. **Finish:** Color casehardened.
Price: $2,200.00

REMINGTON MODEL 7600 PUMP ACTION
Calibers: .270 Win., .30-06, .308. **Barrels:** 22 in. round tapered or 18.5 in. (Carbine). **Weight:** 7.5 lbs. **Length:** 42.6 in. overall. **Stock:** Cut-checkered walnut pistol grip and fore-end, Monte Carlo with full cheekpiece. Satin or high-gloss finish. **Sights:** Gold bead front sight on matte ramp, open step adjustable sporting rear. **Features:** Redesigned and improved version of the Model 760. Detachable 4-round magazine. Crossbolt safety. Receiver tapped for scope mount. Introduced 1981.
Price: 7600 ....$918.00

Prices given are believed to be accurate at time of publication however, many factors affect retail pricing so exact prices are not possible.

74TH EDITION, 2020 ✦ **363**

ROSSI R92 LEVER-ACTION CARBINE
Calibers: .38 Special/.357 Magnum, .44 Magnum., .44-40 Win., .45 Colt. **Barrels:** 16or 20 in. with round barrel, 20 or 24 in. with octagon barrel. **Weight:** 4.8–7 lbs. **Length:** 34–41.5 in. **Features:** Blued or stainless finish. Various options available in selected chamberings (large lever loop, fiber-optic sights, cheekpiece).
Price: Blued **$624.00**
Price: Stainless **$659.00**

UBERTI 1873 SPORTING RIFLE
Calibers: .357 Magnum, .44-40, .45 Colt. **Barrels:** 16.1 in. round, 19 in. round or 20 in., 24.25 in. octagonal. **Weight:** Up to 8.2 lbs. **Length:** Up to 43.3 in. overall. **Stock:** Walnut, straight grip and pistol grip. **Sights:** Blade front adjustable for windage, open rear adjustable for elevation. **Features:** Color casehardened frame, blued barrel, hammer, lever, buttplate, brass elevator. Imported by Stoeger Industries.
Price: Carbine 19-in. bbl. **$1,309.00**
Price: Trapper 16.1-in. bbl. **$1,329.00**
Price: Carbine 18-in. half oct. bbl. **$1,379.00**
Price: Short Rifle 20-in. bbl. **$1,339.00**
Price: Sporting Rifle, 24.25-in. bbl. **$1,339.00**
Price: Special Sporting Rifle, A-grade walnut **$1,449.00**

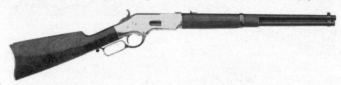

UBERTI 1866 YELLOWBOY CARBINE, SHORT, RIFLE
Calibers: .38 Special, .44-40, .45 Colt. **Barrel:** 24.25 in. octagonal. **Weight:** 8.2 lbs. **Length:** 43.25 in. overall. **Stock:** Walnut. **Sights:** Blade front adjustable for windage, rear adjustable for elevation. **Features:** Frame, buttplate, fore-end cap of polished brass, balance charcoal blued. Imported by Stoeger Industries.
Price: 1866 Yellowboy Carbine, 19-in. round barrel **$1,269.00**
Price: 1866 Yellowboy Short Rifle, 20-in. octagonal barrel ... **$1,269.00**
Price: 1866 Yellowboy Rifle, 24.25-in. octagonal barrel **$1,269.00**

UBERTI 1860 HENRY
Calibers: .44-40, .45 Colt. **Barrel:** 24.25 in. half-octagon. **Weight:** 9.2 lbs. **Length:** 43.75 in. overall. **Stock:** American walnut. **Sights:** Blade front, rear adjustable for elevation. Imported by Stoeger Industries.
Price: 1860 Henry Trapper, 18.5-in. barrel, brass frame **$1,499.00**
Price: 1860 Henry Rifle Iron Frame, 24.25-in. barrel **$1,499.00**

WINCHESTER MODEL 94 SHORT RIFLE
Calibers: .30-30, .38-55, .32 Special. **Barrel:** 20 in. **Weight:** 6.75 lbs. **Sights:** Semi-buckhorn rear, gold bead front. **Stock:** Walnut with straight grip. Fore-end has black grip cap. Also available in Trail's End takedown design in .450 Marlin or .30-30.

Price: **$1,230.00**
Price: (Takedown) **$1,460.00**

WINCHESTER MODEL 94 CARBINE
Same general specifications as M94 Short Rifle except for curved buttplate and fore-end barrel band.
Price: **$1,200.00**

WINCHESTER MODEL 94 SPORTER
Calibers: .30-30, .38-55. **Barrel:** 24 in. **Weight:** 7.5 lbs. **Features:** Same features of Model 94 Short Rifle except for crescent butt and steel buttplate, 24 in. half-round, half-octagon barrel, checkered stock.
Price: **$1,400.00**

WINCHESTER 1873 SHORT RIFLE
Calibers: .357 Magnum, .44-40, .45 Colt. **Capacities:** Tubular magazine holds 10 rounds (.44-40, .45 Colt), 11 rounds (.38 Special). **Barrel:** 20 in. **Weight:** 7.25 lbs. **Sights:** Marble semi-buckhorn rear, gold bead front. Tang is drilled and tapped for optional peep sight. **Stock:** Satin finished, straight-grip walnut with steel crescent buttplate and steel fore-end cap. Tang safety. A modern version of the "Gun That Won the West."
Price: **$1,300.00**
Price: Deluxe Sporting Rifle **$1,800.00**

WINCHESTER MODEL 1886 SHORT RIFLE
Caliber: .45-70. **Barrel:** 24 in. **Weight:** 8.4 lbs. **Sights:** Adjustable buckhorn rear, blade front. **Stock:** Grade 1 walnut with crescent butt.
Price **$1,340.00**

WINCHESTER MODEL 1892 CARBINE
Calibers: .357 Magnum, .44 Magnum, .44-40, .45 Colt. **Barrel:** 20 in. **Weight:** 6 lbs. **Stock:** Satin finished walnut with straight grip, steel fore-end strap. **Sights:** Marble semi-buckhorn rear, gold bead front. Other features include saddle ring and tang safety.
Price: **$1,260.00**
Price: 1892 Short Rifle **$1,070.00**

Prices given are believed to be accurate at time of publication however, many factors affect retail pricing so exact prices are not possible.

ARMALITE AR-30A1 TARGET

Calibers: .300 Win. Mag., .338 Lapua. **Capacity:** 5 rounds. **Barrel:** 26 in., target-grade chrome moly. **Weight:** 12.8 lbs. **Length:** 46 in. **Stock:** Standard fixed with adjustable cheek piece. **Sights:** None. Accessory top rail included. **Features:** Bolt-action rifle. Muzzle brake, ambidextrous magazine release, large ejection port makes single loading easy, V-block patented bedding system, bolt-mounted safety locks firing pin. AR-31 is in .308 Win., accepts AR-10 double-stack magazines, has adjustable pistol grip stock.
Price: $3,460.00
Price: AR-31..$3,460.00

ARMALITE AR-50A1

Caliber: .50 BMG, .416 Barrett. **Capacity:** Bolt-action single-shot. **Barrel:** 30 in. with muzzle brake. National Match model (shown) has 33-in. fluted barrel. **Weight:** 34.1 lbs. **Stock:** Three-section. Extruded fore-end, machined vertical grip, forged and machined buttstock that is vertically adjustable. National Match model (.50 BMG only) has V-block patented bedding system, Armalite Skid System to ensure straight-back recoil.
Price: $3,359.00

BARRETT MODEL 95

Caliber: 50 BMG. **Capacity:** 5-round magazine. **Barrel:** 29 in. **Weight:** 23.5 lbs. **Length:** 45 in. overall. **Stock:** Energy-absorbing recoil pad. **Sights:** Scope optional. **Features:** Bolt-action, bullpup design. Disassembles without tools; extendable bipod legs; match-grade barrel; muzzle brake. Introduced 1995. Made in USA by Barrett Firearms Mfg., Inc.
Price: From..$6,670.00

BARRETT FIELDCRAFT HUNTING RIFLE

Calibers: .22-250 Rem., .243 Win., 6mm Creedmoor, .25-06, 6.5 Creedmoor, 6.5x55, 7mm-08 Rem., .308 Win. .270 Win., .30-06. **Capacity:** 4-round magazine. **Barrel:** 18 (threaded), 21 or 24 inches. **Weight:** 5.2-5.6 lbs. **Features:** Two-position safety, Timney trigger. Receiver, barrels and bolts are scaled for specific calibers. Barrels and action are made from 416 stainless steel and are full-length hand bedded.
Price: ....$1,879.00-$1,929.00

BARRETT MODEL 99 SINGLE SHOT

Calibers: .50 BMG., .416 Barrett. **Barrel:** 33 In. **Weight:** 25 lbs. **Length:** 50.4 in. overall. **Stock:** Anodized aluminum with energy-absorbing recoil pad. **Sights:** None furnished; integral M1913 scope rail. **Features:** Bolt action; detachable bipod; match-grade barrel with high-efficiency muzzle brake. Introduced 1999. Made in USA by Barrett Firearms.
Price: From..$3,999.00-$4,199.00

BARRETT MRAD

Calibers: .260 Rem., 6.5 Creedmoor, .308 Win., .300 Win. Mag., .338 Lapua Magnum. **Capacity:** 10-round magazine. **Barrels:** 20 in., 24 in. or 26 in. fluted or heavy. **Features:** User-interchangeable barrel system, folding stock, adjustable cheekpiece, 5-position length of pull adjustment button, match-grade trigger, 22-in. optics rail.
Price: ....$5,850.00-$6,000.00

BERGARA B-14 SERIES

Calibers: 6.5 Creedmoor, .270 Win., 7mm Rem. Mag., .308 Win., .30-06, .300 Win. Mag. **Barrels:** 22 or 24 in. **Weight:** 7 lbs. **Features:** Synthetic with soft touch finish, recoil pad, swivel studs, adjustable trigger, choice of detachable mag or hinged floorplate. Made in Spain.
Price: $825.00
Price: Walnut Stock (Shown, Top) $945.00
Price: Premier Series, From..$2,190.00
Price: Hunting and Match Rifle (HMR)(Shown, Bottom), From $1,150.00

BERGARA BCR SERIES

Calibers: Most popular calibers from .222 Rem. to .300 Win. Mag. **Barrels:** 18, 22, 24 or 26 in. Various options available.
Price: BCR23 Sport Hunter from $3,950.00
Price: BCR24 Varmint Hunter from $4,100.00
Price: BCR25 Long Range Hunter from $4,350.00
Price: BCR27 Competition from $4,950.00

BLASER R-8 SERIES

Calibers: Available in virtually all standard and metric calibers from .204 Ruger to .500 Jeffery. Straight-pull bolt action. **Barrels:** 20.5, 23, or 25.75 in. **Weights:** 6.375-8.375 lbs. **Lengths:** 40 in. overall (22 in. barrel). **Stocks:** Synthetic or Turkish walnut. **Sights:** None furnished; drilled and tapped for scope mounting. **Features:** Thumb-activated safety slide/cocking mechanism; interchangeable barrels and bolt heads. Many optional features. Imported from Germany by Blaser USA.
Price: From..$3,787.00

BROWNING AB3 COMPOSITE STALKER

Calibers: .243, 6.5 Creedmoor, .270 Win., .270 WSM, 7mm-08, 7mm Rem.

Mag., .30-06, .300 Win. Mag., .300 WSM or .308 Win. **Barrels:** 22 in, 26 in. for magnums. **Weights:** 6.8–7.4 lbs. **Stock:** Matte black synthetic. **Sights:** None. Picatinny rail scope mount included.

Price: $600.00
Price: Micro Stalker $600.00
Price: Hunter..$670.00

BROWNING X-BOLT HUNTER

Calibers: .223, .22-250, .243 Win., 6mm Creedmoor, 6.5 Creedmoor, .25-06 Rem., .270 Win., .270 WSM, .280 Rem., 7mm Rem. Mag., 7mm WSM, 7mm-08 Rem., .308 Win., .30-06, .300 Win. Mag., .300 WSM, .325 WSM, .338 Win. Mag., .375 H&H Mag. **Barrels:** 22 in., 23 in., 24 in., 26 in., varies by model. Matte blued or stainless free-floated barrel, recessed muzzle crown. **Weights:** 6.3–7 lbs. **Stocks:** Hunter and Medallion models have black walnut stocks; Composite Stalker and Stainless Stalker models have composite stocks. Inflex Technology recoil pad. **Sights:** None, drilled and tapped receiver, X-Lock scope mounts. **Features:** Adjustable three-lever Feather Trigger system, polished hard-chromed steel components, factory pre-set at 3.5 lbs., alloy trigger housing. Bolt unlock button, detachable rotary magazine, 60-degree bolt lift, three locking lugs, top-tang safety, sling swivel studs. Introduced 2008.

Price: Standard calibers $900.00
Price: Magnum calibers $950.00
Price: Left-hand models............................$940.00–$980.00

BROWNING X-BOLT MICRO MIDAS

Calibers: .243 Win., 6mm Creedmoor, 6.5 Creedmoor, 7mm-08 Rem., .308 Win., .22-250 Rem. .270 WSM, .300 WSM. **Barrel:** 20 in. **Weight:** 6 lbs.,1 oz. **Length:** 37.625–38.125 in. overall. **Stock:** Satin finish checkered walnut or composite. **Sights:** Hooded front and adjustable rear. **Features:** Steel receiver with low-luster blued finish. Glass bedded, drilled and tapped for scope mounts. Barrel is free-floating and hand chambered with target crown. Bolt-action with adjustable Feather Trigger and detachable rotary magazine. Compact 12.5 in. length of pull for smaller shooters. This model has all the same features as the full-size model with sling swivel studs installed and Inflex Technology recoil pad. (Scope and mounts not included).
Price: $860.00

BROWNING X-BOLT MEDALLION

Calibers: Most popular calibers from .223 Rem. to .375 H&H. **Barrels:** 22, 24 or 26 in. free-floated. **Features:** Engraved receiver with polished blue finish, gloss finished and checkered walnut stock with rosewood grip and fore-end caps, detachable rotary magazine. Medallion Maple model has AAA-grade maple stock.
Price: $1,040.00
Price: Medallion Maple $1,070.00

BROWNING X-BOLT ECLIPSE HUNTER

Calibers: Most popular calibers from .223 Rem. to .300 WSM. Same general features of X-Bolt series except for its laminated thumbhole stock. Varmint and Target models have 26-in. bull barrels.
Price: $1,200.00
Price: Varmint and Target models....................$1,430.00

BROWNING X-BOLT HELL'S CANYON

Calibers: .22 Nosler, 6mm Creedmoor, .243 Win., 26 Nosler, 6.5 Creedmoor, .270 Win., .270 WSM, 7mm-08 Rem., 7mm Rem. Mag., .308 Win., .30-06, .300 Win. Mag., .300 WSM. **Barrels:** 22–26-in. fluted and free-floating with muzzle brake or thread protector. **Stock:** A-TACS AU Camo composite with checkered grip panels. **Features:** Detachable rotary magazine, adjustable trigger, Cerakote Burnt Bronze finish on receiver and barrel.
Price: ....$1,260.00–$1,320.00

BROWNING X-BOLT WHITE GOLD

Calibers: Eighteen popular calibers from .223 Rem. to .338 Win. Mag. Same general features of X-Bolt series plus polished stainless steel barrel, receiver, bolt and trigger. Gloss-finished finely checkered walnut Monte Carlo-style stock with rosewood grip and fore-end caps.
Price: ....$1,420.00–$1,540.00

BROWNING X-BOLT PRO SERIES

Calibers: 6mm Creedmoor, 6.5 Creedmoor, 26 Nosler, 28 Nosler, .270 Win., 7mm Rem. Mag., .308 Win., .30-06., .300 Win. Mag. Detachable rotary magazine. **Barrels:** 22–26 in. Stainless steel, fluted with threaded/removable muzzle brake. **Weights:** 6–7.5 lbs. **Finish:** Cerakote Burnt Bronze. **Stock:** Second generation carbon fiber with palm swell, textured gripping surfaces. Adjustable trigger, top tang safety, sling swivel studs. Long Range has heavy sporter-contour barrel, proprietary lapping process.
Price: X-Bolt Pro..$2,070.00–$2,130.00
Price: X-Bolt Pro Long Range ....$2,100.00–$2,180.00
Price: X-Bolt Pro Tungsten ....$2,070.00–$2,130.00

BUSHMASTER BA50 BOLT-ACTION

Caliber: .50 Browning BMG. **Capacity:** 10-round magazine. **Barrels:** 30 in. (rifle), 22 in. (carbine). **Weight:** 30 lbs. (rifle), 27 lbs. (carbine). **Length:** 58 in. overall (rifle), 50 in. overall (carbine). **Features:** Free-floated Lothar Walther barrel with muzzle brake, Magpul PRS adjustable stock.
Price: $5,657.00

CHEYTAC M-200

Caliber: 357 CheyTac, .408 CheyTac. **Capacity:** 7-round magazine. **Barrel:** 30 in. **Length:** 55 in. stock extended. **Weight:** 27 lbs. (steel barrel); 24 lbs. (carbon-fiber barrel). **Stock:** Retractable. **Sights:** None, scope rail provided. **Features:** CNC-machined receiver, attachable Picatinny rail M-1913, detachable barrel, integral bipod, 3.5-lb. trigger pull, muzzle brake. Made in USA by CheyTac, LLC.
Price: From...$11,700.00

Prices given are believed to be accurate at time of publication however, many factors affect retail pricing so exact prices are not possible.

COOPER FIREARMS OF MONTANA

This company manufacturers bolt-action rifles in a variety of styles and in almost any factory or wildcat caliber. Features of the major model sub-category/styles are listed below. Several other styles and options are available. Classic: Available in all models. AA Claro walnut stock with 4-panel hand checkering, hand-rubbed oil-finished wood, Pachmayr pad, steel grip cap and standard sling swivel studs. Barrel is chrome-moly premium match grade Wilson Arms. All metal work has matte finish. Custom Classic: Available in all models. AAA Claro walnut stock with shadow-line beaded cheek-piece, African ebony tip, Western fleur wrap-around hand checkering, hand-rubbed oil-finished wood, Pachmayr pad, steel grip cap and standard sling swivel studs. Barrel is chrome-moly premium match grade Wilson Arms. All metal work has high gloss finish. Western Classic: Available in all models. AAA+ Claro walnut stock. Selected metal work is highlighted with case coloring. Other features same as Custom Classic. Mannlicher: Available in all models. Same features as Western Classic with full-length stock having multi-point wrap-around hand checkering. Varminter: Available in Models 21, 22, 38, 52, 54 and 57-M. Same features as Classic except heavy barrel and stock with wide fore-end, hand-checkered grip.

COOPER MODEL 21

Calibers: Virtually any factory or wildcat chambering in the .223 Rem. family is available including: .17 Rem., .19-223, Tactical 20, .204 Ruger, .222 Rem., .222 Rem. Mag., .223 Rem, .223 Rem AI, 6x45, 6x47. Single shot. **Barrels:** 22–24 in. for Classic configurations, 24–26 in. for Varminter configurations. **Weights:** 6.5–8.0 lbs., depending on type. **Stock:** AA-AAA select claro walnut, 20 LPI checkering. **Sights:** None furnished. **Features:** Three front locking-lug, bolt-action, single-shot. Action: 7.75 in. long, Sako extractor. Button ejector. Fully adjustable single-stage trigger. Options include wood upgrades, case-color metalwork, barrel fluting, custom LOP, and many others.

Price: Classic	$2,495.00
Price: Custom Classic	$2,995.00
Price: Western Classic	$3,795.00
Price: Varminter	$2,495.00
Price: Mannlicher	$4,395.00

COOPER MODEL 22

Calibers: Virtually any factory or wildcat chambering in the mid-size cartridge length including: .22-250 Rem., .22 250 Rem. AI, .25-06 Rem., .25-06 Rem. AI, .243 Win., .243 Win. AI, .220 Swift, .250/3000 AI, .257 Roberts, .257 Roberts AI, 7mm-08 Rem., 6mm Rem., .260 Rem., 6x284, 6.5x284, .22 BR, 6mm BR, .308 Win. Single shot. **Barrels:** 24 in. or 26 in. stainless match in Classic configurations. 24 in. or 26 in. in Varminter configurations. **Weight:** 7.5–8.0 lbs. depending on type. **Stock:** AA-AAA select claro walnut, 20 LPI checkering. **Sights:** None furnished. **Features:** Three front locking-lug bolt-action single shot. Action: 8.25 in. long, Sako-style extractor. Button ejector. Fully adjustable single-stage trigger. Options include wood upgrades, case-color metalwork, barrel fluting, custom LOP, and many others.

Price: Classic	$2,495.00
Price: Custom Classic	$2,995.00
Price: Western Classic	$3,795.00
Price: Varminter	$2,495.00
Price: Mannlicher	$4,395.00

COOPER MODEL 38

Calibers: .22 Hornet family of cartridges including the .17 Squirrel, .17 He Bee, .17 Ackley Hornet, .17 Mach IV, .19 Calhoon, .20 VarTarg, .221 Fireball, .22 Hornet, .22 K-Hornet, .22 Squirrel, .218 Bee, .218 Mashburn Bee. Single shot. **Barrels:** 22 in. or 24 in. in Classic configurations, 24 in. or 26 in. in Varminter configurations. **Weights:** 6.5–8.0 lbs. depending on type. **Stock:** AA-AAA select claro walnut, 20 LPI checkering. **Sights:** None furnished. **Features:** Three front locking-lug bolt-action single shot. Action: 7 in. long, Sako-style extractor. Button ejector. Fully adjustable single-stage trigger. Options include wood upgrades, case-color metalwork, barrel fluting, custom LOP, and many others.

Price: Classic	$2,225.00
Price: Custom Classic	$2,595.00
Price: Western Classic	$3,455.00

Price: Varminter	$2,225.00
Price: Mannlicher	$4,395.00

COOPER MODEL 52

Calibers: .30-06, .270 Win., .280 Rem, .25-06, .284 Win., .257 Weatherby Mag., .264 Win. Mag., .270 Weatherby Mag., 7mm Remington Mag., 7mm Weatherby Mag., 7mm Shooting Times Westerner, .300 Holland & Holland, .300 Win. Mag., .300 Weatherby Mag., .308 Norma Mag., 8mm Rem. Mag., .338 Win. Mag., .340 Weatherby V. Three-shot magazine. **Barrels:** 22 in. or 24 in. in Classic configurations, 24 in. or 26 in. in Varminter configurations. **Weight:** 7.75–8 lbs. depending on type. **Stock:** AA-AAA select claro walnut, 20 LPI checkering. **Sights:** None furnished. **Features:** Three front locking-lug bolt-action single shot. Action: 7 in. long, Sako style extractor. Button ejector. Fully adjustable single-stage trigger. Options include wood upgrades, case color metalwork, barrel fluting, custom LOP, and many others.

Price: Classic	$2,495.00
Price: Custom Classic	$3,335.00
Price: Western Classic	$3,995.00
Price: Jackson Game	$2,595.00
Price: Jackson Hunter	$2,595.00
Price: Excalibur	$2,595.00
Price: Mannlicher	$4,755.00
Price: Open Country Long Range	$3,795.00-4,155.00
Price: Timberline, Synthetic Stock	$2,595.00
Price: Raptor, Synthetic tactical stock	$2,755.00

COOPER MODEL 54

Calibers: .22-250, .243 Win., .250 Savage, .260 Rem., 7mm-08, .308 Win. and similar length cartridges. Features are similar to those of the Model 52.

Price: Classic	$2,495.00
Price: Custom Classic	$3,355.00
Price: Western Classic	$3,995.00
Price: Jackson Game	$2,595.00
Price: Jackson Hunter	$2,595.00
Price: Excalibur	$2,595.00
Price: Mannlicher	$4,995.00

CZ 527 LUX BOLT-ACTION

Calibers: .17 Hornet, .204 Ruger, .22 Hornet, .222 Rem., .223 Rem. **Capacity:** 5-round magazine. **Barrels:** 23.5 in. standard or heavy. **Weight:** 6 lbs., 1 oz. **Length:** 42.5 in. overall. **Stock:** European walnut with Monte Carlo. **Sights:** Hooded front, open adjustable rear. **Features:** Improved mini-Mauser action with non-rotating claw extractor; single set trigger; grooved receiver. Imported from the Czech Republic by CZ-USA.

Price: Brown laminate stock	$733.00
Price: Model FS, full-length stock, cheekpiece	$827.00

CZ 527 AMERICAN BOLT-ACTION

Similar to the CZ 527 Lux except has classic-style stock with 18 LPI checkering; free-floating barrel; recessed target crown on barrel. No sights furnished. Introduced 1999. Imported from the Czech Republic by CZUSA.

Price: From	$733.00

CZ 527 AMERICAN SUPPRESSOR READY

Calibers: .223 Rem., 6.5 Grendel, .300 Blackout, 7.62x39mm. 5-shot capacity. **Barrel:** 16.5 in. **Stock:** Synthetic American style. **Weight:** 5.9 lbs. No sights furnished. Integrated 16mm scope bases.

Price: From	$766.00

Prices given are believed to be accurate at time of publication however, many factors affect retail pricing so exact prices are not possible.

74TH EDITION, 2020 ✛ **367**

CZ 550 FS MANNLICHER

Calibers: .22-250 Rem., .243 Win., 6.5x55, 7x57, 7x64, .308 Win., 9.3x62, .270 Win., 30-06. **Barrel:** Free-floating; recessed target crown. **Weight:** 7.48 lbs. **Length:** 44.68 in. overall. **Stock:** American classic-style stock with 18 LPI checkering or FS (Mannlicher). **Sights:** No sights furnished. **Features:** Improved Mauser-style action with claw extractor, fixed ejector, square bridge dovetailed receiver; single set trigger. Introduced 1999. Imported from the Czech Republic by CZ-USA.

Price: FS (full stock) $894.00
Price: American, from $827.00

CZ 550 SAFARI MAGNUM/AMERICAN SAFARI MAGNUM

Similar to CZ 550 American Classic. **Calibers:** .375 H&H Mag., .416 Rigby, .458 Win. Mag., .458 Lott. Overall length is 46.5 in. **Barrel:** 25 in. **Weight:** 9.4 lbs., 9.9 lbs (American). **Features:** Hooded front sight, express rear with one standing, two folding leaves. Imported from the Czech Republic by CZ-USA.

Price: Safari Magnum $1,215.00
Price: American Safari Field .... **$1,215.00–$1,348.00**

CZ 550 MAGNUM H.E.T.

High Energy Tactical model similar to CZ 550 American Classic. **Caliber:** .338 Lapua. **Length:** 52 in. **Barrel:** 28 in. **Weight:** 14 lbs. **Features:** Adjustable sights, satin blued barrel. Imported from the Czech Republic by CZ-USA.

Price: $3,929.00

CZ 550 ULTIMATE HUNTING

Similar to CZ 550 American Classic. **Caliber:** .300 Win Mag. **Length:** 44.7 in. **Barrel:** 23.6 in. **Weight:** 7.7 lbs. **Stock:** Kevlar. **Features:** Nightforce 5.5-20x50 scope included. Imported from the Czech Republic by CZ-USA.

Price: $3,458.00

CZ 557

Calibers: .243 Win., 6.5x55, .270 Win., .308 Win., .30-06. **Capacity:** 5+1. **Barrel:** 20.5 in. **Stock:** Satin finished walnut or Manners carbon fiber with textured grip and fore-end. **Sights:** None on Sporter model. **Features:** Forged steel receiver has integral scope mounts. Magazine has hinged floorplate. Trigger is adjustable. Push-feed action features short extractor and plunger style ejector. Varmint model (.243, .308) has 25.6-in. barrel, detachable box magazine.

Price: Sporter, walnut stock $832.00
Price: Synthetic stock $779.00
Price: Varmint model...$865.00

DAKOTA 76 TRAVELER TAKEDOWN

Calibers: .257 Roberts, .25-06 Rem., 7x57, .270 Win., .280 Rem., .30-06, .338-06, .35 Whelen (standard length); 7mm Rem. Mag., .300 Win. Mag., .338 Win. Mag., .416 Taylor, .458 Win. Mag. (short magnums); 7mm, .300, .330, .375 Dakota Magnums. **Barrel:** 23 in. **Weight:** 7.5 lbs. **Length:** 43.5 in. overall. **Stock:** Medium fancy-grade walnut in classic style. Checkered grip and fore-end; solid buttpad. **Sights:** None furnished; drilled and tapped for scope mounts. **Features:** Threadless disassembly. Uses modified Model 76 design with many features of the Model 70 Winchester. Left-hand model also available. Introduced 1989. African chambered for .338 Lapua Mag., .404 Jeffery, .416 Rigby, .416 Dakota, .450 Dakota, 4-round magazine, select wood, two stock cross-bolts. 24-in. barrel. Weighs 9-10 lbs. Ramp front sight, standing leaf rear. Introduced 1989. Made in USA by Dakota Arms, Inc.

Price: Traveler...$7,240.00
Price: Safari Traveler...$9,330.00
Price: African Traveler $10,540.00

DAKOTA 76 CLASSIC

Caliber: .257 Roberts, .270 Win., .280 Rem., .30-06, 7mm Rem. Mag., .338 Win. Mag., .300 Win. Mag., .375 H&H, .458 Win. Mag. **Barrel:** 23 in. **Weight:** 7.5 lbs. **Length:** 43.5 in. overall. **Stock:** Medium fancy-grade walnut in classic style. Checkered pistol grip and fore-end; solid buttpad. **Sights:** None furnished; drilled and tapped for scope mounts. **Features:** Has many features of the original Winchester Model 70. One-piece rail trigger guard assembly; steel grip cap. Model 70-style trigger. Many options available. Left-hand rifle available at same price. Introduced 1988. From Dakota Arms, Inc.

Price: From...$6,030.00
Price: Professional Hunter.....................................$7,995.00
Price: Safari Grade...$8,010.00

DAKOTA MODEL 97

Calibers: .22-250, .375 Dakota Mag. **Barrels:** 22 in., 24 in. **Weight:** 6.1–6.5 lbs. **Length:** 43 in. overall. **Stock:** Fiberglass. **Sights:** Optional. **Features:** Matte blue finish, black stock. Right-hand action only. Introduced 1998. Made in USA by Dakota Arms, Inc.

Price: From $3,720.00
Price: All Weather (stainless)................................$4,050.00
Price: Outfitter Takedown $5,150.00
Price: Varminter...$4,820.00

FRANCHI MOMENTUM

Calibers: .243 Win., 6.5 Creedmoor, .270 Win., .308 Win., .30-06, .300 Win. Mag. **Barrels:** 22 or 24 in. **Weights:** 6.5–7.5 lbs. **Stock:** Black synthetic with checkered gripping surface, recessed sling swivel studs, TSA recoil pad. **Sights:** None. **Features:** Available with Burris Fullfield II 3-9X40mm scope.

Price: Varminter..$609.00
Price: With Burris 3-9X scope...............................$729.00

HOWA M-1500 RANCHLAND COMPACT

Calibers: .223 Rem., .22-250 Rem., .243 Win., .308 Win. and 7mm-08. **Barrel:** 20 in. #1 contour, blued finish. **Weight:** 7 lbs. **Stock:** Hogue Overmolded in black, OD green, Coyote Sand colors. 13.87-in. LOP. **Sights:** None furnished; drilled and tapped for scope mounting. **Features:** Three-position safety, hinged floorplate, adjustable trigger, forged one-piece bolt, M-16-style extractor, forged flat-bottom receiver. Also available with Nikko-Stirling Nighteater 3-9x42 riflescope. Introduced in 2008. Imported from Japan by Legacy Sports International.

Price: Rifle Only $652.00
Price: Rifle with 3-9x42 Nighteater scope.......................$762.00

HOWA/HOGUE KRYPTEK RIFLE

Calibers: Most popular calibers from .204 Ruger to .375 Ruger. **Barrel:** 20, 22 or 24 in., blue or stainless. **Stock:** Hogue overmolded in Kryptek Camo. **Features:** Three-position safety, two-stage match trigger, one-piece bolt with two locking lugs.

Price: $672.00
Price: Magnum calibers $700.00
Price: Stainless from $736.00

HOWA ALPINE MOUNTAIN RIFLE

Calibers: .243 Win., 6.5 Creedmoor, 7mm-08, .308 Win. **Barrel:** 20 in. **Weight:** 5.7 lbs. **Stock:** OD Green synthetic. **Features:** Two-stage HACT trigger, Cerakote finish on barrel and action, Pachmyr Decelerator pad.

Price: Stainless, From $1,188.00

H-S PRECISION PRO-SERIES 2000

Calibers: 30 different chamberings including virtually all popular calibers. Made in hunting, tactical and competition styles with many options. **Barrels:** 20 in., 22 in., 24 in. or 26 in. depending on model and caliber. Hunting models include the Pro-Hunter Rifle (PHR) designed for magnum calibers with built-in recoil reducer and heavier barrel; Pro-Hunter Lightweight (PHL) with slim, fluted barrel; Pro-Hunter Sporter (SPR) and Pro-Hunter Varmint (VAR). Takedown, Competition and Tactical variations are available. **Stock:** H-S Precision synthetic stock in many styles and colors with full-length bedding block chassis system. Made in USA

Prices given are believed to be accurate at time of publication however, many factors affect retail pricing so exact prices are not possible.

Price: PHR...$3,795.00
Price: PHL..$3,895.00
Price: SPR..$3,495.00
Price: SPL Sporter $3,595.00
Price: VAR...$3,595.00
Price: PTD Hunter Takedown...................$3,595.00
Price: STR Short Tactical $3,895.00
Price: HTR Heavy Tactical $3,895.00
Price: Competition $3,895.00

KENNY JARRETT RIFLES

Calibers: Custom built in virtually any chambering including .223 Rem., .243 Improved, .243 Catbird, 7mm-08 Improved, .280 Remington, .280 Ackley Improved, 7mm Rem. Mag., .284 Jarrett, .30-06 Springfield, .300 Win. Mag., .300 Jarrett, .323 Jarrett, .338 Jarrett, .375 H&H, .416 Rem., .450 Rigby, other modern cartridges. Numerous options regarding barrel type and weight, stock styles and material. **Features:** Tri-Lock receiver. Talley rings and bases. Accuracy guarantees and custom loaded ammunition. Newest series is the Shikar featuring 28-year aged American Black walnut hand-checkered stock with Jarrett-designed stabilizing aluminum chassis. Accuracy guaranteed to be .5 MOA with standard calibers, .75 MOA with magnums.
Price: Shikar Series $10,320.00
Price: Signature Series $8,320.00
Price: Long Ranger Series $8,320.00
Price: Ridge Walker Series $8,320.00
Price: Wind Walker $8,320.00
Price: Original Beanfield (customer's receiver) $6,050.00
Price: Professional Hunter $11,070.00
Price: SA/Custom $7,000.00

KIMBER MODEL 8400

Calibers: .25-06 Rem., .270 Win., 7mm, .30-06, .300 Win. Mag., .338 Win. Mag., or .325 WSM. **Capacity:** 4. **Barrel:** 24 in. **Weights:** 6 lbs., 3 oz.–6 lbs., 10 oz. **Length:** 43.25 in. **Stocks:** Claro walnut or Kevlar-reinforced fiberglass. **Sights:** None; drilled and tapped for bases. **Features:** Mauser claw extractor, two-position wing safety, action bedded on aluminum pillars and fiberglass, free-floated barrel, match-grade adjustable trigger set at 4 lbs., matte or polished blue or matte stainless finish. Introduced 2003. Sonora model (2008) has brown laminated stock, hand-rubbed oil finish, chambered in .25-06 Rem., .30-06, and .300 Win. Mag. Weighs 8.5 lbs., measures 44.50 in. overall length. Front swivel stud only for bipod. Stainless steel bull barrel, 24 in. satin stainless steel finish. Made in USA by Kimber Mfg. Inc.
Price: Classic $1,223.00
Price: Classic Select Grade, French walnut stock (2008) $1,427.00
Price: SuperAmerica, AAA walnut stock $2,240.00
Price: Patrol Tactical $2,447.00
Price: Montana $1,427.00

KIMBER MODEL 8400 CAPRIVI

Similar to Model 8400. **Calibers:** .375 H&H, .416 Remington and .458 Lott. **Capacity:** 4-round magazine. **Stock:** Claro walnut or Kevlar-reinforced fiberglass. Features twin steel crossbolts in stock, AA French walnut, pancake cheekpiece, 24 LPI wrap-around checkering, ebony fore-end tip, hand-rubbed oil finish, barrel-mounted sling swivel stud. **Features:** Bolt-action rifle. 3-leaf express sights. Howell-type rear sling swivel stud and a Pachmayr Decelerator recoil pad in traditional orange color. Introduced 2008. Made in USA by Kimber Mfg. Inc.
Price: From $3,263.00

KIMBER MODEL 8400 TALKEETNA

Similar to Model 8400. **Caliber:** .375 H&H. **Capacity:** 4-round magazine. **Weight:** 8 lbs. **Length:** 44.5 in. **Stock:** Synthetic. **Features:** Free-floating match-grade barrel with tapered match-grade chamber and target crown, three-position wing safety acts directly on the cocking piece for greatest security, and Pachmayr Decelerator. Made in USA by Kimber Mfg. Inc
Price: $2,175.00

KIMBER MODEL 84M

Calibers: .22-250 Rem., .204 Ruger, .223 Rem., .243 Win., 6.5 Creedmoor, .257 Roberts., .260 Rem., 7mm-08 Rem., .308 Win., .300 AAC Blackout.

Capacity: 5. **Barrels:** 22 in., 24 in., 26 in. **Weight:** 4 lbs., 13 oz.–8 lbs. **Lengths:** 41–45 in. **Stock:** Claro walnut, checkered with steel grip cap; synthetic or gray laminate. **Sights:** None; drilled and tapped for bases. **Features:** Mauser claw extractor, three-position wing safety, action bedded on aluminum pillars, free-floated barrel, match-grade trigger set at 4 lbs., matte blue finish. Includes cable lock. Introduced 2001. Montana (2008) has synthetic stock, Pachmayr Decelerator recoil pad, stainless steel 22-in. sporter barrel. Adirondack has Kevlar white/black Optifade Forest camo stock, 18-in. barrel with threaded muzzle, weighs less than 5 lbs. Made in USA by Kimber Mfg. Inc.
Price: Classic $1,223.00
Price: Varmint $1,291.00
Price: Montana $1,427.00
Price: Mountain Ascent $2,040.00
Price: SuperAmerica $2,240.00

KIMBER MODEL 84M HUNTER

Calibers: .243 Win., .257 Roberts., 6.5 Creedmoor, 7mm-08, .280 Ackley Imp., .308 Win. **Capacity:** 3 + 1, removable box type. **Barrel:** 22 in. **Weight:** 6.5 lbs. **Stock:** FDE Polymer with recoil pad, pillar bedding. **Finish:** Stainless. Other features include Mauser-type claw extractor, M70-type 3-position safety, adjustable trigger.
Price: $973.00

KIMBER MODEL 84L CLASSIC

Calibers: .270 Win., .30-06. **Capacity:** 5-round magazine. **Features:** Bolt-action rifle. 24-in. sightless matte blue sporter barrel; hand-rubbed A-grade walnut stock with 20 LPI panel checkering; pillar and glass bedding; Mauser claw extractor; 3-position M70-style safety; adjustable trigger.
Price: $1,427.00

KIMBER ADVANCED TACTICAL SOC/SRC II

Calibers: 6.5 Creedmoor, .308 Win. SRC chambered only in .308. **Capacity:** 5-round magazine. **Barrel:** 22-in. (SOC) stainless steel, (18 in. (SRC) with threaded muzzle. **Stock:** Side-folding aluminum with adjustable comb. **Features:** Stainless steel action, matte black or Flat Dark Earth finish. 3-position Model 70-type safety.
Price: $2,449.00

MAUSER M-03 SERIES

Calibers: .243, 6.5x55SE, .270 Win., 7x64mm, 7mm Rem. Mag., .308 Win., .30-06, .300 Win Mag., 8x57mm IS, .338 Win. Mag. 9.3x62mm. **Capacity:** 5-round magazine. **Barrels:** 22 in., 18.5 in. (Trail Model). **Stock:** Grade 2 walnut with ebony tip, or synthetic. **Features:** Classic Mauser design with Mag Safe magazine lock, adjustable rear and ramp front sights.
Price: Extreme (synthetic) $3,745.00
Price: Pure (walnut) $4,941.00
Price: Trail (polymer w/orange pads) $4,410.00

MAUSER M-12 PURE

Calibers: .22-250, .243, 6.5x55SE, .270 Win., 7x64mm, 7mm Rem. Mag., .308 Win., .30-06, .300 Win Mag., 8x57mm IS, .338 Win. Mag. 9.3x62mm. **Capacity:** 5-round magazine. **Barrel:** 22 in. **Sights:** Adjustable rear, blade front. **Stock:** Walnut with ebony fore-end tip.
Price: $1,971.00

MAUSER M-18

Calibers: .243, .270 Win., 7mm Rem. Mag., .308 Win., .30-06, .300 Win Mag. **Capacity:** 5-round magazine. **Barrel:** 21.75 or 24.5 in. **Weight:** 6.5 lbs. **Stock:** Polymer 2 with grip inlays. **Features:** Adjustable trigger, 3-position safety, recessed 3-lug bolt head chiseled from full diameter body.
Price: $699.00

MERKEL RX HELIX
Calibers: .223 Rem., .243 Rem., 6.5x55, 7mm-08, .308 Win., .270 Win., .30-06, 9.3x62, 7mm Rem. Mag., .300 Win. Mag., .270 WSM, .300 WSM, .338 Win. Mag. **Features:** Straight-pull bolt action. Synthetic stock on Explorer model. Walnut stock available in several grades. Factory engraved models available. Takedown system allows switching calibers in minutes.
Price: Explorer, synthetic stock, From $3,360.00
Price: Walnut stock, From $3,870.00

MOSSBERG MVP SERIES
Caliber: .223/5.56 NATO. **Capacity:** 10-round AR-style magazines. **Barrels:** 16.25-in. medium bull, 20-in. fluted sporter. **Weight:** 6.5–7 lbs. **Stock:** Classic black textured polymer. **Sights:** Adjustable folding rear, adjustable blade front. **Features:** Available with factory mounted 3-9x32 scope, (4-16x50 on Varmint model). FLEX model has 20-in. fluted sporter barrel, FLEX AR-style 6-position adjustable stock. Varmint model has laminated stock, 24-in. barrel. Thunder Ranch model has 18-in. bull barrel, OD Green synthetic stock.
Price: Patrol Model..$732.00
Price: Patrol Model w/scope $863.00
Price: FLEX Model $764.00
Price: FLEX Model w/scope $897.00
Price: Thunder Ranch Model $755.00
Price: Predator Model $732.00
Price: Predator Model w/scope $872.00
Price: Varmint Model...$753.00
Price: Varmint Model w/scope $912.00
Price: Long Range Rifle (LR) $974.00

MOSSBERG PATRIOT
Calibers: .22-250, .243 Win., .25-06, .270 Win., 7mm-08, .7mm Rem., .308 Win., .30-06, .300 Win. Mag., .38 Win. Mag., .375 Ruger. **Capacities:** 4- or 5-round magazine. **Barrels:** 22-in. sporter or fluted. **Stock:** Walnut, laminate, camo or synthetic black. **Weights:** 7.5–8 lbs. **Finish:** Matte blued. **Sights:** Adjustable or none. Some models available with 3-9x40 scope. Other features include patented Lightning Bolt Action Trigger adjustable from 2 to 7 pounds, spiral-fluted bolt. Not all variants available in all calibers. Introduced in 2015.
Price: Walnut stock..$438.00
Price: Walnut with premium Vortex Crossfire scope $649.00
Price: Synthetic stock $396.00
Price: Synthetic stock with standard scope $436.00
Price: Laminate stock w/iron sights $584.00
Price: Deer THUG w/Mossy Oak Infinity Camo stock $500.00
Price: Bantam, From $396.00

MOSSBERG PATRIOT NIGHT TRAIN
Calibers: .308 Win. or .300 Win. Mag. **Features:** Tactical model with Silencerco Saker Muzzle brake, 6-24x50 scope with tactical turrets, green synthetic stock with Neoprene comb-raising kit. **Weight:** 9 lbs.
Price: Night Train with 6-24x50 scope $811.00

NESIKA SPORTER RIFLE
Calibers: .260 Rem., 6.5x284, 7mm-08, .280 Rem., 7mm Rem. Mag., 308 Win., .30-06, .300 Win. Mag. **Barrels:** 24 or 26 in. Douglas air-gauged stainless. **Stock:** Composite with aluminum bedding block. **Sights:** None, Leupold QRW bases. **Weight:** 8 lbs. **Features:** Timney trigger set at 3 pounds, receiver made from 15-5 stainless steel, one-piece bolt from 4340 CM steel. Guaranteed accuracy at 100 yards.
Price: $3,499.00
Price: Long Range w/heavy bbl., varmint stock..............................$3,999.00
Price: Tactical w/28î bbl., muzzle brake, adj. stock $4,499.00

NEW ULTRA LIGHT ARMS
Calibers: Custom made in virtually every current chambering. **Barrel:** Douglas, length to order. **Weights:** 4.75–7.5 lbs. **Length:** Varies. **Stock:** Kevlar graphite composite, variety of finishes. **Sights:** None furnished; drilled and tapped for scope mounts. **Features:** Timney trigger, hand-lapped action, button-rifled barrel, hand-bedded action, sling-swivel studs, optional Jewell trigger. Made in USA by New Ultra Light Arms.
Price: Model 20 Ultimate Mountain Rifle $3,500.00
Price: Model 20 Ultimate Varmint Rifle $3,500.00
Price: Model 24 Ultimate Plains Rifle...$3,600.00
Price: Model 28 Ultimate Alaskan Rifle..$3,900.00
Price: Model 40 Ultimate African Rifle..$3,900.00

NOSLER MODEL 48 SERIES
Calibers: Offered in most popular calibers including .280 Ackley Improved and 6.5-284 wildcats. **Barrel:** 24 in. Long Range 26 in. **Weight:** 7.25–8 lbs. **Stock:** Walnut or composite. Custom Model is made to order with several optional features.
Price: Heritage $2,035.00
Price: Custom Model from $2,595.00
Price: Long Range $2,675.00

REMINGTON MODEL 700 CDL CLASSIC DELUXE
Calibers: .243 Win., .270 Win., 7mm-08 Rem., 7mm Rem. Mag., .30-06, .300 Win. Mag. **Barrels:** 24 in. or 26-in. round tapered. **Weights:** 7.4–7.6 lbs. **Lengths:** 43.6–46.5 in. overall. **Stocks:** Straight-comb American walnut stock, satin finish, checkering, right-handed cheekpiece, black fore-end tip and grip cap, sling swivel studs. **Sights:** None. **Features:** Satin blued finish, jeweled bolt body, drilled and tapped for scope mounts. Hinged-floorplate magazine capacity: 4, standard calibers; 3, magnum calibers. SuperCell recoil pad, cylindrical receiver, integral extractor. Introduced 2004. CDL SF (stainless fluted) chambered for .260 Rem., .257 Wby. Mag., .270 Win., .270 WSM, 7mm-08 Rem., 7mm Rem. Mag., .30-06, .300 WSM. Left-hand versions introduced 2008 in six calibers. Made in U.S. by Remington Arms Co., Inc.
Price: Standard Calibers, From ....**$1,029.00–$1,089.00**
Price: CDL SF, From **$1,226.00**

REMINGTON MODEL 700 BDL
Calibers: .243 Win., .270 Win., 7mm Rem. Mag., .30-06, **Barrels:** 22 in., 24 in., 26-in. round tapered. **Weights:** 7.25–7.4 lbs. **Lengths:** 41.6–46.5 in. overall. **Stock:** Walnut. Gloss-finish pistol grip stock with skip-line checkering, black forend tip and grip cap with white line spacers. Quick-release floorplate. **Sights:** Gold bead ramp front; hooded ramp, removable step-adjustable rear with windage screw. **Features:** Side safety, receiver tapped for scope mounts, matte receiver top, quick detachable swivels.
Price: Standard Calibers $994.00

REMINGTON MODEL 700 SPS
Calibers: .22-250 Rem., 6.8 Rem SPC, .223 Rem., .243 Win., .270 Win., .270

Prices given are believed to be accurate at time of publication however, many factors affect retail pricing so exact prices are not possible.

CENTERFIRE RIFLES Bolt Action

WSM, 7mm-08 Rem., 7mm Rem. Mag., 7mm Rem. Ultra Mag., .30-06, .308 Win., .300 WSM, .300 Win. Mag., .300 Rem. Ultra Mag. Barrels: 20 in., 24 in. or 26 in. carbon steel. Weights: 7–7.6 lbs. Lengths: 39.6–46.5 in. overall. Stock: Black synthetic, sling swivel studs, SuperCell recoil pad. Woodtech model has walnut decorated synthetic stock with overmolded grip patterns. Camo stock available. Sights: None. Barrel: Bead-blasted 416 stainless steel. Features: Introduced 2005. SPS Stainless replaces Model 700 BDL Stainless Synthetic. Plated internal fire control component. SPS DM features detachable box magazine. SPS Varmint includes X-Mark Pro trigger, 26-in. heavy contour barrel, vented beavertail fore-end, dual front sling swivel studs. Made in U.S. by Remington Arms Co., Inc.
Price: From .... $724.00–$838.00

REMINGTON 700 SPS TACTICAL
Calibers: .223 .300 AAC Blackout and .308 Win. Features: 20-in. heavy-contour tactical-style barrel; dual-point pillar bedding; black synthetic stock with Hogue overmoldings; semi-beavertail fore-end; X-Mark Pro adjustable trigger system; satin black oxide metal finish; hinged floorplate magazine; SuperCell recoil pad.
Price: From .... $788.00–$842.00

REMINGTON MODEL 700 VLS
Calibers: .204 Ruger, .223 Rem., .22-250 Rem., .243 Win., .308 Win. Barrel: 26-in. heavy contour barrel (0.820-in. muzzle O.D.), concave target-style barrel crown. Weight: 9.4 lbs. Length: 45.75 in. overall. Stock: Brown laminated stock, satin finish, with beavertail fore-end, grip cap, rubber buttpad. Sights: None. Features: Introduced 1995.
Price: $1,056.00

REMINGTON MODEL 700 SENDERO SF II
Calibers: .25-06 Rem., .264 Win. Mag., 7mm Rem. Mag., 7mm Rem. Ultra Mag, .300 Win. Mag., .300 Rem. Ultra Mag. Barrel: Satin stainless 26-in. heavy contour fluted. Weight: 8.5 lbs. Length: 45.75 in. overall. Stock: Black composite reinforced with aramid fibers, beavertail fore-end, palm swell. Sights: None. Features: Aluminum bedding block. Drilled and tapped for scope mounts, hinged floorplate magazines. Introduced 1996. Made in U.S. by Remington Arms Co., Inc.
Price: $1,500.00

REMINGTON MODEL 700 VTR SERIES
Calibers: .204 Ruger, .22-250, .223 Rem., .260 Rem., .308 Win. Barrel: 22-in. triangular counterbored with integrated muzzle brake. Weight: 7.5 lbs. Length: 41.625 in. overall. Features: FDE stock with black overmold strips and carbon steel barrel, or with black stock with gray grips and stainless barrel. ented semi-beavertail fore-end, tactical-style dual swivel mounts for bipod, matte blue on exposed metal surfaces.
Price: From $930.00

REMINGTON MODEL 700 VARMINT SF
Calibers: .22-250, .223, .220 Swift, .308 Win. Barrel: 26-in. stainless steel fluted. Weight: 8.5 lbs. Length: 45.75 in. Features: Synthetic stock with ventilated forend, stainless steel/trigger guard/floorplate, dual tactical swivels for bipod attachment.
Price: $991.00

REMINGTON MODEL 700 MOUNTAIN SS
Calibers: 6.5 Creedmoor, .25-06, .270 Win., .280 Rem., 7mm-08, .308 Win., .30-06. Barrel: 22 in. Length: 40.6 in. Weight: 6.5 lbs. Features: Satin stainless finish, Bell & Carlson Aramid Fiber stock.
Price: From.. $1,152.00

REMINGTON MODEL 700 XCR TACTICAL
Calibers: .308 Win., .300 Win. Mag., 338 Lapua Mag. Detachable box magazine on Lapua model. Barrel: 26-in. varmint contour, fluted and free floating. Features: Tactical, long-range precision rifle with Bell & Carlson Tactical stock in OD Green, full-length aluminum bedding, adjustable X-Mark Pro trigger. Muzzle brake on .338 Lapua model.
Price: $1,540.00
Price: .338 Lapua $2,515.00

REMINGTON MODEL 700 AWR
Calibers: .270 Win., .30-06, .300 Win. Mag., .300 Rem. Ultra Mag., .338 RUM, .338 Win. Mag. Barrel: 24- or 26-in. free floating. Features: Adjustable trigger, fiberglass stock. American Wilderness Rifle.
Price: $1,150.00

REMINGTON MODEL 700 LONG RANGE
Calibers: .25-06 Rem., 7mm Rem. Mag., .30-06, .300 Win. Mag., .300 Rem. Ultra Mag. Barrel: 26-in. heavy contour with concave target-style crown. Weight: 9 lbs. Features: Bell and Carlson M40 tactical stock, externally adjustable trigger, aluminum bedding block.
Price: $880.00

REMINGTON MODEL 783
Calibers: .223 Rem., .22-250, .243 Win., .270 Win., 7mm Rem. Mag., .308 Win., .30-06, .300 Win. Mag. Barrel: 22 in. Stock: Synthetic. Weight: 7–7.25 lbs. Finish: Matte black. Features: Adjustable trigger with two-position trigger-block safety, magnum contour button-rifle barrel, cylindrical receiver with minimum-size ejection port, pillar-bedded stock, detachable box magazine, 90-degree bolt throw.
Price: $399.00
Price: Compact with 18.25- or 20-in. bbl. $399.00

REMINGTON MODEL SEVEN CDL
Calibers: .243, .260 Rem., 7mm-08, .308 Win. Barrel: 20 in. Weight: 6.5 lbs. Length: 39.25 in. Stock: Walnut with black fore-end tip, satin finish. Features: Lightweight barrel has 16.5-in. barrel with threaded muzzle, synthetic camo stock, is available in .300 AAC Blackout chambering.
Price: CDL $1,039.00
Price: Synthetic stock $731.00
Price: Synthetic stock/stainless $838.00
Price: Lightweight/threaded $795.00

REMINGTON 40-XB TACTICAL
Caliber: .308 Win. Features: Stainless steel bolt with Teflon coating; hinged floorplate; adjustable trigger; 27.25-in. tri-fluted 1:14 in. twist barrel; H-S Precision Pro Series tactical stock, black color with dark green spiderweb; two front swivel studs; one rear swivel stud; vertical pistol grip. From the Remington Custom Shop.
Price: $3,195.00

REMINGTON 40-X TIR
Caliber: .308 Win. Features: Adjustable trigger, 24-in. match-grade, hand-lapped barrel, AAC 51T muzzle brake adaptor, H-S Precision PST tactical stock with adjustable length-of-pull and cheek piece, vertical pistol grip, clip-slotted Picatinny rail. Target Interdiction Rifle from the Remington Custom Shop.
Price: $4,095.00

<footer>
Prices given are believed to be accurate at time of publication however, many factors affect retail pricing so exact prices are not possible.

</footer>

CENTERFIRE RIFLES Bolt Action

REMINGTON 40-XB RANGEMASTER
Calibers: Almost any caliber from .22 BR Rem. to .300 Rem. Ultra Mag. Single-shot or repeater. **Features:** Stainless steel bolt with Teflon coating; hinged floorplate; adjustable trigger; 27.25-in. tri-fluted 1:14 in. twist barrel; walnut stock. From the Remington Custom Shop.
Price: $2,595.00
Price: Repeater $2,717.00

REMINGTON 40-XS TACTICAL SERIES
Caliber: .338 Lapua Magnum. **Features:** 416 stainless steel Model 40-X 24-in. 1:12 in. twist barreled action; black polymer coating; McMillan A3 series stock with adjustable length of pull and adjustable comb; adjustable trigger and Sunny Hill heavy-duty, all-steel trigger guard; Tactical Weapons System has Harris bi-pod with quick adjust swivel lock, Leupold Mark IV 3.5-10x40 long range M1 scope with Mil-Dot reticle, Badger Ordnance all-steel Picatinny scope rail and rings, military hard case, Turner AWS tactical sling. From the Remington Custom Shop.
Price: .308 Win. $4,400.00
Price: .338 Lapua $4,995.00
Price: Tactical Weapons System, From $7,695.00

ROCK ISLAND ARMORY TCM
Caliber: .22 TCM. **Capacity:** 5-round magazine, interchangeable with .22 TCM 17-round pistol magazine. **Barrel:** 22.75 in. **Weight:** 6 lbs. **Features:** Introduced in 2013. Manufactured in the Philippines and imported by Armscor Precision International.
Price: $450.00

RUGER PRECISION RIFLE
Calibers: 6mm Creedmoor, 6.5 Creedmoor, 6.5 PRC, .300 PRC, .308 Win., .300 Win. Mag., .338 Lapua Mag. **Capacity:** 10-round magazine. **Barrel:** Medium contour 20 in. (.308), 24 in. (6mm, 6.5), 26 in. (PRC & Magnums). **Stock:** Folding with adjustable length of pull and comb height. Soft rubber buttplate, sling attachment points, Picatinny bottom rail. **Weight:** 9.7–11 lbs. **Features:** Three lug one-piece CNC-machined bolt with oversized handle, dual cocking cams; multi-magazine interface works with Magpul, DPMS, SR-25, M110, AICS and some M14 magazines; CNC-machined 4140 chrome-moly steel upper; Ruger Marksman adjustable trigger with wrench stored in bolt shroud; comes with two 10-round Magpul magazines. Introduced in 2016.
Price: .308, Creedmoor and PRC calibers $1,599.00
Price: With muzzle brake $1,799.00
Price: Magnum calibers $2,099.00

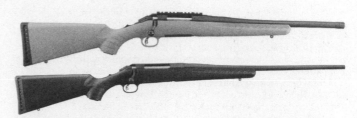

RUGER AMERICAN RIFLE
Calibers: .22-250, .243, 7mm-08, .308, .270 Win., .30-06, .300 Win. Mag, .350 Legend, .450 Bushmaster. **Capacity:** 4-round rotary magazine. **Barrels:** 22 in. or 18 in. (Compact). **Length:** 42.5 in. **Weight:** 6.25 lbs. **Stock:** Black composite. **Finish:** Matte black or matte stainless (All Weather model). **Features:** Tang safety, hammer-forged free-floating barrel. Available with factory mounted Redfield Revolution 4x scope. Ranch model has Flat Dark Earth composite stock, Predator has Moss Green composite stock, both chambered in several additional calibers to standard model.
Price: Standard or compact..$489.00
Price: With scope..$639.00
Price: Ranch or Predator model $529.00
Price: .300 Win. Mag. $699.00

RUGER GUNSITE SCOUT RIFLE
Caliber: .308 Win. **Capacity:** 10-round magazine. **Barrel:** 16.5 in. **Weight:** 7 lbs. **Length:** 38–39.5 in. **Stock:** Black laminate. **Sights:** Front post sight and rear adjustable. **Features:** Gunsite Scout Rifle is a credible rendition of Col. Jeff Cooper's "fighting carbine" scout rifle. The Ruger Gunsite Scout Rifle is a platform in the Ruger M77 family. While the Scout Rifle has M77 features such as controlled round feed and integral scope mounts (scope rings included), the 10-round detachable box magazine is the first clue this isn't your grandfather's Ruger rifle. The Ruger Gunsite Scout Rifle has a 16.5-in. medium contour, cold hammer-forged, alloy steel barrel with a Mini-14 protected nonglare post front sight and receiver mounted, adjustable ghost ring rear sight for out-of-the-box usability. A forward-mounted Picatinny rail offers options in mounting an assortment of optics, including scout scopes available from Burris and Leupold, for "both eyes open" sighting and super-fast target acquisition.
Price: $1,139.00
Price: (stainless) $1,199.00

RUGER MODEL 77 SERIES
Calibers: .17 Hornet, .22 Hornet, .357 Magnum, .44 Magnum. **Capacities:** 4–6 rounds. **Barrel:** 18.5 in. (.357 and .44 Mag,), 20 or 24 in. (.17 Hornet and .22 Hornet). **Weight:** 5.5–7.5 lbs. **Stock:** American walnut, black synthetic, Next G1 Vista Camo or Green Mountain laminate.
Price: 77/17, Green Mtn. laminate stock...........................$969.00
Price: 77/22, Green Mtn. laminate stock...........................$969.00
Price: 77/22, walnut stock...$939.00
Price: 77/357, 77/44, black synthetic stock........................$999.00
Price: 77/44, Next G1 Vista camo..................................$1,060.00

RUGER GUIDE GUN
Calibers: .30-06, .300 Win. Mag., .338 Win. Mag., .375 Ruger, .416 Ruger. **Capacities:** 3 or 4 rounds. **Barrel:** 20 in. with barrel band sling swivel and removable muzzle brake. **Weights:** 8–8.12 pounds. **Stock:** Green Mountain laminate. **Finish:** Hawkeye matte stainless. **Sights:** Adjustable rear, bead front. Introduced 2013.
Price: $1,269.00

Prices given are believed to be accurate at time of publication however, many factors affect retail pricing so exact prices are not possible.

RUGER HAWKEYE

Calibers: .204 Ruger, .223 Rem., .243 Win., .270 Win., 6.5 Creedmoor, 7mm/08, 7mm Rem. Mag., .308 Win., .30-06, .300 Win. Mag., .338 Win. Mag., .375 Ruger, .416 Ruger. **Capacities:** 4-round magazine, except 3-round magazine for magnums; 5-round magazine for .204 Ruger and .223 Rem. **Barrels:** 22 in., 24 in. **Weight:** 6.75–8.25 lbs. **Length:** 42–44.4 in. overall. **Stock:** American walnut, laminate or synthetic. FTW has camo stock, muzzle brake. Long Range Target has adjustable target stock, heavy barrel. **Sights:** None furnished. Receiver has Ruger integral scope mount base, Ruger 1 in. rings. **Features:** Includes Ruger LC6 trigger, new red rubber recoil pad, Mauser-type controlled feeding, claw extractor, 3-position safety, hammer-forged steel barrels, Ruger scope rings. Walnut stocks have wrap-around cut checkering on the forearm, and more rounded contours on stock and top of pistol grips. Matte stainless all-weather version features synthetic stock. Hawkeye African chambered in .375 Ruger, .416 Ruger and has 23-in. blued barrel, checkered walnut stock, windage-adjustable shallow V-notch rear sight, white bead front sight. Introduced 2007.

Price: Standard, right- and left-hand	$939.00
Price: Compact	$939.00
Price: Laminate Compact	$999.00
Price: Compact Magnum	$969.00
Price: VT Varmint Target	$1,139.00
Price: Predator	$1,139.00
Price: African with muzzle brake	$1,279.00
Price: FTW Hunter	$1,279.00
Price: Long Range Target	$1,279.00

SAKO TRG-22 TACTICAL RIFLE

Calibers: 6.5 Creedmoor, .308 Winchester (TRG-22). For TRG-22A1 add .260 Rem. TRG-42 only available in .300 Win. Mag., or .338 Lapua. **Features:** Target-grade Cr-Mo or stainless barrels with muzzle brake; three locking lugs; 60-degree bolt throw; adjustable two-stage target trigger; adjustable or folding synthetic stock; receiver-mounted integral 17mm axial optics rails with recoil stop-slots; tactical scope mount for modern three-turret tactical scopes (30 and 34 mm tube diameter); optional bipod. 22A1 has folding stock with two-hinge design, M-LOK fore-end, full aluminum middle chassis.

Price: TRG-22	$3,495.00
Price: TRG-22A1	$6,725.00
Price: TRG-42	$4,550.00

SAKO MODEL 85

Calibers: .22-250 Rem., .243 Win., .25-06 Rem., .260 Rem., 6.5x55mm, .270 Win., .270 WSM, 7mm-08, 7x64, .308 Win., .30-06; 7mm WSM, .300 WSM, .338 Federal, 8x57IS, 9.3x62. **Barrels:** 22.4 in., 22.9 in., 24.4 in. **Weight:** 7.75 lbs. **Length:** NA. **Stock:** Polymer, laminated or high-grade walnut, straight comb, shadow-line cheekpiece. **Sights:** None furnished. **Features:** Controlled-round feeding, adjustable trigger, matte stainless or nonreflective satin blue. Offered in a wide range of variations and models. Introduced 2006. Imported from Finland by Beretta USA.

Price: Grey Wolf	$1,725.00
Price: Black Bear	$1,850.00
Price: Kodiak	$1,950.00
Price: Varmint Laminated	$2,025.00
Price: Classic	$2,275.00
Price: Bavarian	$2,200.00–$2,300.00
Price: Bavarian carbine, Full-length stock	$2,400.00
Price: Brown Bear	$2,175.00

SAKO 85 FINNLIGHT

Similar to the Model 85 but chambered in .243 Win., .25-06, .260 Rem., 6.5 Creedmoor, .270 Win., .270 WSM, .300 WSM, .30-06, .300 WM, .308 Win., 6.5x55mm, 7mm Rem Mag., 7mm-08. **Weights:** 6 lbs., 3 oz.–6 lbs. 13 oz. **Features:** Stainless steel barrel and receiver, black synthetic stock. Finnlight II has composite stock with carbon fiber bedding, adjustable comb.

Price:	$1,800.00
Price: Finnlight II	$2,475.00

SAVAGE AXIS SERIES

Calibers: .243 Win., 6.5 Creedmoor, 7mm-08 Rem., .308 Win., .25-06 Rem., .270 Win, .30-06, .223 Rem., .22-250 Rem. **Barrel:** 22 in. **Weight:** 6.5 lbs. **Length:** 43.875 in. **Stock:** Black synthetic or camo, including pink/black Muddy Girl. **Sights:** Drilled and tapped for scope mounts. Several models come with factory mounted Weaver Kaspa 3-9x40 scope. **Features:** Available with black matte or stainless finish

Price: From	$363.00–$525.00

SAVAGE MODEL 25 VARMINTER

Calibers: .17 Hornet, .22 Hornet, .222 Rem., .204 Ruger, .223 Rem. **Capacity:** 4-round magazine. **Barrel:** 24-in. medium-contour fluted barrel with recessed target crown, free-floating sleeved barrel, dual pillar bedding. **Weight:** 8.25 lbs. **Length:** 43.75 in. overall. **Stock:** Brown laminate with beavertail-style fore-end. Thumbhole stock available. **Sights:** Weaver-style bases installed. **Features:** Diameter-specific action built around the .223 Rem. bolt head dimension. Three locking lugs, 60-degree bolt lift, AccuTrigger adjustable from 2.5–3.25 lbs. Walking Varminter has black synthetic or camo stock, 22-in. barrel. **Weight:** 7.15 lbs. **Length:** 41.75 in. Introduced 2008. Made in USA by Savage Arms, Inc.

Price: From	$774.00–$824.00
Price: Walking Varminter	$619.00–$671.00

SAVAGE CLASSIC SERIES MODEL 14/114

Calibers: .243 Win., 7mm-08 Rem., .308 Win., .270 Win., 7mm Rem. Mag., .30-06, .300 Win. Mag. **Capacities:** 3- or 4-round magazine. **Barrels:** 22 in. or 24 in. **Weight:** 7–7.5 lbs. **Length:** 41.75–43.75 in. overall (Model 14 short action); 43.25–45.25 in. overall (Model 114 long action). **Stock:** Satin lacquer American walnut with ebony fore-end, wraparound checkering, Monte Carlo comb and cheekpiece. **Sights:** None furnished. Receiver drilled and tapped for scope mounting. **Features:** AccuTrigger, matte blued barrel and action, hinged floorplate.

Price: From	$979.00

Prices given are believed to be accurate at time of publication however, many factors affect retail pricing so exact prices are not possible.

74TH EDITION, 2020 ⊕ 373

SAVAGE MODEL 12 VARMINT/TARGET SERIES

Calibers: .204 Ruger, .223 Rem., .22-250 Rem. **Capacity:** 4-shot magazine. **Barrel:** 26 in. stainless barreled action, heavy fluted, free-floating and button-rifled barrel. **Weight:** 10 lbs. **Length:** 46.25 in. overall. **Stock:** Dual pillar bedded, low profile, black synthetic or laminated stock with extra-wide beavertail fore-end. **Sights:** None furnished; drilled and tapped for scope mounting. **Features:** Recessed target-style muzzle. AccuTrigger, oversized bolt handle, detachable box magazine, swivel studs. Model 112BVSS has heavy target-style prone laminated stock with high comb, Wundhammer palm swell, internal box magazine. Model 12VLP DBM has black synthetic stock, detachable magazine, and additional chamberings in .243, .308 Win., .300 Win. Mag. Model 12FV has blued receiver. Model 12BTCSS has brown laminate vented thumbhole stock. Made in USA by Savage Arms, Inc.

Price: 12 FCV	**$780.00**
Price: 12 BVSS	**$1,146.00**
Price: 12 Varminter Low Profile (VLP)	**$1,181.00**
Price: 12 Long Range Precision	**$1,288.00**
Price: 12 BTCSS Thumbhole stock	**$1,293.00**
Price: 12 Long Range Precision Varminter	**$1,554.00**
Price: 12 F Class	**$1,648.00**
Price: 12 Palma	**$2,147.00**

SAVAGE MODEL 11/111 HUNTER SERIES

Calibers: .223 Rem., .22-250 Rem., .243 Win., 6.5 Creedmoor, .260 Rem., 6.5x284 Norma, .338 Lapua, 7mm-08 Rem., .308 Win. **Capacities:** 2- or 4-round magazine; .25-06 Rem., .270 Win., 7mm Rem. Mag., .30-06, .300 Win. Mag., (long action Model 111), 3- or 4-round magazine. **Barrels:** 20 in., 22 in. or 24 in.; blued free-floated barrel. **Weights:** 6.5–6.75 lbs. **Lengths:** 41.75–43.75 in. overall (Model 11); 42.5–44.5 in. overall (Model 111). **Stock:** Graphite/fiberglass filled composite or hardwood. **Sights:** Ramp front, open fully adjustable rear; drilled and tapped for scope mounting. **Features:** Three-position top tang safety, double front locking lugs. Introduced 1994. Made in USA by Savage Arms, Inc.

Price: From .... **$684.00–$1,421.00**

SAVAGE MODEL 10 GRS

Calibers: 6.5 Creedmoor, .308 Win. **Stock:** Synthetic with adjustable comb, vertical pistol grip. **Sights:** None. Picatinny rail atop receiver. **Features:** Designed primarily for Law Enforcement. Detachable box magazine.

Price: **$1,450.00**

SAVAGE MODEL 10FP/110FP LAW ENFORCEMENT SERIES

Calibers: .223 Rem., .308 Win. (Model 10), 4-round magazine; .25-06 Rem., .300 Win. Mag., (Model 110), 3- or 4-round magazine. **Barrel:** 24 in.; matte blued free-floated heavy barrel and action. **Weight:** 6.5–6.75 lbs. **Length:** 41.75–43.75 in. overall (Model 10); 42.5–44.5 in. overall (Model 110). **Stock:** Black graphite/fiberglass composition, pillar-bedded, positive checkering. **Sights:** None furnished. Receiver drilled and tapped for scope mounting. **Features:** Black matte finish on all metal parts. Double swivel studs on the fore-end for sling and/or bipod mount. Right- or left-hand. Model 110FP introduced 1990. Model 10FP introduced 1998. Model 10FCP HS has HS Precision black synthetic tactical stock with molded alloy bedding

system, Leupold 3.5-10x40 black matte scope with Mil Dot reticle, Farrell Picatinny Rail Base, flip-open lens covers, 1.25-in. sling with QD swivels, Harris bipod, Storm heavy-duty case. Made in USA by Savage Arms, Inc.

Price: Model 10FCP McMillan, McMillan fiberglass tactical stock..	**$1,591.00**
Price: Model 10FCP-HS HS Precision, HS Precision tactical stock...	**$1,315.00**
Price: Model 10FCP	**$925.00**
Price: Model 10FLCP, left-hand model, standard stock or Accu-Stock	**$975.00**
Price: Model 10FCP SR	**$785.00**
Price: Model 10 Precision Carbine	**$952.00**

SAVAGE 110 BA STEALTH

Calibers: .300 win, Mag., or .338 Lapua Mag. **Capacities:** Detachable 5- or 6-round box magazine. **Barrel:** 24 in. with threaded muzzle. **Stock:** Fab Defense GLR Shock buttstock, M-LOK fore-end. **Weight:** 11.125 lbs. **Features:** Adjustable AccuTrigger, Picatinny rail. Stealth Evolution has fluted heavy barrel, 10-round magazine, adjustable length of pull stock, Flat Dark Earth finish.

Price: Stealth	**$1,484.00**
Price: Stealth, .338 Lapua	**$1,624.00**
Price: Evolution	**$1,999.00**
Price: Evolution, .338 Lapua	**$2,149.00**

SAVAGE MODEL 10 PREDATOR HUNTER

Calibers: .204 Ruger. .223, .22-250, .243, .260 Rem., 6.5 Creedmoor, 6.5x284 Norma. **Barrel:** 22 in. medium-contour. **Weight:** 7.25 lbs. **Length:** 43 in. overall. **Stock:** Synthetic with Mossy Oak Max-1 Camo coverage. **Features:** AccuTrigger, oversized bolt handle, right or left-hand action.

Price: **$999.00**

SAVAGE MODEL 110 PREDATOR

Calibers: .204 Ruger. .223, .22-250, .243, .260 Rem., 6.5 Creedmoor. **Capacity:** 4-round magazine. **Barrels:** 22 or 24 in. threaded heavy contour. **Weight:** 8.5 lbs. **Stock:** AccuStock with Mossy Oak Max-1 camo finish, soft grip surfaces, adjustable length of pull.

Price: **$899.00**

SAVAGE MODEL 110 HUNTER SERIES

Calibers: .204 Ruger. .223, .22-250, .243, .25-06, .260 Rem., 6.5 Creedmoor, .270 Win., 7mm-08 Rem., .280 Ackley Imp., .308 Win., .30-06, .300 Win. Mag. **Capacities:** 3- or 4-round magazine. **Barrels:** 22 or 24. in. **Weight:** 8.5 lbs. **Stock:** AccuStock with gray finish, soft-grip surfaces, adjustable length of pull.

Price: Hunter	**$749.00**
Price: Bear Hunter (.300 WSM, .338 Fed., .375 Ruger	**$999.00**
Price: Hog Hunter (20 in. bbl. open sights)	**$594.00**
Price: Brush Hunter (20-in. bbl., .338 Win., .375 Rug.)	**$784.00**
Price: Long Range Hunter (26 in. bbl., muzzle brake)	**$1,099.00**

SAVAGE MODEL 110 TACTICAL

Caliber: .308 Win. **Capacity:** 10-round magazine. **Barrels:** 20 or 24 in. threaded and fluted heavy contour. **Weight:** 8.65 lbs. **Stock:** AccuStock with soft-grip surfaces, AccuFit system. **Features:** Top Picatinny rail, right- or left-hand operation.

Price:	**$784.00**
Price: Tactical Desert (6mm, 6.5 Creedmoor, FDE finish	**$769.00**

SAVAGE MODEL 12 PRECISION TARGET SERIES BENCHREST
Calibers: .308 Win., 6.5x284 Norma, 6mm Norma BR. **Barrel:** 29-in. ultra-heavy. **Weight:** 12.75 lbs. **Length:** 50 in. overall. **Stock:** Gray laminate. **Features:** New Left-Load, Right-Eject target action, Target AccuTrigger adjustable from approx. 6 oz. to 2.5 lbs. oversized bolt handle, stainless extra-heavy free-floating and button-rifled barrel.
Price: $1,629.00

SAVAGE MODEL 12 PRECISION TARGET PALMA
Similar to Model 12 Benchrest but in .308 Win. only, 30-in. barrel, multi-adjustable stock, weighs 13.3 lbs.
Price: $2,147.00

SAVAGE MODEL 12 F CLASS TARGET RIFLE
Similar to Model 12 Benchrest but chambered in 6 Norma BR, 30-in. barrel, weighs 13.3 lbs.
Price: $1,648.00

SAVAGE MODEL 12 F/TR TARGET RIFLE
Similar to Model 12 Benchrest but in .308 Win. only, 30-in. barrel, weighs 12.65 lbs.
Price: $1,538.00

SAVAGE MODEL 112 MAGNUM TARGET
Caliber: .338 Lapua Magnum. Single shot. **Barrel:** 26-in. heavy with muzzle brake. **Stock:** Wood laminate. **Features:** AccuTrigger, matte black finish, oversized bolt handle, pillar bedding.
Price: $1,177.00

STEYR PRO HUNTER
Similar to the Classic Rifle except has ABS synthetic stock with adjustable butt spacers, straight comb without cheekpiece, palm swell, Pachmayr 1 in. swivels. Special 10-round magazine conversion kit available. Introduced 1997. Imported from Austria by Steyr Arms, Inc.
Price: From..................................$1,150.00–$1,377.00

STEYR SCOUT
Calibers: .223, .243, 7mm-08, .308 Win. **Capacity:** 5- or 10-shot magazine. **Barrel:** 19 in. fluted. **Weight:** 6.5 lbs. **Length:** NA. **Stock:** Gray Zytel. **Sights:** Pop-up front and rear. **Features:** Luggage case, scout sling, two stock spacers, two magazines. Introduced 1998. Imported from Austria by Steyr Arms, Inc.
Price: $1,725.00

STEYR SSG08
Calibers: .243 Win., 7.62x51 NATO (.308Win), 7.62x63B (.300 Win Mag)., .338 Lapua Mag. **Capacity:** 10-round magazine. **Barrels:** 20, 23.6 or 25.6 in. **Stock:** Dural aluminum folding stock black with .280 mm long UIT-rail

and various Picatinny rails. **Sights:** Front post sight and rear adjustable. **Features:** High-grade aluminum folding stock, adjustable cheekpiece and buttplate with height marking, and an ergonomical exchangeable pistol grip. Versa-Pod, muzzle brake, Picatinny rail, UIT rail on stock and various Picatinny rails on fore-end, and a 10-round HC-magazine. SBS rotary bolt action with four frontal locking lugs, arranged in pairs. Cold-hammer-forged barrels are available in standard or compact lengths.
Price: $5,899.00

STEYR SM 12
Calibers: .243, 6.5x55SE, .270 Win., 7mm-08 Rem., .308 Win., .30-06, .300 Win. Mag, .300 WSM, 9.3x62mm. **Barrels:** 20-in. blue or 25-in. stainless. **Stock:** Walnut with checkered grip and fore-end. Available in half or full-length configurations. **Sights:** Adjustable rear, ramp front with bead. Stainless barrel has no sights. **Features:** Sling swivels, Bavarian cheekpiece, hand-cocking system operated by thumb manually cocks firing mechanism.
Price: Standard-length stock.............................$2,545.00
Price: Full length (Mannlicher) $2,750.00

THOMPSON/CENTER VENTURE
Calibers: .270 Win., 7mm Rem. Mag., .30-06, .300 Win. Mag. **Capacity:** 3-round magazine. **Barrel:** 24 In., 20 in. (Compact). **Weight:** 7.5 lbs. **Stock:** Composite. **Sights:** None, Weaver-style base. **Features:** Standard-length action with Nitride fat bolt design, externally adjustable trigger, two-position safety, textured grip. Introduced 2009.
Price: $537.00

THOMPSON/CENTER VENTURE MEDIUM ACTION
Calibers: .204, .22-250, .223, .243, 7mm-08, .308 and 30TC. **Capacity:** 3+1 detachable nylon box magazine. **Features:** Bolt-action rifle with a 24-in. crowned medium weight barrel, classic-styled composite stock with inlaid traction grip panels, adjustable 3.5- to 5-pound trigger along with a drilled and tapped receiver (bases included). **Weight:** 7 lbs. **Length:** 43.5 in.
Price: $537.00

THOMPSON/CENTER VENTURE PREDATOR PDX
Calibers: .204, .22-250, .223, .243, .308. **Weight:** 8 lbs. **Length:** 41.5 in. **Features:** Bolt-action rifle similar to Venture medium action but with heavy, deep-fluted 22-in. barrel and Max-1 camo finish overall.
Price: From..$638.00

THOMPSON/CENTER LONG RANGE RIFLE
Calibers: .243 Win., 6.5 Creedmoor, .308 Win. **Capacity:** 10-round magazine. **Barrel:** 20 in. (.308), 22 in. (6.5), 24 in. (.243). Fluted and threaded with muzzle brake. **Weight:** 11-12 lbs. **Stock:** Composite black with adjustable cheek piece and buttplate, built-in Magpul M-LOK accessory slots. **Finish:** Black or Flat Dark Earth. **Features:** Picatinny-style rail, adjustable trigger, Caldwell Pic Rail XLA bipod. From the T/C Performance Center.
Price: $1,211.00

Prices given are believed to be accurate at time of publication however, many factors affect retail pricing so exact prices are not possible.

74TH EDITION, 2020 ✦ **375**

THOMPSON/CENTER COMPASS
Calibers: .204 Ruger, .223 Rem, .22-250 Rem., .243 Win., 6.5 Creedmoor, .270 Win., 7mm-08 Rem., 7mm Rem. Mag., .308 Win., .30-06, .300 Win. Mag. **Capacity:** 4-5-round detachable magazine. **Barrel:** Match-grade 22 in., (24 in. magnums.) with threaded muzzle. **Weight:** 7 ¼-7 1/2 lbs. Stock: Composite black with textured grip panels.
Price: From...$399.00

TIKKA T3X SERIES Calibers: Virtually any popular chambering including .204 Ruger .222 Rem., .223 Rem., .243 Win., .25-06, 6.5x55 SE, .260 Rem, .270 Win., .260 WSM, 7mm-08, 7mm Rem. Mag., .308 Win., .30-06, .300 Win. Mag., .300 WSM. **Barrels:** 20, 22.4, 24.3 in. **Stock:** Checkered walnut, laminate or modular synthetic with interchangeable pistol grips. Newly designed recoil pad. **Features:** Offered in a variety of different models with many options. Left-hand models available. One minute-of-angle accuracy guaranteed. Introduced in 2016. Made in Finland by Sako. Imported by Beretta USA.
Price: Hunter from $875.00
Price: Lite from (shown) $725.00
Price: Varmint from $950.00
Price: Laminate stainless $1,050.00
Price: Forest.. $1,000.00
Price: Tac A1 (shown)...................................... $1,899.00
Price: Compact Tactical Rifle, From................. $1,150.00

WEATHERBY MARK V
This classic action goes back more than 60 years to the late '50s. Several significant changes were made to the original design in 2016. Stocks have a slimmer fore-end and smaller grip, which has an added palm swell. The new LXX trigger is adjustable down to 2.5 lbs. and has precision ground and polished surfaces and a wider trigger face. All new Mark V rifles come with sub-MOA guarantee. Range Certified (RC) models are range tested and come with a certified ballistic data sheet and RC engraved floorplate. Calibers: Varies depending on model. Barrels: 22 in., 24 in., 26 in., 28 in. Weight: 5 3/4 to 10 lbs. Stock: Varies depending on model. Sights: None furnished. Features: Deluxe version comes in all Weatherby calibers plus .243 Win., .270 Win., 7mm-08 Rem., .30-06, .308 Win. Lazermark same as Mark V Deluxe except stock has extensive oak leaf pattern laser carving on pistol grip and fore-end; chambered in Wby. Magnums .257, .270 Win., 7mm., .300, .340, with 26 in. barrel. Sporter is same as the Mark V Deluxe without the embellishments. Metal has low-luster blue, stock is Claro walnut with matte finish, Monte Carlo comb, recoil pad. Chambered for these Wby. Mags: .257, .270 Win., 7mm, .300, .340. Other chamberings: 7mm Rem. Mag., .300 Win. Introduced 1993. Six Mark V models come with synthetic stocks. Ultra Lightweight rifles weigh 5.75 to 6.75 lbs.; 24 in., 26 in. fluted stainless barrels with recessed target crown; Bell & Carlson stock with CNC-machined aluminum bedding plate and tan "spider web" finish, skeletonized handle and sleeve. Available in .243 Win., .25-06 Rem., .270 Win., 7mm-08 Rem., 7mm Rem. Mag., .280 Rem, .308 Win., .30-06, .300 Win. Mag. Wby. Mag chamberings: .240, .257, .270 Win., 7mm, .300. Accumark uses Mark V action with heavy-contour

26 in. and 28 in. stainless barrels with black oxidized flutes, muzzle diameter of .705 in. No sights, drilled and tapped for scope mounting. Stock is composite with matte gel-coat finish, full-length aluminum bedding block. Weighs 8.5 lbs. Chambered for these Wby. Mags: .240, .257, .270, 7mm, .300, .340, .338-378, .30-378. Other chamberings: 6.5 Creedmoor, .270 Win., .308 Win., 7mm Rem. Mag., .300 Win. Mag. Altitude has 22-, 24-, 26-, 28-in. fluted stainless steel barrel, Monte Carlo carbon fiber composite stock with raised comb, Kryptek Altitude camo. Tacmark has 28-in. free floated fluted barrel with Accubrake, fully adjustable stock, black finish. Safari Grade has fancy grade checkered French walnut stock with ebony fore-end and grip cap, adjustable express rear and hooded front sights, from the Weatherby Custom Shop. Camilla series is lightweight model designed to fit a woman's anatomy. Offered in several variations chambered for .240 Wby. Mag., 6.5 Creedmoor, .270 Win., .308 Win., .30-06. Arroyo is available in Weatherby Magnums from .240 to .338-378, plus 6.5 Creedmoor, .300 Win. Mag., and .338 Lapua Mag. Finish is two-tone Cerakote with Brown Sand and FDE added flutes. Carbonmark has 26in. Proof Research carbon fiber threaded barrel and is chambered for .257 and .300 Wby. Mags. Outfitter is chambered for .240-.300 Wby. Magnums plus most popular calibers. Stock has Spiderweb accents. KCR model comes with Krieger Custom Match-grade barrel in .257, 6.5-300, .300 and .30-378 Wby. Magnums. Altitude is lightweight model (5 ¾-6 ¾ lbs.) and comes in Wby. Magnums from .240 to.300, plus 6.5 Creedmoor, .270 Win., .308, .30-06. Dangerous Game Rifle is offered in all Wby. Magnums from .300 to .450, plus .375 H&H. Hand laminated Monte Carlo composite stock. All Weatherby Mark V rifles are made in Sheridan, Wyoming.
Price: Mark V Deluxe $2,700.00
Price: Mark V Lazermark.................................. $2,800.00
Price: Mark V Sporter $1,800.00
Price: Mark V Ultra Lightweight $2,300.00
Price: Mark V Accumark .... $2,300.00–$2,700.00
Price: Mark V Altitude .... $3,000.00–$3,700.00
Price: Mark V Safari Grade Custom............ $6,900.00–$7,600.00
Price: Mark V Tacmark.................................... $4,100.00
Price: Mark V Camilla Series............ $2,300.00–$2,700.00
Price: Mark V Arroyo.. $2,800.00
Price: Mark V Carbonmark $4,100.00
Price: Mark V Outfitter .... $2,600-$2,800.00*
Price: Mark V Krieger Custom Rifle (KCR)....... $3,600-$4,100.00*
Price: Mark V Altitude $2,700.00*
Price: Mark V Dangerous Game Rifle $3,600.00
***Add $500 for optional Range Certified (RC) model with guaranteed sub-MOA accuracy certificate and target.**

WEATHERBY VANGUARD II SERIES
Calibers: Varies depending on model. Most Weatherby Magnums and many standard calibers. **Barrels:** 20, 24, or 26 in. **Weights:** 7.5–8.75 lbs. **Lengths:** 44–46.75 in. overall. **Stock:** Raised comb, Monte Carlo, injection-molded composite stock. **Sights:** None furnished. **Features:** One-piece forged, fluted bolt body with three gas ports, forged and machined receiver, adjustable trigger, factory accuracy guarantee. Vanguard Stainless has 410-Series stainless steel barrel and action, bead blasted matte metal finish. Vanguard Deluxe has raised comb, semi-fancy-grade Monte Carlo walnut stock with maplewood spacers, rosewood fore-end and grip cap, polished action with high-gloss blued metalwork. Sporter has Monte Carlo walnut stock with satin urethane finish, fineline diamond point checkering, contrasting rosewood fore-end tip, matte-blued metalwork. Sporter SS metalwork is 410 Series bead-blasted stainless steel. Vanguard Youth/Compact has 20 in. No. 1 contour barrel, short action, scaled-down nonreflective matte black hardwood stock with 12.5-in. length of pull, and full-size, injection-molded composite stock. Chambered for .223 Rem., .22-250 Rem., .243 Win., 7mm-08 Rem., .308 Win. Weighs 6.75 lbs.; OAL 38.9 in. Sub-MOA Matte and Sub-MOA Stainless models have pillar-bedded Fiberguard composite stock (Aramid, graphite unidirectional fibers and fiberglass) with 24-in. barreled action; matte black metalwork, Pachmayr Decelerator recoil pad. Sub-MOA Stainless metalwork is 410 Series bead-blasted stainless steel. Sub-MOA Varmint guaranteed to shoot 3-shot group of .99 in. or less when used with specified Weatherby factory or premium (non-Weatherby calibers) ammunition. Hand-laminated, tan Monte Carlo composite stock with black spiderwebbing; CNC-machined aluminum bedding block, 22 in. No. 3 contour barrel, recessed target crown. Varmint Special has tan injection-molded Monte Carlo composite stock, pebble grain finish, black spiderwebbing. 22 in. No. 3 contour barrel (.740-in. muzzle dia.), bead blasted matte black finish, recessed target crown. Back

Prices given are believed to be accurate at time of publication however, many factors affect retail pricing so exact prices are not possible.

Country has two-stage trigger, pillar-bedded Bell & Carlson stock, 24-in. fluted barrel, three-position safety.

Price: Vanguard Synthetic $649.00
Price: Vanguard Stainless $799.00
Price: Vanguard Deluxe, 7mm Rem. Mag., .300 Win. Mag.............$1,149.00
Price: Vanguard Sporter $849.00
Price: Vanguard Youth/Compact..$599.00
Price: Vanguard S2 Back Country $1,399.00
Price: Vanguard RC (Range Certified)......................................$1,199.00
Price: Vanguard Varmint Special $849.00
Price: Camilla (designed for women shooters) $849.00
Price: Lazerguard (Laser carved AA-grade walnut stock)..............$1,199.00
Price: H-Bar (tactical series) from ....**$1,149.00–$1,449.00**
Price: Weatherguard $749.00
Price: Modular Chassis $1,519.00
Price: Dangerous Game Rifle (DGR) .375 H&H........................$1,299.00
Price: Safari (.375 or .30-06) $1,199.00
Price: First Lite Fusion Camo $1,099.00
Price: Badlands Camo $849.00
Price: Accuguard $1,099.00
Price: Select $599.00
Price: Wilderness...$999.00

WINCHESTER MODEL 70 SUPER GRADE

Calibers: .270 Win., .270 WSM, 7mm Rem. Mag., .30-06, .300 Win Mag., .300 WSM, .338 Win. Mag. **Capacities:** 5 rounds (short action) or 3 rounds (long action). **Barrels:** 24 in. or 26 in. blued. **Weights:** 8–8.5 lbs. **Features:** Full fancy Grade IV/V walnut stock with shadow-line cheekpiece, controlled round feed with claw extractor, Pachmayr Decelerator pad. No sights but drilled and tapped for scope mounts.
Price: ....**$1,440.00–$1,480.00**

WINCHESTER MODEL 70 ALASKAN

Calibers: .30 06, .300 Win. Mag., .338 Win. Mag., .375 H&H Magnum. **Barrel:** 25 in **Weight:** 8.8 lbs. **Sights:** Folding adjustable rear, hooded brass bead front. **Stock:** Satin finished Monte Carlo with cut checkering. **Features:** Integral recoil lug, Pachmayr Decelerator recoil pad.
Price: $1,400.00

WINCHESTER MODEL 70 COYOTE LIGHT SUPRESSOR READY

Calibers: .22-250, .243 Win., .308 Win., .270 WSM, .300 WSM and .325 WSM. **Capacities:** 5-round magazine (3-round mag. in .270 WSM, .300 WSM and .325 WSM). **Barrel:** 22-in. fluted stainless barrel (24 in. in .270 WSM, .300 WSM and .325 WSM). **Threaded for suppressor or other muzzle device. Weight:** 7.5 lbs. **Length:** NA. **Features:** Composite Bell and Carlson stock, Pachmayr Decelerator pad. Controlled round feeding. No sights but drilled and tapped for mounts.
Price: ....**$1,270.00–$1,310.00**

WINCHESTER MODEL 70 FEATHERWEIGHT

Calibers: .22-250, .243, 6.5 Creedmoor, 7mm-08, .308, .270 WSM, 7mm WSM, .300 WSM, .325 WSM, .25-06, .270, .30-06, 7mm Rem. Mag., .300 Win. Mag., .338 Win. Mag. **Capacities:** 5 rounds (short action) or 3 rounds (long action). **Barrels:** 22-in. blued (24 in. in magnum chamberings). **Weights:** 6.5–7.25 lbs. **Length:** NA. **Features:** Satin-finished checkered Grade I walnut stock, controlled round feeding. Pachmayr Decelerator pad. No sights but drilled and tapped for scope mounts.
Price: $1,010.00
Price: Magnum calibers...$1,050.00
Price: Featherweight Stainless ....$1,210.00-**$1,250.00**

WINCHESTER MODEL 70 SPORTER

Calibers: .270 WSM, 7mm WSM, .300 WSM, .325 WSM, .25-06, .270, .30-06, 7mm Rem. Mag., .300 Win. Mag., .338 Win. Mag. **Capacities:** 5 rounds (short action) or 3 rounds (long action). **Barrels:** 22 in., 24 in. or 26 in. blued. **Weights:** 6.5–7.25 lbs. **Length:** NA. **Features:** Satin-finished checkered Grade I walnut stock with sculpted cheekpiece, controlled round feeding. Pachmayr Decelerator pad. No sights but drilled and tapped for scope mounts.
Price: $1,010.00

WINCHESTER MODEL 70 SAFARI EXPRESS

Calibers: .375 H&H Magnum, .416 Remington, .458 Win. Mag. **Barrel:** 24 in. **Weight:** 9 lbs. **Sights:** Fully adjustable rear, hooded brass bead front. **Stock:** Satin finished Monte Carlo with cut checkering, deluxe cheekpiece. **Features:** Forged steel receiver with double integral recoil lugs bedded front and rear, dual steel crossbolts, Pachmayr Decelerator recoil pad.
Price: $1,560.00

WINCHESTER XPR

Calibers: .243, 6.5 Creedmoor, 270 Win., .270 WSM, 7mm-08, 7mm Rem. Mag., .308 Win., .30-06, .300 Win. Mag., .300 WSM, .325 WSM, .338 Win. Mag.,.350 Legend. **Capacities:** Detachable box magazine holds 3 to 5 rounds. **Barrels:** 24 or 26 in. **Stock:** Black polymer with Inflex Technology recoil pad. **Weight:** Approx. 7 lbs. **Finish:** Matte blue. **Features:** Bolt unlock button, nickel coated Teflon bolt.
Price: $549.99
Price: Mossy Oak Break-Up Country camo stock................$600.00
Price: With Vortex II 3-9x40 scope......................................$710.00
Price: XPR Hunter Camo (shown)..$600.00
Price: Sporter w/Grade 1 walnut stock..............................$600.00
Price: True Timber Strata Camo $600.00
Price: Thumbhole Varmint Suppressor Ready $800.00

WINCHESTER XPC

Caliber: .243, 6.5 Creedmoor, 308 Winchester. **Capacity:** 3. **Barrel:** 20 in., free floating with target crown, threading for suppressor or muzzle brake. **Stock:** Cerakote fully machined alloy chassis frame, Magpul PRS Gen III fully adjustable buttstock. **Weight:** 10 lbs. **Length:** 40 in. **Features:** MOA Trigger System, two-position thumb safety. Full length Picatinny rail, M-LOK on fore-end and buttstock for attaching accessories.
Price: $1,600.00

ARMALITE AR-50
Caliber: .50 BMG **Barrel:** 31 in. **Weight:** 33.2 lbs. **Length:** 59.5 in. **Stock:** Synthetic. **Sights:** None furnished. **Features:** A single-shot bolt-action rifle designed for long-range shooting. Available in left-hand model. Made in USA by Armalite.
Price: $3,359.00

BALLARD 1875 1 1/2 HUNTER
Caliber: Various calibers. **Barrel:** 26–30 in. **Weight:** NA **Length:** NA. **Stock:** Hand-selected classic American walnut. **Sights:** Blade front, Rocky Mountain rear. **Features:** Color casehardened receiver, breechblock and lever. Many options available. Made in USA by Ballard Rifle & Cartridge Co.
Price: $3,250.00

BALLARD 1875 #3 GALLERY SINGLE SHOT
Caliber: Various calibers. **Barrel:** 24–28 in. octagonal with tulip. **Weight:** NA. **Length:** NA. **Stock:** Hand-selected classic American walnut. **Sights:** Blade front, Rocky Mountain rear. **Features:** Color casehardened receiver, breechblock and lever. Many options available. Made in USA by Ballard Rifle & Cartridge Co.
Price: $3,300.00

BALLARD 1875 #4 PERFECTION
Caliber: Various calibers. **Barrels:** 30 in. or 32 in. octagon, standard or heavyweight. **Weights:** 10.5 lbs. (standard) or 11.75 lbs. (heavyweight bbl.) **Length:** NA. **Stock:** Smooth walnut. **Sights:** Blade front, Rocky Mountain rear. **Features:** Rifle or shotgun-style buttstock, straight grip action, single- or double-set trigger, "S" or right lever, hand polished and lapped Badger barrel. Made in USA by Ballard Rifle & Cartridge Co.
Price: $3,950.00

BALLARD 1875 #7 LONG RANGE
Calibers: .32-40, .38-55, .40-65, .40-70 SS, .45-70 Govt., .45-90, .45-110. **Barrels:** 32 in., 34 in. half-octagon. **Weight:** 11.75 lbs. **Length:** NA. **Stock:** Walnut; checkered pistol grip shotgun butt, ebony fore-end cap. **Sights:** Globe front. **Features:** Designed for shooting up to 1,000 yards. Standard or heavy barrel; single or double-set trigger; hard rubber or steel buttplate. Introduced 1999. Made in USA by Ballard Rifle & Cartridge Co.
Price: From..$3,600.00

BALLARD 1875 #8 UNION HILL
Calibers: Various calibers. **Barrel:** 30-in. half-octagon. **Weight:** About 10.5 lbs. **Length:** NA. **Stock:** Walnut; pistol grip butt with cheekpiece. **Sights:** Globe front. **Features:** Designed for 200-yard offhand shooting. Standard or heavy barrel; double-set triggers; full loop lever; hook Schuetzen buttplate. Introduced 1999. Made in USA by Ballard Rifle & Cartridge Co.
Price: From..$4,175.00

BALLARD MODEL 1885 LOW WALL SINGLE SHOT RIFLE
Caliber: Various calibers. **Barrels:** 24–28 in. **Weight:** NA. **Length:** NA. **Stock:** Hand-selected classic American walnut. **Sights:** Blade front, sporting rear. **Features:** Color casehardened receiver, breechblock and lever. Many options available. Made in USA by Ballard Rifle & Cartridge Co.
Price: $3,300.00

BALLARD MODEL 1885 HIGH WALL STANDARD SPORTING SINGLE SHOT
Calibers: Various calibers. **Barrels:** Lengths to 34 in. **Weight:** NA. **Length:** NA. **Stock:** Straight-grain American walnut. **Sights:** Buckhorn or flattop rear, blade front. **Features:** Faithful copy of original Model 1885 High Wall; parts interchange with original rifles; variety of options available. Introduced 2000. Made in USA by Ballard Rifle & Cartridge Co.
Price: $3,300.00

BALLARD MODEL 1885 HIGH WALL SPECIAL SPORTING SINGLE SHOT
Calibers: Various calibers. **Barrels:** 28–30 in. octagonal. **Weight:** NA. **Length:** NA. **Stock:** Hand-selected classic American walnut. **Sights:** Blade front, sporting rear. **Features:** Color casehardened receiver, breechblock and lever. Many options available. Made in USA by Ballard Rifle & Cartridge Co.
Price: $3,600.00

BROWN MODEL 97D SINGLE SHOT
Calibers: Available in most factory and wildcat calibers from .17 Ackley Hornet to .375 Winchester. **Barrels:** Up to 26 in., air-gauged match grade. **Weight:** About 5 lbs., 11 oz. **Stock:** Sporter style with pistol grip, cheekpiece and Schnabel fore-end. **Sights:** None furnished; drilled and tapped for scope mounting. **Features:** Falling-block action gives rigid barrel-receiver matting; polished blue/black finish. Hand-fitted action. Standard and custom made-to-order rifles with many options. Made in USA by E. Arthur Brown Co., Inc.
Price: Standard model $1,695.00

C. SHARPS ARMS MODEL 1875 TARGET & SPORTING RIFLE
Calibers: .38-55, .40-65, .40-70 Straight or Bottlenecks, .45-70, .45-90. **Barrel:** 30-in. heavy tapered round. **Weight:** 11 lbs. **Length:** NA. **Stock:** American walnut. **Sights:** Globe with post front sight. **Features:** Long Range Vernier tang sight with windage adjustments. Pistol grip stock with cheek rest; checkered steel buttplate. Introduced 1991. From C. Sharps Arms Co.
Price: Without sights $1,425.00
Price: With blade front & buckhorn rear barrel sights $1,525.00
Price: With standard tang & globe w/post & ball front sights $1,725.00
Price: With deluxe vernier tang & globe w/spirit level &
      aperture sights $1,825.00
Price: With single set trigger, add $125.00

C. SHARPS ARMS 1875 CLASSIC SHARPS
Similar to New Model 1875 Sporting Rifle except 26 in., 28 in. or 30 in. full octagon barrel, crescent buttplate with toe plate, Hartford-style fore-end with cast German silver nose cap. Blade front sight, Rocky Mountain buckhorn rear. Weighs 10 lbs. Introduced 1987. From C. Sharps Arms Co.
Price: $1,775.00

C. SHARPS ARMS 1874 BRIDGEPORT SPORTING
Calibers: .38-55 to .50-3.25. **Barrel:** 26 in., 28 in., 30-in. tapered octagon. **Weight:** 10.5 lbs. **Length:** 47 in. **Stock:** American black walnut; shotgun butt with checkered steel buttplate; straight grip, heavy fore-end with Schnabel tip. **Sights:** Blade front, buckhorn rear. Drilled and tapped for tang sight. **Features:** Double-set triggers. Made in USA by C. Sharps Arms.
Price: $1,995.00

C. SHARPS ARMS NEW MODEL 1885 HIGHWALL
Calibers: .22 LR, .22 Hornet, .219 Zipper, .25-35 WCF, .32-40 WCF, .38-55 WCF, .40-65, .30-40 Krag, .40-50 ST or BN, .40-70 ST or BN, .40-90 ST or BN, .45-70 Govt. 2-1/10 in. ST, .45-90 2-4/10 in. ST, .45-100 2-6/10 in. ST, .45-110 2-7/8 in. ST, .45-120 3-1/4 in. ST. **Barrels:** 26 in., 28 in., 30 in., tapered full octagon. **Weight:** About 9 lbs., 4 oz. **Length:** 47 in. overall. **Stock:** Oil-finished American walnut; Schnabel-style fore-end. **Sights:** Blade front, buckhorn rear. Drilled and tapped for optional tang sight. **Features:** Single trigger; octagonal receiver top; checkered steel buttplate; color casehardened receiver and buttplate, blued barrel. Many options available. Made in USA by C. Sharps Arms Co.
Price: From..$1,975.00

     Prices given are believed to be accurate at time of publication however, many factors affect retail pricing so exact prices are not possible.

C. SHARPS ARMS 1885 HIGHWALL SCHUETZEN RIFLE
Calibers: .30-30, .32-40, .38-55, .40-50. **Barrels:** 24, 26, 28 or 30 in. Full tapered octagon. **Stock:** Straight grain American walnut with oil finish, pistol grip, cheek rest. **Sights:** Globe front with aperture set, long-range fully adjustable tang sight with Hadley eyecup. **Finish:** Color casehardened receiver group, buttplate and bottom tang, matte blue barrel. Single set trigger.
Price: From..$2,875.00

CIMARRON BILLY DIXON 1874 SHARPS SPORTING
Calibers: .45-70, .45-90, .50-70. **Barrel:** 32-in. tapered octagonal. **Weight:** NA. **Length:** NA. **Stock:** European walnut. **Sights:** Blade front, Creedmoor rear. **Features:** Color casehardened frame, blued barrel. Hand-checkered grip and fore-end; hand-rubbed oil finish. Made by Pedersoli. Imported by Cimarron F.A. Co.
Price: From..$2,141.70
Price: Officer's Trapdoor Carbine w/26-in. round barrel..............$2,616.00

CIMARRON MODEL 1885 HIGH WALL
Calibers: .38-55, .40-65, .45-70 Govt., .45-90, .45-120, .30-40 Krag, .348 Winchester, .405 Winchester. **Barrel:** 30-in. octagonal. **Weight:** NA. **Length:** NA. **Stock:** European walnut. **Sights:** Bead front, semi-buckhorn rear. **Features:** Replica of the Winchester 1885 High Wall rifle. Color case-hardened receiver and lever, blued barrel. Curved buttplate. Optional double-set triggers. Introduced 1999. Imported by Cimarron F.A. Co.
Price: From $1,097.00
Price: With pistol grip, adj. sights, From $1,277.00
Price: Deluxe model, double-set triggers $1,450.00

CIMARRON MODEL 1885 LOW WALL
Calibers: .22 Hornet, .32-20, .38-40, .44-40, .45 Colt. **Barrel:** 30-in. octagonal. **Weight:** NA. **Length:** NA. **Stock:** European walnut. **Sights:** Bead front, semi-buckhorn rear. **Features:** Replica of the Winchester 1885 Low Wall rifle. Color casehardened receiver, blued barrel. Curved buttplate. Optional double-set triggers. Introduced 1999. Imported by Cimarron F.A. Co.
Price: From $1,039.00

CIMARRON ADOBE WALLS ROLLING BLOCK
Caliber: .45-70 Govt. **Barrel:** 30-in. octagonal. **Weight:** 10.33 lbs. **Length:** NA. **Stock:** Hand-checkered European walnut. **Sights:** Bead front, semi-buckhorn rear. **Features:** Color casehardened receiver, blued barrel. Curved buttplate. Double-set triggers. Made by Pedersoli. Imported by Cimarron F.A. Co.
Price: From $1,740.00

DAKOTA ARMS MODEL 10
Calibers: Most rimmed and rimless commercial calibers. **Barrel:** 23 in. **Weight:** 6 lbs. **Length:** 39.5 in. overall. **Stock:** Medium fancy grade walnut in classic style. Standard or full-length Mannlicher-style. Checkered grip and fore-end. **Sights:** None furnished. Drilled and tapped for scope mounting. **Features:** Falling block action with underlever. Top tang safety. Removable trigger plate for conversion to single set trigger. Introduced 1990. Made in USA by Dakota Arms.
Price: From..$5,260.00
Price: Deluxe from $6,690.00

DAKOTA ARMS SHARPS
Calibers: Virtually any caliber from .17 Ackley Hornet to .30-40 Krag. **Features:** 26-in. octagon barrel, XX-grade walnut stock with straight grip and tang sight. Many options and upgrades are available.
Price: From $4,490.00

EMF PREMIER 1874 SHARPS
Calibers: .45-70, .45-110, .45-120. **Barrel:** 32 in., 34 in.. **Weight:** 11–13 lbs. **Length:** 49 in., 51 in. overall. **Stock:** Pistol grip, European walnut. **Sights:** Blade front, adjustable rear. **Features:** Superb quality reproductions of the 1874 Sharps Sporting Rifles; casehardened locks; double-set triggers; blue barrels. Imported from Pedersoli by EMF.
Price: Business Rifle..$1,585.00
Price: Down Under Sporting Rifle, Patchbox, heavy barrel $2,405.00
Price: Silhouette, pistol-grip..$1,899.90
Price: Super Deluxe Hand Engraved $3,600.00
Price: Competition Rifle..$2,200.00

H&R BUFFALO CLASSIC
Calibers: .45 Colt or .45-70 Govt. **Barrel:** 32 in. heavy. **Weight:** 8 lbs. **Length:** 46 in. overall. **Stock:** Cut-checkered American black walnut. **Sights:** Williams receiver sight; Lyman target front sight with 8 aperture inserts. **Features:** Color casehardened Handi-Rifle action with exposed hammer; color casehardened crescent buttplate; 19th-century checkering pattern. Introduced 1995. Made in USA by H&R 1871, Inc.
Price: Buffalo Classic Rifle..$479.00

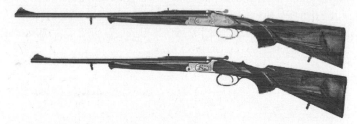

KRIEGHOFF HUBERTUS SINGLE-SHOT
Calibers: .222, .22-250, .243 Win., .270 Win., .308 Win., .30-06, 5.6x50R Mag., 5.6x52R, 6x62R Freres, 6.5x57R, 6.5x65R, 7x57R, 7x65R, 8x57JRS, 8x75RS, 9.3x74R, 7mm Rem. Mag., .300 Win. Mag. **Barrels:** 23.5 in. Shorter lengths available. **Weight:** 6.5 lbs. **Length:** 40.5 in. **Stock:** High-grade walnut. **Sights:** Blade front, open rear. **Features:** Break-open loading with manual cocking lever on top tang; takedown; extractor; Schnabel forearm; many options. Imported from Germany by Krieghoff International Inc.
Price: Hubertus single shot, From..$7,295.00
Price: Hubertus, magnum calibers $8,295.00

Prices given are believed to be accurate at time of publication however, many factors affect retail pricing so exact prices are not possible.

74TH EDITION, 2020 ✦ 379

MERKEL K1 MODEL LIGHTWEIGHT STALKING
Calibers: .243 Win., .270 Win., 7x57R, .308 Win., .30-06, 7mm Rem. Mag., .300 Win. Mag., 9.3x74R. **Barrel:** 23.6 in. **Weight:** 5.6 lbs. unscoped. **Stock:** Satin-finished walnut, fluted and checkered; sling-swivel studs. **Sights:** None (scope base furnished). **Features:** Franz Jager single-shot break-open action, cocking/uncocking slide-type safety, matte silver receiver, selectable trigger pull weights, integrated, quick detach 1 in. or 30mm optic mounts (optic not included). Extra barrels are an option. Imported from Germany by Merkel USA.
Price: Jagd Stalking Rifle $3,795.00
Price: Jagd Stutzen Carbine $4,195.00
Price: Extra barrels $1,195.00

MILLER ARMS
Calibers: Virtually any caliber from .17 Ackley Hornet to .416 Remington. Falling block design with 24-in. premium match-grade barrel, express sights, XXX-grade walnut stock and fore-end with 24 LPI checkering. Made in several styles including Classic, Target and Varmint. Many options and upgrades are available. From Dakota Arms.
Price: From $5,590.00

ROSSI SINGLE-SHOT SERIES
Calibers: .223 Rem., .243 Win., .44 Magnum. **Barrel:** 22 in. **Weight:** 6.25 lbs. **Stocks:** Black Synthetic Synthetic with recoil pad and removable cheek piece. **Sights:** Adjustable rear, fiber optic front, scope rail. Some models have scope rail only. **Features:** Single-shot break open, positive ejection, internal transfer bar mechanism, manual external safety, trigger block system, Taurus Security System, Matte blue finish.
Price: $238.00

RUGER NO. 1 SERIES
This model is currently available only in select limited editions and chamberings each year. Features common to most variants of the No. 1 include a falling block mechanism and under lever, sliding tang safety, integral scope mounts machined on the steel quarter rib, sporting-style recoil pad, grip cap and sling swivel studs. Chamberings for 2018 and 2019 were .450 Bushmaster and .450 Marlin. In addition, many calibers are offered by Ruger distributors Lipsey's and Talo, usually limited production runs of approximately 250 rifles, including .204 Ruger, .22 Hornet, 6.5 Creedmoor, .250 Savage, .257 Roberts, .257 Weatherby Mag. and .30-30. For availability of specific variants and calibers contact **www.lipseysguns.com** or **www.taloinc.com.**
Price: ....$1,899.00-$2,115.00

SHILOH CO. SHARPS 1874 LONG RANGE EXPRESS
Calibers: .38-55, .40-50 BN, .40-70 BN, .40-90 BN, .40-70 ST, .40-90 ST, .45-70 Govt. ST, .45-90 ST, .45-110 ST, .50-70 ST, .50-90 ST. **Barrel:** 34-in. tapered octagon. **Weight:** 10.5 lbs. **Length:** 51 in. overall. **Stock:** Oil-finished walnut (upgrades available) with pistol grip, shotgun-style butt, traditional cheek rest, Schnabel fore-end. **Sights:** Customer's choice. **Features:** Re-creation of the Model 1874 Sharps rifle. Double-set triggers. Made in USA by Shiloh Rifle Mfg. Co.
Price: $2,059.00
Price: Sporter Rifle No. 1 (similar to above except with 30-in. barrel, blade front, buckhorn rear sight) $2,059.00
Price: Sporter Rifle No. 3 (similar to No. 1 except straight-grip stock, standard wood) $1,949.00

SHILOH CO. SHARPS 1874 QUIGLEY
Calibers: .45-70 Govt., .45-110. **Barrel:** 34-in. heavy octagon. **Stock:** Military-style with patch box, standard-grade American walnut. **Sights:** Semi-buckhorn, interchangeable front and midrange vernier tang sight with windage. **Features:** Gold inlay initials, pewter tip, Hartford collar, case color or antique finish. Double-set triggers.
Price: $3,533.00

SHILOH CO. SHARPS 1874 SADDLE
Calibers: .38-55, .40-50 BN, .40-65 Win., .40-70 BN, .40-70 ST, .40-90 BN, .40-90 ST, .44-77 BN, .44-90 BN, .45-70 Govt. ST, .45-90 ST, .45-100 ST, .45-110 ST, .45-120 ST, .50-70 ST, .50-90 ST. **Barrels:** 26 in. full or half octagon. **Stock:** Semi-fancy American walnut. Shotgun style with cheek rest. **Sights:** Buckhorn and blade. **Features:** Double-set trigger, numerous custom features can be added.
Price: $2,044.00

SHILOH CO. SHARPS 1874 MONTANA ROUGHRIDER
Calibers: .38-55, .40-50 BN, .40-65 Win., .40-70 BN, .40-70 ST, .40-90 BN, .40-90 ST, .44-77 BN, .44-90 BN, .45-70 Govt. ST, .45-90 ST, .45-100 ST, .45-110 ST, .45-120 ST, .50-70 ST, .50-90 ST. **Barrels:** 30 in. full or half octagon. **Stock:** American walnut in shotgun or military style. **Sights:** Buckhorn and blade. **Features:** Double-set triggers, numerous custom features can be added.
Price: $2,059.00

SHILOH CO. SHARPS CREEDMOOR TARGET
Calibers: .38-55, .40-50 BN, .40-65 Win., .40-70 BN, .40-70 ST, .40-90 BN, .40-90 ST, .44-77 BN, .44-90 BN, .45-70 Govt. ST, .45-90 ST, .45-100 ST, .45-110 ST, .45-120 ST, .50-70 ST, .50-90 ST. **Barrel:** 32 in. half round-half octagon. **Stock:** Extra fancy American walnut. Shotgun style with pistol grip. **Sights:** Customer's choice. **Features:** Single trigger, AA finish on stock, polished barrel and screws, pewter tip.
Price: $3,105.00

THOMPSON/CENTER ENCORE PRO HUNTER PREDATOR RIFLE
Calibers: .204 Ruger, .223 Remington, .22-250 and .308 Winchester. **Barrel:** 28-in. deep-fluted interchangeable. **Length:** 42.5 in. **Weight:** 7.75 lbs. **Stock:** Composite buttstock and fore-end with non-slip inserts in cheekpiece, pistol grip and fore-end. Realtree Advantage Max-1 camo finish overall. Scope is not included.
Price: $882.00

THOMPSON/CENTER G2 CONTENDER
Calibers: .204 Ruger, .223 Rem., 6.8 Rem. 7-30 Waters, .30-30 Win. **Barrel:** 23-in. interchangeable with blued finish. **Length:** 36.75 in. **Stock:** Walnut. **Sights:** None. Weight: 5.5 pounds. Reintroduced in 2015. Interchangeable barrels available in several centerfire and rimfire calibers.
Price: $769.00

UBERTI 1874 SHARPS SPORTING
Caliber: .45-70 Govt. **Barrels:** 30 in., 32 in., 34 in. octagonal. **Weight:** 10.57 lbs. with 32 in. barrel. **Lengths:** 48.9 in. with 32 in. barrel. **Stock:** Walnut. **Sights:** Dovetail front, Vernier tang rear. **Features:** Cut checkering, case-colored finish on frame, buttplate, and lever. Imported by Stoeger Industries.
Price: Standard Sharps $1,919.00
Price: Special Sharps.. $2,019.00
Price: Deluxe Sharps $3,269.00
Price: Down Under Sharps................................. $2,719.00
Price: Long Range Sharps $2,719.00
Price: Buffalo Hunter Sharps $2,620.00
Price: Sharps Cavalry Carbine $2,020.00
Price: Sharps Extra Deluxe................................ $5,400.00
Price: Sharps Hunter $1,699.00

UBERTI 1885 HIGH-WALL SINGLE-SHOT
Calibers: .45-70 Govt., .45-90, .45-120. **Barrels:** 28–32 in. **Weights:** 9.3–9.9 lbs. **Lengths:** 44.5–47 in. overall. **Stock:** Walnut stock and fore-end. **Sights:** Blade front, fully adjustable open rear. **Features:** Based on Winchester High-Wall design by John Browning. Color casehardened frame and lever, blued barrel and buttplate. Imported by Stoeger Industries.
Price: From.................................. $1,079.00–$1,279.00

UBERTI SPRINGFIELD TRAPDOOR RIFLE/CARBINE
Caliber: .45-70 Govt., single shot **Barrel:** 22 or 32.5 in. **Features:** Blued steel receiver and barrel, casehardened breechblock and buttplate. **Sights:** Creedmoor style.
Price: Springfield Trapdoor Carbine, 22 in. barrel $1,749.00
Price: Springfield Trapdoor Army, 32.5 in. barrel $2,019.00

Prices given are believed to be accurate at time of publication however, many factors affect retail pricing so exact prices are not possible.

74TH EDITION, 2020 ⟡ 381

BERETTA S686/S689 O/U RIFLE SERIES
Calibers: .30-06, 9.3x74R. **Barrels:** 23 in. O/U boxlock action. Single or double triggers. EELL Grade has better wood, moderate engraving.
Price: ....$4,200.00–$9,000.00
Price: EELL Diamond Sable grade, From $12,750.00

BRNO MODEL 802 COMBO GUN
Calibers/Gauges: .243 Win., .308 or .30-06/12 ga. Over/Under. **Barrels:** 23.6 in. **Weight:** 7.6 lbs. **Length:** 41 in. **Stock:** European walnut. **Features:** Double trigger, shotgun barrel is improved-modified chokes. Imported by CZ USA.
Price: $2,087.00

BRNO EFFECT
Caliber: .30-06 Single Shot...$1,585.00

BRNO STOPPER
Caliber: .458 Win. Over/Under $5,554.00
Caliber: .458 Win. Over/Under hand engraved $8,072.00

FAUSTI CLASS EXPRESS
Calibers: .30-06, .30R Blaser, 8x57 JRS, 9.3x74R, .444 Marlin, .45-70 Govt. Over/Under. **Barrels:** 24 in. **Weight:** 7.5 lbs. **Length:** 41 in. **Stock:** Oil-finished Grade A walnut. Pistol grip, Bavarian or Classic. **Sights:** Folding leaf rear, fiber optic front adjustable for elevation. **Features:** Inertia single or double trigger, automatic ejectors. Made in Italy and imported by Fausti USA.
Price: $4,990.00
Price: SL Express w/hand engraving, AA wood..............................$7,600.00

HOENIG ROTARY ROUND ACTION DOUBLE
Calibers: Most popular calibers. Over/Under design. **Barrels:** 22–26 in. **Stock:** English Walnut; to customer specs. **Sights:** Swivel hood front with button release (extra bead stored in trap door grip cap), express-style rear on quarter-rib adjustable for windage and elevation; scope mount. **Features:** Round action opens by rotating barrels, pulling forward. Inertia extractor system, rotary safety blocks strikers. Single lever quick-detachable scope mount. Simple takedown without removing fore-end. Introduced 1997. Custom rifle made in USA by George Hoenig.
Price: From.. $22,500.00

HOENIG ROTARY ROUND ACTION COMBINATION
Calibers: Most popular calibers and shotgun gauges. Over/Under design with rifle barrel atop shotgun barrel. **Barrel:** 26 in. **Weight:** 7 lbs. **Stock:** English Walnut to customer specs. **Sights:** Front ramp with button release blades. Foldable aperture tang sight windage and elevation adjustable. Quarter-rib with scope mount. **Features:** Round action opens by rotating barrels, pulling forward. Inertia extractor; rotary safety blocks strikers. Simple takedown without removing forend. Custom rifle made in USA by George Hoenig.
Price: From.. $27,500.00

HOENIG VIERLING FOUR-BARREL COMBINATION
Calibers/gauges: Two 20-gauge shotgun barrels with one rifle barrel chambered for .22 Long Rifle and another for .223 Remington. Custom rifle made in USA by George Hoenig.
Price: 50,000.00

KRIEGHOFF CLASSIC DOUBLE
Calibers: 7x57R, 7x65R, .308 Win., .30-06, 8x57 JRS, 8x75RS, 9.3x74R, .375NE, .500/.416NE, .470NE, .500NE. **Barrel:** 23.5 in. **Weight:** 7.3–11 lbs. **Stock:** High grade European walnut. Standard model has conventional rounded cheekpiece, Bavaria model has Bavarian-style cheekpiece. **Sights:** Bead front with removable, adjustable wedge (.375 H&H and below), standing leaf rear on quarter-rib. **Features:** Boxlock action; double triggers; short opening angle for fast loading; quiet extractors; sliding, self-adjusting

wedge for secure bolting; Purdey-style barrel extension; horizontal firing pin placement. Many options available. Introduced 1997. Imported from Germany by Krieghoff International.
Price: $10,995.00
Price: Engraved sideplates, add $4,000.00
Price: Extra set of rifle barrels, add................................$6,300.00
Price: Extra set of 20-ga., 28 in. shotgun barrels, add...................$4,400.00

KRIEGHOFF CLASSIC BIG FIVE DOUBLE RIFLE
Similar to the standard Classic except available in .375 H&H, .375 Flanged Mag. N.E., .416 Rigby, .458 Win., 500/416 NE, 470 NE, 500 NE. Has hinged front trigger, nonremovable muzzle wedge, Universal Trigger System, Combi Cocking Device, steel trigger guard, specially weighted stock bolt for weight and balance. Many options available. Introduced 1997. Imported from Germany by Krieghoff International.
Price: $13,995.00
Price: Engraved sideplates, add $4,000.00
Price: Extra set of 20-ga. shotgun barrels, add...............................$5,000.00
Price: Extra set of rifle barrels, add................................$6,300.00

MERKEL BOXLOCK DOUBLE
Calibers: 5.6x52R, .243 Winchester, 6.5x55, 6.5x57R, 7x57R, 7x65R, .308 Win., .30-06, 8x57 IRS, 9.3x74R. **Barrel:** 23.6 in. **Weight:** 7.7 oz. **Length:** NA. **Stock:** Walnut, oil finished, pistol grip. **Sights:** Fixed 100 meter. **Features:** Anson & Deeley boxlock action with cocking indicators, double triggers, engraved color casehardened receiver. Introduced 1995. Imported from Germany by Merkel USA.
Price: Model 140-2, From Approx $13,255.00
Price: Model 141 Small Frame SXS Rifle; built on smaller frame, chambered for 7mm Mauser, .30-06, or 9.3x74R From Approx.. ....$11,825.00
Price: Model 141 Engraved; fine hand-engraved hunting scenes on silvered receiver From Approx. $13,500.00

Prices given are believed to be accurate at time of publication however, many factors affect retail pricing so exact prices are not possible.

BROWNING BUCK MARK SEMI-AUTO

Caliber: .22 LR. **Capacity:** 10+1. **Action:** A rifle version of the Buck Mark Pistol; straight blowback action; machined aluminum receiver with integral rail scope mount; manual thumb safety. **Barrel:** Recessed crowns. **Stock:** Stock and forearm with full pistol grip. **Features:** Action lock provided. Introduced 2001. Four model name variations for 2006, as noted below. **Sights:** FLD Target, FLD Carbon, and Target models have integrated scope rails. Sporter has Truglo/Marble fiber-optic sights. Imported from Japan by Browning.
Price: FLD Target, 5.5 lbs., bull barrel, laminated stock......................**$720.00**
Price: Target, 5.4 lbs., blued bull barrel, wood stock **$700.00**
Price: Sporter, 4.4 lbs., blued sporter barrel w/sights **$700.00**

BROWNING SA-22 SEMI-AUTO 22

Caliber: .22 LR. **Capacity:** Tubular magazine in buttstock holds 11 rounds. **Barrel:** 19.375 in. **Weight:** 5 lbs. 3 oz. **Length:** 37 in. overall. **Stock:** Checkered select walnut with pistol grip and semi-beavertail fore-end. **Sights:** Gold bead front, folding leaf rear. **Features:** Engraved receiver with polished blue finish; crossbolt safety; easy takedown for carrying or storage. The Grade VI is available with either grayed or blued receiver with extensive engraving with gold-plated animals: right side pictures a fox and squirrel in a woodland scene; left side shows a beagle chasing a rabbit. On top is a portrait of the beagle. Stock and fore-end are of high-grade walnut with a double-bordered cut checkering design. Introduced 1956. Made in Belgium until 1974. Currently made in Japan by Miroku.
Price: Grade I, scroll-engraved blued receiver **$700.00**
Price: Grade II, octagon barrel **$1,000.00**
Price: Grade VI BL, gold-plated engraved blued receiver **$1,640.00**

CITADEL M-1 CARBINE

Caliber: .22LR. **Capacity:** 10-round magazine. **Barrel:** 18 in. **Weight:** 4.8 lbs. **Length:** 35 in. **Stock:** Wood or synthetic in black or several camo patterns. **Features:** Built to the exacting specifications of the G.I. model used by U.S. infantrymen in both WWII theaters of battle and in Korea. Used by officers as well as tankers, drivers, artillery crews, mortar crews, and other personnel. Weight, barrel length and OAL are the same as the "United States Carbine, Caliber .30, M1," its official military designation. Made in Italy by Chiappa. Imported by Legacy Sports.
Price: Synthetic stock, black. **$316.00**
Price: Synthetic stock, camo. **$368.00**
Price: Wood stock. **$400.00**

CZ MODEL 512

Calibers: .22 LR/.22 WMR. **Capacity:** 5-round magazines. **Barrel:** 20.5 in. **Weight:** 5.9 lbs. **Length:** 39.3 in. **Stock:** Beech. **Sights:** Adjustable. **Features:** The modular design is easily maintained, requiring only a coin as a tool for field stripping. The action of the 512 is composed of an aluminum alloy upper receiver that secures the barrel and bolt assembly and a fiberglass reinforced polymer lower half that houses the trigger mechanism and detachable magazine. The 512 shares the same magazines and scope rings with the CZ 455 bolt-action rifle.
Price: .22 LR **$495.00**
Price: .22 WMR **$526.00**

EXCEL ARMS MR-22

Caliber: .22 WMR. **Capacity:** 9-shot magazine. **Barrel:** 18 in. fluted stainless steel bull barrel. **Weight:** 8 lbs. **Length:** 32.5 in. overall. **Grips:** Textured black polymer. **Sights:** Fully adjustable target sights. **Features:** Made from 17-4 stainless steel, aluminum shroud w/Weaver rail, manual safety, firing-pin block, last-round bolt-hold-open feature. Four packages with various equipment available. American made, lifetime warranty. Comes with one 9-round stainless steel magazine and a California-approved cable lock. Introduced 2006. Made in USA by Excel Arms.
Price: MR-22 .22 WMR **$538.00**

H&K 416-22

Caliber: .22 LR. **Capacity:** 10- or 20-round magazine. **Features:** Blowback semi-auto rifle styled to resemble H&K 416 with metal upper and lower receivers; rail interface system; retractable stock; pistol grip with storage compartment; on-rail sights; rear sight adjustable for wind and elevation; 16.1-in. barrel. Also available in pistol version with 9-in. barrel. Made in Germany by Walther under license from Heckler & Koch and imported by Umarex.
Price: **$599.00**

H&K MP5 A5

Caliber: .22 LR. **Capacity:** 10- or 25-round magazine. **Features:** Blowback semi-auto rifle styled to resemble H&K MP5 with metal receiver; compensator; bolt catch; NAVY pistol grip; on-rail sights; rear sight adjustable for wind and elevation; 16.1-in. barrel. Also available in pistol version with 9-in. barrel. Also available with SD-type fore-end. Made in Germany by Walther under license from Heckler & Koch. Imported by Umarex.
Price: **$499.00**
Price: MP5 SD...**$599.00**

HENRY U.S. SURVIVAL AR-7 22

Caliber: .22 LR. **Capacity:** 8-shot magazine. **Barrel:** 16 in. steel lined. **Weight:** 2.25 lbs. **Stock:** ABS plastic. **Sights:** Blade front on ramp, aperture rear. **Features:** Takedown design stores barrel and action in hollow stock. Light enough to float on water. Dark gray or camo finish. Comes with two magazines. Introduced 1998. From Henry Repeating Arms Co.
Price: H002B Black finish **$305.00**
Price: H002C Camo finish **$368.00**

KEL-TEC SU-22CA

Caliber: .22 LR. **Capacity:** 26-round magazine. **Barrel:** 16.1 in. **Weight:** 4 lbs. **Length:** 34 in. **Features:** Blowback action, crossbolt safety, adjustable front and rear sights with integral Picatinny rail. Threaded muzzle.
Price: **$547.00**

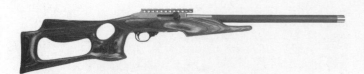

MAGNUM RESEARCH MLR22 SERIES

Calibers: .22 WMR or .22 LR. **Capacity:** 10-shot magazine. **Barrel:** 17 in. graphite. **Weight:** 4.45 lbs. **Length:** 35.5 in. overall. **Stock:** Hogue OverMolded synthetic or Laminated Thumbhole (Barracuda model). **Sights:** Integral scope base. **Features:** French grey anodizing, match bolt, target trigger. .22 LR rifles use factory Ruger 10/22 magazines. 4-5 lbs. average trigger pull. Barracuda model has Laminated Thumbhole stock, 19-in. barrel. Introduced: 2007. From Magnum Research, Inc.

Price: .22 LR Hogue OverMolded stock..............................$669.00
Price: .22 LR Barracuda w/Thumbhole stock....................$819.00
Price: .22 WMR Hogue OverMolded stock $791.00
Price: .22 WMR Barracuda w/Thumbhole stock.................$935.00

MARLIN MODEL 60

Caliber: .22 LR. **Capacity:** 14-round tubular magazine. **Barrel:** 19 in. round tapered. **Weight:** About 5.5 lbs. **Length:** 37.5 in. overall. **Stock:** Press-checkered, laminated Maine birch with Monte Carlo, full pistol grip; black synthetic or Realtree Camo. **Sights:** Ramp front, open adjustable rear. Matted receiver is grooved for scope mount. **Features:** Last-shot bolt hold-open. Available with factory mounted 4x scope.

Price: Laminate $209.00
Price: Model 60C camo $246.00
Price: Synthetic $201.00

MARLIN MODEL 60SS SELF-LOADING RIFLE

Same as the Model 60 except breech bolt, barrel and outer magazine tube are made of stainless steel; most other parts are either nickel-plated or coated to match the stainless finish. Monte Carlo stock is of black/gray Maine birch laminate, and has nickel-plated swivel studs, rubber buttpad. Introduced 1993.

Price: $315.00

MARLIN 70PSS PAPOOSE STAINLESS

Caliber: .22 LR. **Capacity:** 7-shot magazine. **Barrel:** 16.25 in. stainless steel, Micro-Groove rifling. **Weight:** 3.25 lbs. **Length:** 35.25 in. overall. **Stock:** Black fiberglass-filled synthetic with abbreviated fore-end, nickel-plated swivel studs, molded-in checkering. **Sights:** Ramp front with orange post, cut-away Wide Scan hood; adjustable open rear. Receiver grooved for scope mounting. **Features:** Takedown barrel; crossbolt safety; manual bolt hold-open; last shot bolt hold-open; comes with padded carrying case. Introduced 1986. Made in USA by Marlin.

Price: $345.00

MARLIN MODEL 795

Caliber: .22. **Capacity:** 10-round magazine. **Barrel:** 18 in. with 16-groove Micro-Groove rifling. **Sights:** Ramp front sight, adjustable rear. Receiver grooved for scope mount. **Stock:** Black synthetic, hardwood, synthetic thumbhole, solid pink, pink camo, or Mossy Oak New Break-up camo finish. **Features:** Last shot hold-open feature. Introduced 1997. SS is similar to Model 795 except stainless steel barrel. Most other parts nickel-plated. Adjustable folding semi-buckhorn rear sights, ramp front high-visibility post and removable cutaway wide scan hood. Made in USA by Marlin Firearms Co.

Price: $183.00
Price: Stainless $262.00

MOSSBERG BLAZE SERIES

Caliber: .22 LR. **Capacities:** 10 or 25 rounds. **Barrel:** 16.5 in. **Sights:** Adjustable. **Weights:** 3.5–4.75 lbs. **Features:** A series of lightweight polymer rifles with several finish options and styles. Green Dot Combo model has Dead Ringer greet dot sight. Blaze 47 has AK-profile with adjustable fiber optic rear and raised front sight, ambidextrous safety, and a choice of wood or synthetic stock.

Price: $210.00
Price: Muddy Girl camo $269.00
Price: Green Dot Combo $281.00
Price: Wildfire camo $269.00
Price: Kryptek Highlander camo $283.00
Price: Blaze 47 wood stock $420.00

MOSSBERG MODEL 702 PLINKSTER

Caliber: .22 LR. **Capacity:** 10-round magazine. **Barrel:** 18 in. free-floating. **Weights:** 4.1–4.6 lbs. **Sights:** Adjustable rifle. Receiver grooved for scope mount. **Stock:** Wood or black synthetic. **Features:** Ergonomically placed magazine release and safety buttons, crossbolt safety, free gun lock. Made in USA by O.F. Mossberg & Sons, Inc.

Price: From $190.00

MOSSBERG MODEL 715T SERIES

Caliber: .22 LR. **Capacity:** 10- or 25-round magazine. **Barrel:** 16.25 or 18 in. with A2-style muzzle brake. **Weight:** 5.5 lbs. **Features:** AR style offered in several models. Flattop or A2 style carry handle.

Price: Black finish $326.00
Price: Black finish, Red Dot sight $375.00
Price: Muddy Girl camo $438.00

REMINGTON MODEL 552 BDL DELUXE SPEEDMASTER

Calibers: .22 Short (20 rounds), Long (17) or LR (15) tubular magazine. **Barrel:** 21-in. round tapered. **Weight:** 5.75 lbs. **Length:** 40 in. overall. **Stock:** Walnut. Checkered grip and fore-end. **Sights:** Adjustable rear, ramp front. **Features:** Positive crossbolt safety in trigger guard, receiver grooved for tip-off mount. Operates with .22 Short, Long or Long Rifle cartridges. Classic design introduced in 1957.

Price: $707.00

REMINGTON 597

Calibers: .22 LR, 10 rounds; or .22 WMR, 8 rounds. **Barrel:** 20 in. **Weight:** 5.5 lbs. **Length:** 40 in. overall. **Stock:** Black synthetic or camo coverage in several patterns. TVP has laminated, contoured thumbhole stock. **Sights:** Big game. **Features:** Matte black metal finish or stainless, nickel-plated bolt. Receiver is grooved and drilled and tapped for scope mounts. Introduced 1997. Made in USA by Remington.

Price: Standard model, synthetic stock $213.00
Price: Synthetic w/Scope $257.00
Price: Heavy Barrel $254.00
Price: Camo from $306.00

ROSSI RS22

Caliber: .22 LR. **Capacity:** 10-round detachable magazine. **Barrel:** 18 in. **Weight:** 4.1 lbs. **Length:** 36 in. **Stock:** Black synthetic with impressed checkering. **Sights:** Adjustable fiber optic rear, hooded fiber optic front. Made in Brazil, imported by Rossi USA.
Price: Standard model, synthetic stock $139.00

RUGER 10/22 AUTOLOADING CARBINE

Caliber: .22 LR. **Capacity:** 10-round rotary magazine. **Barrel:** 18.5 in. round tapered (16.12 in. compact model). **Weight:** 5 lbs. (4.5, compact). **Length:** 37.25 in., 34 in. (compact) overall. **Stock:** American hardwood with pistol grip and barrel band, or synthetic. **Sights:** Brass bead front, folding leaf rear adjustable for elevation. **Features:** Available with satin black or stainless finish on receiver and barrel. Detachable rotary magazine fits flush into stock, crossbolt safety, receiver tapped and grooved for scope blocks or tip-off mount. Scope base adaptor furnished with each rifle. Made in USA by Sturm, Ruger & Co.
Price: Wood stock..$309.00
Price: Synthetic stock $309.00
Price: Stainless, synthetic stock $339.00
Price: Compact model, fiber-optic front sight $359.00
Price: Go Wild Rockstar Camo..............................$399.00
Price: Collector's Series Man's Best Friend $399.00
Price: Weaver 3-9x Scope $399.00

RUGER 10/22 TAKEDOWN RIFLE

Caliber: .22 LR. **Capacity:** 10-round rotary magazine. **Barrels:** 18.5 in. stainless, or 16.6 in. satin black threaded with suppressor. Easy takedown feature enables quick separation of the barrel from the action by way of a recessed locking lever, for ease of transportation and storage. **Stock:** Black synthetic. **Sights:** Adjustable rear, gold bead front. **Weight:** 4.66 pounds. Comes with backpack carrying bag.
Price: Stainless $439.00
Price: Satin black w/flash suppressor....................$459.00
Price: Threaded barrel $629.00
Price: With Silent-SR suppressor..........................$1,078.00

RUGER 10/22 SPORTER

Same specifications as 10/22 Carbine except has American walnut stock with hand-checkered pistol grip and fore-end, straight buttplate, sling swivels, 18.9-in. barrel, and no barrel band.
Price: $419.00

RUGER 10/22 TARGET LITE

Features a 16 1/8-in. heavy, hammer-forged threaded barrel with tight chamber dimensions, black or red/black laminate stock with thumbhole and adjustable length-of-pull, BX Trigger with 2.5-3 lbs. pull weight, minimal overtravel and positive reset.
Price: $649.00

SAVAGE A17 SERIES

Calibers: .17 HMR, . **Capacity:** 10-round rotary magazine. **Barrel:** 22 in. **Weight:** 5.4–5.6 lbs. **Features:** Delayed blowback action, Savage AccuTrigger, synthetic or laminated stock. Target model has heavy barrel, sporter or thumbhole stock. Introduced in 2016.
Price: Standard model $473.00
Price: Sporter (Gray laminate stock) $574.00
Price: Target Sporter...$571.00
Price: Target Thumbhole $631.00

SAVAGE A22 SERIES

Caliber: .22 LR, .22 WMR. **Capacity 10-round magazine.** Similar to A17 series except for caliber.
Price: $284.00
Price: A22 SS stainless barrel $419.00
Price: Target Thumbhole stock, heavy barrel $449.00
Price: Pro Varmint w/Picatinny rail, heavy bbl., target stock.............$409.00
Price: 22 WMR $479.00

SAVAGE MODEL 64G

Caliber: .22 LR. **Capacity:** 10-round magazine. **Barrels:** 20 in., 21 in. **Weight:** 5.5 lbs. **Lengths:** 40 in., 41 in. **Stock:** Walnut-finished hardwood with Monte Carlo-type comb, checkered grip and fore-end. **Sights:** Bead front, open adjustable rear. Receiver grooved for scope mounting. Thumb-operated rotating safety. Blue finish. 64 SS has stainless finish. Side ejection, bolt hold-open device. Introduced 1990. Made in Canada, from Savage Arms.
Price: 64 G $221.00
Price: 64 F $175.00
Price: 64 FSS $264.00
Price: 64 TR-SR $360.00
Price: FVXP w/3-9x Bushnell scope.........................$269.00

SMITH & WESSON M&P15-22 SERIES

Caliber: .22 LR. **Capacities:** 10- or 25-round magazine. **Barrel:** 15.5 in., 16 in. or 16.5 in. **Stock:** 6-position telescoping or fixed. **Features:** A rimfire version of AR-derived M&P tactical autoloader. Operates with blowback action. Quad-mount Picatinny rails, plain barrel or compensator, alloy upper and lower, matte black metal finish. Kryptek Highlander or Muddy Girl camo finishes available.
Price: Standard $449.00
Price: Kryptek Highlander or Muddy Girl camo..................$499.00
Price: MOE Model with Magpul sights, stock and grip........$609.00
Price: Performance Center upgrades, threaded barrel.......$789.00
Price: M&P 15 Sport w/Crimson Trace Red Dot sight........$759.00

THOMPSON/CENTER T/CR22

Caliber: .22 LR. **Capacities:** 10-round rotary magazine. **Barrel:** 20 in. stainless steel, threaded muzzle. **Stock:** Hogue overmolded sculpted and ambidextrous thumbhole. **Features:** Picatinny top rail, sling swivel studs, push-button safety, fully machined aluminum receiver with hole to allow cleaning from rear. From the Smith & Wesson Performance Center.
Price: $497.00

BROWNING BL-22
Caliber: .22 LR. **Capacity:** Tubular magazines, 15+1. **Action:** Short-throw lever action, side ejection. Rack-and-pinion lever. **Barrel:** Recessed muzzle. **Stock:** Walnut, two-piece straight-grip Western style. **Trigger:** Half-cock hammer safety; fold-down hammer. **Sights:** Bead post front, folding-leaf rear. Steel receiver grooved for scope mount. **Weight:** 5–5.4 lbs. **Length:** 36.75–40.75 in. overall. **Features:** Action lock provided. Introduced 1996. FLD Grade II Octagon has octagonal 24-in. barrel, silver nitride receiver with scroll engraving, gold-colored trigger. FLD Grade I has satin-nickel receiver, blued trigger, no stock checkering. FLD Grade II has satin-nickel receivers with scroll engraving; gold-colored trigger, cut checkering. Both introduced 2005. Grade I has blued receiver and trigger, no stock checkering. Grade II has gold-colored trigger, cut checkering, blued receiver with scroll engraving. Imported from Japan by Browning.

Price: BL-22 Grade I/II, From .... $620.00–$700.00
Price: BL-22 FLD Grade I/II, From .... $660.00–$750.00
Price: BL-22 FLD, Grade II Octagon $980.00

HENRY LEVER-ACTION RIFLES
Caliber: .22 Long Rifle (15 shot), .22 Magnum (11 shots), .17 HMR (11 shots). **Barrel:** 18.25 in. round. **Weight:** 5.5–5.75 lbs. **Length:** 34 in. overall (.22 LR). **Stock:** Walnut. **Sights:** Hooded blade front, open adjustable rear. **Features:** Polished blue finish; full-length tubular magazine; side ejection; receiver grooved for scope mounting. Introduced 1997. Made in USA by Henry Repeating Arms Co.

Price: H001 Carbine .22 LR $378.00
Price: H001L Carbine .22 LR, Large Loop Lever.................. $394.00
Price: H001Y Youth model (33 in. overall, 11-round .22 LR) $378.00
Price: H001M .22 Magnum, 19.25 in. octagonal barrel, deluxe
    walnut stock $525.00
Price: H001V .17 HMR, 20 in. octagonal barrel,
    Williams Fire Sights $578.00

HENRY LEVER-ACTION OCTAGON FRONTIER MODEL
Same as lever rifles except chambered in .17 HMR, .22 Short/Long/LR, .22 Magnum. **Barrel:** 20 in. octagonal. **Sights:** Marble's fully adjustable semi-buckhorn rear, brass bead front. **Weight:** 6.25 lbs. Made in USA by Henry Repeating Arms Co.

Price: H001T Lever Octagon .22 S/L/R $473.00
Price: H001TM Lever Octagon .22 Magnum, .17 HMR $578.00

HENRY GOLDEN BOY SERIES
Calibers: .17 HMR, .22 LR (16-shot), .22 Magnum. **Barrel:** 20 in. octagonal. **Weight:** 6.25 lbs. **Length:** 38 in. overall. **Stock:** American walnut. **Sights:** Blade front, open rear. **Features:** Brasslite receiver, brass buttplate, blued barrel and lever. Introduced 1998. Made in USA from Henry Repeating Arms Co.

Price: H004 .22 LR.. $578.00
Price: H004M .22 Magnum $625.00
Price: H004V .17 HMR $641.00
Price: H004DD .22 LR Deluxe, engraved receiver............ $1,575.00-1,654.00

HENRY SILVER BOY
Calibers: 17 HMR, .22 S/L/LR, .22 WMR. **Capacities:** Tubular magazine. 12 rounds (.17 HMR and .22 WMR), 16 rounds (.22 LR), 21 rounds (.22 Short). **Barrel:** 20 in. **Stock:** American walnut with curved buttplate. **Finish:** Nickel receiver, barrel band and buttplate. **Sights:** Adjustable buckhorn rear, bead front. Silver Eagle model has engraved scroll pattern from early original Henry rifle. Offered in same calibers as Silver Boy. Made in USA from Henry Repeating Arms Company.

Price: .22 S/L/LR $630.00
Price: .22 WMR.. $682.00
Price: .17 HMR... $709.00
Price: Silver Eagle.................................... $892.00–$945.00

HENRY PUMP ACTION
Caliber: .22 LR. **Capacity:** 15 rounds. **Barrel:** 18.25 in. **Weight:** 5.5 lbs. **Length:** NA. **Stock:** American walnut. **Sights:** Bead on ramp front, open adjustable rear. **Features:** Polished blue finish; receiver grooved for scope mount; grooved slide handle; two barrel bands. Introduced 1998. Made in USA from Henry Repeating Arms Co.

Price: H003T .22 LR... $578.00
Price: H003TM .22 Magnum $620.00

MOSSBERG MODEL 464 RIMFIRE
Caliber: .22 LR. **Capacity:** 14-round tubular magazine. **Barrel:** 20-in. round blued. **Weight:** 5.6 lbs. **Length:** 35.75 in. overall. **Features:** Adjustable sights, straight grip stock, plain hardwood straight stock and fore-end. Lever-action model.

Price: $503.00
Price: SPX Tactical model, adjustable synthetic stock $525.00

REMINGTON 572 BDL DELUXE FIELDMASTER PUMP
Calibers: .22 Short (20), .22 Long (17) or .22 LR (15), tubular magazine. **Barrel:** 21 in. round tapered. **Weight:** 5.5 lbs. **Length:** 40 in. overall. **Stock:** Walnut with checkered pistol grip and slide handle. **Sights:** Big game. **Features:** Crossbolt safety; removing inner magazine tube converts rifle to single shot; receiver grooved for tip-off scope mount. Another classic rimfire, this model has been in production since 1955.

Price: $723.00

ANSCHUTZ MODEL 64 MP
Caliber: .22 LR. **Capacity:** 5-round magazine. **Barrel:** 25.6-in. heavy match. **Weight:** 9 lbs. **Stock:** Multipurpose hardwood with beavertail fore-end. **Sights:** None. Drilled and tapped for scope or receiver sights. **Features:** Model 64S BR (benchrest) has 20-in. heavy barrel, adjustable two-stage match-grade trigger, flat beavertail stock. Imported from Germany by Steyr Arms.

Price: $1,399.00

ANSCHUTZ 1416D/1516D CLASSIC
Calibers: .22 LR (1416D888), .22 WMR (1516D). **Capacity:** 5-round magazine. **Barrel:** 22.5 in. **Weight:** 6 lbs. **Length:** 41 in. overall. **Stock:** European hardwood with walnut finish; classic style with straight comb, checkered pistol grip and fore-end. **Sights:** Hooded ramp front, folding leaf rear.

Features: Uses Match 64 action. Adjustable single-stage trigger. Receiver grooved for scope mounting. Imported from Germany by Steyr Arms.
Price: 1416D .22 LR **$1,199.00**
Price: 1416D Classic left-hand **$1,249.00**
Price: 1516D .22 WMR **$1,249.00**
Price: 1416D, thumbhole stock **$1,649.00**

ANSCHUTZ 1710D CUSTOM
Caliber: .22 LR. **Capacity:** 5-round magazine. **Barrels:** 23.75- or 24.25-in. heavy contour. **Weights:** 6.5–7.375 lbs. **Length:** 42.5 in. overall. **Stock:** Select European walnut. **Sights:** Hooded ramp front, folding leaf rear; drilled and tapped for scope mounting. **Features:** Match 54 action with adjustable single-stage trigger; roll-over Monte Carlo cheekpiece, slim fore-end with Schnabel tip, Wundhammer palm swell on pistol grip, rosewood grip cap with white diamond insert; skip-line checkering on grip and fore-end. Introduced 1988. Imported from Germany by Steyr Arms.
Price: From **$2,195.00**

BROWNING T-BOLT RIMFIRE
Calibers: .22 LR, .17 HMR, .22 WMR. **Capacity:** 10-round rotary box double helix magazine. **Barrel:** 22 in. free floating, semi-match chamber, target muzzle crown. **Weight:** 4.8 lbs. **Length:** 40.1 in. overall. **Stock:** Walnut, maple or composite. **Sights:** None. **Features:** Straight-pull bolt action, three-lever trigger adjustable for pull weight, dual action screws, sling swivel studs. Crossbolt lockup, enlarged bolt handle, one-piece dual extractor with integral spring and red cocking indicator band, gold-tone trigger. Top-tang, thumb-operated two-position safety, drilled and tapped for scope mounts. Varmint model has raised Monte Carlo comb, heavy barrel, wide forearm. Introduced 2006. Imported from Japan by Browning. Left-hand models added in 2009.
Price: .22 LR, From .... **$750.00–$780.00**
Price: Composite Target .... **$780.00–$800.00**
Price: .17 HMR/.22 WMR, From .... **$790.00–$830.00**

COOPER MODEL 57-M REPEATER
Calibers: .22 LR, .22 WMR, .17 HMR, .17 Mach. **Barrel:** 22 in. or 24 in. **Weight:** 6.5–7.5 lbs. **Stock:** Claro walnut, 22 LPI hand checkering. **Sights:** None furnished. **Features:** Three rear locking lug, repeating bolt-action with 5-round magazine for .22 LR; 4-round magazine for .22 WMR and 17 HMR. Fully adjustable trigger. Left-hand models add $150 to base rifle price. 0.250-in. group rimfire accuracy guarantee at 50 yards; 0.5-in. group centerfire accuracy guarantee at 100 yards. Options include wood upgrades, case-color metalwork, barrel fluting, custom LOP, and many others.
Price: Classic **$2,495.00**
Price: Custom Classic **$2,995.00**
Price: Western Classic **$3,795.00**
Price: Schnabel **$2,595.00**
Price: Jackson Squirrel **$2,595.00**
Price: Jackson Hunter **$2,455.00**
Price: Mannlicher **$4,755.00**

CZ 457 AMERICAN
Calibers: .17 HMR, .22 LR, .22 WMR. **Capacity:** 5-round detachable magazine. **Barrel:** 24.8 in. **Weight:** 6.2 lbs. **Stock:** Turkish walnut American style with

high flat comb. **Sights:** None. Integral 11mm dovetail scope base. **Features:** Adjustable trigger, push-to-fire safety, interchangeable barrel system.
Price: **$476.00**
Price: .17 HMR .22 WMR **$496.00**
Price: Varmint model................................ **$660.00–$762.00**

CHIPMUNK SINGLE SHOT
Caliber: .22 Short, Long and Long Rifle or .22 WMR. Manually cocked single-shot bolt-action youth gun. **Barrel:** 16.125 in. blued or stainless. **Weight:** 2.6 lbs. **Length:** 30 in., LOP 11.6 in. **Stock:** Synthetic, American walnut or laminate. Barracuda model has ergonomic thumbhole stock with raised comb, accessory rail. **Sights:** Adjustable rear peep, fixed front. From Keystone Sporting Arms.
Price: Synthetic .... **$163.00–$250.00**
Price: Walnut .... **$209.00–$270.00**
Price: Barracuda .... **$258.00–$294.00**

CRICKETT SINGLE SHOT
Caliber: .22 Short, Long and Long Rifle or .22 WMR. Manually cocked single-shot bolt-action. Similar to Chipmunk but with more options and models. **Barrel:** 16.125 in. blued or stainless. **Weight:** 3 lbs. **Length:** 30 in., LOP 11.6 in. **Stock:** Synthetic, American walnut or laminate. Available in wide range of popular camo patterns and colors. **Sights:** Adjustable rear peep, fixed front. Drilled and tapped for scope mounting using special Chipmunk base. Alloy model has AR-style buttstock, XBR has target stock and bull barrel, Precision Rifle has bipod and fully adjustable thumbhole stock.
Price: Alloy **$300.00**
Price: XBR .... **$300.00–$400.00**
Price: Precision Rifle .... **$316.00–$416.00**
Price: Adult Rifle .... **$240.00–$280.00**

HENRY MINI BOLT YOUTH RIFLE
Caliber: .22 LR, single-shot youth gun. **Barrel:** 16 in. stainless, 8-groove rifling. **Weight:** 3.25 lbs. **Length:** 30 in., LOP 11.5 in. **Stock:** Synthetic, pistol grip, wraparound checkering and beavertail forearm. Available in black finish or bright colors. **Sights:** William Fire sights. **Features:** One-piece bolt configuration manually operated safety.
Price: **$289.00**

MARLIN MODEL XT-17 SERIES
Caliber: .17 HRM. **Capacity:** 4- and 7-round, two magazines included. **Barrel:** 22 in. **Weight:** 6 lbs. **Stock:** Black synthetic with palm swell, stippled grip areas, or walnut-finished hardwood with Monte Carlo comb. Laminated stock available. **Sights:** Adjustable rear, ramp front. Drilled and tapped for scope mounts. **Features:** Adjustable trigger. Blue or stainless finish.
Price: .... **$269.00–$429.00**

MARLIN MODEL XT-22 SERIES
Calibers: .22 Short, .22 Long, .22 LR. **Capacities:** Available with 7-shot detachable box magazine or tubular magazine (17 to 22 rounds). **Barrels:** 22 in. Varmint model has heavy barrel. **Weight:** 6 lbs. **Stock:** Black synthetic, walnut-finished hardwood, walnut or camo. Tubular model available with two-tone brown laminated stock. **Finish:** Blued or stainless. **Sights:** Adjustable rear, ramp front. Some models have folding rear sight with a hooded or high-visibility orange front sight. **Features:** Pro-Fire Adjustable Trigger, Micro-Groove rifling, thumb safety with red cocking indicator. The XT-22M series is chambered for .22 WMR. Made in USA by Marlin Firearms Co.
Price: From .... **$221.00–$340.00**
Price: XT-22M .... **$240.00–$270.00**

MEACHAM LOW-WALL
Calibers: Any rimfire cartridge. **Barrels:** 26–34 in. **Weight:** 7-15 lbs. **Sights:** none. Tang drilled for Win. base, .375 in. dovetail slot front. **Stock:** Fancy eastern walnut with cheekpiece; ebony insert in forearm tip. **Features:** Exact copy of 1885 Winchester. With most Winchester factory options available including double-set triggers. Introduced 1994. Made in USA by Meacham T&H Inc.
Price: From...**$4,999.00**

MOSSBERG MODEL 817
Caliber: .17 HMR. **Capacity:** 5-round magazine. **Barrel:** 21-in. free-floating bull barrel, recessed muzzle crown. **Weight:** 4.9 lbs. (black synthetic), 5.2 lbs. (wood). **Stock:** Black synthetic or wood; length of pull, 14.25 in. **Sights:** Factory-installed Weaver-style scope bases. **Features:** Blued or brushed chrome metal finishes, crossbolt safety, gun lock. Introduced 2008. Made in USA by O.F. Mossberg & Sons, Inc.
Price: .... **$230.00–$274.00**

MOSSBERG MODEL 801/802
Caliber: .22 LR **Capacity:** 10-round magazine. **Barrel:** 18 in. free-floating. Varmint model has 21-in. heavy barrel. **Weight:** 4.1–4.6 lbs. **Sights:** Adjustable rifle. Receiver grooved for scope mount. **Stock:** Black synthetic. **Features:** Ergonomically placed magazine release and safety buttons, crossbolt safety, free gun lock. 801 Half Pint has 12.25-in. LOP, 16-in. barrel and weighs 4 lbs. Hardwood stock; removable magazine plug.
Price: Plinkster **$242.00**
Price: Half Pint **$242.00**
Price: Varmint **$242.00**

NEW ULTRA LIGHT ARMS 20RF
Caliber: .22 LR, single-shot or repeater. **Barrel:** Douglas, length to order. **Weight:** 5.25 lbs. **Length:** Varies. **Stock:** Kevlar/graphite composite, variety of finishes. **Sights:** None furnished; drilled and tapped for scope mount. **Features:** Timney trigger, hand-lapped action, button-rifled barrel, hand-bedded action, recoil pad, sling-swivel studs, optional Jewell trigger. Made in USA by New Ultra Light Arms.
Price: 20 RF single shot...**$1,800.00**
Price: 20 RF repeater **$1,850.00**

RUGER AMERICAN RIMFIRE RIFLE
Calibers: .17 HMR, .22 LR, .22 WMR. **Capacity:** 10-round rotary magazine. **Barrels:** 22-in., or 18-in. threaded. **Sights:** Williams fiber optic, adjustable. **Stock:** Composite with interchangeable comb adjustments, sling swivels. Adjustable trigger.
Price: **$359.00**

RUGER PRECISION RIMFIRE RIFLE
Calibers: .17 HMR, .22 LR, .22 HMR. **Capacity:** 9 to 15-round magazine. **Barrel:** 18 in. threaded. **Weight:** 6.8 lbs. **Stock:** Quick-fit adjustable with AR-pattern pistol grip, free-floated handguard with Magpul M-LOK slots. **Features:** Adjustable trigger, oversized bolt handle, Picatinny scope base.
Price: **$529.00**

SAVAGE MARK II BOLT-ACTION
Calibers: .22 LR, .17 HMR. **Capacity:** 10-round magazine. **Barrel:** 20.5 in. **Weight:** 5.5 lbs. **Length:** 39.5 in. overall. **Stock:** Camo, laminate, thumbhole or OD Green stock available **Sights:** Bead front, open adjustable rear. Receiver grooved for scope mounting. **Features:** Thumb-operated rotating safety. Blue finish. Introduced 1990. Made in Canada, from Savage Arms, Inc.
Price: .... **$228.00–$280.00**
Price: Varmint w/heavy barrel **$242.00**
Price: Camo stock **$280.00**
Price: OD Green stock..**$291.00**
Price: Multi-colored laminate stock **$529.00**
Price: Thumbhole laminate stock **$469.00**

SAVAGE MARK II-FSS STAINLESS RIFLE
Similar to the Mark II except has stainless steel barreled action and black

synthetic stock with positive checkering, swivel studs, and 20.75-in. free-floating and button-rifled barrel with magazine. Weighs 5.5 lbs. Introduced 1997. Imported from Canada by Savage Arms, Inc.
Price: **$336.00**

SAVAGE MODEL 93G MAGNUM BOLT ACTION
Caliber: .22 WMR. **Capacity:** 5-round magazine. **Barrel:** 20.75 in. **Weight:** 5.75 lbs. **Length:** 39.5 in. overall. **Stock:** Walnut-finished hardwood with Monte Carlo-type comb, checkered grip and fore-end. **Sights:** Bead front, adjustable open rear. Receiver grooved for scope mount. **Features:** Thumb-operated rotary safety. Blue finish. Introduced 1994. Made in Canada, from Savage Arms.
Price: Model 93G **$285.00**
Price: Model 93F (as above with black graphite/fiberglass stock) **$364.00**
Price: Model 93 BSEV, thumbhole stock **$646.00**

SAVAGE MODEL 93FSS MAGNUM RIFLE
Similar to Model 93G except stainless steel barreled action and black synthetic stock with positive checkering. Weighs 5.5 lbs. Introduced 1997. Imported from Canada by Savage Arms, Inc.
Price: **$353.00**

SAVAGE MODEL 93FVSS MAGNUM
Similar to Model 93FSS Magnum except 21-in. heavy barrel with recessed target-style crown, satin-finished stainless steel barreled action, black graphite/fiberglass stock. Drilled and tapped for scope mounting; comes with Weaver-style bases. Introduced 1998. Imported from Canada by Savage Arms, Inc.
Price: **$364.00**

SAVAGE B-MAG
Caliber: .17 Win. Super Magnum. **Capacity:** 8-round rotary magazine. **Stock:** Synthetic. **Weight:** 4.5 pounds. Chambered for new Winchester .17 Super Magnum rimfire cartridge that propels a 20-grain bullet at approximately 3,000 fps. **Features:** Adjustable AccuTrigger, rear locking lugs, new and different bolt-action rimfire design that cocks on close of bolt. New in 2013.
Price: **$402.00**
Price: Stainless steel receiver and barrel **$440.00**
Price: Heavy Bbl. Laminate stock **$589.00**

SAVAGE BRJ SERIES
Similar to Mark II, Model 93 and Model 93R17 rifles but features spiral fluting pattern on a heavy barrel, blued finish and Royal Jacaranda wood laminate stock.
Price: Mark II BRJ, .22 LR **$519.00**
Price: Model 93 BRJ, .22 Mag...**$542.00**
Price: Model 93 R17 BRJ, .17 HMR **$542.00**

SAVAGE TACTICAL RIMFIRE SERIES
Similar to Savage Model BRJ series semi-auto rifles but with matte finish and a tactical-style wood stock.
Price: Mark II TR, .22 LR **$533.00**
Price: Mark II TRR, .22 LR, three-way accessory rail **$627.00**
Price: Model 93R17 TR, .17 HMR **$558.00**
Price: Model 93R17 TRR, .17 HMR, three-way accessory rail **$654.00**

SAVAGE B SERIES
Calibers: .17 HMR, .22 LR, 22 WMR. **Capacity:** 10-round rotary magazine. **Barrel:** 21 in. (16.25 in. threaded heavy barrel on Magnum FV-SR Model). **Stock:** Black synthetic with target-style vertical pistol grip. **Weight:** 6 lbs. Features include top tang safety, Accutrigger. Introduced in 2017.
Price: From... **$281.00–$445.00**

SAVAGE MODEL 42
Calibers/Gauges: Break-open over/under design with .22 LR or .22 WMR barrel over a .410 shotgun barrel. Under-lever operation. **Barrel:** 20 in. **Stock:** Synthetic black matte. **Weight:** 6.1 lbs. **Sights:** Adjustable rear, bead front. Updated variation of classic Stevens design from the 1940s.
Price **$509.00**

Prices given are believed to be accurate at time of publication however, many factors affect retail pricing so exact prices are not possible.

ANSCHUTZ 1903 MATCH

Caliber: .22 LR. **Capacity:** Single-shot. **Barrel:** 21.25 in. **Weight:** 8 lbs. **Length:** 43.75 in. overall. **Stock:** Walnut-finished hardwood with adjustable cheekpiece; stippled grip and fore-end. **Sights:** None furnished. **Features:** Uses Anschutz Match 64 action. A medium weight rifle for intermediate and advanced Junior Match competition. Available from Champion's Choice.
Price: Right-hand **$1,195.00**

ANSCHUTZ 64-MP R SILHOUETTE

Caliber: .22 LR. **Capacity:** 5-round magazine. **Barrel:** 21.5-in. medium heavy; 0.875-in. diameter. **Weight:** 8 lbs. **Length:** 39.5 in. overall. **Stock:** Walnut-finished hardwood, silhouette-type. **Sights:** None furnished. **Features:** Uses Match 64 action. Designed for metallic silhouette competition. Stock has stippled checkering, contoured thumb groove with Wundhammer swell. Two-stage #5098 trigger. Slide safety locks sear and bolt. Introduced 1980. Available from Champion's Choice.
Price: 64-MP R **$1,100.00**
Price: 64-S BR Benchrest **$1,399.00**

ANSCHUTZ 2007 MATCH RIFLE

Uses same action as the Model 2013 but has a lighter barrel. European walnut stock in right-hand, true left-hand or extra-short models. Sights optional. Available with 19.6-in. barrel with extension tube, or 26 in., both in stainless or blued. Introduced 1998. Available from Champion's Choice.
Price: Right-hand, blued, no sights................................ **$2,795.00**

ANSCHUTZ 1827BT FORTNER BIATHLON

Caliber: .22 LR. **Capacity:** 5-round magazine. **Barrel:** 21.7 in. **Weight:** 8.8 lbs. with sights. **Length:** 40.9 in. overall. **Stock:** European walnut with cheekpiece, stippled pistol grip and fore-end. **Sights:** Optional globe front specially designed for Biathlon shooting, micrometer rear with hinged snow cap. **Features:** Uses Super Match 54 action and nine-way adjustable trigger; adjustable wooden buttplate, biathlon butthook, adjustable hand-stop rail. Uses Anschutz/Fortner system straight-pull bolt action, blued or stainless steel barrel. Introduced 1982. Available from Champion's Choice.
Price: From.. **$3,450.00**

ANSCHUTZ SUPER MATCH SPECIAL MODEL 2013

Caliber: .22 LR. **Capacity:** single-shot. **Barrel:** 25.9 in. **Weight:** 13 lbs. **Length:** 41.7–42.9 in. **Stock:** Adjustable aluminum. **Sights:** None furnished. **Features:** 2313 aluminum-silver/blue stock, 500mm barrel, fast lock time, adjustable cheekpiece, heavy action and muzzle tube, with handstop and standing riser block. Introduced in 1997. Available from Champion's Choice.
Price: From **$4,295.00**

ANSCHUTZ 1912 SPORT

Caliber: .22 LR. **Barrel:** 26 in. match. **Weight:** 11.4 lbs. **Length:** 41.7 in. overall. **Stock:** Non-stained thumbhole stock adjustable in length with adjustable buttplate and cheekpiece adjustment. Flat fore-end raiser block 4856 adjustable in height. Hook buttplate. **Sights:** None furnished. **Features:** in. Free rifle in. for women. Smallbore model 1907 with 1912 stock: Match 54 action. Delivered with: Hand stop 6226, fore-end raiser block 4856, screwdriver, instruction leaflet with test target. Available from Champion's Choice.
Price: **$2,995.00**

ANSCHUTZ 1913 SUPER MATCH RIFLE

Same as the Model 1911 except European walnut International-type stock with adjustable cheekpiece, or color laminate, both available with straight or lowered fore-end, adjustable aluminum hook buttplate, adjustable hand stop, weighs 13 lbs., 46 in. overall. Stainless or blued barrel. Available from Champion's Choice.
Price: Right-hand, blued, no sights, walnut stock............ **$3,799.00**

ANSCHUTZ 1907 STANDARD MATCH RIFLE

Same action as Model 1913 but with 0.875-in. diameter 26-in. barrel (stainless or blues). **Length:** 44.5 in. overall. **Weight:** 10.5 lbs. **Stock:**

Choice of stock configurations. Vented fore-end. Designed for prone and position shooting ISU requirements; suitable for NRA matches. Also available with walnut flat-forend stock for benchrest shooting. Available from Champion's Choice.
Price: Right-hand, blued, no sights................................ **$2,385.00**

ARMALITE M15 A4 CARBINE 6.8 & 7.62X39

Calibers: 6.8 Rem., 7.62x39. **Barrel:** 16 in. chrome-lined with flash suppressor. **Weight:** 7 lbs. **Length:** 26.6 in. **Features:** Front and rear picatinny rails for mounting optics, two-stage tactical trigger, anodized aluminum/phosphate finish.
Price: **$1,107.00**

BUSHMASTER A2/A3 TARGET

Calibers: 5.56 NATO, .223 Rem. **Capacity:** 30-round magazine. **Barrels:** 20 in., 24 in. **Weight:** 8.43 lbs. (A2); 8.78 lbs. (A3). **Length:** 39.5 in. overall (20 in. barrel). **Stock:** Black composition; A2 type. **Sights:** Adjustable post front, adjustable aperture rear. **Features:** Patterned after Colt M-16A2. Chrome-lined barrel with manganese phosphate exterior. Available in stainless barrel. Made in USA by Bushmaster Firearms Co.
Price: A2 .... **$969.00**
Price: A3 with carrying handle **$999.00**

REMINGTON 40-XB RANGEMASTER TARGET

Calibers: 15 calibers from .22 BR Remington to .300 Win. Mag. **Barrel:** 27.25 in. **Weight:** 11.25 lbs. **Length:** 47 in. overall. **Stock:** American walnut, laminated thumbhole or Kevlar with high comb and beavertail fore-end stop. Rubber nonslip buttplate. **Sights:** None. Scope blocks installed. **Features:** Adjustable trigger. Stainless barrel and action. Receiver drilled and tapped for sights. Model 40-XB Tactical (2008) chambered in .308 Win., comes with guarantee of 0.75-in. maximum 5-shot groups at 100 yards. **Weight:** 10.25 lbs. Includes Teflon-coated stainless button-rifled barrel, 1:14 in. twist, 27.25-in. long, three longitudinal flutes. Bolt-action repeater, adjustable 40-X trigger and precision machined aluminum bedding block. Stock is H-S Precision Pro Series synthetic tactical stock, black with green web finish, vertical pistol grip. From Remington Custom Shop.
Price: 40-XB KS, aramid fiber stock, single shot **$2,863.00**
Price: 40-XB KS, aramid fiber stock, repeater **$3,014.00**
Price: 40-XB Tactical .308 Win. **$2,992.00**

REMINGTON 40-XBBR KS

Calibers: Five calibers from .22 BR to .308 Win. **Barrel:** 20 in. (light varmint class), 24 in. (heavy varmint class). **Weight:** 7.25 lbs. (light varmint class); 12 lbs. (heavy varmint class). **Length:** 38 in. (20-in. bbl.), 42 in. (24 in. bbl.). **Stock:** Aramid fiber. **Sights:** None. Supplied with scope blocks. **Features:** Unblued benchrest with stainless steel barrel, trigger adjustable from 1.5 lbs. to 3.5 lbs. Special 2-oz. trigger extra cost. Scope and mounts extra. From Remington Custom Shop.
Price: Single shot **$3,950.00**

SAKO TRG-22 BOLT-ACTION
Calibers: .308 Win., .260 Rem, 6.5 Creedmoor, .300 Win Mag, .338 Lapua. **Capacity:** 5-round magazine. **Barrel:** 26 in. **Weight:** 10.25 lbs. **Length:** 45.25 in. overall. **Stock:** Reinforced polyurethane with fully adjustable cheekpiece and buttplate. **Sights:** None furnished. Optional quick-detachable, one-piece scope mount base, 1 in. or 30mm rings. **Features:** Resistance-free bolt, free-floating heavy stainless barrel, 60-degree bolt lift. Two-stage trigger is adjustable for length, pull, horizontal or vertical pitch. TRG-42 has similar features but has long action and is chambered for .338 Lapua. Imported from Finland by Beretta USA.
Price: TRG-22 .... **$3,495.00**
Price: TRG-22 with folding stock **$6,400.00**
Price: TRG-42 .... **$4,445.00**
Price: TRG-42 with folding stock **$7,400.00**

SPRINGFIELD ARMORY M1A SUPER MATCH
Caliber: .308 Win. **Barrel:** 22 in., heavy Douglas Premium. **Weight:** About 11 lbs. **Length:** 44.31 in. overall. **Stock:** Heavy walnut competition stock with longer pistol grip, contoured area behind the rear sight, thicker butt and fore-end, glass bedded. **Sights:** National Match front and rear. **Features:** Has figure-eight-style operating rod guide. Introduced 1987. From Springfield Armory.
Price: Approx **$3,250.00**

SPRINGFIELD ARMORY M1A/M-21 TACTICAL MODEL
Similar to M1A Super Match except special sniper stock with adjustable cheekpiece and rubber recoil pad. Weighs 11.6 lbs. From Springfield Armory.
Price: **$3,619.00**
Price: Krieger stainless barrel **$4,046.00**

TIME PRECISION .22 RF BENCH REST
Caliber: .22 LR. **Capacity:** Single-shot. **Barrel:** Shilen match-grade stainless. **Weight:** 10 lbs. with scope. **Length:** NA. **Stock:** Fiberglass. Pillar bedded. **Sights:** None furnished. **Features:** Shilen match trigger removable trigger bracket, full-length steel sleeve, aluminum receiver. Introduced 2008. Made in USA by Time Precision.
Price: From **$2,200.00**

ACCU-TEK AT-380 II ACP
Caliber: 380 ACP. **Capacity:** 6-round magazine. **Barrel:** 2.8 in. **Weight:** 23.5 oz. **Length:** 6.125 in. overall. **Grips:** Textured black composition. **Sights:** Blade front,rear adjustable for windage. **Features:** Made from 17-4 stainless steel, has an exposed hammer, manual firing-pin safety block and trigger disconnect. Magazine release located on the bottom of the grip. American made, lifetime warranty. Comes with two 6-round stainless steel magazines and a California-approved cable lock. Introduced 2006. Made in USA by Excel Industries.
Price: Satin stainless $289.00

ACCU-TEK HC-380
Similar to AT-380 II except has a 13-round magazine.
Price: $330.00

ACCU-TEK LT-380
Similar to AT-380 II except has a lightweight aluminum frame. **Weight:** 15 ounces.
Price: $324.00

AMERICAN CLASSIC 1911-A1 II SERIES
Caliber: .45 ACP, 9mm, .38 Super. **Capacity:** 8+1 magazine **Barrel:** 5 in. **Grips:** Checkered walnut. **Sights:** Novak-style rear, fixed front. **Finish:** Blue or hard chromed. Other variations include Trophy model with checkered mainspring housing, fiber optic front sight, hard-chrome finish.
Price: .... $609.00–$819.00

AMERICAN CLASSIC COMMANDER
Caliber: .45 ACP. Same features as 1911-A1 model except is Commander size with 4.25-in. barrel.
Price: .... $624.00–$795.00

AMERICAN CLASSIC AMIGO SERIES
Caliber: .45 ACP. **Capacity:** 7+1. Same features as Commander size with 3.6-in. bull barrel and Officer-style frame.
Price: .... $714.00-$813.00

AMERICAN TACTICAL IMPORTS MILITARY 1911
Caliber: .45 ACP. **Capacity:** 7+1 magazine. **Barrel:** 5 in. **Grips:** Textured mahogany. **Sights:** Fixed military style. **Finish:** Blue. Also offered in Commander and Officer's sizes and Enhanced model with additional features.
Price: .... $500.00–$899.00

AMERICAN TACTICAL IMPORTS GSG 1911
Caliber: .22 LR. **Capacity:** 10+1 magazine. **Weight:** 34 oz. Other features and dimensions similar to centerfire 1911.
Price: $299.95

AUTO-ORDNANCE 1911A1
Caliber: 45 ACP. **Capacity:** 7-round magazine. **Barrel:** 5 in. **Weight:** 39 oz. **Length:** 8.5 in. overall. **Grips:** Brown checkered plastic with medallion. **Sights:** Blade front, rear drift adjustable for windage. **Features:** Same specs as 1911A1 military guns-parts interchangeable. Frame and slide blued; each radius has non-glare finish. Introduced 2002. Made in USA by Kahr Arms
Price: 1911BKO Parkerized, plastic grips $673.00
Price: 1911BKOW Black matte finish, wood grips $689.00
Price: 1911BKOWWC1 Victory Girls Special $750.00

BAER 1911 BOSS .45
Caliber: .45 ACP. **Capacity:** 8+1 capacity. **Barrel:** 5 in. **Weight:** 37 oz. **Length:** 8.5 in. overall. **Grips:** Premium Checkered Coçobolo Grips. **Sights:** Low-Mount LBC Adj. Sight, Red Fiber Optic Front. **Features:** Speed Trigger, Beveled Mag Well, Rounded for Tactical. Rear cocking serrations on the slide, Baer fiber optic front sight (red), flat mainspring housing, checkered at 20 LPI, extended combat safety, Special tactical package, chromed complete lower, blued slide, (2) 8-round premium magazines.
Price: $2,636.00

Prices given are believed to be accurate at time of publication however, many factors affect retail pricing so exact prices are not possible.

74TH EDITION, 2020 ⊕ **391**

BAER 1911 CUSTOM CARRY

Caliber: .45 ACP. **Capacity:** 7- or 10-round magazine. **Barrel:** 5 in. **Weight:** 37 oz. **Length:** 8.5 in. overall. **Grips:** Checkered walnut. **Sights:** Baer improved ramp-style dovetailed front, Novak low-mount rear. **Features:** Baer forged NM frame, slide and barrel with stainless bushing. Baer speed trigger with 4-lb. pull. Partial listing shown. Made in USA by Les Baer Custom, Inc.

Price: Custom Carry 5, blued $2,190.00
Price: Custom Carry 5, stainless $2,290.00
Price: Custom Carry 5, 9mm or .38 Super $2,625.00
Price: Custom Carry 4 Commanche-length, blued $2,190.00
Price: Custom Carry 4 Commanche-length, .38 Super $2,550.00

BAER 1911 PREMIER II

Calibers: .38 Super, .45 ACP. **Capacity:** 7- or 10-round magazine. **Barrel:** 5 in. **Weight:** 37 oz. **Length:** 8.5 in. overall. **Grips:** Checkered rosewood, double diamond pattern. **Sights:** Baer dovetailed front, low-mount Bo-Mar rear with hidden leaf. **Features:** Baer NM forged steel frame and barrel with stainless bushing, deluxe Commander hammer and sear, beavertail grip safety with pad, extended ambidextrous safety; flat mainspring housing; 30 LPI checkered front strap. Made in USA by Les Baer Custom, Inc.

Price: 5 in. .45 ACP $2,2,245.00
Price: 5 in. .38 Super, 9mm $2,968.00
Price: 6 in. .45 ACP, .38 Super, 9mm .... $2,461.00-$2,925.00
Price: Super-Tac, .45 ACP, .38 Super $2,729.00-3,917.00
Price: 6-in Hunter 10mm $3090.00

BAER 1911 S.R.P.

Caliber: .45 ACP. **Barrel:** 5 in. **Weight:** 37 oz. **Length:** 8.5 in. overall. **Grips:** Checkered walnut. **Sights:** Trijicon night sights. **Features:** Similar to the F.B.I. contract gun except uses Baer forged steel frame. Has Baer match barrel with supported chamber, complete tactical action. Has Baer Ultra Coat finish. Introduced 1996. Made in USA by Les Baer Custom, Inc.

Price: Government or Commanche Length $2,925.00

BAER 1911 STINGER

Calibers: .45 ACP or .38 Super. **Capacity:** 7-round magazine. **Barrel:** 5 in. **Weight:** 34 oz. **Length:** 8.5 in. overall. **Grips:** Checkered cocobolo. **Sights:** Baer dovetailed front, low-mount Bo-Mar rear with hidden leaf. **Features:** Baer NM frame. Baer Commanche slide, Officer's style grip frame, beveled mag well. Made in USA by Les Baer Custom, Inc.

Price: .45 ACP .... $2,307.00–$2,379.00
Price: .38 Super $2,925.00

BAER HEMI 572

Caliber: .45 ACP. Based on Les Baer's 1911 Premier I pistol and inspired by Chrysler 1970 Hemi Cuda muscle car. **Features:** Double serrated slide, Baer fiber optic front sight with green insert, VZ black recon grips with hex-head screws, hard chrome finish on all major components, Dupont S coating on barrel, trigger, hammer, ambi safety and other controls.

Price: $2,770.00

BAER ULTIMATE MASTER COMBAT

Calibers: .45 ACP or .38 Super. A full house competition 1911 offered in 8 variations including 5 or 6-inch barrel, PPC Distinguished or Open class, Bullseye Wadcutter class and others. Features include double serrated slide, fitted slide to frame, checkered front strap and trigger guard, serrated rear of slide, extended ejector, tuned extractor, premium checkered grips, blued finish and two 8-round magazines.

Price: Compensated .45 .... $3,131.00
Price: Compensated .38 Super $3,234.00

BAER 1911 MONOLITH S

Calibers: .45 ACP, .38 Super, 9mm, .40 S&W. A full house competition 1911 offered in 14 variations. Unique feature is extra-long dust cover that

matches the length of the slide and reduces muzzle flip. Features include flat-bottom double serrated slide, low mount LBC adjustable sight with hidden rear leaf, dovetail front sight, flat serrated mainspring housing, premium checkered grips, blued finish and two 8-round magazines.

Price: .45 .... From $2,419.00
Price: .38 Super, .40 S&W .... From $2,790.00

BAER KENAI SPECIAL

Caliber: 10mm. **Capacity:** 9-round magazine. **Barrel:** 5 in. **Features:** Hard-chrome finish, double serrated slide, Baer fiber optic front sight with green or red insert, low-mount LBC adjustable rear sight, Baer black recon grips, special bear paw logo, flat serrated mainspring housing, lowered and flared ejection port, extended safety.

Price: $3,630.00

BAER GUNSITE PISTOL

Calibers: .45 ACP. **Capacity:** 8-round magazine. **Barrel:** 5 in. **Features:** double serrated slide, fitted slide to frame, flat serrated mainspring housing, flared and lowered ejection port, extended tactical thumb safety, fixed rear sight, dovetail front sight with night sight insert, all corners rounded, extended ejector, tuned extractor, premium checkered grips, blued finish and two 8-round magazines. Gunsite Raven logo on grips and slide.

Price: $2,255.00

BERETTA M92/96 A1 SERIES

Calibers: 9mm, .40 S&W. **Capacities:** 15-round magazine; .40 S&W, 12 rounds (M96 A1). **Barrel:** 4.9 in. **Weight:** 33-34 oz. **Length:** 8.5 in. **Sights:** Fiber optic front, adjustable rear. **Features:** Same as other models in 92/96 family except for addition of accessory rail.

Price: $775.00

BERETTA MODEL 92FS

Caliber: 9mm. **Capacity:** 10-round magazine. **Barrels:** 4.9 in., 4.25 in. (Compact). **Weight:** 34 oz. **Length:** 8.5 in. overall. **Grips:** Checkered black plastic. **Sights:** Blade front, rear adjustable for windage. Tritium night sights available. **Features:** Double action. Extractor acts as chamber loaded indicator, squared trigger guard, grooved front and backstraps, inertia firing pin. Matte or blued finish. Introduced 1977. Made in USA

Price: $699.00
Price: Inox $850.00

BERETTA MODEL 92G ELITE

Calibers: 9mm. **Capacities:** 15-round magazine. **Barrel:** 4.7 in. **Weight:** 33 oz. **Length:** 8.5 in. **Sights:** Fiber optic front, square notch rear. **Features:**

M9A1 frame with M9A3 slide, front and rear serrations, ultra-thin VZ/LTT G10 grips, oversized mag release button, skeletonized trigger, ships with three magazines.
Price: $1,100.00

BERETTA M9 .22 LR
Caliber: .22 LR. **Capacity:** 10 or 15-round magazine. **Features:** Black Brunitron finish, interchangeable grip panels. Similar to centerfire 92/M9 with same operating controls, lighter weight (26 oz.).
Price: $430.00

BERETTA MODEL PX4 STORM
Calibers: 9mm, 40 S&W. **Capacities:** 17 (9mm Para.); 14 (40 S&W). **Barrel:** 4 in. **Weight:** 27.5 oz. **Grips:** Black checkered w/3 interchangeable backstraps. **Sights:** 3-dot system coated in Superluminova; removable front and rear sights. **Features:** DA/SA, manual safety/hammer decocking lever (ambi) and automatic firing pin block safety. Picatinny rail. Comes with two magazines (17/10 in 9mm Para. and 14/10 in 40 S&W). Removable hammer unit. American made by Beretta. Introduced 2005.
Price: 9mm or .40 .... $650.00
Price: .45 ACP $700.00
Price: .45 ACP SD (Special Duty) $1,150.00

BERETTA MODEL PX4 STORM SUB-COMPACT
Calibers: 9mm, 40 S&W. **Capacities:** 13 (9mm); 10 (40 S&W). **Barrel:** 3 in. **Weight:** 26.1 oz. **Length:** 6.2 in. overall. **Grips:** NA. **Sights:** NA. **Features:** Ambidextrous manual safety lever, interchangeable backstraps included, lock breech and tilt barrel system, stainless steel barrel, Picatinny rail.
Price: $650.00

BERETTA MODEL APX SERIES
Calibers: 9mm, 40 S&W. **Capacities:** 10, 17 (9mm); 10, 15 (40 S&W). **Barrel:** 4.25 or 3.7 in. (Centurion). **Weight:** 28, 29 oz. **Length:** 7.5 in. Sights: Fixed. **Features:** Striker fired, 3 interchangeable backstraps included, reversible mag release button, ambidextrous slide stop. Centurion is mid-size with shorter grip and barrel. Magazine capacity is two rounds shorter than standard model.
Price: $575.00

BERETTA MODEL M9
Caliber: 9mm. **Capacity:** 15. **Barrel:** 4.9 in. **Weights:** 32.2-35.3 oz. **Grips:** Plastic. **Sights:** Dot and post, low profile, windage adjustable rear. **Features:** DA/SA, forged aluminum alloy frame, delayed locking-bolt system, manual safety doubles as decocking lever, combat-style trigger guard, loaded chamber indicator. Comes with two magazines (15/10). American made by Beretta. Introduced 2005.
Price: $675.00

BERETTA MODEL M9A1
Caliber: 9mm. **Capacity:** 15. **Barrel:** 4.9 in. **Weights:** 32.2-35.3 oz. **Grips:** Plastic. **Sights:** Dot and post, low profile, windage adjustable rear. **Features:** Same as M9, but also includes integral Mil-Std-1913 Picatinny rail, has checkered front and backstrap. Comes with two magazines (15/10). American made by Beretta. Introduced 2005.
Price: $775.00

BERETTA M9A3
Caliber: 9mm. **Capacity:** 10 or 15. **Features:** Same general specifications as M9A1 with safety lever able to be converted to decocker configuration. Flat Dark Earth finish. Comes with three magazines, Vertec-style thin grip.
Price: $1,100.00

BERETTA BU9 NANO
Caliber: 9mm. **Capacity:** 6- or 8-round magazine. **Barrel:** 3.07 in. **Weight:** 17.7 oz. **Length:** 5.7 in. overall. **Grips:** Polymer. **Sights:** 3-dot low profile. **Features:** Double-action only, striker fired. Replaceable grip frames. Polymer frames offered in black, RE Blue, FDE, Rosa or Sniper Grey colors.
Price: $450.00

BERETTA PICO
Caliber: .380 ACP. **Capacity:** 6-round magazine. **Barrel:** 2.7 in. **Weight:** 11.5 oz. **Length:** 5.1 in. overall. **Grips:** Integral with polymer frame. Interchangeable backstrap. **Sights:** White outline rear. **Features:** Adjustable, quick-change. Striker-fired, double-action only operation. Ambidextrous magazine release and slide release. Available with Black, RE Blue, FDE or Lavender frame. Ships with two magazines, one flush, one with grip extension. Made in the USA.
Price: $300.00

BERSA THUNDER 45 ULTRA COMPACT
Caliber: .45 ACP. **Barrel:** 3.6 in. **Weight:** 27 oz. **Length:** 6.7 in. overall. **Grips:** Anatomically designed polymer. **Sights:** White outline rear. **Features:** Double

action; firing pin safeties, integral locking system. Available in matte or duo-tone. Introduced 2003. Imported from Argentina by Eagle Imports, Inc.
Price: Thunder 45, matte blue $500.00

BERSA THUNDER 380 SERIES
Caliber: .380 ACP. **Capacity:** 7 rounds. **Barrel:** 3.5 in. **Weight:** 23 oz. **Length:** 6.6 in. overall. **Features:** Otherwise similar to Thunder 45 Ultra Compact. 380 DLX has 9-round capacity. 380 Concealed Carry has 8-round capacity. Imported from Argentina by Eagle Imports, Inc.
Price: Thunder Matte $335.00
Price: Thunder Satin Nickel $355.00
Price: Thunder Duo-Tone $355.00
Price: Thunder Duo-Tone with Crimson Trace Laser Grips $555.00
Price: Thunder CC Duo-Tone with aluminum frame $346.00

BERSA THUNDER 9 ULTRA COMPACT/40 SERIES
Calibers: 9mm, 40 S&W. **Barrel:** 3.5 in. **Weight:** 24.5 oz. **Length:** 6.6 in. overall. **Features:** Otherwise similar to Thunder 45 Ultra Compact. 9mm Para. High Capacity model has 17-round capacity. 40 High Capacity model has 13-round capacity. Imported from Argentina by Eagle Imports, Inc.
Price: $500.00

BERSA THUNDER 22
Caliber: .22 LR. **Capacity:** 10-round magazine. **Weight:** 19 oz. **Features:** Similar to Thunder .380 Series except for caliber. Alloy frame and slide. Finish: Matte black, satin nickel or duo-tone.
Price: $320.00

BROWNING 1911-22 BLACK LABEL
Caliber: .22 LR. **Capacity:** 10-round magazine. **Barrels:** 4.25 in. or 3.625 in. (Compact model). **Weight:** 14 oz. overall. **Features:** Other features are similar to standard 1911-22 except for this model's composite/polymer frame, extended grip safety, stippled black laminated grip, skeleton trigger and hammer. Available with accessory rail (shown). Suppressor Ready model has threaded muzzle protector, 4.875-inch barrel.
Price: $640.00
Price: With Rail.. $720.00
Price: Suppressor Ready model... $800.00

BERSA THUNDER PRO XT
Caliber: 9mm. **Capacity:** 17-round magazine. **Barrel:** 5 in. **Weight:** 34 oz. **Grips:** Checkered black polymer. **Sights:** Adjustable rear, dovetail fiber optic front. **Features:** Available with matte or duo-tone finish. Traditional double/single action design developed for competition. Comes with five magazines.
Price: $923.00

BROWNING 1911-22 COMPACT
Caliber: .22 LR **Capacity:** 10-round magazine. **Barrel:** 3.625 in. **Weight:** 15 oz. **Length:** 6.5 in. overall. **Grips:** Brown composite. **Sights:** Fixed. **Features:** Slide is machined aluminum with alloy frame and matte blue finish. Blowback action and single action trigger with manual thumb and grip safeties. Works, feels and functions just like a full-size 1911. It is simply scaled down and chambered in the best of all practice rounds: .22 LR for focus on the fundamentals.
Price: $600.00

BROWNING 1911-22 POLYMER DESERT TAN
Caliber: .22 LR. **Capacity:** 10-round magazine. **Barrels:** 4.25 in. or 3.625 in. **Weight:** 13–14 oz. overall. **Features:** Other features are similar to standard 1911-22 except for this model's composite/polymer frame. Also available with pink composite grips.
Price: $580.00

BROWNING 1911-22 A1
Caliber: .22 LR, **Capacity:** 10-round magazine. **Barrel:** 4.25 in. **Weight:** 16 oz. **Length:** 7.0625 in. overall. **Grips:** Brown composite. **Sights:** Fixed. **Features:** Slide is machined aluminum with alloy frame and matte blue finish. Blowback action and single action trigger with manual thumb and grip safeties. Works, feels and functions just like a full-size 1911. It is simply scaled down and chambered in the best of all practice rounds: .22 LR for focus on the fundamentals.
Price: $600.00

BROWNING 1911-380
Caliber: .380 ACP. **Capacity:** 8-round magazine. **Barrels:** 4.25 in. or 3.625 in. (Compact). **Weight:** 16 to 17.5 oz. **Features:** Aluminum or stainless slide, polymer frame with or without rail. Features are virtually identical to those on the 1911-22. 1911-380 Pro has three-dot combat or night sights, G10 grips, accessory rail. Medallion Pro has checkered walnut grips.
Price: $670.00
Price: Pro, Medallion Pro....................................... $800.00–$910.00

Prices given are believed to be accurate at time of publication however, many factors affect retail pricing so exact pricing is not possible.

74TH EDITION, 2020 ✦ **395**

BROWNING BUCK MARK CAMPER UFX

Caliber: .22 LR. **Capacity:** 10-round magazine. **Barrel:** 5.5-in. tapered bull. **Weight:** 34 oz. **Length:** 9.5 in. overall. **Grips:** Overmolded Ultragrip Ambidextrous. **Sights:** Pro-Target adjustable rear, ramp front. **Features:** Matte blue receiver, matte blue or stainless barrel.
Price: Camper UFX... $390.00
Price: Camper UFX stainless $430.00

BROWNING BUCK MARK HUNTER

Caliber: .22 LR. **Capacity:** 10-round magazine. **Barrel:** 7.25-in. heavy tapered bull. **Weight:** 38 oz. **Length:** 11.3 in. overall. **Grips:** Cocobolo target. **Sights:** Pro-Target adjustable rear, Tru-Glo/Marble's fiber-optic front. Integral scope base on top rail. Scope in photo not included. **Features:** Matte blue.
Price: $500.00

BROWNING BUCK PRACTICAL URX

Caliber: .22 LR. **Capacity:** 10-round magazine. **Barrels:** 5.5-in. tapered bull or 4-in. slab-sided (Micro). **Weight:** 34 oz. **Length:** 9.5 in. overall. **Grips:** Ultragrip RX Ambidextrous. **Sights:** Pro-Target adjustable rear, Tru-Glo/Marble's fiber-optic front. **Features:** Matte gray receiver, matte blue barrel.
Price: $479.00
Price: Stainless $470.00
Price: Micro $470.00

BROWNING BUCK MARK MEDALLION ROSEWOOD

Caliber: .22 LR. **Capacity:** 10-round magazine. **Barrel:** 5.5-in. **Grips:** Laminate rosewood colored with gold Buckmark. **Sights:** Pro-Target adjustable rear, TruGlo/Marble's fiber-optic front. **Finish:** Matte black receiver, blackened stainless barrel with polished flats. Gold-plated trigger.
Price: $510.00

BROWNING BUCK MARK CONTOUR STAINLESS URX

Caliber: .22 LR. **Capacity:** 10-round magazine. **Barrel:** 5.5 or 7.25-in. special contour. **Grips:** Checkered, textured. **Sights:** Pro-Target adjustable rear, Pro-Target front. Integral scope base on top rail. **Finish:** Matte black receiver, blackened stainless barrel with polished flats. Gold-plated trigger.
Price: $550.00

BROWNING BUCK MARK FIELD TARGET SUPPRESSOR READY

Caliber: .22 LR. **Capacity:** 10-round magazine. **Barrel:** 5.5-in. heavy bull, suppressor ready. **Grips:** Cocobolo target. **Sights:** Pro-Target adjustable rear, Tru-Glo/Marble's fiber-optic front. Integral scope base on top rail. Scope in photo not included. **Features:** Matte blue.
Price: $600.00

CHIAPPA 1911-22

Caliber: .22 LR. **Capacity:** 10-round magazine. **Barrel:** 5 in. **Weight:** 33.5 oz. **Length:** 8.5 in. **Grips:** Two-piece wood. **Sights:** Fixed. **Features:** A faithful replica of the famous John Browning 1911A1 pistol. Fixed barrel design. Available in black, OD green or tan finish. Target and Tactical models have adjustable sights.
Price: From .... $269.00–$408.00

CHIAPPA M9-22 STANDARD

Caliber: .22 LR. **Barrel:** 5 in. **Weight:** 2.3 lbs. **Length:** 8.5 in. **Grips:** Black molded plastic or walnut. **Sights:** Fixed front sight and windage adjustable rear sight. **Features:** The M9 9mm has been a U.S. standard-issue service pistol since 1990. Chiappa's M9-22 is a replica of this pistol in 22 LR. The M9-22 has the same weight and feel as its 9mm counterpart but has an affordable 10-shot magazine for the .22 Long Rifle cartridge, which makes it a true rimfire reproduction. Comes standard with steel trigger, hammer assembly and a 1/2x28 threaded barrel.
Price: $339.00

CHIAPPA M9-22 TACTICAL

Caliber: .22 LR. **Barrel:** 5 in. **Weight:** 2.3 lbs. **Length:** 8.5 in. **Grips:** Black molded plastic. **Sights:** Fixed front sight and Novak-style rear sights. **Features:** The M9-22 Tactical model comes with a faux suppressor (this ups the "cool factor" on the range and extends the barrel to make it even more accurate). It also has a 1/2x28 thread adaptor that can be used with a legal suppressor.
Price: $419.00

CHRISTENSEN ARMS 1911 SERIES

Calibers: .45 ACP, 9mm. **Barrels:** 4.25 in., 5 or 5.5 in. **Features:** Models are offered with aluminum, stainless steel or titanium frame with hand-fitted slide, match-grade barrel, tritium night sights and G10 Operator grip panels.
Price: Aluminum frame $1,995.00
Price: Stainless $2,895.00
Price: Titanium .... $4,795.00–$5,095.00

CITADEL M-1911

Calibers: .45 ACP, 9mm. **Capacity:** 7 (.45), 8 (9mm). **Barrels:** 5 or 3.5 in. **Weight:** 2.3 lbs. **Length:** 8.5 in. **Grips:** Cocobolo. **Sights:** Low-profile combat fixed rear, blade front. **Finish:** Matte black. **Features:** Extended grip safety, lowered and flared ejection port, beveled mag well, Series 70 firing system. Built by Armscor (Rock Island Armory) in the Philippines and imported by Legacy Sports.
Price: $599.00

CIMARRON MODEL 1911

Caliber: .45 ACP. **Barrel:** 5 in. **Weight:** 37.5 oz. **Length:** 8.5 in. overall. **Grips:** Checkered walnut. **Features:** A faithful reproduction of the original pattern of the Model 1911 with Parkerized finish and lanyard ring. Polished or nickel finish available.
Price: $571.00
Price: Polished blue or nickel $800.00

CIMARRON MODEL 1911 WILD BUNCH

Caliber: .45 ACP. **Barrel:** 5 in. **Weight:** 37.5 oz. **Length:** 8.5 in. overall. **Grips:** Checkered walnut. **Features:** Original WWI 1911 frame with flat mainspring housing, correct markings, polished blue finish, comes with tanker shoulder holster.
Price: $956.00

COBRA ENTERPRISES FS32, FS380

Calibers: .32 ACP or .380 ACP. **Capacity:** 7 rounds. **Barrel:** 3.5 in. **Weight:** 2.1 lbs. **Length:** 6.375 in. overall. **Grips:** Black molded synthetic integral with frame. **Sights:** Fixed. Made in USA by Cobra Enterprises of Utah, Inc.
Price: .... $138.00–$250.00

COBRA ENTERPRISES PATRIOT SERIES

Calibers: .380, 9mm or .45 ACP. **Capacities:** 6-, 7- or 10-round magazine. **Barrel:** 3.3 in. **Weight:** 20 oz. **Length:** 6 in. overall. **Grips:** Black polymer. **Sights:** Fixed. **Features:** Bright chrome, satin nickel or black finish. Made in USA by Cobra Enterprises of Utah, Inc.
Price: .... $349.00–$395.00

COBRA DENALI

Caliber: .380 ACP. **Capacity:** 5 rounds. **Barrel:** 2.8 in. **Weight:** 22 oz. **Length:** 5.4 in. **Grips:** Black molded synthetic integral with frame. **Sights:** Fixed. **Features:** Made in USA by Cobra Enterprises of Utah, Inc.
Price: $179.00

COLT MODEL 1991 MODEL O

Caliber: .45 ACP. **Capacity:** 7-round magazine. **Barrel:** 5 in. **Weight:** 38 oz. **Length:** 8.5 in. overall. **Grips:** Checkered black composition. **Sights:** Ramped blade front, fixed square notch rear, high profile. **Features:** Matte finish. Continuation of serial number range used on original G.I. 1911A1 guns. Comes with one magazine and molded carrying case. Introduced 1991. Series 80 firing system.
Price: Blue $799.00
Price: Stainless $879.00

COLT XSE SERIES MODEL O COMBAT ELITE

Caliber: .45 ACP. **Capacity:** 8-round magazine. **Barrel:** 5 in. **Grips:** Checkered, double-diamond rosewood. **Sights:** Three white-dot Novak. **Features:** Brushed stainless receiver with blued slide; adjustable, two-cut aluminum trigger; extended ambidextrous thumb safety; upswept beavertail with palm swell; elongated slot hammer.
Price: $1,100.00

COLT LIGHTWEIGHT COMMANDER

Calibers: .45 ACP, 8-shot, 9mm (9 shot). **Barrel:** 4.25 in. **Weight:** 26 oz. alloy frame, 33 oz. (steel frame). **Length:** 7.75 in. overall. **Grips:** G10 Checkered Black Cherry. **Sights:** Novak White Dot front, Low Mount Carry rear. **Features:** Blued slide, black anodized frame. Aluminum alloy frame.
Price: $999.00
Price: Combat Commander w/steel frame $949.00

Prices given are believed to be accurate at time of publication however, many factors affect retail pricing so exact prices are not possible.

74TH EDITION, 2020 ✦ **397**

COLT DEFENDER
Caliber: .45 ACP (7-round magazine), 9mm (8-round). **Barrel:** 3 in. **Weight:** 22.5 oz. **Length:** 6.75 in. overall. **Grips:** Pebble-finish rubber wraparound with finger grooves. **Sights:** White dot front, snag-free Colt competition rear. **Features:** Stainless or blued finish; aluminum frame; combat-style hammer; Hi-Ride grip safety, extended manual safety, disconnect safety. Introduced 1998. Made in USA by Colt's Mfg. Co., Inc.
Price: Stainless $999.00
Price: Blue $999.00

COLT SERIES 70
Caliber: .45 ACP. **Barrel:** 5 in. **Weight:** 37.5 oz. **Length:** 8.5 in. **Grips:** Rosewood with double diamond checkering pattern. **Sights:** Fixed. **Features:** Custom replica of the Original Series 70 pistol with a Series 70 firing system, original roll marks. Introduced 2002. Made in USA by Colt's Mfg. Co., Inc.
Price: Blued $899.00
Price: Stainless $979.00

COLT 38 SUPER CUSTOM SERIES
Caliber: .38 Super. **Barrel:** 5 in. **Weight:** 36.5 oz. **Length:** 8.5 in. **Grips:** Wood with double diamond checkering pattern. **Finish:** Bright stainless. **Sights:** 3-dot. **Features:** Beveled magazine well, standard thumb safety and service-style grip safety, flat mainspring housing. Introduced 2003. Made in USA. by Colt's Mfg. Co., Inc.
Price: $1,549.00

COLT MUSTANG XSP
Caliber: .380 ACP. **Features:** Similar to Mustang Pocketlite except has polymer frame, black diamond or bright stainless slide, squared trigger guard, accessory rail, electroless nickel finished controls.
Price: Bright Stainless $528.00
Price: Black Diamond-Like Carbon finish $672.00

COLT RAIL GUN
Caliber: .45 ACP. **Capacity:** (8+1). **Barrel:** 5 in. **Weight:** 40 oz. **Length:** 8.5 in. **Grips:** Rosewood double diamond. **Sights:** White dot front and Novak rear. **Features:** 1911-style semi-auto. Stainless steel frame and slide, front and rear slide serrations, skeletonized trigger, integral accessory rail, Smith & Alexander upswept beavertail grip palm swell safety, tactical thumb safety, National Match barrel.
Price: $1,199.00

COLT M45A1 MARINE PISTOL
Caliber: .45 ACP. Variant of Rail Gun series with features of that model plus Decobond Brown Coating, dual recoil springs system, Novak tritium front and rear 3-dot sights. Selected by U.S. Marine Corps as their Close Quarters Battle Pistol (CQBP).
Price: $1,699.00

COLT DELTA ELITE
Caliber: 10 mm. **Capacity:** 8+1. **Barrel:** 5 in. **Grips:** Black composite with Delta Medallions. **Sights:** Novak Low Mount Carry rear, Novak White Dot front. **Finish:** Two-tone stainless frame, black matte slide. **Features:** Upswept beavertail safety, extended thumb safety, 3-hole aluminum trigger.
Price: $1,199.00

COLT MUSTANG POCKETLITE
Caliber: .380 ACP. **Capacity:** 6-round magazine. **Barrel:** 2.75 in. **Weight:** 12.5 oz. **Length:** 5.5 in. **Grips:** Black composite. **Finish:** Brushed stainless. **Features:** Thumb safety, firing-pin safety block. Introduced 2012.
Price: $699.00

COLT MUSTANG LITE
Caliber: .380 ACP. Similar to Mustang Pocketlite except has black polymer frame.
Price: $599.00

COLT SPECIAL COMBAT GOVERNMENT CARRY MODEL
Calibers: .45 ACP (8+1), .38 Super (9+1). **Barrel:** 5 in. **Weight:** NA. **Length:** 8.5 in. **Grips:** Black/silver synthetic. **Sights:** Novak front and rear night sights. **Features:** 1911-style semi-auto. Skeletonized three-hole trigger, slotted hammer, Smith & Alexander upswept beavertail grip palm swell safety and extended magazine well, Wilson tactical ambidextrous safety. Available in blued, hard chrome, or blued/satin-nickel finish, depending on chambering. Marine pistol has desert tan Cerakote stainless steel finish, lanyard loop.
Price: $2,095.00

COLT GOVERNMENT MODEL 1911A1 .22
Caliber: .22 LR. **Capacity:** 12-round magazine. **Barrel:** 5 in. **Weight:** 36 oz.
Features: Made in Germany by Walther under exclusive arrangement with Colt Manufacturing Company. Blowback operation. All other features identical to original, including manual and grip safeties, drift-adjustable sights.
Price: $399.00

COLT COMPETITION PISTOL
Calibers: .45 ACP, .38 Super or 9mm Para. Full-size Government Model with 5-inch national match barrel, dual-spring recoil operating system, adjustable rear and fiber optic front sights, custom G10 Colt logo grips blued or stainless steel finish.
Price: Blued finish $949.00
Price: Stainless steel $999.00
Price: 38 Super $1,099.00

COLT SERIES 70 NATIONAL MATCH GOLD CUP
Caliber: .45 ACP. **Barrel:** 5 in. national match. **Weight:** 37 oz. **Length:** 8.5 in.
Grips: Checkered walnut with gold medallions. **Sights:** Adjustable Bomar rear, target post front. **Finish:** blued. **Features:** Flat top slide, flat mainspring housing. Wide three-hole aluminum trigger.
Price: $1,299.00

COLT GOLD CUP TROPHY
Calibers: .45 ACP or 9mm. Updated version of the classic Colt target and service pistol first introduced in the late 1950s to give shooters a serious competition pistol out of the box. Features include an undercut trigger guard, upswept beavertail grip safety and dual-spring recoil system. Checkering on the front and rear of the grip strap is 25 LPI with blue G10 grips. The new Gold Cup Trophy is built on the Series 70 firing system. Re-introduced to the Colt catalog in 2017.
Price: $1,699.00

CZ 75 B
Calibers: 9mm, .40 S&W. **Capacity:** 16-round magazine (9mm), 10-round (.40). **Barrel:** 4.7 in. **Weight:** 34.3 oz. **Length:** 8.1 in. overall. **Grips:** High impact checkered plastic. **Sights:** Square post front, rear adjustable for windage; 3-dot system. **Features:** Single action/double action; firing pin block safety; choice of black polymer, matte or high-polish blue finishes. All-steel frame. B-SA is a single action with a drop-free magazine. Imported from the Czech Republic by CZ-USA.
Price: 75 B $625.00
Price: 75 B, stainless $783.00
Price: 75 B-SA $661.00

CZ 75 BD DECOCKER
Similar to the CZ 75B except has a decocking lever in place of the safety lever. All other specifications are the same. Introduced 1999. Imported from the Czech Republic by CZ-USA.
Price: 9mm, black polymer $612.00

CZ 75 B COMPACT
Similar to the CZ 75 B except has 14-round magazine in 9mm, 3.9-in. barrel and weighs 32 oz. Has removable front sight, non-glare ribbed slide top. Trigger guard is squared and serrated; combat hammer. Introduced 1993. Imported from the Czech Republic by CZ-USA.
Price: 9mm, black polymer $631.00
Price: 9mm, dual tone or satin nickel $651.00
Price: 9mm. D PCR Compact, alloy frame $651.00

CZ P-07

Calibers: .40 S&W, 9mm. **Capacity:** 15 (9mm), 12 (.40). **Barrel:** 3.8 in. **Weight:** 27.2 oz. **Length:** 7.3 in. overall. **Grips:** Polymer black Polycoat. **Sights:** Blade front, fixed groove rear. **Features:** The ergonomics and accuracy of the CZ 75 with a totally new trigger system. The new Omega trigger system simplifies the CZ 75 trigger system, uses fewer parts and improves the trigger pull. In addition, it allows users to choose between using the handgun with a decocking lever (installed) or a manual safety (included) by a simple parts change. The polymer frame design and a new sleek slide profile (fully machined from bar stock) reduce weight, making the P-07 a great choice for concealed carry.
Price: $524.00

CZ P-09 DUTY

Calibers: 9mm, .40 S&W. **Capacity:** 19 (9mm), 15 (.40). **Features:** High-capacity version of P-07. Accessory rail, interchangeable grip backstraps, ambidextrous decocker can be converted to manual safety.
Price: $544.00
Price: Suppressor ready $629.00

CZ 75 TACTICAL SPORT

Similar to the CZ 75 B except the CZ 75 TS is a competition ready pistol designed for IPSC standard division (USPSA limited division). Fixed target

sights, tuned single-action operation, lightweight polymer match trigger with adjustments for take-up and overtravel, competition hammer, extended magazine catch, ambidextrous manual safety, checkered walnut grips, polymer magazine well, two-tone finish. Introduced 2005. Imported from the Czech Republic by CZ-USA.
Price: 9mm, 20-shot mag. $1,837.00
Price: .40 S&W, 16-shot mag. $1,837.00

CZ 75 SP-01

Similar to NATO-approved CZ 75 Compact P-01 model. Features an integral 1913 accessory rail on the dust cover, rubber grip panels, black Polycoat finish, extended beavertail, new grip geometry with checkering on front and back straps, and double or single action operation. Introduced 2005. The Shadow variant designed as an IPSC "production" division competition firearm. Includes competition hammer, competition rear sight and fiber-optic front sight, modified slide release, lighter recoil and mainspring for use with "minor power factor" competition ammunition. Includes Polycoat finish and slim walnut grips. Finished by CZ Custom Shop. Imported from the Czech Republic by CZ-USA.
Price: SP-01 Standard $680.00
Price: SP-01 Shadow Target II $1,638.00

CZ 97 B

Caliber: .45 ACP. **Capacity:** 10-round magazine. **Barrel:** 4.85 in. **Weight:** 40 oz. **Length:** 8.34 in. overall. **Grips:** Checkered walnut. **Sights:** Fixed. **Features:** Single action/double action; full-length slide rails; screw-in barrel bushing; linkless barrel; all-steel construction; chamber loaded indicator; dual transfer bars. Introduced 1999. Imported from the Czech Republic by CZ-USA.
Price: Black polymer $707.00
Price: Glossy blue $727.00

CZ 97 BD DECOCKER

Similar to the CZ 97 B except has a decocking lever in place of the safety lever. Tritium night sights. Rubber grips. All other specifications are the same. Introduced 1999. Imported from the Czech Republic by CZ-USA.
Price: $816.00

CZ 2075 RAMI

Calibers: 9mm. **Barrel:** 3 in. **Weight:** 25 oz. **Length:** 6.5 in. overall. **Grips:** Rubber. **Sights:** Blade front with dot, white outline rear drift adjustable for windage. **Features:** Single action/double action; alloy frame, steel slide; has laser sight mount. Rami BD has decocking system. Imported from the Czech Republic by CZ-USA.
Price: Rami Standard $632.00
Price: Rami Decocker version $699.00

CZ P-01

Caliber: 9mm. **Capacity:** 14-round magazine. **Barrel:** 3.85 in. **Weight:** 27 oz. **Length:** 7.2 in. overall. **Grips:** Checkered rubber. **Sights:** Blade front with dot, white outline rear drift adjustable for windage. **Features:** Based on the CZ 75, except with forged aircraft-grade aluminum alloy frame. Hammer forged barrel, decocker, firing-pin block, M3 rail, dual slide serrations, squared trigger guard, re-contoured trigger, lanyard loop on butt. Serrated front and backstrap. Introduced 2006. Imported from the Czech Republic by CZ-USA.
Price: CZ P-01 .... $680.00

CZ SCORPION EVO

Caliber: 9mm. **Capacity:** 20-round magazine. **Features:** Semi-automatic version of CZ Scorpion Evo submachine gun. Ambidextrous controls, adjustable sights, accessory rails.
Price: $849.00

DAN WESSON DW RZ-10

Caliber: 10mm. **Capacity:** 9-round magazine. **Barrel:** 5 in. **Grips:** Diamond checkered cocobolo. **Sights:** Bo-Mar-style adjustable target sight. **Weight:** 38.3 oz. **Length:** 8.8 in. overall. **Features:** Stainless steel frame and serrated slide. Series 70-style 1911, stainless steel frame, forged stainless steel slide. Commander style match hammer. Reintroduced 2005. Made in USA by Dan Wesson Firearms, distributed by CZ-USA.
Price: 10mm, 8+1 .... $1,480.00

DAN WESSON DW RZ-45 HERITAGE

Caliber: .45 ACP. **Capacity:** 7-round magazine. **Weight:** 36 oz. **Length:** 8.8 in. overall. Similar to the RZ-10 Auto except in .45 ACP.
Price: 10mm, 8+1 .... $1,428.00

DAN WESSON SPECIALIST

Caliber: .45 ACP. **Capacity:** 8-round magazine. **Barrel:** 5 in. **Grips:** G10 VZ Operator II. **Sights:** Single amber tritium dot rear, green lamp with white target ring front sight. **Features:** Integral Picatinny rail, 25 LPI frontstrap checkering, undercut trigger guard, ambidextrous thumb safety, extended mag release and detachable two-piece mag well.
Price: $1,701.00

DAN WESSON V-BOB

Caliber: .45 ACP. **Capacity:** 8-round magazine. **Barrel:** 4.25 in. **Weight:** 34 oz. **Length:** 8 in. **Grips:** Slim Line G10. **Sights:** Heinie Ledge Straight-Eight Night Sights. **Features:** Black matte or stainless finish. Bobtail forged grip frame with 25 LPI checkering front and rear.
Price: $2,077.00

DAN WESSON POINTMAN

Calibers: 9mm, .38 Super, .45 ACP. **Capacity:** 8 or 9-round magazine. **Barrel:** 5 in. **Length:** 8.5 in. **Grips:** Double-diamond cocobolo. **Sights:** Adjustable rear and fiber optic front. **Features:** Undercut trigger guard, checkered front strap, serrated rib on top of slide.
Price: .45, .38 Super $1,597.00
Price: 9mm $1,558.00

DAN WESSON A2

Caliber: .45 ACP. **Capacity:** 8-round magazine capacity. Limited production model based on traditional 1911A1 design. **Features:** Modern fixed combat sights, lowered/flared ejection port, double-diamond walnut grips. Introduced 2017.
Price: $1,363.00

DAN WESSON VIGIL

Caliber: 9mm, .45 ACP. **Capacity:** 8 (.45) or 9 (9mm). **Barrel:** 4.25 or 5 in. **Features:** Forged aluminum frame with stainless round-top slide, serrated tactical rear and tritium front sight, checkered frontstrap and backstrap, walnut grips with rounded butt.
Price: $1,298.00

DAN WESSON WRAITH

Caliber: .45 ACP, 9m, 10mm. **Capacity:** 8 (.45), 9 (.40), 10 (9mm). **Barrel:** 5.75, threaded. **Finish:** Distressed Duty. **Features:** High profile fixed combat sights, lowered/flared ejection port, G10 grips, extended controls and grip safety.
Price: $2,077.00

DESERT EAGLE 1911 G
Caliber: .45 ACP. **Capacity:** 8-round magazine. **Barrels:** 5 in. or 4.33 in. (DE1911C Commander size), or 3.0 in. (DE1911U Undercover). **Grips:** Double diamond checkered wood. **Features:** Extended beavertail grip safety, checkered flat mainspring housing, skeletonized hammer and trigger, extended mag release and thumb safety, stainless full-length guide road, enlarged ejection port, beveled mag well and high-profile sights. Comes with two 8-round magazines.
Price: $904.00
Price: Undercover... $1,019.00

DESERT EAGLE MARK XIX
Calibers: .357 Mag., 9 rounds; .44 Mag., 8 rounds; .50 AE, 7 rounds. **Barrels:** 6 in., 10 in., interchangeable. **Weight:** 62 oz. (.357 Mag.); 69 oz. (.44 Mag.); 72 oz. (.50 AE) **Length:** 10.25-in. overall (6-in. bbl.). **Grips:** Polymer; rubber available. **Sights:** Blade-on-ramp front, combat-style rear. Adjustable available. **Features:** Interchangeable barrels; rotating three-lug bolt; ambidextrous safety; adjustable trigger. Military epoxy finish. Satin, bright nickel, chrome, brushed, matte or black-oxide finishes available. 10-in. barrel extra. Imported from Israel by Magnum Research, Inc.
Price: .... $1,572.00–$2,060.00

BABY DESERT EAGLE III
Calibers: 9mm, .40 S&W, .45 ACP. **Capacities:** 10-, 12- or 15-round magazines. **Barrels:** 3.85 in. or 4.43 in. **Weights:** 28–37.9 oz. **Length:** 7.25–8.25 overall. **Grips:** Ergonomic polymer. **Sights:** White 3-dot system. **Features:** Choice of steel or polymer frame with integral rail; slide-mounted decocking safety. Upgraded design of Baby Eagle II series.
Price: .... $646.00–$691.00

DESERT EAGLE L5/L6
Caliber: .357 Magnum, .44 Magnum, .50 AE. **Capacity:** 7, 8 or 9+1. **Barrel:** 5 in. or 6 in (L6). **Weight:** 50 to 70 oz. **Length:** 9.7 in. (L5), 10.8, (L6). **Features:** Steel barrel, aluminum frame and stainless steel slide with full Weaver-style accessory rail and integral muzzle brake. Gas-operated rotating bolt, single-action trigger, fixed sights.
Price: From $1,790.00

DIAMONDBACK DB380
Caliber: .380 ACP. **Capacity:** 6+1. **Barrel:** 2.8 in. **Weight:** 8.8 oz. **Features:** ZERO-Energy striker firing system with a mechanical firing pin block, steel magazine catch, windage-adjustable sights. Frames available with several color finish options.
Price: .... $290.00–$350.00

DIAMONDBACK DB9
Caliber: 9mm. **Capacity:** 6+1. **Barrel:** 3 in. **Weight:** 11 oz. **Length:** 5.60 in. **Features:** Other features similar to DB380 model.
Price: .... $290.00–$350.00

DIAMONDBACK DB FS NINE
Caliber: 9mm. **Capacity:** 15+1. **Barrel:** 4.75 in. **Weight:** 21.5 oz. **Length:** 7.8 in. **Features:** Double-action, striker-fired model with polymer frame and stainless steel slide. Flared mag well, extended magazine base pad, ergonomically contoured grip, fixed 3-dot sights, front and rear slide serrations, integral MIL-STD 1913 Picatinny rail.
Price: $483.00

DOUBLESTAR 1911 SERIES
Caliber: .45 ACP. **Capacity:** 8-round magazine. **Barrels:** 3.5 in., 4.25 in., 5 in. **Weights:** 33–40 oz. **Grips:** Cocobolo wood. **Sights:** Novak LoMount 2 white-dot rear, Novak white-dot front. **Features:** Single action, M1911-style with forged frame and slide of 4140 steel, stainless steel barrel machined from bar stock by Storm Lake, funneled mag well, accessory rail, black Nitride finish. Optional features include bobtail grip frame, accessory rail.
Price: .... $1,364.00–$2,242.00

EAA WITNESS FULL SIZE
Calibers: 9mm, .38 Super. **Capacity:** 18-round magazine; .40 S&W, 10mm, 15-round magazine; .45 ACP, 10-round magazine. **Barrel:** 4.5 in. **Weight:** 35.33 oz. **Length:** 8.1 in. overall. **Grips:** Checkered rubber. **Sights:** Undercut blade front, open rear adjustable for windage. **Features:** Double-action/single-action trigger system; round trigger guard; frame-mounted safety. Available with steel or polymer frame. Also available with interchangeable .45 ACP and .22 LR slides. Steel frame introduced 1991. Polymer frame introduced 2005. Imported from Italy by European American Armory.
Price: Steel frame $699.00
Price: Polymer frame $589.00

EAA WITNESS COMPACT
Caliber: 9mm. **Capacity:** 14-round magazine; .40 S&W, 10mm, 12-round magazine; .45 ACP, 8-round magazine. **Barrel:** 3.6 in. **Weight:** 30 oz. **Length:** 7.3 in. overall. **Features:** Available with steel or polymer frame (shown). All polymer frame Witness pistols are capable of being converted to other calibers. Otherwise similar to full-size Witness. Imported from Italy by European American Armory.
Price: Polymer frame $589.00
Price: Steel frame $699.00

EAA WITNESS-P CARRY
Caliber: 9mm. **Capacity:** 17-round magazine; 10mm, 15-round magazine; .45 ACP, 10-round magazine. **Barrel:** 3.6 in. **Weight:** 27 oz. **Length:** 7.5 in. overall. **Features:** Otherwise similar to full-size Witness. Polymer frame introduced 2005. Imported from Italy by European American Armory.
Price: $711.00

EAA WITNESS PAVONA COMPACT POLYMER
Calibers: .380 ACP (13-round magazine), 9mm (13) or .40 S&W (9). **Barrel:** 3.6 in. **Weight:** 30 oz. **Length:** 7 in. overall. **Features:** Designed primarily for women with fine-tuned recoil and hammer springs for easier operation, a polymer frame with integral checkering, contoured lines and in black, charcoal, blue, purple or magenta with silver or gold sparkle.
Price: .... $476.00–$528.00

EAA WITNESS ELITE 1911
Caliber: .45 ACP. **Capacity:** 8-round magazine. **Barrel:** 5 in. **Weight:** 32 oz. **Length:** 8.58 in. overall. **Features:** Full-size 1911-style pistol with either steel or polymer frame. Also available in Commander or Officer's models with 4.25- or 3.5-in. barrel, polymer frame.
Price: $580.00
Price: Commander or Officer's Model................................. $627.00
Price: Steel frame $895.00

EAA SAR B6P
Caliber: 9mm. Based on polymer frame variation of CZ 75 design. Manufactured by Sarsilmaz in Turkey. Features similar to Witness series.
Price: .... $407.00–$453.00

EAA SAR K2-45

Caliber: .45 ACP. **Barrel:** 4.7 in. **Weight:** 2.5 lbs. **Features:** Similar to B6P with upgraded features. Built by Sarsilmaz for the Turkish military. Features include a cocked and locked carry system, ergonomically designed grip, steel frame and slide construction, adjustable rear sight, extended beaver tail, serrated trigger guard and frame, removable dove-tail front sight, auto firing pin block and low barrel axis for reduced felt recoil.
Price: $849.00

EAA MC 1911 SERIES

Caliber: .45 ACP, 9mm. **Capacity:** 8-round magazine, 9+1 (9mm).
Barrel: 5, 4.4, or 3.4 in. **Weight:** 26-39 oz. **Sights:** Novak-style rear, fixed front. **Features:** 1911-style pistol with either steel or polymer frame, ambidextrous safety, extended beavertail. Available in full-size, Commander or Officer's models. Manufactured by Girsan in Turkey.
Price: .... $572.00-$694.00

ED BROWN CLASSIC CUSTOM

Caliber: .45 ACP, 9mm, .38 Super. **Capacity:** 7-round magazine. **Barrel:** 5 in. **Weight:** 40 oz. **Grips:** Cocobolo wood. **Sights:** Bo-Mar adjustable rear, dovetail front. **Features:** Single action, M1911 style, custom made to order, stainless frame and slide available. Special mirror-finished slide.
Price: From $3,695.00

ED BROWN KOBRA CARRY

Caliber: .45 ACP. **Capacity:** 7-round magazine. **Barrels:** 4.25 in. **Weight:** 34 oz. **Grips:** Hogue exotic wood. **Sights:** Ramp, front; fixed Novak low-mount night sights, rear. **Features:** Snakeskin pattern serrations on forestrap and mainspring housing, dehorned edges, beavertail grip safety.
Price: .45 ACP From... $2,995.00
Price: 9 mm From... $3,095.00
Price: .38 Super From... $3,095.00

ED BROWN KOBRA CARRY LIGHTWEIGHT

Caliber: .45 ACP, 9mm, .38 Super. **Capacity:** 7-round magazine. **Barrel:** 4.25 in. (Commander model slide). **Weight:** 27 oz. **Grips:** Hogue exotic wood. **Sights:** 10-8 Performance U-notch plain black rear sight with .156-in. notch for fast acquisition of close targets. Fixed dovetail front night sight with high-visibility white outlines. **Features:** Aluminum frame and bobtail housing. Matte finished Gen III coated slide for low glare, with snakeskin on rear of slide only. Snakeskin pattern serrations on forestrap and mainspring housing, dehorned edges, beavertail grip safety. LW insignia on slide, which stands for Lightweight.
Price: Kobra Carry Lightweight $3,495.00

ED BROWN EXECUTIVE SERIES

Similar to other Ed Brown products, but with 25-LPI checkered frame and mainspring housing. Various finish, sight and grip options.
Price: .... $3,170.00-$3,880.00

ED BROWN SPECIAL FORCES

Similar to other Ed Brown products, but with ChainLink treatment on forestrap and mainspring housing. Entire gun coated with Gen III finish. Square cut serrations on rear of slide only. Dehorned. Introduced 2006. Available with various finish, sight and grip options.
Price: From .... $2,770.00–$4,775.00

ED BROWN CCO SERIES

Caliber: .45 ACP, 9mm, .38 Super. **Capacity:** 7-round magazine. **Barrel:** 4.25 in. Built on Officer's size frame with Commander slide. **Features:** Snakeskin metal treatment on mainspring housing, front strap and slide, round butt housing, concealed-carry beavertail grip safety, fixed black rear sight, high visibility fiber optic front. Lightweight aluminum version available.
Price: From .... $3,070.00–$3,585.00

EXCEL ARMS MP-22

Caliber: .22 WMR. **Capacity:** 9-round magazine. **Barrel:** 8.5-in. bull barrel. **Weight:** 54 oz. **Length:** 12.875 in. overall. **Grips:** Textured black composition. **Sights:** Fully adjustable target sights. **Features:** Made from 17-4 stainless steel, comes with aluminum rib, integral Weaver base, internal hammer, firing pin block. American made, lifetime warranty. Comes with two 9-round stainless steel magazines and a California-approved cable lock. .22 WMR Introduced 2006. Made in USA by Excel Arms.
Price: $477.00

EXCEL ARMS MP-5.7
Caliber: 5.7x28mm. **Capacity:** 9-round magazine. **Features:** Blowback action. Other features similar to MP-22. Red-dot optic sights, scope and rings are optional.
Price: $615.00
Price: With optic sights.................................... $685.00
Price: With scope and rings............................. $711.00

FIRESTORM 380
Caliber: .380 ACP. **Capacity:** 7+1. **Barrel:** 3.5 in. **Weight:** 20 oz. **Length:** 6.6 in. **Sights:** Fixed, white outline system. **Grips:** Rubber. **Finish:** Black matte. **Features:** Traditional DA/SA operation.
Price: $270.00

FMK 9C1 G2
Caliber: 9mm. **Capacity:** 10+1 or 14+1. **Barrel:** 4 in. **Overall length:** 6.85 in. **Weight:** 23.45 oz. **Finish:** Black, Flat Dark Earth or pink. **Sights:** Interchangeable Glock compatible. **Features:** Available in either single action or double action only. Polymer frame, high-carbon steel slide, stainless steel barrel. Very low bore axis and shock absorbing backstrap are said to result in low felt recoil. DAO model has Fast Action Trigger (FAT) with shorter pull and reset. Made in the USA.
Price: $409.95

FN FNS SERIES
Caliber: 9mm. **Capacity:** 17-round magazine, .40 S&W (14-round magazine). **Barrels:** 4 in. or 3.6 in. (Compact). **Weights:** 25 oz. (9mm), 27.5 oz. (.40). **Length:** 7.25 in. **Grips:** Integral polymer with two interchangeable backstrap inserts. **Features:** Striker fired, double action with manual safety, accessory rail, ambidextrous controls, 3-dot night sights.
Price: $599.00

FN FNX SERIES
Calibers: 9mm, .40 S&W. **Capacities:** 17-round magazine, .40 S&W (14 rounds), .45 ACP (10 or 14 rounds). **Barrels:** 4 in. (9mm and .40), 4.5 in. .45. **Weights:** 22–32 oz. (.45). **Lengths:** 7.4, 7.9 in. (.45). **Features:** DA/SA operation with decocking/manual safety lever. Has external extractor with loaded-chamber indicator, front and rear cocking serrations, fixed 3-dot combat sights.
Price: 9mm, .40 .... $699.00
Price: .45 ACP $824.00

FN FNX .45 TACTICAL
Similar to standard FNX .45 except with 5.3-in. barrel with threaded muzzle, polished chamber and feed ramp, enhanced high-profile night sights, slide cut and threaded for red-dot sight (not included), MIL-STD 1913 accessory rail, ring-style hammer.
Price: $1,349.00

FN FIVE-SEVEN
Caliber: 5.7x28mm. **Capacity:** 10- or 20-round magazine. **Barrel:** 4.8 in. **Weight:** 23 oz. **Length:** 8.2 in. **Features:** Adjustable three-dot system. Single-action polymer frame, chambered for low-recoil 5.7x28mm cartridge.
Price: $1,435.00

GLOCK 17/17C
Caliber: 9mm. **Capacities:** 17/19/33-round magazines. **Barrel:** 4.49 in. **Weight:** 22.04 oz. (without magazine). **Length:** 7.32 in. overall. **Grips:** Black polymer. **Sights:** Dot on front blade, white outline rear adjustable for windage. **Features:** Polymer frame, steel slide; double-action trigger with Safe Action system; mechanical firing pin safety, drop safety; simple takedown without tools; locked breech, recoil operated action. ILS designation refers to Internal Locking System. Adopted by Austrian armed forces 1983. NATO approved 1984. Model 17L has 6-inch barrel, ported or non-ported, slotted and relieved slide, checkered grip with finger grooves, no accessory rail. Imported from Austria by Glock, Inc. USA.
Price: From $599.00
Price: 17L $750.00
Price: 17 Gen 4 .... $649.00
Price: 17 Gen 5 .... $699.99

GLOCK GEN4 SERIES
In 2010, a new series of Generation 4 pistols was introduced with several improved features. These included a multiple backstrap system offering three different size options, short, medium or large frame; reversible and enlarged magazine release; dual recoil springs; and RTF (Rough Textured Finish) surface. Some recent models are only available in Gen 4 configuration.

GEN 5 SERIES
A new frame design was introduced in 2017 named Generation 5. The finger grooves were removed for more versatility and the user can customize the grip by using different backstraps, as with the Gen 4 models. A flared mag well and a cutout at the front of the frame give the user more speed during reloading. There is a reversible and enlarged magazine catch, changeable by users, as well as the ambidextrous slide stop lever to accommodate left- and right-handed operators. The rifling and crown of the barrel are slightly modified for increased precision. As of 2019, Gen 5 variants are available in Glock Models 17, 19, 26, 34 and 45.

Prices given are believed to be accurate at time of publication however, many factors affect retail pricing so exact prices are not possible.

74TH EDITION, 2020 ✦ 405

GLOCK 19/19C
Caliber: 9mm. **Capacities:** 15/17/19/33-round magazines. **Barrel:** 4.02 in. **Weight:** 20.99 oz. (without magazine). **Length:** 6.85 in. overall. Compact version of Glock 17. Imported from Austria by Glock, Inc.
Price: **$599.00**
Price: 19 Gen 4 .... **$649.00**
Price: 19 Gen 5 .... **$749.00**

GLOCK 20/20C 10MM
Caliber: 10mm. **Capacity:** 15-round magazine. **Barrel:** 4.6 in. **Weight:** 27.68 oz. (without magazine). **Length:** 7.59 in. overall. **Features:** Otherwise similar to Model 17. Imported from Austria by Glock, Inc. Introduced 1990.
Price: From **$637.00**
Price: 20 Gen 4 .... **$687.00**

GLOCK MODEL 20 SF SHORT FRAME
Caliber: 10mm. **Barrel:** 4.61 in. with hexagonal rifling. **Weight:** 27.51 oz. **Length:** 8.07 in. overall. **Sights:** Fixed. **Features:** Otherwise similar to the Model 20 but with short-frame design, extended sight radius.
Price: **$637.00**

GLOCK 21/21C
Caliber: .45 ACP. **Capacity:** 13-round magazine. **Barrel:** 4.6 in. **Weight:** 26.28 oz. (without magazine). **Length:** 7.59 in. overall. **Features:** Otherwise similar to the Model 17. Imported from Austria by Glock, Inc. Introduced 1991. SF version has tactical rail, smaller diameter grip, 10-round magazine capacity. Introduced 2007.
Price: From **$637.00**
Price: 21 Gen 4 .... **$687.00**

GLOCK 22/22C
Caliber: .40 S&W. **Capacities:** 15/17-round magazine. **Barrel:** 4.49 in. **Weight:** 22.92 oz. (without magazine). **Length:** 7.32 in. overall. **Features:** Otherwise similar to Model 17, including pricing. Imported from Austria by Glock, Inc. Introduced 1990.
Price: From **$599.00**
Price: 22C **$649.00**
Price: 22 Gen 4 .... **$649.00**

GLOCK 23/23C
Caliber: .40 S&W. **Capacities:** 13/15/17-round magazine. **Barrel:** 4.02 in. **Weight:** 21.16 oz. (without magazine). **Length:** 6.85 in. overall. **Features:** Otherwise similar to the Model 22, including pricing. Compact version of Glock 22. Imported from Austria by Glock, Inc. Introduced 1990.

Price: **$599.00**
Price: 23C Compensated **$621.00**
Price: 23 Gen 4 .... **$649.00**

GLOCK 24/24C
Caliber: .40 S&W. **Capacities:** 10/15/17 or 22-round magazine. **Features:** Similar to Model 22 except with 6.02-inch barrel, ported or non-ported, trigger pull recalibrated to 4.5 lbs.
Price: From **$750.00**

GLOCK 26
Caliber: 9mm. **Capacities:** 10/12/15/17/19/33-round magazine. **Barrel:** 3.46 in. **Weight:** 19.75 oz. **Length:** 6.29 in. overall. Subcompact version of Glock 17. Imported from Austria by Glock, Inc.
Price: **$599.00**
Price: 26 Gen 4 .... **$649.00**
Price: 26 Gen 5 .... **$749.00**

GLOCK 27
Caliber: .40 S&W. **Capacities:** 9/11/13/15/17-round magazine. **Barrel:** 3.46 in. **Weight:** 19.75 oz. (without magazine). **Length:** 6.29 overall. **Features:** Otherwise similar to the Model 22, including pricing. Subcompact version of Glock 22. Imported from Austria by Glock, Inc. Introduced 1996.
Price: From **$599.00**
Price: 27 Gen 4 .... **$649.00**

GLOCK 29 GEN 4
Caliber: 10mm. **Capacities:** 10/15-round magazine. **Barrel:** 3.78 in. **Weight:** 24.69 oz. (without magazine). **Length:** 6.77 in. overall. **Features:** Otherwise similar to the Model 20, including pricing. Subcompact version of the Glock 20. Imported from Austria by Glock, Inc. Introduced 1997.
Price: Fixed sight **$637.00**

GLOCK MODEL 29 SF SHORT FRAME
Caliber: 10mm. **Barrel:** 3.78 in. with hexagonal rifling. **Weight:** 24.52 oz. **Length:** 6.97 in. overall. **Sights:** Fixed. **Features:** Otherwise similar to the Model 29 but with short-frame design, extended sight radius.
Price: **$637.00**

GLOCK 30 GEN 4
Caliber: .45 ACP. **Capacities:** 9/10/13-round magazines. **Barrel:** 3.78 in. **Weight:** 23.99 oz. (without magazine). **Length:** 6.77 in. overall. **Features:** Otherwise similar to the Model 21, including pricing. Subcompact version of the Glock 21. Imported from Austria by Glock, Inc. Introduced 1997. SF version has tactical rail, octagonal rifled barrel with a 1:15.75 rate of twist, smaller diameter grip, 10-round magazine capacity. Introduced 2008.
Price: **$637.00**
Price: 30 SF (short frame) **$637.00**

GLOCK 30S
Caliber: .45 ACP. **Capacity:** 10-round magazine. **Barrel:** 3.78 in. **Weight:** 20 oz. **Length:** 7 in. **Features:** Variation of Glock 30 with a Model 36 slide on a Model 30SF frame (short frame).
Price: **$637.00**

GLOCK 31/31C
Caliber: .357 Auto. **Capacities:** 15/17-round magazine. **Barrel:** 4.49 in. **Weight:** 23.28 oz. (without magazine). **Length:** 7.32 in. overall. **Features:** Otherwise similar to the Model 17. Imported from Austria by Glock, Inc.
Price: From **$599.00**
Price: 31 Gen 4 .... **$649.00**

GLOCK 32/32C
Caliber: .357 Auto. **Capacities:** 13/15/17-round magazine. **Barrel:** 4.02 in. **Weight:** 21.52 oz. (without magazine). **Length:** 6.85 in. overall. **Features:** Otherwise similar to the Model 31. Compact. Imported from Austria by Glock, Inc.
Price: $599.00
Price: 32 Gen 4 .... $649.00

GLOCK 33
Caliber: .357 Auto. **Capacities:** 9/11/13/15/17-round magazine. **Barrel:** 3.46 in. **Weight:** 19.75 oz. (without magazine). **Length:** 6.29 in. overall. **Features:** Otherwise similar to the Model 31. Subcompact. Imported from Austria by Glock, Inc.
Price: From $599.00
Price: 33 Gen 4 .... $614.00

GLOCK 34
Caliber: 9mm. **Capacities:** 17/19/33-round magazine. **Barrel:** 5.32 in. **Weight:** 22.9 oz. **Length:** 8.15 in. overall. **Features:** Competition version of Glock 17 with extended barrel, slide, and sight radius dimensions. Available with MOS (Modular Optic System).
Price: From $679.00
Price: MOS $840.00
Price: 34 Gen 4 .... $729.00
Price: 34 Gen 5 .... $899.00

GLOCK 35
Caliber: .40 S&W. **Capacities:** 15/17-round magazine. **Barrel:** 5.32 in. **Weight:** 24.52 oz. (without magazine). **Length:** 8.15 in. overall. **Sights:** Adjustable. **Features:** Otherwise similar to the Model 22. Competition version of the Glock 22 with extended barrel, slide and sight radius dimensions. Available with MOS (Modular Optic System). Introduced 1996.
Price: From $679.00
Price: MOS $840.00
Price: 35 Gen 4 .... $729.00

GLOCK 36
Caliber: .45 ACP. **Capacity:** 6-round magazine. **Barrel:** 3.78 in. **Weight:** 20.11 oz. (without magazine). **Length:** 6.77 overall. **Sights:** Fixed. **Features:** Single-stack magazine, slimmer grip than Glock 21/30. Subcompact. Imported from Austria by Glock, Inc. Introduced 1997.
Price: $637.00

GLOCK 37
Caliber: .45 GAP. **Capacity:** 10-round magazine. **Barrel:** 4.49 in. **Weight:** 25.95 oz. (without magazine). **Length:** 7.32 overall. **Features:** Otherwise similar to the Model 17. Imported from Austria by Glock, Inc. Introduced 2005.
Price: $614.00
Price: 37 Gen 4 .... $664.00

GLOCK 38
Caliber: .45 GAP. **Capacities:** 8/10-round magazine. **Barrel:** 4.02 in. **Weight:** 24.16 oz. (without magazine). **Length:** 6.85 overall. **Features:** Otherwise similar to the Model 37. Compact. Imported from Austria by Glock, Inc.
Price: $614.00

GLOCK 39
Caliber: .45 GAP. **Capacities:** 6/8/10-round magazine. **Barrel:** 3.46 in. **Weight:** 19.33 oz. (without magazine). **Length:** 6.3 overall. **Features:** Otherwise similar to the Model 37. Subcompact. Imported from Austria by Glock, Inc.
Price: $614.00

GLOCK 40 GEN 4
Caliber: 10mm. **Features:** Similar features as the Model 41 except for 6.01-in. barrel. Includes MOS optics.
Price: $840.00

GLOCK 41 GEN 4
Caliber: .45 ACP. **Capacity:** 13-round magazine. **Barrel:** 5.31 in. **Weight:** 27 oz. **Length:** 8.9 in. overall. **Features:** This is a long-slide .45 ACP Gen4 model introduced in 2014. Operating features are the same as other Glock models. Available with MOS (Modular Optic System).
Price: $749.00
Price: MOS $840.00

GLOCK 42 GEN 4
Caliber: .380 ACP. **Capacity:** 6-round magazine. **Barrel:** 3.25 in. **Weight:** 13.8 oz. **Length:** 5.9 in. overall. **Features:** This single-stack, slimline sub-compact is the smallest pistol Glock has ever made. This is also the first Glock pistol made in the USA.
Price: $499.00

GLOCK 43 GEN 4
Caliber: 9mm. **Capacity:** 6+1. **Barrel:** 3.39 in. **Weight:** 17.95 oz. **Length:** 6.26 in. **Height:** 4.25 in. **Width:** 1.02 in. **Features:** Newest member of Glock's Slimline series with single-stack magazine.
Price: $599.00

GLOCK 43X
Caliber: 9mm. **Capacity:** 17+1. **Barrel:** 4.02 in. **Weight:** 24.5 oz. **Length:** 7.4 in. **Height:** 5.5 in. **Width:** 1.3 in. Combines compact slide with full-size frame.
Price: **$580.00**

GLOCK 45
Caliber: 9mm. **Capacity:** 10+1. **Barrel:** 3.41 in. **Weight:** 18.7 oz. **Length:** 6.5 in. **Height:** 5.04 in. **Width:** 1.1 in. Combines Glock 43 short and slim dimensions with extended frame size of G48.
Price: **$580.00**

GLOCK 48 GEN 4
Caliber: 9mm. **Capacity:** 10. **Barrel:** 3.41 in. **Weight:** 18.7 oz. **Length:** 6.05 in. **Height:** 5.04 in. **Width:** 1.1 in. **Features:** Silver-colored PVD coated slide with front serrations. Similar length and height as Model 19 with width reduced to 1.1 inch.
Price: **$580.00**

GRAND POWER P-1 MK7
Caliber: 9mm. **Capacity:** 15+1 magazine. **Barrel:** 3.7 in. **Weight:** 26 oz. **Features:** Compact DA/SA pistol featuring frame-mounted safety, steel slide and frame and polymer grips. Offered in several variations and sizes. Made in Slovakia
Price: **$449.99**

GUNCRAFTER INDUSTRIES
Calibers: 9mm, .38 Super, .45 ACP or .50 GI. **Capacity:** 7- or 8-round magazine. **Features:** 1911-style series of pistols best known for the proprietary .50 GI chambering. Offered in approximately 30 1911 variations. No. 1 has 5-inch heavy match-grade barrel, Parkerized or hard chrome finish, checkered grips and frontstrap, numerous sight options. Other models include Commander-style, Officer's Model, Long Slide w/6-inch barrel and several 9mm and .38 Super versions.
Price: .... **$2,795.00–$5,195.00**

HECKLER & KOCH USP
Calibers: 9mm, .40 S&W, .45 ACP. **Capacities:** 15-round magazine; .40 S&W, 13-shot magazine; 45 ACP, 12-shot magazine. **Barrels:** 4.25–4.41 in. **Weight:** 1.65 lbs. **Length:** 7.64–7.87 in. overall. **Grips:** Non-slip stippled black polymer. **Sights:** Blade front, rear adjustable for windage. **Features:** New HK design with polymer frame, modified Browning action with recoil reduction system, single control lever. Special "hostile environment" finish on all metal parts. Available in SA/DA, DAO, left- and right-hand versions. Introduced 1993. .45 ACP Introduced 1995. Imported from Germany by Heckler & Koch, Inc.
Price: USP .45 .... **$1,199.00**
Price: USP .40 and USP 9mm **$952.00**

HECKLER & KOCH USP COMPACT
Calibers: 9mm, .357 SIG, .40 S&W, .45 ACP. **Capacities:** 13-round magazine; .40 S&W and .357 SIG, 12-shot magazine; .45 ACP, 8-shot magazine. **Features:** Similar to the USP except the 9mm, .357 SIG and .40 S&W have 3.58-in. barrels, measure 6.81 in. overall and weigh 1.47 lbs. (9mm). Introduced 1996. .45 ACP measures 7.09 in. overall. Introduced 1998. Imported from Germany by Heckler & Koch, Inc.
Price: USP Compact .45 .... **$1,040.00**
Price: USP Compact 9mm, .40 S&W **$992.00**

HECKLER & KOCH USP45 TACTICAL
Calibers: .40 S&W, .45 ACP. **Capacities:** 13-round magazine; .45 ACP, 12-round magazine. **Barrels:** 4.90-5.09 in. **Weight:** 1.9 lbs. **Length:** 8.64 in. overall. **Grips:** Non-slip stippled polymer. **Sights:** Blade front, fully adjustable target rear. **Features:** Has extended threaded barrel with rubber O-ring; adjustable trigger; extended magazine floorplate; adjustable trigger stop; polymer frame. Introduced 1998. Imported from Germany by Heckler & Koch, Inc.
Price: USP Tactical .45 .... **$1,352.00**
Price: USP Tactical .40 .... **$1,333.00**

HECKLER & KOCH USP COMPACT TACTICAL
Caliber: .45 ACP. **Capacity:** 8-round magazine. **Features:** Similar to the USP Tactical except measures 7.72 in. overall, weighs 1.72 lbs. Introduced 2006. Imported from Germany by Heckler & Koch, Inc.
Price: USP Compact Tactical **$1,352.00**

HECKLER & KOCH HK45
Caliber: .45 ACP. **Capacity:** 10-round magazine. **Barrel:** 4.53 in. **Weight:** 1.73 lbs. **Length:** 7.52 in. overall. **Grips:** Ergonomic with adjustable grip panels. **Sights:** Low profile, drift adjustable. **Features:** Polygonal rifling, ambidextrous controls, operates on improved Browning linkless recoil system. Available in Tactical and Compact variations. Tactical models come with threaded barrel, adjustable TruGlo high-profile sights, Picatinny rail.
Price: HK45 .... **$819.00**
Price: HK45 Tactical **$919.00-999.00**

Prices given are believed to be accurate at time of publication however, many factors affect retail pricing so exact prices are not possible.

HECKLER & KOCH MARK 23 SPECIAL OPERATIONS

Caliber: .45 ACP. **Capacity:** 12-round magazine. **Barrel:** 5.87 in. **Weight:** 2.42 lbs. **Length:** 9.65 in. overall. **Grips:** Integral with frame; black polymer. **Sights:** Blade front, rear drift adjustable for windage; 3-dot. **Features:** Civilian version of the SOCOM pistol. Polymer frame; double action; exposed hammer; short recoil, modified Browning action. Introduced 1996. Imported from Germany by Heckler & Koch, Inc.
Price: **$2,299.00**

HECKLER & KOCH P30 AND P30L

Calibers: 9mm, .40 S&W. **Capacities:** 13- or 15-round magazines. **Barrels:** 3.86 in. or 4.45 in. (P30L) **Weight:** 26–27.5 oz. **Length:** 6.95, 7.56 in. overall. **Grips:** Interchangeable panels. **Sights:** Open rectangular notch rear sight with contrast points. **Features:** Ergonomic features include a special grip frame with interchangeable backstrap inserts and lateral plates, allowing the pistol to be individually adapted to any user. Browning-type action with modified short recoil operation. Ambidextrous controls include dual slide releases, magazine release levers and a serrated decocking button located on the rear of the frame (for applicable variants). A Picatinny rail molded into the front of the frame. The extractor serves as a loaded-chamber indicator.
Price: P30 .... **$1,099.00**
Price: P30L Variant 2 Law Enforcement Modification
(LEM) enhanced DAO **$1,149.00**
Price: P30L Variant 3 Double Action/Single Action
(DA/SA) with Decocker **$1,108.00**

HECKLER & KOCH P2000

Calibers: 9mm, .40 S&W. **Capacities:** 13-round magazine; .40 S&W, 12-shot magazine. **Barrel:** 3.62 in. **Weight:** 1.5 lbs. **Length:** 7 in. overall. **Grips:** Interchangeable panels. **Sights:** Fixed Patridge style, drift adjustable for windage, standard 3-dot. **Features:** Incorporates features of HK USP Compact pistol, including Law Enforcement Modification (LEM) trigger, double-action hammer system, ambidextrous magazine release, dual slide-release levers, accessory mounting rails, recurved, hook trigger guard, fiber-reinforced polymer frame, modular grip with exchangeable backstraps, nitro-carburized finish, lock-out safety device. Introduced 2003. Imported from Germany by Heckler & Koch, Inc.
Price: **$799.00**

HECKLER & KOCH P2000 SK

Calibers: 9mm, .357 SIG, .40 S&W. **Capacities:** 10-round magazine; .40 S&W and .357 SIG, 9-round magazine. **Barrel:** 3.27 in. **Weight:** 1.3 lbs. **Length:** 6.42 in. overall. **Sights:** Fixed Patridge style, drift adjustable. **Features:** Standard accessory rails, ambidextrous slide release, polymer frame, polygonal bore profile. Smaller version of P2000. Introduced 2005. Imported from Germany by Heckler & Koch, Inc.
Price: **$799.00**

HECKLER & KOCH VP9/VP 40

Calibers: 9mm, .40 S&W. **Capacities:** 10- or 15-round magazine. .40 S&W (10 or 13). **Barrel:** 4.09 in. **Weight:** 25.6 oz. **Length:** 7.34 in. overall. **Sights:** Fixed 3-dot, drift adjustable. **Features:** Striker-fired system with HK enhanced light pull trigger. Ergonomic grip design with interchangeable backstraps and side panels. VP9SK is compact model with 3.4-in. barrel.
Price: **$719.00**

HI-POINT FIREARMS MODEL 9MM COMPACT

Caliber: 9mm. **Capacity:** 8-round magazine. **Barrel:** 3.5 in. **Weight:** 25 oz. **Length:** 6.75 in. overall. **Grips:** Textured plastic. **Sights:** Combat-style adjustable 3-dot system; low profile. **Features:** Single-action design; frame-mounted magazine release; polymer frame offered in black or several camo finishes. Scratch-resistant matte finish. Introduced 1993. Comps are similar except they have a 4-in. barrel with muzzle brake/compensator. Compensator is slotted for laser or flashlight mounting. Introduced 1998. Made in USA by MKS Supply, Inc.
Price: C-9 9mm **$199.00**

HI-POINT FIREARMS MODEL 380 POLYMER

Caliber: .380 ACP. **Capacities:** 10- and 8-round magazine. **Weight:** 25 oz. **Features:** Similar to the 9mm Compact model except chambered for adjustable 3-dot sights. Polymer frame with black or camo finish. Action locks open after last shot. Trigger lock.
Price: CF-380 .... **$179.00**

Prices given are believed to be accurate at time of publication however, many factors affect retail pricing so exact prices are not possible.

74TH EDITION, 2020 ✦ **409**

HI-POINT FIREARMS 40 AND 45 SW/POLYMER

Calibers: .40 S&W, .45 ACP. **Capacities:** .40 S&W, 8-round magazine; .45 ACP, 9 rounds. **Barrel:** 4.5 in. **Weight:** 32 oz. **Length:** 7.72 in. overall. **Sights:** Adjustable 3-dot. **Features:** Polymer frames, offered in black or several camo finishes, last round lock-open, grip-mounted magazine release, magazine disconnect safety, integrated accessory rail, trigger lock. Introduced 2002. Made in USA by MKS Supply, Inc.
Price: $219.00

KAHR CM SERIES

Calibers: 9mm, .40 S&W, .45 ACP. **Capacities:** 9mm (6+1), .40 S&W (6+1). .45 ACP (5+1). CM45 Model is shown. **Barrels:** 3 in., 3.25 in. (45) **Weights:** 15.9–17.3 oz. **Length:** 5.42 in. overall. **Grips:** Textured polymer with integral steel rails molded into frame. **Sights:** CM9093, Pinned in polymer sight; PM9093, drift-adjustable, white bar-dot combat. **Features:** A conventional rifled barrel instead of the match-grade polygonal barrel on Kahr's PM series; the CM slide stop lever is MIM (metal-injection-molded) instead of machined; the CM series slide has fewer machining operations and uses simple engraved markings instead of roll marking. The CM series are shipped with one magazine instead of two. The slide is machined from solid 416 stainless with a matte finish, each gun is shipped with one 6-round stainless steel magazine with a flush baseplate. Magazines are U.S.-made, plasma welded, tumbled to remove burrs and feature Wolff springs. The magazine catch in the polymer frame is all metal and will not wear out on the stainless steel magazine after extended use.
Price: $460.00

ITHACA 1911

Caliber: .45 ACP. **Capacity:** 7-round capacity. **Barrels:** 4.25 or 5 in. **Weight:** 35 or 40 oz. **Sights:** Fixed combat or fully adjustable target. **Grips:** Checkered cocobolo with Ithaca logo. Classic 1911A1 style with enhanced features including match-grade barrel, lowered and flared ejection port, extended beavertail grip safety, hand-fitted barrel bushing, two-piece guide rod, checkered front strap.
Price: $1,575.00
Price: Hand fit $2,375.00

IVER JOHNSON EAGLE

Calibers: 9mm, .45 ACP, 10mm. **Features:** Series of 1911-style pistols made in typical variations including full-size (Eagle), Commander (Hawk), Officer's (Thrasher) sizes.
Price: .... $532.00–$959.00

KAHR CT 9/40/45 SERIES
Calibers: 9mm, .40 S&W, .45 ACP. **Capacities:** 9mm (8+1), .40 S&W (6+1) .45 ACP (7+1). **Barrel:** 4 in. **Weights:** 20–25 oz. **Length:** 5.42 in. overall. **Grips:** Textured polymer with integral steel rails molded into frame. **Sights:** Drift adjustable, white bar-dot combat. **Features:** Same as Kahr CM Series.
Price: $460.00

KAHR CT 380
Caliber: .380 ACP. **Capacity:** (7+1). **Barrel:** 3 in. **Weight:** 14 oz. Other features similar to CT 9/40/45 models.
Price: $419.00

KAHR K SERIES
Calibers: K9: 9mm, 7-shot; K40: .40 S&W, 6-shot magazine. **Barrel:** 3.5 in. **Weight:** 25 oz. **Length:** 6 in. overall. **Grips:** Wraparound textured soft polymer. **Sights:** Blade front, rear drift adjustable for windage; bar-dot combat style. **Features:** Trigger-cocking double-action mechanism with passive firing pin block. Made of 4140 ordnance steel with matte black finish. Contact maker for complete price list. Introduced 1994. Made in USA by Kahr Arms.
Price: K9093C K9, matte stainless steel $855.00
Price: K9093NC K9, matte stainless steel w/tritium
    night sights $985.00
Price: K9094C K9 matte blackened stainless steel $891.00
Price: K9098 K9 Elite 2003, stainless steel $932.00
Price: K4043 K40, matte stainless steel $855.00
Price: K4043N K40, matte stainless steel w/tritium
    night sights $985.00
Price: K4044 K40, matte blackened stainless steel $891.00
Price: K4048 K40 Elite 2003, stainless steel $932.00

KAHR MK SERIES MICRO
Similar to the K9/K40 except is 5.35 in. overall, 4 in. high, with a 3.08 In. barrel. Weighs 23.1 oz. Has snag-free bar-dot sights, polished feed ramp, dual recoil spring system, DAO trigger. Comes with 5-round flush baseplate and 6-shot grip extension magazine. Introduced 1998. Made in USA by Kahr Arms.
Price: M9093 MK9, matte stainless steel $911.00
Price: M9093N MK9, matte stainless steel, tritium
    night sights $1,017.00
Price: M9098 MK9 Elite 2003, stainless steel $991.00
Price: M4043 MK40, matte stainless steel $911.00
Price: M4043N MK40, matte stainless steel, tritium
    night sights $1,115.00
Price: M4048 MK40 Elite 2003, stainless steel $991.00

KAHR P SERIES
Calibers: .380 ACP, 9mm, .40 S&W, 45 ACP. **Capacity:** 7-shot magazine. **Features:** Similar to K9/K40 steel frame pistol except has polymer frame, matte stainless steel slide. Barrel length 3.5 in.; overall length 5.8 in.; weighs 17 oz. Includes two 7-shot magazines, hard polymer case, trigger lock. Introduced 2000. Made in USA by Kahr Arms.
Price: KP9093 9mm $762.00
Price: KP4043 .40 S&W $762.00
Price: KP4543 .45 ACP $829.00
Price: KP3833 .380 ACP (2008) $667.00

KAHR KP GEN 2 PREMIUM SERIES
Calibers: 9mm, .45 ACP. **Capacities:** KP9 9mm (7-shot magazine), KP45 .45 ACP (6 shots). **Barrel:** 3.5 in. **Features:** Black polymer frame, matte stainless slide, Tru-Glo Tritium fiber optic sights, short trigger, accessory rail.
Price: .... $833.00-$1,101.00

KAHR TP GEN 2 PREMIUM SERIES
Calibers: 9mm, .45 ACP. **Capacities:** TP9 9mm (8-shot magazine), TP45 .45 ACP (7 or 8 shots). **Barrels:** 4, 5, or 6 in. **Features:** Model with 4-inch barrel has features similar to KP GEN 2. The 5-inch model has front and rear slide

serrations, white 3-dot sights, mount for reflex sights. The 6-inch model has the same features plus comes with Leupold Delta Point Reflex sight.
Price: $976.00
Price: 5-inch bbl $1,015.00
Price: 6-inch bbl $1,566.00

KAHR PM SERIES
Calibers: 9mm, .40 S&W, .45 ACP. **Capacity:** 7-round magazine. **Features:** Similar to P-Series pistols except has smaller polymer frame (Polymer Micro). Barrel length 3.08 in.; overall length 5.35 in.; weighs 17 oz. Includes two 7-shot magazines, hard polymer case, trigger lock. Introduced 2000. Made in USA by Kahr Arms.
Price: PM9093 PM9 .... $810.00
Price: PM4043 PM40 .... $810.00
Price: PM4543 PM45 .... $880.00

KAHR T SERIES
Calibers: 9mm, .40 S&W. **Capacities:** T9: 9mm, 8-round magazine; T40: .40 S&W, 7-round magazine. **Barrel:** 4 in. **Weight:** 28.1–29.1 oz. **Length:** 6.5 in. overall. **Grips:** Checkered Hogue Pau Ferro wood grips. **Sights:** Rear: Novak low-profile 2-dot tritium night sight, front tritium night sight. **Features:** Similar to other Kahr makes, but with longer slide and barrel upper, longer butt. Trigger cocking DAO; locking breech; Browning-type recoil lug; passive striker block; no magazine disconnect. Comes with two magazines. Introduced 2004. Made in USA by Kahr Arms.
Price: KT9093 T9 matte stainless steel $857.00
Price: KT9093-NOVAK T9, "Tactical 9," Novak night sight $980.00
Price: KT4043 40 S&W $857.00

Prices given are believed to be accurate at time of publication however, many factors affect retail pricing so exact prices are not possible.

74TH EDITION, 2020 ⊕ **411**

KAHR CW SERIES
Caliber: 9mm, .40 S&W, .45 ACP. **Capacities:** 9mm, 7-round magazine; .40 S&W and .45 ACP, 6-round magazine. **Barrels:** 3.5 and 3.64 in. **Weight:** 17.7–18.7 oz. **Length:** 5.9–6.36 in. overall. **Grips:** Textured polymer. Similar to P-Series, but CW Series have conventional rifling, metal-injection-molded slide stop lever, no front dovetail cut, one magazine. CW40 introduced 2006. Made in USA by Kahr Arms. Several optional finishes available.
Price: .... **$449.00-$495.00**

KAHR P380
Caliber: .380 ACP. **Capacity:** 6+1. **Features:** Very small DAO semi-auto pistol. Features include 2.5-in. Lothar Walther barrel; black polymer frame with stainless steel slide; drift adjustable white bar/dot combat/sights; optional tritium sights; two 6+1 magazines. Overall length 4.9 in., weight 10 oz. without magazine.
Price: Standard sights **$667.00**
Price: Night sights... **$792.00**

KAHR CW380
Caliber: .380 ACP. **Capacity:** 6-round magazine. **Barrel:** 2.58 in. **Weight:** 11.5 oz. **Length:** 4.96 in. **Grips:** Textured integral polymer. **Sights:** Fixed white-bar combat style. **Features:** DAO. Black or purple polymer frame, stainless slide.
Price: **$419.00**

KAHR TIG SPECIAL EDITION
Caliber: 9mm. **Capacity:** 8 rounds. **Weight:** 18.5 oz. **Barrel:** 4 in. (Sub-compact model). **Features:** Limited Special Edition to support Beyond the Battlefield Foundation founded by John "Tig" Tiegen and his wife to provide support for wounded veterans. Tiegen is one of the heroes of the Benghazi attack in 2012. Kryptek Typhon finish on frame, black Teracote finish on slide engraved with Tiegen signature, Tig logo and BTB logo. Production will be limited to 1,000 pistols. Part of the proceeds from the sale of each firearm will be donated to the Beyond the Battlefield Foundation by Kahr Firearms Group.
Price: **$541.00**

KEL-TEC P-11
Caliber: 9mm. **Capacity:** 10-round magazine. **Barrel:** 3.1 in. **Weight:** 14 oz. **Length:** 5.6 in. overall. **Grips:** Checkered black polymer. **Sights:** Blade front, rear adjustable for windage. **Features:** Ordnance steel slide, aluminum frame. DAO trigger mechanism. Introduced 1995. Made in USA by Kel-Tec CNC Industries, Inc.
Price: From **$340.00**

KEL-TEC PF-9
Caliber: 9mm. **Capacity:** 7 rounds. **Weight:** 12.7 oz. **Sights:** Rear sight adjustable for windage and elevation. **Barrel:** 3.1 in. **Length:** 5.85 in. **Features:** Barrel, locking system, slide stop, assembly pin, front sight, recoil springs and guide rod adapted from P-11. Trigger system with integral hammer block and the extraction system adapted from P-3AT. Mil-Std-1913 Picatinny rail. Made in USA by Kel-Tec CNC Industries, Inc.
Price: From **$356.00**

KEL-TEC P-32
Caliber: .32 ACP. **Capacity:** 7-round magazine. **Barrel:** 2.68. **Weight:** 6.6 oz. **Length:** 5.07 overall. **Grips:** Checkered composite. **Sights:** Fixed. **Features:** Double-action-only mechanism with 6-lb. pull; internal slide stop. Textured composite grip/frame.
Price: From **$326.00**

KEL-TEC P-3AT
Caliber: .380 ACP. **Capacity:** 7-round magazine **Weight:** 7.2 oz. **Length:** 5.2. **Features:** Lightest .380 ACP made; aluminum frame, steel barrel.
Price: From **$331.00**

KEL-TEC PLR-16

Caliber: 5.56mm NATO. **Capacity:** 10-round magazine. **Weight:** 51 oz. **Sights:** Rear sight adjustable for windage, front sight is M-16 blade. **Barrel:** 9.2 in. **Length:** 18.5 in. **Features:** Muzzle is threaded 1/2x28 to accept standard attachments such as a muzzle brake. Except for the barrel, bolt, sights and mechanism, the PLR-16 pistol is made of high-impact glass fiber reinforced polymer. Gas-operated semi-auto. Conventional gas-piston operation with M-16 breech locking system. MIL-STD-1913 Picatinny rail. Made in USA by Kel-Tec CNC Industries, Inc.
Price: Blued **$682.00**

KEL-TEC PLR-22

Caliber: .22 LR. **Capacity:** 26-round magazine. **Length:** 18.5 in. overall. 40 oz. **Features:** Semi-auto pistol based on centerfire PLR-16 by same maker. Blowback action. Open sights and Picatinny rail for mounting accessories; threaded muzzle.
Price: **$400.00**

KEL-TEC PMR-30

Caliber: .22 Magnum (.22WMR). **Capacity:** 30 rounds. **Barrel:** 4.3 in. **Weight:** 13.6 oz. **Length:** 7.9 in. overall. **Grips:** Glass reinforced Nylon (Zytel). **Sights:** Dovetailed aluminum with front & rear fiber optics. **Features:** Operates on a unique hybrid blowback/locked-breech system. It uses a double-stack magazine of a new design that holds 30 rounds and fits completely in the grip of the pistol. Dual opposing extractors for reliability, heel magazine release to aid in magazine retention, Picatinny accessory rail under the barrel, Urethane recoil buffer, captive coaxial recoil springs. The barrel is fluted for light weight and effective heat dissipation. PMR30 disassembles for cleaning by removal of a single pin.
Price: **$455.00**

KIMBER MICRO CDP

Caliber: .380 ACP. **Capacity:** 6-round magazine. **Barrel:** 2.75 in. **Weight:** 17 oz. **Grips:** Double diamond rosewood. Mini 1911-style single action with no grip safety.
Price: **$869.00**

KIMBER MICRO CRIMSON CARRY

Caliber: .380 ACP. **Capacity:** 6-round magazine. **Barrel:** 2.75 in. **Weight:** 13.4 oz. **Length:** 5.6 in **Grips:** Black synthetic, double diamond. **Sights:** Fixed low profile. **Finish:** Matte black. **Features:** Aluminum frame with satin silver finish, steel slide, carry-melt treatment, full-length guide rod, rosewood Crimson Trace Lasergrips.
Price: **$839.00**

KIMBER MICRO TLE

Caliber: .380 ACP. **Features:** Similar to Micro Crimson Carry. **Features:** Black slide and frame. Green and black G10 grips.
Price: **$734.00**

KIMBER MICRO RAPTOR

Caliber: .380 ACP **Capacity:** 6-round magazine. **Sights:** Tritium night sights. **Finish:** Stainless. **Features:** Variation of Micro Carry with Raptor-style scalloped "feathered" slide serrations and grip panels.
Price: **$842.00**

KIMBER COVERT SERIES

Caliber: .45 ACP **Capacity:** 7-round magazine. **Barrels:** 3, 4 or 5 in. **Weight:** 25–31 oz. **Grips:** Crimson Trace laser with camo finish. **Sights:** Tactical wedge 3-dot night sights. **Features:** Made in the Kimber Custom Shop. **Finish:** Kimber Gray frame, matte black slide, black small parts. Carry Melt treatment. Available in three frame sizes: Custom, Pro and Ultra.
Price: **$1,457.00**

KIMBER CUSTOM II

Caliber: 9mm, .45 ACP. **Barrel:** 5 in. **Weight:** 38 oz. **Length:** 8.7 in. overall. **Grips:** Checkered black rubber, walnut, rosewood. **Sights:** Dovetailed front and rear, Kimber low profile adjustable or fixed sights. **Features:** Slide, frame and barrel machined from steel or stainless steel. Match-grade barrel, chamber and trigger group. Extended thumb safety, beveled magazine well, beveled front and rear slide serrations, high ride beavertail grip safety, checkered flat mainspring housing, kidney cut under trigger guard, high cut grip, match-grade stainless steel barrel bushing, polished breechface, Commander-style hammer, lowered and flared ejection port, Wolff springs, bead blasted black oxide or matte stainless finish. Introduced in 1996. Made in USA by Kimber Mfg., Inc.
Price: Custom II **$871.00**

Prices given are believed to be accurate at time of publication however, many factors affect retail pricing so exact prices are not possible.

74TH EDITION, 2020 ⊕ **413**

KIMBER CUSTOM TLE II
Caliber: .45 ACP or 10mm. **Features:** TLE (Tactical Law Enforcement) version of Custom II model plus night sights, frontstrap checkering, threaded barrel, Picatinny rail.
Price: .45 ACP **$1,007.00**
Price: 10mm **$1,028.00**

KIMBER STAINLESS II
Same features as Custom II except has stainless steel frame.
Price: Stainless II .45 ACP **$998.00**
Price: Stainless II 9mm **$1,016.00**
Price: Stainless II .45 ACP w/night sights................... **$1,141.00**
Price: Stainless II Target .45 ACP (stainless, adj. sight) **$1,108.00**

KIMBER RAPTOR II
Caliber: .45 ACP. **Capacities:** .45 ACP (8-round magazine, 7-round (Ultra and Pro models). **Barrels:** 3, 4 or 5 in. **Weight:** 25–31 oz. **Grips:** Thin milled rosewood. **Sights:** Tactical wedge 3-dot night sights. **Features:** Made in the Kimber Custom Shop. Matte black or satin silver finish. Available in three frame sizes: Custom (shown), Pro and Ultra.
Price: .... **$1,192.00–$1,464.00**

KIMBER PRO CARRY II
Calibers: 9mm, .45 ACP. **Features:** Similar to Custom II, has aluminum frame, 4-in. bull barrel fitted directly to the slide without bushing. Introduced 1998. Made in USA by Kimber Mfg., Inc.
Price: Pro Carry II, .45 ACP **$837.00**
Price: Pro Carry II, 9mm **$857.00**
Price: Pro Carry II w/night sights **$977.00**

KIMBER SAPPHIRE PRO II
Caliber: 9mm. **Capacity:** 9-round magazine. **Features:** Similar to Pro Carry II, 4-inch match-grade barrel. Striking two-tone appearance with satin silver aluminum frame and high polish bright blued slide. Grips are blue/black G-10 with grooved texture. Fixed Tactical Edge night sights. From the Kimber Custom Shop.
Price: **$1,652.00**

KIMBER ULTRA CARRY II
Calibers: 9mm, .45 ACP. **Features:** Lightweight aluminum frame, 3-in. match-grade bull barrel fitted to slide without bushing. Grips 0.4-in. shorter. Light recoil spring. Weighs 25 oz. Introduced in 1999. Made in USA by Kimber Mfg., Inc.
Price: Stainless Ultra Carry II .45 ACP **$919.00**
Price: Stainless Ultra Carry II 9mm **$1,016.00**
Price: Stainless Ultra Carry II .45 ACP with night sights **$1,039.00**

KIMBER GOLD MATCH II
Caliber: .45 ACP. **Features:** Similar to Custom II models. Includes stainless steel barrel with match-grade chamber and barrel bushing, ambidextrous thumb safety, adjustable sight, premium aluminum trigger, hand-checkered double diamond rosewood grips. Barrel hand-fitted for target accuracy. Made in USA by Kimber Mfg., Inc.
Price: Gold Match II .45 ACP... **$1,393.00**
Price: Gold Match Stainless II .45 ACP **$1,574.00**

KIMBER CDP II SERIES
Calibers: 9mm, .45 ACP. **Features:** Similar to Custom II but designed for concealed carry. Aluminum frame. Standard features include stainless steel slide, fixed Meprolight tritium 3-dot (green) dovetail-mounted night sights, match-grade barrel and chamber, 30 LPI frontstrap checkering, two-tone finish, ambidextrous thumb safety, hand-checkered double diamond rosewood grips. Introduced in 2000. Made in USA by Kimber Mfg., Inc.
Price: Ultra CDP II 9mm (2008) **$1,359.00**
Price: Ultra CDP II .45 ACP **$1,318.00**
Price: Compact CDP II .45 ACP **$1,318.00**
Price: Pro CDP II .45 ACP **$1,318.00**
Price: Custom CDP II (5-in. barrel, full length grip) **$1,318.00**

Trace laser grips; tritium 3-dot night sights.
Price: $1,603.00

KIMBER CDP
Calibers: 9mm, .45 ACP. **Barrel:** 3, 4 or 5 in. **Weight:** 25–31 oz. **Features:** Aluminum frame, stainless slide, 30 LPI checkering on backstrap and trigger guard, low profile tritium night sights, Carry Melt treatment. **Sights:** Hand checkered rosewood or Crimson Trace Lasergrips. Introduced in 2017.
Price: **$1,173.00**
Price: With Crimson Trace Lasergrips................................. **$1,473.00**

KIMBER ECLIPSE II SERIES
Calibers: .38 Super, 10 mm, .45 ACP. **Features:** Similar to Custom II and other stainless Kimber pistols. Stainless slide and frame, black oxide, two-tone finish. Gray/black laminated grips. 30 LPI frontstrap checkering. All models have night sights; Target versions have Meprolight adjustable Bar/Dot version. Made in USA by Kimber Mfg., Inc.
Price: Eclipse Ultra II (3-in. barrel, short grip) **$1,350.00**
Price: Eclipse Pro II (4-in. barrel, full-length grip) **$1,350.00**
Price: Eclipse Custom II 10mm **$1,350.00**
Price: Eclipse Target II (5-in. barrel, full-length grip,
        adjustable sight) **$1,393.00**

KIMBER TACTICAL ENTRY II
Caliber: 45 ACP. **Capacity:** 7-round magazine. **Barrel:** 5 in. **Weight:** 40 oz. **Length:** 8.7 in. overall. **Features:** 1911-style semi-auto with checkered frontstrap, extended magazine well, night sights, heavy steel frame, tactical rail.
Price: **$1,490.00**

KIMBER TACTICAL CUSTOM HD II
Caliber: .45 ACP. **Capacity:** 7-round magazine. **Barrel:** 5 in. match-grade. **Weight:** 39 oz. **Length:** 8.7 in. overall. **Features:** 1911-style semiauto with night sights, heavy steel frame.
Price: **$1,387.00**

KIMBER ULTRA CDP II
Calibers: 9mm, .45 ACP. **Capacities:** 7-round magazine (9 in 9mm). **Features:** Compact 1911-style pistol; ambidextrous thumb safety; carry melt profiling; full-length guide rod; aluminum frame with stainless slide; satin silver finish; checkered frontstrap; 3-inch barrel; rosewood double diamond Crimson

KIMBER STAINLESS ULTRA TLE II
Caliber: .45 ACP. **Capacity:** 7-round magazine. **Features:** 1911-style semi-auto pistol. Features include full-length guide rod; aluminum frame with stainless slide; satin silver finish; checkered frontstrap; 3-in. barrel; tactical gray double diamond grips; tritium 3-dot night sights.
Price: **$1,136.00**

KIMBER ROYAL II
Caliber: .45 ACP. **Capacity:** 7-round magazine. **Barrel:** 5 in. **Weight:** 38 oz. **Length:** 8.7 in. overall. **Grips:** Solid bone-smooth. **Sights:** Fixed low profile. **Features:** A classic full-size pistol wearing a charcoal blue finish complimented with solid bone grip panels. Front and rear serrations. Aluminum match-grade trigger with a factory setting of approximately 4–5 pounds.
Price: **$1,785.00**

Prices given are believed to be accurate at time of publication however, many factors affect retail pricing so exact prices are not possible.

74TH EDITION, 2020 ✦ **415**

KIMBER MASTER CARRY SERIES
Caliber: .45 ACP. **Capacity:** 8-round magazine, 9mm (Pro only). **Barrels:** 5 in. (Custom), 4 in. (Pro), 3 in. (Ultra) **Weight:** 25–30 oz. **Grips:** Crimson Trace Laser. **Sights:** Fixed low profile. **Features:** Matte black KimPro slide, aluminum round heel frame, full-length guide rod.
Price: **$1,497.00**

KIMBER WARRIOR SOC
Caliber: .45 ACP. **Capacity:** 7-round magazine. **Barrel:** 5 in threaded for suppression. **Sights:** Fixed Tactical Wedge tritium. **Finish:** Dark Green frame, Flat Dark Earth slide. **Features:** Full-size 1911 based on special series of pistols made for USMC. Service melt, ambidextrous safety.
Price: **$1,392.00**

KIMBER KHX SERIES
Calibers: .45 ACP, 9mm. **Capacity:** 8+1. **Features:** This series is offered in Custom, Pro and Ultra sizes. **Barrels:** 5-, 4- or 3-inch match-grade stainless steel. **Weights:** 25–38 oz. **Finishes:** Stainless steel frame and slide with matte black KimPro II finish. Stepped hexagonal slide and top-strap serrations. **Sights:** Green and red fiber optic and Hogue Laser Enhanced MagGrip G10 grips and matching mainspring housings. Pro and Ultra models have rounded heel frames. Optics Ready (OR) models available in Custom and Pro sizes with milled slide that accepts optics plates for Vortex, Trijicon and Leupold red-dot sights.
Price: Custom OR .45 ACP **$1,087.00**
Price: Custom OR 9mm **$1,108.00**
Price: Custom, Pro or Ultra .45....................... **$1,259.00**
Price: Custom, Pro or Ultra 9mm **$1,279.00**

KIMBER SUPER JAGARE
Caliber: 10mm. **Capacity:** 8+1. **Barrel:** 6 in, ported. **Weight:** 42 oz. **Finish:** Stainless steel KimPro, Charcoal gray frame, diamond-like carbon coated slide. Slide is ported. **Sights:** Delta Point Pro Optic. **Grips:** Micarta. Frame has rounded heel, high cut trigger guard. Designed for hunting.
Price: **$2,688.00**

KIMBER AEGIS ELITE SERIES
Calibers: 9mm, .45 ACP. **Features:** Offered in Custom, Pro and Ultra sizes with 5-, 4.25- or 3-in. barrels. Sights: Green or red fiber optic or Vortex Venom red dot on OI (Optics Installed) models (shown). Grips: G10. Features: Satin finish stainless steel frame, matte black or gray slide, front and rear AEX slide serrations.
Price: .45 ACP **$1,021.00**
Price: 9mm **$1,041.00**
Price: .45 OI.. **$1,375.00**
Price: 9mm OI... **$1,395.00**

KIMBER EVO SERIES
Caliber: 9mm. **Capacity:** 7 rounds. **Barrel:** 3.16 in. **Sights:** Tritium night sights. **Weight:** 19 oz. **Grips:** G10. **Features:** Offered in TLE, CDP, Two Tone variants with stainless slide, aluminum frame.
Price: TLE.. **$925.00**
Price: CDP... **$949.00**
Price: Two Tone **$856.00**

Prices given are believed to be accurate at time of publication however, many factors affect retail pricing so exact prices are not possible.

LIONHEART LH9 MKII

Caliber: 9mm. **Capacities:** 15-round magazine. LH9C Compact, 10 rounds. **Barrel:** 4.1 in. **Weight:** 26.5 oz. **Length:** 7.5 in **Grips:** One-piece black polymer with textured design. **Sights:** Fixed low profile. Novak LoMount sights available. **Finish:** Cerakote Graphite Black or Patriot Brown. **Features:** Hammer-forged heat-treated steel slide, hammer-forged aluminum frame. Double-action PLUS action.
Price: **$695.00**
Price: Novak sights **$749.00**

LLAMA MAX-1

Calibers: .38 Super, .45 ACP. **Barrel:** 5 in. **Weight:** 37 oz. **Sights:** Mil-spec. fixed. **Features:** Standard size and features of the 1911A1 full-size model. Lowered ejection port, matte blue or hard chrome finish. Imported from the Philippines by Eagle Imports. Introduced in 2016.
Price: **$565.00**

LLAMA MICRO MAX

Caliber: .380 ACP. **Capacity:** 7-round magazine. **Weight:** 23 oz. **Sights:** Novak style rear, fiber optic front. **Grips:** Wood or black synthetic. **Features:** A compact 1911-style pistol with 3.75-in. barrel. Skeletonized hammer and trigger, double slide serrations, comes with two 7-shot magazines. Imported from the Philippines by Eagle Imports.
Price: **$468.00**

MAC 3011 SSD TACTICAL

Caliber: .45 ACP. **Capacity:** 14+1 magazine. **Barrel:** 5-in. match-grade bull. **Sights:** Bomar-type fully adjustable rear, dovetail front. **Weight:** 46 oz. **Finish:** Blue. **Grips:** Aluminum. **Features:** Checkered frontstrap serrations, skeletonized trigger and hammer, flared and lowered ejection port, ambidextrous safety. Imported from the Philippines by Eagle Imports.
Price: **$1,136.00**

MAC 1911 BOB CUT

Caliber: .45 ACP. **Capacity:** 8+1 magazine. **Barrel:** 4.25 in. Commander-size 1911 design. **Sights:** Novak type fully adjustable rear, dovetail front. **Weight:** 34.5 oz. **Finish:** Blue or hard chrome. **Grips:** Custom hardwood. **Features:** Stippled frontstrap, skeletonized trigger and hammer, flared and lowered ejection port, bobtail grip frame. Imported from the Philippines by Eagle Imports.
Price: **$902.00**

MAC 1911 BULLSEYE

Caliber: .45 ACP **Capacity:** 8+1 magazine. **Barrel:** 6-in. match-grade bull. **Sights:** Bomar-type fully adjustable rear, dovetail front. **Weight:** 46 oz. **Finish:** Blue or hard chrome. **Grips:** Hardwood. **Features:** Checkered frontstrap, skeletonized trigger and hammer, flared and lowered ejection port, wide front and rear slide serrations. Imported from the Philippines by Eagle Imports.
Price: **$1,219.00**

MOSSBERG MC1SC

Caliber: 9mm **Capacity:** 6+1 magazine. **Barrel:** 3.4 in. **Sights:** Three white-dot, snag free. TruGlo tritium Pro sights or Viridian E-Series Red Laser available as option. **Weight:** 22 oz., loaded. **Grips:** Integral with aggressive texturing and with palm swell. **Features:** Glass-reinforced polymer frame, stainless steel slide with multi-angle front and rear serrations, flat-profile trigger with integrated blade safety, ships with one 6-round and one 7-round magazine. Optional cross-bolt safety. Centennial Limited Edition (1,000 units) has 24k gold accents, tritium nitride finish on barrel, polished slide.

Price: $421.00
Price: Viridian laser sight $514.00
Price: TruGlo tritium sights............................. $526.00
Price: Centennial Limited Edition $686.00

NIGHTHAWK CUSTOM T4

Calibers: 9mm, .45 ACP **Capacities:** .45 ACP, 7- or 8-round magazine; 9mm, 9 or 10 rounds; 10mm, 9 or 10 rounds. **Barrels:** 3.8, 4.25 or 5 in. **Weights:** 28–41 ounces, depending on model. **Features:** Manufacturer of a wide range of 1911-style pistols in Government Model (full-size), Commander and Officer's frame sizes. Shown is T4 model, introduced in 2013 and available only in 9mm.

Price: From .... $3,495.00–$3,695.00

NIGHTHAWK CUSTOM GRP

Calibers: 9mm, 10mm, .45 ACP. **Capacity:** 8-round magazine. **Features:** Global Response Pistol (GRP). Black, Sniper Gray, green, Coyote Tan or Titanium Blue finish. Match-grade barrel and trigger, choice of Heinie or Novak adjustable night sights.

Price: $3,095.00

NIGHTHAWK CUSTOM SHADOW HAWK

Caliber: 9mm. **Barrels:** 5 in. or 4.25 in. **Features:** Stainless steel frame with black Nitride finish, flat-faced trigger, high beavertail grip safety, checkered frontstrap, Heinie Straight Eight front and rear titanium night sights.

Price: $3,795.00

NIGHTHAWK CUSTOM WAR HAWK

Caliber: .45 ACP. **Barrels:** 5 in. or 4.25 in. **Features:** One-piece mainspring housing and mag well, Everlast Recoil System, Hyena Brown G10 grips.

Price: $3,895.00

NIGHTHAWK CUSTOM BOB MARVEL 1911

Calibers: 9mm or .45 ACP. **Barrel:** 4.25-in. bull barrel. **Features:** Everlast Recoil System, adjustable sights, match trigger, black Melonite finish.

Price: $4,395.00

NIGHTHAWK CUSTOM DOMINATOR

Caliber: .45 ACP. **Capacity:** 8-round magazine. **Features:** Stainless frame, black Perma Kote slide, cocobolo double-diamond grips,, front and rear slide serrations, adjustable sights.

Price: $3,699.00

NIGHTHAWK CUSTOM SILENT HAWK

Caliber: .45 ACP. **Capacity:** 8-round magazine. **Barrel:** 4.25 in. **Features:** Commander recon frame, G10 black and gray grips. Designed to match Silencerco silencer, not included with pistol.

Price: $4,295.00

NIGHTHAWK CUSTOM HEINIE LONG SLIDE

Calibers: 10mm, .45 ACP. **Barrel:** Long slide 6-in. **Features:** Cocobolo wood grips, black Perma Kote finish, adjustable or fixed sights, frontstrap checkering.

Price: $3,895.00

NIGHTHAWK CUSTOM BORDER SPECIAL

Caliber: .45 ACP **Capacity:** 8+1 magazine. **Barrel:** 4.25-in. match grade. **Weight:** 34 oz. **Sights:** Heinie Black Slant rear, gold bead front. **Grips:** Cocobolo double diamond. **Finish:** Cerakote Elite Midnight black. **Features:** Commander-size steel frame with bobtail concealed carry grip. Scalloped frontstrap and mainspring housing. Serrated slide top. Rear slide serrations only. Crowned barrel flush with bushing.

Price: $3,699.00

NIGHTHAWK VIP BLACK

Caliber: .45 ACP. **Capacity:** 8+1 magazine. Hand built with all Nighthawk 1911 features plus deep hand engraving throughout, black DLC finish, custom vertical frontstrap and mainspring serrations, 14k solid gold bead front sight, crowned barrel, giraffe bone grips, custom walnut hardwood presentation case.

Price: $7,999.00

NORTH AMERICAN ARMS GUARDIAN DAO

Calibers: .25 NAA, .32 ACP, .380 ACP, .32 NAA. **Capacity:** 6-round magazine. **Barrel:** 2.49 in. **Weight:** 20.8 oz. **Length:** 4.75 in. overall. **Grips:** Black polymer. **Sights:** Low-profile fixed. **Features:** DAO mechanism. All stainless steel construction. Introduced 1998. Made in USA by North American Arms. The .25 NAA is based on a bottle-necked .32 ACP case, and the .32 NAA is on a bottle-necked .380 ACP case. Custom model has roll-engraved slide, high-polish features, choice of grips.

Price: .25 NAA, .32 ACP $409.00
Price: .32 NAA, .380 ACP $486.00
Price: Engraved Custom Model ....$575.00-$625.00

PHOENIX ARMS HP22, HP25

Calibers: .22 LR, .25 ACP. **Capacities:** .22 LR, 10-shot (HP22), .25 ACP, 10-shot (HP25). **Barrel:** 3 in. **Weight:** 20 oz. **Length:** 5.5 in. overall. **Grips:** Checkered composition. **Sights:** Blade front, adjustable rear. **Features:** Single action, exposed hammer; manual hold-open; button magazine release. Available in satin nickel,matte blue finish. Introduced 1993. Made in USA by Phoenix Arms.

Price: With gun lock $162.00
Price: HP Range kit with 5-in. bbl., locking case and
    accessories (1 Mag) $207.00
Price: HP Deluxe Range kit with 3- and 5-in. bbls., 2 mags, case $248.00

REMINGTON R1
Caliber: .45 ACP. **Capacity:** 7-round magazine. **Barrels:** 5 in. (Full-size); 4.25 in. (Commander). **Weight:** 38.5 oz., 31 oz. (Ultralite). **Grips:** Double diamond walnut. **Sights:** Fixed, dovetail front and rear, 3-dot. **Features:** Flared and lowered ejection port. Comes with two magazines.
Price: Full-size or Commander $774.00
Price: Stainless $837.00
Price: Ultralite Commander... $849.00

REMINGTON R1 LIMITED
Calibers: 9mm, .40 S&W, .45 ACP (Double-stack only). **Capacity:** 19+1 magazine. **Barrel:** 5 in. **Grips:** G10 VZ Operator. **Weight:** 38 oz. **Features:** Stainless steel frame and slide. Double Stack Model has 19-shot capacity.
Price: $1,250.00
Price: Limited Double Stack.. $1,310.00

REMINGTON R1 RECON
Calibers: 9mm, .45 ACP. **Barrel:** 4.25-in. match grade. **Features:** Double-stack stainless steel frame and slide. G10 VZ Operator grips, skeletonized trigger, ambidextrous safety, PVD coating, Tritium night sights, wide front and rear serrations, checkered mainspring housing and frontstrap.
Price: $1,275.00

REMINGTON R1 TACTICAL
Caliber: .45 ACP. **Barrel:** 5-in. **Sights:** Trijicon night sights. **Features:** Single- or double-stack frame. Threaded barrel available on double-stack model. Adjustable trigger. Other features same as Recon.
Price: $1,250.00
Price: Threaded barrel.. $1,275.00

REMINGTON R1 HUNTER
Caliber: 10mm. **Capacity:** 8-round magazine. **Barrel:** 6-in. match grade. **Sights:** Fully adjustable. **Finish:** Stainless steel. Comes with two 8-shot magazines, Operator II VZ G10 grips.
Price: $1,310.00

REMINGTON R1 ENHANCED
Calibers: .45 ACP, 9mm. **Capacities:** Same features as standard R1 except 8-shot magazine (.45), 9-shot (9mm). Stainless satin black oxide finish, wood laminate grips and adjustable rear sight. Other features include forward slide serrations, fiber optic front sight. Available with threaded barrel.
Price: $903.00
Price: Stainless $990.00
Price: Threaded barrel.. $959.00
Price: With Crimson Trace Laser Sight... $1,129.00
Price: Enhanced Double Stack $999.00

REMINGTON R1 CARRY
Caliber: .45 ACP. **Capacity:** 8-round magazine. **Barrel:** 5 in. or 4.25 in. (Carry Commander). **Weight:** 35–39 oz. **Grips:** Cocobolo. **Sights:** Novak-type drift-adjustable rear, tritium-dot front sight. **Features:** Skeletonized trigger. Comes with one 8- and one 7-round magazine.
Price: $1,067.00

REMINGTON RM380
Caliber: .380 ACP. **Capacity:** 6-round magazine. **Barrel:** 2.9 in. **Length:** 5.27 in. **Height:** 3.86 in. **Weight:** 12.2 oz. **Sights:** Fixed and contoured. **Grips:** Glass-filled nylon with replaceable panels. **Features:** Double-action-only operation, all-metal construction with aluminum frame, stainless steel barrel, light dual recoil spring system, extended beavertail. Executive has brushed stainless slide, black frame, laminate Macassar exotic ebony grips.
Price: Light blue/black two-tone $348.00
Price: Executive $405.00
Price: Black finish $436.00
Price: With Crimson Trace Laser Sight................................. $638.00

REMINGTON RP9/RP45
Calibers: 9mm, .45 ACP. **Capacities:** 10- or 18-round magazine. **Barrel:** 4.5 in. **Weight:** 26.4 oz. **Sights:** Drift adjustable front and rear. **Features:** Striker-fired polymer frame model with Picatinny rail. Interchangeable backstraps. Smooth, light trigger pull with short reset, trigger safety. Easy loading double-stack magazine.
Price: $418.00

REMINGTON R51
Caliber: 9mm. **Capacity:** 7-round magazine. **Barrel:** 3.4 in. **Sights:** Fixed low profile. **Weight:** 22 oz. **Features:** Skeletonized trigger with crisp, light pull. Aluminum frame with black stainless slide. Redesigned and improved variation of 2014 model, which was recalled. Reintroduced in 2017.
Price: $448.00
Price: Smoke/Silver Two Tone finish.................................... $460.00
Price: Crimson Trace Laser Grips $648.00

REPUBLIC FORGE 1911
Calibers: .45 ACP, 9mm, .38 Super, .40 S&W, 10mm. **Features:** A manufacturer of custom 1911-style pistols offered in a variety of configurations, finishes and frame sizes, including single- and double-stack models with many options. Made in Texas.
Price: From $2,795.00

ROBERTS DEFENSE 1911 SERIES
Caliber: .45 ACP. **Capacity:** 8-round magazine. **Barrels:** 5, 4.25 or 3.5 in. **Weights:** 26–38 oz. **Sights:** Novak-type drift-adjustable rear, tritium-dot or fiber optic front sight. **Features:** Skeletonized trigger. Offered in four model variants with many custom features and options. Made in Wisconsin by Roberts Defense.
Price: Recon.. $2,370.00
Price: Super Grade $2,270.00
Price: Operator.. $2,350.00

ROCK ISLAND ARMORY 1911A1-45 FSP
Calibers: 9mm, .38 Super, .45 ACP. **Capacities:** .45 ACP (8 rounds), 9mm Parabellum, .38 Super (9 rounds). **Features:** 1911-style semi-auto pistol. Hard rubber grips, 5-inch barrel, blued, Duracoat or two-tone finish, drift-adjustable sights. Nickel finish or night sights available.
Price: From $592.00

ROCK ISLAND ARMORY 1911A1-FS MATCH
Caliber: .45 ACP. **Barrels:** 5 in. or 6 in. **Features:** 1911 match-style pistol. Features fiber optic front and adjustable rear sights, skeletonized trigger and hammer, extended beavertail, double diamond checkered walnut grips.
Price: $877.00

ROCK ISLAND ARMORY 1911A1-.22 TCM
Caliber: .22 TCM. **Capacity:** 17-round magazine. **Barrel:** 5 in. **Weight:** 36 oz. **Length:** 8.5 in. **Grips:** Polymer. **Sights:** Adjustable rear. **Features:** Chambered for high velocity .22 TCM rimfire cartridge. Comes with interchangeable 9mm barrel.
Price: From $806.00

ROCK ISLAND ARMORY PRO MATCH ULTRA "BIG ROCK"
Caliber: 10mm. **Capacity:** 8- or 16-round magazine. **Barrel:** 6 in. **Weight:** 40 oz. **Length:** 8.5 in. **Grips:** VZ G10. **Sights:** Fiber optic front, adjustable rear. **Features:** Two magazines, upper and lower accessory rails, extended beavertail safety.
Price: $1,187.00
Price: High capacity model.. $1,340.00

ROCK ISLAND ARMORY MAP & MAPP
Caliber: 9mm, .22 TCM. **Capacity:** 16-round magazine. **Barrel:** 3.5 (MAPP) or 4 in (MAP). Browning short recoil action-style pistols with: integrated front sight; snag-free rear sight; single- & double-action trigger; standard or ambidextrous rear safety; polymer frame with accessory rail.
Price: From $429.00

ROCK ISLAND ARMORY XT22
Calibers: .22 LR, .22 Magnum. **Capacities:** 10- or 15-round magazine. **Barrel:** 5 in. **Weight:** 38 oz. **Features:** The XT-22 is the only .22 1911 with a forged 4140 steel slide and a one piece 4140 chrome moly barrel. Available as a .22/.45 ACP combo.
Price: $600.00
Price: .22 LR/.45 combo $900.00

ROCK ISLAND ARMORY BABY ROCK 380
Caliber: .380 ACP. **Capacity:** 7-round magazine. **Features:** Blowback operation. An 85 percent-size version of 1911-A1 design with features identical to full-size model.
Price: $460.00

ROCK RIVER ARMS LAR-15/LAR-9
Calibers: .223/5.56mm NATO, 9mm. **Barrels:** 7 in., 10.5 in. Wilson chrome moly, 1:9 twist, A2 flash hider, 1/2x28 thread. **Weights:** 5.1 lbs. (7-in. barrel), 5.5 lbs. (10.5-in. barrel). **Length:** 23 in. overall. **Stock:** Hogue rubber grip.

Sights: A2 front. **Features:** Forged A2 or A4 upper, single stage trigger, aluminum free-float tube, one magazine. Similar 9mm Para. LAR-9 also available. From Rock River Arms, Inc.
Price: LAR-15 7 in. A2 AR2115 .... **$1,175.00**
Price: LAR-15 10.5 in. A4 AR2120 .... **$1,055.00**
Price: LAR-9 7 in. A2 9mm2115 .... **$1,320.00**

ROCK RIVER ARMS TACTICAL PISTOL
Caliber: .45 ACP. **Features:** Standard-size 1911 pistol with rosewood grips, Heinie or Novak sights, Black Cerakote finish.
Price: **$2,200.00**

ROCK RIVER ARMS LIMITED MATCH
Calibers: .45 ACP, 40 S&W, .38 Super, 9mm. **Barrel:** 5 in. **Sights:** Adjustable rear, blade front. **Finish:** Hard chrome. **Features:** National Match frame with beveled magazine well, front and rear slide serrations, Commander Hammer, G10 grips.
Price: **$3,600.00**

ROCK RIVER ARMS CARRY PISTOL
Caliber: .45 ACP. **Barrel:** 5 in. **Sights:** Heinie. **Finish:** Parkerized. **Grips:** Rosewood. **Weight:** 39 oz.
Price: **$1,600.00**

ROCK RIVER ARMS 1911 POLY
Caliber: .45 ACP. **Capacity:** 7-round magazine. **Barrel:** 5 in. **Weight:** 33 oz. **Sights:** Fixed. **Features:** Full-size 1911-style model with polymer frame and steel slide.
Price: **$925.00**

RUGER AMERICAN PISTOL
Calibers: 9mm, .45 ACP. **Capacities:** 10 or 17 (9mm), 10 (.45 ACP). **Barrels:** 4.2 in. (9), 4.5 in. (.45). **Lengths:** 7.5 or 8 in. **Weights:** 30–31.5 oz. **Sights:** Novak LoMount Carry 3-Dot. **Finish:** Stainless steel slide with black Nitride finish. **Grip:** One-piece ergonomic wrap-around module with adjustable palm swell and trigger reach. **Features:** Short take-up trigger with positive re-set, ambidextrous mag release and slide stop, integrated trigger safety, automatic sear block system, easy takedown. Introduced in 2016.
Price: **$579.00**

RUGER AMERICAN COMPACT PISTOL
Caliber: 9mm. **Barrel:** 3.5 in. **Features:** Compact version of American Pistol with same general specifications.
Price: **$579.00**

RUGER SR9 /SR40
Calibers: 9mm, .40 S&W. **Capacities:** 9mm (17-round magazine), .40 S&W (15). **Barrel:** 4.14 in. **Weights:** 26.25, 26.5 oz. **Grips:** Glass-filled nylon in two color options — black or OD Green, w/flat or arched reversible backstrap. **Sights:** Adjustable 3-dot, built-in Picatinny-style rail. **Features:** Semi-auto in six configurations, striker-fired, through-hardened stainless steel slide brushed or blackened stainless slide with black grip frame or blackened stainless slide with OD Green grip frame, ambidextrous manual 1911-style safety, ambi. mag release, mag disconnect, loaded chamber indicator, Ruger cam block design to absorb recoil, comes with two magazines. 10-shot mags available. Introduced 2008. Made in USA by Sturm, Ruger & Co.
Price: SR9 (17-Round), SR9-10 (SS) **$569.00**

RUGER SR9C/SR40C COMPACT
Calibers: 9mm, .40 S&W. **Capacities:** 10- and 17-round magazine. **Barrels:** 3.4 in. (SR9C), 3.5 in. (SR40C). **Weight:** 23.4 oz. **Features:** Features include 1911-style ambidextrous manual safety; internal trigger bar interlock and striker blocker; trigger safety; magazine disconnector; loaded chamber indicator; two magazines, one 10-round and the other 17-round; 3.5-in. barrel; 3-dot sights; accessory rail; brushed stainless or blackened alloy finish.
Price: **$569.00**

RUGER SECURITY-9
Caliber: 9mm. **Capacity:** 10- or 15-round magazine. **Barrel:** 4 or 3.4 in. **Weight:** 21 oz. **Sights:** Drift-adjustable 3-dot. Viridian E-Series Red Laser available. Striker-fired polymer-frame compact model. Uses the same Secure Action as LCP II. Bladed trigger safety plus external manual safety.
Price: **$379.00**
Price: Viridian Laser sight **$439.00**

RUGER SR45
Caliber: .45 ACP. **Capacity:** 10-round magazine. **Barrel:** 4.5 in. **Weight:** 30 oz. **Length:** 8 in. **Grips:** Glass-filled nylon with reversible flat/arched backstrap. **Sights:** Adjustable 3-dot. **Features:** Same features as SR9.
Price: $569.00

RUGER LC9S
Caliber: 9mm. **Capacity:** 7+1. **Barrel:** 3.12 in. **Grips:** Glass-filled nylon. **Sights:** Adjustable 3-dot. **Features:** Brushed stainless slide, black glass-filled grip frame, blue alloy barrel finish. Striker-fired operation with smooth trigger pull. Integral safety plus manual safety. Aggressive frame checkering with smooth "melted" edges. Slightly larger than LCS380. LC9S Pro has no manual safety.
Price: $479.00

RUGER LC380
Caliber: .380 ACP. Other specifications and features identical to LC9.
Price: $479.00
Price: LaserMax laser grips $529.00
Price: Crimson Trace Laserguard $629.00

RUGER LCP
Caliber: .380. **Capacity:** 6-round magazine. **Barrel:** 2.75 in. **Weight:** 9.4 oz. **Length:** 5.16 in. **Grips:** Glass-filled nylon. **Sights:** Fixed, drift adjustable or integral Crimson Trace Laserguard.
Price: Blued $259.00
Price: Stainless steel slide $289.00
Price: Viridian-E Red Laser sight $349.00
Price: Custom w/drift adjustable rear sight $269.00

RUGER LCP II
Caliber: .380. **Capacity:** 6-round magazine. **Barrel:** 2.75 in. **Weight:** 10.6 oz. **Length:** 5.16 in. **Grips:** Glass-filled nylon. **Sights:** Fixed. **Features:** Last round fired holds action open. Larger grip frame surface provides better recoil distribution. Finger grip extension included. Improved sights for superior visibility. Sights are integral to the slide, hammer is recessed within slide.
Price: $349.00

RUGER EC9S
Caliber: 9mm. **Capacity:** 7-shot magazine. **Barrel:** 3.125 in. Striker-fired polymer frame. **Weight:** 17.2 oz.
Price: $299.00

RUGER CHARGER
Caliber: .22 LR. **Capacity:** 15-round BX-15 magazine. **Features:** Based on famous 10/22 rifle design with pistol grip stock and fore-end, scope

rail, bipod. Black laminate stock. Silent-SR Suppressor available. Add $449. NFA regulations apply. Reintroduced with improvements and enhancements in 2015.

Price: Standard **$309.00**
Price: Takedown **$419.00**

RUGER MK IV COMPETITION

RUGER 22/45 MARK IV

RUGER MARK IV TARGET

RUGER 22/45 MARK IV PISTOL

Caliber: .22 LR. **Features:** Similar to other .22 Mark IV autos except has Zytel grip frame that matches angle and magazine latch of Model 1911 .45 ACP pistol. Available in 4.4-, 5.5-in. bull barrels. Comes with extra magazine, plastic case, lock. Molded polymer or replaceable laminate grips. **Weight:** 25–33 oz. **Sights:** Adjustable. Updated design of Mark III with one-button takedown. Introduced 2016.

Price: **$409.00**
Price: 4.4-in. bull threaded barrel w/rails **$529.00**
Price: Lite w/aluminum frame, rails **$549.00**

RUGER MARK IV SERIES

Caliber: .22 LR. **Capacity:** 10-round magazine. **Barrels:** 5.5 in, 6.875 in. Target model has 5.5-in. bull barrel, Hunter model 6.88-in. fluted bull, Competition model 6.88-in. slab-sided bull. **Weight:** 33–46 oz. **Grips:** Checkered or target laminate. **Sights:** Adjustable rear, blade or fiber-optic front (Hunter). **Features:** Updated design of Mark III series with one-button takedown. Introduced 2016. Modern successor of the first Ruger pistol of 1949.

Price: Standard **$449.00**
Price: Target (blue) **$529.00**
Price: Target (stainless) **$689.00**
Price: Hunter .... **$769.00–$799.00**
Price: Competition **$749.00**

RUGER SR22

Caliber: .22 LR. **Capacity:** 10-round magazine. **Barrel:** 3.5 in. **Weight:** 17.5 oz. **Length:** 6.4 in. **Sights:** Adjustable 3-dot. **Features:** Ambidextrous manual safety/decocking lever and mag release. Comes with two interchangeable rubberized grips and two magazines. Black or silver anodize finish. Available with threaded barrel.

Price: Black **$439.00**
Price: Silver **$459.00**
Price: Threaded barrel **$479.00**

Prices given are believed to be accurate at time of publication however, many factors affect retail pricing so exact prices are not possible.

74TH EDITION, 2020 ⬩ **423**

RUGER SR1911
Caliber: .45. **Capacity:** 8-round magazine. **Barrel:** 5 in. (3.5 in. Officer Model) **Weight:** 39 oz. **Length:** 8.6 in., 7.1 in. **Grips:** Slim checkered hardwood. **Sights:** Novak LoMount Carry rear, standard front. **Features:** Based on Series 70 design. Flared and lowered ejection port. Extended mag release, thumb safety and slide-stop lever, oversized grip safety, checkered backstrap on the flat mainspring housing. Comes with one 7-round and one 8-round magazine.
Price: $939.00

RUGER SR1911 CMD
Caliber: .45 ACP. **Barrel:** 4.25 in. **Weight:** 29.3 (aluminum), 36.4 oz. (stainless). **Features:** Commander-size version of SR1911. Other specifications and features are identical to SR1911. Lightweight Commander also offered in 9mm.
Price: Low glare stainless $939.00
Price: Anodized aluminum two-tone....................................... $979.00

RUGER SR1911 COMPETITION
Calibers: 9mm. **Capacities:** .10+1. **Barrel:** 5 in. **Weight:** 39 oz. **Sights:** Fiber optic front, adjustable target rear. **Grips:** Hogue Piranha G10 Deluxe checkered. **Features:** Skeletonized hammer and trigger, satin stainless finish, hand-fitted frame and slide, competition trigger, competition barrel with polished feed ramp. From Ruger Competition Shop. Introduced in 2016.
Price: $2,499.00

RUGER SR1911 OFFICER
Caliber: .45 ACP, 9mm. **Capacity:** 8-round magazine. **Barrel:** 3.6 in. **Weight:** 27 oz. **Features:** Compact variation of SR1911 Series. Black anodized aluminum frame, stainless slide, skeletonized trigger, Novak 3-dot Night Sights, G10 deluxe checkered G10 grips.
Price: $979.00

RUGER SR1911 TARGET
Calibers: 9mm, 10mm, .45 ACP. **Capacities:** .45 and 10mm (8-round magazine), 9mm (9 shot). **Barrel:** 5 in. **Weight:** 39 oz. **Sights:** Bomar adjustable. **Grips:** G10 Deluxe checkered. **Features:** Skeletonized hammer and trigger, satin stainless finish. Introduced in 2016.
Price: $1,019.00

SCCY CPX
Caliber: 9mm. **Capacity:** 10-round magazine. **Barrel:** 3.1 in. **Weight:** 15 oz. **Length:** 5.7 in. overall. **Grips:** Integral with polymer frame. **Sights:** 3-dot system, rear adjustable for windage. **Features:** Zytel polymer frame, steel slide, aluminum alloy receiver machined from bar stock. DAO with consistent 9-pound trigger pull. Concealed hammer. Available with (CPX-1) or without (CPX-2) manual thumb safety. Introduced 2014. CPX-3 is chambered for .380 ACP. Made in USA by SCCY Industries.
Price: CPX-1 .... $284.00
Price: CPX-2 .... $270.00
Price: CPX-3 .... $305.00

SEECAMP LWS 32/380 STAINLESS DA
Calibers: .32 ACP, .380 ACP. **Capacity:** 6-round magazine. **Barrel:** 2 in., integral with frame. **Weight:** 10.5 oz. **Length:** 4.125 in. overall. **Grips:** Glass-filled nylon. **Sights:** Smooth, no-snag, contoured slide and barrel top. **Features:** Aircraft quality 17-4 PH stainless steel. Inertia-operated firing pin. Hammer fired DAO. Hammer automatically follows slide down to safety rest position after each shot, no manual safety needed. Magazine safety disconnector. Polished stainless. Introduced 1985. From L.W. Seecamp.
Price: .32 .... $446.25
Price: .380 .... $795.00

SIG SAUER P220

Caliber: .45 ACP, 10mm. **Capacity:** 7- or 8-round magazine. **Barrel:** 4.4 in. **Weight:** 27.8 oz. **Length:** 7.8 in. overall. **Grips:** Checkered black plastic. **Sights:** Blade front, drift adjustable rear for windage. Optional Siglite night sights. **Features:** Double action. Stainless steel slide, Nitron finish, alloy frame, M1913 Picatinny rail; safety system of decocking lever, automatic firing pin safety block, safety intercept notch, and trigger bar disconnector. Squared combat-type trigger guard. Slide stays open after last shot. Introduced 1976. P220 SAS Anti-Snag has dehorned stainless steel slide, front Siglite night sight, rounded trigger guard, dust cover, Custom Shop wood grips. Equinox line is Custom Shop product with Nitron stainless slide with a black hard-anodized alloy frame, brush-polished flats and nickel accents. Truglo tritium fiber-optic front sight, rear Siglite night sight, gray laminated wood grips with checkering and stippling. From SIG Sauer, Inc.

Price:	$1,087.00
Price: P220 Elite Stainless	$1,450.00
Price: Hunter SAO	$1,629.00
Price: Legion 45 ACP	$1,413.00
Price: Legion 10mm	$1,904.00

SIG SAUER 1911

Calibers: .45 ACP, .40 S&W. **Capacities:** .45 ACP, .40 S&W. 8- and 10-round magazine. **Barrel:** 5 in. **Weight:** 40.3 oz. **Length:** 8.65 in. overall. **Grips:** Checkered wood grips. **Sights:** Novak night sights. Blade front, drift adjustable rear for windage. **Features:** Single-action 1911. Hand-fitted dehorned stainless steel frame and slide; match-grade barrel, hammer/sear set and trigger; 25-LPI front strap checkering, 20-LPI mainspring housing checkering. Beavertail grip safety with speed bump, extended thumb safety, firing pin safety and hammer intercept notch. Introduced 2005. XO series has contrast sights, Ergo Grip XT textured polymer grips. STX line available from Sig Sauer Custom Shop; two-tone 1911, non-railed, Nitron slide, stainless frame, burled maple grips. Polished cocking serrations, flat-top slide, mag well. Carry line has Siglite night sights, lanyard attachment point, gray diamondwood or rosewood grips, 8+1 capacity. Compact series has 6+1 capacity, 7.7 OAL, 4.25-in. barrel, slim-profile wood grips, weighs 30.3 oz. Ultra Compact in 9mm or .45 ACP has 3.3-in. barrel, low-profile night sights, slim-profile gray diamondwood or rosewood grips. 6+1 capacity. 1911 C3 is a 6+1 compact .45 ACP, rosewood custom wood grips, two-tone and Nitron finishes. Weighs 30 oz. unloaded, lightweight alloy frame. Length is 7.7 in. Now offered in more than 30 different models with numerous options for frame size, grips, finishes, sight arrangements and other features. From SIG Sauer, Inc.

Price: Nitron	$1,174.00
Price: Tacops	$1,221.00
Price: XO Black	$1,010.00
Price: STX	$1,244.00
Price: Nightmare	$1,244.00
Price: Carry Nightmare	$1,195.00
Price: Compact C3	$1,010.00
Price: Ultra Compact	$1,119.00
Price: Max	$1,663.00
Price: Spartan	$1,397.00
Price: Super Target	$1,609.00
Price: Traditional Stainless Match Elite	$1,164.00
Price: We the People	$1,481.00
Price: Select	$1,234.00
Price: Stand Commemorative (Honored Veterans, C.O.P.S.)	$1,279.00

SIG SAUER P225 A-1

Caliber: 9mm. **Capacity:** 8-round magazine. **Barrels:** 3.6 or 5 in. **Weight:** 30.5 oz. **Features:** Shorter and slim-profile version of P226 with enhanced short reset trigger, single-stack magazine.

Price:	$1,122.00
Price: Night sights	$1,236.00

SIG SAUER SP2022

Calibers: 9mm, .40 S&W. **Capacities:** 10-, 12-, or 15-round magazines. **Barrel:** 3.9 in. **Weight:** 30.2 oz. **Length:** 7.4 in. overall. **Grips:** Composite and rubberized one-piece. **Sights:** Blade front, rear adjustable for windage. **Features:** Polymer frame, stainless steel slide; integral frame accessory rail; replaceable steel frame rails; left- or right-handed magazine release, two interchangeable grips.
Price: $642.00

SIG SAUER P238

Caliber: .380 ACP. **Capacity:** 6-round magazine. **Barrel:** 2.7 in. **Weight:** 15.4 oz. **Length:** 5.5 in. overall. **Grips:** Hogue G-10 and Rosewood grips. **Sights:** Contrast/Siglite night sights. **Features:** All-metal beavertail-style frame.
Price: $723.00
Price: Desert Tan $738.00
Price: Polished $798.00
Price: Rose Gold $932.00
Price: Emperor Scorpion $801.00

SIG SAUER P226

Calibers: 9mm, .40 S&W. **Barrel:** 4.4 in. **Length:** 7.7 in. overall. **Features:** Similar to the P220 pistol except has 4.4-in. barrel, measures 7.7 in. overall, weighs 34 oz. DA/SA or DAO. Many variations available. Snap-on modular grips. Legion series has improved short reset trigger, contoured and shortened beavertail, relieved trigger guard, higher grip, other improvements. From SIG Sauer, Inc.
Price: From $1,087.00
Price: Elite Stainless.................................... $1,481.00
Price: Legion $1,428.00
Price: Legion RX w/Romeo 1 Reflex sight........ $1,685.00
Price: MK25 Navy Version $1,187.00

SIG SAUER P227

Caliber: .45 ACP. **Capacity:** 10-round magazine. **Features:** Same general specifications and features as P226 except chambered for .45 ACP and has double-stack magazine.
Price: .... $1,087.00–$1,350.00

SIG SAUER P229 DA

Caliber: Similar to the P220 except chambered for 9mm (10- or 15-round magazines), .40 S&W, (10- or 12-round magazines). **Barrels:** 3.86-in. barrel, 7.1 in. overall length and 3.35 in. height. **Weight:** 32.4 oz. **Features:** Introduced 1991. Snap-on modular grips. Frame made in Germany, stainless steel slide assembly made in U.S.; pistol assembled in U.S. Many variations available. Legion series has improved short reset trigger, contoured and shortened beavertail, relieved trigger guard, higher grip, other improvements. Select has Nitron slide, Select G10 grips, Emperor Scorpion has accessory rail, FDE finish, G10 Piranha grips.
Price: P229, From $1,085.00
Price: P229 Emperor Scorpion $1,282.00
Price: P229 Legion $1,413.00
Price: P229 Select... $1,195.00

SIG SAUER P320

Calibers: 9mm, .357 SIG, .40 S&W, .45 ACP. **Capacities:** 15 or 16 rounds (9mm), 13 or 14 rounds (.357 or .40). **Barrels:** 3.6 in. (Subcompact), 3.9 in. (Carry model) or 4.7 in. (Full size). **Weights:** 26–30 oz. **Lengths:** 7.2 or 8.0 in overall. **Grips:** Interchangeable black composite. **Sights:** Blade front, rear adjustable for windage. Optional Siglite night sights. **Features:** Striker-fired DAO, Nitron finish slide, black polymer frame. Frame size and calibers are interchangeable. Introduced 2014. Made in USA by SIG Sauer, Inc.
Price: Full size $679.00
Price: Carry (shown) $679.00

SIG SAUER P320 SUBCOMPACT

Calibers: 9mm, .40 S&W. **Barrel:** 3.6 in. **Features:** Accessory rail. Other features similar to Full-Size and Carry models.
Price: $679.00

SIG SAUER MODEL 320 RX

Caliber: 9mm. **Capacity:** 17-round magazine. **Barrels:** 4.7 in. or 3.9 in. **Features:** Full and Compact size models with ROMEO1 Reflex sight, accessory rail, stainless steel frame and slide. XFive has improved control ergonomics, bull barrel, 21-round magazines.
Price: $952.00
Price: XFive.. $1,005.00

Prices given are believed to be accurate at time of publication however, many factors affect retail pricing so exact prices are not possible.

SIG SAUER P365
Caliber: 9mm. **Barrel:** 3.1 in. **Weight:** 17.8 oz. **Features:** Micro-compact striker-fired model with 10-round magazine, stainless steel frame and slide, XRAY-3 day and night sights fully textured polymer grip.
Price: $599.00

SIG SAUER MPX
Calibers: 9mm, .357 SIG, .40 S&W. **Capacities:** 10, 20 or 30 rounds. **Barrel:** 8 in. **Weight:** 5 lbs **Features:** Semi-auto AR-style gun with closed, fully locked short-stroke pushrod gas system.
Price: From $2,016.00

SIG SAUER P938
Calibers: 9mm, .22 LR. **Capacities:** 9mm (6-shot mag.), .22 LR (10-shot mag.). **Barrel:** 3.0 in. **Weight:** 16 oz. **Length:** 5.9 in. **Grips:** Rosewood, Blackwood, Hogue Extreme, Hogue Diamondwood. **Sights:** Siglite night sights or Siglite rear with Tru-Glo front. **Features:** Slightly larger version of P238.
Price: .... $760.00–$1,195.00
Price: .22 LR.. $656.00

SMITH & WESSON M&P SERIES
Calibers: .22 LR, 9mm, .40 S&W. **Capacities, full-size models:** 12 rounds (.22), 17 rounds (9mm), 15 rounds (.40). **Compact models:** 12 (9mm), 10 (.40). **Barrels:** 4.25, 3.5 in. **Weights:** 24, 22 oz. **Lengths:** 7.6, 6.7 in. **Grips:** Polymer with three interchangeable palm swell grip sizes. **Sights:** 3 white-dot system with low-profile rear. **Features:** Zytel polymer frame with stainless steel slide, barrel and structural components. VTAC (Viking Tactics) model has Flat Dark Earth finish, VTAC Warrior sights. Compact models available with Crimson Trace Lasergrips. Numerous options for finishes, sights, operating controls.
Price: $569.00
Price: (VTAC)... $799.00
Price: (Crimson Trace) .... $699.00–$829.00
Price: M&P 22 .... $389.00–$419.00

SMITH & WESSON M&P 45
Caliber: .45 ACP. **Capacity:** 8 or 10 rounds. **Barrel length:** 4 or 4.5 in. **Weight:** 26, 28 or 30 oz. **Features:** Available with or without thumb safety. **Finish:** Black or Dark Earth Brown. **Features:** M&P model offered in three frame sizes.
Price: .... $599.00–$619.00

Price: Threaded barrel kit......**$719.00SMITH & WESSON M&P M2.0 SERIES**
Calibers: 9mm, .40 S&W, .45 ACP. **Capacities:** 17 rounds (9mm), 15 rounds (.40), 10 rounds (.45). **Barrels:** 4.0 (Compact), 4.25, 4.5 or 4.6 in. (.45 only). **Weights:** 25 –27 oz. **Finishes:** Armornite Black or Flat Dark Earth. **Grip:** Textured polymer with 4 interchangeable modular inserts. Second Generation of M&P Pistol series. Introduced in 2017.
Price: $599.00
Price: Compact $569.00

SMITH & WESSON M&P 9/40 SHIELD
Calibers: 9mm, .40 S&W. **Capacities:** 7- and 8-round magazine (9mm); 6-round and 7-round magazine (.40). **Barrel:** 3.1 in. **Length:** 6.1 in. **Weight:** 19 oz. **Sights:** 3-white-dot system with low-profile rear. **Features:** Ultra-compact, single-stack variation of M&P series. Available with or without thumb safety. Crimson Trace Green Laserguard available.
Price: $449.00
Price: CT Green Laserguard $589.00

SMITH & WESSON M&P 45 SHIELD
Caliber: .45 ACP. **Barrel:** 3.3 in. Ported model available. **Weight:** 20–23 oz. **Sights:** White dot or tritium night sights. Comes with one 6-round and one 7-round magazine.
Price: $479.00
Price: Tritium night sights...................................... $579.00
Price: Ported barrel $609.00

SMITH & WESSON MODEL SD9 VE/SD40 VE
Calibers: .40 S&W, 9mm. **Capacities:** 10+1, 14+1 and 16+1 **Barrel:** 4 in. **Weight:** 39 oz. **Length:** 8.7 in. **Grips:** Wood or rubber. **Sights:** Front: Tritium Night Sight, Rear: Steel Fixed 2-Dot. **Features:** SDT (Self Defense Trigger) for optimal, consistent pull first round to last, standard Picatinny-style rail, slim ergonomic textured grip, textured finger locator and aggressive front and backstrap texturing with front and rear slide serrations.
Price: $389.00

Prices given are believed to be accurate at time of publication however, many factors affect retail pricing so exact prices are not possible.

74TH EDITION, 2020 ⊕ **427**

SPHINX SDP

Caliber: 9mm. **Capacity:** 15-shot magazine. **Barrel:** 3.7 in. **Weight:** 27.5 oz. **Length:** 7.4 in. **Sights:** Defiance Day & Night Green fiber/tritium front, tritium 2-dot red rear. **Features:** DA/SA with ambidextrous decocker, integrated slide position safety, aluminum MIL-STD 1913 Picatinny rail, Blued alloy/steel or stainless. Aluminum and polymer frame, machined steel slide. Offered in several variations. Made in Switzerland and imported by Kriss USA.
Price: From **$999.00**

SMITH & WESSON MODEL SW1911

Calibers: .45 ACP, 9mm. **Capacities:** 8 rounds (.45), 7 rounds (subcompact .45), 10 rounds (9mm). **Barrels:** 3, 4.25, 5 in. **Weights:** 26.5–41.7 oz. **Lengths:** 6.9–8.7 in. **Grips:** Wood, wood laminate or synthetic. Crimson Trace Lasergrips available. **Sights:** Low-profile white dot, tritium night sights or adjustable. **Finish:** Black matte, stainless or two-tone. **Features:** Offered in three different frame sizes. Skeletonized trigger. Accessory rail on some models. Compact models have round-butt frame. Pro Series have 30 LPI checkered frontstrap, oversized external extractor, extended mag well, full-length guide rod, ambidextrous safety.
Price: Standard Model E Series, From **$979.00**
Price: Crimson Trace grips **$1,149.00**
Price: Pro Series .... **$1,459.00–$1,609.00**
Price: Scandium Frame E Series **$1,449.00**

SMITH & WESSON BODYGUARD 380

Caliber: .380 Auto. **Capacity:** 6+1. **Barrel:** 2.75 in. **Weight:** 11.85 oz. **Length:** 5.25 in. **Grips:** Polymer. **Sights:** Integrated laser plus drift-adjustable front and rear. **Features:** The frame of the Bodyguard is made of reinforced polymer, as is the magazine base plate and follower, magazine catch and trigger. The slide, sights and guide rod are made of stainless steel, with the slide and sights having a Melonite hardcoating.
Price: **$449.00**

SPRINGFIELD ARMORY EMP ENHANCED MICRO

Calibers: 9mm, 40 S&W. **Capacity:** 9-round magazine. **Barrel:** 3-inch stainless steel match grade, fully supported ramp, bull. **Weight:** 26 oz. **Length:** 6.5 in. overall. **Grips:** Thinline cocobolo hardwood. **Sights:** Fixed low-profile combat rear, dovetail front, 3-dot tritium. **Features:** Two 9-round stainless steel magazines with slam pads, long aluminum match-grade trigger adjusted to 5 to 6 lbs., forged aluminum alloy frame, black hardcoat anodized finish; dual spring full-length guide rod, forged satin-finish stainless steel slide. Introduced 2007. Champion has 4-inch barrel, fiber optic front sight, three 10-round magazines, Bi-Tone finish.
Price: .... **$1,104.00–$1,249.00**
Price: Champion **$1,179.00**

Prices given are believed to be accurate at time of publication however, many factors affect retail pricing so exact prices are not possible.

SPRINGFIELD ARMORY XD SERIES

Calibers: 9mm, .40 S&W, .45 ACP. **Barrels:** 3, 4, 5 in. **Weights:** 20.5-31 oz.
Lengths: 6.26-8 overall. **Grips:** Textured polymer. **Sights:** Varies by model;
Fixed sights are dovetail front and rear steel 3-dot units. **Features:** Three sizes
in X-Treme Duty (XD) line: Sub-Compact (3-in. barrel), Service (4-in. barrel),
Tactical (5-in. barrel). Three ported models available. Ergonomic polymer
frame, hammer-forged barrel, no-tool disassembly, ambidextrous magazine
release, visual/tactile loaded chamber indicator, visual/tactile striker status
indicator, grip safety, XD gear system included. Compact is shipped with
one extended magazine (13) and one compact magazine (10). XD Mod.2
Sub-Compact has newly contoured slide and redesigned serrations, stippled
grip panels, fiber-optic front sight. OSP has Vortex Venom Red Dot sight, and
suppressor-height sights that co-witness with red dot. Non-threaded barrel is
also included.

Price: Sub-Compact OD Green 9mm/40 S&W, fixed sights $508.00
Price: Compact .45 ACP, 4 barrel, Bi-Tone finish $607.00
Price: Service Black 9mm/.40 S&W, fixed sights $541.00
Price: Service Black .45 ACP, external thumb safety $638.00
Price: V 10 Ported Black 9mm/.40 S&W $608.00
Price: XD Mod.2 .... $565.00
Price: XD OSP w/Vortex Venom Red Dot Sight $958.00

SPRINGFIELD ARMORY XD(M) SERIES

Calibers: 9mm, .40 S&W, .45 ACP. **Barrels:** 3.8 or 4.5 In. **Sights:** Fiber optic
front with interchangeable red and green filaments, adjustable target rear.
Grips: Integral polymer with three optional backstrap designs. **Features:**
Variation of XD design with Improved ergonomics, deeper and longer slide
serrations, slightly modified grip contours and texturing. Black polymer
frame, forged steel slide. Black and two-tone finish options.
Price: .... $623.00–$779.00

SPRINGFIELD ARMORY MIL-SPEC 1911A1

Caliber: .45 ACP. **Capacity:** 7-round magazine. **Barrel:** 5 in. **Weights:** 35.6–39
oz. **Lengths:** 8.5–8.625 in. overall. **Finish:** Stainless steel. **Features:** Similar to
Government Model military .45.
Price: Mil-Spec Parkerized, 7+1, 35.6 oz. $785.00
Price: Mil-Spec Stainless Steel, 7+1, 36 oz. $889.00

SPRINGFIELD ARMORY RANGE OFFICER

Calibers: 9mm, .45 ACP. **Barrels:** 5-in. stainless match grade. Compact model has 4 in. barrel. **Sights:** Adjustable target rear, post front. **Grips:** Double diamond checkered walnut. **Weights:** 40 oz., 28 oz. (compact). **Features:** Operator model has fiber optic sights.

Price:	**$936.00**
Price: Compact	**$899.00**
Price: Stainless finish...	**$1,045.00**
Price: Operator..	**$1,029.00**
Price: Elite Operator...	**$1,145.00**

SPRINGFIELD ARMORY 1911 LOADED

Caliber: .45 ACP. **Capacity:** 7-round magazine. **Barrel:** 5 in. **Weight:** 34 oz. **Length:** 8.6 in. overall. Similar to Mil-Spec 1911A1 with the following additional features: Lightweight Delta hammer, extended and ergonomic beavertail safety, ambidextrous thumb safety, and other features depending on the specific model. MC, Marine, LB and Lightweight models have match-grade barrels, low-profile 3-dot combat sights.

Price: Parkerized..	**$950.00**
Price: Stainless	**$1,004.00**
Price: MC Operator (shown).....................................	**$1,308.00**
Price: Marine Operator	**$1,308.00**
Price: LB Operator	**$1,409.00**
Price: Lightweight Operator	**$1,210.00**
Price: 10mm TRP (Trijicon RMR Red Dot sight	**$2,238.00**

SPRINGFIELD ARMORY TACTICAL RESPONSE

Caliber: .45 ACP, 10mm. **Features:** Similar to 1911A1, except checkered frontstrap and main-spring housing, Novak Night Sight combat rear sight and matching dove-tailed front sight, tuned, polished extractor, oversize barrel link; lightweight speed trigger and combat action job, match barrel and

bushing, extended ambidextrous thumb safety and fitted beavertail grip safety. Checkered Cocobolo wood grips, comes with two Wilson 7-shot magazines. Frame is engraved "Tactical" both sides of frame with "TRP" Introduced 1998. TRP-Pro Model meets FBI specifications for SWAT Hostage Rescue Team.

Price:	**$1,646.00**
Price: Operator with adjustable Trijicon night sights........	**$1,730.00**

SPRINGFIELD ARMORY RANGE OFFICER

Calibers: 9mm, .45 ACP. **Barrels:** 5-in. stainless match grade. Compact model has 4 in. barrel. **Sights:** Adjustable target rear, post front. **Grips:** Double diamond checkered walnut. **Weights:** 40 oz., 28 oz. (compact). **Features:** Operator model has fiber optic sights.

Price:	**$936.00**
Price: Compact	**$899.00**
Price: Stainless finish...	**$1,045.00**
Price: Operator..	**$1,029.00**
Price: Elite Operator...	**$1,145.00**

SPRINGFIELD ARMORY CHAMPION OPERATOR LIGHTWEIGHT

Caliber: .45 ACP. **Barrel:** 4-in. stainless match-grade bull barrel. **Sights:** 3-dot Tritium combat profile. **Grips:** Double diamond checkered cocobolo with Cross Cannon logo. **Features:** Alloy frame with integral rail, extended ambi thumb safety and trigger, lightweight Delta hammer.

Price:	**$1,050.00**

SPRINGFIELD ARMORY 911

Caliber: .380 ACP. **Barrel:** 2.7-in. stainless steel. **Sights:** 3-dot Tritium combat profile. Viridian Green Laser available. **Weight:** 12.6 oz. **Length:** 6.5 in. **Grips:** Grooved Hogue G10. **Features:** Alloy frame, stainless steel slide.

Price:	**$599.00**
Price: Viridian Laser	**$809.00**

SPRINGFIELD ARMORY 911 9MM

Caliber: 9mm. **Barrel:** 3-in. stainless steel. **Sights:** Pro-Glo Tritium/luminescent front, white-dot outlined Tritium rear. **Weight:** 15.3 oz. **Length:** 5.9 in. **Grips:** Thin-line G10. **Features:** Alloy frame, stainless steel slide.

Price:	**$659.00**
Price: Viridian Laser	**$849.00**

Prices given are believed to be accurate at time of publication however, many factors affect retail pricing so exact prices are not possible.

STEYR M-A1 SERIES
Calibers: 9mm, .40 S&W. **Capacities:** 9mm (15 or 17-round capacity) or .40 S&W (10-12). **Barrels:** 3.5 in. (MA-1), 4.5 in. (L-A1), 3 in. (C-A1). **Weight:** 27 oz. **Sights:** Fixed with white outline triangle. **Grips:** Black synthetic. Ergonomic low-profile for reduced muzzle lift. **Features:** DAO striker-fired operation.
Price: M-A1..$575.00
Price: C-A1 compact model...$575.00
Price: L-A1 full-size model..$575.00
Price: S-A1 subcompact model.......................................$575.00

STOEGER COMPACT COUGAR
Caliber: 9mm. **Capacity:** 13+1. **Barrel:** 3.6 in. **Weight:** 32 oz. **Length:** 7 in. **Grips:** Wood or rubber. **Sights:** Quick read 3-dot. **Features:** DA/SA with a matte black finish. The ambidextrous safety and decocking lever is easily accessible to the thumb of a right- or left-handed shooter.
Price: $469.00

STI INTERNATIONAL
This company manufactures a wide selection of 1911-style semi-auto pistols chambered in .45 ACP, 9mm, .357 SIG, 10mm and .38 Super. Barrel lengths are offered from 3.0 to 6.0 in. Listed here are several of the company's more than 20 current models. Numerous finish, grip and sight options are available.
Price: 5.0 Trojan $1,499.00
Price: 5.0 Apeiro...$2,999.00
Price: Costa Carry Comp..$3,699.00
Price: H.O.S.T. Single stack..$2,699.00
Price: H.O.S.T. Double stack.......................................$3,199.00
Price: Stacatto Series From...$1,499.00
Price: DVC 3-Gun..$2,999.00

Price: DVC Limited..$3,199.00
Price: DVC Open...$3,999.00
Price: HEXTAC Series $2,199.00
Price: Stacatto Series $1,499.99

TAURUS CURVE
Caliber: .380 ACP. **Capacity:** 6+1. **Barrel:** 2.5 in. **Weight:** 10.2 oz. **Length:** 5.2 in. **Features:** Unique curved design to fit contours of the body for comfortable concealed carry with no visible "printing" of the firearm. Double-action only. Light and laser are integral with frame.
Price: $404.00

TAURUS G2S
Caliber: 9mm. **Capacity:** 6+1. **Barrel:** 3.2 in. **Weight:** 20 oz. **Length:** 6.3 in. **Sights:** Adjustable rear, fixed front. **Features:** Double/Single Action, polymer frame in blue with matte black or stainless slide, accessory rail, manual and trigger safeties.
Price: $317.00
Price: Two tone with stainless slide................................$333.00

TAURUS TH9
Caliber: 9mm. **Capacity:** 16+1. **Barrel:** 4.3 in. **Weight:** 28 oz. **Length:** 7.7 in. **Sights:** Novak drift adjustable. **Features:** Full-size 9mm double-stack model with SA/DA action. Polymer frame has integral grips with finger grooves and stippling panels. Compact model has 3.8-in barrel, 6.8-in overall length.
Price: $377.00

TAURUS MODEL 1911
Calibers: 9mm, .45 ACP. **Capacities:** .45 ACP 8+1, 9mm 9+1. **Barrel:** 5 in. **Weight:** 33 oz. **Length:** 8.5 in. **Grips:** Checkered black. **Sights:** Heinie straight 8. **Features:** SA. Blued, stainless steel, duotone blue and blue/gray finish. Standard/Picatinny rail, standard frame, alloy frame and alloy/Picatinny rail. Introduced in 2007. Imported from Brazil by Taurus International.
Price: 1911B, Blue $633.00
Price: 1911B, Walnut grips...$685.00
Price: 1911SS, Stainless Steel......................................$752.00
Price: 1911SS-1, Stainless Steel w/rail...........................$769.00
Price: 1911 DT, Duotone Blue $727.00

TAURUS MODEL 92
Caliber: 9mm. **Capacity:** 10- or 17-round magazine. **Barrel:** 5 in. **Weight:** 34 oz. **Length:** 8.5 in. overall. **Grips:** Checkered rubber, rosewood, mother of pearl. **Sights:** Fixed notch rear. 3-dot sight system. Also offered with micrometer-click adjustable night sights. **Features:** DA, ambidextrous 3-way hammer drop safety, allows cocked and locked carry. Blued, stainless steel, blued with gold highlights, stainless steel with gold highlights, forged aluminum frame, integral key-lock. .22 LR conversion kit available. Imported from Brazil by Taurus International.
Price: 92B $433.00
Price: 92SS $550.00

TAURUS SPECTRUM
Caliber: .380. **Barrel:** 2.8 in. **Weight:** 10 oz. **Length:** 5.4 in. **Sights:** Low-profile integrated with slide. **Features:** Polymer frame with stainless steel slide. Many finish combinations with various bright colors. Made in the USA. Introduced in 2017.
Price: .... $289.00–$305.00

TRISTAR 100 /120 SERIES
Calibers: 9mm, .40 S&W (C-100 only). **Capacities:** 15 (9mm), 11 (.40). **Barrels:** 3.7–4.7 in. **Weights:** 26–30 oz. **Grips:** Checkered polymer. **Sights:** Fixed. **Finishes:** Blue or chrome. **Features:** Alloy or steel frame. SA/DA. A series of pistols based on the CZ 75 design. Imported from Turkey.
Price: From .... $460.00–$490.00

TURNBULL MODEL 1911
Caliber: .45 ACP. **Features:** An accurate reproduction of 1918-era Model 1911 pistol. Forged slide with appropriate shape and style. Late-style sight with semi-circle notch. Early-style safety lock with knurled undercut thumb piece. Short, wide checkered spur hammer. Hand-checkered double-diamond American Black Walnut grips. Hand polished with period correct Carbonia charcoal bluing. Custom made to order with many options. Made in the USA by Doug Turnbull Manufacturing Co.
Price: From $2,625.00

WALTHER P99 AS
Calibers: 9mm, .40 S&W. **Capacities:** 15 or 10 rounds (9mm), 10 or 8 rounds (.40). **Barrels:** 3.5 or 4 in. **Weights:** 21–26 oz. **Lengths:** 6.6–7.1 in. **Grips:** Polymer with interchangeable backstrap inserts. **Sights:** Adjustable rear, blade front with three interchangeable inserts of different heights. **Features:** Offered in two frame sizes, standard and compact. DA with trigger safety, decocker, internal striker safety, loaded chamber indicator. Made in Germany.
Price: $629.00

WALTHER PK380
Caliber: .380 ACP. **Capacity:** 8-round magazine. **Barrel:** 3.66 in. **Weight:** 19.4 oz. **Length:** 6.5 in. **Sights:** Three-dot system, drift adjustable rear. **Features:** DA with external hammer, ambidextrous mag release and manual safety. Picatinny rail. Black frame with black or nickel slide.
Price: $399.00
Price: Nickel slide $449.00

WALTHER PPK, PPK/S
Caliber: .380 ACP. **Capacities:** 6+1 (PPK), 7+1 (PPK/s). **Barrel:** 3.3 in. **Weight:** 21-26 oz. **Length:** 6.1 in. **Grips:** Checkered plastic. **Sights:** Fixed. New production in 2019. Made in Fort Smith, AR with German-made slide.
Price: $749.00

WALTHER PPQ M2
Calibers: 9mm, .40 S&W, .45 ACP, .22 LR. **Capacities:** 9mm, (15-round magazine), .40 S&W (11). .45 ACP, 22 LR (PPQ M2 .22). **Barrels:** 4 or 5 in. **Weight:** 24 oz. **Lengths:** 7.1, 8.1 in. **Sights:** Drift-adjustable. **Features:** Quick Defense trigger, firing pin block, ambidextrous slidelock and mag release, Picatinny rail. Comes with two extra magazines, two interchangeable frame backstraps and hard

Prices given are believed to be accurate at time of publication however, many factors affect retail pricing so exact pricing is not possible.

case. Navy SD model has threaded 4.6-in. barrel. M2 .22 has aluminum slide, blowback operation, weighs 19 ounces.

Price: 9mm, .40 .... $649.00–$749.00
Price: M2 .22 .... $429.00
Price: .45 .... $699.00–$799.00

Features: A rimfire version of the Walther P99 pistol, available in nickel slide with black frame, Desert Camo or Digital Pink Camo frame with black slide.

Price: From $379.00
Price: Nickel slide/black frame, or black slide/camo frame $449.00

WALTHER CCP
Caliber: 9mm. **Capacity:** 8-round magazine. **Barrel:** 3.5 in. **Weight:** 22 oz. **Length:** 6.4 in. **Features:** Thumb-operated safety, reversible mag release, loaded chamber indicator. Delayed blowback gas-operated action provides less recoil and muzzle jump, and easier slide operation. Available in all black or black/stainless two-tone finish.
Price: From .... $469.00–$499.00

WALTHER CREED
Caliber: 9mm. **Capacity:** 16+1. **Barrel:** 4 in. **Weight:** 27 oz. **Sights:** 3-dot system. Features: Polymer frame with ergonomic grip, Picatinny rail, pre-cocked DA trigger, front and rear slide serrations with non-slip surface. Comes with two magazines. Similar to the discontinued PPX. Made in Germany.
Price: $399.00

WALTHER PPS
Calibers: 9mm, 40 S&W. **Capacities:** 6-, 7-, 8-round magazines for 9mm; 5-, 6-, 7-round magazines for 40 S&W. **Barrel:** 3.2 in. **Weight:** 19.4 oz. **Length:** 6.3 in. overall. **Stocks:** Stippled black polymer. **Sights:** Picatinny-style accessory rail, 3-dot low-profile contoured sight. **Features:** PPS — "Polizeipistole Schmal" or Police Pistol Slim. Measures 1.04-in. wide. Ships with 6- and 7-round magazines. Striker-fired action, flat slide stop lever, alternate backstrap sizes. QuickSafe feature decocks striker assembly when backstrap is removed. Loaded chamber indicator. Introduced 2008.
Price: $629.00

WILSON COMBAT ELITE SERIES
Calibers: 9mm, .38 Super, .40 S&W; .45 ACP. **Barrel:** Compensated 4.1-in. hand-fit, heavy flanged cone match grade. **Weight:** 36.2 oz. **Length:** 7.7 in. overall. **Grips:** Cocobolo. **Sights:** Combat Tactical yellow rear tritium inserts, brighter green tritium front insert. **Features:** High-cut frontstrap, 30 LPI checkering on frontstrap and flat mainspring housing, High-Ride Beavertail grip safety. Dehorned, ambidextrous thumb safety, extended ejector, skeletonized ultra light hammer, ultralight trigger, Armor-Tuff finish on frame and slide. Introduced 1997. Made in USA by Wilson Combat. This manufacturer offers more than 100 different 1911 models ranging in price from about $2,800 to $5,000. XTAC and Classic 6-in. models shown. Prices show a small sampling of available models.
Price: Classic, From $3,300.00
Price: CQB, From $2,865.00
Price: Hackathorn Special $3,750.00
Price: Tactical Carry $3,750.00
Price: Tactical Supergrade $5,045.00
Price: Bill Wilson Carry Pistol $3,850.00
Price: Ms. Sentinel $3,875.00
Price: Hunter 10mm, .460 Rowland $4,100.00
Price: Beretta Brigadier Series, From $1,195.00
Price: X-Tac Series, From $2,760.00
Price: Texas BBQ Special, From $4,960.00

WALTHER P22
Caliber: .22 LR. **Barrels:** 3.4, 5 in. **Weights:** 19.6 oz. (3.4), 20.3 oz. (5). **Lengths:** 6.26, 7.83 in. **Sights:** Interchangeable white dot, front, 2-dot adjustable, rear.

BAER 1911 ULTIMATE MASTER COMBAT

Calibers: .38 Super, 400 Cor-Bon, .45 ACP (others available). **Capacity:** 10-shot magazine. **Barrels:** 5, 6 in. Baer National Match. **Weight:** 37 oz. **Length:** 8.5 in. overall. **Grips:** Checkered cocobolo. **Sights:** Baer dovetail front, low-mount Bo-Mar rear with hidden leaf. **Features:** Full-house competition gun. Baer forged NM blued steel frame and double serrated slide; Baer triple port, tapered cone compensator; fitted slide to frame; lowered, flared ejection port; Baer reverse recoil plug; full-length guide rod; recoil buff; beveled magazine well; Baer Commander hammer, sear; Baer extended ambidextrous safety, extended ejector, checkered slide stop, beavertail grip safety with pad, extended magazine release button; Baer speed trigger. Made in USA by Les Baer Custom, Inc.

Price: .45 ACP Compensated $3,240.00
Price: .38 Super Compensated $3,390.00
Price: 5-in. Standard barrel $3,040.00
Price: 5-in. barrel .38 Super or 9mm $3,140.00
Price: 6-in. barrel $3,234.00
Price: 6-in. barrel .38 Super or 9mm $3,316.00

BAER 1911 NATIONAL MATCH HARDBALL

Caliber: .45 ACP. **Capacity:** 7-round magazine. **Barrel:** 5 in. **Weight:** 37 oz. **Length:** 8.5 in. overall. **Grips:** Checkered walnut. **Sights:** Baer dovetail front with under-cut post, low-mount Bo-Mar rear with hidden leaf. **Features:** Baer NM forged steel frame, double serrated slide and barrel with stainless bushing; slide fitted to frame; Baer match trigger with 4-lb. pull; polished feed ramp, throated barrel; checkered frontstrap, arched mainspring housing; Baer beveled magazine well; lowered, flared ejection port; tuned extractor; Baer extended ejector, checkered slide stop; recoil buff. Made in USA by Les Baer Custom, Inc.

Price: $2,379.00

BAER 1911 PPC OPEN CLASS

Caliber: .45 ACP, 9mm. **Barrel:** 6 in, fitted to frame. **Sights:** Adjustable PPC rear, dovetail front. **Grips:** Checkered Cocobola. **Features:** Designed for NRA Police Pistol Combat matches. Lowered and flared ejection port, extended ejector, polished feed ramp, throated barrel, frontstrap checkered at 30 LPI, flat serrated mainspring housing, Commander hammer, front and rear slide serrations. 9mm has supported chamber.

Price: $2,775.00
Price: 9mm w/supported chamber $3,187.00

BAER 1911 BULLSEYE WADCUTTER

Similar to National Match Hardball except designed for wadcutter loads only. Polished feed ramp and barrel throat; Bo-Mar rib on slide; full-length recoil rod; Baer speed trigger with 3.5-lb. pull; Baer deluxe hammer and sear; Baer beavertail grip safety with pad; flat mainspring housing checkered 20 LPI. Blue finish; checkered walnut grips. Made in USA by Les Baer Custom, Inc.

Price: From $2,461.00

COLT GOLD CUP NM SERIES

Caliber: .45 ACP, 9mm, .38 Super. **Capacity:** 8-round magazine. **Barrel:** 5-inch National Match. **Weight:** 37 oz. **Length:** 8.5. **Grips:** Checkered wraparound rubber composite with silver-plated medallions or checkered walnut grips with gold medallions. **Sights:** Target post dovetail front, Bomar fully adjustable rear. **Features:** Adjustable aluminum wide target trigger, beavertail grip safety, full-length recoil spring and target recoil spring, available in blued finish or stainless steel.

Price: (blued) $1,299.00
Price: (stainless) $1,350.00
Price: Gold Cup Lite $1,199.00
Price: Gold Cup Trophy $1,699.00

COLT COMPETITION PISTOL

Calibers: .45 ACP, 9mm or .38 Super. **Capacities:** 8 or 9-shot magazine. **Barrel:** 5 in. National Match. **Weight:** 39 oz. **Length:** 8.5 in. **Grips:** Custom Blue Colt G10. **Sights:** Novak adjustable rear, fiber optic front. A competition-ready pistol out of the box at a moderate price. Blue or satin nickel finish. Series 80 firing system. O Series has stainless steel frame and slide with Cerakote gray frame and black slide, competition trigger, gray/black G-10 grips, front and rear slide serrations.

Price: .... $949.00–$1,099.00
Price: Competition O series.. $2,499.00

CZ 75 TS CZECHMATE

Caliber: 9mm. **Capacity:** 20-round magazine. **Barrel:** 130mm. **Weight:** 1360 g **Length:** 266mm overall. **Features:** The handgun is custom built, therefore the quality of workmanship is fully comparable with race pistols built directly to IPSC shooters' wishes. Individual parts and components are excellently match fitted, broke-in and tested. Every handgun is outfitted with a four-port compensator, nut for shooting without a compensator, the slide stop with an extended finger piece, the slide stop without a finger piece, ergonomic grip panels from aluminum with a new type pitting and side mounting provision with the C-More red-dot sight. For shooting without a red-dot sight there is included a standard target rear sight of Tactical Sports type, package contains also the front sight.

Price: $3,416.00

CZ 75 TACTICAL SPORTS

Calibers: 9mm, .40 S&W. **Capacities:** 17-20-round magazines. **Barrel:** 114mm. **Weight:** 1270 g **Length:** 225mm overall. **Features:** Semi-automatic handgun with a locked breech. This model is designed for competition shooting in accordance with world IPSC (International Practical Shooting Confederation) rules and regulations. The CZ 75 TS pistol model design stems from the standard CZ 75 model. However, this model features a number of special modifications, which are usually required for competitive handguns: SA trigger mechanism, match trigger made of plastic featuring option for trigger travel adjustments before discharge (using upper screw), and for overtravel (using bottom screw). The adjusting screws are set by the manufacturer — sporting hammer specially adapted for a reduced trigger pull weight, an extended magazine catch, grip panels made of walnut, guiding tunnel made of plastic for quick inserting of the magazine into pistol's frame. Glossy blued slide, silver Polycoat frame. Packaging includes 3 magazines.
Price: **$1,837.00**

DAN WESSON CHAOS
Caliber: 9mm. **Capacity:** 21-round magazine. **Barrel:** 5 in. **Weight:** 3.20 lbs. **Length:** 8.75 in. overall. **Features:** A double-stack 9mm designed for 3-Gun competition.
Price: **$3,829.00**

DAN WESSON HAVOC
Calibers: 9mm, .38 Super. **Capacity:** 21-round magazine. **Barrel:** 4.25 in. **Weight:** 2.20 lbs. **Length:** 8 in. overall. **Features:** The Havoc is based on an "All Steel" Hi-capacity version of the 1911 frame. It comes ready to compete in Open IPSC/USPSA division. The C-more mounting system offers the lowest possible mounting configuration possible, enabling extremely fast target acquisition. The barrel and compensator arrangement pair the highest level of accuracy with the most effective compensator available.
Price: **$4,299.00**

DAN WESSON MAYHEM
Caliber: .40 S&W. **Capacity:** 18-round magazine. **Barrel:** 6 in. **Weight:** 2.42 lbs. **Length:** 8.75 in. overall. **Features:** The Mayhem is based on an "All-Steel" Hi-capacity version of the 1911 frame. It comes ready to compete in Limited IPSC/USPSA division or fulfill the needs of anyone looking for a superbly accurate target-grade 1911. The 6-in. bull barrel and tactical rail add to the static weight, or "good weight." A 6-in. long slide for added sight radius and enhanced pointability, but that would add to the "bad weight" so the

6-in. slide has been lightened to equal the weight of a 5 in. The result is a 6 in. long slide that balances and feels like a 5 in. but shoots like a 6 in. The combination of the all-steel frame with industry leading parts delivers the most well-balanced, softest shooting 6-in. limited gun on the market.
Price: **$3,899.00**

DAN WESSON TITAN
Caliber: 10mm. **Capacity:** 21-round magazine. **Barrel:** 4.25 in. **Weight:** 1.62 lbs. **Length:** 8 in. overall. **Features:** The Titan is based on an "All Steel" Hi-capacity version of the 1911 frame. The rugged HD night sights are moved forward and recessed deep into the slide yielding target accuracy and extreme durability. The Snake Scale serrations' aggressive 25 LPI checkering, and the custom competition G-10 grips ensure controllability even in the harshest of conditions. The combination of the all-steel frame, bull barrel and tactical rail enhance the balance and durability of this formidable target-grade Combat handgun.
Price: **$3,829.00**

DAN WESSON DISCRETION
Caliber: .45 ACP. **Capacity:** 8-round magazine. **Barrel:** 5.75 in. Match-grade stainless extended and threaded. **Weight:** 2.6 lbs. **Features:** Ported slide, serrated trigger, competition hammer, high tritium sights for sighting over the top of most suppressors.
Price: **$2,142.00**

EAA WITNESS ELITE GOLD TEAM
Calibers: 9mm, 9x21, .38 Super, .40 S&W, .45 ACP. **Barrel:** 5.1 in. **Weight:** 44 oz. **Length:** 10.5 in. overall. **Grips:** Checkered walnut, competition-style. **Sights:** Square post front, fully adjustable rear. **Features:** Triple-chamber cone compensator; competition SA trigger; extended safety and magazine release; competition hammer; beveled magazine well; beavertail grip. Hand-fitted major components. Hard chrome finish. Match-grade barrel. From EAA Custom Shop. Introduced 1992. Limited designed for IPSC Limited Class competition. Features include full-length dust-cover frame, funneled magazine well, interchangeable front sights. Stock (2005) designed for IPSC Production Class competition. Match introduced 2006. Made in Italy, imported by European American Armory.
Price: Gold Team **$2,406.00**
Price: Stock, 4.5 in. barrel, hard-chrome finish **$1,263.00**
Price: Limited Custom Xtreme.. **$2,502.00**
Price: Witness Match Xtreme.. **$2,335.00**
Price: Witness Stock III Xtreme **$2,252.00**

Prices given are believed to be accurate at time of publication however, many factors affect retail pricing so exact prices are not possible.

74TH EDITION, 2020 ⊕ **435**

FREEDOM ARMS MODEL 83 .22 FIELD GRADE SILHOUETTE CLASS

Caliber: .22 LR. **Capacity:** 5-round cylinder. **Barrel:** 10 in. **Weight:** 63 oz. **Length:** 15.5 in. overall. **Grips:** Black Micarta. **Sights:** Removable Patridge front blade; Iron Sight Gun Works silhouette rear click-adjustable for windage and elevation (optional adj. front sight and hood). **Features:** Stainless steel, matte finish, manual sliding-bar safety system; dual firing pins, lightened hammer for fast lock time, pre-set trigger stop. Introduced 1991. Made in USA by Freedom Arms.
Price: Silhouette Class **$2,762.00**

FREEDOM ARMS MODEL 83 CENTERFIRE SILHOUETTE MODELS

Calibers: 357 Mag., .41 Mag., .44 Mag. **Capacity:** 5-round cylinder. **Barrel:** 10 in., 9 in. (.357 Mag. only). **Weight:** 63 oz. (41 Mag.). **Length:** 15.5 in., 14.5 in. (.357 only). **Grips:** Pachmayr Presentation. **Sights:** Iron Sight Gun Works silhouette rear sight, replaceable adjustable front sight blade with hood. **Features:** Stainless steel, matte finish, manual sliding-bar safety system. Made in USA by Freedom Arms.
Price: Silhouette Models, From **$2,460.00**

KIMBER SUPER MATCH II

Caliber: .45 ACP. **Capacity:** 8-round magazine. **Barrel:** 5 in. **Weight:** 38 oz. **Length:** 8.7 in. overall. **Grips:** Rosewood double diamond. **Sights:** Blade front, Kimber fully adjustable rear. **Features:** Guaranteed to shoot 1-in. groups at 25 yards. Stainless steel frame, black KimPro slide; two-piece magazine well; premium aluminum match-grade trigger; 30 LPI frontstrap checkering; stainless match-grade barrel; ambidextrous safety; special Custom Shop markings. Introduced 1999. Made in USA by Kimber Mfg., Inc.
Price: **$2,313.00**

RUGER MARK IV TARGET

Caliber: .22 LR. **Capacity:** 10-round magazine. **Barrel:** 5.5-in. heavy bull. **Weight:** 35.6 oz. **Grips:** Checkered synthetic or laminate. **Sights:** .125 blade front, micro-click rear, adjustable for windage and elevation. **Features:** Loaded Chamber indicator; integral lock, magazine disconnect. Plastic case with lock included.
Price: (blued) **$529.00**
Price: (stainless) **$689.00**

SMITH & WESSON MODEL 41 TARGET

Caliber: .22 LR. **Capacity:** 10-round magazine. **Barrels:** 5.5 in., 7 in. **Weight:** 41 oz. (5.5-in. barrel). **Length:** 10.5 in. overall (5.5-in. barrel). **Grips:** Checkered walnut with modified thumb rest, usable with either hand. **Sights:** .125 in. Patridge on ramp base; micro-click rear-adjustable for windage and elevation. **Features:** .375 in. wide, grooved trigger; adjustable trigger stop drilled and tapped.
Price: .... **$1,369.00–$1,619.00**

STI APEIRO

Calibers: 9mm, .40 S&W, .45 ACP. **Features:** 1911-style semi-auto pistol with Schuemann "Island" barrel; patented modular steel frame with polymer grip; high capacity double-stack magazine; stainless steel ambidextrous thumb safeties and knuckle relief high-rise beavertail grip safety; unique sabertooth rear cocking serrations; 5-inch fully ramped, fully supported "Island" bull barrel, with the sight milled in to allow faster recovery to point of aim; custom engraving on the polished sides of the (blued) stainless steel slide; stainless steel mag well; STI adjustable rear sight and Dawson fiber optic front sight; blued frame.
Price: **$2,999.00**

STI DVC P

Calibers: 9mm, .45 ACP. **Barrel:** 5.0 in., compensated. **Sights:** HOST rear with Fiber Optic front. **Grip:** Gen II 2011 Double Stack. **Features:** Diamond Like Carbon Black finish, Dawson Precision Tool-Less guide rod, railed frame.
Price: **$3,999.00**

STI DVC O

Calibers: 9mm, .38 Super. **Barrel:** 5.4 in., TX2 Compensated, TiN coated. **Sights:** Frame mounted C-More RTS2. **Grip:** Gen II 2011. **Finish:** Hard chrome with Black DLC Barrel. **Features:** 2.5-lb trigger, ambidextrous safety, Dawson Precision Tool-Less guide rod.
Price: **$3,999.00**

STI DVC S

Calibers: 9mm, .38 Super. **Barrel:** 4.15 in., TX1 Compensated. **Sights:** Frame mounted C-More RTS2. **Grip:** Gen II 2011. **Finish:** Hard chrome or Black DLC with TiN or DLC Barrel. **Features:** 2.5-lb trigger, ambidextrous safety, Dawson Precision Tool-Less guide rod.
Price: **$3,999.00**

STI TROJAN

Calibers: 9mm, .45 ACP. **Barrel:** 5 in. **Weight:** 36 oz. **Length:** 8.5 in. **Grips:** Rosewood. **Sights:** STI front with STI adjustable rear. **Features:** Stippled frontstrap, flat-top slide, one-piece steel guide rod.
Price: (Trojan 5) **$1,499.00**

CHARTER ARMS BULLDOG

Caliber: .44 Special. **Capacity:** 5-round cylinder. **Barrel:** 2.5 in. **Weight:** 21 oz. **Sights:** Blade front, notch rear. **Features:** Soft-rubber pancake-style grips, shrouded ejector rod, wide trigger and hammer spur. American made by Charter Arms.
Price: Blued $409.00
Price: Stainless $422.00
Price: Target Bulldog, 4.2-in. barrel, 23 oz. $479.00
Price: Black Nitride finish $443.00

CHARTER ARMS CRIMSON UNDERCOVER

Caliber: .38 Special +P. **Capacity:** 5-round cylinder. **Barrel:** 2 in. **Weight:** 16 oz. **Grip:** Crimson Trace. **Sights:** Fixed. **Features:** Stainless finish and frame. American made by Charter Arms.
Price: $577.00

CHARTER ARMS BOOMER

Caliber: .44 Special. **Capacity:** 5-round cylinder. **Barrel:** 2 in., ported. **Weight:** 20 oz. **Grips:** Full rubber combat. **Sights:** Fixed.
Price: Blued $443.00

CHARTER ARMS POLICE BULLDOG

Caliber: .38 Special. **Capacity:** 6-round cylinder. **Barrel:** 4.2 in. **Weight:** 26 oz. **Sights:** Blade front, notch rear. Large frame version of Bulldog design.
Price: Blued $408.00

CHARTER ARMS OFF DUTY

Caliber: .38 Special. **Barrel:** 2 in. **Weight:** 12.5 oz. **Sights:** Blade front, notch rear. **Features:** 5-round cylinder, aluminum casting, DAO with concealed hammer. Also available with semi-concealed hammer. American made by Charter Arms.
Price: Aluminum $404.00
Price: Crimson Trace Laser grip $657.00

CHARTER ARMS MAG PUG

Caliber: .357 Mag. **Capacity:** 5-round cylinder. **Barrel:** 2.2 in. **Weight:** 23 oz. **Sights:** Blade front, notch rear. **Features:** American made by Charter Arms.
Price: Blued or stainless $400.00
Price: 4.4-in. full-lug barrel.. $470.00
Price: Crimson Trace Laser Grip................................... $609.00

CHARTER ARMS CHIC LADY & CHIC LADY DAO

Caliber: .38 Special. **Capacity:** 5-round cylinder. **Barrel:** 2 in. **Weight:** 12 oz. **Grip:** Combat. **Sights:** Fixed. **Features:** 2-tone pink or lavender & stainless with aluminum frame. American made by Charter Arms.
Price: Chic Lady $473.00
Price: Chic Lady DAO $483.00

CHARTER UNDERCOVER LITE

Caliber: .38 Special +P. **Capacity:** 5-round cylinder. **Barrel:** 2 in. **Weight:** 12 oz. **Grip:** Full. **Sights:** Fixed. **Features:** 2-tone pink & stainless with aluminum frame. Constructed of tough aircraft-grade aluminum and steel, the Undercover Lite offers rugged reliability and comfort. This ultra-lightweight 5-shot .38 Special features a 2-in. barrel, fixed sights and traditional spurred hammer. American made by Charter Arms.
Price: $397.00

CHARTER ARMS PITBULL

Calibers: 9mm, 40 S&W, .45 ACP. **Capacity:** 5-round cylinder. **Barrel:** 2.2 in. **Weights:** 20–22 oz. **Sights:** Fixed rear, ramp front. **Grips:** Rubber. **Features:** Matte stainless steel frame or Nitride frame. Moon clips not required for 9mm, .45 ACP.
Price: 9mm $502.00
Price: .40 S&W $489.00
Price: .45 ACP $489.00
Price: 9mm Black Nitride finish $522.00
Price: .40, .45 Black Nitride finish............................ $509.00

Prices given are believed to be accurate at time of publication however, many factors affect retail pricing so exact prices are not possible.

74TH EDITION, 2020 ◈ 437

CHARTER ARMS SOUTHPAW
Caliber: .38 Special +P. **Capacity:** 5-round cylinder. **Barrel:** 2 in. **Weight:** 12 oz. **Grips:** Rubber Pachmayr style. **Features:** Snubnose, matte black aluminum alloy frame with stainless steel cylinder. Cylinder latch and crane assembly are on right side of frame for convenience of left-hand shooters.
Price: **$419.00**

CHARTER ARMS PATHFINDER
Calibers: .22 LR or .22 Mag. **Capacity:** 6-round cylinder. **Barrel:** 2 in., 4 in. **Weights:** 20 oz. (12 oz. Lite model). **Grips:** Full. **Sights:** Fixed or adjustable (Target). **Features:** Stainless finish and frame.
Price .22 LR **$365.00**
Price .22 Mag **$367.00**
Price: Lite **$379.00**
Price: Target **$409.00**

CHARTER ARMS UNDERCOVER
Caliber: .38 Special +P. **Capacity:** 6-round cylinder. **Barrel:** 2 in. **Weight:** 12 oz. **Sights:** Blade front, notch rear. **Features:** American made by Charter Arms.
Price: Blued **$346.00**

CHARTER ARMS UNDERCOVER SOUTHPAW
Caliber: .38 Spec. +P. **Capacity:** 5-round cylinder. **Barrel:** 2 in. **Weight:** 12 oz. **Sights:** NA. **Features:** Cylinder release is on the right side and the cylinder opens to the right side. Exposed hammer for both SA and DA. American made by Charter Arms.
Price: **$419.00**

CHIAPPA RHINO
Calibers: .357 Magnum, 9mm, .40 S&W. **Features:** 2-, 4-, 5- or 6-inch barrel; fixed or adjustable sights; visible hammer or hammerless design. **Weights:** 24–33 oz. Walnut or synthetic grips with black frame; hexagonal-shaped cylinder. Unique design fires from bottom chamber of cylinder.
Price: From .... $1,090.00-**$1,465.00**

COBRA SHADOW
Caliber: .38 Special +P. **Capacity:** 5 rounds. **Barrel:** 1.875 in. **Weight:** 15 oz. Aluminum frame with stainless steel barrel and cylinder. **Length:** 6.375 in. **Grips:** Rosewood, black rubber or Crimson Trace Laser. **Features:** Black anodized, titanium anodized or custom colors including gold, red, pink and blue.
Price: **$369.00**
Price: Rosewood grips **$434.00**
Price: Crimson Trace Laser grips **$625.00**

COLT COBRA
Caliber: .38 Special. **Capacity:** 6 rounds. **Sights:** Fixed rear, fiber optic red front. **Grips:** Hogue rubbed stippled with finger grooves. **Weight:** 25 oz. **Finish:** Matte stainless. Same name as classic Colt model made from 1950–1986 but totally new design. Introduced in 2017. King Cobra has a heavy-duty frame and 3-inch barrel.
Price: **$699.00**
Price: King Cobra **$899.00**

COLT NIGHT COBRA
Caliber; .38 Special. **Capacity:** 6 rounds. **Grips:** Black synthetic VC G10. **Sight:** Tritium front night sight. DAO operation with bobbed hammer. Features a linear leaf spring design for smooth DA trigger pull.
Price: **$899.00**

COMANCHE II-A
Caliber: .38 Special. **Capacity:** 6-round cylinder. **Barrels:** 3 or 4 in. **Weights:** 33, 35 oz. **Lengths:** 8, 8.5 in. overall. **Grips:** Rubber. **Sights:** Fixed. **Features:** Blued finish, alloy frame. Distributed by SGS Importers.
Price: **$220.00**

DAN WESSON 715
Caliber: .357 Magnum. **Capacity:** 6-round cylinder. **Barrel:** 6-inch heavy barrel with full lug. **Weight:** 38 oz. **Lengths:** 8, 8.5 in. overall. **Grips:** Hogue rubber with finger grooves. **Sights:** Adjustable rear, interchangeable front blade. **Features:** Stainless steel. Interchangeable barrel assembly. Reintroduced in 2014. 715 Pistol Pack comes with 4-, 6- and 8-in. interchangeable barrels.
Price: From **$1,558.00**
Price: Pistol Pack **$1,999.00**

EAA WINDICATOR
Calibers: .38 Special, .357 Mag **Capacity:** 6-round cylinder. **Barrels:** 2 in., 4 in. **Weight:** 30 oz. (4 in.). **Length:** 8.5 in. overall (4 in. bbl.). **Grips:** Rubber with finger grooves. **Sights:** Blade front, fixed rear. **Features:** Swing-out cylinder; hammer block safety; blue or nickel finish. Introduced 1991. Imported from Germany by European American Armory.

Price: .38 Spec. from	**$354.00**
Price: .357 Mag, steel frame from	**$444.00**

KORTH SKYHAWK
Caliber: 9mm. **Barrels:** 2 or 3 in. **Sights:** Adjustable rear with gold bead front. **Grips:** Hogue with finger grooves. **Features:** Polished trigger, skeletonized hammer. Imported by Nighthawk Custom.

Price:	**$1,699.00**

KIMBER K6S
Caliber: .357 Magnum. **Capacity:** 6-round cylinder. **Barrel:** 2-inch full lug. **Grips:** Gray rubber. **Finish:** Satin stainless. Kimber's first revolver, claimed to be world's lightest production 6 shot .357 Magnum. DAO design with non-stacking match-grade trigger. Introduced 2016. CDP model has laminated checkered rosewood grips, Tritium night sights, two-tone black DLC/brushed stainless finish, match grade trigger.

Price:	**$878.00**
Price: 3-in. Barrel	**$899.00**
Price: Deluxe Carry w/Medallion grips	**$1,088.00**
Price: Custom Defense Package	**$1,155.00**
Price: Crimson Trace Laser Grips	**$1,177.00**
Price: TLE	**$999.00**
Price: DA/SA	**$949.00**

KORTH USA
Calibers: .22 LR, .22 WMR, .32 S&W Long, .38 Special, .357 Mag., 9mm. **Capacity:** 6-shot. **Barrels:** 3, 4, 5.25, 6 in. **Weights:** 36–52 oz. **Grips:** Combat, Sport: Walnut, Palisander, Amboina, Ivory. **Finish:** German Walnut, matte with oil finish, adjustable ergonomic competition style. **Sights:** Adjustable Patridge (Sport) or Baughman (Combat), interchangeable and adjustable rear w/Patridge front (Target) in blue and matte. **Features:** DA/SA, 3 models, over 50 configurations, externally adjustable trigger stop and weight, interchangeable cylinder, removable wide-milled trigger shoe on Target model. Deluxe models are highly engraved editions. Available finishes include high polish blued finish, plasma coated in high polish or matte silver, gold, blue or charcoal. Many deluxe options available. From Korth USA.

Price: From	**$8,000.00**
Price: Deluxe Editions, from	**$12,000.00**

RUGER GP-100
Calibers: .357 Mag., .327 Federal Mag, .44 Special **Capacities:** 6- or 7-round cylinder, .327 Federal Mag (7-shot), .44 Special (5-shot), .22 LR, (10-shot). **Barrels:** 3-in. full shroud, 4-in. full shroud, 6-in. full shroud. (.44 Special offered only with 3-in. barrel.) **Weights:** 36–45 oz. **Sights:** Fixed; adjustable on 4- and 6-in. full shroud barrels. **Grips:** Ruger Santoprene Cushioned Grip with Goncalo Alves inserts. **Features:** Uses action, frame features of both the Security-Six and Redhawk revolvers. Full-length, short ejector shroud. Satin blue and stainless steel.

Price: Blued	**$769.00**
Price: Satin stainless	**$799.00**
Price: .22 LR	**$829.00**
Price: .44 Spl.	**$829.00**
Price: 7-round cylinder, 327 Fed or .357 Mag	**$899.00**

Prices given are believed to be accurate at time of publication however, many factors affect retail pricing so exact prices are not possible.

74TH EDITION, 2020 ✛ **439**

RUGER GP-100 MATCH CHAMPION
Calibers: 10mm Magnum, .357 Mag. **Capacity:** 6-round cylinder. **Barrel:** 4.2-in. half shroud, slab-sided. **Weight:** 38 oz. **Sights:** Fixed rear, fiber optic front. **Grips:** Hogue Stippled Hardwood. **Features:** Satin stainless steel finish.
Price: Blued $969.00

RUGER LCRX
Calibers: .38 Special +P, 9mm, .327 Fed. Mag., .22 WMR. **Barrels:** 1.875 in. or 3 in. **Features:** Similar to LCR except this model has visible hammer, adjustable rear sight. The 3-inch barrel model has longer grip. 9mm comes with three moon clips.
Price: $579.00
Price: .327 Mag., .357 Mag., 9mm $669.00

RUGER LCR
Calibers: .22 LR (8-round cylinder), .22 WMR, .327 Fed. Mag, .38 Special and .357 Mag., 5-round cylinder. **Barrel:** 1.875 in. **Weights:** 13.5–17.10 oz. **Length:** 6.5 in. overall. **Grips:** Hogue Tamer or Crimson Trace Lasergrips. **Sights:** Pinned ramp front, U-notch integral rear. **Features:** The Ruger Lightweight Compact Revolver (LCR), a 13.5 ounce, small frame revolver with a smooth, easy-to-control trigger and highly manageable recoil.
Price: .22 LR, .22 WMR, .38 Spl., iron sights $579.00
Price: 9mm, .327, .357, iron sights..................................... $669.00
Price: .22 LR, .22WMR, .38 Spl. Crimson Trace Lasergrip $859.00
Price: 9mm, .327, .357, Crimson Trace Lasergrip $949.00

RUGER SP-101
Calibers: .22 LR (8 shot); .327 Federal Mag. (6-shot), 9mm, .38 Spl, .357 Mag. (5-shot). **Barrels:** 2.25, 3 1/16, 4.2 in (.22 LR, .327 Mag., .357 Mag). **Weights:** 25–30 oz. **Sights:** Adjustable or fixed, rear; fiber-optic or black ramp front. **Grips:** Ruger Cushioned Grip with inserts. **Features:** Compact, small frame, double-action revolver. Full-length ejector shroud. Stainless steel only.
Price: Fixed sights $719.00
Price: Adjustable rear, fiber optic front sights $769.00
Price: .327 Fed Mag 3-in bbl $769.00
Price: .327 Fed Mag $749.00

RUGER REDHAWK
Calibers: .44 Rem. Mag., .45 Colt and .45 ACP/.45 Colt combo. **Capacity:** 6-round cylinder. **Barrels:** 2.75, 4.2, 5.5, 7.5 in. (.45 Colt in 4.2 in. only.) **Weight:** 54 oz. (7.5 bbl.). **Length:** 13 in. overall (7.5-in. barrel). **Grips:** Square butt cushioned grip panels. TALO Distributor exclusive 2.75-in. barrel stainless model has round butt, wood grips. **Sights:** Interchangeable Patridge-type front, rear adjustable for windage and elevation. **Features:** Stainless steel, brushed satin finish, blued ordnance steel. 9.5 sight radius. Introduced 1979.
Price: $1,079.00
Price: Hunter Model 7.5-in. bbl. $1,159.00
Price: TALO 2.75 in. model $1,069.00

RUGER SUPER REDHAWK
Calibers: 10mm, .44 Rem. Mag., .454 Casull, .480 Ruger. **Capacities:** 5- or 6-round cylinder. **Barrels:** 2.5 in. (Alaskan), 5.5 in., 6.5 in. (10mm), 7.5 in. or 9.5 in. **Weight:** 44–58 oz. **Length:** 13 in. overall (7.5-in. barrel). **Grips:** Hogue Tamer Monogrip. **Features:** Similar to standard Redhawk except has heavy extended frame with Ruger Integral Scope Mounting System on wide topstrap. Wide hammer spur lowered for better scope clearance. Incorporates mechanical design features and improvements of GP-100. Ramp front sight base has Redhawk-style interchangeable insert sight blades, adjustable rear sight. Alaskan model has 2.5-inch barrel. Satin stainless steel and low-glare stainless finishes. Introduced 1987.
Price: .44 Magnum, 10mm $1,159.00
Price: .454 Casull, .480 Ruger $1,199.00
Price: Alaskan, .44 Mag, .454 Casull, .480 Ruger $1,189.00

SMITH & WESSON GOVERNOR
Calibers: .410 Shotshell (2.5 in.), .45 ACP, .45 Colt. **Capacity:** 6 rounds. **Barrel:** 2.75 in. **Length:** 7.5 in., (2.5 in. barrel). **Grip:** Synthetic. **Sights:** Front: Dovetailed tritium night sight or black ramp, rear: fixed. **Grips:** Synthetic. **Finish:** Matte black or matte silver (Silver Edition). **Weight:** 29.6 oz. **Features:** Capable of chambering a mixture of .45 Colt, .45 ACP and .410 gauge 2.5-inch shotshells, the Governor is suited for both close and distant encounters, allowing users to customize the load to their preference. Scandium alloy frame, stainless steel cylinder. Packaged with two full moon clips and three 2-shot clips.
Price: $869.00
Price: w/Crimson Trace Laser Grip $1,179.00

SMITH & WESSON J-FRAME

The J-frames are the smallest Smith & Wesson wheelguns and come in a variety of chamberings, barrel lengths and materials as noted in the individual model listings.

SMITH & WESSON 60LS/642LS LADYSMITH

Calibers: .38 Special +P, .357 Mag. **Capacity:** 5-round cylinder. **Barrels:** 1.875 in. (642LS); 2.125 in. (60LS) **Weights:** 14.5 oz. (642LS); 21.5 oz. (60LS); **Length:** 6.6 in. overall (60LS). **Grips:** Wood. **Sights:** Black blade, serrated ramp front, fixed notch rear. 642 CT has Crimson Trace Laser Grips. **Features:** 60LS model has a Chiefs Special-style frame. 642LS has Centennial-style frame, frosted matte finish, smooth combat wood grips. Introduced 1996. Comes in a fitted carry/ storage case. Introduced 1989. Made in USA by Smith & Wesson.

Price: (642LS) **$499.00**
Price: (60LS) **$759.00**
Price: (642 CT) **$699.00**

SMITH & WESSON MODEL 63

Caliber: .22 LR **Capacity:** 8-round cylinder. **Barrel:** 3 in. **Weight:** 26 oz. **Length:** 7.25 in. overall. **Grips:** Black synthetic. **Sights:** Hi-Viz fiber optic front sight, adjustable black blade rear sight. **Features:** Stainless steel construction throughout. Made in USA by Smith & Wesson.

Price: **$769.00**

SMITH & WESSON MODELS 637 CT/638 CT

Similar to Models 637, 638 and 642 but with Crimson Trace Laser Grips.
Price: **$699.00**

SMITH & WESSON MODEL 317 AIRLITE

Caliber: .22 LR. **Capacity:** 8-round cylinder. **Barrel:** 1.875 in. **Weight:** 10.5 oz. **Length:** 6.25 in. overall (1.875-in. barrel). **Grips:** Rubber. **Sights:** Serrated ramp front, fixed notch rear. **Features:** Aluminum alloy, carbon and stainless steels, Chiefs Special-style frame with exposed hammer. Smooth combat trigger. Clear Cote finish. Model 317 Kit Gun has adjustable rear sight, fiber optic front. Introduced 1997.
Price: **$759.00**

SMITH & WESSON MODEL 442/637/638/642 AIRWEIGHT

Caliber: .38 Special +P. **Capacity:** 5-round cylinder. **Barrels:** 1.875 in., 2.5 in. **Weight:** 15 oz. **Length:** 6.375 in. overall. **Grips:** Soft rubber. **Sights:** Fixed, serrated ramp front, square notch rear. **Features:** A family of J-frame .38 Special revolvers with aluminum-alloy frames. Model 637; Chiefs Special-style frame with exposed hammer. Introduced 1996. Models 442, 642; Centennial-style frame, enclosed hammer. Model 638, Bodyguard style, shrouded hammer. Comes in a fitted carry/storage case. Introduced 1989. Made in USA by Smith & Wesson.

Price: From **$469.00**
Price: Laser Max Frame Mounted Red Laser sight **$539.00**

SMITH & WESSON MODEL 340/340PD AIRLITE SC CENTENNIAL

Calibers: .357 Mag., 38 Special +P. **Capacity:** 5-round cylinder. **Barrel:** 1.875 in. **Weight:** 12 oz. **Length:** 6.375 in. overall (1.875-in. barrel). **Grips:** Rounded butt rubber. **Sights:** Black blade front, rear notch **Features:** Centennial-style frame, enclosed hammer. Internal lock. Matte silver finish. Scandium alloy frame, titanium cylinder, stainless steel barrel liner. Made in USA by Smith & Wesson.
Price: **$1,019.00**

SMITH & WESSON MODEL 351PD

Caliber: .22 Mag. **Capacity:** 5-round cylinder. **Barrel:** 1.875 in. **Weight:** 10.6 oz. **Length:** 6.25 in. overall (1.875-in. barrel). **Sights:** HiViz front sight, rear notch. **Grips:** Wood. **Features:** 7-shot, aluminum-alloy frame. Chiefs Special-style frame with exposed hammer. Nonreflective matte-black finish. Internal lock. Made in USA by Smith & Wesson.
Price: **$759.00**

Prices given are believed to be accurate at time of publication however, many factors affect retail pricing so exact prices are not possible.

SMITH & WESSON MODEL 360/360PD AIRLITE CHIEF'S SPECIAL
Calibers: .357 Mag., .38 Special +P. **Capacity:** 5-round cylinder. **Barrel:** 1.875 in. **Weight:** 12 oz. **Length:** 6.375 in. overall (1.875-in. barrel). **Grips:** Rounded butt rubber. **Sights:** Red ramp front, fixed rear notch. **Features:** Chief's Special-style frame with exposed hammer. Internal lock. Scandium alloy frame, titanium cylinder, stainless steel barrel. Model 360 has unfluted cylinder. Made in USA by Smith & Wesson.
Price: 360 .... $770.00
Price: 360PD $1,019.00

SMITH & WESSON BODYGUARD 38
Caliber: .38 Special +P. **Capacity:** 5-round cylinder. **Barrel:** 1.9 in. **Weight:** 14.3 oz. **Length:** 6.6 in. **Grip:** Synthetic. **Sights:** Front: Black ramp, Rear: fixed, integral with backstrap. Plus: Integrated laser sight. **Finish:** Matte black. **Features:** The first personal protection series that comes with an integrated laser sight.
Price: $539.00

SMITH & WESSON MODEL 640 CENTENNIAL DA ONLY
Calibers: .357 Mag., .38 Special +P. **Capacity:** 5-round cylinder. **Barrel:** 2.125 in. **Weight:** 23 oz. **Length:** 6.75 in. overall. **Grips:** Uncle Mike's Boot grip. **Sights:** Tritium Night Sights. **Features:** Stainless steel. Fully concealed hammer, snag-proof smooth edges. Internal lock.
Price: $839.00

SMITH & WESSON MODEL 649 BODYGUARD
Caliber: .357 Mag., .38 Special +P. **Capacity:** 5-round cylinder. **Barrel:** 2.125 in. **Weight:** 23 oz. **Length:** 6.625 in. overall. **Grips:** Uncle Mike's Combat. **Sights:** Black pinned ramp front, fixed notch rear. **Features:** Stainless steel construction, satin finish. Internal lock. Bodyguard style, shrouded hammer. Made in USA by Smith & Wesson.
Price: $729.00

SMITH & WESSON K-FRAME/L-FRAME
The K-frame series are mid-size revolvers and the L-frames are slightly larger.

SMITH & WESSON MODEL 10 CLASSIC
Caliber: .38 Special. **Capacity:** 6-round cylinder. **Features:** Bright blued steel frame and cylinder, checkered wood grips, 4-inch barrel and fixed sights. The oldest model in the Smith & Wesson line, its basic design goes back to the original Military & Police Model of 1905.
Price: $739.00

SMITH & WESSON MODEL 17 MASTERPIECE CLASSIC
Caliber: .22 LR. **Capacity:** 6-round cylinder. **Barrel:** 6 in. **Weight:** 40 oz. **Grips:** Checkered wood. **Sights:** Pinned Patridge front, micro-adjustable rear. Updated variation of K-22 Masterpiece of the 1930s.
Price: $989.00

SMITH & WESSON MODEL 19 CLASSIC
Caliber: .357 Magnum. **Capacity:** 6-round cylinder **Barrel:** 4.25 in. **Weight:** 37.2 oz. **Grips:** Walnut. **Sights:** Adjustable rear, red ramp front. **Finish:** Polished blue. Classic-style thumbpiece. Reintroduced 2019.
Price: $826.00

SMITH & WESSON MODEL 48 CLASSIC
Same specifications as Model 17 except chambered in .22 Magnum (.22 WMR) and is available with a 4- or 6-inch barrel.
Price: .... $949.00–$989.00

SMITH & WESSON MODEL 64/67
Caliber: .38 Special +P. **Capacity:** 6-round cylinder **Barrel:** 3 in. **Weight:** 33 oz. **Length:** 8.875 in. overall. **Grips:** Soft rubber. **Sights:** Fixed, .125-in. serrated ramp front, square notch rear. Model 67 is similar to Model 64 except for adjustable sights. **Features:** Satin finished stainless steel, square butt.
Price: From .... $689.00–$749.00

SMITH & WESSON MODEL 66
Caliber: .357 Magnum. **Capacity:** 6-round cylinder. **Barrel:** 4.25 in. **Weight:** 36.6 oz. **Grips:** Synthetic. **Sights:** White outline adjustable rear, red ramp front. **Features:** Return in 2014 of the famous K-frame "Combat Magnum" with stainless finish.
Price: $849.00

Prices given are believed to be accurate at time of publication however, many factors affect retail pricing so exact prices are not possible.

74TH EDITION, 2020 ✦ **443**

SMITH & WESSON MODEL 69
Caliber: .44 Magnum. **Capacity:** 5-round cylinder. **Barrel:** 4.25 in. **Weight:** 37 oz. **Grips:** Checkered wood. **Sights:** White outline adjustable rear, red ramp front. **Features:** L-frame with stainless finish, 5-shot cylinder, introduced in 2014.
Price: $989.00

SMITH & WESSON MODEL 610
Caliber: 10mm. Will also fire .40 S&W. **Capacity:** 6-round cylinder. 3 moon clips provided. **Barrel:** 4 or 6.5 in. **Weight:** 43–50 oz. **Length:** 11.125 in. **Grips:** Synthetic. **Sights:** Black blade adjustable front, white outline adjustable rear. **Finish:** Stainless steel.
Price: $929.00

SMITH & WESSON MODEL 617
Caliber: .22 LR. **Capacity:** 10-round cylinder. **Barrel:** 6 in. **Weight:** 44 oz. **Length:** 11.125 in. **Grips:** Soft rubber. **Sights:** Patridge front, adjustable rear. Drilled and tapped for scope mount. **Features:** Stainless steel with satin finish. Introduced 1990.
Price: From $829.00

SMITH & WESSON MODEL 686/686 PLUS
Caliber: .357 Mag/.38 Special. **Capacity:** 6 (686) or 7 (Plus). **Barrels:** 6 in. (686), 3 or 6 in. (686 Plus), 4 in. (SSR). **Weight:** 35 oz. (3 in. barrel). **Grips:** Rubber. Sights: White outline adjustable rear, red ramp front. Features: Satin stainless frame and cylinder. Stock Service Revolver (SSR) has tapered underlug, interchangeable front sight, high-hold ergonomic wood grips, chamfered charge holes, custom barrel w/recessed crown, bossed mainspring.
Price: 686 .... $829.00
Price: Plus $849.00
Price: SSR $999.00

SMITH & WESSON MODEL 986 PRO
Caliber: 9mm. **Capacity:** 7-round cylinder **Barrel:** 5-in. tapered underlug. **Features:** SA/DA L-frame revolver chambered in 9mm. Features similar to 686 PLUS Pro Series with 5-inch tapered underlug barrel, satin stainless finish, synthetic grips, adjustable rear and Patridge blade front sight.
Price: $1,149.00

SMITH & WESSON M&P R8
Caliber: .357 Mag. **Capacity:** 8-round cylinder. **Barrel:** 5-in. half lug with accessory rail. **Weight:** 36.3 oz. **Length:** 10.5 in. **Grips:** Black synthetic. **Sights:** Adjustable v-notch rear, interchangeable front. **Features:** Scandium alloy frame, stainless steel cylinder.
Price: $1,329.00

SMITH & WESSON N-FRAME
These large-frame models introduced the .357, .41 and .44 Magnums to the world.

SMITH & WESSON MODEL 25 CLASSIC
Calibers: .45 Colt or .45 ACP. **Capacity:** 6-round cylinder. **Barrel:** 6.5 in. **Weight:** 45 oz. **Grips:** Checkered wood. **Sights:** Pinned Patridge front, micro-adjustable rear.
Price: $1,019.00

SMITH & WESSON MODEL 27 CLASSIC
Caliber: .357 Magnum. **Capacity:** 6-round cylinder. **Barrels:** 4 or 6.5 in. **Weight:** 41.2 oz. **Grips:** Checkered wood. **Sights:** Pinned Patridge front, micro-adjustable rear. Updated variation of the first magnum revolver, the .357 Magnum of 1935.
Price: (4 in.) $1,019.00
Price: (6.5 in.) $1,059.00

SMITH & WESSON MODEL 29 CLASSIC
Caliber: .44 Magnum **Capacity:** 6-round cylinder. **Barrel:** 4 or 6.5 in. **Weight:** 48.5 oz. **Length:** 12 in. **Grips:** Altamont service walnut. **Sights:** Adjustable white-outline rear, red ramp front. **Features:** Carbon steel frame, polished-blued or nickel finish. Has integral key lock safety feature to prevent accidental discharges. Original Model 29 made famous by "Dirty Harry" character played in 1971 by Clint Eastwood.
Price: .... $999.00–$1,169.00

SMITH & WESSON MODEL 57 CLASSIC
Caliber: .41 Magnum. **Capacity:** 6-round cylinder. **Barrel:** 6 in. **Weight:** 48 oz. **Grips:** Checkered wood. **Sights:** Pinned red ramp, micro-adjustable rear.
Price: $1,009.00

SMITH & WESSON MODEL 329PD ALASKA BACKPACKER
Caliber: .44 Magnum. **Capacity:** 6-round cylinder. **Barrel:** 2.5 in. **Weight:** 26 oz. **Length:** 9.5 in. **Grips:** Synthetic. **Sights:** Adj. rear, HiViz orange-dot front. **Features:** Scandium alloy frame, blue/black finish, stainless steel cylinder.
Price: From $1,159.00

Prices given are believed to be accurate at time of publication however, many factors affect retail pricing so exact prices are not possible.

SMITH & WESSON MODEL 625/625JM

Caliber: .45 ACP. **Capacity:** 6-round cylinder. **Barrels:** 4 in., 5 in. **Weight:** 43 oz. (4-in. barrel). **Length:** 9.375 in. overall (4-in. barrel). **Grips:** Soft rubber; wood optional. **Sights:** Patridge front on ramp, S&W micrometer click rear adjustable for windage and elevation. **Features:** Stainless steel construction with .400-in. wide semi-target hammer, .312-in. smooth combat trigger; full lug barrel. Glass beaded finish. Introduced 1989. Jerry Miculek Professional (JM) Series has .265-in. wide grooved trigger, special wooden Miculek Grip, five full moon clips, gold bead Patridge front sight on interchangeable front sight base, bead blast finish. Unique serial number run. Mountain Gun has 4-in. tapered barrel, drilled and tapped, Hogue Rubber Monogrip, pinned black ramp front sight, micrometer click-adjustable rear sight, satin stainless frame and barrel weighs 39.5 oz.
Price: 625 or 625JM **$1,074.00**

SMITH & WESSON MODEL 629

Calibers: .44 Magnum, .44 S&W Special. **Capacity:** 6-round cylinder. **Barrels:** 4 in., 5 in., 6.5 in. **Weight:** 41.5 oz. (4-in. bbl.). **Length:** 9.625 in. overall (4-in. bbl.). **Grips:** Soft rubber; wood optional. **Sights:** .125-in. red ramp front, white outline rear, internal lock, adjustable for windage and elevation. Classic similar to standard Model 629, except Classic has full-lug 5-in. barrel, chamfered front of cylinder, interchangeable red ramp front sight with adjustable white outline rear, Hogue grips with S&W monogram, drilled and tapped for scope mounting. Factory accurizing and endurance packages. Introduced 1990. Classic Power Port has Patridge front sight and adjustable rear sight. Model 629CT has 5-in. barrel, Crimson Trace Hoghunter Lasergrips, 10.5 in. OAL, 45.5 oz. weight. Introduced 2006.
Price: From **$949.00**

SMITH & WESSON X-FRAME

These extra-large X-frame S&W revolvers push the limits of big-bore handgunning.

SMITH & WESSON MODEL 500

Caliber: 500 S&W Magnum. **Capacity:** 5-round cylinder. **Barrels:** 4 in., 6.5 in., 8.375 in. **Weight:** 72.5 oz. **Length:** 15 in. (8.375-in. barrel). **Grips:** Hogue Sorbothane Rubber. **Sights:** Interchangeable blade, front, adjustable rear. **Features:** Recoil compensator, ball detent cylinder latch, internal lock. 6.5-in.-barrel model has orange-ramp dovetail Millett front sight, adjustable black rear sight, Hogue Dual Density Monogrip, .312-in. chrome trigger with overtravel stop, chrome tear-drop hammer, glass bead finish. 10.5-in.-barrel model has red ramp front sight, adjustable rear sight, .312-in. chrome trigger with overtravel stop, chrome teardrop hammer with pinned sear, hunting sling. Compensated Hunter has .400-in. orange ramp dovetail front sight, adjustable black blade rear sight, Hogue Dual Density Monogrip, glass bead finish w/black clear coat. Made in USA by Smith & Wesson.
Price: From **$1,299.00**

SMITH & WESSON MODEL 460V

Caliber: 460 S&W Magnum (Also chambers .454 Casull, .45 Colt). **Capacity:** 5-round cylinder. **Barrels:** 7.5 in., 8.375-in. gain-twist rifling. **Weight:** 62.5 oz. **Length:** 11.25 in. **Grips:** Rubber. **Sights:** Adj. rear, red ramp front. **Features:** Satin stainless steel frame and cylinder, interchangeable compensator. 460XVR (X-treme Velocity Revolver) has black blade front sight with interchangeable green Hi-Viz tubes, adjustable rear sight. 7.5-in.-barrel version has Lothar-Walther barrel, 360-degree recoil compensator, tuned Performance Center action, pinned sear, integral Weaver base, non-glare surfaces, scope mount accessory kit for mounting full-size scopes, flashed-chromed hammer and trigger, Performance Center gun rug and shoulder sling. Interchangeable Hi-Viz green dot front sight, adjustable black rear sight, Hogue Dual Density Monogrip, matte-black frame and shroud finish with glass-bead cylinder finish, 72 oz. Compensated Hunter has teardrop chrome hammer, .312-in. chrome trigger, Hogue Dual Density Monogrip, satin/matte stainless finish, HiViz interchangeable front sight, adjustable black rear sight. XVR introduced 2006.
Price: 460V **$1,369.00**
Price: 460XVR, from **$1,369.00**

SUPER SIX CLASSIC BISON BULL

Caliber: .45-70 Government. **Capacity:** 6-round cylinder. **Barrel:** 10in. octagonal with 1:14 twist. **Weight:** 6 lbs. **Length:** 17.5 in. overall. **Grips:** NA. **Sights:** Ramp front sight with dovetailed blade, click-adjustable rear. **Features:** Manganese bronze frame. Integral scope mount, manual cross bolt safety.
Price: **$1,500.00**

TAURUS MODEL 17 TRACKER

Caliber: .17 HMR. **Capacity:** 7-round cylinder. **Barrel:** 6.5 in. **Weight:** 45.8 oz. **Grips:** Rubber. **Sights:** Adjustable. **Features:** Double action, matte stainless, integral key-lock.
Price: From **$539.00**

TAURUS MODEL 992 TRACKER

Calibers: .22 LR with interchangeable .22 WMR cylinder. **Capacity:** 9-round cylinder. **Barrel:** 4 or 6.5 in with ventilated rib. **Features:** Adjustable rear sight, blued or stainless finish.
Price: Blue **$640.00**
Price: Stainless **$692.00**

TAURUS MODEL 44SS

Caliber: .44 Magnum. **Capacity:** 5-round cylinder. **Barrel:** Ported, 4, 6.5, 8.4 in. **Weight:** 34 oz. **Grips:** Rubber. **Sights:** Adjustable. **Features:** Double action. Integral key-lock. Introduced 1994. Finish: Matte stainless. Imported from Brazil by Taurus International Manufacturing, Inc.
Price: From .... **$648.00-$664.00**

Prices given are believed to be accurate at time of publication however, many factors affect retail pricing so exact prices are not possible.

74TH EDITION, 2020 ⊕ **445**

TAURUS MODEL 65
Caliber: .357 Magnum. **Capacity:** 6-round cylinder. **Barrel:** 4-in. full underlug. **Weight:** 38 oz. **Length:** 10.5 in. overall. **Grips:** Soft rubber. **Sights:** Fixed. **Features:** Double action, integral key-lock. Matte blued or stainless. Imported by Taurus International.
Price: Blued $539.00
Price: Stainless $591.00

TAURUS MODEL 66
Similar to Model 65, 4 in. or 6 in. barrel, 7-round cylinder, adjustable rear sight. Integral key-lock action. Imported by Taurus International.
Price: Blue $599.00
Price: Stainless $652.00

TAURUS MODEL 82 HEAVY BARREL
Caliber: .38 Special. **Capacity:** 6-round cylinder. **Barrel:** 4 in., heavy. **Weight:** 36.5 oz. **Length:** 9.25 in. overall. **Grips:** Soft black rubber. **Sights:** Serrated ramp front, square notch rear. **Features:** Double action, solid rib, integral key-lock. Imported by Taurus International.
Price: From $521.00

TAURUS MODEL 85FS
Caliber: .38 Special. **Capacity:** 5-round cylinder. **Barrel:** 2 in. **Weights:** 17–24.5 oz., titanium 13.5–15.4 oz. **Grips:** Rubber, rosewood or mother of pearl. **Sights:** Ramp front, square notch rear. **Features:** Spurred hammer. Blued, matte stainless, blue with gold accents, stainless with gold accents; rated for +P ammo. Integral keylock. Some models have titanium frame. Introduced 1980. Imported by Taurus International.
Price: From $379.00

TAURUS MODEL 856 ULTRALIGHT
Caliber: .38 Special. **Capacity:** 6-round cylinder. **Barrel:** 2 in. Matte black or stainless. **Weights:** 15.7 oz., titanium 13.5–15.4 oz. **Grips:** Rubber, rosewood or mother of pearl. **Sights:** Serrated ramp front, square notch rear. **Features:** Aluminum frame, matte black or stainless cylinder, azure blue, bronze, burnt orange or rouge finish.
Price: .... $364.00-$461.00

TAURUS 380 MINI
Caliber: .380 ACP. **Capacity:** 5-round cylinder w/moon clip. **Barrel:** 1.75 in. **Weight:** 15.5 oz. **Length:** 5.95 in. **Grips:** Rubber. **Sights:** Adjustable rear, fixed front. **Features:** DAO. Available in blued or stainless finish. Five Star (moon) clips included.
Price: Blued $478.00
Price: Stainless $514.00

TAURUS MODEL 45-410 JUDGE
Calibers: 2.5-in. .410/.45 Colt, 3-in. .410/.45 Colt. **Barrels:** 3 in., 6.5 in. (blued finish). **Weights:** 35.2 oz., 22.4 oz. **Length:** 7.5 in. **Grips:** Ribber rubber. **Sights:** Fiber Optic. **Features:** DA/SA. Matte stainless and ultra-lite stainless finish. Introduced in 2007. Imported from Brazil by Taurus International.
Price: From $511.00

TAURUS JUDGE PUBLIC DEFENDER POLYMER
Caliber: .45 Colt/.410 (2.5 in.). **Capacity:** 5-round cylinder. **Barrel:** 2.5-in. **Weight:** 27 oz. **Features:** SA/DA revolver with 5-round cylinder; polymer frame; Ribber rubber-feel grips; fiber-optic front sight; adjustable rear sight; blued or stainless cylinder; shrouded hammer with cocking spur; blued finish.
Price: From $469.00

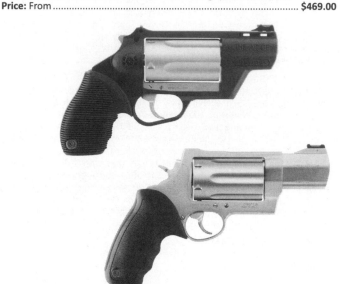

TAURUS RAGING JUDGE MAGNUM
Calibers: .454 Casull, .45 Colt, 2.5-in. and 3-in. .410. **Barrels:** 3 or 6 in. **Features:** SA/DA revolver with fixed sights with fiber-optic front; blued or stainless steel finish; vent rib for scope mounting (6-in. only); cushioned Raging Bull grips.
Price: $1,168.00

TAURUS MODEL 627 TRACKER
Caliber: .357 Magnum. **Capacity:** 7-round cylinder. **Barrels:** 4 or 6.5 in. **Weights:** 28.8, 41 oz. **Grips:** Rubber. **Sights:** Fixed front, adjustable rear. **Features:** Double-action. Stainless steel, Shadow Gray or Total Titanium; vent rib (steel models only); integral key-lock action. Imported by Taurus International.
Price: From $577.00

Prices given are believed to be accurate at time of publication however, many factors affect retail pricing so exact prices are not possible.

TAURUS MODEL 444 ULTRA-LIGHT
Caliber: .44 Magnum. **Capacity:** 5-round cylinder. **Barrels:** 2.5 or 4 in. **Weight:** 28.3 oz. **Grips:** Cushioned inset rubber. **Sights:** Fixed red-fiber optic front, adjustable rear. **Features:** UltraLite titanium blue finish, titanium/alloy frame built on Raging Bull design. Smooth trigger shoe, 1.760-in. wide, 6.280-in. tall. Barrel rate of twist 1:16, 6 grooves. Introduced 2005. Imported by Taurus International.
Price: $944.00

TAURUS RAGING HUNTER
Caliber: .44 Magnum. **Capacity:** 6-round cylinder. **Barrel:** 8.375 in. **Sights:** Adjustable rear, fixed front. **Grips:** Soft rubber with cushioned inset. **Weight:** 55 oz. **Features:** DA, ventilated rib. Imported by Taurus International.
Price: $919.00

TAURUS MODEL 605 PLY
Caliber: .357 Magnum. **Capacity:** 5-round cylinder. **Barrel:** 2 in. **Weight:** 20 oz. **Grips:** Rubber. **Sights:** Fixed. **Features:** Polymer frame steel cylinder. Blued or stainless. Introduced 1995. Imported by Taurus International.
Price: Blued $393.00
Price: Stainless $410.00

TAURUS MODEL 905
Caliber: 9mm. **Capacity:** 5-round cylinder. **Barrel:** 2 in. **Features:** Small-frame revolver with rubber boot grips, fixed sights, choice of exposed or concealed hammer. Blued or stainless finish.
Price: Blued $531.00
Price: Stainless $583.00

TAURUS MODEL 444/454 RAGING BULL SERIES
Calibers: .44 Magnum, .454 Casull. **Barrels:** 2.25 in., 5 in., 6.5 in., 8.375 in. **Weight:** 53–63 oz. **Length:** 12 in. overall (6.5 in. barrel). **Grips:** Soft black rubber. **Sights:** Patridge front, adjustable rear. **Features:** DA, ventilated rib, integral key-lock. Most models have ported barrels. Introduced 1997. Imported by Taurus International.
Price: 444 .... $900.00
Price: 454 .... $1,204.00.

TAURUS MODEL 692
Calibers: .38 Special/.357 Magnum or 9mm. **Capacity:** 7-round cylinder. **Barrels:** 3 or 6.5 in, ported. **Sights:** Adjustable rear, fixed front. **Grip:** "Ribber" textured. **Finish:** Matte blued or stainless. **Features:** Caliber can be changed with a swap of the cylinders which are non-fluted.
Price: $659.00

Prices given are believed to be accurate at time of publication however, many factors affect retail pricing so exact prices are not possible.

74TH EDITION, 2020 ⊕ **447**

CIMARRON 1872 OPEN TOP

Calibers: .38, .44 Special, .44 Colt, .44 Russian, .45 LC, .45 S&W Schofield. **Barrels:** 5.5 in. and 7.5 in. **Grips:** Walnut. **Sights:** Blade front, fixed rear. **Features:** Replica of first cartridge-firing revolver. Blued finish; Navy-style brass or steel Army-style frame. Introduced 2001 by Cimarron F.A. Co.
Price: Navy model $529.00
Price: Army $550.00

CIMARRON 1875 OUTLAW

Calibers: .357 Magnum, .38 Special, .44 W.C.F., .45 Colt, .45 ACP. **Barrels:** 5.5 in. and 7.5 in. **Weight:** 2.5–2.6 lbs. **Grip:** 1-piece walnut. **Features:** Standard blued finish with color casehardened frame. Replica of 1875 Remington model. Available with dual .45 Colt/.45 ACP cylinder.
Price: $578.00
Price: Dual Cyl. $686.00

CIMARRON MODEL 1890

Caliber: .357 Magnum, .38 Special, .44 W.C.F., .45 Colt, .45 ACP. **Barrel:** 5.5 in. **Weight:** 2.4-2.5 lbs. **Grip:** 1-piece walnut. **Features:** Standard blued finish with standard blue frame. Replica of 1890 Remington model. Available with dual .45 Colt/.45 ACP cylinder.
Price: $606.00
Price: Dual Cylinder $702.00

CIMARRON BISLEY MODEL SINGLE-ACTION

Calibers: .357 Magnum, .44 WCF, .44 Special, .45. **Features:** Similar to Colt Bisley, special grip frame and trigger guard, knurled wide-spur hammer, curved trigger. Introduced 1999. Imported by Cimarron F.A. Co.
Price: From $636.00

CIMARRON LIGHTNING SA

Calibers: .22 LR, .32-20/32 H&R dual cyl. combo, .38 Special, .41 Colt. **Barrels:** 3.5 in., 4.75 in., 5.5 in. **Grips:** Smooth or checkered walnut. **Sights:** Blade front. **Features:** Replica of the Colt 1877 Lightning DA. Similar to Cimarron Thunderer, except smaller grip frame to fit smaller hands. Standard blued, charcoal blued or nickel finish with forged, old model, or color casehardened frame. Dual cylinder model available with .32-30/.32 H&R chambering. Introduced 2001. From Cimarron F.A. Co.
Price: From .... $503.00–$565.00
Price: .32-20/.32 H&R dual cylinder...................................... $649.00

CIMARRON MODEL P SAA

Calibers: .32 WCF, .38 WCF, .357 Magnum, .44 WCF, .44 Special, .45 Colt and .45 ACP. **Barrels:** 4.75, 5.5, 7.5 in. **Weight:** 39 oz. **Length:** 10 in. overall (4.75-in. barrel). **Grips:** Walnut. **Sights:** Blade front. **Features:** Old model black-powder frame with Bullseye ejector, or New Model frame. Imported by Cimarron F.A. Co.
Price: From $550.00

CIMARRON MODEL "P" JR.

Calibers: .22 LR, .32-20, .32 H&R, 38 Special **Barrels:** 3.5, 4.75, 5.5 in. **Grips:** Checkered walnut. **Sights:** Blade front. **Features:** Styled after 1873 Colt Peacemaker, except 20 percent smaller. Blue finish with color case-hardened frame; Cowboy action. Introduced 2001. From Cimarron F.A. Co.
Price: From $480.00

CIMARRON ROOSTER SHOOTER

Calibers: .357, .45 Colt and .44 W.C.F. **Barrel:** 4.75 in. **Weight:** 2.5 lbs. **Grip:** 1-piece orange finger grooved. **Features:** A replica of John Wayne's Colt Single Action Army model used in many of his great Westerns including his Oscar-winning performance in "True Grit," where he brings the colorful character Rooster Cogburn to life.
Price: $909.00

CIMARRON THUNDERER

Calibers: .357 Magnum, .44 WCF, .45 Colt. **Capacity:** 6-round cylinder. **Features:** Doc Holiday combo comes with leather shoulder holster, ivory handled dagger. Gun and knife have matching serial numbers. Made by Uberti.
Price: From .... $575.00–$948.00
Price: Combo $1,559.00

CIMARRON FRONTIER

Calibers: .357 Magnum, .44 WCF, .45 Colt. **Barrels:** 3.5, 4.75, 5.5 or 7.5 in. **Features:** Basic SAA design. Choice of Old Model or Pre-War frame. Blued or stainless finish. Available with Short Stroke action.
Price: Blued $530.00
Price: Stainless $723.00
Price: Short Stroke Action $598.00

CIMARRON U.S.V. ARTILLERY MODEL SINGLE-ACTION

Caliber: .45 Colt. **Barrel:** 5.5 in. **Weight:** 39 oz. **Length:** 11.5 in. overall. **Grips:** Walnut. **Sights:** Fixed. **Features:** U.S. markings and cartouche, casehardened frame and hammer. Imported by Cimarron F.A. Co.
Price: Blued finish.. $594.00
Price: Original finish $701.00

CIMARRON BAD BOY

Caliber: .44 Magnum. **Features:** Single Action Army-style revolver with 6- or 8-in. octagon barrel, standard blued finish, smooth walnut one-piece grip, flat-top frame with adjustable rear sight. Introduced 2018.
Price: $688.00

COLT NEW FRONTIER

Calibers: .357 Magnum, .44 Special and .45 Colt. **Barrels:** 4.75 in., 5.5 in., and 7.5 in. **Grip:** Walnut. **Features:** From 1890 to 1898, Colt manufactured a variation of the venerable Single Action Army with a uniquely different profile. The "Flattop Target Model" was fitted with an adjustable leaf rear sight and blade front sights. Colt has taken this concept several steps further to bring shooters a reintroduction of a Colt classic. The New Frontier has that sleek flattop design with an adjustable rear sight for windage and elevation and a target ready ramp-style front sight. The guns are meticulously finished in Colt Royal Blue on both the barrel and cylinder, with a case-colored frame. Additional calibers available through Colt Custom Shop.
Price: $1,899.00

COLT SINGLE ACTION ARMY

Calibers: .357 Magnum, .45 Colt. **Capacity:** 6-round cylinder. **Barrels:** 4.75, 5.5, 7.5 in. **Weight:** 40 oz. (4.75 in. barrel). **Length:** 10.25 in. overall (4.75-in. barrel). **Grips:** Black Eagle composite. **Sights:** Blade front, notch rear. **Features:** Available in full nickel finish with nickel grip medallions, or Royal Blue with color casehardened frame. Reintroduced 1992. Additional calibers available through Colt Custom Shop.
Price: Blued $1,599.00
Price: Nickel... $1,799.00

EAA BOUNTY HUNTER SA

Calibers: .22 LR/.22 WMR, .357 Mag., .44 Mag., .45 Colt. **Capacities:** 6. 10-round cylinder available for .22LR/.22WMR. **Barrels:** 4.5 in., 7.5 in. **Weight:** 2.5 lbs. **Length:** 11 in. overall (4.625 in. barrel). **Grips:** Smooth walnut. **Sights:** Blade front, grooved topstrap rear. **Features:** Transfer bar safety; 3-position hammer; hammer-forged barrel. Introduced 1992. Imported by European American Armory
Price: Centerfire, blued or case-hardened $478.00
Price: Centerfire, nickel $515.00
Price: .22 LR/.22 WMR, blued $343.00
Price: .22LR/.22WMR, nickel $380.00
Price: .22 LR/.22WMR, 10-round cylinder $465.00

EMF 1875 OUTLAW

Calibers: .357 Magnum, .44-40, .45 Colt. **Barrels:** 7.5 in., 9.5 in. **Weight:** 46 oz. **Length:** 13.5 in. overall. **Grips:** Smooth walnut. **Sights:** Blade front, fixed groove rear. **Features:** Authentic copy of 1875 Remington with firing pin in hammer; color casehardened frame, blued cylinder, barrel, steel backstrap and trigger guard. Also available in nickel, factory engraved. Imported by E.M.F. Co.
Price: All calibers $520.00
Price: Laser Engraved $800.00

Prices given are believed to be accurate at time of publication however, many factors affect retail pricing so exact prices are not possible.

74TH EDITION, 2020 ✦ **449**

EMF 1873 GREAT WESTERN II

Calibers: .357 Magnum, .45 Colt, .44/40. **Barrels:** 3.5 in., 4.75 in., 5.5 in., 7.5 in. **Weight:** 36 oz. **Length:** 11 in. (5.5-in. barrel). **Grips:** Walnut. **Sights:** Blade front, notch rear. **Features:** Authentic reproduction of the original 2nd Generation Colt single-action revolver. Standard and bone casehardening. Coil hammer spring. Hammer-forged barrel. Alchimista has case-hardened frame, brass backstrap, longer and wider 1860 grip.

Price: 1873 Californian .... **$545.00–$560.00**
Price: 1873 Custom series, bone or nickel, ivory-like grips **$689.90**
Price: 1873 Stainless steel, ivory-like grips **$589.90**
Price: 1873 Paladin **$560.00**
Price: Deluxe Californian with checkered walnut grips stainless.......... **$780.00**
Price: Buntline **$605.00**
Price: Alchimista.. **$675.00**

EMF 1873 DAKOTA II

Caliber: .357 Magnum, 45 Colt. **Barrel:** 4.75 in. **Grips:** Walnut. **Finish:** black.
Price: **$460.00**

FREEDOM ARMS MODEL 83 PREMIER GRADE

Calibers: .357 Magnum, 41 Magnum, .44 Magnum, .454 Casull, .475 Linebaugh, .500 Wyo. Exp. **Capacity:** 5-round cylinder. **Barrels:** 4.75 in., 6 in., 7.5 in., 9 in. (.357 Mag. only), 10 in. (except .357 Mag. and 500 Wyo. Exp.) **Weight:** 53 oz. (7.5-in. bbl. in .454 Casull). **Length:** 13 in. (7.5 in. bbl.). **Grips:** Impregnatedhardwood. **Sights:** Adjustable rear with replaceable front sight. Fixed rear notch and front blade. **Features:** Stainless steel construction with brushed finish; manual sliding safety bar. Micarta grips optional. 500 Wyo. Exp. Introduced 2006. Lifetime warranty. Made in USA by Freedom Arms, Inc.
Price: From **$2,738.00**

FREEDOM ARMS MODEL 83 FIELD GRADE

Calibers: .22 LR, .357 Magnum, .41 Magnum, .44 Magnum, .454 Casull, .475 Linebaugh, .500 Wyo. Exp. **Capacity:** 5-round cylinder. **Barrels:** 4.75 in., 6 in., 7.5 in., 9 in. (.357 Mag. only), 10 in. (except .357 Mag. and .500 Wyo. Exp.) **Weight:** 56 oz. (7.5-in. bbl. in .454 Casull). **Length:** 13.1 in. (7.5 in. bbl.).

Grips: Pachmayr standard, impregnated hardwood or Micarta optional. **Sights:** Adjustable rear with replaceable front sight. Model 83 frame. All stainless steel. Introduced 1988. Made in USA by Freedom Arms Inc.
Price: From **$2,332.00**

FREEDOM ARMS MODEL 97 PREMIER GRADE

Calibers: .17 HMR, .22 LR, .32 H&R, .327 Federal, .357 Magnum, 6 rounds; .41 Magnum, .44 Special, .45 Colt. **Capacity:** 5-round cylinder. **Barrels:** 4.25 in., 5.5 in., 7.5 in., 10 in. (.17 HMR, .22 LR, .32 H&R). **Weight:** 40 oz. (5.5 in. .357 Mag.). **Length:** 10.75 in. (5.5 in. bbl.). **Grips:** Impregnated hardwood; Micarta optional. **Sights:** Adjustable rear, replaceable blade front. Fixed rear notch and front blade. **Features:** Stainless steel construction, brushed finish, automatic transfer bar safety system. Introduced in 1997. Lifetime warranty. Made in USA by Freedom Arms.
Price: From **$2,148.00**

HERITAGE ROUGH RIDER

Calibers: .22 LR, 22 LR/22 WMR combo, .357 Magnum .44-40, .45 Colt. **Capacity:** 6-round cylinder. **Barrels:** 3.5 in., 4.75 in., 5.5 in., 7.5 in. **Weights:** 31–38 oz. **Grips:** Exotic cocobolo laminated wood or mother of pearl; bird's head models offered. **Sights:** Blade front, fixed rear. Adjustable sight on 4.75 in. and 5.5 in. models. **Features:** Hammer block safety. Transfer bar with Big Bores. High polish blue, black satin, silver satin, casehardened and stainless finish. Introduced 1993. Made in USA by Heritage Mfg., Inc.
Price: Rimfire calibers, From **$200.00**
Price: Centerfire calibers, From... **$450.00**

MAGNUM RESEARCH BFR SINGLE ACTION
Calibers: .44 Magnum, .444 Marlin, .45-70, .45 Colt/.410, .450 Marlin, .454 Casull, .460 S&W Magnum, .480 Ruger/.475 Linebaugh, .500 Linebaugh, .500 JRH, .500 S&W, .30-30. **Barrels:** 6.5 in., 7.5 in. and 10 in. **Weights:** 3.6–5.3 lbs. **Grips:** Black rubber. **Sights:** Rear sights are the same configuration as the Ruger revolvers. Many aftermarket rear sights will fit the BFR. Front sights are machined by Magnum in four heights and anodized flat black. The four heights accommodate all shooting styles, barrel lengths and calibers. All sights are interchangeable with each BFR's. **Features:** Crafted in the USA, the BFR single-action 5-shot stainless steel revolver frames are CNC machined inside and out from a pre-heat treated investment casting. This is done to prevent warping and dimensional changes or shifting that occurs during the heat treat process. Magnum Research designed the frame with large calibers and substantial recoil in mind, built to close tolerances to handle the pressure of true big-bore calibers. The BFR is equipped with a transfer bar safety feature that allows the gun to be carried safely with all five chambers loaded.
Price: ....$1,218.00-$1,302.00

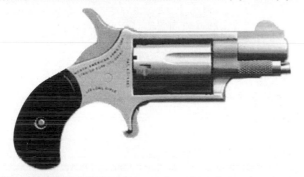

NORTH AMERICAN ARMS MINI
Calibers: .22 Short, 22 LR, 22 WMR. **Capacity:** 5-round cylinder. **Barrels:** 1.125 in., 1.625 in. **Weight:** 4–6.6 oz. **Length:** 3.625 in., 6.125 in. overall. **Grips:** Laminated wood. **Sights:** Blade front, notch fixed rear. **Features:** All stainless steel construction. Polished satin and matte finish. Engraved models available. From North American Arms.
Price: .22 Short, .22 LR $226.00
Price: .22 WMR $236.00

NORTH AMERICAN ARMS MINI-MASTER
Calibers: .22 LR, .22 WMR. **Capacity:** 5-round cylinder. **Barrel:** 4 in. **Weight:** 10.7 oz. **Length:** 7.75 in. overall. **Grips:** Checkered hard black rubber. **Sights:** Blade front, white outline rear adjustable for elevation, or fixed. **Features:** Heavy vented barrel; full-size grips. Non-fluted cylinder. Introduced 1989.
Price: ....$284.00–$349.00

NORTH AMERICAN ARMS BLACK WIDOW
Similar to Mini-Master, 2-in. heavy vent barrel. Built on .22 WMR frame. Non-fluted cylinder, black rubber grips. Available with Millett low-profile fixed sights or Millett sight adjustable for elevation only. Overall length 5.875 in., weighs 8.8 oz. From North American Arms.
Price: Adjustable sight, .22 LR or .22 WMR $352.00
Price: Fixed sight, .22 LR or .22 WMR $288.00

NORTH AMERICAN ARMS "THE EARL" SINGLE-ACTION
Calibers: .22 Magnum with .22 LR accessory cylinder. **Capacity:** 5-round cylinder. **Barrel:** 4 in. octagonal. **Weight:** 6.8 oz. **Length:** 7.75 in. overall. **Grips:** Wood. **Sights:** Barleycorn front and fixed notch rear. **Features:** Single-action mini-revolver patterned after 1858-style Remington percussion revolver. Includes a spur trigger and a faux loading lever that serves as cylinder pin release.
Price: ....$298.00, $332.00 (convertible)

RUGER NEW MODEL SINGLE-SIX SERIES
Calibers: .22 LR, .17 HMR. Convertible and Hunter models come with extra cylinder for .22 WMR. **Capacity:** 6. **Barrels:** 4.62 in., 5.5 in., 6.5 in. or 9.5 in. **Weight:** 35–42 oz. **Finish:** Blued or stainless. **Grips:** Black checkered hard rubber, black laminate or hardwood (stainless model only). Single-Six .17 Model available only with 6.5-in. barrel, blue finish, rubber grips. Hunter Model available only with 7.5-in. barrel, black laminate grips and stainless finish.
Price: (blued) $629.00
Price: (stainless) $699.00

RUGER SINGLE-TEN AND RUGER SINGLE-NINE SERIES
Calibers: .22 LR, .22 WMR. **Capacities:** 10 (.22 LR Single-Ten), 9 (.22 Mag Single-Nine). **Barrels:** 5.5 in. (Single-Ten), 6.5 in. (Single-Nine). **Weight:** 38–39 oz. **Grips:** Hardwood Gunfighter. **Sights:** Williams Adjustable Fiber Optic.
Price: $699.00

RUGER NEW MODEL BLACKHAWK/ BLACKHAWK CONVERTIBLE
Calibers: .30 Carbine, .357 Magnum/.38 Special, .41 Magnum, .44 Special, .45 Colt. **Capacity:** 6-round cylinder. **Barrels:** 4.625 in., 5.5 in., 6.5 in., 7.5 in. (.30 carbine and .45 Colt). **Weights:** 36–45 oz. **Lengths:** 10.375 in. to 13.5 in. **Grips:** Rosewood or black checkered. **Sights:** .125-in. ramp front, micro-click rear adjustable for windage and elevation. **Features:** Rosewood grips, Ruger transfer bar safety system, independent firing pin, hardened chrome-moly steel frame, music wire springs through-out. Case and lock included. Convertibles come with extra cylinder.
Price: (blued) $669.00
Price: (Convertible, .357/9mm) $749.00
Price: (Convertible, .45 Colt/.45 ACP) $749.00
Price: (stainless, .357 only) $799.00

Prices given are believed to be accurate at time of publication however, many factors affect retail pricing so exact pricing is not possible.

74TH EDITION, 2020 ✦ **451**

RUGER BISLEY SINGLE ACTION
Calibers: .44 Magnum. and .45 Colt. **Barrel:** 7.5-in. barrel. **Length:** 13.5 in. **Weight:** 48–51 oz. Similar to standard Blackhawk, hammer is lower with smoothly curved, deeply checkered wide spur. The trigger is strongly curved with wide smooth surface. Longer grip frame. Adjustable rear sight, ramp-style front. Unfluted cylinder and roll engraving, adjustable sights. Plastic lockable case. Orig. fluted cylinder introduced 1985; discontinued 1991. Unfluted cylinder introduced 1986.
Price: $899.00

RUGER NEW VAQUERO SINGLE-ACTION
Calibers: .357 Magnum, .45 Colt. **Capacity:** 6-round cylinder. **Barrel:** 4.625 in., 5.5 in., 7.5 in. **Weight:** 39–45 oz. **Length:** 10.5 in. overall (4.625 in. barrel). **Grips:** Rubber with Ruger medallion. **Sights:** Fixed blade front, fixed notch rear. **Features:** Transfer bar safety system and loading gate interlock. Blued model color casehardened finish on frame, rest polished and blued. Engraved model available. Gloss stainless. Introduced 2005.
Price: $829.00

RUGER NEW MODEL BISLEY VAQUERO
Calibers: .357 Magnum, .45 Colt. **Capacity:** 6-round cylinder. **Barrel:** 5.5-in. **Length:** 11.12 in. **Weight:** 45 oz. **Features:** Similar to New Vaquero but with Bisley-style hammer and grip frame. Simulated ivory grips, fixed sights.
Price: $899.00

RUGER NEW MODEL SUPER BLACKHAWK
Caliber: .44 Magnum/.44 Special. **Capacity:** 6-round cylinder. **Barrel:** 4.625 in., 5.5 in., 7.5 in., 10.5 in. bull. **Weight:** 45–55 oz. **Length:** 10.5 in. to 16.5 in. overall. **Grips:** Rosewood. **Sights:** .125-in. ramp front, micro-click rear adjustable for windage and elevation. **Features:** Ruger transfer bar safety system, fluted or unfluted cylinder, steel grip and cylinder frame, round or square back trigger guard, wide serrated trigger, wide spur hammer. With case and lock.
Price: $829.00

RUGER NEW BEARCAT SINGLE-ACTION
Caliber: .22 LR. **Capacity:** 6-round cylinder. **Barrel:** 4 in. **Weight:** 24 oz. **Length:** 9 in. overall. **Grips:** Smooth rosewood with Ruger medallion. **Sights:** Blade front, fixed notch rear. Distributor special edition available with adjustable sights. **Features:** Reintroduction of the Ruger Bearcat with slightly lengthened frame, Ruger transfer bar safety system. Available in blued finish only. Rosewood grips. Introduced 1996 (blued), 2003 (stainless). With case and lock.
Price: SBC-4, blued $639.00
Price: KSBC-4, satin stainless $689.00

RUGER NEW MODEL SUPER BLACKHAWK HUNTER
Caliber: .44 Magnum. **Capacity:** 6-round cylinder. **Barrel:** 7.5 in., full-length solid rib, unfluted cylinder. **Weight:** 52 oz. **Length:** 13.625 in. **Grips:** Black laminated wood. **Sights:** Adjustable rear, replaceable front blade. **Features:** Reintroduced Ultimate SA revolver. Includes instruction manual, high-impact case, set of medium scope rings, gun lock, ejector rod as standard. Bisley-style frame available.
Price: (Hunter, Bisley Hunter) $959.00

Prices given are believed to be accurate at time of publication however, many factors affect retail pricing so exact prices are not possible.

TAYLOR'S CATTLEMAN SERIES
Calibers: .357 Magnum or 45 Colt. **Barrels:** 4.75 in., 5.5 in., or 7.5 in. **Features:** Series of Single Action Army-style revolvers made in many variations.
Price: Gunfighter w/blued & color case finish......................................$556.00
Price: Stainless $720.00
Price: Nickel...$672.00
Price: Charcoal blued $647.00
Price: Bird's Head 3.5- or 4.5-in. bbl., walnut grips $603.00
Price: Engraved (shown)...$925.00

UBERTI 1851–1860 CONVERSION
Calibers: .38 Special, .45 Colt. **Capacity:** 6-round engraved cylinder. **Barrels:** 4.75 in., 5.5 in., 7.5 in., 8 in. **Weight:** 2.6 lbs. (5.5-in. bbl.). **Length:** 13 in. overall (5.5-in. bbl.). **Grips:** Walnut. **Features:** Brass backstrap, trigger guard; color casehardened frame, blued barrel, cylinder. Introduced 2007.
Price: 1851 Navy $569.00
Price: 1860 Army $589.00

UBERTI 1873 CATTLEMAN SINGLE-ACTION
Caliber: .45 Colt. **Capacity:** 6-round cylinder. **Barrels:** 4.75 in., 5.5 in., 7.5 in. **Weight:** 2.3 lbs. (5.5-in. bbl.). **Length:** 11 in. overall (5.5-in. bbl.). **Grips:** Styles: Frisco (pearl styled); Desperado (buffalo horn styled); Chisholm (checkered walnut); Gunfighter (black checkered), Cody (ivory styled), one-piece walnut. **Sights:** Blade front, groove rear. **Features:** Steel or brass backstrap, trigger guard; color casehardened frame, blued barrel, cylinder. NM designates New Model plunger-style frame; OM designates Old Model screw cylinder pin retainer.
Price: 1873 Cattleman Frisco $869.00
Price: 1873 Cattleman Desperado (2006) $889.00
Price: 1873 Cattleman Chisholm (2006) $599.00
Price: 1873 Cattleman NM, blued 4.75 in. barrel $669.00
Price: 1873 Cattleman NM, Nickel finish, 7.5 in. barrel $689.00
Price: 1873 Cattleman Cody $899.00

UBERTI 1871–1872 OPEN TOP
Calibers: .38 Special, .45 Colt. **Capacity:** 6-round engraved cylinder. **Barrels:** 4.75 in., 5.5 in., 7.5 in. **Weight:** 2.6 lbs. (5.5-in. bbl.). **Length:** 13 in. overall (5.5-in. bbl.). **Grips:** Walnut. **Features:** Blued backstrap, trigger guard; color casehardened frame, blued barrel, cylinder. Introduced 2007.
Price: .... $539.00–$569.00

UBERTI 1873 CATTLEMAN BIRD'S HEAD SINGLE ACTION
Calibers: .357 Magnum, .45 Colt. **Capacity:** 6-round cylinder. **Barrels:** 3.5 in., 4 in., 4.75 in., 5.5 in. **Weight:** 2.3 lbs. (5.5-in. bbl.). **Length:** 10.9 in. overall (5.5-in. bbl.). **Grips:** One-piece walnut. **Sights:** Blade front, groove rear. **Features:** Steel or brass backstrap, trigger guard; color casehardened frame, blued barrel, fluted cylinder.
Price: $569.00

UBERTI CATTLEMAN .22
Caliber: .22 LR. **Capacity:** 6- or 12-round cylinder. **Barrel:** 5.5 in. **Grips:** One-piece walnut. **Sights:** Fixed. **Features:** Blued and casehardened finish, steel or brass backstrap/trigger guard.
Price: (brass backstrap, trigger guard) $539.00
Price: (steel backstrap, trigger guard) $559.00
Price: (12-round model, steel backstrap, trigger guard) $589.00

UBERTI 1873 BISLEY SINGLE-ACTION

Calibers: .357 Magnum, .45 Colt (Bisley); .22 LR and .38 Special. (Stallion), both with 6-round fluted cylinder. **Barrels:** 4.75 in., 5.5 in., 7.5 in. **Weight:** 2–2.5 lbs. **Length:** 12.7 in. overall (7.5-in. barrel). **Grips:** Two-piece walnut. **Sights:** Blade front, notch rear. **Features:** Replica of Colt's Bisley Model. Polished blued finish, color casehardened frame. Introduced 1997.
Price: 1873 Bisley, 7.5-in. barrel $619.00

UBERTI 1873 BUNTLINE AND REVOLVER CARBINE SINGLE-ACTION

Caliber: .357 Magnum, .44-40, .45 Colt. **Capacity:** 6. **Barrel:** 18 in. **Length:** 22.9–34 in. **Grips:** Walnut pistol grip or rifle stock. **Sights:** Fixed or adjustable.
Price: 1873 Revolver Carbine, 18-in. bbl., 34 in. OAL $729.00
Price: 1873 Cattleman Buntline Target, 18-in. bbl. 22.9 in. OAL $639.00

UBERTI OUTLAW, FRONTIER, AND POLICE

Caliber: .45 Colt. **Capacity:** 6-round cylinder. **Barrels:** 5.5 in., 7.5 in. **Weight:** 2.5–2.8 lbs. **Length:** 10.8 in. to 13.6 in. overall. **Grips:** Two-piece smooth walnut. **Sights:** Blade front, notch rear. **Features:** Cartridge version of 1858 Remington percussion revolver. Nickel and blued finishes. Fluted cylinder.
Price: 1875 Outlaw, nickel finish $609.00
Price: 1875 Frontier, blued finish $609.00
Price: 1890 Police, blued finish $599.00

UBERTI 1870 SCHOFIELD-STYLE TOP BREAK

Calibers: .38 Special, .44 Russian, .44-40, .45 Colt. **Capacity:** 6-round cylinder. **Barrels:** 3.5 in., 5 in., 7 in. **Weight:** 2.4 lbs. (5-in. barrel) **Length:** 10.8 in. overall (5-in. barrel). **Grips:** Two-piece smooth walnut or pearl. **Sights:** Blade front, notch rear. **Features:** Replica of Smith & Wesson Model 3 Schofield. Single-action, top break with automatic ejection. Polished blued finish (first model). Introduced 1994.
Price: .... $1,189.00-$1,599.00

AMERICAN DERRINGER MODEL 1
Calibers: All popular handgun calibers plus .45 Colt/.410 Shotshell. **Capacity:** 2, (.45-70 model is single shot). **Barrel:** 3 in. **Overall length:** 4.82 in. **Weight:** 15 oz. **Features:** Manually operated hammer-block safety automatically disengages when hammer is cocked. Texas Commemorative has brass frame and is available in .38 Special, .44-40. or .45 Colt.
Price: .... $635.00–$735.00
Price: Texas Commemorative $835.00

AMERICAN DERRINGER MODEL 8
Calibers: .45 Colt/.410 shotshell. **Capacity:** 2. **Barrel:** 8 in. **Weight:** 24 oz.
Price: $915.00
Price: High polish finish $1,070.00

AMERICAN DERRINGER DA38
Calibers: .38 Special, .357 Magnum, 9mm Luger. **Barrel:** 3.3 in. **Weight:** 14.5 oz. **Features:** DA operation with hammer-block thumb safety. Barrel, receiver and all internal parts are made from stainless steel.
Price: .... $690.00–$740.00

BOND ARMS TEXAS DEFENDER DERRINGER
Calibers: Available in more than 10 calibers, from .22 LR to .45 LC/.410 shotshells. **Barrel:** 3 in. **Weight:** 20 oz. **Length:** 5 in. **Grips:** Rosewood. **Sights:** Blade front, fixed rear. **Features:** Interchangeable barrels, stainless steel firing pins, cross-bolt safety, automatic extractor for rimmed calibers. Stainless steel construction, brushed finish. Right or left hand.
Price: $543.00
Price: Interchangeable barrels, .22 LR thru .45 LC, 3 in. $139.00
Price: Interchangeable barrels, .45 LC, 3.5 in. .... $159.00–$189.00

BOND ARMS RANGER II
Caliber: .45 LC/.410 shotshells or .357 Magnum/.38 Special. **Barrel:** 4.25 in. **Weight:** 23.5 oz. **Length:** 6.25 in. **Features:** This model has a trigger guard. Intr. 2011. From Bond Arms.
Price: $673.00

BOND ARMS CENTURY 2000 DEFENDER
Calibers: .45 LC/.410 shotshells. or .357 Magnum/.38 Special. **Barrel:** 3.5 in. **Weight:** 21 oz. **Length:** 5.5 in. **Features:** Similar to Defender series.
Price: $517.00

BOND ARMS COWBOY DEFENDER
Calibers: From .22 LR to .45 LC/.410 shotshells. **Barrel:** 3 in. **Weight:** 19 oz. **Length:** 5.5 in. **Features:** Similar to Defender series. No trigger guard.
Price: $493.00

BOND ARMS SNAKE SLAYER
Calibers: .45 LC/.410 shotshell (2.5 in. or 3 in.). **Barrel:** 3.5 in. **Weight:** 21 oz. **Length:** 5.5 in. **Grips:** Extended rosewood. **Sights:** Blade front, fixed rear. **Features:** Single-action; interchangeable barrels; stainless steel firing pin. Introduced 2005.
Price: $603.00

BOND ARMS SNAKE SLAYER IV
Calibers: .45 LC/.410 shotshell (2.5 in. or 3 in.). **Barrel:** 4.25 in. **Weight:** 22 oz. **Length:** 6.25 in. **Grips:** Extended rosewood. **Sights:** Blade front, fixed rear. **Features:** Single-action; interchangeable barrels; stainless steel firing pin. Introduced 2006.
Price: $648.00

COBRA BIG-BORE DERRINGERS
Calibers: .22 WMR, .32 H&R Mag., .38 Special, 9mm Para., .380 ACP. **Barrel:** 2.75 in. **Weight:** 14 oz. **Length:** 4.65 in. overall. **Grips:** Textured black or white synthetic or laminated rosewood. **Sights:** Blade front, fixed notch rear. **Features:** Alloy frame, steel-lined barrels, steel breechblock. Plunger-type safety with integral hammer block. Black, chrome or satin finish. Introduced 2002. Made in USA by Cobra Enterprises of Utah, Inc.
Price: $187.00

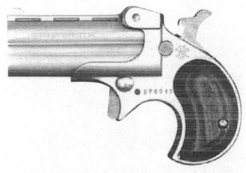

COBRA STANDARD SERIES DERRINGERS
Calibers: .22 LR, .22 WMR, .25 ACP, .32 ACP. **Barrel:** 2.4 in. **Weight:** 9.5 oz. **Length:** 4 in. overall. **Grips:** Laminated wood or pearl. **Sights:** Blade front, fixed notch rear. **Features:** Choice of black powder coat, satin nickel or chrome finish. Introduced 2002. Made in USA by Cobra Enterprises of Utah, Inc.
Price: $169.00

COBRA LONG-BORE DERRINGERS
Calibers: .22 WMR, .38 Special, 9mm. **Barrel:** 3.5 in. **Weight:** 16 oz. **Length:** 5.4 in. overall. **Grips:** Black or white synthetic or rosewood. **Sights:** Fixed. **Features:** Chrome, satin nickel, or black Teflon finish. Introduced 2002. Made in USA by Cobra Enterprises of Utah, Inc.
Price: $187.00

COBRA TITAN .45 LC/.410 DERRINGER
Calibers: .45 LC, .410 or 9mm, 2-round capacity. **Barrel:** 3.5 in. **Weight:** 16.4 oz. **Grip:** Rosewood. **Features:** Standard finishes include: satin stainless, black stainless and brushed stainless. Made in USA by Cobra Enterprises of Utah, Inc.
Price: $399.00

COMANCHE SUPER SINGLE-SHOT
Calibers: .45 LC/.410 **Barrel:** 10 in. **Sights:** Adjustable. **Features:** Blue finish, not available for sale in CA, MA. Distributed by SGS Importers International, Inc.
Price: $240.00

DOUBLETAP DERRINGER
Calibers: .45 Colt or 9mm **Barrel:** 3 in. **Weight:** 12 oz. **Length:** 5.5 in. **Sights:** Adjustable. **Features:** Over/under, two-barrel design. Rounds are fired individually with two separate trigger pulls. Tip-up design, aluminum frame.
Price: $499.00

HEIZER PS1 POCKET SHOTGUN
Calibers: .45 Colt or .410 shotshell. Single-shot. **Barrel:** Tip-up, 3.25 in. **Weight:** 22 oz. **Length:** 5.6 in. **Width:** .742 in **Height:** 3.81 in. **Features:** Available in several finishes. Standard model is matte stainless or black. Also offered in Hedy Jane series for the women in pink or in two-tone combinations of stainless and pink, blue, green, purple. Includes interchangeable AR .223 barrel. Made in the USA by Heizer Industries.
Price: $499.00

HEIZER POCKET AR
Caliber: .223 Rem./5.56 NATO. Single shot. **Barrel:** 3.75 in., ported or non-ported. **Length:** 6.375 in. **Weight:** 23 oz. **Features:** Similar to PS1 pocket shotgun but chambered for .223/5.56 rifle cartridge.
Price: $339.00

HEIZER PAK1
Caliber: 7.2x39. Similar to Pocket AR but chambered for 7.62x39mm. Single shot. **Barrel:** 3.75 in., ported or unported. **Length:** 6.375 in. **Weight:** 23 oz.
Price: $339.00

HENRY MARE'S LEG

Calibers: .22 LR, .22 WMR, .357 Magnum, .44 Magnum, .45 Colt. **Capacities:** 10 rounds (.22 LR), 8 rounds (.22 WMR), 5 rounds (others). **Barrel:** 12.9 in. **Length:** 25 in. **Weight:** 4.5 lbs. (rimfire) to 5.8 lbs. (centerfire calibers). **Features:** Lever-action operation based on Henry rifle series and patterned after gun made famous in Steve McQueen's 1950s TV show, "Wanted: Dead or Alive." Made in the USA.
Price: .22 LR **$462.00**
Price: .22 WMR **$473.00**
Price: Centerfire calibers **$1,024.00**

MAXIMUM SINGLE-SHOT

Calibers: .22 LR, .22 Hornet, .22 BR, .22 PPC, 223 Rem., .22-250, 6mm BR, 6mm PPC, .243, .250 Savage, 6.5mm-35M, .270 MAX, .270 Win., 7mm TCU, 7mm BR, 7mm-35, 7mm INT-R, 7mm-08, 7mm Rocket, 7mm Super-Mag., .30 Herrett, .30 Carbine, .30-30, .308 Win., 30x39, .32-20, .350 Rem. Mag., .357 Mag., .357 Maximum, .358 Win., .375 H&H, .44 Mag., .454 Casull. **Barrel:** 8.75 in., 10.5 in., 14 in. **Weight:** 61 oz. (10.5 in. bbl.); 78 oz. (14-in. bbl.). **Length:** 15 in., 18.5 in. overall (with 10.5- and 14-in. bbl., respectively). **Grips:** Smooth walnut stocks and fore-end. Also available with 17-finger-groove grip. **Sights:** Ramp front, fully adjustable open rear. **Features:** Falling block action; drilled and tapped for M.O.A. scope mounts; integral grip frame/receiver; adjustable trigger; Douglas barrel (interchangeable). Introduced 1983. Made in USA by M.O.A. Corp.
Price: **$1,062.00**

ROSSI MATCHED PAIR, "DUAL THREAT PERFORMER"

Calibers: .22LR, .44 Magnum, .223, .243. .410, 20 gauge, single shot. Interchangeable rifle and shotgun barrels In various combinations. **Sights:** Fiber optic front sights, adjustable rear. **Features:** Two-in-one pistol system with single-shot simplicity. Removable choke and cushioned grip with a Taurus Security System.
Price: .22/.410 from **$345.00**

THOMPSON/CENTER ENCORE PRO HUNTER

Calibers: .223, .308. Single shot, break-open design. **Barrel:** 15 in. **Weight:** 4.25–4.5 lbs. **Grip:** Walnut on blued models, rubber on stainless. Matching fore-end. **Sights:** Adjustable rear, ramp front. **Features:** Interchangeable barrels, adjustable trigger. Pro Hunter has "Swing Hammer" to allow reaching the hammer when the gun is scoped. Other Pro Hunter features include fluted barrel.
Price: From **$779.00**

THOMPSON/CENTER G2 CONTENDER

Calibers: .22 LR or .357 Magnum. A second generation Contender pistol maintaining the same barrel interchangeability with older Contender barrels and their corresponding forends (except Herrett fore-end). The G2 frame will not accept old-style grips due to the change in grip angle. Incorporates an automatic hammer block safety with built-in interlock. Features include trigger adjustable for overtravel, adjustable rear sight; ramp front sight blade, blued steel finish.
Price: From **$729.00**

Prices given are believed to be accurate at time of publication however, many factors affect retail pricing so exact prices are not possible.

74TH EDITION, 2020 ⊕ **457**

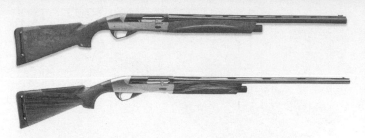

Barrel: 24 in. Weight: 6-7 lbs. Stock: 12 ga. model has ComfortTech with pistol grip, Bottomland/Cerakote finish. 20 ga. has standard stock with Realtree APG finish. Features: From the Benelli Performance Shop.
Price: 20 ga. standard stock $3,199.00
Price: 12 ga. pistol grip stock $3,399.00

BENELLI ETHOS

Gauges: 12 ga., 20 ga., 28 ga. 3 in. Capacity: 4+1. Barrel: 26 in. or 28 in. (Full, Mod., Imp. Cyl., Imp. Mod., Cylinder choke tubes). Weights: 6.5 lbs. (12 ga.), 5.3–5.7 (20 & 28 ga.). Length: 49.5 in. overall (28 in. barrel). Stock: Select AA European walnut with satin finish. Sights: Red bar fiber optic front, with three interchangeable inserts, metal middle bead. Features: Utilizes Benelli's Inertia Driven system. Recoil is reduced by Progressive Comfort recoil reduction system within the buttstock. Twelve and 20-gauge models cycle all 3-inch loads from light 7/8 oz. up to 3-inch magnums. Also available with nickel-plated engraved receiver. Imported from Italy by Benelli USA, Corp.
Price: $1,999.00
Price: Engraved nickel-plated (shown)...$2,149.00
Price: 20 or 28 ga. (engraved, nickel plated only)...........................$2,149.00

BENELLI ETHOS SPORT

Gauges: 12 ga., 20 ga., 28 ga. 3 in. Capacity: 4+1. Barrel: Ported, 28 in. or 30 in. (12 ga. only). Full, Mod., Imp. Cyl., Imp. Mod., Cylinder extended choke tubes. Wide rib. Other features similar to Ethos model.
Price: $2,269.00

BENELLI ULTRA LIGHT

Gauges: 12 ga., 20 ga., 28 ga. 3 in. chamber (12, 20), 2 3/4 in. (28). Barrels: 24 in., 26 in. Mid-bead sight. Weights: 5.2–6 lbs. Features: Similar to Legacy line. Drop adjustment kit allows the stock to be custom fit without modifying the stock. WeatherCoat walnut stock. Lightened receiver, shortened magazine tube, carbon-fiber rib and grip cap. Introduced 2008. Imported from Italy by Benelli USA, Corp.
Price: 12 and 20 ga. $1,699.00
Price: 28 ga. $1,799.00

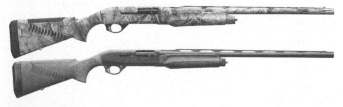

BENELLI M2 FIELD

Gauges: 20 ga., 12 ga., 3 in. chamber. Barrels: 21 in., 24 in., 26 in., 28 in. Weights: 5.4–7.2 lbs. Length: 42.5–49.5 in. overall. Stock: Synthetic, Advantage Max-4 HD, Advantage Timber HD, APG HD. Sights: Red bar. Features: Uses the Inertia Driven bolt mechanism. Vent rib. Comes with set of five choke tubes. Imported from Italy by Benelli USA.
Price: Synthetic stock 12 ga. $1,499.00
Price: Camo stock 12 ga. $1,549.00
Price: Synthetic stock 20 ga. $1,499.00
Price: Camo stock 20 ga. $1,599.00
Price: Rifled slug ....$1,469.00–$1,589.00
Price: Left-hand 12 ga. $1,409.00
Price: Left-hand model 20 ga. $1,519.00
Price: Tactical, from $1,249.00

BENELLI M2 TURKEY EDITION

Gauges: 12 ga. and 20 ga., Full, Imp. Mod, Mod., Imp. Cyl., Cyl. choke tubes.

BENELLI MONTEFELTRO

Gauges: 12 ga. and 20 ga. Full, Imp. Mod, Mod., Imp. Cyl., Cyl. choke tubes. Barrels: 24 in., 26 in., 28 in., 30 in. (Sporting). Weights: 5.3–7.1 lbs. Stock: Checkered walnut with satin finish. Lengths: 43.6–49.5 in. overall. Features: Burris FastFire II sight. Uses the Inertia Driven rotating bolt system with a simple inertia recoil design. Finish is blued. Introduced 1987.
Price: Standard Model $1,129.00
Price: Silver $1,779.00
Price: Sporting $1,329.00

BENELLI SUPER BLACK EAGLE III

Gauge: 12 ga., 3 1/2 inch. Latest evolution of Super Black Eagle. ComforTech stock with adjustable comb, 22 synthetic chevrons, gel recoil pad. Offered with several camo finishes, black synthetic or satin walnut. Left-hand model available. Introduced in 2017.
Price: $1,899.00
Price: Camo finish $1,999.00
Price: Rifle Slug $1,499.00

BENELLI SUPERSPORT & SPORT II

Gauges: 20 ga., 12 ga., 3-in. chamber. Capacity: 4+1. Barrels: 28 in., 30 in., ported, 10mm sporting rib. Weight: 7.2–7.3 lbs. Lengths: 49.6–51.6 in. Stock: Carbon fiber, ComforTech (Supersport) or walnut (Sport II). Sights: Red bar front, metal midbead. Sport II is similar to the Legacy model except has nonengraved dual tone blued/silver receiver, ported wide-rib barrel, adjustable buttstock, and functions with all loads. Walnut stock with satin finish. Introduced 1997. Features: Designed for high-volume sporting clays. Inertia-driven action, Extended CrioChokes. Ported. Imported from Italy by Benelli USA.
Price: SuperSport $2,199.00
Price: Sport II $1,899.00

BENELLI VINCI

Gauge: 12 ga., 3-in. Barrels: 26- or 28-inch ribbed. Tactical model available with 18.5-in. barrel. Finishes: Black, MAX-4HD or APG HD; synthetic contoured stocks; optional Steady-Grip model. Weight: 6.7–6.9 lbs. Features: Gas-operated action. Modular disassembly; interchangeable choke tubes. Picatinny rail, pistol grip, ghost ring sight.
Price: ....$1,349.00–$1,469.00

BENELLI SUPER VINCI

Gauge: 12 ga.. 2 3/4 in., 3 in. and 3 1/2 in. Capacity: 3+1. Barrels: 26 in., 28 in. Weights: 6.9–7 lbs. Lengths: 48.5–50.5 in. Stock: Black synthetic, Realtree Max4 and Realtree APG. Features: Crio Chokes: C,IC,M,IM,F. Length of Pull: 14.375 in. Drop at Heel: 2 in. Drop at Comb: 1.375 in. Sights: Red bar front sight and metal bead mid-sight. Minimum recommended load: 3-dram, 1 1/8 oz. loads (12 ga.). Receiver drilled and tapped for scope mounting. Imported from Italy by Benelli USA., Corp.
Price: Black Synthetic Comfortech $1,799.00
Price: Camo $1,899.00

BERETTA A300 OUTLANDER

Gauge: 12 ga., 3-in. Capacity: 3+1. Operates with 2 3/4-in. shells. Barrel: 28 in. with Mobilechoke system. Stock: Synthetic, camo or wood. Weight: 7.1 pounds. Features: Based on A400 design but at a lower price.
Price: ....$775.00–$850.00

Prices given are believed to be accurate at time of publication however, many factors affect retail pricing so exact prices are not possible.

BERETTA A350 XTREMA

Gauge: 12 ga., 3 1/2-in. **Capacity:** 3+1. Operates with 3- and 2 3/4-in. shells. **Barrel:** 24 in. or 28 in. with Optima Choke HP system. **Stock:** Synthetic, camo or wood. **Weight:** 7-7 3/4 pounds. Adjustable buttstock.
Price: Max 5 Waterfowl...$1,150.00
Price: Turkey w/Mossy Oak Obsession camo..................$1,365.00

BERETTA A400 XTREME PLUS MAX

Gauge: 12 ga., 3 1/2-in. **Capacity:** 3+1. Also operates with 3- and 2 3/4-in. shells. **Barrel:** 26, 28 or 30 in. with five Black Edition Extended choke tubes. **Stock:** Kick-Off Mega and Kick-Off 3 with soft comb. **Finish:** Realtree Max-5. **Weight:** 7-7 3/4 pounds.
Price: $1,900.00

BERETTA A400 XPLOR UNICO

Gauge: 12 ga.. 2 3/4 to 3 1/2-inch shells. **Barrels:** 26- or 28-inch "Steelium" with interchangeable choke tubes. **Features:** Self-regulation gas-operated shotgun. Optional Kick-Off hydraulic damper. Anodized aluminum receiver; sculpted, checkered walnut buttstock and fore-end.
Price: $1,755.00
Price: With Kick-Off recoil reduction system................$1,855.00

BERETTA A400 XCEL SPORTING

Gauge: 12 ga. 3-in. chamber. **Barrels:** 28 in., 30 in. 32 in. **Weight:** 7.5 lbs. **Stock:** Walnut and polymer. **Features:** Gas operated. In addition to A400 specifications and features, the Sporting model has aqua blue receiver. Optional Gun Pod electronic system gives digital readout of air temperature, ammunition pressure, number of rounds fired.
Price: $1,745.00
Price: With Kick-Off system....................................$1,845.00

BERETTA A400 XPLOR ACTION

Gauges: 12 ga., 20 (3 in.) or 28 ga. (2 3/4-in. chamber). **Barrels:** 28 in., 30 in. **Weight:** 5.3 (28 ga.) to 6.7 lbs. **Stock:** Walnut and polymer combination. **Features:** Gas-operating Blink operating system can reportedly fire 4 rounds in less than one second. Kick-Off hydraulic recoil reduction system reduces felt recoil up to 70 percent.
Price: $1,600.00
Price: With Kick-Off system....................................$1,700.00

BROWNING A5

Gauges: 12 ga., 3 or 3 1/2; 16 ga., 2 3/4 in. (Sweet Sixteen). **Barrels:** 26 in., 28 in. or 30 in. **Weights:** 5 3/4 to 7 lbs. **Lengths:** 47.25–51.5 in. **Stock:** Gloss finish walnut with 22 LPI checkering, black synthetic or camo. Adjustable for cast and drop. **Features:** Operates on Kinematic short-recoil system, totally different than the classic Auto-5 long-recoil action manufactured from 1903–1999. Lengthened forcing cone, three choke tubes (IC, M, F), flat ventilated rib, brass bead front sight, ivory middle bead. Available in Mossy Oak Duck Blind or Break-up Infinity camo. Ultimate Model has satin finished aluminum alloy receiver with light engraving of pheasants on left side, mallards on the right. Gloss blued finish, Grade III oil-finished walnut stock. Wicked Wing has Cerakote Burnt Bronze finish on receiver and barrel, Mossy Oak Shadow Grass Blades camo on stock.
Price: A5 Hunter...$1,670.00
Price: A5 Hunter 3 1/2 in. $1,800.00
Price: A5 Stalker (synthetic) $1,540.00
Price: A5 Stalker 3 1/2 in. $1,670.00
Price: A5 Ultimate $2,030.00
Price: A5 Sweet Sixteen..$1,740.00
Price: A5 Wicked Wing $1,870.00
Price: A5 Wicked Wing 3 1/2 in................................$2,000.00

BROWNING MAXUS HUNTER

Gauges: 12 ga., 3 in. and 3 1/2 in. **Barrels:** 26 in., 28 in. and 30 in. Flat ventilated rib with fixed cylinder choke; stainless steel; matte finish. **Weight:** 7 lbs. 2 oz. **Length:** 40.75 in. **Stock:** Gloss finish walnut stock with close radius pistol grip, sharp 22 LPI checkering, Speed Lock Forearm, shim adjustable for length of pull, cast and drop. **Features:** Vector Pro-lengthened forcing cone, three Invector-Plus choke tubes, Inflex Technology recoil pad, ivory front bead sight, One 1/4 in. stock spacer. Strong, lightweight aluminum alloy receiver with durable satin nickel finish & laser engraving (pheasant on the right, mallard on the left). All-Purpose Hunter has Mossy Oak Break-Up Country Camo, Duratouch coated composite stock. Wicked Wing has Cerakote Burnt Bronze finish on receiver and barrel, Mossy Oak Shadow Grass Blades camo on stock.
Price: 3 in. $1,590.00
Price: 3 1/2 in. $1,740.00
Price: All-Purpose Hunter.......................................$1,780.00
Price: Maxus Wicked Wing.....................................$1,900.00

BROWNING MAXUS SPORTING

Gauge: 12 ga., 3 in. **Barrels:** 28 in., 30 in. flat ventilated rib. **Weight:** 7 lbs. 2 oz. **Length:** 49.25 in.–51.25 in. **Stock:** Gloss finish high grade walnut stock with close radius pistol grip, Speed Lock forearm, shim adjustable for length of pull, cast and drop. **Features:** Laser engraving of game birds transforming into clay birds on the lightweight alloy receiver. Quail are on the right side, and a mallard duck on the left. The Power Drive Gas System reduces recoil and cycles a wide array of loads. It's available in a 28 in. or 30 in. barrel length. The high-grade walnut stock and forearm are generously checkered, finished with a deep, high gloss. The stock is adjustable and one .250-in. stock spacer is included. For picking up either clay or live birds quickly, the HiViz Tri-Comp fiber-optic front sight with mid-bead ivory sight does a great job, gathering light on the most overcast days. Vector Pro-lengthened forcing cone, five Invector-Plus choke tubes, Inflex Technology recoil pad, HiViz Tri-Comp fiber-optic front sight, ivory mid-bead sight, one .250-in. stock spacer.
Price: $1,800.00
Price: Golden Clays $2,100.00

BROWNING MAXUS SPORTING CARBON FIBER

Gauge: 12 ga., 3 in. **Barrels:** 28 in., 30 in. flat ventilated rib. **Weights:** 6 lbs. 15 oz.–7 lbs. **Length:** 49.25–51.25 in. **Stock:** Composite stock with close radius pistol grip, Speed Lock forearm, textured gripping surfaces, shim adjustable for length of pull, cast and drop, carbon fiber finish, Dura-Touch Armor Coating. **Features:** Strong, lightweight aluminum alloy, carbon fiber finish on top and bottom. The stock is finished with Dura-Touch Armor Coating for a secure, non-slip grip when the gun is wet. It has the Browning exclusive Magazine Cut-Off, a patented Turn-Key Magazine Plug and Speed Load Plus. Deeply finished look of carbon fiber and Dura-Touch Armor Coating. Vector Pro-lengthened forcing cone, five Invector-Plus choke tubes, Inflex Technology recoil pad, HiViz Tri-Comp fiber-optic front sight, ivory mid-bead sight, one .250-in. stock spacer.
Price: $1,590.00

BROWNING GOLD LIGHT 10 GAUGE

Gauge: 10 ga. 3 1/2 in. **Capacity:** 4 rounds. **Barrels:** 24 (NWTF), 26 or 28 in. **Stock:** Composite with Dura-Cote Armor coating. Mossy Oak camo (Break-Up Country or Shadow Grass Blades). **Weight:** Approx. 9.5 pounds. Gas operated action, aluminum receiver, three standard Invector choke tubes. Receiver is drilled and tapped for scope mount. National Wild Turkey Foundation model has Hi-Viz 4-in-1 fiber optic sight, NWTF logo on buttstock.

Price: Mossy Oak Camo finishes..$1,780.00
Price: NWTF Model..$1,900.00

BROWNING SILVER

Gauges: 12 ga., 3 in. or 3 1/2 in.; 20 ga., 3 in. chamber. **Barrels:** 26 in., 28 in., 30 in. Invector Plus choke tubes. **Weights:** 7 lbs., 9 oz. (12 ga.), 6 lbs., 7 oz. (20 ga.). **Stock:** Satin finish walnut or composite. **Features:** Active Valve gas system, semi-humpback receiver. Invector Plus choke system, three choke tubes. Imported by Browning.

Price: Silver Field, 12 ga...$1,070.00
Price: Silver Field, 20 ga...$1,140.00
Price: Black Lightning, 12 ga...$1,140.00
Price: Silver Field Composite, 12 ga., 3 in. $1,000.00
Price: Silver Field Composite, 12 ga., 3 1/2 in...............................$1,070.00
Price: Silver Field Rifled Deer Matte, 20 ga...................................$1,200.00

CHARLES DALY MODEL 600

Gauges: 12 ga. or 20 ga. (3 in.) or 28 ga. (2 3/4 in.). **Capacity:** 5+1. **Barrels:** 26 in., 28 in. (20 and 28 ga.), 26 in., 28 in. or 30 in. (12 ga.). Three choke tubes provided (Rem-Choke pattern). **Stock:** Synthetic, wood or camo. **Features:** Comes in several variants including Field, Sporting Clays, Tactical and Trap. Left-hand models available. Uses gas-assisted recoil operation. Imported from Turkey.

Price: Field 12, 20 ga...$480.00
Price: Field 28 ga...$531.00
Price: Sporting $858.00
Price: Tactical $685.00

CHARLES DALY MODEL 635 MASTER MAG

Gauge: 12 ga., 3 1/2 in. **Barrels:** 24 in., 26 in., 28 in. Ported. **Stock:** Synthetic with full camo coverage. **Features:** Similar to Model 600 series.

Price: From..$665.00

CZ MODEL 712/720

Gauges: 12 ga., 20 ga. **Capacity:** 4+1. **Barrel:** 26 in. **Weight:** 6.3 lbs. **Stock:** Turkish walnut with 14.5 in. length of pull. **Features:** Chrome-lined barrel with 3-inch chamber, ventilated rib, five choke tubes. Matte black finish.

Price: 712 12 ga. ....$499.00–$699.00
Price: 720 20 ga..$516.00–$599.00

CZ MODEL 1012

Gauges: 12 ga. **Capacity:** 4+1. **Barrel:** 28 in. **Weight:** 6.5 lbs. **Stock:** Turkish walnut with 14.5 in. length of pull. **Features:** Inertia-operated action, chrome-lined barrel with 3-inch chamber, ventilated rib, five choke tubes, matte black finish.

Price: 712 12 ga..$659.00

ESCORT WATERFOWL EXTREME SEMI-AUTO

Gauges: 12 ga. or 20 ga., 2 3/4 in. through 3 1/2 in. **Capacity:** 5+1. **Barrel:** 28 in. **Weight:** 7.4 lbs. **Length:** 48 in. **Stock:** Composite stock with close radius pistol grip; Speed Lock forearm; textured gripping surfaces; shim adjustable for length of pull, cast and drop; Realtree Max4 or AP camo finish; Dura-Touch Armor Coating. **Sights:** HiVis MagniSight fiber-optic, magnetic sight to enhance sight acquisition in lowlight conditions. **Features:** The addition of non-slip grip pads on the fore-end and pistol grip provide a superior hold in all weather conditions. Smart-Valve gas pistons regulate gas blowback to cycle every round — from 2 3/4-inch range loads through 3 1/2-inch heavy magnums. Escorts also have Fast-loading systems that allow one-handed round changes without changing aiming position. Left-hand models available at no increase in price.

Price: Black/Synthetic $551.00
Price: Realtree Camo $736.00
Price: 3 1/2-in. Black/Synthetic $649.00
Price: 3 1/2-in. Realtree Camo $815.00

FABARM XLR5 VELOCITY AR

Gauge: 12 ga. **Barrels:** 30 or 32 in. **Weight:** 8.25 lbs. **Features:** Gas-operated model designed for competition shooting. Unique adjustable rib that allows a more upright shooting position. There is also an adjustable trigger shoe, magazine cap adjustable weight system. Five interchangeable choke tubes. Imported from Italy by Fabarm USA.

Price: From..$2,755.00–$3,300.00
Price: FR Sporting ....$1,990.00–$2,165.00
Price: LR (Long Rib) ....$2,260.00–$2,800.00

FRANCHI AFFINITY

Gauges: 12 ga., 20 ga. Three-inch chamber also handles 2 3/4-inch shells. **Barrels:** 26 in., 28 in., 30 in. (12 ga.), 26 in. (20 ga.). 30-in. barrel available only on 12-ga. Sporting model. **Weights:** 5.6–6.8 pounds. **Stocks:** Black synthetic or Realtree Camo. Left-hand versions available. Catalyst model has stock designed for women.

Price: Synthetic $789.00
Price: Synthetic left-hand action...$899.00
Price: Camo $949.00
Price: Compact $849.00
Price: Catalyst $969.00
Price: Sporting $1,149.00
Price: Companion $1,599.00

MOSSBERG 930

Gauge: 12 ga., 3 in. **Capacity:** 4-shell magazine. **Barrels:** 24 in., 26 in., 28 in., over-bored to 10-gauge bore dimensions; factory ported, Accu-Choke tubes. **Weight:** 7.5 lbs. **Length:** 44.5 in. overall (28-in. barrel). **Stock:** Walnut or synthetic. Adjustable stock drop and cast spacer system. **Sights:** Turkey Taker fiber-optic, adjustable windage and elevation. Front bead fiber-optic front on waterfowl models. **Features:** Self-regulating gas system, dual gas-vent system and piston, EZ-Empty magazine button, cocking indicator. Interchangeable Accu-Choke tube set (IC, Mod, Full) for waterfowl and field models. XX-Full turkey Accu-Choke tube included with turkey models. Ambidextrous thumb-operated safety, Uni-line stock and receiver. Receiver drilled and tapped for scope base attachment, free gun lock. Introduced 2008. From O.F. Mossberg & Sons, Inc.

Price: Turkey, From $630.00
Price: Waterfowl, From $619.00
Price: Combo, From $693.00
Price: Field, From $560.00
Price: Slugster, From $678.00
Price: Turkey Pistolgrip; Mossy Oak Infinity Camo $735.00
Price: Tactical; 18.5-in. tactical barrel, black synthetic stock
and matte black finish $878.00
Price: SPX; no muzzle brake, M16-style front sight,
ghost ring rear sight, pistol grip stock, 8-shell
extended magazine $1,046.00
Price: Home Security/Field Combo; 18.5 in. Cylinder bore barrel
and 28 in. ported Field barrel; black synthetic stock and
matte black finish $693.00
Price: High Performance (13-round magazine).................... $974.00

MOSSBERG MODEL 935 MAGNUM
Gauge: 12 ga. 3 in. and 3 1/2-in., interchangeable. **Barrels:** 22 in., 24 in., 26 in., 28in. **Weights:** 7.25–7.75 lbs. **Lengths:** 45–49 in. overall. **Stock:** Synthetic. **Features:** Gas-operated semi-auto models in blued or camo finish. Fiber-optics sights, drilled and tapped receiver, interchangeable Accu-Mag choke tubes.
Price: 935 Magnum Turkey Pistol grip; full pistol grip stock $924.00
Price: 935 Magnum Grand Slam: 22 in. barrel $756.00
Price: 935 Magnum Waterfowl: 26 in. or 28 in. barrel .... $660.00-$735.00
Price: 935 Pro Series Waterfowl $875.00

MOSSBERG SA-20
Gauge: 20 or 28 ga. **Barrels:** 20 in. (Tactical), 26 in. or 28 in. **Weight:** 5.5–6 lbs. **Stock:** Black synthetic. Gas operated action, matte blue finish. Tactical model has ghost-ring sight, accessory rail.
Price: 20 ga. From .... $592.00–$664.00
Price: 28 ga. From .... $588.00–$675.00

REMINGTON MODEL 11-87 SPORTSMAN
Gauges: 12 ga., 20 ga., 3 in. **Barrels:** 26 in., 28 in., RemChoke tubes. Standard contour, vent rib. **Weights:** 7.75–8.25 lbs. **Lengths:** 46–48 in. overall. **Stock:** American walnut with satin finish. **Sights:** Single bead front. **Features:** Matte-black metal finish, magazine cap swivel studs.
Price: $816.00
Price: Mossy Oak New Break-Up camo $88.00

REMINGTON MODEL 1100 CLASSIC
Gauges: 12 ga., 20 ga. or 28 ga. **Barrels:** 28 in. (12 ga.), 26 in. (20), 25 in. (28). **Features:** Part of the Remington American Classics Collection honoring Remington's most enduring firearms. American walnut B-grade stock with classic white line spacer and grip caps, ventilated recoil pad the white line spacer and white diamond grip cap. Machine-cut engraved receiver has tasteful scroll pattern with gold inlay retriever and "American Classic" label. Limited availability.
Price: $1,686.00

REMINGTON MODEL 1100 200TH YEAR ANNIVERSARY
Gauge: 12 ga. **Barrel:** 28 in. **Features:** C-grade American walnut stock with *fleur-de-lis* checkering. Receiver has classic engraving pattern, gold inlay. Limited edition of 2,016 guns to honor the Remington company's 200th anniversary — the oldest firearms manufacturer in the USA. Limited availability.
Price: $1,999.00

REMINGTON MODEL 1100 COMPETITION MODELS
Gauges: .410 bore, 28 ga., 20 ga., 12 ga. **Barrels:** 26 in., 27 in., 28 in., 30 in. light target contoured vent rib barrel with twin bead target sights. **Stock:**

Semi-fancy American walnut stock and fore-end, cut checkering, high gloss finish. **Features:** Classic Trap has 30-inch barrel and weighs approximately 8.25 pounds. Sporting Series is available in all four gauges with 28-inch barrel in 12 and 20 gauge, 27 in. in 28 and .410. **Weights:** 6.25–8 pounds. Competition Synthetic model has synthetic stock with adjustable comb, case and length. Five Briley Target choke tubes. High-gloss blued barrel, Nickel-Teflon finish on receiver and internal parts. **Weight:** 8.1 pounds.
Price: Classic Trap $1,334.00
Price: Sporting Series, From $1,252.00
Price: Competition Synthetic: $1,305.00

REMINGTON VERSA MAX SERIES
Gauge: 12 ga., 2 3/4 in., 3 in., 3 1/2 in. **Barrels:** 26 in. and 28 in. flat ventilated rib. **Weights:** 7.5–7.7 lbs. **Length:** 40.25 in. **Stock:** Synthetic. **Features:** Reliably cycles 12-gauge rounds from 2 3/4 in. to 3 1/2 in. magnum. Versaport gas system regulates cycling pressure based on shell length. Reduces recoil to that of a 20-gauge. Self-cleaning. Continuously cycled thousands of rounds in torture test. Synthetic stock and fore-end with grey overmolded grips. Drilled and tapped receiver. Enlarged trigger guard opening and larger safety for easier use with gloves. TriNyte Barrel and Nickel Teflon plated internal components offer extreme corrosion resistance. Includes 5 Flush Mount Pro Bore Chokes (Full, Mod, Imp Mod Light Mod, IC)
Price: Sportsman, From $1,066.00
Price: Synthetic, From $1,427.00
Price: Tactical, From $1,456.00
Price: Waterfowl, From $1,765.00
Price: Camo, From $1,664.00

REMINGTON MODEL V3
Gauge: 12 ga., 3 in. **Capacity:** 3+1 magazine. **Barrels:** 26 or 28 in. **Features:** The newest addition to the Remington shotgun family operates on an improved VersaPort gas system, claimed to offer the least recoil of any 12-ga. autoloader. Operating system is located in front of the receiver instead of the fore-end, resulting in better weight distribution than other autoloaders, and improved handling qualities. **Stock:** Walnut, black synthetic, or camo. Designed to function with any 2 3/4- or 3-in. ammo. Made in the USA by Remington.
Price: Synthetic black.. $895.00
Price: Walnut or camo $995.00

SKB MODEL IS300
Gauge: 12 ga., 2-3/4- and 3-in. loads. **Capacity:** 4+1 magazine. **Barrels:** 26 in., 28 in. or 30 in. with 3 choke tubes IC, M, F. **Stock:** Black synthetic, oil-finished walnut or camo. **Weight:** 6.7–7.3 pounds. **Features:** Inertia-driven operating system. Target models have adjustable stock dimensions including cast and drop. Made in Turkey and imported by GU, Inc.
Price: Synthetic $625.00
Price: Walnut or Camo Field $715.00
Price: Walnut Target $870.00
Price: RS300 Target with adjustable stock...................... $1,000.00

SKB MODEL HS 300
Gauges: 12 ga. or 20 ga. **Barrel:** 26 or 28 in. **Stock:** Checkered walnut or camo finish. **Weight:** 7 lbs. **Features:** Gas-operated design. Introduced in 2017.
Price: Walnut stock... $750.00
Price: Camo stock $780.00

STOEGER MODEL 3000
Gauge: 12 ga., 2 3/4- and 3-in. loads. Minimum recommended load 3-dram, 1 1/8 ounces. **Capacity:** 4+1 magazine. Inertia-driven operating system. **Barrels:** 26 or 28 in. with 3 choke tubes IC, M, XF. **Weights:** 7.4–7.5 lbs. **Finish:** Black synthetic or camo (Realtree APG or Max-4). M3K model is designed for 3-Gun competition and has synthetic stock, 24-in. barrel, modified loading port.
Price: Synthetic $599.00

Prices given are believed to be accurate at time of publication however, many factors affect retail pricing so exact prices are not possible.

74TH EDITION, 2020 ✛ **461**

Price: Walnut or Camo $649.00
Price: M3K $699.00
Price: 3000R rifled slug model $649.00

STOEGER MODEL 3020
Gauge: 20 ga., 2 3/4- or 3-in. loads. **Features:** This model has the same general specifications as the Model 3000 except for its chambering and weight of 5.5 to 5.8 pounds.
Price: Synthetic $599.00
Price: Camo $649.00

STOEGER MODEL 3500
Gauge: 12 ga. 2 3/4-, 3- and 3 1/2-in. loads. Minimum recommended load 3-dram, 1-1/8 ounces. **Barrels:** 24 in., 26 in. or 28 in. Choke tubes for IC, M, XF. **Weights:** 7.4–7.5 pounds. **Finish:** Satin walnut, black synthetic or camo (Realtree APG or Max-4). **Features:** Other features similar to Model 3000.
Price: Synthetic $679.00
Price: Camo $799.00
Price: Satin Walnut (shown) $769.00

TRISTAR VIPER G2
Gauges: 12 ga., 20 ga. 2 3/4 in. or 3 in. interchangeably. Capacity: 5-round magazine. **Barrels:** 26 in., 28 in. (carbon fiber only offered in 12-ga. 28 in. and 20-ga. 26 in.). **Stock:** Wood, black synthetic, Mossy Oak Duck Blind camouflage, faux carbon fiber finish (2008) with the new Comfort Touch technology. **Features:** Magazine cutoff, vent rib with matted sight plane, brass front bead (camo models have fiber-optic front sight), shot plug included, and 3 Beretta-style choke tubes (IC, M, F). Viper synthetic, Viper camo have swivel studs. Five-year warranty. Viper Youth models have shortened length of pull and 24 in. barrel. Sporting model has ported barrel, checkered walnut stock with adjustable comb. Imported by Tristar Sporting Arms Ltd.
Price: From...$549.00
Price: Camo models, From $640.00
Price: Silver Model..$670.00–$715.00
Price: Youth Model $565.00
Price: Sporting Model..$825.00

TRISTAR VIPER MAX
Gauge: 12. 3 1/2 in. **Barrel:** 24–30 in., threaded to accept Benelli choke tubes. Gas-operated action. Offered in several model variants. Introduced in 2017.
Price: ....$630.00-$730.00

WEATHERBY SA-SERIES
Gauges: 12 ga., 20 ga., 3 in. **Barrels:** 26 in., 28 in. flat ventilated rib. **Weight:** 6.5 lbs. **Stock:** Wood and synthetic. **Features:** The SA-08 is a reliable workhorse that lets you move from early season dove loads to late fall's heaviest waterfowl loads in no time. Available with wood and synthetic stock options in 12- and 20-gauge models, including a scaled-down youth model to fit 28 ga. Comes with 3 application-specific choke tubes (SK/IC/M). Made in Turkey.
Price: SA-08 Synthetic $649.00
Price: SA-08 Synthetic Youth $649.00
Price: SA-08 Deluxe $849.00

WEATHERBY SA-459
Gauges: 12 ga., 20 ga., 3 in. **Capacities:** 5 or 8 round. **Barrels:** 18.5 in. (Tactical) or 21.25 in. (Turkey). **Features:** Tactical model has Picatinny rail, pistol grip synthetic stock, ghost ring rear and M16-type front sight. Turkey model has fiber optic front sight, Realtree Xtra Green camo finish full coverage.
Price: Tactical model...$699.00

Price: Turkey model...$799.00

WEATHERBY 18-I
Gauges: 12 ga., 20 ga., 3 in. **Capacities:** 4+1. **Barrels:** 26 or 28 in. **Stock:** Synthetic, camo or walnut. **Features:** Inertia-operated system. Mossy Oak Shadow Grass or Realtree Max-5 camo full coverage.
Price: Synthetic...$1,099.00
Price: Waterfowler camo $1,199.00
Price: Deluxe model walnut stock....................................$1,899.00

WINCHESTER SUPER X3
Gauge: 12 ga., 3 in. and 3 1/2 in. **Barrels:** 26 in., 28 in., .742-in. back-bored; Invector Plus choke tubes. **Weights:** 7–7.25 lbs. **Stock:** Composite, 14.25 in. x 1.75 in. x 2 in. Mossy Oak New Break-Up camo with Dura-Touch Armor Coating. Pachmayr Decelerator buttpad with hard heel insert, customizable length of pull. **Features:** Alloy magazine tube, gunmetal grey Perma-Cote UT finish, self-adjusting Active Valve gas action, lightweight recoil spring system. Electroless nickel-plated bolt, three choke tubes, two length-of-pull stock spacers, drop and cast adjustment spacers, sling swivel studs. Introduced 2006. Made in Belgium, assembled in Portugal.
Price: Field $1,140.00
Price: Sporting, adj. comb...$1,700.00
Price: Long Beard, pistol grip camo stock........................$1,270.00
Price: Composite Sporting...$1,740.00

WINCHESTER SUPER X4
Gauge: 12 ga., 3 in. and 3 1/2 in. **Capacity:** 4-round magazine. **Barrels:** 22 in., 24 in., 26 in. or 28 in. Invector Plus Flush choke tubes. **Weight:** 6 lbs. 10 oz. **Stock:** Synthetic with rounded pistol grip and textured gripping surfaces, or satin finished checkered grade II/III Turkish walnut. Length-of-pull spacers. Several camo finishes available. **Features:** TruGlo fiber optic front sight, Inflex Technology recoil pad, active valve system, matte blue barrel, matte black receiver. Offered in Standard, Field, Compact, Waterfowl, Cantilever Buck, Cantilever Turkey models.
Price: Synthetic...$940.00
Price: Field, From ....$940.00–$1,070.00
Price: Upland Field $1,100.00
Price: Waterfowl Hunter ....$940.00–$1,070.00
Price: Hybrid Hunter...$1,040.00
Price: NWTF Cantilever Turkey, Mossy Oak Obsession $1,070.00

BENELLI SUPERNOVA

Gauge: 12 ga. 3 1/2 in. **Capacity:** 4-round magazine. **Barrels:** 24 in., 26 in., 28 in. **Lengths:** 45.5–49.5 in. **Stock:** Synthetic; Max 4, Timber, APG HD (2007). **Sights:** Red bar front, metal midbead. **Features:** 2 3/4 in., 3 in. chamber (3 1/2 in. 12 ga. only). Montefeltro rotating bolt design with dual action bars, magazine cutoff, synthetic trigger assembly, adjustable combs, shim kit, choice of buttstocks. Introduced 2006. Imported from Italy by Benelli USA.

Price: **$549.00**
Price: Camo stock **$669.00**
Price: Rifle slug model .... **$829.00–$929.00**
Price: Tactical model.............................. **$519.00–$549.00**

BENELLI NOVA

Gauges: 12 ga., 20 ga. **Capacity:** 4-round magazine. **Barrels:** 24 in., 26 in., 28 in. **Stock:** Black synthetic, Max-4, Timber and APG HD. **Sights:** Red bar. **Features:** 2 3/4 in., 3 in. (3 1/2 in. 12 ga. only). Montefeltro rotating bolt design with dual action bars, magazine cut-off, synthetic trigger assembly. Introduced 1999. Field & Slug Combo has 24 in. barrel and rifled bore; open rifle sights; synthetic stock; weighs 8.1 lbs. Imported from Italy by Benelli USA.

Price: Field Model.. **$449.00**
Price: Max-5 camo stock **$559.00**
Price: H20 model, black synthetic, matte nickel finish **$669.00**
Price: Tactical, 18.5-in. barrel, Ghost Ring sight **$459.00**
Price: Black synthetic youth stock, 20 ga. **$469.00**

BROWNING BPS

Gauges: 10 ga., 12 ga., 3 1/2 in.; 12 ga., 16 ga., or 20 ga., 3 in. (2 3/4 in. in target guns), 28 ga., 2 3/4 in., 5-shot magazine, .410, 3 in. chamber. **Barrels:** 10 ga. 24 in. Buck Special, 28 in., 30 in., 32 in. Invector; 12 ga., 20 ga. 22 in., 24 in., 26 in., 28 in., 30 in., 32 in. (Imp. Cyl., Mod. or Full), .410 26 in. (Imp. Cyl., Mod. and Full choke tubes). Also available with Invector choke tubes, 12 or 20 ga. Upland Special has 22-in. barrel with Invector tubes. BPS 3 in. and 3 1/2 in. have back-bored barrel. **Weight:** 7 lbs., 8 oz. (28 in. barrel). **Length:** 48.75 in. overall (28 in. barrel). **Stock:** 14.25 in. x 1.5 in. x 2.5 in. Select walnut, semi-beavertail fore-end, full pistol grip stock. **Features:** All 12 ga. 3 in. guns except Buck Special and game guns have back-bored barrels with Invector Plus choke tubes. Bottom feeding and ejection, receiver top safety, high post vent rib. Double action bars eliminate binding. Vent rib barrels only. All 12 and 20 ga. guns with 3 in. chamber available with fully engraved receiver flats at no extra cost. Each gauge has its own unique game scene. Introduced 1977. Stalker is same gun as the standard BPS except all exposed metal parts have a matte blued finish and the stock has a black finish with a black recoil pad. Available in 10 ga. (3 1/2 in.)

and 12 ga. with 3 in. or 3 1/2 in. chamber, 22 in., 28 in., 30 in. barrel with Invector choke system. Introduced 1987. Rifled Deer Hunter is similar to the standard BPS except has newly designed receiver/magazine tube/barrel mounting system to eliminate play, heavy 20.5-in. barrel with rifle-type sights with adjustable rear, solid receiver scope mount, "rifle" stock dimensions for scope or open sights, sling swivel studs. Gloss or matte finished wood with checkering, polished blue metal. Medallion model has additional engraving on receiver, polished blue finish, AA/AAA grade walnut stock with checkering. All-Purpose model has Realtree AP camo on stock and fore-end, HiVis fiber optic sights. Introduced 2013. Imported from Japan by Browning.

Price: Field, Stalker models, From .... **$600.00–$700.00**
Price: Camo coverage **$820.00**
Price: Deer Hunter **$830.00**
Price: Deer Hunter Camo **$870.00**
Price: Magnum Hunter (3 1/2 in.) .... **$800.00–$1,030.00**
Price: Medallion **$830.00**
Price: Trap **$840.00**

BROWNING BPS 10 GAUGE SERIES

Similar to the standard BPS except completely covered with Mossy Oak Shadow Grass camouflage. Available with 26- and 28-in. barrel. Introduced 1999. Imported by Browning

Price: Mossy Oak camo **$950.00**
Price: Synthetic stock, Stalker **$800.00**

BROWNING BPS NWTF TURKEY SERIES

Similar to the standard BPS except has full coverage Mossy Oak Break-Up Infinity camo finish on synthetic stock, fore-end and exposed metal parts. Offered in 12 ga., 3 in. or 3 1/2 in., or 10 ga. 24-in. bbl. has extra-full choke tube and HiViz fiber-optic sights. Introduced 2001. From Browning.

Price: 12 ga., 3 in. **$950.00**
Price: 3 1/2 in. **$1,030.00**

BROWNING BPS MICRO MIDAS

Gauges: 12 ga., 20 ga., 28 ga. or .410 bore. **Barrels:** 24 or 26 in. Three Invector choke tubes for 12 and 20 ga., standard tubes for 28 ga. and .410. **Stock:** Walnut with pistol grip and recoil pad. Satin finished and scaled down to fit smaller statured shooters. Length of pull is 13.25 in. Two spacers included for stock length adjustments. **Weights:** 7–7.8 lbs.
Price: .... **$700.00–$740.00**

BROWING BPS HIGH CAPACITY

Gauge: .410 bore. 3 in. **Capacity:** 5-round magazine. **Barrel:** 20 in. fixed Cylinder choke; stainless Steel; Matte finish. **Weight:** 6 lbs. **Length:** 40.75 in. **Stock:** Black composite on All Weather with matte finish. **Features:** Forged and machined steel; satin nickel finish. Bottom ejection; dual steel action bars; top tang safety. HiViz Tactical fiber-optic front sight; stainless internal mechanism; swivel studs installed.
Price: Synthetic **$800.00**

CHARLES DALY 300 SERIES

Gauges: 12 ga., 20 ga. or 28 ga. 3 in. and 2 3/4-in. shells (12 ga. and 20 ga.), 2 3/4 in. (28 ga.). Model 335 Master Mag is chambered for 12-ga. 3 1/2-inch shells. **Barrels:** 24 in., 26 in., 28 in. and 30 in., depending upon specific model. Ventilated rib. Three choke tubes (REM-Choke pattern) are provided. **Stock:** Synthetic, walnut or camo. **Weights:** 7–8 lbs. Left-hand models available. Imported from Turkey.

Price: Field .... **$365.00–$495.00**
Price: Tactical .... **$354.00–$503.00**
Price: Turkey **$553.00**

CZ 612

Gauge: 12 ga. Chambered for all shells up to 3 1/2 in. **Capacity:** 5+1, magazine plug included with Wildfowl Magnum. **Barrels:** 18.5 in. (Home Defense), 20 in. (HC-P), 26 in. (Wildfowl Mag.) **Weights:** 6–6.8 pounds. **Stock:** Polymer. **Finish:** Matte black or full camo (Wildfowl Mag.) HC-P model has pistol grip stock, fiber optic front sight and ghost-ring rear. Home Defense Combo comes with extra 26-in. barrel.

Price: Wildfowl Magnum **$428.00**
Price: Home Defense .... **$304.00–$409.00**
Price: Target **$549.00**

CZ MODEL 620/628 Field Select

Gauges: 20 ga. or 28 ga. **Barrel:** 28 inches. **Weight:** 5.4 lbs. **Features:** Similar to Model 612 except for chambering. Introduced in 2017.
Price: **$429.00**

ESCORT PUMP SERIES

Gauges: 12 ga., 20 ga.; 3 in. **Barrels:** 18 in. (AimGuard, Home Defense and MarineGuard), 22 in. (Youth Pump), 26 in., and 28 in. lengths. **Weight:** 6.7-7.0 lbs. **Stock:** Polymer in black, Shadow Grass camo or Obsession camo finish. Two adjusting spacers included. Youth model has Trio recoil pad. **Sights:** Bead or Spark front sights, depending on model. AimGuard and MarineGuard models have blade front sights. **Features:** Black-chrome or dipped camo metal parts, top of receiver dovetailed for sight mounts, gold plated trigger, trigger guard safety, magazine cutoff. Three choke tubes (IC, M, F) except AimGuard/MarineGuard which are cylinder bore. Models include: FH, FH Youth, AimGuard and Marine Guard. Introduced in 2003. Imported from Turkey by Legacy Sports International.

Price: $379.00
Price: Youth model $393.00
Price: Model 87 w/wood stock.. $350.00
Price: Home Defense (18-in. bbl.) $400.00

HARRINGTON & RICHARDSON (H&R) PARDNER PUMP

Gauges: 12 ga., 20 ga. 3 in. **Barrels:** 21–28 in. **Weight:** 6.5–7.5 lbs. **Stock:** Synthetic or hardwood. Ventilated recoil pad and grooved fore-end. **Features:** Steel receiver, double action bars, cross-bolt safety, easy takedown, ventilated rib, screw-in choke tubes.

Price: From.. $231.00–$259.00

IAC MODEL 97T TRENCH GUN

Gauge: 12 ga., 2 3/4 in. **Barrel:** 20 in. with cylinder choke. **Stock:** Hand rubbed American walnut. **Features:** Replica of Winchester Model 1897 Trench Gun. Metal handguard, bayonet lug. Imported from China by Interstate Arms Corp.

Price: $465.00

IAC HAWK SERIES

Gauge: 12, 2 3/4 in. **Barrel:** 18.5 in. with cylinder choke. **Stock:** Synthetic. **Features:** This series of tactical/home defense shotguns is based on the Remington 870 design. 981 model has top Picatinny rail and bead front sight. 982 has adjustable ghost ring sight with post front. 982T has same sights as 982 plus a pistol grip stock. Imported from China by Interstate Arms Corporation.

Price: 981 .... $275.00
Price: 982 .... $285.00
Price: 982T $300.00

ITHACA MODEL 37 FEATHERLIGHT

Gauges: 12 ga., 20 ga., 16 ga., 28 ga. **Capacity:** 4+1. **Barrels:** 26 in., 28 in. or 30 in. with 3-in. chambers (12 and 20 ga.), plain or ventilated rib. **Weights:** 6.1–7.6 lbs. **Stock:** Fancy-grade black walnut with Pachmayr Decelerator recoil pad. Checkered fore-end made of matching walnut. **Features:** Receiver machined from a single block of steel or aluminum. Barrel is steel shot compatible. Three Briley choke tubes provided. Available in several variations including turkey, home defense, tactical and high-grade.

Price: 12 ga., 16 ga. or 20 ga. From $895.00
Price: 28 ga. From..$1,149.00
Price: Turkey Slayer w/synthetic stock, From $925.00

Price: Trap Series 12 ga... $1,020.00
Price: Waterfowl...$885.00
Price: Home Defense 18- or 20-in. bbl............................$784.00

ITHACA DEERSLAYER III SLUG

Gauges: 12 ga., 20 ga. 3 in. **Barrel:** 26 in. fully rifled, heavy fluted with 1:28 twist for 12 ga. 1:24 for 20 ga. **Weights:** 8.14–9.5 lbs. with scope mounted. **Length:** 45.625 in. overall. **Stock:** Fancy black walnut stock and fore-end. **Sights:** NA. **Features:** Updated, slug-only version of the classic Model 37. Bottom ejection, blued barrel and receiver.

Price: $1,350.00

MAVERICK ARMS MODEL 88

Gauges: 12 ga., 20 ga. 3 in. **Barrels:** 26 in. or 28 in., Accu-Mag choke tubes for steel or lead shot. **Weight:** 7.25 lbs. **Stock:** Black synthetic with recoil pad. **Features:** Crossbolt safety, aluminum alloy receiver. Economy model of Mossberg Model 500 series. Available in several variations including Youth, Slug and Special Purpose (home defense) models.

Price: .... $231.00-$259.00

MOSSBERG MODEL 835 ULTI-MAG

Gauge: 12 ga., 3 1/2 in. **Barrels:** Ported 24 in. rifled bore, 24 in., 28 in., Accu-Mag choke tubes for steel or lead shot. Combo models come with interchangeable second barrel. **Weight:** 7.75 lbs. **Length:** 48.5 in. overall. **Stock:** 14 in. x 1.5 in. x 2.5 in. Dual Comb. Cut-checkered hardwood or camo synthetic; both have recoil pad. **Sights:** White bead front, brass mid-bead; fiber-optic rear. **Features:** Shoots 2 3/4-, 3- or 3 1/2-in. shells. Back-bored and ported barrel to reduce recoil, improve patterns. Ambidextrous thumb safety, twin extractors, dual slide bars. Mossberg Cablelock included. Introduced 1988.

Price: Turkey .... $601.00–$617.00
Price: Waterfowl .... $518.00–$603.00
Price: Turkey/Deer combo... $661.00–$701.00
Price: Turkey/Waterfowl combo $661.00
Price: Tactical Turkey...$652.00

MOSSBERG MODEL 500 SPORTING SERIES

Gauges: 12 ga., 20 ga., .410 bore, 3 in. **Barrels:** 18.5 in. to 28 in. with fixed or Accu-Choke, plain or vent rib. Combo models come with interchangeable second barrel. **Weight:** 6.25 lbs. (.410), 7.25 lbs. (12). **Length:** 48 in. overall (28-in. barrel). **Stock:** 14 in. x 1.5 in. x 2.5 in. Walnut-stained hardwood, black synthetic, Mossy Oak Advantage camouflage. Cut-checkered grip and fore-end. **Sights:** White bead front, brass mid-bead; fiber-optic. **Features:** Ambidextrous thumb safety, twin extractors, disconnecting safety, dual action bars. Quiet Carry fore-end. Many barrels are ported. FLEX series has many modular options and accessories including barrels and stocks. From Mossberg. Left-hand versions (L-series) available in most models.

Price: Turkey, From $486.00
Price: Waterfowl, From $537.00
Price: Combo, From $593.00
Price: FLEX Hunting $702.00
Price: FLEX All Purpose $561.00
Price: Field, From $419.00
Price: Slugster, From $447.00
Price: FLEX Deer/Security combo................................. $787.00
Price: Home Security 410 .... $477.00
Price: Tactical.. $486.00-$602.00

SHOTGUNS Pumps

MOSSBERG MODEL 500 SUPER BANTAM PUMP
Same as the Model 500 Sporting Pump except 12 or 20 ga., 22-in. vent rib Accu-Choke barrel with choke tube set; has 1 in. shorter stock, reduced length from pistol grip to trigger, reduced fore-end reach. Introduced 1992.
Price: **$419.00**
Price: Combo with extra slug barrel, camo finish **$549.00**

MOSSBERG 510 MINI BANTAM
Gauges: 20 ga., .410 bore, 3 in. **Barrel:** 18.5 in. vent-rib. **Weight:** 5 lbs. **Length:** 34.75 in. **Stock:** Synthetic with optional Mossy Oak Break-Up Infinity, Muddy Girl pink/black camo. **Features:** Available in either 20 ga. or .410 bore, the Mini features an 18.5-in. vent-rib barrel with dual bead sights. Parents don't have to worry about their young shooter growing out of this gun too quick, the adjustable classic stock can be adjusted from 10.5 to 11.5-in. length of pull so the Mini can grow with your youngster. This adjustability also helps provide a proper fit for young shooters and allowing for a more safe and enjoyable shooting experience.
Price: From .... **$419.00–$466.00**

MOSSBERG SHOCKWAVE SERIES
Gauges: 12, 20 ga. or .410 cylinder bore, 3-inch chamber. **Barrel:** 14 3/8, 18.5 in. **Weight:** 5 – 5.5 lbs. **Length:** 26.4 - 30.75 in. **Stock:** Synthetic or wood. Raptor bird's-head type pistol grip. Nightstick has wood stock and fore-end.
Price: From **$455.00**
Price: Ceracote finish **$504.00**
Price: Nightstick (shown **$539.00**
Price: Mag-Fed **$721.00**
Price: SPX w/heatshield **$560.00**

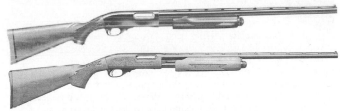

REMINGTON MODEL 870 WINGMASTER
Gauge: 12 ga., 20 ga., 28 ga., .410 bore. **Barrel:** 25 in., 26 in., 28 in., 30 in. (RemChokes). **Weight:** 7.25 lbs. **Lengths:** 46–48 in. **Stock:** Walnut, hardwood. **Sights:** Single bead (Twin bead Wingmaster). **Features:** Light contour barrel. Double action bars, cross-bolt safety, blue finish. LW is 28 ga. and .410 bore only, 25-in. vent rib barrel with RemChoke tubes, high-gloss wood finish. Gold-plated trigger, American B Grade or Claro walnut stock and fore-end, high-gloss finish, *fleur-de-lis* checkering. A classic American shotgun first introduced in 1950.
Price: From **$847.00**

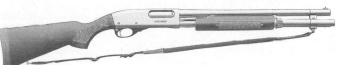

REMINGTON MODEL 870 TAC-14
Similar to 870 Wingmaster except has Raptor pistol grip, synthetic or hardwood grip fore-end. Has 18-in. plain barrel (cyl.), bead front sight, 7-round magazine. Marine Magnum has electroless nickel-plated finish on all metal parts including inside receiver and barrel. Special Purpose model has full-length synthetic stock.
Price: **$443.00**
Price: DM Detachable magazine model **$559.00**
Price: Marine Magnum **$841.00**
Price: Marine Magnum Special Purpose **$841.00**

REMINGTON MODEL 870 CLASSIC TRAP
Similar to Model 870 Wingmaster except has 30-in. vent rib, light contour barrel, singles, mid- and long-handicap choke tubes, semi-fancy American walnut stock, high-polish blued receiver with engraving. Chamber 2.75 in. From Remington Arms Co.
Price: **$1,120.00**

REMINGTON MODEL 870 EXPRESS
Similar to Model 870 Wingmaster except laminate, synthetic black, or camo stock with solid, black recoil pad and pressed checkering on grip and fore-end. Outside metal surfaces have black oxide finish. Comes with 26- or 28-in. vent rib barrel with mod. RemChoke tube. ShurShot Turkey (2008) has ShurShot synthetic pistol-grip thumbhole design, extended fore-end, Mossy Oak Obsession camouflage, matte black metal finish, 21-in. vent rib barrel, twin beads, Turkey Extra Full Rem Choke tube. Receiver drilled and tapped for mounting optics. ShurShot FR CL (Fully Rifled Cantilever, 2008) includes compact 23-in. fully rifled barrel with integrated cantilever scope mount.
Price: .... **$417.00–$629.00**

REMINGTON MODEL 870 EXPRESS SUPER MAGNUM
Similar to Model 870 Express except 28-in. vent rib barrel with 3 1/2-in. chamber, vented recoil pad. Introduced 1998. Model 870 Express Super Magnum Waterfowl (2008) is fully camouflaged with Mossy Oak Duck Blind pattern, 28-inch vent rib Rem Choke barrel, "Over Decoys" Choke tube (.007 in.) fiber-optic HiViz single bead front sight; front and rear sling swivel studs, padded black sling.
Price: **$469.00**

Prices given are believed to be accurate at time of publication however, many factors affect retail pricing so exact prices are not possible.

74TH EDITION, 2020 ✧ **465**

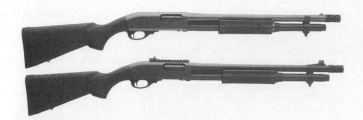

REMINGTON MODEL 870 EXPRESS TACTICAL

Similar to Model 870 but in 12 ga. only (2 3/4 in. and 3 in. interchangeably) with 18.5-in. barrel, Tactical RemChoke extended/ported choke tube, black synthetic buttstock and fore-end, extended magazine tube, gray powder coat finish overall. 38.5 in. overall length. Weighs 7.5 lbs.
Price: **$601.00**
Price: Model 870 TAC Desert Recon; desert camo stock
    and sand-toned metal surfaces **$692.00**
Price: Tactical Magpul **$898.00**

REMINGTON 870 EXPRESS SYNTHETIC TURKEY CAMO

Gauge: 12 ga., 2 3/4 and 3 in. **Features:** Pump-action shotgun. 21-inch vent rib bead-sighted barrel; standard Express finish on barrel and receiver; Turkey Extra Full RemChoke; synthetic stock with integrated sling swivel attachment.
Price: **$492.00**

REMINGTON 870 DM SERIES

Gauge: 12 ga. (2 3/4 in. and 3 in. interchangeably). **Capacity:** Detachable 6-round magazine. **Barrel:** 18.5-in. cylinder bore. **Stock:** Hardwood or black synthetic with textured gripping surfaces. Tac-14 DM model features short pistol grip buttstock and 14-inch barrel.
Price: **$559.00**

REMINGTON 870 SUPER MAG TURKEY-PREDATOR CAMO WITH SCOPE

Gauge: 12 ga., 2 3/4 to 3 1/2 in. **Features:** Pump-action shotgun. 20-in. barrel; TruGlo red/green selectable illuminated sight mounted on pre-installed Weaver-style rail; black padded sling; Wingmaster HDTurkey/Predator RemChoke; full Mossy Oak Obsession camo coverage; ShurShot pistol grip stock with black overmolded grip panels; TruGlo 30mm Red/Green Dot Scope pre-mounted.
Price: **$710.00**

REMINGTON MODEL 870 SPS SHURSHOT SYNTHETIC SUPER SLUG

Gauge: 12 ga.; 2 3/4 in. and 3 in. interchangeable. **Barrel:** 25.5-in. extra-heavy, fully rifled pinned to receiver. **Weight:** 7.875 lbs. **Length:** 47 in. overall. **Features:** Pump-action model based on 870 platform. SuperCell recoil pad. Drilled and tapped for scope mounts with Weaver rail included. Matte black metal surfaces, ShurShot pistol grip buttstock with Mossy Oak Treestand camo.
Price: **$829.00**
Price: 870 SPS ShurShot Synthetic Turkey; adjustable
    sights and APG HD camo buttstock and fore-end **$681.00**

STEVENS MODEL 320

Gauges: 12 ga., or 20 ga. with 3-in. chamber. **Capacity:** 5+1. **Barrels:** 18.25 in., 20 in., 22 in., 26 in. or 28 in. with interchangeable choke tubes. Features include all-steel barrel and receiver; bottom-load and ejection design; black synthetic stock.
Price: Security Model **$276.00**
Price: Field Model 320 with 28-inch barrel **$251.00**
Price: Combo Model with Field and Security barrels **$307.00**

STOEGER P3000

Gauge: 12 ga. 3-in. **Barrels:** 18.5 in., 26 in., 28 in., with ventilated rib. **Weight:** 6.5–7 lbs. **Stock:** Black synthetic. Camo finish available. Defense Model available with or without pistol grip.
Price: **$299.00**
Price: Camo finish **$399.00**
Price: Defense model w/pistol grip **$349.00**

REMINGTON 870 EXPRESS SYNTHETIC SUPER MAG TURKEY-WATERFOWL CAMO

Gauge: 12 ga., 2 3/4 to 3 1/2 in. **Features:** Pump-action shotgun. Full Mossy Oak Bottomland camo coverage; 26-inch barrel with HiViz fiber-optics sights; Wingmaster HD Waterfowl and Turkey Extra Full RemChokes; SuperCell recoil pad; drilled and tapped receiver.
Price: **$629.00**

WINCHESTER SUPER X (SXP)

Gauges: 12 ga., 3 in. or 3 1/2 in. chambers; 20 ga., 3 in. **Barrels:** 18 in., 26 in., 28 in. Barrels .742-in. back-bored, chrome plated; Invector Plus choke tubes. **Weights:** 6.5–7 lbs. **Stocks:** Walnut or composite. **Features:** Rotary bolt, four lugs, dual steel action bars. Walnut Field has gloss-finished walnut stock and forearm, cut checkering. Black Shadow Field has composite stock and forearm, non-glare matte finish barrel and receiver. SXP Defender has composite stock and forearm, chromed plated, 18-in. cylinder choked barrel, non-glare metal surfaces, five-shot magazine, grooved forearm. Some models offered in left-hand versions. Reintroduced 2009. Made in USA by Winchester Repeating Arms Co.
Price: Black Shadow Field, 3 in. **$380.00**
Price: Black Shadow Field, 3 1/2 in. **$430.00**
Price: SXP Defender .... **$350.00–$400.00**
Price: Waterfowl Hunter 3 in. **$460.00**
Price: Waterfowl Hunter 3 1/2 in. **$500.00**
Price: Turkey Hunter 3 1/2 in. **$520.00**
Price: Black Shadow Deer **$520.00**
Price: Trap **$480.00**
Price: Field, walnut stock............................... **$400.00–$430.00**

Prices given are believed to be accurate at time of publication however, many factors affect retail pricing so exact prices are not possible.

BARRETT SOVEREIGN ALBANY
Gauges: 12 ga., 20 ga., 28 ga. 3 in. (2 3/4 for 28 ga.) **Barrels:** 26 in., 28 in. or 30 in. **Stock:** Checkered grade AAA Turkish walnut with rounded Prince of Wales pistol grip. **Features:** Receiver scaled to individual gauges. Round body boxlock design, ornamental sideplates, coin-finished receiver. Introduced in 2016. Imported from Italy by Barrett Firearms.
Price: 12 or 20 ga. $5,700.00
Price: 28 ga. $6,150.00

BARRET SOVEREIGN BX-PRO
Gauge: 12 ga. **Barrels:** 30 in., 32 in. with 6 extended choke tubes. Ventilated rib tapered from 10mm to 7mm. **Stock:** A+ grade walnut with rounded Prince of Wales pistol grip. Cast-off comb and toe for right-handed shooters Length of pull: 14.5 inches. Adjustable comb. Right-hand palm swell.
Features: Automatic ejectors, single selective trigger, coin finished and engraved receiver. Imported from Fausti of Italy by Barrett Firearms.
Price: $3,075.00

BARRET SOVEREIGN RUTHERFORD
Gauges: 12 ga., 16 ga., 20 ga., 28 ga. **Barrels:** 26 in., 28 in. with 5 choke tubes. Chamber lengths are 3-in. for 12 and 20 ga., 2 ¾ in. for 16 ga. and 28 ga. **Stock:** A+ grade with cut checkering, red recoil pad, and rounded Prince of Wales pistol grip. **Features:** Receivers are sized to individual gauge, automatic ejectors, single selective trigger, coin finished receiver. Imported from Fausti of Italy by Barrett Firearms.
Price: 12, 20 ga. $2,200.00
Price: 16, 28 ga. $2,520.00

BENELLI 828U
Gauges: 12 ga. 3 in. **Barrels:** 26 in., 28 in. **Weights:** 6.5–7 lbs. **Stock:** AA-grade satin walnut, fully adjustable for both drop and cast. **Features:** New patented locking system allows use of aluminum frame. Features include carbon fiber rib, fiber-optic sight, removable trigger group, and Benelli's Progressive Comfort recoil reduction system.
Price: Matte black...$2,699.00
Price: Nickel $3,199.00

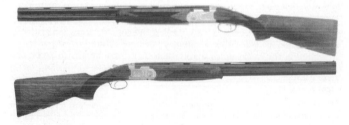

BERETTA 686/687 SILVER PIGEON SERIES
Gauges: 12 ga., 20 ga., 28 ga., 3 in. (2 3/4 in. 28 ga.). .410 bore, 3 in. **Barrels:** 26 in., 28 in. **Weight:** 6.8 lbs. **Stock:** Checkered walnut. **Features:** Interchangeable barrels (20 ga. and 28 ga.), single selective gold-plated trigger, boxlock action, auto safety, Schnabel fore-end.
Price: 686 Silver Pigeon Grade I $2,350.00
Price: 686 Silver Pigeon Grade I, Sporting $2,400.00
Price: 687 Silver Pigeon Grade III $3,430.00
Price: 687 Silver Pigeon Grade V $4,075.00

BERETTA MODEL 687 EELL
Gauges: 12 ga., 20 ga., 28 ga., 410 bore. **Features:** Premium-grade model with decorative sideplates featuring lavish hand-chased engraving with a classic game scene enhanced by detailed leaves and flowers that also cover the trigger guard, trigger plate and fore-end lever. Stock has high-grade, specially selected European walnut with fine-line checkering. Offered in three action sizes with scaled-down 28 ga. and .410 receivers. Combo models are available with extra barrel sets in 20/28 or 28/.410.
Price: $7,995.00
Price: Combo model $9,695.00

BERETTA MODEL 690
Gauge: 12 ga. 3 in. **Barrels:** 26 in., 28 in., 30 in. with OptimaChoke HP

system. **Features:** Similar to the 686/687 series with minor improvements. Stock has higher grade oil-finished walnut. Re-designed barrel/fore-end attachment reduces weight.
Price: ....$2,650.00–$3,100.00

BERETTA MODEL 692 SPORTING
Gauge: 12 ga., 3 in. **Barrels:** 30 in. with long forcing cones of approximately 14 in.. Skeet model available with 28- or 30-in. barrel, Trap model with 30 in or 32 in. Receiver is .50-in. wider than 682 model for improved handling. **Stock:** Hand rubbed oil finished select walnut with Schnabel fore-end. Features include selective single adjustable trigger, manual safety, tapered 8mm to 10mm rib.
Price: $4,800.00
Price: Skeet $5,275.00
Price: Trap..$5,600.00

BERETTA DT11
Gauge: 12 ga. 3 in. **Barrels:** 30 in., 32 in., 34 in. Top rib has hollowed bridges. **Stock:** Hand-checkered buttstock and fore-end. Hand-rubbed oil, Tru-Oil or wax finish. Adjustable comb on skeet and trap models. **Features:** Competition model offered in Sporting, Skeet and Trap models. Newly designed receiver, top lever, safety/selector button.
Price: Sporting, From $8,650.00
Price: Skeet, From $8,650.00
Price: Trap, From $8,999.00

BLASER F3 SUPERSPORT
Gauge: 12 ga., 3 in. **Barrel:** 32 in. **Weight:** 9 lbs. **Stock:** Adjustable semi-custom, Turkish walnut wood grade: 4. **Features:** The latest addition to the F3 family is the F3 SuperSport. The perfect blend of overall weight, balance and weight distribution make the F3 SuperSport the ideal competitor. Briley Spectrum-5 chokes, free-floating barrels, adjustable barrel hanger system on o/u, chrome plated barrels full length, revolutionary ejector ball system, barrels finished in a powder coated nitride, selectable competition trigger.
Price: SuperSport, From $9,076.00
Price: Competition Sporting................................$7,951.00
Price: Superskeet..$9,076.00
Price: American Super Trap $9,530.00

Prices given are believed to be accurate at time of publication however, many factors affect retail pricing so exact prices are not possible.

74TH EDITION, 2020 ⟡ **467**

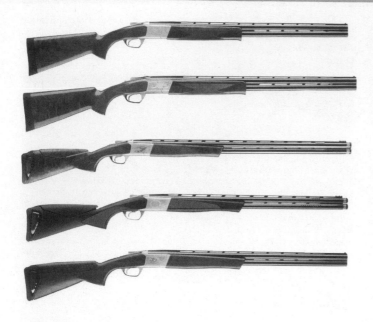

BROWNING CYNERGY

Gauges: .410 bore, 12 ga., 20 ga., 28 ga. **Barrels:** 26 in., 28 in., 30 in., 32 in. **Stocks:** Walnut or composite. **Sights:** White bead front most models; HiViz Pro-Comp sight on some models; mid bead. **Features:** Mono-Lock hinge, recoil-reducing interchangeable Inflex recoil pad, silver nitride receiver; striker-based trigger, ported barrel option. Imported from Japan by Browning.

Price: Field Grade Model, 12 ga.	**$1,910.00**
Price: CX composite	**$1,710.00**
Price: CX walnut stock	**$1,780.00**
Price: Field, small gauges	**$1,940.00**
Price: Ultimate Turkey, Mossy Oak Breakup camo	**$2,390.00**

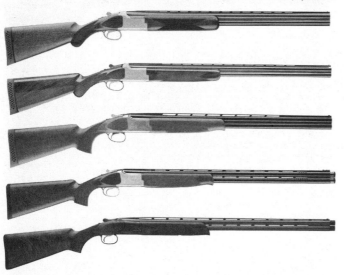

BROWNING CITORI SERIES

Gauges: 12 ga., 20 ga., 28 ga., .410 bore. **Barrels:** 26 in., 28 in. in 28 ga. and .410 bore. Offered with Invector choke tubes. All 12- and 20-ga. models have back-bored barrels and Invector Plus choke system. **Weights:** 6 lbs., 8 oz. (26 in. .410) to 7 lbs., 13 oz. (30 in. 12 ga.). **Length:** 43 in. overall (26-in. bbl.). **Stock:** Dense walnut, hand checkered, full pistol grip, beavertail fore-end. Field-type recoil pad on 12 ga. field guns and trap and skeet models. **Sights:** Medium-raised beads, German nickel silver. **Features:** Barrel selector integral with safety, automatic ejectors, three-piece takedown. Imported from Japan by Browning.

Price: White Lightning	**$2,670.00**
Price: Feather Lightning	**$2,870.00**
Price: Gran Lightning	**$3,300.00**

Price: Crossover (CX)	**$2,140.00**
Price: Crossover (CX) w/adjustable comb	**$2,560.00**
Price: Crossover (CXS)	**$2,140.00**
Price: Crossover Target (CXT)	**$2,260.00**
Price: Crossover Target (CXT) w/adjustable comb	**$2,660.00**
Price: Crossover (CXS)	**$2,190.00**
Price: Crossover (CXS) w/adjustable comb	**$2,590.00**
Price: Crossover (CXS Micro)	**$2,140.00**

BROWNING 725 CITORI

Gauges: 12 ga., 20 ga., 28 ga. or .410 bore. **Barrels:** 26 in., 28 in., 30 in. **Weights:** 5.7–7.6 lbs. **Length:** 43.75–50 in. **Stock:** Gloss oil finish, grade II/III walnut. **Features:** New receiver that is significantly lower in profile than other 12-gauge Citori models. Mechanical trigger, Vector Pro lengthened forcing cones, three Invector-DS choke tubes, silver nitride finish with high relief engraving.

Price: 725 Field (12 ga. or 20 ga.)	**$2,560.00**
Price: 725 Field (28 ga. or .410 bore)	**$2,590.00**
Price: 725 Field Grade VI	**$6,000.00**
Price: 725 Feather (12 ga. or 20 ga.)	**$2,670.00**
Price: 725 Sporting, From	**$3,270.00**
Price: 725 Sporting w/adjustable comb	**$3,600.00**
Price: 725 Sporting Golden Clays	**$5,440.00**
Price: 725 Trap, From	**$3,400.00**

CAESAR GUERINI

Gauges: 12 ga., 20 ga., 28 ga., also 20/28 gauge combo. Some models are available in .410 bore. **Barrels:** All standard lengths from 26–32 inches. **Weights:** 5.5–8.8 lbs. **Stock:** High-grade walnut with hand-rubbed oil finish. **Features:** A wide range of over/under models designed for the field, sporting clays, skeet and trap shooting. The models listed below are representative of some of the different models and variants. Many optional features are offered including high-grade wood and engraving, and extra sets of barrels. Made it Italy and imported by Caesar Guerini USA.

Price: Summit Sporting	**$3,995.00**
Price: Summit Limited	**$4,895.00**
Price: Summit Ascent	**$5,135.00**
Price: Tempio	**$4,325.00**
Price: Ellipse	**$4,650.00**
Price: Ellipse Curve	**$7,500.00**
Price: Ellipse EVO Sporting	**$6,950.00**
Price: Magnus, from	**$5,075.00**
Price: Maxum, from	**$6,825.00**
Price: Forum, from	**$11,500.00**
Price: Woodlander	**$3,795.00**
Price: Invictus Sporting, from	**$7,400.00**
Price: Maxum Trap	**$9,295.00**
Price: Maxum Sporting	**$7,150.00**

CONNECTICUT SHOTGUN A10 AMERICAN

Gauges: 12 ga., 20 ga., 28 ga., .410 bore. 2 3/4, 3 in. Sidelock design. **Barrels:** 26 in., 28 in., 30 in. or 32 in. with choice of fixed or interchangeable chokes. **Weight:** 6.3 lbs. **Stock:** Hand rubbed oil finish, hand checkered at 24 LPI. Black, English or Turkish walnut offered in numerous grades. Pistol or Prince of Wales grip, short or long tang. **Features:** Low-profile, shallow frame full sidelock. Single-selective trigger, automatic ejectors. Engraved models available. Made in the USA by Connecticut Shotgun Mfg. Co.

Price: 12 ga., From	**$9,999.00**
Price: Smaller ga., From	**$11,900.00**
Price: Sporting Clays	**$14,950.00**

Prices given are believed to be accurate at time of publication however, many factors affect retail pricing so exact prices are not possible.

CONNECTICUT SHOTGUN MODEL 21 O/U
Gauge: 20 ga., 3 in. **Barrels:** 26–32 in. chrome-lined, back-bored with extended forcing cones. **Weight:** 6.3 lbs. **Stock:** A Fancy (2X) American walnut, standard point checkering, choice of straight or pistol grip. Higher grade walnut is optional. **Features:** The over/under version of Conn. Shotgun's replica of the Winchester Model 21 side-by-side, built using the same machining, tooling, techniques and finishes. Low-profile shallow frame with blued receiver. Pigeon and Grand American grades are available. Made in the USA by Connecticut Shotgun Mfg. Co.
Price: From...$4,545.00

CZ REDHEAD PREMIER
Gauges: 12 ga., 20 ga., (3 in. chambers), 28 ga. (2 3/4 in.). **Barrel:** 28 in. **Weight:** 7.4 lbs. **Length:** NA. **Stock:** Round-knob pistol grip, Schnabel fore-end, Turkish walnut. **Features:** Single selective triggers and extractors (12 & 20 ga.), screw-in chokes (12 ga., 20 ga., 28 ga.) choked IC and Mod (.410), coin-finished receiver, multi chokes. From CZ-USA.
Price: Deluxe $953.00
Price: Mini (28 ga., .410 bore) $1,057.00
Price: Target $1,389.00

CZ SUPER SCROLL COMBO
Gauges: 20 and 28 combo. **Barrels:** 30 in. for both gauges with five choke tubes for each set. **Stock:** Grave V Turkish walnut with Schnabel fore-end, rounded grip. **Weight:** 6.7 pounds. **Features:** Ornate hand-engraved scrollwork on receiver, faux sideplates, trigger guard and mono-block. Comes in a custom-fitted aluminum case.
Price: $3,899.00

CZ UPLAND STERLING
Gauge: 12 ga., 3 in. **Barrels:** 28 in. with ventilated rib, fiber optic sight, five choke tubes. **Stock:** Turkish walnut with stippled gripping surfaces. **Weight:** 7.5 pounds. Lady Sterling has smaller stock dimensions.
Price: $999.00
Price: Lady Sterling $1,321.00

CZ WINGSHOOTER ELITE
Gauge: 12 ga., 20 ga., 2 3/4 in. **Barrel:** 28 in. flat ventilated rib. **Weight:** 6.3 lbs. **Length:** 45.5 in. **Stock:** Turkish walnut. **Features:** This colorful Over/Under shotgun has old world craftsmanship but with a new stylish look. This elegant hand engraved work of art is available in four gauges and its eye-catching engraving will stand alone in the field or range. 12- and 20-ga. models have auto ejectors, while the 28 ga. and .410 have extractors only. Heavily engraved scroll work with special side plate design, mechanical selective triggers, box Lock frame design, 18 LPI checkering, coil spring operated hammers, chrome lined, 5 interchangeable choke tubes and special engraved skeleton butt plate.
Price: 12 ga. or 20 ga. $1,059.00

FAUSTI CLASS ROUND BODY
Gauges: 16 ga., 20 ga., 28 ga.. **Barrels:** 28 or 30 in. **Weights:** 5.8–6.3 lbs. **Lengths:** 45.5–47.5 in. **Stock:** Turkish walnut Prince of Wales style with oil finish. Features include automatic ejectors, single selective trigger, laser-engraved receiver.
Price: From...$4,199.00

FAUSTI CALEDON
Gauges: 12 ga., 16 ga., 20 ga., 28 ga. and .410 bore. **Barrels:** 26 in., 28 in., 30 in. **Weights:** 5.8–7.3 lbs. **Stock:** Turkish walnut with oil finish, round pistol grip. **Features:** Automatic ejectors, single selective trigger, laser-engraved receiver. Coin finish receiver with gold inlays.

Price: 12 ga. or 20 ga. $1,999.00
Price: 16 ga., 28 ga., .410 bore $2,569.00

FAUSTI MAGNIFICENT
Gauges: 12 ga., 16 ga., 20 ga., 28 ga., .410 bore. **Barrels:** 26 in., 28 in., 30 in. **Stock:** AAA-Grade oil finished walnut. **Features:** Frame size scaled to gauge. Laser deep sculpted engraving coin finished receiver with gold inlays. Automatic ejectors, single selective trigger.
Price: 12 ga. $4,999.00
Price: Smaller ga. $5,559.00

FRANCHI INSTINCT SERIES
Gauges: 12 ga., 20 ga., 3 in. **Barrels:** 26 in., 28 in. **Weight:** 5.3–6.4 lbs. **Lengths:** 42.5–44.5 in. **Stock:** AA-grade satin walnut (LS), A-grade (L) with rounded pistol grip and recoil pad. Single trigger, automatic ejectors, tang safety, choke tubes. L model has steel receiver, SL has aluminum alloy receiver. Sporting model has higher grade wood, extended choke tubes. Catalyst model is designed for women, including stock dimensions for cast, drop, pitch, grip and length of pull.
Price: L $1,299.00
Price: SL $1,599.00
Price: Sporting $1,999.00
Price: Catalyst $1,469.00

KOLAR SPORTING CLAYS
Gauge: 12 ga., 2 3/4 in. **Barrels:** 30 in., 32 in., 34 in.; extended choke tubes. **Stock:** 14.625 in. x 2.5 in. x 1.875 in. x 1.375 in. French walnut. Four stock versions available. **Features:** Single selective trigger, detachable, adjustable for length; overbored barrels with long forcing cones; flat tramline rib; matte blue finish. Made in U.S. by Kolar.
Price: Standard $11,995.00
Price: Prestige $14,190.00
Price: Elite Gold $16,590.00
Price: Legend $17,090.00
Price: Select $22,590.00
Price: Custom..Price on request

KOLAR AAA COMPETITION TRAP
Gauge: 12 ga. Similar to the Sporting Clays gun except has 32 in. O/U 34 in. Unsingle or 30 in. O/U 34 in. Unsingle barrels as an over/under, unsingle, or combination set. Stock dimensions are 14.5 in. x 2.5 in. x 1.5 in., American or French walnut; step parallel rib standard. Contact maker for full listings. Made in USA by Kolar.
Price: Single bbl., From......................................$8,495.00
Price: O/U, From...$11,695.00

KOLAR AAA COMPETITION SKEET
Similar to the Sporting Clays gun except has 28 in. or 30 in. barrels with Kolarite AAA sub-gauge tubes; stock of American or French walnut with matte finish; flat tramline rib; under barrel adjustable for point of impact. Many options available. Contact maker for complete listing. Made in USA by Kolar.
Price: Max Lite, From......................................$13,995.00

KRIEGHOFF K-80 SPORTING CLAYS
Gauge: 12 ga. **Barrels:** 28 in., 30 in., 32 in., 34 in. with choke tubes. **Weight:** About 8 lbs. **Stock:** #3 Sporting stock designed for gun-down shooting. **Features:** Standard receiver with satin nickel finish and classic scroll engraving. Selective mechanical trigger adjustable for position. Choice of tapered flat or 8mm parallel flat barrel rib. Free-floating barrels. Aluminum case. Imported from Germany by Krieghoff International, Inc.
Price: Standard grade with five choke tubes, From......................$12,395.00

Prices given are believed to be accurate at time of publication however, many factors affect retail pricing so exact prices are not possible.

74ᵀᴴ EDITION, 2020 ◆ 469

SHOTGUNS Over/Unders

KRIEGHOFF K-80 SKEET
Gauge: 12 ga., 2 3/4 in. **Barrels:** 28 in., 30 in., 32 in., (skeet & skeet), optional choke tubes. **Weight:** About 7.75 lbs. **Stock:** American skeet or straight skeet stocks, with palm-swell grips. Walnut. **Features:** Satin gray receiver finish. Selective mechanical trigger adjustable for position. Choice of ventilated 8mm parallel flat rib or ventilated 8–12mm tapered flat rib. Introduced 1980. Imported from Germany by Krieghoff International, Inc.
Price: Standard, skeet chokes **$11,795.00**

KRIEGHOFF K-80 TRAP
Gauge: 12 ga., 2 3/4 in. **Barrels:** 30 in., 32 in. (Imp. Mod. & Full or choke tubes). **Weight:** About 8.5 lbs. **Stock:** Four stock dimensions or adjustable stock available; all have palm-swell grips. Checkered European walnut. **Features:** Satin nickel receiver. Selective mechanical trigger, adjustable for position. Ventilated step rib. Introduced 1980. Imported from Germany by Krieghoff International, Inc.
Price: K-80 O/U (30 in., 32 in., Imp. Mod. & Full), From **$11,795.00**
Price: K-80 Unsingle (32 in., 34 in., Full), standard, From **$13,995.00**
Price: K-80 Combo (two-barrel set), standard, From **$17,995.00**

KRIEGHOFF K-20
Similar to the K-80 except built on a 20-ga. frame. Designed for skeet, sporting clays and field use. Offered in 20 ga., 28 ga. and .410; **Barrels:** 28 in., 30 in. and 32 in. Imported from Germany by Krieghoff International Inc.
Price: K-20, 20 ga., From **$11,695.00**
Price: K-20, 28 ga., From **$12,395.00**
Price: K-20, .410, From **$12,395.00**

LEBEAU-COURALLY BOSS-VEREES
Gauges: 12 ga., 20 ga., 2 3/4 in. **Barrels:** 25–32 in. **Weight:** To customer specifications. **Stock:** Exhibition-quality French walnut. **Features:** Boss-type sidelock with automatic ejectors; single or double triggers; chopper lump barrels. A custom gun built to customer specifications. Imported from Belgium by Wm. Larkin Moore.
Price: From **$96,000.00**

MERKEL MODEL 2001EL O/U
Gauges: 12 ga., 20 ga., 3 in., 28 ga. 2-3/4 in. chambers. **Barrels:** 12 ga. 28 in.; 20 ga., 28 ga. 26.75 in. **Weight:** About 7 lbs. (12 ga.). **Stock:** Oil-finished walnut; English or pistol grip. **Features:** Self-cocking Blitz boxlock action with cocking indicators; Kersten double cross-bolt lock; silver-grayed receiver with engraved hunting scenes; coil spring ejectors; single selective or double triggers. Imported from Germany by Merkel USA.
Price: **$13,255.00**

MERKEL MODEL 2000CL
Similar to Model 2001EL except scroll-engraved casehardened receiver; 12 ga., 20 ga., 28 ga. Imported from Germany by Merkel USA.
Price: **$12,235.00**

MOSSBERG SILVER RESERVE II
Gauge: 12 ga., 3 in. **Barrels:** 28 in. with ventilated rib, choke tubes. **Stock:** Select black walnut with satin finish. **Sights:** Metal bead. Available with extractors or automatic ejectors. Also offered in Sport model with ported barrels with wide rib, fiber optic front and middle bead sights. Super Sport has extra wide high rib, optional adjustable comb.
Price: Field **$773.00**
Price: Sport **$950.00**
Price: Sport w/ejectors................................ **$1,070.00**
Price: Super Sport w/ejectors **$1,163.00**
Price: Super Sport w/ejectors, adj. comb **$1,273.00**

PERAZZI MX8/MX8 TRAP/SKEET
Gauge: 12 ga., 20 ga. 2 3/4 in. **Barrels:** Trap: 29.5 in. (Imp. Mod. & Extra Full), 31.5 in. (Full & Extra Full). Choke tubes optional. Skeet: 27.625 in. (skeet & skeet). **Weights:** About 8.5 lbs. (trap); 7 lbs., 15 oz. (skeet). **Stock:** Interchangeable and custom made to customer specs. **Features:** Has

detachable and interchangeable trigger group with flat V springs. Flat .4375 in. vent rib. Many options available. Imported from Italy by Perazzi USA, Inc.
Price: Trap, From **$11,760.00**
Price: Skeet, From **$11,760.00**

PERAZZI MX8
Gauge: 12 ga., 20 ga. 2 3/4 in. **Barrels:** 28.375 in. (Imp. Mod. & Extra Full), 29.50 in. (choke tubes). **Weight:** 7 lbs., 12 oz. **Stock:** Special specifications. **Features:** Has single selective trigger; flat .4375 in. x .3125 in. vent rib. Many options available. Imported from Italy by Perazzi USA, Inc.
Price: Standard, From **$11,760.00**
Price: Sporting, From **$11,760.00**
Price: SC3 Grade (variety of engraving patterns), From **$21,000.00**
Price: SCO Grade (more intricate engraving/inlays), From **$36,000.00**

PERAZZI MX12 HUNTING
Gauge: 12 ga., 2 3/4 in. **Barrels:** 26.75 in., 27.5 in., 28.375 in., 29.5 in. (Mod. & Full); choke tubes available in 27.625 in., 29.5 in. only (MX12C). **Weight:** 7 lbs., 4 oz. **Stock:** To customer specs; interchangeable. **Features:** Single selective trigger; coil springs used in action; Schnabel fore-end tip. Imported from Italy by Perazzi USA, Inc.
Price: From **$12,700.00**
Price: MX12C (with choke tubes), From **$12,700.00**

PERAZZI MX20 HUNTING
Gauges: 20 ga., 28 ga., .410 with 2 3/4 in. or 3 in. chambers. **Barrel:** 26 in. standard barrel choked Mod. & Full. **Weight:** 6 lbs., 6 oz. Features: Similar to the MX12 except 20 ga. frame size. Non-removable trigger group. Imported from Italy by Perazzi USA, Inc.
Price: From **$12,700.00**
Price: MX20C (with choke tubes), From **$13,700.00**

PERAZZI MX2000S
Gauges: 12 ga., 20 ga. **Barrels:** 29.5 in., 30.75 in., 31.5 in. with fixed I/M and Full chokes, or interchangeable. Competition model with features similar to MX8.
Price: **$13,200.00**

PERAZZI MX15 UNSINGLE TRAP
Gauge: 12 ga. **Barrel:** 34 in. with fixed Full choke. **Features:** Bottom single barrel with 6-notch adjustable rib, adjustable stock, drop-out trigger or interchangeable. Competition model with features similar to MX8.
Price: **$9,175.00**

PIOTTI BOSS
Gauges: 12 ga., 16 ga., 20 ga., 28 ga., .410 bore. **Barrels:** 26–32 in., chokes as specified. **Weight:** 6.5–8 lbs. **Stock:** Dimensions to customer specs. Best quality figured walnut. **Features:** Essentially a custom-made gun with many options. Introduced 1993. SportingModel is production model with many features of custom series Imported from Italy by Wm. Larkin Moore.
Price: From....................................... **$78,000.00**
Price: Sporting Model.................................... **$27,200.00**

RIZZINI AURUM
Gauges: 12 ga., 16 ga., 20 ga., 28 ga., .410 bore. **Barrels:** 26, 28, 29 and 30, set of five choke tubes. **Weight:** 6.25 to 6.75 lbs. (Aurum Light 5.5 to 6.5 lbs.) **Stock:** Select Turkish walnut with Prince of Wales grip, rounded fore-end. Hand checkered with polished oil finish. **Features:** Boxlock low-profile action, single selective trigger, automatic ejectors, engraved game scenes in relief, light coin finish with gold inlay. Aurum Light has alloy receiver.
Price: 12, 16, 20 ga.................................. **$3,425.00**
Price: 28, .410 bore.................................. **$3,625.00**
Price: Aurum Light 12, 16, 20 ga..................... **$3,700.00**
Price: Aurum Light 28, .410 bore..................... **$3,900.00**

RIZZINI ARTEMIS
Gauges: 12 ga., 16 ga., 20 ga., 28 ga., .410 bore. Same as Upland EL model

Prices given are believed to be accurate at time of publication however, many factors affect retail pricing so exact prices are not possible.

except dummy sideplates with extensive game scene engraving. Fancy European walnut stock. Fitted case. Introduced 1996. Imported from Italy by Fierce Products and by Wm. Larkin Moore & Co.
Price: From **$3,975.00**
Price: Artemis Light **$4,395.00**

RIZZINI FIERCE 1 COMPETITION
Gauges: 12 ga., 20 ga., 28 ga. **Barrels:** 28, 30 and 32 in. Five extended completion choke tubes. **Weight:** 6.6 to 8.1 lbs. **Stock:** Select Turkish walnut, hand checkered with polished oil finish. **Features:** Available in trap, skeet or sporting models. Adjustable stock and rib available. Boxlock low-profile action, single selective trigger, automatic ejectors, engraved game scenes in relief, light coin finish with gold inlay. Aurum Light has alloy receiver.
Price: From **$4,260.00**

SKB 590 FIELD
Gauges: 12 ga., 20 ga., 3 in. **Barrels:** 26 in., 28 in., 30 in. Three SKB Competition choke tubes (IC, M, F). Lengthened forcing cones. **Stock:** Oil finished walnut with Pachmayr recoil pad. **Weight:** 7.1–7.9 lbs. **Sights:** NA. **Features:** Boxlock action, bright blue finish with laser engraved receiver. Automatic ejectors, single trigger with selector switch incorporated in thumb-operated tang safety. Youth Model has 13 in. length of pull. Imported from Turkey by GU, Inc.
Price: **$1,300.00**

SKB 90TSS
Gauges: 12 ga., 20 ga., 2 3/4 in. **Barrels:** 28 in., 30 in., 32 in. Three SKB Competition choke tubes (SK, IC, M for Skeet and Sporting Models; IM, M, F for Trap). Lengthened forcing cones. **Stock:** Oil finished walnut with Pachmayr recoil pad. **Weight:** 7.1–7.9 lbs. **Sights:** Ventilated rib with target sights. **Features:** Boxlock action, bright blue finish with laser engraved receiver. Automatic ejectors, single trigger with selector switch incorporated in thumb-operated tang safety. Sporting and Trap models have adjustable comb and buttpad system. Imported from Turkey by GU, Inc.
Price: Skeet **$1,470.00**
Price: Sporting Clays, Trap **$1,800.00**

STEVENS MODEL 555
Gauges: 12 ga., 20 ga., 28 ga., .410; 2 3/4 and 3 in. **Barrels:** 26 in., 28 in. **Weights:** 5.5–6 lbs. **Features:** Five screw-in choke tubes with 12 ga., 20 ga., and 28 ga.; .410 has fixed M/IC chokes. Turkish walnut stock and Schnabel fore-end. Single selective mechanical trigger with extractors.
Price: **$705.00**
Price: Enhanced Model **$879.00**

STOEGER CONDOR
Gauge: 12 ga., 20 ga., 2 3/4 in., 3 in.; 16 ga., .410. **Barrels:** 22 in., 24 in., 26 in., 28 in., 30 in. **Weights:** 5.5–7.8 lbs. **Sights:** Brass bead. **Features:** IC, M, or F screw-in choke tubes with each gun. Oil finished hardwood with pistol grip and fore-end. Auto safety, single trigger, automatic extractors.
Price: From .... **$449.00–$669.00**
Price: Combo with 12 and 20 ga. barrel sets **$899.00**
Price: Competition **$669.00**

TRISTAR HUNTER EX
Gauge: 12 ga., 20 ga., 28 ga., .410. **Barrels:** 26 in., 28 in. **Weights:** 5.7 lbs. (.410); 6.0 lbs. (20, 28), 7.2–7.4 lbs. (12). Chrome-lined steel mono-block barrel, five Beretta-style choke tubes (SK, IC, M, IM, F). **Length:** NA. **Stock:** Walnut, cut checkering. 14.25 in. x 1.5 in. x 2.375 in. **Sights:** Brass front sight. **Features:** All have extractors, engraved receiver, sealed actions, self-adjusting locking bolts, single selective trigger, ventilated rib. 28 ga. and .410 built on true frames. Five-year warranty. Imported from Italy by Tristar Sporting Arms Ltd.
Price: From .... **$640.00–$670.00**

TRISTAR SETTER
Gauge: 12 ga., 20 ga., 3-in. **Barrels:** 28 in. (12 ga.), 26 in. (20 ga.) with ventilated rib, three Beretta-style choke tubes. **Weights:** 6.3–7.2 pounds.

Stock: High gloss wood. Single selective trigger, extractors.
Price: .... **$535.00-$565.00**
Price: Sporting Model .... **$824.00-$915.00**

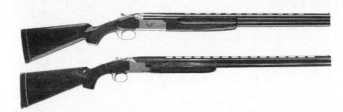

WINCHESTER MODEL 101
Gauge: 12 ga., 2 3/4 in., 3 in. **Barrels:** 28 in., 30 in., 32 in., ported, Invector Plus choke system. **Weights:** 7 lbs. 6 oz.–7 lbs. 12. oz. **Stock:** Checkered high-gloss grade II/III walnut stock, Pachmayr Decelerator sporting pad. **Features:** Chrome-plated chambers; back-bored barrels; tang barrel selector/safety; Signature extended choke tubes. Model 101 Field comes with solid brass bead front sight, three tubes, engraved receiver. Model 101 Sporting has adjustable trigger, 10mm runway rib, white mid-bead, Tru-Glo front sight, 30 in. and 32 in. barrels. Model 101 Pigeon Grade Trap has 10mm steel runway rib, mid-bead sight, interchangeable fiber-optic front sight, porting and vented side ribs, adjustable trigger shoe, fixed raised comb or adjustable comb, Grade III/IV walnut, 30 in. or 32 in. barrels, molded ABS hard case. Reintroduced 2008. Made in Belgium by FN. Winchester 150th Anniversary Commemorative model has grade IV/V stock, deep relief scrolling on a silver nitride finish receiver.
Price: Field **$1,900.00**
Price: Sporting **$2,380.00**
Price: Pigeon Grade Trap **$2,520.00**
Price: Pigeon Grade Trap w/adj. comb **$2,680.00**

ARRIETA SIDELOCK DOUBLE

Gauges: 12 ga., 16 ga., 20 ga., 28 ga., .410 bore. **Barrels:** Length and chokes to customer specs. **Weight:** To customer specs. **Stock:** To customer specs. Straight English with checkered butt (standard), or pistol grip. Select European walnut with oil finish. **Features:** Essentially custom gun with myriad options. H&H pattern hand-detachable sidelocks, selective automatic ejectors, double triggers (hinged front) standard. Some have self-opening action. Finish and engraving to customer specs. Imported from Spain by Quality Arms, Wm. Larking Moore and others.
Price: Model 557 .... **$6,970.00**
Price: Model 570 .... **$7,350.00**
Price: Model 578 .... **$12,200.00**
Price: Model 600 Imperial **$14,125.00**
Price: Model 803 .... **$17,000.00**
Price: Model 931 .... **$40,000.00**

AYA MODEL 4/53

Gauges: 12 ga., 16 ga., 20 ga., 28 ga., 410 bore. **Barrels:** 26 in., 27 in., 28 in., 30 in. **Weights:** To customer specifications. **Length:** To customer specifications. **Features:** Hammerless boxlock action; double triggers; light scroll engraving; automatic safety; straight grip oil finished walnut stock; checkered butt. Made in Spain. Imported by New England Custom Gun Service.
Price: **$5,500.00**
Price: No. 2 .... **$7,000.00**
Price: No. 2 Rounded Action **$7,400.00**

AYA MODEL ADARRA

Gauges: 12 ga., 16 ga., 20 ga., 28 ga., 410 bore. **Barrel:** 26 in., 28 in. **Weight:** Approx. 6.7 lbs. **Features:** Hammerless boxlock action; double triggers; light scroll engraving; automatic safety; straight grip oil finished walnut stock; checkered butt. Made in Spain. Imported by New England Custom Gun Service.
Price: **$6,000.00**

BARRETT SOVEREIGN BELTRAMI

Gauges: 12 ga., 20 ga. or 28 ga. 3 in. (2 3/4 for 28 ga.). **Barrels:** 26 in., 28 in. or 30 in. **Stock:** Checkered grade AAA Turkish walnut with straight grip. **Features:** Boxlock design, ornamental sideplates, coin-finished receiver. Receiver scaled to individual gauges. Imported from Italy by Barrett Firearms.
Price: 12 ga. or 20 ga. **$6,150.00**
Price: 28 ga. **$6,550.00**

BERETTA 486 PARALELLO

Gauges: 12 ga., 20 ga., 3 in., or 28 ga. 2 3/4 in. **Barrels:** 26 in., 28 in., 30 in. **Weight:** 7.1 lbs. **Stock:** English-style straight grip, splinter fore-end. Select European walnut, checkered, oil finish. **Features:** Round action, Optima-Choke Tubes. Automatic ejection or mechanical extraction. Firing-pin block safety, manual or automatic, open top-lever safety. Imported from Italy by Beretta USA
Price: From.. **$5,350.00**

CIMARRON 1878 COACH GUN

Gauge: 12 ga. 3 in. **Barrels:** 20 in., 26 in. **Weights:** 8–9 lbs. **Stock:** Hardwood. External hammers, double triggers. **Finish:** Blue, Cimarron "USA," Cimarron "Original."
Price: Blue .... **$597.00 (20 in.)–$623.00 (26 in.)**

CIMARRON DOC HOLLIDAY MODEL

Gauge: 12 ga. **Barrels:** 20 in., cylinder bore. **Stock:** Hardwood with rounded pistol grip. **Features:** Double triggers, hammers, false sideplates.
Price: **$1,581.00**

CONNECTICUT SHOTGUN MANUFACTURING CO. RBL

Gauges: 12 ga., 16 ga., 20 ga.. **Barrels:** 26 in., 28 in., 30 in., 32 in. **Weight:** NA. **Length:** NA. **Stock:** NA. **Features:** Round-action SxS shotguns made in the USA. Scaled frames, five TruLock choke tubes. Deluxe fancy grade walnut buttstock and fore-end. Quick Change recoil pad in two lengths.

Various dimensions and options available depending on gauge.
Price: 12 ga. **$3,795.00**
Price: 16 ga. **$3,795.00**
Price: 20 ga. Special Custom Model **$7,995.00**

CONNECTICUT SHOTGUN MANUFACTURING CO. MODEL 21

Gauges: 12 ga., 16 ga., 20 ga., 28 ga., .410 bore. **Features:** A faithful re-creation of the famous Winchester Model 21. Many options and upgrades are available. Each frame is machined from specially produced proof steel. The 28 ga. and .410 guns are available on the standard frame or on a newly engineered small frame. These are custom guns and are made to order to the buyer's individual specifications, wood, stock dimensions, barrel lengths, chokes, finishes and engraving.
Price: 12 ga., 16 ga. or 20 ga., From **$15,000.00**
Price: 28 ga. or .410, From **$18,000.00**

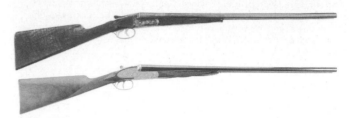

CZ SHARP-TAIL

Gauges: 12 ga., 20 ga., 28 ga., .410. (5 screw-in chokes in 12 and 20 ga. and fixed chokes in IC and Mod in .410). **Barrels:** 26 in. or 28 in. **Weight:** 6.5 lbs. **Stock:** Hand-checkered Turkish walnut with straight English-style grip and single selective trigger.
Price: Sharp-Tail **$1,022.00**
Price: Sharp-Tail Target **$1,298.00**

CZ HAMMER COACH

Gauge: 12 ga., 3 in. **Barrel:** 20 in. **Weight:** 6.7 lbs. **Features:** Following in the tradition of the guns used by the stagecoach guards of the 1880s, this cowboy gun features double triggers, 19th-century color casehardening and fully functional external hammers.
Price: **$922.00**
Price: Classic model w/30-in. bbls. **$963.00**

EMF MODEL 1878 WYATT EARP

Gauge: 12. **Barrel:** 20 in.. **Weight:** 8 lbs. **Length:** 37 in. overall. **Stock:** Smooth walnut with steel butt place. **Sights:** Large brass bead. **Features:** Colt-style exposed hammers rebounding type; blued receiver and barrels; cylinder bore. Based on design of Colt Model 1878 shotgun. Made in Italy by Pedersoli.
Price: **$1,590.00**
Price: Hartford Coach Model................................... **$1,150.00**

FAUSTI DEA SERIES

Gauges: 12 ga., 16 ga., 20 ga., 28 ga., .410. **Barrels:** 26 in., 28 in., 30 in. **Weight:** 6–6.8 lbs. **Stock:** AAA walnut, oil finished. Straight grip, checkered butt, classic fore-end. **Features:** Automatic ejectors, single non-selective trigger. Duetto model is in 28 ga. with extra set of .410 barrels. Made in Italy and imported by Fausti, USA.
Price: 12 ga. or 20 ga. **$3,718.00**
Price: 16 ga., 28 ga., .410.. **$4,990.00**
Price: Duetto **$5,790.00**

FOX, A.H.

Gauges: 16 ga., 20 ga., 28 ga., .410. **Barrels:** Length and chokes to customer specifications. Rust-blued Chromox or Krupp steel. **Weight:** 5.5–6.75 lbs. **Stock:** Dimensions to customer specifications. Hand-checkered Turkish Circassian walnut with hand-rubbed oil finish. Straight, semi or full pistol grip; splinter, Schnabel or beavertail fore-end; traditional pad, hard rubber buttplate or skeleton butt. **Features:** Boxlock action with automatic ejectors; double or Fox single selective trigger. Scalloped, rebated and color case-hardened receiver; hand finished and hand-engraved. Grades differ in engraving, inlays, grade of wood, amount of hand finishing. Introduced 1993. Made in U.S. by Connecticut Shotgun Mfg.
Price: CE Grade **$19,500.00**
Price: XE Grade **$22,000.00**

Price: DE Grade...$25,000.00
Price: FE Grade...$30,000.00
Price: 28 ga./.410 CE Grade $21,500.00
Price: 28 ga./.410 XE Grade $24,000.00
Price: 28 ga./.410 DE Grade $27,000.00
Price: 28 ga./.410 FE Grade $32,000.00

GARBI MODEL 101

Gauges: 12 ga., 16 ga., 20 ga., 28 ga. **Barrels:** 26 in., 28 in., choked to customer specs. **Weights:** 5.5–7.5 lbs. **Stock:** 14.5 in. x 2.25 in. x 1.5 in. Select European walnut. Straight grip, checkered butt, classic fore-end. **Features:** Sidelock action, automatic ejectors, double triggers standard. Color casehardened action, coin finish optional. Single trigger; beavertail fore-end, etc. optional. Hand engraved with scroll engraving. Imported from Spain by Wm. Larkin Moore.
Price: From...$17,000.00

GARBI MODEL 103A, 103B

Similar to the Garbi Model 101 except has Purdey-type fine scroll and rosette engraving. Model 103B has nickel-chrome steel barrels, H&H-type easy opening mechanism; other mechanical details remain the same. Imported from Spain by Wm. Larkin Moore.
Price: Model 103A, From......................$23,000.00
Price: Model 103B, From......................$26,500.00

GARBI MODEL 200

Similar to the Garbi Model 101 except has heavy-duty locks, magnum proofed. Very fine Continental-style floral and scroll engraving, well figured walnut stock. Other mechanical features remain the same. Imported from Spain by Wm. Larkin Moore.
Price: $27,000.00

MERKEL MODEL 147SL

H&H style sidelock action with cocking indicators, ejectors. Silver-grayed receiver and sideplates have arabesque engraving, fine hunting scene engraving. Limited edition. Imported from Germany by Merkel USA.
Price: Model 147SL $13,255.00

MERKEL MODEL 280EL, 360EL

Similar to Model 47E except smaller frame. Greener crossbolt with double under-barrel locking lugs, fine engraved hunting scenes on silver-grayed receiver, luxury-grade wood, Anson and Deeley boxlock action. H&H ejectors, single-selective or double triggers. Introduced 2000. Imported from Germany by Merkel USA.
Price: Model 280EL (28 ga., 28 in. barrel, Imp. Cyl.
    and Mod. chokes) $8,870.00
Price: Model 360EL (.410, 28 in. barrel, Mod. and Full chokes).......$8,870.00

MERKEL MODEL 280SL AND 360SL

Similar to Model 280EL and 360EL except has sidelock action, double triggers, English-style arabesque engraving. Introduced 2000. Imported from Germany by Merkel USA.
Price: Model 280SL (28 ga., 28 in. barrel, Imp. Cyl.
    and Mod. chokes) $13,255.00
Price: Model 360SL (.410, 28 in. barrel, Mod. and Full chokes) $13,255.00

MERKEL MODEL 1620

Gauge: 16 ga. **Features:** Greener crossbolt with double under-barrel locking lugs, scroll-engraved casehardened receiver, Anson and Deeley boxlock action, Holland & Holland ejectors, English-style stock, single selective or double triggers, or pistol grip stock with single selective trigger. Imported from Germany by Merkel USA.
Price: Model 1620EL $8,870.00
Price: Model 1620EL Combo; 16- and 20-ga. two-barrel set $13,255.00

MERKEL MODEL 40E

Gauges: 12 ga., 20 ga. **Barrels:** 28 in. (12 ga.), 26.75 in. (20 ga.). **Weight:** 6.2 lbs. **Features:** Anson & Deeley locks, Greener-style crossbolt, automatic ejectors, choice of double or single trigger, blue finish, checkered walnut stock with cheekpiece.
Price: $4,795.00

PIOTTI KING NO. 1

Gauges: 12 ga., 16 ga., 20 ga., 28 ga., .410. **Barrels:** 25–30 in. (12 ga.), 25–28 in. (16 ga., 20 ga., 28 ga., .410). To customer specs. Chokes as specified. **Weight:** 6.5–8 lbs. (12 ga. to customer specs.). **Stock:** Dimensions to customer specs.

Finely figured walnut; straight grip with checkered butt with classic splinter fore-end and hand-rubbed oil finish standard. Pistol grip, beavertail fore-end. **Features:** Holland & Holland pattern sidelock action, automatic ejectors. Double trigger; non-selective single trigger optional. Coin finish standard; color case-hardened optional. Top rib; level, file-cut; concave, ventilated optional. Very fine, full coverage scroll engraving with small floral bouquets. Imported from Italy by Wm. Larkin Moore.
Price: From...$42,800.00

PIOTTI LUNIK SIDE-BY-SIDE SHOTGUN

Similar to the Piotti King No. 1 in overall quality. Has Renaissance-style large scroll engraving in relief. Best quality Holland & Holland-pattern sidelock ejector double with chopper lump (demi-bloc) barrels. Other mechanical specifications remain the same. Imported from Italy by Wm. Larkin Moore.
Price: From... $46,000.00

PIOTTI PIUMA

Gauges: 12 ga., 16 ga., 20 ga., 28 ga., .410. **Barrels:** 25–30 in. (12 ga.), 25–28 in. (16 ga., 20 ga., 28 ga., .410). **Weights:** 5.5–6.25 lbs. (20 ga.). **Stock:** Dimensions to customer specs. Straight grip stock with walnut checkered butt, classic splinter fore-end, hand-rubbed oil finish are standard; pistol grip, beavertail fore-end, satin luster finish optional. **Features:** Anson & Deeley boxlock ejector double with chopper lump barrels. Level, file-cut rib, light scroll and rosette engraving, scalloped frame. Double triggers; single non-selective optional. Coin finish standard, color case-hardened optional. Imported from Italy by Wm. Larkin Moore.
Price: From..$25,000.00

SAVAGE FOX A-GRADE

Gauge: 12 or 20. **Barrels:** 26 or 28 in. with solid rib and IC, M, and F choke tubes. **Features:** Straight-grip American walnut stock with splinter fore-end, oil finish and cut checkering. Anson & Deeley-style boxlock action, Holland & Holland-style ejectors, double triggers and brass bead sight. A re-creation of the famous Fox double gun, presented by Savage and made at the Connecticut Shotgun Manufacturing Co. plant.
Price: From...$5,375.00

SKB 200 SERIES

Gauges: 12 ga., 20 ga., .410, 3 in.; 28 ga., 2 3/4 in. **Barrels:** 26 in., 28 in. Five choke tubes provided (F, IM, M, IC, SK). **Stock:** Hand checkered and oil finished Turkish walnut. Prince of Wales grip and beavertail fore-end. **Weight:** 6–7 lbs. **Sights:** Brass bead. **Features:** Boxlock with platform lump barrel design. Polished bright blue finish with charcoal color case hardening on receiver. Manual safety, automatic ejectors, single selective trigger. 200 HR target model has high ventilated rib, full pistol grip. 250 model has decorative color casehardened sideplates. Imported from Turkey by GU, Inc.
Price: 12 ga., 20 ga...$2,100.00
Price: 28 ga., .410...$2,250.00
Price: 200 28 ga./.410 Combo $3,300.00
Price: 200 HR 12 ga., 20 ga.............................$2,500.00
Price: 200 HR 28 ga., .410..............................$2,625.00
Price: 200 HR 28 ga./.410 combo $3,600.00
Price: 250 12 ga., 20 ga..................................$2,600.00
Price: 250 28 ga., .410......................................$2,725.00
Price: 250 28 ga./.410 Combo..........................$3,700.00

SKB 7000SL SIDELOCK

Gauges: 12 ga., 20 ga. **Barrels:** 28 in., 30 in. Five choke tubes provided (F, IM, M, IC, SK). **Stock:** Premium Turkish walnut with hand-rubbed oil finish, fine-line hand checkering, Prince of Wales grip and beavertail fore-end. **Weights:** 6–7 lbs. **Sights:** Brass bead. **Features:** Sidelock design with Holland & Holland style seven-pin removable locks with safety sears. Bison Bone Charcoal casehardening, hand engraved sculpted sidelock receiver. Manual safety, automatic ejectors, single selective trigger. Available by special order only. Imported from Turkey by GU, Inc.
Price: From...$6,500.00

STOEGER UPLANDER

Gauges: 12 ga., 20 ga., .410, 3 in.; 28 ga., 2 3/4. **Barrels:** 22 in., 24 in., 26 in., 28 in. **Weights:** 6.5–7.3 lbs. **Sights:** Brass bead. **Features:** Double trigger, IC & M choke tubes included with gun. Other choke tubes available. Tang auto safety, extractors, black plastic buttplate. Imported by Benelli USA.

Price: Standard $449.99
Price: Supreme (single trigger, AA-grade wood) $549.99
Price: Longfowler (12 ga., 30-in. bbl.) $449.99
Price: Home Defense (20 or 12 ga., 20-in. bbl., tactical sights) $499.00
Price: Double Defense (20 ga.) fiber-optic sight, accessory rail $499.00

STOEGER COACH GUN

Gauges: 12 ga., 20 ga., 2 3/4 in., 3 in. **Barrel:** 20 in. **Weight:** 6.5 lbs. **Stock:** Brown hardwood, classic beavertail fore-end. **Sights:** Brass bead. **Features:** Double or single trigger, IC & M choke tubes included, others available. Tang auto safety, extractors, black plastic buttplate. Imported by Benelli USA.

Price: From...$549.00

BROWNING BT-99 TRAP
Gauge: 12 ga. **Barrels:** 30 in., 32 in., 34 in. **Stock:** Walnut; standard or adjustable. **Weights:** 7 lbs. 11 oz.–9 lbs. **Features:** Back-bored single barrel; interchangeable chokes; beavertail forearm; extractor only; high rib.
Price: BT-99 w/conventional comb, 32- or 34-in. barrel.................**$1,470.00**
Price: BT-99 w/adjustable comb, 32- or 34-in. barrel......................**$1,840.00**
Price: BT-99 Max High Grade w/adjustable comb, 32- or
    34-in. barrel..**$5,340.00**

HENRY .410 LEVER-ACTION SHOTGUN
Gauge: .410, 2 1/2 in. **Capacity:** 5. **Barrels:** 20 or 24 in. with either no choke (20 in.) or full choke (24 in.). **Stock:** American walnut. **Sights:** Gold bead front only. **Finish:** Blued. Introduced in 2017. **Features:** Design is based on the Henry .45-70 rifle.
Price: 20-in. bbl..**$893.00**
Price: 24-in. bbl..**$947.00**

HENRY SINGLE-SHOT SHOTGUN
Gauges: 12 ga., 20 ga. or .410 bore, 3 1/2 in. (12 ga.), 3 in. (20 ga. and 410). **Barrels:** 26 or 28 in. with either modified choke tube (12 ga., 20 ga., compatible with Rem-Choke tubes) or fixed full choke (.410). **Stock:** American walnut, straight or pistol grip. **Sights:** Gold bead front only. **Weight:** 6.33 lbs. **Finish:** Blued or brass receiver. **Features:** Break-open single-shot design. Introduced in 2017.
Price: **$448.00**
Price: Brass receiver, straight grip..**$576.00**

KRIEGHOFF K-80 SINGLE BARREL TRAP GUN
Gauge: 12 ga., 2 3/4 in. **Barrel:** 32 in., 34 in. Unsingle. Fixed Full or choke tubes. **Weight:** About 8.75 lbs. **Stock:** Four stock dimensions or adjustable stock available. All hand-checkered European walnut. **Features:** Satin nickel finish. Selective mechanical trigger adjustable for finger position. Tapered step vent rib. Adjustable point of impact.
Price: Standard Grade Full Unsingle, From **$12,995.00**

KRIEGHOFF KX-6 SPECIAL TRAP GUN
Gauge: 12 ga., 2 3/4 in. **Barrel:** 32 in., 34 in.; choke tubes. **Weight:** About 8.5 lbs. **Stock:** Factory adjustable stock. European walnut. **Features:** Ventilated tapered step rib. Adjustable position trigger, optional release trigger. Fully adjustable rib. Satin gray electroless nickel receiver. Fitted aluminum case. Imported from Germany by Krieghoff International, Inc.
Price: **$5,995.00**

LJUTIC MONO GUN SINGLE BARREL
Gauge: 12 ga. **Barrel:** 34 in., choked to customer specs; hollow-milled rib, 35.5-in. sight plane. **Weight:** Approx. 9 lbs. **Stock:** To customer specs. Oil finish, hand checkered. **Features:** Custom gun. Pull or release trigger; removable trigger guard contains trigger and hammer mechanism; Ljutic pushbutton opener on front of trigger guard. From Ljutic Industries.
Price: Std., med. or Olympic rib, custom bbls., fixed choke. **$7,495.00**
Price: Stainless steel mono gun..**$8,495.00**

LJUTIC LTX PRO 3 DELUXE MONO GUN
Deluxe, lightweight version of the Mono gun with high-quality wood, upgrade checkering, special rib height, screw-in chokes, ported and cased.
Price: **$8,995.00**
Price: Stainless steel model...**$9,995.00**

ROSSI CIRCUIT JUDGE
Revolving shotgun chambered in .410 (2 1/2- or 3-in./.45 Colt. Based on Taurus Judge handgun. Features include 18.5-in. barrel; fiber-optic front sight; 5-round cylinder; hardwood Monte Carlo stock.
Price: From...**$689.00**

TAR-HUNT RSG-12 PROFESSIONAL RIFLED SLUG GUN
Gauge: 12 ga., 2 3/4 in., 3 in., **Capacity:** 1-round magazine. **Barrel:** 23 in., fully rifled with muzzle brake. **Weight:** 7.75 lbs. **Length:** 41.5 in. overall. **Stock:** Matte black McMillan fiberglass with Pachmayr Decelerator pad. **Sights:** None furnished; comes with Leupold windage or Weaver bases. **Features:** Uses rifle-style action with two locking lugs; two-position safety; Shaw barrel; single-stage, trigger; muzzle brake. Many options available. All models have area-controlled feed action. Introduced 1991. Made in U.S. by Tar-Hunt Custom Rifles, Inc.
Price: 12 ga. Professional model **$3,495.00**
Price: Left-hand model **$3,625.00**

TAR-HUNT RSG-20 MOUNTAINEER SLUG GUN
Similar to the RSG-12 Professional except chambered for 20 ga. (2 3/4 in. and 3 in. shells); 23 in. Shaw rifled barrel, with muzzle brake; two-lug bolt; one-shot blind magazine; matte black finish; McMillan fiberglass stock with Pachmayr Decelerator pad; receiver drilled and tapped for Rem. 700 bases. Right- or left-hand versions. Weighs 6.5 lbs. Introduced 1997. Made in USA by Tar-Hunt Custom Rifles, Inc.
Price: **$3,495.00**

BENELLI M2 TACTICAL

Gauge: 12 ga., 2 3/4 in., 3 in. **Capacity:** 5-round magazine. **Barrel:** 18.5 in. IC, M, F choke tubes. **Weight:** 6.7 lbs. **Length:** 39.75 in. overall. **Stock:** Black polymer. Standard or pistol grip. **Sights:** Rifle type ghost ring system, tritium night sights optional. **Features:** Semi-auto inertia recoil action. Cross-bolt safety; bolt release button; matte-finish metal. Introduced 1993. Imported from Italy by Benelli USA.
Price: From.. **$1,239.00–$1,359.00**

BENELLI M3 TACTICAL

Gauge: 12 ga., 3 in. **Barrel:** 20 in. **Stock:** Black synthetic w/pistol grip. **Sights:** Ghost ring rear, ramp front. Convertible dual-action operation (semi-auto or pump).
Price: **$1,599.00**

BENELLI M4 TACTICAL

Gauge: 12 ga., 3 in. **Barrel:** 18.5 in. **Weight:** 7.8 lbs. **Length:** 40 in. overall. **Stock:** Synthetic. **Sights:** Ghost Ring rear, fixed blade front. **Features:** Auto-regulating gas-operated (ARGO) action, choke tube, Picatinny rail, standard and collapsible stocks available, optional LE tactical gun case. Introduced 2006.
Price: From... **$1,999.00**
Price: M4 H20 Cerakote Finish **$2,269.00**

BENELLI NOVA TACTICAL

Gauge: 12 ga., 3 in. **Barrel:** 18.5 in. **Stock:** Black synthetic standard or pistol grip. **Sights:** Ghost ring rear, ramp front. Pump action.
Price: From... **$439.00**

BENELLI VINCI TACTICAL

Gauge: 12 ga., 3 in. **Barrel:** 18.5 in. Semi-auto operation. **Stock:** Black synthetic. **Sights:** Ghost ring rear, ramp front.
Price: **$1,349.00**
Price: ComforTech stock **$1,469.00**

KEL-TEC KSG BULL-PUP TWIN-TUBE

Gauge: 12 ga. **Capacity:** 13+1. **Barrel:** 18.5 in. **Overall Length:** 26.1 in. **Weight:** 8.5 lbs. (loaded). **Features:** Pump-action shotgun with two magazine tubes. The shotgun bears a resemblance to the South African designed Neostead pump-action gun. The operator is able to move a switch located near the top of the grip to select the right or left tube, or move the switch to the center to eject a shell without chambering another round. Optional accessories include a factory installed Picatinny rail with flip-up sights and a pistol grip. KSG-25 has 30-in. barrel and 20-round capacity magazine tubes.
Price: **$990.00**
Price: KSG-25 .... **$1400.00**

MOSSBERG MODEL 500 SPECIAL PURPOSE

Gauges: 12 ga., 20 ga., .410, 3 in. **Barrels:** 18.5 in., 20 in. (Cyl.). **Weight:** 7 lbs. **Stock:** Walnut-finished hardwood or black synthetic. **Sights:** Metal bead front. **Features:** Slide-action operation. Available in 6- or 8-round models. Top-mounted safety, double action slide bars, swivel studs, rubber recoil pad. Blue, Parkerized, Marinecote finishes. Mossberg Cablelock included. The HS410 Home Security model chambered for .410 with 3 in. chamber; has pistol grip fore-end, thick recoil pad, muzzle brake and has special spreader choke on the 18.5-in. barrel. Overall length is 37.5 in. Blued finish; synthetic field stock. Mossberg Cablelock and video included. Mariner model has Marinecote metal

finish to resist rust and corrosion. Synthetic field stock; pistol grip kit included. 500 Tactical 6-shot has black synthetic tactical stock. Introduced 1990.
Price: 500 Mariner... **$636.00**
Price: HS410 Home Security... **$477.00**
Price: Home Security 20 ga. **$631.00**
Price: FLEX Tactical.. **$672.00**
Price: 500 Chainsaw pistol grip only; removable top handle **$547.00**
Price: JIC (Just In Case)... **$500.00**
Price: Thunder Ranch **$553.00**

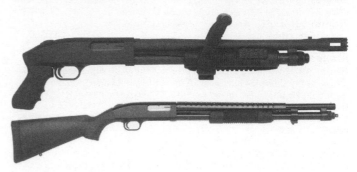

MOSSBERG MODEL 590 SPECIAL PURPOSE

Gauges: 12 ga., 20 ga., .410 3 in. **Capacity:** 9-round magazine. **Barrel:** 20 in. (Cyl.). **Weight:** 7.25 lbs. **Stock:** Synthetic field or Speedfeed. **Sights:** Metal bead front or Ghost Ring. **Features:** Slide action. Top-mounted safety, double slide action bars. Comes with heat shield, bayonet lug, swivel studs, rubber recoil pad. Blue, Parkerized or Marinecote finish. Shockwave has 14-inch heavy walled barrel, Raptor pistol grip, wrapped fore-end and is fully BATFE compliant. Magpul model has Magpul SGA stock with adjustable comb and length of pull. Mossberg Cablelock included. From Mossberg.
Price: From... **$559.00**
Price: Flex Tactical **$672.00**
Price: Tactical Tri-Rail Adjustable **$879.00**
Price: Mariner... **$756.00**
Price: Shockwave... **$455.00-$721.00**
Price: MagPul 9-shot **$836.00**

MOSSBERG 930 SPECIAL PURPOSE SERIES

Gauge: 12 ga., 3 in. **Barrel:** 18.5-28 in. flat ventilated rib. **Weight:** 7.3 lbs. **Length:** 49 in.. **Stock:** Composite stock with close radius pistol grip; Speed Lock forearm; textured gripping surfaces; shim adjustable for length of pull, cast and drop; Mossy Oak Bottomland camo finish; Dura-Touch Armor Coating. **Features:** 930 Special Purpose shotguns feature a self-regulating gas system that vents excess gas to aid in recoil reduction and eliminate stress on critical components. All 930 autoloaders chamber both 2 3/4 inch and 3-in. 12-ga. shotshells with ease — from target loads, to non-toxic magnum loads, to the latest sabot slug ammo. Magazine capacity is 7+1 on models with extended magazine tube, 4+1 on models without. To complete the package, each Mossberg 930 includes a set of specially designed spacers for quick adjustment of the horizontal and vertical angle of the stock, bringing a custom-feel fit to every shooter. All 930 Special Purpose models feature a drilled and tapped receiver, factory-ready for Picatinny rail, scope base or optics installation. 930 SPX models conveniently come with a factory-mounted Picatinny rail and LPA/M16-Style Ghost Ring combination sight right out of the box. Other sighting options include a basic front bead, or white-dot front sights. Mossberg 930 Special Purpose shotguns are available in a variety of configurations; 5-round tactical barrel, 5-round with muzzle brake, 8-round pistol-grip, and even a 5-round security/field combo.
Price: Tactical 5-Round.. **$612.00**
Price: Home Security **$662.00**
Price: Standard Stock... **$787.00**
Price: Pistol Grip 8-Round..**$1,046.00**
Price: 5-Round Combo w/extra 18.5-in. barrel **$693.00**

Prices given are believed to be accurate at time of publication however, many factors affect retail pricing so exact prices are not possible.

REMINGTON 870 DM SERIES
Gauge: 12 ga. (2 3/4 in., 3 in. interchangeably) **Barrel:** 18.5-in. cylinder bore. Detachable 6-round magazine. **Stock:** Hardwood or black synthetic with textured gripping surfaces. Tac-14 DM model features short pistol grip buttstock and 14-in. barrel.
Price: **$529.00**

REMINGTON MODEL 870 PUMP TACTICAL SHOTGUNS
Gauges: 12 ga., 2 3/4 or 3 in. **Barrels:** 18 in., 20 in., 22 in. (Cyl or IC). **Weight:** 7.5–7.75 lbs. **Length:** 38.5–42.5 in. overall. **Stock:** Black synthetic, synthetic Speedfeed IV full pistol-grip stock, or Knoxx Industries SpecOps stock w/ recoil-absorbing spring-loaded cam and adjustable length of pull (12 in. to 16 in., 870 only). **Sights:** Front post w/dot. **Features:** R3 recoil pads, LimbSaver technology to reduce felt recoil, 2-, 3- or 4-round extensions based on barrel length; matte-olive-drab barrels and receivers. Standard synthetic-stocked version is equipped with 22-in. barrel and four-round extension. Introduced 2006. From Remington Arms Co.
Price: 870 Express Tactical Knoxx 20 ga. **$555.00**
Price: 870 Express Magpul **$898.00**
Price: 870 Special Purpose Marine (nickel)....................... **$841.00**

REMINGTON 870 EXPRESS TACTICAL
Gauge: 12 ga., 2 3/4 and 3 in. **Features:** Pump-action shotgun; 18.5-in. barrel; extended ported Tactical RemChoke; SpeedFeed IV pistol-grip stock with SuperCell recoil pad; fully adjustable XS Ghost Ring Sight rail with removable white bead front sight; 7-round capacity with factory-installed 2-shot extension; drilled and tapped receiver; sling swivel stud.
Price: From.. **$600.00**

REMINGTON 887 NITRO MAG TACTICAL
Gauge: 12 ga., 2 3/4 to 3 1/2 in. **Features:** Pump-action shotgun,18.5-in. barrel with ported, extended tactical RemChoke; 2-shot magazine extension; barrel clamp with integral Picatinny rails; ArmorLokt coating; synthetic stock and fore-end with specially contour grip panels.
Price: **$534.00**

TACTICAL RESPONSE STANDARD MODEL
Gauge: 12 ga., 3 in. **Capacity:** 7-round magazine. **Barrel:** 18 in. (Cyl.). **Weight:** 9 lbs. **Length:** 38 in. overall. **Stock:** Fiberglass-filled polypropylene with non-snag recoil absorbing butt pad. Nylon tactical fore-end houses flashlight. **Sights:** Trak-Lock ghost ring sight system. Front sight has Tritium insert. **Features:** Highly modified Remington 870P with Parkerized finish. Comes with nylon three-way adjustable sling, high visibility non-binding follower, high-performance magazine spring, Jumbo Head safety, and Side Saddle extended 6-shotshell carrier on left side of receiver. Introduced 1991. From Scattergun Technologies, Inc.
Price: Standard model, From.. **$1,540.00**
Price: Border Patrol model, From **$1,135.00**
Price: Professional Model 13-in. bbl. (Law enf., military only)........ **$1,550.00**

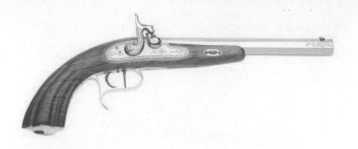

CHIAPPA LE PAGE PERCUSSION DUELING PISTOL

Caliber: .45. **Barrel:** 10 in. browned octagon, rifled. **Weight:** 2.5 lbs. **Length:** 16.6 in. overall. **Stock:** Walnut, rounded, fluted butt. **Sights:** Blade front, open-style rear. **Features:** Double set trigger. Bright barrel, silver-plated brass furniture. External ramrod. Made by Chiappa.
Price: Chiappa 940.001 ....$779.00

CVA OPTIMA PISTOL

Caliber: .50. **Barrel:** 14 in., 1:28-in. twist, Cerakote finish. **Weight:** 3.7 lbs. **Length:** 19 in. **Stock:** Black synthetic, Realtree Xtra Green. **Sights:** Scope base mounted. **Features:** Break-open action, all stainless construction, aluminum ramrod, quick-removal breech plug for 209 primer. From CVA.
Price: PP222SM Stainless/Realtree Xtra, rail mount $354.00
Price: PP221SM Stainless/black, rail mount.......................................$307.00

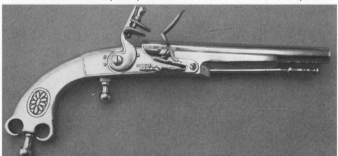

DIXIE MURDOCK SCOTTISH HIGHLANDER'S PISTOL

Caliber: .352. **Barrel:** 7.5 in., blued steel finish, round. **Weight:** 3.75 lbs. **Length:** 18.25 in. overall. **Stock:** Steel frame. **Sights:** None. **Features:** Flintlock, steel ramrod. An exact copy of an Alexander Murdock Scottish pistol of the 1770s. Made in India. Imported by Dixie Gun Works.

Price: Dixie Gun Works FH1040..$425.00

DIXIE MODEL 1855 U.S. DRAGOON PISTOL

Caliber: .58. **Barrel:** 12 in., bright finish, round. **Weight:** 2.25 lbs. **Length:** 16.75 in. overall. **Stock:** Walnut. **Sights:** Fixed rear and front sights. **Features:** Percussion, swivel-style, steel ramrod. Made by Palmetto Arms. Imported by Dixie Gun Works.
Price: Dixie Gun Works PH1000 ....$650.00

LYMAN PLAINS PISTOL

Caliber: .50 or .54. **Barrel:** 8 in.; 1:30-in. twist, both calibers. **Weight:** 3.1 lb. **Length:** 15 in. overall. **Stock:** Walnut. **Sights:** Blade front, square-notch rear adjustable for windage. **Features:** Polished brass triggerguard and ramrod tip, color case-hardened coil spring lock, spring-loaded trigger, stainless steel nipple, blackened iron furniture. Hooked patent breech, detachable belt hook. Introduced 1981. From Lyman Products.
Price: 6010608 .50-cal...$426.95
Price: 6010609 .54-cal...$426.95
Price: 6010610 .50-cal Kit..$349.95
Price: 6010611 .54-cal. Kit...$349.95

PEDERSOLI CARLETON UNDERHAMMER MATCH PERCUSSION PISTOL

Caliber: .36. **Barrel:** 9.5 in., browned octagonal, rifled. **Weight:** 2.25 lbs. **Length:** 16.75 in. overall. **Stock:** Walnut. **Sights:** Blade front, open rear, adjustable for elevation. **Features:** Percussion, under-hammer ignition, adjustable trigger, no half cock. No ramrod. Made by Pedersoli. Imported by Dixie Gun Works.
Price: Dixie Gun Works FH0332..$925.00

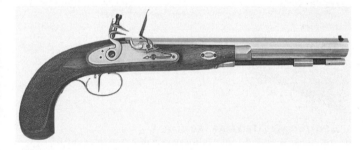

PEDERSOLI CHARLES MOORE ENGLISH DUELING PISTOL

Caliber: .45. **Barrel:** 11 in., 1:18 twist **Weight:** 2.5 lbs. **Length:** 16.5 in. overall. **Stock:** Walnut. **Sights:** Fixed. **Features:** Flintlock or percussion. Single set, adjustable trigger. Blued barrel and lock, steel furniture left in the white. Wooden ramrod. Replica of a fine British dueling pistol made by Charles Moore in London. Made by Pedersoli. Imported by Dixie Gun Works.
Price: Dixie Gun Works Flintlock FH0237 .... $795.00
Price: Dixie Gun Works Percussion PH0501 .... $610.00

PEDERSOLI FRENCH AN IX NAPOLEONIC PISTOL

Caliber: .69. **Barrel:** 8.25 in. **Weight:** 3 lbs. **Length:** 14 in. overall. **Stock:** Walnut. **Sights:** None. **Features:** Flintlock, case-hardened lock, brass furniture, buttcap, lock marked "Imperiale de S. Etienne." Steel ramrod. Made by Pedersoli. Imported by Dixie Gun Works.
Price: Dixie Gun Works FH0890..$740.00

PEDERSOLI FRENCH AN IX GENDARMERIE NAPOLEONIC PISTOL

Caliber: .69. **Barrel:** 5.25 in. **Weight:** 3 lbs. **Length:** 14 in. overall. **Stock:** Walnut. **Sights:** None. **Features:** Flintlock, case-hardened lock, brass furniture, buttcap, lock marked "Imperiale de S. Etienne." Steel ramrod. Imported by Dixie Gun Works.
Price: Dixie Gun Works Gendarmerie FHO954....................................$725.00

PEDERSOLI FRENCH AN XIII NAPOLEONIC PISTOL
Caliber: .69. **Barrel:** 8.25 in. **Weight:** 3 lbs. **Length:** 14 in. overall. **Stock:** Walnut half-stock. **Sights:** None. **Features:** Flintlock, case-hardened lock, brass furniture, butt cap, lock marked "Imperiale de S. Etienne." Steel ramrod. Made by Pedersoli. Imported by Dixie Gun Works.
Price: Dixie Gun Works AN XIII FHO895 .... **$725.00**

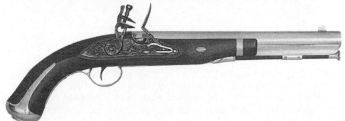

PEDERSOLI HARPER'S FERRY 1805 PISTOL
Caliber: .58. **Barrel:** 10 in. **Weight:** 2.5 lbs. **Length:** 16 in. overall. **Stock:** Walnut. **Sights:** Fixed. **Features:** Flintlock or percussion. Case-hardened lock, brass-mounted German silver-colored barrel. Wooden ramrod. Replica of the first U.S. government made flintlock pistol. Made by Pedersoli. Imported by Dixie Gun Works.
Price: Dixie Gun Works Flint RH0225 .... **$565.00**
Price: Dixie Gun Works Flint Kit RH0411 .... **$450.00**
Price: Dixie Gun Works Percussion RH0951 .... **$565.00**
Price: Dixie Gun Works Percussion Kit RH0937 .... **$395.00**

PEDERSOLI HOWDAH HUNTER PISTOLS
Caliber: .50, 20 gauge, .58. **Barrels:** 11.25 in., blued, rifled in .50 and .58 calibers. **Weight:** 4.25 to 5 lbs. **Length:** 17.25 in. **Stock:** American walnut with checkered grip. **Sights:** Brass bead front sight. **Features:** Blued barrels, swamped barrel rib, engraved, color case-hardened locks and hammers, captive steel ramrod. Available with detachable shoulder stock, case, holster and mold. Made by Pedersoli. Imported by Dixie Gun Works, Cabela's, Taylor's and others.
Price: Dixie Gun Works, 50X50, PH0572 .... **$895.00**
Price: Dixie Gun Works, 58XD58, PH09024 .... **$895.00**
Price: Dixie Gun Works, 20X20 gauge, PH0581 .... **$850.00**
Price: Dixie Gun Works, 50X20 gauge, PH0581 .... **$850.00**
Price: Dixie Gun Works, 50X50, Kit, PK0952 .... **$640.00**
Price: Dixie Gun Works, 50X20, Kit, PK1410 .... **$675.00**
Price: Dixie Gun Works, 20X20, Kit, PK0954 .... **$640.00**

PEDERSOLI KENTUCKY PISTOL
Caliber: .45, .50, .54. **Barrel:** 10.33 in. **Weight:** 2.5 lbs. **Length:** 15.4 in. overall. **Stock:** Walnut with smooth rounded birds-head grip. **Sights:** Fixed. **Features:** Available in flint or percussion ignition in various calibers. Case-hardened lock, blued barrel, drift-adjustable rear sights, blade front. Wooden ramrod. Kit guns of all models available from Dixie Gun Works. Made by Pedersoli. Imported by Dixie Gun Works, EMF and others.
Price: Dixie Gun Works .45 Percussion, PH0440 .... **$395.00**
Price: Dixie Gun Works.45 Flint, PH0430 .... **$437.00**
Price: Dixie Gun Works .45 Flint, Kit FH0320 .... **$325.00**

Price: Dixie Gun Works .50 Flint, PH0935 .... **$495.00**
Price: Dixie Gun Works .50 Percussion, PH0930 .... **$450.00**
Price: Dixie Gun Works .54 Flint, PH0080 .... **$495.00**
Price: Dixie Gun Works .54 Percussion, PH0330 .... **$450.00**
Price: Dixie Gun Works .54 Percussion, Kit PK0436 .... **$325.00**
Price: Dixie Gun Works .45, Navy Moll, brass buttcap, Flint PK0436 ...... **$650.00**
Price: .45, Navy Moll, brass buttcap, Percussion PK0903 .... **$595.00**

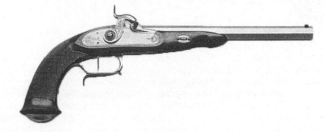

PEDERSOLI LE PAGE PERCUSSION DUELING PISTOL
Caliber: .44. **Barrel:** 10 inches, browned octagon, rifled. **Weight:** 2.5 lbs. **Length:** 16.75 inches overall. **Stock:** Walnut, rounded checkered butt. **Sights:** Blade front, open-style rear. **Features:** Single set trigger, external ramrod. Made by Pedersoli. Imported by Dixie Gun Works.
Price: Dixie, Pedersoli, PH0431 .... **$950.00**
Price: Dixie, International, Pedersoli, PH0231 .... **$1,250.00**

PEDERSOLI MAMELOUK
Caliber: .57. **Barrel:** 7-5/8 in., bright. **Weight:** 1.61 lbs. **Length:** 13 in. overall. **Stock:** Walnut, with brass end cap and medallion. **Sights:** Blade front. **Features:** Flint, lanyard ring, wooden ramrod. Made by Pedersoli. Available on special order from IFG (Italian Firearms Group)
Price: .... **TBD at time of order**

PEDERSOLI MANG TARGET PISTOL
Caliber: .38. **Barrel:** 11.5 in., octagonal, browned; 1:15-in. twist. **Weight:** 2.5 lbs. **Length:** 17. in. overall. **Stock:** Walnut with fluted grip. **Sights:** Blade front, open rear adjustable for windage. **Features:** Browned barrel, polished breech plug, remainder color case-hardened. Made by Pedersoli. Imported by Dixie Gun Works.
Price: PH0503 .... **$1,795.00**

Prices given are believed to be accurate at time of publication however, many factors affect retail pricing so exact prices are not possible.

74TH EDITION, 2020 ✛ **479**

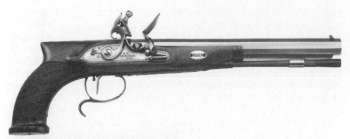

PEDERSOLI MORTIMER TARGET PISTOL
Caliber: .44. **Barrel:** 10 in., bright octagonal on Standard, browned on Deluxe, rifled. **Weight:** 2.55 lbs. **Length:** 15.75 in. overall. **Stock:** Walnut, checkered saw-handle grip on Deluxe. **Sights:** Blade front, open-style rear. **Features:** Percussion or flint, single set trigger, sliding hammer safety, engraved lock on Deluxe. Wooden ramrod. Made by Pedersoli. Imported by Dixie Gun Works.
Price: Dixie, Flint, FH0316 .... $1,175.00
Price: Dixie, Percussion, PH0231 .... $1,095.00
Price: Dixie, Deluxe, FH0950 .... $2,220.00

PEDERSOLI PHILADELPHIA DERRINGER
Caliber: .45. **Barrel:** 3.1 in., browned, rifled. **Weight:** 0.5 lbs. **Length:** 6.215 in. **Stock:** European walnut checkered. **Sights:** V-notch rear, blade front. **Features:** Back-hammer percussion lock with engraving, single trigger. Made by Pedersoli. Imported by Dixie Gun Works.
Price: Dixie, PH0913 . ... $550.00
Price: Dixie, Kit PK0863 . ... $385.00

PEDERSOLI QUEEN ANNE FLINTLOCK PISTOL
Caliber: .50. **Barrel:** 7.5 in., smoothbore. **Stock:** Walnut. **Sights:** None. **Features:** Flintlock, German silver-colored steel barrel, fluted brass triggerguard, brass mask on butt. Lockplate left in the white. No ramrod. Introduced 1983. Made by Pedersoli. Imported by Dixie Gun Works.
Price: Dixie, RH0211 .... $495.00
Price: Dixie, Kit, FH0421 .... $375.00

PEDERSOLI REMINGTON RIDER DERRINGER
Caliber: 4.3 mm (BB lead balls only). **Barrel:** 2.1 in., blued, rifled. **Weight:** 0.25 lbs. **Length:** 4.75 in. **Grips:** All-steel construction. **Sights:** V-notch rear, bead front. **Features:** Fires percussion cap only – no powder. Available as case-hardened frame or polished white. Made by Pedersoli. Imported by Dixie Gun Works.
Price: Dixie, Case-hardened PH0923. .... $210.00

PEDERSOLI SCREW BARREL PISTOL
Caliber: .44. **Barrel:** 2.35 in., blued, rifled. **Weight:** 0.5 lbs. **Length:** 6.5 in. **Grips:** European walnut. **Sights:** None. **Features:** Percussion, boxlock with center hammer, barrel unscrews for loading from rear, folding trigger, external hammer, combination barrel and nipple wrench furnished. Made by Pedersoli. Imported by Dixie Gun Works.
Price: Dixie, PH0530. .... $225.00
Price: Dixie, PH0545. .... $175.00

TRADITIONS KENTUCKY PISTOL
Caliber: .50. **Barrel:** 10 in., 1:20 in. twist. **Weight:** 2.75 lbs. **Length:** 15 in. **Stock:** Hardwood full stock. **Sights:** Brass blade front, square notch rear adjustable for windage. **Features:** Polished brass finger spur-style trigger guard, stock cap and ramrod tip, color case-hardened leaf spring lock, spring-loaded trigger, No. 11 percussion nipple, brass furniture. From Traditions, and as kit from Bass Pro and others.
Price: P1060 Finished $244.00
Price: KPC50602 Kit $209.00

TRADITIONS TRAPPER PISTOL
Caliber: .50. **Barrel:** 9.75 in., octagonal, blued, hooked patent breech, 1:20 in. twist. **Weight:** 2.75 lbs. **Length:** 15.5 in. **Stock:** Hardwood, modified saw-handle style grip, halfstock. **Sights:** Brass blade front, rear sight adjustable for windage and elevation. **Features:** Percussion or flint, double set triggers, polished brass triggerguard, stock cap and ramrod tip, color case-hardened leaf spring lock, spring-loaded trigger, No. 11 percussion nipple, brass furniture. From Traditions and as a kit from Bass Pro and others.
Price: P1100 Finished, percussion...................................... $329.00
Price: P1090 Finished, flint $369.00
Price: KPC51002 Kit, percussion $299.00
Price: KPC50902 Kit, flint $359.00

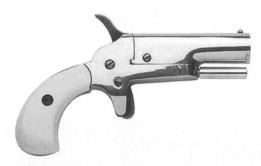

TRADITIONS VEST POCKET DERRINGER
Caliber: .31. **Barrel:** 2.35 in., round brass, smoothbore. **Weight:** .75 lbs. **Length:** 4.75 in. **Grips:** Simulated ivory. **Sights:** Front bead. **Features:** Replica of riverboat gambler's derringer. No. 11 percussion cap nipple, brass frame and barrel, spur trigger, external hammer. From Traditions.
Price: P1381, Brass $194.00
Price: Dixie, White, PH0920. .... $175.00

PIETTA TEXAS PATTERSON PERCUSSION REVOLVER

Caliber: .36. **Barrel:** 9 in. tapered octagon. **Weight:** 2.75 lbs. **Length:** 13.75 in. **Grips:** One-piece walnut. **Sights:** Brass pin front, hammer notch rear. **Features:** Folding trigger, blued steel furniture, frame and barrel; engraved scene on cylinder. Ramrod: Loading tool provided. **Made by Pietta.** Imported by E.M.F, Dixie Gun Works.
Price: EMF PF36ST36712 .... **$610.00**

NORTH AMERICAN COMPANION PERCUSSION REVOLVER

Caliber: .22. **Barrel:** 1-1/8 in. **Weight:** 5.1 oz. **Length:** 4 in. overall. **Grips:** Laminated wood. **Sights:** Blade front, notch rear. **Features:** All stainless steel construction. Uses No. 11 percussion caps. Comes with bullets, powder measure, bullet seater, leather clip holster, gun rag. Long Rifle frame. Introduced 1996. Made in U.S. by North American Arms.
Price: NAA-22LR-CB Long Rifle frame................................... **$251.00**

PIETTA 1851 NAVY MODEL PERCUSSION REVOLVER

Caliber: .36, .44, 6-shot. **Barrel:** 7.5 in. **Weight:** 44 oz. **Length:** 13 in. overall. **Grips:** Walnut. **Sights:** Post front, hammer notch rear. **Features:** Available in brass-framed and steel-framed models. Made by Pietta. Imported by EMF, Dixie Gun Works, Cabela's, Cimarron, Taylor's, Traditions and others.
Price: Brass frame EMF PF51BR36712 .... **$230.00**
Price: Steel frame EMF PF51CH36712................................. **$275.00**

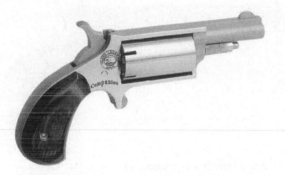

NORTH AMERICAN SUPER COMPANION PERCUSSION REVOLVER

Caliber: .22. **Barrel:** 1-5/8 in. **Weight:** 7.2 oz. **Length:** 5-1/8 in. **Grips:** Laminated wood. **Sights:** Blade font, notched rear. **Features:** All stainless steel construction. No. 11 percussion caps. Comes with bullets, powder measure, bullet seater, leather clip holster, gun rag. Introduced 1996. Larger "Magnum" frame. Made in U.S. by North American Arms.
Price: NAA-Mag-CB Magnum frame................................... **$296.00**

PEDERSOLI REMINGTON PATTERN TARGET REVOLVER

Caliber: .44. **Barrel:** 8 in., tapered octagon progressive twist. **Weight:** 2.75 lbs. **Length:** 13-3/4 in. overall. **Grips:** One-piece hardwood. **Sights:** V-notch on top strap, blued steel blade front. **Features:** Brass trigger guard, Non-reflective coating on the barrel and a wear resistant coating on the cylinder, blued steel frame, case-hardened hammer, trigger and loading lever. Made by Pedersoli. Imported by EMF, Dixie Gun Works, Cabela's and others.
Price: EMF Steel Frame PF58ST448................................. **$1,010.00**

PIETTA 1851 NAVY LONDON MODEL PERCUSSION REVOLVER

Caliber: .36, 6-shot. **Barrel:** 7.5 in. **Weight:** 44 oz. **Length:** 13 in. overall. **Grips:** Walnut. **Sights:** Post front, hammer notch rear. **Features:** steel frame and steel trigger guard and back strap. Available with oval trigger guard or squared back trigger guard. Made by Pietta. Imported by EMF, Dixie, Gun Works, Cabela's, Cimarron, Taylor's, Traditions and others.
Price: EMF PF51CHS36712 .... **$275.00**

Prices given are believed to be accurate at time of publication however, many factors affect retail pricing so exact prices are not possible.

74TH EDITION, 2020 ✦ **481**

PIETTA 1851 NAVY SHERIFF'S MODEL PERCUSSION REVOLVER

Caliber: .44, 6-shot. **Barrel:** 5.5 in. **Weight:** 40 oz. **Length:** 11 in. overall. **Grips:** Walnut. **Sights:** Post front, hammer notch rear. **Features:** Available in brass-framed and steel-framed models. Made by Pietta. Imported by EMF, Dixie, Gun Works, Cabela's.
Price: Brass frame EMF PF51BR44512 ....**$235.00**
Price: Steel frame EMF PF51CH44512................................**$275.00**

PIETTA 1851 NAVY CAPTAIN SCHAEFFER MODEL PERCUSSION REVOLVER

Caliber: .36, 6-shot. **Barrel:** 4 in. **Weight:** 40 oz. **Length:** 9.5 in. overall. **Grips:** Grips Ultra-ivory (polymer). **Sights:** Post front, hammer notch rear. **Features:** Polished steel finish, completely laser engraved. Made by Pietta. Imported by EMF
Price: EMF PF51LESS36312UI..**$395.00**

PIETTA 1851 NAVY YANK PEPPERBOX MODEL PERCUSSION REVOLVER

Caliber: .36, 6-shot. **Barrel:** No Barrel. **Weight:** 36 oz. **Length:** 7 in. overall. **Grips:** One-piece walnut. **Sights:** Post front, hammer notch rear. **Features:** There is no barrel. Rounds fire directly out of the chambers of the elongated cylinder. Made by Pietta. Imported by EMF, Dixie Gun Works and Taylor's & Co.
Price: EMF PF51PEPPER36 ....**$235.00**

PIETTA 1851 NAVY BUNTLINE MODEL PERCUSSION REVOLVER

Caliber: .44, 6-shot. **Barrel:** 12 in. **Weight:** 36 oz. **Length:** 18.25 in. overall. **Grips:** Walnut. **Sights:** Post front, hammer notch rear. **Features:** Available in

brass-framed and steel-framed models. Made by Pietta. Imported by EMF, Dixie Gun Works (Brass only).
Price: Brass frame EMF PF51BR4412 ....**$245.00**
Price: Steel frame EMF PF51CH4412............................**$295.00**

PIETTA 1851 NAVY SNUBNOSE MODEL PERCUSSION REVOLVER

Caliber: .44, 6-shot. **Barrel:** 3 in. **Weight:** 36 oz. **Length:** 8.25 in. overall. **Grips:** Birds-head grip frame, one-piece checkered walnut. **Sights:** Post front, hammer notch rear. **Features:** Color case-hardened, steel-frame. Made by Pietta. Imported by Dixie Gun Works.
Price: Dixie SS1249 ....**$395.00**

PIETTA 1860 ARMY MODEL PERCUSSION REVOLVER

Caliber: .44. **Barrel:** 8 in. **Weight:** 2.75 lbs. **Length:** 13.25 in. overall. **Grips:** One-piece walnut. **Sights:** Brass blade front, hammer notch rear. **Features:** Models available with either case-hardened, steel frame, brass trigger guard, or brass frame, trigger guard and backstrap. EMF also offers a model with a silver finish on all the metal. Made by Pietta. Imported by EMF, Cabela's, Dixie Gun Works, Taylor's and others.
Price: EMF Brass Frame PF60BR448............................**$260.00**
Price: EMF Steel Frame PF60CH448.............................**$295.00**
Price: EMF Steel Frame Old Silver finish PF60OS448 ....**$325.00**
Price: EMF Steel Frame Old Silver finish Deluxe Engraved PF60CHES448 ....**$350.00**

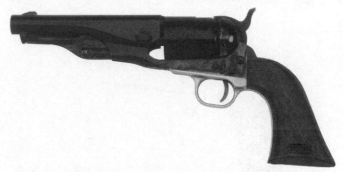

PIETTA 1860 ARMY SHERIFF'S MODEL PERCUSSION REVOLVER

Caliber: .44. **Barrel:** 5.5in. **Weight:** 40 oz. **Length:** 11.5 in. overall. **Grips:** One-piece walnut. **Sights:** Brass blade front, hammer notch rear. **Features:** Case-hardened, steel frame, brass trigger guard. Made by Pietta. Imported by EMF, Cabela's, Dixie Gun Works and others.
Price: EMF PF60CH44512 ....**$295.00**

PIETTA 1860 ARMY SNUBNOSE MODEL PERCUSSION REVOLVER

Caliber: .44. **Barrel:** 3 in. **Weight:** 36 oz. **Length:** 8.25 in. overall. **Grips:** Birds-head grip frame, one-piece, checkered walnut. **Sights:** Brass blade front, hammer notch rear. **Features:** Fluted cylinder, case-hardened, steel frame, brass trigger guard, Made by Pietta. Imported by EMF.
Price: EMF PF51CHLG44212CW **$385.00**

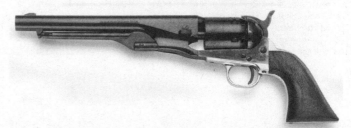

PIETTA NAVY 1861 PERCUSSION REVOLVER

Caliber: .36. **Barrel:** 8 in. **Weight:** 2.75 lbs. **Length:** 13.25 in. overall. **Grips:** One-piece walnut. **Sights:** Brass blade front, hammer notch rear. **Features:** Steel,

Prices given are believed to be accurate at time of publication however, many factors affect retail pricing so exact prices are not possible.

case-hardened frame, brass-grip frame, or steel-grip frame (London Model), case-hardened creeping loading lever. Made by Pietta. Imported by EMF, Dixie Gun Works, Cabela's and others.
Price: EMF with brass triggerguard PF61CH368CIV **$300.00**
Price: EMF with steel triggerguard PF61CH368 .... **$300.00**

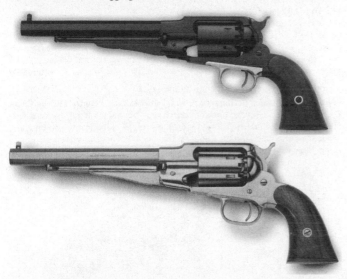

PIETTA 1858 REMINGTON ARMY REVOLVER
Caliber: .44. **Barrel:** 8 in., tapered octagon. **Weight:** 2.75 lbs. **Length:** 13.5 in. overall. **Grips:** Two-piece walnut. **Sights:** V-notch on top strap, blued steel blade front. **Features:** Brass triggerguard, blued steel backstrap and frame, case-hardened hammer and trigger. Also available, a brass framed model, and an all stainless steel model. Made by Pietta. Imported by EMF, Dixie Gun Works, Cabela's and others.
Price: EMF Steel Frame PF58ST448 .... **$290.00**
Price: EMF Brass Frame PF58BR448 .... **$250.00**
Price: EMF Stainless Steel PF58SS448 .... **$430.00**

PIETTA 1858 REMINGTON TARGET REVOLVER
Caliber: .44. **Barrel:** 8 in., tapered octagon. **Weight:** 2.75 lbs. **Length:** 13.5 in. overall. **Grips:** Two-piece walnut. **Sights:** Adjustable rear, ramped blade front. **Features:** Brass triggerguard, blued steel frame, case-hardened hammer, and trigger. Also available, a brass-framed model. Made by Pietta. Imported by EMF, Dixie Gun Works, Cabela's and others.
Price: EMF PF58STT448 .... **$350.00**

PIETTA 1858 REMINGTON SHIRIFF'S MODEL REVOLVER
Caliber: .36 and .44. **Barrel:** 5.5in., tapered octagon. **Weight:** 2.75 lbs. **Length:** 11.5 in. overall. **Grips:** Two-piece checkered walnut. **Sights:** V-notch

on top strap, blued steel blade front. **Features:** Brass triggerguard, blued steel backstrap and frame, case-hardened hammer and trigger. Also available in a color case-hardened-framed model, and in an all stainless steel model. Made by Pietta. Imported by EMF, and others.
Price: EMF Blued Steel Frame PF58ST36612 .... **$290.00**
Price: EMF Color Case-Hardened frame PF58CH44512CW **$395.00**
Price: EMF Stainless Steel PF58SS44512CW **$490.00**

PIETTA 1858 REMINGTON BUFFALO BILL COMMEMORATIVE REVOLVER
Caliber: .44. **Barrel:** 8 in., tapered octagon. **Weight:** 2.75 lbs. **Length:** 13-3/4 in. overall. **Grips:** Two-piece walnut. **Sights:** V-notch on top strap, blued steel blade front. **Features:** Gold-filled engraving over dark blue steel. A higher-grade gun commemorating the life of Buffalo Bill Cody. Made by Pietta. Imported by EMF.
Price: EMF PF58BB448 .... **$695.00**

PIETTA REMINGTON BELT MODEL REVOLVER
Caliber: .36. **Barrel:** 6.5 in., octagon. **Weight:** 44 oz. **Length:** 12.5 in. overall. **Grips:** Two-piece walnut. **Sights:** V-notch on top strap, blued steel blade front. **Features:** Brass triggerguard, blued steel backstrap and frame, case-hardened hammer and trigger. Made by Pietta. Imported by Dixie Gun Works.
Price: Dixie RH0214 .... **$295.00**

PIETTA 1863 REMINGTON POCKET MODEL REVOLVER
Caliber: .31, 5-shot. **Barrel:** 3.5 In. **Weight:** 1 lb. **Length:** 7.6 in. **Grips:** Two-piece walnut. **Sights:** Pin front, groove-in-frame rear. **Features:** Spur trigger, iron-, brass- or nickel-plated frame. Made by Pietta. Imported by EMF (Steel Frame), Dixie Gun Works, Taylor's and others.
Price: Brass frame, Dixie PH0407 .... **$260.00**
Price: Steel frame, Dixie PH0370 .... **$295.00**
Price: Nickel-plated, Dixie PH0409 .... **$315.00**

DANCE AND BROTHERS PERCUSSION REVOLVER
Caliber: .44. **Barrel:** 7.4 in., round. **Weight:** 2.5 lbs. **Length:** 13 in. overall. **Grips:** One-piece walnut. **Sights:** Brass blade front, hammer notch rear. **Features:** Reproduction of the C.S.A. revolver. Brass trigger guard. Color case-hardened frame Made by Pietta. Imported by Dixie Gun Works and others.
Price: Dixie Gun Works RH0344 .... $350.00

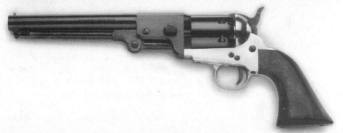

GRISWOLD AND GUNNISON PERCUSSION REVOLVER
Caliber: .36. **Barrel:** 7.5 in., round. **Weight:** 2.5 lbs. **Length:** 13.25 in. **Grips:** One-piece walnut. **Sights:** Fixed. **Features:** Reproduction of the C.S.A. revolver. Brass frame and triggerguard. Made by Pietta. Imported by EMF, Cabela's and others.
Price: EMF PF51BRGG36712 .... $235.00

PIETTA LEMATT REVOLVER
Caliber: .44/20 Ga. **Barrel:** 6.75 in. (revolver); 4-7/8 in. (single shot). **Weight:** 3 lbs., 7 oz. **Length:** 14 in. overall. **Grips:** Hand-checkered walnut. **Sights:** Post front, hammer notch rear. **Features:** Exact reproduction with all-steel construction; 44-cal., 9-shot cylinder, 20-gauge single barrel; color case-hardened hammer with selector; spur triggerguard; ring at butt; lever-type barrel release. Made by Pietta. Imported by EMF, Dixie Gun Works and others.
Price: EMF Navy PFLMSTN44634 .... $1,075.00
Price: EMF Cavalry PFLMST44712 .... $1,100.00
Price: EMF Army PFLMSTA44634 .... $1,100.00

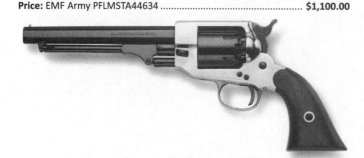

PIETTA SPILLER & BURR PERCUSSION REVOLVER
Caliber: .36. **Barrel:** 7 in., octagon. **Weight:** 2.5 lbs. **Length:** 12.5 in. overall. **Grips:** Two-piece walnut. **Sights:** V-notch on top strap, blued steel blade

front. **Features:** Reproduction of the C.S.A. revolver. Brass frame and trigger guard. Also available as a kit. Made by Pietta. Imported by Dixie Gun Works, Traditions, Midway USA and others.
Price: Dixie RH0120 .... $275.00
Price: Dixie kit RH0300 .... $235.00

PIETTA STARR DOUBLE-ACTION ARMY REVOLVER
Caliber: .44. **Barrel:** 6 in. tapered round. **Weight:** 3 lbs. **Length:** 11.75 in. **Grips:** One-piece walnut. **Sights:** Hammer notch rear, dovetailed front. **Features:** Double-action mechanism, round tapered barrel, all blued frame and barrel. Made by Pietta. Imported by Dixie Gun Works and others.
Price: Dixie RH460 .... $565.00

PIETTA STARR SINGLE-ACTION ARMY REVOLVER
Caliber: .44. **Barrel:** 8 in. tapered round. **Weight:** 3 lbs. **Length:** 13.5 in. **Grips:** One-piece walnut. **Sights:** Hammer notch rear, dovetailed front. **Features:** Single-action mechanism, round tapered barrel, all blued frame and barrel. Made by Pietta. Imported by Cabela's, Dixie Gun Works and others.
Price: Dixie RH460 .... $550.00

PIETTA 1873 PERCUSSION REVOLVER
Caliber: .44. **Barrel:** 5.5 in. **Weight:** 40 oz. **Length:** 11.25 in. overall. **Grips:** One-piece walnut. **Sights:** V-notch on top strap, blued steel blade front. **Features:** A cap-and-ball version of the Colt Single Action Army revolver. Made by Pietta. Imported by EMF, Cabela's, Dixie Gun Works and others.
Price: EMF PF73CHS434NM $360.00

UBERTI 1847 WALKER PERCUSSION REVOLVER
Caliber: .44. **Barrel:** 9 in. **Weight:** 4.5 lbs. **Length:** 15.7 in. overall. **Grips:** One-piece hardwood. **Sights:** Brass blade front, hammer notch rear. **Features:** Copy of Sam Colt's first U.S. contract revolver. Engraved cylinder, case-hardened hammer and loading lever. Blued finish. Made by Uberti. Imported by Cabela's, Cimarron, Dixie Gun Works, EMF, Taylor's, Uberti U.S.A. and others.
Price: Uberti USA, standard model, blued steel 340200 .... $429.00

Prices given are believed to be accurate at time of publication however, many factors affect retail pricing so exact prices are not possible.

DRAGOON PERCUSSION REVOLVERS
Caliber: .44. **Barrel:** 7.5 in. **Weight:** 4.1 lbs. **Grips:** One-piece walnut. **Sights:** Brass blade front, hammer notch rear. **Features:** Four models of the big .44 caliber revolvers that followed the massive Walker model and pre-dated the sleek 1860 Army model. Blued barrel, backstrap and trigger guard. Made by Uberti. Imported by Uberti USA, Dixie Gun Works, Taylor's and others.
Price: Uberti USA, Whitneyville Dragoon 340830 .... **$429.00**
Price: Uberti USA, First Model Dragoon 340800 .... **$429.00**
Price: Uberti USA, Second Model Dragoon 340810 .... **$429.00**
Price: Uberti USA, Third Model Dragoon 340860 .... **$429.00**

UBERTI 1849 POCKET MODEL WELLS FARGO PERCUSSION REVOLVER
Caliber: .31. **Barrel:** 4 in., seven-groove, RH twist. **Weight:** About 24 oz. **Grips:** One-piece walnut. **Sights:** Brass pin front, hammer notch rear. **Features:** Unfluted cylinder with stagecoach holdup scene, cupped cylinder pin, no grease grooves, one safety pin on cylinder and slot in hammer face. Made by Uberti. Imported by Uberti USA, Cimarron, Dixie Gun Works and others.
Price: Uberti USA 340350 .... **$349.00**

UBERTI 1849 WELLS FARGO PERCUSSION REVOLVER
Caliber: .31. **Barrel:** 4 in.; seven-groove; RH twist. **Weight:** About 24 oz. **Grips:** One-piece walnut. **Sights:** Brass pin front, hammer notch rear. **Features:** No loading lever, Unfluted cylinder with stagecoach holdup scene, cupped cylinder pin, no grease grooves, one safety pin on cylinder and slot in hammer face. Made by Uberti. Imported by Uberti USA, Cimarron, Dixie Gun Works and others.
Price: Uberti USA 340380 .... **$349.00**

UBERTI NAVY MODEL 1851 PERCUSSION REVOLVER
Caliber: .36, 6-shot. **Barrel:** 7.5 in. **Weight:** 44 oz. **Length:** 13 in. overall. **Grips:** One-piece walnut. **Sights:** Post front, hammer notch rear. **Features:** Brass backstrap and trigger guard, or steel backstrap and trigger guard (London Model), engraved cylinder with navy battle scene; case-hardened hammer, loading lever. Made by Uberti and Pietta. Imported by Uberti USA, Cabela's, Cimarron, and others.
Price: Uberti USA Brass grip assembly 340000 .... **$329.00**
Price: Uberti USA London Model 340050 .... **$369.00**

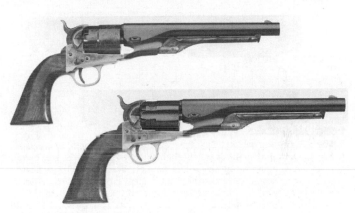

UBERTI 1860 ARMY REVOLVER
Caliber: .44. **Barrel:** 8 in. **Weight:** 44 oz. **Length:** 13.25 in. overall. **Grips:** One-piece walnut. **Sights:** Brass blade front, hammer notch rear. **Features:** Steel or case-hardened frame, brass triggerguard, case-hardened creeping loading lever. Many models and finishes are available for this pistol. Made by Uberti. Imported by Cabela's, Cimarron, Dixie Gun Works, EMF, Taylor's, Uberti U.S.A. and others.
Price: Uberti USA, roll engraved cylinder 340400 .... **$349.00**
Price: Uberti USA, full fluted cylinder 340410 .... **$369.00**

UBERTI NAVY 1861 PERCUSSION REVOLVER
Caliber: .36 **Barrel:** 7.5 in. **Weight:** 44 oz. **Length:** 13.25 in. overall. **Grips:** One-piece walnut. **Sights:** Brass blade front, hammer notch rear. **Features:** Brass backstrap and trigger guard, or steel backstrap and trigger guard (London Model), engraved cylinder with navy battle scene; case-hardened hammer, loading lever. Made by Uberti. Imported by Uberti USA, Cabela's, Cimarron, Dixie Gun Works, Taylor's and others.
Price: Uberti USA Brass grip assembly 340630 .... **$349.00**
Price: Uberti USA London Model 340500 .... **$349.00**

Prices given are believed to be accurate at time of publication however, many factors affect retail pricing so exact prices are not possible.

74TH EDITION, 2020 ✦ **485**

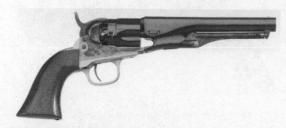

UBERTI 1862 POLICE PERCUSSION REVOLVER

Caliber: .36, 5-shot. **Barrel:** 5.5 in., 6.5 in., 7.5 in. **Weight:** 26 oz. **Length:** 12 in. overall (6.5 in. bbl.). **Grips:** One-piece walnut. **Sights:** Fixed. **Features:** Round tapered barrel; half-fluted and rebated cylinder; case-hardened frame, loading lever and hammer; brass trigger guard and backstrap. Made by Uberti. Imported by Cimarron, Dixie Gun Works, Taylor's, Uberti U.S.A. and others.
Price: Uberti USA 340700 .... $369.00

UBERTI 1862 POCKET NAVY PERCUSSION REVOLVER

Caliber: .36, 5-shot. **Barrel:** 5.5 in., 6.5 in. **Weight:** 26 oz. **Length:** 12 in. overall (6.5 in. bbl.). **Grips:** One-piece walnut. **Sights:** Fixed. **Features:** Octagon barrel; case-hardened frame, loading lever and hammer; silver or brass trigger guard and backstrap; also available in an all stainless steel version. Made by Uberti. Imported by Uberti USA, Cimarron, Dixie Gun Works, Taylor's and others.
Price: Uberti USA 340750 .... $369.00

UBERTI LEACH AND RIGDON PERCUSSION REVOLVER

Caliber: .36. **Barrel:** 7.5 in., octagon to round. **Weight:** 2.75 lbs. **Length:** 13 in. **Grips:** One-piece walnut. **Sights:** Hammer notch and pin front. **Features:** Steel frame. Reproduction of the C.S.A. revolver. Brass backstrap and trigger guard. Made by Uberti. Imported by Uberti USA, Dixie Gun Works and others.
Price: Uberti USA 340030 .... $349.00

UBERTI NEW ARMY REMINGTON PERCUSSION REVOLVER

Caliber: .44, 6-shot. **Barrel:** Tapered octagon 8 in. **Weight:** 32 oz. **Length:** Standard 13.5 in. **Grips:** Two-piece walnut. **Sights:** Standard blade front, groove-in-frame rear; adjustable on some models. **Features:** Many variations of this gun are available. Target Model (Uberti U.S.A.) has fully adjustable target rear sight, target front, .36 or .44. Made by Uberti. Imported by Uberti USA, Cimarron F.A. Co., Taylor's and others.
Price: Uberti USA Steel frame, 341000 .... $369.00
Price: Uberti USA Stainless, 341020 .... $449.00

ARMI SPORT ENFIELD THREE-BAND P1853 RIFLE
Caliber: .58. **Barrel:** 39 in. **Weight:** 10.25 lbs. **Length:** 52 in. overall. **Stock:** European walnut. **Sights:** Blade front, flip-up rear with elevator marked to 800 yards. **Features:** Reproduction of the original three-band rifle. Percussion musket-cap ignition. Blued barrel with steel barrelbands, brass furniture. Case-hardened lock. Lockplate marked "London Armory Co. and Crown." Made by Euro Arms, Armi Sport (Chiappa). Imported by Dixie Gun Works and others.
Price: Dixie Gun Works rifled bore PR1130 ....$895.00
Price: Dixie Gun Work smooth bore PR1052.......................................$750.00

CVA ACCURA IN-LINE BREAK-ACTION RIFLE
Caliber: .50. **Barrel:** 28 in. fluted. **Weight:** 7.5 lbs. **Length:** Standard 45 in. **Stock:** Ambidextrous solid composite in standard or thumbhole. **Sights:** Adj. fiber-optic. **Features:** Break-action, quick-release breech plug, aluminum loading rod, cocking spur, lifetime warranty. By CVA.
Price: CVA PR3120NM (Accura MR Nitride with Black Stocks
    and Scope Mount)..$493.00

CVA ACCURA V2 LR NITRIDE "SPECIAL EDITION" IN-LINE BREAK-ACTION RIFLE
Caliber: .50. **Barrel:** 30 in. fluted. **Weight:** 7.5 lbs. **Length:** Standard 45 in. **Stock:** Ambidextrous solid composite. **Sights:** Adj. fiber-optic. **Features:** Break-action, quick-release breech plug, aluminum loading rod, cocking spur, equipped with a genuine, Nitride treated, 30-inch Bergara Barrel, and a deep pistol grip stock decorated in APG camo. Lifetime warranty. By CVA.
Price: CVA PR6124NM $449.95

CVA ACCURA MR (MOUNTAIN RIFLE) IN-LINE BREAK-ACTION RIFLE
Caliber: .50. **Barrel:** 25 in. **Weight:** 6.35 lbs. **Length:** Standard 45 in. **Stock:** Ambidextrous solid composite. **Sights:** DuraSight DEAD-ON One-Piece Scope Mount. **Features:** Break-action, quick-release breech plug, aluminum loading rod, cocking spur, and a deep pistol grip stock decorated in Realtree APG camo. Lifetime warranty. By CVA.
Price: CVA PR3121SNM $546.00

CVA OPTIMA IN-LINE BREAK-ACTION RIFLE
Caliber: .50. **Barrel:** 26 in., stainless steel. **Weight:** 6.65 lbs. **Length:** 41in. **Stock:** Ambidextrous solid composite. Available in pistol grip or thumbhole configurations. **Sights:** DuraSight DEAD-ON One-Piece Scope Mount. **Features:** Ambidextrous with rubber grip panels in black or Realtree APG camo, crush-zone recoil pad, reversible hammer spur, quake claw sling. Lifetime warranty. By CVA.
Price: CVA PR2020SM.. $371.00

CVA WOLF IN-LINE BREAK-ACTION RIFLE
Caliber: .50 **Barrel:** 24 in. **Weight:** 6.23 lbs. **Stock:** Ambidextrous composite. **Sights:** Dead-On Scope Mounts or Fiber Optic. **Features:** Break-action, quick-release breech plug for 209 primer, aluminum loading road, cocking spur. Lifetime warranty. By CVA.
Price: CVA PR2112SM (.50-cal, stainless/Realtree Hardwoods HD,
    scope mount)..$289.50
Price: CVA PR2112S (50-cal, stainless/Realtree Hardwoods HD,
    fib. opt. sight) $289.50
Price: CVA PR2110SM (.50-cal, stainless/black, scope mount) $240.50

DIXIE DELUXE CUB RIFLE
Caliber: .32, .36. **Barrel:** 28 in. octagonal. **Weight:** 6.5 lbs. **Length:** 44 in. overall. **Stock:** Walnut. **Sights:** Fixed. **Features:** Each gun available in either flint or percussion ignition. Short rifle for small game and beginning shooters. Brass patchbox and furniture. Made by Pedersoli for Dixie Gun Works.
Price: Dixie Gun Works (.32-cal. flint) PR3130....................................$890.00
Price: Dixie Gun Works (.36-cal. flint) FR3135.....................................$890.00
Price: Dixie Gun Works (.32-cal. Percussion kit) PK3360.....................$690.00
Price: Dixie Gun Works (.36-cal. Percussion kit) PK3365.....................$690.00
Price: Dixie Gun Works (.32-cal. Flint kit) PK3350...............................$710.00
Price: Dixie Gun Works (.36-cal. Flint kit) PK335.................................$710.00
Price: Dixie Gun Works (.32-cal. percussion) PR3140...........................$850.00
Price: Dixie Gun Works (.36-cal. percussion) PR3145...........................$850.00

DIXIE PENNSYLVANIA RIFLE
Caliber: .45 and .50. **Barrel:** 41.5 in. octagonal, .45/1:48, .50/1:56 in. twist. **Weight:** 8.5, 8.75 lbs. **Length:** 56 in. overall. **Stock:** European walnut, full-length stock. **Sights:** Notch rear, blade front. **Features:** Flintlock or percussion, brass patchbox, double-set triggers. Also available as kit guns for both calibers and ignition systems. Made by Pedersoli for Dixie Gun Works.
Price: Dixie Gun Works (.45-cal. flint) FR1060................................$1,100.00
Price: Dixie Gun Works (.50-cal. flint) FR3200................................$1,100.00
Price: Dixie Gun Works (.45-cal. Percussion kit) PR1075....................$910.00
Price: Dixie Gun Works (.50-cal. Percussion kit) PK3365....................$910.00
Price: Dixie Gun Works (.45-cal. Flint kit) FR1065.............................$910.00
Price: Dixie Gun Works (.50-cal. Flint kit) FK3420.............................$910.00
Price: Dixie Gun Works (.45-cal. percussion) FR1070.......................$1,050.00
Price: Dixie Gun Works (.50-cal. percussion) PR3205.......................$1,050.00

EUROARMS 1803 HARPER'S FERRY FLINTLOCK RIFLE
Caliber: .54. **Barrel:** 35.5 in., smoothbore. **Weight:** 9.5 lbs. **Length:** 50.5 in. overall. **Stock:** Half-stock, walnut w/oil finish. **Sights:** Blade front, notched rear. **Features:** Color case-hardened lock, browned barrel, with barrel key. Made by Euroarms. Imported by Dixie Gun Works.
Price: Dixie Gun Works FR0171 ....$795.00

EUROARMS J.P. MURRAY ARTILLERY CARBINE
Caliber: .58. **Barrel:** 23.5 in. **Weight:** 8 lbs. **Length:** 39.5 in. **Stock:** European walnut. **Sights:** Blade front, fixed notch rear. **Features:** Percussion musket-cap ignition. Reproduction of the original Confederate carbine. Lock marked "J.P. Murray, Columbus, Georgia." Blued barrel. Made by Euroarms. Imported by Dixie Gun Works and others.
Price: Dixie, Gun Works PR0173...$1,100.00

EUROARMS ENFIELD MUSKETOON P1861

Caliber: .58. **Barrel:** 24 in. **Weight:** 9 lbs. **Length:** 40 in. overall. **Stock:** European walnut. **Sights:** Blade front, flip-up rear with elevator marked to 700 yards. **Features:** Reproduction of the original cavalry version of the Enfield rifle. Percussion musket-cap ignition. Blued barrel with steel barrelbands, brass furniture. Case-hardened lock. Euroarms version marked London Armory with crown. Pedersoli version has Birmingham stamp on stock and Enfield and Crown on lockplate. Made by Euroarms. Imported by Dixie Gun Works and others.
Price: Dixie Gun Works PR0343 ....$1,050.00

KNIGHT 500 IN-LINE RIFLE

Caliber: .50. **Barrel:** 28 in., custom Green Mountain. **Weight:** 10 lbs. **Length:** 46 in. overall. **Stock:** Boyd's custom stock with integrated aluminum bedding **Sights:** Not included. **Features:** Competition-grade muzzleloader that can be used as a hunting rifle, handcrafted Green Mountain barrel, the stock also features an adjustable cheek piece that gives you a clear view down range. Made in U.S. by Knight Rifles.
Price: Muzzleloaders.com MMTE758TAR....................... Starting at $2,080.99

KNIGHT BIGHORN IN-LINE RIFLE

Caliber: .50. **Barrel:** 26 in., 1:28 in. twist. **Weight:** 7 lbs. 3 oz. **Length:** 44.5 in. overall. **Stock:** G2 straight or thumbhole, Carbon Knight straight or thumbhole or black composite thumbhole with recoil pad, sling swivel studs. **Ramrod:** Carbon core with solid brass extendable jag. **Sights:** Fully adjustable metallic fiber optic. **Features:** Uses four different ignition systems (included): #11 nipple, musket nipple, bare 208 shotgun primer and 209 Extreme shotgun primer system (Extreme weatherproof full plastic jacket system); vented breech plug, striker fired with one-piece removable hammer assembly. With recommended loads, guaranteed to have 4-inch, three-shot groups at 200 yards. Also available as Western gun with exposed ignition. Made in U.S. by Knight Rifles.
Price: Muzzleloaders.com MBH706C $646.99

KNIGHT DISC EXTREME

Caliber: .50, .52. **Barrel:** 26 in., fluted stainless, 1:28 in. twist. **Weight:** 7 lbs. 14 oz. to 8 lbs. **Length:** 45 in. overall. **Stock:** Carbon Knight straight or thumbhole with blued or SS; G2 thumbhole; left-handed Nutmeg thumbhole. **Ramrod:** Solid brass extendable jag. **Sights:** Fully adjustable metallic fiber optics. **Features:** Bolt-action rifle, full plastic jacket ignition system, #11 nipple, musket nipple, bare 208 shotgun primer. With recommended loads, guaranteed to have 4-inch, three-shot groups at 200 yards. Also available as Western gun with exposed ignition. Made in U.S. by Knight Rifles.
Price: Muzzleloaders.com MDE706SMX ....Starting at $721.99

KNIGHT LITTLEHORN IN-LINE RIFLE

Caliber: .50. **Barrel:** 22 in., 1:28 in. twist. **Weight:** 6.7 lbs. **Length:** 39 in. overall. **Stock:** 12.5-in. length of pull, G2 straight or pink Realtree AP HD. **Ramrod:** Carbon core with solid brass extendable jag. **Sights:** Fully adjustable Williams fiber optic. **Features:** Uses four different ignition systems (included): Full Plastic Jacket, #11 nipple, musket nipple or bare 208 shotgun primer; vented breech plug, striker-fired with one-piece removable hammer assembly. **Finish:** Stainless steel. With recommended loads, guaranteed to have 4-inch, three-shot groups at 200 yards. Also available as Western gun with exposed ignition. Made in U.S. by Knight Rifles.
Price: Muzzleloaders.com MLHW702C ....Starting at $390.00

KNIGHT MOUNTAINEER IN-LINE RIFLE

Caliber: .45, .50, .52. **Barrel:** 27 in. fluted stainless steel, free floated. **Weight:** 8 lbs. (thumbhole stock), 8.3 lbs. (straight stock). **Length:** 45.5 inches. **Sights:** Fully adjustable metallic fiber optic. **Features:** Bolt-action rifle, adjustable match-grade trigger, aluminum ramrod with carbon core, solid brass extendable jag, vented breech plug. **Ignition:** Full plastic jacket, #11 nipple, musket nipple, bare 208 shotgun primer. With recommended loads, guaranteed to have 4-inch, three-shot groups at 200 yards. Also available as Western gun with exposed ignition. Made in U.S. by Knight Rifles.
Price: Muzzleloaders.com MMT707SNMNT ....Starting at $1,016.99

KNIGHT TK-2000 IN-LINE SHOTGUN

Gauge: 12. **Barrel:** 26 inches. **Choke:** Extra-full and improved cylinder available. **Stock:** Realtree Xtra Green straight or thumbhole. **Weight:** 7.7 pounds. **Sights:** Williams fully adjustable rear, fiber-optic front. **Features:** Striker-fired action, receiver is drilled and tapped for scope, adjustable trigger, removable breech plug, double-safety system. **Ignition:** #209 primer with Full Plastic Jacket, musket cap or No. 11. Striker-fired with one-piece removable hammer assembly. Made in U.S. by Knight Rifles.
Price: Muzzleloaders.com MTK2000SXG............................Starting at $742.99

KNIGHT ULTRA-LITE IN-LINE RIFLE

Caliber: .45 or .50. **Barrel:** 24 in. **Stock:** Black, tan or olive-green Kevlar spider web. **Weight:** 6 lbs. **Features:** Bolt-action rifle. **Ramrod:** Carbon core with solid brass extendable jag. **Sights:** With or without Williams fiber-optic sights, drilled and tapped for scope mounts. **Finish:** Stainless steel. **Ignition:** 209 Primer with Full Plastic Jacket, musket cap or #11 nipple, bare 208 shotgun primer; vented breech plug. With recommended loads, guaranteed to have 4-inch, three-shot groups at 200 yards. Also available as Western version with exposed ignition. Made in U.S. by Knight Rifles.
Price: Muzzleloaders.com MULE704TNT ....Starting at $1,217.99

KNIGHT VISION IN-LINE RIFLE

Caliber: .50. **Barrel:** 24 in. **Length:** 44 in. **Stock:** Black composite. **Weight:** 7.9 lbs. **Features:** Break-open rifle with carbon-steel barrel and all-new machined steel action. With recommended loads, guaranteed to have 4-inch, three-shot groups at 200 yards. **Ramrod:** Carbon core with solid brass extendable jag. **Ignition:** Full Plastic Jacket. **Sights:** Weaver sight bases attached, and Williams fiber-optic sights provided. **Finish:** Blued steel. Made in U.S. by Knight Rifles.
Price: Muzzleloaders.com MKVE04XT... ....Starting at $346.99

KNIGHT WOLVERINE IN-LINE RIFLE

Caliber: .50. **Barrel:** 22 in. stainless steel, 1:28 in. twist. **Weight:** 6.9 lbs. **Length:** 40.5 overall. **Stock:** Realtree Hardwoods straight, CarbonKnight straight. **Ramrod:** Carbon core with solid brass extendable jag. **Sights:** Fully adjustable Williams fiber optic. **Features:** Ignition systems (included): #11 nipple, musket nipple, bare 208 shotgun primer; vented breech plug, striker-fired with one-piece removable hammer assembly. **Finish:** Stainless steel. With recommended loads, guaranteed to have 4-inch, three-shot groups at 200 yards. Also available as Western gun with exposed ignition. Made in U.S. by Knight Rifles.
Price: Muzzleloaders.com MWS702XT... ....Starting at $395.99

BLACKPOWDER Muskets & Rifles

LYMAN DEERSTALKER RIFLE
Caliber: .50, .54. **Barrel:** 28 in. octagon, 1:48 in. twist. **Weight:** 10.8 lbs. **Length:** 45 in. overall. **Stock:** European walnut with black rubber recoil pad. **Sights:** Lyman's high visibility, fiber-optic sights. **Features:** Fast-twist rifling for conical bullets. Blackened metal parts to eliminate glare, stainless steel nipple. Hook breech, single trigger, coil spring lock. Steel barrel rib and ramrod ferrules. From Lyman.
Price: Muzzleloaders.com 6033146/7. 50-cal /.54-cal. flint............... **$448.00**
Price: Muzzleloaders.com 6033140/7 .50-cal /.54-cal. percussion **$398.00**

LYMAN GREAT PLAINS RIFLE
Caliber: .50, .54. **Barrel:** 32 in., 1:60 in. twist. **Weight:** 11.6 lbs. **Stock:** Walnut. **Sights:** Steel blade front, buckhorn rear adjustable for windage and elevation, and fixed notch primitive sight included. **Features:** Percussion or flint ignition. Blued steel furniture. Stainless steel nipple. Coil spring lock, Hawken-style triggerguard and double-set triggers. Round thimbles recessed and sweated into rib. Steel wedge plates and toe plate. Introduced 1979. From Lyman.
Price: 6031102/3 .50-cal./.54-cal percussion......................................**$784.95**
Price: 6031105/6 .50-cal./.54-cal flintlock **$839.95**
Price: 6031125/6 .50-ca./.54-cal left-hand percussion **$824.95**
Price: 6031137 .50-cal. left-hand flintlock **$859.95**
Price: 6031111/2 .50/.54-cal. percussion kit.....................................**$639.95**
Price: 6031114/5 .50/.54-cal. flintlock kit..**$689.95**

LYMAN GREAT PLAINS HUNTER MODEL
Similar to Great Plains model except 1:32 in. twist, shallow-groove barrel for conicals or sabots, and comes drilled and tapped for Lyman 57GPR peep sight.
Price: 6031120/1 .50-cal./.54-cal percussion.......................................**$791.95**
Price: 6031148/9 .50-cal/.54-cal flintlock **$839.95**
Price: 6031112 .50-cal/.54-cal percussion kit **$669.95**
Price: 6031115 .50-cal/.54-cal flintlock kit..**$729.95**

LYMAN TRADE RIFLE
Caliber: .50, .54. **Barrel:** 28 in. octagon, 1:48 in. twist. **Weight:** 10.8 lbs. **Length:** 45 in. overall. **Stock:** European walnut. **Sights:** Blade front, open rear adjustable for windage, or optional fixed sights. **Features:** Fast-twist rifling for conical bullets. Polished brass furniture with blue steel parts, stainless steel nipple. Hook breech, single trigger, coil spring percussion lock. Steel barrel rib and ramrod ferrules. Introduced 1980. From Lyman.
Price: 6032125/6 .50-cal./.54-cal. percussion.....................................**$565.00**
Price: 6032129/30 .50-cal./.54-cal. flintlock **$583.00**

PEDERSOLI 1777 CHARLEVILLE MUSKET
Caliber: .69. **Barrel:** 44.75 in. round, smoothbore. **Weight:** 10.5 lbs. **Length:** 57 in. **Stock:** European walnut, fullstock. **Sights:** Steel stud on upper barrelband. **Features:** Flintlock using one-inch flint. Steel parts all polished armory bright, brass furniture. Lock marked Charleville. Made by Pedersoli. Imported by Cabela's, Dixie Gun Works, others.
Price: Dixie Gun Works FR0930 .... **$1,450.00**

PEDERSOLI 1795 SPRINGFIELD MUSKET
Caliber: .69. **Barrel:** 44.75 in., round, smoothbore. **Weight:** 10.5 lbs. **Length:** 57.25 in. **Stock:** European walnut, fullstock. **Sights:** Brass stud on upper barrelband. **Features:** Flintlock using one-inch flint. Steel parts all polished armory bright, brass furniture. Lock marked US Springfield. Made by Pedersoli. Imported by Cabela's, Dixie Gun Works, others.
Price: Dixie Gun Works FR3210 .... **$1,495.00**

PEDERSOLI POTSDAM 1809 PRUSSIAN MUSKET
Caliber: .75. **Barrel:** 41.2 in. round, smoothbore. **Weight:** 9 lbs. **Length:** 56 in. **Stock:** European walnut, fullstock. **Sights:** Brass lug on upper barrelband. **Features:** Flintlock using one-inch flint. Steel parts all polished armory bright, brass furniture. Lock marked "Potsdam over G.S." Made by Pedersoli. Imported by Dixie Gun Works.
Price: Dixie Gun Works FR3175 .... **$1,575.00**

PEDERSOLI 1816 FLINTLOCK MUSKET
Caliber: .69. **Barrel:** 42 in., smoothbore. **Weight:** 9.75 lbs. **Length:** 56-7/8 in. overall. **Stock:** Walnut w/oil finish. **Sights:** Blade front. **Features:** All metal finished in "National Armory Bright," three barrel bands w/springs, steel ramrod w/button-shaped head. Made by Pedersoli. Imported by Dixie Gun Works.
Price: Dixie Gun Works PR3180, Percussion conversion **$1,495.00**

PEDERSOLI 1841 MISSISSIPPI RIFLE
Caliber: .54, .58. **Barrel:** 33 inches. **Weight:** 9.5 lbs. **Length:** 48.75 in. overall. **Stock:** European walnut. **Sights:** Blade front, notched rear. **Features:** Percussion musket-cap ignition. Reproduction of the original one-band rifle with large brass patchbox. Color case-hardened lockplate with browned barrel. Made by Pedersoli. Imported by Dixie Gun Works, Cabela's and others.
Price: Dixie Gun Works PR0870 (.54 caliber)....................................**$1,200.00**
Price: Dixie Gun Works PR3470 (.58 caliber)....................................**$1,100.00**

PEDERSOLI 1854 LORENZ RIFLE
Caliber: .54. **Barrel:** 37 in. **Weight:** 9 lbs. **Length:** 49 in. overall. **Stock:** European walnut. **Sights:** Blade front, rear steel open, flip-up style. **Features:** Percussion musket-cap ignition. Armory bright lockplate marked "Konigi. Wurt Fabrik." Armory bright steel barrel. Made by Pedersoli. Imported by Dixie Gun Works.
Price: Dixie Gun Works PR3156...**$1,500.00**

PEDERSOLI 1857 MAUSER RIFLE
Caliber: .54. **Barrel:** 39.75 in. **Weight:** 9.5 lbs. **Length:** 52 in. overall. **Stock:** European walnut. **Sights:** Blade front, rear steel adjustable for windage and elevation. **Features:** Percussion musket-cap ignition. Color case-hardened lockplate marked "Konigi. Wurt Fabrik." Armory bright steel barrel. Made by Pedersoli. Imported by Dixie Gun Works.
Price: Dixie Gun Works PR1330...**$1,695.00**

PEDERSOLI 1861 RICHMOND MUSKET
Caliber: .58. **Barrel:** 40 inches. **Weight:** 9.5 lbs. **Length:** 55.5 in. overall. **Stock:** European walnut. **Sights:** Blade front, three-leaf military rear. **Features:** Reproduction of the original three-band rifle. Percussion musket-cap ignition. Lock marked C. S. Richmond, Virginia. Armory bright. Made by Pedersoli. Imported by Dixie Gun Works and others.
Price: Dixie Gun Works PR4095...**$1,150.00**

PEDERSOLI 1861 SPRINGFIELD RIFLE
Caliber: .58. **Barrel:** 40 inches. **Weight:** 10 lbs. **Length:** 55.5 in. overall. **Stock:** European walnut. **Sights:** Blade front, three-leaf military rear. **Features:** Reproduction of the original three-band rifle. Percussion musket-cap ignition. Lockplate marked 1861 with eagle and U.S. Springfield. Armory bright steel. Made by Armi Sport/Chiappa, Pedersoli. Imported by Cabela's, Dixie Gun Works, others.
Price: Cabela's **$1,199.99**

Prices given are believed to be accurate at time of publication however, many factors affect retail pricing so exact pricing are not possible.

74TH EDITION, 2020 ⊕ **489**

PEDERSOLI BAKER CAVALRY SHOTGUN

Gauge: 20. **Barrels:** 11.25 inches. **Weight:** 5.75 pounds. **Length:** 27.5 in. overall. **Stock:** American walnut. **Sights:** Bead front. **Features:** Reproduction of shotguns carried by Confederate cavalry. Single non-selective trigger, back-action locks. No. 11 percussion musket-cap ignition. Blued barrel with steel furniture. Case-hardened lock. Pedersoli also makes a 12-gauge coach-length version of this back-action-lock shotgun with 20-inch barrels, and a full-length version in 10, 12 and 20 gauge. Made by Pedersoli. Imported by Cabela's and others.
Price: Cabela's $1,099.99

PEDERSOLI BRISTLEN MORGES AND WAADTLANDER TARGET RIFLES

Caliber: .44, .45. **Barrel:** 29.5 in. tapered octagonal, hooked breech. **Weight:** 15.5 lbs. **Length:** 48.5 in. overall. **Stock:** European walnut, halfstock with hooked buttplate and detachable palm rest. **Sights:** Creedmoor rear on Morges, Swiss Diopter on Waadtlander, hooded front sight notch. **Features:** Percussion back-action lock, double set, double-phase triggers, one barrel key, muzzle protector. Specialized bullet molds for each gun. Made by Pedersoli. Imported by Dixie Gun Works and others.
Price: Dixie Gun Works, .44 Bristlen Morges PR0165 .... $2,995.00
Price: Dixie Gun Works, .45 Waadtlander PR0183 .... $2,995.00

PEDERSOLI BROWN BESS

Caliber: .75. **Barrel:** 42 in., round, smoothbore. **Weight:** 9 lbs. **Length:** 57.75 in. **Stock:** European walnut, fullstock. **Sights:** Steel stud on front serves as bayonet lug. **Features:** Flintlock using one-inch flint with optional brass flash guard (SCO203), steel parts all polished armory bright, brass furniture. Lock marked Grice, 1762 with crown and GR. Made by Pedersoli. Imported by Cabela's, Dixie Gun Works, others.
Price: Dixie Gun Works Complete Gun FR0810 .... $1,350.00
Price: Dixie Gun Works Kit Gun FR0825 .... $1,050.00
Price: Dixie Gun Works Trade Gun, 30.5-in. barrel FR0665 .... $1,495.00
Price: Dixie Gun Works Trade Gun Kit FR0600 .... $975.00

PEDERSOLI COOK & BROTHER CONFEDERATE CARBINE/ARTILLERY/RIFLE

Caliber: .58 **Barrel:** 24/33/39 inches. **Weight:** 7.5/8.4/8.6 lbs. **Length:** 40.5/48/54.5 in. **Stock:** Select oil-finished walnut. **Features:** Percussion musket-cap ignition. Color case-hardened lock, browned barrel. Buttplate, triggerguard, barrelbands, sling swivels and nose cap of polished brass. Lock marked with stars and bars flag on tail and Athens, Georgia. Made by Pedersoli. Imported by Dixie Gun Works, others.
Price: Dixie Gun Works Carbine PR0830 ....$995.00
Price: Dixie Gun Works Artillery/Rifle PR32165 .... $995.00

PEDERSOLI COUNTRY HUNTER

Caliber: .50. **Barrel:** 26 in. octagonal. **Weight:** 6 lbs. **Length:** 41.75 in. overall. **Stock:** European walnut, halfstock. **Sights:** Rear notch, blade front. **Features:** Percussion, one barrel key. Made by Pedersoli. Imported by Dixie Gun Works.
Price: Cherry's Fine Guns Percussion, .50 .... $675.00
Price: Cherry's Fine Guns Flint, .50.. $688.00

PEDERSOLI ENFIELD MUSKETOON P1861

Caliber: .58. **Barrel:** 33 in. **Weight:** 9 lbs. **Length:** 35 in. overall. **Stock:** European walnut. **Sights:** Blade front, flip-up rear with elevator marked to 700 yards. **Features:** Reproduction of the original cavalry version of the Enfield rifle. Percussion musket-cap ignition. Blued barrel with steel barrelbands, brass furniture. Case-hardened lock. Euroarms version marked London Armory with crown. Pedersoli version has Birmingham stamp on stock and Enfield and Crown on lockplate. Made by Euroarms, Pedersoli. Imported by Cabela's and others.
Price: Cabela's $1,099.99

PEDERSOLI FRONTIER RIFLE

Caliber: .32, .36, .45, .50, .54. **Barrel:** 39 in., octagon, 1:48 twist. **Weight:** 7.75 lbs. **Length:** 54.5 in. overall. **Stock:** American black walnut. **Sights:** Blade front, rear drift adjustable for windage. **Features:** Color case-hardened lockplate and cock/hammer, brass triggerguard and buttplate; double set, double-phased triggers. Made by Pedersoli. Imported by Dixie Gun Works, and by Cabela's (as the Blue Ridge Rifle).
Price: Cabela's Percussion $599.99
Price: Cabela's Flintlock $649.99

PEDERSOLI ENFIELD THREE-BAND P1853 RIFLE

Caliber: .58. **Barrel:** 39 in. **Weight:** 10.25 lbs. **Length:** 52 in. overall. **Stock:** European walnut. **Sights:** Blade front, flip-up rear with elevator marked to 800 yards. **Features:** Reproduction of the original three-band rifle. Percussion musket-cap ignition. Blued barrel with steel barrelbands, brass furniture. Case-hardened lock. Lockplate marked "London Armory Co. and Crown." Made by Pedersoli. Imported by Cabela's.
Price: Cabela's $1,149.99

PEDERSOLI INDIAN TRADE MUSKET

Gauge: 20. **Barrel:** 36 in., octagon to round, smoothbore. **Weight:** 7.25 lbs. **Length:** 52 in. overall. **Stock:** American walnut. **Sights:** Blade front sight, no rear sight. **Features:** Flintlock. Kits version available. Made by Pedersoli. Imported by Dixie Gun Works.
Price: Dixie Gun Works, FR3170 .... $1,095.00
Price: Dixie Gun Works Kit, FK3370 .... $995.00

PEDERRSOLI JAEGER RIFLE

Caliber: .54. **Barrel:** 27.5 in. octagon, 1:24 in. twist. **Weight:** 8.25 lbs. **Length:** 43.5 in. overall. **Stock:** American walnut; sliding wooden patchbox on butt. **Sights:** Notch rear, blade front. **Features:** Flintlock or percussion. Conversion kits available, and recommended converting percussion guns to flintlocks using kit LO1102 at $209.00. Browned steel furniture. Made by Pedersoli. Imported by Dixie Gun Works.
Price: Dixie Gun Works Percussion, PR0835 .... $1,350.00
Price: Dixie Gun Works Flint, PR0835 .... $1,450.00
Price: Dixie Gun Works Percussion, kit gun, PK0146 .... $1,075.00
Price: Dixie Gun Works Flint, kit gun, PKO143 .... $1,100.00

PEDERSOLI KENTUCKY RIFLE

Caliber: .32, .45 and .50. **Barrel:** 35.5 in. octagonal. **Weight:** 7.5 (.50 cal.) to 7.75 lbs. (.32 cal.) **Length:** 51 in. overall. **Stock:** European walnut, full-length stock. **Sights:** Notch rear, blade front. **Features:** Flintlock or percussion, brass patchbox, double-set triggers. Also available as kit guns for all calibers and ignition systems. Made by Pedersoli. Imported by Dixie Gun Works.
Price: Dixie Gun Works Percussion, .32, PR3115 .... $750.00
Price: Dixie Gun Works Flint, .32, FR3100 .... $775.00
Price: Dixie Gun Works Percussion, .45, FR3120 .... $750.00
Price: Dixie Gun Works Flint, .45, FR3105 .... $775.00
Price: Dixie Gun Works Percussion, .50, FR3125 .... $750.00
Price: Dixie Gun Works Flint, .50, FR3110 .... $775.00

Prices given are believed to be accurate at time of publication however, many factors affect retail pricing so exact prices are not possible.

PEDERSOLI KODIAK DOUBLE RIFLES AND COMBINATION GUN.

Caliber: .50, .54 and .58. **Barrel:** 28.5 in.; 1:24/1:24/1:48 in. twist. **Weight:** 11.25/10.75/10 lbs. **Stock:** Straight grip European walnut. **Sights:** Two adjustable rear, steel ramp with brass bead front. **Features:** Percussion ignition, double triggers, sling swivels. A .72-caliber express rifle and a .50-caliber/12-gauge shotgun combination gun are also available. Blued steel furniture. Stainless steel nipple. Made by Pedersoli. Imported by Dixie Gun Works and some models by Cabela's and others.

Price: Dixie Gun Works Rifle 50X50 PR0970......................$1,525.00
Price: Dixie Gun Works Rifle 54X54 PR0975 ....$1,525.00
Price: Dixie Gun Works Rifle 58X58 PR0980......................$1,525.00
Price: Dixie Gun Works Combo 50X12 gauge PR0990 ....$1,350.00
Price: Dixie Gun Works Express Rifle .72 caliber PR0916 ....$1,550.00

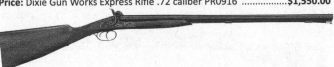

PEDERSOLI MAGNUM PERCUSSION SHOTGUN & COACH GUN

Gauge: 10, 12, 20 **Barrel:** Chrome-lined blued barrels, 25.5 in. Imp. Cyl. and Mod. **Weight:** 7.25, 7, 6.75 lbs. **Length:** 45 in. overall. **Stock:** Hand-checkered walnut, 14-in. pull. **Features:** Double triggers, light hand engraving, case-hardened locks, sling swivels. Made by Pedersoli. From Dixie Gun Works, others.

Price: Dixie Gun Works 10-ga. PS1030 ....$1,250.00
Price: Dixie Gun Works 10-ga. kit PS1040 ....$975.00
Price: Dixie Gun Works 12-ga. PS0930 ....$1,175.00
Price: Dixie Gun Works 12-ga. kit PS0940 ....$875.00
Price: Dixie Gun Works 12-ga. Coach gun, CylXCyl, PS0914 ....$1,150.00
Price: Dixie Gun Works 20-ga. PS0334 ....$1,175.00

PEDERSOLI MORTIMER RIFLE & SHOTGUN

Caliber: .54, 12 gauge. **Barrel:** 36 in., 1:66 in. twist, and cylinder bore. **Weight:** 10 lbs. rifle, 9 lbs. shotgun. **Length:** 52.25 in. **Stock:** Halfstock walnut. **Sights:** Blued steel rear with flip-up leaf, blade front. **Features:** Percussion and flint ignition. Blued steel furniture. Single trigger. Lock with hammer safety and "waterproof pan" marked Mortimer. A percussion .45-caliber target version of this gun is available with a peep sight on the wrist, and a percussion shotgun version is also offered. Made by Pedersoli. Imported by Dixie Gun Works.

Price: Dixie Gun Works Flint Rifle, FR0151 ....$1,575.00
Price: Dixie Gun Works Flint Shotgun FS0155 ....$1,525.00

PEDERSOLI OLD ENGLISH SHOTGUN

Gauge: 12 **Barrels:** Browned, 28.5 in. Cyl. and Mod. **Weight:** 7.5 lbs. **Length:** 45 in. overall. **Stock:** Hand-checkered American maple, cap box, 14-in. pull. **Features:** Double triggers, light hand engraving on lock, cap box and tang, swivel studs for sling attachment. Made by Pedersoli. From Dixie Gun Works, others.
Price: Dixie Gun Works PR4090 ....$1,750.00

PEDERSOLI ROCKY MOUNTAIN & MISSOURI RIVER HAWKEN RIFLES

Caliber: .54 Rocky Mountain, .45 and .50 in Missouri River. **Barrel:** 34.75 in. octagonal with hooked breech; Rocky Mountain 1:65 in. twist; Missouri River 1:47 twist in .45 cal., and 1:24 twist in .50 cal. **Weight:** 10 lbs. **Length:** 52 in. overall. **Stock:** Maple or walnut, halfstock. **Sights:** Rear buckhorn with push elevator, silver blade front. **Features:** Available in Percussion, with brass furniture and double triggers. Made by Pedersoli. Imported by Dixie Gun Works and others.

Price: Dixie Gun Works Rocky Mountain, Maple PR3430 ....$1,395.00
Price: Dixie Gun Works Rocky Mountain, Walnut PR3435 ....$1,195.00
Price: Dixie Gun Works Missouri River, .50 Walnut PR3415 ....$1,275.00
Price: Dixie Gun Works Missouri River, .45 Walnut PR3405 ....$1,275.00

PEDERSOLI PENNSYLVANIA RIFLE

Caliber: .32, .45 and .50. **Barrel:** 41.5 in. browned, octagonal, 1:48 in. twist. **Weight:** 8.25 lbs. **Length:** 56 in. overall. **Stock:** American walnut. **Sights:** Rear semi-buckhorn with push elevator, steel blade front. **Features:** Available in flint or percussion, with brass furniture, and double triggers. Also available as a kit. Made by Pedersoli. Imported by Dixie Gun Works and others.

Price: Dixie Gun Works Flint .32 FR3040 ....$950.00
Price: Dixie Gun Works Percussion .32 PR3055...................$900.00
Price: Dixie Gun Works Flint .45 PR3045 ....$950.00
Price: Dixie Gun Works Percussion .45 PR3060....................$900.00
Price: Dixie Gun Works Flint .50 PR3050 ....$950.00
Price: Dixie Gun Works Percussion .50 PR3065...................$900.00
Price: Dixie Gun Works Flint Kit .32 FK3260 ....$750.00
Price: Dixie Gun Works Percussion kit .32 PK3275 ....$695.00
Price: Dixie Gun Works Flint kit .45 FK3265 ....$750.00
Price: Dixie Gun Works Percussion kit .45 PR3280 ....$695.00
Price: Dixie Gun Works Flint kit .50 FK3270 ....$750.00
Price: Dixie Gun Works Percussion kit .50 PK3285 ....$695.00

PEDERSOLI SHARPS NEW MODEL 1859 MILITARY RIFLE AND CARBINE

Caliber: .54. **Barrel:** 30 in., 6-groove, 1:48 in. twist. **Weight:** 9 lbs. **Length:** 45.5 in. overall. **Stock:** Oiled walnut. **Sights:** Blade front, ladder-style rear. **Features:** Blued barrel, color case-hardened barrelbands, receiver, hammer, nose cap, lever, patchbox cover and buttplate. Introduced in 1995. Rifle made by Pedersoli. Rifle imported from Italy by Dixie Gun Works and others.

Price: Dixie Gun Work Rifle PR0862 ....$1,650.00
Price: Dixie Gun Work Carbine (22-in. barrel) PR0982 ....$1,400.00

PEDERSOLI SHARPS MODEL 1863 SPORTING RIFLE

Caliber: .45. **Barrel:** 32 in., octagon, 6-groove, 1:18 in. twist. **Weight:** 10.75 lbs. **Length:** 49 in. overall. **Stock:** Oiled walnut. **Sights:** Silver blade front, flip-up rear. **Features:** Browned octagon barrel, color case-hardened receiver, hammer and buttplate. Rifle made by Pedersoli. Imported by Dixie Gun Works and others.

Price: Dixie Gun Work Rifle PR5001 ....$1,500.00

PEDERSOLI SHARPS CONFEDERATE CARBINE

Caliber: .54. **Barrel:** 22 in., 6-groove, 1:48 in. twist. **Weight:** 8 lbs. **Length:** 39 in. overall. **Stock:** Oiled walnut. **Sights:** Blade front, dovetailed rear. **Features:** Browned barrel, color case-hardened receiver, hammer, and lever. Brass buttplate and barrel bands. Rifle made by Pedersoli. Imported by Dixie Gun Works and others.

Price: Dixie Gun Work Carbine PR3380 ....$1,395.00

PEDERSOLI TRADITIONAL HAWKEN TARGET RIFLE

Caliber: .50 and .54. **Barrel:** 29.5 in. octagonal, 1:48 in. twist. **Weight:** 9 or 8.5 lbs. **Length:** 45.5 in. overall. **Stock:** European walnut, halfstock. **Sights:** Rear click adjustable for windage and elevation, blade front. **Features:** Percussion and flintlock, brass patchbox, double-set triggers, one barrel key. Flint gun available for left-handed shooters. Both flint and percussion guns available as kit guns. Made by Pedersoli. Imported by Dixie Gun Works.

Price: Dixie Gun Works Percussion, .50 PR0502...................$650.00
Price: Dixie Gun Works Percussion, .54 PR0507...................$650.00
Price: Dixie Gun Works Flint, .50 FR1332 ....$725.00
Price: Dixie Gun Works Flint, .54 FR3515 ....$725.00

PEDERSOLI TRYON RIFLE

Caliber: .50. **Barrel:** 32 in. octagonal, 1:48 in. twist. **Weight:** 9.5 lbs. **Length:** 49 in. overall. **Stock:** European walnut, halfstock. **Sights:** Elevation-adjustable rear with stair-step notches, blade front. **Features:** Percussion, brass patchbox, double-set triggers, two barrel keys. Made by Pedersoli. Imported by Dixie Gun Works.

Price: Percussion, PR0860...........................$1,100.00

PEDERSOLI VOLUNTEER RIFLE

Caliber: .451. **Barrel:** 33 in., round interior bore 1:21 in. twist. **Weight:** 9.5 lbs. **Length:** 49 in. **Stock:** Oiled Grade 1 American walnut. **Sights:** Blade front, ladder-style rear. **Features:** Checkered stock wrist and fore-end. Blued barrel, steel ramrod, bone charcoal case-hardened receiver and hammer. Designed for .451 conical bullets. Compare to hexagonal-bored Whitworth Rifle below. Hand-fitted and finished.
Price: Dixie Gun Works PR3150...... .... **$1,295.00**

PEDERSOLI WHITWORTH RIFLE

Caliber: .451. **Barrel:** 36 in., hexagonal interior bore 1:20 in. twist. **Weight:** 9.6 lbs. **Length:** 52.5 in. **Stock:** Oiled Grade 1 American walnut. **Sights:** Blade front, ladder-style rear. **Features:** Checkered stock wrist and fore-end. Blued barrel, steel ramrod, bone charcoal case-hardened receiver and hammer. Designed for .451 conical hexagonal bullet. Compare to round-bored Volunteer Rifle above. Hand-fitted to original specifications using original Enfield arsenal gauges.
Price: Dixie Gun Works PR3256...... .... **$1,750.00**

PEDERSOLI ZOUAVE RIFLE

Caliber: .58 percussion. **Barrel:** 33 inches. **Weight:** 9.5 lbs. **Length:** 49 inches. **Stock:** European walnut. **Sights:** Blade front, three-leaf military rear. **Features:** Percussion musket-cap ignition. One-piece solid barrel and bolster. Brass-plated patchbox. Made in Italy by Pedersoli. Imported by Dixie Gun Works, others.
Price: Dixie Gun Works PF0340. ....**$975.00**

REMINGTON MODEL 700 ULTIMATE MUZZLELOADER

Caliber: .50 percussion. **Barrel:** 26 in., 1:26 in. twist, satin stainless steel, fluted. **Length:** 47 in. **Stock:** Bell & Carlson black synthetic. **Sights:** None on synthetic-stocked model. **Ramrod:** Stainless steel. **Weight:** 8.5 lbs. **Features:** Remington single shot Model 700 bolt action, re-primable cartridge-case ignition using Remington Magnum Large Rifle Primer, sling studs.
Price: 86960 Starting at **$1,015.00**

THOMPSON/CENTER IMPACT MUZZLELOADING RIFLE

Caliber: .50. **Barrel:** 26 in., 1:28 twist, Weather Shield finish. **Weight:** 6.5 lbs. **Length:** 41.5 in. **Stock:** Straight Realtree Hardwoods HD or black composite. **Features:** Sliding-hood, break-open action, #209 primer ignition, removable breech plug, synthetic stock adjustable from 12.5 to 13.5 in., adjustable fiber-optic sights, aluminum ramrod, camo, QLA relieved muzzle system.
Price: .50-cal Stainless/Realtree Hardwoods, Weather Shield **$324.00**
Price: .50-cal Blued/Black/scope, case............................ ....**$263.99**

THOMPSON/CENTER PRO HUNTER FX

Caliber: .50 as muzzleloading barrel. **Barrel:** 26 in., Weather Shield with relieved muzzle on muzzleloader; interchangeable with 14 centerfire calibers. **Weight:** 7 lbs. **Length:** 40.5 in. overall. **Stock:** Interchangeable American walnut butt and fore-end, black composite, FlexTech recoil-reducing camo stock as thumbhole or straight, rubber over-molded stock and fore-end. **Ramrod:** Solid aluminum. **Sights:** Tru-Glo fiber-optic front and rear. **Features:** Blue or stainless steel. Uses the frame of the Encore centerfire pistol; break-open design using triggerguard spur; stainless steel universal breech plug; uses #209 shotshell primers. Made in U.S. by Thompson/Center Arms.
Price: .50-cal Stainless/Black FlexTech Stock Model 5800................... **$649.00**
Price: .50-cal Stainless/Engraved frame FlexTech RT-AP camo.............**$709.00**

THOMPSON/CENTER TRIUMPH BONE COLLECTOR

Caliber: .50. **Barrel:** 28 in., Weather Shield coated. **Weight:** 6.5 lbs. Overall: 42 in. **Stock:** FlexTech recoil-reducing. Black composite or Realtree AP HD camo straight, rubber over-molded stock and fore-end. **Sights:** Fiber optic. **Ramrod:** Solid aluminum. **Features:** Break-open action. Quick Detachable Speed Breech XT plug, #209 shotshell primer ignition, easy loading QLA relieved muzzle. Made in U.S. by Thompson/Center Arms. Available from Cabela's, Bass Pro.
Price: .50-cal Synthetic Realtree AP, fiber optics.... .... **$720.00**
Price: .50-cal Synthetic/Weather Shield Black...................................**$638.00**
Price: .50-cal. Weather Shield/AP Camo...**$679.00**
Price: .50 cal. Silver Weather Shield/AP Camo......................................**$689.00**

THOMPSON/CENTER STRIKE

Caliber: .50. **Barrel:** 24 or 20 in., nitride finished, tapered barrel. **Weight:** 6.75 or 6.25 lbs. **Length:** 44 in. or 40 in. **Stock:** Walnut, black synthetic, G2-Vista Camo. **Finish:** Armornite nitride. **Features:** Break-open action, sliding hammerless cocking mechanism, optional pellet or loose powder primer holders, easily removable breech plugs retained by external collar, aluminum frame with steel mono-block to retain barrel, recoil pad. **Sights:** Williams fiber-optic sights furnished, drilled and tapped for scope. Made in the U.S. by Thompson/Center.
Price: .50 cal. 24-in. barrel, black synthetic stock **$499.00**
Price: .50 cal. 24-in. barrel, walnut stock **$599.00**
Price: .50 cal. 24-in. barrel, G2 camo stock **$549.00**

TRADITIONS BUCKSTALKER IN-LINE RIFLE

Caliber: .50. **Barrel:** 24 in., Cerakote finished, Accelerator Breech Plug. **Weight:** 6 lbs. **Length:** 40 in. **Stock:** Synthetic, G2 Vista camo or black. **Sights:** Fiber-optic rear. **Features:** Break-open action, matte-finished action and barrel. **Ramrod:** Solid aluminum. Imported by Traditions.
Price: R72003540 .50-cal. Youth Synthetic stock/blued........................**$219.00**
Price: R72103540 .50-cal. Synthetic stock/Cerakote **$329.00**
Price: R5-72003540 .50-cal. Synthetic stock/blued, scope.................**$294.00**
Price: R5-72103547 .50-cal. Synthetic stock/Cerakote, scope **$369.00**

BLACKPOWDER Muskets & Rifles

TRADITIONS CROCKETT RIFLE
Caliber: .32. **Barrel:** 32 in., 1:48 in. twist. **Weight:** 6.75 lbs. **Length:** 49 in. overall. **Stock:** Beech, inletted toe plate. **Sights:** Blade front, fixed rear. **Features:** Set triggers, hardwood halfstock, brass furniture, color case-hardened lock. Percussion. Imported by Traditions.
Price: R26128101 .32-cal. Percussion, finished $543.00
Price: RK52628100 .32-cal. Percussion, kit... $479.00

TRADITIONS EVOLUTION BOLT-ACTION BLACKPOWDER RIFLE
Caliber: .50 percussion. **Barrel:** 26 in., 1:28 in. twist, Cerakote finished barrel and action. **Length:** 39 in. **Sights:** Steel Williams fiber-optic sights. **Weight:** 7 to 7.25 lbs. **Length:** 45 in. overall. **Features:** Bolt action, cocking indicator, thumb safety, shipped with adaptors for No. 11 caps, musket caps and 209 shotgun-primer ignition, sling swivels. Ramrod: Aluminum, sling studs. Available with exposed ignition as a Northwest gun. Imported by Traditions.
Price: R67113350 .50-cal. synthetic black, Cerakote........................... $250.00
Price: R67113353 .50-cal. synthetic Realtree AP camo...... ....$299.00

TRADITIONS HAWKEN WOODSMAN RIFLE
Caliber: .50. **Barrel:** 28 in., blued, 15/16 in. flats. **Weight:** 7 lbs., 11 oz. **Length:** 44.5 in. overall. **Stock:** Walnut stained hardwood. **Sights:** Beaded blade front hunting-style open rear adjustable for windage and elevation. **Features:** Brass patchbox and furniture. Double-set triggers. Flint or percussion. Imported by Traditions.
Price: R2390801 .50-cal. Flintlock $544.00
Price: R24008 .50-cal. Percussion $499.00

TRADITIONS KENTUCKY RIFLE
Caliber: .50. **Barrel:** 33.5 in., 7/8 in. flats, 1:66 in. twist. **Weight:** 7 lbs. **Length:** 49 in. overall. **Stock:** Beech, inletted toe plate. **Sights:** Blade front, fixed rear. **Features:** Full-length, two-piece stock; brass furniture; color case-hardened lock. Flint or percussion. Imported by Traditions.
Price: R2010 .50-cal. Flintlock,1:66 twist $509.00
Price: R2020 .50-cal. Percussion, 1:66 twist....................................... $449.00
Price: KRC52206 .50-cal. Percussion, kit... $343.00

TRADITIONS PA PELLET FLINTLOCK
Caliber: .50. **Barrel:** 26 in., blued, 1:28 in. twist., Cerakote. **Weight:** 7 lbs. **Length:** 45 in. **Stock:** Hardwood, synthetic and synthetic break-up, sling swivels. Fiber-optic sights. **Features:** New flintlock action, removable breech plug, available as left-hand model with hardwood stock. Imported by Traditions.
Price: R3800501 .50-cal. Hardwood, blued, fib. opt $519.00
Price: R3890501 .50-cal. Hardwood, left-hand, blued $529.00
Price: R3800550 .50-cal. Synthetic/blued, fib. opt............................... $497.00

TRADITIONS PENNSYLVANIA RIFLE
Caliber: .50. **Barrel:** 40.25 in., 7/8 in. flats, 1:66 in. twist, octagon. **Weight:** 9 lbs. **Length:** 57.5 in. overall. **Stock:** Walnut. **Sights:** Blade front, adjustable rear. **Features:** Single-piece walnut stock, brass patchbox and ornamentation. Double-set triggers. Flint or percussion. Imported by Traditions.
Price: R2090 .50-cal. Flintlock $865.00
Price: R2100 .50-cal. Percussion... $834.00

TRADITIONS PURSUIT ULTRALIGHT MUZZLELOADER
Caliber: .50. **Barrel:** 26 in., chromoly tapered, fluted barrel with premium Cerakote finish, Accelerator Breech Plug. **Weight:** 5.5 lbs. **Length:** 42 in. **Stock:** Rubber over-molded Soft Touch camouflage, straight and thumbhole stock options. **Sights:** Optional 3-9x40 scope with medium rings and bases, mounted and bore-sighted by a factory-trained technician. **Features:** Break-open action, Williams fiber-optic sights. Imported by Traditions.
Price: Pursuit G4 Ultralight .50 Cal. Select Hardwoods/
Cerakote R741101NS...$469.00
Price: Pursuit G4 Ultralight .50 Cal. Mossy Oak Break Up Country Camo/
Cerakote R7411416..$404.00
Price: Pursuit G4 Ultralight .50 Cal. Mossy Oak Break Up Country/Cerakote/
Scope/Carrying Case.... .... $479.00

TRADITIONS TRACKER IN-LINE RIFLE
Caliber: .50. **Barrel:** 24 in., blued or Cerakote, 1:28 in. twist. **Weight:** 6 lbs., 4 oz. **Length:** 43 in. **Stock:** Black synthetic. Ramrod: Synthetic, high-impact polymer. **Sights:** Lite Optic blade front, adjustable rear. **Features:** Striker-fired action, thumb safety, adjustable trigger, rubber buttpad, sling swivel studs. Takes 150 grains of Pyrodex pellets, one-piece musket cap and 209 ignition systems. Drilled and tapped for scope. Legal for use in Northwest. Imported by Traditions.
Price: R44003470 .50-cal. Synthetic/blued $184.00

TRADITIONS VORTEK STRIKERFIRE
Caliber: .50 **Barrel:** 28 in., chromoly, tapered, fluted barrel. **Weight:** 6.25 lbs. **Length:** 44 in. **Stock:** Over-molded soft-touch straight stock, removable buttplate for in-stock storage. **Finish:** Premium Cerakote and Realtree Xtra. **Features:** Break-open action, sliding hammerless cocking mechanism, drop-out trigger assembly, speed load system, Accelerator Breech Plug, recoil pad. **Sights:** Optional 3-9x40 muzzleloader scope. Imported by Traditions.
Price: Vortek StrikerFire with Nitride Coating Mossy Oak
Break-Up Country Camo..... ....$583.00
Price: Vortek StrikerFire with 3-9x40 Sig Sauer Whisky 3 Scope,
Sling & Case...$756.00

TRADITIONS VORTEK STRIKERFIRE LDR
Caliber: .50. **Barrel:** 30 in., chromoly, tapered, fluted barrel. **Weight:** 6.8 lbs. **Length:** 46 in. **Stock:** Over-molded soft-touch straight stock, removable buttplate for in-stock storage. **Finish:** Premium Cerakote and Realtree Xtra. **Features:** Break-open action, sliding hammerless cocking mechanism, drop-out trigger assembly, speed load system, Accelerator Breech Plug, recoil pad. **Sights:** Optional 3-9x40 muzzleloader scope. Imported by Traditions.
Price: R491140WA Synthetic/black Hogue Over-mold,
        Cerakote barrel, no sights..$499.00

WOODMAN ARMS PATRIOT
Caliber: .45, .50. **Barrel:** 24 in., nitride-coated, 416 stainless, 1:24 twist in .45, 1:28 twist in .50. **Weight:** 5.75 lbs. **Length:** 43-in. Stocks: Laminated, walnut or hydrographic dipped, synthetic black, over-molded soft-touch straight stock. **Finish:** Nitride black and black anodized. **Features:** Break-open action, hammerless cocking mechanism, match-grade patented trigger assembly, speed load system, recoil pad. **Sights:** Picatinny rail with built-in rear and 1-inch or 30 mm scope mounts, red fiber-optic front bead.
Price: Patriot .45 or .50-cal...$899.00

UBERTI 1858 NEW ARMY REMINGTON TARGET CARBINE REVOLVER
Caliber: .44, 6-shot. **Barrel:** Tapered octagon, 18 in. **Weight:** 70.4 oz. **Length:** Standard 35.3 in. **Stock:** Walnut. **Sights:** Standard blade front, adjustable rear. **Features:** Replica of Remington's revolving rifle of 1866. Made by Uberti. Imported by Uberti USA, Cimarron F.A. Co., Taylor's and others.
Price: Uberti USA, 341200.. $559.00

AIR ARMS ALFA PROJ COMPETITION PCP PISTOL
Caliber: .177 pellets. **Barrel:** Rifled. **Weight:** 1.94 lbs. **Length:** 15.5 inches. **Power:** Pre-charged pneumatic. **Sights:** Front post, fully adjustable rear blade, **Features:** 10-Meter competition class pistol, highly adjustable trigger, **Velocity:** 500 fps.
Price: $879.99

AIRFORCE TALON P

AIRFORCE TALON P PCP AIR PISTOL
Caliber: .25. **Barrel:** Rifled 12.0 in. **Weight:** 3.5 lbs. **Length:** 24.2 in. **Sights:** None, grooved for scope. **Features:** Quick-detachable air tank with adjustable power. Match-grade Lothar Walther, massive power output in a highly compact size, two-stage trigger. **Velocity:** 400-900 fps.
Price: $479.95

AIR VENTURI V10 MATCH AIR PISTOL
Caliber: .177 pellets. **Barrel:** Rifled. **Weight:** 1.95 lbs. **Length:** 12.6 in. **Power:** Single stroke pneumatic. **Sights:** Front post, fully adjustable rear blade, **Features:** 10-Meter competition class pistol, fully adjustable trigger, 1.5-lb. trigger pull **Velocity:** 400 fps.
Price: $300.00

ASG STI DUTY ONE CO2 BB PISTOL
Caliber: .177 steel BBs. **Barrel:** Smoothbore **Weight:** 1.82 lbs. **Length:** 8.66 in. **Power:** CO2. **Sights:** Fixed. **Features:** Blowback, accessory rail, and metal slide. **Velocity:** 383 fps.
Price: $120.00

ATAMAN AP16 REGULATED COMPACT AIR PISTOL, SILVER
Caliber: .22 pellets. **Barrel:** Rifled Match Barrel **Weight:** 1.76 lbs. **Length:** 12.0 in.

Power: Pre-Charged Pneumatic. **Sights:** Fixed Front Ramp, Adjustable Rear Notch. **Features:** 7-round Rotary Magazine, 300 Bar Max Fill, Regulated for hunting power, exceptional build quality, available in satin and blued finishes **Velocity:** 590 fps.
Price: $1,049.99

ATAMAN AP16 REGULATED STANDARD AIR PISTOL
Caliber: .22 pellets. **Barrel:** Rifled Match Barrel **Weight:** 2.2 lbs. **Length:** 14.37 in. **Power:** Pre-Charged Pneumatic. **Sights:** Fixed Front Ramp, Adjustable Rear Notch. **Features:** 7-round Rotary Magazine, 300 Bar Max Fill, Regulated for hunting power, exceptional build quality, **Velocity:** 656 fps.
Price: $1,049.99

BEEMAN P17 AIR PISTOL
Caliber: .177 pellets. **Barrel:** Rifled. **Weight:** 1.7 lbs. **Length:** 9.6 in. **Power:** Single stroke pneumatic. **Sights:** Front and rear fiber-optic sights, rear sight fully adjustable. **Features:** Exceptional trigger, Grooved for scope mounting with dry-fire feature for practice. **Velocity:** 410 fps.
Price: $44.99

BEEMAN P1 MAGNUM AIR PISTOL
Caliber: .177, .20, .22. pellets. **Barrel:** Rifled. **Weight:** 2.5 lbs. **Length:** 11 in. **Power:** Single stroke, spring-piston. **Grips:** Checkered walnut. **Sights:** Blade front, square notch rear with click micrometer adjustments for windage and elevation. Grooved for scope mounting. **Features:** Dual power for .177 and 20 cal.; Compatible with all Colt 45 auto grips. Dry-firing feature for practice. **Velocity:** varies by caliber and power setting.
Price: .... $529.95–$564.95

BEEMAN P3 PNEUMATIC AIR PISTOL
Caliber: .177. pellets. **Barrel:** Rifled **Weight:** 1.7 lbs. **Length:** 9.6 in. **Power:** Single-stroke pneumatic. **Sights:** Front and rear fiber-optic sights, rear sight fully adjustable. **Features:** Grooved for scope mounting, exceptional trigger, automatic safety. **Velocity:** 410 fps.
Price: $289.95

BEEMAN P11 AIR PISTOL
Caliber: .177, .22. **Barrel:** Rifled. **Weight:** 2.6 lbs. **Length:** 10.75 in. **Power:** Single-stroke pneumatic with high and low settings. **Sights:** Front ramp sight, fully adjustable rear sight. **Features:** 2-stage adjustable trigger and automatic safety. **Velocity:** Up to 600 fps in .177 caliber and Up to 460 fps in .22 caliber.
Price: .... $614.95–$634.95

BENJAMIN MARAUDER PCP PISTOL
Caliber: .22 **Barrel:** Rifled. **Weight:** 2.7-3 lbs. **Length:** Pistol length 18 in./ Carbine length 29.75 in. **Power:** Pre-charged pneumatic **Sights:** None. Grooved for optics. **Features:** Multi-shot (8-round rotary magazine) bolt action, shrouded steel barrel, two-stage adjustable trigger, includes both pistol grips and a carbine stock and is built in America. **Velocity:** 700 fps.
Price: $500.00

BENJAMIN MARAUDER WOODS WALKER PCP PISTOL
Caliber: .22 **Barrel:** Rifled. **Weight:** 2.7 lbs. **Length:** Pistol length 18 in./Carbine length 29.75 in. **Power:** Pre-charged pneumatic **Sights:** Includes CenterPoint Multi-TAC Quick Aim Sight. **Features:** Multi-shot (8-round rotary magazine) bolt action, shrouded steel barrel, two-stage adjustable trigger, includes both pistol grips and a carbine stock and is built in America. **Velocity:** 700 fps.
Price: $550.00

BENJAMIN TRAIL MARK II NP AIR PISTOL
Caliber: .177 pellets. **Barrel:** Rifled. **Weight:** 3.43 lbs. **Length:** 16 in. **Power:** Single cock, nitro piston. **Sights:** Fiber-optic front, fully adjustable rear. **Features:** Grooved for scope, **Velocity:** To 625 fps.
Price: $99.99

BERETTA APX BLOWBACK AIR PISTOL
Caliber: .177 steel BBs. **Barrel:** Smoothbore. **Weight:** 1.47 lbs. **Length:** 7.48 in. **Power:** CO2. **Sights:** Fixed. **Features:** Highly accurate replica action pistol, 19-shot capacity, front accessory rail, metal and ABS plastic construction. **Velocity:** 400 fps.
Price: $65.00

BERETTA MODEL 84FS

BERETTA M84FS AIR PISTOL
Caliber: .177 steel BBs. **Barrel:** Smoothbore **Weight:** 1.4 lbs. **Length:** 7 in. **Power:** CO2. **Sights:** Fixed. **Features:** Highly realistic replica action pistol, blowback operation, full metal construction. **Velocity:** To 360 fps.
Price: $85.55

BERETTA PX4 CO2 PISTOL
Caliber: .177 pellet /.177 steel BBs. **Barrel:** Rifled **Weight:** 1.6 lbs. **Length:** 7.6 in. **Power:** CO2. **Sights:** Blade front sight and fixed rear sight. **Features:** Semi-automatic, 16-shot capacity with maximum of 40-shots per fill, dual ammo capable. **Velocity:** To 380 fps.
Price: $101.64

BERETTA ELITE II CO2 PISTOL
Caliber: .177 steel BBs. **Barrel:** Smoothbore **Weight:** 1.5 lbs. **Length:** 8.5 in. **Power:** CO2. **Sights:** Blade front sight and fixed rear sight. **Features:** Semi-automatic, 19-shot capacity. **Velocity:** Up to 410 fps.
Price: $49.99

BERETTA M9A3 FULL AUTO BB PISTOL
Caliber: .177 steel BBs. **Barrel:** Smoothbore **Weight:** NA. **Length:** NA. **Power:** CO2. **Sights:** Blade front sight and fixed rear sight. **Features:** Can operate as semi-automatic or fully automatic, full size 18-shot magazine, blowback slide, single/double action, ambidextrous safety. **Velocity:** To 380 fps.
Price: $124.99

BERETTA 92A1 CO2 FULL AUTO BB PISTOL
Caliber: .177 steel BBs. **Barrel:** Smoothbore **Weight:** 2.4 lbs. **Length:** 8.5 in. **Power:** CO2. **Sights:** Fixed. **Features:** Highly realistic replica action pistol, 18-shot semi-automatic, full metal construction, selectable fire semi-automatic & full-automatic. **Velocity:** To 330 fps.
Price: $139.09

BERETTA 92FS CO2 PELLET GUN
Caliber: .177 pellets. **Barrel:** Rifled **Weight:** 2.75 lbs. **Length:** 8.0 in. **Power:** CO2. **Sights:** Fixed front sight, rear adjustable for windage. **Features:** Highly realistic replica-action pistol, 8-shot semi-automatic, full metal construction, available in various finishes and grips. **Velocity:** To 425 fps.
Price: .... $224.00-$288.00

BERSA THUNDER 9 PRO BB PISTOL
Caliber: .177 steel BBs. **Barrel:** Smoothbore. **Weight:** 1.17 lbs. **Length:** 7.56 in. **Power:** CO2. **Sights:** Fixed, three-white-dot system. **Features:** Highly realistic replica action pistol, 19-shot semi-automatic, composite/synthetic construction. **Velocity:** To 400 fps.
Price: $79.95

BERSA BP9CC DUAL TONE BLOWBACK AIR PISTOL
Caliber: .177 steel BBs. **Barrel:** Smoothbore. **Weight:** 1.35 lbs. **Length:** 6.61 in. **Power:** CO2. **Sights:** Fixed three-dot system. **Features:** Blowback, metal slide, weaver accessory rail. **Velocity:** 350 fps.
Price: $119.95

BLACK OPS 1911 FULL METAL CO2 BLOWBACK AIR
Caliber: .177 steel BBs. **Barrel:** Smoothbore **Weight:** 1.80 lbs. **Length:** 8.6 in. **Power:** CO2. **Sights:** Fixed blade and ramp. **Features:** Highly realistic replica-action pistol, 17-shot semi-automatic, full metal construction **Velocity:** To 320 fps.
Price: $119.99

BROWNING 800 EXPRESS AIR PISTOL BROWNING 800 EXPRESS
Caliber: .177 pellets. **Barrel:** Rifled **Weight:** 3.9 lbs. **Length:** 18 in. **Power:** Single cock, spring-piston. **Sights:** Fiber-optic front sight and adjustable fiber-optic rear sight. **Features:** Automatic safety, 11mm dovetail rail scope mounting possible. **Velocity:** 700 fps.
Price: $168.00

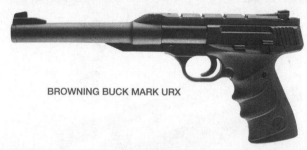

BROWNING BUCK MARK URX

BROWNING BUCK MARK URX AIR PISTOL BROWNING BUCK MARK AIR PISTOL
Caliber: .177 pellets. **Barrel:** Rifled **Weight:** 1.5 lbs. **Length:** 12.0 in. **Power:** Single cock, spring-piston. **Sights:** Front ramp sight, fully adjustable rear notch sight. **Features:** Weaver rail for scope mounting, light cocking force. **Velocity:** 360 fps.
Price: $45.00

CHIAPPA FAS 6044 PNEUMATIC PISTOL
Caliber: .177 pellets. **Barrel:** Rifled. **Weight:** 2 lbs. **Length:** 11.0 in. **Power:** Single stroke pneumatic. **Sights:** Fully adjustable target rear sight. **Features:** Walnut ambidextrous grip, fully adjustable trigger. **Velocity:** 330 fps.
Price: $469.00

COLT PYTHON

COLT PYTHON CO2 PISTOL
Caliber: .177 steel BBs. **Barrel:** Smoothbore **Weight:** 2.6 lbs. **Length:** 11.25 in. **Power:** CO2. **Sights:** Fixed. **Features:** High-quality replica, swing-out cylinder, removable casings and functioning ejector, multiple finishes other options. **Velocity:** To 400 fps.
Price: $149.99

COLT PYTHON 6-INCH CO2 PISTOL
Caliber: .177 steel BBs. **Barrel:** Smoothbore. **Weight:** 1.1 lbs. **Length:** 11.5 in. **Power:** CO2. **Sights:** Fixed front sight, rear sight adjustable for windage and elevation. **Features:** High-quality replica, removable 10-round clip. **Velocity:** To 410 fps.
Price: $50.00

COLT DEFENDER

COLT DEFENDER BB PISTOL
Caliber: .177 steel BBs. **Barrel:** Smoothbore **Weight:** 1.6 lbs. **Length:** 6.75 in. **Power:** CO2. **Sights:** Fixed with blade ramp front sight. **Features:** Semi-automatic, 16-shot capacity, all metal construction, realistic weight and feel. **Velocity:** 410 fps.
Price: **$75.00**

COLT 1911 SPECIAL COMBAT CLASSIC BB PISTOL
Caliber: .177 steel BBs. **Barrel:** Smoothbore. **Weight:** 2.05 lbs. **Length:** 8.58 in. **Power:** CO2. **Sights:** Blade front sight and adjustable rear sight. **Features:** Semi-automatic, 20-shot capacity, realistic action, weight and feel. **Velocity:** 400 fps.
Price: **$120.00**

COLT 1911 A1 CO2 PELLET PISTOL
Caliber: .177 pellets. **Barrel:** Rifled **Weight:** 2.4 lbs. **Length:** 9.0 in. **Power:** CO2. **Sights:** Blade ramp front sight and adjustable rear sight. **Features:** Semi-automatic, 8-shot capacity, all metal construction, realistic weight and feel. **Velocity:** 425 fps.
Price: **$259.99**

COLT COMMANDER CO2 PISTOL
Caliber: .177 steel BBs. **Barrel:** Smoothbore. **Weight:** 2.1 lbs. **Length:** 8.5 in. **Power:** CO2. **Sights:** Blade front sight and fixed rear sight. **Features:** Semi-automatic, blowback action, 18-shot capacity, highly realistic replica pistol. **Velocity:** 325 fps.
Price: **$119.99**

COLT PEACEMAKER SAA CO2 REVOLVER, NICKEL
Caliber: .177 steel BBs. **Barrel:** Smoothbore. **Weight:** 2.1 lbs. **Length:** 11 in. **Power:** CO2. **Sights:** Blade front sight and fixed rear sight. **Features:** Full metal revolver with manual safety, realistic loading, 6 individual shells, highly accurate, full metal replica pistol, multiple finishes, grips and custom engraved, special editions available. **Velocity:** 410 fps.
Price: **$149.99**

COLT SAA CO2 PELLET REVOLVER, NICKEL
Caliber: .177 pellets. **Barrel:** Rifled. **Weight:** 2.1 lbs. **Length:** 11 in. **Power:** CO2. **Sights:** Blade front sight and fixed rear sight. **Features:** Full metal revolver with manual safety, realistic loading, 6 individual shells, highly accurate, full metal replica pistol, multiple finishes and grips available. **Velocity:** 380 fps.
Price: **$179.99**

JOHN WAYNE "DUKE" COLT SINGLE ACTION ARMY CO2 PELLET REVOLVER
Caliber: .177 steel BBs. **Barrel:** Smoothbore. **Weight:** 2.1 lbs. **Length:** 11 in. **Power:** CO2. **Sights:** Blade front sight and fixed rear sight. **Features:** Officially licensed "John Wayne Duke" imagery and signature, full metal revolver with manual safety, realistic loading, 6 individual shells, highly accurate, full metal replica pistol, multiple finishes and grips available. **Velocity:** 380 fps.
Price: **$159.99**

COMETA INDIAN AIR PISTOL, NICKEL/BLACK
Caliber: .177 pellets. **Barrel:** Rifled. **Weight:** 2.43 lbs. **Length:** 10.43 in. **Power:** Spring Powered. **Sights:** Blade front sight and adjustable rear sight. **Features:** Single shot, cold-hammered forged barrel, textured grips. **Velocity:** 492 fps.
Price: .... **$189.95–$219.95**

CROSMAN 2240
Caliber: .22. **Barrel:** Rifled. **Weight:** 1.8 lbs. **Length:** 11.13 in. **Power:** CO2. **Sights:** Blade front, rear adjustable. **Features:** Single shot bolt action, ambidextrous grip, all metal construction. **Velocity:** 460 fps.
Price: **$87.60**

CROSMAN 2300S TARGET PISTOL
Caliber: .177 pellets. **Barrel:** Rifled. **Weight:** 2.66 lbs. **Length:** 16 in. **Power:** CO2. **Sights:** Front fixed sight and Williams notched rear sight. **Features:** Meets IHMSA rules for Production Class Silhouette Competitions. Lothar Walter match-grade barrel, adjustable trigger, adjustable hammer, stainless steel bolt, 60 shots per CO2 cartridge. **Velocity:** 520 fps.
Price: **$274.95**

CROSMAN 2300T
Caliber: .177 pellets. **Barrel:** Rifled. **Weight:** 2.66 lbs. **Length:** 13.25 in. **Power:** CO2. **Sights:** fixed front sight and LPA rear sight. **Features:** Single-shot, bolt action, adjustable trigger, designed for shooting clubs and organizations that teach pistol shooting and capable of firing 40 shots per CO2 cartridge. **Velocity:** 420 fps.
Price: **$190.00**

CROSMAN 1701P SILHOUETTE PCP AIR PISTOL
Caliber: .177 pellets. **Barrel:** Rifled Lothar Walther Match. **Weight:** 2.5 lbs. **Length:** 14.75 in. **Power:** Pre-charged Pneumatic. **Sights:** fixed front sight rear sight not included. **Features:** Adjustable trigger, designed for shooting silhouette competition, 50 shots per fill. **Velocity:** 450 fps.
Price: **$374.95**

CROSMAN 1720T PCP TARGET PISTOL
Caliber: .177 pellets. **Barrel:** Rifled Lothar Walther Match. **Weight:** 2.96 lbs. **Length:** 18.00 in. **Power:** Pre-charged Pneumatic. **Sights:** Not included **Features:** Adjustable trigger, designed for shooting silhouettes, fully shrouded barrel, 50 shots per fill. **Velocity:** 750 fps.
Price: **$500.00**

CROSMAN SR .357 Revolver
Caliber: .177 steel BBs. **Barrel:** Smoothbore. **Weight:** 2 lbs. **Length:** 11.5 in. **Power:** CO2. **Sights:** Blade front, rear adjustable. **Features:** Semi-auto 6-round revolver styling and finger-molded grip design. Multiple finishes and configurations available. **Velocity:** 450 fps.
Price: .... **$99.99–$129.99**

CROSMAN SNR.357S DUAL AMMO CO2 REVOLVER
Caliber: .177 steel BBs/.177 pellets. **Barrel:** Smoothbore **Weight:** 2.00 lbs. **Length:** 11.73 in. **Power:** CO2. **Sights:** Adjustable rear sight, Fixed Front Blade. **Features:** Full metal revolver in "stainless steel" finish. Comes with shells for BBs and .177 lead pellets **Velocity:** 400 fps. with steel BBs.
Price: **$149.99**

CROSMAN TRIPLE THREAT CO2 REVOLVER
Caliber: .177 steel BBs/.177 pellets. **Barrel:** Rifled. **Weight:** Variable. **Length:** Variable. **Power:** CO2. **Sights:** Adjustable rear sight. **Features:** Comes with three barrels (3 in., 6 in., and 8 in.) and six-shot BB clip and 10-shot .177 lead pellet clip, single/double action, die cast full metal frame. **Velocity:** Up to 425 fps. with steel BBs.
Price: **$99.99**

CROSMAN C11 CO2 BB GUN
Caliber: .177 steel BBs. **Barrel:** Smoothbore **Weight:** 1.4 lbs. **Length:** 7.0 in. **Power:** CO2. **Sights:** Fixed. **Features:** Compact semi-automatic BB pistol, front accessory rail. **Velocity:** 480 fps.
Price: $49.99

CROSMAN P10KT CO2 BB Pistol
Caliber: .177 steel BBs. **Barrel:** Smoothbore. **Weight:** 1.1 lbs. **Length:** 6.9 in. **Power:** CO2. **Sights:** Fixed. **Features:** 20-round drop-out magazine, accessory rail. **Velocity:** 480 fps.
Price: $59.99

CROSMAN ICEMAN DUAL AMMO CO2 PISTOL
Caliber: .177 BBs or .177 pellets. **Barrel:** Rifled. **Weight:** 0.8 lbs. **Length:** 7.75 in. **Power:** CO2. **Sights:** Windage adjustable rear. **Features:** Eight-shot rotary clip, accessory rail, single or double action. **Velocity:** 400-475 fps.
Price: $69.99

CROSMAN MK45 BB PISTOL
Caliber: .177 steel BBs. **Barrel:** Smoothbore. **Weight:** 1.1 lbs. **Length:** 7.5 in. **Power:** CO2. **Sights:** Fixed. **Features:** 20-round drop-out magazine, accessory rail. **Velocity:** 480 fps.
Price: $49.99

CROSMAN MAKO BB PISTOL
Caliber: .177 BBs. **Barrel:** Smoothbore. **Weight:** 1.7 lbs. **Length:** 8.6 in. **Power:** CO2. **Sights:** Fiber optic. Blowback action, tricolor, accessory rail. **Velocity:** 425 fps.
Price: $79.99

CROSMAN C41 CO2 BB PISTOL
Caliber: .177 steel BBs. **Barrel:** Smoothbore **Weight:** 2 lbs. **Length:** 6.75 in. **Power:** CO2. **Sights:** Fixed. **Features:** Compact, realistic weight and feel. **Velocity:** To 450 fps.
Price: $64.95

CROSMAN PFM16 FULL METAL CO2 BB PISTOL
Caliber: .177 steel BBs. **Barrel:** Smoothbore **Weight:** 1.6 lbs. **Length:** 6.5 in. **Power:** CO2. **Sights:** Fixed. **Features:** Compact semi-automatic BB pistol, full metal construction, 20-shot capacity, kit includes: co2, BBs, and holster. **Velocity:** 400 fps.
Price: $59.99

CROSMAN PFAM9B
Caliber: .177 steel BBs. **Barrel:** Smoothbore. **Weight:** 1.6 lbs. **Length:** 6.5 in. **Power:** CO2. **Sights:** Fixed. **Features:** Full metal construction, full, auto, blowback slide, 20-shot capacity. **Velocity:** 400 fps.
Price: $129.99

CROSMAN AMERICAN CLASSIC 1377C / PC77, BLACK
Caliber: .177 pellets. **Barrel:** Rifled **Weight:** 2 lbs. **Length:** 13.63 in. **Power:** Multi-pump pneumatic. **Sights:** Front fixed sight and adjustable rear sight. **Features:** Single shot, bolt action. **Velocity:** 600 fps.
Price: $64.99

CROSMAN AMERICAN CLASSIC 1322 AIR PISTOL, BLACK
Caliber: .22. **Barrel:** Rifled **Weight:** 2 lbs. **Length:** 13.63 in. **Power:** Multi-pump pneumatic. **Sights:** Front Blade & Ramp. **Features:** Single shot, bolt action. **Velocity:** To 460 fps.
Price: $79.99

CROSMAN VIGILANTE CO2 REVOLVER
Caliber: .177 steel BBs/.177 pellets. **Barrel:** Rifled. **Weight:** 2 lbs. **Length:** 11.38 in. **Power:** CO2. **Sights:** Blade front, rear adjustable. **Features:** Single- and double-action revolver (10-shot pellet/6-shot BBs) synthetic frame and finger-molded grip design. **Velocity:** 465 fps.
Price: $59.99

CROSMAN GI MODEL 1911 CO2 BLOWBACK BB PISTOL
Caliber: .177 steel BBs. **Barrel:** Smoothbore. **Weight:** 1.88 lbs. **Length:** 8.63 in. **Power:** CO2. **Sights:** Rear Fixed sights Front Blade. **Features:** Full metal replica with realistic blowback, 20-round capacity, double-action only. **Velocity:** 450 fps.
Price: $99.99

CZ P-09 DUTY CO2 PISTOL
Caliber: .177 BBs/.177 flat-head pellets. **Barrel:** Rifled. **Weight:** 1.6 lbs. **Length:** 8.2 in. **Power:** CO2. **Sights:** Three-dot fixed sights. **Features:** Blowback action, manual safety, double-action-only trigger, 16-round capacity in a 2x8 shot stick magazine, Weaver-style accessory rail, threaded muzzle, blue or two-tone finish, ambidextrous safety with decocker. **Velocity:** 492 fps.
Price: $104.95

CZ-75 CO2 PISTOL
Caliber: .177 BBs. **Barrel:** Smooth. **Weight:** 2.1 lbs. **Length:** 8.2 in. **Power:** CO2. **Sights:** Fixed sights. **Features:** Blowback action, manual safety, full metal construction, single-action trigger, removable 17-round BB magazine, Weaver-style accessory rail, also available as a non-blowback compact version. **Velocity:** 312 fps.
Price: $159.95

CZ 75 SP-01 SHADOW CO2 BB PISTOL
Caliber: .177 steel BBs. **Barrel:** Smoothbore threaded for barrel extension. **Power:** CO2. **Weight:** 1.3 lbs. **Length:** 8.4 in. **Sights:** Fiber-optic front and rear. **Features:** Non-blowback, double action, accessory rail, 21-round capacity, also available in a heavier-weight, blowback version. **Velocity:** 380 fps.
Price: $59.95

CZ 75 P-07 DUTY PISTOL
Caliber: .177 steel BBs. **Barrel:** Smoothbore. **Weight:** 1.81 lbs. **Length:** 7.5 in. **Power:** CO2. **Sights:** Fixed. **Features:** Full metal construction, accessory rail, blowback, 20-round dropout magazine, threaded barrel, blue or two-tone finish, also available in a non-blowback, lower-priced version. **Velocity:** 342 fps.
Price: $109.95

CZ 75D COMPACT CO2 BB PISTOL
Caliber: .177 steel BBs. **Barrel:** Smoothbore. **Weight:** 1.5 lbs. **Length:** 7.4 in. **Power:** CO2. **Sights:** Adjustable rear sight and blade front sight. **Features:** Compact design, non-blowback action, blue or two-tone finish, accessory rail. **Velocity:** 380 fps.
Price: $79.95

DAISY POWERLINE 340 AIR PISTOL
Caliber: .177 steel BBs. **Barrel:** Smoothbore. **Weight:** 1.0 lbs. **Length:** 8.5 in. **Power:** Single cock, spring-piston. **Sights:** Rear sight Fixed **Front blade.** **Features:** Spring-air action, 200-shot BB reservoir with a 13-shot Speed-load Clip located in the grip. **Velocity:** 240 fps.
Price: $24.99

DAISY POWERLINE 415 CO2 BB PISTOL
Caliber: .177 steel BBs. **Barrel:** Smoothbore. **Weight:** 1.0 lbs. **Length:** 8.6 in. **Power:** CO2. **Sights:** Front blade, Rear fixed open rear. **Features:** Semi-automatic 21-shot BB pistol. **Velocity:** 500 fps.
Price: $39.99

DAISY POWERLINE 5170

DAISY POWERLINE 5170 AIRSTRIKE
Caliber: .177 steel BBs. **Barrel:** Smoothbore. **Weight:** 1.0 lbs. **Length:** 9.5 in. **Power:** CO2. **Sights:** Blade and ramp front, Fixed rear. **Features:** Semi-automatic, 21-shot capacity, upper and lower weaver rails for mounting sights and other accessories. **Velocity:** 520 fps.
Price: $59.99

DAISY POWERLINE 5501
Caliber: .177 steel BBs. **Barrel:** Smoothbore. **Weight:** 1.0 lbs. **Length:** 6.8 in. **Power:** CO2. **Sights:** Blade and ramp front, Fixed rear. **Features:** CO2 semi-automatic blowback action. 15-shot clip. **Velocity:** 430 fps.
Price: $89.99

DAN WESSON 2.5 in./4 in./6 in./8 in. PELLET REVOLVER
Caliber: .177 BBs or .177 pellets. **Barrel:** Smoothbore (BB version) or Rifled (Pellet version). **Weights:** 1.65–2.29 lbs. **Lengths:** 8.3–13.3 in. **Power:** CO2. **Sights:** Blade front and adjustable rear sight. **Features:** Highly realistic replica revolver with swing-out, six-shot cylinder, Weaver-style scope rail, multiple finishes and grip configurations, 6 realistic cartridges, includes a speed loader. **Velocities:** 318–426 fps.
Price: .... $159.95–$199.95

DAN WESSON 715 2.5 in./4 in./6 in. REVOLVER
Caliber: .177 BBs or .177 pellets. **Barrel:** Smoothbore (BB Version) or Rifled (Pellet version). **Weights:** 2.2–2.7 lbs. **Lengths:** 8.3–11.7 in. **Power:** CO2. **Sights:** Blade front and adjustable rear sight. **Features:** Highly realistic replica revolver, accessory rail, multiple finishes and grip configurations, six realistic cartridges, includes a speed loader. **Velocities:** 318–426 fps.
Price: .... $150.00–$199.95

DAN WESSON VALOR 1911 PISTOL
Caliber: .177 pellets. **Barrel:** Rifled. **Weight:** 2.2 lbs. **Length:** 8.7 in. **Power:** CO2. **Sights:** Fixed. **Features:** Non-blowback, full metal construction, 12-round capacity in two six-round drum magazines. **Velocities:** 332 fps.
Price: $145.99

DIANA RWS LP 8
Caliber: .177 pellets. **Barrel:** Rifled. **Weight:** 3.20 lbs. **Length:** 7.00 in. **Power:** Spring powered. **Sights:** Fixed front sight with fully adjustable rear sight. **Features:** Powerful spring-powered air pistol, single cock delivers full power, exceptional design and build quality. **Velocity:** 700 fps.
Price: $329.95

EVANIX HUNTING MASTER AR6 AIR PISTOL
Caliber: .177, .22, .25. **Barrel:** Rifled. **Weight:** 3.05 lbs. **Length:** 17.3 in. overall. **Power:** Pre-charged Pneumatic. **Sights:** Adjustable rear, blade front. **Features:** Checkered hardwood grips, 6-shot repeater with rotary magazine, single or double action, receiver grooved for scope **Velocity:** .22 cal. with 3,000 psi charge: 922 fps–685 fps.
Price: $659.99

EVANIX REX P AIR PISTOL
Calibers: .177, .22, .302 (7.67mm), .35 (9mm), .45. **Barrel:** Rifled. **Weight:** 4.00 lbs. **Length:** 20.7 in. overall. **Power:** Pre-charged Pneumatic. **Sights:** None. **Features:** Extremely compact and massively powerful, capable of putting out well over 120 ft-lbs at the muzzle in .45 caliber, truly effective hunting power in a tiny package **Velocity:** .22, 900 fps/.25, 810 fps/.35, 700 fps/.45, 635 fps.
Price: ....$699.99–$799.99

FEINWERKBAU P11 PICCOLO AIR PISTOL
Caliber: .177 pellets. **Barrel:** Rifled. **Weight:** 1.6 lbs. **Length:** 13.58 in. **Power:** Pre-charged pneumatic. **Sights:** Front post, fully adjustable rear blade, **Features:** 10-Meter competition class pistol, meets ISSF requirements, highly adjustable match trigger, **Velocity:** 492 fps.
Price: $1,600.00

FEINWERKBAU P8X PCP 10-METER AIR PISTOL
Caliber: .177 pellets. **Barrel:** Rifled. **Weight:** 2.09 lbs. **Length:** 16.33 in. **Power:** Pre-charged pneumatic. **Sights:** Front post, fully adjustable rear blade. **Features:** 10-Meter competition class pistol with highly customizable grip system, meets ISSF requirements, highly adjustable match trigger. **Velocity:** 508 fps.
Price: $2,073.89

GAMO C-15 BONE COLLECTOR CO2 Pistol
Caliber: .177 BB/.177 pellets. **Barrel:** Smooth. **Weight:** 1.5 lbs. **Length:** 10 in. **Power:** CO2. **Sights:** Fixed. **Features:** Blowback action, approximately 80 shots per CO2 cylinder, single/double action, manual safety, has two side-by-side eight-shot magazines **Velocity:** 450 fps with PBA pellets.
Price: $79.99

GAMO P-900 IGT AIR PISTOL
Caliber: .177 pellets. **Barrel:** Rifled. **Weight:** 1.3 lbs. **Length:** 12.6 in. **Power:** Single cock, gas-pistol. **Sights:** Fiber-optic front and fully adjustable fiber-optic rear sight. **Features:** Break-barrel single-shot, ergonomic design, rubberized grip. **Velocity:** 508 fps.
Price: $79.95

GAMO P-25 AIR PISTOL
Caliber: .177 pellets. **Barrel:** Rifled. **Weight:** 1.5 lbs. **Length:** 7.75 in. **Power:** CO2. **Sights:** Fixed. **Features:** Semi-automatic, 16-shot capacity, realistic blowback action. **Velocity:** 450 fps.
Price: $109.95

GAMO PR-776 CO2 REVOLVER
Caliber: .177 pellets. **Barrel:** Rifled. **Weight:** 2.29 lbs. **Length:** 11.5 in. **Power:** CO2. **Sights:** Fixed front sight with fully adjustable rear sight. **Features:** All metal frame, comes with two 8-shot clips, double- and single-action **Velocity:** 438 fps.
Price: $120.00

GAMO PT-85 CO2 PISTOL
Caliber: .177 pellets. **Barrel:** Rifled. **Weight:** 1.5 lbs. **Length:** 7.8 in. **Power:** CO2. **Sights:** Fixed. **Features:** Semi-automatic, 16-shot capacity, realistic blowback action **Velocity:** 450 fps.
Price: $119.95

GAMO PT-85 BLOWBACK TACTICAL CO2 AIR PISTOL
Caliber: .177 pellets. **Barrel:** Rifled. **Weight:** 3.3 lbs. **Length:** 14.93 in. **Power:** CO2. **Sights:** Fixed/Red-dot optical sight included. **Features:** Semi-automatic design, compensator, rifled steel barrel, manual safety, 16-shot double magazine, quad rail, laser and light included. **Velocity:** 560 fps.
Price: $159.99

GLETCHER STECHKIN APS BLOWBACK CO2 BB PISTOL
Caliber: .177 steel BBs. **Barrel:** Smoothbore. **Weight:** 2.3 lbs. **Length:** 8.88 in. **Power:** CO2. **Sights:** Fixed **Features:** Full metal frame, highly realistic replica, 22-round magazine, double action and single action. **Velocities:** 361–410 fps.
Price: $129.95

GLETCHER GRACH NBB CO2 BB PISTOL
Caliber: .177 steel BBs. **Barrel:** Smoothbore. **Weight:** 2.12 lbs. **Length:** 7.75 in. **Power:** CO2. **Sights:** Fixed **Features:** Full metal frame, highly realistic replica, 18-round magazine, double action and single action. **Velocity:** 361 fps.
Price: $129.95

GLETCHER NGT F CO2 BB REVOLVER
Caliber: .177 steel BBs. **Barrel:** Smoothbore. **Weight:** 1.54 lbs. **Length:** 9.00 in. **Power:** CO2. **Sights:** Fixed **Features:** Full metal frame, highly realistic replica, 7-shot cylinder with realistic "shells," double action and single action, available in blued and polished silver finishes. **Velocity:** 403 fps..
Price: .... $107.99–$124.99

GLOCK 17 GEN3/GEN 4
Caliber: .177 BBs. **Barrel:** Smoothbore. **Weight:** 1.6 lbs. **Length:** 7.75 in. Power: CO2. **Sights:** Fixed **Features:** Blowback action, metal slide and magazine, 18 BB capacity, manual safety, double-action trigger, replica of the Glock 17 firearm. **Velocity:** 365 fps..
Price: $109.99-129.99

GLOCK 19 GEN3
Caliber: .177 BBs. **Barrel:** Smoothbore. **Weight:** 1.6 lbs. **Length:** 7.25 in. **Power:** CO2. **Sights:** Fixed **Features:** Non-blowback action, manual safety, 16 BB capacity, integrated Weaver-style accessory rail, double-action trigger, replica of the Glock 19 firearm. **Velocity:** 410 fps.
Price: $79.95

HATSAN USA MOD 25 SUPERCHARGER VORTEX PISTOL

HATSAN MODEL 25 SUPERCHARGER VORTEX AIR PISTOL
Caliber: .177 or .22 pellets. **Barrel:** Rifled. **Weight:** 3.9 lbs. **Length:** 20 in. **Power:** Single cock, air-piston **Sights:** Fiber-optic front and fully adjustable fiber-optic rear Sight. **Features:** Molded right-handed grips, left-handed grips available, fully adjustable "Quattro" trigger, integrated anti-recoil system, threaded muzzle. **Velocity:** 700 fps with lead pellets.
Price: $189.99

HATSAN USA AT P1 QUIET ENERGY PCP PISTOL

HATSAN USA AT P1 QUIET ENERGY PCP PISTOL
Calibers: .177, .22, .25. **Barrel:** Rifled. **Weight:** 4.7 lbs. **Length:** 23.2 in. **Power:** Pre-charged pneumatic. **Sights:** N/A. Grooved for scope mounting. **Features:** Multi-shot magazine feed, integrated suppressor, muzzle energy suitable for pest control and small game hunting. **Velocity:** .177, 870 fps/.22, 780 fps/.25, 710 fps.
Price: $479.99

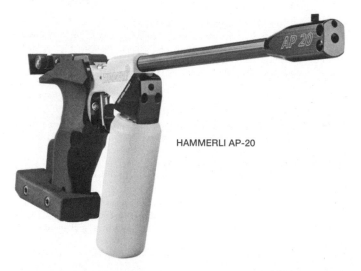

HAMMERLI AP-20

HAMMERLI AP-20 AIR PISTOL
Caliber: .177 pellets. **Barrel:** Rifled. **Weight:** 1.92 lbs. **Length:** 16.34 in. **Power:** Pre-charged pneumatic. **Sights:** Fully adjustable micrometer. **Features:** 2-stage adjustable trigger factory set to 500 grams pull weight, single shot, bolt action, up to 120 shots per fill. **Velocity:** 492 fps.
Price: $999.99

HATSAN SORTIE AIR PISTOL
Caliber: .177, .22, or .25 pellets. **Barrel:** Rifled. **Weight:** 4.4 lbs. **Length:** 15.5 in. Power: Pre-charged pneumatic. **Sights:** Fiber-optic front and fully adjustable rear sight. **Features:** Polymer grips, semi-automatic action, fully shrouded barrel, rotary magazine, Picatinny rail. Velocity with lead pellets: 850 fps (.177), 700 fps (.22), 625 fps (.25).
Price: $579.99

H&K VP9 BB CO2 PISTOL
Caliber: .177 steel BBs. **Barrel:** Smoothbore. **Weight:** 1.42 lbs. **Length:** 7.2 in. Power: CO2. **Sights:** Fixed. **Features:** Highly realistic replica, blowback action, integrated front weaver accessory rail, 18-round magazine. **Velocity:** 350 fps.
Price: $89.99

H&K P30 BB CO2 PISTOL
Caliber: .177 BB/.177 pellet. **Barrel:** Rifled. **Weight:** 1.7 lbs. **Length:** 7.1 in. Power: CO2. **Sights:** Front and rear windage adjustable. **Features:** Highly realistic replica, blowback action, integrated front weaver accessory rail, eight-pellet rotary magazine, drop out 15-BB magazine, double/single action. **Velocity:** 360 fps.
Price: $249.99

H&K USP CO2 BB PISTOL
Caliber: .177 steel BBs. **Barrel:** Smoothbore. **Weight:** 1.35 lbs. **Length:** 7.5 in. **Power:** CO2. **Sights:** Fixed **Features:** Highly realistic replica, integrated front weaver accessory rail, 22-round magazine, double action only. **Velocity:** 360 fps.
Price: **$60.00**

HK45 CO2 BB PISTOL
Caliber: .177 steel BBs. **Barrel:** Smoothbore. **Weight:** 1.4 lbs. **Length:** 8.0 in. **Power:** CO2. **Sights:** Fixed. **Features:** Highly realistic replica, integrated front weaver accessory rail, 20-shot capacity, double-action only. **Velocity:** 400 fps.
Price: **$54.99**

ISSC M-22 CO2 AIR PISTOL
Caliber: .177 steel BBs. **Barrel:** Smoothbore. **Weight:** 1.3 lbs. **Length:** 6.75 in. **Power:** CO2. **Sights:** Fixed front sight and adjustable rear sight. **Features:** Realistic replica, integrated front weaver accessory rail, 18-shot capacity, metal slide with blowback action. **Velocity:** 400 fps.
Price: **$110.00**

MARKSMAN 1010 Classic
Caliber: .177 steel BBs, .177 darts. **Barrel:** Smoothbore. **Weight:** 1.0 lbs. **Length:** (not provided). **Power:** Spring-piston. **Sights:** Blade front, adjustable rear. **Features:** 18-shot BB reservoir. **Velocity:** 200 fps.
Price: **$29.75**

MORINI MOR-162EL AIR PISTOL
Caliber: .177 pellets. **Barrel:** Rifled. **Weight:** 2.25 lbs. **Length:** 16.14 in. **Power:** Pre-charged pneumatic. **Sights:** Front post, rear adjustable for windage. **Features:** Adjustable electronic trigger, single-shot bolt action, extreme match grade accuracy, over 200 regulated shots per 200 bar fill. **Velocity:** 500 fps.
Price: **$2,200.00**

REMINGTON 1875 CO2 REVOLVER
Caliber: .177 steel BBs/.177 pellet. **Barrel:** Smoothbore. **Weight:** 2.3 lbs. **Length:** 13.1 in. **Power:** CO2. **Sights:** Fixed. **Features:** Metal construction, nickel finish, faux ivory grip, single action, functional load gate, hammer and extractor. **Velocity:** Up to 450 fps.
Price: **$149.99**

REMINGTON 1911 RAC
CO2 BB PISTOL

REMINGTON 1911 RAC CO2 BB PISTOL
Caliber: .177 steel BBs. **Barrel:** Smoothbore. **Weight:** 2.0 lbs. **Length:** 8.0 in. **Power:** CO2. **Sights:** Fixed. **Features:** All metal, blowback, extremely realistic replica pistol, bottom weaver/picatinny accessory rail. **Velocity:** 320 fps.
Price: **$111.98**

SCHOFIELD NO. 3 REVOLVER, FULL METAL
Caliber: .177 steel BBs or .177 pellets. **Barrel:** Smoothbore. **Weight:** 2.4 lbs. **Length:** 12.5 in. **Power:** CO2. **Sights:** Fixed. **Features:** Highly detailed replica revolver, 6-shot capacity, realistic reusable cartridges, available in black and nickel finishes. **Velocity:** 430 fps.
Price: .... **$159.95–$169.95**

SIG SAUER X-FIVE ASP .177 CO2 PISTOL
Caliber: .177 pellets. **Barrel:** Smoothbore. **Weight:** 2.75 lbs. **Length:** 9.75 in. **Power:** CO2. **Sights:** Fixed. **Features:** Realistic replica action pistol, 18-shot capacity, front accessory rail, full metal construction, metal slide with blowback action. **Velocity:** 300 fps.
Price: **$159.95**

SIG SAUER 1911 METAL BLOWBACK CO2 BB PISTOL
Caliber: .177 steel BBs. **Barrel:** Smoothbore. **Weight:** 2.0 lbs. **Length:** 8.7 in. **Power:** CO2. **Sights:** Adjustable. **Features:** Extremely Realistic replica action pistol, 20-shot capacity, front accessory rail, black or silver finish, full metal construction, metal slide with blowback action. **Velocity:** 430 fps.
Price: **$139.95**

Prices given are believed to be accurate at time of publication however, many factors affect retail pricing so exact prices are not possible.

74TH EDITION, 2020 ⊕ **501**

SIG SAUER P226 CO2 PELLET PISTOL
Caliber: .177 pellets. **Barrel:** Rifled. **Weight:** 2.35 lbs. **Length:** 8.25 in. **Power:** CO2. **Sights:** Fixed. **Features:** Highly detailed replica action pistol, 16-shot capacity, front accessory rail, full metal construction, metal slide with blowback action, available in dark earth and black. **Velocity:** 450 fps.
Price: **$109.99**

SIG SAUER P320 CO2 PISTOL
Caliber: .177 BBs/.177 pellets. **Barrel:** Rifled. **Weight:** 2.2 lbs. **Length:** 9.6 in. **Power:** CO2. **Sights:** Fixed, white dot. **Features:** 30-round belt-fed magazine, front accessory rail, polymer frame, metal slide with blowback action, black or coyote tan finish. **Velocity:** 430 fps.
Price: **$119.99**

SIG SAUER MAX MICHEL 1911 FULL METAL CO2 BB PISTOL
Caliber: .177 steel BBs. **Barrel:** Smoothbore. **Weight:** 2.6 lbs. **Length:** 8.7 in. **Power:** CO2. **Sights:** Fixed. **Features:** Replica action pistol, 16-shot capacity, front accessory rail, all metal construction, metal slide with blowback action. **Velocity:** 410 fps.
Price: **$109.95**

SMITH & WESSON 586 & 686
Caliber: .177 pellets. **Barrel:** Rifled. **Weights:** Model 586 4 in. 2.50 lbs. / Model 586 & 686 6 in. 2.8 lbs. **Length:** Model 586 4-in. barrel - 9.5 in. - Model 586, 6 in. barrel - 11.50 in. / Model 686 6 in. barrel - 11.5 in. **Power:** CO2. **Sights:** Fixed front, adjustable rear **Features:** Extremely accurate, full metal, replica revolvers.
Price: 586 4-in. barrel. Velocity - 400 fps **$300.00**
Price: 586 6-in. barrel. Velocity - 425 fps **$295.95**
Price: 686 6-in. barrel. Velocity - 425 fps **$329.95**

SMITH & WESSON M&P CO2 PISTOL
Caliber: .177 steel BBs. **Barrel:** Smoothbore. **Weight:** 1.5 lbs. **Lengths:** 7.5 in. **Power:** CO2. **Sights:** Blade front and ramp rear fiber optic. **Features:** Integrated accessory rail, removable 19-shot BB magazine, double-action only, synthetic frame available in dark earth brown or black color. **Velocity:** 300–480 fps.
Price: **$50.00**

SMITH & WESSON M&P 40
CO2 BB PISTOL

SMITH & WESSON M&P 40 CO2 BB PISTOL
Caliber: .177 steel BBs. **Barrel:** Smoothbore. **Weight:** 1.61 lbs. **Length:** 7.75 in. **Power:** CO2. **Sights:** Fixed. **Features:** All-metal replica action pistol, blowback, 15-shot semi-automatic. **Velocity:** 300 fps.
Price: **$119.99**

SMITH & WESSON M&P 45 CO2 PISTOL
Caliber: .177 steel BBs, .177 pellets. **Barrel:** Rifled. **Weight:** 1.35 lbs. **Length:** 8.1 in. **Power:** CO2. **Sights:** Fixed front sight, fully adjustable rear sight. **Features:** Double and single action, 8-shot semi-automatic. **Velocity:** 370 fps.
Price: **$80.00**

SMITH & WESSON 327 TRR8 CO2 BB PISTOL
Caliber: .177 steel BBs. **Barrel:** Smoothbore. **Weight:** 2.0 lbs. **Length:** 12 in. **Power:** CO2. **Sights:** Fiber-optic front sight, fully adjustable fiber-optic rear sight. **Features:** High-quality replica, top-mounted weaver scope rail, weaver accessory rail under the barrel, swing-out cylinder, removable casings and functioning ejector. **Velocity:** 400 fps.
Price: **$120.00**

STEYR M9-A1 PISTOL
Caliber: .177 BBs. **Barrel:** Smoothbore. **Weight:** 1.2 lbs. **Length:** 7.5 in. **Power:** CO2. **Sights:** Fixed. **Features:** Non-blowback, accessory rail, metal slide, two-tone or blue finish, 19-round capacity. **Velocity:** 449 fps.
Price: .... **$59.95 (blue); 99.95 (two-tone)**

STI DUTY ONE CO2 BB PISTOL
Caliber: .177 steel BBs. **Barrel:** Smoothbore. **Weight:** 1.8 lbs. **Length:** 8.8 in. **Power:** CO2. **Sights:** Fixed. **Features:** Blowback, accessory rail, metal slide, threaded barrel, 20-round magazine. **Velocity:** 397 fps.
Price: **$99.95**

TANFOGLIO WITNESS 1911 CO2 BB PISTOL, BROWN GRIPS
Caliber: .177 steel BBs. **Barrel:** Smoothbore. **Weight:** 1.98 lbs. **Length:** 8.6 in. **Power:** CO2. **Sights:** Fixed. **Features:** Often recognized as the "standard" for 1911 replica action pistols, 18-shot capacity, full metal construction with metal slide with blowback action. **Velocity:** 320 fps.
Price: $119.99

TANFOGLIO GOLD CUSTOM CO2 BLOWBACK BB PISTOL
Caliber: .177 steel BBs. **Barrel:** Smoothbore. **Weight:** 3.05 lbs. **Length:** 9.84 in. **Power:** CO2. **Sights:** None, weaver rail for optics. **Features:** Officially licensed, highly detailed replica action pistol, 20-shot capacity, custom accessory rail for dot sights and other optics, full metal construction with metal slide with blowback action, single action only. **Velocity:** 330 fps.
Price: $189.95

UMAREX LEGENDS MAKAROV ULTRA BLOWBACK CO2 BB PISTOL
Caliber: .177 steel BBs. **Barrel:** Smoothbore. **Weight:** 1.40 lbs. **Length:** 6.38 in. **Power:** CO2. **Sights:** Fixed. **Features:** Highly realistic replica, all-metal construction with blowback action, semi-automatic and fully-automatic capable, 16-round capacity. **Velocity:** 350 fps.
Price: $119.95

UMAREX LEGENDS M712 FULL-AUTO CO2 BB PISTOL
Caliber: .177 steel BBs. **Barrel:** Smoothbore. **Weight:** 3.10 lbs. **Length:** 12.00 in. **Power:** CO2. **Sights:** Fixed front sight with rear sight adjustable for elevation. **Features:** Highly realistic replica that functions as the original, all-metal construction with blowback action, semi-automatic and fully-automatic capable, 18-round capacity. **Velocity:** 360 fps.
Price: $149.99

UMAREX LEGENDS P08 BLOWBACK CO2 BB PISTOL
Caliber: .177 steel BBs. **Barrel:** Smoothbore. **Weight:** 1.90 lbs. **Length:** 8.75 in. **Power:** CO2. **Sights:** Fixed. **Features:** Highly realistic replica that functions as the original, all-metal construction with blowback action, 21-round capacity. **Velocity:** 300 fps.
Price: $149.99

UMAREX BRODAX BB
Caliber: .177 steel BBs. **Barrel:** Smoothbore. **Weight:** 1.52 lbs. **Length:** 10.0 in. **Power:** CO2. **Sights:** Fixed. **Features:** Aggressively styled BB revolver, 10-shot capacity, top accessory rail, front accessory rail, synthetic construction. **Velocity:** 375 fps.
Price: $42.99

UMAREX MORPH 3X CO2 BB PISTOL/RIFLE
Caliber: .177 steel BBs. **Barrel:** Smoothbore. **Weight:** 2.5 lbs. **Length:** Up to 38.5 in. **Power:** CO2. **Sights:** Fixed fiber optic. **Features:** Convertible from pistol to short carbine to full rifle, 30-shot capacity, semi-automatic repeater, weaver top rail for optics. **Velocity:** 380 fps as pistol/600 fps as rifle.
Price: $90.00

UMAREX STRIKE POINT PELLET MULTI-PUMP AIR PISTOL
Caliber: .177 pellets. **Barrel:** Rifled. **Weight:** 2.6 lbs. **Length:** 14.00 in. **Power:** Multi-pump pneumatic. **Sights:** Adjustable rear sight, fixed fiber-optic front sight. **Features:** Variable power based on number of pumps, bolt action, includes integrated "silenceair" moderator for quite shooting. **Velocity:** Up to 650 fps.
Price: $59.99

UMAREX TREVOX AIR PISTOL
Caliber: .177 pellets. **Barrel:** Rifled. **Weight:** 3.5 lbs. **Length:** 18.25 in. **Power:** Gas Piston. **Sights:** Adjustable rear sight, fixed fiber-optic front sight. **Features:** full power from a single cock, suitable for target practice and plinking, includes integrated "silenceair" moderator for quite shooting. **Velocity:** 540 fps.
Price: $89.95

Prices given are believed to be accurate at time of publication however, many factors affect retail pricing so exact prices are not possible.

74TH EDITION, 2020 ⊕ **503**

UMAREX XBG CO2 PISTOL
Caliber: .177 steel BBs. **Barrel:** Smoothbore. **Weight:** 0.7 lbs. **Length:** 6.75 in. **Power:** CO2. **Sights:** Fixed. **Features:** 19-shot capacity, under barrel accessory rail, double-action only. **Velocity:** 410 fps.
Price: $32.00

MINI UZI CARBINE
Caliber: .177 steel BBs. **Barrel:** Smoothbore. **Weight:** 2.45 lbs. **Length:** 23.5 in. **Power:** CO2. **Sights:** Fixed. **Features:** Realistic replica airgun, 28-shot capacity, foldable stock, semi-automatic with realistic blowback system, heavy bolt provides realistic "kick" when firing. **Velocity:** 390 fps.
Price: $120.95

UZI CO2 BB SUBMACHINE GUN
Caliber: .177 steel BBs. **Barrel:** Smoothbore. **Weight:** 4.85 lbs. **Length:** 23.5 in. **Power:** CO2. **Sights:** Fixed. **Features:** Realistic replica airgun, 25-shot capacity, foldable stock, semi-automatic and fully-automatic selectable fire, realistic blowback system. **Velocity:** 360 fps.
Price: $199.99

WALTHER CP88, BLUED, 4-INCH BARREL
Caliber: .177 pellets. **Barrel:** Rifled. **Weight:** 2.3 lbs. **Length:** 7 in. **Power:** CO2. **Sights:** Blade ramp front sight and adjustable rear sight. **Features:** Manual safety, semi-auto repeater, single or double action, available in multiple finishes and grip materials, 8-shot capacity. **Velocity:** 400 fps.
Price: .... $229.99–$300.00

WALTHER CP88, BLUED, 6-INCH BARREL
Caliber: .177 pellets. **Barrel:** Rifled. **Weight:** 2.5 lbs. **Length:** 9 in. **Power:** CO2. **Sights:** Blade ramp front sight and adjustable rear sight. **Features:** Manual safety, Semi-auto repeater, single or double action, available in multiple finishes and grip materials, 8-shot capacity. **Velocity:** 450 fps.
Price: .... $229.95–$329.99

WALTHER CP99 CO2 GUN, BLACK
Caliber: .177 pellets. **Barrel:** Rifled **Weight:** 1.6 lbs. **Length:** 7.1 in. **Power:** CO2. **Sights:** Fixed front and fully adjustable rear sight. **Features:** Extremely realistic replica pistol, single and double action, 8-shot rotary magazine. **Velocity:** 360 fps.
Price: $200.00

WALTHER CP99 COMPACT

WALTHER CP99 COMPACT & COMPACT NICKEL
Caliber: .177 steel BBs. **Barrel:** Smoothbore. **Weight:** 1.7 lbs. **Length:** 6.6 in. **Power:** CO2. **Sights:** Fixed front and rear. **Features:** Extremely realistic replica pistol, semi-automatic 18-shot capacity, available in various configurations including a nickel slide. **Velocity:** 345 fps.
Price: ....$100.00–$105.99

WALTHER PPQ

WALTHER PPQ / P99 Q CO2 PISTOL
Caliber: .177 steel BBs, .177 pellets. **Barrel:** Rifled **Weight:** 1.37 lbs. **Length:** 7.0 in. **Power:** CO2. **Sights:** Fixed front and fully adjustable rear sight. **Features:** Extremely realistic replica pistol, semi-automatic 8-shot rotary magazine. **Velocity:** 360 fps.
Price: $70.00

WALTHER P38 CO2 BB PISTOL
Caliber: .177 steel BBs. **Barrel:** Smoothbore. **Weight:** 1.9 lbs. **Length:** 8.5 in. **Power:** CO2. **Sights:** Fixed. **Features:** Authentic replica action pistol, blowback action, semi-automatic 20-shot magazine. **Velocity:** 400 fps.
Price: $120.00

Prices given are believed to be accurate at time of publication however, many factors affect retail pricing so exact prices are not possible.

WALTHER PPK/S CO2 PISTOL
Caliber: .177 steel BBs. **Barrel:** Smoothbore. **Weight:** 3.7 lbs. **Length:** 6.1 in. **Power:** CO2. **Sights:** Fixed. **Features:** Authentic replica action pistol, blowback slide locks back after last shot, stick-style magazine with 15-shot capacity. **Velocity:** 295 fps.
Price: $85.60

WALTHER PPS

WALTHER PPS CO2 PISTOL
Caliber: .177 steel BBs. **Barrel:** Smoothbore. **Weight:** 1.2 lbs. **Length:** 6.38 in. **Power:** CO2. **Sights:** Fixed. **Features:** Authentic replica action pistol, blowback action, semi-automatic 18-shot capacity. **Velocity:** 350 fps.
Price: $89.99

WEBLEY AND SCOTT MKVI REVOLVER
Caliber: .177 pellets. **Barrel:** Rifled. **Weight:** 2.4 lbs. **Length:** 11.25 in. **Power:** CO2. **Sights:** Fixed. **Features:** Authentic replica pistol, single/double action, can be field-stripped, full metal construction, six-shot capacity, available in silver or distressed finish. **Velocity:** 400 fps.
Price: $199.99

WEIHRAUCH HW 75
Caliber: .177 pellets. **Barrel:** Rifled. **Weight:** 2.34 lbs. **Length:** 11.0 in. **Power:** Spring-powered. **Sights:** Fixed front sight with fully adjustable rear sight. **Features:** Single shot, designed precision shooting, beautifully crafted German airgun, two-stage adjustable trigger. **Velocity:** 410 fps.
Price: $516.99

WEIHRAUCH HW 40 AIR PISTOL
Caliber: .177, .20, .22. **Barrel:** Rifled. **Weight:** 1.7 lbs. **Length:** 9.5 in. **Power:** Single-stroke spring piston. **Sights:** Fiber-optic, fully adjustable. **Features:** Automatic safety, two-stage trigger, single shot. **Velocity:** 400 fps..
Price: $252.00

WEIHRAUCH HW 44 AIR PISTOL, FAC VERSION
Caliber: .177, .22. **Barrel:** Rifled. **Weight:** 2.9 lbs. **Length:** 19 in. **Power:** Pre-charged pneumatic. **Sights:** None. **Features:** Ambidextrous safety, two-stage adjustable match trigger, built in suppressor, Weaver-style scope rail, 10-shot magazine, built-in air cartridge with quick fill, internal pressure gauge. **Velocity:** 750 (.177), 570 (.22) fps.
Price: $1,049.99

WEIHRAUCH HW 45 AIR PISTOL
Caliber: .177, .20, .22. **Barrel:** Rifled. **Weight:** 2.5 lbs. **Length:** 10.9 in. **Power:** Single-stroke spring piston. **Sights:** Fiber-optic, fully adjustable. **Features:** Automatic safety, two-stage trigger, single shot, two power levels, blued or two tone. **Velocity:** 410/558 (.177), 394/492 (.20), 345/427 (.22) fps.
Price: $516.00

WEIHRAUCH HW 70 AIR PISTOL
Caliber: .177. **Barrel:** Rifled. **Weight:** 2.4 lbs. **Length:** 12.6 in. **Power:** Single-stroke spring piston. **Sights:** Micrometer adjustable rear. **Features:** Ambidextrous, adjustable match-type trigger, single shot. **Velocity:** 410 fps.
Price: $334.95

WEIHRAUCH HW 75 AIR PISTOL
Caliber: .177. **Barrel:** Rifled. **Weight:** 2.3 lbs. **Length:** 11 in. **Power:** Single-stroke spring piston. **Sights:** Micrometer adjustable rear. **Features:** Ambidextrous, adjustable match-type trigger, single shot. **Velocity:** 410 fps.
Price: $544.99

WINCHESTER MODEL 11

WINCHESTER MODEL 11 BB PISTOL
Caliber: .177 steel BBs. **Barrel:** Smoothbore. **Weight:** 1.9 lbs. **Length:** 8.5 in. **Power:** CO2. **Sights:** Fixed. **Features:** All-metal replica action pistol, blowback action, 4-lb. 2-stage trigger, semi-automatic 15-shot capacity. **Velocity:** 410 fps.
Price: $110.00

Prices given are believed to be accurate at time of publication however, many factors affect retail pricing so exact prices are not possible.

74TH EDITION, 2020 ✛ **505**

AIR ARMS TX200 MKIII AIR RIFLE
Calibers: .177, .22. **Barrel:** Rifled, Lothar Walter match-grade, 13.19 in. **Weight:** 9.3 lbs. **Length:** 41.34 in. **Power:** Single cock, spring-piston. **Stock:** Various; right- and left-handed versions, multiple wood options. **Sights:** 11mm dovetail. **Features:** Fixed barrel, heirloom quality craftsmanship, holds the record for the most winning spring powered airgun in international field target competitions. **Velocities:** .177, 930 fps/.22, 755 fps.
Price: ....$699.99–$829.99

AIR ARMS PRO-SPORT
Calibers: .177, .22. **Barrel:** Rifled, Lothar Walter match-grade, 9.5 in. **Weight:** 9.03 lbs. **Length:** 40.5 in. **Power:** Single cock, spring-piston **Stock:** Various; right-and left-handed versions, multiple wood options. **Sights:** 11mm dovetail. **Features:** Fixed barrel, Heirloom quality craftsmanship, unique inset cocking arm. **Velocities:** .177, 950 fps/.22, 750 fps.
Price: $824.99–879.99

AIR ARMS S510 XTRA FAC PCP AIR RIFLE
Calibers: .177, .22, .25. **Barrel:** Rifled, Lothar Walter match-grade, 19.45 in. **Weight:** 7.55 lbs. **Length:** 43.75 in. **Power:** Pre-charged pneumatic. **Stock:** Right-handed, multiple wood options. **Sights:** 11mm dovetail. **Features:** Side-lever action, 10-round magazine, shrouded barrel, variable power, Heirloom quality craftsmanship **Velocities:** .177, 1,050 fps/.22, 920 fps/.25, 850 fps.
Price: $1,299.99

AIR ARMS S510 ULTIMATE SPORTER
Calibers: .177, .22, .25. **Barrel:** Rifled, Lothar Walter match-grade, 19.5 in. **Weight:** 8.6 lbs. **Length:** 44.25 in. **Power:** Pre-charged pneumatic. **Stock:** Fully adjustable, ambidextrous laminate stock. **Sights:** 11mm dovetail. **Features:** Side-lever action, 10-shot magazine, integrated suppressor, variable power, Heirloom quality craftsmanship. **Velocities:** .177, 1,050 fps/.22, 920 fps/.25, 850 fps.
Price: $1,699.99

AIR ARMS S200 FT
Caliber: .177 pellets. **Barrel:** Rifled, match-grade, 19.09 in. **Weight:** 6.17 lbs. **Length:** 35.7 in. **Power:** Pre-charged pneumatic. **Stock:** Ambidextrous hardwood stock. **Sights:** 11mm dovetail. **Features:** Single-shot, designed for international field target competition. **Velocity:** 800 fps.
Price: $699.99

AIR ARMS T200
Caliber: .177 pellets. **Barrel:** Hammer-forged, rifled 19.1 in. **Weight:** 6.6 lbs. **Length:** 35.5 in. **Power:** Pre-charged pneumatic. **Stock:** Hardwood. **Sights:** Globe front sight, fully adjustable diopter rear sight. **Features:** Aluminum muzzle brake, two-stage adjustable trigger, removable air tank, single shot, grooved receiver, made by CZ. **Velocity:** 575 fps.
Price: $650.00

AIR ARMS FTP 900 FIELD TARGET PCP AIR RIFLE
Caliber: .177. **Barrel:** Rifled, Lothar Walter match-grade, 19.0 in. **Weight:** 11.00 lbs. **Length:** 42.50 in. **Power:** Pre-charged pneumatic **Stock:** Fully adjustable competition style, available in right- or left-handed laminate stock. **Sights:** 11mm dovetail. **Features:** Side-lever action, single shot for maximum accuracy, integrated muzzle break, heirloom quality craftsmanship, regulated for supreme shot consistency, delivers up to 100 shots per fill. **Velocity:** 800 fps.
Price: $3,029.99

AIR ARMS GALAHAD RIFLE REG FAC
Calibers: .22, .25. **Barrel:** Rifled, Lothar Walter match-grade, 19.4 in. **Weight:** 8.6 lbs. **Length:** 35.5 in. **Power:** Pre-charged pneumatic. **Stock:** Ambidextrous bullpup stock available in "soft touch" synthetic over beech or walnut. **Sights:** 11mm dovetail. **Features:** Moveable side-lever action, 10-shot magazine, available with integrated moderator, variable power with integrated regulator, Heirloom quality craftsmanship. **Velocity:** .22, 900 fps/.25, 800 fps.
Price: ....$1699.99–$1849.00

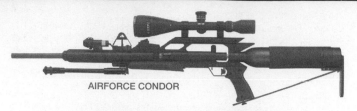

AIRFORCE CONDOR

AIRFORCE CONDOR/CONDOR SS RIFLE
Calibers: .177, .20, .22, .25. **Barrel:** Rifled, Lothar Walther match-grade, 18 or 24 in. **Weight:** 6.1 lbs. **Length:** 38.1-38.75 in. **Power:** Pre-charged pneumatic. **Stock:** Synthetic pistol grip, tank acts as buttstock. **Sights:** Grooved for scope mounting. **Features:** Single shot, adjustable power, automatic safety, large 490cc tank volume, extended scope rail allows easy mounting of the largest air-gun scopes, optional CO2 power system available, manufactured in the USA by AirForce Airguns. **Velocities:** .177, 1,450 fps/.20, 1,150 fps/.22, 1,250 fps/.25, 1,100 fps.
Price: $744.95

AIRFORCE EDGE 10-METER AIR RIFLE
Caliber: .177. **Barrel:** Rifled, Lothar Walther match-grade, 12 in. **Weight:** 6.1 lbs. **Length:** 40.00 in. **Power:** Pre-charged pneumatic. **Stock:** Synthetic pistol grip, tank acts as buttstock. **Sights:** Match front globe and rear micrometer adjustable diopter sight. **Features:** Single shot, automatic safety, two-stage adjustable trigger, accepted by CMP for completive shooting, available in multiple colors and configurations, manufactured in the USA by AirForce Airguns. **Velocity:** .530 fps.
Price: $694.95

AIRFORCE ESCAPE/SS/UL AIR RIFLE
Calibers: .22, .25. **Barrel:** Rifled, Lothar Walther match-grade, 12, 18 or 24 in. **Weight:** 4.3-5.3 lbs. **Length:** 32.3-39.00 in. **Power:** Pre-charged pneumatic. **Stock:** Synthetic pistol grip, tank acts as buttstock. **Sights:** Grooved for scope mounting. **Features:** Single shot, adjustable power, automatic safety, extended scope rail allows easy mounting of the largest airgun scopes, manufactured in the USA by AirForce Airguns. **Velocities:** .22, 1,300 fps/.25, 1,145 fps.
Price: ....$642.95-$694.95

AIRFORCE TALON PCP AIR RIFLE
Calibers: .177, .22, .25. **Barrel:** Rifled, Lothar Walther match-grade, 18 in. **Weight:** 5.5 lbs. **Length:** 32.6 in. **Power:** Pre-charged pneumatic, **Stock:** Synthetic pistol grip, tank acts as buttstock. **Sights:** Grooved for scope mounting. **Features:** Single shot, adjustable power, automatic safety, large 490cc tank volume, extended scope rail allows easy mounting of the largest airgun scopes, optional CO2 power system available, manufactured in the USA by AirForce Airguns. **Velocities:** .177, 1,100 fps/.22, 950 fps/.25, 850 fps.
Price: $609.95

AIRFORCE TALON SS PCP AIR RIFLE
Calibers: .177, .20, .22, .25. **Barrel:** Rifled, Lothar Walther match-grade, 12 in. **Weight:** 5.25 lbs. **Length:** 32.75 in. **Power:** Pre-charged pneumatic. **Stock:** Synthetic pistol grip, tank acts as buttstock. **Sights:** Grooved for scope mounting. **Features:** Fully shrouded barrel with integrated suppressor, single shot, adjustable power, automatic safety, large 490cc tank volume, extended scope rail allows easy mounting of the largest airgun scopes, multiple color options available, optional CO2 power system available, manufactured in the USA by AirForce Airguns. **Velocities:** .177, 1,000 fps/.20, 800 fps/.22, 800 fps/.25, 665 fps.
Price: $652.95

AIRFORCE TEXAN / TEXAN SS AIR RIFLE
Calibers: .30, .35, .45. **Barrel:** Rifled, 34.00 in. **Weight:** 7.65 lbs. **Length:** 48.00 in. **Power:** Pre-charged pneumatic. **Stock:** Synthetic pistol grip, tank acts as buttstock. **Sights:** Grooved for scope mounting. **Features:** Delivers massive energy and long-range accuracy, two-stage non-adjustable trigger, very easy to cock, open receiver accepts a vast selection of off the shelf or custom cast ammunition, available in a fully shrouded suppressed model, manufactured in the USA by AirForce Airguns. **Velocities:** .30, 1,100 fps, 300 ft-lbs/.35, 1,000 fps, 350 ft-lbs/.45, 1,000 fps 500 ft-lbs.
Price: ....$1,054.95–$1210.95

AIRFORCE INTERNATIONAL ORION AIR RIFLE
Calibers: .177, .22, .25. **Barrel:** Hammer forged barrel, 18.5 in. **Weight:** 7.25 lbs. **Length:** 41.00 in. **Power:** Pre-charged pneumatic. **Stock:** Right-handed hardwood stock with adjustable cheek riser. **Sights:** 11mm dovetail for scope mounting. **Features:** Multi-shot magazine varies on caliber, side-lever action, adjustable power and adjustable trigger. **Velocities:** .177, 1,000 fps/.22, 800 fps/.25, 600 fps.
Price: $629.95

AIRFORCE INTERNATIONAL MODEL 94 SPRING AIR RIFLE
Calibers: .177, .22, 25. **Barrel:** Rifled, hammer forged, 18.75 in. **Weight:** 7.5 lbs. **Length:** 44.9 in. **Power:** Spring piston. **Stock:** Synthetic with textured grip and forearm. **Sights:** Fixed fiber-optic front and fully adjustable fiber-optic rear. **Features:** Single shot, adjustable two-stage trigger, 32-pound cocking effort, integral muzzle brake. Velocities: 1100 fps (.177)/900 fps (.22)/700 fps (.25).
Price: $249.95

AIRFORCE INTERNATIONAL MODEL 95 SPRING AIR RIFLE
Calibers: .177, .22. **Barrel:** Rifled, hammer forged. **Weight:** 7.25 lbs. **Length:** 44.9 in. **Power:** Spring piston. **Stock:** Hardwood stock with checkering on grip and forearm. **Sights:** None, 11mm dovetail for scope mounting. **Features:** Single shot, adjustable trigger, 32-pound cocking effort. Velocities: .177, 980 fps/.22, 835 fps.
Price: $315.95

AIR VENTURI WING SHOT AIR SHOTGUN
Caliber: .50. **Barrel:** Smoothbore 22.5 in. **Weight:** 7.4 lbs. **Length:** 43.0 in. **Power:** Pre-charged pneumatic. **Stock:** Ambidextrous wood stock. **Sights:** Fixed bead shotgun-style sight. **Features:** 244cc reservoir delivers several powerful shots, shoots shot cartridges and round balls, exceptionally reliable. **Velocity:** 1,130 fps.
Price: $849.99

ANSCHUTZ 9015 AIR RIFLE
Caliber: .177. **Barrel:** Rifled, 16.5 in. **Weight:** Variable from 8.1 to 11 pounds. **Length:** Variable from 39.0 to 47 in. **Power:** Pre-charged pneumatic. **Stock:** Fully adjustable variable composition. **Sights:** Fully adjustable target sights with interchangeable inserts. **Features:** Single shot, ambidextrous grip, adjustable match trigger, exchangeable air cylinder with integrated manometer, approximately 200 shots per fill, available with a bewildering array of options. **Velocity:** 560 fps.
Price: .... $2,545.00 - $5,350.00

ASG TAC-4.5 CO2 BB RIFLE
Caliber: .177 steel BBs. **Barrel:** Smoothbore. **Weight:** 3.5 lbs. **Length:** 36.0 in. **Power:** CO2 **Stock:** Synthetic thumbhole stock. **Sights:** Fixed fiber-optic front sight and fully adjustable fiber-optic rear sight/weaver rail for optics. **Features:** Semi-automatic action, includes bi-pod, 21-shot capacity. **Velocity:** 417 fps.
Price: $119.99

ATAMAN M2R CARBINE AIR RIFLE
Calibers: .177, .22, .25, .30, .35. **Barrel:** Lothar Walther rifled match-grade, 20.47 in. **Weight:** 8.82 lbs. **Length:** 43.31 in. **Power:** Pre-charged pneumatic. **Stock:** Ambidextrous stock available in various configurations and finishes. **Sights:** weaver rails for scope mounting. **Features:** Multi-shot side-lever action, shot capacity varies on caliber, adjustable match trigger, finely tuned regulator matched to optimal velocity in each caliber for maximum accuracy. **Velocities:** .177, 980 fps/.22, 980 fps/.25, 980 fps/.30, 984 fps/.35, 900 fps.
Price: .... $1429.99–$1649.99

ATAMAN M2R BULLPUP TYPE 1 & 2 AIR RIFLE
Calibers: .22, .25, .35. **Barrel:** Lothar Walther rifled match-grade, 20.47 in. **Weight:** 8.81 lbs. **Length:** 32.38 in. **Power:** Pre-charged pneumatic. **Stock:** Ambidextrous bullpup stock available in walnut or "soft touch" synthetic. **Sights:** Weaver rails for scope mounting. **Features:** Multi-shot side level action, shot capacity varies on caliber, adjustable match trigger, side-lever action, finely tuned regulator matched to optimal velocity in each caliber for maximum accuracy. **Velocities:** .22, 980 fps/.25, 980 fps/.35, 900 fps.
Price: $1429.99–1649.99

ATAMAN M2R CARBINE ULTRA COMPACT AIR RIFLE
Caliber: .22. **Barrel:** Lothar Walther rifled match-grade, 15.39 in. **Weight:** 6.17 lbs. **Length:** 36.48 in. **Power:** Pre-charged pneumatic. **Stock:** Ambidextrous adjustable/foldable stock available in walnut or "soft touch" synthetic. **Sights:** Weaver rails for scope mounting. **Features:** Multi-shot side-lever action, 10-shot capacity, adjustable match trigger, finely tuned regulator matched to optimal velocity. **Velocity:** 850 fps.
Price: $1,319.99

BEEMAN RS-2 DUAL-CALIBER GAS RAM AIR RIFLE COMBO
Calibers: .177, .22. **Barrel:** Rifled. **Weight:** 6.9 lbs. **Length:** 45.5 in. **Power:** Break-barrel, gas-piston. **Stock:** Ambidextrous hardwood stock. **Sights:** Fiber-optic front and rear, includes 4x32 scope and rings. **Features:** Single-shot, easily exchangeable .177 and .22 cal. barrels, two-stage trigger. **Velocities:** .177, 1,000 fps/.22, 830 fps.
Price: $179.99

BEEMAN QUIET TEK DC DUAL CALIBER GAS RAM AIR RIFLE COMBO
Calibers: .177, .22. **Barrel:** Rifled. **Weight:** 6.7 lbs. **Length:** 47 in. **Power:** Break-barrel, spring-piston. **Stock:** Ambidextrous synthetic stock. **Sights:** None, grooved for scope mounting, includes 4x32 scope and rings. **Features:** Integrated suppressor, single shot, easily exchangeable .177- and .22-cal. barrels, two-stage trigger. **Velocities:** .177, 1,000 fps/.22, 830 fps.
Price: $179.99

BEEMAN R7 AIR RIFLE
Calibers: .177, .20. **Barrel:** Rifled 13.5 in. **Weight:** 6.1 lbs. **Length:** 37 in. **Power:** Break-barrel, spring-piston. **Stock:** Ambidextrous walnut-stained beech, cut-checkered pistol grip, Monte Carlo comb and rubber buttpad. **Sights:** None, grooved for scope. **Features:** German quality, limited lifetime warranty, highly adjustable match grade trigger, very easy to cock and shoot, extremely accurate. **Velocities:** .177, 700 fps/.20, 620 fps.
Price: .... $329.99–$379.99

BEEMAN R9 AIR RIFLE
Calibers: .177, .20, .22. **Barrel:** Rifled 16.33 in. **Weight:** 7.3 lbs. **Length:** 43 in. **Power:** Break-barrel, spring-piston. **Stock:** Ambidextrous walnut-stained beech, cut-checkered pistol grip, Monte Carlo comb and rubber buttpad. **Sights:** None, grooved for scope. **Features:** German quality, limited lifetime warranty, highly adjustable match-grade trigger, extremely accurate. **Velocities:** .177, 935 fps/.20, 800 fps/.22, 740 fps.
Price: .... $439.99–$479.99

BEEMAN RAM AIR RIFLE COMBO, RS2 TRIGGER
Calibers: .177, .22. **Barrel:** Rifled 20 in. **Weight:** 7.9 lbs. **Length:** 46.5 in. **Power:** Break-barrel, spring-piston. **Stock:** Ambidextrous hardwood stock. **Sights:** None, grooved for scope mounting, includes 3-9x32 scope and rings. **Features:** Muzzle brake for extra cocking leverage, single-shot, adjustable two-stage trigger. **Velocities:** .177, 1,000 fps/.22, 850 fps.
Price: $220.00

BEEMAN WOLVERINE CARBINE COMBO AIR RIFLE
Caliber: .177 pellets. **Barrel:** Rifled. **Weight:** 8.5 lbs. **Length:** 45.5 in. **Power:** Break-barrel, spring-piston. **Stock:** Ambidextrous synthetic stock. **Sights:** Fiber-optic front sight, fully adjustable fiber-optic rear sight, grooved for scope, includes 4x32 scope and mounts. **Features:** Single-shot, two-stage trigger. **Velocity:** 1,000 fps.
Price: $129.99

BEEMAN GUARDIAN COMBO AIR RIFLE

Caliber: .177 pellets. **Barrel:** Rifled. **Weight:** 5.85 lbs. **Length:** 37 in. **Power:** Break-barrel, spring-piston. **Stock:** Monte Carlo-style synthetic stock. **Sights:** None, grooved for scope, includes mounted 4x20 scope and mounts. **Features:** Lightweight youth airgun. **Velocity:** 550 fps.
Price: $59.99

BEEMAN SPORTSMAN RANGER COMBO AIR RIFLE

Caliber: .177 pellets. **Barrel:** Rifled. **Weight:** 4.15 lbs. **Length:** 40 in. **Power:** Break-barrel, spring-piston. **Stock:** Lightweight skeleton, synthetic stock. **Sights:** None, grooved for scope, includes 4x20 scope and mounts. **Features:** Lightweight youth airgun. **Velocity:** 480 fps.
Price: $79.99

BEEMAN SILVER KODIAK X2 COMBO AIR RIFLE

Calibers: .177, .22. **Barrel:** Rifled. **Weight:** 8.75 lbs. **Length:** 47.75 in. **Power:** Break-barrel, spring-piston. **Stock:** Ambidextrous synthetic stock. **Sights:** None includes 4x32 scope and rings. **Features:** Satin finish nickel plated receiver and barrels, single-shot, easily exchangeable .177 and .22 cal barrels, two-stage trigger. **Velocities:** .177, 1,000 fps/.22, 830 fps.
Price: $169.99

BENJAMIN 392 / 397 AIR RIFLE

Calibers: .177, .22. **Barrel:** Rifled 19.25 in. **Weight:** 5.5 lbs. **Length:** 36.25 in. **Power:** Multi-pump Pneumatic. **Stock:** Ambidextrous wood or synthetic stock. **Sights:** Front ramp and adjustable rear sight. **Features:** Multi-pump system provides variable power, single-shot bolt action. **Velocities:** .177, 800 fps/.20, 685 fps.
Price: ....$200.00-$249.99

BENJAMIN ARMADA, BASE, TACTICAL, & MAGPUL EDITION AIR RIFLE

BENJAMIN ARMADA

Calibers: .177, .22, .25. **Barrel:** Rifled, 20 in. **Weight:** 7.3 lbs. (10.3 lbs. with scope and bipod). **Length:** 42.8 in. **Power:** Pre-charged pneumatic. **Stock:** Adjustable mil-spec AR-15-style buttstock, all metal M-LOK compatible handguard with 15 in. of picatinny rail space. **Sights:** None, weaver/Picatinny rail for scope mounting. **Features:** Fully shrouded barrel with integrated suppressor, dampener device, bolt action, multi shot, choked barrel for maximum accuracy. **Velocities:** .177, 1,100 fps/.22, 1,000 fps/.25, 900 fps.
Price: $649.99

BENJAMIN BULLDOG .357 BULLPUP

BENJAMIN BULLDOG .357 BULLPUP

Caliber: .357. **Barrel:** Rifled 28 in. **Weight:** 7.7 lbs. **Length:** 36 in. **Power:** Pre-charged pneumatic. **Stock:** Synthetic bullpup stock with pistol grip. **Sights:** Full top Picatinny rail. **Features:** Innovative bullpup design, massive power output of up to 180 ft-lbs, 5-shot magazine, shrouded barrel for noise reduction, large cylinder delivers up to 10 usable shots, available in multiple bundled configurations and stock finishes. **Velocity:** Up to 900 fps based on the weight of the projectile.
Price: ....$849.99-$1,099.99

BENJAMIN DISCOVERY PCP AIR RIFLE AND PUMP

Calibers: .177, .22. **Barrel:** Rifled 24.25 in. **Weight:** 5.2 lbs. **Length:** 39.0 in. **Power:** Pre-Charged Pneumatic/CO2. **Stock:** Ambidextrous hardwood stock. **Sights:** Front fiber-optic and adjustable rear fiber-optic sight/grooved 11mm dovetail for scope mounting. **Features:** Dual fuel allows this to run on HPA or bulk fill CO2, turn-key PCP package with included 3-stage hand pump, built in pressure gauge. **Velocities:** .177, 1,000 fps/.22, 900 fps.
Price: $479.99

BENJAMIN FORTITUDE GEN 2 PCP RIFLE

Calibers: .177 or .22. **Barrel:** Rifled 24.25 in. **Weight:** 5.3 lbs. **Length:** 42.6 in. **Power:** Pre-charged pneumatic. **Stock:** Synthetic, ambidextrous. **Sights:** None, grooved 11mm dovetail for scope mounting. **Features:** Shrouded barrel with integrated suppressor, 10-shot rotary magazine, 3,000 PSI pressure gauge with regulator, 60 to 200 shots per fill, adjustable hammer spring. **Velocity:** 950 fps (.177), 850 fps (.22).
Price: $399.99

BENJAMIN MAG-FIRE MISSION/NOMAD/ULTRA Series

Caliber: .177 or .22. **Barrel:** Rifled. **Weight:** 9 lbs. **Length:** 45.5 in. **Power:** Break-barrel, second-generation gas-piston. **Stock:** Synthetic or wood stock. **Sights:** None, Picatinny rail for scope mounting, includes CenterPoint 4x32 scope and mounts. **Features:** Sound suppression, 10-shot magazine that is autoloading with each break of the barrel, adjustable two-stage trigger, sling mounts. **Velocity:** 1,400 fps (.177), 1100 fps (.22).
Price: $149-179.00

BENJAMIN MARAUDER PCP AIR RIFLE

Caliber: .177, .22, .25. **Barrel:** Rifled 20 in. **Weight:** Synthetic 7.3 lbs./Hardwood 8.2 lbs. **Length:** 42.8 in. **Power:** Pre-charged pneumatic. **Stock:** Ambidextrous stock available in hardwood or synthetic, adjustable cheek riser. **Sights:** None, grooved for scope mounting. **Features:** Multi-shot bolt action, 10-shot in .177 and .22, 8-shot in .25, user-adjustable performance settings for power and shot count, reversible bolt handle. Also available with options such as an integrated regulator for shot-to-shot consistency, a Picatinny rail and a Lothar Walther barrel. **Velocities:** .177, 1,100 fps/.22, 1,000 fps/.25, 900 fps.
Price: ....$579.99–$599.99

BENJAMIN MAYHEM STEALTH BREAK BARREL RIFLE

Calibers: .177, .22. **Barrel:** Rifled. **Weight:** 7.4 lbs. **Length:** 46.5 in. **Power:** Break-barrel, Nitro-Piston Elite. **Stock:** Synthetic with soft-touch inserts. **Sights:** Adjustable rear, comes with a CenterPoint 3-9x32 scope and

Picatinny rail. **Features:** SBD sound suppression, sling mounts, single-shot, adjustable two-stage trigger. **Velocities:** 1,400 fps (.177), 1100 fps (.22).
Price: $299.95

BENJAMIN PROWLER BREAK BARREL RIFLE
Calibers: .177, .22. **Barrel:** Rifled. **Weight:** 6.4 lbs. **Length:** 45 in. **Power:** Break-barrel, Nitro-Piston. **Stock:** Ambidextrous synthetic. **Sights:** None, comes with a CenterPoint 4x32 scope. **Features:** Reduced recoil, 35-pound cocking effort, single-shot, adjustable two-stage trigger. **Velocities:** 1,200 fps (.177), 950 fps (.22).
Price: $149.95

BENJAMIN TRAIL STEALTH NITRO PISTON 2 (NP2) BREAK BARREL AIR RIFLE
Calibers: .177, .22. **Barrel:** Rifled 15.75 in. **Weight:** 8.3 lbs. **Length:** 46.25 in. **Power:** Break-barrel, 2nd generation gas-piston. **Stock:** Ambidextrous thumbhole stock available in wood and synthetic options as well as multiple finishes and patterns. **Sights:** None, picatinny rail for scope mounting, multiple Crosman CenterPoint scope options available as factory bundles. **Features:** Very quiet due to the shrouded barrel with integrated suppressor, extremely easy cocking, single-shot, advanced adjustable two-stage trigger, innovative sling mounts for optional Benjamin break-barrel rifle sling. **Velocities:** .177, 1,400 fps/.22, 1,100 fps.
Price: ....$295.95–$349.95

BENJAMIN TRAIL NITRO PISTON 2 (NP2) SBD BREAK BARREL AIR RIFLE
Calibers: .177, .22. **Barrel:** Rifled 15.75 in. **Weight:** 8.3 lbs. **Length:** 45.6 in. **Power:** Break-barrel, 2nd generation gas-piston. **Stock:** Ambidextrous thumbhole stock available in wood and synthetic options as well as multiple finishes and patterns. **Sights:** None, Picatinny rail for scope mounting, multiple Crosman CenterPoint scope options available as factory bundles. **Features:** Newly introduced SBD integrated suppressor does not interfere with scope sight picture, extremely easy cocking, single-shot, advanced adjustable two-stage trigger, innovative sling mounts for optional Benjamin break-barrel rifle sling. **Velocities:** .177, 1,400 fps/.22, 1,100 fps.
Price: ....$299.95–$339.99

BENJAMIN MAXIMUS PCP AIR RIFLE
Calibers: .177, .22. **Barrel:** Rifled 26.25 in. **Weight:** 5.0 lbs. **Length:** 41.7 in. **Power:** Pre-Charged Pneumatic. **Stock:** Ambidextrous synthetic stock. **Sights:** Front Fiber-optic and adjustable rear fiber-optic sight/grooved 11mm dovetail for scope mounting. **Features:** HPA required only 2000 psi to operate, built in pressure gauge. **Velocities:** .177, 1,000 fps/.22, 850 fps.
Price: $219.99

BENJAMIN VARMINT POWER PACK
Caliber: .22. **Barrel:** Rifled. **Weight:** 7.38 lbs. **Length:** 44.5 in. **Power:** Break-barrel, gas piston. **Stock:** Ambidextrous synthetic stock. **Sights:** none, Weaver rail for scope mounting, includes a Crosman CenterPoint 4x32 scope with laser and light attachments complete with intermittent pressure switches. **Features:** Shrouded barrel, easy cocking, single-shot, adjustable two-stage trigger. **Velocity:** 950 fps.
Price: $249.95

BENJAMIN WILDFIRE SEMI-AUTOMATIC PCP AIR RIFLE
Caliber: .177. **Barrel:** Rifled 20.39 in. **Weight:** 3.69 lbs. **Length:** 36.88 in. **Power:** Pre-Charged Pneumatic. **Stock:** Ambidextrous synthetic stock. **Sights:** Front fiber-optic and adjustable rear sight/grooved 11mm dovetail for scope mounting. **Features:** HPA required only 2000 psi to operate, built in pressure gauge, 12-shot semi-automatic system, double-action only. **Velocity:** .177, 800 fps.
Price: $199.99

BERETTA CX4 STORM

BERETTA CX4 STORM
Caliber: .177 pellets. **Barrel:** Rifled 17.5 in. **Weight:** 5.25 lbs. **Length:** 30.75 in. **Power:** CO2. **Stock:** Synthetic thumbole. **Sights:** Adjustable front and rear. **Features:** Multi-shot semi-automatic with 30-round belt-fed magazine, highly realistic replica, utilizes large 88/90 gram disposable CO2 canisters for high shot count and uninterrupted shooting sessions. Available bundled with a Walther red-dot optics. **Velocity:** 600 fps.
Price: ....$375.95–$400.00

BLACK OPS TACTICAL SNIPER GAS-PISTON AIR RIFLE
Calibers: .177, .22. **Barrel:** Rifled. **Weight:** 9.6 lbs. **Length:** 44.0 in. **Power:** Break-barrel, gas-piston. **Stock:** Ambidextrous pistol grip synthetic stock. **Sights:** none, Weaver rail for scope mounting, includes a 4x32 scope. **Features:** Muzzle break helps with cocking force, single-shot, single cock delivers maximum power, adjustable single-stage trigger. **Velocity:** .177, 1,250 fps/.22, 1,000 fps.
Price: ....$179.99–$199.99

BLACK OPS JUNIOR SNIPER AIR RIFLE COMBO
Caliber: .177 steel BBs, .117 pellets. **Barrel:** Rifled. **Weight:** 4.41 lbs. **Length:** 39.37in. **Power:** Multi-pump pneumatic. **Stock:** Ambidextrous pistol grip synthetic stock. **Sights:** Fiber-optic front and rear fiber-optic sights, 11mm rail for scope mounting, includes a 4-15 scope. **Features:** Multi-pump system delivers variable power, single-shot, single cock delivers maximum power, adjustable single-stage trigger. **Velocity:** 675 fps.
Price: $69.99

BROWNING LEVERAGE AIR RIFLE
Calibers: .177, .22. **Barrel:** Rifled 18.9 in. **Weight:** 8.6 lbs. **Length:** 44.8 in. **Power:** Under-lever cock, spring-piston **Stock:** Hardwood right handed with raised cheekpiece. **Sights:** Front fiber-optic sight and fully adjustable rear fiber-optic sight, Weaver/Picatinny rail for scope mounting, includes 3-9x40 scope. **Features:** Fixed barrel accuracy, easy cocking, two-stage trigger. **Velocities:** .177, 1,000 fps/.22, 800 fps.
Price: $230.00

BSA METEOR EVO AIR RIFLE
Calibers: .177, .22. **Barrel:** Rifled 17.5 in. **Weight:** 6.1 lbs. **Length:** 43.5 in. **Power:** Break-barrel, spring-piston. **Stock:** Ambidextrous beech stock. **Sights:** Front fiber-optic sight and fully adjustable rear fiber-optic sight grooved for scope mounting. **Features:** European quality, fitted with BSA-Made cold hammer forged barrel known for precision and accuracy, adjustable two-stage trigger, single-shot, manufactured to stringent quality control and testing. **Velocities:** .177, 950 fps/.22, 722 fps.
Price: $199.99

BSA R-10 SE PCP AIR RIFLE

Calibers: .177, .22. **Barrel:** Rifled, BSA-made cold hammer forged precision barrel, 19 in. **Weight:** 7.3 lbs. **Length:** 44 in. **Power:** Pre-charged pneumatic. **Stock:** Available right- or left-hand, walnut, laminate, camo or black synthetic. **Sights:** None, grooved for scope mounting. **Features:** Multi-shot bolt action, 10-shot magazine (eight-shot for .25 caliber), fully regulated valve for maximum accuracy and shot consistency, free-floating, shrouded barrel, also available with lower power/velocity and as a shorter carbine. Velocities: 1,000 fps (.177)/980 fps (.22).
Price: **$1,399.99**

BSA BUCCANEER SE AIR RIFLE

Calibers: .177, .22. **Barrel:** Rifled, BSA-made cold hammer forged precision barrel, 24 in. **Weight:** 7.7 lbs. **Length:** 42.5 in. **Stock:** Ambidextrous beech stock or hardwood stock wrapped in innovative black soft-touch. **Sights:** None, grooved for scope mounting. **Features:** Multi-shot bolt action, 10-shot magazine, enhanced valve system for maximum shot count and consistency, integrated suppressor, adjustable two-stage trigger. **Velocities:** .177, 1,000 fps/.22, 800 fps.
Price: ....**$649.99–$749.99**

BSA DEFIANT BULLPUP AIR RIFLE

Calibers: .177, .22. **Barrel:** Rifled, cold hammer forged precision barrel, 18.5 in. **Weight:** 9 lbs. **Length:** 31 in. **Power:** Pre-charged pneumatic. **Stock:** Ambidextrous walnut, black soft-touch or black pepper laminate with adjustable buttpad. **Sights:** None, grooved for scope mounting. **Features:** Multi-shot bolt action, two 10-shot magazines, enhanced valve system for maximum shot count and consistency, integrated suppressor, adjustable two-stage trigger. Velocities: .177, 825 fps /.22. 570 fps.
Price: ....**$NA**

BSA GOLD STAR SE HUNTER FIELD TARGET PCP AIR RIFLE

Caliber: .177. **Barrel:** Rifled, BSA-made enhanced cold hammer forged precision barrel, 15.2 in. **Weight:** 7 lbs. **Length:** 35.8 in. **Power:** Pre-charged pneumatic. **Stock:** Highly adjustable gray laminate field target competition stock. **Sights:** None, grooved for scope mounting. **Features:** Multi-shot boltaction, 10-shot magazine, fully regulated valve for maximum accuracy and shot consistency, 70 consistent shots per charge, free-floating barrel with 1/2 UNF threaded muzzle, includes adjustable air stripper, adjustable match-grade trigger. **Velocity:** 800 fps.
Price: **$1,949.95**

BSA SCORPION 1200 SE
AIR RIFLE

BSA SCORPION 1200 SE AIR RIFLE

Calibers: .177, .22. **Barrel:** Rifled, BSA-made cold hammer forged free-floating

shrouded recision barrel, 24 in. **Weight:** 87.5 lbs. **Length:** 44.5 in. **Power:** Pre-charged pneumatic. **Stock:** Ambidextrous synthetic. **Sights:** None, grooved for scope mounting. **Features:** Multi-shot bolt action, 10-shot magazine, enhanced valve system for maximum shot count and consistency up to 80 shots in .177, 45 in .22, adjustable two-stage trigger. **Velocities:** .177, 1,200 fps/.22, 1000 fps.
Price: **$979.95**

BSA ULTRA XL AIR RIFLE

Calibers: .177, .22. **Barrel:** Rifled, BSA-made cold hammer forged precision barrel, 15.2 in. **Weight:** 7.3 lbs. **Length:** 35.4 in. **Power:** Pre-charged pneumatic. **Stock:** Ambidextrous, thumbhole, adjustable cheek piece, wood. **Sights:** None, grooved for scope mounting. **Features:** 10-shot magazine, fully regulated valve for maximum accuracy and shot consistency, free-floating, shrouded barrel, single-stage adjustable trigger, removable muzzle brake, also available as the JSR version for smaller framed shooters. Velocities: .177, 700 fps/.22, 570 fps.
Price: ....**$NA**

CROSMAN CHALLENGER PCP COMPETITION

CROSMAN CHALLENGER PCP COMPETITION AIR RIFLE

Caliber: .177. **Barrel:** Match-grade Lothar Walther rifled barrel. **Weight:** 7.3 lbs. **Length:** 41.75 in. **Power:** Pre-charged pneumatic/CO2. **Stock:** Highly adjustable synthetic competition stock. **Sights:** Globe front sight and Precision Diopter rear sight. **Features:** Innovative dual fuel design allows this rifle to run on HPA or CO2, single-shot, adjustable match-grade trigger, approved by the Civilian Marksmanship Program (CMP) for 3-position air rifle Sporter Class competition. **Velocity:** 530 fps.
Price: **$629.99**

CROSMAN GENESIS NP AIR RIFLE

Caliber: .22. **Barrel:** Rifled. **Weight:** 7.44 lbs. **Length:** 44.5 in. **Power:** Break-barrel, gas-piston. **Stock:** Ambidextrous wood stock with dual raised cheekpieces and checkered grip and forearm. **Sights:** None, Weaver/Picatinny rail for scope mounting, includes 4x32 scope and rings. **Features:** Shrouded barrel with integrated suppressor, extremely easy cocking, single-shot, adjustable two-stage trigger, innovative sling mounts for optional Benjamin break-barrel rifle sling. **Velocity:** 950 fpsPrice: **$229.99**

CROSMAN M4-177

CROSMAN M4-177 (various styles and kits available)

Caliber: .177 steel BBs, .177 pellets. **Barrel:** Rifled 17.25 in. **Weight:** 3.75 lbs. **Length:** 33.75 in. **Power:** Multi-pump pneumatic. **Stock:** M4-style adjustable plastic stock. **Sights:** Weaver/Picatinny rail for scope mounting and flip-up sights. Bundled packages include various included sighting options. **Features:** Single-shot bolt action, lightweight and very accurate, multiple colors available. "Ready to go" kits available complete with ammo, safety glasses, targets and extra 5-shot pellet magazines. **Velocity:** 660 fps.
Price: ....**$110.00–$149.95**

CROSMAN MODEL 760 PUMPMASTER AIR RIFLE

Caliber: .177 steel BBs, .177 pellets. **Barrel:** Rifled 16.75 in. **Weight:** 2.75 lbs. **Length:** 33.5 in. **Power:** Multi-pump pneumatic. **Stock:** Ambidextrous plastic stock. **Sights:** Blade and ramp, rear sight adjustable for elevation, grooved for scope mounting. **Features:** Single-shot pellet, BB repeater, bolt action, lightweight, accurate and easy to shoot. Multiple colors available and configurations available. "Ready to go" kits available complete with ammo, safety glasses, targets and extra 5-shot pellet magazines. **Velocity:** 625 fps.
Price: ....**$50.00–$60.00**

CROSMAN OPTIMUS AIR RIFLE
Caliber: .177, .22. **Barrel:** Rifled. **Weight:** 6.5 lbs. **Length:** 43 in. **Power:** Break-barrel. **Stock:** Ambidextrous wood. **Sights:** Fiber-optic with adjustable rear sight, dovetail for scope mounting, includes CenterPoint 4x32 scope and rings. **Features:** Single-shot, adjustable two-stage trigger. Velocities: 1,200 fps (.177)/950 fps (.22).
Price: $145.00

CROSMAN QUEST AIR RIFLE
Caliber: .177, .22. **Barrel:** Rifled 15.75 in. **Weight:** 7.8 lbs. **Length:** 45.5 in. **Power:** Break-barrel, Nitro-Piston. **Stock:** Synthetic. **Sights:** None, dovetail for scope mounting, includes CenterPoint 4x32 scope and rings. **Features:** SBD sound suppression, single-shot, adjustable two-stage trigger. Velocities: 1,400 fps (.177)/1,100 fps (.22) with alloy pellet.
Price: $184.99

CROSMAN REPEATAIR 1077 AIR RIFLE
Caliber: .177 pellets. **Barrel:** Rifled 20.38 in. **Weight:** 3.75 lbs. **Length:** 36.88 in. **Power:** CO2. **Stock:** Ambidextrous plastic stock. **Sights:** Blade and ramp, rear sight adjustable for windage and elevation, grooved for scope mounting. **Features:** Multi-shot, semi-automatic, 12-shot magazine, lightweight, fun and easy to shoot. "Ready to go" kits available complete with ammo, CO2, targets, target trap, etc. **Velocity:** 625 fps.
Price: ....$69.99-$115.99

CROSMAN 2100B CLASSIC AIR RIFLE
Caliber: .177 steel BBs, .177 pellets. **Barrel:** Rifled 20.84 in. **Weight:** 4.81 lbs. **Length:** 39.75 in. **Power:** Multi-pump pneumatic. **Stock:** Ambidextrous plastic stock with simulated wood grain. **Sights:** Blade and ramp, rear sight adjustable for windage and elevation, grooved for scope mounting. **Features:** Adult-size inexpensive airgun, single-shot, bolt action, lightweight, accurate and easy to shoot. **Velocity:** 755 fps.
Price: $79.95

CROSMAN SHOCKWAVE NP AIR RIFLE
Calibers: .177, .22. **Barrel:** Rifled 15.00 in. **Weight:** 6.0 lbs. **Length:** 43.5 in. **Power:** Break-barrel, gas-piston. **Stock:** Ambidextrous synthetic with dual raised cheekpieces. **Sights:** Front fiber-optic sight and fully adjustable fiber-optic rear sight, Weaver/Picatinny rail for scope mounting, includes 4x32 scope and rings. **Features:** Single-shot, includes bipod, adjustable two-stage trigger. **Velocities:** .177, 1,200 fps/.22, 950 fps.
Price: $149.99

CROSMAN TYRO AIR RIFLE
Calibers: .177. **Barrel:** Rifled. **Weight:** 4.9 lbs. **Length:** 37.5 in. **Power:** Break-barrel, spring-piston. **Stock:** Synthetic thumbhole with spacers to adjust length of pull. **Sights:** Front fiber-optic sight and adjustable rear sight. **Features:** Single shot, sized for smaller shooters. Velocities: 720 fps with alloy pellet.
Price: $105.99

CROSMAN TR77 NPS/MTR77 AIR RIFLE
Caliber: .177 pellets. **Barrel:** Rifled 12 in. **Weight:** 5.8 lbs. **Length:** 40 in. **Power:** Break-barrel, gas-piston. **Stock:** Ambidextrous synthetic skeleton stock or MSR-style stock with carry handle and incorporated rear sight. **Sights:** Fixed sights (MTR77) or none, grooved for scope mounting (TR77), available with a CenterPoint 4x32 scope and rings. **Features:** Aggressive styling, single-shot, adjustable two-stage trigger. **Velocity:** 1,200 fps.
Price: ....$159.99-$245.99

DAISY 1938 RED RYDER

DAISY 1938 RED RYDER AIR RIFLE
Caliber: .177 steel BBs. **Barrel:** Smoothbore 10.85 in. **Weight:** 2.2 lbs. **Length:** 35.4 in. **Power:** Single-cock, lever action, spring-piston. **Stock:** Solid wood stock and fore-end. **Sights:** Blade front sight, adjustable rear sight. **Features:**

650 BB reservoir, single-stage trigger, designed for all day fun and backyard plinking, exceptional first airgun for young shooters. **Velocity:** 350 fps.
Price: $56.99

DAISY AVANTI MODEL 887 GOLD MEDALIST COMPETITION
Caliber: .177 pellets. **Barrel:** Rifled, match-grade Lothar Walther barrel, 20.88 in. **Weight:** 6.9 lbs. **Length:** 38.5 in. **Power:** CO2. **Stock:** Ambidextrous laminated wood stock. **Sights:** Globe front sight and Precision Diopter rear sight. **Features:** Precision bored and crowned barrel for match accuracy, bulk fill CO2 is capable of up to 300 shots, additional inserts available for front sight, ideal entry level rifle for all 10-meter shooting disciplines. **Velocity:** 500 fps.
Price: $563.99

DAISY MODEL 599 COMPETITION AIR RIFLE
Caliber: .177 pellets. **Barrel:** Rifled, cold hammer forged BSA barrel, 20.88 in. **Weight:** 7.1 lbs. **Length:** 34.35-37.25 in. **Power:** Pre-charged pneumatic. **Stock:** Ambidextrous beech wood stock with vertical and length-of-pull adjustment, adjustable comb. **Sights:** Hooded front and diopter rear sight. **Features:** Trigger weight adjustable down to 1.5 lbs., rotating trigger adjustment for positioning right or left, straight pull T-bolt handle, removable power cylinder. **Velocity:** 520 fps.
Price: $595

DAISY MODEL 25 PUMP GUN
Caliber: .177 steel BBs. **Barrel:** Smoothbore. **Weight:** 3 lbs. **Length:** 37 in. **Power:** pump action, spring-air. **Stock:** Solid wood buttstock. **Sights:** Fixed front and rear sights. **Features:** 50 shot BB reservoir, removable screw out shot tube, decorative engraving on receiver, rear sight can be flipped over to change from open to peep sight. **Velocity:** 350 fps.
Price: $47.99

DAISY MODEL 74 CO2 RIFLE
Caliber: .177 steel BBs. **Barrel:** Smoothbore. **Weight:** 2 lbs. **Length:** 35.5 in. **Power:** CO2. **Stock:** Synthetic. **Sights:** Fixed front and adjustable rear. **Features:** 200 round BB reservoir, 15-shot internal magazine, designed for all-day fun and backyard plinking. **Velocity:** 350 fps.
Price: $59.99

DAISY MODEL 105 BUCK AIR RIFLE
Caliber: .177 steel BBs. **Barrel:** Smoothbore 7.97 in. **Weight:** 1.6 lbs. **Length:** 29.8 in. **Power:** Single-cock, lever action, spring-piston. **Stock:** Solid wood buttstock. **Sights:** Fixed front and rear sights. **Features:** 400 BB reservoir, single-stage trigger, designed for all day fun and backyard plinking. **Velocity:** 275 fps.
Price: $35.99

DAISY MODEL 763 ELITE

DAISY MODEL 753S MATCH GRADE AVANTI
Caliber: .177 pellets. **Barrel:** Rifled, Lothar Walther, 19.5 in. **Weight:** 7.3 lbs. **Length:** 38.5 in. **Power:** Single-stroke pneumatic. **Stock:** Ambidextrous wood stock & Synthetic stock available. **Sights:** Globe front sight and Precision Diopter rear sight. **Features:** Full-size wood stock, additional inserts available for front sight, fully self-contained power system, excellent "first" rifle for all 10-meter shooting disciplines. **Velocity:** 495 fps.
Price: ....$300.00-$469.99

DAISY PINK 1998 BB GUN
Caliber: .177, steel BBs. **Barrel:** Smoothbore 10.85 in. **Weight:** 2.2 lbs. **Length:** 35.4 in. **Power:** Single-cock, lever action, spring-piston. **Stock:** Solid wood stock and forearm painted pink. **Sights:** Blade front sight, adjustable rear sight. **Features:** 650 BB reservoir, single-stage trigger, designed for all day fun and backyard plinking, great option for young ladies just starting out. **Velocity:** 350 fps.
Price: $47.99

Prices given are believed to be accurate at time of publication however, many factors affect retail pricing so exact prices are not possible.

74TH EDITION, 2020 ✧ **511**

DAISY POWERLINE MODEL 880 AIR RIFLE
Caliber: .177 steel BBs, .177 pellets. **Barrel:** Rifled, 21 in. **Weight:** 3.1 lbs. **Length:** 37.6 in. **Power:** Multi-pump pneumatic. **Stock:** Synthetic. **Sights:** Fiber-optic front sight, rear sight adjustable for elevation, grooved for scope mounting. **Features:** Single-shot pellet, 50 shot BB, lightweight, accurate and easy to shoot. **Velocity:** 800 fps (BBs), 665 fps (pellets).
Price: $49.95

DAISY POWERLINE MODEL 35 AIR RIFLE
Caliber: .177 steel BBs, .177 pellets. **Barrel:** Smoothbore. **Weight:** 2.25 lbs. **Length:** 34.5 in. **Power:** Multi-pump pneumatic. **Stock:** Ambidextrous plastic stock, available in black and pink camo. **Sights:** Blade and ramp, rear sight adjustable for elevation, grooved for scope mounting. **Features:** Single-shot pellet, BB rep, lightweight, accurate and easy to shoot. **Velocity:** 625 fps.
Price: .... $41.99–$69.95

DAISY POWERLINE 901 AIR RIFLE
Caliber: .177 steel BBs, .177 pellets. **Barrel:** Rifled 20.8 in. **Weight:** 3.2 lbs. **Length:** 37.75 in. **Power:** Multi-pump pneumatic **Stock:** Ambidextrous black wood grain plastic stock. **Sights:** Front fiber-optic sight, rear blade sight adjustable for elevation, grooved for scope mounting. **Features:** Full-size adult airgun, single-shot pellet, BB repeater, bolt action, lightweight, accurate and easy to shoot. "Ready to go" kit available complete with ammo, safety glasses, shatterblast targets, 4x15 scope and mounts. **Velocity:** 750 fps.
Price: ....$71.99–$95.99

DAYSTATE HUNTSMAN REGAL XL AIR RIFLE
Calibers: .177, .22, .25. **Barrel:** Rifled 17 in. **Weight:** 6.17 lbs. **Length:** 40.0 in. **Power:** Pre-charged pneumatic. **Stock:** Right-handed Monte Carlo hardwood. **Sights:** None, 11mm grooved dovetail for scope mounting. **Features:** Features the exceptional pedigree of the finest European airguns, 10-shot rotary magazine, rear bolt action, adjustable trigger, fully moderated barrel. **Velocity:** (not provided).
Price: $1,208.90

DAYSTATE RED WOLF RIFLE
Calibers: .177, .22, .25. **Barrel:** Match grade rifled Lothar Walther 17 in. **Weight:** 7.5 lbs. **Length:** 39 in. **Power:** Pre-charged pneumatic. **Stock:** Fully adjustable walnut. **Sights:** None, 11mm grooved dovetail for scope mounting. **Features:** Three individual programmed energy and velocity settings, computer controlled state-of-the-art MCT firing system, LCD screen displays air pressure, battery state, number of shots fired. Ten-shot magazine, fully adjustable trigger from ounces to pounds, stock provides cheek-piece adjustments for height, left and right canting as well as buttpad adjustment for up, down, left and right. **Velocity:** NA.
Price: $2,899.99

DAYSTATE TSAR TARGET RIFLE
Calibers: .177 pellet. **Barrel:** Match grade rifled Lothar Walther 20.5 in. **Weight:** 9.9 lbs. **Length:** 39 in. **Power:** Pre-charged pneumatic. **Stock:** Laminate. **Sights:** None, 11mm grooved dovetail for scope mounting. **Features:** Adjustable cheek rest and buttpad, five-level adjustable multi-sear trigger, fully moderated barrel, designed for field target competition, side lever cocking system allows for dry-firing practice. **Velocity:** (not provided).
Price: $2,935.90

DIANA AR8 N-TEC AIR RIFLE
Calibers: .177, .22. **Barrel:** Rifled 19.5 in. **Weight:** 8.45 lbs. **Length:** 48.0 in. **Power:** Break-barrel, German gas-piston. **Stock:** Ambidextrous synthetic thumbhole stock. **Sights:** Front post and fully adjustable rear sight, grooved for scope mounting.

Features: European quality, exceptional two-stage adjustable match trigger, single-shot, German manufactured to stringent quality control and testing, limited lifetime warranty. The new N-TEC gas-piston power plant boasts smoother cocking and shooting, making the N-TEC line of Diana guns the most refined Diana airguns to date. **Velocities:** .177, 1,320 fps/.22, 975 fps.
Price: $399.99

DIANA 240 CLASSIC AIR RIFLE
Caliber: .177. **Barrel:** Rifled 16.5 in. **Weight:** 5.0 lbs. **Length:** 40 in. **Power:** Break-barrel, spring-piston. **Stock:** Ambidextrous beech stock. **Sights:** Front fiber-optic sight and fully adjustable rear fiber-optic sight, grooved for scope mounting. **Features:** European quality, exceptional two-stage adjustable trigger, single-shot, German manufactured to stringent quality control and testing, limited lifetime warranty. Various bundled configurations available. **Velocity:** .177, 580 fps.
Price: $219.99

DIANA Mauser K98 AIR RIFLE
Calibers: .177, .22. **Barrel:** Rifled 18.0 in. **Weight:** 9.5 lbs. **Length:** 44 in. **Power:** Break-barrel, spring-piston. **Stock:** Authentic Mauser K98 hardwood stock. **Sights:** Front post and fully adjustable rear sight, 11mm dovetail grooved for scope mounting. **Features:** European quality, fixed barrel with underlever cocking, exceptional two-stage adjustable match trigger, single-shot, German manufactured to stringent quality control and testing, limited lifetime warranty. **Velocities:** .177, 1,150 fps/.22, 850 fps.
Price: $469.99

DIANA RWS 34P STRIKER COMBO
Calibers: .177, .22. **Barrel:** Rifled 19.0 in. **Weight:** 7.75 lbs. **Length:** 46 in. **Power:** Break-barrel, spring-piston. **Stock:** Ambidextrous beech or synthetic stock. **Sights:** Front fiber-optic sight and fully adjustable rear fiber-optic sight, grooved for scope mounting. **Features:** European quality, exceptional two-stage adjustable match trigger, single-shot, German manufactured to stringent quality control and testing, limited lifetime warranty. Various bundled configurations available. **Velocity:** .177, 1,000 fps/.22, 800 fps.
Price: $399.99

DIANA MODEL 340
AIR RIFLE

DIANA 340 N-TEC PREMIUM AIR RIFLE
Calibers: .177, .22. **Barrel:** Rifled 19.5 in. **Weight:** 7.9 lbs. **Length:** 46 in. **Power:** Break-barrel, German gas-piston. **Stock:** Ambidextrous beech stock. **Sights:** Front fiber-optic sight and fully adjustable rear fiber-optic sight, grooved for scope mounting. **Features:** European quality, exceptional two-stage adjustable match trigger, single-shot, German manufactured to stringent quality control and testing, limited lifetime warranty. The new N-TEC gas-piston power plant boasts smoother cocking and shooting, making the N-TEC line of Diana guns the most refined Diana airguns to date. Various bundled configurations available. **Velocities:** .177, 1,000 fps/.22, 800 fps.
Price: $449.99

DIANA RWS 350 MAGNUM
Calibers: .177, .22. **Barrel:** Rifled 19.25 in. **Weight:** 8.2 lbs. **Length:** 48 in. **Power:** Break-barrel, spring-piston. **Stock:** Right handed beech stock with grip and forearm checkering. **Sights:** Post and globe front sight and fully adjustable rear sight, grooved for scope mounting. **Features:** European quality, exceptional two-stage adjustable match trigger, single-shot, German manufactured to stringent quality control and testing, limited lifetime warranty. Various bundled configurations available. **Velocities:** .177, 1,250 fps/.22, 1,000 fps.
Price: $499.95

Prices given are believed to be accurate at time of publication however, many factors affect retail pricing so exact prices are not possible.

DIANA 350 N-TEC MAGNUM PREMIUM AIR RIFLE
Calibers: .177, .22. **Barrel:** Rifled 19.5 in. **Weight:** 6.7 lbs. **Length:** 48.5 in. **Power:** Break-barrel, German gas-piston. **Stock:** Ambidextrous stock, available in beech and synthetic options. **Sights:** Front post and fully adjustable rear sight, grooved for scope mounting. **Features:** European quality, exceptional two-stage adjustable match trigger, single-shot, German manufactured to stringent quality control and testing, limited lifetime warranty. The new N-TEC gas-piston power plant boasts smoother cocking and shooting, making the N-TEC line of Diana guns the most refined Diana airguns to date. **Velocities:** .177, 1,250 fps/.22, 1,000 fps.
Price: $499.99

DIANA MODEL 48 AIR RIFLE

DIANA MODEL RWS 48 AIR RIFLE, T06 TRIGGER
Calibers: .177, .22. **Barrel:** Rifled 17 in. **Weight:** 8.5 lbs. **Length:** 42.13 in. **Power:** Single-cock, side-lever, spring-piston. **Stock:** Ambidextrous beech thumbhole stock. **Sights:** Blade front sight, fully adjustable rear sight, grooved for scope mounting. **Features:** European quality, exceptional two-stage match trigger, single-shot, German manufactured to stringent quality control and testing, limited lifetime warranty. **Velocities:** .177, 1,100 fps/.22, 900 fps.
Price: $529.95

DIANA 460 MAGNUM
Calibers: .177, .22. **Barrel:** Rifled 18.44 in. **Weight:** 8.3 lbs. **Length:** 45 in. **Power:** Under-lever, spring-piston. **Stock:** Right-hand hardwood stock with grip and fore-end checkering. **Sights:** Post front sight and fully adjustable rear sight, grooved for scope mounting. **Features:** European quality, exceptional two-stage adjustable match trigger, single-shot, German manufactured to stringent quality control and testing, limited lifetime warranty. Various bundled configurations available. **Velocity:** .177, 1,200 fps/.22, 1,000 fps.
Price: $599.95

DIANA 56 TARGET HUNTER AIR RIFLE
Calibers: .177, .22. **Barrel:** Rifled 17.3 in. **Weight:** 11.1 lbs. **Length:** 44 in. **Power:** Single-cock, side-lever, spring-piston. **Stock:** Ambidextrous beech thumbhole stock. **Sights:** None, grooved for scope mounting. **Features:** European quality, exceptional two-stage match trigger, single-shot, German manufactured to stringent quality control and testing. **Velocities:** .177, 1,100 fps/.22, 890 fps.
Price: ....$799.99-$999.99

DIANA STORMRIDER GEN 2 PCP RIFLE
Calibers: .177, .22. **Barrel:** Rifled 19 in. **Weight:** 5.0 lbs. **Length:** 40.5 in. **Power:** Pre-charged pneumatic. **Stock:** Checkered beech stock. **Sights:** Blade front, fully adjustable rear, 11 mm dovetail grove. **Features:** Entry level PCP rifle, nine-shot (.177) or seven-shot (.22) capacity, adjustable two-stage trigger, built-in muzzle brake, integrated pressure gauge. Velocities: 1,050 fps (.177)/900 fps (.22).
Price: $219.99

DPMS CLASSIC A4 NITRO PISTON AIR RIFLE
Caliber: .177 pellets. **Barrel:** Rifled 15 in. **Weight:** 7 lbs. **Length:** 40 in. **Power:** Break-barrel, gas-piston. **Stock:** Ambidextrous AR-15-styled stock. **Sights:** none, Weaver/Picatinny rail for flip-up sights and scope mounting, includes 4x32 scope and rings. **Features:** Aggressive and realistic AR-15 styling. Sling mounts, single-shot, adjustable two-stage trigger. **Velocity:** 1,200 fps.
Price: $229.95

DPMS SBR FULL AUTO BB RIFLE
Caliber: .177 BB. **Barrel:** Smoothbore. **Weight:** 6.2 lbs. **Length:** 26.5 in. **Power:** CO2. **Stock:** Adjustable six-position buttstock with AR compatible pistol grip. **Sights:** Folding BUIS front and rear with Picatinny rail. **Features:** Blowback action, quad rail forearm for accessory mounting, 25-round drop-out magazine, fully auto with up to 1,400 rounds per minute. **Velocity:** 430 fps.
Price: $199.99

EVANIX RAINSTORM II PCP AIR RIFLE
Calibers: .22, .25, .30, .35 (9mm). **Barrel:** Rifled, 17.00 in. **Weight:** 7.2 lbs. **Length:** 39.00 in. overall. **Power:** Pre-charged Pneumatic. **Stock:** Ambidextrous beech thumbhole stock. **Sights:** None, grooved 11mm dovetail for scope mounting **Features:** Multi shot side-lever action, shot count varies based on caliber, very well made and versatile hunting airgun. **Velocities:** .22, 1,176 fps/.25, 910 fps/.30, 910 fps/.35, 800 fps.
Price: $799.99-999.99

EVANIX REX AIR RIFLE
Calibers: .22, .25, .35 (9mm), .45. **Barrel:** Rifled, 19.68 in. **Weight:** 5.51 lbs. **Length:** 35.82 in. overall. **Power:** Pre-charged Pneumatic. **Sights:** weaver rail for scope mounting **Features:** Lightweight, compact and massively powerful, single shot, capable of putting out well over 200 foot pounds at the muzzle in .45 caliber, truly effective hunting power in a compact package **Velocities:** .22, 1,080 fps/.25, 970 fps/.35, 860 fps/.45, 700 fps.
Price: $699.99-799.99

FEINWERKBAU 500 AIR RIFLE
Caliber: .177. **Barrel:** Rifled 13.8 in. **Weight:** 7.05 lbs. **Length:** 43.7 in. **Power:** Pre-charged pneumatic. **Stock:** Ambidextrous beech stock with adjustable cheekpiece and buttstock. **Sights:** Globe front sight and diopter rear. **Features:** Meets requirements for ISSF competition, trigger-pull weight adjusts from 3.9 to 7.8 ounces, bolt action, competition grade airgun. **Velocity:** 574 fps.
Price: $1,650

FEINWERKBAU 800X FIELD TARGET AIR RIFLE
Caliber: .177. **Barrel:** Rifled 16.73 in. **Weight:** 11.7–15.05 lbs. **Length:** 49.76 in. **Power:** Pre-charged pneumatic. **Stock:** Highly adaptable field target competition stock **Sights:** None, 11mm grooved for scope mounting. **Features:** Designed from airguns featuring Olympic accuracy, this field target variant is designed to win., 5-way adjustable match trigger, bolt action, competition grade airgun **Velocity:** 825 fps.
Price: $3,799.99

FEINWERKBAU P75 BIATHLON AIR RIFLE
Caliber: .177. **Barrel:** Rifled 16.73 in. **Weight:** 9.26 lbs. **Length:** 42.91 in. **Power:** Pre-charged pneumatic. **Stock:** Highly adaptable laminate wood competition stock **Sights:** Front globe with aperture inserts and diopter micrometer rear. **Features:** 5-shot bolt action, competition grade airgun, inspired from airguns featuring Olympic accuracy, 5-way adjustable match trigger. **Velocity:** 564 fps.
Price: $3,254.95

FEINWERKBAU SPORT AIR RIFLE
Caliber: .177. **Barrel:** Rifled 18.31 in. **Weight:** 8.27 lbs. **Length:** 44.84 in. **Power:** Spring-piston break barrel. **Stock:** Ambidextrous wood stock with dual raised cheekpieces. **Sights:** Front globe, fully adjustable rear sight, grooved for scope mounting. **Features:** Lightweight, single-shot, easy cocking, adjustable two-stage trigger. **Velocity:** .177, 850 fps.
Price: $999.99

FX CROWN AIR RIFLE
Calibers: .177, .22, .25, .30. **Barrel:** Rifled 19-23.5 in. **Weight:** 6.5 - 7.5 lbs. **Length:** 38.5 - 43 in. **Power:** Pre-charged pneumatic. **Stock:** Ambidextrous stock in walnut, laminate or synthetic. **Sights:** None, 11mm grooved for scope mounting. **Features:** Smooth Twist X barrels can be swapped to change not only caliber but also twist rate, adjustable 15-ounce two-stage trigger, externally adjustable regulator, adjustable power wheel and hammer spring, removable carbon fiber tank, dual air-pressure gauges, multiple-shot magazine (14 to 18 shots depending on caliber). Velocities: .177, 1,000 fps/.22, 920 fps/.25, 900 fps/.30, 870 fps.
Price: $1,799.99-1,999.99

Prices given are believed to be accurate at time of publication however, many factors affect retail pricing so exact prices are not possible.

74TH EDITION, 2020 ⬩ **513**

FX IMPACT AIR RIFLE

Calibers: .25, .30. **Barrel:** Rifled 24.4 in. **Weight:** 7.0 lbs. **Length:** 34.0 in. **Power:** Pre-charged pneumatic. **Stock:** Compact bullpup stock in various materials and finishes **Sights:** None, 11mm grooved for scope mounting. **Features:** Premium airgun brand known for exceptional build quality and accuracy, regulated for consistent shots, adjustable two-stage trigger, FX smooth twist barrel, multi-shot side lever action, fully moderated barrel, highly adjustable and adaptable air rifle system. **Velocities:** .25, 900 fps/.30, 870 fps.
Price: **$2,198.99**

FX WILDCAT AIR RIFLE

Calibers: .22, .25. **Barrel:** Rifled 19.7 in. **Weight:** 6.1 lbs. **Length:** 26.5 in. **Power:** Pre-charged pneumatic. **Stock:** Compact bullpup stock in various materials and finishes. **Sights:** None, 11mm grooved for scope mounting. **Features:** Premium airgun brand known for exceptional build quality and accuracy, regulated for consistent shots, adjustable two-stage trigger, FX smooth twist barrel, multi-shot side lever action, fully moderated barrel. **Velocity:** .22, 1,200 fps/.25, 900 fps.
Price: **$1,499.99–1,899.99**

FX .30 BOSS AIR RIFLE

Caliber: .30. **Barrel:** Rifled 24.4 in. **Weight:** 7.0 lbs. **Length:** 47.5 in. **Power:** Pre-charged pneumatic. **Stock:** Right-handed Monte Carlo Stock available in various materials and finishes. **Sights:** None. 11mm grooved for scope mounting. **Features:** Premium airgun brand known for exceptional build quality and accuracy, regulated for consistent shots, adjustable two-stage trigger, FX smooth twist barrel, multi-shot side lever action, fully moderated barrel. **Velocities:** .22, 1,200 fps/.25, 900 fps.
Price: .... **$1949.99–$2399.99**

GAMO COYOTE WHISPER PCP AIR RIFLE

Calibers: .177, .22. **Barrel:** Cold hammer-forged match-grade rifled barrel, 24.5 in. **Weight:** 6.6 lbs. **Length:** 42.9 in. **Power:** Pre-charged pneumatic. **Stock:** Ambidextrous hardwood stock. **Sights:** None, grooved for scope mounting, **Features:** European class airgun, highly accurate and powerful, adjustable two-stage trigger, integrated moderator, 10-shot bolt action. **Velocities:** .177, 1,200 fps/.22, 1,000 fps.
Price: **$559.99**

GAMO MAGNUM AIR RIFLE

Calibers: .177, .22. **Barrel:** Rifled 21.3 in. **Weight:** 6.88 lbs. **Length:** 48.0 in. **Power:** Break-barrel, gas-piston. **Stock:** Ambidextrous composite thumbhole stock. **Sights:** Fiber-optic front sight and fully adjustable fiber-optic rear sight, grooved for scope mounting, includes 3-9x40AO scope and mounts. **Features:** Most powerful break barrel from Gamo USA, single-shot, adjustable two-stage trigger. **Velocity:** .177, 1,650 fps/.22, 1,300 fps.
Price: **$299.99**

GAMO RECON G2 WHISPER YOUTH AIR RIFLE

Caliber: .177 pellets. **Barrel:** Rifled 18 in. **Weight:** 4.4 lbs. **Length:** 41 in. **Power:** Break-barrel, gas-piston. Stock: Ambidextrous synthetic. **Sights:** Adjustable rear, also includes a quick-aid electronic dot sight. **Features:** Very lightweight, single-shot, easy cocking, adjustable two-stage trigger, fluted barrel, nonremovable noise dampener. **Velocity:** 750 fps.
Price: **$79.99**

GAMO SWARM MAXXIM MULTI-SHOT AIR RIFLE

Calibers: .177, .22. **Barrel:** Rifled 19.9 in. **Weight:** 5.64 lbs. **Length:** 45.3 in. **Power:** Break-barrel, gas-piston. **Stock:** Ambidextrous lightweight composite stock. **Sights:** None, grooved for scope mounting, includes recoil-reducing rail, 3-9x32 scope and mounts. **Features:** New for 2017, loaded with patented features including an ingenious 10-shot multi-shot system allows for automatic loading with each cock of the barrel, easy cocking, adjustable two-stage trigger, all-weather fluted barrel, features integrated suppressor technology. **Velocities:** .177, 1,300 fps/.22, 975 fps.
Price: **$199.99**

GAMO SWARM MAGNUM MULTI-SHOT AIR RIFLE

Caliber: .22. **Barrel:** Rifled 21.3 in. **Weight:** 6.88 lbs. **Length:** 49.2 in. **Power:** Break-barrel, gas-piston. **Stock:** Ambidextrous lightweight composite stock. **Sights:** None, grooved for scope mounting, includes recoil-reducing rail, 3-9x32 scope and mounts. **Features:** New for 2018, loaded with patented features including an ingenious 10-shot multi-shot system allows for automatic loading with each cock of the barrel, easy cocking, adjustable two-stage trigger, steel barrel, features integrated suppressor technology. **Velocity:** 1,300 fps.
Price: **$279.99**

GAMO URBAN PCP AIR RIFLE

Caliber: .22. **Barrel:** Cold hammer forged match grade rifled barrel. **Weight:** 6.7 lbs. **Length:** 42.0 in. **Power:** Pre-charged pneumatic. **Stock:** Ambidextrous composite thumbhole stock. **Sights:** None, grooved for scope mounting, **Features:** European class airgun, highly accurate and powerful, adjustable two-stage trigger, integrated moderator, 10-shot bolt action. **Velocity:** 800 fps.
Price: **$450.00**

GAMO TC35 AIR RIFLE

Caliber: .35. **Barrel:** rifled, 14.96 in. **Weight:** 6.0 lbs. **Length:** 35.88 in. **Power:** Pre-charged pneumatic. **Stock:** Ambidextrous. **Sights:** None, weaver rail for scope mounting, **Features:** Very light and yet very powerful producing up to 170 ft-lbs of muzzle energy, adjustable trigger, two power settings, shrouded barrel, single-shot action allows for an extremely wide range of ammo choices.
Price: **$1,099.99**

GAMO TC45 AIR RIFLE

Caliber: .45. **Barrel:** rifled, 24.24 in. **Weight:** 8.0 lbs. **Length:** 47.13 in. **Power:** Pre-charged pneumatic. **Stock:** Ambidextrous. **Sights:** None, weaver rail for scope mounting. **Features:** Very light and yet very powerful producing over 400 ft-lbs of muzzle energy shooting 350-grain cast slugs, adjustable trigger, two power settings, shrouded barrel, single shot action allows for an extremely wide range of ammo choices.
Price: **$1,099.99**

GAMO VARMINT HUNTER HP AIR RIFLE

Caliber: .177 pellets. **Barrel:** Rifled 18 in. **Weight:** 6.61 lbs. **Length:** 43.78 in. **Power:** Break-barrel, spring-piston. **Stock:** Ambidextrous lightweight composite with dual raised cheekpieces. **Sights:** None, grooved for scope mounting, includes recoil-reducing rail, 4x32 scope and mounts, laser and light with intermittent pressure switches included. **Features:** Lightweight, single-shot, easy cocking, adjustable two-stage trigger, all-weather fluted barrel. **Velocity:** 1,400 fps.
Price: **$309.99**

GAMO WHISPER FUSION AIR RIFLE, IGT

Calibers: .177, .22. **Barrel:** Rifled 18 in. **Weight:** 8 lbs. **Length:** 43 in. **Power:** Break-barrel, gas-piston. **Stock:** Ambidextrous lightweight composite stock with adjustable cheekpiece. **Sights:** Globe fiber-optic front sight and fully adjustable fiber-optic rear sight, grooved for scope mounting, includes recoil reducing rail, 3-9x40 scope and heavy-duty mount. **Features:** Integrated Gamo "Whisper" noise dampening system and bull barrel noise suppression system for maximum stealth, lightweight, single-shot, easy cocking, adjustable two-stage trigger. **Velocities:** .177, 1,300 fps/.22, 975 fps.
Price: **$249.99**

HAMMERLI 850 AIR MAGNUM

Calibers: .177, .22. **Barrel:** Rifled 23.62 in. **Weight:** 5.65 lbs. **Length:** 41 in. **Power:** CO_2. **Stock:** Ambidextrous lightweight composite stock with dual raised cheekpieces. **Sights:** Globe fiber-optic front sight and fully adjustable

fiber-optic rear sight, grooved for scope mounting. **Features:** Multi-shot bolt action, 8-shot rotary magazine, utilizes 88-gram disposable CO2 canisters delivering up to 200 shots per cartridge. Extremely accurate, very easy to shoot. German manufacturing. **Velocities:** .177, 760 fps/.22, 655 fps.
Price: **$349.99**

HAMMERLI AR20 SILVER AIR RIFLE
Calibers: .177. **Barrel:** Rifled Lothar Walther 19.7 in. **Weight:** 8.75 lbs. **Length:** 41.65-43.66 in. **Power:** Pre-charged pneumatic. **Stock:** Ambidextrous aluminum stock with vertically adjustable buttpad and spacers for adjusting length. **Sights:** Globe front sight and fully adjustable diopter rear sight, grooved for scope mounting. **Features:** Single shot, ambidextrous cocking piece, removable aluminum air cylinder, meets ISSF requirements, stock is available in several colors. **Velocity:** 557 fps.
Price: **$995.95**

HATSAN USA EDGE CLASS AIRGUNS
Calibers: .177, .22, .25. **Barrel:** Rifled 17.7 in. **Weight:** 6.4–6.6 lbs. **Length:** 43 in. **Power:** Break-barrel, spring-piston and gas-spring variations. **Stock:** Multiple synthetic and synthetic skeleton stock options. Available in different colors such as black, muddy girl camo, moon camo, etc. **Sights:** Fiber-optic front sight and fully adjustable fiber-optic rear sight, grooved for scope mounting, includes 3-9x32 scope and mounts. **Features:** European manufacturing with German steel, single-shot, adjustable two-stage trigger, performance tested at the factory with lead pellets for accurate velocity specifications. **Velocities:** .177, 1,000 fps/.22, 800 fps/.25, 650 fps.
Price: .... **$150.00–$180.00**

HATSAN USA AIRMAX PCP AIR RIFLE
Calibers: .177, .22, .25. **Barrel:** Rifled 23.0 in. **Weight:** 10.8 lbs. **Length:** 37 in. **Power:** Pre-charged pneumatic. **Stock:** Ambidextrous wood bullpup stock. **Sights:** None, combination Picatinny rail and 11mm dovetail for scope mounting. **Features:** Multi-shot side-lever action, 10-shot .177 and .22 magazines/9-shot .25 magazine, "Quiet Energy" barrel shroud with integrated suppressor, removable air cylinder, fully adjustable two-stage "Quattro" trigger, "EasyAdjust" elevation comb, sling swivels, includes two magazines. **Velocities:** .177, 1,170 fps/.22, 1,070 fps/.25, 970 fps.
Price: **$799.99**

HATSAN USA BULLBOSS QE AIR RIFLE
Calibers: .177, .22, .25. **Barrel:** Rifled 23.0 in. **Weight:** 8.6 lbs. **Length:** 36.8 in. **Power:** Pre-charged pneumatic. **Stock:** Ambidextrous synthetic bullpup stock **Sights:** None, innovative dual rail 11mm dovetail and Weaver compatible for scope mounting. **Features:** Multi-shot side-lever action, 10-shot .177 and .22 magazines/9-shot .25 magazine, "Quiet Energy" barrel shroud with integrated suppressor, European manufacturing with German steel, removable air cylinder, fully adjustable two-stage "Quattro" trigger, performance tested at the factory with lead pellets for accurate velocity specifications. **Velocities:** .177, 1,170 fps/.22, 1,070 fps/.25, 970 fps.
Price: **$899.99**

HATSAN USA BARRAGE SEMI-AUTOMATIC PCP AIR RIFLE
Calibers: .177, .22 .25. **Barrel:** Rifled, 19.7 in. **Weight:** 10.1 lbs. **Length:** 40.9 in. **Power:** Pre-charged pneumatic. **Stock:** Ambidextrous adjustable synthetic

thumbhole stock with integrated magazine storage. **Sights:** None, innovative dual rail 11mm dovetail and Weaver compatible for scope mounting. **Features:** Air-driven true semi-automatic action, 14 shots in .177 and 12 shots in .22, "Quiet Energy" barrel shroud with integrated suppressor, 500 cc cylinder with 250BAR capacity, European manufacturing with German steel, performance tested at the factory with lead pellets for accurate velocity specifications. **Velocities:** .177, 1,100 fps/.22, 1,000 fps/.25, 900 fps.
Price: .... **$1,099.99–$1,199.99**

HATSAN USA BULLMASTER SEMI-AUTOMATIC PCP AIR RIFLE
Calibers: .177, .22, .25. **Barrel:** Rifled, 19.7 in. **Weight:** 10.3 lbs. **Length:** 30.9 in. **Power:** Pre-charged pneumatic. **Stock:** Ambidextrous adjustable synthetic bullpup stock with integrated magazine storage. **Sights:** None, innovative dual rail 11mm dovetail and Weaver compatible for scope mounting. **Features:** Air-driven true semi-automatic action, 14 shots in .177 and 12 shots in .22, "Quiet Energy" barrel shroud with integrated suppressor, 500 cc cylinder with 250BAR capacity, European manufacturing with German steel, performance tested at the factory with lead pellets for accurate velocity specifications. **Velocities:** .177, 1,100 fps/.22, 1,000 fps/.25 900 fps.
Price: **$1,099.99–1,199.99**

HATSAN USA BULLY (BULLPUP) PCP AIR RIFLE
Calibers: .177, .22, .25, .30, .35, .45. **Barrel:** Rifled 23 in. **Weight:** 13 lbs. **Length:** 48.4 in. **Power:** Pre-charged pneumatic. **Stock:** Adjustable synthetic all-weather bullpup stock with, sling mounts. **Sights:** None, innovative dual rail 11mm dovetail and Weaver compatible for scope mounting. **Features:** Available in 6 calibers, 500cc of air via carbon fiber reservoir, multi-shot side-lever action, 17-shot .177 magazine, 14-shot .22 magazine, 13-shot .25 magazine, 10-shot .30 magazine, 9-shot .35 magazine, 7-shot .45 magazine. "Quiet Energy" barrel shroud with integrated suppressor, European manufacturing with German steel, fully adjustable two-stage "Quattro" trigger, performance tested at the factory with lead pellets for accurate velocity specifications. **Velocities:** .177, 1,450 fps/.22, 1,300 fps/.25, 1,200 fps/.30, 1,070 fps/.35, 910 fps/.45, 850 fps.
Price: **$899.99**

HATSAN USA FLASH QE PCP
Calibers: .177, .22, .25. **Barrel:** Rifled, 17.7 in. **Weight:** 5.9 lbs. **Length:** 42.3 in. **Power:** Pre-charged pneumatic. **Stock:** Ambidextrous synthetic thumbhole stock **Sights:** None, innovative dual rail 11mm dovetail and Weaver compatible for scope mounting. **Features:** Very lightweight, multi-shot side-lever action, multi-shot magazine (shot count varies by caliber). "Quiet Energy" barrel shroud with integrated suppressor, European manufacturing with German steel, fully adjustable two-stage "Quattro" trigger, performance tested at the factory with lead pellets for accurate velocity specifications. **Velocities:** .177, 1,250 fps/.22, 1,100 fps/.25, 900 fps.
Price: **$309.99**

Prices given are believed to be accurate at time of publication however, many factors affect retail pricing so exact prices are not possible.

74TH EDITION, 2020 ✛ **515**

HATSAN USA MOD 135
QE VORTEX AIRGUN

HATSAN USA FLASHPUP QE PCP
Calibers: .177, .22, .25. **Barrel:** Rifled, 19.4 in. **Weight:** 6.1 lbs. **Length:** 32.0 in. **Power:** Pre-charged pneumatic. **Stock:** Ambidextrous hardwood bullpup stock **Sights:** None, innovative dual rail 11mm dovetail and Weaver compatible for scope mounting. **Features:** Very lightweight, multi-shot side-lever action, multi-shot magazine (shot count varies by caliber). "Quiet Energy" barrel shroud with integrated suppressor, European manufacturing with German steel, fully adjustable two-stage "Quattro" trigger, performance tested at the factory with lead pellets for accurate velocity specifications. **Velocity:** .177, 1,250 fps/.22, 1,100 fps/.25, 900 fps.
Price: $439.99

HATSAN USA GLADIUS AIRGUN (LONG VERSION)
Calibers: .177, .22, .25. **Barrel:** Rifled, 23.0 in. **Weight:** 10.6 lbs. **Length:** 38 in. **Power:** Pre-charged pneumatic. **Stock:** Ambidextrous adjustable synthetic bullpup stock with integrated magazine storage **Sights:** None, innovative dual rail 11mm dovetail and Weaver compatible for scope mounting. **Features:** 6 way variable power, multi-shot side-lever action, 10-shot .177 and .22 magazines / 9-shot .25 magazine, "Quiet Energy" barrel shroud with integrated suppressor, European manufacturing with German steel, removable air cylinder, fully adjustable two-stage "Quattro" trigger, performance tested at the factory with lead pellets for accurate velocity specifications. **Velocities:** .177, 1,070 fps/.22, 970 fps/.25, 870 fps.
Price: $909.99

HATSAN USA MOD 87 QE VORTEX AIRGUN

HATSAN USA MOD 87 QE VORTEX AIR RIFLE
Calibers: .177, .22, .25. **Barrel:** Rifled 10.6 in. **Weight:** 7.4 lbs. **Length:** 44.5 in. **Power:** Break-barrel, gas-spring. **Stock:** Synthetic all-weather stock with adjustable cheekpiece. **Sights:** Fiber-optic front sight and fully adjustable fiber-optic rear sight, grooved for scope mounting, includes 3-9x32 scope and mounts. **Features:** "Quiet Energy" barrel shroud with integrated suppressor, European manufacturing with German steel, single-shot, fully adjustable two-stage "Quattro" trigger, performance tested at the factory with lead pellets for accurate velocity specifications. **Velocities:** .177, 1,000 fps/.22, 800 fps/.25, 650 fps.
Price: $204.99

HATSAN USA MOD 125 SNIPER VORTEX AIRGUN

HATSAN USA MOD 125 SNIPER VORTEX AIR RIFLE
Calibers: .177, .22, .25. **Barrel:** Rifled 19.6 in. **Weight:** 9 lbs. **Length:** 48.8 in. **Power:** Break-barrel, gas-spring. **Stock:** Synthetic all-weather stock with adjustable cheekpiece, available in black or camo options. **Sights:** Fiber-optic front sight and fully adjustable fiber-optic rear sight, grooved for scope mounting, includes 3-9x32 scope and mounts. **Features:** Integrated suppressor, European manufacturing with German steel, single-shot, fully adjustable two-stage "Quattro" trigger, performance tested at the factory with lead pellets for accurate velocity specifications. **Velocities:** .177, 1,250 fps/.22, 1,000 fps/.25, 750 fps.
Price: ....$299.99-$379.99

HATSAN USA MOD 135 QE VORTEX AIR RIFLE
Calibers: .177, .22, .25, .30. **Barrel:** Rifled 10.6 in. **Weight:** 9.9 lbs. **Length:** 47.2 in. **Power:** Break-barrel, gas-spring. **Stock:** Turkish walnut stock with grip and fore-end checkering, adjustable buttplate and cheekpiece. **Sights:** Fiber-optic front sight and fully adjustable fiber-optic rear sight, innovative dual rail 11mm dovetail and Weaver compatible for scope mounting. **Features:** The most powerful break barrel in the world. Worlds first "big-bore" break-barrel airgun, "Quiet Energy" barrel shroud with integrated suppressor, European manufacturing with German steel, single-shot, fully adjustable two-stage "Quattro" trigger, performance tested at the factory with lead pellets for accurate velocity specifications. **Velocities:** .177, 1,250 fps/.22, 1,000 fps/.25, 750 fps/.30, 550 fps.
Price: $299.99-329.99

HATSAN USA MOD "TORPEDO" 150 SNIPER VORTEX AIRGUN
Calibers: .177, .22, .25. **Barrel:** Rifled 13 in. **Weight:** 9.4 lbs. **Length:** 48.4 in. **Power:** Under-lever, gas-spring. **Stock:** Synthetic all-weather stock with adjustable cheekpiece. **Sights:** Fiber-optic front sight and fully adjustable fiber-optic rear sight, innovative dual rail 11mm dovetail and Weaver compatible for scope mounting. **Features:** Integrated suppressor, enhanced fixed barrel accuracy, European manufacturing with German steel, single-shot, fully adjustable two-stage "Quattro" trigger, performance tested at the factory with lead pellets for accurate velocity specifications. **Velocities:** .177, 1,250 fps/.22, 1,000 fps/.25, 750 fps.
Price: $359.99

HATSAN USA AT44 QE PCP AIRGUN

HATSAN USA AT44 QE PCP AIRGUN
Calibers: .177, .22, .25. **Barrel:** Rifled 19.5 in. **Weight:** 8 lbs. **Length:** 45.4 in. **Power:** Pre-charged pneumatic. **Stock:** Various configurations, synthetic all-weather stock with front accessory rail and sling mounts. Turkish hardwood with sling mounts, full tactical stock with soft rubber grip inserts, adjustable buttstock and cheek riser. **Sights:** None, innovative dual rail 11mm dovetail and Weaver compatible for scope mounting. **Features:** Multi-shot side-lever action, 10-shot .177 and .22 magazines / 9-shot .25 magazine. "Quiet Energy" barrel shroud with integrated suppressor, European manufacturing with German steel, removable air cylinder, fully adjustable two-stage "Quattro" trigger, performance tested at the factory with lead pellets for accurate velocity specifications. **Velocities:** .177, 1,070 fps/.22, 970 fps/.25, 870 fps.
Price: $599.00

HATSAN USA BT BIG BORE CARNIVORE BIG BORE QE AIR RIFLE
Calibers: .30, .35. **Barrel:** Rifled 23 in. **Weight:** 9.3 lbs. **Length:** 48.9 in. **Power:** Pre-charged pneumatic. **Stock:** Synthetic all-weather stock with sling mounts, front accessory rail, adjustable cheekpiece and buttpad. **Sights:** None, innovative dual rail 11mm dovetail and Weaver compatible for scope mounting. **Features:** Multi-shot bolt action, 6-shot .35 magazine / 7-shot .30 magazine. "Quiet Energy" barrel shroud with integrated suppressor, European manufacturing with German steel, removable air cylinder, fully adjustable two-stage "Quattro" trigger, performance tested at the factory with lead pellets for accurate velocity specifications. **Velocities:** .30, 860 fps/.35, 730 fps.
Price: $754.99

HATSAN USA GALATIAN QE AIR RIFLE
Calibers: .177, .22, .25. **Barrel:** Rifled 17.7 in. **Weight:** 8.6 lbs. **Length:** 43.3 in. **Power:** Pre-charged pneumatic. **Stock:** Synthetic all-weather stock with extra mag storage, sling mounts, tri-rail front accessory rails, adjustable cheek riser and buttstock. **Sights:** None, innovative dual rail 11mm dovetail and Weaver compatible

for scope mounting. **Features:** Multi-shot side-lever action, 17-shot .177 magazine, 14-shot .22 magazine, 13-shot .25 magazine. "Quiet Energy" barrel shroud with integrated suppressor, European manufacturing with German steel, removable air cylinder, fully adjustable two-stage "Quattro" trigger, performance tested at the factory with lead pellets for accurate velocity specifications. **Velocities:** .177, 1,130 fps./.22, 1,050 fps./.25, 950 fps.
Price: **$999.99**

HATSAN USA HERCULES QE AIR RIFLE
Calibers: .177, .22, .25, .30, .35, .45. **Barrel:** Rifled 23 in. **Weight:** 13 lbs. **Length:** 48.4 in. **Power:** Pre-charged pneumatic. **Stock:** Fully adjustable synthetic all-weather stock with, sling mounts. **Sights:** None, innovative dual rail 11mm dovetail and Weaver compatible for scope mounting. **Features:** Available in 6 calibers, 1000cc of air on board provides industry leading shot count and energy on target. Multi-shot side-lever action, 17-shot .177 magazine, 14-shot .22 magazine, 13-shot .25 magazine, 10-shot .30 magazine, 9-shot .35 magazine, 7-shot .45 magazine. "Quiet Energy" barrel shroud with integrated suppressor, European manufacturing with German steel, fully adjustable two-stage "Quattro" trigger, performance tested at the factory with lead pellets for accurate velocity specifications. **Velocities:** .177, 1,300 fps/.22, 1,230 fps/.25, 1,200 fps/.30, 1,070 fps/.35, 930 fps/.45, 810 fps.
Price: **$1,399.99**

HATSAN USA VECTIS LEVER ACTION PCP AIR RIFLE
Calibers: .177, .22, .25. **Barrel:** Rifled 17.7 in. **Weight:** 7.1 lbs. **Length:** 41.3 in. **Power:** Pre-charged pneumatic. **Stock:** Synthetic all-weather stock. **Sights:** Fiber-optic front and rear, combination dual 11mm dovetail and Weaver compatible for scope mounting. **Features:** Multi-shot lever action, 14-shot .177 magazine, 12-shot .22 magazine, 10-shot .25 magazine. "Quiet Energy" barrel shroud with integrated suppressor, fully adjustable two-stage "Quattro" trigger, Picatinny under barrel accessory rail. **Velocities:** .177, 1,150 fps/.22, 1,000 fps/.25, 900 fps.
Price: **$399.99**

KALIBR CRICKET BULLPUP PCP AIR RIFLE
Caliber: .22. **Barrel:** Rifled 17.5 in. **Weight:** 6.95 lbs. **Length:** 27.0 in. **Power:** Pre-charged pneumatic. **Stock:** Ambidextrous bullpup stock available in various materials. **Sights:** None, weaver rail for scope mounting. **Features:** Multi-shot side-lever action, 14-shot magazine, shrouded barrel with integrated suppression technology, adjustable two-stage trigger. **Velocity:** .22, 925 fps.
Price: .... **$1,629.00–$1,835.00**

KRAL ARMS PUNCHER MEGA WALNUT SIDELEVER PCP AIR RIFLE
Calibers: .177, .22, .25. **Barrel:** Rifled 21.0 in. **Weight:** 8.35 lbs. **Length:** 42.0 in. **Power:** Pre-charged pneumatic. **Stock:** Ambidextrous stock available in synthetic with adjustable cheek piece, and Turkish walnut. **Sights:** None, 11mm grooved dovetail for scope mounting. **Features:** Multi-shot side-lever action, 14-shot .177 magazine, 12-shot .22 magazine, 10-shot .25 magazine, half shrouded barrel with integrated suppression technology, available in blue and satin marine finish, adjustable two-stage trigger. **Velocities:** .177, 1,070 fps/.22, 975 fps/.25, 825 fps.
Price: **$599.99**

KRAL ARMS PUNCHER PRO PCP AIR RIFLE
Calibers: .177, .22, .25. **Barrel:** Rifled 22.8 in. **Weight:** 8.6 lbs. **Length:** 41.3 in. **Power:** Pre-charged pneumatic. **Stock:** Monte Carlo hardwood right-handed stock. **Sights:** None, 11mm grooved dovetail for scope mounting. **Features:** Multi-shot rear bolt action, 14-shot .177 magazine, 12-shot .22 magazine, 10-shot .25 magazine, half shrouded barrel with integrated suppression technology,

two-stage adjustable trigger. **Velocities:** .177, 1,070 fps/.22, 975 fps/.25, 825 fps.
Price: **$599.99**

KRAL ARMS PUNCHER BREAKER SILENT SYNTHETIC SIDELEVER PCP AIR RIFLE
Calibers: .177, .22, .25. **Barrel:** Rifled 21.0 in. **Weight:** 7.4 lbs. **Length:** 29.0 in. **Power:** Pre-charged pneumatic. **Stock:** Ambidextrous bullpup stock available in synthetic and Turkish walnut. **Sights:** None, 11mm grooved dovetail for scope mounting. **Features:** Multi-shot side-lever action, 14-shot .177 magazine, 12-shot .22 magazine, 10-shot .25 magazine, half shrouded barrel with integrated suppression technology, available in blue and satin marine finish, adjustable two-stage trigger. **Velocities:** .177, 1,100 fps/.22, 975 fps/.25, 825 fps.
Price: **$549.99**

KRAL ARMS PUNCHER BIG MAX PCP AIR RIFLE
Calibers: .177, .22, .25. **Barrel:** Rifled 22.0 in. **Weight:** 9.5 lbs. **Length:** 42.1 in. **Power:** Pre-charged pneumatic. **Stock:** Ambidextrous Turkish walnut pistol grip. **Sights:** None, 11mm grooved dovetail for scope mounting. **Features:** Multi-shot side-lever action, 14-shot .177 magazine, 12-shot .22 magazine, 10-shot .25 magazine, shrouded barrel, adjustable two-stage trigger, massive dual air reservoirs with total of 850 CC. **Velocities:** .177, 1,070 fps/.22, 975 fps/.25, 825 fps.
Price: **$779.99**

KRAL ARMS PUNCHER PITBULL PCP AIR RIFLE
Calibers: .177, .22, .25. **Barrel:** Rifled 23.0 in. **Weight:** 8.65 lbs. **Length:** 42.3 in. **Power:** Pre-charged pneumatic. **Stock:** Ambidextrous Turkish walnut pistol grip. **Sights:** None, 11mm grooved dovetail for scope mounting. **Features:** Multi-shot side-lever action, 14-shot .177 magazine, 12-shot .22 magazine, 10-shot .25 magazine, shrouded barrel, adjustable two-stage trigger, massive dual air reservoirs with total of 755 CC. **Velocities:** .177, 1,070 fps/.22, 975 fps/.25, 825 fps.
Price: **$749.99**

KRAL ARMS N-07 BREAKBARREL AIR RIFLE, WOOD OR SKULL
Calibers: .177, .22, .25. **Barrel:** Rifled, 17.9 in. **Weight:** 7.49–7.85 lbs. **Length:** 47.6 in. **Power:** Break-barrel, spring-piston **Stock:** Available in ambidextrous wood and various synthetic options. **Sights:** Fiber-optic front sight and fully adjustable fiber-optic rear sight, 11mm grooved dovetail for scope mounting. **Features:** Single-shot, full power with just one cock of the barrel, two-stage trigger. **Velocities:** .177, 1,200 fps/.22, 1,000 fps/.25, 750 fps.
Price: ....**$179.99–$199.99**

KRAL ARMS N-11 BREAKBARREL AIR RIFLE, BLACK
Calibers: .177, .22, .25. **Barrel:** Rifled, 15.7 in. **Weight:** 7.82 lbs. **Length:** 49.0 in. **Power:** Break-barrel, spring-piston **Stock:** Available in ambidextrous thumbhole synthetic options. **Sights:** Fiber-optic front sight and fully adjustable fiber-optic rear sight, 11mm grooved dovetail for scope mounting. **Features:** Muzzle break suppressor for quite shooting and easier cocking, single-shot, full power with just one cock of the barrel, two-stage trigger. **Velocities:** .177, 1,200 fps/.22, 950 fps./.25, 750 fps.
Price: **$179.99**

Prices given are believed to be accurate at time of publication however, many factors affect retail pricing so exact prices are not possible.

74TH EDITION, 2020 ⊕ **517**

REMINGTON EXPRESS

REMINGTON EXPRESS HUNTER AIR RIFLE W/SCOPE COMBOS
Caliber: .177 or .22. **Barrel:** Rifled, 19 in. **Weight:** 8 lbs. **Length:** 45 in. **Power:** Break-barrel, spring-piston **Stock:** Available in ambidextrous wood with grip and fore-end checkering and textured synthetic options. **Sights:** Fiber-optic front sight and fully adjustable fiber-optic rear sight, grooved for scope mounting, includes 4x32 scope and mounts. **Features:** Single-shot, two-stage trigger. **Velocity:** 1,000 fps (.177), 800 fps (.22).
Price: $159.99

REMINGTON 725 VTR AIR RIFLE
Caliber: .25. **Barrel:** Rifled. **Weight:** 10.5 lbs. **Length:** 48 in. **Power:** Break-barrel, spring-piston. **Stock:** Ambidextrous, synthetic. **Sights:** None, grooved for scope mounting, includes 4x32 scope and mounts. **Features:** Single-shot, bull barrel, Picatinny rail. **Velocity:** 900 fps with alloy pellet.
Price: $249.99

REMINGTON R1100 AIR RIFLE
Caliber: .177 BB or pellet. **Barrel:** Rifled. **Weight:** NA. **Length:** NA. **Power:** Multi-pump pneumatic. **Stock:** Synthetic. **Sights:** Fixed front and adjustable rear. **Features:** Single-shot pellet, 1,000 shot BB, youth rifle. **Velocity:** 645 fps with BB.
Price: $259.99

RUGER 10/22 CO2 RIFLE
Calibers: .177 pellets. **Barrel:** Rifled 18 in. **Weight:** 4.5 lbs. **Length:** 37.1 in. **Power:** Two 12-gram CO_2 cylinders. **Stock:** Synthetic stock. **Sights:** Rear sight adjustable for elevation, accepts aftermarket rail. **Features:** 10-shot Ruger-style rotary magazine, bolt cocks rifle, 3-pound single-action trigger pull, sling attachments. **Velocity:** 650 fps.
Price: $149.95

RUGER AIR MAGNUM COMBO

RUGER AIR MAGNUM COMBO
Calibers: .177, .22. **Barrel:** Rifled 19.5 in. **Weight:** 9.5 lbs. **Length:** 48.5 in. **Power:** Break-barrel, spring-piston. **Stock:** Ambidextrous Monte Carlo synthetic stock with textured grip and fore-end. **Sights:** Fiber-optic front sight and fully adjustable fiber-optic rear sight, Weaver scope rail, includes 4x32 scope and mounts. **Features:** Single-shot, two-stage trigger. **Velocities:** .177, 1,400 fps/.22, 1,200 fps.
Price: $220.00

RUGER BLACKHAWK COMBO
Caliber: .177 pellets. **Barrel:** Rifled 18.7 in. **Weight:** 6.95 lbs. **Length:** 44.8 in.

Power: Break-barrel, spring-piston. **Stock:** Ambidextrous synthetic stock with checkering on the grip and fore-end. **Sights:** Fiber-optic front sight and fully adjustable fiber-optic rear sight, grooved for scope mounting, includes 4x32 scope and mounts. **Features:** Single-shot, two-stage trigger. **Velocity:** 1,000 fps.
Price: $130.00

RUGER EXPLORER
Caliber: .177 pellets. **Barrel:** Rifled 15 in. **Weight:** 4.45 lbs. **Length:** 37.12 in. **Power:** Break-barrel, spring-piston **Stock:** Ambidextrous synthetic skeleton stock. **Sights:** Fiber-optic front sight and fully adjustable fiber-optic rear sight, grooved for scope mounting. **Features:** Designed as an entry level youth break-barrel rifle, easy to shoot and accurate, single-shot, two-stage trigger. **Velocity:** 495 fps.
Price: $79.99

RUGER TARGIS HUNTER AIR RIFLE COMBO
Caliber: .22. **Barrel:** Rifled 18.7 in. **Weight:** 9.85 lbs. **Length:** 44.85 in. **Power:** Break-barrel, spring-piston. **Stock:** Ambidextrous synthetic stock with texture grip and fore-end, includes rifle sling. **Sights:** Fiber-optic front sight and fully adjustable fiber-optic rear sight, picatinny optics rail, includes 3-9x40AO scope and mounts. **Features:** Integrated "SilencAIR" suppressor, single-shot, two-stage trigger. **Velocity:** 1,000 fps.
Price: $210.00

RUGER TARGIS AIR RIFLE
Caliber: .177. **Barrel:** Rifled 18.7 in. **Weight:** 9.85 lbs. **Length:** 44.85 in. **Power:** Break-barrel, spring-piston, single-shot. **Stock:** Black colored synthetic with ventilated comb. **Sights:** Fiber-optic front sight and adjustable rear sight with Weaver/Picatinny rail system. **Features:** Two-stage trigger with 3.3-lb. trigger pull weight and rubber buttplate. **Velocities:** 1,200 fps with alloy pellets and 1,000 fps with lead pellets.
Price: $175.95

SENECA BIG BORE 44 909 LIGHT HUNTER 500CC TANK
Caliber: .45. **Barrel:** Rifled 21.65 in. **Weight:** 8.5 lbs. **Length:** 42.1 in. **Power:** Pre-charged pneumatic. **Stock:** Right-handed wood stock. **Sights:** Fixed front sight with fully adjustable rear sight. **Features:** Massive 500cc reservoir delivers several powerful shots, delivers well over 200 ft-lbs at the muzzle, long-range hunting accuracy, exceptionally reliable. **Velocity:** 730 fps.
Price: $729.99

SENECA DRAGON FLY MULTI-PUMP AIR RIFLE
Calibers: .177, .22. **Barrel:** Rifled 21.7 in. **Weight:** 6.65 lbs. **Length:** 38.5 in. **Power:** Multi-Pump pneumatic. **Stock:** Ambidextrous wood stock. **Sights:** Fixed front sight with fully adjustable rear sight. **Features:** No recoil for maximum precision, variable power based on number of pumps, bolt action, single shot and multi-shot capability. **Velocities:** .177, 800 fps/.22 630 fps.
Price: $219.99

SENECA RECLUSE AIR RIFLE
Caliber: .35 (9mm). **Barrel:** Rifled 21.60 in. **Weight:** 7.5 lbs. **Length:** 42.1 in. **Power:** Pre-charged pneumatic. **Stock:** Right-handed wood stock. **Sights:** Fixed front sight with fully adjustable rear sight. **Features:** Massive 500cc reservoir delivers several powerful shots, delivers well over 150 ft-lbs at the muzzle, long-range hunting accuracy, exceptionally reliable. **Velocity:** 983 fps.
Price: $699.95

SIG SAUER MCX CO2 RIFLE & SCOPE, BLACK
Caliber: .177. **Barrel:** Rifled 17.7 in. **Weight:** 7.9 lbs. **Length:** 34.7 in. **Power:** CO_2. **Stock:** Synthetic stock, various color options. **Sights:** Varies with model, weaver rail system for iron sight systems, red dot systems, and traditional scope mounting. **Features:** 30-round semi-auto, reliable belt fed magazine system, available in various colors and sighting combination, very realistic replica.

Velocity: 700 fps.
Price: $269.99

SIG SAUER MPX CO2 RIFLE, DOT SIGHT, BLACK
Caliber: .177. **Barrel:** Rifled 8 in. **Weight:** 6.6 lbs. **Length:** 25.8 in. **Power:** CO2. **Stock:** Synthetic stock, various color options. **Sights:** Varies with model, weaver rail system for iron sight systems, red dot systems, and traditional scope mounting. **Features:** 30-round semi-auto, reliable belt fed magazine system, available in various colors and sighting combination, very realistic replica. **Velocity:** 575 fps.
Price: $245.95

SIG SAUER ASP20 RIFLE
Caliber: .177 or .22 pellets. **Barrel:** Rifled 13.8 in. **Weight:** 8.5 pounds. **Length:** 45.6 in. **Power:** Break barrel. **Stock:** Black-stained beech wood. **Sights:** None, Picatinny rail. **Features:** Two-stage Matchlite trigger adjustable from 2.5 to 4 pounds, integrated suppressor, 33-pound cocking effort. **Velocity:** 1,021 fps (.177), 841 fps (.22).
Price: $399.99

STOEGER ARMS A30 S2 AIR RIFLE COMBO
Calibers: .177, .22. **Barrel:** Rifled 16.5 in. **Weight:** 8.2 lbs. **Length:** 42.5 in. **Power:** Break-barrel, gas-piston **Stock:** Ambidextrous synthetic stock with textured grip and fore-end. **Sights:** None, picatinny optics rail, includes 4x32 scope and mounts. **Features:** Single-shot, two-stage trigger. **Velocities:** .177, 1,200 fps/.22, 1,000 fps.
Price: $220.00

STOEGER ARMS X20S2 SUPPRESSOR AIR RIFLE
Calibers: .177, .22. **Barrel:** Rifled 16.5 in. **Weight:** 7 lbs. **Length:** 43 in. **Power:** Break-barrel, spring-piston. **Stock:** Ambidextrous Monte Carlo synthetic stock. **Sights:** None, grooved for scope mounting, includes compact 4x32 scope and mounts. **Features:** Industry leading dual-stage noise reduction technology makes the X20s perhaps the quietest spring-powered magnum airgun on the market. Single-shot, two-stage trigger. **Velocity:** .177, 1,200 fps/.22, 1,000 fps.
Price: $199.99

UMAREX EMBARK AIR RIFLE
Caliber: .177. **Barrel:** Rifled 15 in. **Weight:** 4.45 **Length:** 37.25 in. **Power:** Spring piston. **Stock:** Ambidextrous neon green thumbhole synthetic. **Sights:** Fully adjustable micrometer rear, grooved 11mm dovetail for scope mounting. **Features:** Official air rifle for the Student Air Rifle program, 12-inch length of pull, muzzle brake, 16.5-pound cocking effort, 4.25-pound trigger pull, automatic safety. **Velocity:** 510 fps.
Price: $95.00

UMAREX FUSION CO2 AIR RIFLE
Caliber: .177. **Barrel:** Rifled 17.13 in. **Weight:** 5.71 lbs. **Length:** 40.1 in. **Power:** CO2 **Stock:** Ambidextrous synthetic. **Sights:** None, grooved 11mm dovetail for scope mounting, includes 4x32 and mounts. **Features:** Single-shot bolt action, includes integrated suppressor. **Velocity:** 750 fps.
Price: $180.99

UMAREX GAUNTLET PCP AIR RIFLE, SYNTHETIC STOCK
Caliber: .177, .22., .25 **Barrel:** Rifled 23.5 in. **Weight:** 8.5 lbs. **Length:** 46 in. **Power:** Pre-charged pneumatic. **Stock:** Ambidextrous synthetic. **Sights:** None, grooved 11mm dovetail for scope mounting. **Features:** Removable regulated bottle, multi-shot bolt action, fully shrouded and moderated, adjustable two-stage trigger, first production PCP with these high-end features at this low price point. **Velocities:** .177, 1,000 fps/.22, 900 fps.
Price: $299.99

UMAREX HAMMER AIR RIFLE
Caliber: .50. **Barrel:** Rifled 29.5 in. **Weight:** 8.5 **Length:** 43.75 in. **Power:** Pre-charged pneumatic. **Stock:** Nymax synthetic. **Sights:** None, Picatinny rail for scope mounting. **Features:** Fires three full-power shots, 2-pound straight pull bolt cocks rifle and advances the magazine, 4,500-psi. built-in carbon-fiber tank with quick disconnect Foster fitting, trigger-block safety, will not fire without magazine, Magpul AR grip, full-length composite barrel shroud, comes with two double-chamber magazines. **Velocities:** 1,130 fps (180-grain non-lead bullet), 760 fps (550-grain lead slug).
Price: $799.99

UMAREX SYNERGIS UNDER LEVER AIR RIFLE
Caliber: .177 pellets. **Barrel:** Rifled. **Weight:** 8.3 lbs. **Length:** 45.3 in. **Power:** Gas piston under lever. **Stock:** Synthetic. **Sights:** None, Picatinny rail for scope mounting. **Features:** 12-shot repeater, fixed barrel, removable magazine, integrated suppressor. **Velocity:** 1,000 fps.
Price: $169.00

UMAREX THROTTLE AIR RIFLE COMBO, GAS PISTON
Calibers: .177, .22. **Barrel:** Rifled 15.9 in. **Weight:** 8.3 lbs. **Length:** 45.3 in. **Power:** Break-barrel, gas-piston. **Stock:** Ambidextrous synthetic. **Sights:** None, Weaver rail for scope mounting, includes 3-9x32 AO scope and mounts. **Features:** Single shot, includes integrated suppressor, features new "STOPSHOX" anti-recoil feature. **Velocities:** .177, 1,200 fps/.22, 1,000 fps.
Price: $183.99

WALTHER LG400 UNIVERSAL AIR RIFLE, AMBI GRIP
Caliber: .177. **Barrel:** Advanced match-grade rifled barrel 16.53 in. **Weight:** 8.6 lbs. **Length:** 43.7 in. **Power:** Pre-charged pneumatic. **Stock:** Ambidextrous competition, highly adjustable wood stock. **Sights:** Olympic-grade, match Diopter/Micrometer adjustable sights. **Features:** True professional class 10-meter target rifle, meets ISSF requirements. **Velocity:** 557 fps.
Price: $2,500.00

WALTHER MAXIMATHOR AIR RIFLE
Calibers: .22, .25. **Barrel:** Advanced match-grade rifled barrel, 23.5 in. **Weight:** 9.6 lbs. **Length:** 41.75 in. **Power:** Pre-charged pneumatic. **Stock:** Ambidextrous wood stock. **Sights:** None, grooved 11mm dovetail for scope mounting. **Features:** Bolt action 8-shot magazine, pure hunting PCP with range and accuracy. **Velocities:** .22, 1,260 fps/.25, 1,000 fps.
Price: $802.49

WALTHER LEVER ACTION

WALTHER LEVER ACTION CO2 RIFLE, BLACK
Caliber: .177. **Barrel:** Rifled 18.9 in. **Weight:** 6.2 lbs. **Length:** 39.2 in. **Power:** CO2 **Stock:** Ambidextrous wood stock. **Sights:** Blade front sight, adjustable rear sight. **Features:** Lever-action repeater, 8-shot rotary magazine, great wild west replica airgun. **Velocity:** 600 fps.
Price: $500.00

WALTHER 1250 DOMINATOR COMBO AIR RIFLE
Calibers: .177, .22. **Barrel:** Rifled 23.62 in. **Weight:** 8 lbs. **Length:** 40.94 in. **Power:** Pre-charged pneumatic. **Stock:** Ambidextrous synthetic stock with dual raised cheekpieces. **Sights:** None, grooved for scope mounting, includes 8-32x56 side focus mil-dot scope and mounts. **Features:** German-engineered and manufactured, bolt-action repeater, 8-shot rotary magazine, adjustable two-stage trigger. Ships with hard case, bipod and muzzle brake. **Velocities:** .177, 1,200 fps/.22, 1,000 fps.
Price: $949.99

WALTHER LG300-XT JUNIOR AIR RIFLE, LAMINATED STOCK
Caliber: .177. **Barrel:** Advanced match-grade rifled barrel, 16.54 in. **Weight:** 7.72 lbs. **Length:** 39.76 in. **Power:** Pre-charged pneumatic. **Stock:** Ambidextrous highly adjustable competition laminate wood stock. **Sights:** Olympic-grade, match Diopter/Micrometer adjustable sights. **Features:** 10-meter competition target rifle, meets ISSF requirements, removable air cylinder delivers up to 400 shots per fill. **Velocity:** 570 fps.
Price: $1,725.95

WALTHER ROTEK AIR RIFLE
Calibers: .177, .22. **Barrel:** Rifled Lothar Walther 19.7 in. **Weight:** 8 lbs. **Length:** 41 in. **Power:** Pre-charged pneumatic. **Stock:** Ambidextrous Minelli beech with checkered forearm and grip. **Sights:** None, 11 mm dovetail grooved for scope mounting. **Features:** 1/2 UNF threaded muzzle, eight-shot rotary clip, vibration reduction system, two-stage adjustable match trigger. **Velocities:** 1,000 fps (.177)/900 fps (.22).
Price: $759.99

WALTHER TERRUS AIR RIFLE
Calibers: .177, .22. **Barrel:** Rifled 17.75 in. **Weight:** 7.52 lbs. **Length:** 44.25 in. **Power:** Single-cock, spring-piston. **Stock:** Ambidextrous beech and synthetic stock options available. **Sights:** Front fiber-optic sight and fully adjustable rear fiber-optic sight, grooved for scope mounting. **Features:** German engineered and manufactured, very easy cocking and shooting, 1/2 UNF threaded muzzle, single-shot, two-stage target trigger, limited lifetime warranty. **Velocities:** .177, 1,050 fps /.22, 800 fps.
Price: ....$279.95–$329.95

WEBLEY VMX QUANTUM SPRING PISTON RIFLE

Calibers: .177, .22 pellet. **Barrel:** Rifled, 16.9 in. **Weight:** 6.4 lbs. **Length:** 42.9 in. **Power:** Spring-piston. **Stock:** Synthetic with textured forearm and pistol grip. **Sights:** None, 11 mm grooved dovetail for sighting equipment. **Features:** Over-sleeved silencer allows for quiet shots, automatic safety, two-stage trigger. **Velocity:** 1,000 fps (.177)/820 fps (.22).
Price: .... $NA

WEIHRAUCH HW50S SPRING PISTON RIFLE
Calibers: .177, .22. **Barrel:** Rifled, 15.5 in. **Weight:** 6.8 lbs. **Length:** 40.5 in. **Power:** Spring-piston. **Stock:** Checkered beech wood. **Sights:** Front globe and adjustable rear. **Features:** Single shot, 24-pound cocking effort, two-stage adjustable Rekord trigger. **Velocity:** 820 fps (.177), 574 fps (.22).
Price: $367.99

WEIHRAUCH HW90 SPRING PISTON RIFLE
Calibers: .177, .22, .25. **Barrel:** Rifled, 19.7 in. **Weight:** 6.8 lbs. **Length:** 45.3 in. **Power:** Spring-piston. **Stock:** Checkered beech wood. **Sights:** Front globe and adjustable rear, 11 mm dovetail for scope mounting. **Features:** Single shot, 46-pound cocking effort, two-stage adjustable Rekord trigger. **Velocity:** 1,050 fps (.177), 853 fps (.22), 625 fps (.25).
Price: $682.49

WEIHRAUCH HW97K/KT AIR RIFLE
Calibers: .177, .20, .22, .25. **Barrel:** Rifled, 11.81 in. **Weight:** 8.8 lbs. **Length:** 40.1 in. **Power:** Under-lever, spring-piston. **Stock:** Various, beech wood, blue-gray laminated, or synthetic, with or without thumbhole. **Sights:** None, grooved for scope. **Features:** Silver or blue finish, highly adjustable match-grade trigger. Extremely accurate fixed-barrel design. **Velocity:** 820 fps (.177), 755 fps (.22).
Price: ....$749.95-$890.00

WEIHRAUCH HW100 S FSB PRECHARGE PNEUMATIC AIR RIFLE
Caliber: .177. **Barrel:** Rifled, 23.63 in. **Weight:** 8.6 lbs. **Length:** 42.13 in. **Power:** Pre-charged pneumatic. **Stock:** Right-handed hardwood stock. **Sights:** Grooved for scope mounting. **Features:** Multi-shot side lever, 14-round magazine, shrouded barrel. **Velocity:** 1,135 fps.
Price: $1,769.95

WINCHESTER 77XS MULTI-PUMP AIR RIFLE
Caliber: .177 steel BBs, .177 Pellet. **Barrel:** Rifled 20.8 in. **Weight:** 3.1 lbs. **Length:** 37.6 in. **Power:** Multi-pump pneumatic. **Stock:** Ambidextrous synthetic thumbhole stock. **Sights:** Blade front sight, adjustable rear sight, grooved for scope mounting, includes 4x32 scope and mounts. **Features:** Single-shot pellet, 50-round BB repeater, bolt action, lightweight, accurate and easy to shoot. **Velocity:** 800 fps.
Price: $129.99

WINCHESTER 500S AIR RIFLE
Caliber: .177. **Barrel:** Rifled. **Weight:** 6 lbs. **Length:** 39.38 in. **Power:** Break-barrel, spring-piston. **Stock:** Ambidextrous synthetic stock with textured grip and fore-end. **Sights:** Fiber-optic front sight and fully adjustable fiber-optic rear sight, grooved for scope mounting. **Features:** Easy cocking, designed for younger

shooters, single-shot. **Velocity:** 490 fps.
Price: $119.99

WINCHESTER 1100SS AIR RIFLE

Caliber: .177. **Barrel:** Rifled. **Weight:** 8.5 lbs. **Length:** 46.25 in. **Power:** Break-barrel, spring-piston. **Stock:** Ambidextrous synthetic stock, textured grip and fore-end. **Sights:** Fixed front sight and fully adjustable rear sight, grooved for scope mounting, includes 4x32 scope and mounts. **Features:** Single-shot, aggressive pricing. **Velocity:** 1,100 fps.
Price: $129.99

WINCHESTER 1250SS/WS AIR RIFLE

Caliber: .177. **Barrel:** Rifled **Weight:** 8.7 lbs. **Length:** 46.5 in. **Power:** Break-barrel, spring-piston. **Stock:** Ambidextrous wood or synthetic thumbhole stock. **Sights:** Fixed fiber-optic front sight and fully adjustable fiber-optic rear sight, grooved for scope mounting, includes 3-9x32 scope and mounts. **Features:** Integrated suppressor, single-shot, includes web sling, integrated bipod. **Velocity:** 1,250 fps.
Price: $179.99

WINCHESTER 1400CS AIR RIFLE, MOSSY OAK CAMO

Caliber: .177. **Barrel:** Rifled. **Weight:** 9 lbs. **Length:** 51.2 in. **Power:** Break-barrel, spring-piston. **Stock:** Ambidextrous synthetic thumbhole Mossy Oak camo pattern stock. **Sights:** None, grooved for scope mounting, includes 3-9x32 scope and mounts. **Features:** Single-shot, includes web sling, integrated bipod. **Velocity:** 1,400 fps.
Price: $229.99

WINCHESTER 1052SS AIR RIFLE COMBO

Caliber: .22. **Barrel:** Rifled. **Weight:** 8.2 lbs. **Length:** 46.25 in. **Power:** Break-barrel, spring-piston. **Stock:** Ambidextrous synthetic thumbhole stock. **Sights:** None, grooved for scope mounting, includes 3-9x32 scope and mounts. **Features:** Single-shot, includes web sling, all-weather fluted barrel jacket. **Velocity:** 1,000 fps.
Price: $199.99

WINCHESTER MODEL 70

Calibers: .35, .45. **Barrel:** Rifled, 20.87 in. **Weight:** 9.0 lbs. **Length:** 41.75 in. **Power:** Pre-charged pneumatic. **Stock:** Right handed hardwood. **Sights:** None, grooved for scope mounting. **Features:** Multi-Shot big bore (6 shots .35 / 5 shots .45), highly stable shot strings for maximum accuracy, traditional Winchester styling, .35 produces up to 134 ft-lbs, .45 produces over 200 ft-lbs. **Velocities:** .35, 865 fps/.45, 803 fps.
Price: $799.99

Many manufacturers do not supply suggested retail prices. Others did not get their pricing to us before press time. All pricing can vary dependent on the exact brand and style of ammo selected and/or the retail outlet from which you make your purchase. Pricing has been rounded to the nearest dollar and represents our best estimate of average pricing.
An * after the cartridge means these loads are available with Nosler Partition or Swift A-Frame bullets. Listed pricing may or may not reflect this bullet type.
** = these are packed 50 to box, all others are 20 to box. Wea. Mag.= Weatherby Magnum. Spfd. = Springfield. A-Sq. = A-Square. N.E.=Nitro Express.

Cartridge	Bullet Wgt. Grs.	VELOCITY (fps)					ENERGY (ft. lbs.)					TRAJ. (in.)				Est. Price/box
		Muzzle	100 yds.	200 yds.	300 yds.	400 yds.	Muzzle	100 yds.	200 yds.	300 yds.	400 yds.	100 yds.	200 yds.	300 yds.	400 yds.	
17, 22																
17 Hornet	15.5	3860	2924	2159	1531	1108	513	294	160	81	42	1.4	0.0	-9.1	-33.7	NA
17 Hornet	20	3650	3078	2574	2122	1721	592	421	294	200	131	1.10	0.0	-6.4	-20.6	NA
17 Hornet	25	3375	2842	2367	1940	1567	632	448	311	209	136	1.4	0	24.8	56.3	NA
17 Remington Fireball	20	4000	3380	2840	2360	1930	710	507	358	247	165	1.6	1.5	-2.8	-13.5	NA
17 Remington Fireball	25	3850	3280	2780	2330	1925	823	597	429	301	206	0.9	0.0	-5.4	NA	NA
17 Remington	20	4200	3544	2978	2477	2029	783	558	394	272	183	0	-1.3	-6.6	-17.6	NA
17 Remington	25	4040	3284	2644	2086	1606	906	599	388	242	143	+2.0	+1.7	-4.0	-17.0	$17
4.6x30 H&K	30	2025	1662	1358	1135	1002	273	184	122	85	66	0	-12.7	-44.5	—	NA
4.6x30 H&K	40	1900	1569	1297	1104	988	320	218	149	108	86	0	-14.3	-39.3	—	NA
204 Ruger (Hor)	24	4400	3667	3046	2504	2023	1032	717	494	334	218	0.6	0	-4.3	-14.3	NA
204 Ruger (Fed)	32 Green	4030	3320	2710	2170	1710	1155	780	520	335	205	0.9	0.0	-5.7	-19.1	NA
204 Ruger	32	4125	3559	3061	2616	2212	1209	900	666	486	348	0	-1.3	-6.3	—	NA
204 Ruger	32	4225	3632	3114	2652	2234	1268	937	689	500	355	.6	0.0	-4.2	-13.4	NA
204 Ruger	40	3900	3451	3046	2677	2336	1351	1058	824	636	485	.7	0.0	-4.5	-13.9	NA
204 Ruger	45	3625	3188	2792	2428	2093	1313	1015	778	589	438	1.0	0.0	-5.5	-16.9	NA
5.45x39mm	60	2810	2495	2201	1927	1677	1052	829	645	445	374	1.0	0.0	-9.2	-27.7	NA
221 Fireball	40	3100	2510	1991	1547	1209	853	559	352	212	129	0	-4.1	-17.3	-45.1	NA
221 Fireball	50	2800	2137	1580	1180	988	870	507	277	155	109	+0.0	-7.0	-28.0	0.0	$14
22 Hornet (Fed)	30 Green	3150	2150	1390	990	830	660	310	130	65	45	0.0	-6.6	-32.7	NA	NA
22 Hornet	34	3050	2132	1415	1017	852	700	343	151	78	55	+0.0	-6.6	-15.5	-29.9	NA
22 Hornet	35	3100	2278	1601	1135	929	747	403	199	100	67	+2.75	0.0	-16.9	-60.4	NA
22 Hornet	40	2800	2397	2029	1698	1413	696	510	366	256	177	0	-4.6	-17.8	-43.1	NA
22 Hornet	45	2690	2042	1502	1128	948	723	417	225	127	90	+0.0	-7.7	-31.0	0.0	$27**
218 Bee	46	2760	2102	1550	1155	961	788	451	245	136	94	+0.0	-7.2	-29.0	0.0	$46**
222 Rem.	35	3760	3125	2574	2085	1656	1099	759	515	338	213	1.0	0.0	-6.3	-20.8	NA
222 Rem.	50	3345	2930	2553	2205	1886	1242	953	723	540	395	1.3	0	-6.7	-20.6	NA
222 Remington	40	3600	3117	2673	2269	1911	1151	863	634	457	324	+1.07	0.0	-6.13	-18.9	NA
222 Remington	50	3140	2602	2123	1700	1350	1094	752	500	321	202	+2.0	-0.4	-11.0	-33.0	$11
222 Remington	55	3020	2562	2147	1773	1451	1114	801	563	384	257	+2.0	-0.4	-11.0	-33.0	$12
222 Rem. Mag.	40	3600	3140	2726	2347	2000	1150	876	660	489	355	1.0	0	-5.7	-17.8	NA
222 Rem. Mag.	50	3340	2917	2533	2179	1855	1238	945	712	527	382	1.3	0	-6.8	-20.9	NA
222 Rem. Mag.	55	3240	2748	2305	1906	1556	1282	922	649	444	296	+2.0	-0.2	-9.0	-27.0	$14
22 PPC	52	3400	2930	2510	2130	NA	1335	990	730	525	NA	+2.0	1.4	-5.0	0.0	NA
223 Rem.	35	3750	3206	2725	2291	1899	1092	799	577	408	280	1.0	0	-5.7	-18.1	NA
223 Rem.	35	4000	3353	2796	2302	1861	1243	874	607	412	269	0.8	0	-5.3	-17.3	NA
223 Rem.	64	2750	2368	2018	1701	1427	1074	796	578	411	289	2.4	0	-11	-34.1	NA
223 Rem.	75	2790	2562	2345	2139	1943	1296	1093	916	762	629	1.5	0	-8.2	-24.1	NA
223 Remington	40	3650	3010	2450	1950	1530	1185	805	535	340	265	+2.0	+1.0	-6.0	-22.0	$14
223 Remington	40	3800	3305	2845	2424	2044	1282	970	719	522	371	0.84	0.0	-5.34	-16.6	NA
223 Remington (Rem)	45 Green	3550	2911	2355	1865	1451	1259	847	554	347	210	2.5	2.3	-4.3	-21.1	NA
223 Remington	50	3300	2874	2484	2130	1809	1209	917	685	504	363	1.37	0.0	-7.05	-21.8	NA
223 Remington	52/53	3330	2882	2477	2106	1770	1305	978	722	522	369	+2.0	+0.6	-6.5	-21.5	$14
223 Remington (Win)	55 Green	3240	2747	2304	1905	1554	1282	921	648	443	295	1.9	0.0	-8.5	-26.7	NA
223 Remington	55	3240	2748	2305	1906	1556	1282	922	649	444	296	+2.0	-0.2	-9.0	-27.0	$12
223 Remington	60	3100	2712	2355	2026	1726	1280	979	739	547	397	+2.0	+0.2	-8.0	-24.7	$16
223 Remington	62	3000	2700	2410	2150	1900	1240	1000	800	635	495	1.60	0.0	-7.7	-22.8	NA
223 Remington	64	3020	2621	2256	1920	1619	1296	977	723	524	373	+2.0	-0.2	-9.3	-23.0	$14
223 Remington	69	3000	2720	2460	2210	1980	1380	1135	925	750	600	+2.0	+0.8	-5.8	-17.5	$15
223 Remington	75	2790	2554	2330	2119	1926	1296	1086	904	747	617	2.37	0.0	-8.75	-25.1	NA
223 Rem. Super Match	75	2930	2694	2470	2257	2055	1429	1209	1016	848	703	1.20	0.0	-6.9	-20.7	NA
223 Remington	77	2750	2584	2354	2169	1992	1293	1110	948	804	679	1.93	0.0	-8.2	-23.8	NA
223 WSSM	55	3850	3438	3064	2721	2402	1810	1444	1147	904	704	0.7	0.0	-4.4	-13.6	NA
223 WSSM	64	3600	3144	2732	2356	2011	1841	1404	1061	789	574	1.0	0.0	-5.7	-17.7	NA
5.56 NATO	55	3130	2740	2382	2051	1750	1196	917	693	514	372	1.1	0	-7.3	-23.0	NA
5.56 NATO	75	2910	2676	2543	2242	2041	1410	1192	1002	837	693	1.2	0	-7.0	-21.0	NA
224 Wea. Mag.	55	3650	3192	2780	2403	2057	1627	1244	943	705	516	+2.0	+1.2	-4.0	-17.0	$32

Cartridge	Bullet Wgt. Grs.	VELOCITY (fps)					ENERGY (ft. lbs.)					TRAJ. (in.)				Est. Price/box
		Muzzle	100 yds.	200 yds.	300 yds.	400 yds.	Muzzle	100 yds.	200 yds.	300 yds.	400 yds.	100 yds.	200 yds.	300 yds.	400 yds.	
22 Nosler	55	3350	2965	2615	2286	1984	1370	1074	833	638	480	0	-2.5	-10.1	-24.4	
22 Nosler	77	2950	2672	2410	2163	1931	1488	1220	993	800	637	0	-3.4	-12.8	-29.7	
224 Valkyrie	90	2700	2542	2388	2241	2098	1457	1291	1140	1003	880	1.9	0	-8.1	-23.2	NA
224 Valkyrie	75	3000	2731	2477	2237	2010	1499	1242	1022	833	673	1.6	0	-7.3	-21.5	NA
224 Valkyrie	60	3300	2930	2589	2273	1797	1451	1144	893	688	522	1.3	0	-6.5	-19.8	NA
225 Winchester	55	3570	3066	2616	2208	1838	1556	1148	836	595	412	+2.0	+1.0	-5.0	-20.0	$19
22-250 Rem.	35	4450	3736	3128	2598	2125	1539	1085	761	524	351	6.5	0	-4.1	-13.4	NA
22-250 Rem.	40	4000	3320	2720	2200	1740	1420	980	660	430	265	+2.0	+1.8	-3.0	-16.0	$14
22-250 Rem.	40	4150	3553	3033	2570	2151	1530	1121	817	587	411	0.6	0	-4.4	-14.2	NA
22-250 Rem.	45 Green	4000	3293	2690	2159	1696	1598	1084	723	466	287	1.7	1.7	-3.2	-15.7	NA
22-250 Rem.	50	3725	3264	2641	2455	2103	1540	1183	896	669	491	0.89	0.0	-5.23	-16.3	NA
22-250 Rem.	52/55	3680	3137	2656	2222	1832	1654	1201	861	603	410	+2.0	+1.3	-4.0	-17.0	$13
22-250 Rem.	60	3600	3195	2826	2485	2169	1727	1360	1064	823	627	+2.0	+2.0	-2.4	-12.3	$19
22-250 Rem.	64	3425	2988	2591	2228	1897	1667	1269	954	705	511	1.2	0	-6.4	-20.0	NA
220 Swift	40	4200	3678	3190	2739	2329	1566	1201	904	666	482	+0.51	0.0	-4.0	-12.9	NA
220 Swift	50	3780	3158	2617	2135	1710	1586	1107	760	506	325	+2.0	+1.4	-4.4	-17.9	$20
220 Swift	50	3850	3396	2970	2576	2215	1645	1280	979	736	545	0.74	0.0	-4.84	-15.1	NA
220 Swift	50	3900	3420	2990	2599	2240	1688	1298	992	750	557	0.7	0	-4.7	-14.5	NA
220 Swift	55	3800	3370	2990	2630	2310	1765	1390	1090	850	650	0.8	0.0	-4.7	-14.4	NA
220 Swift	55	3650	3194	2772	2384	2035	1627	1246	939	694	506	+2.0	+2.0	-2.6	-13.4	$19
220 Swift	60	3600	3199	2824	2475	2156	1727	1364	1063	816	619	+2.0	+1.6	-4.1	-13.1	$19
22 Savage H.P.	70	2868	2510	2179	1874	1600	1279	980	738	546	398	0	-4.1	-15.6	-37.1	NA
22 Savage H.P.	71	2790	2340	1930	1570	1280	1225	860	585	390	190	+2.0	-1.0	-10.4	-35.7	NA
6mm (24)																
6mm BR Rem.	100	2550	2310	2083	1870	1671	1444	1185	963	776	620	+2.5	-0.6	-11.8	0.0	$22
6mm Norma BR	107	2822	2667	2517	2372	2229	1893	1690	1506	1337	1181	+1.73	0.0	-7.24	-20.6	NA
6mm Creedmoor	108	2786	2618	2456	2299	2140	1861	1643	1446	1267	1106	1.5	0	-6.6	-18.9	$26
6mm PPC	70	3140	2750	2400	2070	NA	1535	1175	895	665	NA	+2.0	+1.4	-5.0	0.0	NA
243 Winchester	55	4025	3597	3209	2853	2525	1978	1579	1257	994	779	+0.6	0.0	-4.0	-12.2	NA
243 Win.	58	3925	3465	3052	2676	2330	1984	1546	1200	922	699	0.7	0	-4.4	-13.8	NA
243 Winchester	60	3600	3110	2660	2260	1890	1725	1285	945	680	475	+2.0	+1.8	-3.3	-15.5	$17
243 Win.	70	3400	3020	2672	2350	2050	1797	1418	1110	858	653	0	-2.5	-9.7	—	NA
243 Winchester	70	3400	3040	2700	2390	2100	1795	1435	1135	890	685	1.1	0.0	-5.9	-18.0	NA
243 Winchester	75/80	3350	2955	2593	2259	1951	1993	1551	1194	906	676	+2.0	+0.9	-5.0	-19.0	$16
243 Win.	80	3425	3081	2763	2468	2190	2084	1686	1357	1082	852	1.1	0	6.7	-17.1	NA
243 Win.	87	2800	2574	2359	2155	1961	1514	1280	1075	897	743	1.9	0	-8.1	-23.8	NA
243 Win.	95	3185	2908	2649	2404	2172	2140	1784	1480	1219	995	1.3	0	-6.3	-18.6	NA
243 W. Superformance	80	3425	3080	2760	2463	2184	2083	1684	1353	1077	847	1.1	0.0	-5.7	-17.1	NA
243 Winchester	85	3320	3070	2830	2600	2380	2080	1770	1510	1280	1070	+2.0	+1.2	-4.0	14.0	$10
243 Winchester	90	3120	2871	2635	2411	2199	1946	1647	1388	1162	966	1.4	0.0	-6.4	-18.8	NA
243 Winchester*	100	2960	2697	2449	2215	1993	1945	1615	1332	1089	882	+2.5	+1.2	-6.0	-20.0	$16
243 Winchester	105	2920	2689	2470	2261	2062	1988	1686	1422	1192	992	+2.5	+1.6	-5.0	-18.4	$21
243 Light Mag.	100	3100	2839	2592	2358	2138	2133	1790	1491	1235	1014	+1.5	0.0	-6.8	-19.8	NA
243 WSSM	55	4060	3628	3237	2880	2550	2013	1607	1280	1013	794	0.6	0.0	-3.9	-12.0	NA
243 WSSM	95	3250	3000	2763	2538	2325	2258	1898	1610	1359	1140	1.2	0.0	-5.7	-16.9	NA
243 WSSM	100	3110	2838	2583	2341	2112	2147	1789	1481	1217	991	1.4	0.0	-6.6	-19.7	NA
6mm Remington	80	3470	3064	2694	2352	2036	2139	1667	1289	982	736	+2.0	+1.1	-5.0	-17.0	$16
6mm R. Superformance	95	3235	2955	2692	2443	3309	2207	1841	1528	1259	1028	1.2	0.0	-6.1	-18.0	NA
6mm Remington	100	3100	2829	2573	2332	2104	2133	1777	1470	1207	983	+2.5	+1.6	5.0	-17.0	$16
6mm Remington	105	3060	2822	2596	2381	2177	2105	1788	1512	1270	1059	+2.5	+1.1	-3.3	-15.0	$21
240 Wea. Mag.	87	3500	3202	2924	2663	2416	2366	1980	1651	1370	1127	+2.0	+2.0	-2.0	-12.0	$32
240 Wea. Mag.	100	3150	2894	2653	2425	2207	2202	1860	1563	1395	1082	1.3	0	-6.3	-18.5	NA
240 Wea. Mag.	100	3395	3106	2835	2581	2339	2559	2142	1785	1478	1215	+2.5	+2.8	-2.0	-11.0	$43
25-20 Win.	86	1460	1194	1030	931	858	407	272	203	165	141	0.0	-23.5	0.0	0.0	$32**
25-45 Sharps	87	3000	2677	2385	2112	1859	1739	1384	1099	862	668	1.1	0	-7.4	-22.6	$25
25-35 Win.	117	2230	1866	1545	1282	1097	1292	904	620	427	313	+2.5	-4.2	-26.0	0.0	$24
250 Savage	100	2820	2504	2210	1936	1684	1765	1392	1084	832	630	+2.5	+0.4	-9.0	-28.0	$17
257 Roberts	100	2980	2661	2363	2085	1827	1972	1572	1240	965	741	+2.5	-0.8	-5.2	-21.6	$20
257 Roberts	122	2600	2331	2078	1842	1625	1831	1472	1169	919	715	+2.5	0.0	-10.6	-31.4	$21
257 Roberts+P	100	3000	2758	2529	2312	2105	1998	1689	1421	1187	984	1.5	0	-7.0	-20.5	NA
257 Roberts+P	117	2780	2411	2071	1761	1488	2009	1511	1115	806	576	+2.5	-0.2	-10.2	-32.6	$18
257 Roberts+P	120	2780	2560	2360	2160	1970	2060	1750	1480	1240	1030	+2.5	+1.2	-6.4	-23.6	$22

Cartridge	Bullet Wgt. Grs.	VELOCITY (fps)					ENERGY (ft. lbs.)					TRAJ. (in.)				Est. Price/box
		Muzzle	100 yds.	200 yds.	300 yds.	400 yds.	Muzzle	100 yds.	200 yds.	300 yds.	400 yds.	100 yds.	200 yds.	300 yds.	400 yds.	
257 R. Superformance	117	2946	2705	2478	2265	2057	2253	1901	1595	1329	1099	1.1	0.0	-5.7	-17.1	NA
25-06 Rem.	87	3440	2995	2591	2222	1884	2286	1733	1297	954	686	+2.0	+1.1	-2.5	-14.4	$17
25-06 Rem.	90	3350	3001	2679	2378	2098	2243	1790	1434	1130	879	1.2	0	-6.0	-18.3	NA
25-06 Rem.	90	3440	3043	2680	2344	2034	2364	1850	1435	1098	827	+2.0	+1.8	-3.3	-15.6	$17
25-06 Rem.	100	3230	2893	2580	2287	2014	2316	1858	1478	1161	901	+2.0	+0.8	-5.7	-18.9	$17
25-06 Rem.	117	2990	2770	2570	2370	2190	2320	2000	1715	1465	1246	+2.5	+1.0	-7.9	-26.6	$19
25-06 Rem.*	120	2990	2730	2484	2252	2032	2382	1985	1644	1351	1100	+2.5	+1.2	-5.3	-19.6	$17
25-06 Rem.	122	2930	2706	2492	2289	2095	2325	1983	1683	1419	1189	+2.5	+1.8	-4.5	-17.5	$23
25-06 R. Superformance	117	3110	2861	2626	2403	2191	2512	2127	1792	1500	1246	1.4	0.0	-6.4	-18.9	NA
25 WSSM	85	3470	3156	2863	2589	2331	2273	1880	1548	1266	1026	1.0	0.0	-5.2	-15.7	NA
25 WSSM	115	3060	2844	2639	2442	2254	2392	2066	1778	1523	1398	1.4	0.0	-6.4	-18.6	NA
25 WSSM	120	2990	2717	2459	2216	1987	2383	1967	1612	1309	1053	1.6	0.0	-7.4	-21.8	NA
257 Wea. Mag.	87	3825	3456	3118	2805	2513	2826	2308	1870	1520	1220	+2.0	+2.7	-0.3	-7.6	$32
257 Wea. Mag.	90	3550	3184	2848	2537	2246	2518	2026	1621	1286	1008	1.0	0	-5.3	-16.0	NA
257 Wea. Mag.	100	3555	3237	2941	2665	2404	2806	2326	1920	1576	1283	+2.5	+3.2	0.0	-8.0	$32
257 Wea. Mag.	110	3330	3069	2823	2591	2370	2708	2300	1947	1639	1372	1.1	0	-5.5	-16.1	NA
257 Scramjet	100	3745	3450	3173	2912	2666	3114	2643	2235	1883	1578	+2.1	+2.77	0.0	-6.93	NA
6.5																
6.5 Grendel	123	2590	2420	2256	2099	1948	1832	1599	1390	1203	1037	1.8	0	-8.6	-25.1	NA
6.5x47 Lapua	123	2887	NA	2554	NA	2244	2285	NA	1788	NA	1380	NA	4.53	0.0	-10.7	NA
6.5x50mm Jap.	139	2360	2160	1970	1790	1620	1720	1440	1195	985	810	+2.5	-1.0	-13.5	0.0	NA
6.5x50mm Jap.	156	2070	1830	1610	1430	1260	1475	1155	900	695	550	+2.5	-4.0	-23.8	0.0	NA
6.5x52mm Car.	139	2580	2360	2160	1970	1790	2045	1725	1440	1195	985	+2.5	0.0	-9.9	-29.0	NA
6.5x52mm Car.	156	2430	2170	1930	1700	1500	2045	1630	1285	1005	780	+2.5	-1.0	-13.9	0.0	NA
6.5x52mm Carcano	160	2250	1963	1700	1467	1271	1798	1369	1027	764	574	+3.8	0.0	-15.9	-48.1	NA
6.5x55mm Swe.	93	2625	2350	2090	1850	1630	1425	1140	905	705	550	2.4	0.0	-10.3	-31.1	NA
6.5x55mm Swe.	123	2750	2570	2400	2240	2080	2065	1810	1580	1370	1185	1.9	0.0	-7.9	-22.9	NA
6.5x55mm Swe.*	139/140	2850	2640	2440	2250	2070	2525	2170	1855	1575	1330	+2.5	+1.6	-5.4	-18.9	$18
6.5x55mm Swe.	140	2550	NA	NA	NA	NA	2020	NA	NA	NA	NA	0.0	0.0	0.0	0.0	$18
6.5x55mm Swe.	140	2735	2563	2397	2237	2084	2325	2041	1786	1556	1350	1.9	0	-8.0	-22.9	NA
6.5x55mm Swe.	156	2650	2370	2110	1870	1650	2425	1950	1550	1215	945	+2.5	0.0	-10.3	-30.6	NA
260 Rem.	100	3200	2917	2652	2402	2165	2273	1889	1561	1281	1041	1.3	0	-6.3	-18.6	NA
260 Rem.	130	2800	2613	2433	2261	2096	2262	1970	1709	1476	1268	1.8	0	-7.7	-22.2	NA
260 Remington	125	2875	2669	2473	2285	2105	2294	1977	1697	1449	1230	1.71	0.0	-7.4	-21.4	NA
260 Remington	140	2750	2544	2347	2158	1979	2351	2011	1712	1448	1217	+2.2	0.0	-8.6	-24.6	NA
6.5 Creedmoor	120	3020	2815	2619	2430	2251	2430	2111	1827	1574	1350	1.4	0.0	-6.5	-18.9	NA
6.5 Creedmoor	120	3050	2850	2659	2476	2300	2479	2164	1884	1634	1310	1.4	0	-6.3	-18.3	NA
6.5 Creedmoor	140	2550	2380	2217	2060	1910	2021	1761	1527	1319	1134	2.3	0	-9.4	-27.0	NA
6.5 Creedmoor	140	2710	2557	2410	2267	2129	2283	2033	1805	1598	1410	1.9	0	-7.9	-22.6	NA
6.5 Creedmoor	140	2820	2654	2494	2339	2190	2472	2179	1915	1679	1467	1.7	0.0	-7.2	-20.6	NA
6.5 C. Superformance	129	2950	2756	2570	2392	2221	2492	2175	1892	1639	1417	1.5	0.0	-6.8	-19.7	NA
6.5x52R	117	2208	1856	1544	1287	1104	1267	895	620	431	317	0	-8.7	-32.2	—	NA
6.5x57	131	2543	2295	2060	1841	1638	1882	1532	1235	986	780	0	-5.1	-18.5	-42.1	NA
6.5 PRC	143	2960	2808	2661	2519	2381	2782	2503	2248	2014	1800	1.5	0	-6.4	-18.2	NA
6.5 PRC	147	2910	2775	2645	2518	2395	2764	2514	2281	2069	1871	1.5	0	-6.5	-18.4	NA
6.5-284 Norma	142	3025	2890	2758	2631	2507	2886	2634	2400	2183	1982	1.13	0.0	-5.7	-16.4	NA
6.5-284 Norma	156	2790	2531	2287	2056	-	2697	2220	1812	1465	-	1.9	0	-8.6	-	NA
6.71 (264) Phantom	120	3150	2929	2718	2517	2325	2645	2286	1969	1698	1440	+1.3	0.0	-6.0	-17.5	NA
6.5 Rem. Mag.	120	3210	2905	2621	2353	2102	2745	2248	1830	1475	1177	+2.5	+1.7	-4.1	-16.3	Disc.
264 Win. Mag.	100	3400	3104	2828	2568	2322	2566	2139	1775	1464	1197	1.1	0	-5.4	-16.1	NA
264 Win. Mag.	125	3200	2978	2767	2566	2373	2841	2461	2125	1827	1563	1.2	0	-5.8	-16.8	NA
264 Win. Mag.	130	3100	2900	2709	2526	2350	2773	2427	2118	1841	1594	1.3	0	-6.1	-17.6	NA
264 Win. Mag.	140	3030	2782	2548	2326	2114	2854	2406	2018	1682	1389	+2.5	+1.4	-5.1	-18.0	$24
6.5 Nosler	129	3400	3213	3035	2863	2698	3310	2957	2638	2348	2085	0.9	0	-4.7	-13.6	NA
6.5 Nosler	140	3300	3118	2943	2775	2613	3119	2784	2481	2205	1955	1.0	0	-5.0	-14.6	NA
6.71 (264) Blackbird	140	3480	3261	3053	2855	2665	3766	3307	2899	2534	2208	+2.4	+3.1	0.0	-7.4	NA
6.5-300 Weatherby Magnum	127	3531	3309	3099	2898	2706	-	3088	2707	2368	2065	0	-1.68	-6.98	-16.43	NA
6.5-300 Weatherby Magnum	130	3476	3267	3084	2901	2726	-	3097	2746	2430	2145	0	-1.74	-7.14	-16.68	NA
6.5-300 Weatherby Magnum	140	3395	3122	2866	2624	2394	-	3030	2552	2139	1781	0	-2.04	-8.24	-19.36	NA
6.8 REM SPC	90	2840	2444	2083	1756	1469	1611	1194	867	616	431	2.2	0	-3.9	-32.0	NA
6.8 REM SPC	110	2570	2338	2118	1910	1716	1613	1335	1095	891	719	2.4	0.0	-6.3	-20.8	NA
6.8 REM SPC	120	2460	2250	2051	1863	1687	1612	1349	1121	925	758	2.3	0	-10.5	-31.1	NA

Cartridge	Bullet Wgt. Grs.	VELOCITY (fps)					ENERGY (ft. lbs.)					TRAJ. (in.)				Est. Price/box
		Muzzle	100 yds.	200 yds.	300 yds.	400 yds.	Muzzle	100 yds.	200 yds.	300 yds.	400 yds.	100 yds.	200 yds.	300 yds.	400 yds.	
6.8mm Rem.	115	2775	2472	2190	1926	1683	1966	1561	1224	947	723	+2.1	0.0	-3.7	-9.4	NA
27																
270 Win. (Rem.)	115	2710	2482	2265	2059	NA	1875	1485	1161	896	NA	0.0	4.8	-17.3	0.0	NA
270 Win.	120	2675	2288	1935	1619	1351	1907	1395	998	699	486	2.6	0	-12.0	-37.4	NA
270 Win.	140	2940	2747	2563	2386	2216	2687	2346	2042	1770	1526	1.8	0	-6.8	-19.8	NA
270 Win. Supreme	130	3150	2881	2628	2388	2161	2865	2396	1993	1646	1348	1.3	0.0	-6.4	-18.9	NA
270 Win. Supreme	150	2930	2693	2468	2254	2051	2860	2416	2030	1693	1402	1.7	0.0	-7.4	-21.6	NA
270 W. Superformance	130	3200	2984	2788	2582	2393	2955	2570	2228	1924	1653	1.2	0.0	-5.7	-16.7	NA
270 Winchester	100	3430	3021	2649	2305	1988	2612	2027	1557	1179	877	+2.0	+1.0	-4.9	-17.5	$17
270 Winchester	130	3060	2776	2510	2259	2022	2702	2225	1818	1472	1180	+2.5	+1.4	-5.3	-18.2	$17
270 Winchester	135	3000	2780	2570	2369	2178	2697	2315	1979	1682	1421	+2.5	+1.4	-6.0	-17.6	$23
270 Winchester*	140	2940	2700	2480	2260	2060	2685	2270	1905	1590	1315	+2.5	+1.8	-4.6	-17.9	$20
270 Winchester*	150	2850	2585	2336	2100	1879	2705	2226	1817	1468	1175	+2.5	+1.2	-6.5	-22.0	$17
270 WSM	130	3275	3041	2820	2609	2408	3096	2669	2295	1564	1673	1.1	0.0	-5.5	-16.1	NA
270 WSM	140	3125	2865	2619	2386	2165	3035	2559	2132	1769	1457	1.4	0.0	-6.5	-19.0	NA
270 WSM	150	3000	2795	2599	2412	2232	2997	2601	2250	1937	1659	1.5	0	-6.6	-19.2	NA
270 WSM	150	3120	2923	2734	2554	2380	3242	2845	2490	2172	1886	1.3	0.0	-5.9	-17.2	NA
270 Wea. Mag.	100	3760	3380	3033	2712	2412	3139	2537	2042	1633	1292	+2.0	+2.4	-1.2	-10.1	$32
270 Wea. Mag.	130	3375	3119	2878	2649	2432	3287	2808	2390	2026	1707	+2.5	-2.9	-0.9	-9.9	$32
270 Wea. Mag.	130	3450	3194	2958	2732	2517	3435	2949	2525	2143	1828	1.0	0	-4.9	-14.5	NA
270 Wea. Mag.*	150	3245	3036	2837	2647	2465	3507	3070	2681	2334	2023	+2.5	+2.6	-1.8	-11.4	$47
7mm																
7mm BR	140	2216	2012	1821	1643	1481	1525	1259	1031	839	681	+2.0	-3.7	-20.0	0.0	$23
275 Rigby	140	2680	2455	2242	2040	1848	2233	1874	1563	1292	1062	2.2	0	-9.1	-26.5	NA
7mm Mauser*	139/140	2660	2435	2221	2018	1827	2199	1843	1533	1266	1037	+2.5	0.0	-9.6	-27.7	$17
7mm Mauser	139	2740	2556	2379	2209	2046	2317	2016	1747	1506	1292	1.9	0	-8.1	-23.3	NA
7mm Mauser	154	2690	2490	2300	2120	1940	2475	2120	1810	1530	1285	+2.5	+0.8	-7.5	-23.5	$17
7mm Mauser	175	2440	2137	1857	1603	1382	2313	1774	1340	998	742	+2.5	-1.7	-10.1	0.0	$17
7x30 Waters	120	2700	2300	1930	1600	1330	1940	1405	990	685	470	+2.5	-0.2	-12.3	0.0	$18
7mm-08 Rem.	120	2675	2435	2207	1992	1790	1907	1579	1298	1057	854	2.2	0	-9.4	-27.5	NA
7mm-08 Rem.	120	3000	2725	2467	2223	1992	2398	1979	1621	1316	1068	+2.0	0.0	-7.6	-22.3	$18
7mm-08 Rem.	139	2840	2608	2387	2177	1978	2489	2098	1758	1463	1207	1.8	0	-7.9	-23.2	NA
7mm-08 Rem.*	140	2860	2625	2402	2189	1988	2542	2142	1793	1490	1228	+2.5	+0.8	-6.9	-21.9	$18
7mm-08 Rem.	154	2715	2510	2315	2128	1950	2520	2155	1832	1548	1300	+2.5	+1.0	-7.0	-22.7	$23
7-08 R. Superformance	139	2950	2857	2571	2393	2222	2686	2345	2040	1768	1524	1.5	0.0	-6.8	-19.7	NA
7x64mm	173	2526	2260	2010	1777	1565	2452	1962	1552	1214	941	0	-5.3	-19.3	-44.4	NA
7x64mm Bren.	140	2950	2710	2483	2266	2061	2705	2283	1910	1597	1320	1.6	0.0	-2.9	-7.3	$24.50
7x64mm Bren.	154	2820	2610	2420	2230	2050	2720	2335	1995	1695	1430	+2.5	+1.4	-5.7	-19.9	NA
7x64mm Bren.*	160	2850	2669	2495	2327	2166	2885	2530	2211	1924	1667	+2.5	+1.6	-4.8	-17.8	$24
7x64mm Bren.	175	2650	2445	2248	2061	1883	2728	2322	1964	1650	1378	2.2	0	-9.1	-26.4	$24.50
7x65mmR	173	2608	2337	2082	1844	1626	2613	2098	1666	1307	1015	0	-4.9	-17.9	-41.9	NA
275 Rigby	139	2680	2456	2242	2040	1848	2217	1861	1552	1284	1054	2.2	0	-9.1	-26.5	NA
284 Winchester	150	2860	2595	2344	2108	1886	2724	2243	1830	1480	1185	+2.5	+0.8	-7.3	-23.2	$24
280 R. Superformance	139	3090	2890	2699	2516	2341	2946	2578	2249	1954	1691	1.3	0.0	-6.1	-17.7	NA
280 Rem.	139	3090	2891	2700	2518	2343	2947	2579	2250	1957	1694	1.3	0	-6.1	-17.7	NA
280 Remington	140	3000	2758	2528	2309	2102	2797	2363	1986	1657	1373	+2.5	+1.4	-5.2	-18.3	$17
280 Remington*	150	2890	2624	2373	2135	1912	2781	2293	1875	1518	1217	+2.5	+0.8	-7.1	-22.6	$17
280 Remington	160	2840	2637	2442	2556	2078	2866	2471	2120	1809	1535	+2.5	+0.8	-6.7	-21.0	$20
280 Remington	165	2820	2510	2220	1950	1701	2913	2308	1805	1393	1060	+2.5	+0.4	-8.8	-26.5	$17
280 Ack. Imp.	140	3150	2946	2752	2566	2387	3084	2698	2354	2047	1772	1.3	0	-5.8	-17.0	NA
280 Ack. Imp.	150	2900	2712	2533	2360	2194	2800	2450	2136	1855	1603	1.6	0	-7.0	-20.3	NA
280 Ack. Imp.	160	2950	2751	2561	2379	2205	3091	2686	2331	2011	1727	1.5	0	-6.9	-19.9	NA
7x61mm S&H Sup.	154	3060	2720	2400	2100	1820	3200	2520	1965	1505	1135	+2.5	+1.8	-5.0	-19.8	NA
7mm Dakota	160	3200	3001	2811	2630	2455	3637	3200	2808	2456	2140	+2.1	+1.9	-2.8	-12.5	NA
7mm Rem. Mag.	139	3190	2986	2791	2605	2427	3141	2752	2405	2095	1817	1.2	0	-5.7	-16.5	NA
7mm Rem. Mag. (Rem.)	140	2710	2482	2265	2059	NA	2283	1915	1595	1318	NA	0.0	-4.5	-1.57	0.0	NA
7mm Rem. Mag.*	139/140	3150	2930	2710	2510	2320	3085	2660	2290	1960	1670	+2.5	+2.4	-2.4	-12.7	$21
7mm Rem. Mag.	150/154	3110	2830	2568	2320	2085	3221	2667	2196	1792	1448	+2.5	+1.6	-4.6	-16.5	$21
7mm Rem. Mag.*	160/162	2950	2730	2520	2320	2120	3090	2650	2250	1910	1600	+2.5	+1.8	-4.4	-17.8	$34
7mm Rem. Mag.	165	2900	2699	2507	2324	2147	3081	2669	2303	1978	1689	+2.5	+1.2	-5.9	-19.0	$28
7mm Rem Mag.	175	2860	2645	2440	2244	2057	3178	2718	2313	1956	1644	+2.5	+1.0	-6.5	-20.7	$21
7 R.M. Superformance	139	3240	3033	2836	2648	2467	3239	2839	2482	2163	1877	1.1	0.0	-5.5	-15.9	NA

Cartridge	Bullet Wgt. Grs.	VELOCITY (fps)					ENERGY (ft. lbs.)					TRAJ. (in.)				Est. Price/box
		Muzzle	100 yds.	200 yds.	300 yds.	400 yds.	Muzzle	100 yds.	200 yds.	300 yds.	400 yds.	100 yds.	200 yds.	300 yds.	400 yds.	
7 R.M. Superformance	154	3100	2914	2736	2565	2401	3286	2904	2560	2250	1970	1.3	0.0	-5.9	-17.2	NA
7mm Rem. SA ULTRA MAG	140	3175	2934	2707	2490	2283	3033	2676	2277	1927	1620	1.3	0.0	-6	-17.7	NA
7mm Rem. SA ULTRA MAG	150	3110	2828	2563	2313	2077	3221	2663	2188	1782	1437	2.5	2.1	-3.6	-15.8	NA
7mm Rem. SA ULTRA MAG	160	2850	2676	2508	2347	2192	2885	2543	2235	1957	1706	1.7	0	-7.2	-20.7	NA
7mm Rem. SA ULTRA MAG	160	2960	2762	2572	2390	2215	3112	2709	2350	2029	1743	2.6	2.2	-3.6	-15.4	NA
7mm WSM	140	3225	3008	2801	2603	2414	3233	2812	2438	2106	1812	1.2	0.0	-5.6	-16.4	NA
7mm WSM	160	2990	2744	2512	2081	1883	3176	2675	2241	1864	1538	1.6	0.0	-7.1	-20.8	NA
7mm Wea. Mag.	139	3300	3091	2891	2701	2519	3361	2948	2580	2252	1958	1.1	0	-5.2	-15.2	NA
7mm Wea. Mag.	140	3225	2970	2729	2501	2283	3233	2741	2315	1943	1621	+2.5	+2.0	-3.2	-14.0	$35
7mm Wea. Mag.	140	3340	3127	2925	2732	2546	3467	3040	2659	2320	2016	0	-2.1	-8.2	-19	NA
7mm Wea. Mag.	150	3175	2957	2751	2553	2364	3357	2913	2520	2171	1861	0	-2.5	-9.6	-22	NA
7mm Wea. Mag.	154	3260	3023	2799	2586	2382	3539	3044	2609	2227	1890	+2.5	+2.8	-1.5	-10.8	$32
7mm Wea. Mag.*	160	3200	3004	2816	2637	2464	3637	3205	2817	2469	2156	+2.5	+2.7	-1.5	-10.6	$47
7mm Wea. Mag.	165	2950	2747	2553	2367	2189	3188	2765	2388	2053	1756	+2.5	+1.8	-4.2	-16.4	$43
7mm Wea. Mag.	175	2910	2693	2486	2288	2098	3293	2818	2401	2033	1711	+2.5	+1.2	-5.9	-19.4	$35
7.21(.284) Tomahawk	140	3300	3118	2943	2774	2612	3386	3022	2693	2393	2122	2.3	3.2	0.0	-7.7	NA
7mm STW	140	3300	3086	2889	2697	2513	3384	2966	2594	2261	1963	0	-2.1	-8.5	-19.6	NA
7mm STW	140	3325	3064	2818	2585	2364	3436	2918	2468	2077	1737	+2.3	+1.8	-3.0	-13.1	NA
7mm STW	150	3175	2957	2751	2553	2364	3357	2913	2520	2171	1861	0	-2.5	-9.6	-22	NA
7mm STW	175	2900	2760	2625	2493	2366	3267	2960	2677	2416	2175	0	-3.1	-11.2	-24.9	NA
7mm STW Supreme	160	3150	2894	2652	2422	2204	3526	2976	2499	2085	1727	1.3	0.0	-6.3	-18.5	NA
7mm Rem. Ultra Mag.	140	3425	3184	2956	2740	2534	3646	3151	2715	2333	1995	1.7	1.6	-2.6	-11.4	NA
7mm Rem. Ultra Mag.	160	3225	3035	2854	2680	2512	3694	3273	2894	2551	2242	0	-2.3	-8.8	-20.2	NA
7mm Rem. Ultra Mag.	174	3040	2896	2756	2621	2490	3590	3258	2952	2669	2409	0	-2.6	-9.9	-22.2	NA
7mm Firehawk	140	3625	3373	3135	2909	2695	4084	3536	3054	2631	2258	+2.2	+2.9	0.0	-7.03	NA
7.21 (.284) Firebird	140	3750	3522	3306	3101	2905	4372	3857	3399	2990	2625	1.6	2.4	0.0	-6.0	NA
.28 Nosler	160	3300	3114	2930	2753	2583	3883	3444	3049	2693	2371	1.1	0	-5.1	-14.9	$78
30																
300 ACC Blackout	110	2150	1886	1646	1432	1254	1128	869	661	501	384	0	-8.3	-29.6	-67.8	NA
300 AAC Blackout	125	2250	2031	1826	1636	1464	1404	1145	926	743	595	0	-7	-24.4	-54.8	NA
300 AAC Blackout	220	1000	968	-	-	-	488	457	-	-	-	0	-	-	-	-
30 Carbine	110	1990	1567	1236	1035	923	977	600	373	262	208	0.0	-13.5	0.0	0.0	$28**
30 Carbine	110	2000	1601	1279	1067	—	977	626	399	278	—	0	-12.9	-47.2	—	NA
300 Whisper	110	2375	2094	1834	1597	NA	1378	1071	822	623	NA	3.2	0.0	-13.6	NA	NA
300 Whisper	208	1020	988	959	NA	NA	480	451	422	NA	NA	0.0	-34.10	NA	NA	NA
303 Savage	190	1890	1612	1327	1183	1055	1507	1096	794	591	469	+2.5	-7.6	0.0	0.0	$24
30 Remington	170	2120	1822	1555	1328	1153	1696	1253	913	666	502	+2.5	-4.7	-26.3	0.0	$20
7.62x39mm Rus.	123	2360	2049	1764	1511	1296	1521	1147	850	623	459	3.4	0	-14.7	-44.7	NA
7.62x39mm Rus.	123/125	2300	2030	1780	1550	1350	1445	1125	860	655	500	+2.5	-2.0	-17.5	0.0	$13
30-30 Win.	55	3400	2693	2085	1570	1187	1412	886	521	301	172	+2.0	0.0	-10.2	-35.0	$18
30-30 Win.	125	2570	2090	1660	1320	1080	1830	1210	770	480	320	-2.0	-2.6	-19.9	0.0	$13
30-30 Win.	140	2500	2198	1918	1662	—	1943	1501	1143	858	—	2.9	0	-12.4	—	NA
30-30 Win.	150	2390	2040	1723	1447	1225	1902	1386	989	697	499	0.0	-7.5	-27.0	-63.0	NA
30-30 Win. Supreme	150	2480	2095	1747	1446	1209	2049	1462	1017	697	487	0.0	-6.5	-24.5	0.0	NA
30-30 Win.	160	2300	1997	1719	1473	1268	1879	1416	1050	771	571	+2.5	-2.9	-20.2	0.0	$18
30-30 Win. Lever Evolution	160	2400	2150	1916	1699	NA	2046	1643	1304	1025	NA	3.0	0.2	-12.1	NA	NA
30-30 PMC Cowboy	170	1300	1198	1121	—	—	638	474	—	—	—	0.0	-27.0	0.0	0.0	NA
30-30 Win.*	170	2200	1895	1619	1381	1191	1827	1355	989	720	535	+2.5	-5.8	-23.6	0.0	$13
300 Savage	150	2630	2354	2094	1853	1631	2303	1845	1462	1143	886	+2.5	-0.4	-10.1	-30.7	$17
300 Savage	150	2740	2499	2272	2056	1852	2500	2081	1718	1407	1143	2.1	0	-8.8	-25.8	NA
300 Savage	180	2350	2137	1935	1754	1570	2207	1825	1496	1217	985	+2.5	-1.6	-15.2	0.0	$17
30-40 Krag	180	2430	2213	2007	1813	1632	2360	1957	1610	1314	1064	+2.5	-1.4	-13.8	0.0	$18
7.65x53mm Arg.	180	2590	2390	2200	2010	1830	2685	2280	1925	1615	1345	+2.5	0.0	-27.6	0.0	NA
7.5x53mm Argentine	150	2785	2519	2269	2032	1814	2583	2113	1714	1376	1096	+2.0	0.0	-8.8	-25.5	NA
308 Marlin Express	140	2800	2532	2279	2040	1818	2437	1992	1614	1294	1207	2.0	0	-8.7	-25.8	NA
308 Marlin Express	160	2660	2430	2226	2026	1836	2513	2111	1761	1457	1197	3.0	1.7	-6.7	-23.5	NA
307 Winchester	150	2760	2321	1924	1575	1289	2530	1795	1233	826	554	+2.5	-1.5	-13.6	0.0	Disc.
7.5x55 Swiss	180	2650	2450	2250	2060	1880	2805	2390	2020	1700	1415	+2.5	+0.6	-8.1	-24.9	NA
7.5x55mm Swiss	165	2720	2515	2319	2132	1954	2710	2317	1970	1665	1398	+2.0	0.0	-8.5	-24.6	NA
30 Remington AR	123/125	2800	2465	2154	1867	1606	2176	1686	1288	967	716	2.1	0.0	-9.7	-29.4	NA
308 Winchester	55	3770	3215	2726	2286	1888	1735	1262	907	638	435	-2.0	+1.4	-3.8	-15.8	$22
308 Win.	110	3165	2830	2520	2230	1960	2447	1956	1551	1215	938	1.4	0	-6.9	-20.9	NA

Cartridge	Bullet Wgt. Grs.	VELOCITY (fps)					ENERGY (ft. lbs.)					TRAJ. (in.)				Est. Price/box
		Muzzle	100 yds.	200 yds.	300 yds.	400 yds.	Muzzle	100 yds.	200 yds.	300 yds.	400 yds.	100 yds.	200 yds.	300 yds.	400 yds.	
308 Win. PDX1	120	2850	2497	2171	NA	NA	2164	1662	1256	NA	NA	0.0	-2.8	NA	NA	NA
308 Winchester	150	2820	2533	2263	2009	1774	2648	2137	1705	1344	1048	+2.5	+0.4	-8.5	-26.1	$17
308 W. Superformance	150	3000	2772	2555	2348	1962	2997	2558	2173	1836	1540	1.5	0.0	-6.9	-20.0	NA
308 Win.	155	2775	2553	2342	2141	1950	2650	2243	1887	1577	1308	1.9	0	-8.3	-24.2	NA
308 Win.	155	2850	2640	2438	2247	2064	2795	2398	2047	1737	1466	1.8	0	-7.5	-22.1	NA
308 Winchester	165	2700	2440	2194	1963	1748	2670	2180	1763	1411	1199	+2.5	0.0	-9.7	-28.5	$20
308 Winchester	168	2680	2493	2314	2143	1979	2678	2318	1998	1713	1460	+2.5	0.0	-8.9	-25.3	$18
308 Win. Super Match	168	2870	2647	2462	2284	2114	3008	2613	2261	1946	1667	1.7	0.0	-7.5	-21.6	NA
308 Win. (Fed.)	170	2000	1740	1510	NA	NA	1510	1145	860	NA	NA	0.0	0.0	0.0	0.0	NA
308 Winchester	178	2620	2415	2220	2034	1857	2713	2306	1948	1635	1363	+2.5	0.0	-9.6	-27.6	$23
308 Win. Super Match	178	2780	2609	2444	2285	2132	3054	2690	2361	2064	1797	1.8	0.0	-7.6	-21.9	NA
308 Winchester*	180	2620	2393	2178	1974	1782	2743	2288	1896	1557	1269	+2.5	-0.2	-10.2	-28.5	$17
30-06 Spfd.	55	4080	3485	2965	2502	2083	2033	1483	1074	764	530	+2.0	+1.9	-2.1	-11.7	$22
30-06 Spfd. (Rem.)	125	2660	2335	2034	1757	NA	1964	1513	1148	856	NA	0.0	-5.2	-18.9	0.0	NA
30-06 Spfd.	125	2700	2412	2143	1891	1660	2023	1615	1274	993	765	2.3	0	-9.9	-29.5	NA
30-06 Spfd.	125	3140	2780	2447	2138	1853	2736	2145	1662	1279	953	+2.0	+1.0	-6.2	-21.0	$17
30-06 Spfd.	150	2910	2617	2342	2083	1853	2820	2281	1827	1445	1135	+2.5	+0.8	-7.2	-23.4	$17
30-06 Superformance	150	3080	2848	2617	2417	2216	3159	2700	2298	1945	1636	1.4	0.0	-6.4	-18.9	NA
30-06 Spfd.	152	2910	2654	2413	2184	1968	2858	2378	1965	1610	1307	+2.5	+1.0	-6.6	-21.3	$23
30-06 Spfd.*	165	2800	2534	2283	2047	1825	2872	2352	1909	1534	1220	+2.5	+0.4	-8.4	-25.5	$17
30-06 Spfd.	168	2710	2522	2346	2169	2003	2739	2372	2045	1754	1497	+2.5	+0.4	-8.0	-23.5	$18
30-06 M1 Garand	168	2710	2523	2343	2171	2006	2739	2374	2048	1758	1501	2.3	0	-8.6	-24.6	NA
30-06 Spfd. (Fed.)	170	2000	1740	1510	NA	NA	1510	1145	860	NA	NA	0.0	0.0	0.0	0.0	NA
30-06 Spfd.	178	2720	2511	2311	2121	1939	2924	2491	2111	1777	1486	+2.5	+0.4	-8.2	-24.6	$23
30-06 Spfd.*	180	2700	2469	2250	2042	1846	2913	2436	2023	1666	1362	-2.5	0.0	-9.3	-27.0	$17
30-06 Superformance	180	2820	2630	2447	2272	2104	3178	2764	2393	2063	1769	1.8	0.0	-7.6	-21.9	NA
30-06 Spfd.	220	2410	2130	1870	1632	1422	2837	2216	1708	1301	988	+2.5	-1.7	-18.0	0.0	$17
30-06 High Energy	180	2880	2690	2500	2320	2150	3315	2880	2495	2150	1845	+1.7	0.0	-7.2	-21.0	NA
30 T/C	150	2920	2696	2483	2280	2087	2849	2421	2054	1732	1450	1.7	0	-7.3	-21.3	NA
30 T/C Superformance	150	3000	2772	2555	2348	2151	2997	2558	2173	1836	1540	1.5	0.0	-6.9	-20.0	NA
30 T/C Superformance	165	2850	2644	2447	2258	2078	2975	2560	2193	1868	1582	1.7	0.0	7.6	-22.0	NA
300 Rem SA Ultra Mag	150	3200	2901	2622	2359	2112	3410	2803	2290	1854	1485	1.3	0.0	-6.4	-19.1	NA
300 Rem SA Ultra Mag	165	3075	2792	2527	2276	2040	3464	2856	2339	1898	1525	1.5	0.0	-7	20.7	NA
300 Rem SA Ultra Mag	180	2960	2761	2571	2389	2214	3501	3047	2642	2280	1959	2.6	2.2	-3.6	-15.4	NA
300 Rem. SA Ultra Mag	200	2800	2644	2494	2348	2208	3841	3104	2761	2449	2164	0	-3.5	-12.5	-27.9	NA
7.82 (308) Patriot	150	3250	2999	2762	2537	2323	3519	2997	2542	2145	1798	+1.2	0.0	-5.8	-16.9	NA
300 RCM	150	3265	3023	2794	2577	2369	3550	3043	2600	2211	1870	1.2	0	5.6	16.5	NA
300 RCM Superformance	150	3310	3065	2833	2613	2404	3648	3128	2673	2274	1924	1.1	0.0	-5.4	-16.0	NA
300 RCM Superformance	165	3185	2964	2753	2552	2360	3716	3217	2776	2386	2040	1.2	0.0	-5.8	-17.0	NA
300 RCM Superformance	180	3040	2840	2649	2466	2290	3693	3223	2804	2430	2096	1.4	0.0	-6.4	-18.5	NA
300 WSM	150	3300	3061	2834	2619	2414	3628	3121	2676	2285	1941	1.1	0.0	-5.4	-15.9	NA
300 WSM	180	2970	2741	2524	2317	2120	3526	3005	2547	2147	1797	1.6	0.0	-7.0	-20.5	NA
300 WSM	180	3010	2923	2734	2554	2380	3242	2845	2490	2172	1886	1.3	0	-5.9	-17.2	NA
300 WSM	190	2875	2729	2588	2451	2010	3486	3142	2826	2535	2269	0	3.2	-11.5	-25.7	NA
308 Norma Mag.	180	2975	2787	2608	2435	2269	3536	3105	2718	2371	2058	0	-3	-11.1	-25.0	NA
308 Norma Mag.	180	3020	2820	2630	2440	2270	3645	3175	2755	2385	2050	+2.5	+2.0	-3.5	-14.8	NA
300 Dakota	200	3000	2824	2656	2493	2336	3996	3542	3131	2760	2423	+2.2	+1.5	-4.0	-15.2	NA
300 H&H Mag.	180	2870	2678	2494	2318	2148	3292	2866	2486	2147	1844	1.7	0	-7.3	-21.6	NA
300 H&H Magnum*	180	2880	2640	2412	2196	1990	3315	2785	2325	1927	1583	+2.5	+0.8	-6.8	-21.7	$24
300 H&H Mag.	200	2750	2596	2447	2303	2164	3357	2992	2659	2355	2079	1.8	0	-7.6	-21.8	NA
300 H&H Magnum	220	2550	2267	2002	1757	NA	3167	2510	1958	1508	NA	-2.5	-0.4	-12.0	0.0	NA
300 Win. Mag.	150	3290	2951	2636	2342	2068	3605	2900	2314	1827	1424	+2.5	+1.9	-3.8	-15.8	$22
300 WM Superformance	150	3400	3150	2914	2690	2477	3850	3304	2817	2409	2043	1.0	0.0	-5.1	-15.0	NA
300 Win. Mag.	165	3100	2877	2665	2462	2269	3522	3033	2603	2221	1897	+2.5	+2.4	-3.0	-16.9	$24
300 Win. Mag.	178	2900	2760	2568	2375	2191	3509	3030	2606	2230	1897	+2.5	+1.4	-5.0	-17.6	$29
300 Win. Mag.	178	2960	2770	2588	2413	2245	3463	3032	2647	2301	1992	1.5	0	-6.7	-19.4	NA
300 WM Super Match	178	2960	2770	2587	2412	2243	3462	3031	2645	2298	1988	1.5	0.0	-6.7	-19.4	NA
300 Win. Mag.*	180	2960	2745	2540	2344	2157	3501	3011	2578	2196	1859	+2.5	+1.2	-5.5	-18.5	$22
300 WM Superformance	180	3130	2927	2732	2546	2366	3917	3424	2983	2589	2238	1.3	0.0	-5.9	-17.3	NA
300 Win. Mag.	190	2885	1691	2506	2327	2156	3511	3055	2648	2285	1961	+2.5	+1.2	-5.7	-19.0	$26
300 Win. Mag.	195	2930	2760	2596	2438	2286	3717	3297	2918	2574	2262	1.5	0	-6.7	-19.4	NA
300 Win. Mag.*	200	2825	2595	2376	2167	1970	3545	2991	2508	2086	1742	-2.5	+1.6	-4.7	-17.2	$36

Cartridge	Bullet Wgt. Grs.	VELOCITY (fps)					ENERGY (ft. lbs.)					TRAJ. (in.)				Est. Price/box
		Muzzle	100 yds.	200 yds.	300 yds.	400 yds.	Muzzle	100 yds.	200 yds.	300 yds.	400 yds.	100 yds.	200 yds.	300 yds.	400 yds.	
300 Win. Mag.	220	2680	2448	2228	2020	1823	3508	2927	2424	1993	1623	+2.5	0.0	-9.5	-27.5	$23
30 Nosler	180	3200	3004	2815	2635	2462	4092	3606	3168	2774	2422	0	-2.4	-9.1	-20.9	NA
30 Nosler	210	3000	2868	2741	2617	2497	4196	3836	3502	3193	2906	0	-2.7	-10.1	-22.5	NA
300 Rem. Ultra Mag.	150	3450	3208	2980	2762	2556	3964	3427	2956	2541	2175	1.7	1.5	-2.6	-11.2	NA
300 Rem. Ultra Mag.	150	2910	2686	2473	2279	2077	2820	2403	2037	1716	1436	1.7	0.0	-7.4	-21.5	NA
300 Rem. Ultra Mag.	165	3350	3099	2862	2938	2424	4110	3518	3001	2549	2152	1.1	0	-5.3	-15.6	NA
300 Rem. Ultra Mag.	180	3250	3037	2834	2640	2454	4221	3686	3201	2786	2407	2.4	0.0	-3.0	-12.7	NA
300 Rem. Ultra Mag.	180	2960	2774	2505	2294	2093	3501	2971	2508	2103	1751	2.7	2.2	-3.8	-16.4	NA
300 Rem. Ultra Mag.	200	3032	2791	2562	2345	2138	4083	3459	2916	2442	2030	1.5	0.0	-6.8	-19.9	NA
300 Rem. Ultra Mag.	210	2920	2790	2665	2543	2424	3975	3631	3311	3015	2740	1.5	0	-6.4	-18.1	NA
30 Nosler	180	3200	3004	2815	2635	2462	4092	3606	3168	2774	2422	0	-2.4	-9.1	-20.9	NA
30 Nosler	210	3000	2868	2741	2617	2497	4196	3836	3502	3193	2906	0	-2.7	-10.1	-22.5	NA
300 Wea. Mag.	100	3900	3441	3038	2652	2305	3714	2891	2239	1717	1297	+2.0	+2.6	-0.6	-8.7	$32
300 Wea. Mag.	150	3375	3126	2892	2670	2459	3794	3255	2786	2374	2013	1.0	0	-5.2	-15.3	NA
300 Wea. Mag.	150	3600	3307	3033	2776	2533	4316	3642	3064	2566	2137	+2.5	+3.2	0.0	-8.1	$32
300 Wea. Mag.	165	3140	2921	2713	2515	2325	3612	3126	2697	2317	1980	1.3	0	-6.0	-17.5	NA
300 Wea. Mag.	165	3450	3210	3000	2792	2593	4360	3796	3297	2855	2464	+2.5	+3.2	0.0	-7.8	NA
300 Wea. Mag.	178	3120	2902	2695	2497	2308	3847	3329	2870	2464	2104	+2.5	-1.7	-3.6	-14.7	$43
300 Wea. Mag.	180	3330	3110	2910	2710	2520	4430	3875	3375	2935	2540	+1.0	0.0	-5.2	-15.1	NA
300 Wea. Mag.	190	3030	2830	2638	2455	2279	3873	3378	2936	2542	2190	+2.5	+1.6	-4.3	-16.0	$38
300 Wea. Mag.	220	2850	2541	2283	1964	1736	3967	3155	2480	1922	1471	+2.5	+0.4	-8.5	-26.4	$35
300 Pegasus	180	3500	3319	3145	2978	2817	4896	4401	3953	3544	3172	+2.28	+2.89	0.0	-6.79	NA
300 Norma Magnum	215	3017	2881	2748	2618	2491	4346	3963	3605	3272	2963	NA	NA	NA	NA	$85
300 Norma Magnum	230	2934	2805	2678	2555	2435	4397	4018	3664	3334	3028	NA	NA	NA	NA	$85
300 Norma Magnum	225	2850	2731	2615	2502	2392	4058	3726	3417	3128	2859	1.6	0	-6.7	-18.9	NA
31																
32-20 Win.	100	1210	1021	913	834	769	325	231	185	154	131	0.0	-32.3	0.0	0.0	$23**
303 British	150	2685	2441	2211	1993	1789	2401	1985	1628	1323	1066	2.2	0	-9.3	-27.4	NA
303 British	180	2460	2124	1817	1542	1311	2418	1803	1319	950	687	+2.5	-1.8	-16.8	0.0	$18
303 Light Mag.	150	2830	2570	2325	2094	1884	2667	2199	1800	1461	1185	+2.0	0.0	-8.4	-24.6	NA
7.62x54mm Rus.	146	2950	2730	2520	2320	NA	2820	2415	2055	1740	NA	+2.5	+2.0	-4.4	-17.7	NA
7.62x54mm Rus.	174	2800	2607	2422	2245	2075	3029	2626	2267	1947	1664	1.8	0	-7.8	-22.4	NA
7.62x54mm Rus.	180	2580	2370	2180	2000	1820	2650	2250	1900	1590	1100	+2.5	0.0	-9.8	-28.5	NA
7.7x58mm Jap.	150	2640	2399	2170	1954	1752	2321	1916	1568	1271	1022	+2.3	0.0	-9.7	-28.5	NA
7.7x58mm Jap.	180	2500	2300	2100	1920	1750	2490	2105	1770	1475	1225	+2.5	0.0	-10.4	-30.2	NA
8mm																
8x56 R	205	2400	2188	1987	1797	1621	2621	2178	1796	1470	1196	+2.9	0.0	-11.7	-34.3	NA
8x57mm JS Mau.	165	2850	2520	2210	1930	1670	2965	2330	1795	1360	1015	+2.5	+1.0	-7.7	0.0	NA
32 Win. Special	165	2410	2145	1897	1669	NA	2128	1685	1318	1020	NA	2.0	0.0	-13.0	-19.9	NA
32 Win. Special	170	2250	1921	1626	1372	1175	1911	1393	998	710	521	+2.5	-3.5	-22.9	0.0	$14
8mm Mauser	170	2360	1969	1622	1333	1123	2102	1464	993	671	476	+2.5	-3.1	-22.2	0.0	$18
8mm Mauser	196	2500	2338	2182	2032	1888	2720	2379	2072	1797	1552	2.4	0	-9.8	-27.9	NA
325 WSM	180	3060	2841	2632	2432	2242	3743	3226	2769	2365	2009	+1.4	0.0	-6.4	-18.7	NA
325 WSM	200	2950	2753	2565	2384	2210	3866	3367	2922	2524	2170	+1.5	0.0	-6.8	-19.8	NA
325 WSM	220	2840	2605	2382	2169	1968	3941	3316	2772	2300	1893	+1.8	0.0	-8.0	-23.3	NA
8mm Rem. Mag.	185	3080	2761	2464	2186	1927	3896	3131	2494	1963	1525	+2.5	+1.4	-5.5	-19.7	$30
8mm Rem. Mag.	220	2830	2581	2346	2123	1913	3912	3254	2688	2201	1787	+2.5	+0.6	-7.6	-23.5	Disc.
33																
338 Federal	180	2830	2590	2350	2130	1930	3200	2670	2215	1820	1480	1.8	0.0	-8.2	-23.9	NA
338 Marlin Express	200	2565	2365	2174	1992	1820	2922	2484	2099	1762	1471	3.0	1.2	-7.9	-25.9	NA
338 Federal	185	2750	2550	2350	2160	1980	3105	2660	2265	1920	1615	1.9	0.0	-8.3	-24.1	NA
338 Federal	210	2630	2410	2200	2010	1820	3225	2710	2265	1880	1545	2.3	0.0	-9.4	-27.3	NA
338 Federal MSR	185	2680	2459	2230	2020	1820	2950	2460	2035	1670	1360	2.2	0.0	-9.2	-26.8	NA
338-06	200	2750	2553	2364	2184	2011	3358	2894	2482	2118	1796	+1.9	0.0	-8.22	-23.6	NA
330 Dakota	250	2900	2719	2545	2378	2217	4668	4103	3595	3138	2727	+2.3	+1.3	-5.0	-17.5	NA
338 Lapua	250	2900	2685	2481	2285	2098	4668	4002	2416	2899	2444	1.7	0	-7.3	-21.3	NA
338 Lapua	250	2963	2795	2640	2493	NA	4842	4341	3881	3458	NA	+1.9	0.0	-7.9	0.0	NA
338 Lapua	285	2745	2616	2491	2369	2251	4768	4331	3926	3552	3206	1.8	0	-7.4	-21	NA
338 Lapua	300	2660	2544	2432	2322	-	4715	4313	3940	3592	-	1.9	0	-7.8	-	NA
338 RCM Superformance	185	2980	2755	2542	2338	2143	3647	3118	2653	2242	1887	1.5	0.0	-6.9	-20.3	NA
338 RCM Superformance	200	2950	2744	2547	2358	2177	3846	3342	2879	2468	2104	1.6	0.0	-6.9	-20.1	NA
338 RCM Superformance	225	2750	2575	2407	2245	2089	3778	3313	2894	2518	2180	1.9	0.0	-7.9	-22.7	NA

Cartridge	Bullet Wgt. Grs.	VELOCITY (fps)					ENERGY (ft. lbs.)					TRAJ. (in.)				Est. Price/box
		Muzzle	100 yds.	200 yds.	300 yds.	400 yds.	Muzzle	100 yds.	200 yds.	300 yds.	400 yds.	100 yds.	200 yds.	300 yds.	400 yds.	
338 WM Superformance	185	3080	2850	2632	2424	2226	3896	3337	2845	2413	2034	1.4	0.0	-6.4	-18.8	NA
338 Win. Mag.	200	3030	2820	2620	2429	2246	4077	3532	3049	2621	2240	1.4	0	-6.5	-18.9	NA
338 Win. Mag.*	210	2830	2590	2370	2150	1940	3735	3130	2610	2155	1760	+2.5	+1.4	-6.0	-20.9	$33
338 Win. Mag.*	225	2785	2517	2266	2029	1808	3871	3165	2565	2057	1633	+2.5	+0.4	-8.5	-25.9	$27
338 WM Superformance	225	2840	2758	2582	2414	2252	4318	3798	3331	2911	2533	1.5	0.0	-6.8	-19.5	NA
338 Win. Mag.	230	2780	2573	2375	2186	2005	3948	3382	2881	2441	2054	+2.5	+1.2	-6.3	-21.0	$40
338 Win. Mag.*	250	2660	2456	2261	2075	1898	3927	3348	2837	2389	1999	+2.5	+0.2	-9.0	-26.2	$27
338 Ultra Mag.	250	2860	2645	2440	2244	2057	4540	3882	3303	2794	2347	1.7	0.0	-7.6	-22.1	NA
338 Lapua Match	250	2900	2760	2625	2494	2366	4668	4229	3825	3452	3108	1.5	0.0	-6.6	-18.8	NA
338 Lapua Match	285	2745	2623	2504	2388	2275	4768	4352	3966	3608	3275	1.8	0.0	-7.3	-20.8	NA
33 Nosler	225	3025	2856	2687	2525	2369	4589	4074	3608	3185	2803	0	-2.8	-10.4	-23.4	NA
33 Nosler	265	2775	2661	2547	2435	2326	4543	4167	3816	3488	3183	0	-3.4	-12.2	-26.8	NA
33 Nosler	300	2550	2445	2339	2235	2134	4343	3981	3643	3327	3033	0	-4.3	-15	-32.6	NA
8.59(.338) Galaxy	200	3100	2899	2707	2524	2347	4269	3734	3256	2829	2446	3	3.8	0.0	-9.3	NA
340 Wea. Mag.*	210	3250	2991	2746	2515	2295	4924	4170	3516	2948	2455	+2.5	+1.9	-1.8	-11.8	$56
340 Wea. Mag.*	250	3000	2806	2621	2443	2272	4995	4371	3812	3311	2864	+2.5	+2.0	-3.5	-14.8	$56
338 A-Square	250	3120	2799	2500	2220	1958	5403	4348	3469	2736	2128	+2.5	+2.7	-1.5	-10.5	NA
338-378 Wea. Mag.	225	3180	2974	2778	2591	2410	5052	4420	3856	3353	2902	3.1	3.8	0.0	-8.9	NA
338 Titan	225	3230	3010	2800	2600	2409	5211	4524	3916	3377	2898	+3.07	+3.8	0.0	-8.95	NA
338 Excalibur	200	3600	3361	3134	2920	2715	5755	5015	4363	3785	3274	+2.23	+2.87	0.0	-6.99	NA
338 Excalibur	250	3250	2922	2618	2333	2066	5863	4740	3804	3021	2370	+1.3	0.0	-6.35	-19.2	NA
34, 35																
348 Winchester	200	2520	2215	1931	1672	1443	2820	2178	1656	1241	925	+2.5	-1.4	-14.7	0.0	$42
357 Magnum	158	1830	1427	1138	980	883	1175	715	454	337	274	0.0	-16.2	-33.1	0.0	$25**
35 Remington	150	2300	1874	1506	1218	1039	1762	1169	755	494	359	+2.5	-4.1	-26.3	0.0	$16
35 Remington	200	2080	1698	1376	1140	1001	1921	1280	841	577	445	+2.5	-6.3	-17.1	-33.6	$16
35 Remington	200	2225	1963	1722	1505	—	2198	1711	1317	1006	—	3.8	0	-15.6	—	NA
35 Rem. Lever Evolution	200	2225	1963	1721	1503	NA	2198	1711	1315	1003	NA	3.0	-1.3	-17.5	NA	NA
356 Winchester	200	2460	2114	1797	1517	1284	2688	1985	1434	1022	732	+2.5	-1.8	-15.1	0.0	$31
356 Winchester	250	2160	1911	1682	1476	1299	2591	2028	1571	1210	937	+2.5	-3.7	-22.2	0.0	$31
358 Winchester	200	2475	2180	1906	1655	1434	2720	2110	1612	1217	913	2.9	0	-12.6	-37.9	NA
358 Winchester	200	2490	2171	1876	1619	1379	2753	2093	1563	1151	844	+2.5	-1.6	-15.6	0.0	$31
358 STA	275	2850	2562	2292	2039	NA	4958	4009	3208	2539	NA	+1.9	0.0	-8.6	0.0	NA
350 Rem. Mag.	200	2710	2410	2130	1870	1631	3261	2579	2014	1553	1181	+2.5	-0.2	-10.0	-30.1	$33
35 Wholen	200	2675	2378	2100	1842	1606	3177	2510	1958	1506	1145	+2.5	-0.2	-10.3	-31.1	$20
35 Whelen	200	2910	2585	2283	2001	1742	3760	2968	2314	1778	1347	1.9	0	-8.6	26.0	NA
35 Whelen	225	2500	2300	2110	1930	1770	3120	2650	2235	1870	1560	+2.6	0.0	-10.2	-29.9	NA
35 Whelen	250	2400	2197	2005	1823	1652	3197	2680	2230	1844	1515	+2.5	-1.2	-13.7	0.0	$20
350 Norma Mag.	250	2800	2510	2230	1970	1730	4350	3480	2750	2145	1655	+2.5	+1.0	-7.6	-25.2	NA
358 STA	275	2850	2562	229*2	2039	1764	4959	4009	3208	2539	1899	+1.9	0.0	-8.58	-26.1	NA
9.3mm																
9.3x57mm Mau.	232	2362	2058	1778	1528	NA	2875	2182	1630	1203	NA	0	-6.8	-24.6	NA	NA
9.3x57mm Mau.	286	2070	1810	1590	1390	1110	2710	2090	1600	1220	955	+2.5	-2.6	-22.5	0.0	NA
370 Sako Mag.	286	3550	2370	2200	2040	2880	4130	3570	3075	2630	2240	2.4	0.0	-9.5	-27.2	NA
9.3x62mm	232	2625	2302	2002	1728	-	2551	2731	2066	1539	-	2.6	0	-11.3	-	NA
9.3x62mm	250	2550	2376	2208	2048	—	3609	3133	2707	2328	—	0	-5.4	-17.9	—	NA
9.3x62mm	286	2360	2155	1961	1778	1608	3537	2949	2442	2008	1642	0	-6.0	-21.1	-47.2	NA
9.3x62mm	286	2400	2163	1941	1733	—	3657	2972	2392	1908	—	0	-6.7	-22.6	—	NA
9.3x64mm	286	2700	2505	2318	2139	1968	4629	3984	3411	2906	2460	+2.5	+2.7	-4.5	-19.2	NA
9.3x72mmR	193	1952	1610	1326	1120	996	1633	1112	754	538	425	0	-12.1	-44.1	—	NA
9.3x74mmR	250	2550	2376	2208	2048	—	3609	3133	2707	2328	—	0	-5.4	-17.9	—	NA
9.3x74Rmm	286	2360	2136	1924	1727	1545	3536	2896	2351	1893	1516	0.0	-6.1	-21.7	-49.0	NA
375																
375 Winchester	200	2200	1841	1526	1268	1089	2150	1506	1034	714	527	+2.5	-4.0	-26.2	0.0	$27
375 Winchester	250	1900	1647	1424	1239	1103	2005	1506	1126	852	676	+2.5	-6.9	-33.3	0.0	$27
376 Steyr	225	2600	2331	2078	1842	1625	3377	2714	2157	1694	1319	2.5	0.0	-10.6	-31.4	NA
376 Steyr	270	2600	2372	2156	1951	1759	4052	3373	2787	2283	1855	2.3	0.0	-9.9	-28.9	NA
375 Dakota	300	2600	2316	2051	1804	1579	4502	3573	2800	2167	1661	+2.4	0.0	-11.0	-32.7	NA
375 N.E. 2-1/2"	270	2000	1740	1507	1310	NA	2398	1815	1362	1026	NA	+2.5	-6.0	-30.0	0.0	NA
375 Flanged	300	2450	2150	1886	1640	NA	3998	3102	2369	1790	NA	+2.5	-2.4	-17.0	0.0	NA
375 Ruger	250	2890	2675	2471	2275	2088	4636	3973	3388	2873	2421	1.7	0	-7.4	-21.5	NA
375 Ruger	260	2900	2703	2514	2333	—	4854	4217	3649	3143	—	0	-4.0	-13.4	—	NA

Cartridge	Bullet Wgt. Grs.	VELOCITY (fps)					ENERGY (ft. lbs.)					TRAJ. (in.)				Est. Price/box
		Muzzle	100 yds.	200 yds.	300 yds.	400 yds.	Muzzle	100 yds.	200 yds.	300 yds.	400 yds.	100 yds.	200 yds.	300 yds.	400 yds.	
375 Ruger	270	2840	2600	2372	2156	1951	4835	4052	3373	2786	2283	1.8	0.0	-8.0	-23.6	NA
375 Ruger	300	2660	2344	2050	1780	1536	4713	3660	2800	2110	1572	2.4	0.0	-10.8	-32.6	NA
375 Flanged NE	300	2400	2103	1829	NA	NA	3838	2947	2228	NA	NA	0	-6.4	-	-	NA
375 H&H Magnum	250	2890	2675	2471	2275	2088	4636	3973	3388	2873	2421	1.7	0	-7.4	-21.5	NA
375 H&H Magnum	250	2670	2450	2240	2040	1850	3955	3335	2790	2315	1905	+2.5	-0.4	-10.2	-28.4	NA
375 H&H Magnum	270	2690	2420	2166	1928	1707	4337	3510	2812	2228	1747	+2.5	0.0	-10.0	-29.4	$28
375 H&H Mag.	270	2800	2562	2337	2123	1921	4700	3936	3275	2703	2213	1.9	0	-8.3	-24.3	NA
375 H&H Magnum*	300	2530	2245	1979	1733	1512	4263	3357	2608	2001	1523	+2.5	-1.0	-10.5	-33.6	$28
375 H&H Mag.	300	2660	2345	2052	1782	1539	4713	3662	2804	2114	1577	2.4	0	-10.8	-32.6	NA
375 H&H Hvy. Mag.	270	2870	2628	2399	2182	1976	4937	4141	3451	2150	1845	+1.7	0.0	-7.2	-21.0	NA
375 H&H Hvy. Mag.	300	2705	2386	2090	1816	1568	4873	3793	2908	2195	1637	+2.3	0.0	-10.4	-31.4	NA
375 H&H Mag.	350	2300	2052	1821	-	-	4112	3273	2578	-	-	0	-6.7	-	-	NA
375 Rem. Ultra Mag.	270	2900	2558	2241	1947	1678	5041	3922	3010	2272	1689	1.9	2.7	-8.9	-27.0	NA
375 Rem. Ultra Mag.	260	2950	2750	2560	2377	—	5023	4367	3783	3262	—	0	-3.8	-12.9	—	NA
375 Rem. Ultra Mag.	300	2760	2505	2263	2035	1822	5073	4178	3412	2759	2210	2.0	0.0	-8.8	-26.1	NA
375 Wea. Mag.	260	3000	2798	2606	2421	—	5195	4520	3920	3384	—	0	-3.6	-12.4	—	NA
375 Wea. Mag.	300	2700	2420	2157	1911	1685	4856	3901	3100	2432	1891	+2.5	-.04	-10.7	0.0	NA
378 Wea. Mag.	260	3100	2894	2697	2509	—	5547	4834	4199	3633	—	0	-4.2	-14.6	—	NA
378 Wea. Mag.	270	3180	2976	2781	2594	2415	6062	5308	4635	4034	3495	+2.5	+2.6	-1.8	-11.3	$71
378 Wea. Mag.	300	2929	2576	2252	1952	1680	5698	4419	3379	2538	1881	+2.5	+1.2	-7.0	-24.5	$77
375 A-Square	300	2920	2626	2351	2093	1850	5679	4594	3681	2917	2281	+2.5	+1.4	-6.0	-21.0	NA
38-40 Win.	180	1160	999	901	827	764	538	399	324	273	233	0.0	-33.9	0.0	0.0	$42**

40, 41

Cartridge	Bullet Wgt. Grs.	Muzzle	100 yds.	200 yds.	300 yds.	400 yds.	Muzzle	100 yds.	200 yds.	300 yds.	400 yds.	100 yds.	200 yds.	300 yds.	400 yds.	Est. Price/box
400 A-Square DPM	400	2400	2146	1909	1689	NA	5116	2092	3236	2533	NA	2.98	0.0	-10.0	NA	NA
400 A-Square DPM	170	2980	2463	2001	1598	NA	3352	2289	1512	964	NA	2.16	0.0	-11.1	NA	NA
408 CheyTac	419	2850	2752	2657	2562	2470	7551	7048	6565	6108	5675	-1.02	0.0	1.9	4.2	NA
405 Win.	300	2200	1851	1545	1296		3224	2282	1589	1119		4.6	0.0	-19.5	0.0	NA
450/400-3"	400	2050	1815	1595	1402	NA	3732	2924	2259	1746	NA	0.0	NA	-33.4	NA	NA
416 Ruger	400	2400	2151	1917	1700	NA	5116	4109	3264	2568	NA	0.0	-6.0	-21.6	0.0	NA
416 Dakota	400	2450	2294	2143	1998	1859	5330	4671	4077	3544	3068	+2.5	-0.2	-10.5	-29.4	NA
416 Taylor	375	2350	2021	1722	na	na	4600	3403	2470	NA	NA	0	-7	NA	NA	NA
416 Taylor	400	2350	2117	1896	1693	NA	4905	3980	3194	2547	NA	+2.5	-1.2	15.0	0.0	NA
416 Hoffman	400	2380	2145	1923	1718	1529	5031	4087	3285	2620	2077	+2.5	-1.0	-14.1	0.0	NA
416 Rigby	350	2600	2449	2303	2162	2026	5253	4661	4122	3632	3189	+2.5	-1.8	-10.2	-26.0	NA
416 Rigby	400	2370	2210	2050	1900	NA	4990	4315	3720	3185	NA	+2.5	-0.7	-12.1	0.0	NA
416 Rigby	400	2400	2115	1851	1611	—	5115	3973	3043	2305	—	0	-6.5	-21.8	—	NA
416 Rigby	400	2415	2156	1915	1691	—	5180	4130	3256	2540	—	0	-6.0	-21.6	—	NA
416 Rigby	410	2370	2110	1870	1640	NA	5115	4050	3165	2455	NA	+2.5	-2.4	-17.3	0.0	$110
416 Rem. Mag.*	350	2520	2270	2034	1814	1611	4935	4004	3216	2557	2017	+2.5	-0.8	-12.6	-35.0	$82
416 Rem. Mag.	400	2400	2142	1901	1679	—	5116	4076	3211	2504	—	3.1	0	-12.7	—	NA
416 Rem. Mag.	450	2150	1925	1716	-	-	4620	3702	2942	-	-	0	-7.8	-	-	NA
416 Wea. Mag.*	400	2700	2397	2115	1852	1613	6474	5104	3971	3047	2310	+2.5	0.0	-10.1	-30.4	$96
10.57 (416) Meteor	400	2730	2532	2342	2161	1987	6621	5695	4874	4147	3508	+1.9	0.0	-8.3	-24.0	NA
500/416 N.E.	400	2300	2092	1895	1712	—	4697	3887	3191	2602	—	0	-7.2	-24.0	—	NA
500/416 N.E.	410	2325	2062	1817	-	-	4620	3735	2996	NA	NA	0	-6.7	-	-	NA
404 Jeffrey	400	2150	1924	1716	1525	NA	4105	3289	2614	2064	NA	+2.5	-4.0	-22.1	0.0	NA
404 Jeffrey	400	2300	2053	1823	1611	—	4698	3743	2950	2306	—	0	-6.8	-24.1	—	NA
404 Jeffery	400	2350	2020	1720	1458	—	4904	3625	2629	1887	—	0	-6.5	-21.8	—	NA
404 Jeffery	450	2150	1946	1755	-	-	4620	3784	3078	-	-	0	-7.6	-	-	NA

425, 44

Cartridge	Bullet Wgt. Grs.	Muzzle	100 yds.	200 yds.	300 yds.	400 yds.	Muzzle	100 yds.	200 yds.	300 yds.	400 yds.	100 yds.	200 yds.	300 yds.	400 yds.	Est. Price/box
425 Express	400	2400	2160	1934	1725	NA	5115	4145	3322	2641	NA	+2.5	-1.0	-14.0	0.0	NA
44-40 Win.	200	1190	1006	900	822	756	629	449	360	300	254	0.0	-33.3	0.0	0.0	$36**
44 Rem. Mag.	210	1920	1477	1155	982	880	1719	1017	622	450	361	0.0	-17.6	0.0	0.0	$14
44 Rem. Mag.	240	1760	1380	1114	970	878	1650	1015	661	501	411	0.0	-17.6	0.0	0.0	$13
444 Marlin	240	2350	1815	1377	1087	941	2942	1753	1001	630	472	+2.5	-15.1	-31.0	0.0	$22
444 Marlin	265	2120	1733	1405	1160	1012	2644	1768	1162	791	603	+2.5	-6.0	-32.2	0.0	Disc.
444 Mar. Lever Evolution	265	2325	1971	1652	1380	NA	3180	2285	1606	1120	NA	3.0	-1.4	-18.6	NA	NA
444 Mar. Superformance	265	2400	1976	1603	1298	NA	3389	2298	1512	991	NA	4.1	0.0	-17.8	NA	NA

45

Cartridge	Bullet Wgt. Grs.	Muzzle	100 yds.	200 yds.	300 yds.	400 yds.	Muzzle	100 yds.	200 yds.	300 yds.	400 yds.	100 yds.	200 yds.	300 yds.	400 yds.	Est. Price/box
45-70 Govt.	250	2025	1616	1285	1068	—	2276	1449	917	634	—	6.1	0	-27.2	—	NA
45-70 Govt.	300	1810	1497	1244	1073	969	2182	1492	1031	767	625	0.0	-14.8	0.0	0.0	$21
45-70 Govt. Supreme	300	1880	1558	1292	1103	988	2355	1616	1112	811	651	0.0	-12.9	-46.0	-105.0	NA

Cartridge	Bullet Wgt. Grs.	VELOCITY (fps)					ENERGY (ft. lbs.)					TRAJ. (in.)				Est. Price/box
		Muzzle	100 yds.	200 yds.	300 yds.	400 yds.	Muzzle	100 yds.	200 yds.	300 yds.	400 yds.	100 yds.	200 yds.	300 yds.	400 yds.	
45-70 Govt.	325	2000	1685	1413	1197	—	2886	2049	1441	1035	—	5.5	0	-23.0	—	NA
45-70 Lever Evolution	325	2050	1729	1450	1225	NA	3032	2158	1516	1083	NA	3.0	-4.1	-27.8	NA	NA
45-70 Govt. CorBon	350	1800	1526	1296			2519	1810	1307			0.0	-14.6	0.0	0.0	NA
45-70 Govt.	405	1330	1168	1055	977	918	1590	1227	1001	858	758	0.0	-24.6	0.0	0.0	$21
45-70 Govt. PMC Cowboy	405	1550	1193	—	—	—	1639	1280	—	—	—	0.0	-23.9	0.0	0.0	NA
45-70 Govt. Garrett	415	1850	—	—	—	—	3150	—	—	—	—	3.0	-7.0	0.0	0.0	NA
45-70 Govt. Garrett	530	1550	1343	1178	1062	982	2828	2123	1633	1327	1135	0.0	-17.8	0.0	0.0	NA
450 Bushmaster	250	2200	1831	1508	1480	1073	2686	1860	1262	864	639	0.0	-9.0	-33.5	0.0	NA
450 Marlin	325	2225	1887	1587	1332	—	3572	2570	1816	1280	—	4.2	0	-18.1	—	NA
450 Marlin	360	2100	1774	1488	1254	1089	3427	2446	1720	1222	922	0.0	-9.7	-35.2	0.0	NA
450 Mar. Levor Evolution	325	2225	1887	1585	1331	NA	3572	2569	1813	1278	NA	3.0	-2.2	-21.3	NA	NA
457 Wild West Magnum	350	2150	1718	1348	NA		3645	2293	1413	NA	NA	0.0	-10.5	NA	NA	NA
450/500 N.E.	400	2050	1820	1609	1420	—	3732	2940	2298	1791	—	0	-9.7	-32.8	—	NA
450 N.E. 3-1/4"	465	2190	1970	1765	1577	NA	4952	4009	3216	2567	NA	+2.5	-3.0	-20.0	0.0	NA
450 N.E.	480	2150	1881	1635	1418	—	4927	3769	2850	2144	—	0	-8.4	-29.8	—	NA
450 N.E. 3-1/4"	500	2150	1920	1708	1514	NA	5132	4093	3238	2544	NA	+2.5	-4.0	-22.9	0.0	NA
450 No. 2	465	2190	1970	1765	1577	NA	4952	4009	3216	2567	NA	+2.5	-3.0	-20.0	0.0	NA
450 No. 2	500	2150	1920	1708	1514	NA	5132	4093	3238	2544	NA	+2.5	-4.0	-22.9	0.0	NA
450 Ackley Mag.	465	2400	2169	1950	1747	NA	5947	4857	3927	3150	NA	+2.5	-1.0	-13.7	0.0	NA
450 Ackley Mag.	500	2320	2081	1855	1649	NA	5975	4085	3820	3018	NA	+2.5	-1.2	-15.0	0.0	NA
450 Rigby	500	2350	2139	1939	1752	—	6130	5079	4176	3408	—	0	-6.8	-22.9	—	NA
450 Rigby	550	2100	1887	1690	–	–	5387	4311	3425	-	-	0	-8.3	–	–	NA
458 Win. Magnum	400	2380	2170	1960	1770	NA	5030	4165	3415	2785	NA	+2.5	-0.4	-13.4	0.0	$73
458 Win. Magnum	465	2220	1999	1791	1601	NA	5088	4127	3312	2646	NA	+2.5	-2.0	-17.7	0.0	NA
458 Win. Magnum	500	2040	1823	1623	1442	1237	4620	3689	2924	2308	1839	+2.5	-3.5	-22.0	0.0	$61
458 Win. Mag.	500	2140	1880	1643	1432	—	5084	3294	2996	2276	—	0	-8.4	-29.8	—	NA
458 Win. Magnum	510	2040	1770	1527	1319	1157	4712	3547	2640	1970	1516	+2.5	-4.1	-25.0	0.0	$41
458 Lott	465	2380	2150	1932	1730	NA	5848	4773	3855	3091	NA	+2.5	-1.0	-14.0	0.0	NA
458 Lott	500	2300	2029	1778	1551	—	5873	4569	3509	2671	—	0	-7.0	-25.1	—	NA
458 Lott	500	2300	2062	1838	1633	NA	5873	4719	3748	2960	NA	+2.5	-1.6	-16.4	0.0	NA
460 Short A-Sq.	500	2420	2175	1943	1729	NA	6501	5250	4193	3319	NA	+2.5	-0.8	12.8	0.0	NA
460 Wea. Mag.	500	2700	2404	2128	1869	1635	8092	6416	5026	3878	2969	+2.5	+0.6	-8.9	-28.0	$72

475

Cartridge	Bullet Wgt. Grs.	Muzzle	100 yds.	200 yds.	300 yds.	400 yds.	Muzzle	100 yds.	200 yds.	300 yds.	400 yds.	100 yds.	200 yds.	300 yds.	400 yds.	Est. Price/box
500/465 N.E.	480	2150	1917	1703	1507	NA	4926	3917	3089	2419	NA	+2.5	-4.0	-22.2	0.0	NA
470 Rigby	500	2150	1940	1740	1560	NA	5130	4170	3360	2695	NA	+2.5	-2.8	-19.4	0.0	NA
470 Nitro Ex.	480	2190	1954	1735	1536	NA	5111	4070	3210	2515	NA	+2.5	-3.5	-20.8	0.0	NA
470 N.E.	500	2150	1885	1643	1429	—	5132	3945	2998	2267	—	0	-0.9	30.8	—	NA
470 Nitro Ex.	500	2150	1890	1650	1440	1270	5130	3965	3040	2310	1790	+2.5	-4.3	-24.0	0.0	$177
475 No. 2	500	2200	1955	1728	1522	NA	5375	4243	3316	2573	NA	+2.5	-3.2	-20.9	0.0	NA

50, 58

Cartridge	Bullet Wgt. Grs.	Muzzle	100 yds.	200 yds.	300 yds.	400 yds.	Muzzle	100 yds.	200 yds.	300 yds.	400 yds.	100 yds.	200 yds.	300 yds.	400 yds.	Est. Price/box
50 Alaskan	450	2000	1729	1492	NA	NA	3997	2987	2224	NA	NA	0.0	-11.25	NA	NA	NA
500 Jeffery	570	2300	1979	1688	1434	—	6094	4058	3608	2604	—	0	-8.2	-28.6	—	NA
505 Gibbs	525	2300	2063	1840	1637	NA	6166	4922	3948	3122	NA	+2.5	-3.0	-18.0	0.0	NA
505 Gibbs	570	2100	1893	1701	-	-	5583	4538	3664	-	-	0	-8.1	-	-	NA
505 Gibbs	600	2100	1899	1711	-	-	5877	4805	3904	-	-	0	-8.1	-	-	NA
500 N.E.	570	2150	1889	1651	1439	—	5850	4518	3450	2621	—	0	-8.9	-30.6	—	NA
500 N.E.-3"	570	2150	1928	1722	1533	NA	5850	4703	3752	2975	NA	+2.5	-3.7	-22.0	0.0	NA
500 N.E.-3"	600	2150	1927	1721	1531	NA	6158	4947	3944	3124	NA	+2.5	-4.0	-22.0	0.0	NA
495 A-Square	570	2350	2117	1896	1693	NA	5850	4703	3752	2975	NA	+2.5	-1.0	-14.5	0.0	NA
495 A-Square	600	2280	2050	1833	1635	NA	6925	5598	4478	3562	NA	+2.5	-2.0	-17.0	0.0	NA
500 A-Square	600	2380	2144	1922	1766	NA	7546	6126	4920	3922	NA	+2.5	-3.0	-17.0	0.0	NA
500 A-Square	707	2250	2040	1841	1567	NA	7947	6530	5318	4311	NA	+2.5	-2.0	-17.0	0.0	NA
500 BMG PMC	660	3080	2854	2639	2444	2248	13688		500 yd. zero			+3.1	+3.9	+4.7	+2.8	NA
577 Nitro Ex.	750	2050	1793	1562	1360	NA	6990	5356	4065	3079	NA	+2.5	-5.0	-26.0	0.0	NA
577 Tyrannosaur	750	2400	2141	1898	1675	NA	9591	7633	5996	4671	NA	+3.0	0.0	-12.9	0.0	NA

600, 700

Cartridge	Bullet Wgt. Grs.	Muzzle	100 yds.	200 yds.	300 yds.	400 yds.	Muzzle	100 yds.	200 yds.	300 yds.	400 yds.	100 yds.	200 yds.	300 yds.	400 yds.	Est. Price/box
600 N.E.	900	1950	1680	1452	NA	NA	7596	5634	4212	NA	NA	+5.6	0.0	0.0	0.0	NA
700 N.E.	1200	1900	1676	1472	NA	NA	9618	7480	5774	NA	NA	+5.7	0.0	0.0	0.0	NA

50 BMG

Cartridge	Bullet Wgt. Grs.	Muzzle	100 yds.	200 yds.	300 yds.	400 yds.	Muzzle	100 yds.	200 yds.	300 yds.	400 yds.	100 yds.	200 yds.	300 yds.	400 yds.	Est. Price/box
50 BMG	624	2952	2820	2691	2566	2444	12077	11028	10036	9125	8281	0	-2.9	-10.6	-23.5	NA
50 BMG Match	750	2820	2728	2637	2549	2462	13241	12388	11580	10815	10090	1.5	0.0	-6.5	-18.3	NA

Centerfire Handgun Cartridge Ballistics & Prices

Notes: Blanks are available in 32 S&W, 38 S&W and 38 Special. "V" after barrel length indicates test barrel was vented to produce ballistics similar to a revolver with a normal barrel-to-cylinder gap. Ammo prices are per 50 rounds except when marked with an ** which signifies a 20 round box; *** signifies a 25-round box. Not all loads are available from all ammo manufacturers. Listed loads are those made by Remington, Winchester, Federal, and others. DISC. is a discontinued load. Prices are rounded to the nearest whole dollar and will vary with brand and retail outlet.

Cartridge	Bullet Wgt. Grs.	VELOCITY (fps)			ENERGY (ft. lbs.)			Mid-Range Traj. (in.)		Bbl. Lgth. (in).	Est. Price/ box
		Muzzle	50 yds.	100 yds.	Muzzle	50 yds.	100 yds.	50 yds.	100 yds.		
22, 25											
221 Rem. Fireball	50	2650	2380	2130	780	630	505	0.2	0.8	10.5"	$15
25 Automatic	35	900	813	742	63	51	43	NA	NA	2"	$18
25 Automatic	45	815	730	655	65	55	40	1.8	7.7	2"	$21
25 Automatic	50	760	705	660	65	55	50	2.0	8.7	2"	$17
30											
7.5mm Swiss	107	1010	NA	NA	240	NA	NA	NA	NA	NA	NEW
7.62x25 Tokarev	85	1647	1458	1295	512	401	317	0	-3.2	4.75	
7.62mmTokarev	87	1390	NA	NA	365	NA	NA	0.6	NA	4.5"	NA
7.62 Nagant	97	790	NA	NA	134	NA	NA	NA	NA	NA	NEW
7.63 Mauser	88	1440	NA	NA	405	NA	NA	NA	NA	NA	NEW
30 Luger	93	1220	1110	1040	305	255	225	0.9	3.5	4.5"	$34
30 Carbine	110	1790	1600	1430	785	625	500	0.4	1.7	10"	$28
30-357 AeT	123	1992	NA	NA	1084	NA	NA	NA	NA	10"	NA
32											
32 NAA	80	1000	933	880	178	155	137	NA	NA	4"	NA
32 S&W	88	680	645	610	90	80	75	2.5	10.5	3"	$17
32 S&W Long	98	705	670	635	115	100	90	2.3	10.5	4"	$17
32 Short Colt	80	745	665	590	100	80	60	2.2	9.9	4"	$19
32 H&R	80	1150	1039	963	235	192	165	NA	NA	4"	NA
32 H&R Magnum	85	1100	1020	930	230	195	165	1.0	4.3	4.5"	$21
32 H&R Magnum	95	1030	940	900	225	190	170	1.1	4.7	4.5"	$19
327 Federal Magnum	85	1400	1220	1090	370	280	225	NA	NA	4-V	NA
327 Federal Magnum	100	1500	1320	1180	500	390	310	-0.2	-4.50	4-V	NA
32 Automatic	60	970	895	835	125	105	95	1.3	5.4	4"	$22
32 Automatic	60	1000	917	849	133	112	96			4"	NA
32 Automatic	65	950	890	830	130	115	100	1.3	5.6	NA	NA
32 Automatic	71	905	855	810	130	115	95	1.4	5.8	4"	$19
8mm Lebel Pistol	111	850	NA	NA	180	NA	NA	NA	NA	NA	NEW
8mm Steyr	112	1080	NA	NA	290	NA	NA	NA	NA	NA	NEW
8mm Gasser	126	850	NA	NA	200	NA	NA	NA	NA	NA	NEW
9mm, 38											
380 Automatic	60	1130	960	NA	170	120	NA	1.0	NA	NA	NA
380 Automatic	75	950	NA	NA	183	NA	NA	NA	NA	3"	$33
380 Automatic	85/88	990	920	870	190	165	145	1.2	5.1	4"	$20
380 Automatic	90	1000	890	800	200	160	130	1.2	5.5	3.75"	$10
380 Automatic	95/100	955	865	785	190	160	130	1.4	5.9	4"	$20
38 Super Auto +P	115	1300	1145	1040	430	335	275	0.7	3.3	5"	$26
38 Super Auto +P	125/130	1215	1100	1015	425	350	300	0.8	3.6	5"	$26
38 Super Auto +P	147	1100	1050	1000	395	355	325	0.9	4.0	5"	NA
38 Super Auto +P	115	1130	1016	938	326	264	225	1	-9.5	-	NA
9x18mm Makarov	95	1000	930	874	211	182	161	NA	NA	4"	NEW
9x18mm Ultra	100	1050	NA	NA	240	NA	NA	NA	NA	NA	NEW
9x21	124	1150	1050	980	365	305	265	NA	NA	4"	NA
9x21 IMI	123	1220	1095	1010	409	330	281	-3.15	—	5.0	NA
9x23mm Largo	124	1190	1055	966	390	306	257	0.7	3.7	4"	NA
9x23mm Win.	125	1450	1249	1103	583	433	338	0.6	2.8	NA	NA
9mm Steyr	115	1180	NA	NA	350	NA	NA	NA	NA	NA	NEW
9mm Luger	80	1445	–	–	–	385	–	–	–	–	NA
9mm Luger	88	1500	1190	1010	440	275	200	0.6	3.1	4"	$24
9mm Luger	90	1360	1112	978	370	247	191	NA	NA	4"	$26
9mm Luger	92	1325	1117	991	359	255	201	-3.2	—	4.0	NA
9mm Luger	95	1300	1140	1010	350	275	215	0.8	3.4	4"	NA
9mm Luger	100	1180	1080	NA	305	255	NA	0.9	NA	4"	NA
9mm Luger Guard Dog	105	1230	1070	970	355	265	220	NA	NA	4"	NA
9mm Luger	115	1155	1045	970	340	280	240	0.9	3.9	4"	$21

Cartridge	Bullet Wgt. Grs.	VELOCITY (fps)			ENERGY (ft. lbs.)			Mid-Range Traj. (in.)		Bbl. Lgth. (in).	Est. Price/ box
		Muzzle	50 yds.	100 yds.	Muzzle	50 yds.	100 yds.	50 yds.	100 yds.		
9mm Luger	123/125	1110	1030	970	340	290	260	1.0	4.0	4"	$23
9mm Luger	124	1150	1040	965	364	298	256	-4.5	—	4.0	NA
9mm Luger	135	1010	960	918	306	276	253	—	—	4.0	NA
9mm Luger	140	935	890	850	270	245	225	1.3	5.5	4"	$23
9mm Luger	147	990	940	900	320	290	265	1.1	4.9	4"	$26
9mm Luger +P	90	1475	NA	NA	437	NA	NA	NA	NA	NA	NA
9mm Luger +P	115	1250	1113	1019	399	316	265	0.8	3.5	4"	$27
9mm Federal	115	1280	1130	1040	420	330	280	0.7	3.3	4"V	$24
9mm Luger Vector	115	1155	1047	971	341	280	241	NA	NA	4"	NA
9mm Luger +P	124	1180	1089	1021	384	327	287	0.8	3.8	4"	NA
38											
38 S&W	146	685	650	620	150	135	125	2.4	10.0	4"	$19
38 S&W Short	145	720	689	660	167	153	140	-8.5	—	5.0	NA
38 Short Colt	125	730	685	645	150	130	115	2.2	9.4	6"	$19
39 Special	100	950	900	NA	200	180	NA	1.3	NA	4"V	NA
38 Special	110	945	895	850	220	195	175	1.3	5.4	4"V	$23
38 Special	110	945	895	850	220	195	175	1.3	5.4	4"V	$23
38 Special	130	775	745	710	175	160	120	1.9	7.9	4"V	$22
38 Special Cowboy	140	800	767	735	199	183	168			7.5" V	NA
38 (Multi-Ball)	140	830	730	505	215	130	80	2.0	10.6	4"V	$10**
38 Special	148	710	635	565	165	130	105	2.4	10.6	4"V	$17
38 Special	158	755	725	690	200	185	170	2.0	8.3	4"V	$18
38 Special +P	95	1175	1045	960	290	230	195	0.9	3.9	4"V	$23
38 Special +P	110	995	925	870	240	210	185	1.2	5.1	4"V	$23
38 Special +P	125	975	929	885	264	238	218	1	5.2	4"	NA
38 Special +P	125	945	900	860	250	225	205	1.3	5.4	4"V	#23
38 Special +P	120	945	910	870	255	235	215	1.3	5.3	4"V	$11
38 Special +P	130	925	887	852	247	227	210	1.3	5.50	4"V	NA
38 Special +P	147/150	884	NA	NA	264	NA	NA	NA	NA	4"V	$27
38 Special +P	158	890	855	825	280	255	240	1.4	6.0	4"V	$20
357											
357 SIG	115	1520	NA	NA	593	NA	NA	NA	NA	NA	NA
357 SIG	124	1450	NA	NA	578	NA	NA	NA	NA	NA	NA
357 SIG	125	1350	1190	1080	510	395	325	0.7	3.1	4"	NA
357 SIG	135	1225	1112	1031	450	371	319	—	—	4.0	NA
357 SIG	147	1225	1132	1060	490	418	367	—	—	4.0	NA
357 SIG	150	1130	1030	970	420	355	310	0.9	4.0	NA	NA
356 TSW	115	1520	NA	NA	593	NA	NA	NA	NA	NA	NA
356 TSW	124	1450	NA	NA	578	NA	NA	NA	NA	NA	NA
356 TSW	135	1280	1120	1010	490	375	310	0.8	3.5	NA	NA
356 TSW	147	1220	1120	1040	485	410	355	0.8	3.5	5"	NA
357 Mag., Super Clean	105	1650									NA
357 Magnum	110	1295	1095	975	410	290	230	0.8	3.5	4"V	$25
357 (Med.Vel.)	125	1220	1075	985	415	315	270	0.8	3.7	4"V	$25
357 Magnum	125	1450	1240	1090	585	425	330	0.6	2.8	4"V	$25
357 Magnum	125	1500	1312	1163	624	478	376	—	—	8.0	NA
357 (Multi-Ball)	140	1155	830	665	420	215	135	1.2	6.4	4"V	$11**
357 Magnum	140	1360	1195	1075	575	445	360	0.7	3.0	4"V	$25
357 Magnum FlexTip	140	1440	1274	1143	644	504	406	NA	NA	NA	NA
357 Magnum	145	1290	1155	1060	535	430	360	0.8	3.5	4"V	$26
357 Magnum	150/158	1235	1105	1015	535	430	360	0.8	3.5	4"V	$25
357 Mag. Cowboy	158	800	761	725	225	203	185				NA
357 Magnum	165	1290	1189	1108	610	518	450	0.7	3.1	8-3/8"	NA
357 Magnum	180	1145	1055	985	525	445	390	0.9	3.9	4"V	$25
357 Magnum	180	1180	1088	1020	557	473	416	0.8	3.6	8"V	NA
357 Mag. CorBon F.A.	180	1650	1512	1386	1088	913	767	1.66	0.0	NA	NA
357 Mag. CorBon	200	1200	1123	1061	640	560	500	3.19	0.0	NA	NA
357 Rem. Maximum	158	1825	1590	1380	1170	885	670	0.4	1.7	10.5"	$14**
40, 10mm											
40 S&W	120	1150	—	—	352	—	—	—	—	—	$38
40 S&W	125	1265	1102	998	444	337	276	-3.0	—	4.0	NA

Cartridge	Bullet Wgt. Grs.	VELOCITY (fps)			ENERGY (ft. lbs.)			Mid-Range Traj. (in.)		Bbl. Lgth. (in).	Est. Price/ box
		Muzzle	50 yds.	100 yds.	Muzzle	50 yds.	100 yds.	50 yds.	100 yds.		
40 S&W	135	1140	1070	NA	390	345	NA	0.9	NA	4"	NA
40 S&W Guard Dog	135	1200	1040	940	430	325	265	NA	NA	4"	NA
40 S&W	155	1140	1026	958	447	362	309	0.9	4.1	4"	$14***
40 S&W	165	1150	NA	NA	485	NA	NA	NA	NA	4"	$18***
40 S&W	175	1010	948	899	396	350	314	—	—	4.0	NA
40 S&W	180	985	936	893	388	350	319	1.4	5.0	4"	$14***
40 S&W	180	1000	943	896	400	355	321	4.52	—	4.0	NA
40 S&W	180	1015	960	914	412	368	334	1.3	4.5	4"	NA
400 Cor-Bon	135	1450	NA	NA	630	NA	NA	NA	NA	5"	NA
10mm Automatic	155	1125	1046	986	436	377	335	0.9	3.9	5"	$26
10mm Automatic	155	1265	1118	1018	551	430	357	—	—	5.0	NA
10mm Automatic	170	1340	1165	1145	680	510	415	0.7	3.2	5"	$31
10mm Automatic	175	1290	1140	1035	650	505	420	0.7	3.3	5.5"	$11**
10mm Auto. (FBI)	180	950	905	865	361	327	299	1.5	5.4	4"	$16**
10mm Automatic	180	1030	970	920	425	375	340	1.1	4.7	5"	$16**
10mm Auto H.V.	180	1240	1124	1037	618	504	430	0.8	3.4	5"	$27
10mm Automatic	200	1160	1070	1010	495	510	430	0.9	3.8	5"	$14**
10.4mm Italian	177	950	NA	NA	360	NA	NA	NA	NA	NA	NEW
41 Action Exp.	180	1000	947	903	400	359	326	0.5	4.2	5"	$13**
41 Rem. Magnum	170	1420	1165	1015	760	515	390	0.7	3.2	4"V	$33
41 Rem. Magnum	175	1250	1120	1030	605	490	410	0.8	3.4	4"V	$14**
41 (Med. Vel.)	210	965	900	840	435	375	330	1.3	5.4	4"V	$30
41 Rem. Magnum	210	1300	1160	1060	790	630	535	0.7	3.2	4"V	$33
41 Rem. Magnum	240	1250	1151	1075	833	706	616	0.8	3.3	6.5V	NA
44											
44 S&W Russian	247	780	NA	NA	335	NA	NA	NA	NA	NA	NA
44 Special	210	900	861	825	360	329	302	5.57	—	6.0	NA
44 Special FTX	165	900	848	802	297	263	235	NA	NA	2.5"	NA
44 S&W Special	180	980	NA	NA	383	NA	NA	NA	NA	6.5"	NA
44 S&W Special	180	1000	935	882	400	350	311	NA	NA	7.5"V	NA
44 S&W Special	200	875	825	780	340	302	270	1.2	6.0	6"	$13**
44 S&W Special	200	1035	940	865	475	390	335	1.1	4.9	6.5"	$13**
44 S&W Special	240/246	755	725	695	310	285	265	2.0	8.3	6.5"	$26
44-40 Win.	200	722	698	676	232	217	203	-3.4	-23.7	4.0	NA
44-40 Win.	205	725	689	655	239	216	195	—	—	7.5	NA
44-40 Win.	210	725	698	672	245	227	210	-11.6	—	5.5	NA
44-40 Win.	225	725	697	670	263	243	225	-3.4	-23.8	4.0	NA
44-40 Win. Cowboy	225	750	723	695	281	261	242				NA
44 Rem. Magnum	180	1610	1365	1175	1035	745	550	0.5	2.3	4"V	$18**
44 Rem. Magnum	200	1296	1193	1110	747	632	548	-.5	-6.2	6.0	NA
44 Rem. Magnum	200	1400	1192	1053	870	630	492	0.6	NA	6.5"	$20
44 Rem. Magnum	200	1500	1332	1194	999	788	633	—	—	7.5	NA
44 Rem. Magnum	210	1495	1310	1165	1040	805	635	0.6	2.5	6.5"	$18**
44 Rem. Mag. FlexTip	225	1410	1240	1111	993	768	617	NA	NA	NA	NA
44 (Med. Vel.)	240	1000	945	900	535	475	435	1.1	4.8	6.5"	$17
44 R.M. (Jacketed)	240	1180	1080	1010	740	625	545	0.9	3.7	4"V	$18**
44 R.M. (Lead)	240	1350	1185	1070	970	750	610	0.7	3.1	4"V	$29
44 Rem. Magnum	250	1180	1100	1040	775	670	600	0.8	3.6	6.5"V	$21
44 Rem. Magnum	250	1250	1148	1070	867	732	635	0.8	3.3	6.5"V	NA
44 Rem. Magnum	275	1235	1142	1070	931	797	699	0.8	3.3	6.5"	NA
44 Rem. Magnum	300	1150	1083	1030	881	781	706	—	—	7.5	NA
44 Rem. Magnum	300	1200	1100	1026	959	806	702	NA	NA	7.5"	$17
44 Rem. Magnum	330	1385	1297	1220	1406	1234	1090	1.83	0.00	NA	NA
44 Webley	262	850	—	—	—	—	—	—	—	—	NA
440 CorBon	260	1700	1544	1403	1669	1377	1136	1.58	NA	10"	NA
45, 50											
450 Short Colt/450 Revolver	226	830	NA	NA	350	NA	NA	NA	NA	NA	NEW
45 S&W Schofield	180	730	NA	NA	213	NA	NA	NA	NA	NA	NA
45 S&W Schofield	230	730	NA	NA	272	NA	NA	NA	NA	NA	NA
45 G.A.P.	165	1007	936	879	372	321	283	-1.4	-11.8	5.0	NA
45 G.A.P.	185	1090	970	890	490	385	320	1.0	4.7	5"	NA

Cartridge	Bullet Wgt. Grs.	VELOCITY (fps)			ENERGY (ft. lbs.)			Mid-Range Traj. (in.)		Bbl. Lgth. (in).	Est. Price/ box
		Muzzle	50 yds.	100 yds.	Muzzle	50 yds.	100 yds.	50 yds.	100 yds.		
45 G.A.P.	230	880	842	NA	396	363	NA	NA	NA	NA	NA
45 Automatic	150	1050	NA	NA	403	NA	NA	NA	NA	NA	$40
45 Automatic	165	1030	930	NA	385	315	NA	1.2	NA	5"	NA
45 Automatic Guard Dog	165	1140	1030	950	475	390	335	NA	NA	5"	NA
45 Automatic	185	1000	940	890	410	360	325	1.1	4.9	5"	$28
45 Auto. (Match)	185	770	705	650	245	204	175	2.0	8.7	5"	$28
45 Auto. (Match)	200	940	890	840	392	352	312	2.0	8.6	5"	$20
45 Automatic	200	975	917	860	421	372	328	1.4	5.0	5"	$18
45 Automatic	230	830	800	675	355	325	300	1.6	6.8	5"	$27
45 Automatic	230	880	846	816	396	366	340	1.5	6.1	5"	NA
45 Automatic +P	165	1250	NA	NA	573	NA	NA	NA	NA	NA	NA
45 Automatic +P	185	1140	1040	970	535	445	385	0.9	4.0	5"	$31
45 Automatic +P	200	1055	982	925	494	428	380	NA	NA	5"	NA
45 Super	185	1300	1190	1108	694	582	504	NA	NA	5"	NA
45 Win. Magnum	230	1400	1230	1105	1000	775	635	0.6	2.8	5"	$14**
45 Win. Magnum	260	1250	1137	1053	902	746	640	0.8	3.3	5"	$16**
45 Win. Mag. CorBon	320	1150	1080	1025	940	830	747	3.47			NA
455 Webley MKII	262	850	NA	NA	420	NA	NA	NA	NA	NA	NA
45 Colt FTX	185	920	870	826	348	311	280	NA	NA	3"V	NA
45 Colt	200	1000	938	889	444	391	351	1.3	4.8	5.5"	$21
45 Colt	225	960	890	830	460	395	345	1.3	5.5	5.5"	$22
45 Colt + P CorBon	265	1350	1225	1126	1073	884	746	2.65	0.0		NA
45 Colt + P CorBon	300	1300	1197	1114	1126	956	827	2.78	0.0		NA
45 Colt	250/255	860	820	780	410	375	340	1.6	6.6	5.5"	$27
454 Casull	250	1300	1151	1047	938	735	608	0.7	3.2	7.5"V	NA
454 Casull	260	1800	1577	1381	1871	1436	1101	0.4	1.8	7.5"V	NA
454 Casull	300	1625	1451	1308	1759	1413	1141	0.5	2.0	7.5"V	NA
454 Casull CorBon	360	1500	1387	1286	1800	1640	1323	2.01	0.0		NA
460 S&W	200	2300	2042	1801	2350	1851	1441	0	-1.60	NA	NA
460 S&W	260	2000	1788	1592	2309	1845	1464	NA	NA	7.5"V	NA
460 S&W	250	1450	1267	1127	1167	891	705	NA	NA	8.375-V	NA
460 S&W	250	1900	1640	1412	2004	1494	1106	0	-2.75	NA	NA
460 S&W	300	1750	1510	1300	2040	1510	1125	NA	NA	8.4-V	NA
460 S&W	395	1550	1389	1249	2108	1691	1369	0	-4.00	NA	NA
475 Linebaugh	400	1050	1217	1119	1618	1315	1112	NA	NA	NA	NA
480 Ruger	325	1350	1191	1076	1315	1023	835	2.6	0.0	7.5"	NA
50 Action Exp.	300	1475	1251	1092	1449	1043	795		-	6"	NA
50 Action Exp.	325	1400	1209	1075	1414	1055	835	0.2	2.3	6"	$24**
500 S&W	275	1665	1392	1183	1693	1184	854	1.5	NA	8.375	NA
500 S&W	300	1950	1653	1396	2533	1819	1298	—	—	8.5	NA
500 S&W	325	1800	1560	1350	2340	1755	1315	NA	NA	8.4-V	NA
500 S&W	350	1400	1231	1106	1523	1178	951	NA	NA	10"	NA
500 S&W	400	1675	1472	1299	2493	1920	1499	1.3	NA	8.375	NA
500 S&W	440	1625	1367	1169	2581	1825	1337	1.6	NA	8.375	NA
500 S&W	500	1300	1178	1085	1876	1541	1308	—	—	8.5	NA
500 S&W	500	1425	1281	1164	2254	1823	1505	NA	NA	10"	NA

Note: The actual ballistics obtained with your firearm can vary considerably from the advertised ballistics.
Also, ballistics can vary from lot to lot with the same brand and type load.

Rimfire Ammunition Ballistics

Cartridge	Bullet Wt. Grs.	Velocity (fps) 22-1/2" Bbl.		Energy (ft. lbs.) 22-1/2" Bbl.		Mid-Range Traj. (in.)	Muzzle Velocity
		Muzzle	100 yds.	Muzzle	100 yds.	100 yds.	6" Bbl.
17 Aguila	20	1850	1267	NA	NA	NA	NA
17 Hornady Mach 2	15.5	2050	1450	149	75	NA	NA
17 Hornady Mach 2	17	2100	1530	166	88	0.7	NA
17 HMR Lead Free	15.5	2550	1901	NA	NA	.90	NA
17 HMR TNT Green	16	2500	1642	222	96	NA	NA
17 HMR	17	2550	1902	245	136	NA	NA
17 HMR	17	2650	NA	NA	NA	NA	NA
17 HMR	20	2375	1776	250	140	NA	NA
17 Win. Super Mag.	20 Tipped	3000	2504	400	278	0.0	NA
17 Win. Super Mag.	20 JHP	3000	2309	400	237	0.0	NA
17 Win. Super Mag.	25 Tipped	2600	2230	375	276	0.0	NA
5mm Rem. Rimfire Mag.	30	2300	1669	352	188	NA	24
22 Short Blank	—	—	—	—	—	—	—
22 Short CB	29	727	610	33	24	NA	706
22 Short Target	29	830	695	44	31	6.8	786
22 Short HP	27	1164	920	81	50	4.3	1077
22 Colibri	20	375	183	6	1	NA	NA
22 Super Colibri	20	500	441	11	9	NA	NA
22 Long CB	29	727	610	33	24	NA	706
22 Long HV	29	1180	946	90	57	4.1	1031
22 LR Pistol Match	40	1070	890	100	70	4.6	940
22 LR Shrt. Range Green	21	1650	912	127	NA	NA	NA
CCI Quiet 22 LR	40	710	640	45	36	NA	NA
22 LR Sub Sonic HP	38	1050	901	93	69	4.7	NA
22 LR Segmented HP	40	1050	897	98	72	NA	NA
22 LR Standard Velocity	40	1070	890	100	70	4.6	940
22 LR AutoMatch	40	1200	990	130	85	NA	NA
22 LR HV	40	1255	1016	140	92	3.6	1060
22 LR Silhoutte	42	1220	1003	139	94	3.6	1025
22 SSS	60	950	802	120	86	NA	NA
22 LR HV HP	40	1280	1001	146	89	3.5	1085
22 Velocitor GDHP	40	1435	–	–	–	NA	NA
22LR CCI Copper	21	1850	–	–	–	–	–
22 LR Segmented HP	37	1435	1080	169	96	2.9	NA
22 LR Hyper HP	32/33/34	1500	1075	165	85	2.8	NA
22 LR Expediter	32	1640	NA	191	NA	NA	NA
22 LR Stinger HP	32	1640	1132	191	91	2.6	1395
22 LR Lead Free	30	1650	NA	181	NA	NA	NA
22 LR Hyper Vel	30	1750	1191	204	93	NA	NA
22 LR Shot #12	31	950	NA	NA	NA	NA	NA
22 WRF LFN	45	1300	1015	169	103	3	NA
22 Win. Mag. Lead Free	28	2200	NA	301	NA	NA	NA
22 Win. Mag.	30	2200	1373	322	127	1.4	1610
22 Win. Mag. V-Max BT	33	2000	1495	293	164	0.60	NA
22 Win. Mag. JHP	34	2120	1435	338	155	1.4	NA
22 Win. Mag. JHP	40	1910	1326	324	156	1.7	1480
22 Win. Mag. FMJ	40	1910	1326	324	156	1.7	1480
22 Win. Mag. Dyna Point	45	1550	1147	240	131	2.60	NA
22 Win. Mag. JHP	50	1650	1280	300	180	1.3	NA
22 Win. Mag. Shot #11	52	1000	–	NA	–	–	NA

Shotshell Loads & Prices

NOTES: * = 10 rounds per box. ** = 5 rounds per box. Pricing variations and number of rounds per box can occur with type and brand of ammunition. Listed pricing is the average nominal cost for load style and box quantity shown. Not every brand is available in all shot size variations. Some manufacturers do not provide suggested list prices. All prices rounded to nearest whole dollar. The price you pay will vary dependent upon outlet of purchase. # = new load spec this year; "C" indicates a change in data.

Dram Equiv.	Shot Ozs.	Load Style	Shot Sizes	Brands	Avg. Price/box	Velocity (fps)
10 Gauge 3-1/2" Magnum						
Max	2-3/8	magnum blend	5, 6, 7	Hevi-shot	NA	1200
4-1/2	2-1/4	premium	BB, 2, 4, 5, 6	Win., Fed., Rem.	$33	1205
Max	2	premium	4, 5, 6	Fed., Win.	NA	1300
4-1/4	2	high velocity	BB, 2, 4	Rem.	$22	1210
Max	18 pellets	premium	00 buck	Fed., Win.	$7**	1100
Max	1-7/8	Bismuth	BB, 2, 4	Bis.	NA	1225
Max	1-3/4	high density	BB, 2	Rem.	NA	1300
4-1/4	1-3/4	steel	TT, T, BBB, BB, 1, 2, 3	Win., Rem.	$27	1260
Mag	1-5/8	steel	T, BBB, BB, 2	Win.	$27	1285
Max	1-5/8	Bismuth	BB, 2, 4	Bismuth	NA	1375
Max	1-1/2	hypersonic	BBB, BB, 2	Rem.	NA	1700
Max	1-1/2	heavy metal	BB, 2, 3, 4	Hevi-Shot	NA	1500
Max	1-1/2	steel	T, BBB, BB, 1, 2, 3	Fed.	NA	1450
Max	1-3/8	steel	T, BBB, BB, 1, 2, 3	Fed., Rem.	NA	1500
Max	1-3/8	steel	T, BBB, BB, 2	Fed., Win.	NA	1450
Max	1-3/4	slug, rifled	slug	Fed.	NA	1280
Max	24 pellets	Buckshot	1 Buck	Fed.	NA	1100
Max	54 pellets	Super-X	4 Buck	Win.	NA	1150
12 Gauge 3-1/2" Magnum						
Max	2-1/4	premium	4, 5, 6	Fed., Rem., Win.	$13*	1150
Max	2	Lead	4, 5, 6	Fed.	NA	1300
Max	2	Copper plated turkey	4, 5	Rem.	NA	1300
Max	18 pellets	premium	00 buck	Fed., Win., Rem.	$7**	1100
Max	1-7/8	Wingmaster HD	4, 6	Rem.	NA	1225
Max	1-7/8	heavyweight	5, 6	Fed.	NA	1300
Max	1-3/4	high density	BB, 2, 4, 6	Rem.		1300
Max	1-7/8	Bismuth	BB, 2, 4	Bis.	NA	1225
Max	1-5/8	blind side	Hex, 1, 3	Win.	NA	1400
Max	1-5/8	Hevi-shot	T	Hevi-shot	NA	1350
Max	1-5/8	Wingmaster HD	T	Rem.	NA	1350
Max	1-5/8	high density	BB, 2	Fed.	NA	1450
Max	1-5/8	Blind side	Hex, BB, 2	Win.	NA	1400
Max	1-5/8	high density	BB, 2	Fed.	NA	1450
Max	1-5/8	Blind side	Hex, BB, 2	Win.	NA	1400
Max	1-3/8	Heavyweight	2, 4, 6	Fed.	NA	1450
Max	1-3/8	steel	T, BBB, BB, 2, 4	Fed., Win., Rem.	NA	1450
Max	1-1/2	FS steel	BBB, BB, 2	Fed.	NA	1500
Max	1-1/2	Supreme H-V	BBB, BB, 2, 3	Win.	NA	1475
12 Gauge 3-1/2" Magnum (cont.)						
Max	1-3/8	H-speed steel	BB, 2	Rem.	NA	1550
Max	1-1/4	Steel	BB, 2	Win.	NA	1625
Max	24 pellets	Premium	1 Buck	Fed.	NA	1100
Max	54 pellets	Super-X	4 Buck	Win.	NA	1050
12 Gauge 3" Magnum						
Max	1-3/4	turkey	4, 5, 6	Fed., Fio., Win., Rem.	NA	1300
Max	1-3/4	high density	BB, 2, 4	Rem.	NA	1450
Max	1-5/8	high density	BB, 2	Fed.	NA	1450
Max	1-5/8	Wingmaster HD	4, 6	Rem.	NA	1227
Max	1-5/8	high velocity	4, 5, 6	Fed.	NA	1350
4	1-5/8	premium	2, 4, 5, 6	Win., Fed., Rem.	$18	1290
Max	1-1/2	Wingmaster HD	T	Rem.	NA	1300
Max	1-1/2	Hevi-shot	T	Hevi-shot	NA	1300
Max	1-1/2	high density	BB, 2, 4	Rem.	NA	1300
Max	1-1/2	slug	slug	Bren.	NA	1604
Max	1-5/8	Bismuth	BB, 2, 4, 5, 6	Bis.	NA	1250
4	24 pellets	buffered	1 buck	Win., Fed., Rem.	$5**	1040
4	15 pellets	buffered	00 buck	Win., Fed., Rem.	$6**	1210
4	10 pellets	buffered	000 buck	Win., Fed., Rem.	$6**	1225
4	41 pellets	buffered	4 buck	Win., Fed., Rem.	$6**	1210
Max	1-3/8	heavyweight	5, 6	Fed.	NA	1300
Max	1-3/8	high density	B, 2, 4, 6	Rem. Win.	NA	1450
Max	1-3/8	slug	slug	Bren.	NA	1476
Max	1-3/8	blind side	Hex, 1, 3, 5	Win.	NA	1400
Max	1-1/4	slug, rifled	slug	Fed.	NA	1600
Max	1-3/16	saboted	slug	Bren.	NA	1476
Max	7/8	slug, rifled	slug	Rem.	NA	1875
Max	1-1/8	low recoil	BB	Fed.	NA	850
Max	1-1/8	steel	BB, 2, 3, 4	Fed., Win., Rem.	NA	1550
Max	1-1/16	high density	2, 4	Win.	NA	1400
Max	1	steel	4, 6	Fed.	NA	1330
Max	1-3/8	buckhammer	slug	Rem.	NA	1500
Max	1	TruBall slug	slug	Fed.	NA	1700
Max	1	slug, rifled	slug, magnum	Win., Rem.	$5**	1760
Max	1-3/8	buckhammer	slug	Rem.	NA	1500
Max	1	saboted slug	slug	Rem., Win., Fed.	$10**	1550

12 Gauge 3" Magnum (cont.)

Dram Equiv.	Shot Ozs.	Load Style	Shot Sizes	Brands	Avg. Price/box	Velocity (fps)
Max	385 grs.	partition gold	slug	Win.	NA	2000
Max	1-1/8	Rackmaster	slug	Win.	NA	1700
Max	300 grs.	XP3	slug	Win.	NA	2100
3-5/8	1-3/8	steel	BBB, BB, 1, 2, 3, 4	Win., Fed., Rem.	$19	1275
Max	1-1/8	snow goose FS	BB, 2, 3, 4	Fed.	NA	1635
Max	1-1/8	steel	BB, 2, 4	Rem.	NA	1500
Max	1-1/8	steel	T, BBB, BB, 2, 4, 5, 6	Fed., Win.	NA	1450
Max	1-1/8	steel	BB, 2	Fed.	NA	1400
Max	1-1/8	FS lead	3, 4	Fed.	NA	1600
Max	1-3/8	Blind side	Hex, BB, 2	Win.	NA	1400
4	1-1/4	steel	T, BBB, BB, 1, 2, 3, 4, 6	Win., Fed., Rem.	$18	1400
Max	1-1/4	FS steel	BBB, BB, 2	Fed.	NA	1450

12 Gauge 2-3/4"

Dram Equiv.	Shot Ozs.	Load Style	Shot Sizes	Brands	Avg. Price/box	Velocity (fps)
Max	1-5/8	magnum	4, 5, 6	Win., Fed.	$8*	1250
Max	1-3/8	lead	4, 5, 6	Fiocchi	NA	1485
Max	1-3/8	turkey	4, 5, 6	Fio.	NA	1250
Max	1-3/8	steel	4, 5, 6	Fed.	NA	1400
Max	1-3/8	Bismuth	BB, 2, 4, 5, 6	Bis.	NA	1300
3-3/4	1-1/2	magnum	BB, 2, 4, 5, 6	Win., Fed., Rem.	$16	1260
Max	1-1/4	blind side	Hex, 2, 5	Win.	NA	1400
Max	1-1/4	Supreme H-V	4, 5, 6, 7-1/2	Win. Rem.	NA	1400
3-3/4	1-1/4	high velocity	BB, 2, 4, 5, 6, 7-1/2, 8, 9	Win., Fed., Rem., Fio.	$13	1330
Max	1-1/4	high density	B, 2, 4	Win.	NA	1450
Max	1-1/4	high density	4, 6	Rem.	NA	1325
3-1/4	1-1/4	standard velocity	6, 7-1/2, 8, 9	Win., Fed., Rem., Fio.	$11	1220
Max	1-1/8	Hevi-shot	5	Hevi-shot	NA	1350
3-1/4	1-1/8	standard velocity	4, 6, 7-1/2, 8, 9	Win., Fed., Rem., Fio.	$9	1255
Max	1-1/8	steel	2, 4	Rem.	NA	1390
Max	1	steel	BB, 2	Fed.	NA	1450
3-1/4	1	standard velocity	6, 7-1/2, 8	Rem., Fed., Fio., Win.	$6	1290
3-1/4	1-1/4	target	7-1/2, 8, 9	Win., Fed., Rem.	$10	1220
3	1-1/8	spreader	7-1/2, 8, 8-1/2, 9	Fio.	NA	1200
3	1-1/8	target	7-1/2, 8, 9, 7-1/2x8	Win., Fed., Rem., Fio.	$7	1200
2-3/4	1-1/8	target	7-1/2, 8, 8-1/2, 9, 7-1/2x8	Win., Fed., Rem., Fio.	$7	1145
2-3/4	1-1/8	low recoil	7-1/2, 8	Rem.	NA	1145
2-1/2	26 grams	low recoil	8	Win.	NA	980

12 Gauge 2-3/4" (cont.)

Dram Equiv.	Shot Ozs.	Load Style	Shot Sizes	Brands	Avg. Price/box	Velocity (fps)
2-1/4	1-1/8	target	7-1/2, 8, 8-1/2, 9	Rem., Fed.	$7	1080
Max	1	spreader	7-1/2, 8, 8-1/2, 9	Fio.	NA	1300
3-1/4	28 grams (1 oz)	target	7-1/2, 8, 9	Win., Fed., Rem., Fio.	$8	1290
3	1	target	7-1/2, 8, 8-1/2, 9	Win., Fio.	NA	1235
2-3/4	1	target	7-1/2, 8, 8-1/2, 9	Fed., Rem., Fio.	NA	1180
3-1/4	24 grams	target	7-1/2, 8, 9	Fed., Win., Fio.	NA	1325
3	7/8	light	8	Fio.	NA	1200
3-3/4	8 pellets	buffered	000 buck	Win., Fed., Rem.	$4**	1325
4	12 pellets	premium	00 buck	Win., Fed., Rem.	$5**	1290
3-3/4	9 pellets	buffered	00 buck	Win., Fed., Rem., Fio.	$19	1325
3-3/4	12 pellets	buffered	0 buck	Win., Fed., Rem.	$4**	1275
4	20 pellets	buffered	1 buck	Win., Fed., Rem.	$4**	1075
3-3/4	16 pellets	buffered	1 buck	Win., Fed., Rem.	$4**	1250
4	34 pellets	premium	4 buck	Fed., Rem.	$5**	1250
3-3/4	27 pellets	buffered	4 buck	Win., Fed., Rem., Fio.	$4**	1325
		PDX1	1 oz. slug, 3-00 buck	Win.	NA	1150
Max	1 oz	segmenting, slug	slug	Win.	NA	1600
Max	1	saboted slug	slug	Win., Fed., Rem.	$10**	1450
Max	1-1/4	slug, rifled	slug	Fed.	NA	1520
Max	1-1/4	slug	slug	Lightfield		1440
Max	1-1/4	saboted slug	attached sabot	Rem.	NA	1550
Max	1	slug, rifled	slug, magnum	Rem., Fio.	$5**	1680
Max	1	slug, rifled	slug	Win., Fed., Rem.	$4**	1610
Max	1	sabot slug	slug	Sauvestre		1640
Max	7/8	slug, rifled	slug	Rem.	NA	1800
Max	400	plat. tip	sabot slug	Win.	NA	1700
Max	385 grains	Partition Gold Slug	slug	Win.	NA	1900
Max	385 grains	Core-Lokt bonded	sabot slug	Rem.	NA	1900
Max	325 grains	Barnes Sabot	slug	Fed.	NA	1900
Max	300 grains	SST Slug	sabot slug	Hornady	NA	2050
Max	3/4	Tracer	#8 + tracer	Fio.	NA	1150
Max	130 grains	Less Lethal	.73 rubber slug	Lightfield	NA	600
Max	3/4	non-toxic	zinc slug	Win.	NA	NA

Dram Equiv.	Shot Ozs.	Load Style	Shot Sizes	Brands	Avg. Price/ box	Velocity (fps)
12 Gauge 2-3/4" *(cont.)*						
3	1-1/8	steel target	6-1/2, 7	Rem.	NA	1200
2-3/4	1-1/8	steel target	7	Rem.	NA	1145
3	1#	steel	7	Win.	$11	1235
3-1/2	1-1/4	steel	T, BBB, BB, 1, 2, 3, 4, 5, 6	Win., Fed., Rem.	$18	1275
3-3/4	1-1/8	steel	BB, 1, 2, 3, 4, 5, 6	Win., Fed., Rem., Fio.	$16	1365
3-3/4	1	steel	2, 3, 4, 5, 6, 7	Win., Fed., Rem., Fio.	$13	1390
Max	7/8	steel	7	Fio.	NA	1440
12 Gauge 2-3/4" *(cont.)*						
Max	1-1/8	steel target	6-1/2, 7	Rem.	NA	1200
Max	1-1/8	steel target	7	Rem.	NA	1145
Max	1#	steel	7	Win.	$11	1235
16 Gauge 2-3/4"						
3-1/4	1-1/4	magnum	2, 4, 6	Fed., Rem.	$16	1260
3-1/4	1-1/8	high velocity	4, 6, 7-1/2	Win., Fed., Rem., Fio.	$12	1295
Max	1-1/8	Bismuth	4, 5	Bis.	NA	1200
2-3/4	1-1/8	standard velocity	6, 7-1/2, 8	Fed., Rem., Fio.	$9	1185
2-1/2	1	dove	6, 7-1/2, 8, 9	Fio., Win.	NA	1165
Max	1	Bismuth	4, 6	Rio	NA	1200
Max	15/16	steel	2, 4	Fed., Rem.	NA	1300
Max	7/8	steel	2, 4	Win.	$16	1300
3	12 pellets	buffered	1 buck	Win., Fed., Rem.	$4**	1225
Max	4/5	slug, rifled	slug	Win., Fed., Rem.	$4**	1570
Max	.92	sabot slug	slug	Sauvestre	NA	1560
20 Gauge 3" Magnum						
3	1-1/4	premium	2, 4, 5, 6, 7-1/2	Win., Fed., Rem.	$15	1185
Max	1-1/4	Wingmaster HD	4, 6	Rem.	NA	1185
3	1-1/4	turkey	4, 6	Fio.	NA	1200
Max	1-1/4	Hevi-shot	2, 4, 6	Hevi-shot	NA	1250
Max	1-1/8	high density	4, 6	Rem.	NA	1300
Max	18 pellets	buck shot	2 buck	Fed.	NA	1200

Dram Equiv.	Shot Ozs.	Load Style	Shot Sizes	Brands	Avg. Price/ box	Velocity (fps)
Max	24 pellets	buffered	3 buck	Win.	$5**	1150
20 Gauge 3" Magnum *(cont.)*						
2-3/4	20 pellets	buck	3 buck	Rem.	$4**	1200
Max	1	hypersonic	2, 3, 4	Rem.	NA	Rem.
3-1/4	1	steel	1, 2, 3, 4, 5, 6	Win., Fed., Rem.	$15	1330
Max	1	blind side	Hex, 2, 5	Win.	NA	1300
Max	7/8	steel	2, 4	Win.	NA	1300
Max	7/8	FS lead	3, 4	Fed.	NA	1500
Max	1-1/16	high density	2, 4	Win.	NA	1400
Max	1-1/16	Bismuth	2, 4, 5, 6	Bismuth	NA	1250
Mag	5/8	saboted slug	275 gr.	Fed.	NA	1900
Max	3/4	TruBall slug	slug	Fed.	NA	1700
20 Gauge 2-3/4"						
2-3/4	1-1/8	magnum	4, 6, 7-1/2	Win., Fed., Rem.	$14	1175
2-3/4	1	high velocity	4, 5, 6, 7-1/2, 8, 9	Win., Fed., Rem., Fio.	$12	1220
Max	1	Bismuth	4, 6	Bis.	NA	1200
Max	1	Hevi-shot	5	Hevi-shot	NA	1250
Max	1	Supreme H-V	4, 6, 7-1/2	Win. Rem.	NA	1300
Max	1	FS lead	4, 5, 6	Fed.	NA	1350
Max	7/8	Steel	2, 3, 4	Fio.	NA	1500
2-1/2	1	standard velocity	6, 7-1/2, 8	Win., Rem., Fed., Fio.	$6	1165
2-1/2	7/8	clays	8	Rem.	NA	1200
2-1/2	7/8	promotional	6, 7-1/2, 8	Win., Rem., Fio.	$6	1210
2-1/2	1	target	8, 9	Win., Rem.	$8	1165
Max	7/8	clays	7-1/2, 8	Win.	NA	1275
2-1/2	7/8	target	8, 9	Win., Fed., Rem.	$8	1200
Max	3/4	steel	2, 4	Rem.	NA	1425
2-1/2	7/8	steel - target	7	Rem.	NA	1200
1-1/2	7/8	low recoil	8	Win.	NA	980
Max	1	buckhammer	slug	Rem.	NA	1500
Max	5/8	Saboted Slug	Copper Slug	Rem.	NA	1500
Max	20 pellets	buffered	3 buck	Win., Fed.	$4	1200

Dram Equiv.	Shot Ozs.	Load Style	Shot Sizes	Brands	Avg. Price/box	Velocity (fps)
Max	5/8	slug, saboted	slug	Win.,	$9**	1400
2-3/4	5/8	slug, rifled	slug	Rem.	$4**	1580
Max	3/4	saboted slug	copper slug	Fed., Rem.	NA	1450
Max	3/4	slug, rifled	slug	Win., Fed., Rem., Fio.	$4**	1570

20 Gauge 2-3/4" (cont.)

Dram Equiv.	Shot Ozs.	Load Style	Shot Sizes	Brands	Avg. Price/box	Velocity (fps)
Max	.9	sabot slug	slug	Sauvestre		1480
Max	260 grains	Partition Gold Slug	slug	Win.	NA	1900
Max	260 grains	Core-Lokt Ultra	slug	Rem.	NA	1900
Max	260 grains	saboted slug	platinum tip	Win.	NA	1700
Max	3/4	steel	2, 3, 4, 6	Win., Fed., Rem.	$14	1425
Max	250 grains	SST slug	slug	Hornady	NA	1800
Max	1/2	rifled, slug	slug	Rem.	NA	1800
Max	67 grains	Less lethal	2/.60 rubber balls	Lightfield	NA	900

28 Gauge 3"

Dram Equiv.	Shot Ozs.	Load Style	Shot Sizes	Brands	Avg. Price/box	Velocity (fps)
Max	7/8	tundra tungsten	4, 5, 6	Fiocchi	NA	TBD

28 Gauge 2-3/4"

Dram Equiv.	Shot Ozs.	Load Style	Shot Sizes	Brands	Avg. Price/box	Velocity (fps)
2	1	high velocity	6, 7-1/2, 8	Win.	$12	1125
2-1/4	3/4	high velocity	6, 7-1/2, 8, 9	Win., Fed., Rem., Fio.	$11	1295
2	3/4	target	8, 9	Win., Fed., Rem.	$9	1200
Max	3/4	sporting clays	7-1/2, 8-1/2	Win.	NA	1300
Max	3/4	Bismuth	5, 7	Rio	NA	1250
Max	5/8	steel	6, 7	NA	NA	1300
Max	5/8	slug		Bren.	NA	1450

410 Bore 3"

Dram Equiv.	Shot Ozs.	Load Style	Shot Sizes	Brands	Avg. Price/box	Velocity (fps)
Max	11/16	high velocity	4, 5, 6, 7-1/2, 8, 9	Win., Fed., Rem., Fio.	$10	1135
Max	9/16	Bismuth	5, 7	Rio	NA	1175
Max	3/8	steel	6	NA	NA	1400
		judge	5 pellets 000 Buck	Fed.	NA	960
		judge	9 pellets #4 Buck	Fed.	NA	1100
Max	Mixed	Per. Defense	3DD/12BB	Win.	NA	750

410 Bore 2-1/2"

Dram Equiv.	Shot Ozs.	Load Style	Shot Sizes	Brands	Avg. Price/box	Velocity (fps)
Max	1/2	high velocity	4, 6, 7-1/2	Win., Fed., Rem.	$9	1245
Max	1/5	slug, rifled	slug	Win., Fed., Rem.	$4**	1815
1-1/2	1/2	target	8, 8-1/2, 9	Win., Fed., Rem., Fio.	$8	1200
Max	1/2	sporting clays	7-1/2, 8, 8-1/2	Win.	NA	1300
Max		Buckshot	5-000 Buck	Win.	NA	1135
		judge	12-bb's, 3 disks	Win.	NA	TBD
Max	Mixed	Per. Defense	4DD/16BB	Win.	NA	750
Max	42 grains	Less lethal	4/.41 rubber balls	Lightfield	NA	1150

THE 2020 GUN DIGEST
web directory

AMMUNITION AND COMPONENTS

2 Monkey Trading **www.2monkey.com**

2nd Amendment Ammunition **www.secondammo.com**

Accurate Reloading Powders **www.accuratepowder.com**

Advanced Tactical **www.advancedtactical.com**

Aguila Ammunition **www.aguilaammo.com**

Alexander Arms **www.alexanderarms.com**

Alliant Powder **www.alliantpowder.com**

American Copper Bullets
        www.americancopperbulletscorp.com

American Derringer Co. **www.amderringer.com**

American Eagle **www.federalpremium.com**

American Pioneer Powder **www.americanpioneerpowder.com**

American Specialty Ammunition
        www.americanspecialityammo.com

Ammo Depot **www.ammodepot.com**

Ammo Importers **www.ammoimporters.com**

Ammo-Up **www.ammoupusa.com**

Applied Ballistics Munitions **www.buyabmammo.com**

Arizona Ammunition, Inc. **www.arizonaammunition.net**

Armscor **www.armscor.com**

ASYM Precision Ammunition **www.asymammo.com**

Atesci **www.atesci.com**

Australian Munitions **www.australian-munitions.com**

B&T (USA) **www.bt-ag.ch**

Ballistic Products Inc. **www.ballisticproducts.com**

Barnes Bullets **www.barnesbullets.com**

Baschieri & Pellagri **www.baschieri-pellagri.com**

Berger Bullets, Ltd. **www.bergerbullets.com**

Berry's Mfg., Inc. **www.berrysmfg.com**

Big Bore Express **www.powerbeltbullets.com**

Bishop Ammunition and Firearms. **www.bishopammunition.com**

Black Hills Ammunition, Inc. **www.black-hills.com**

BlackHorn209 **www.blackhorn209.com**

Brenneke of America Ltd. **www.brennekeusa.com**

Browning **www.browning.com**

Buffalo Arms **www.buffaloarms.com**

Buffalo Bore Ammunition **www.buffalobore.com**

Buffalo Cartridge Co. **www.buffalocartridge.com**

Calhoon, James, Bullets **www.jamescalhoon.com**

Cartuchos Saga **www.saga.es**

Cast Performance Bullet **www.grizzlycartridge.com**

CCI **www.cci-ammunition.com**

Century International Arms **www.centuryarms.com**

Cheaper Than Dirt **www.cheaperthandirt.com**

Cheddite France **www.cheddite.com**

Claybuster Wads **www.claybusterwads.com**

Combined Tactical Systems **www.combinedsystems.com**

Cor-Bon/Glaser **www.corbon.com**

Creedmoor Sports **www.creedmoorsports.com**

Custom Cartridge **www.customcartridge.com**

Cutting Edge Bullets **www.cuttingedgebullets.com**

Dakota Arms **www.dakotaarms.com**

DDupleks, Ltd. **www.ddupleks.com**

Dead Nuts Manufacturing **www.deadnutsmfg.us**

Defense Technology Corp. **www.defense-technology.com**

Denver Bullets **www.denverbullets.com**

Desperado Cowboy Bullets **www.cowboybullets.com**

Dillon Precision **www.dillonprecision.com**

Double Tap Ammunition **www.doubletapammo.net**

Down Range Mfg. **www.downrangemfg.com**

Dynamic Research Technologies **www.drtammo.com**

E. Arthur Brown Co. **www.wabco.com**

EcoSlug **www.eco-slug.com**

Eley Ammunition **www.eley.co.uk**

Environ-Metal **www.hevishot.com**

Estate Cartridge **www.estatecartridge.com**

Federal Cartridge Co. **www.federalpremium.com**

Fiocchi of America **www.fiocchiusa.com**

G2 Research **www.g2rammo.com**

Gamebore Cartridge **www.gamebore.com**

GaugeMate **www.gaugemate.com**

Glaser Safety Slug, Inc. **www.corbon.com**

GOEX Inc. **www.goexpowder.com**

Graf & Sons **www.grafs.com**

Grizzly Cartridge Co. **www.grizzlycartridge.com**

Haendler & Natermann **www.hn-sport.de**

Harvester Muzzleloading **www.harvestermuzzleloading.com**

Hawk Bullets **www.hawkbullets.com**

Herter's Ammunition **www.cabelas.com**

Hevi.Shot www.hevishot.com
High Precision Down Range www.hprammo.com
Hodgdon Powder www.hodgdon.com
Hornady www.hornady.com
HSM Ammunition www.thehuntingshack.com
Huntington Reloading Products www.huntingtons.com
IMI Systems www.imisystems.com
IMR Smokeless Powders www.imrpowder.com
Inceptor Ammunition www.inceptorammo.com
International Cartridge Corp www.iccammo.com
I.O. Inc. www.ioinc.us
J&G Sales www.jgsales.com
James Calhoon www.jamescalhoon.com
Kent Cartridge America www.kentgamebore.com
Knight Bullets www.benchrest.com/knight/
Kraken Ballistics www.krakenballistics.com
Lapua www.lapua.com
Lawrence Brand Shot www.lawrencebrandshot.com
Lazzeroni Arms www.lazzeroni.com
Leadheads Bullets www.proshootpro.com
Lehigh Defense www.lehighdefense.com
Lightfield Ammunition Corp www.litfld.com
Lyman www.lymanproducts.com
Magnum Muzzleloading Products www.mmpsabots.com
Magnus Bullets www.magnusbullets.com
MagSafe Ammo www.magsafeonline.com
Magtech www.magtechammunition.com
Meister Bullets www.meisterbullets.com
Midway USA www.midwayusa.com
Mitchell's Mausers www.mauser.org
National Bullet Co. www.nationalbullet.com
Navy Arms www.navyarms.com
Nobel Sport www.nobelsportammo.com
Norma www.norma.cc
North Fork Technologies www.northforkbullets.com
Nosler Bullets, Inc. www.nosler.com
Old Western Scrounger www.ows-ammo.com
Pattern Control www.patterncontrol.com
PCP Ammunition www.pcpammo.com
Piney Mountain Ammunition
            www.pineymountainammunitionco.com
PMC www.pmcammo.com
PolyCase Ammunition www.polycaseammo.com
Polywad www.polywad.com
PowerBelt Bullets www.powerbeltbullets.com
PPU Ammunition www.prvipartizan.com
PR Bullets www.prbullet.com
Precision Delta www.precisiondelta.com
Precision Reloading www.precisionreloading.com
Pro Load Ammunition www.proload.com
Prvi Partizan Ammunition www.prvipartizan.com

Quality Cartridge www.qual-cart.com
Rainier Ballistics www.rainierballistics.com
Ram Shot Powder www.ramshot.com
Rare Ammunition www.rareammo.com
Reloading Specialties Inc. www.reloadingspecialtiesinc.com
Remington www.remington.com
Rio Ammunition www.rioammo.com
Rocky Mountain Cartridge www.rockymountaincartride.com
Sauvestre Ammunition www.centuryarms.com
SBR Ammunition www.sbrammunition.com
Schuetzen Powder www.schuetzenpowder.com
Sellier & Bellot www.sellier-bellot.cz
Shilen www.shilen.com
Sierra www.sierrabullets.com
SIG Sauer www.sigammo.com
Silver State Armory www.ssarmory.com
Simunition www.simunition.com
SinterFire, Inc. www.sinterfire.com
Spectra Shot www.spectrashot.com
Speer Ammunition www.speer-ammo.com
Speer Bullets www.speer-bullets.com
Sporting Supplies Int'l Inc. www.wolfammo.com
Starline www.starlinebrass.com
Stealth Gunpowder www.stealthgunpowder.com
Super Vel www.supervelammunition.com
Swift Bullets Co. www.swiftbullets.com
Tannerite www.tannerite.com
Tascosa Cartridge Co. www.tascosacartridge.com
Ted Nugent Ammunition www.americantactical.us
Ten-X Ammunition www.tenxammo.com
Top Brass www.topbrass-inc.com
TulAmmo www.tulammousa.com
Velocity Tactics www.velocitytactics.com
Vihtavuori www.vihtavuori.com
Weatherby www.weatherby.com
Western Powders Inc. www.westernpowders.com
Widener's Reloading & Shooters Supply www.wideners.com
Winchester Ammunition www.winchester.com
Windjammer Tournament Wads www.windjammer-wads.com
Wolf Ammunition www.wolfammo.com
Woodleigh Bullets www.woodleighbullets.com.au
Xtreme Bullets www.xtremebullets.com
Zanders Sporting Goods www.gzanders.com

CASES, SAFES, GUN LOCKS, AND CABINETS

Ace Case Co. www.acecase.com
AG English Sales Co. www.agenglish.com
ALEON www.aleoncase.com
American Security Products www.amsecusa.com

Americase **www.americase.com**
Assault Systems **www.elitesurvival.com**
Avery Outdoors, Inc. **www.averyoutdoors.com**
Birchwood Casey **www.birchwoodcasey.com**
Bore-Stores **www.borestores.com**
Boyt Harness Co. **www.boytharness.com**
Gardall Safes **www.gardall.com**
Campbell Industrial Supply **www.gun-racks.com**
Cannon Safe Co. **www.cannonsafe.com**
Eversafe **www.eversafetech.com**
Fort Knox Safes **www.ftknox.com**
Franzen Security Products **www.securecase.com**
Goldenrod Dehumidifiers **www.goldenroddehumidifiers.com**
Gunlocker Phoenix USA Inc. **www.gunlocker.com**
Gun Storage Solutions **www.storemoreguns.com**
GunVault **www.gunvault.com**
Hakuba USA Inc. **www.hakubausa.com**
Heritage Safe Co. **www.heritagesafe.com**
Homak Safes **www.homak.com**
Hunter Company **www.huntercompany.com**
Kalispel Case Line **www.kalispelcaseline.net**
Lakewood Products **www.lakewoodproducts.com**
Liberty Safe & Security **www.libertysafe.com**
Morton Enterprises **www.uniquecases.com**
New Innovative Products **www.starlightcases.com**
Pelican Products **www.pelican.com**
Phoenix USA Inc. **www.gunlocker.com**
Plano Molding Co. **www.planomolding.com**
Plasticase, Inc. **www.nanuk.com**
Rhino Safe **www.rhinosafe.com**
Rotary Gun Racks **www.gun-racks.com**
Sack-Ups **www.sackups.com**
Safe Tech, Inc. **www.safrgun.com**
Securecase **www.securecase.com**
Sentry Safe **www.sentrysafe.com**
Shot Lock Corp. **www.shotlock.com**
SKB Cases **www.skbcases.com**
Smart Lock Technology Inc. **www.smartlock.com**
Snap Safe **www.snapsafe.com**
Sportsmans Steel Safe Co. **www.sportsmansteelsafes.com**
Stack-On Safes **www.stackon.com**
Starlight Cases **www.starlightcases.com**
Stealth Safe **www.stealthtac.com**
Strong Case **www.strongcasebytnb.com**
Technoframes **www.technoframes.com**
The Gun Box **www.thegunbox.com**
Titan Gun Safes **www.titangunsafes.com**
Tracker Safe **www.trackersafe.com**
Tuffy Security Products **www.tuffyproducts.com**
T.Z. Case Int'l **www.tzcase.com**
U.S. Explosive Storage **www.usexplosivestorage.com**

Vanguard World **www.vanguardworld.com**
Versatile Rack Co. **www.versatilegunrack.com**
V-Line Industries **www.vlineind.com**
Winchester Safes **www.winchestersafes.com**
Ziegel Engineering **www.ziegeleng.com**

CHOKE DEVICES, RECOIL REDUCERS, SUPPRESSORS AND ACCURACY DEVICES

ACT Tactical **www.blackwidowshooters.com**
AO Safety Peltor **www.aosafety.com**
Advanced Armament Corp. **www.advanced-armament.com**
Alpha Dog Silencers **www.alphadogsilencers.com**
100 Straight Products **www.100straight.com**
Briley Mfg. **www.briley.com**
Carlson's **www.choketube.com**
Colonial Arms **www.colonialarms.com**
Comp-N-Choke **www.comp-n-choke.com**
Elite Iron **www.eliteiron.net**
Gemtech **www.gem-tech.com**
Great Lakes Tactical **www.gltactical.com**
Horizon Firearms **www.iotaoutdoors.com**
KDF, Inc. **www.kdfguns.com**
KG Industries **www.kgcoatings.com**
Kick's Industries **www.kicks-ind.com**
LimbSaver **www.limbsaver.com**
Lyman Products **www.lymanproducts.com**
Mag-Na-Port Int'l Inc. **www.magnaport.com**
Mesa Tactical **www.mesatactical.com**
Metro Gun **www.metrogun.com**
NG2 Defense **www.ng2defense.com**
Operators Suppressor Systems **www.osssuppressors.com**
OSS Suppressors **www.osssuppressors.com**
Patternmaster Chokes **www.patternmaster.com**
Poly-Choke **www.polychoke.com**
Precision Armament **www.precisionarmament.com**
SilencerCo **www.silencerco.com**
Silencer Shop **www.silencershop.com**
Sims Vibration Laboratory **www.limbsaver.com**
SRT Arms **www.srtarms.com**
SureFire **www.surefire.com**
Teague Precision Chokes **www.teaguechokes.com**
Truglo **www.truglo.com**
Trulock Tool **www.trulockchokes.com**
Vais Arms, Inc. **www.muzzlebrakes.com**
Vaultek **www.vaulteksafe.com**

CHRONOGRAPHS AND BALLISTIC SOFTWARE

Barnes Ballistic Program **www.barnesbullets.com**
Ballisticard Systems **www.ballisticards.com**
Competition Electronics **www.competitionelectronics.com**
Competitive Edge Dynamics **www.cedhk.com**
Hodgdon Shotshell Program **www.hodgdon.com**
Lee Shooter Program **www.leeprecision.com**
NECO **www.neconos.com**
Oehler Research Inc. **www.oehler-research.com**
PACT **www.pact.com**
ProChrony **www.competitionelectronics.com**
Quickload **www.neconos.com**
RCBS Load **www.rcbs.com**
Shooting Chrony **www.shootingchrony.com**
Sierra Infinity Ballistics Program **www.sierrabullets.com**
Winchester Ballistics Calculator **www.winchester.com**

CLEANING PRODUCTS

Accupro **www.accupro.com**
Ballistol USA **www.ballistol.com**
Barrel Buddy **www.barrelbuddy.com**
Birchwood Casey **www.birchwoodcasey.com**
Bore Tech **www.boretech.com**
Break-Free, Inc. **www.break-free.com**
Bruno Shooters Supply **www.brunoshooters.com**
Butch's Bore Shine **www.butchsboreshine.com**
C.J. Weapons Accessories **www.cjweapons.com**
Clenzoil **www.clenzoil.com**
Corrosion Technologies **www.corrosionx.com**
Dewey Mfg. **www.deweyrods.com**
Dry Vapor Cleaner **www.dryvaporcleaner.com**
DuraCoat **www.lauerweaponry.com**
Emby Enterprises **www.alltemptacticallube.com**
Extreme Gun Care **www.extremeguncare.com**
G96 **www.g96.com**
Gun Butter **www.gunbutter.com**
Gun Cleaners **www.guncleaners.com**
Gunslick Gun Care **www.gunslick.com**
Gunzilla **www.topduckproducts.com**
Hoppes **www.hoppes.com**
Hydrosorbent Products **www.dehumidify.com**
Inhibitor VCI Products **www.theinhibitor.com**
Jag Brush **www.jagbrush.com**
KG Industries **www.kgcoatings.com**
L&R Ultrasonics **www.ultrasonics.com**
Lyman **www.lymanproducts.com**
Mil-Comm Products **www.mil-comm.com**
Montana X-Treme **www.montanaxtreme.com**
MPT Industries **www.mptindustries.com**

Mpro7 Gun Care **www.mp7.com**
NFUSED Weapons Cleaner **www.Nfused.com**
Old West Snake Oil **www.oldwestsnakeoil.com**
Otis Technology, Inc. **www.otisgun.com**
Outers **www.outers-guncare.com**
Pro Gun Cleaning **www.proultrasonics.com**
Prolix Lubricant **www.prolixlubricant.com**
Pro-Shot Products **www.proshotproducts.com**
Rigel Products **www.rigelproducts.com**
Sagebrush Products **www.sagebrushproducts.com**
Sentry Solutions Ltd. **www.sentrysolutions.com**
Shooters Choice Gun Care **www.shooters-choice.com**
Slip 2000 **www.slip2000.com**
Southern Bloomer Mfg. **www.southernbloomer.com**
Stony Point Products **www.unclemikes.com**
Top Duck Products, LLC **www.topduckproducts.com**
Triangle Patch **www.trianglepatch.com**
Wipe-Out **www.sharpshootr.com**
World's Fastest Gun Bore Cleaner **www.michaels-oregon.com**

FIREARM AUCTION SITES

Alderfer Auction **www.alderferauction.com**
Amoskeag Auction Co. **www.amoskeagauction.com**
Antique Guns **www.antiqueguns.com**
Auction Arms **www.auctionarms.com**
Batterman's Auctions **www.battermans.com**
Bonhams & Butterfields **www.bonhams.com/usarms**
Cowan's **www.cowans.com**
Fontaine's Auction Gallery **www.fontainesauction.net**
Guns America **www.gunsamerica.com**
Gun Broker **www.gunbroker.com**
Guns International **www.gunsinternational.com**
Heritage Auction Galleries **www.ha.com**
Little John's Auction Service **www.littlejohnsauctionservice.net**
Lock, Stock & Barrel Investments **www.lsbauctions.com**
Morphy Auctions **www.morphyauctions.com**
Poulin Auction Co. **www.poulinantiques.com**
Rock Island Auction Co. **www.rockislandauction.com**
Wallis & Wallis **www.wallisandwallis.org**

FIREARM MANUFACTURERS AND IMPORTERS

Accu-Tek **www.accu-tekfirearms.com**
Accuracy Int'l North America **www.accuracyinternational.com**
Adcor Defense **www.adcorindustries.com**
AGP Arms In. **www.agparms.com**
AIM **www.aimsurplus.com**
AirForce Airguns **www.airforceairguns.com**
Air Gun Inc. **www.airrifle-china.com**

Air Ordnance/Tippmann Armory **www.tippmannarmory.com**

Airguns of Arizona **www.airgunsofarizona.com**

Alexander Arms **www.alexanderarms.com**

America Remembers **www.americaremembers.com**

American Airsoft Factory **www.americanairsoftfactory.com**

American Classic **www.americanclassic1911.com**

American Derringer Corp. **www.amderringer.com**

American Rifle Co. **www.americanrifle.com**

American Spirit Arms **www.americanspirtarms.com**

American Tactical Imports **www.americantactical.us**

American Classic **www.eagleimportsinc.com**

American Western Arms **www.awaguns.com**

Angstadt Arms **www.angstadtarms.com**

Anschutz **www.anschutz-sporters.com**

AR-7 Industries **www.ar-7.com**

Ares Defense Systems **www.aresdefense.com**

Armalite **www.armalite.com**

Armi Sport **www.armisport.com**

Armscor Precision Internationl **www.armscor.com**

Armscorp USA Inc. **www.armscorpusa.com**

Arrieta **www.arrietashotguns.com**

Arsenal Inc. **www.arsenalinc.com**

Atlanta Cutlery Corp. **www.atlantacutlery.com**

Atlas Gun Works **www.atlas-gunworks.com**

ATA Arms **www.ataarms.com**

Auto-Ordnance Corp. **www.tommygun.com**

AYA **www.aya-fineguns.com**

B&T (USA) **www.bt-ag.ch**

Ballard Rifles **www.ballardrifles.com**

Barrett Firearms Mfg. **www.barrettrifles.com**

Bat Machine Co. **www.batmachine.com**

Battle Arms Development **www.battlearmsdevelopment.com**

Bear Creek Arsenal **www.bearcreekarsenal.com**

Beeman Precision Airguns **www.beeman.com**

Benelli USA Corp. **www.benelliusa.com**

Benjamin Sheridan **www.crosman.com**

Beretta U.S.A. **www.berettausa.com**

Bergara Rifles **www.bergararifles.com**

Bernardelli **www.bernardelli.com**

Bersa **www.bersa.com**

Bighorn Arms **www.bighornarms.com**

Big Horn Armory **www.bighornarmory.com**

Bishop Ammunition and Firearms. **www.bishopammunition.com**

Blaser Jagdwaffen Gmbh **www.blaser.de**

Bleiker **www.bleiker.ch**

Bond Arms **www.bondarms.com**

Borden Rifles, Inc. **www.bordenrifles.com**

Boss & Co. **www.bossguns.co.uk**

Bowen Classic Arms **www.bowenclassicarms.com**

Breda **www.bredafucili.com**

Briley Mfg. **www.briley.com**

BRNO Arms **www.cz-usa.com**

Brown, E. Arthur **www.eabco.com**

Brown, Ed Products **www.edbrown.com**

Brown, McKay **www.mckaybrown.com**

Browning **www.browning.com**

BRP Corp. **www.brpguns.com**

BUL Ltd. **www.bultransmark.com**

Bushmaster Firearms **www.bushmaster.com**

BWE Firearms **www.bwefirearms.com**

Cabot Guns **www.cabotguns.com**

Caesar Guerini USA **www.gueriniusa.com**

Calico **www.calicoweaponsystems.com**

Caracal **www.caracal-usa.com**

Carolina Arms Group **www.carolinaarmsgroup.com**

Caspian Arms, Ltd. **www.caspianarmsltd.com**

CDNN Sports **www.cdnnsports.com**

Century Arms **www.centuryarms.com**

Champlin Firearms **www.champlinarms.com**

Charles Daly **www.charlesdaly.com**

Charter Arms **www.charterfirearms.com**

CheyTac USA **www.cheytac.com**

Chiappa Firearms **www.chiappafirearms.com**

Christensen Arms **www.christensenarms.com**

Cimarron Firearms Co. **www.cimarron-firearms.com**

CK Arms/Freedom Gunworks **www.ckarms.com**

Clark Custom Guns **www.clarkcustomguns.com**

CMMG **www.cmmginc.com**

Cobalt Kinetics **www.cobaltarms.com**

Cobra Enterprises **www.cobrapistols.net**

Cogswell & Harrison **www.cogswellandharrison.com**

Collector's Armory, Ltd. **www.collectorsarmory.com**

Colt's Mfg Co. **www.colt.com**

Comanche **www.eagleimportsinc.com**

Connecticut Shotgun Mfg. Co. **www.connecticutshotgun.com**

Connecticut Valley Arms **www.cva.com**

Coonan, Inc. **www.coonaninc.com**

Cooper Firearms **www.cooperfirearms.com**

Core Rifle Systems **www.core15.com**

Corner Shot **www.cornershot.com**

CPA Rifles **www.singleshotrifles.com**

Crickett Rifles **www.crickett.com**

Crosman **www.crosman.com**

CVA **www.cva.com**

Cylinder & Slide Shop **www.cylinder-slide.com**

Czechp Int'l **www.czechpoint-usa.com**

CZ USA **www.cz-usa.com**

Daisy Mfg Co. **www.daisy.com**

Daniel Defense **www.danieldefense.com**

Dan Wesson **www.danwessonfirearms.com**

Dakota Arms Inc. **www.dakotaarms.com**

Davidsons **www.davidsonsinc.com**

Desert Eagle **www.magnumresearch.com**
Detonics USA **www.detonicsdefense.com**
Devil Dog Arms **www.devildogarms.com**
Diamondback **www.diamondbackamerica.com**
Diana **www.diana-airguns.de**
Dixie Gun Works **www.dixiegunworks.com**
Double D Armory **www.ddarmory.com**
DoubleStar **www.star15.co**
Downsizer Corp. **www.downsizer.com**
DPMS, Inc. **www.dpmsinc.com**
DSA Inc. **www.dsarms.com**
Dumoulin **www.dumoulin-herstal.com**
EAA Corp. **www.eaacorp.com**
Eagle Imports, Inc. **www.eagleimportsinc.com**
Ed Brown Products **www.edbrown.com**
EMF Co. **www.emf-company.com**
Empty Shell **www.emptyshell.com**
EMTAN **www.emtan.co.il**
E.R. Shaw **www.ershawbarrels.com**
European American Armory Corp. **www.eaacorp.com**
Evans, William **www.williamevans.com**
Excel Arms **www.excelarms.com**
F-1 Firearms **www.f-1firearms.com**
Fabarm **www.fabarm.com**
Fausti USA **www.faustiusa.com**
FightLite Industries **www.fightlite.com**
Flint River Armory **www.flintriverarmory.com**
Flodman Guns **www.flodman.com**
FMK **www.fmkfirearms.com**
FN Herstal **www.fnherstal.com**
FN America **www.fnamerica.com**
FNH USA **www.fnhusa.com**
Franchi **www.franchiusa.com**
Franklin Armory **www.franklinarmory.com**
Freedom Arms **www.freedomarms.com**
Freedom Group, Inc. **www.freedom-group.com**
Galazan **www.connecticutshotgun.com**
Gambo Renato **www.renatogamba.it**
Gamo **www.gamo.com**
Gary Reeder Custom Guns **www.reedercustomguns.com**
German Sport Guns **www.german-sport-guns.com**
Gibbs Rifle Company **www.gibbsrifle.com**
Girsan Firearms **www.girsan.com.tr/en**
Glock **www.glock.com**
Griffin & Howe **www.griffinhowe.com**
Gunbroker.com **www.gunbroker.com**
Guncrafter Industries **www.guncrafterindustries.com**
Gun Room Co. **www.onlylongrange.com**
Hammerli **www.carl-walther.com**
Harpers Ferry Armory **www.harpersferryarmory.com**
Hardened Arms **www.hardenedarms.com**

Hatsan USA **www.hatsanUSA.com**
Heckler and Koch **www.hk-usa.com**
Heizer Defense **www.heizerdefense.com**
Henry Repeating Arms Co. **www.henryrepeating.com**
Heritage Mfg. **www.heritagemfg.com**
High Standard Mfg. **www.highstandard.com**
Hi-Point Firearms **www.hi-pointfirearms.com**
Holland & Holland **www.hollandandholland.com**
Honor Defense **www.honordefense.com**
Horizon Firearms **www.horizonfirearms.com**
Howa **www.howausa.com**
H&R 1871 Firearms **www.hr1871.com**
H-S Precision **www.hsprecision.com**
Hunters Lodge Corp. **www.hunterslodge.com**
Hudson Manufacturing **www.hudsonmfg.com**
Inland Arms **www.inland-mfg.com**
International Military Antiques, Inc. **www.ima-usa.com**
Inter Ordnance **www.interordnance.com**
ISSC, LLC **www.issc-austria.com**
Ithaca Gun Co. **www.ithacagun.com**
Iver Johnson Arms **www.iverjohnsonarms.com**
IWI US Inc. **www.iwi.us**
Izhevsky Mekhanichesky Zavod **www.baikalinc.ru**
James River Armory **www.jamesriverarmory.com**
Jarrett Rifles, Inc. **www.jarrettrifles.com**
Jesse James Firearms **www.jjfu.com**
J&G Sales, Ltd. **www.jgsales.com**
Johannsen Express Rifle **www.johannsen-jagd.de**
JP Enterprises, Inc. **www.jprifles.com**
Kahr Arms/Auto-Ordnance **www.kahr.com**
Kalashnikov USA **www.kalashnikov-usa.com**
KDF, Inc. **www.kdfguns.com**
KE Arms **www.kearms.com**
Keystone Sporting Arms **www.keystonesportingarmsllc.com**
Kifaru **www.kifaru.net**
Kimber **www.kimberamerica.com**
Kingston Armory **www.kingstonarmory.com**
Knight's Armament Co. **www.knightarmco.com**
Knight Rifles **www.knightrifles.com**
Kodiak Defence **www.kodiakdefence.com**
Kolar **www.kolararms.com**
Korth **www.korthwaffen.de**
Krebs Custom Guns **www.krebscustom.com**
Krieghoff Int'l **www.krieghoff.com**
Kriss **www.kriss-usa.com**
KY Imports, Inc. **www.kyimports.com**
K-VAR **www.k-var.com**
Larue **www.laruetactical.com**
Layke Tactical **www.layketactical.com**
Lazzeroni Arms Co. **www.lazzeroni.com**
Legacy Sports International **www.legacysports.com**

Legendary Arms Works **www.legendaryarmsworks.com**
Les Baer Custom, Inc. **www.lesbaer.com**
Lewis Machine & Tool Co. **www.lewismachine.net**
Linebaugh Custom Sixguns **www.customsixguns.com**
Lionheart **www.lionheartindustries.com**
Lipsey's **www.lipseys.com**
Ljutic **www.ljuticgun.com**
Llama **www.eagleimportsinc.com**
LMT Defense **www.lmtdefense.com**
Lone Star Armory **www.lonestararmory.us**
Longthorne Gunmakers **www.longthorneguns.com**
LRB Arms **www.lrbarms.com**
Lyman **www.lymanproducts.com**
LWRC Int'l **www.lwrci.com**
MAC **www.eagleimportsinc.com**
Magnum Research **www.magnumresearch.com**
Majestic Arms **www.majesticarms.com**
Marksman Products **www.marksman.com**
Marlin **www.marlinfirearms.com**
MasterPiece Arms **www.masterpiecearms.com**
Mauser **www.mauser.com**
McMillan Firearms **www.mcmillanfirearms.com**
Meacham Rifles **www.meachamrifles.com**
Mean Arms **www.meanarms.com**
Merkel USA **www-die-jagd.de**
Metro Arms **www.metroarms.com**
Midland Arms **www.shootmidland.com**
Midwest Industries **www.midwestindustriesinc.com**
Milkor USA **www.milkorusainc.com**
Miltech **www.miltecharms.com**
MOA Maximum **www.moaguns.com**
MOA Precision **www.moaprecision.com**
Modern Weapon Systems **www.modernweaponsystems.com**
Molot Oruzhie **www.fimegroup.com**
Montana Rifle Co. **www.montanarifleco.com**
Mossberg **www.mossberg.com**
MSR Distribution Co. **www.msrdistribution.com**
Navy Arms **www.navyarms.com**
Nemo Arms **www.nemoarms.com**
New England Arms Corp. **www.newenglandarms.com**
New England Custom Gun **www.newenglandcustomgun.com**
New Ultra Light Arms **www.newultralight.com**
Nighthawk Custom **www.nighthawkcustom.com**
North American Arms **www.northamericanarms.com**
Nosler **www.nosler.com**
O.F. Mossberg & Sons **www.mossberg.com**
Ohio Ordnance Works **www.ohioordnanceworks.com**
Olympic Arms **www.olyarms.com**
Osprey Defense **www.gaspiston.com**
Panther Arms **www.dpmsinc.com**
Pedersoli Davide & Co. **www.davide-pedersoli.com**

Perazzi **www.perazzi.com**
Pietta **www.pietta.it**
Piotti **www.piotti.com/en**
Pistol Dynamics **www.pistoldynamics.com**
PKP Knife-Pistol **www.sanjuanenterprise.com**
Power Custom **www.powercustom.com**
Precision Firearms **www.precisionfirearms.com**
Precision Global Arms **www.precisionglobalarms.com**
Precision Small Arm Inc. **www.precisionsmallarms.com**
Primary Weapons Systems **www.primaryweapons.com**
Proof Research **www.proofresearch.com**
PTR 91, Inc. **www.ptr91.com**
Purdey & Sons **www.purdey.com**
Pyramyd Air **www.pyramydair.com**
Quarter Minute Magnums **www.quarterminutemagnums.com**
Radian Weapons **www.radianweapons.com**
Radical Firearms **www.radicalfirearms.com**
Remington **www.remington.com**
Republic Forge **www.republicforge.com**
Rifles Inc. **www.riflesinc.com**
Rigby **www.johnrigbyandco.co**
Ritter & Stark **www.ritterstark.com**
Riverman Gun Works **www.rivermangunworks.com**
Rizzini USA **www.rizziniusa.com**
RM Equipment, Inc. **www.40mm.com**
Robar Companies, Inc. **www.robarguns.com**
Roberts Defense **www.robertsdefense.com**
Robinson Armament Co. **www.robarm.com**
Rock Island Armory **www.armscor.com**
Rock River Arms, Inc. **www.rockriverarms.com**
Rossi Arms **www.rossiusa.com**
RUAG Ammotec **www.ruag.com**
Ruger **www.ruger.com**
Sabatti SPA **www.sabatti.it**
Safety Harbor Firearms **www.safetyharborfirearms.com**
Sarco **www.sarcoinc.com**
Sarsilmaz Silah San **www.sarsilmaz.com**
Sauer & Sohn **www.sauer.de**
Savage Arms Inc. **www.savagearms.com**
Scattergun Technologies Inc. **www.wilsoncombat.com**
SCCY Firearms **www.sccy.com**
Schmeisser Gmbh **www.schmeisser-germany.de**
SD Tactical Arms **www.sdtacticalarms.com**
Searcy Enterprises **www.searcyent.com**
Seecamp **www.seecamp.com**
Shadow Systems **www.shadowsystemscorp.com**
Shaw Barrels **www.ershawbarrels.com**
Shilen Rifles **www.shilen.com**
Shiloh Rifle Mfg. **www.shilohrifle.com**
Sig Sauer, Inc. **www.sigsauer.com**
Simpson Ltd. **www.simpsonltd.com**

SKB Shotguns **www.skbshotguns.com**
Smith & Wesson **www.smith-wesson.com**
Snowy Mountain Rifles **www.snowymountainrifles.com**
Southeast Arms, Inc. **www.southeastarms.ne**
Sovereign Shotguns **www.barrettrifles.com**
Springfield Armory **www.springfield-armory.com**
SPS **www.eagleimportsinc.com**
SSK Industries **www.sskindustries.com**
Stag Arms **www.stagarms.com**
Stevens **www.savagearms.com**
Steyr Arms, Inc. **www.steyrarms.com**
STI International **www.stiguns.com**
Stoeger Industries **www.stoegerindustries.com**
Strayer-Voigt Inc. **www.sviguns.com**
Sturm, Ruger & Company **www.ruger.com**
Surgeon Rifles **www.surgeonrifles.com**
Tactical Solutions **www.tacticalsol.com**
Tanfoglio Fratelli SNC **www.tanfoglio.it**
Tar-Hunt Slug Guns, Inc. **www.tarhunt.com**
Taser Int'l **www.taser.com**
Taurus **www.taurususa.com**
Taylor's Firearms **www.taylorsfirearms.com**
Tempco Mfg. Co. **www.tempcomfg.com**
Thompson/Center Arms **www.tcarms.com**
Tikka **www.tikka.fi**
Time Precision **www.benchrest.com/timeprecision**
Tippman Arms **www.tippmann.com**
TNW, Inc. **www.tnwfirearms.com**
Traditions **www.traditionsfirearms.com**
Tristar Sporting Arms **www.tristarsportingarms.com**
Turnbull Mfg. Co. **www.turnbullmfg.com**
Uberti **www.ubertireplicas.com**
Ultra Light Arms **www.newultralight.com**
Umarex **www.umarex.com**
U.S. Armament Corp. **www.usarmamentcorp.com**
Uselton Arms, Inc. **www.useltonarmsinc.com**
Valkyrie Arms **www.valkyriearms.com**
Vektor Arms **www.vektorarms.com**
Verney-Carron **www.verney-carron.com**
Volquartsen Custom Ltd. **www.volquartsen.com**
Warrior **www.warrior.co**
Walther Arms **www.waltherarms.com**
Weapon Depot **www.weapondepot.com**
Weatherby **www.weatherby.com**
Webley and Scott Ltd. **www.webley.co.uk**
Westley Richards **www.westleyrichards.com**
Wild West Guns **www.wildwestguns.com**
William Larkin Moore & Co. **www.williamlarkinmoore.com**
Wilson Combat **www.wilsoncombat.com**
Winchester Rifles and Shotguns **www.winchesterguns.com**
Zastava Arms **www.zastavaarmsusa.com**

GUN PARTS, BARRELS, AFTERMARKET ACCESSORIES

100 Straight Products **www.100straight.com**
300 Below **www.300below.com**
Accuracy International of North America
www.accuracyinternational.us
Accuracy Speaks, Inc. **www.accuracyspeaks.com**
Accuracy Systems **www.accuracysystemsinc.com**
Accurate Airguns **www.accurateairguns.com**
Advantage Arms **www.advantagearms.com**
AG Composites **www.agcomposites.com**
Aim Surplus **www.aimsurplus.com**
American Spirit Arms Corp. **www.americanspiritarms.com**
Amhurst-Depot **www.amherst-depot.com**
Apex Gun Parts **www.apexgunparts.com**
Armaspec **www.armaspec.com**
Armatac Industries **www.armatac.com**
Arthur Brown Co. **www.eabco.com**
Asia Sourcing Corp. **www.asiasourcing.com**
Barnes Precision Machine **www.barnesprecision.com**
Bar-Sto Precision Machine **www.barsto.com**
Bellm TC's **www.bellmtcs.com**
Belt Mountain Enterprises **www.beltmountain.com**
Bergara Barrels **www.bergarabarrels.com**
Beyer Barrels **www.beyerbarrels.com**
Bighorn Arms **www.bighornarms.com**
Bill Wiseman & Co. **www.wisemanballistics.com**
Bluegrass Gun Works **www.rocksolidind.com**
Bravo Company USA **www.bravocompanyusa.com**
Briley **www.briley.com**
Brownells **www.brownells.com**
B-Square **www.b-square.com**
Buffer Tech **www.buffer-tech.com**
Bullberry Barrel Works **www.bullberry.com**
Bulldog Barrels **www.bulldogbarrels.com**
Bullet Central **www.bulletcentral.com**
Bushmaster Firearms/Quality Parts **www.bushmaster.com**
Butler Creek Corp **www.butlercreek.com**
Cape Outfitters Inc. **www.capeoutfitters.com**
Cavalry Arms **www.cavalryarms.com**
Caspian Arms Ltd. **www.caspianarms.com**
CDNN Sports **www.cdnnsports.com**
Cheaper Than Dirt **www.cheaperthandirt.com**
Chesnut Ridge **www.chestnutridge.com/**
Choate Machine & Tool Co. **www.riflestock.com**
Christie's Products **www.1022cental.com**
CJ Weapons Accessories **www.cjweapons.com**
Colonial Arms **www.colonialarms.com**
Comp-N-Choke **www.comp-n-choke.com**
Criterion Barrels **www.criterionbarrels.com**

Custom Gun Rails **www.customgunrails.com**
Cylinder & Slide Shop **www.cylinder-slide.com**
Dave Manson Precision Reamers **www.mansonreamers.com**
DC Machine **www.dcmachine.net**
DTF Industries **www.dtfindustries.com**
Digi-Twist **www.fmtcorp.com**
Dixie Gun Works **www.dixiegun.com**
DPMS **www.dpmsinc.com**
D.S. Arms **www.dsarms.com**
E. Arthur Brown Co. **www.eabco.com**
Ed Brown Products **www.edbrown.com**
EFK/Fire Dragon **www.efkfiredragon.com**
E.R. Shaw **www.ershawbarrels.com**
FJ Fedderson Rifle Barrels **www.gunbarrels.net**
FTF Industries **www.ftfindustries.com**
Fulton Armory **www.fulton-armory.com**
Galazan **www.connecticutshotgun.com**
Gemtech **www.gem-tech.com**
Gentry, David **www.gentrycustom.com**
GG&G **www.gggaz.com**
Great Lakes Tactical **www.gltactical.com**
Green Mountain Rifle Barrels **www.gmriflebarrel.com**
Gun Parts Corp. **www.gunpartscorp.com**
Guntec USA **www.guntecusa.com**
Harris Engineering **www.harrisbipods.com**
Hart Rifle Barrels **www.hartbarrels.com**
Hastings Barrels **www.hastingsbarrels.com**
Heinie Specialty Products **www.heinie.com**
High Performance Firearms/Hiperfire **www.hiperfire.com**
HKS Products **www.hksspeedloaders.com**
Holland Shooters Supply **www.hollandguns.com**
H-S Precision **www.hsprecision.com**
Horizon Firearms **www. iotaoutdoors.com**
I.M.A. **www.ima-usa.com**
International Barrels **www.internationbarrels.com**
Iron City Rifle Works **www.ironcityrifle.com**
Jarvis, Inc. **www.jarvis-custom.com**
J&T Distributing **www.jtdistributing.com**
JP Enterprises **www.jprifles.com**
Keng's Firearms Specialties **www.versapod.com**
KCI USA **www.kcius.com**
KFS Industries **www.kfsindustries.com**
KG Industries **www.kgcoatings.com**
Kick Eez **www.kickeezproducts.com**
Kidd Triggers **www.coolguyguns.com**
Kinetic Development **www.keneticdg.com**
KM Tactical **www.kmtactical.net**
Knoxx Industries **www.impactguns.com**
Krieger Barrels **www.kriegerbarrels.com**
K-VAR Corp. **www.k-var.com**
LaRue Tactical **www.laruetactical.com**

Les Baer Custom, Inc. **www.lesbaer.com**
Lilja Barrels **www.riflebarrels.com**
Lone Wolf Dist. **www.lonewolfdist.com**
Lothar Walther Precision Tools **www.lothar-walther.com**
M&A Parts, Inc. **www.mapartsinc.com**
Magna-Matic Defense **www.magna-matic-defense.com**
Magpul Industries Corp. **www.magpul.com**
Majestic Arms **www.majesticarms.com**
MarColMar Firearms **www.marcolmarfirearms.com**
MEC-GAR USA **www.mec-gar.com**
Mech Tech Systems **www.mechtechsys.com**
Mesa Tactical **www.mesatactical.com**
Midway USA **www.midwayusa.com**
Model 1 Sales **www.model1sales.com**
New England Custom Gun Service
        www.newenglandcustomgun.com
NIC Industries **www.nicindustries.com**
North Mfg. Co. **www.rifle-barrels.com**
Numrich Gun Parts Corp. **www.e-gunparts.com**
Osprey Defense LLC **www.gaspiston.com**
Pac-Nor Barrels **www.pac-nor.com**
Power Custom, Inc. **www.powercustom.com**
Precision Reflex **www.pri-mounts.com**
Promag Industries **www.promagindustries.com**
RCI-XRAIL **www.xrailbyrci.com**
Red Star Arms **www.redstararms.com**
River Bank Armory **www.riverbankarmory.com**
Riverman Gun Works **www.rivermangunworks.com**
Rock Creek Barrels **www.rockcreekbarrels.com**
Royal Arms Int'l **www.royalarms.com**
R.W. Hart **www.rwhart.com**
Sage Control Ordnance **www.sageinternationalltd.com**
Sarco Inc. **www.sarcoinc.com**
Scattergun Technologies Inc. **www.wilsoncombat.com**
Schuemann Barrels **www.schuemann.com**
Score High Gunsmithing **www.scorehi.com**
Shaw Barrels **www.ershawbarrels.com**
Shilen **www.shilen.com**
SIG Sauer **www.sigsauer.com**
SilencerCo **www.silencerco.com**
Sims Vibration Laboratory **www.limbsaver.com**
Smith & Alexander Inc. **www.smithandalexander.com**
Sprinco USA **www.sprinco.com**
Springfield Sporters, Inc. **www.ssporters.com**
STI Int'l **www.stiguns.com**
Stiller Actions **www.stilleractions.com**
S&S Firearms **www.ssfirearms.com**
SSK Industries **www.sskindustries.com**
Sun Devil Mfg. **www.sundevilmfg.com**
Sunny Hill Enterprises **www.sunny-hill.com**
Tac Star **www.lymanproducts.com**

Tactical Innovations **www.tacticalinc.com**
Tactical Solutions **www.tacticalsol.com**
Tapco **www.tapco.com**
Triple K Manufacturing Co. Inc. **www.triplek.com**
Uintah Precision **www.uintahprecision.com**
Ultimak **www.ultimak.com**
Verney-Carron SA **www.verney-carron.com**
Vintage Ordnance **www.vintageordnance.com**
Vltor Weapon Systems **www.vltor.com**
Volquartsen Custom Ltd. **www.volquartsen.com**
W.C. Wolff Co. **www.gunsprings.com**
Weigand Combat Handguns **www.jackweigand.com**
Western Gun Parts **www.westerngunparts.com**
Wilson Arms **www.wilsonarms.com**
Wilson Combat **www.wilsoncombat.com**
WMD Guns **www.wmdguns.com**
XLR Industries **www.xlrindustries.com**
Xtreme Precision **www.ar15xtreme.com**

GUNSMITHING SUPPLIES AND INSTRUCTION

4-D Products **www.4-dproducts.com**
American Gunsmithing Institute **www.americangunsmith.com**
Baron Technology **www.baronengraving.com**
Battenfeld Technologies **www.btibrands.com**
Bellm TC's **www.bellmtcs.com**
Blue Ridge Machinery & Tools **www.blueridgemachinery.com**
Brownells, Inc. **www.brownells.com**
B-Square Co. **www.b-square.com**
Cerakote Firearm Coatings **www.ncindustries.com**
Clymer Mfg. Co. **www.clymertool.com**
Dem-Bart **www.dembartco.com**
Doug Turnbull Restoration **www.turnbullrestoration.com**
Du-Lite Corp. **www.dulite.com**
DuraCoat Firearm Finishes **www.lauerweaponry.com**
Dvorak Instruments **www.dvorakinstruments.com**
Gradiant Lens Corp. **www.gradientlens.com**
Grizzly Industrial **www.grizzly.com**
Gunline Tools **www.gunline.com**
Harbor Freight **www.harborfreight.com**
JGS Precision Tool Mfg. LLC **www.jgstools.com**
JME Innovations **www.jmeinnovations.com**
Mag-Na-Port International **www.magnaport.com**
Manson Precision Reamers **www.mansonreamers.com**
Midway USA **www.midwayusa.com**
Murray State College **www.mscok.edu**
New England Custom Gun Service
        www.newenglandcustomgun.com
Olympus America Inc. **www.olympus.com**
Pacific Tool & Gauge **www.pacifictoolandgauge.com**

Penn Foster Career School **www.pennfoster.edu**
Pennsylvania Gunsmith School **www.pagunsmith.edu**
Piedmont Community College **www.piedmontcc.edu**
Precision Metalsmiths, Inc. **www.precisionmetalsmiths.com**
Sonoran Desert Institute **www.sdi.edu**
Trinidad State Junior College **www.trinidadstate.edu**
Wright Armory **www.wrightarmory.com**

HANDGUN GRIPS

Ajax Custom Grips, Inc. **www.ajaxgrips.com**
Altamont Co. **www.altamontco.com**
Aluma Grips **www.alumagrips.com**
Barami Corp. **www.hipgrip.com**
Crimson Trace Corp. **www.crimsontrace.com**
Decal Grip **www.decalgrip.com**
Eagle Grips **www.eaglegrips.com**
Falcon Industries **www.ergogrips.net**
Handgun Grips **www.handgungrips.com**
Herrett's Stocks **www.herrettstocks.com**
Hogue Grips **www.hogueinc.com**
Kirk Ratajesak **www.kgratajesak.com**
N.C. Ordnance **www.gungrip.com**
Nill-Grips USA **www.nill-grips.com**
Pachmayr **www.pachmayr.com**
Pearce Grips **www.pearcegrip.com**
Rio Grande Custom Grips **www.riograndecustomgrips.com**
Talon Grips **www.talongrips.com**
Uncle Mike's **www.unclemikes.com**

HOLSTERS AND LEATHER PRODUCTS

Active Pro Gear **www.activeprogear.com**
Akah **www.akah.de**
Aker Leather Products **www.akerleather.com**
Alessi Distributor R&F Inc. **www.alessigunholsters.com**
Alien Gear Holsters **www.aliengearholsters.com**
Armor Holdings **www.holsters.com**
Bagmaster **www.bagmaster.com**
Barranti Leather **www.barrantileather.com**
Bianchi International **www.safariland.com/our-brands/bianchi**
Black Dog Machine **www.blackdogmachinellc.net**
Blackhawk Outdoors **www.blackhawk.com**
Blackhills Leather **www.blackhillsleather.com**
Boyt Harness Co. **www.boytharness.com**
Bravo Concealment **www.bravoconcealment.com**
Brigade Gun Leather **www.brigadegunleather.com**
C&G Holsters **www.candgholsters.com**
Clipdraw **www.clipdraw.com**
Comp-Tac Victory Gear **www.comp-tac.com**
Concealed Carrie **www.concealedcarrie.com**

Concealment Shop Inc. **www.theconcealmentshop.com**
Coronado Leather Co. **www.coronadoleather.com**
Creedmoor Sports, Inc. **www.creedmoorsports.com**
Cross Breed Holsters **www.crossbreedholsters.com**
Deep Conceal **www.deepconceal.com**
Defense Security Products **www.thunderwear.com**
Dene Adams **www.deneadams.com**
DeSantis Holster **www.desantisholster.com**
Dillon Precision **www.dillonprecision.com**
Don Hume Leathergoods, Inc. **www.donhume.com**
DSG Holsters **www.dssgarms.com**
Duty Smith **www.dutysmith.com**
Elite Survival **www.elitesurvival.com**
El Paso Saddlery **www.epsaddlery.com**
Fobus USA **www.fobusholster.com**
Frontier Gun Leather **www.frontiergunleather.com**
Galco **www.usgalco.com**
Gilmore's Sports Concepts **www.gilmoresports.com**
Gould & Goodrich **www.gouldusa.com**
GS Holsters **www.gsholsters.com**
High Noon Holsters **www.highnoonholsters.com**
High Threat Concealment **www.highthreatconcealmcnt.com**
Holsters.com **www.holsters.com**
Houston Gun Holsters **www.houstongunholsters.com**
Hunter Co. **www.huntercompany.com**
JBP/Master's Holsters **www.jbpholsters.com**
Just Holster It **www.justholsterit.com**
KJ Leather **www.kbarjleather.com**
KNJ **www.knjmfg.com**
Kramer Leather **www.kramerleather.com**
K-Rounds Holsters **www.krounds.com**
Lady Conceal Purses **www.itsinthebagboutique.com**
L.A.G. Tactical **www.lagtactical.com**
Master's Holsters **www.holsterama.com**
Mernickle Holsters **www.mernickleholsters.com**
Milt Sparks Leather **www.miltsparks.com**
Miss Concealed **www.missconcealed.com**
Mitch Rosen Extraordinary Gunleather **www.mitchrosen.com**
N82 Tactical **www.n82tactical.com**
Pacific Canvas & Leather Co.
　　　　www.pacificcanvasandleather.com
Pager Pal **www.pagerpal.com**
Phalanx Corp. **www.smartholster.com**
Purdy Gear **www.purdygear.com**
Safariland Ltd. Inc. **www.safariland.com**
Shooting Systems Group Inc. **www.shootingsystems.com**
Sneaky Pete Holsters **www.sneakypete.com**
Skyline Tool Works **www.clipdraw.com**
Stellar Rigs **www.stellarrigs.com**
Talon Holsters **www.talonholsters.com**
Tex Shoemaker & Sons **www.texshoemaker.com**

The Outdoor Connection **www.outdoorconnection.com**
Tuff Products **www.tuffproducts.com**
Triple K Manufacturing Co. **www.triplek.com**
Urban Carry Holsters **www.urbancarryholsters.com**
Wilson Combat **www.wilsoncombat.com**
Wright Leatherworks **www.wrightleatherworks.com**

MISCELLANEOUS SHOOTING PRODUCTS

10-24 Products **www.10-24products.com**
3TS **www.3TS.us**
ADCO Sales **www.adcosales.com**
ADL Training Solutions **www.adlsmartshooting.com**
American Body Armor **www.americanbodyarmor.com**
American Speedloaders **www.americanspeedloaders.com**
AMI Defense **www.amidefense.com**
Ammo-Up **www.ammoupusa.com**
Angel Armor **www.angelarmor.com**
Armor Advantage **www.armoradvantage.com**
Azimuth Technology **www.azimuthtechnology.com**
Battenfeld Technologies **www.btibrands.com**
Beartooth **www.beartoothproducts.com**
Burnham Brothers **www.burnhambrothers.com**
Collectors Armory **www.collectorsarmory.com**
Dead Ringer Hunting **www.deadringerhunting.com**
Deben Group Industries Inc. **www.deben.com**
E.A.R., Inc. **www.earinc.com**
ESP **www.espamerica.com**
Global Gun Safety **www.globalgunsafety.com**
GSM Outdoors **www.gsmoutdoors.com**
GunSkins **www.gunskins.com**
Gunstands **www.gunstands.com**
Horizon Firearms **www.iotaoutdoors.com**
Howard Leight Hearing Protectors **www.howardleight.com**
Hunters Specialities **www.hunterspec.com**
Johnny Stewart Wildlife Calls **www.hunterspec.com**
Joseph Chiarello Gun Insurance **www.guninsurance.com**
Mec-Gar USA **www.mec-gar.com**
Merit Corporation **www.meritcorporation.com**
Michaels of Oregon Co. **www.michaels-oregon.com**
Midway USA **www.midwayusa.com**
MT2, LLC **www.mt2.com**
MTM Case-Gard **www.mtmcase-gard.com**
Natchez Shooters Supplies **www.natchezss.com**
Oakley, Inc. **www.usstandardissue.com**
Outdoor Connection **www.outdoorconnection.com**
Peregrine Outdoor Products **www.perregrinefieldgear.com**
Plano Molding **www.planomolding.com**
Practical Air Rifle Training Systems **www.smallarms.com**
Pro-Ears **www.pro-ears.com**
Quantico Tactical **www.quanticotactical.com**

Santa Cruz Gunlocks **www.santacruzgunlocks.com**
Sergeants Gun Cleaner **www.sergeantsguncleaner.com**
Second Chance Body Armor Inc. **www.secondchance.com**
SilencerCo **www.silencerco.com**
Smart Lock Technologies **www.smartlock.com**
SportEAR **www.sportear.com**
Surefire **www.surefire.com**
Taser Int'l **www.taser.com**
THRiL **www.thrilusa.com**
UniqueTek, Inc. **www.uniquetek.com**
Walker's Game Ear Inc. **www.walkersgameear.com**

MUZZLELOADING FIREARMS AND PRODUCTS

American Pioneer Powder **www.americanpioneerpowder.com**
Armi Sport **www.armisport.com**
Barnes Bullets **www.barnesbullets.com**
Black Powder Products **www.bpiguns.com**
Buckeye Barrels **www.buckeyebarrels.com**
Cabin Creek Muzzleloading **www.cabincreek.net**
CVA **www.cva.com**
Caywood Gunmakers **www.caywoodguns.com**
Davide Perdsoli & Co. **www.davide-pedersoli.com**
Dixie Gun Works, Inc. **www.dixiegun.com**
Goex Black Powder **www.goexpowder.com**
Green Mountain Rifle Barrel Co. **www.gmriflebarrel.com**
Gunstocks Plus **www.gunstocksplus.com**
Gun Works **www.thegunworks.com**
Honorable Company of Horners **www.hornguild.org**
Hornady **www.hornady.com**
Jedediah Starr Trading Co. **www.jedediah-starr.com**
Jim Chambers Flintlocks **www.flintlocks.com**
Knight Rifles **www.knightrifles.com**
Knob Mountain **www.knobmountainmuzzleloading.com**
The Leatherman **www.blackpowderbags.com**
Log Cabin Shop **www.logcabinshop.com**
L&R Lock Co. **www.lr-rpl.com**
Lyman **www.lymanproducts.com**
Muzzleload Magnum Products **www.mmpsabots.com**
Navy Arms **www.navyarms.com**
Nosler, Inc. **www.nosler.com**
Palmetto Arms **www.palmetto.it**
Pecatonica River **www.longrifles-pr.com**
Pietta **www.pietta.it**
Powerbelt Bullets **www.powerbeltbullets.com**
Precision Rifle Dead Center Bullets **www.prbullet.com**
R.E. Davis Co. **www.redaviscompany.com**
Rightnour Mfg. Co. Inc. **www.rmcsports.com**
Savage Arms, Inc. **www.savagearms.com**
Schuetzen Powder **www.schuetzenpowder.com**

TDC **www.tdcmfg.com**
Tennessee Valley Muzzleloading
      www.tennessevalleymuzzleloading.com
Thompson Center Arms **www.tcarms.com**
Tiger Hunt Stocks **www.gunstockwood.com**
Track of the Wolf **www.trackofthewolf.com**
Traditions Performance Muzzleloading
      www.traditionsfirearms. com
Turnbull Restoration & Mfg. **www.turnbullmfg.com**
Vernon C. Davis & Co. **www.stonewallcreekoutfitters.com**

PUBLICATIONS, VIDEOS AND CDs

Arms and Military Press **www.skennerton.com**
A&J Arms Booksellers **www.ajarmsbooksellers.com**
American Cop **www.americancopmagazine.com**
American Gunsmithing Institute **www.americangunsmith.com**
American Handgunner **www.americanhandgunner.com**
American Hunter **www.nrapublications.org**
American Pioneer Video **www.americanpioneervideo.com**
American Rifleman **www.nrapublications.org**
Athlon Outdoors **www.athlonoptics.com**
Backwoodsman **www.backwoodsmanmag.com**
Blue Book Publications **www.bluebookinc.com**
Combat Handguns **www.combathandguns.com**
Concealed Carry **www.uscca.us**
Cornell Publications **www.cornellpubs.com**
Deer & Deer Hunting **www.deeranddeerhunting.com**
Field & Stream **www.fieldandstream.com**
Firearms News **www.firearmsnews.com**
FMG Publications **www.fmgpubs.com**
Fouling Shot **www.castbulletassoc.org**
Fur-Fish-Game **www.furfishgame.com**
George Shumway Publisher **www.shumwaypublisher.com**
Grays Sporting Journal **www.grayssportingjournal.com**
Gun Digest, The Magazine **www.gundigest.com**
Gun Digest Books **www.gundigeststore.com**
Gun Dog **www.gundogmag.com**
Gun Mag **www.thegunmag.com**
Gun Tests **www.gun-tests.com**
Gun Video **www.gunvideo.com**
Gun World **www.gunworld.com**
Guns & Ammo **www.gunsandammo.com**
GUNS Magazine **www.gunsmagazine.com**
Guns of the Old West **www.gunsoftheoldwest.com**
Handloader **www.riflemagazine.com**
Handguns **www.handguns.com**
Hendon Publishing Co. **www.hendonpub.com**
Heritage Gun Books **www.gunbooks.com**
Law and Order **www.hendonpub.com**
Man at Arms **www.manatarmsbooks.com**

Muzzle Blasts **www.nmlra.org**
Muzzleloader **www.muzzleloadermag.com**
North American Whitetail **www.northamericanwhitetail.com**
On-Target Productions **www.ontargetdvds.com**
Outdoor Channel **www.outdoorchannel.com**
Outdoor Life **www.outdoorlife.com**
Petersen's Hunting **www.petersenshunting.com**
Police and Security News **www.policeandsecuritynews.com**
Police Magazine **www.policemag.com**
Primitive Arts Video **www.primitiveartsvideo.com**
Pursuit Channel **www.pursuitchannel.com**
Recoil Gun Magazine **www.recoilweb.com**
Rifle Magazine **www.riflemagazine.com**
Rifle Shooter Magazine **www.rifleshootermag.com**
Safari Press Inc. **www.safaripress.com**
Shoot! Magazine **www.shootmagazine.com**
Shooting Illustrated **www.nrapublications.org**
Shooting Industry **www.shootingindustry.com**
Shooting Times Magazine **www.shootingtimes.com**
Shooting Sports Retailer **www.shootingsportsretailer.com**
Shooting Sports USA **www.nrapublications.org**
Shop Deer Hunting **www.shopdeerhunting.com**
Shotgun Report **www.shotgunreport.com**
Shotgun Sports Magazine **www.shotgunsportsmagazine.com**
Single Shot Exchange **www.singleshotexchange.com**
Single Shot Rifle Journal **www.assra.com**
Skyhorse Publishing **www.skyhorsepublishing.com**
Small Arms Review **www.smallarmsreview.com**
Sporting Classics **www.sportingclassics.com**
Sports Afield **www.sportsafield.com**
Sportsman Channel **www.thesportsmanchannel.com**
Sportsmen on Film **www.sportsmenonfilm.com**
Standard Catalog of Firearms **www.gundigeststore.com**
Successful Hunter **www.riflemagazine.com**
SWAT Magazine **www.swatmag.com**
Trapper & Predator Caller **www.trapperpredatorcaller.com**
Turkey & Turkey Hunting **www.turkeyandturkeyhunting.com**
Varmint Hunter **www.varminthunter.com**
VSP Publications **www.gunbooks.com**
Wildfowl **www.wildfowlmag.com**

RELOADING TOOLS

21st Century Shooting **www.xxicsi.com**
Ballisti-Cast Mfg. **www.ballisti-cast.com**
Battenfeld Technologies **www.btibrands.com**
Black Hills Shooters Supply **www.bhshooters.com**
Bruno Shooters Supply **www.brunoshooters.com**
Buffalo Arms **www.buffaloarms.com**
CabineTree **www.castingstuff.com**
Camdex, Inc. **www.camdexloader.com**

CH/4D Custom Die **www.ch4d.com**
Corbin Mfg & Supply Co. **www.corbins.com**
Dillon Precision **www.dillonprecision.com**
Forster Precision Products **www.forsterproducts.com**
Gracey Trimmer **www.matchprep.com**
Harrell's Precision **www.harrellsprec.com**
Hornady **www.hornady.com**
Hunter's Supply, Inc. **www.hunters-supply.com**
Huntington Reloading Products **www.huntingtons.com**
J & J Products Co. **www.jandjproducts.com**
Lead Bullet Technology **www.lbtmoulds.com**
Lee Precision, Inc. **www.leeprecision.com**
L.E. Wilson **www.lewilson.com**
Little Crow Gun Works **www.littlecrowgunworks.com**
Littleton Shotmaker **www.littletonshotmaker.com**
Load Data **www.loaddata.com**
Lyman **www.lymanproducts.com**
Mayville Engineering Co. (MEC) **www.mecreloaders.com**
Midway USA **www.midwayusa.com**
Montana Bullet Works **www.montanabulletworks.com**
NECO **www.neconos.com**
NEI **www.neihandtools.com**
Neil Jones Custom Products **www.neiljones.com**
New Lachaussee SA **www.lachaussee.com**
Ponsness/Warren **www.reloaders.com**
Precision Reloading **www.precisionreloading.com**
Quinetics Corp. **www.quineticscorp.com**
RCBS **www.rcbs.com**
Redding Reloading Equipment **www.redding-reloading.com**
Sinclair Int'l Inc. **www.sinclairintl.com**
Stealth Gunpowder **www.stealthgunpowder.com**
Stoney Point Products Inc. **www.stoneypoint.com**
Vickorman Seating Die **www.castingstuff.com**

RESTS — BENCH, PORTABLE, ATTACHABLE

AOA Tactical **www.aoatactical.com**
Accu-Shot **www.accu-shot.com**
Battenfeld Technologies **www.btibrands.com**
Bench Master **www.bench-master.com**
B-Square **www.b-square.com**
Center Mass, Inc. **www.centermassinc.com**
Desert Mountain Mfg. **www.benchmasterusa.com**
DOA Tactical **www.doatactical.com**
Harris Engineering Inc. **www.harrisbipods**
KFS Industries **www.versapod.com**
Level-Lok **www.levellok.com**
Midway **www.midwayusa.com**
Rotary Gun Racks **www.gun-racks.com**
R.W. Hart **www.rwhart.com**

Sinclair Intl, Inc. **www.sinclairintl.com**
Shooting Bench USA **www.shootingbenchusa.com**
Stoney Point Products **www.stoneypoint.com**
Target Shooting **www.targetshooting.com**
SCOPES, SIGHTS, MOUNTS AND ACCESSORIES
Accumount **www.accumounts.com**
Accusight **www.accusight.com**
Advantage Tactical Sight **www.advantagetactical.com**
Aimpoint **www.aimpoint.com**
Aim Shot, Inc. **www.aimshot.com**
Aimsight **www.aimsightusa.com**
Aimtech Mount Systems **www.aimtech-mounts.com**
Alpen Outdoor Corp. **www.alpenoutdoor.com**
American Technologies Network, Corp. **www.atncorp.com**
AmeriGlo, LLC **www.ameriglo.net**
ArmaLaser **www.armalaser.com**
Amerigun USA **www.amerigunusa.com**
Armament Technology, Inc. **www.armament.com**
ARMS **www.armsmounts.com**
Athlon Optics **www.athlonoptics.com**
ATN **www.atncorp.com**
Badger Ordnance **www.badgerordnance.com**
Barrett **www.barrettrifles.com**
Beamshot-Quarton **www.beamshot.com**
BKL Technologies, Inc. **www.bkltech.com**
BSA Optics **www.bsaoptics.com**
B-Square **www.b-square.com**
Burris **www.burrisoptics.com**
Bushnell Performance Optics **www.bushnell.com**
Carl Zeiss Optical Inc. **www.zeiss.com**
CenterPoint Precision Optics **www.centerpointoptics.com**
Centurion Arms **www.centurionarms.com**
C-More Systems **www.cmore.com**
Conetrol Scope Mounts **www.conetrol.com**
Crimson Trace Corp. **www.crimsontrace.com**
D&L Sports **www.disports.com**
DuraSight Scope Mounting Systems **www.durasight.com**
DYX International **www.dyxint.com**
EasyHit, Inc. **www.easyhit.com**
EAW **www.eaw.de**
Elcan Optical Technologies **www.elcan. com**
Electro-Optics Technologies **www.eotech.com**
Elusive Technologies **www.elusivetechnologies.com**
EoTech **www.eotechinc.com**
Eurooptik Ltd. **www.eurooptik.com**
Field Sport Inc. **www.fieldsportinc.com**
German Precision Optics **www.gpo-usa.com**
GG&G **www.gggaz.com**
Gilmore Sports **www.gilmoresports.com**
Gradient Lens Corp. **www.gradientlens.com**
Guangzhou Bosma Corp. **www.bosmaoptics.com**

Hahn Precision **www.hahn-precision.com**
Hawke Sport Optics **www.hawkeoptics.com**
Hi-Lux Optics **www.hi-luxoptics.com**
HIVIZ **www.hivizsights.com**
Horus Vision **www.horusvision.com**
Huskemaw Optics **www.huskemawoptics.com**
Insight **www.insighttechnology.com**
Ironsighter Co. **www.ironsighter.com**
Kahles **www.kahlesusa.com**
KenSight **www.kensight.com**
Knight's Armament **www.knightarmco.com**
Konus **www.konus.com**
Kruger Optical **www.krugeroptical.com**
LaRue Tactical **www.laruetactical.com**
Lasergrips **www.crimsontrace.com**
LaserLyte **www.laserlytesights.com**
LaserMax Inc. **www.lasermax.com**
Laser Products **www.surefire.com**
Leapers, Inc. **www.leapers.com**
Leatherwood **www.hi-luxoptics.com**
Leica Camera Inc. **www.leica-camera.com**
Leupold **www.leupold.com**
Lewis Machine and Tool **www.lmtdefense.com**
LightForce/NightForce USA **www.nightforceoptics.com**
LUCID LLC **www.mylucidgear.com**
Luna Optics **www.lunaoptics.com**
Lyman **www.lymanproducts.com**
Lynx **www.b-square.com**
Matech **www.matech.net**
Marble's Gunsights **www.marblearms.com**
Meopta **www.meopta.com**
Meprolight **www.meprolight.com**
Mini-Scout-Mount **www.amegaranges.com**
Minox USA **www.minox.com**
Montana Vintage Arms **www.montanavintagearms.com**
Mounting Solutions Plus **www.mountsplus.com**
NAIT **www.nait.com**
Newcon International Ltd. **www.newcon-optik.com**
NG2 Defense **www.ng2defense.com**
Night Force Optics **www.nightforceoptics.com**
Night Ops Tactical **www.nightopstactical.com**
Night Optics USA, Inc. **www.nightoptics.com**
Night Owl Optics **www.nightowloptics.com**
Night Vision Inc. **www.nvincorporated.com**
Nikon Inc. **www.nikonhunting.com**
Nitehog **www.nitehog.com**
Nite Site LLC **www.darkwidowgear.com**
North American Integrated Technologies **www.nait.com**
Novak Sights **www.novaksights.com**
N-Vision Optics **www.nvisionoptics.com**
O.K. Weber, Inc. **www.okweber.com**

Optolyth-Optic **www.optolyth.de**
Photonis **www.photonis.com**
Precision Reflex **www.pri-mounts.com**
Pride Fowler, Inc. **www.rapidreticle.com**
Primary Arms Optics **www.primaryarmsoptics.com**
Redfield **www.redfield.com**
Schmidt & Bender **www.schmidtundbender.de**
Scopecoat **www.scopecoat.com**
Scopelevel **www.scopelevel.com**
SIG Sauer **www.sigsauer.com**
Sightmark **www.sightmark.com**
Simmons **www.simmonsoptics.com**
S&K **www.scopemounts.com**
Springfield Armory **www.springfield-armory.com**
Steiner Optik **www.steiner-optics.com**
Sun Optics USA **www.sunopticsusa.com**
Sure-Fire **www.surefire.com**
SWATSCOPE **www.swatscope.com**
Talley Mfg. Co. **www.talleyrings.com**
Steve Earle Scope Blocks **www.steveearleproducts.com**
Swarovski Optik **www.swarovskioptik.com**
Tacomhq **www.tacomhq.com**
Tasco **www.tasco.com**
Tech Sights **www.tech-sights.com**
Torrey Pines Logic **www.tplogic.com**
Trijicon Inc. **www.trijicon.com**
Trinity Force **www.trinityforce.com**
Triumph Systems **www.triumph-systems.com**
Troy Industries **www.troyind.com**
Truglo Inc. **www.truglo.com**
Ultimak **www.ultimak.com**
UltraDot **www.ultradotusa.com**
U.S. Night Vision **www.usnightvision.com**
U.S. Optics Technologies Inc. **www.usoptics.com**
Valdada-IOR Optics **www.valdada.com**
Viridian Green Laser Sights **www.viridiangreenlaser.com**
Vortex Optics **www.vortexoptics.com**
Warne **www.warnescopemounts.com**
Weaver Scopes **www.weaveroptics.com**
Wilcox Industries Corp **www.wilcoxind.com**
Williams Gun Sight Co. **www.williamsgunsight.com**
Wilson Combat **www.wilsoncombat.com**
XS Sight Systems **www.xssights.com**
Zeiss **www.zeiss.com**

SHOOTING ORGANIZATIONS, SCHOOLS AND MUSEUMS

Amateur Trapshooting Assoc. **www.shootata.com**
American Custom Gunmakers Guild **www.acgg.org**
American Gunsmithing Institute **www.americangunsmith.com**
American Pistolsmiths Guild **www.americanpistol.com**
American Single Shot Rifle Assoc. **www.assra.com**
American Snipers **www.americansnipers.org**
Assoc. of Firearm & Tool Mark Examiners **www.afte.org**
Aurora Sportsman's Club **www.aurorasc.orc**
Autry National Center of the American West **www.theautry.org**
BATFE **www.atf.gov**
Boone and Crockett Club **www.boone-crockett.org**
Browning Collectors Association **www.browningcollectors.com**
Buffalo Bill Center of the West **www.centerofthewest.org**
Buckmasters, Ltd. **www.buckmasters.com**
Cast Bullet Assoc. **www.castbulletassoc.org**
Citizens Committee for the Right to Keep & Bear Arms **www. ccrkba.org**
Civilian Marksmanship Program **www.odcmp.com**
Colorado School of Trades **www.schooloftrades.edu**
Contemporary Longrifle Assoc. **www.longrifle.com**
Colt Collectors Assoc. **www.coltcollectors.com**
Cylinder & Slide Pistolsmithing Schools **www.cylinder-slide. com**
Ducks Unlimited **www.ducks.org**
4-H Shooting Sports Program **www.4-hshootingsports.org**
Fifty Caliber Shooters Assoc. **www.fcsa.org**
Firearms Coalition **www.nealknox.com**
Fox Collectors Association **www.foxcollectors.com**
Front Sight Firearms Training Institute **www.frontsight.com**
Garand Collectors Assoc. **www.thegca.org**
German Gun Collectors Assoc. **www.germanguns.com**
Gibbs Military Collectors Club **www.gibbsrifle.com**
Gun Clubs **www.associatedgunclubs.org**
Gun Owners Action League **www.goal.org**
Gun Owners of America **www.gunowners.org**
Gun Trade Asssoc. Ltd. **www.gtaltd.co.uk**
Gunsite Training Center, Inc. **www.gunsite.com**
Hunting and Shooting Sports Heritage Fund **www.hsshf.org**
I.C.E. Training **www.icetraining.us**
International Ammunition Assoc. **www.cartridgecollectors.org**
IWA **www.iwa.info**
International Defensive Pistol Assoc. **www.idpa.com**
International Handgun Metallic Silhouette Assoc. **www.ihmsa.org**
International Hunter Education Assoc. **www.ihea.com**
International Single Shot Assoc. **www.issa-schuetzen.org**
Ithaca Owners **www.ithacaowners.com**
Jews for the Preservation of Firearms Ownership **www.jpfo.org**
L.C. Smith Collectors Assoc. **www.lcsmith.org**
Lefever Arms Collectors Assoc. **www.lefevercollectors.com**
Mannlicher Collectors Assoc. **www.mannlicher.org**
Marlin Firearms Collectors Assoc. **www.marlin-collectors.com**
Mule Deer Foundation **www.muledeer.org**
Muzzle Loaders Assoc. of Great Britain **www.mlagb.com**
National 4-H Shooting Sports **www.4-hshootingsports.org**

National Association of Sporting Goods Wholesalers
www.nasgw.org
National Benchrest Shooters Assoc. **www.nbrsa.com**
National Defense Industrial Assoc. **www.ndia.org**
National Cowboy & Western Heritage Museum
www.nationalcowboymuseum.org
National Firearms Museum **www.nramuseum.org**
National Mossberg Collectors Assoc.
www.mossbergcollectors.org
National Muzzle Loading Rifle Assoc. **www.nmlra.org**
National Rifle Association **www.nra.org**
National Rifle Association ILA **www.nraila.org**
National Shooting Sports Foundation **www.nssf.org**
National Tactical Officers Assoc. **www.ntoa.org**
National Wild Turkey Federation **www.nwtf.com**
NICS/FBI **www.fbi.gov**
North American Hunting Club **www.huntingclub.com**
Order of Edwardian Gunners (Vintagers) **www.vintagers.org**
Outdoor Industry Foundation
www.outdoorindustryfoundation.org
Parker Gun Collectors Assoc. **www.parkerguns.org**
Pennsylvania Gunsmith School **www.pagunsmith.com**
Pheasants Forever **www.pheasantsforever.org**
Piedmont Community College **www.piedmontcc.edu**
Quail & Upland Wildlife Federation **www.quwf.net**
Quail Forever **www.quailforever.org**
Remington Society of America **www.remingtonsociety.com**
Right To Keep and Bear Arms **www.rkba.org**
Rocky Mountain Elk Foundation **www.rmef.org**
Ruffed Grouse Society **www.ruffedgrousesociety.org**
Ruger Collectors Assoc. **www.rugercollectorsassociation.com**
Ruger Owners & Collectors Society **www.rugersociety.com**
SAAMI **www.saami.org**
Safari Club International **www.scifirstforhunters.org**
Sako Collectors Club **www.sakocollectors.com**
Scholastic Clay Target Program
www.sssfonline.org/scholasti-clay-target-program
Scholastic Shooting Sports Foundation **www.sssfonline.org**
Second Amendment Foundation **www.saf.org**
Shooting for Women Alliance
www.shootingforwomenalliance.com
SHOT Show **www.nssf.org**
Sig Sauer Academy **www.sigsauer.com**
Single Action Shooting Society **www.sassnet.com**
Smith & Wesson Collectors Assoc. **www.theswca.org**
L.C. Smith Collectors Assoc. **www.lcsmith.org**
Steel Challenge Pistol Tournament **www.steelchallenge.com**
Students for Second Amendment **www.sf2a.org**
Sturgis Economic Development Corp.
www.sturgisdevelopment.com
Suarez Training **www.warriortalk.com**

Tactical Defense Institute **www.tdiohio.com**
Tactical Life **www.tactical-life.com**
Thompson/Center Assoc. **www.thompsoncenterassociation.org**
Thunder Ranch **www.thunderranchinc.com**
Trapshooters Homepage **www.trapshooters.com**
Trinidad State Junior College **www.trinidadstate.edu**
United Sportsmen's Youth Foundation **www.usyf.com**
Universal Shooting Academy
www.universalshootingacademy.com
U.S. Concealed Carry Association **www.uscca.us**
U.S. Fish and Wildlife Service **www.fws.gov**
U.S. Practical Shooting Assoc. **www.uspsa.org**
U.S. Sportsmen's Alliance **www.ussportsmen.org**
USA Shooting **www.usashooting.com**
Weatherby Collectors Assoc. **www.weatherbycollectors.com**
Wild Sheep Foundation **www.wildsheepfoundation.org**
Winchester Arms Collectors Assoc.
www.winchestercollector.com

STOCKS, GRIPS, FOREARMS

10/22 Fun Gun **www.1022fungun.com**
Advanced Technology **www.atigunstocks.com**
AG Composites **www.agcomposites.com**
Battenfeld Technologies **www.btibrands.com**
Bell & Carlson, Inc. **www.bellandcarlson.com**
Butler Creek Corp **www.butlercreek.com**
Cadex **www.vikingtactics.com**
Calico Hardwoods, Inc. **www.calicohardwoods.com**
Choate Machine **www.riflestock.com**
Command Arms **www.commandarms.com**
C-More Systems **www.cmore.com**
D&L Sports **www.dlsports.com**
E. Arthur Brown Co. **www.eabco.com**
Fajen **www.battenfeldtechnologies.com**
Grip Pod **www.grippod.com**
Gun Stock Blanks **www.gunstockblanks.com**
Herrett's Stocks **www.herrettstocks.com**
High Tech Specialties **www.hightech-specialties.com**
Hogue Grips **www.getgrip.com**
Knight's Mfg. Co. **wwwknightarmco.com**
Knoxx Industries **www.blackhawk.com**
KZ Tactical **www.kleyzion.com**
LaRue Tactical **www.laruetactical.com**
Lewis Machine & Tool **www.lewismachine.net**
Magpul **www.magpul.com**
Manners Composite Stocks **www.mannersstocks.com**
McMillan Fiberglass Stocks **www.mcmfamily.com**
Phoenix Technology/Kicklite **www.kicklitestocks.com**
Precision Gun Works **www.precisiongunstocks.com**
Ram-Line **www.outers-guncare.com**

Richards Microfit Stocks **www.rifle-stocks.com**
Rimrock Rifle Stock **www.bordenrifles.com**
Royal Arms Gunstocks **www.royalarmsgunstocks.com**
Speedfeed **www.safariland.com**
Tango Down **www.tangodown.com**
TAPCO **www.tapco.com**
Stocky's **www.stockysstocks.com**
Surefire **www.surefire.com**
Tiger-Hunt Curly Maple Gunstocks **www.gunstockwood.com**
UTG Pro **www.leapers.com**
Wenig Custom Gunstocks Inc. **www.wenig.com**
Wilcox Industries **www.wilcoxind.com**
Yankee Hill **www.yhm.net**

TARGETS AND RANGE EQUIPMENT

Action Target Co. **www.actiontarget.com**
Advanced Training Systems **www.atsusa.biz**
Alco Target **www.alcotarget.com**
Arntzen Targets **www.arntzentargets.com**
Birchwood Casey **www.birchwoodcasey.com**
Caswell Meggitt Defense Systems **www.mds-caswell.com**
Champion Traps & Targets **www.championtarget.com**
Custom Metal Products **www.custommetalprod.com**
Firebird Targets **www.firebirdtargets.com**
HD Targets **www.hdtargets.com**
Laser Ammo USA **www.laser-ammo.com**
Laser Shot **www.lasershot.com**
MGM Targets **www.mgmtargets.com**
MTM Products **www.mtmcase-gard.com**
National Muzzleloading Rifle Assoc. **www.nmlra.org**
National Target Co. **www.nationaltarget.com**
Newbold Target Systems **www.newboldtargets.com**
Oehler Research **www.oehler-research.com**
Paragon Tactical **www.paragontactical.com**
PJL Targets **www.pjltargets.com**
Range Systems **www.range-systems.com**
Savage Range Systems **www.savagerangesystems.com**
ShatterBlast Targets **www.daisy.com**
Splatter Pro Targets **www.splatterprotargets.com**
Super Trap Bullet Containment Systems **www.supertrap.com**
Targetvision **www.targetvisioncam.com**
Thompson Target Technology **www.thompsontarget.com**
Thundershot Exploding Targets **www.gryphonenergetics.com**
Unique Tek **www.uniquetek.com**
Visible Impact Targets **www.crosman.com**
White Flyer **www.whiteflyer.com**

TRAP AND SKEET SHOOTING EQUIPMENT AND ACCESSORIES

Atlas Trap Co **www.atlastraps.com**
Auto-Sporter Industries **www.auto-sporter.com**
Do-All Traps, Inc. **www.doalloutdoors.com**
Gamaliel Shooting Supply **www.gamaliel.com**
Howell Shooting Supplies **www.howellshootingsupplies.com**
Laporte America **www.laporteamerica.com**
Promatic, Inc. **www.promatic.biz**
White Flyer **www.whiteflyer.com**

TRIGGERS

American Trigger Corp. **www.americantrigger.com**
Brownells **www.brownells.com**
CMC Triggers **www.cmctriggers.com**
Huber Concepts **www.huberconcepts.com**
Jard, Inc. **www.jardinc.com**
Kidd Triggers **www.coolguyguns.com**
Shilen **www.shilen.com**
Spec-Tech Industries, Inc. **www.spec-tech-industries.com**
Timney Triggers **www.timneytriggers.com**
Williams Trigger Specialties **www.williamstriggers.com**

MAJOR SHOOTING WEBSITES AND LINKS

24 Hour Campfire **www.24hourcampfire.com**
Accurate Shooter **www.6mmbr.com**
Alphabetic Index of Links **www.gunsgunsguns.com**
Ammo Guide **www.ammoguide.com**
Auction Arms **www.auctionarms.com**
Benchrest Central **www.benchrest.com**
Big Game Hunt **www.biggamehunt.net**
Bullseye Pistol **www.bullseyepistol.com**
Firearms History **www.researchpress.co.uk**
Glock Talk **www.glocktalk.com**
Gun Broker Auctions **www.gunbroker.com**
Gun Blast **www.gunblast.com**
Gun Boards **www.gunboards.com**
Gun Digest **www. gundigest.com**
Guns & Ammo Forum **www.gunsandammo.com**
GunsAmerica **www.gunsamerica.com**
Gun Shop Finder **www.gunshopfinder.com**
Guns and Hunting **www.gunsandhunting.com**
Hunt and Shoot (NSSF) **www.huntandshoot.org**
Keep and Bear Arms **www.keepandbeararms.com**
Leverguns **www.leverguns.com**
Load Swap **www.loadswap.com**
Long Range Hunting **www.longrangehunting.com**

Real Guns **www.realguns.com**
Ruger Forum **www.rugerforum.com**
Savage Shooters **www.savageshooters.com**
Shooters Forum **www.shootersforum.com**
Shotgun Sports Resource Guide **www.shotgunsports.com**
Shotgun World **www.shotgunworld.com**
Sniper's Hide **www.snipershide.com**
Sportsman's Web **www.sportsmansweb.com**
Tactical-Life **www.tactical-life.com**
The Gun Room **www.doublegun.com**
Wing Shooting USA **www.wingshootingusa.org**

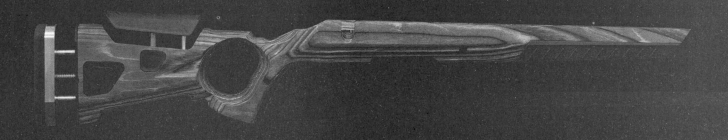